Praise for *Ways of Reading*

"I've had the most successful writing classes of my teaching career using *Ways of Reading*. The students are given difficult work, and that challenge rewards them and gives them a true sense of accomplishment."

—Susan Glassow, *Lane Community College*

"The readings are ambitious and demanding. The assignment sequences are a strength of *Ways of Reading*. They are thought through and through yet allow great latitude."

—Anne Trubek, *Oberlin College*

"*Ways of Reading* includes complex, challenging essays that require my students to read and reread, to push themselves to become more active in the interpretation process. The book provides an entry into the world of academic writing, the kind of writing that students will be expected to read and write about as they proceed in college."

—Steven Scherwatsky, *Merrimack College*

"These essays provide excellent topics, profound discussions, energizing styles. My students can read for content, for form, and for enjoyment. Few readers do this."

—Mada Morgan, *Southern Oregon University*

"*Ways of Reading* contains excellent texts, all of which are intellectually challenging and multifaceted, and none of which provide easy 'conclusions.' The book is well organized and introduced."

—David A. Griffith, *University of Pittsburgh*

"The 'Making Connections' questions are phenomenal."

—Susan M. Corbin, *El Camino College*

"The great strength of *Ways of Reading* is that it presumes that first-year college students can read, understand, and write about complex writers and topics. Students will be challenged, but they will also be rewarded for their critical engagement with these pieces."

—Matt Hill, *Michigan Technological University*

"The sequences provide an inexperienced teacher with direction."

—Derek Driedger, *University of North Dakota*

"This text continues to offer some of the most challenging and interesting reading selections available in a composition text. It offers teachers an opportunity to teach writing and challenge minds with powerful, complex essays."

—Will Hochman, *Southern Connecticut State University*

"I like the 'push and shove' approach to reading and writing because it teaches students the value of being in academia."

—Elena V. Rodionova, *University of North Dakota*

"The readings are substantial, challenging, and 'real'; students know that they are doing serious scholarly work. The questions for reading and writing are likewise demanding, well-designed, and amazingly dependable to promote fruitful class discussion."

—Noreen T. O'Connor, *Georgetown University*

"The intrinsic strength of *Ways of Reading* is the fact that it doesn't condescend to students; it treats them as real scholars and thinkers—something I find particularly important for community college students, who are often treated as less capable and not worthy of higher-order thinking and efforts."

—Paul Almonte, *Salt Lake Community College*

"The assignment sequences do a great deal in terms of stimulating students to regard all the reading they do as part of a conversation among writers, rather than a summary response to required texts."

—Andrew Mossin, *Rutgers University*

WAYS OF READING

An Anthology for Writers

Sixth Edition

David Bartholomae

UNIVERSITY OF PITTSBURGH

Anthony Petrosky

UNIVERSITY OF PITTSBURGH

BEDFORD/ST. MARTIN'S

Boston ◆ New York

For Bedford/St. Martin's
Developmental Editor: John Sullivan
Production Editor: Lori Chong Roncka
Production Supervisor: Maria R. Gonzalez
Marketing Manager: Brian Wheel
Editorial Assistant: Caroline Thompson
Production Assistants: Thomas P. Crehan and Kendra LeFleur
Copyeditor: Tara L. Masih
Text Design: Anna George
Cover Design: Claire Jarvis
Cover Art: Robert Rauschenberg, *Per Diem (Arcadian Retreats)*, fresco. © Robert
   Rauschenberg/Licensed by VAGA, New York, NY.
Composition: Pine Tree Composition, Inc.
Printing and Binding: Haddon Craftsmen, Inc., an R.R. Donnelley & Sons
   Company

President: Charles H. Christensen
Editorial Director: Joan E. Feinberg
Editor in Chief: Karen S. Henry
Director of Marketing: Karen Melton
Director of Editing, Design, and Production: Marcia Cohen
Managing Editor: Elizabeth M. Schaaf

Library of Congress Control Number: 2001095036

Manufactured in the United States of America.
6   5   4   3   2   1
f   e   d   c   b   a

For information, write: Bedford/St. Martin's,
75 Arlington Street, Boston, MA 02116
(617-399-4000)

ISBN: 0–312–25897–6

ACKNOWLEDGMENTS

Gloria Anzaldúa, "Entering into the Serpent" and "How to Tame a Wild Tongue." From *Border-
   lands/La frontera: The New Mestiza*. Copyright © 1987 by Gloria Anzaldúa. Reprinted by permission
   of Aunt Lute Books.
James Baldwin, "Notes of a Native Son." From *Notes of a Native Son* by James Baldwin. Copyright ©
   1955, renewed 1983, by James Baldwin. Reprinted by permission of Beacon Press, Boston.
Walter Benjamin, "The Work of Art in the Age of Mechanical Reproduction." From *Illuminations* by
   Walter Benjamin, copyright © 1955 by Suhrkamp Verlag, Frankfurt a.M. English translation by
   Harry Zohn copyright © 1968 and renewed 1996 by Harcourt, Inc. Reprinted by permission of
   Harcourt, Inc.

*Acknowledgments and copyrights are continued at the back of the book on pages 914–15, which constitute an
extension of the copyright page. It is a violation of the law to reproduce these selections by any means whatsoever without the written permission of the copyright holder.*

Preface

Ways of Reading is designed for a course where students are given the opportunity to work on what they read, and to work on it by writing. When we began developing such courses, we realized the problems our students had when asked to write or talk about what they read were not "reading problems," at least not as these are strictly defined. Our students knew how to move from one page to the next. They could read sentences. They had, obviously, been able to carry out many of the versions of reading required for their education—skimming textbooks, cramming for tests, strip-mining books for term papers.

Our students, however, felt powerless in the face of serious writing, in the face of long and complicated texts—the kinds of texts we thought they should find interesting and challenging. We thought (as many teachers have thought) that if we just, finally, gave them something good to read—something rich and meaty—they would change forever their ways of thinking about English. It didn't work, of course. The issue is not only *what* students read, but what they can learn to *do* with what they read. We learned that the problems our students had lay not in the reading material (it was too hard) or in the students (they were poorly prepared) but in the classroom—in the ways we and they imagined what it meant to work on an essay.

There is no better place to work on reading than in a writing course, and this book is intended to provide occasions for readers to write. You will find a number of distinctive features in *Ways of Reading*. For one thing, it contains selections you don't usually see in a college reader: long, powerful, mysterious pieces like John Berger's "Ways of Seeing," Susan Griffin's "Our Secret," Adrienne Rich's "When We Dead Awaken: Writing as Re-Vision," Clifford Geertz's "Deep Play: Notes on the Balinese Cockfight," Mary Louise Pratt's "Arts of the Contact Zone," John Edgar Wideman's "Our Time," W. J. T. Mitchell's "The Photographic Essay: Four Case Studies," and Michel Foucault's "Panopticism." These are the sorts of readings we talk about when we talk with our colleagues. We have learned that we can talk about them with our students as well.

When we chose the essays, we were looking for "readable" texts—that is, texts that leave some work for a reader to do. We wanted selections that invite students to be active, critical readers, that present powerful readings of common experience, that open up the familiar world and make it puzzling, rich, and problematic. We wanted to choose selections that invite students to be active readers and to take responsibility for their acts of interpretation. So we avoided the short set-pieces you find in so many anthologies. In a sense, those short selections misrepresent the act of reading. They can be read in a single sitting; they make arguments that can be easily paraphrased; they solve all the problems they raise; they wrap up Life and put it into a box; and so they turn reading into an act of appreciation, where the most that seems to be required is a nod of the head. And they suggest that a writer's job is to do just that, to write a piece that is similarly tight and neat and self-contained. We wanted to avoid pieces that were so plainly written or tightly bound that there was little for students to do but "get the point."

We learned that if our students had reading problems when faced with long and complex texts, the problems lay in the way they imagined a reader—the role a reader plays, what a reader does, why a reader reads (if not simply to satisfy the requirements of a course). When, for example, our students were puzzled by what they read, they took this as a sign of failure. ("It doesn't make any sense," they would say, as though the sense were supposed to be waiting on the page, ready for them the first time they read through.) And our students were haunted by the thought that they couldn't remember everything they had read (as though one could store all of Geertz's "Deep Play" in memory); or if they did remember bits and pieces, they felt that the fragmented text they possessed was evidence that they could not do what they were supposed to do. Our students were confronting the experience of reading, in other words, but they were taking the problems of reading—problems all readers face—and concluding that there was nothing for them to do but give up.

As expert readers, we have all learned what to do with a complex text. We know that we can go back to a text; we don't have to remember it—in fact, we've learned to mark up a text to ease that re-entry. We know that a reader is a person who puts together fragments. Those coherent readings we construct begin with confusion and puzzlement, and we construct those readings by writing and rewriting—by working on a text.

These are the lessons our students need to learn, and this is why a course in reading is also a course in writing. Our students need to learn that there is something they can do once they have first read through a complicated text; successful reading is not just a matter of "getting" an essay the first time. In a very real sense, you can't begin to feel the power a reader has until you realize the problems, until you realize that no one "gets" Geertz or Rich or Griffin or Wideman all at once. You work on what you read, and then what you have at the end is something that is yours, something you made. And this is what the teaching apparatus in *Ways of Reading* is designed to do. In a sense, it says to students, "OK, let's get to work on these essays; let's see what you can make of them."

This, then, is the second distinctive feature you will find in *Ways of Reading*: reading and writing assignments designed to give students access to the essays. After each selection, for example, you will find "Questions for a Second Reading." We wanted to acknowledge that rereading is a natural way of carrying out the work of a reader, just as rewriting is a natural way of completing the work of a writer. It is not something done out of despair or as a punishment for not getting things right the first time. The questions we have written highlight what we see as central textual or interpretive problems. Geertz, for example, divides his essay into seven sections, each written in a different style. By going back through the essay with this in mind and by asking what Geertz is doing in each case (what his method is and what it enables him to accomplish), a student is in a position to see the essay as the enactment of a method and not just as a long argument with its point hidden away at the end. These questions might serve as preparations for class discussion or ways of directing students' work in journals. Whatever the case, they both honor and direct the work of rereading.

Each selection is also followed by two sets of writing assignments, "Assignments for Writing" and "Making Connections." The first set directs students back into the work they have just read. While the assignments vary, there are some basic principles behind them. They ask students to work on the essay by focusing on difficult or problematic moments in the text; they ask students to work on the author's examples, extending and testing his or her methods of analysis; or they ask students to apply the method of the essay (its way of seeing and understanding the world) to settings or experiences of their own. Students are asked, for example, to give a "Geertzian" reading to scenes from their own immediate culture (the behavior of people at a shopping mall, characteristic styles of dress), and they are asked to imagine that they are working alongside Geertz and making his project their own. Or they are asked to consider the key examples in Rich's "When We Dead Awaken" (poems from various points in her career) to see how as writers they might use the key terms of her argument ("structures of oppression," "renaming") in representing their own experience. The last assignments—"Making Connections"—invite students to read one essay in the context of another, to see, for example, if Pratt's account of the "literate arts of the contact zone" can be used to frame a reading of Gloria Anzaldúa's prose, Harriet Jacobs's narrative, or Paulo Freire's account of education. In a sense, then, the essays are offered as models, but not as "prose models" in the strictest sense. What they model is a way of seeing or reading the world, of both imagining problems and imagining methods to make those problems available to a writer.

At the end of the book, we have included several longer assignment sequences and a goodly number of shorter sequences. In some cases these incorporate single assignments from earlier in the book; in most cases they involve students in projects that extend anywhere from two to three weeks for the shorter sequences to an entire semester's worth of work for the longer ones. Almost all the sequences include several of the essays in the anthology and require a series of separate drafts and revisions. In academic life, readers seldom read single essays in isolation, as though one were "finished" with Geertz after a week or two. Rather, they read with a purpose—with a project in mind or a problem to solve. The assignment sequences are designed to give students a feel for the rhythm and texture of an extended academic project. They offer, that is, one more way of reading and writing. Because these sequences lead students through intellectual projects proceeding from one week to the next, they enable them to develop authority as specialists, to feel the difference between being an expert and being a "common" reader on a single subject. And, with the luxury of time available for self-reflection, students can look back on what they have done, not only to revise what they know, but also to take stock and comment on the value and direction of their work.

Because of their diversity, it is difficult to summarize the assignment sequences. Perhaps the best way to see what we have done is to turn to the back of the book and look at them. They are meant to frame a project for students but to leave open possibilities for new directions. You should feel free to add or drop readings, to mix sequences, and to revise the assignments to fit your course and your schedule.

You will also notice that there are few "glosses" appended to the essays. We have not added many editors' notes to define difficult words or to identify names or allusions to other authors or artists. We've omitted them because their presence suggests something we feel is false about reading. They suggest that good readers know all the words or pick up all the allusions or recognize every name that is mentioned. This is not true. Good readers do what they can and try their best to fill in the blanks; they ignore seemingly unimportant references and look up the important ones. There is no reason for students to feel they lack the knowledge necessary to complete a reading of these texts. We have translated foreign phrases and glossed some technical terms, but we have kept the selections as clean and open as possible.

We have been asked on several occasions whether the readings aren't finally just too hard for students. The answer is no. Students will have to work on the selections, but that is the point of the course and the reason, as we said before, why a reading course is also a course in writing. College students want to believe that they can strike out on their own, make their mark, do something they have never done before. They want to *be* experts, not just hear from them. This is the great pleasure, as well as the great challenge, of undergraduate instruction. It is not hard to convince students they ought to be able to speak alongside of (or even speak back to) Clifford Geertz, Adrienne Rich, or James Baldwin. And, if a teacher is patient and forgiving—willing, that is, to let a student work out a reading of Walker Percy, willing to keep from saying, "No, that's not it," and filling the silence with the "right" reading—then students can, with care and assistance, learn to speak for themselves. It takes a certain kind of classroom, to be sure. A teacher who teaches this book will have to be comfortable turning the essays over to the students, even with the knowledge that they will not do immediately on their own what a professional could do—at least not completely, or with the same grace and authority.

In our own teaching, we have learned that we do not have to be experts on every figure or every area of inquiry represented in this book. And, frankly, that has come as a great relief. We can have intelligent, responsible conversations about Geertz's "Deep Play" without being experts on Geertz or on anthropology or ethnography. We needed to prepare ourselves to engage and direct students as readers, but we did not have to prepare ourselves to lecture on Foucault or Rich, or poststructuralism, documentary studies, or American feminism. The classes we have been teaching, and they have been some of the most exciting we have ever taught, have been classes where students—together and with their instructors—work on what these essays might mean.

So here we are, imagining students working shoulder to shoulder with Geertz and Rich and Foucault, even talking back to them as the occasion arises. There is a wonderful Emersonian bravado in all this. But such is the case with strong and active readers. If we allow students to work on powerful texts, they will want to share the power. This is the heady fun of academic life, the real pleasure of thinking, reading, and writing. There is no reason to keep it secret from our students.

Note to the Sixth Edition.   The sixth edition of *Ways of Reading* contains seven new selections by James Baldwin, Walter Benjamin, Simon Frith, Marianne Hirsch, Patricia Nelson Limerick, Alice Munro, and Edward Said, and we've added more poetry by Adrienne Rich.

Our principle of selection remains the same—we were looking for "readable" texts, pieces that instructors and students would find challenging and compelling, pieces that offer powerful readings of ordinary experience, pieces worth extended work.

We revised the assignment sequences, some to incorporate the new selections, others because, after teaching them again, we thought about them differently. The sequences that were most radically changed are

"Autobiographical Explorations (II)," "On Difficulty," "Reading Culture (II)," and "Working with the Past (II)." We have continued to offer sequences focusing on autobiographical writing and the personal essay. While there have always been assignments in *Ways of Reading* that ask students to use their experience as subject matter, these assignments invite students to look critically and historically at the genre and insist that reading and thinking can *also* be represented as part of one's "personal" experience. The sequence on documentary projects extends the study of images from advertising and painting to those in works like *Let Us Now Praise Famous Men* and *After the Last Sky: Palestinian Lives*. Teaching these as examples of reading and writing projects has taught us that they have much to offer that students can study and imitate. We have revised the sequence on "Close Reading/Close Writing" and remain convinced that this kind of work helps students to think about sentences in useful ways. And we have continued to focus attention on prose models that challenge conventional forms and idioms, that complicate the usual ways of thinking about and representing knowledge and experience. There are several assignment sequences that ask students to write as though they too could participate in such revisionary work.

We continue to offer a number of shorter "minisequences." The shortest of these might engage a class for two to three weeks, the longest for a month or two. We wrote these minisequences at the request of instructors who wanted more flexibility and a wider range of projects to offer their students.

We've also updated *Resources for Teaching* WAYS OF READING, by including an essay we've written for composition directors on using *Ways of Reading* as a unit adoption in a large program as well as a new essay by an experienced instructor on problems specific to teaching the materials in *Ways of Reading*. We continue to offer essays by graduate students; these essays give advice on how to work with the book. They stand as examples of the kinds of papers graduate students might write when they use *Ways of Reading* in conjunction with a teaching seminar. They stand best, however, as examples of graduate students speaking frankly to other graduate students about teaching and about this book.

With our colleagues, we have taught most of the selections in this book, including the new ones. Several of us worked together to prepare the assignment sequences; most of these, too, have been tested in class. As we have traveled around giving talks, we've met many people who have used *Ways of Reading*. We have been delighted to hear them talk about how it has served their teaching, and we have learned much from their advice and example. It is an unusual and exciting experience to see our course turned into a text, to see our work read, critiqued, revised, and expanded. We have many people to thank. The list that follows can't begin to name all those to whom we owe a debt. And it can't begin to express our gratitude.

Acknowledgments.   We owe much to the friendship and wisdom of our colleagues at the University of Pittsburgh. There are old friends and colleagues with whom we have worked for a very long time: Ellen Bishop, Jean Ferguson Carr, Steve Carr, Nick Coles, Kathryn Flannery, Paul Kameen, Margaret Marshall, Mariolina Salvatori, and Jim Seitz. We also want to thank students and colleagues who gave particular help and attention to the work in preparation of the Sixth Edition: Molly Brown, John Champagne, Malkiel Choseed, Ashley Currier, Jean Grace, David Griffith, Lorraine Higgins, Linda Huff, Aitor Ibarrola, Deane Kern, Geeta Khothari, Jennifer Lee, Dana Och, Juli Parrish, Richard Purcell, Tanya Reyes, Suzette Roth, Lauren Skrabala, Patricia Sullivan, Steve Sutherland, Jocelyn Trachtenberg, Jennifer Trainor, Henry Veggian, Ellen Wadey, Stacey Waite, Chris Warnick, Kathleen Welsch, Matt Willen, and Lois Williams. Deborah Galle helped significantly with the research for the headnotes.

And we owe much to colleagues at other schools who have followed our work with interest and offered their support and criticism. We are grateful for the notes, letters, and student papers.

We were fortunate to have a number of outstanding reviewers on the project. We would first like to thank those who did in-depth reviews of the fifth edition: Paul Almonte, Salt Lake Community College; Carla Copenhaven, University of California–Irvine; Judith Goleman, University of Massachusetts–Boston; Kathleen Kelly, Northeastern University; Carole Kley, Princeton University; Thomas Recchio, University of Connecticut; James Seitz, University of Pittsburgh; Gail Stygall, University of Washington; Stephen Sutherland, University of Missouri–Columbia; Sheila Walsh, Northeastern University; Kathleen Welsch, Clarion University; and Matthew Willen, Indiana University of Pennsylvania.

We also owe thanks to a group who reviewed our manual, *Resources for Teaching WAYS OF READING:* Lisa Bickmore, Salt Lake Community College; Pam Dane, Lane Community College; Thomas Recchio, University of Connecticut; Mary Peters Rodeback, University of Oregon; and Sheila Walsh, Northestern University.

A number of reviewers examined our new selections, and we are grateful for their help: Carolyn Allen, University of Washington; Carol Bott, University of Miami; John Champagne, Pennsylvania State University, The Behrend College; Hugh English, Queens College, City University of New York; Kathryn Flannery, University of Pittsburgh; Alfred Guy, New York University; Will Hochman, Southern Connecticut State University; Andrew Mossin, Rutgers University–New Brunswick; Thomas Recchio, University of Connecticut; Stephanie Roach, University of Connecticut; Dawn Skorczewski, Emerson College; Stephen Sutherland, University of Missouri–Columbia; Sheila Walsh, Northeastern University; and Matthew Willen, Indiana University of Pennsylvania.

We would also like to thank those who responded to our questionnaire: Jeff Abernathy, Illinois College; Paul Almonte, Salt Lake Community College; Kristin Arola, Michigan Technological University; Susan Aylworth, California State University–Chico; Richard Braverman, Columbia University; Molly Brown, University of Pittsburgh; John Champagne, Pennsylvania State University, The Behrend College; Susan Corbin,

Michigan Technological University; Jeff E. Cravello, California State University–Pomona; Ashley Currier, University of Pittsburgh; Pam Dane, Lane Community College; Carole Deletiner, New York University; Derek Driedger, University of North Dakota; Susan Eldridge, University of Massachusetts–Boston; Benjamin Fisher, Rowan University; Gregory W. Fowler, Pennsylvania State University–Erie; Susan Glassow, Lane Community College; Maggie Gordon, University of Mississippi; David A. Griffith, University of Pittsburgh; Matt Hill, Michigan Technological University; Will Hochman, Southern Connecticut State University; Cris Hollingsworth, Rutgers University; Anne Jurecic, Rutgers University and Raritan Valley Community College; Deane Lindsey Kern, University of Pittsburgh; Martin Klammer, Luther College; Sharon Kubasak, Baldwin-Wallace College; Ralph Leary, Clarion University; Joseph Lisowski, Rutgers University; Tom Lombardo, Glendale Community College; Jaime Lynn Longo, Temple University; Mada Petranovich Morgan, Southern Oregon University; Andrew Mossin, Rutgers University; Dana C. Och, University of Pittsburgh; Noreen O'Connor, Georgetown University; Douglas F. Rice, Kent State University–Salem; Lori Robison, University of South Carolina–Lancaster; Elena Rodionova, University of North Dakota; Steven Scherwatsky, Merrimack College; Roger Schmidt, Idaho State University; Roberta Schreyer, SUNY–Potsdam; Dawn Skorczewski, Emerson College; Kathleen St. Peters, St. Louis University; Lauren Skrabala, University of Pittsburgh; Elisa B. Stone, Salt Lake Community College; Linda Breton Tredennick, University of Oregon; Anne Trubek, Oberlin College; Kathryn Valentine, Michigan Technological University; Henry Veggian, University of Pittsburgh; Ellen Placey Wadey, University of Pittsburgh; Stacey Waite, University of Pittsburgh; John Walter, St. Louis University; and Eric Wolfe, University of South Carolina–Lancaster.

Chuck Christensen of Bedford/St. Martin's remains the best in the business. He is on the eve of retirement. We wish him the very best in his new life. Joan Feinberg helped to shape this project from its very beginning. She is a fine and thoughtful friend as well as a fine and thoughtful editor. John Sullivan joined the group for the Fifth Edition. He had taught from an earlier edition of *Ways of Reading* and had, for us, a wonderful sense of the book's approach to reading, writing, and teaching. John is organized, resourceful, generous, quick to offer suggestions and to take on extra work. He soon became as much a collaborator as an editor. His care and dedication held everything together at times when we were falling apart. It was a real pleasure to work with him. Chris Stripinis and Ruth Gordon handled permissions. Caroline Thompson helped locate books, readings, and material for the headnotes and later edited *Resources for Teaching* WAYS OF READING. Lori Chong Roncka expertly guided the manuscript through production. Tara L. Masih was an excellent copyeditor, sensitive to the quirks of our prose and attentive to detail.

And, finally, we are grateful to Joyce and Ellen, and to Jesse, Dan, Kate, Matthew, and Ben, for their love and support.

Contents

SEQUENCE SIX   *The Documentary Tradition   836*

COLES   *The Tradition: Fact and Fiction*

MITCHELL   *The Photographic Essay: Four Case Studies*

SAID   *States*

HIRSCH   *Projected Memory: Holocaust Photographs in Personal and Public Fantasy*

Assignments

SEQUENCE SEVEN   *Experimental Readings and Writings   842*

GRIFFIN   *Our Secret*

HIRSCH   *Projected Memory: Holocaust Photographs in Personal and Public Fantasy*

WIDEMAN   *Our Time*

ANZALDÚA   *Entering into the Serpent; How to Tame a Wild Tongue*

Assignments

SEQUENCE EIGHT   *Experts and Expertise   849*

MITCHELL   *The Photographic Essay: Four Case Studies*

RICH   *When We Dead Awaken: Writing as Re-Vision*

GEERTZ   *Deep Play: Notes on the Balinese Cockfight*

WIDEMAN   *Our Time*

PERCY   *The Loss of the Creature*

Assignments

Assignments

SEQUENCE SIXTEEN   *Working with the Past (II)*   *904*

MUNRO *The Albanian Virgin*
BALDWIN *Notes of a Native Son*
SAID *States*
BENJAMIN *The Work of Art in the Age of Mechanical Reproduction*

Assignments

SEQUENCE SEVENTEEN   *Writing History*   *907*

LIMERICK *Haunted America*
TOMPKINS *"Indians": Textualism, Morality, and the Problem of History*

Assignments

SEQUENCE EIGHTEEN   *Writing Projects*   *910*

SAID *States*
MUNRO *The Albanian Virgin*
BALDWIN *Notes of a Native Son*
RICH *When We Dead Awaken: Writing as Re-Vision*

Assignments

WAYS OF READING

An Anthology for Writers

Introduction:
Ways of Reading

Making a Mark

*R*EADING involves a fair measure of push and shove. You make your mark on a book and it makes its mark on you. Reading is not simply a matter of hanging back and waiting for a piece, or its author, to tell you what the writing has to say. In fact, one of the difficult things about reading is that the pages before you will begin to speak only when the authors are silent and you begin to speak in their place, sometimes for them—doing their work, continuing their projects—and sometimes for yourself, following your own agenda.

This is an unusual way to talk about reading, we know. We have not mentioned finding information or locating an author's purpose or identifying main ideas, useful though these skills are, because the purpose of our book is to offer you occasions to imagine other ways of reading. We think of reading as a social interaction—sometimes peaceful and polite, sometimes not so peaceful and polite.

We'd like you to imagine that when you read the works we've collected here, somebody is saying something to you, and we'd like you to imagine that you are in a position to speak back, to say something of your own in turn. In other words, we are not presenting our book as a miniature library (a place to find information) and we do not think of you, the reader, as a term-paper writer (a person looking for information to write down on three-by-five cards).

When you read, you hear an author's voice as you move along; you believe a person with something to say is talking to you. You pay attention, even when you don't completely understand what is being said, trusting that it will all make sense in the end, relating what the author says to what you already know or expect to hear or learn. Even if you don't quite grasp everything you are reading at every moment (and you won't), and even if you don't remember everything you've read (no reader does—at least not in long, complex pieces), you begin to see the outlines of the author's project, the patterns and rhythms of that particular way of seeing and interpreting the world.

When you stop to talk or write about what you've read, the author is silent; you take over—it is your turn to write, to begin to respond to what the author said. At that point this author and his or her text become something you construct out of what you remember or what you notice as you go back through the text a second time, working from passages or examples but filtering them through your own predisposition to see or read in particular ways.

In "The Achievement of Desire," one of the essays in this book, Richard Rodriguez tells the story of his education, of how he was drawn to imitate his teachers because of his desire to think and speak like them. His is not a simple story of hard work and success, however. In a sense, Rodriguez's education gave him what he wanted—status, knowledge, a way of understanding himself and his position in the world. At the same time, his education made it difficult to talk to his parents, to share their point of view; and to a degree, he felt himself becoming consumed by the powerful ways of seeing and understanding represented by his reading and his education. The essay can be seen as Rodriguez's attempt to weigh what he had gained against what he had lost.

If ten of us read his essay, each would begin with the same words on the page, but when we discuss the chapter (or write about it), each will retell and interpret Rodriguez's story differently; we will emphasize different sections—some, for instance, might want to discuss the strange way Rodriguez learned to read, others might be taken by his difficult and changing relations to his teachers, and still others might want to think about Rodriguez's remarks about his mother and father.

Each of us will come to his or her own sense of what is significant, of what the point is, and the odds are good that what each of us makes of the essay will vary from one to another. Each of us will understand Rodriguez's story in his or her own way, even though we read the same piece. At the same time, if we are working with Rodriguez's essay (and not putting it aside or ignoring its peculiar way of thinking about education), we will be working within a framework he has established, one that makes education stand, metaphorically, for a complicated interplay between permanence and change, imitation and freedom, loss and achievement.

In "The Achievement of Desire," Rodriguez tells of reading a book by Richard Hoggart, *The Uses of Literacy*. He was captivated by a section of this book in which Hoggart defines a particular kind of student, the "scholarship boy." Here is what Rodriguez says:

> Then one day, leafing through Richard Hoggart's *The Uses of Literacy*, I found, in his description of the scholarship boy, myself. For the first time I realized that there were other students like me, and so I was able to frame the meaning of my academic success, its consequent price—the loss.

For Rodriguez, this phrase, "scholarship boy," became the focus of Hoggart's book. Other people, to be sure, would read that book and take different phrases or sections as the key to what Hoggart has to say. Some might argue that Rodriguez misread the book, that it is really about something else, about British culture, for example, or about the class system in England. The power and value of Rodriguez's reading, however, are represented by what he was able to *do* with what he read, and what he was able to do was not record information or summarize main ideas but, as he says, "frame the meaning of my academic success." Hoggart provided a frame, a way for Rodriguez to think and talk about his own history as a student. As he goes on in his essay, Rodriguez not only uses this frame to talk about his experience, but he resists it, argues with it. He casts his experience in Hoggart's terms but then makes those terms work for him by seeing both what they can and what they cannot do. This combination of reading, thinking, and writing is what we mean by *strong reading*, a way of reading we like to encourage in our students.

When we have taught "The Achievement of Desire" to our students, it has been almost impossible for them not to see themselves in Rodriguez's description of the scholarship boy (and this was true of students who were not minority students and not literally on scholarships). They, too, have found a way of framing (even inventing) their own lives as students—students whose histories involve both success and loss. When we have asked our students to write about this essay, however, some students have argued, and quite convincingly, that Rodriguez had either to abandon his family and culture or to remain ignorant. Other students have argued equally convincingly that Rodriguez's anguish was destructive and self-serving, that he was trapped into seeing his situation in terms that he might have replaced with others. He did not necessarily have to turn his back on his family. Some have contended that Rodriguez's problems with his family had nothing to do with what he says about education, that he himself shows how imitation need not blindly lead a person away from his culture, and these student essays, too, have been convincing.

Reading, in other words, can be the occasion for you to put things together, to notice this idea or theme rather than that one, to follow a writer's announced or secret ends while simultaneously following your own. When this happens, when you forge a reading of a story or an essay, you make your mark on it, casting it in your terms. But the story makes its mark on you as well, teaching you not only about a subject (Rodriguez's struggles with his teachers and his parents, for example) but about a way of seeing and understanding a subject. The text provides the opportunity for you to see through someone else's powerful language, to imagine your own familiar settings through the images, metaphors, and ideas of others. Rodriguez's essay, in other words, can make its mark on readers, but they, too, if they are strong, active readers, can make theirs on it.

Readers learn to put things together by writing. It is not something you can do, at least not to any degree, while you are reading. It requires that you work on what you have read, and that work best takes shape when you sit down to write. We will have more to say about this kind of thinking in a later section of the introduction, but for now let us say that writing gives you a way of going to work on the text you have read. To write about a story or essay, you go back to what you have read to find phrases or passages that define what for you are the key moments, that help you interpret sections that seem difficult or troublesome or mysterious. If you are writing an essay of your own, the work that you are doing gives a purpose and a structure to that rereading.

Writing also, however, gives you a way of going back to work on the text of your own reading. It allows you to be self-critical. You can revise not just to make your essay neat or tight or tidy but to see what kind of reader you have been, to examine the pattern and consequences in the choices you have made. Revision, in other words, gives you the chance to work on your essay, but it also gives you an opportunity to work on your reading—to qualify or extend or question your interpretation of, say, "The Achievement of Desire."

We can describe this process of "re-vision," or re-seeing, fairly simply. You should not expect to read "The Achievement of Desire" once and completely understand the essay or know what you want to say. You will work out what you have to say while you write. And once you have constructed a reading—once you have completed a draft of your essay, in other words—you can step back, see what you have done, and go back to work on it. Through this activity—writing and rewriting—we have seen our students become strong, active, and critical readers.

Not everything a reader reads is worth that kind of effort. The pieces we have chosen for this book all provide, we feel, powerful ways of seeing (or framing) our common experience. The selections cannot be quickly summarized. They are striking, surprising, sometimes troubling in how they challenge common ways of seeing the world. Some of them (we're thinking of pieces by Walter Benjamin, Michel Foucault, Clifford Geertz, and Adrienne Rich) have captured and altered the way our culture sees and understands daily experience. The essays have changed the ways people think and write. In fact, every selection in the book is one that has given us, our students, and our colleagues that dramatic experience, almost like a discovery, when we suddenly saw things as we had never seen them before and, as a consequence, we had to work hard to understand what had happened and how our thinking had changed.

If we recall, for example, the first time we read Susan Griffin's "Our Secret" or John Edgar Wideman's "Our Time," we know that they have radically shaped our thinking. We carry these essays with us in our minds, mulling over them, working through them, hearing Griffin and Wideman in sentences we write or sentences we read; we introduce the essays in classes we teach whenever we can; we are surprised, reading them for the third or fourth time, to find things we didn't see before. It's not that we failed to "get" these essays the first time around. In fact, we're not sure we have captured them yet, at least not in any final sense, and we disagree in basic ways about what Griffin and Wideman are saying or about how these essays might best be used. Essays like these are not the sort that you can "get" like a loaf of bread at the store. We're each convinced that the essays are ours in that we know best what's going on in them, and yet we have also become theirs, creatures of these essays, because of the ways they have come to dominate our seeing, talking, reading, and writing. This captivity is something we welcome, yet it is also something we resist.

Our experience with these texts is a remarkable one and certainly hard to provide for others, but the challenges and surprises are reasons we read—we hope to be taken and changed in just these ways. Or, to be more accurate, it is why we read outside the daily requirements to keep up with the news or conduct our business. And it is why we bring reading into our writing courses.

Ways of Reading

Before explaining how we organized this book, we would like to say more about the purpose and place of the kind of strong, aggressive, labor-intensive reading we've been referring to.

Readers face many kinds of experiences, and certain texts are written with specific situations in mind and invite specific ways of reading. Some texts, for instance, serve very practical purposes—they give directions or information. Others, like the short descriptive essays often used in English textbooks and anthologies, celebrate common ways of seeing and thinking and ask primarily to be admired. These texts seem self-contained; they announce their own meanings with little effort and ask little from the reader, making it clear how they want to be read and what they have to say. They ask only for a nod of the head or for the reader to take notes and give a sigh of admiration ("yes, that was very well said"). They are clear and direct. It is as though the authors could anticipate all the questions their essays might raise and solve all the problems a reader might imagine. There is not much work for a reader to do, in other words, except, perhaps, to take notes and, in the case of textbooks, to work step-by-step, trying to re-member as much as possible.

This is how assigned readings are often presented in university class-rooms. Introductory textbooks (in biology or business, for instance) are good examples of books that ask little of readers outside of note-taking and memorization. In these texts the writers are experts and your job, as novice, is to digest what they have to say. And, appropriately, the task set before you is to summarize—so you can speak again what the author said, so you can better remember what you read. Essay tests are an example of the writing tasks that often follow this kind of reading. You might, for in-stance, study the human nervous system through textbook readings and lectures and then be asked to write a summary of what you know from both sources. Or a teacher might ask you during a class discussion to para-phrase a paragraph from a textbook describing chemical cell communica-tion to see if you understand what you've read.

Another typical classroom form of reading is reading for main ideas. With this kind of reading you are expected to figure out what most people (or most people within a certain specialized group of readers) would take as the main idea of a selection. There are good reasons to read for main ideas. For one, it is a way to learn how to imagine and anticipate the val-ues and habits of a particular group—test-makers or, if you're studying business, Keynesian economists, perhaps. If you are studying business, to continue this example, you must learn to notice what Keynesian econo-mists notice—for instance, when they analyze the problems of growing government debt—to share key terms, to know the theoretical positions they take, and to adopt for yourself their common examples and interpre-tations, their jargon, and their established findings.

There is certainly nothing wrong with reading for information or read-ing to learn what experts have to say about their fields of inquiry. These are not, however, the only ways to read, although they are the ones most often taught. Perhaps because we think of ourselves as writing teachers, we are concerned with presenting other ways of reading in the college and university curriculum.

A danger arises in assuming that reading is only a search for informa-tion or main ideas. There are ways of thinking through problems and working with written texts which are essential to academic life, but which are not represented by summary and paraphrase or by note-taking and essay exams.

Student readers, for example, can take responsibility for determining the meaning of the text. They can work as though they were doing some-thing other than finding ideas already there on the page and they can be guided by their own impressions or questions as they read. We are not, now, talking about finding hidden meanings. If such things as hidden meanings can be said to exist, they are hidden by readers' habits and prej-udices (by readers' assumptions that what they read should tell them what they already know), or by readers' timidity and passivity (by their unwillingness to take the responsibility to speak their minds and say what they notice).

Reading to locate meaning in the text places a premium on memory, yet a strong reader is not necessarily a person with a good memory. This point may seem minor, but we have seen too many students haunted because they could not remember everything they read or retain a complete essay in their minds. A reader could set herself the task of remembering as much as she could from Walker Percy's "The Loss of the Creature," an essay filled with stories about tourists at the Grand Canyon and students in a biology class, but a reader could also do other things with that essay; a reader might figure out, for example, how both students and tourists might be said to have a common problem seeing what they want to see. Students who read Percy's essay as a memory test end up worrying about bits and pieces (bits and pieces they could go back and find if they had to) and turn their attention away from the more pressing problem of how to make sense of a difficult and often ambiguous essay.

A reader who needs to have access to something in the essay can use simple memory aids. A reader can go back and scan, for one thing, to find passages or examples that might be worth reconsidering. Or a reader can construct a personal index, making marks in the margin or underlining passages that seem interesting or mysterious or difficult. A mark is a way of saying, "This is something I might want to work on later." If you mark the selections in this book as you read them, you will give yourself a working record of what, at the first moment of reading, you felt might be worth a second reading.

If Percy's essay presents problems for a reader, they are problems of a different order from summary and recall. The essay is not the sort that tells you what it says. You would have difficulty finding one sentence that sums up or announces, in a loud and clear voice, what Percy is talking about. At the point you think Percy is about to summarize, he turns to one more example that complicates the picture, as though what he is discussing defies his attempts to sum things up. Percy is talking about tourists and students, about such things as individual "sovereignty" and our media culture's "symbolic packages," but if he has a point to make, it cannot be stated in a sentence or two.

In fact, Percy's essay is challenging reading in part because it does not have a single, easily identifiable main idea. A reader could infer that it has several points to make, none of which can be said easily and some of which, perhaps, are contradictory. To search for information, or to ignore the rough edges in search of a single, paraphrasable idea, is to divert attention from the task at hand, which is not to remember what Percy says but to speak about the essay and what it means to you, the reader. In this sense, the Percy essay is not the sum of its individual parts; it is, more accurately, what its readers make of it.

A reader could go to an expert on Percy to solve the problem of what to make of the essay—perhaps to a teacher, perhaps to a book in the library. And if the reader pays attention, he could remember what the expert said or she could put down notes on paper. But in doing either, the reader only rehearses what he or she has been told, abandoning the responsibility to make the essay meaningful. There are ways of reading, in other words, in which Percy's essay "The Loss of the Creature" is not what it means to the experts but what it means to you as a reader willing to take the chance to construct a reading. You can be the authority on Percy; you don't have to turn to others. The meaning of the essay, then, is something you develop as you go along, something for which you must take final responsibility. The meaning is forged from reading the essay, to be sure, but it is determined by what you do with the essay, by the connections you can make and your explanation of why those connections are important, and by your account of what Percy might mean when he talks about "symbolic packages" or a "loss of sovereignty" (phrases Percy uses as key terms in the essay). This version of Percy's essay will finally be yours; it will not be exactly what Percy said. (Only his words in the order he wrote them would say exactly what he said.) You will choose the path to take through his essay and support it as you can with arguments, explanations, examples, and commentary.

If an essay or a story is not the sum of its parts but something you as a reader create by putting together those parts that seem to matter personally, then the way to begin, once you have read a selection in this collection, is by reviewing what you recall, by going back to those places that stick in your memory—or, perhaps, to those sections you marked with checks or notes in the margins. You begin by seeing what you can make of these memories and notes. You should realize that with essays as long and complex as those we've included in this book, you will never feel, after a single reading, as though you have command of everything you read. This is not a problem. After four or five readings (should you give any single essay that much attention), you may still feel that there are parts you missed or don't understand. This sense of incompleteness is part of the experience of reading, at least the experience of reading serious work. And it is part of the experience of a strong reader. No reader could retain one of these essays in her mind, no matter how proficient her memory or how experienced she might be. No reader, at least no reader we would trust, would admit that he understood everything that Michel Foucault or Adrienne Rich or Edward Said had to say. What strong readers know is that they have to begin, and they have to begin regardless of their doubts or hesitations. What you have after your first reading of an essay is a starting place, and you begin with your marked passages or examples or notes, with questions to answer, or with problems to solve. Strong readings, in other words, put a premium on individual acts of attention and composition.

Strong Readers, Strong Texts

We chose pieces for this book that invite strong readings. Our selections require more attention (or a different form of attention) than a written summary, a reduction to gist, or a recitation of main ideas. They are not "easy" reading. The challenges they present, however, do not make them inaccessible to college students. The essays are not specialized studies; they have interested, pleased, or piqued general and specialist audiences alike. To say that they are challenging is to say, then, that they leave some work for a reader to do. They are designed to teach a reader new ways to read (or to step outside habitual ways of reading), and they anticipate readers willing to take the time to learn. These readers need not be experts on the subject matter. Perhaps the most difficult problem for students is to believe that this is true.

You do not need experts to explain these stories and essays, although you could probably go to the library and find an expert guide to most of the selections we've included. Let's take, for example, Adrienne Rich's "When We Dead Awaken: Writing as Re-Vision." This essay looks at the history of women's writing (and at Rich's development as a poet). It argues that women have been trapped within a patriarchal culture—speaking in men's voices and telling stories prepared by men—and, as a consequence, according to Rich, "We need to know the writing of the past, and know it differently than we have ever known it; not to pass on a tradition but to break its hold over us."

You could go to the library to find out how Rich is regarded by experts, by literary critics or feminist scholars, for example; you could learn how her work fits into an established body of work on women's writing and the representation of women in modern culture. You could see what others have said about the writers she cites: Virginia Woolf, Jane Austen, and Elizabeth Bishop. You could see how others have read and made use of Rich's essay. You could see how others have interpreted the poems she includes as part of her argument. You could look for standard definitions of key terms like "patriarchy" or "formalism."

Though it is often important to seek out other texts and to know what other people are saying or have said, it is often necessary and even desirable to begin on your own. Rich can also be read outside any official system of interpretation. She is talking, after all, about our daily experience. And when she addresses the reader, she addresses a person—not a term-paper writer. When she says, "We need to know the writing of the past, and know it differently than we have ever known it," she means us and what we know and how we know what we know. (The "we" of her essay could be said to refer most accurately to women readers, leading men to feel the kind of exclusion women must feel when the reader is always "he.")

The question, then, is not what Rich's words might mean to a literary critic, or generally to those who study contemporary American culture.

The question is what you, the reader, can make of those words given your own experience, your goals, and the work you do with what she has written. In this sense, "When We Dead Awaken" is not what it means to others (those who have already decided what it means) but what it means to you, and this meaning is something you compose when you write about the essay; it is your account of what Rich says and how what she says might be said to make sense.

A teacher, poet, and critic we admire, I. A. Richards, once said, "Read as though it made sense and perhaps it will." To take command of complex material like the selections in this book, you need not subordinate yourself to experts; you can assume the authority to provide such a reading on your own. This means you must allow yourself a certain tentativeness and recognize your limits. You should not assume that it is your job to solve the problems between men and women. You can speak with authority while still acknowledging that complex issues *are* complex.

There is a paradox here. On the one hand, the essays are rich, magnificent, too big for anyone to completely grasp all at once, and before them, as before inspiring spectacles, it seems appropriate to stand humbly, admiringly. And yet, on the other hand, a reader must speak with authority.

In "The American Scholar," Ralph Waldo Emerson says, "Meek young men grow up in libraries, believing it their duty to accept the views, which Cicero, which Locke, which Bacon, have given, forgetful that Cicero, Locke, and Bacon were only young men in libraries when they wrote these books." What Emerson offers here is not a fact but an attitude. There is creative reading, he says, as well as creative writing. It is up to you to treat authors as your equals, as people who will allow you to speak too. At the same time, you must respect the difficulty and complexity of their texts and of the issues and questions they examine. Little is to be gained, in other words, by turning Rich's essay into a message that would fit on a poster in a dorm room: "Be Yourself" or "Stand on Your Own Two Feet."

Reading with and against the Grain

Reading, then, requires a difficult mix of authority and humility. On the one hand, a reader takes charge of a text; on the other, a reader gives generous attention to someone else's (a writer's) key terms and methods, commits his time to her examples, tries to think in her language, imagines that this strange work is important, compelling, at least for the moment.

Most of the questions in *Ways of Reading* will have you moving back and forth in these two modes, reading with and against the grain of a text, reproducing an author's methods, questioning his or her direction and authority. With the essay "When We Dead Awaken," for example, we have asked students to give a more complete and detailed reading of Rich's poems (the poems included in the essay) than she does, to put her terms to work, to extend her essay by extending the discussion of her examples.

We have asked students to give themselves over to her essay—recognizing that this is not necessarily an easy thing to do. Or, again in Rich's name, we have asked students to tell a story of their own experience, a story similar to the one she tells, one that can be used as an example of the ways a person is positioned by a dominant culture. Here we are saying, in effect, read your world in Rich's terms. Notice what she would notice. Ask the questions she would ask. Try out her conclusions.

To read generously, to work inside someone else's system, to see your world in someone else's terms—we call this "reading with the grain." It is a way of working *with* a writer's ideas, in conjunction with someone else's text. As a way of reading, it can take different forms. In the reading and writing assignments that follow the selections in this book, you will sometimes be asked to summarize and paraphrase, to put others' ideas into your terms, to provide your account of what they are saying. This is a way of getting a tentative or provisional hold on a text, its examples and ideas; it allows you a place to begin to work. And sometimes you will be asked to extend a writer's project—to add your examples to someone else's argument, to read your experience through the frame of another's text, to try out the key terms and interpretive schemes in another writer's work. In the assignments that follow the Rich essay, for example, students are asked both to reproduce her argument and to extend her terms to examples from their own experience.

We have also asked students to read against the grain, to read critically, to turn back, for example, *against* Rich's project, to ask questions they believe might come as a surprise, to look for the limits of her vision, to provide alternate readings of her examples, to find examples that challenge her argument, to engage her, in other words, in dialogue. How might her poems be read to counter what she wants to say about them? If her essay argues for a new language for women, how is this language represented in the final poem or the final paragraphs, when the poem seems unreadable and the final paragraph sounds familiarly like the usual political rhetoric? If Rich is arguing for a collective movement, a "we" represented by the "we" of her essay, who is included and who is excluded by the terms and strategies of her writing? To what degree might you say that this is a conscious or necessary strategy?

Many of the essays in this book provide examples of writers working against the grain of common sense or everyday language. This is true of John Berger, for example, who redefines the "art museum" against the way it is usually understood. It is true of John Edgar Wideman, who reads against his own text while he writes it—asking questions that disturb the story as it emerges on the page. It is true of Harriet Jacobs, Patricia Nelson Limerick, and Simon Frith, whose writings show the signs of their efforts to work against the grain of the standard essay, habitual ways of representing what it means to know something, to be somebody, to speak before others.

[handwritten marginalia:] This is how I have changed

[handwritten marginalia:] This allowed reading me to think outside the box

This, we've found, is the most difficult work for students to do, this work against the grain. For good reasons and bad, students typically define their skill by reproducing rather than questioning or revising the work of their teachers (or the work of those their teachers ask them to read). It is important to read generously and carefully and to learn to submit to projects that others have begun. But it is also important to know what you are doing—to understand where this work comes from, whose interests it serves, how and where it is kept together by will rather than desire, and what it might have to do with you. To fail to ask the fundamental questions—Where am I in this? How can I make my mark? Whose interests are represented? What can I learn by reading with or against the grain?—to fail to ask these questions is to mistake skill for understanding, and it is to misunderstand the goals of a liberal education. All of the essays in this book, we would argue, ask to be read, not simply reproduced; they ask to be read and to be read with a difference. Our goal is to make that difference possible.

Reading and Writing:
The Questions and Assignments

Strong readers, we've said, remake what they have read to serve their own ends, putting things together, figuring out how ideas and examples relate, explaining as best they can material that is difficult or problematic, translating phrases like Richard Rodriguez's "scholarship boy" into their own terms. At these moments, it is hard to distinguish the act of reading from the act of writing. In fact, the connection between reading and writing can be seen as almost a literal one, since the best way you can show your reading of a rich and dense essay like "The Achievement of Desire" is by writing down your thoughts, placing one idea against another, commenting on what you've done, taking examples into account, looking back at where you began, perhaps changing your mind, and moving on.

Readers, however, seldom read a single essay in isolation, as though their only job were to arrive at some sense of what an essay has to say. Although we couldn't begin to provide examples of all the various uses of reading in academic life, it is often the case that readings provide information and direction for investigative projects, whether they are philosophical or scientific in nature. The reading and writing assignments that follow each selection in this book are designed to point you in certain directions, to give you ideas and projects to work with, and to challenge you to see one writer's ideas through another's.

Strong readers often read critically, weighing, for example, an author's claims and interpretations against evidence—evidence provided by the author in the text, evidence drawn from other sources, or the evidence that is assumed to be part of a reader's own knowledge and experience. Critical reading can produce results as far-reaching as a biochemist publicly challenging the findings and interpretations in an article on cancer research in the *New England Journal of Medicine* or as quiet as a student offering a personal interpretation of a story in class discussion.

You will find that the questions we have included in our reading and writing assignments often direct you to test what you think an author is saying by measuring it against your own experience. Paulo Freire, for example, in "The 'Banking' Concept of Education" talks about the experience of the student, and one way for you to develop or test your reading of his essay is to place what he says in the context of your own experience, searching for examples that are similar to his and examples that differ from his. If the writers in this book are urging you to give strong readings of your common experience, you have access to what they say because they are talking not only to you but about you. Freire has a method that he employs when he talks about the classroom—one that compares "banking" education with "problem-posing" education. You can try out his method and his terms on examples of your own, continuing his argument as though you were working with him on a common project. Or you can test his argument as though you want to see not only where and how it will work but where and how it will not.

You will also find questions that ask you to extend the argument of the essay by looking in detail at some of the essay's own examples. John Berger, for example, gives a detailed analysis of two paintings by Frans Hals in "Ways of Seeing." Other paintings in the essay he refers to only briefly. One way of working on his essay is to look at the other examples, trying to do with them what he has done for you earlier.

Readers, as we have said, seldom read an essay in isolation, as though, having once worked out a reading of Adrienne Rich's "When We Dead Awaken: Writing as Re-Vision," they could go on to something else, something unrelated. It is unusual for anyone, at least in an academic setting, to read in so random a fashion. Readers read most often because they have a project in hand—a question they are working on or a problem they are trying to solve. For example, if as a result of reading Rich's essay you become interested in the difference between women's writing and men's writing, and you begin to notice things you would not have noticed before, then you can read other essays in the book through this frame. If you have a project in mind, that project will help determine how you read these other essays. Sections of an essay that might otherwise seem unimportant suddenly become important—Gloria Anzaldúa's unusual prose style, or the moments when Harriet Jacobs addresses the "women of the North." Rich may enable you to read Jacobs's narrative differently. Jacobs may spur you to rethink Rich.

In a sense, then, you do have the chance to become an expert reader, a reader with a project in hand, one who has already done some reading, who has watched others at work, and who has begun to develop a method of analysis and a set of key terms. You might read Jacobs's narrative "Incidents in the Life of a Slave Girl," for example, in the context of Mary Louise Pratt's discussion of "autoethnography," or you might read the selections by Gloria Anzaldúa, James Baldwin, and John Edgar Wideman as offering differing accounts of racism in America. Imagining yourself operating alongside some of the major figures in contemporary thought can be great fun and heady work—particularly when you have the occasion to speak back to them.

In every case, then, the material we provide to direct your work on the essay, story, or poem will have you constructing a reading, but then doing something with what you have read—using the selection as a frame through which you can understand (through which you can "read") your own experience, the examples of others, or the ideas and methods of other writers.

You may find that you have to alter your sense of who a writer is and what a writer does as you work on your own writing. Writers are often told that they need to begin with a clear sense of what they want to do and what they want to say. The writing assignments we've written, we believe, give you a sense of what you want (or need) to do. We define a problem for you to work on, and the problem will frame the task for you. You will have to decide where you will go in the texts you have read to find materials to work with, the primary materials that will give you a place to begin as you work on your essay. It would be best, however, if you did not feel that you need to have a clear sense of what you want to say before you begin. You may begin to develop a sense of what you want to say while you are writing—as you begin, for example, to examine how and why Anzaldúa's prose could be said to be difficult to read, and what that difficulty might enable you to say about what Anzaldúa expects of a reader. It may also be the case, however, that the subjects you will be writing about are too big for you to assume that you need to have all the answers or that it is up to you to have the final word or to solve the problems once and for all. When you work on your essays, you should cast yourself in the role of one who is exploring a question, examining what might be said, and speculating on possible rather than certain conclusions. If you consider your responses to be provisional, examples of what might be said by a bright and serious student at this point in time, you will be in a position to learn more, as will those who read what you write. Think of yourself, then, as a writer intent on opening a subject up rather than closing one down.

Let us turn briefly now to the three categories of reading and writing assignments you will find in the book.

Questions for a Second Reading

Immediately following each selection are questions designed to guide your second reading. You may, as we've said, prefer to follow your own instincts as you search for the materials to build your understanding of the essay or story. These questions are meant to assist that process or develop those instincts. Most of the essays and stories in the book are longer and more difficult than those you may be accustomed to reading. They are difficult enough that any reader would have to reread them and work to understand them; these questions are meant to suggest ways of beginning that work.

The second reading questions characteristically ask you to consider the relations between ideas and examples in what you have read or to test specific statements in the essays against your own experience (so that you can get a sense of the author's habit of mind, his or her way of thinking about subjects that are available to you, too). Some turn your attention to what we take to be key terms or concepts, asking you to define these terms by observing how the writer uses them throughout the essay.

These are the questions that seemed "natural" to us; they reflect our habitual way of reading and, we believe, the general habits of mind of the academic community. These questions have no simple answers; you will not find a correct answer hidden somewhere in the selection. In short, they are not the sorts of questions asked on SAT or ACT exams. They are real questions, questions that ask about the basic methods of an essay or about the issues the essay raises. They pose problems for interpretation or indicate sections where, to our minds, there is some interesting work for a reader to do. They are meant to reveal possible ways of reading the text, not to indicate that there is only one correct way, and that we have it.

You may find it useful to take notes as you read through each selection a second time, perhaps in a journal you can keep as a sourcebook for more formal written work.

Assignments for Writing

This book actually offers three different kinds of writing assignments: assignments that ask you to write about a single essay or story, assignments that ask you to read one selection through the frame of another, and longer sequences of assignments that define a project within which three or four of the selections serve as primary sources. All of these assignments serve a dual purpose. Like the second reading questions, they suggest a way for you to reconsider the stories or essays; they give you access from a different perspective. The assignments also encourage you to be a strong reader and actively interpret what you have read. In one way or another, they all invite you to use a story or an essay as a way of framing experience, as a source of terms and methods to enable you to interpret something else—some other text, events and objects around you, or your own memories and experience. The assignment sequences can be found at the end of the book. The others (titled "Assignments for Writing" and "Making Connections") come immediately after each selection.

"Assignments for Writing" ask you to write about a single selection. Although some of these assignments call for you to paraphrase or reconstruct difficult passages, most ask you to interpret what you have read with a specific purpose in mind. The work you are to do is generally of two sorts. For most of the essays, one question asks you to interpret a moment from your own experience through the frame of the essay. This, you will remember, is the use that Rodriguez made of Richard Hoggart's *The Uses of Literacy*.

Other assignments, however, ask you to turn an essay back on itself or to extend the conclusions of the essay by reconsidering the examples the writer has used to make his or her case. Adrienne Rich's essay "When We Dead Awaken: Writing as Re-Vision" is built around a series of poems she wrote at various stages in her career. She says that the development represented by these poems reflects her growing understanding of the problems women in a patriarchal society have in finding a language for their own experience. She presents the poems as examples but offers little detailed discussion of them. One of the assignments, then, asks you to describe the key differences in these poems. It next asks you to comment on the development of her work and to compare your account of that development with hers.

In her essay, Rich also says that writing is "renaming." This is an interesting and, one senses, a potentially powerful term. For it to be useful, however, a reader must put it to work, to see what results when you accept the challenge of the essay and think about writing as renaming. Another assignment, then, asks you to apply this term to one of her poems and to discuss the poem as an act of renaming. The purpose of this assignment is not primarily to develop your skill as a reader of poems but to develop your sense of the method and key terms of Rich's argument.

A note on the writing assignments: When we talk with teachers and students using *Ways of Reading*, we are often asked about the wording of these assignments. The assignments are long. The wording is often unusual, unexpected. The assignments contain many questions, not simply one. The directions seem indirect, confusing. "Why?" we're asked. "How should we work with these?" When we write assignments, our goal is to point students toward a project, to provide a frame for their reading, a motive for writing, a way of asking certain kinds of questions. In that sense, the assignments should not be read as a set of directions to be followed literally. In fact, they are written to resist that reading, to forestall a writer's desire to simplify, to be efficient, to settle for the first clear line toward the finish. We want to provide a context to suggest how readers and writers might take time, be thoughtful. And we want the projects students work on to become their own. We hope to provoke varied responses, to leave the final decisions to the students. So the assignments try to be open and suggestive rather than narrow and direct. We ask lots of questions, but students don't need to answer them all (or any of them) once they begin to write. Our questions are meant to suggest ways of questioning, starting points. "What do you want?" Our own students ask this question. We want writers to make the most they can of what they read, including our questions and assignments.

Making Connections

The connections questions will have you work with two or more readings at a time. These are not so much questions that ask you to compare or contrast the essays or stories as they are directions on how you might use one text as the context for interpreting another. Mary Louise Pratt, for example, in "Arts of the Contact Zone" looks at the work of a South American native, an Inca named Guaman Poma, writing in the seventeenth century to King Philip III of Spain. His work, she argues, can be read as a moment of contact, one in which different cultures and positions of power come together in a single text—in which a conquered person responds to the ways he is represented in the mind and the language of the conqueror. Pratt's reading of Guaman Poma's letter to King Philip, and the terms she uses to describe the way she reads it, provides a powerful context for a reader looking at essays by other writers, like Harriet Jacobs or Gloria Anzaldúa, for whom the "normal" or "standard" language of American culture is difficult, troubling, unsatisfactory, or incomplete. There are, then, assignments that ask you both to extend and to test Pratt's reading through your reading of alternative texts. In another assignment, you are asked to consider different ways of writing "history," writing about the past, by looking at the work of two very different writers: John Edgar Wideman, a fiction writer who turns his hand to "real life" when he writes about his brother and his family, and Patricia Nelson Limerick, a professional historian who writes not only about the American West but also about the writing of the American West, about how the American West has been written into popular culture and the popular imagination.

The purpose of all these assignments is to demonstrate how the work of one author can be used as a frame for reading and interpreting the work of another. This can be exciting work, and it demonstrates a basic principle of liberal arts education: students should be given the opportunity to adopt different points of view, including those of scholars and writers who have helped to shape modern thought. These kinds of assignments give you the chance, even as a <u>novice,</u> to try your hand at the work of professionals.

The Assignment Sequences

The assignment sequences are more broad-ranging versions of the making connections assignments; in the sequences, several reading and writing assignments are linked and directed toward a single goal. They allow you to work on projects that require more time and incorporate more readings than would be possible in a single assignment. And they encourage you to develop your own point of view in concert with those of the professionals who wrote the essays and stories you are reading.

The assignments in a sequence build on one another, each relying on the ones before. A sequence will usually make use of four or five reading selections. The first is used to introduce an area of study or inquiry as well as to establish a frame of reference, a way of thinking about the subject. In the sequence titled "The Aims of Education," you begin with an essay by Paulo Freire. Freire, a Marxist educator, takes a standard account of education (in which students are said to be "given" knowledge by a teacher) and, as he says, "problematizes" that account, opens it up to question, by arguing that such classrooms only reproduce the powerlessness students will face in the larger society. The goal of the sequence is to provide a point for you to work from, one that you can open up to question. Subsequent assignments ask you to develop examples from your own schooling as you work through other accounts of education in, for example, Adrienne Rich's "When We Dead Awaken," Mary Louise Pratt's "Arts of the Contact Zone," or Susan Griffin's "Our Secret."

The sequences allow you to participate in an extended academic project, one in which you take a position, revise it, look at a new example, hear what someone else has to say, revise it again, and see what conclusions you can draw about your subject. These projects always take time— they go through stages and revisions as a writer develops a command over his or her material, pushing against habitual ways of thinking, learning to examine an issue from different angles, rejecting quick conclusions, seeing the power of understanding that comes from repeated effort, and feeling the pleasure writers take when they find their own place in the context of others whose work they admire. This is the closest approximation we can give you of the rhythm and texture of academic life, and we offer our book as an introduction to its characteristic ways of reading, thinking, and writing.

The Readings

GLORIA
ANZALDÚA

*G*LORIA ANZALDÚA *grew up in southwest Texas, the physical and cultural borderland between the United States and Mexico, an area she has called "una herida abierta," an open wound, "where the Third World grates against the first and bleeds." Defining herself as lesbian, feminist, Chicana—a representative of the new* mestiza—*she has dramatically revised the usual narrative of American autobiography. "I am a border woman," she says. "I grew up between two cultures, the Mexican (with a heavy Indian influence) and the Anglo (as a member of a colonized people in our own territory). I have been straddling that* tejas-Mexican *border, and others, all my life." Cultural, physical, spiritual, sexual, linguistic—the borderlands defined by Anzaldúa extend beyond geography. "In fact," she says, "the Borderlands are present where two or more cultures edge each other, where people of different races occupy the same territory, where under, lower, middle, and upper classes touch, where the space between two individuals shrinks with intimacy." In a sense, her writing argues against the concept of an "authentic," unified, homogeneous culture, the pure "Mexican experience," a nostalgia that underlies much of the current interest in "ethnic" literature.*

In the following selections, which represent two chapters from her book Borderlands/La frontera: The New Mestiza *(1987), Anzaldúa mixes genres, moving between poetry and prose, weaving stories with sections that resemble the work of a cultural or political theorist. She tells us a story about her childhood, her*

21

culture, and her people that is at once both myth and history. Her prose, too, is mixed, shifting among Anglo-American English, Castilian Spanish, Tex-Mex, Northern Mexican dialect, and Nahuatl (Aztec), speaking to us in the particular mix that represents her linguistic heritage: "Presently this infant language, this bastard language, Chicano Spanish, is not approved by any society. But we Chicanos no longer feel that we need to beg entrance, that we need always to make the first overture—to translate to Anglos, Mexicans, and Latinos, apology blurting out of our mouths with every step. Today we ask to be met halfway. This book is our invitation to you." The book is an invitation, but not always an easy one. The chapters that follow make a variety of demands on the reader. The shifting styles, genres, and languages can be confusing or disturbing, but this is part of the effect of Anzaldúa's prose, part of the experience you are invited to share.

In a chapter from the book that is not included here, Anzaldúa gives this account of her writing:

> In looking at this book that I'm almost finished writing, I see a mosaic pattern (Aztec-like) emerging, a weaving pattern, thin here, thick there. I see a preoccupation with the deep structure, the underlying structure, with the gesso underpainting that is red earth, black earth. . . . This almost finished product seems an assemblage, a montage, a beaded work with several leitmotifs and with a central core, now appearing, now disappearing in a crazy dance. The whole thing has had a mind of its own, escaping me and insisting on putting together the pieces of its own puzzle with minimal direction from my will.

Beyond her prose, she sees the competing values of more traditionally organized narratives, "art typical of Western European cultures, [which] attempts to manage the energies of its own internal system. . . . It is dedicated to the validation of itself. Its task is to move humans by means of achieving mastery in content, technique, feeling. Western art is always whole and always 'in power.'"

Anzaldúa's prose puts you, as a reader, on the borderland; in a way, it recreates the position of the mestiza. As you read, you will need to meet this prose halfway, generously, learning to read a text that announces its difference.

In addition to Borderlands/La frontera, Anzaldúa has edited Haciendo Caras: Making Face/Making Soul (1990) and coedited an anthology, This Bridge Called My Back: Writings by Radical Women of Color (1983). She has published a book for children, Prietita and the Ghost Woman (1996), which retells traditional Mexican folktales from a feminist perspective. A collection of interviews, Interviews/Entrevistas, was published in 2000.

Entering into the Serpent

Sueño con serpientes, con serpientes del mar,
Con cierto mar, ay de serpientes sueño yo.
Largas, transparentes, en sus barrigas llevan
Lo que puedan arebatarle al amor.
Oh, oh, oh, la mató y aparese una mayor.
Oh, con mucho más infierno en digestión.

I dream of serpents, serpents of the sea,
A certain sea, oh, of serpents I dream.
Long, transparent, in their bellies they carry
All that they can snatch away from love.
Oh, oh, oh, I kill one and a larger one appears.
Oh, with more hellfire burning inside!

— SILVIO RODRÍGUES,
"Sueño con serpientes"[1]

In the predawn orange haze, the sleepy crowing of roosters atop the trees. *No vayas al escusado en lo oscuro.* Don't go to the outhouse at night, Prieta, my mother would say. *No se te vaya a meter algo pour allá.* A snake will crawl into your *nalgas*,[2] make you pregnant. They seek warmth in the cold. *Dicen que las culebras* like to suck *chiches*,[3] can draw milk out of you.

En el escusado in the half-light spiders hang like gliders. Under my bare buttocks and the rough planks the deep yawning tugs at me. I can see my legs fly up to my face as my body falls through the round hole into the sheen of swarming maggots below. Avoiding the snakes under the porch I walk back into the kitchen, step on a big black one slithering across the floor.

Ella tiene su tono[4]

Once we were chopping cotton in the fields of Jesus Maria Ranch. All around us the woods. *Quelite*[5] towered above me, choking the stubby cotton that had outlived the deer's teeth.

I swung *el ázadón*[6] hard. *El quelite* barely shook, showered nettles on my arms and face. When I heard the rattle the world froze.

I barely felt its fangs. Boot got all the *veneno*.[7] My mother came shrieking, swinging her hoe high, cutting the earth, the writhing body.

I stood still, the sun beat down. Afterwards I smelled where fear had been: back of neck, under arms, between my legs, I felt its heat slide down my body. I swallowed the rock it had hardened into.

23

When Mama had gone down the row and was out of sight, I took out my pocketknife. I made an X over each prick. My body followed the blood, fell onto the soft ground. I put my mouth over the red and sucked and spit between the rows of cotton.

I picked up the pieces, placed them end on end. *Culebra de cascabel.*[8] I counted the rattlers: twelve. It would shed no more. I buried the pieces between the rows of cotton.

That night I watched the window sill, watched the moon dry the blood on the tail, dreamed rattler fangs filled my mouth, scales covered my body. In the morning I saw through snake eyes, felt snake blood course through my body. The serpent, *mi tono,* my animal counterpart. I was immune to its venom. Forever immune.

Snakes, *víboras:* since that day I've sought and shunned them. Always when they cross my path, fear and elation flood my body. I know things older than Freud, older than gender. She—that's how I think of *la Víbora,* Snake Woman. Like the ancient Olmecs, I know Earth is a coiled Serpent. Forty years it's taken me to enter into the Serpent, to acknowledge that I have a body, that I am a body and to assimilate the animal body, the animal soul.

Coatlalopeuh, She Who Has Dominion over Serpents

Mi mamagrande Ramona toda su vida mantuvo un altar pequeño en la esquina del comedor. Siempre tenía las velas prendidas. Allí hacía promesas a la Virgen de Guadalupe. My family, like most Chicanos, did not practice Roman Catholicism but a folk Catholicism with many pagan elements. *La Virgen de Guadalupe*'s Indian name is *Coatlalopeuh.* She is the central deity connecting us to our Indian ancestry.

Coatlalopeuh is descended from, or is an aspect of, earlier Mesoamerican fertility and Earth goddesses. The earliest is *Coatlicue,* or "Serpent Skirt." She had a human skull or serpent for a head, a necklace of human hearts, a skirt of twisted serpents, and taloned feet. As creator goddess, she was mother of the celestial deities, and of *Huitzilopochtli* and his sister, *Coyolxauhqui,* She with Golden Bells, Goddess of the Moon, who was decapitated by her brother. Another aspect of *Coatlicue* is *Tonantsi.*[9] The Totonacs, tired of the Aztec human sacrifices to the male god, *Huitzilopochtli,* renewed their reverence for *Tonantsi* who preferred the sacrifice of birds and small animals.[10]

The male-dominated Azteca-Mexica culture drove the powerful female deities underground by giving them monstrous attributes and by substituting male deities in their place, thus splitting the female Self and the female deities. They divided her who had been complete, who possessed both upper (light) and underworld (dark) aspects. *Coatlicue,* the Serpent goddess, and her more sinister aspects, *Tlazolteotl* and *Cihuacoatl,* were "darkened" and disempowered much in the same manner as the Indian *Kali.*

Tonantsi—split from her dark guises, *Coatlicue, Tlazolteotl,* and *Cihuacoatl*—became the good mother. The Nahuas, through ritual and prayer, sought to oblige *Tonantsi* to ensure their health and the growth of their crops. It was she who gave *México* the cactus plant to provide her people with milk and pulque. It was she who defended her children against the wrath of the Christian God by challenging God, her son, to produce mother's milk (as she had done) to prove that his benevolence equalled his disciplinary harshness.[11]

After the Conquest, the Spaniards and their Church continued to split *Tonantsi/Guadalupe.* They desexed *Guadalupe,* taking *Coatlalopeuh,* the serpent/sexuality, out of her. They completed the split begun by the Nahuas by making *la Virgen de Guadalupe/Virgen María* into chaste virgins and *Tlazolteotl/Coatlicue/la Chingada* into *putas;* into the Beauties and the Beasts. They went even further; they made all Indian deities and religious practices the work of the devil.

Thus *Tonantsi* became *Guadalupe,* the chaste protective mother, the defender of the Mexican people.

> *El nueve de diciembre del año 1531*
> *a las cuatro de la madrugada*
> *un pobre indio que se llamaba Juan Diego*
> *iba cruzando el cerro de Tepeyác*
> *cuando oyó un cantó de pájaro.*
> *Alzó al cabeza vío que en la cima del cerro*
> *estaba cubierta con una brillante nube blanca.*
> *Parada en frente del sol*
> *sobre una luna creciente*
> *sostenida por un ángel*
> *estaba una azteca*
> *vestida en ropa de india.*
> *Nuestra Señora María de Coatlalopeuh*
> *se le apareció.*
> *"Juan Diegito, El-que-habla-como-un-águila,"*
> *la Virgen le dijo en el lenguaje azteca.*
> *"Para hacer mi altar este cerro eligo.*
> *Dile a tu gente que yo soy la madre de Dios,*
> *a los indios yo les ayudaré.*
> *Estó se lo contó a Juan Zumarraga*
> *pero el obispo no le creyo.*
> *Juan Diego volvió, lleño su tilma*[12]
> *con rosas de castilla*
> *creciendo milagrosamiente en la nieve.*
> *Se las llevó al obispo,*
> *y cuando abrío su tilma*
> *el retrato de la Virgen*
> *ahí estaba pintado.*

Guadalupe appeared on December 9, 1531, on the spot where the Aztec goddess, *Tonantsi* ("Our Lady Mother"), had been worshiped by the Nahuas and where a temple to her had stood. Speaking Nahua, she told Juan Diego, a poor Indian crossing Tepeyac Hill, whose Indian name was *Cuautlaohuac* and who belonged to the *mazehual* class, the humblest within the Chichimeca tribe, that her name was *María Coatlalopeuh*. *Coatl* is the Nahuatl word for serpent. *Lopeuh* means "the one who has dominion over serpents." I interpret this as "the one who is at one with the beasts." Some spell her name *Coatlaxopeuh* (pronounced *"Cuatlashupe"* in Nahuatl) and say that *"xopeuh"* means "crushed or stepped on with disdain." Some say it means "she who crushed the serpent," with the serpent as the symbol of the indigenous religion, meaning that her religion was to take the place of the Aztec religion.[13] Because *Coatlalopeuh* was homophonous to the Spanish *Guadalupe*, the Spanish identified her with the dark Virgin, *Guadalupe*, patroness of West Central Spain.[14]

From that meeting, Juan Diego walked away with the image of *la Virgen* painted on his cloak. Soon after, Mexico ceased to belong to Spain, and *la Virgen de Guadalupe* began to eclipse all the other male and female religious figures in Mexico, Central America, and parts of the U.S. Southwest. *"Desde entonces para el mexicano ser Guadalupano es algo esencial/*Since then for the Mexican, to be a *Guadalupano* is something essential."[15]

Mi Virgen Morena	My brown virgin
Mi Virgen Ranchera	my country virgin
Eres nuestra Reina	you are our queen
México es tu tierra	Mexico is your land
Y tú su bandera.	and you its flag.
	– "La Virgen Ranchera"[16]

In 1660 the Roman Catholic Church named her Mother of God, considering her synonymous with *la Virgen María;* she became *la Santa Patrona de los mexicanos.* The role of defender (or patron) has traditionally been assigned to male gods. During the Mexican Revolution, Emiliano Zapata and Miguel Hidalgo used her image to move *el pueblo mexicano* toward freedom. During the 1965 grape strike in Delano, California, and in subsequent Chicano farmworkers' marches in Texas and other parts of the Southwest, her image on banners heralded and united the farmworkers. *Pachucos* (zoot suiters) tattoo her image on their bodies. Today, in Texas and Mexico she is more venerated than Jesus or God the Father. In the Lower Rio Grande Valley of south Texas it is *la Virgen de San Juan de los Lagos* (an aspect of *Guadalupe*) that is worshiped by thousands every day at her shrine in San Juan. In Texas she is considered the patron saint of Chicanos. *Cuando Carito, mi hermanito,* was missing in action and, later, wounded in Viet Nam, *mi mamá* got on her knees *y le prometío a Ella que si su hijito volvía vivo* she would crawl on her knees and light novenas in her honor.

• • •

Today, *la Virgen de Guadalupe* is the single most potent religious, political, and cultural image of the Chicano/*mexicano*. She, like my race, is a synthesis of the old world and the new, of the religion and culture of the two races in our psyche, the conquerors and the conquered. She is the symbol of the *mestizo* true to his or her Indian values. *La cultura chicana* identifies with the mother (Indian) rather than with the father (Spanish). Our faith is rooted in indigenous attributes, images, symbols, magic, and myth. Because *Guadalupe* took upon herself the psychological and physical devastation of the conquered and oppressed *indio*, she is our spiritual, political, and psychological symbol. As a symbol of hope and faith, she sustains and insures our survival. The Indian, despite extreme despair, suffering, and near genocide, has survived. To Mexicans on both sides of the border, *Guadalupe* is the symbol of our rebellion against the rich, upper and middle class; against their subjugation of the poor and the *indio.*

Guadalupe unites people of different races, religions, languages: Chicano protestants, American Indians, and whites. "*Nuestra abogada siempre serás*/Our *mediatrix* you will always be." She mediates between the Spanish and the Indian cultures (or three cultures as in the case of *mexicanos* of African or other ancestry) and between Chicanos and the white world. She mediates between humans and the divine, between this reality and the reality of spirit entities. *La Virgen de Guadalupe* is the symbol of ethnic identity and of the tolerance for ambiguity that Chicanos-*mexicanos*, people of mixed race, people who have Indian blood, people who cross cultures, by necessity possess.

La gente Chicana tiene tres madres. All three are mediators: *Guadalupe,* the virgin mother who has not abandoned us, *la Chingada (Malinche),* the raped mother whom we have abandoned, and *la Llorona,* the mother who seeks her lost children and is a combination of the other two.

Ambiguity surrounds the symbols of these three "Our Mothers." *Guadalupe* has been used by the Church to mete out institutionalized oppression: to placate the Indians and *mexicanos* and Chicanos. In part, the true identity of all three has been subverted—*Guadalupe* to make us docile and enduring, *la Chingada* to make us ashamed of our Indian side, and *la Llorona* to make us long-suffering people. This obscuring has encouraged the *virgen/puta* (whore) dichotomy.

Yet we have not all embraced this dichotomy. In the U.S. Southwest, Mexico, Central and South America the *indio* and the *mestizo* continue to worship the old spirit entities (including *Guadalupe*) and their supernatural power, under the guise of Christian saints.[17]

> Las invoco diosas mías, ustedes las indias
> sumergidas en mi carne que son mis sombras.
> Ustedes que persisten mudas en sus cuevas.
> Ustedes Señoras que ahora, como yo,
>   están en desgracia.

For Waging War Is My Cosmic Duty:
The Loss of the Balanced Oppositions and the
Change to Male Dominance

Therefore I decided to leave
The country [Aztlán],
Therefore I have come as one charged with a special duty,
Because I have been given arrows and shields,
For waging war is my duty,
And on my expeditions I
Shall see all the lands,
I shall wait for the people and meet them
In all four quarters and I shall give them
Food to eat and drinks to quench their thirst,
For here I shall unite all the different peoples!
                              — HUITZILOPOCHTLI
                    speaking to the Azteca-Mexica[18]

Before the Aztecs became a militaristic, bureaucratic state where male predatory warfare and conquest were based on patrilineal nobility, the principle of balanced opposition between the sexes existed.[19] The people worshiped the Lord and Lady of Duality, *Ometecuhtli* and *Omecihuatl.* Before the change to male dominance, *Coatlicue,* Lady of the Serpent Skirt, contained and balanced the dualities of male and female, light and dark, life and death.

The changes that led to the loss of the balanced oppositions began when the Azteca, one of the twenty Toltec tribes, made the last pilgrimage from a place called Aztlán. The migration south began about the year A.D. 820. Three hundred years later the advance guard arrived near Tula, the capital of the declining Toltec empire. By the eleventh century, they had joined with the Chichimec tribe of Mexitin (afterwards called Mexica) into one religious and administrative organization within Aztlán, the Aztec territory. The Mexitin, with their tribal god *Tetzauhteotl Huitzilopochtli* (Magnificent Humming Bird on the Left), gained control of the religious system.[20] (In some stories *Huitzilopochtli* killed his sister, the moon goddess *Malinalxoch,* who used her supernatural power over animals to control the tribe rather than wage war.)

Huitzilopochtli assigned the Azteca-Mexica the task of keeping the human race (the present cosmic age called the Fifth Sun, *El Quinto Sol*) alive. They were to guarantee the harmonious preservation of the human race by unifying all the people on earth into one social, religious, and administrative organ. The Aztec people considered themselves in charge of regulating all earthly matters.[21] Their instrument: controlled or regulated war to gain and exercise power.

After one hundred years in the central plateau, the Azteca-Mexica went to Chapultepec, where they settled in 1248 (the present site of the park on the outskirts of Mexico City). There, in 1345, the Azteca-Mexica chose the site of their capital, Tenochtitlan.[22] By 1428, they dominated the Central Mexican lake area.

The Aztec ruler, *Itzcoatl*, destroyed all the painted documents (books called codices) and rewrote a mythology that validated the wars of conquest and thus continued the shift from a tribe based on clans to one based on classes. From 1429 to 1440, the Aztecs emerged as a militaristic state that preyed on neighboring tribes for tribute and captives.[23] The "wars of flowers" were encounters between local armies with a fixed number of warriors, operating within the Aztec World, and, according to set rules, fighting ritual battles at fixed times and on predetermined battlefields. The religious purpose of these wars was to procure prisoners of war who could be sacrificed to the deities of the capturing party. For if one "fed" the gods, the human race would be saved from total extinction. The social purpose was to enable males of noble families and warriors of low descent to win honor, fame, and administrative offices, and to prevent social and cultural decadence of the elite. The Aztec people were free to have their own religious faith, provided it did not conflict too much with the three fundamental principles of state ideology: to fulfill the special duty set forth by *Huitzilopochtli* of unifying all peoples, to participate in the wars of flowers, and to bring ritual offerings and do penance for the purpose of preventing decadence.[24]

Matrilineal descent characterized the Toltecs and perhaps early Aztec society. Women possessed property, and were curers as well as priestesses. According to the codices, women in former times had the supreme power in Tula, and in the beginning of the Aztec dynasty, the royal blood ran through the female line. A council of elders of the Calpul headed by a supreme leader, or *tlactlo,* called the father and mother of the people, governed the tribe. The supreme leader's vice-emperor occupied the position of "Snake Woman" or *Cihuacoatl,* a goddess.[25] Although the high posts were occupied by men, the terms referred to females, evidence of the exalted role of women before the Aztec nation became centralized. The final break with the democratic Calpul came when the four Aztec lords of royal lineage picked the king's successor from his siblings or male descendants.[26]

La Llorona's wailing in the night for her lost children has an echoing note in the wailing or mourning rites performed by women as they bid their sons, brothers, and husbands good-bye before they left to go to the "flowery wars." Wailing is the Indian, Mexican, and Chicana woman's feeble protest when she has no other recourse. These collective wailing rites may have been a sign of resistance in a society which glorified the warrior and war and for whom the women of the conquered tribes were booty.[27]

In defiance of the Aztec rulers, the *macehuales* (the common people) continued to worship fertility, nourishment, and agricultural female deities, those of crops and rain. They venerated *Chalchiuhtlicue* (goddess of sweet or inland water), *Chicomecoatl* (goddess of food), and *Huixtocihuatl* (goddess of salt).

Nevertheless, it took less than three centuries for Aztec society to change from the balanced duality of their earlier times and from the egalitarian traditions of a wandering tribe to those of a predatory state. The nobility kept the tribute, the commoner got nothing, resulting in a class split. The conquered tribes hated the Aztecs because of the rape of their women and the heavy taxes levied on them. The *Tlaxcalans* were the Aztec's bitter enemies and it was they who helped the Spanish defeat the Aztec rulers, who were by this time so unpopular with their own common people that they could not even mobilize the populace to defend the city. Thus the Aztec nation fell not because *Malinali (la Chingada)* interpreted for and slept with Cortés, but because the ruling elite had subverted the solidarity between men and women and between noble and commoner.[28]

Sueño con serpientes

Coatl.   In pre-Columbian America the most notable symbol was the serpent. The Olmecs associated womanhood with the Serpent's mouth which was guarded by rows of dangerous teeth, a sort of *vagina dentate.* They considered it the most sacred place on earth, a place of refuge, the creative womb from which all things were born and to which all things returned. Snake people had holes, entrances to the body of the Earth Serpent; they followed the Serpent's way, identified with the Serpent deity, with the mouth, both the eater and the eaten. The destiny of humankind is to be devoured by the Serpent.[29]

Dead,
the doctor by the operating table said.
I passed between the two fangs,
the flickering tongue.
Having come through the mouth of the serpent,
swallowed,
I found myself suddenly in the dark,
sliding down a smooth wet surface
down down into an even darker darkness.
Having crossed the portal, the raised hinged mouth,
having entered the serpent's belly,
now there was no looking back, no going back.

Why do I cast no shadow?
Are there lights from all sides shining on me?
Ahead, ahead,
curled up inside the serpent's coils,
the damp breath of death on my face.
I knew at that instant; something must change
or I'd die.
Algo tenía que cambiar.

After each of my four bouts with death I'd catch glimpses of an otherworld Serpent. Once, in my bedroom, I saw a cobra the size of the room, her hood expanding over me. When I blinked she was gone. I realized she was, in my psyche, the mental picture and symbol of the instinctual in its collective impersonal, prehuman. She, the symbol of the dark sexual drive, the chthonic (underworld), the feminine, the serpentine movement of sexuality, of creativity, the basis of all energy and life.

The Presences

> She appeared in white, garbed in white,
> standing white, pure white.
> — BERNARDINO DE SAHAGÚN[30]

On the gulf where I was raised, *en el Valle del Río Grande* in South Texas—that triangular piece of land wedged between the river *y el golfo* which serves as the Texas-U.S./Mexican border—is a Mexican *pueblito* called Hargill (at one time in the history of this one-grocery-store, two-service-stations town there were thirteen churches and thirteen *cantinas*). Down the road, a little ways from our house, was a deserted church. It was known among the *mexicanos* that if you walked down the road late at night you would see a woman dressed in white floating about, peering out the church window. She would follow those who had done something bad or who were afraid. *Los mexicanos* called her *la Jila*. Some thought she was *la Llorona*. She was, I think, *Cihuacoatl*, Serpent Woman, ancient Aztec goddess of the earth, of war and birth, patron of midwives, and antecedent of *la Llorona*. Covered with chalk, *Cihuacoatl* wears a white dress with a decoration half red and half black. Her hair forms two little horns (which the Aztecs depicted as knives) crossed on her forehead. The lower part of her face is a bare jawbone, signifying death. On her back she carries a cradle, the knife of sacrifice swaddled as if it were her papoose, her child.[31] Like *la Llorona*, *Cihuacoatl* howls and weeps in the night, screams as if demented. She brings mental depression and sorrow. Long before it takes place, she is the first to predict something is to happen.

Back then, I, an unbeliever, scoffed at these Mexican superstitions as I was taught in Anglo school. Now, I wonder if this story and similar ones were the culture's attempts to "protect" members of the family, especially girls, from "wandering." Stories of the devil luring young girls away and having his way with them discouraged us from going out. There's an ancient Indian tradition of burying the umbilical cord of an infant girl under the house so she will never stray from it and her domestic role.

> *A mis ancas caen los cueros de culebra,*
> *cuatro veces por año los arrastro,*
> *me tropiezo y me caigo*
> *y cada vez que miro una culebra le pregunto*
> *¿Qué traes conmigo?*

Four years ago a red snake crossed my path as I walked through the woods. The direction of its movement, its pace, its colors, the "mood" of the trees and the wind and the snake—they all "spoke" to me, told me things. I look for omens everywhere, everywhere catch glimpses of the patterns and cycles of my life. Stones "speak" to Luisah Teish, a Santera; trees whisper their secrets to Chrystos, a Native American. I remember listening to the voices of the wind as a child and understanding its messages. *Los espíritus* that ride the back of the south wind. I remember their exhalation blowing in through the slits in the door during those hot Texas afternoons. A gust of wind raising the linoleum under my feet, buffeting the house. Everything trembling.

We're not supposed to remember such otherworldly events. We're supposed to ignore, forget, kill those fleeting images of the soul's presence and of the spirit's presence. We've been taught that the spirit is outside our bodies or above our heads somewhere up in the sky with God. We're supposed to forget that every cell in our bodies, every bone and bird and worm has spirit in it.

Like many Indians and Mexicans, I did not deem my psychic experiences real. I denied their occurrences and let my inner senses atrophy. I allowed white rationality to tell me that the existence of the "other world" was mere pagan superstition. I accepted their reality, the "official" reality of the rational, reasoning mode which is connected with external reality, the upper world, and is considered the most developed consciousness—the consciousness of duality.

The other mode of consciousness facilitates images from the soul and the unconscious through dreams and the imagination. Its work is labeled "fiction," make-believe, wish-fulfillment. White anthropologists claim that Indians have "primitive" and therefore deficient minds, that we cannot think in the higher mode of consciousness—rationality. They are fascinated by what they call the "magical" mind, the "savage" mind, the *participation mystique* of the mind that says the world of the imagination—the world of the soul—and of the spirit is just as real as physical reality.[32] In trying to become "objective," Western culture made "objects" of things and people when it distanced itself from them, thereby losing "touch" with them. This dichotomy is the root of all violence.

Not only was the brain split into two functions but so was reality. Thus people who inhabit both realities are forced to live in the interface between the two, forced to become adept at switching modes. Such is the case with the *india* and the *mestiza.*

Institutionalized religion fears trafficking with the spirit world and stigmatizes it as witchcraft. It has strict taboos against this kind of inner knowledge. It fears what Jung calls the Shadow, the unsavory aspects of ourselves. But even more it fears the suprahuman, the god in ourselves.

"The purpose of any established religion . . . is to glorify, sanction, and bless with a superpersonal meaning all personal and interpersonal activities. This occurs through the 'sacraments,' and indeed through most religious rites."[33] But it sanctions only its own sacraments and rites. Voodoo, Santeria, Shamanism, and other native religions are called cults and their beliefs are called mythologies. In my own life, the Catholic Church fails to give meaning to my daily acts, to my continuing encounters with the "other world." It and other institutionalized religions impoverish all life, beauty, pleasure.

The Catholic and Protestant religions encourage fear and distrust of life and of the body; they encourage a split between the body and the spirit and totally ignore the soul; they encourage us to kill off parts of our-selves. We are taught that the body is an ignorant animal; intelligence dwells only in the head. But the body is smart. It does not discern between external stimuli and stimuli from the imagination. It reacts equally viscer-ally to events from the imagination as it does to "real" events.

So I grew up in the interface trying not to give countenance to *el mal aigre,*[34] evil nonhuman, noncorporeal entities riding the wind, that could come in through the window, through my nose with my breath. I was not supposed to believe in *susto,* a sudden shock or fall that frightens the soul out of the body. And growing up between such opposing spiritualities how could I reconcile the two, the pagan and the Christian?

No matter to what use my people put the supranatural world, it is evident to me now that the spirit world, whose existence the whites are so adamant in denying, does in fact exist. This very minute I sense the presence of the spirits of my ancestors in my room. And I think *la Jila* is *Cihuacoatl,* Snake Woman; she is *la Llorona,* Daughter of Night, trav-eling the dark terrains of the unknown searching for the lost parts of herself. I remember *la Jila* following me once, remember her eerie lament. I'd like to think that she was crying for her lost children, *los* Chicanos/*mexicanos.*

La facultad

La facultad is the capacity to see in surface phenomena the meaning of deeper realities, to see the deep structure below the surface. It is an instant "sensing," a quick perception arrived at without conscious reasoning. It is an acute awareness mediated by the part of the psyche that does not speak, that communicates in images and symbols which are the faces of feelings, that is, behind which feelings reside/hide. The one possessing this sensitivity is excruciatingly alive to the world.

Those who are pushed out of the tribe for being different are likely to become more sensitized (when not brutalized into insensitivity). Those who do not feel psychologically or physically safe in the world are more apt to develop this sense. Those who are pounced on the most have it the strongest—the females, the homosexuals of all races, the darkskinned, the outcast, the persecuted, the marginalized, the foreign.

When we're up against the wall, when we have all sorts of oppressions coming at us, we are forced to develop this faculty so that we'll know when the next person is going to slap us or lock us away. We'll sense the rapist when he's five blocks down the street. Pain makes us acutely anx-ious to avoid more of it, so we hone that radar. It's a kind of survival tactic that people, caught between the worlds, unknowingly cultivate. It is latent in all of us.

I walk into a house and I know whether it is empty or occupied. I feel the lingering charge in the air of a recent fight or lovemaking or depression. I sense the emotions someone near is emitting—whether friendly or threatening. Hate and fear—the more intense the emotion, the greater my reception of it. I feel a tingling on my skin when someone is staring at me or thinking about me. I can tell how others feel by the way they smell, where others are by the air pressure on my skin. I can spot the love or greed or generosity lodged in the tissues of another. Often I sense the direction of and my distance from people or objects—in the dark, or with my eyes closed, without looking. It must be a vestige of a proximity sense, a sixth sense that's lain dormant from long-ago times.

Fear develops the proximity sense aspect of *la facultad*. But there is a deeper sensing that is another aspect of this faculty. It is anything that breaks into one's everyday mode of perception, that causes a break in one's defenses and resistance, anything that takes one from one's habitual grounding, causes the depths to open up, causes a shift in perception. This shift in perception deepens the way we see concrete objects and people; the senses become so acute and piercing that we can see through things, view events in depth, a piercing that reaches the underworld (the realm of the soul). As we plunge vertically, the break, with its accompanying new seeing, makes us pay attention to the soul, and we are thus carried into awareness—an experiencing of soul (Self).

We lose something in this mode of initiation, something is taken from us: our innocence, our unknowing ways, our safe and easy ignorance. There is a prejudice and a fear of the dark, chthonic (underworld), material such as depression, illness, death, and the violations that can bring on this break. Confronting anything that tears the fabric of our everyday mode of consciousness and that thrusts us into a less literal and more psychic sense of reality increases awareness and *la facultad*.

NOTES

[1] From the song *"Sueño con serpientes"* by Silvio Rodrígues, from the album *Días y flores.* Translated by Barbara Dane with the collaboration of Rina Benmauor and Juan Flores.

[2] *Nalgas:* vagina, buttocks.

[3] *Dicen que las culebras like to suck chiches:* they say snakes like to suck women's teats.

[4] *Ella tiene su tono:* she has supernatural power from her animal soul, the *tono.*

[5] *Quelite:* weed.

[6] *Ázadón:* hoe.

[7] *Veneno:* venom, poison.

[8] *Culebra de cascabel:* rattlesnake.

[9] In some Nahuatl dialects *Tonantsi* is called *Tonatzin,* literally "Our Holy Mother." *"Tonan* was a name given in Nahuatl to several mountains, these being the congelations of the Earth Mother at spots convenient for her worship." The Mexica considered the mountain mass southwest of Chapultepec to be their mother. Burr Cartwright Brundage, *The Fifth Sun: Aztec Gods, Aztec World* (Austin, TX: University of Texas Press, 1979), 154, 242.

[10] Ena Campbell, "The Virgin of Guadalupe and the Female Self-image: A Mexican Case History," *Mother Worship: Themes and Variations,* James J. Preston, ed. (Chapel Hill, NC: University of North Carolina Press, 1982), 22.

[11] Alan R. Sandstrom, "The Tonantsi Cult of the Eastern Nahuas," *Mother Worship: Themes and Variations,* James J. Preston, ed.

[12] *Una tela tejida con asperas fibras de agave:* it is an oblong cloth that hangs over the back and ties together across the shoulders.

[13] Andres Gonzales Guerrero, Jr., *The Significance of Nuestra Señora de Guadalupe and La Raza Cósmica in the Development of a Chicano Theology of Liberation* (Ann Arbor, MI: University Microfilms International, 1984), 122.

[14] *Algunos dicen que Guadalupe es una palabra derivada del lenguaje arabe que significa "Río Oculto."* Tomie de Paola, *The Lady of Guadalupe* (New York, NY: Holiday House, 1980), 44.

[15] *"Desde el cielo una hermosa mañana,"* from *Propios de la misa de Nuestra Señora de Guadalupe,* Guerrero, 124.

[16] From *"La Virgen Ranchera,"* Guerrero, 127.

[17] *La Virgin María* is often equated with the Aztec *Teleoinam,* the Maya *Ixchel,* the Inca *Mamacocha,* and the Yoruba *Yemayá.*

[18] Geoffrey Parrinder, ed., *World Religions: From Ancient History to the Present* (New York, NY: Facts on File Publications, 1971), 72.

[19] Lévi-Strauss's paradigm which opposes nature to culture and female to male has no such validity in the early history of our Indian forebears. June Nash, "The Aztecs and the Ideology of Male Dominance," *Signs* (Winter, 1978), 349.

[20] Parrinder, 72.

[21] Parrinder, 77.

[22] Nash, 352.

[23] Nash, 350, 355.

[24] Parrinder, 355.

[25] Jacques Soustelle, *The Daily Life of the Aztecs on the Eve of the Spanish Conquest* (New York, NY: Macmillan Publishing Company, 1962). Soustelle and most other historians got their information from the Franciscan father, Bernardino de Sahagún, chief chronicler of Indian religious life.

[26] Nash, 252–253.

[27] Nash, 358.

[28] Nash, 361–362.

[29] Karl W. Luckert, *Olmec Religion: A Key to Middle America and Beyond* (Norman, OK: University of Oklahoma Press, 1976), 68, 69, 87, 109.

[30] Bernardino de Sahagún, *General History of the Things of New Spain* (Florentine Codex), Vol. I Revised, trans. Arthur Anderson and Charles Dibble (Sante Fe, NM: School of American Research, 1950), 11.

[31] The Aztecs muted Snake Woman's patronage of childbirth and vegetation by placing a sacrificial knife in the empty cradle she carried on her back (signifying a child who died in childbirth), thereby making her a devourer of sacrificial victims. Snake Woman had the ability to change herself into a serpent or into a lovely young woman to entice young men, who withered away and died after intercourse with her. She was known as a witch and a shape-shifter. Brundage, 168–171.

[32] Anthropologist Lucien Levy-Bruhl coined the word *participation mystique.* According to Jung, "It denotes a peculiar kind of psychological connection . . . [in which] the subject cannot clearly distinguish himself from the object but is bound to it by a direct relationship which amounts to partial identity." Carl Jung, "Definitions," in *Psychological Types, The Collected Works of C. G. Jung,* Vol. 6 (Princeton, NJ: Princeton University Press, 1953), par. 781.

[33] I have lost the source of this quote. If anyone knows what it is, please let the publisher know. [Author's note]

[34] Some *mexicanos* and Chicanos distinguish between *aire,* air, and *mal aigre,* the evil spirits which reside in the air.

How to Tame a Wild Tongue

"We're going to have to control your tongue," the dentist says, pulling out all the metal from my mouth. Silver bits plop and tinkle into the basin. My mouth is a motherlode.

The dentist is cleaning out my roots. I get a whiff of the stench when I gasp. "I can't cap that tooth yet, you're still draining," he says.

"We're going to have to do something about your tongue," I hear the anger rising in his voice. My tongue keeps pushing out the wads of cotton, pushing back the drills, the long thin needles. "I've never seen anything as strong or as stubborn," he says. And I think, how do you tame a wild tongue, train it to be quiet, how do you bridle and saddle it? How do you make it lie down?

> Who is to say that robbing a people of
> its language is less violent than war?
> — RAY GWYN SMITH[1]

I remember being caught speaking Spanish at recess—that was good for three licks on the knuckles with a sharp ruler. I remember being sent to the corner of the classroom for "talking back" to the Anglo teacher when all I was trying to do was tell her how to pronounce my name. "If you want to be American, speak 'American.' If you don't like it, go back to Mexico where you belong."

"I want you to speak English. *Pa' hallar buen trabajo tienes que saber hablar el inglés bien. Qué vale toda tu educación si todavía hablas inglés con un 'accent,'*" my mother would say, mortified that I spoke English like a Mexican. At Pan American University, I and all Chicano students were required to take two speech classes. Their purpose: to get rid of our accents.

Attacks on one's form of expression with the intent to censor are a violation of the First Amendment. *El Anglo con cara de inocente nos arrancó la lengua.* Wild tongues can't be tamed, they can only be cut out.

Overcoming the Tradition of Silence

Ahogadas, escupimos el oscuro.
Peleando con nuestra propia sombra
el silencio nos sepulta.

En boca cerrada no entran moscas. "Flies don't enter a closed mouth" is a saying I kept hearing when I was a child. *Ser habladora* was to be a gossip and a liar, to talk too much. *Muchachitas bien criadas,* well-bred girls don't answer back. *Es una falta de respeto* to talk back to one's mother or father. I remember one of the sins I'd recite to the priest in the confession box the few times I went to confession: talking back to my mother, *hablar pa' 'tras, repelar. Hociocona, repelona, chismosa,* having a big mouth, questic rying tales are all signs of being *mal criada.* In my culture th words that are derogatory if applied to women—I've never he applied to men.

The first time I heard two women, a Puerto Rican and a Cuban, say the word *"nosotras,"* I was shocked. I had not known the word existed. Chicanas use *nosotros* whether we're male or female. We are robbed of our female being by the masculine plural. Language is a male discourse.

> And our tongues have become
> dry   the wilderness has
> dried out our tongues   and
> we have forgotten speech.
> — IRENA KLEPFISZ[2]

Even our own people, other Spanish speakers *nos quieren poner candados en la boca.* They would hold us back with their bag of *reglas de academia.*

Oyé como ladra:
el lenguaje de la frontera

Quien tiene boca se equivoca.
– Mexican saying

"*Pocho,* cultural traitor, you're speaking the oppressor's language by speaking English, you're ruining the Spanish language," I have been accused by various Latinos and Latinas. Chicano Spanish is considered by the purist and by most Latinos deficient, a mutilation of Spanish.

But Chicano Spanish is a border tongue which developed naturally. Change, *evolución, enriquecimiento de palabras nuevas por invención o adopción* have created variants of Chicano Spanish, *un nuevo lenguaje. Un lenguaje que corresponde a un modo de vivir.* Chicano Spanish is not incorrect, it is a living language.

For a people who are neither Spanish nor live in a country in which Spanish is the first language; for a people who live in a country in which English is the reigning tongue but who are not Anglo; for a people who cannot entirely identify with either standard (formal, Castilian) Spanish nor standard English, what recourse is left to them but to create their own language? A language which they can connect their identity to, one capable of communicating the realities and values true to themselves—a language with terms that are neither *español ni inglés,* but both. We speak a patois, a forked tongue, a variation of two languages.

Chicano Spanish sprang out of the Chicanos' need to identify ourselves as a distinct people. We needed a language with which we could communicate with ourselves, a secret language. For some of us, language is a homeland closer than the Southwest—for many Chicanos today

live in the Midwest and the East. And because we are a complex, heterogeneous people, we speak many languages. Some of the languages we
speak are

1. Standard English
2. Working-class and slang English
3. Standard Spanish
4. Standard Mexican Spanish
5. North Mexican Spanish dialect
6. Chicano Spanish (Texas, New Mexico, Arizona, and California have
   regional variations)
7. Tex-Mex
8. *Pachuco* (called *caló*)

My "home" tongues are the languages I speak with my sister and
brothers, with my friends. They are the last five listed, with 6 and 7 being
closest to my heart. From school, the media, and job situations, I've picked
up standard and working-class English. From Mamagrande Locha and
from reading Spanish and Mexican literature, I've picked up Standard
Spanish and Standard Mexican Spanish. From *los recién llegados*, Mexican
immigrants, and *braceros*, I learned the North Mexican dialect. With Mexicans I'll try to speak either Standard Mexican Spanish or the North Mexican dialect. From my parents and Chicanos living in the Valley, I picked
up Chicano Texas Spanish, and I speak it with my mom, younger brother
(who married a Mexican and who rarely mixes Spanish with English),
aunts, and older relatives.

With Chicanas from *Nuevo México* or *Arizona* I will speak Chicano
Spanish a little, but often they don't understand what I'm saying. With
most California Chicanas I speak entirely in English (unless I forget).
When I first moved to San Francisco, I'd rattle off something in Spanish,
unintentionally embarrassing them. Often it is only with another Chicana
tejano that I can talk freely.

Words distorted by English are known as anglicisms or *pochismos*. The
pocho is an anglicized Mexican or American of Mexican origin who speaks
Spanish with an accent characteristic of North Americans and who dis-
torts and reconstructs the language according to the influence of English.[3]
Tex-Mex, or Spanglish, comes most naturally to me. I may switch back
and forth from English to Spanish in the same sentence or in the same
word. With my sister and my brother Nune and with Chicano *tejano* contemporaries I speak in Tex-Mex.

From kids and people my own age I picked up *Pachuco*. *Pachuco* (the
language of the zoot suiters) is a language of rebellion, both against Standard Spanish and Standard English. It is a secret language. Adults of the
culture and outsiders cannot understand it. It is made up of slang words
from both English and Spanish. *Ruca* means girl or woman, *vato* means

guy or dude, *chale* means no, *simón* means yes, *churro* is sure, talk is *periquiar*, *pigionear* means petting, *que gacho* means how nerdy, *ponte águila* means watch out, death is called *la pelona*. Through lack of practice and not having others who can speak it, I've lost most of the *Pachuco* tongue.

Chicano Spanish

Chicanos, after 250 years of Spanish/Anglo colonization, have developed significant differences in the Spanish we speak. We collapse two adjacent vowels into a single syllable and sometimes shift the stress in certain words such as *maíz/maiz, cohete/cuete*. We leave out certain consonants when they appear between vowels: *lado/lao, mojado/mojao*. Chicanos from South Texas pronounce *f* as *j* as in *jue (fue)*. Chicanos use "archaisms," words that are no longer in the Spanish language, words that have been evolved out. We say *semos, truje, haiga, ansina,* and *naiden*. We retain the "archaic" *j*, as in *jalar*, that derives from an earlier *h* (the French *halar* or the Germanic *halon* which was lost to standard Spanish in the sixteenth century), but which is still found in several regional dialects such as the one spoken in South Texas. (Due to geography, Chicanos from the Valley of South Texas were cut off linguistically from other Spanish speakers. We tend to use words that the Spaniards brought over from Medieval Spain. The majority of the Spanish colonizers in Mexico and the Southwest came from Extremadura—Hernán Cortés was one of them—and Andalucía. Andalucians pronounce *ll* like a *y*, and their *d*'s tend to be absorbed by adjacent vowels: *tirado* becomes *tirao*. They brought *el lenguaje popular, dialectos y regionalismos*.)[4]

Chicanos and other Spanish speakers also shift *ll* to *y* and *z* to *s*.[5] We leave out initial syllables, saying *tar* for *estar*, *toy* for *estoy*, *hora* for *ahora* (*cubanos* and *puertorriqueños* also leave out initial letters of some words). We also leave out the final syllable such as *pa* for *para*. The intervocalic *y*, the *ll* as in *tortilla, ella, botella*, gets replaced by *tortia* or *toriya, ea, botea*. We add an additional syllable at the beginning of certain words: *atocar* for *tocar, agastar* for *gastar*. Sometimes we'll say *lavaste las vacijas*, other times *lavates* (substituting the *ates* verb endings for the *aste*).

We use anglicisms, words borrowed from English: *bola* from ball, *carpeta* from carpet, *máchina de lavar* (instead of *lavadora*) from washing machine. Tex-Mex argot, created by adding a Spanish sound at the beginning or end of an English word such as *cookiar* for cook, *watchar* for watch, *parkiar* for park, and *rapiar* for rape, is the result of the pressures on Spanish speakers to adapt to English.

We don't use the word *vosotros/as* or its accompanying verb form. We don't say *claro* (to mean yes), *imagínate*, or *me emociona*, unless we picked up Spanish from Latinas, out of a book, or in a classroom. Other Spanish-speaking groups are going through the same, or similar, development in their Spanish.

Linguistic Terrorism

Deslenguadas. Somos los del español deficiente. We are your linguistic nightmare, your linguistic aberration, your linguistic *mestisaje*, the subject of your *burla.* Because we speak with tongues of fire we are culturally crucified. Racially, culturally, and linguistically *somos huérfanos*—we speak an orphan tongue.

Chicanas who grew up speaking Chicano Spanish have internalized the belief that we speak poor Spanish. It is illegitimate, a bastard language. And because we internalize how our language has been used against us by the dominant culture, we use our language differences against each other.

Chicana feminists often skirt around each other with suspicion and hesitation. For the longest time I couldn't figure it out. Then it dawned on me. To be close to another Chicana is like looking into the mirror. We are afraid of what we'll see there. *Pena.* Shame. Low estimation of self. In childhood we are told that our language is wrong. Repeated attacks on our native tongue diminish our sense of self. The attacks continue throughout our lives.

Chicanas feel uncomfortable talking in Spanish to Latinas, afraid of their censure. Their language was not outlawed in their countries. They had a whole lifetime of being immersed in their native tongue; generations, centuries in which Spanish was a first language, taught in school, heard on radio and TV, and read in the newspaper.

If a person, Chicana or Latina, has a low estimation of my native tongue, she also has a low estimation of me. Often with *mexicanas y latinas* we'll speak English as a neutral language. Even among Chicanas we tend to speak English at parties or conferences. Yet, at the same time, we're afraid the other will think we're *agringadas* because we don't speak Chicano Spanish. We oppress each other trying to out-Chicano each other, vying to be the "real" Chicanas, to speak like Chicanos. There is no one Chicano language just as there is no one Chicano experience. A monolingual Chicana whose first language is English or Spanish is just as much a Chicana as one who speaks several variants of Spanish. A Chicana from Michigan or Chicago or Detroit is just as much a Chicana as one from the Southwest. Chicano Spanish is as diverse linguistically as it is regionally.

By the end of this century, Spanish speakers will comprise the biggest minority group in the United States, a country where students in high schools and colleges are encouraged to take French classes because French is considered more "cultured." But for a language to remain alive it must be used.[6] By the end of this century English, and not Spanish, will be the mother tongue of most Chicanos and Latinos.

So, if you want to really hurt me, talk badly about my language. Ethnic identity is twin skin to linguistic identity—I am my language. Until I can take pride in my language, I cannot take pride in myself. Until I can accept as legitimate Chicano Texas Spanish, Tex-Mex, and all the other languages I speak, I cannot accept the legitimacy of myself. Until I am free to write bilingually and to switch codes without having always to translate, while I still have to speak English or Spanish when I would rather speak Spanglish, and as long as I have to accommodate the English speaker rather than having them accommodate me, my tongue will be illegitimate.

I will no longer be made to feel ashamed of existing. I will have my voice: Indian, Spanish, white. I will have my serpent's tongue—my woman's voice, my sexual voice, my poet's voice. I will overcome the tradition of silence.

> My fingers
> move sly against your palm
> Like women everywhere, we speak in code. . . .
> — MELANIE KAYE/KANTROWITZ[7]

"Vistas," corridos, y comida: My Native Tongue

In the 1960s, I read my first Chicano novel. It was *City of Night* by John Rechy, a gay Texan, son of a Scottish father and a Mexican mother. For days I walked around in stunned amazement that a Chicano could write and could get published. When I read *I Am Joaquín*[8] I was surprised to see a bilingual book by a Chicano in print. When I saw poetry written in Tex-Mex for the first time, a feeling of pure joy flashed through me. I felt like we really existed as a people. In 1971, when I started teaching High School English to Chicano students, I tried to supplement the required texts with works by Chicanos, only to be reprimanded and forbidden to do so by the principal. He claimed that I was supposed to teach "American" and English literature. At the risk of being fired, I swore my students to secrecy and slipped in Chicano short stories, poems, a play. In graduate school, while working toward a Ph.D., I had to "argue" with one adviser after the other, semester after semester, before I was allowed to make Chicano literature an area of focus.

Even before I read books by Chicanos or Mexicans, it was the Mexican movies I saw at the drive-in—the Thursday night special of $1.00 a carload—that gave me a sense of belonging. *"Vámonos a las vistas,"* my mother would call out and we'd all—grandmother, brothers, sister, and cousins—squeeze into the car. We'd wolf down cheese and bologna white bread sandwiches while watching Pedro Infante in melodramatic tearjerkers like *Nosotros los pobres,* the first "real" Mexican movie (that was not an imitation of European movies). I remember seeing *Cuando los hijos se van* and surmising that all Mexican movies played up the love a mother has for her children and what ungrateful sons and daughters suffer when they are not devoted to their mothers. I remember the singing-type "westerns" of Jorge Negrete and Miquel Aceves Mejía. When watching Mexican movies, I felt a sense of homecoming as well as alienation. People who were to amount to something didn't go to Mexican movies, or *bailes*, or tune their radios to *bolero, rancherita,* and *corrido* music.

The whole time I was growing up, there was *norteño* music sometimes called North Mexican border music, or Tex-Mex music, or Chicano music, or *cantina* (bar) music. I grew up listening to *conjuntos*, three- or four-piece bands made up of folk musicians playing guitar, *bajo sexto*, drums, and button accordion, which Chicanos had borrowed from the German immigrants who had come to Central Texas and Mexico to farm and build breweries. In the Rio Grande Valley, Steven Jordan and Little Joe Hernández were popular, and Flaco Jiménez was the accordion king. The rhythms of Tex-Mex music are those of the polka, also adapted from the Germans, who in turn had borrowed the polka from the Czechs and Bohemians.

I remember the hot, sultry evenings when *corridos*—song of love and death on the Texas-Mexican borderlands—reverberated out of cheap amplifiers from the local *cantinas* and wafted in through my bedroom window.

Corridos first became widely used along the South Texas/Mexican border during the early conflict between Chicanos and Anglos. The *corridos* are usually about Mexican heroes who do valiant deeds against the Anglo oppressors. Pancho Villa's song, *"La cucaracha,"* is the most famous one. *Corridos* of John F. Kennedy and his death are still very popular in the Valley. Older Chicanos remember Lydia Mendoza, one of the great border *corrido* singers who was called *la Gloria de Tejas.* Her *"El tango negro,"* sung during the Great Depression, made her a singer of the people. The ever-present *corridos* narrated one hundred years of border history, bringing news of events as well as entertaining. These folk musicians and folk songs are our chief cultural mythmakers, and they made our hard lives seem bearable.

I grew up feeling ambivalent about our music. Country-western and rock-and-roll had more status. In the fifties and sixties, for the slightly educated and *agringado* Chicanos, there existed a sense of shame at being caught listening to our music. Yet I couldn't stop my feet from thumping to the music, could not stop humming the words, nor hide from myself the exhilaration I felt when I heard it.

There are more subtle ways that we internalize identification, especially in the forms of images and emotions. For me food and certain smells are tied to my identity, to my homeland. Woodsmoke curling up to an immense blue sky; woodsmoke perfuming my grandmother's clothes, her skin. The stench of cow manure and the yellow patches on the ground; the crack of a .22 rifle and the reek of cordite. Homemade white cheese sizzling in a pan, melting inside a folded *tortilla.* My sister Hilda's hot, spicy *menudo, chile colorado* making it deep red, pieces of *panza* and hominy floating on top. My brother Carito barbequing *fajitas* in the backyard. Even now and 3,000 miles away, I can see my mother spicing the ground beef, pork, and venison with *chile*. My mouth salivates at the thought of the hot steaming *tamales* I would be eating if I were home.

Si le preguntas a mi mamá, "¿Qué eres?"

> Identity is the essential core of who
> we are as individuals, the conscious
> experience of the self inside.
> 　　　　　　　　－ GERSHEN KAUFMAN[9]

Nosotros los Chicanos straddle the borderlands. On one side of us, we are constantly exposed to the Spanish of the Mexicans, on the other side we hear the Anglos' incessant clamoring so that we forget our language. Among ourselves we don't say *nosotros los americanos, o nosotros los españoles, o nosotros los hispanos.* We say *nosotros los mexicanos* (by *mexicanos* we do not mean citizens of Mexico; we do not mean a national identity, but a racial one). We distinguish between *mexicanos del otro lado* and *mexicanos de este lado.* Deep in our hearts we believe that being Mexican has nothing to do with which country one lives in. Being Mexican is a state of soul—not one of mind, not one of citizenship. Neither eagle nor serpent, but both. And like the ocean, neither animal respects borders.

> *Dime con quien andas y te diré quien eres.*
> (Tell me who your friends are and I'll tell you who you are.)
> 　　　　　　　　－ Mexican saying

Si le preguntas a mi mamá, "¿Qué eres?" te dirá, "Soy mexicana." My brothers and sister say the same. I sometimes will answer *"soy mexicana"* and at others will say *"soy Chicana" o "soy tejana."* But I identified as *"Raza"* before I ever identified as *"mexicana"* or "Chicana."

As a culture, we call ourselves Spanish when referring to ourselves as a linguistic group and when copping out. It is then that we forget our predominant Indian genes. We are 70–80 percent Indian.[10] We call ourselves Hispanic[11] or Spanish-American or Latin American or Latin when linking ourselves to other Spanish-speaking peoples of the Western hemisphere and when copping out. We call ourselves Mexican-American[12] to signify we are neither Mexican nor American, but more the noun "American" than the adjective "Mexican" (and when copping out).

Chicanos and other people of color suffer economically for not acculturating. This voluntary (yet forced) alienation makes for psychological conflict, a kind of dual identity—we don't identify with the Anglo-American cultural values and we don't totally identify with the Mexican cultural values. We are a synergy of two cultures with various degrees of Mexicanness or Angloness. I have so internalized the borderland conflict that sometimes I feel like one cancels out the other and we are zero, nothing, no one. *A veces no soy nada ni nadie. Pero hasta cuando no lo soy, lo soy.*

When not copping out, when we know we are more than nothing, we call ourselves Mexican, referring to race and ancestry; *mestizo* when affirming both our Indian and Spanish (but we hardly ever own our Black) ancestry; Chicano when referring to a politically aware people born and/or raised in the United States; *Raza* when referring to Chicanos; *tejanos* when we are Chicanos from Texas.

Chicanos did not know we were a people until 1965 when Cesar Chavez and the farmworkers united and *I Am Joaquín* was published and *la Raza Unida* party was formed in Texas. With that recognition, we became a distinct people. Something momentous happened to the Chicano soul—we became aware of our reality and acquired a name and a language (Chicano Spanish) that reflected that reality. Now that we had a name, some of the fragmented pieces began to fall together—who we were, what we were, how we had evolved. We began to get glimpses of what we might eventually become.

Yet the struggle of identities continues, the struggle of borders is our reality still. One day the inner struggle will cease and a true integration take place. In the meantime, *tenémos que hacer la lucha. ¿Quién está protegiendo los ranchos de mi gente? ¿Quién está tratando de cerrar la fisura entre la india y el blanco en nuestra sangre? El Chicano, si, el Chicano que anda como un ladrón en su propia casa.*

Los Chicanos, how patient we seem, how very patient. There is the quiet of the Indian about us.[13] We know how to survive. When other races have given up their tongue we've kept ours. We know what it is to live under the hammer blow of the dominant *norteamericano* culture. But more than we count the blows, we count the days the weeks the years the centuries the aeons until the white laws and commerce and customs will rot in the deserts they've created, lie bleached. *Humildes* yet proud, *quietos* yet wild, *nosotros los mexicanos-Chicanos* will walk by the crumbling ashes as we go about our business. Stubborn, persevering, impenetrable as stone, yet possessing a malleability that renders us unbreakable, we, the *mestizas* and *mestizos*, will remain.

NOTES

[1] Ray Gwyn Smith, *Moorland Is Cold Country*, unpublished book.

[2] Irena Klepfisz, *"Di rayze aheym/*The Journey Home," in *The Tribe of Dina: A Jewish Women's Anthology*, Melanie Kaye/Kantrowitz and Irena Klepfisz, eds. (Montpelier, VT: Sinister Wisdom Books, 1986), 49.

[3] R. C. Ortega, *Dialectología Del Barrio*, trans. Hortencia S. Alwan (Los Angeles, CA: R. C. Ortega Publisher & Bookseller, 1977), 132.

[4] Eduardo Hernandéz-Chávez, Andrew D. Cohen, and Anthony F. Beltramo, *El Lenguaje de los Chicanos: Regional and Social Characteristics of Language Used by Mexican Americans* (Arlington, VA: Center for Applied Linguistics, 1975), 39.

[5] Hernandéz-Chávez, xvii.

[6] Irena Klepfisz, "Secular Jewish Identity: Yidishkayt in America," in *The Tribe of Dina*, Kaye/Kantrowitz and Klepfisz, eds., 43.

[7] Melanie Kaye/Kantrowitz, "Sign," in *We Speak in Code: Poems and Other Writings* (Pittsburgh, PA: Motheroot Publications, Inc., 1980), 85.

[8]Rodolfo Gonzales, *I Am Joaquín/Yo Soy Joaquín* (New York, NY: Bantam Books, 1972). It was first published in 1967.

[9]Gershen Kaufman, *Shame: The Power of Caring* (Cambridge, MA: Schenkman Books, Inc., 1980), 68.

[10]John R. Chávez, *The Lost Land: The Chicano Images of the Southwest* (Albuquerque, NM: University of New Mexico Press, 1984), 88–90.

[11]"Hispanic" is derived from *Hispanis* (*España*, a name given to the Iberian Peninsula in ancient times when it was a part of the Roman Empire) and is a term designated by the U.S. government to make it easier to handle us on paper.

[12]The Treaty of Guadalupe Hidalgo created the Mexican-American in 1848.

[13]Anglos, in order to alleviate their guilt for dispossessing the Chicano, stressed the Spanish part of us and perpetrated the myth of the Spanish Southwest. We have accepted the fiction that we are Hispanic, that is Spanish, in order to accommodate ourselves to the dominant culture and its abhorrence of Indians. Chávez, 88–91.

•   •   •   •   •   •   •   •   •   •   •

QUESTIONS FOR A SECOND READING

1. The most immediate challenge to many readers of these chapters will be the sections that are written in Spanish. Part of the point of a text that mixes languages is to give non-Spanish-speaking readers the feeling of being lost, excluded, left out. What is a reader to do with this prose? One could learn Spanish and come back to reread, but this is not a quick solution and, according to Anzaldúa, not even a completely satisfactory one, since some of her Spanish is drawn from communities of speakers not represented in textbooks and classes.

    So how do you read this text if you don't read Spanish? Do you ignore the words? sound them out? improvise? Anzaldúa gives translations of some words or phrases, but not all. Which ones does she translate? Why? Reread these chapters with the goal of explaining how you handled Anzaldúa's polyglot style.

2. These chapters are made up of shorter sections written in a variety of styles (some as prose poems, some with endnotes, some as stories). And, while the sections are obviously ordered, the order is not a conventional argumentative one. The text is, as Anzaldúa says elsewhere in her book, "an assemblage, a montage, a beaded work, . . . a crazy dance":

    > In looking at this book that I'm almost finished writing, I see a mosaic pattern (Aztec-like) emerging, a weaving pattern, thin here, thick there. . . . This almost finished product seems an assemblage, a montage, a beaded work with several leitmotifs and with a central core, now appearing, now disappearing in a crazy dance. The whole thing has had a mind of its own, escaping me and insisting on putting together the pieces of its own puzzle with minimal direction from my will. It is a rebellious, willful entity, a precocious girl-child forced to grow up too quickly, rough, unyielding, with pieces of feather sticking out here and there, fur, twigs, clay. My child, but not for much longer. This female being is angry, sad, joyful, is Coatlicue, dove, horse, serpent, cactus. Though it is

a flawed thing—clumsy, complex, groping, blind thing, for me it is alive, infused with spirit. I talk to it; it talks to me.

This is not, in other words, a conventional text; it makes unexpected demands on a reader. As you reread, mark sections you could use to talk about how, through the text, Anzaldúa invents a reader and/or a way of reading. Who is Anzaldúa's ideal reader? What does he or she need to be able to do?

3. Although Anzaldúa's text is not a conventional one, it makes an argument and proposes terms and examples for its readers to negotiate. How might you summarize Anzaldúa's argument in these two chapters? How do the individual chapters mark stages or parts of her argument? How might you explain the connections between the chapters? As you reread this selection, mark those passages where Anzaldúa seems to you to be creating a case or argument. What are its key terms? its key examples? its conclusions?

ASSIGNMENTS FOR WRITING

1. Anzaldúa has described her text as a kind of crazy dance (see the second "Question for a Second Reading"); it is, she says, a text with a mind of its own, "putting together the pieces of its own puzzle with minimal direction from my will." Hers is a prose full of variety and seeming contradictions; it is a writing that could be said to represent the cultural "crossroads" which is her experience/sensibility.

As an experiment whose goal is the development of an alternate (in Anzaldúa's terms, a mixed or *mestiza*) understanding, write an autobiographical text whose shape and motives could be described in her terms: a mosaic, woven, with numerous overlays; a montage, a beaded work, a crazy dance, drawing on the various ways of thinking, speaking, understanding that might be said to be part of your own mixed cultural position, your own mixed sensibility.

To prepare for this essay, think about the different positions you could be said to occupy, the different voices that are part of your background or present, the competing ways of thinking that make up your points of view. Imagine that your goal is to present your world and your experience to those who are not necessarily prepared to be sympathetic or to understand. And, following Anzaldúa, you should work to construct a mixed text, not a single unified one. This will be hard, since you will be writing what might be called a "forbidden" text, one you have not been prepared to write.

2. In *"La conciencia de la mestiza*/Towards a New Consciousness," the last essaylike chapter in her book (the remaining chapters are made up of poems), Anzaldúa steps forward to define her role as writer and yours as reader. She says, among other things,

> Many women and men of color do not want to have any dealings with white people. . . . Many feel that whites should help their own people rid themselves of race hatred and fear first. I, for one, choose to use some of my energy to serve as mediator. I think we need to allow whites to be our allies. Through our literature, art, *corridos*, and folk-

tales we must share our history with them so when they set up com-
mittees to help Big Mountain Navajos or the Chicano farmworkers or
los Nicaragüenses they won't turn people away because of their racial
fears and ignorances. They will come to see that they are not helping us
but following our lead.

Individually, but also as a racial entity, we need to voice our needs.
We need to say to white society: We need you to accept the fact that Chicanos are different, to acknowledge your rejection and negation of us. We
need you to own the fact that you looked upon us as less than human, that
you stole our lands, our personhood, our self-respect. We need you to
make public restitution: to say that, to compensate for your own sense of
defectiveness, you strive for power over us, you erase our history and our
experience because it makes you feel guilty—you'd rather forget your
brutish acts. To say you've split yourself from minority groups, that you
disown us, that your dual consciousness splits off parts of yourself, transferring the "negative" parts onto us. . . . To say that you are afraid of us,
that to put distance between us, you wear the mask of contempt. Admit that Mexico is your double, that she exists in the shadow of this country, that we are irrevocably tied to her. Gringo, accept the doppelganger
in your psyche. By taking back your collective shadow the intracultural
split will heal. And finally, tell us what you need from us.

This is only a part of the text—one of the ways it defines the roles of
reader and writer—but it is one that asks to be taken account of, with its
insistent list of what a white reader must do and say. (Of course not every
reader is white, and not all white readers are the same. What Anzaldúa is
defining here is a "white" way of reading.)

Write an essay in which you tell a story of reading, the story of your
work with the two chapters of *Borderlands/La frontera* reprinted here.
Think about where you felt at home with the text and where you felt lost,
where you knew what you were doing and where you needed help; think
about the position (or positions) you have taken as a reader and how it
measures up against the ways Anzaldúa has figured you in the text, the
ways she has anticipated a response, imagined who you are and how you
habitually think and read.

3. In "How to Tame a Wild Tongue" (p. 36), Anzaldúa says, "I will no
   longer be made to feel ashamed of existing. I will have my voice: Indian,
   Spanish, white. I will have my serpent's tongue—my woman's voice, my
   sexual voice, my poet's voice." Anzaldúa speaks almost casually about
   "having her voice," not a single, "authentic" voice, but one she names in
   these terms: Indian, Spanish, white; woman, lesbian, poet. What is
   "voice" as defined by these chapters? Where does it come from? What
   does it have to do with the act of writing or the writer?

   As you reread these chapters, mark those passages that you think best
   represent Anzaldúa's voices. Using these passages as examples, write an
   essay in which you discuss how these voices are different—both different
   from one another and different from a "standard" voice (as a "standard"
   voice is imagined by Anzaldúa). What do these voices represent? How do
   they figure in your reading? in her writing?

4. Anzaldúa's writing is difficult to categorize as an essay or a story or a
   poem; it has all of these within it. The writing may appear to have been
   just put together, but it is more likely that it was carefully crafted to

represent the various voices Anzaldúa understands to be a part of her. She speaks directly about her voices—her woman's voice, her sexual voice, her poet's voice; her Indian, Spanish, and white voices on page 41 of "How to Tame a Wild Tongue."

Following Anzaldúa, write an argument of your own, one that requires you to use a variety of voices, in which you carefully present the various voices that you feel are a part of you or a part of the argument.

When you have completed this assignment, write a two-page essay in which you explain why the argument you made might be worth a reader's attention.

MAKING CONNECTIONS

1. In "Arts of the Contact Zone" (p. 605), Mary Louise Pratt talks about the "autoethnographic" text, "a text in which people undertake to describe themselves in ways that engage with representations others have made of them," and about "transculturation," the "processes whereby members of subordinated or marginal groups select and invent from materials transmitted by a dominant or metropolitan culture."

   Write an essay in which you present a reading of these two chapters as an example of an autoethnographic and/or transcultural text. You should imagine that you are writing to someone who is not familiar with either Pratt's argument or Anzaldúa's book. Part of your work, then, is to present Anzaldúa's text to readers who don't have it in front of them. You have the example of Pratt's reading of Guaman Poma's *New Chronicle and Good Government*. And you have her discussion of the "literate arts of the contact zone." Think about how Anzaldúa's text might be similarly read, and about how her text does and doesn't fit Pratt's description. Your goal should be to add an example to Pratt's discussion and to qualify it, to give her discussion a new twist or spin now that you have had a chance to look at an additional example.

2. Both Adrienne Rich in "When We Dead Awaken: Writing as Re-Vision" (p. 627) and Gloria Anzaldúa in these two chapters could be said to be writing about the same issues—writing, identity, gender, history. Both texts contain an argument; both, in their peculiar styles, enact an argument—they demonstrate how and why one might need to revise the usual ways of writing. Identify what you understand to be the key points, the key terms, and the key examples in each selection.

   Beginning with the passages you have identified, write an essay in which you examine the similarities and differences in these two texts. Look particularly for the differences, since they are harder to find and harder to explain. Consider the selections as marking different positions on writing, identity, politics, history. How might you account for these differences (if they represent more than the fact that different people are likely to differ)? How are these differences significant?

JAMES
BALDWIN

*J*AMES BALDWIN *was born into poverty in Harlem in 1924; he died in 1987 in France, where he had spent most of his adult life as an expatriate writer. "Once I found myself on the other side of the ocean," Baldwin said, "I could see where I came from very clearly, and I could see that I carried myself, which is my home, with me. You can never escape that. I am the grandson of a slave, and I am a writer. I must deal with both."*

As a writer, among his chosen tasks, he took on the responsibility of speaking as a black American (and as a gay black American) about the "Negro problem in America." He did this as a playwright and poet, but most significantly through a series of novels, including Go Tell It on the Mountain *(1953),* Giovanni's Room *(1956),* Another Country *(1962),* Tell Me How Long the Train's Been Gone *(1968),* If Beale Street Could Talk *(1974),* Just Above My Head *(1979), and* Harlem Quartet *(1987). And he did it as a prolific essayist, writing for American journals and magazines, including* Harper's Magazine, *the* Partisan Review, Esquire, *and* The New Yorker. *His essays have been collected in several widely read volumes, including* Notes of a Native Son *(1955),* Nobody Knows My Name: More Notes of a Native Son *(1961),* The Fire Next Time *(1963),* No Name in the Street *(1972),* The Devil Finds Work *(1976), and* The Evidence of Things Not Seen. *A selection from his essays was recently published by the Library of America (1998).*

The essay that follows, "Notes of a Native Son," was written early in Baldwin's career. (It was first published in Harper's Magazine *in November 1955.) It tells the story of his father's death and of the family life that preceded the death. Baldwin had started to write quite early. In a brief autobiographical sketch published in 1955, he said, "I began plotting novels at about the time I learned to read. . . . I read just about everything I could get my hands on—except the Bible, probably because it was the only book I was encouraged to read." He wrote stories and poems, including a short story published in his church newspaper. At fourteen he became a preacher at the Fireside Pentecostal Assembly; at seventeen he stopped preaching, having lost faith that the church was serving the fundamental needs of his community.*

After high school he worked in the defense industry, a story he includes in the following essay. In 1944 he met Richard Wright, author of the novel Native Son *and one of the most widely read and influential African American intellectuals of the 1940s. Wright helped Baldwin win a fellowship, and with that money Baldwin followed Wright to Paris to work on a novel. (Wright had moved to Paris the year before.) Baldwin developed a difficult relationship with Wright, the successful writer of one generation before. He was a figure Baldwin needed to struggle against, reject, and (in his ambition, at least) surpass. In an odd and difficult essay titled, "Alas, Poor Richard," Baldwin wrote, "I had made a pilgrimage to meet him because he was the greatest black writer in the world for me. In* Uncle Tom's Children, *in* Native Son, *and, above all, in* Black Boy, *I found expressed, for the first time in my life, the sorrow, the rage, and the murderous bitterness which was eating up my life and the lives of those around me. His work was an immense liberation and revelation for me. He became my ally and my witness, and alas! my father."*

In 1946 Baldwin returned to the United States: "The fellowship was over, the novel turned out to be unsalable, and I started waiting on tables in a Village restaurant and writing book reviews—mostly, as it turned out, about the Negro problem, concerning which the color of my skin made me automatically an expert." Writing book reviews was the beginning, he said, of his career as an essayist. Later he stated, "I was a black kid and was expected to write from that perspective. Yet I had to realize the black perspective was dictated by the white imagination. Since I wouldn't write from the perspective, essentially, of the victim, I had to find what my own perspective was and then use it. I couldn't talk about 'them' and 'us.' So I had to use 'we' and let the reader figure out who 'we' is."

Baldwin returned again to the United States in 1957, spurred by the revived civil rights movement, and he became one of the most prominent intellectuals writing on the inevitability of racial tension, the possibility of racial understanding, and the consequences of continued conflict. In the essay "Split at the Root," Adrienne Rich said, "Reading James Baldwin's early essays, in the fifties, had stirred me with a sense that apparently 'given' situations like racism could be analyzed and described and that this could lead to action, to change." His collection The Fire Next Time *(1963) is a crucial document for any student of American race relations.*

In the 1955 autobiographical sketch, Baldwin said:

> *One of the difficulties about being a Negro writer (and this is not spe-cial pleading, since I don't mean to suggest that he has it worse than anybody else) is that the Negro problem is written about so widely. The bookshelves groan under the weight of information, and everyone therefore considers himself informed. And this information, further-more, operates usually (generally, popularly) to reenforce traditional attitudes. Of traditional attitudes there are only two—For or Against—and I, personally, find it difficult to say which attitude has caused me the most pain. I am speaking as a writer; from a social point of view I am perfectly aware that the change from ill-will to good-will, however motivated, however imperfect, however expressed, is better than no change at all.*
>
> *But it is part of the business of the writer—as I see it—to exam-ine attitudes, to go beneath the surface, to tap the source. From this point of view the Negro problem is nearly inaccessible. It is not only written about so widely; it is written about so badly. It is quite pos-sible to say that the price a Negro pays for becoming articulate is to find himself, at length, with nothing to be articulate about. ("You taught me language," says Caliban to Prospero, "and my profit on 't is I know how to curse.") Consider: the tremendous social activity that this problem generates imposes on whites and Negroes alike the necessity of looking forward, of working to bring about a better day. This is fine, it keeps the waters troubled; it is all, indeed, that has made possible the Negro's progress. Nevertheless, social affairs are not, generally speaking, the writer's prime concern, whether they ought to be or not; it is absolutely necessary that he establish between himself and these affairs a distance which will allow, at least, for clar-ity, so that before he can look forward in any meaningful sense, he must first be allowed to take a long look back. In the context of the Negro problem, neither whites nor blacks, for excellent reasons of their own, have the faintest desire to look back; but I think that the past is all that makes the present coherent, and further, that the past will remain horrible for exactly as long as we refuse to assess it honestly.*

In "Notes of a Native Son," Baldwin writes about his father and his family's his-tory, set in relation to the history of the United States—slavery, black migration to the North, the experience of black soldiers in World War II, race riots in Detroit and in Harlem. It certainly has the quality of honesty; it is, in its assessment of fa-ther and son, frank and difficult; in its range and ambition, it is a remarkable achievement. One question to ask, as you read it, is whether it was, for Baldwin, a looking back to the past to make the present coherent.

Notes of a Native Son

On the 29th of July, in 1943, my father died. On the same day, a few hours later, his last child was born. Over a month before this, while all our energies were concentrated in waiting for these events, there had been, in Detroit, one of the bloodiest race riots of the century. A few hours after my father's funeral, while he lay in state in the undertaker's chapel, a race riot broke out in Harlem. On the morning of the 3rd of August, we drove my father to the graveyard through a wilderness of smashed plate glass.

The day of my father's funeral had also been my nineteenth birthday. As we drove him to the graveyard, the spoils of injustice, anarchy, discontent, and hatred were all around us. It seemed to me that God himself had devised, to mark my father's end, the most sustained and brutally dissonant of codas. And it seemed to me, too, that the violence which rose all about us as my father left the world had been devised as a corrective for the pride of his eldest son. I had declined to believe in that apocalypse which had been central to my father's vision; very well, life seemed to be saying, here is something that will certainly pass for an apocalypse until the real thing comes along. I had inclined to be contemptuous of my father for the conditions of his life, for the conditions of our lives. When his life had ended I began to wonder about that life and also, in a new way, to be apprehensive about my own.

I had not known my father very well. We had got on badly, partly because we shared, in our different fashions, the vice of stubborn pride. When he was dead I realized that I had hardly ever spoken to him. When he had been dead a long time I began to wish I had. It seems to be typical of life in America, where opportunities, real and fancied, are thicker than anywhere else on the globe, that the second generation has no time to talk to the first. No one, including my father, seems to have known exactly how old he was, but his mother had been born during slavery. He was of the first generation of free men. He, along with thousands of other Negroes, came North after 1919 and I was part of that generation which had never seen the landscape of what Negroes sometimes call the Old Country.

He had been born in New Orleans and had been a quite young man there during the time that Louis Armstrong, a boy, was running errands for the dives and honky-tonks of what was always presented to me as one of the most wicked of cities—to this day, whenever I think of New Orleans, I also helplessly think of Sodom and Gomorrah. My father never mentioned Louis Armstrong, except to forbid us to play his records; but there was a picture of him on our wall for a long time. One of my father's strong-willed female relatives had placed it there and forbade my father to take it down. He never did, but he eventually maneuvered her out of the house and when, some years later, she was in trouble and near death, he refused to do anything to help her.

He was, I think, very handsome. I gather this from photographs and from my own memories of him, dressed in his Sunday best and on his way to preach a sermon somewhere, when I was little. Handsome, proud, and ingrown, "like a toe-nail," somebody said. But he looked to me, as I grew older, like pictures I had seen of African tribal chieftains: he really should have been naked, with war-paint on and barbaric mementos, standing among spears. He could be chilling in the pulpit and indescribably cruel in his personal life and he was certainly the most bitter man I have ever met; yet it must be said that there was something else in him, buried in him, which lent him his tremendous power and, even, a rather crushing charm. It had something to do with his blackness, I think—he was very black—with his blackness and his beauty, and with the fact that he knew that he was black but did not know that he was beautiful. He claimed to be proud of his blackness but it had also been the cause of much humiliation and it had fixed bleak boundaries to his life. He was not a young man when we were growing up and he had already suffered many kinds of ruin; in his outrageously demanding and protective way he loved his children, who were black like him and menaced, like him; and all these things sometimes showed in his face when he tried, never to my knowledge with any success, to establish contact with any of us. When he took one of his children on his knee to play, the child always became fretful and began to cry; when he tried to help one of us with our homework the absolutely unabating tension which emanated from him caused our minds and our tongues to become paralyzed, so that he, scarcely knowing why, flew into a rage and the child, not knowing why, was punished. If it ever entered his head to bring a surprise home for his children, it was, almost unfailingly, the wrong surprise and even the big watermelons he often brought home on his back in the summertime led to the most appalling scenes. I do not remember, in all those years, that one of his children was ever glad to see him come home. From what I was able to gather of his early life, it seemed that this inability to establish contact with other people had always marked him and had been one of the things which had driven him out of New Orleans. There was something in him, therefore, groping and tentative, which was never expressed and which was buried with him. One saw it most clearly when he was facing new people and hoping to impress them. But he never did, not for long. We went from church to smaller and more improbable church, he found himself in less and less demand as a minister, and by the time he died none of his friends had come to see him for a long time. He had lived and died in an intolerable bitterness of spirit and it frightened me, as we drove him to the graveyard through those unquiet, ruined streets, to see how powerful and overflowing this bitterness could be and to realize that this bitterness now was mine.

When he died I had been away from home for a little over a year. In that year I had had time to become aware of the meaning of all my father's bitter warnings, had discovered the secret of his proudly pursed lips and rigid carriage: I had discovered the weight of white people in the world. I saw that this had been for my ancestors and now would be for me an awful thing to live with and that the bitterness which had helped to kill my father could also kill me.

He had been ill a long time—in the mind, as we now realized, reliving instances of his fantastic intransigence in the new light of his affliction and endeavoring to feel a sorrow for him which never, quite, came true. We had not known that he was being eaten up by paranoia, and the discovery that his cruelty, to our bodies and our minds, had been one of the symptoms of his illness was not, then, enough to enable us to forgive him. The younger children felt, quite simply, relief that he would not be coming home anymore. My mother's observation that it was he, after all, who had kept them alive all these years meant nothing because the problems of keeping children alive are not real for children. The older children felt, with my father gone, that they could invite their friends to the house without fear that their friends would be insulted or, as had sometimes happened with me, being told that their friends were in league with the devil and intended to rob our family of everything we owned. (I didn't fail to wonder, and it made me hate him, what on earth we owned that anybody else would want.)

His illness was beyond all hope of healing before anyone realized that he was ill. He had always been so strange and had lived, like a prophet, in such unimaginably close communion with the Lord that his long silences which were punctuated by moans and hallelujahs and snatches of old songs while he sat at the living-room window never seemed odd to us. It was not until he refused to eat because, he said, his family was trying to poison him that my mother was forced to accept as a fact what had, until then, been only an unwilling suspicion. When he was committed, it was discovered that he had tuberculosis and, as it turned out, the disease of his mind allowed the disease of his body to destroy him. For the doctors could not force him to eat, either, and, though he was fed intravenously, it was clear from the beginning that there was no hope for him.

In my mind's eye I could see him, sitting at the window, locked up in his terrors; hating and fearing every living soul including his children who had betrayed him, too, by reaching towards the world which had despised him. There were nine of us. I began to wonder what it could have felt like for such a man to have had nine children whom he could barely feed. He used to make little jokes about our poverty, which never, of course, seemed very funny to us; they could not have seemed very funny to him, either, or else our all too feeble response to them would never have caused such rages. He spent great energy and achieved, to our chagrin, no small amount of success in keeping us away from the people who surrounded us, people who had all-night rent parties to which we listened when we should have been sleeping, people who cursed and drank and flashed razor blades on Lenox Avenue. He could not understand why, if they had so much energy to spare, they could not use it to make their lives better. He treated almost everybody on our block with a most uncharitable asperity and neither they, nor, of course, their children were slow to reciprocate.

The only white people who came to our house were welfare workers and bill collectors. It was almost always my mother who dealt with them, for my father's temper, which was at the mercy of his pride, was never to be trusted. It was clear that he felt their very presence in his home to be a violation: this was conveyed by his carriage, almost ludicrously stiff, and by his voice, harsh and vindictively polite. When I was around nine or ten I wrote a play which was directed by a young, white schoolteacher, a woman, who then took an interest in me, and gave me books to read and, in order to corroborate my theatrical bent, decided to take me to see what she somewhat tactlessly referred to as "real" plays. Theater-going was forbidden in our house, but, with the really cruel intuitiveness of a child, I suspected that the color of this woman's skin would carry the day for me. When, at school, she suggested taking me to the theater, I did not, as I might have done if she had been a Negro, find a way of discouraging her, but agreed that she should pick me up at my house one evening. I then, very cleverly, left all the rest to my mother, who suggested to my father, as I knew she would, that it would not be very nice to let such a kind woman make the trip for nothing. Also, since it was a schoolteacher, I imagine that my mother countered the idea of sin with the idea of "education," which word, even with my father, carried a kind of bitter weight.

Before the teacher came my father took me aside to ask *why* she was coming, what *interest* she could possibly have in our house, in a boy like me. I said I didn't know but I, too, suggested that it had something to do with education. And I understood that my father was waiting for me to say something—I didn't quite know what; perhaps that I wanted his protection against this teacher and her "education." I said none of these things and the teacher came and we went out. It was clear, during the brief interview in our living room, that my father was agreeing very much against his will and that he would have refused permission if he had dared. The fact that he did not dare caused me to despise him: I had no way of knowing that he was facing in that living room a wholly unprecedented and frightening situation.

Later, when my father had been laid off from his job, this woman became very important to us. She was really a very sweet and generous woman and went to a great deal of trouble to be of help to us, particularly during one awful winter. My mother called her by the highest name she knew: she said she was a "christian." My father could scarcely disagree but during the four or five years of our relatively close association he never trusted her and was always trying to surprise in her open, Midwestern face the genuine, cunningly hidden, and hideous motivation. In later years, particularly when it began to be clear that this "education" of mine was going to lead me to perdition, he became more explicit and warned me that my white friends in high school were not really my friends and that I would see, when I was older, how white people would do anything to keep a Negro down. Some of them could be nice, he admitted, but none of them were to be trusted and most of them were not even nice. The best thing was to have as little to do with them as possible. I did not feel this way and I was certain, in my innocence, that I never would.

But the year which preceded my father's death had made a great change in my life. I had been living in New Jersey, working in defense plants, working and living among southerners, white and black. I knew about the south, of course, and about how southerners treated Negroes and how they expected them to behave, but it had never entered my mind that anyone would look at me and expect *me* to behave that way. I learned in New Jersey that to be a Negro meant, precisely, that one was never looked at but was simply at the mercy of the reflexes the color of one's skin caused in other people. I acted in New Jersey as I had always acted, that is as though I thought a great deal of myself—I had to *act* that way— with results that were, simply, unbelievable. I had scarcely arrived before I had earned the enmity, which was extraordinarily ingenious, of all my superiors and nearly all my co-workers. In the beginning, to make matters worse, I simply did not know what was happening. I did not know what I had done, and I shortly began to wonder what *anyone* could possibly do, to bring about such unanimous, active, and unbearably vocal hostility. I knew about jim-crow but I had never experienced it. I went to the same self-service restaurant three times and stood with all the Princeton boys before the counter, waiting for a hamburger and coffee; it was always an extraordinarily long time before anything was set before me; but it was not until the fourth visit that I learned that, in fact, nothing had ever been set before me: I had simply picked something up. Negroes were not served there, I was told, and they had been waiting for me to realize that I was always the only Negro present. Once I was told this, I determined to go there all the time. But now they were ready for me and, though some dreadful scenes were subsequently enacted in that restaurant, I never ate there again.

It was the same story all over New Jersey, in bars, bowling alleys, diners, places to live. I was always being forced to leave, silently, or with mutual imprecations. I very shortly became notorious and children giggled behind me when I passed and their elders whispered or shouted—they really believed that I was mad. And it did begin to work on my mind, of course; I began to be afraid to go anywhere and to compensate for this I went places to which I really should not have gone and where, God knows, I had no desire to be. My reputation in town naturally enhanced my reputation at work and my working day became one long series of acrobatics designed to keep me out of trouble. I cannot say that these acrobatics succeeded. It began to seem that the machinery of the organization I worked for was turning over, day and night, with but one aim: to eject me. I was fired once, and contrived, with the aid of a friend from New York, to get back on the payroll; was fired again, and bounced back again. It took a while to fire me for the third time, but the third time took. There were no loopholes anywhere. There was not even any way of getting back inside the gates.

That year in New Jersey lives in my mind as though it were the year during which, having an unsuspected predilection for it, I first contracted some dread, chronic disease, the unfailing symptom of which is a kind of blind fever, a pounding in the skull and fire in the bowels. Once this disease is contracted, one can never be really carefree again, for the fever, without an instant's warning, can recur at any moment. It can wreck more important things than race relations. There is not a Negro alive who does not have this rage in his blood—one has the choice, merely, of living with it consciously or surrendering to it. As for me, this fever has recurred in me, and does, and will until the day I die.

My last night in New Jersey, a white friend from New York took me to the nearest big town, Trenton, to go to the movies and have a few drinks. As it turned out, he also saved me from, at the very least, a violent whipping. Almost every detail of that night stands out very clearly in my memory. I even remember the name of the movie we saw because its title impressed me as being so patly ironical. It was a movie about the German occupation of France, starring Maureen O'Hara and Charles Laughton and called *This Land Is Mine.* I remember the name of the diner we walked into when the movie ended: it was the "American Diner." When we walked in the counterman asked what we wanted and I remember answering with the casual sharpness which had become my habit: "We want a hamburger and a cup of coffee, what do you think we want?" I do not know why, after a year of such rebuffs, I so completely failed to anticipate his answer, which ways, of course, "We don't serve Negroes here." This reply failed to discompose me, at least for the moment. I made some sardonic comment about the name of the diner and we walked out into the streets.

This was the time of what was called the "brown-out," when the lights in all American cities were very dim. When we re-entered the streets something happened to me which had the force of an optical illusion, or a nightmare. The streets were very crowded and I was facing north. People were moving in every direction but it seemed to me, in that instant, that all of the people I could see, and many more than that, were moving toward me, against me, and that everyone was white. I remember how their faces gleamed. And I felt, like a physical sensation, a *click* at the nape of my neck as though some interior string connecting my head to my body had been cut. I began to walk. I heard my friend call after me, but I ignored him. Heaven only knows what was going on in his mind, but he had the good sense not to touch me—I don't know what would have happened if he had—and to keep me in sight. I don't know what was going on in my mind, either; I certainly had no conscious plan. I wanted to do something to crush these white faces, which were crushing me. I walked for perhaps a block or two until I came to an enormous, glittering, and fashionable restaurant in which I knew not even the intercession of the Virgin would cause me to be served. I pushed through the doors and took the first vacant seat I saw, at a table for two, and waited.

I do not know how long I waited and I rather wonder, until today, what I could possibly have looked like. Whatever I looked like, I frightened the waitress who shortly appeared, and the moment she appeared all of my fury flowed towards her. I hated her for her white face, and for her great, astounded, frightened eyes. I felt that if she found a black man so frightening I would make her fright worth-while.

She did not ask me what I wanted, but repeated, as though she had learned it somewhere, "We don't serve Negroes here." She did not say it with the blunt, derisive hostility to which I had grown so accustomed, but, rather, with a note of apology in her voice, and fear. This made me colder and more murderous than ever. I felt I had to do something with my hands. I wanted her to come close enough for me to get her neck between my hands.

So I pretended not to have understood her, hoping to draw her closer. And she did step a very short step closer, with her pencil poised incongruously over her pad, and repeated the formula: ". . . don't serve Negroes here."

Somehow, with the repetition of that phrase, which was already ringing in my head like a thousand bells of a nightmare, I realized that she would never come any closer and that I would have to strike from a distance. There was nothing on the table but an ordinary water-mug half full of water, and I picked this up and hurled it with all my strength at her. She ducked and it missed her and shattered against the mirror behind the bar. And, with that sound, my frozen blood abruptly thawed, I returned from wherever I had been, I *saw,* for the first time, the restaurant, the people with their mouths open, already, as it seemed to me, rising as one man, and I realized what I had done, and where I was, and I was frightened. I rose and began running for the door. A round, potbellied man grabbed me by the nape of the neck just as I reached the doors and began to beat me about the face. I kicked him and got loose and ran into the streets. My friend whispered, *"Run!"* and I ran.

My friend stayed outside the restaurant long enough to misdirect my pursuers and the police, who arrived, he told me, at once. I do not know what I said to him when he came to my room that night. I could not have said much. I felt, in the oddest, most awful way, that I had somehow betrayed him. I lived it over and over and over again, the way one relives an automobile accident after it has happened and one finds oneself alone and safe. I could not get over two facts, both equally difficult for the imagination to grasp, and one was that I could have been murdered. But the other was that I had been ready to commit murder. I saw nothing very clearly but I did see this: that my life, my *real* life, was in danger, and not from anything other people might do but from the hatred I carried in my own heart.

II

I had returned home around the second week in June—in great haste because it seemed that my father's death and my mother's confinement were both but a matter of hours. In the case of my mother, it soon became clear that she had simply made a miscalculation. This had always been her tendency and I don't believe that a single one of us arrived in the world, or has since arrived anywhere else, on time. But none of us dawdled so intolerably about the business of being born as did my baby sister. We sometimes amused ourselves, during those endless, stifling weeks, by picturing the baby sitting within in the safe, warm dark, bitterly regretting the necessity of becoming a part of our chaos and stubbornly putting it off as long as possible. I understood her perfectly and congratulated her on showing such good sense so soon. Death, however, sat as purposefully at my father's bedside as life stirred within my mother's womb and it was harder to understand why he so lingered in that long shadow. It seemed that he had bent, and for a long time, too, all of his energies towards dying. Now death was ready for him but my father held back.

All of Harlem, indeed, seemed to be infected by waiting. I had never before known it to be so violently still. Racial tensions throughout this country were exacerbated during the early years of the war, partly because the labor market brought together hundreds of thousands of ill-prepared people and partly because Negro soldiers, regardless of where they were born, received their military training in the south. What happened in defense plants and army camps had repercussions, naturally, in every Negro ghetto. The situation in Harlem had grown bad enough for clergymen, policemen, educators, politicians, and social workers to assert in one breath that there was no "crime wave" and to offer, in the very next breath, suggestions as to how to combat it. These suggestions always seemed to involve playgrounds, despite the fact that racial skirmishes were occurring in the playgrounds, too. Playground or not, crime wave or not, the Harlem police force had been augmented in March, and the unrest grew—perhaps, in fact, partly as a result of the ghetto's instinctive hatred of policemen. Perhaps the most revealing news item, out of the steady parade of reports of muggings, stabbings, shootings, assaults, gang wars, and accusations of police brutality, is the item concerning six Negro girls who set upon a white girl in the subway because, as they all too accurately put it, she was stepping on their toes. Indeed she was, all over the nation.

I had never before been so aware of policemen, on foot, on horseback, on corners, everywhere, always two by two. Nor had I ever been so aware of small knots of people. They were on stoops and on corners and in doorways, and what was striking about them, I think, was that they did not seem to be talking. Never, when I passed these groups, did the usual sound of a curse or a laugh ring out and neither did there seem to be any hum of gossip. There was certainly, on the other hand, occurring between them communication extraordinarily intense. Another thing that was striking was the unexpected diversity of the people who made up these groups. Usually, for example, one would see a group of sharpies standing on the street corner, jiving the passing chicks; or a group of older men, usually, for some reason, in the vicinity of a barber shop, discussing baseball scores, or the numbers, or making rather chilling observations about women they had known. Women, in a general way, tended to be seen less often together—unless they were church women, or very young girls, or prostitutes met together for an unprofessional instant. But that summer I saw the strangest combinations: large, respectable, churchly matrons standing on the stoops or the corners with their hair tied up, together with a girl in sleazy satin whose face bore the marks of gin and the razor, or heavy-set, abrupt, no-nonsense older men, in company with the most disreputable and fanatical "race" men, or these same "race" men with the sharpies, or these sharpies with the churchly women. Seventh Day Adventists and Methodists and Spiritualists seemed to be hobnobbing with Holyrollers and they were all, alike, entangled with the most flagrant disbelievers; something heavy in their stance seemed to indicate that they had all, incredibly, seen a common vision, and on each face there seemed to be the same strange, bitter shadow.

The churchly women and the matter-of-fact, no-nonsense men had children in the Army. The sleazy girls they talked to had lovers there, the sharpies and the "race" men had friends and brothers there. It would have demanded an unquestioning patriotism, happily as uncommon in this country as it is undesirable, for these people not to have been disturbed by the bitter letters they received, by the newspaper stories they read, not to have been enraged by the posters, then to be found all over New York, which described the Japanese as "yellow-bellied Japs." It was only the "race" men, to be sure, who spoke ceaselessly of being revenged—how this vengeance was to be exacted was not clear—for the indignities and dangers suffered by Negro boys in uniform; but everybody felt a directionless, hopeless bitterness, as well as that panic which can scarcely be suppressed when one knows that a human being one loves is beyond one's reach, and in danger. This helplessness and this gnawing uneasiness does something, at length, to even the toughest mind. Perhaps the best way to sum all this up is to say that the people I knew felt, mainly, a peculiar kind of relief when they knew that their boys were being shipped out of the south, to do battle overseas. It was, perhaps, like feeling that the most dangerous part of a dangerous journey had been passed and that now, even if death should come, it would come with honor and without the complicity of their countrymen. Such a death would be, in short, a fact with which one could hope to live.

It was on the 28th of July, which I believe was a Wednesday, that I visited my father for the first time during his illness and for the last time in his life. The moment I saw him I knew why I had put off this visit so long. I had told my mother that I did not want to see him because I hated him. But this was not true. It was only that I *had* hated him and I wanted to hold on to this hatred. I did not want to look on him as a ruin: it was not a ruin I had hated. I imagine that one of the reasons people cling to their hates so stubbornly is because they sense, once hate is gone, that they will be forced to deal with pain.

We traveled out to him, his older sister and myself, to what seemed to be the very end of a very Long Island. It was hot and dusty and we wrangled, my aunt and I, all the way out, over the fact that I had recently begun to smoke and, as she said, to give myself airs. But I knew that she wrangled with me because she could not bear to face the fact of her brother's dying. Neither could I endure the reality of her despair, her unstated bafflement as to what had happened to her brother's life, and her own. So we wrangled and I smoked and from time to time she fell into a heavy reverie. Covertly, I watched her face, which was the face of an old woman; it had fallen in, the eyes were sunken and lightless; soon she would be dying, too.

In my childhood—it had not been so long ago—I had thought her beautiful. She had been quick-witted and quick-moving and very generous with all the children and each of her visits had been an event. At one time one of my brothers and myself had thought of running away to live with her. Now she could no longer produce out of her handbag some unexpected and yet familiar delight. She made me feel pity and revulsion and fear. It was awful to realize that she no longer caused me to feel affection. The closer we came to the hospital the more querulous she became and at the same time, naturally, grew more dependent on me. Between pity and guilt and fear I began to feel that there was another me trapped in my skull like a jack-in-the-box who might escape my control at any moment and fill the air with screaming.

She began to cry the moment we entered the room and she saw him lying there, all shriveled and still, like a little black monkey. The great, gleaming apparatus which fed him and would have compelled him to be still even if he had been able to move brought to mind, not beneficence, but torture; the tubes entering his arm made me think of pictures I had seen when a child, of Gulliver, tied down by the pygmies on that island. My aunt wept and wept, there was a whistling sound in my father's throat; nothing was said; he could not speak. I wanted to take his hand, to say something. But I do not know what I could have said, even if he could have heard me. He was not really in that room with us, he had at last really embarked on his journey; and though my aunt told me that he said he was going to meet Jesus, I did not hear anything except that whistling in his throat. The doctor came back and we left, into that unbearable train again, and home. In the morning came the telegram saying that he was dead. Then the house was suddenly full of relatives, friends, hysteria, and confusion and I quickly left my mother and the children to the care of those impressive women, who, in Negro communities at least, automatically appear at times of bereavement armed with lotions, proverbs, and patience, and an ability to cook. I went downtown. By the time I returned, later the same day, my mother had been carried to the hospital and the baby had been born.

III

For my father's funeral I had nothing black to wear and this posed a nagging problem all day long. It was one of those problems, simple, or impossible of solution, to which the mind insanely clings in order to avoid the mind's real trouble. I spent most of that day at the downtown apartment of a girl I knew, celebrating my birthday with whiskey and wondering what to wear that night. When planning a birthday celebration one naturally does not expect that it will be up against competition from a funeral and this girl had anticipated taking me out that night, for a big dinner and a night club afterwards. Sometime during the course of that long day we decided that we would go out anyway, when my father's funeral service was over. I imagine *I* decided it, since, as the funeral hour approached, it became clearer and clearer to me that I would not know what to do with myself when it was over. The girl, stifling her very lively concern as to the possible effects of the whiskey on one of my father's chief mourners, concentrated on being conciliatory and practically helpful. She found a black shirt for me somewhere and ironed it and, dressed in the darkest pants and jacket I owned, and slightly drunk, I made my way to my father's funeral.

The chapel was full, but not packed, and very quiet. There were, mainly, my father's relatives, and his children, and here and there I saw faces I had not seen since childhood, the faces of my father's one-time friends. They were very dark and solemn now, seeming somehow to suggest that they had known all along that something like this would happen. Chief among the mourners was my aunt, who had quarreled with my father all his life; by which I do not mean to suggest that her mourning was insincere or that she had not loved him. I suppose that she was one of the few people in the world who had, and their incessant quarreling proved precisely the strength of the tie that bound them. The only other person in the world, as far as I knew, whose relationship to my father rivaled my aunt's in depth was my mother, who was not there.

It seemed to me, of course, that it was a very long funeral. But it was, if anything, a rather shorter funeral than most, nor, since there were no overwhelming, uncontrollable expressions of grief, could it be called—if I dare to use the word—successful. The minister who preached my father's funeral sermon was one of the few my father had still been seeing as he neared his end. He presented to us in his sermon a man whom none of us had ever seen—a man thoughtful, patient, and forbearing, a Christian inspiration to all who knew him, and a model for his children. And no doubt the children, in their disturbed and guilty state, were almost ready to believe this; he had been remote enough to be anything and, anyway, the shock of the incontrovertible, that it was really our father lying up there in that casket, prepared the mind for anything. His sister moaned and this grief-stricken moaning was taken as corroboration. The other faces held a dark, non-committal thoughtfulness. This was not the man they had known, but they had scarcely expected to be confronted with *him*; this was, in a sense, deeper than questions of fact, the man they had not known, and the man they had not known may have been the real one. The real man, whoever he had been, had suffered and now he was dead: this was all that was sure and all that mattered now. Every man in the chapel hoped that when his hour came he, too, would be eulogized, which is to say forgiven, and that all of his lapses, greeds, errors, and strayings from the truth would be invested with coherence and looked upon with charity. This was perhaps the last thing human beings could give each other and it was what they demanded, after all, of the Lord. Only the Lord saw the midnight tears, only He was present when one of His children, moaning and wringing hands, paced up and down the room. When one slapped one's child in anger the recoil in the heart reverberated through heaven and became part of the pain of the universe. And when the children were hungry and sullen and distrustful and one watched them, daily, growing wilder, and further away, and running headlong into danger, it was the Lord who knew what the charged heart endured as the strap was laid to the backside; the Lord alone who knew what one *would* have said if one had had, like the Lord, the gift of the living word. It was the Lord who knew of the impossibility every parent in that room faced: how to prepare the child for the day when the child would be despised and how to *create* in the child—by what means?—a stronger antidote to this poison than one had found for oneself. The avenues, side streets, bars, billiard halls, hospitals, police stations, and even the playgrounds of Harlem—not to mention the houses of correction, the jails, and the morgue—testified to the potency of the poison while remaining silent as to the efficacy of whatever antidote, irresistibly raising the question of whether or not such an antidote existed; raising, which was worse, the question of whether or not an antidote was desirable; perhaps poison should be fought with poison. With these several schisms in the mind and with more terrors in the heart than could be named, it was better not to judge the man who had gone down under an impossible burden. It was better to remember: *Thou knowest this man's fall; but thou knowest not his wrassling.*

While the preacher talked and I watched the children—years of changing their diapers, scrubbing them, slapping them, taking them to school, and scolding them had had the perhaps inevitable result of making me love them, though I am not sure I knew this then—my mind was busily breaking out with a rash of disconnected impressions. Snatches of popular songs, indecent jokes, bits of books I had read, movie sequences, faces, voices, political issues—I thought I was going mad; all these impressions suspended, as it were, in the solution of the faint nausea produced in me by the heat and liquor. For a moment I had the impression that my alcoholic breath, inefficiently disguised with chewing gum, filled the entire chapel. Then someone began singing one of my father's favorite songs and, abruptly, I was with him, sitting on his knee, in the hot, enormous, crowded church which was the first church we attended. It was the Abyssinia Baptist Church on 138th Street. We had not gone there long. With this image, a host of others came. I had forgotten, in the rage of my growing up, how proud my father had been of me when I was little. Apparently, I had had a voice and my father had liked to show me off before the members of the church. I had forgotten what he had looked like when he was pleased but now I remembered that he had always been grinning with pleasure when my solos ended. I even remembered certain expressions on his face when he teased my mother—had he loved her? I would never know. And when had it all begun to change? For now it seemed that he had not always been cruel. I remembered being taken for a haircut and scraping my knee on the footrest of the barber's chair and I remembered my father's face as he soothed my crying and applied the stinging iodine. Then I remembered our fights, fights which had been of the worst possible kind because my technique had been silence.

I remembered the one time in all our life together when we had really spoken to each other.

It was on a Sunday and it must have been shortly before I left home. We were walking, just the two of us, in our usual silence, to or from church. I was in high school and had been doing a lot of writing and I was, at about this time, the editor of the high school magazine. But I had also been a Young Minister and had been preaching from the pulpit. Lately, I had been taking fewer engagements and preached as rarely as possible. It was said in the church, quite truthfully, that I was "cooling off."

My father asked me abruptly, "You'd rather write than preach, wouldn't you?"

I was astonished at his question—because it was a real question. I answered, "Yes."

That was all we said. It was awful to remember that that was all we had *ever* said.

The casket now was opened and the mourners were being led up the aisle to look for the last time on the deceased. The assumption was that the family was too overcome with grief to be allowed to make this journey alone and I watched while my aunt was led to the casket and, muffled in black, and shaking, led back to her seat. I disapproved of forcing the children to look on their dead father, considering that the shock of his death, or, more truthfully, the shock of death as a reality, was already a little more than a child could bear, but my judgment in this matter had been overruled and there they were, bewildered and frightened and very small, being led, one by one, to the casket. But there is also something very gallant about children at such moments. It has something to do with their silence and gravity and with the fact that one cannot help them. Their legs, somehow, seem *exposed,* so that it is at once incredible and terribly clear that their legs are all they have to hold them up.

I had not wanted to go to the casket myself and I certainly had not wished to be led there, but there was no way of avoiding either of these forms. One of the deacons led me up and I looked on my father's face. I cannot say that it looked like him at all. His blackness had been equivocated by powder and there was no suggestion in that casket of what his power had or could have been. He was simply an old man dead, and it was hard to believe that he had ever given anyone either joy or pain. Yet, his life filled that room. Further up the avenue his wife was holding his newborn child. Life and death so close together, and love and hatred, and right and wrong, said something to me which I did not want to hear concerning man, concerning the life of man.

After the funeral, while I was downtown desperately celebrating my birthday, a Negro soldier, in the lobby of the Hotel Braddock, got into a fight with a white policeman over a Negro girl. Negro girls, white policemen, in or out of uniform, and Negro males—in or out of uniform—were part of the furniture of the lobby of the Hotel Braddock and this was certainly not the first time such an incident had occurred. It was destined, however, to receive an unprecedented publicity, for the fight between the policeman and the soldier ended with the shooting of the soldier. Rumor, flowing immediately to the streets outside, stated that the soldier had been shot in the back, an instantaneous and revealing invention, and that the soldier had died protecting a Negro woman. The facts were somewhat different—for example, the soldier had not been shot in the back, and was not dead, and the girl seems to have been as dubious a symbol of womanhood as her white counterpart in Georgia usually is, but no one was interested in the facts. They preferred the invention because this invention expressed and corroborated their hates and fears so perfectly. It is just as well to remember that people are always doing this. Perhaps many of those legends, including Christianity, to which the world clings began their conquest of the world with just some such concerted surrender to distortion. The effect, in Harlem, of this particular legend was like the effect of a lit match in a tin of gasoline. The mob gathered before the doors of the Hotel Braddock simply began to swell and to spread in every direction, and Harlem exploded.

The mob did not cross the ghetto lines. It would have been easy, for example, to have gone over Morningside Park on the west side or to have crossed the Grand Central railroad tracks at 125th Street on the east side, to wreak havoc in white neighborhoods. The mob seems to have been mainly interested in something more potent and real than the white face, that is, in white power, and the principal damage done during the riot of the summer of 1943 was to white business establishments in Harlem. It might have been a far bloodier story, of course, if, at the hour the riot began, these establishments had still been open. From the Hotel Braddock the mob fanned out, east and west along 125th Street, and for the entire length of Lenox, Seventh, and Eighth avenues. Along each of these avenues, and along each major side street—116th, 125th, 135th, and so on— bars, stores, pawnshops, restaurants, even little luncheonettes had been smashed open and entered and looted—looted, it might be added, with more haste than efficiency. The shelves really looked as though a bomb had struck them. Cans of beans and soup and dog food, along with toilet paper, corn flakes, sardines, and milk tumbled every which way, and abandoned cash registers and cases of beer leaned crazily out of the splintered windows and were strewn along the avenues. Sheets, blankets, and clothing of every description formed a kind of path, as though people had dropped them while running. I truly had not realized that Harlem *had* so many stores until I saw them all smashed open; the first time the word *wealth* ever entered my mind in relation to Harlem was when I saw it scattered in the streets. But one's first, incongruous impression of plenty was countered immediately by an impression of waste. None of this was doing anybody any good. It would have been better to have left the plate glass as it had been and the goods lying in the stores.

It would have been better, but it would also have been intolerable, for Harlem had needed something to smash. To smash something is the ghetto's chronic need. Most of the time it is the members of the ghetto who smash each other, and themselves. But as long as the ghetto walls are standing there will always come a moment when these outlets do not work. That summer, for example, it was not enough to get into a fight on Lenox Avenue, or curse out one's cronies in the barber shops. If ever, indeed, the violence which fills Harlem's churches, pool halls, and bars erupts outward in a more direct fashion, Harlem and its citizens are likely to vanish in an apocalyptic flood. That this is not likely to happen is due to a great many reasons, most hidden and powerful among them the Negro's real relation to the white American. This relation prohibits, simply, anything as uncomplicated and satisfactory as pure hatred. In order really to hate white people, one has to blot so much out of the mind—and the heart—that this hatred itself becomes an exhausting and self-destructive pose. But this does not mean, on the other hand, that love comes easily: the white world is too powerful, too complacent, too ready with gratuitous humiliation, and, above all, too ignorant and too innocent for that. One is absolutely forced to make perpetual qualifications and one's own reactions are always canceling each other out. It is this, really, which has driven so many people mad, both white and black. One is always in the position of having to decide between amputation and gangrene. Amputation is swift but time may prove that the amputation was not necessary— or one may delay the amputation too long. Gangrene is slow, but it is impossible to be sure that one is reading one's symptoms right. The idea of going through life as a cripple is more than one can bear, and equally unbearable is the risk of swelling up slowly, in agony, with poison. And the trouble, finally, is that the risks are real even if the choices do not exist.

"But as for me and my house," my father had said, "we will serve the Lord." I wondered, as we drove him to his resting place, what this line had meant for him. I had heard him preach it many times. I had preached it once myself, proudly giving it an interpretation different from my father's. Now the whole thing came back to me, as though my father and I were on our way to Sunday school and I were memorizing the golden text: *And if it seem evil unto you to serve the Lord, choose you this day whom you will serve; whether the gods which your fathers served that were on the other side of the flood, or the gods of the Amorites, in whose land ye dwell: but as for me and my house, we will serve the Lord.* I suspected in these familiar lines a meaning which had never been there for me before. All of my father's texts and songs, which I had decided were meaningless, were arranged before me at his death like empty bottles, waiting to hold the meaning which life would give them for me. This was his legacy: nothing is ever escaped. That bleakly memorable morning I hated the unbelievable streets and the Negroes and whites who had, equally, made them that way. But I knew that it was folly, as my father would have said, this bitterness was folly. It was necessary to hold on to the things that mattered. The dead man mattered, the new life mattered; blackness and whiteness did not matter; to believe that they did was to acquiesce in one's own destruction. Hatred, which could destroy so much, never failed to destroy the man who hated and this was an immutable law.

It began to seem that one would have to hold in the mind forever two ideas which seemed to be in opposition. The first idea was acceptance, the acceptance, totally without rancor, of life as it is, and men as they are: in the light of this idea, it goes without saying that injustice is a commonplace. But this did not mean that one could be complacent, for the second idea was of equal power: that one must never, in one's own life, accept these injustices as commonplace but must fight them with all one's strength. This fight begins, however, in the heart and it now had been laid to my charge to keep my own heart free of hatred and despair. This intimation made my heart heavy and, now that my father was irrecoverable, I wished that he had been beside me so that I could have searched his face for the answers which only the future would give me now.

•   •   •   •   •   •   •   •   •   •   •   •

QUESTIONS FOR A SECOND READING

1. Baldwin is usually considered to be one of the great essayists writing in English in the twentieth century. Irving Howe, a distinguished writer and critic, said that Baldwin brought a "new luster" to the essay as an art form, "a form with possibilities for discursive reflection and concrete drama." And, he said, "The style of these essays is a remarkable instance of the way in which a grave and sustained eloquence . . . can be employed in an age deeply suspicious of rhetorical prowess."

    How does Baldwin organize a reader's efforts to understand what this essay is about? And, at the end, for you as its reader, what *is* it about?

    As you reread, think about style as a formal achievement, as a way of organizing not only the material but also a reader's time and attention. The essay is broken into three sections. How does this sectioning work strategically? And how would you describe (or chart) the organization within each section? And, finally, as the essay is a tool for thinking (for "discursive reflection," the writer's and the reader's), what are the points (the sentences or paragraphs) that allow a way of thinking about the people, places, and actions that provide the drama in this essay? Be prepared to turn to particular pages and lines.

2. Question 1 focuses attention on "style." In an interview, Baldwin was once asked, "What do you think readers hope to find in autobiographies?" The interviewer had been talking to Baldwin about his work, including his essays. Baldwin answered, "Somebody said to me once that it's not so much what happens as who it happens to. The sound of the voice is the key; without that it's false."

    As you reread, prepare yourself to talk in detail about "voice" as it is present in the pages of this essay. And prepare yourself for more than one-word descriptions: "honest," "brave," "angry." Choose four or five passages that seem to you to be exemplary. Be prepared to use them to think out loud about character (how you understand and visualize the person speaking) and point of view (how you understand the position, attitudes, habits, or achievements of mind of the person speaking), and think about language (the idiom and rhythm, the echoes and surprises in the ways the speaker speaks). Are you, for example, asked to think of the voice as distinctively defined by race—a "Negro" voice?

3. Here is a characteristic passage from the first section of "Notes of a Native Son." As you reread it, think of the punctuation as part of an expressive project, part of an attempt to order and arrange and control what must be said but cannot be said easily:

He was not a young man when we were growing up and he had already suffered many kinds of ruin; in his outrageously demanding and protective way he loved his children, who were black like him and menaced, like him; and all these things sometimes showed in his face when he tried, never to my knowledge with any success, to establish contact with any of us. When he took one of his children on his knee to play, the child always became fretful and began to cry; when he tried to help one of us with our homework the absolutely unabating tension which emanated from him caused our minds and our tongues to become paralyzed, so that he, scarcely knowing why, flew into a rage and the child, not knowing why, was punished. (p. 53)

If this is done for effect, what *is* the effect?

One way to work on this question is to write parallel sentences, each with the exact number of words in the same order and with the same punctuation. You can fill in any content you want. Once you get inside the sentences, see where they will lead you (or where you must go).

Another way is to find other passages in Baldwin's essay (perhaps pairs of sentences) that you can set beside the passage above. Be prepared in class to lead a discussion of not only what the words say but what their arrangement says (or seems to say).

4. The essay begins with references to two race riots: one in Detroit in the summer of 1943; one in Harlem, New York City, on August 3 of the same year. Go to the library to find newspaper and magazine accounts of one or both of these events. In the almost sixty years since these events, we have developed a careful way of talking in public about race politics in the United States. Use the media accounts in 1943 to get a sense of the language, the explanations, arguments, and stories available to writers at the time. With these in mind, reread to think about Baldwin in 1955, writing with and against standard ways of thinking and speaking.

ASSIGNMENTS FOR WRITING

1. The title of this essay, "Notes of a Native Son," alludes to *Native Son*, the 1940 novel by Richard Wright. The central character of *Native Son* is Bigger Thomas, an angry young black man who kills two women, one white and one black; his actions ignite a race riot in Chicago. Bigger Thomas is characterized by his inarticulateness, his inability to speak from or about his situation, and his anger. Here is a brief passage from *Native Son*. Bigger Thomas, imprisoned and sentenced to death, is in conversation with his lawyer, Max:

Max opened his mouth to say something and Bigger drowned out his voice. "I ain't trying to forgive nobody and I ain't asking for nobody to forgive me. I ain't going to cry. They wouldn't let me live and I killed. Maybe it ain't fair to kill, and I reckon I really didn't want to kill. But when I think of why all the killing was, I begin to feel what I wanted, what I am. . . ."

Bigger saw Max back away from him with compressed lips. But he felt he had to make Max understand how he saw things now.

> "I didn't want to kill!" Bigger shouted. "But what I killed for, I *am!*
> It must've been pretty deep in me to make me kill! I must have felt it
> awful hard to murder."

One way of reading "Notes of a Native Son" is as a revision of Wright's novel, an attempt to create a counterpoint to Bigger Thomas. Bigger struggles to speak. The narrator in "Notes of a Native Son" speaks at great length and with apparent ease. His anger drives him to speak (and write). "Notes" could be said to represent a narrative where Baldwin, a writer of the next generation, provides a voice for Bigger, for his anger and rage, a voice Max could listen to and understand. It tells a story of a native son, born to poverty and discrimination, that does not end in murder and imprisonment.

The speaker in "Notes of a Native Son," like the "Thoreau" in *Walden,* is one of the exemplary characters of American letters. Write an essay on the character of the speaker, or narrator, in "Notes of a Native Son." What is his story? How does he think and speak? How does he make his way in the world? What promise might he offer to a culture still struggling to understand the position of the black man? Can you think of a comparable voice today, in the twenty-first century?

2. Toward the end of his essay, after talking about the riot in Harlem in 1943, Baldwin says,

> If ever, indeed, the violence which fills Harlem's churches, pool halls, and bars erupts outward in a more direct fashion, Harlem and its citizens are likely to vanish in an apocalyptic flood. That this is not likely to happen is due to a great many reasons, most hidden and powerful among them the Negro's real relation to the white American. This relation prohibits, simply, anything as uncomplicated and satisfactory as pure hatred. (p. 66)

We are still, as a country and as a culture, trying to explain to ourselves the real relationship between white Americans and people we now refer to as "African Americans." Choose any contemporary example that is available to you—writing, music, film, TV—something that you could offer as a parallel attempt to represent the relationship of black to white Americans. Write an essay in which you compare "Notes" with whatever example you have chosen.

Assume that your reader is familiar with neither of your selections. You will need to introduce and present "Notes of a Native Son" (present through summary, paraphrase, and quotation), and you will need to do the same for the example you bring to this project. The point of the comparison (or one of its points) should be to think about the history of the representation of race.

3. Irving Howe, a distinguished writer and critic, said that Baldwin brought a "new luster" to the essay as an art form, "a form with possibilities for discursive reflection and concrete drama." And, he said, "The style of these essays is a remarkable instance of the way in which a grave and sustained eloquence . . . can be employed in an age deeply suspicious of rhetorical prowess."

Write an essay in which you consider and present "Notes of a Native Son" as an example of the essay as a genre. You could imagine that you are writing a review; you could imagine that you are writing for an audience of writers, people like yourself who are studying the arts of nonfiction and trying to imagine its uses and possibilities. You should imagine that you are writing for a reader who may know something about James Baldwin but who doesn't have "Notes" close at hand or firmly in memory. You will need to provide a careful presentation, then, on both what the essay says and what it does (or how it says what it says). And you should be sure to use this occasion to speak for yourself as a writer and on the question of the essay as a genre that might be useful for you and for your generation.

The exercise defined above in the first of the "Questions for a Second Reading" might help you prepare to work on this project.

4. Irving Howe, a distinguished writer and critic, said that Baldwin brought a "new luster" to the essay as an art form, "a form with possibilities for discursive reflection and concrete drama." And, he said, "The style of these essays is a remarkable instance of the way in which a grave and sustained eloquence . . . can be employed in an age deeply suspicious of rhetorical prowess."

"Discursive reflection and concrete drama." "Notes of a Native Son" is a mix of narrative (or story) and argument (or commentary). This is not the kind of argument that works from thesis statement through example to conclusion. It works slowly, indirectly, by accretion and apposition, and with a careful, determined attention to detail. As way of rereading Baldwin's essay, write a Baldwin-like essay of your own.

This is an invitation to carry out a similar project, one that reproduces his method and style, extends his example to a new set of materials. You can choose any subject (or person, or occurrence) as your narrative center; your goal should be to connect the local with the national, the personal history with larger issues or concerns, and to use concrete drama as the occasion for discursive reflection. It is also an invitation to formal experimentation, to try out Baldwin-like sentences, paragraphs, and chapters (or subsections).

5. Baldwin says this about the eulogy at his father's funeral:

> Every man in the chapel hoped that when his hour came he, too, would be eulogized, which is to say forgiven, and that all of his lapses, greeds, errors, and strayings from the truth would be invested with coherence and looked upon with charity. This was perhaps the last thing human beings could give each other and it was what they demanded, after all, of the Lord. (p. 63)

At this moment in the essay a reader is invited to think about "Notes of a Native Son." It is not a eulogy, at least not technically, since it was written long after the funeral and not read at the ceremony. The essay is, among other things, a son's public account of his father.

Write an essay in which you contextualize, examine, and explain Baldwin's representation of his father in "Notes of a Native Son." What does Baldwin say, in the end, about his father? How are we asked to understand this man in relation to his family? to history? What use is Baldwin making of his father and his story?

MAKING CONNECTIONS

1. Toward the end of his essay, after talking about the riot in Harlem in 1943, Baldwin says,

   > If ever, indeed, the violence which fills Harlem's churches, pool halls, and bars erupts outward in a more direct fashion, Harlem and its citizens are likely to vanish in an apocalyptic flood. That this is not likely to happen is due to a great many reasons, most hidden and powerful among them the Negro's real relation to the white American. This relation prohibits, simply, anything as uncomplicated and satisfactory as pure hatred. (p. 66)

   We are still, as a country and as a culture, trying to explain to ourselves the real relationship between white Americans and people we now refer to as "African Americans." *Ways of Reading* contains three other documents that are part of this history: "Incidents in the Life of a Slave Girl" (Harriet Jacobs, p. 428), "In Search of Our Mothers' Gardens" (Alice Walker, p. 739), and "Our Time" (John Edgar Wideman, p. 752).

   Write an essay about one of these as read next to, or through, "Notes of a Native Son." Assume that your reader is familiar with neither of your selections. You will need to introduce and present both documents (present through summary, paraphrase, and quotation). The purpose of the comparison should be to think about the history and the problems of representing what Baldwin refers to as "the Negro's real relation to the white American."

2. Susan Griffin in "Our Secret" (p. 345), Adrienne Rich in "When We Dead Awaken: Writing as Re-Vision" (p. 627), and James Baldwin in "Notes of a Native Son" each use family history to think about and to represent forces beyond the family that shape human life and possibility: war, patriarchy, race. Susan Griffin explains her motives this way, "One can find traces of every life in each life."

   Perhaps. It is a bold step to think that this is true and to believe that one can, or should, write the family into the national or international narrative. Write an essay in which you read "Notes of a Native Son" alongside one of the other two. Your goal is not only to discuss how these writers do what they do, and to what conclusions and to what ends, but also to discuss your sense of what is at stake in such a project. What are the technical issues? How does a skilled writer handle this project? What would lead a writer to write something like this? Would you do it? where and how? for whose benefit?

WALTER BENJAMIN

WALTER BENJAMIN *was born in 1892 in Berlin, Germany. He was raised in a prosperous Jewish family and educated at the universities of Freiburg, Munich, Berlin, and Bern. He had hoped for a university career, but his work was idiosyncratic, running counter to the traditions of German scholarship and, at thirty-three, he was denied a position at Frankfurt. He lived off a stipend from his father and money earned by freelance writing for magazines and newspapers (writing on religion, art, literature, and philosophy). He became interested in the writings of Karl Marx and in communism; his friends, including the German avant-garde playwright, Bertolt Brecht, were leftist intellectuals. In 1927 he traveled to Moscow to learn more about the Soviet state; he did not, however, become a member of the Communist Party, nor was he involved in street-level politics.*

Concerned about the Nazi rise to power, Benjamin left Berlin in 1933 for Paris, where he continued to write and where, in fact, he wrote the essays which have established his reputation today, including the following selection, "The Work of Art in the Age of Mechanical Reproduction" (1936). In Paris, he was supported, in part, by the Frankfurt Institute for Social Research and assisted in his work by his friend and editor, Theodor Adorno. At this point, Benjamin's life took a strange and tragic turn.

In 1940, after the Nazi occupation of Paris, Benjamin fled with a group of refugees to the Pyrenees Mountains on the border of Spain, taking only the manuscripts and papers he could carry, hoping to cross Spain to Portugal and from there to flee by boat to the United States. The refugees were turned back at the border since they did not have the appropriate exit visas. In despair Benjamin took his own life. Those who remained were allowed to cross the border a few weeks later.

"The Work of Art in the Age of Mechanical Reproduction" has become a key essay for those interested in the study of culture. It is not an easy read. It will help to remember the date of its writing, 1936. Benjamin focuses on changes in the ways in which art—music, literature, painting, drama—is produced and made available to a mass audience. He is writing about radio, photography, and film at a time when these media (and the technology supporting them) were not so easily taken for granted. The world he is imagining is in many ways ours, although he cannot imagine television, the Walkman, the Internet. You will need to sense his wonder and ambivalence in the face of technological change, and you will need to be able to think back and forth between the 1930s and the present, and to our own concerns about the effects of mechanical reproduction.

It will also help to have some sense of the terms that ground Benjamin's argument. They come from his reading of Marx and participate in a way of thinking about individual lives and historical change, about modes of production (forms of work) and the social relations they create that are characteristic of Marxist thinking. In the preface to "The Work of Art in the Age of Mechanical Reproduction" (which, like most prefaces, will make much better sense after you have finished the essay), Benjamin says, "The transformation of the superstructure, which takes place far more slowly than that of the substructure, has taken more than half a century to manifest in all areas of culture the change in the conditions of production."

The "substructure," in this form of analysis, can be thought of as economic forces, as work, as the people who are engaged in producing food, clothing, shelter, and the material necessities of life. In Europe by the 1930s, the conditions of work had produced a large working-class urban population (the proletariat), and it was believed that their force and interests would produce a revolution to transform social relations. The "superstructure" can be thought of as the society's way of understanding and regulating itself through education, culture, art, law, religion, philosophy, and politics. Benjamin argues that the ways people produce and consume art are in dramatic transition and that they have not yet caught up with the changes in life at the ground level. The old ways of seeing art, of using art in service of faith and belief, these no longer work; the world is at a moment of transition, he argues, where tradition no longer holds or has power—a painting no longer can mean what it once meant. When Benjamin refers to "dialecticians" or "progressives," he is referring to those who are thinking inside this argument. When he refers to fascists, it is to those with a different argument to make, where order needs to be imposed on history and on the masses from the top down, by force and strict governmental regulation.

It is worth noting that Benjamin is not a systematic, doctrinaire, or rigid Marxist. You will see this as you read the essay. It does not set out to prove anything or to force belief along predictable lines. The political theorist Hannah Arendt, who introduced Benjamin to a wide U.S. readership in the late 1960s, said,

> Benjamin probably was the most peculiar Marxist ever produced by this movement. . . . The theoretical aspect that was bound to fascinate him was the doctrine of the superstructure, which was only briefly sketched by Marx but then assumed a disproportionate role in the movement as it was joined by a disproportionately large number of intellectuals, hence by people who were interested only in the superstructure. Benjamin used this doctrine only as a heuristic-methodological stimulus and was hardly interested in its historical or philosophical background.

Finally, it should help you to know in advance that the essay has an odd and distinctive way of moving from point to point or page to page. It is, for example, important to read all the footnotes. They are very much a part of Benjamin's writing. (They are not "mere" documentation, in other words.) Many of them contain long quotations from other works. Benjamin was a great collector of quotations, notebooks full. Arendt says that these collections could be imagined as Benjamin's primary work; they were not simply devices to support arguments: "The main work consisted in tearing fragments out of their context and arranging them afresh in such a way that they illustrated one another and were able to prove their raison d'être in a free-floating state, as it were. It definitely was a sort of surrealistic montage." And you'll note that the essay is divided into numbered subsections. Each one is its own brief meditation, a moment of attention and assembly, a putting of this together with that (a magician and a surgeon, a painter and a filmmaker); together the numbered sections present an argument and a conclusion, but not in textbook style—dominated by a thesis and moving systematically to final statement. In fact you need to sense, at the end, the difficulty or ambivalence Benjamin expresses in endorsing the new forms of art over the old.

The Work of Art in the Age of Mechanical Reproduction

"Our fine arts were developed, their types and uses were established, in times very different from the present, by men whose power of action upon things was insignificant in comparison with ours. But the amazing growth of our techniques, the adaptability and precision they have attained, the ideas and habits they are creating, make it a certainty that profound changes are impending in the ancient craft of the Beautiful. In all the arts there is a physical component which can no longer be considered or treated as it used to be, which cannot remain unaffected by our modern knowledge and power. For the last twenty years neither matter nor space nor time has been what it was from time immemorial. We must expect great innova-

tions to transform the entire technique of the arts, thereby affecting artistic invention itself and perhaps even bringing about
an amazing change in our very notion of art."[1]
> —PAUL VALÉRY, Pièces sur l'art,
> "La Conquête de l'ubiquité," Paris.

Preface

When Marx undertook his critique of the capitalistic mode of production, this mode was in its infancy. Marx directed his efforts in such a way
as to give them prognostic value. He went back to the basic conditions underlying capitalistic production and through his presentation showed
what could be expected of capitalism in the future. The result was that one
could expect it not only to exploit the proletariat with increasing intensity,
but ultimately to create conditions which would make it possible to abolish capitalism itself.

The transformation of the superstructure, which takes place far more
slowly than that of the substructure, has taken more than half a century
to manifest in all areas of culture the change in the conditions of production. Only today can it be indicated what form this has taken. Certain
prognostic requirements should be met by these statements. However,
theses about the art of the proletariat after its assumption of power or
about the art of a classless society would have less bearing on these
demands than theses about the developmental tendencies of art under
present conditions of production. Their dialectic is no less noticeable in
the superstructure than in the economy. It would therefore be wrong to
underestimate the value of such theses as a weapon. They brush aside a
number of outmoded concepts, such as creativity and genius, eternal
value and mystery—concepts whose uncontrolled (and at present almost
uncontrollable) application would lead to a processing of data in the
Fascist sense. The concepts which are introduced into the theory of art
in what follows differ from the more familiar terms in that they are
completely useless for the purposes of Fascism. They are, on the other
hand, useful for the formulation of revolutionary demands in the politics
of art.

I

In principle a work of art has always been reproducible. Man-made artifacts could always be imitated by men. Replicas were made by pupils in
practice of their craft, by masters for diffusing their works, and, finally, by

---

[1]Quoted from Paul Valéry, *Aesthetics*, "The Conquest of Ubiquity," translated by
Ralph Manheim, p. 225. Pantheon Books, Bollingen Series, New York, 1964. [All notes
are Benjamin's unless otherwise specified.]

third parties in the pursuit of gain. Mechanical reproduction of a work of art, however, represents something new. Historically, it advanced intermittently and in leaps at long intervals, but with accelerated intensity. The Greeks knew only two procedures of technically reproducing works of art: founding and stamping. Bronzes, terra cottas, and coins were the only art works which they could produce in quantity. All others were unique and could not be mechanically reproduced. With the woodcut graphic art became mechanically reproducible for the first time, long before script became reproducible by print. The enormous changes which printing, the mechanical reproduction of writing, has brought about in literature are a familiar story. However, within the phenomenon which we are here examining from the perspective of world history, print is merely a special, though particularly important, case. During the Middle Ages engraving and etching were added to the woodcut; at the beginning of the nineteenth century lithography made its appearance.

With lithography the technique of reproduction reached an essentially new stage. This much more direct process was distinguished by the tracing of the design on a stone rather than its incision on a block of wood or its etching on a copperplate and permitted graphic art for the first time to put its products on the market, not only in large numbers as hitherto, but also in daily changing forms. Lithography enabled graphic art to illustrate everyday life, and it began to keep pace with printing. But only a few decades after its invention, lithography was surpassed by photography. For the first time in the process of pictorial reproduction, photography freed the hand of the most important artistic functions which henceforth devolved only upon the eye looking into a lens. Since the eye perceives more swiftly than the hand can draw, the process of pictorial reproduction was accelerated so enormously that it could keep pace with speech. A film operator shooting a scene in the studio captures the images at the speed of an actor's speech. Just as lithography virtually implied the illustrated newspaper, so did photography foreshadow the sound film. The technical reproduction of sound was tackled at the end of the last century. These convergent endeavors made predictable a situation which Paul Valéry pointed up in this sentence: "Just as water, gas, and electricity are brought into our houses from far off to satisfy our needs in response to a minimal effort, so we shall be supplied with visual or auditory images, which will appear and disappear at a simple movement of the hand, hardly more than a sign" [*op. cit.*, p. 226]. Around 1900 technical reproduction had reached a standard that not only permitted it to reproduce all transmitted works of art and thus to cause the most profound change in their impact upon the public; it also had captured a place of its own among the artistic processes. For the study of this standard nothing is more revealing than the nature of the repercussions that these two different manifestations—the reproduction of works of art and the art of the film—have had on art in its traditional form.

lack presence of time

II

Even the most perfect reproduction of a work of art is lacking in one element: its presence in time and space, its unique existence at the place where it happens to be. This unique existence of the work of art determined the history to which it was subject throughout the time of its existence. This includes the changes which it may have suffered in physical condition over the years as well as the various changes in its ownership.[2] The traces of the first can be revealed only by chemical or physical analyses which it is impossible to perform on a reproduction; changes of ownership are subject to a tradition which must be traced from the situation of the original.

authenticity

miles auothint

The presence of the original is the prerequisite to the concept of authenticity. Chemical analyses of the patina of a bronze can help to establish this, as does the proof that a given manuscript of the Middle Ages stems from an archive of the fifteenth century. The whole sphere of authenticity is outside technical—and, of course, not only technical— reproducibility.[3] Confronted with its manual reproduction, which was usually branded as a forgery, the original preserved all its authority; not so *vis à vis* technical reproduction. The reason is twofold. First, process reproduction is more independent of the original than manual reproduction. For example, in photography, process reproduction can bring out those aspects of the original that are unattainable to the naked eye yet accessible to the lens, which is adjustable and chooses its angle at will. And photographic reproduction, with the aid of certain processes, such as enlargement or slow motion, can capture images which escape natural vision. Secondly, technical reproduction can put the copy of the original into situations which would be out of reach for the original itself. Above all, it enables the original to meet the beholder halfway, be it in the form of a photograph or a phonograph record. The cathedral leaves its locale to be received in the studio of a lover of art; the choral production, performed in an auditorium or in the open air, resounds in the drawing room.

The situations into which the product of mechanical reproduction can be brought may not touch the actual work of art, yet the quality of its pres-

---

[2]Of course, the history of a work of art encompasses more than this. The history of the "Mona Lisa," for instance, encompasses the kind and number of its copies made in the seventeenth, eighteenth, and nineteenth centuries.

[3]Precisely because authenticity is not reproducible, the intensive penetration of certain (mechanical) processes of reproduction was instrumental in differentiating and grading authenticity. To develop such differentiations was an important function of the trade in works of art. The invention of the woodcut may be said to have struck at the root of the quality of authenticity even before its late flowering. To be sure, at the time of its origin a medieval picture of the Madonna could not yet be said to be "authentic." It became "authentic" only during the succeeding centuries and perhaps most strikingly so during the last one.

ence is always depreciated. This holds not only for the art work but also, for instance, for a landscape which passes in review before the spectator in a movie. In the case of the art object, a most sensitive nucleus—namely, its authenticity—is interfered with whereas no natural object is vulnerable on that score. The authenticity of a thing is the essence of all that is transmissible from its beginning, ranging from its substantive duration to its testimony to the history which it has experienced. Since the historical testimony rests on the authenticity, the former, too, is jeopardized by reproduction when substantive duration ceases to matter. And what is really jeopardized when the historical testimony is affected is the authority of the object.[4]

One might subsume the eliminated element in the term "aura" and go on to say: that which withers in the age of mechanical reproduction is the aura of the work of art. This is a symptomatic process whose significance points beyond the realm of art. One might generalize by saying: the technique of reproduction detaches the reproduced object from the domain of tradition. By making many reproductions it substitutes a plurality of copies for a unique existence. And in permitting the reproduction to meet the beholder or listener in his own particular situation, it reactivates the object reproduced. These two processes lead to a tremendous shattering of tradition which is the obverse of the contemporary crisis and renewal of mankind. Both processes are intimately connected with the contemporary mass movements. Their most powerful agent is the film. Its social significance, particularly in its most positive form, is inconceivable without its destructive, cathartic aspect, that is, the liquidation of the traditional value of the cultural heritage. This phenomenon is most palpable in the great historical films. It extends to ever new positions. In 1927 Abel Gance exclaimed enthusiastically: "Shakespeare, Rembrandt, Beethoven will make films . . . all legends, all mythologies and all myths, all founders of religion, and the very religions . . . await their exposed resurrection, and the heroes crowd each other at the gate."[5] Presumably without intending it, he issued an invitation to a far-reaching liquidation.

III

During long periods of history, the mode of human sense perception changes with humanity's entire mode of existence. The manner in which human sense perception is organized, the medium in which it is

---

[4]The poorest provincial staging of *Faust* is superior to a Faust film in that, ideally, it competes with the first performance at Weimar. Before the screen it is unprofitable to remember traditional contents which might come to mind before the stage—for instance, that Goethe's friend Johann Heinrich Merck is hidden in Mephisto, and the like.

[5]Abel Gance, "Le Temps de l'image est venu," *L'Art cinématographique*, Vol. 2, pp. 94 f, Paris, 1927.

accomplished, is determined not only by nature but by historical circumstances as well. The fifth century, with its great shifts of population, saw the birth of the late Roman art industry and the Vienna Genesis, and there developed not only an art different from that of antiquity but also a new kind of perception. The scholars of the Viennese school, Riegl and Wickhoff, who resisted the weight of classical tradition under which these later art forms had been buried, were the first to draw conclusions from them concerning the organization of perception at the time. However far-reaching their insight, these scholars limited themselves to showing the significant, formal hallmark which characterized perception in late Roman times. They did not attempt—and, perhaps, saw no way—to show the social transformations expressed by these changes of perception. The conditions for an analogous insight are more favorable in the present. And if changes in the medium of contemporary perception can be comprehended as decay of the aura, it is possible to show its social causes.

The concept of aura which was proposed above with reference to historical objects may usefully be illustrated with reference to the aura of natural ones. We define the aura of the latter as the unique phenomenon of a distance, however close it may be. If, while resting on a summer afternoon, you follow with your eyes a mountain range on the horizon or a branch which casts its shadow over you, you experience the aura of those mountains, of that branch. This image makes it easy to comprehend the social bases of the contemporary decay of the aura. It rests on two circumstances, both of which are related to the increasing significance of the masses in contemporary life. Namely, the desire of contemporary masses to bring things "closer" spatially and humanly, which is just as ardent as their bent toward overcoming the uniqueness of every reality by accepting its reproduction.[6] Every day the urge grows stronger to get hold of an object at very close range by way of its likeness, its reproduction. Unmistakably, reproduction as offered by picture magazines and newsreels differs from the image seen by the unarmed eye. Uniqueness and permanence are as closely linked in the latter as are transitoriness and reproducibility in the former. To pry an object from its shell, to destroy its aura, is the mark of a perception whose "sense of the universal equality of things" has increased to such a degree that it extracts it even from a unique object by means of reproduction. Thus is manifested in the field of perception what in the theoretical sphere is noticeable in the increasing importance of statistics. The adjustment of reality to the masses and of the

---

[6]To satisfy the human interest of the masses may mean to have one's social function removed from the field of vision. Nothing guarantees that a portraitist of today, when painting a famous surgeon at the breakfast table in the midst of his family, depicts his social function more precisely than a painter of the seventeenth century who portrayed his medical doctors as representing this profession, like Rembrandt in his "Anatomy Lesson."

masses to reality is a process of unlimited scope, as much for thinking as for perception.

IV

The uniqueness of a work of art is inseparable from its being imbedded in the fabric of tradition. This tradition itself is thoroughly alive and extremely changeable. An ancient statue of Venus, for example, stood in a different traditional context with the Greeks, who made it an object of veneration, than with the clerics of the Middle Ages, who viewed it as an ominous idol. Both of them, however, were equally confronted with its uniqueness, that is, its aura. Originally the contextual integration of art in tradition found its expression in the cult. We know that the earliest art works originated in the service of a ritual—first the magical, then the religious kind. It is significant that the existence of the work of art with reference to its aura is never entirely separated from its ritual function.[7] In other words, the unique value of the "authentic" work of art has its basis in ritual, the location of its original use value. This ritualistic basis, however remote, is still recognizable as secularized ritual even in the most profane forms of the cult of beauty.[8] The secular cult of beauty, developed during the Renaissance and prevailing for three centuries, clearly showed that ritualistic basis in its decline and the first deep crisis which befell it. With the advent of the first truly revolutionary means of reproduction, photography, simultaneously with the rise of socialism, art sensed the approaching crisis which has become evident a century later. At the time, art reacted with the doctrine of *l'art pour l'art*,[9] that is, with a theology of art. This gave rise to what might be called a negative theology in the form of the idea of "pure" art, which not only denied any social function of art but also any categorizing by subject matter. (In poetry, Mallarmé was the first to take this position.)

---

[7]The definition of the aura as a "unique phenomenon of a distance however close it may be" represents nothing but the formulation of the cult value of the work of art in categories of space and time perception. Distance is the opposite of closeness. The essentially distant object is the unapproachable one. Unapproachability is indeed a major quality of the cult image. True to its nature, it remains "distant, however close it may be." The closeness which one may gain from its subject matter does not impair the distance which it retains in its appearance.

[8]To the extent to which the cult value of the painting is secularized the ideas of its fundamental uniqueness lose distinctness. In the imagination of the beholder the uniqueness of the phenomena which hold sway in the cult image is more and more displaced by the empirical uniqueness of the creator or of his creative achievement. To be sure, never completely so; the concept of authenticity always transcends mere genuineness. (This is particularly apparent in the collector who always retains some traces of the fetishist and who, by owning the work of art, shares in its ritual power.) Nevertheless, the function of the concept of authenticity remains determinate in the evaluation of art; with the secularization of art, authenticity displaces the cult value of the work.

[9]*l'art pour l'art*   "Art for art's sake." [Editors' note]

An analysis of art in the age of mechanical reproduction must do justice to these relationships, for they lead us to an all-important insight: for the first time in world history, mechanical reproduction emancipates the work of art from its parasitical dependence on ritual. To an ever greater degree the work of art reproduced becomes the work of art designed for reproducibility.[10] From a photographic negative, for example, one can make any number of prints; to ask for the "authentic" print makes no sense. But the instant the criterion of authenticity ceases to be applicable to artistic production, the total function of art is reversed. Instead of being based on ritual, it begins to be based on another practice—politics.

V

Works of art are received and valued on different planes. Two polar types stand out: with one, the accent is on the cult value; with the other, on the exhibition value of the work.[11] Artistic production begins with ceremonial objects destined to serve in a cult. One may assume that what mattered was their existence, not their being on view. The elk portrayed by the man of

---

[10]In the case of films, mechanical reproduction is not, as with literature and painting, an external condition for mass distribution. Mechanical reproduction is inherent in the very technique of film production. This technique not only permits in the most direct way but virtually causes mass distribution. It enforces distribution because the production of a film is so expensive that an individual who, for instance, might afford to buy a painting no longer can afford to buy a film. In 1927 it was calculated that a major film, in order to pay its way, had to reach an audience of nine million. With the sound film, to be sure, a setback in its international distribution occurred at first: audiences became limited by language barriers. This coincided with the Fascist emphasis on national interests. It is more important to focus on this connection with Fascism than on this setback, which was soon minimized by synchronization. The simultaneity of both phenomena is attributable to the depression. The same disturbances which, on a larger scale, led to an attempt to maintain the existing property structure by sheer force led the endangered film capital to speed up the development of the sound film. The introduction of the sound film brought about a temporary relief, not only because it again brought the masses into the theaters but also because it merged new capital from the electrical industry with that of the film industry. Thus, viewed from the outside, the sound film promoted national interests, but seen from the inside it helped to internationalize film production even more than previously.

[11]This polarity cannot come into its own in the aesthetics of Idealism. Its idea of beauty comprises these polar opposites without differentiating between them and consequently excludes their polarity. Yet in Hegel this polarity announces itself as clearly as possible within the limits of Idealism. We quote from his *Philosophy of History:*

> "Images were known of old. Piety at an early time required them for worship, but it could do without *beautiful* images. These might even be disturbing. In every beautiful painting there is also something nonspiritual, merely external, but its spirit speaks to man through its beauty. Worshipping, conversely, is concerned with the work as an object, for it is but a spiritless stupor of the soul. . . . Fine art has arisen . . . in the church . . . , although it has already gone beyond its principle as art."

Likewise, the following passage from *The Philosophy of Fine Art* indicates that Hegel sensed a problem here.

the Stone Age on the walls of his cave was an instrument of magic. He did expose it to his fellow men, but in the main it was meant for the spirits. Today the cult value would seem to demand that the work of art remain hidden. Certain statues of gods are accessible only to the priest in the cella; certain Madonnas remain covered nearly all year round; certain sculptures on medieval cathedrals are invisible to the spectator on ground level. With the emancipation of the various art practices from ritual go increasing opportunities for the exhibition of their products. It is easier to exhibit a portrait bust that can be sent here and there than to exhibit the statue of a divinity that has its fixed place in the interior of a temple. The same holds for the painting as against the mosaic or fresco that preceded it. And even though the public presentability of a mass originally may have been just as great as that of a symphony, the latter originated at the moment when its public presentability promised to surpass that of the mass.

With the different methods of technical reproduction of a work of art, its fitness for exhibition increased to such an extent that the quantitative shift between its two poles turned into a qualitative transformation of its nature. This is comparable to the situation of the work of art in prehistoric times when, by the absolute emphasis on its cult value, it was, first and foremost, an instrument of magic. Only later did it come to be recognized as a work of art. In the same way today, by the absolute emphasis on its exhibition value the work of art becomes a creation with entirely new functions, among

---

"We are beyond the stage of reverence for works of art as divine and objects deserving our worship. The impression they produce is one of a more reflective kind, and the emotions they arouse require a higher test. . . ."—G. W. F. Hegel, *The Philosophy of Fine Art*, trans., with notes, by F. P. B. Osmaston, Vol. 1, p. 12, London, 1920.

The transition from the first kind of artistic reception to the second characterizes the history of artistic reception in general. Apart from that, a certain oscillation between these two polar modes of reception can be demonstrated for each work of art. Take the Sistine Madonna. Since Hubert Grimme's research it has been known that the Madonna originally was painted for the purpose of exhibition. Grimme's research was inspired by the question: What is the purpose of the molding in the foreground of the painting which the two cupids lean upon? How, Grimme asked further, did Raphael come to furnish the sky with two draperies? Research proved that the Madonna had been commissioned for the public lying-in-state of Pope Sixtus. The Popes lay in state in a certain side chapel of St. Peter's. On that occasion Raphael's picture had been fastened in a nichelike background of the chapel, supported by the coffin. In this picture Raphael portrays the Madonna approaching the papal coffin in clouds from the background of the niche, which was demarcated by green drapes. At the obsequies of Sixtus a pre-eminent exhibition value of Raphael's picture was taken advantage of. Some time later it was placed on the high altar in the church of the Black Friars at Piacenza. The reason for this exile is to be found in the Roman rites which forbid the use of paintings exhibited at obsequies as cult objects on the high altar. This regulation devalued Raphael's picture to some degree. In order to obtain an adequate price nevertheless, the Papal See resolved to add to the bargain the tacit toleration of the picture above the high altar. To avoid attention the picture was given to the monks of the far-off provincial town.

which the one we are conscious of, the artistic function, later may be recognized as incidental.[12] This much is certain: today photography and the film are the most serviceable exemplifications of this new function.

VI

In photography, exhibition value begins to displace cult value all along the line. But cult value does not give way without resistance. It retires into an ultimate retrenchment: the human countenance. It is no accident that the portrait was the focal point of early photography. The cult of remembrance of loved ones, absent or dead, offers a last refuge for the cult value of the picture. For the last time the aura emanates from the early photographs in the fleeting expression of a human face. This is what constitutes their melancholy, incomparable beauty. But as man withdraws from the photographic image, the exhibition value for the first time shows its superiority to the ritual value. To have pinpointed this new stage constitutes the incomparable significance of Atget, who, around 1900, took photographs of deserted Paris streets. It has quite justly been said of him that he photographed them like scenes of crime. The scene of a crime, too, is deserted; it is photographed for the purpose of establishing evidence. With Atget, photographs become standard evidence for historical occurrences, and acquire a hidden political significance. They demand a specific kind of approach; free-floating contemplation is not appropriate to them. They stir the viewer; he feels challenged by them in a new way. At the same time picture magazines begin to put up signposts for him, right ones or wrong ones, no matter. For the first time, captions have become obligatory. And it is clear that they have an altogether different character than the title of a painting. The directives which the captions give to those looking at pictures in illustrated magazines soon become even more explicit and more imperative in the film where the meaning of each single picture appears to be prescribed by the sequence of all preceding ones.

VII

The nineteenth-century dispute as to the artistic value of painting versus photography today seems devious and confused. This does not diminish its importance, however; if anything, it underlines it. The dispute was in fact

---

[12]Bertolt Brecht, on a different level, engaged in analogous reflections: "If the concept of 'work of art' can no longer be applied to the thing that emerges once the work is transformed into a commodity, we have to eliminate this concept with cautious care but without fear, lest we liquidate the function of the very thing as well. For it has to go through this phase without mental reservation, and not as noncommittal deviation from the straight path; rather, what happens here with the work of art will change it fundamentally and erase its past to such an extent that should the old concept be taken up again—and it will, why not?—it will no longer stir any memory of the thing it once designated."

the symptom of a historical transformation the universal impact of which was not realized by either of the rivals. When the age of mechanical reproduction separated art from its basis in cult, the semblance of its autonomy disappeared forever. The resulting change in the function of art transcended the perspective of the century; for a long time it even escaped that of the twentieth century, which experienced the development of the film.

Earlier much futile thought had been devoted to the question of whether photography is an art. The primary question—whether the very invention of photography had not transformed the entire nature of art—was not raised. Soon the film theoreticians asked the same ill-considered question with regard to the film. But the difficulties which photography caused traditional aesthetics were mere child's play as compared to those raised by the film. Whence the insensitive and forced character of early theories of the film. Abel Gance, for instance, compares the film with hieroglyphs: "Here, by a remarkable regression, we have come back to the level of expression of the Egyptians. . . . Pictorial language has not yet matured because our eyes have not yet adjusted to it. There is as yet insufficient respect for, insufficient cult of, what it expresses."[13] Or, in the words of Séverin-Mars: "What art has been granted a dream more poetical and more real at the same time! Approached in this fashion the film might represent an incomparable means of expression. Only the most high-minded persons, in the most perfect and mysterious moments of their lives, should be allowed to enter its ambience."[14] Alexandre Arnoux concludes his fantasy about the silent film with the question: "Do not all the bold descriptions we have given amount to the definition of prayer?"[15] It is instructive to note how their desire to class the film among the "arts" forces these theoreticians to read ritual elements into it—with a striking lack of discretion. Yet when these speculations were published, films like *L'Opinion publique* and *The Gold Rush* had already appeared. This, however, did not keep Abel Gance from adducing hieroglyphs for purposes of comparison, nor Séverin-Mars from speaking of the film as one might speak of paintings by Fra Angelico. Characteristically, even today ultra-reactionary authors give the film a similar contextual significance—if not an outright sacred one, then at least a supernatural one. Commenting on Max Reinhardt's film version of *A Midsummer Night's Dream,* Werfel states that undoubtedly it was the sterile copying of the exterior world with its streets, interiors, railroad stations, restaurants, motorcars, and beaches which until now had obstructed the elevation of the film to the realm of art. "The film has not yet realized its true meaning, its real possibilities . . . these consist in its unique faculty to express by natural means and with

---

[13] Abel Gance, *op. cit.*, pp. 100–1.
[14] Séverin-Mars, quoted by Abel Gance, *op. cit.*, p. 100.
[15] Alexandre Arnoux, *Cinéma pris*, 1929, p. 28.

incomparable persuasiveness all that is fairylike, marvelous, super-natural."[16]

VIII

The artistic performance of a stage actor is definitely presented to the public by the actor in person; that of the screen actor, however, is presented by a camera, with a twofold consequence. The camera that presents the performance of the film actor to the public need not respect the performance as an integral whole. Guided by the cameraman, the camera continually changes its position with respect to the performance. The sequence of positional views which the editor composes from the material supplied him constitutes the completed film. It comprises certain factors of movement which are in reality those of the camera, not to mention special camera angles, close-ups, etc. Hence, the performance of the actor is subjected to a series of optical tests. This is the first consequence of the fact that the actor's performance is presented by means of a camera. Also, the film actor lacks the opportunity of the stage actor to adjust to the audience during this performance, since he does not present his performance to the audience in person. This permits the audience to take the position of a critic, without experiencing any personal contact with the actor. The audience's identification with the actor is really an identification with the camera. Consequently, the audience takes the position of the camera; its approach is that of testing.[17] This is not the approach to which cult values may be exposed.

IX

For the film, what matters primarily is that the actor represents himself to the public before the camera, rather than representing someone else. One of the first to sense the actor's metamorphosis by this form of testing was Pirandello. Though his remarks on the subject in his novel *Si Gira* were limited to the negative aspects of the question and to the silent film only, this hardly impairs their validity. For in this respect, the sound film

---

[16]Franz Werfel, "Ein Sommernachstraum, Ein Film von Shakespeare und Reinhardt," *Neues Wiener Journal,* cited in *Lu* 15, November, 1935.

[17]"The film . . . provides—or could provide—useful insight into the details of human actions. . . . Character is never used as a source of motivation; the inner life of the persons never supplies the principal cause of the plot and seldom is its main result." (Bertolt Brecht, *Versuche,* "Der Dreigroschenprozess," p. 268.) The expansion of the field of the testable which mechanical equipment brings about for the actor corresponds to the extraordinary expansion of the field of the testable brought about for the individual through economic conditions. Thus, vocational aptitude tests become constantly more important. What matters in these tests are segmental performances of the individual. The film shot and the vocational aptitude test are taken before a committee of experts. The camera director in the studio occupies a place identical with that of the examiner during aptitude tests.

did not change anything essential. What matters is that the part is acted not for an audience but for a mechanical contrivance—in the case of the sound film, for two of them. "The film actor," wrote Pirandello, "feels as if in exile—exiled not only from the stage but also from himself. With a vague sense of discomfort he feels inexplicable emptiness: his body loses its corporeality, it evaporates, it is deprived of reality, life, voice, and the noises caused by his moving about, in order to be changed into a mute image, flickering an instant on the screen, then vanishing into silence. . . . The projector will play with his shadow before the public, and he himself must be content to play before the camera."[18] This situation might also be characterized as follows: for the first time—and this is the effect of the film—man has to operate with his whole living person, yet forgoing its aura. For aura is tied to his presence; there can be no replica of it. The aura which, on the stage, emanates from Macbeth, cannot be separated for the spectators from that of the actor. However, the singularity of the shot in the studio is that the camera is substituted for the public. Consequently, the aura that envelops the actor vanishes, and with it the aura of the figure he portrays.

It is not surprising that it should be a dramatist such as Pirandello who, in characterizing the film, inadvertently touches on the very crisis in which we see the theater. Any thorough study proves that there is indeed no greater contrast than that of the stage play to a work of art that is completely subject to or, like the film, founded in, mechanical reproduction. Experts have long recognized that in the film "the greatest effects are almost always obtained by 'acting' as little as possible. . . ." In 1932 Rudolf Arnheim saw "the latest trend . . . in treating the actor as a stage prop chosen for its characteristics and . . . inserted at the proper place."[19] With this

---

[18]Luigi Pirandello, *Si Gira,* quoted by Léon Pierre-Quint, "Signification du cinéma," *L'Art cinématographique, op. cit.,* pp. 14–15.

[19]Rudolf Arnheim, *Film als Kunst,* Berlin, 1932, pp. 176 f. In this context certain seemingly unimportant details in which the film director deviates from stage practices gain in interest. Such is the attempt to let the actor play without makeup, as made among others by Dreyer in his *Jeanne d'Arc.* Dreyer spent months seeking the forty actors who constitute the Inquisitors' tribunal. The search for these actors resembled that for stage properties that are hard to come by. Dreyer made every effort to avoid resemblances of age, build, and physiognomy. If the actor thus becomes a stage property, this latter, on the other hand, frequently functions as actor. At least it is not unusual for the film to assign a role to the stage property. Instead of choosing at random from a great wealth of examples, let us concentrate on a particularly convincing one. A clock that is working will always be a disturbance on the stage. There it cannot be permitted its function of measuring time. Even in a naturalistic play, astronomical time would clash with theatrical time. Under these circumstances it is highly revealing that the film can, whenever appropriate, use time as measured by a clock. From this more than from many other touches it may clearly be recognized that under certain circumstances each and every prop in a film may assume important functions. From here it is but one step to Pudovkin's statement that "the playing of an actor which is connected with an object and is built around it . . . is always one of the strongest methods of cinematic construction." (W. Pudovkin, *Filmregie und Filmmanuskript,* Berlin, 1928, p. 126.) The film is the first art form capable of demonstrating how matter plays tricks on man. Hence, films can be an excellent means of materialistic representation.

idea something else is closely connected. The stage actor identifies himself
with the character of his role. The film actor very often is denied this opportunity. His creation is by no means all of a piece; it is composed of
many separate performances. Besides certain fortuitous considerations,
such as cost of studio, availability of fellow players, décor, etc., there are
elementary necessities of equipment that split the actor's work into a series of mountable episodes. In particular, lighting and its installation require the presentation of an event that, on the screen, unfolds as a rapid
and unified scene, in a sequence of separate shootings which may take
hours at the studio; not to mention more obvious montage. Thus a jump
from the window can be shot in the studio as a jump from a scaffold, and
the ensuing flight, if need be, can be shot weeks later when outdoor scenes
are taken. Far more paradoxical cases can easily be construed. Let us assume that an actor is supposed to be startled by a knock at the door. If his
reaction is not satisfactory, the director can resort to an expedient: when
the actor happens to be at the studio again he has a shot fired behind him
without his being forewarned of it. The frightened reaction can be shot
now and be cut into the screen version. Nothing more strikingly shows
that art has left the realm of the "beautiful semblance" which, so far, had
been taken to be the only sphere where art could thrive.

X

The feeling of strangeness that overcomes the actor before the camera,
as Pirandello describes it, is basically of the same kind as the estrangement
felt before one's own image in the mirror. But now the reflected image has
become separable, transportable. And where is it transported? Before the
public.[20] Never for a moment does the screen actor cease to be conscious of
this fact. While facing the camera he knows that ultimately he will face the
public, the consumers who constitute the market. This market, where he
offers not only his labor but also his whole self, his heart and soul, is beyond his reach. During the shooting he has as little contact with it as any
article made in a factory. This may contribute to that oppression, that new

---

[20]The change noted here in the method of exhibition caused by mechanical reproduction applies to politics as well. The present crisis of the bourgeois democracies comprises
a crisis of the conditions which determine the public presentation of the rulers. Democracies exhibit a member of government directly and personally before the nation's representatives. Parliament is his public. Since the innovations of camera and recording
equipment make it possible for the orator to become audible and visible to an unlimited
number of persons, the presentation of the man of politics before camera and recording
equipment becomes paramount. Parliaments, as much as theaters, are deserted. Radio
and film not only affect the function of the professional actor but likewise the function of
those who also exhibit themselves before this mechanical equipment, those who govern.
Though their tasks may be different, the change affects equally the actor and the ruler.
The trend is toward establishing controllable and transferable skills under certain social
conditions. This results in a new selection, a selection before the equipment from which
the star and the dictator emerge victorious.

anxiety which, according to Pirandello, grips the actor before the camera. The film responds to the shriveling of the aura with an artificial build-up of the "personality" outside the studio. The cult of the movie star, fostered by the money of the film industry, preserves not the unique aura of the person but the "spell of the personality," the phony spell of a commodity. So long as the movie-makers' capital sets the fashion, as a rule no other revolutionary merit can be accredited to today's film than the promotion of a revolutionary criticism of traditional concepts of art. We do not deny that in some cases today's films can also promote revolutionary criticism of social conditions, even of the distribution of property. However, our present study is no more specifically concerned with this than is the film production of Western Europe.

It is inherent in the technique of the film as well as that of sports that everybody who witnesses its accomplishments is somewhat of an expert. This is obvious to anyone listening to a group of newspaper boys leaning on their bicycles and discussing the outcome of a bicycle race. It is not for nothing that newspaper publishers arrange races for their delivery boys. These arouse great interest among the participants, for the victor has an opportunity to rise from delivery boy to professional racer. Similarly, the newsreel offers everyone the opportunity to rise from passer-by to movie extra. In this way any man might even find himself part of a work of art, as witness Vertoff's *Three Songs About Lenin* or Ivens' *Borinage.* Any man today can lay claim to being filmed. This claim can best be elucidated by a comparative look at the historical situation of contemporary literature.

For centuries a small number of writers were confronted by many thousands of readers. This changed toward the end of the last century. With the increasing extension of the press, which kept placing new political, religious, scientific, professional, and local organs before the readers, an increasing number of readers became writers—at first, occasional ones. It began with the daily press opening to its readers space for "letters to the editor." And today there is hardly a gainfully employed European who could not, in principle, find an opportunity to publish somewhere or other comments on his work, grievances, documentary reports, or that sort of thing. Thus, the distinction between author and public is about to lose its basic character. The difference becomes merely functional; it may vary from case to case. At any moment the reader is ready to turn into a writer. As expert, which he had to become willy-nilly in an extremely specialized work process, even if only in some minor respect, the reader gains access to authorship. In the Soviet Union work itself is given a voice. To present it verbally is part of a man's ability to perform the work. Literary license is now founded on polytechnic rather than specialized training and thus becomes common property.[21]

---

[21]The privileged character of the respective techniques is lost. Aldous Huxley writes:

"Advances in technology have led . . . to vulgarity . . . . Process reproduction and the rotary press have made possible the indefinite

All this can easily be applied to the film, where transitions that in literature took centuries have come about in a decade. In cinematic practice, particularly in Russia, this change-over has partially become established reality.
Some of the players whom we meet in Russian films are not actors in our
sense but people who portray *themselves*—and primarily in their own work
process. In Western Europe the capitalistic exploitation of the film denies
consideration to modern man's legitimate claim to being reproduced. Under
these circumstances the film industry is trying hard to spur the interest of the
masses through illusion-promoting spectacles and dubious speculations.

XI

The shooting of a film, especially of a sound film, affords a spectacle
unimaginable anywhere at any time before this. It presents a process in
which it is impossible to assign to a spectator a viewpoint which would

---

multiplication of writing and pictures. Universal education and relatively high wages have created an enormous public who know how to
read and can afford to buy reading and pictorial matter. A great industry has been called into existence in order to supply these commodities.
Now, artistic talent is a very rare phenomenon; whence it follows . . .
that, at every epoch and in all countries, most art has been bad. But the
proportion of trash in the total artistic output is greater now than at any
other period. That it must be so is a matter of simple arithmetic. The
population of Western Europe has a little more than doubled during
the last century. But the amount of reading—and seeing—matter has
increased, I should imagine, at least twenty and possibly fifty or even a
hundred times. If there were n men of talent in a population of x millions, there will presumably be $2n$ men of talent among $2x$ millions. The
situation may be summed up thus. For every page of print and pictures
published a century ago, twenty or perhaps even a hundred pages are
published today. But for every man of talent then living, there are now
only two men of talent. It may be of course that, thanks to universal education, many potential talents which in the past would have been still-
born are now enabled to realize themselves. Let us assume, then, that
there are now three or even four men of talent to every one of earlier
times. It still remains true to say that the consumption of reading—and
seeing—matter has far outstripped the natural production of gifted
writers and draughtsmen. It is the same with hearing-matter. Prosper-
ity, the gramophone and the radio have created an audience of hearers
who consume an amount of hearing-matter that has increased out of all
proportion to the increase of population and the consequent natural increase of talented musicians. It follows from all this that in all the arts
the output of trash is both absolutely and relatively greater than it was
in the past; and that it must remain greater for just so long as the world
continues to consume the present inordinate quantities of reading-
matter, seeing-matter, and hearing-matter."—Aldous Huxley, *Beyond
the Mexique Bay. A Traveller's Journal*, London, 1949, pp. 274 ff. First published in 1934.

This mode of observation is obviously not progressive.

exclude from the actual scene such extraneous accessories as camera equipment, lighting machinery, staff assistants, etc.—unless his eye were on a line parallel with the lens. This circumstance, more than any other, renders superficial and significant any possible similarity between a scene in the studio and one on the stage. In the theater one is well aware of the place from which the play cannot immediately be detected as illusionary. There is no such place for the movie scene that is being shot. Its illusionary nature is that of the second degree, the result of cutting. That is to say, in the studio the mechanical equipment has penetrated so deeply into reality that its pure aspect freed from the foreign substance of equipment is the result of a special procedure, namely, the shooting by the specially adjusted camera and the mounting of the shot together with other similar ones. The equipment-free aspect of reality here has become the height of artifice; the sight of immediate reality has become an orchid in the land of technology.

Even more revealing is the comparison of these circumstances, which differ so much from those of the theater, with the situation in painting. Here the question is: How does the cameraman compare with the painter? To answer this we take recourse to an analogy with a surgical operation. The surgeon represents the polar opposite of the magician. The magician heals a sick person by the laying on of hands; the surgeon cuts into the patient's body. The magician maintains the natural distance between the patient and himself; though he reduces it very slightly by the laying on of hands, he greatly increases it by virtue of his authority. The surgeon does exactly the reverse; he greatly diminishes the distance between himself and the patient by penetrating into the patient's body, and increases it but little by the caution with which his hand moves among the organs. In short, in contrast to the magician—who is still hidden in the medical practitioner—the surgeon at the decisive moment abstains from facing the patient man to man; rather, it is through the operation that he penetrates into him.

Magician and surgeon compare to painter and cameraman. The painter maintains in his work a natural distance from reality, the cameraman penetrates deeply into its web.[22] There is a tremendous difference between the pictures they obtain. That of the painter is a total one, that of the cameraman consists of multiple fragments which are assembled under a new law. Thus, for contemporary man the representation of reality by the film is incomparably more significant than that of the painter, since it

---

[22]The boldness of the cameraman is indeed comparable to that of the surgeon. Luc Durtain lists among specific technical sleights of hand those "which are required in surgery in the case of certain difficult operations. I choose as an example a case from otorhino-laryngology; . . . the so-called endonasal perspective procedure; or I refer to the acrobatic tricks of larynx surgery which have to be performed following the reversed picture in the laryngoscope. I might also speak of ear surgery which suggests the precision work of watchmakers. What range of the most subtle muscular acrobatics is required from the man who wants to repair or save the human body! We have only to think of the couching of a cataract where there is virtually a debate of steel with nearly fluid tissue, or of the major abdominal operations (laparotomy)."—Luc Durtain, *op. cit.*

offers, precisely because of the thoroughgoing permeation of reality with mechanical equipment, an aspect of reality which is free of all equipment. And that is what one is entitled to ask from a work of art.

argue
against

XII

Mechanical reproduction of art changes the reaction of the masses toward art. The reactionary attitude toward a Picasso painting changes into the progressive reaction toward a Chaplin movie. The progressive reaction is characterized by the direct, intimate fusion of visual and emotional enjoyment with the orientation of the expert. Such fusion is of great social significance. The greater the decrease in the social significance of an art form, the sharper the distinction between criticism and enjoyment by the public. The conventional is uncritically enjoyed, and the truly new is criticized with aversion. With regard to the screen, the critical and the receptive attitudes of the public coincide. The decisive reason for this is that individual reactions are predetermined by the mass audience response they are about to produce, and this is nowhere more pronounced than in the film. The moment these responses become manifest they control each other. Again, the comparison with painting is fruitful. A painting has always had an excellent chance to be viewed by one person or by a few. The simultaneous contemplation of paintings by a large public, such as developed in the nineteenth century, is an early symptom of the crisis of painting, a crisis which was by no means occasioned exclusively by photography but rather in a relatively independent manner by the appeal of art works to the masses.

Painting simply is in no position to present an object for simultaneous collective experience, as it was possible for architecture at all times, for the epic poem in the past, and for the movie today. Although this circumstance in itself should not lead one to conclusions about the social role of painting, it does constitute a serious threat as soon as painting, under special conditions and, as it were, against its nature, is confronted directly by the masses. In the churches and monasteries of the Middle Ages and at the princely courts up to the end of the eighteenth century, a collective reception of paintings did not occur simultaneously, but by graduated and hierarchized mediation. The change that has come about is an expression of the particular conflict in which painting was implicated by the mechanical reproducibility of paintings. Although paintings began to be publicly exhibited in galleries and salons, there was no way for the masses to organize and control themselves in their reception.[23] Thus the same public

---

[23]This mode of observation may seem crude, but as the great theoretician Leonardo has shown, crude modes of observation may at times be usefully adduced. Leonardo compares painting and music as follows: "Painting is superior to music because, unlike unfortunate music, it does not have to die as soon as it is born. . . . Music which is consumed in the very act of its birth is inferior to painting which the use of varnish has rendered eternal." (Trattato I, 29.)

which responds in a progressive manner toward a grotesque film is bound to respond in a reactionary manner to surrealism.

XIII

The characteristics of the film lie not only in the manner in which man presents himself to mechanical equipment but also in the manner in which, by means of this apparatus, man can represent his environment. A glance at occupational psychology illustrates the testing capacity of the equipment. Psychoanalysis illustrates it in a different perspective. The film has enriched our field of perception with methods which can be illustrated by those of Freudian theory. Fifty years ago, a slip of the tongue passed more or less unnoticed. Only exceptionally may such a slip have revealed dimensions of depth in a conversation which had seemed to be taking its course on the surface. Since the *Psychopathology of Everyday Life* things have changed. This book isolated and made analyzable things which had heretofore floated along unnoticed in the broad stream of perception. For the entire spectrum of optical, and now also acoustical, perception the film has brought about a similar deepening of apperception. It is only an obverse of this fact that behavior items shown in a movie can be analyzed much more precisely and from more points of view than those presented on paintings or on the stage. As compared with painting, filmed behavior lends itself more readily to analysis because of its incomparably more precise statements of the situation. In comparison with the stage scene, the filmed behavior item lends itself more readily to analysis because it can be isolated more easily. The circumstance derives its chief importance from its tendency to promote the mutual penetration of art and science. Actually, of a screened behavior item which is nearly brought out in a certain situation, like a muscle of a body, it is difficult to say which is more fascinating, its artistic value or its value for science. To demonstrate the identity of the artistic and scientific uses of photography which heretofore usually were separated will be one of the revolutionary functions of the film.[24]

By close-ups of the things around us, by focusing on hidden details of familiar objects, by exploring commonplace milieus under the ingenious guidance of the camera, the film, on the one hand, extends our

---

[24]Renaissance painting offers a revealing analogy to this situation. The incomparable development of this art and its significance rested not least on the integration of a number of new sciences, or at least of new scientific data. Renaissance painting made use of anatomy and perspective, of mathematics, meteorology, and chromatology. Valéry writes: "What could be further from us than the strange claim of a Leonardo to whom painting was a supreme goal and the ultimate demonstration of knowledge? Leonardo was convinced that painting demanded universal knowledge, and he did not even shrink from a theoretical analysis which to us is stunning because of its very depth and precision. . . ."—Paul Valéry, *Pièces sur l'art*, "Autour de Corot," Paris, p. 191.

comprehension of the necessities which rule our lives; on the other hand, it manages to assure us of an immense and unexpected field of action. Our taverns and our metropolitan streets, our offices and furnished rooms, our railroad stations and our factories appeared to have us locked up hopelessly. Then came the film and burst this prison-world asunder by the dynamite of the tenth of a second, so that now, in the midst of its far-flung ruins and debris, we calmly and adventurously go traveling. With the close-up, space expands; with slow motion, movement is extended. The enlargement of a snapshot does not simply render more precise what in any case was visible, though unclear: it reveals entirely new structural formations of the subject. So, too, slow motion not only presents familiar qualities of movement but reveals in them entirely unknown ones "which, far from looking like retarded rapid movements, give the effect of singularly gliding, floating, supernatural motions."[25] Evidently a different nature opens itself to the camera than opens to the naked eye—if only because an unconsciously penetrated space is substituted for a space consciously explored by man. Even if one has a general knowledge of the way people walk, one knows nothing of a person's posture during the fractional second of a stride. The act of reaching for a lighter or a spoon is familiar routine, yet we hardly know what really goes on between hand and metal, not to mention how this fluctuates with our moods. Here the camera intervenes with the resources of its lowerings and liftings, its interruptions and isolations, its extensions and accelerations, its enlargements and reductions. The camera introduces us to unconscious optics as does psychoanalysis to unconscious impulses.

XIV

One of the foremost tasks of art has always been the creation of a demand which could be fully satisfied only later.[26] The history of every art form shows critical epochs in which a certain art form aspires to effects

---

[25]Rudolf Arnheim, *loc. cit.,* p. 138.

[26]"The work of art," says André Breton, "is valuable only in so far as it is vibrated by the reflexes of the future." Indeed, every developed art form intersects three lines of development. Technology works toward a certain form of art. Before the advent of the film there were photo booklets with pictures which flitted by the onlooker upon pressure of the thumb, thus portraying a boxing bout or a tennis match. Then there were the slot machines in bazaars; their picture sequences were produced by the turning of a crank.

Secondly, the traditional art forms in certain phases of their development strenuously work toward effects which later are effortlessly attained by the new ones. Before the rise of the movie the Dadaists' performances tried to create an audience reaction which Chaplin later evoked in a more natural way.

Thirdly, unspectacular social changes often promote a change in receptivity which will benefit the new art form. Before the movie had begun to create its public, pictures that were no longer immobile captivated an assembled audience in the so-called *Kaiser-panorama.* Here the public assembled before a screen into which stereoscopes were mounted, one to each beholder. By a mechanical process individual pictures appeared

which could be fully obtained only with a changed technical standard, that is to say, in a new art form. The extravagances and crudities of art which thus appear, particularly in the so-called decadent epochs, actually arise from the nucleus of its richest historical energies. In recent years, such barbarisms were abundant in Dadaism. It is only now that its impulse becomes discernible: Dadaism attempted to create by pictorial—and literary—means the effects which the public today seeks in the film.

Every fundamentally new, pioneering creation of demands will carry beyond its goal. Dadaism did so to the extent that it sacrificed the market values which are so characteristic of the film in favor of higher ambitions—though of course it was not conscious of such intentions as here described. The Dadaists attached much less importance to the sales value of their work than to its uselessness for contemplative immersion. The studied degradation of their material was not the least of their means to achieve this uselessness. Their poems are "word salad" containing obscenities and every imaginable waste product of language. The same is true of their paintings, on which they mounted buttons and tickets. What they intended and achieved was a relentless destruction of the aura of their creations, which they branded as reproductions with the very means of production. Before a painting of Arp's or a poem by August Stramm it is impossible to take time for contemplation and evaluation as one would before a canvas of Derain's or a poem by Rilke. In the decline of middle-class society, contemplation became a school for asocial behavior; it was countered by distraction as a variant of social conduct.[27] Dadaistic activities actually assured a rather vehement distraction my making works of art the center of scandal. One requirement was foremost: to outrage the public.

From an alluring appearance or persuasive structure of sound the work of art of the Dadaists became an instrument of ballistics. It hit the spectator like a bullet, it happened to him, thus acquiring a tactile quality. It promoted a demand for the film, the distracting element of which is also primarily tactile, being based on changes of place and focus which periodically assail the spectator. Let us compare the screen on which a film unfolds with the canvas of a painting. The painting invites the spectator to

---

briefly before the stereoscopes, then made way for others. Edison still had to use similar devices in presenting the first movie strip before the film screen and projection were known. This strip was presented to a small public which stared into the apparatus in which the succession of pictures was reeling off. Incidentally, the institution of the *Kaiserpanorama* shows very clearly a dialectic of the development. Shortly before the movie turned the reception of pictures into a collective one, the individual viewing of pictures in these swiftly outmoded establishments came into play once more with an intensity comparable to that of the ancient priest beholding the statue of a divinity in the cells.

[27]The theological archetype of this contemplation is the awareness of being alone with one's God. Such awareness, in the heyday of the bourgeoisie, went to strengthen the freedom to shake off clerical tutelage. During the decline of the bourgeoisie this awareness had to take into account the hidden tendency to withdraw from public affairs those forces which the individual draws upon in his communion with God.

contemplation; before it the spectator can abandon himself to his associations. Before the movie frame he cannot do so. No sooner has his eye grasped a scene than it is already changed. It cannot be arrested. Duhamel, who detests the film and knows nothing of its significance, though something of its structure, notes this circumstance as follows: "I can no longer think what I want to think. My thoughts have been replaced by moving images."[28] The spectator's process of association in view of these images is indeed interrupted by their constant, sudden change. This constitutes the shock effect of the film, which, like all shocks, should be cushioned by heightened presence of mind.[29] By means of its technical structure, the film has taken the physical shock effect out of the wrappers in which Dadaism had, as it were, kept it inside the moral shock effect.[30]

XV

The mass is a matrix from which all traditional behavior toward works of art issues today in a new form. Quantity has been transmuted into quality. The greatly increased mass of participants has produced a change in the mode of participation. The fact that the new mode of participation first appeared in a disreputable form must not confuse the spectator. Yet some people have launched spirited attacks against precisely this superficial aspect. Among these, Duhamel has expressed himself in the most radical manner. What he objects to most is the kind of participation which the movie elicits from the masses. Duhamel calls the movie "a pastime for helots, a diversion for uneducated, wretched, worn-out creatures who are consumed by their worries . . . , a spectacle which requires no concentration and presupposes no intelligence . . . , which kindles no light in the heart and awakens no hope other than the ridiculous one of someday becoming a 'star' in Los Angeles."[31] Clearly, this is at bottom the same ancient lament that the masses seek distraction whereas art demands concentration from the spectator. That is a commonplace. The question remains whether it provides a platform for the analysis of the film. A

---

[28]Georges Duhamel, *Scènes de la vie future,* Paris, 1930, p. 52.

[29]The film is the art form that is in keeping with the increased threat to his life which modern man has to face. Man's need to expose himself to shock effects is his adjustment to the dangers threatening him. The film corresponds to profound changes in the apperceptive apparatus—changes that are experienced on an individual scale by the man in the street in big-city traffic, on a historical scale by every present-day citizen.

[30]As for Dadaism, insights important for Cubism and Futurism are to be gained from the movie. Both appear as deficient attempts of art to accommodate the pervasion of reality by the apparatus. In contrast to the film, these schools did not try to use the apparatus as such for the artistic presentation of reality, but aimed at some sort of alloy in the joint presentation of reality and apparatus. In Cubism, the premonition that this apparatus will be structurally based on optics plays a dominant part; in Futurism, it is the premonition of the effects of this apparatus which are brought out by the rapid sequence of the film strip.

[31]Duhamel, *op. cit.,* p. 58.

closer look is needed here. Distraction and concentration form polar opposites which may be stated as follows: A man who concentrates before a work of art is absorbed by it. He enters into this work of art the way legend tells of the Chinese painter when he viewed his finished painting. In contrast, the distracted mass absorbs the work of art. This is most obvious with regard to buildings. Architecture has always represented the prototype of a work of art the reception of which is consummated by a collectivity in a state of distraction. The laws of its reception are most instructive.

Buildings have been man's companions since primeval times. Many art forms have developed and perished. Tragedy begins with the Greeks, is extinguished with them, and after centuries its "rules" only are revived. The epic poem, which had its origin in the youth of nations, expires in Europe at the end of the Renaissance. Panel painting is a creation of the Middle Ages, and nothing guarantees its uninterrupted existence. But the human need for shelter is lasting. Architecture has never been idle. Its history is more ancient than that of any other art, and its claim to being a living force has significance in every attempt to comprehend the relationship of the masses to art. Buildings are appropriated in a twofold manner: by use and by perception—or rather, by touch and sight. Such appropriation cannot be understood in terms of the attentive concentration of a tourist before a famous building. On the tactile side there is no counterpart to contemplation on the optical side. Tactile appropriation is accomplished not so much by attention as by habit. As regards architecture, habit determines to a large extent even optical reception. The latter, too, occurs much less through rapt attention than by noticing the object in incidental fashion. This mode of appropriation, developed with reference to architecture, in certain circumstances acquires canonical value. For the tasks which face the human apparatus of perception at the turning points of history cannot be solved by optical means, that is, by contemplation, alone. They are mastered gradually by habit, under the guidance of tactile appropriation.

The distracted person, too, can form habits. More, the ability to master certain tasks in a state of distraction proves that their solution has become a matter of habit. Distraction as provided by art presents a covert control of the extent to which new tasks have become soluble by apperception. Since, moreover, individuals are tempted to avoid such tasks, art will tackle the most difficult and most important ones where it is able to mobilize the masses. Today it does so in the film. Reception in a state of distraction, which is increasing noticeably in all fields of art and is symptomatic of profound changes in apperception, finds in the film its true means of exercise. The film with its shock effect meets this mode of reception halfway. The film makes the cult value recede into the background not only by putting the public in the position of the critic, but also by the fact that at the movies this position requires no attention. The public is an examiner, but an absent-minded one.

Epilogue

The growing proletarianization of modern man and the increasing formation of masses are two aspects of the same process. Fascism attempts to organize the newly created proletarian masses without affecting the property structure which the masses strive to eliminate. Fascism sees its salvation in giving these masses not their right, but instead a chance to express themselves.[32] The masses have a right to change property relations; Fascism seeks to give them an expression while preserving property. The logical result of Fascism is the introduction of aesthetics into political life. The violation of the masses, whom Fascism, with its *Führer* cult, forces to their knees, has its counterpart in the violation of an apparatus which is pressed into the production of ritual values.

All efforts to render politics aesthetic culminate in one thing: war. War and war only can set a goal for mass movements on the largest scale while respecting the traditional property system. This is the political formula for the situation. The technological formula may be stated as follows: Only war makes it possible to mobilize all of today's technical resources while maintaining the property system. It goes without saying that the Fascist apotheosis of war does not employ such arguments. Still, Marinetti says in his manifesto on the Ethiopian colonial war: "For twenty-seven years we Futurists have rebelled against the branding of war as anti-aesthetic. . . . Accordingly we state: . . . War is beautiful because it establishes man's dominion over the subjugated machinery by means of gas masks, terrifying megaphones, flame throwers, and small tanks. War is beautiful because it initiates the dreamt-of metalization of the human body. War is beautiful because it enriches a flowering meadow with the fiery orchids of machine guns. War is beautiful because it combines the gunfire, the cannonades, the cease-fire, the scents, and the stench of putrefaction into a symphony. War is beautiful because it creates new architecture, like that of the big tanks, the geometrical formation flights, the smoke spirals from burning villages, and many others. . . . Poets and artists of Futurism! . . . remember these principles of an aesthetics of war so that your struggle for a new literature and a new graphic art . . . may be illumined by them!"

---

[32]One technical feature is significant here, especially with regard to newsreels, the propagandist importance of which can hardly be overestimated. Mass reproduction is aided especially by the reproduction of masses. In big parades and monster rallies, in sports events, and in war, all of which nowadays are captured by camera and sound recording, the masses are brought face to face with themselves. This process, whose significance need not be stressed, is intimately connected with the development of the techniques of reproduction and photography. Mass movements are usually discerned more clearly by a camera than by the naked eye. A bird's-eye view best captures gatherings of hundreds of thousands. And even though such a view may be as accessible to the human eye as it is to the camera, the image received by the eye cannot be enlarged the way a negative is enlarged. This means that mass movements, including war, constitute a form of human behavior which particularly favors mechanical equipment.

fight against war as beautiful

This manifesto has the virtue of clarity. Its formulations deserve to be accepted by dialecticians. To the latter, the aesthetics of today's war appears as follows: If the natural utilization of productive forces is impeded by the property system, the increase in technical devices, in speed, and in the sources of energy will press for an unnatural utilization, and this is found in war. The destructiveness of war furnishes proof that society has not been mature enough to incorporate technology as its organ, that technology has not been sufficiently developed to cope with the elemental forces of society. The horrible features of imperialistic warfare are attributable to the discrepancy between the tremendous means of production and their inadequate utilization in the process of production—in other words, to unemployment and the lack of markets. Imperialistic war is a rebellion of technology which collects, in the form of "human material," the claims to which society has denied its natural material. Instead of draining rivers, society directs a human stream into a bed of trenches; instead of dropping seeds from airplanes, it drops incendiary bombs over cities; and through gas warfare the aura is abolished in a new way.

"*Fiat ars—pereat mundus*,"[33] says Fascism, and, as Marinetti admits, expects war to supply the artistic gratification of a sense perception that has been changed by technology. This is evidently the consummation of "*l'art pour l'art*." Mankind, which in Homer's time was an object of contemplation for the Olympian gods, now is one for itself. Its self-alienation has reached such a degree that it can experience its own destruction as an aesthetic pleasure of the first order. This is the situation of politics which Fascism is rendering aesthetic. Communism responds by politicizing art.

• • • • • • • • • • • •

QUESTIONS FOR A SECOND READING

1. The preface is tough, a tough beginning. It begins with a reference to Karl Marx and his prediction that capitalism would exploit the proletariat "with increasing intensity," creating the conditions "which would make it possible to abolish capitalism itself." Benjamin argues that "superstructure" changes slowly compared to "substructure," but that it should be possible to predict the changes that will come in art and in perception. The current condition is worth understanding, he argues, since such understanding would serve as a "weapon" in the struggle—it could be used to "formulate revolutionary demands in the politics of art." To think this through, one would need to study the "developmental tendencies of art under present conditions of production." And the results of such a study could brush aside "a number of outmoded concepts, such as creativity

---

[33]*Fiat ars—pereat mundus*   "Let art exist—let the world perish." [Editors' note]

and genius, eternal value and mystery—concepts whose uncontrolled (and at present almost uncontrollable) application would lead to a processing of data in the Fascist sense."

This preface locates Benjamin's project in a discourse familiar to his readers, Marxists thinking in relation to the changes in Europe in the 1930s. It assumes a theoretical frame of reference you most likely don't share. You do, however, share the cultural tradition of movies, paintings, and music that are his points of reference.

As you reread, pay attention to the sentences that refer back to the issues defined in the preface. Be prepared to turn to those sentences in discussion, and be prepared to speak for what the essay says about class struggle, about superstructure and substructure, about the "developmental tendencies of art under the present conditions of production." Your goal should be to bring forward the argument surrounding the discussion of photography and film.

2. If, as Benjamin argues in this preface, "creativity and genius, eternal value and mystery" are "outmoded concepts," what does he (or what does his argument) offer to take their place? As you reread, look to see how, from within the argument of the essay, one might value art and artistic production.

3. One of the interesting features of the essay is the use of footnotes. As you reread, pay particular attention to the way each note functions—functions for you as a reader, functions (or might have functioned) for Benjamin as a writer. Choose one or two that seem to you to be particularly interesting or illustrative and be prepared to present them in class.

As a side note: According to Hannah Arendt, Benjamin's ideal was a work that would consist entirely of quotations, prepared so masterfully that "it could dispense with any accompanying text." She says, "To the extent that an accompanying text by the author proved unavoidable, it was a matter of fashioning it in such a way as to preserve 'the intention of such investigations,' namely, 'to plumb the depths of language and thought by drilling rather than excavating,' so as not to ruin everything with explanations that seek to provide a causal or systematic connection. . . . What mattered to him above all was to avoid anything that might be reminiscent of empathy, as though a given subject of investigation had a message in readiness which easily communicated itself, or could be communicated, to the reader or spectator. . . ."

4. In the epilogue, Benjamin offers two accounts of war. As you reread, look to see how and where the essay prepares a reader for this conclusion. How would you paraphrase the two positions Benjamin presents? And where do you locate Benjamin in the epilogue—what is *he* saying?

ASSIGNMENTS FOR WRITING

1. Benjamin writes in 1936. He is not a visionary and he is not writing science fiction and so he does not imagine all the developments in technical reproduction (and the developmental tendencies of art) that are present in our own historical moment. Write an essay in which you extend "The Work of Art in the Age of Mechanical Reproduction" into the twenty-first

century. You should focus your work in a single area: film and video, painting, architecture, music, or literature and writing. You will need to provide a careful account of Benjamin's argument, focusing close attention on a particular discussion of your genre.

Once you have provided the Benjaminian background, you can see what happens as you work forward to time present. You can imagine that you are extending Benjamin's work, that you are in conversation with it, or that you are putting him to the test. You can, if it makes sense to you, continue in his style—writing short sections, numbered in sequence, with similar internal design.

2. One of the interesting features of the essay is the use of footnotes. Write an essay in which you provide a reader, a reader not familiar with "The Work of Art in the Age of Mechanical Reproduction," with a way of seeing and understanding Benjamin's use of the footnote. And offer this not only as an interesting spectacle but also as evidence of a style of writing or a theory of writing, one that might have potential uses for you and your colleagues.

How do you think Benjamin wrote this—footnotes later, footnotes first, footnotes pulled out of the body of the text? How might a writer be served by this way of writing? What is the effect on a reader? How might this be a strategic move on his part?

3. Benjamin's argument depends upon the concepts of "authenticity" and "aura." He says,

> that which withers in the age of mechanical reproduction is the aura of the work of art. This is a symptomatic process whose significance points beyond the realm of art. One might generalize by saying: the technique of reproduction detaches the reproduced object from the domain of tradition. By making many reproductions it substitutes a plurality of copies for a unique existence. And in permitting the reproduction to meet the beholder or listener in his own particular situation, it reactivates the object reproduced. These two processes led to a tremendous shattering of tradition which is the obverse of the contemporary crisis and renewal of mankind. Both processes are intimately connected with the contemporary mass movements. Their most powerful agent is the film. Its social significance, particularly in its most positive form, is inconceivable without its destructive, cathartic aspect, that is, the liquidation of the traditional value of the cultural heritage. (p. 79)

For this assignment, imagine that you are writing for someone who has not read Benjamin's essay. What is Benjamin saying here? What does this have to do with the essay as a whole? What examples can you bring to bear from the text? It will be important to work with the complete essay and not to take as final (or without further context) things said in earlier pages. What examples does Benjamin prompt from your own field of reference, examples that will help bring Benjamin's argument to a twenty-first century reader?

4. Benjamin writes,

> During long periods of history, the mode of human sense perception changes with humanity's entire mode of existence. The manner in which human sense perception is organized, the medium in which it is accomplished, is determined not only by nature but by historical circumstances as well. (pp. 79–80)

Film, he argues, has begun (in 1936) to change the way we see—the way we see the individual, the actor, time and motion, space. Write a two-part essay (or an essay in which you explore both options):

   a. First, present Benjamin's account of the effects of film. Be sure to fol-low this argument from the beginning to the end of the essay. You should imagine that you are writing for someone who has not read "The Work of Art in the Age of Mechanical Reproduction."

   b. Second, respond on behalf of your generation of viewers—surely more fully formed by film, perhaps more fully aware of the technology and its effects. What, for instance, would your friends say? (In fact, why not try this out on them.) Speaking on behalf of your generation, what can you add as someone who has read Benjamin and thought this through?

5. In the epilogue, Benjamin offers two accounts of war. Write an essay in which you explain the epilogue as a conclusion. Where and how does the essay prepare a reader for this conclusion? It will be important to work with the complete essay and not to take as final (or without further con-text) things said in earlier pages.

    How would you paraphrase the two positions Benjamin presents? And where do you locate Benjamin in the epilogue—what is *he* saying? For this essay, you can imagine a reader who has read "The Work of Art in the Age of Mechanical Reproduction." Your reader will not, however, have the book at hand.

MAKING CONNECTIONS

1. John Berger offers his essay, "Ways of Seeing" (p. 105), as a reading of "The Work of Art in the Age of Mechanical Reproduction." Rather than a footnote or a series of footnotes or passages in quotation, he acknowl-edges Benjamin's precedence and influence by including his picture and a brief reference at the end of his text. It is a lovely gesture.

    After reading "The Work of Art," read "Ways of Seeing" with an eye (or an ear) to where and how it draws upon or speaks back to Benjamin's work. Think not only about the large sweep of the argument, but about particular ideas, terms, or phrases that adhere from or echo or allude to the prior text.

    With this preparation, write an essay in which you present and dis-cuss Berger's use of Benjamin. Where and how does he draw from him? Where and how does he extend, refute, or exceed him? And, from this ex-ample, what conclusions can you draw about the work of scholarship and the relations among scholars?

2. Walker Percy (p. 588) is not a Marxist. He argues on behalf of the individ-ual, not a class. Still, "The Loss of the Creature," like "The Work of Art in the Age of Mechanical Reproduction," is very much concerned with the loss of the category of authenticity as the result of a change in the condi-tions of everyday life, changes related to consumerism, technology, and the rise of the Expert.

Write an essay in which you compare the positions taken by Percy and Benjamin, looking particularly at the differences. It would be best to work with one or two parallel passages, after a general introduction. It would be ambitious but potentially fruitful to try to situate each in relation to their traditions of inquiry, for both were concerned with philosophy, religion, and literature: Did Percy read Benjamin? Were they formed by similar sources? You don't need to do the research, however, to make this a useful exercise. You can use your essay to represent their two positions and then to speak for yourself (or for your class or generation) in response.

3. In "Panopticism" (p. 225), Michel Foucault presents a disciplinary society based on technologies of surveillance. The image (and history) of the Panopticon stands at the center of Foucault's argument; it signals what he refers to as an "inspired" change in disciplinary practices since it "automizes and disindividualizes power." He says, "Power has its principle not so much in a person as in a certain concerned distribution of bodies, surfaces, lights, gazes; in an arrangement whose internal mechanisms produce the relation in which individuals are caught up . . . . Consequently, it does not matter who exercises power" (p. 232).

Benjamin is thinking about a different (a more recent) point in time and different technologies, but he is thinking about power and control and the shaping of minds and lives. At the center of his argument is film: "Thus, for contemporary man the representation of reality by the film is incomparably more significant than that of the painter, since it offers, precisely because of the thoroughgoing permeation of reality with mechanical equipment, an aspect of reality which is free of all equipment" (p. 91). Benjamin is also interested in how power is exerted by art, by images, and by technologies of reproduction over the "masses."

Write an essay in which you consider the different representations of and attitudes toward power in Foucault's "Panopticism" and Benjamin's "The Work of Art in the Age of Mechanical Reproduction."

(handwritten) aura, authority, originality is lost when you put any artwork on shirts, towels, or photo copied to sell. Takes away fr. mystical value.

- Mechanical reproduction → - damaging authority of orig.
  - democratize art
  - art for mass, damage uniquess/authority of Mona Lisa.
  → destroy uniqueness of art

p. 108, art of past mystified...

p. 126
p. 124

JOHN
BERGER

(handwritten)
- art establishment → cult of the original.

Museum   Bulletin board
authority   Democracy.

- mystification → ~~making the cultural look natural.~~
  mate new look as if old. Nostalgia
  Make new look old.

- given to the masses, self-expression accomplished
- democratize: also result in nostalgia info. giving art bogus authority → corporations

JOHN BERGER (b. 1926), like few other art critics, elicits strong and contradictory reactions to his writing. He has been called (sometimes in the same review) "preposterous" as well as "stimulating," "pompous" yet "exciting." He has been accused of falling prey to "ideological excesses" and of being a victim of his own "lack of objectivity," but he has been praised for his "scrupulous" and "cogent" observations on art and culture. He is one of Europe's most influential Marxist critics, yet his work has been heralded and damned by leftists and conservatives alike. Although Berger's work speaks powerfully, its tone is quiet, thoughtful, measured. According to the poet and critic Peter Schjeldahl, "The most mysterious element in Mr. Berger's criticism has always been the personality of the critic himself, a man of strenuous conviction so loath to bully that even his most provocative arguments sit feather-light on the mind."

The first selection is Chapter 1 from Ways of Seeing, a book which began as a series on BBC television. In fact, the show was a forerunner of those encyclopedic television series later popular on public television stations in the United States: Civilization, The Ascent of Man, Cosmos, The Civil War. Berger's show was less glittery and ambitious, but in its way it was more serious in its claims to be educational. As you watched the screen, you saw a series of images (like those in the following text). These were sometimes presented with commentary, but sometimes in silence, so that you constantly saw one image in the context of another—for example, classic presentations of women in oil paintings interspersed with images of women from contemporary art, advertising, movies, and "men's magazines." The goal of the exercise, according to Berger, was to "start a process of questioning," to focus his viewer's attention not on a single painting in isolation but on "ways of seeing" in general, on the ways we have learned to look at and understand the images that surround us, and on the culture that teaches us to see things as we do. The method of Ways of Seeing, a book of art history, was used by Berger in another book, A Seventh Man, to document the situation of the migrant worker in Europe.

After the chapter from Ways of Seeing, we have added two brief passages from a beautiful, slight, and quite compelling book by Berger, And Our Faces, My Heart, Brief as Photos. This book is both a meditation on time and space and a long love letter (if you can imagine such a combination!). At several points in the book, Berger turns his (and his reader's) attention to paintings. We have included two instances, his descriptions of Rembrandt's Woman in Bed and Caravaggio's The Calling of St. Matthew (and we have included reproductions of the paintings). We offer these as supplements to Ways of Seeing, as additional examples of how a writer turns images into words and brings the present to the past.

Berger has written poems, novels, essays, and film scripts, including The Success and Failure of Picasso (1965), A Fortunate Man (1967), G. (1971), and About Looking (1980). He lived and worked in England for years, but he currently lives in Quincy, a small peasant village in Haute-Savoie, France, where he wrote, over the course of several years, a trilogy of books on peasant life, titled Into Their Labours. The first book in the series, Pig Earth (1979), is a collection of essays, poems, and stories set in Haute-Savoie. The second, Once in Europa (1987), consists of five peasant tales that take love as their subject. The third and final book in the trilogy, Lilac and Flag: An Old Wives' Tale of the City, published in 1990, is a novel about the migration of peasants to the city. His most recent books are Photocopies, a collection of short stories (1996); King: A Street Story, a novel (1999); and I Send You This Cadmium Red: A Correspondence between John Berger and John Christie (2000).

Ways of Seeing

Seeing comes before words. The child looks and recognizes before it can speak.

But there is also another sense in which seeing comes before words. It is seeing which establishes our place in the surrounding world; we explain that world with words, but words can never undo the fact that we are surrounded by it. The relation between what we see and what we know is never settled. Each evening we *see* the sun set. We *know* that the earth is turning away from it. Yet the knowledge, the explanation, never quite fits the sight.

The Key of Dreams by Magritte [1898–1967]

The Surrealist painter Magritte commented on this always-present gap between words and seeing in a painting called *The Key of Dreams.*

The way we see things is affected by what we know or what we believe. In the Middle Ages when men believed in the physical existence of Hell the sight of fire must have meant something different from what it means today. Nevertheless their idea of Hell owed a lot to the sight of fire consuming and the ashes remaining—as well as to their experience of the pain of burns.

When in love, the sight of the beloved has a completeness which no words and no embrace can match: a completeness which only the act of making love can temporarily accommodate.

Yet this seeing which comes before words, and can never be quite covered by them, is not a question of mechanically reacting to stimuli. (It can only be thought of in this way if one isolates the small part of the process which concerns the eye's retina.) We only see what we look at. To look is an act of choice. As a result of this act, what we see is brought within our reach—though not necessarily within arm's reach. To touch something is to situate oneself in relation to it. (Close your eyes, move round the room and notice how the faculty of touch is like a static, limited form of sight.) We never look at just one thing; we are always looking at the relation between things and ourselves. Our vision is continually active, continually moving, continually holding things in a circle around itself, constituting what is present to us as we are.

Soon after we can see, we are aware that we can also be seen. The eye of the other combines with our own eye to make it fully credible that we are part of the visible world.

If we accept that we can see that hill over there, we propose that from that hill we can be seen. The reciprocal nature of vision is more fundamental than that of spoken dialogue. And often dialogue is an attempt to verbalize this—an attempt to explain how, either metaphorically or literally, "you see things," and an attempt to discover how "he sees things."

In the sense in which we use the word in this book, all images are man-made [see above]. An image is a sight which has been recreated or reproduced. It is an appearance, or a set of appearances, which has been detached from the place and time in which it first made its appearance and preserved—for a few moments or a few centuries. Every image embodies a way of seeing. Even a photograph. For photographs are not, as is often assumed, a mechanical record. Every time we look at a photograph, we are aware, however slightly, of the photographer selecting that sight from an infinity of other possible sights. This is true even in the most casual family snapshot. The photographer's way of seeing is reflected in his choice of subject. The painter's way of seeing is reconstituted by the marks he makes on the canvas or paper. Yet, although every image embodies a way of seeing, our perception or appreciation of an image depends also upon our own way of seeing. (It may be, for example, that Sheila is one figure among twenty; but for our own reasons she is the one we have eyes for.)

· · ·

Images were first made to conjure up the appearance of something that was absent. Gradually it became evident that an image could outlast what it represented; it then showed how something or somebody had once looked—and thus by implication how the subject had once been seen by other people. Later still the specific vision of the image-maker was also recognized as part of the record. An image became a record of how X had seen Y. This was the result of an increasing consciousness of individuality, accompanying an increasing awareness of history. It would be rash to try to date this last development precisely. But certainly in Europe such consciousness has existed since the beginning of the Renaissance.

No other kind of relic or text from the past can offer such a direct testimony about the world which surrounded other people at other times. In this respect images are more precise and richer than literature. To say this is not to deny the expressive or imaginative quality of art, treating it as mere documentary evidence; the more imaginative the work, the more profoundly it allows us to share the artist's experience of the visible.

Yet when an image is presented as a work of art, the way people look at it is affected by a whole series of learnt assumptions about art. Assumptions concerning:

> Beauty
> Truth
> Genius
> Civilization
> Form
> Status
> Taste, etc.

Many of these assumptions no longer accord with the world as it is. (The world-as-it-is is more than pure objective fact, it includes consciousness.) Out of true with the present, these assumptions obscure the past. They mystify rather than clarify. The past is never there waiting to be discovered, to be recognized for exactly what it is. History always constitutes the relation between a present and its past. Consequently fear of the present leads to mystification of the past. The past is not for living in; it is a well of conclusions from which we draw in order to act. Cultural mystification of the past entails a double loss. Works of art are made unnecessarily remote. And the past offers us fewer conclusions to complete in action.

When we "see" a landscape, we situate ourselves in it. If we "saw" the art of the past, we would situate ourselves in history. When we are prevented from seeing it, we are being deprived of the history which belongs to us. Who benefits from this deprivation? In the end, the art of the past is being mystified because a privileged minority is striving to invent a history which can retrospectively justify the role of the ruling classes, and such a justification can no longer make sense in modern terms. And so, inevitably, it mystifies.

Let us consider a typical example of such mystification. A two-volume study was recently published on Frans Hals.[1] It is the authoritative work

Regents of the Old Men's Alms House by Hals [1580–1666]

Regentesses of the Old Men's Alms House by Hals [1580–1666]

to date on this painter. As a book of specialized art history it is no better and no worse than the average.

The last two great paintings by Frans Hals [above] portray the Governors and the Governesses of an Alms House for old paupers in the Dutch seventeenth-century city of Haarlem. They were officially commissioned portraits. Hals, an old man of over eighty, was destitute. Most of his life he had been in debt. During the winter of 1664, the year he began painting these pictures, he obtained three loads of peat on public charity, otherwise he would have frozen to death. Those who now sat for him were administrators of such public charity.

The author records these facts and then explicitly says that it would be incorrect to read into the paintings any criticism of the sitters. There is no evidence, he says, that Hals painted them in a spirit of bitterness. The author considers them, however, remarkable works of art and explains why. Here he writes of the Regentesses:

> Each woman speaks to us of the human condition with equal importance. Each woman stands out with equal clarity against the *enormous* dark surface, yet they are linked by a firm rhythmical arrangement and the subdued diagonal pattern formed by their heads and hands. Subtle modulations of the *deep,* glowing blacks contribute to the *harmonious fusion* of the whole and form an *unforgettable contrast* with the *powerful* whites and vivid flesh tones where the detached strokes reach *a peak of breadth and strength.* [Berger's italics]

The compositional unity of a painting contributes fundamentally to the power of its image. It is reasonable to consider a painting's composition. But here the composition is written about as though it were in itself the emotional charge of the painting. Terms like *harmonious fusion, unforgettable contrast,* reaching *a peak of breadth and strength* transfer the emotion provoked by the image from the plane of lived experience, to that of disinterested "art appreciation." All conflict disappears. One is left with the unchanging "human condition," and the painting considered as a marvellously made object.

Very little is known about Hals or the Regents who commissioned him. It is not possible to produce circumstantial evidence to establish what their relations were. But there is the evidence of the paintings themselves: the evidence of a group of men and a group of women as seen by another man, the painter. Study this evidence and judge for yourself.

The art historian fears such direct judgement:

> As in so many other pictures by Hals, the penetrating charac-
> terizations almost seduce us into believing that we know the
> personality traits and even the habits of the men and women
> portrayed.

What is this "seduction" he writes of? It is nothing less than the paintings working upon us. They work upon us because we accept the way
Hals saw his sitters. We do not accept this innocently. We accept it in so
far as it corresponds to our own observation of people, gestures, faces, institutions. This is possible because we still live in a society of comparable
social relations and moral values. And it is precisely this which gives
the paintings their psychological and social urgency. It is this—not the
painter's skill as a "seducer"—which convinces us that we *can* know the
people portrayed.

The author continues:

> In the case of some critics the seduction has been a total suc-
> cess. It has, for example, been asserted that the Regent in the
> tipped slouch hat, which hardly covers any of his long, lank
> hair, and whose curiously set eyes do not focus, was shown in
> a drunken state. [below]

This, he suggests, is a libel. He argues that it was a fashion at that time
to wear hats on the side of the head. He cites medical opinion to prove
that the Regent's expression could well be the result of a facial paralysis.
He insists that the painting would have been unacceptable to the Regents

if one of them had been portrayed drunk. One might go on discussing each of these points for pages. (Men in seventeenth-century Holland wore their hats on the side of their heads in order to be thought of as adventurous and pleasure-loving. Heavy drinking was an approved practice. Etcetera.) But such a discussion would take us even farther away from the only confrontation which matters and which the author is determined to evade.

In this confrontation the Regents and Regentesses stare at Hals, a destitute old painter who has lost his reputation and lives off public charity; he examines them through the eyes of a pauper who must nevertheless try to be objective; i.e., must try to surmount the way he sees as a pauper. This is the drama of these paintings. A drama of an "unforgettable contrast."

Mystification has little to do with the vocabulary used. Mystification is the process of explaining away what might otherwise be evident. Hals was the first portraitist to paint the new characters and expressions created by capitalism. He did in pictorial terms what Balzac did two centuries later in literature. Yet the author of the authoritative work on these paintings sums up the artist's achievement by referring to

> Hals's unwavering commitment to his personal vision, which enriches our consciousness of our fellow men and heightens our awe for the ever-increasing power of the mighty impulses that enabled him to give us a close view of life's vital forces.

That is mystification.

In order to avoid mystifying the past (which can equally well suffer pseudo-Marxist mystification) let us now examine the particular relation which now exists, so far as pictorial images are concerned, between the present and the past. If we can see the present clearly enough, we shall ask the right questions of the past.

Today we see the art of the past as nobody saw it before. We actually perceive it in a different way.

This difference can be illustrated in terms of what was thought of as perspective. The convention of perspective, which is unique to European art and which was first established in the early Renaissance, centres everything on the eye of the beholder. It is like a beam from a lighthouse—only instead of light travelling outwards, appearances travel in. The conventions called those appearances *reality*. Perspective makes the single eye the centre of the visible world. Everything converges on to the eye as to the vanishing point of infinity. The visible world is arranged for the spectator as the universe was once thought to be arranged for God.

According to the convention of perspective there is no visual reciprocity. There is no need for God to situate himself in relation to others: he is himself the situation. The inherent contradiction in perspective was that it structured all images of reality to address a single spectator who, unlike God, could only be in one place at a time.

After the invention of the camera this contradiction gradually became apparent.

> I'm an eye. A mechanical eye. I, the machine, show you a world the way only I can see it. I free myself for today and forever from human immobility. I'm in constant movement. I approach and pull away from objects. I creep under them. I move alongside a running horse's mouth. I fall and rise with the falling and rising bodies. This is I, the machine, manoeuvring in the chaotic movements, recording one movement after another in the most complex combinations.
>
> Freed from the boundaries of time and space, I coordinate any and all points of the universe, wherever I want them to be. My way leads towards the creation of a fresh perception of the world. Thus I explain in a new way the world unknown to you.[2]

The camera isolated momentary appearances and in so doing destroyed the idea that images were timeless. Or, to put it another way, the camera showed that the notion of time passing was inseparable from the experience of the visual (except in paintings). What you saw depended upon

Still from *Man with a Movie Camera* by Vertov [1895–1954]

where you were when. What you saw was relative to your position in time and space. It was no longer possible to imagine everything converging on the human eye as on the vanishing point of infinity.

This is not to say that before the invention of the camera men believed that everyone could see everything. But perspective organized the visual field as though that were indeed the ideal. Every drawing or painting that used perspective proposed to the spectator that he was the unique centre of the world. The camera—and more particularly the movie camera—demonstrated that there was no centre.

The invention of the camera changed the way men saw. The visible came to mean something different to them. This was immediately reflected in painting.

For the Impressionists the visible no longer presented itself to man in order to be seen. On the contrary, the visible, in continual flux, became fugitive. For the Cubists the visible was no longer what confronted the single eye, but the totality of possible views taken from points all round the object (or person) being depicted [below].

The invention of the camera also changed the way in which men saw paintings painted long before the camera was invented. Originally paintings were an integral part of the building for which they were designed. Sometimes in an early Renaissance church or chapel one has the feeling that the images on the wall are records of the building's interior life, that together they make up the building's memory—so much are they part of the particularity of the building [p. 115].

The uniqueness of every painting was once part of the uniqueness of the place where it resided. Sometimes the painting was transportable. But it could never be seen in two places at the same time. When the camera re-

Still Life with Wicker Chair by Picasso [1881–1973]

Church of St. Francis at Assisi

produces a painting, it destroys the uniqueness of its image. As a result its meaning changes. Or, more exactly, its meaning multiplies and fragments into many meanings.

This is vividly illustrated by what happens when a painting is shown on a television screen. The painting enters each viewer's house. There it is surrounded by his wallpaper, his furniture, his mementos. It enters the atmosphere of his family. It becomes their talking point. It lends its meaning to their meaning. At the same time it enters a million other houses and, in each of them, is seen in a different context. Because of the camera, the

painting now travels to the spectator rather than the spectator to the painting. In its travels, its meaning is diversified.

One might argue that all reproductions more or less distort, and that therefore the original painting is still in a sense unique. Here [below] is a reproduction of the *Virgin of the Rocks* by Leonardo da Vinci.

Having seen this reproduction, one can go to the National Gallery to look at the original and there discover what the reproduction lacks. Alternatively one can forget about the quality of the reproduction and simply be reminded, when one sees the original, that it is a famous painting of which somewhere one has already seen a reproduction. But in either case the uniqueness of the original now lies in it being *the original of a reproduction.* It is no longer what its image shows that strikes one as unique; its first meaning is no longer to be found in what it says, but in what it is.

This new status of the original work is the perfectly rational consequence of the new means of reproduction. But it is at this point that a process of mystification again enters. The meaning of the original work no longer lies in what it uniquely says but in what it uniquely is. How is its unique existence evaluated and defined in our present culture? It is defined as an object whose value depends upon its rarity. This market is affirmed and gauged by the price it fetches on the market. But because

Virgin of the Rocks by Leonardo da Vinci [1452–1519]. Reproduced by courtesy of the Trustees, The National Gallery, London

it is nevertheless "a work of art"—and art is thought to be greater than commerce—its market price is said to be a reflection of its spiritual value. Yet the spiritual value of an object, as distinct from a message or an example, can only be explained in terms of magic or religion. And since in modern society neither of these is a living force, the art object, the "work of art," is enveloped in an atmosphere of entirely bogus religiosity. Works of art are discussed and presented as though they were holy relics: relics which are first and foremost evidence of their own survival. The past in which they originated is studied in order to prove their survival genuine. They are declared art when their line of descent can be certified.

Before the *Virgin of the Rocks* the visitor to the National Gallery would be encouraged by nearly everything he might have heard and read about the painting to feel something like this: "I am in front of it. I can see it. This painting by Leonardo is unlike any other in the world. The National Gallery has the real one. If I look at this painting hard enough, I should

National Gallery

Virgin of the Rocks by Leonardo da Vinci [1452–1519].
Louvre Museum

somehow be able to feel its authenticity. The *Virgin of the Rocks* by Leonardo da Vinci: it is authentic and therefore it is beautiful."

To dismiss such feelings as naive would be quite wrong. They accord perfectly with the sophisticated culture of art experts for whom the National Gallery catalogue is written. The entry on the *Virgin of the Rocks* is one of the longest entries. It consists of fourteen closely printed pages. They do not deal with the meaning of the image. They deal with who commissioned the painting, legal squabbles, who owned it, its likely date, the families of its owners. Behind this information lie years of research. The aim of the research is to prove beyond any shadow of doubt that the painting is a genuine Leonardo. The secondary aim is to prove that an almost identical painting in the Louvre is a replica of the National Gallery version.

French art historians try to prove the opposite [see p. 117].

The National Gallery sells more reproductions of Leonardo's cartoon of *The Virgin and Child with St. Anne and St. John the Baptist* [below] than any other picture in their collection. A few years ago it was known only to scholars. It became famous because an American wanted to buy it for two and a half million pounds.

Now it hangs in a room by itself. The room is like a chapel. The drawing is behind bullet-proof perspex. It has acquired a new kind of impressiveness. Not because of what it shows—not because of the meaning of its image. It has become impressive, mysterious, because of its market value.

The Virgin and Child with St. Anne and St. John the Baptist
by Leonardo da Vinci [1452–1519]. Reproduced by courtesy of the
Trustees, The National Gallery, London

• • •

The bogus religiosity which now surrounds original works of art, and which is ultimately dependent upon their market value, has become the substitute for what paintings lost when the camera made them reproducible. Its function is nostalgic. It is the final empty claim for the continuing values of an oligarchic, undemocratic culture. If the image is no longer unique and exclusive, the art object, the thing, must be made mysteriously so.

The majority of the population do not visit art museums. The following table shows how closely an interest in art is related to privileged education.

National proportion of art museum visitors according to level of education: Percentage of each educational category who visit art museums

	Greece	Poland	France	Holland		Greece	Poland	France	Holland
With no educational qualification	0.02	0.12	0.15	—	Only secondary education	10.5	10.4	10	20
Only primary education	0.30	1.50	0.45	0.50	Further and higher education	11.5	11.7	12.5	17.3

Source: Pierre Bourdieu and Alain Darbel, *L'Amour de l'art*, Editions de Minuit, Paris 1969, Appendix 5, table 4

The majority take it as axiomatic that the museums are full of holy relics which refer to a mystery which excludes them: the mystery of unaccountable wealth. Or, to put this another way, they believe that original masterpieces belong to the preserve (both materially and spiritually) of the rich. Another table indicates what the idea of an art gallery suggests to each social class.

Of the places listed below which does a museum remind you of most?

	Manual workers	Skilled and white collar workers	Professional and upper managerial
	%	%	%
Church	66	45	30.5
Library	9	34	28
Lecture hall	—	4	4.5
Department store or entrance hall in public building	—	7	2
Church and library	9	2	4.5
Church and lecture hall	4	2	—
Library and lecture hall	—	—	2
None of these	4	2	19.5
No reply	8	4	9
	100 (n = 53)	100 (n = 98)	100 (n = 99)

Source: as above, Appendix 4, table 8

In the age of pictorial reproduction the meaning of paintings is no longer attached to them; their meaning becomes transmittable: that is to say it becomes information of a sort, and, like all information, it is either put to use or ignored; information carries no special authority within itself. When a painting is put to use, its meaning is either modified or totally changed. One should be quite clear about what this involves. It is not a question of reproduction failing to reproduce certain aspects of an image faithfully; it is a question of reproduction making it possible, even inevitable, that an image will be used for many different purposes and that the reproduced image, unlike an original work, can lend itself to them all.

Venus and Mars by Botticelli [1445–1510]. Reproduced by courtesy of the Trustees, The National Gallery, London

Let us examine some of the ways in which the reproduced image lends it-self to such usage.

Reproduction isolates a detail of a painting from the whole. The detail is transformed. An allegorical figure becomes a portrait of a girl [see bottom, p. 120].

When a painting is reproduced by a film camera it inevitably becomes material for the film-maker's argument.

A film which reproduces images of a painting leads the spectator, through the painting, to the film-maker's own conclusions. The painting lends authority to the film-maker. This is because a film unfolds in time and a painting does not. In a film the way one image follows another, their succession, constructs an argument which becomes irreversible. In a painting all its elements are there to be seen simultaneously. The spectator may need time to examine each element of the painting but whenever he reaches a conclusion, the simultaneity of the whole painting is there to reverse or qualify his conclusion. The painting maintains its own authority [below]. Paintings are often reproduced with words around them [see top, p. 122].

Procession to Calvary by Breughel [1525–1569]

This is a landscape of a cornfield with birds flying out of it. Look at it for a moment [below]. Then turn the page [p. 123].

It is hard to define exactly how the words have changed the image but undoubtedly they have. The image now illustrates the sentence.

In this essay each image reproduced has become part of an argument which has little or nothing to do with the painting's original independent meaning. The words have quoted the paintings to confirm their own verbal authority. . . .

Wheatfield with Crows by Van Gogh [1853–1890]

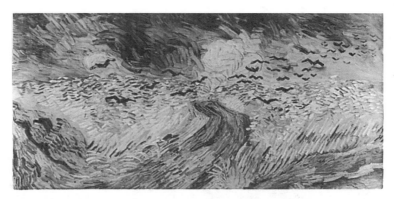

*This is the last picture that Van Gogh painted
before he killed himself.*

Reproduced paintings, like all information, have to hold their own against all the other information being continually transmitted [below].

Consequently a reproduction, as well as making its own references to the image of its original, becomes itself the reference point for other images. The meaning of an image is changed according to what one sees immediately beside it or what comes immediately after it. Such authority as it retains, is distributed over the whole context in which it appears [see p. 124].

Because works of art are reproducible, they can, theoretically, be used by anybody. Yet mostly—in art books, magazines, films, or within gilt frames in living-rooms—reproductions are still used to bolster the illusion that nothing has changed, that art, with its unique undiminished authority, justifies most other forms of authority, that art makes inequality seem

If women knew then... what they know now.

noble and hierarchies seem thrilling. For example, the whole concept of the National Cultural Heritage exploits the authority of art to glorify the present social system and its priorities.

The means of reproduction are used politically and commercially to disguise or deny what their existence makes possible. But sometimes individuals use them differently [p. 125].

Adults and children sometimes have boards in their bedrooms or living-rooms on which they pin pieces of paper: letters, snapshots, reproductions of paintings, newspaper cuttings, original drawings, postcards. On each board all the images belong to the same language and all are more or less equal within it, because they have been chosen in a highly personal way to match and express the experience of the room's inhabitant. Logically, these boards should replace museums.

What are we saying by that? Let us first be sure about what we are not saying.

We are not saying that there is nothing left to experience before original works of art except a sense of awe because they have survived. The way original works of art are usually approached—through museum catalogues, guides, hired cassettes, etc.—is not the only way they might be approached. When the art of the past ceases to be viewed nostalgically, the

works will cease to be holy relics—although they will never re-become what they were before the age of reproduction. We are not saying original works of art are now useless.

Original paintings are silent and still in a sense that information never is. Even a reproduction hung on a wall is not comparable in this respect for in the original the silence and stillness permeate the actual material, the paint, in which one follows the traces of the painter's immediate gestures. This has the effect of closing the distance in time between the painting of the picture and one's own act of looking at it. In this special sense all paintings are contemporary. Hence the immediacy of their testimony. Their historical moment is literally there before our eyes. Cézanne made a similar observation from the painter's point of view. "A minute in the world's life passes! To paint it in its reality, and forget everything for that! To become that minute, to be the sensitive plate . . . give the image of what we see, forgetting everything that has appeared before our time. . . ." What we make of that painted moment when it is before our eyes depends upon what we expect of art, and that in turn depends today upon how we have already experienced the meaning of paintings through reproductions.

Nor are we saying that all art can be understood spontaneously. We are not claiming that to cut out a magazine reproduction of an archaic Greek head, because it is reminiscent of some personal experience, and to pin it to a board beside other disparate images, is to come to terms with the full meaning of that head.

The idea of innocence faces two ways. By refusing to enter a conspiracy, one remains innocent of that conspiracy. But to remain innocent may also be to remain ignorant. The issue is not between innocence and knowledge (or between the natural and the cultural) but between a total approach to art which attempts to relate it to every aspect of experience and the esoteric approach of a few specialized experts who are the clerks of the nostalgia of a ruling class in decline. (In decline, not before the proletariat, but before the new power of the corporation and the state.) The real question is: to whom does the meaning of the art of the past properly belong? to those who can apply it to their own lives, or to a cultural hierarchy of relic specialists?

The visual arts have always existed within a certain preserve; originally this preserve was magical or sacred. But it was also physical: it was the place, the cave, the building, in which, or for which, the work was made. The experience of art, which at first was the experience of ritual, was set apart from the rest of life—precisely in order to be able to exercise power over it. Later the preserve of art became a social one. It entered the culture of the ruling class, whilst physically it was set apart and isolated in their palaces and houses. During all this history the authority of art was inseparable from the particular authority of the preserve.

What the modern means of reproduction have done is to destroy the authority of art and to remove it—or, rather, to remove its images which they reproduce—from any preserve. For the first time ever, images of art have become ephemeral, ubiquitous, insubstantial, available, valueless, free. They surround us in the same way as a language surrounds us. They

Woman Pouring Milk by Vermeer [1632–1675]

~ 𝓃𝒾𝓀𝓊 𝒽𝒶𝓈 𝓅𝓌𝒶

have entered the mainstream of life over which they no longer, in them-selves, have power.

Yet very few people are aware of what has happened because the means of reproduction are used nearly all the time to promote the illusion that nothing has changed except that the masses, thanks to reproductions, can now begin to appreciate art as the cultured minority once did. Under-standably, the masses remain uninterested and sceptical.

If the new language of images were used differently, it would, through its use, confer a new kind of power. Within it we could begin to define our experiences more precisely in areas where words are inadequate. (Seeing comes before words.) Not only personal experience, but also the essential historical experience of our relation to the past: that is to say the experi-ence of seeking to give meaning to our lives, of trying to understand the history of which we can become the active agents.

The art of the past no longer exists as it once did. Its authority is lost. In its place there is a language of images. What matters now is who uses that language for what purpose. This touches upon questions of copy-right for reproduction, the ownership of art presses and publishers, the total policy of public art galleries and museums. As usually presented, these are narrow professional matters. One of the aims of this essay has been to show that what is really at stake is much larger. A people or a class which is cut off from its own past is far less free to choose and to act as a people or class than one that has been able to situate itself in his-tory. This is why—and this is the only reason why—the entire art of the past has now become a political issue.

Many of the ideas in the preceding essay have been taken from another, writ-ten over forty years ago by the German critic and philosopher Walter Benjamin.

His essay was entitled The Work of Art in the Age of Mechanical Repro-duction. *This essay is available in English in a collection called* Illuminations *(Cape, London, 1970).*

NOTES

[1]Seymour Slive, *Frans Hals* (Phaidon, London).

[2]This quotation is from an article written in 1923 by Dziga Vertov, the revolutionary Soviet film director.

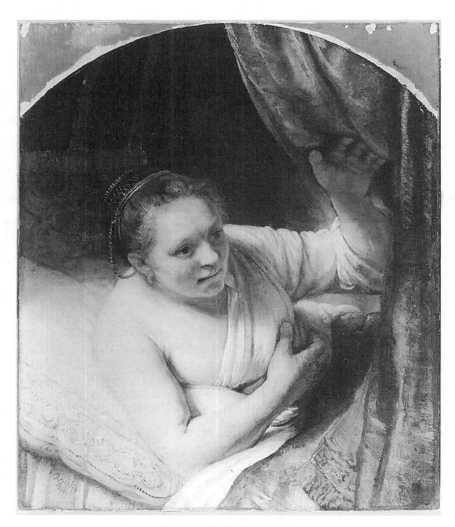

Woman in Bed by Rembrandt

On Rembrandt's *Woman in Bed*

It is strange how art historians sometimes pay so much attention, when trying to date certain paintings, to "style," inventories, bills, auction lists, and so little to the painted evidence concerning the model's age. It is as if they do not trust the painter on this point. For example, when they try to date and arrange in chronological order Rembrandt's paintings of Hendrickje Stoffels. No painter was a greater expert about the process of aging, and no painter has left us a more intimate record of the great love of his life. Whatever the documentary conjectures may allow, the paintings make it clear that the love between Hendrickje and the painter lasted for about twenty years, until her death, six years before his.

She was ten or twelve years younger than he. When she died she was, on the evidence of the paintings, at the very least forty-five, and when he first painted her she could certainly not have been older than twenty-seven. Their daughter, Cornelia, was baptized in 1654. This means that Hendrickje gave birth to their child when she was in her mid-thirties.

The *Woman in Bed* (from Edinburgh) was painted, by my reckoning, a little before or a little after the birth of Cornelia. The historians suggest that it may be a fragment taken from a larger work representing the wedding night of Sarah and Tobias. A biblical subject for Rembrandt was always contemporary. If it is a fragment, it is certain that Rembrandt finished it, and bequeathed it finally to the spectator, as his most intimate painting of the woman he loved.

There are other paintings of Hendrickje. Before the *Bathsheba* in the Louvre, or the *Woman Bathing* in the National Gallery (London), I am wordless. Not because their genius inhibits me, but because the experience from which they derive and which they express—desire experiencing itself as something as old as the known world, tenderness experiencing itself as the end of the world, the eyes' endless rediscovery, as if for the first time, of their love of a familiar body—all this comes before and goes beyond words. No other paintings lead so deftly and powerfully to silence. Yet, in both, Hendrickje is absorbed in her own actions. In the painter's vision of her there is the greatest intimacy, but there is no mutual intimacy between them. They are paintings which speak of his love, not of hers.

In the painting of the *Woman in Bed* there is a complicity between the woman and the painter. This complicity includes both reticence and abandon, day and night. The curtain of the bed, which Hendrickje lifts up with her hand, marks the threshold between daytime and nighttime.

In two years, by daylight, Van Rijn will be declared bankrupt. Ten years before, by daylight, Hendrickje came to work in Van Rijn's house as a nurse for his baby son. In the light of Dutch seventeenth-century accountability and Calvinism, the housekeeper and the painter have distinct and separate responsibilities. Hence their reticence.

At night, they leave their century.

> A necklace hangs loose across her breasts,
> And between them lingers—
>   yet is it a lingering
>   and not an incessant arrival?—
>   the perfume of forever.
>   A perfume as old as sleep,
>   as familiar to the living as to the dead.

Leaning forward from her pillows, she lifts up the curtain with the back of her hand, for its palm, its face, is already welcoming, already making a gesture which is preparatory to the act of touching his head.

She has not yet slept. Her gaze follows him as he approaches. In her face the two of them are reunited. Impossible now to separate the two images: his image of her in bed, as he remembers her: her image of him as she sees him approaching their bed. It is nighttime.

The Calling of St. Matthew by Caravaggio

On Caravaggio's *The Calling of St. Matthew*

One night in bed you asked me who was my favorite painter. I hesitated, searching for the least knowing, most truthful answer. Caravaggio. My own reply surprised me. There are nobler painters and painters of greater breadth of vision. There are painters I admire more and who are more admirable. But there is none, so it seems—for the answer came unpremeditated—to whom I feel closer.

The few canvases from my own incomparably modest life as a painter, which I would like to see again, are those I painted in the late 1940s of the streets of Livorno. This city was then war-scarred and poor, and it was there that I first began to learn something about the ingenuity of the dispossessed. It was there too that I discovered that I wanted as little as possible to do in this world with those who wield power. This has turned out to be a lifelong aversion.

The complicity I feel with Caravaggio began, I think, during that time in Livorno. He was the first painter of life as experienced by the popolaccio, the people of the backstreets, les sans-culottes, the lumpenproletariat, the lower orders, those of the lower depths, the underworld. There is no word in any traditional European language which does not either denigrate or patronize the urban poor it is naming. That is power.

Following Caravaggio up to the present day, other painters—Brower, Ostade, Hogarth, Goya, Géricault, Guttuso—have painted pictures of the same social milieu. But all of them—however great—were genre pictures, painted in order to show others how the less fortunate or the more dangerous lived. With Caravaggio, however, it was not a question of presenting scenes but of seeing itself. He does not depict the underworld for others: his vision is one that he shares with it.

In art-historical books Caravaggio is listed as one of the great innovating masters of chiaroscuro and a forerunner of the light and shade later used by Rembrandt and others. His vision can of course be considered art-historically as a step in the evolution of European art. Within such a perspective *a* Caravaggio was almost inevitable, as a link between the high art of the Counter Reformation and the domestic art of the emerging Dutch bourgeoisie, the form of this link being that of a new kind of space, defined by darkness as well as by light. (For Rome and for Amsterdam damnation had become an everyday affair.)

For the Caravaggio who actually existed—for the boy called Michelangelo born in a village near Bergamo, not far from where my friends, the Italian woodcutters, come—light and shade, as he imagined and saw them, had a deeply personal meaning, inextricably entwined with his desires and his instinct for survival. And it is by this, not by any art-historical logic, that his art is linked with the underworld.

His chiaroscuro allowed him to banish daylight. Shadows, he felt, offered shelter as can four walls and a roof. Whatever and wherever he
painted he really painted interiors. Sometimes—for *The Flight into Egypt* or
one of his beloved John the Baptists—he was obliged to include a landscape in the background. But these landscapes are like rugs or drapes
hung up on a line across an inner courtyard. He only felt at home—no,
that he felt nowhere—he only felt relatively at ease *inside.*

His darkness smells of candles, overripe melons, damp washing waiting to be hung out the next day: it is the darkness of stairwells, gambling
corners, cheap lodgings, sudden encounters. And the promise is not in
what will flare against it, but in the darkness itself. The shelter it offers is
only relative, for the chiaroscuro reveals violence, suffering, longing, mortality, but at least it reveals them intimately. What has been banished,
along with the daylight, are distance and solitude—and both these are
feared by the underworld.

Those who live precariously and are habitually crowded together
develop a phobia about open spaces which transforms their frustrating lack
of space and privacy into something reassuring. He shared those fears.

The Calling of St. Matthew depicts five men sitting round their usual
table, telling stories, gossiping, boasting of what one day they will do,
counting money. The room is dimly lit. Suddenly the door is flung open.
The two figures who enter are still part of the violent noise and light of the
invasion. (Berenson wrote that Christ, who is one of the figures, comes in
like a police inspector to make an arrest.)

Two of Matthew's colleagues refuse to look up, the other two younger
ones stare at the strangers with a mixture of curiosity and condescension.
Why is he proposing something so mad? Who's protecting him, the thin
one who does all the talking? And Matthew, the tax-collector with a shifty
conscience which has made him more unreasonable than most of his colleagues, points at himself and asks: Is it really I who must go? Is it really I
who must follow you?

How many thousands of decisions to leave have resembled Christ's
hand here! The hand is held out towards the one who has to decide, yet it
is ungraspable because so fluid. It orders the way, yet offers no direct support. Matthew will get up and follow the thin stranger from the room,
down the narrow streets, out of the district. He will write his gospel, he
will travel to Ethiopia and the South Caspian and Persia. Probably he will
be murdered.

And behind the drama of this moment of decision in the room at the
top of the stairs, there is a window, giving onto the outside world. Traditionally in painting, windows were treated either as sources of light or as
frames framing nature or framing an exemplary event outside. Not so this
window. No light enters by it. The window is opaque. We see nothing.
Mercifully we see nothing because what is outside is bound to be threatening. It is a window through which only the worst news can come.

•   •   •   •   •   •   •   •   •   •   •   •   •

QUESTIONS FOR A SECOND READING

1. Berger says, "The past is never there waiting to be discovered, to be recognized for exactly what it is. History always constitutes the relation between a present and its past" (p. 108). And he says, "If we 'saw' the art of
   the past, we would situate ourselves in history. When we are prevented
   from seeing it, we are being deprived of the history which belongs to us"
   (p. 108). As you reread this essay, pay particular attention to Berger's uses
   of the word "history." What does it stand for? What does it have to do
   with looking at pictures? How might you define the term if your definition were based on its use in this essay?

   You might take Berger's discussion of the Hals paintings as a case in
   point. What is the relation Berger establishes between the past and the
   present? If he has not "discovered" the past or recognized it for exactly
   what it is, what has Berger done in writing about these paintings? What
   might it mean to say that he has "situated" us in history or has returned
   a history that belongs to us? And in what way might this be said to be a
   political act?

2. Berger argues forcefully that the account of the Hals painting offered by
   the unnamed art historian is a case of "mystification." How would you
   characterize Berger's account of that same painting? Would you say that
   he sees what is "really" there? If so, why wasn't it self-evident? Why does
   it take an expert to see "clearly"? As you read back over the essay, look
   for passages you could use to characterize the way Berger looks at images
   or paintings. If, as he says, "The way we see things is affected by what we
   know or what we believe," what does he know and what does he believe?

ASSIGNMENTS FOR WRITING

1.   We are not saying that there is nothing left to experience before origi-
       nal works of art except a sense of awe because they have survived. The
       way original works of art are usually approached—through museum
       catalogues, guides, hired cassettes, etc.—is not the only way they might
       be approached. When the art of the past ceases to be viewed nostalgi-
       cally, the works will cease to be holy relics—although they will never
       re-become what they were before the age of reproduction. We are not
       saying original works of art are now useless. (pp. 124–25)

   Berger argues that there are barriers to vision, problems in the ways we
   see or don't see original works of art, problems that can be located in and
   overcome by strategies of approach.

   For Berger, what we lose if we fail to see properly is history: "If we
   'saw' the art of the past, we would situate ourselves in history. When we
   are prevented from seeing it, we are being deprived of the history which
   belongs to us." It is not hard to figure out who, according to Berger,

prevents us from seeing the art of the past. He says it is the ruling class. It *is* difficult, however, to figure out what he believes gets in the way and what all this has to do with history.

For this assignment, write an essay explaining what, as you read Berger, it is that gets in the way when we look at paintings, and what it is that we might do to overcome the barriers to vision (and to history). You should imagine that you are writing for someone interested in art, perhaps preparing to go to a museum, but someone who has not read Berger's essay. You will, that is, need to be careful in summary and paraphrase.

2. Berger says that the real question is this: "To whom does the meaning of the art of the past properly belong?" Let's say, in Berger's spirit, that it belongs to you. Look again at the painting by Vermeer, *Woman Pouring Milk*, that is included in "Ways of Seeing" (p. 126). Berger includes the painting but without much discussion, as though he were, in fact, leaving it for you. Write an essay that shows others how they might best understand that painting. You should offer this lesson in the spirit of John Berger. Imagine that you are doing this work for him, perhaps as his apprentice.

3.   Original paintings are silent and still in a sense that information never is. Even a reproduction hung on a wall is not comparable in this respect for in the original the silence and stillness permeate the actual material, the paint, in which one follows the traces of the painter's immediate gestures. This has the effect of closing the distance in time between the painting of the picture and one's own act of looking at it. . . . What we make of that painted moment when it is before our eyes depends upon what we expect of art, and that in turn depends today upon how we have already experienced the meaning of paintings through reproductions. (p. 125)

While Berger describes original paintings as silent in this passage, it is clear that these paintings begin to speak if one approaches them properly, if one learns to ask "the right questions of the past." Berger demonstrates one route of approach, for example, in his reading of the Hals paintings, where he asks questions about the people and objects and their relationships to the painter and the viewer. What the paintings might be made to say, however, depends on the viewer's expectations, his or her sense of the questions that seem appropriate or possible. Berger argues that, because of the way art is currently displayed, discussed, and reproduced, the viewer expects only to be mystified.

For this paper, imagine that you are working against the silence and mystification Berger describes. Go to a museum—or, if that is not possible, to a large-format book of reproductions in the library (or, if that is not possible, to the reproductions in this essay)—and select a painting that seems silent and still, yet invites conversation. Your job is to figure out what sorts of questions to ask, to interrogate the painting, to get it to speak, to engage with the past in some form of dialogue. Write an essay in which you record this process and what you have learned from it. Somewhere in your paper, perhaps at the end, turn back to Berger's essay and speak to it about how this process has or hasn't confirmed what you take to be Berger's expectations.

Note: If possible, include with your essay a reproduction of the painting you select. (Check the postcards at the museum gift shop.) In any event, you want to make sure that you describe the painting in sufficient detail for your readers to follow what you say.

4. In "Ways of Seeing" Berger says

> If the new language of images were used differently, it would, through its use, confer a new kind of power. Within it we could begin to define our experiences more precisely in areas where words are inadequate. . . . Not only personal experience, but also the essential historical experience of our relation to the past: that is to say the experience of seeking to give meaning to our lives, of trying to understand the history of which we can become the active agents. (p. 127)

As a writer, Berger is someone who uses images (including some of the great paintings of the Western tradition) "to define [experience] more precisely in areas where words are inadequate." In a wonderful book, *And our faces, my heart, brief as photos,* a book that is both a meditation on time and space and a long love letter, Berger writes about paintings in order to say what he wants to say to his lover. We have included two examples, descriptions of Rembrandt's *Woman in Bed* and Caravaggio's *The Calling of St. Matthew.*

Read these as examples, as lessons in how and why to look at, to value, to think with, to write about paintings. Then use one or both as a way of thinking about the concluding section of "Ways of Seeing" (pp. 125–27). You can assume that your readers have read Berger's essay but have difficulty grasping what he is saying in that final section, particularly since it is a section that seems to call for action, asking the reader to do something. Of what use might Berger's example be in trying to understand what we might do with and because of paintings?

MAKING CONNECTIONS

1. Walker Percy, in "The Loss of the Creature" (p. 588), like Berger in "Ways of Seeing," talks about the problems people have seeing things. "How can the sightseer recover the Grand Canyon?" Percy asks. "He can recover it in any number of ways, all sharing in common the stratagem of avoiding the approved confrontation of the tour and the Park Service." There is a way in which Berger also tells a story about tourists—tourists going to a museum to see paintings, to buy postcards, gallery guides, reprints, and T-shirts featuring the image of the Mona Lisa. "The way original works of art are usually approached—through museum catalogues, guides, hired cassettes, etc.—is not the only way they might be approached. When the art of the past ceases to be viewed nostalgically, the works will cease to be holy relics—although they will never re-become what they were before the age of reproduction" (p. 124).

Write an essay in which you describe possible "approaches" to a painting in a museum, approaches that could provide for a better understanding or a more complete "recovery" of that painting than would be possible to a casual viewer, to someone who just wandered in, for example, with no strategy in mind. You should think of your essay as providing real advice to a real person. (You might, if you can, work with a particular painting in a particular museum.) What should that person do? How should that person prepare? What would the consequences be?

At least one of your approaches should reflect Percy's best advice to a viewer who wanted to develop a successful strategy, and at least one should represent the best you feel Berger would have to offer. When you've finished explaining these approaches, go on in your essay to examine the differences between those you associate with Percy and those you associate with Berger. What are the key differences? And what do they say about the different ways these two thinkers approach the problem of why we do or do not see that which lies before us?

2. Both John Berger in "Ways of Seeing" and Michel Foucault in "Panopticism" (p. 225) discuss what Foucault calls "power relations." Berger claims that "the entire art of the past has now become a political issue," and he makes a case for the evolution of a "new language of images" that could "confer a new kind of power" if people were to understand history in art. Foucault argues that the Panopticon signals an "inspired" change in power relations. "It is," he says, "an important mechanism, for it automatizes and disindividualizes power. Power has its principle not so much in a person as in a certain concerted distribution of bodies, surfaces, lights, gazes; in an arrangement whose internal mechanisms produce the relation in which individuals are caught up" (p. 232).

Both Berger and Foucault create arguments about power and its methods and goals. As you read through their essays, mark passages you might use to explain how each author thinks about power—where it comes from, who has it, how it works, where you look for it, how you know it when you see it, what it does, where it goes. You should reread the essays as a pair, as part of a single project in which you are seeking to explain theories of power.

Write an essay in which you present and explain "Ways of Seeing" and "Panopticism" as examples of Berger's and Foucault's theories of power and vision. Both Berger and Foucault are arguing against usual understandings of power and knowledge and history. In this sense, their projects are similar. You should be sure, however, to look for differences as well as similarities.

3. Clifford Geertz, in "Deep Play: Notes on the Balinese Cockfight" (p. 305), argues that the cockfights are a "Balinese reading of Balinese experience; a story they tell themselves about themselves." They are not, then, just cockfights. Or, as Geertz says, the cockfights can be seen as texts "saying something of something." Berger's essay, "Ways of Seeing," offers a view of our culture and, in particular, of the way our culture reproduces and uses images from the past. They are placed in museums, on bulletin boards, on T-shirts, and in advertisements. They are described by experts in certain predictable tones or phrases. It is interesting to look at our use of those images as a story we tell ourselves about ourselves, as a practice that says something about something else.

Geertz's analysis of the cockfight demonstrates this way of seeing and interpreting a feature of a culture. Write an essay in which you use Geertz's methods to interpret the examples that Berger provides of the ways our culture reproduces and uses images from the past. If these practices say something about something else, what do they say, and about what do they say it? What story might we be telling ourselves about ourselves?

Note: For this assignment, you should avoid rushing to the conclusion Berger draws—that the story told here is a story about the ruling class and its conspiracy against the proletariat. You should see, that is, what other interpretation you can provide. You may, if you choose, return to Berger's conclusions in your paper, but only after you have worked on some of your own.

SUSAN BORDO

S USAN BORDO *(b. 1947) is the Otis A. Singletary Chair of Humanities at the University of Kentucky. Bordo is a philosopher, and while her work touches on figures and subjects traditional to the study of philosophy (René Descartes, for example), she brings her training to the study of culture, including popular culture and its representations of the body. She is a philosopher, that is, who writes not only about Plato but also about Madonna and O.J.*

In Unbearable Weight: Feminism, Western Culture, and the Body *(1993), the source for the selection that follows, Bordo looks at the complicated cultural forces that have produced our ways of understanding and valuing a woman's body. These powerful forces have shaped not only attitudes and lives but, through dieting, training, and cosmetic surgery, the physical body itself.* Unbearable Weight *was nominated for the 1993 Pulitzer Prize; it won the Association for Women in Psychology's Distinguished Publication Award and was named by the* New York Times *as one of the "Notable Books of 1993." Bordo is also the author of* The Flight to Objectivity: Essays on Cartesianism and Culture *(1987) and* Twilight Zones: The Hidden Life of Cultural Images from Plato to O.J. *(1997); she is coeditor (with Alison Jaggar) of* Gender/Body/ Knowledge: Feminist Reconstruction of Being and Knowing *(1989). Her most recent book is* The Male Body: A New Look at Men in Public and in Private *(1999).*

In "Hunger as Ideology" Bordo looks closely at ideas and images, both past and present, to trace the representation of the female body in relation to what is offered as "true" or "real," "natural" or "normal." She is particularly interested in the culture's assumptions about gender identity, about the differences attributed to men and women in the stories we tell ourselves and the ways we picture our attitudes toward food, eating, cooking, body size, and shape. She provides a powerful example of what it means to read closely, to read images as well as words, and to write that close reading into an extended argument. Bordo's writing is witty, committed, and engaging. It brings the concerns of a philosopher to the materials of everyday life.

Hunger as Ideology

The Woman Who Doesn't Eat Much

In a television commercial, two little French girls are shown dressing up in the feathery finery of their mother's clothes. They are exquisite little girls, flawless and innocent, and the scene emphasizes both their youth and the natural sense of style often associated with French women. (The ad is done in French, with subtitles.) One of the girls, spying a picture of the other girl's mother, exclaims breathlessly, "Your mother, she is so slim, so beautiful! Does she eat?" The daughter, giggling, replies: "Silly, just not so much," and displays her mother's helper, a bottle of FibreThin. "Aren't you jealous?" the friend asks. Dimpling, shy yet self-possessed, deeply knowing, the daughter answers, "Not if I know her secrets."

Admittedly, women are continually bombarded with advertisements and commercials for weight-loss products and programs, but this commercial makes many of us particularly angry. On the most obvious level, the commercial affronts with its suggestion that young girls begin early in learning to control their weight, and with its romantic mystification of diet pills as part of the obscure, eternal arsenal of feminine arts to be passed from generation to generation. This romanticization, as often is the case in American commercials, trades on our continuing infatuation with (what we imagine to be) the civility, tradition, and savoir-faire of "Europe" (seen as the stylish antithesis to our own American clumsiness, aggressiveness, crudeness). The little girls are fresh and demure, in a way that is undefinably but absolutely recognizably "European"—as defined, that is, within the visual vocabulary of popular American culture. And FibreThin, in this commercial, is nothing so crass and "medical" and pragmatic (read: American) as a diet pill, but a mysterious, prized (and, it is implied, age-old) "secret," known only to those with both history and taste.

But we expect such hype from contemporary advertisements. Far more unnerving is the psychological acuity of the ad's focus, not on the size and shape of bodies, but on a certain *subjectivity*, represented by the absent but central figure of the mother, the woman who eats, only "not so much." We never see her picture; we are left to imagine her ideal beauty and slenderness. But what she looks like is not important, in any case; what is important is the fact that she has achieved what we might call a "cool" (that is, casual) relation to food. She is not starving herself (an obsession, indicating the continuing power of food), but neither is she desperately and shamefully binging in some private corner. Eating has become, for her, no big deal. In its evocation of the lovely French mother who doesn't eat much, the commercial's metaphor of European "difference" reveals itself as a means of representing that enviable and truly foreign "other": the woman for whom food is merely ordinary, who can take it or leave it.

Another version, this time embodied by a sleek, fashionable African American woman, playfully promotes Virginia Slims Menthol [Fig. 1, p. 141]. This ad, which appeared in *Essence* magazine, is one of a series specifically targeted at the African American female consumer. In contrast to the Virginia Slims series concurrently appearing in *Cosmo* and *People,* a series which continues to associate the product with historically expanded opportunities for women ("You've come a long way, baby" remains the motif and slogan), Virginia Slims pitches to the *Essence* reader by mocking solemnity and self-importance *after* the realization of those opportunities: "Why climb the ladder if you're not going to enjoy the view?" "Big girls don't cry. They go shopping." And, in the variant depicted in Figure 1: "Decisions are easy. When I get to a fork in the road, I eat."

Arguably, the general subtext meant to be evoked by these ads is the failure of the dominant, white culture (those who *don't* "enjoy the view") to relax and take pleasure in success. The upwardly mobile black consumer, it is suggested, will do it with more panache, with more cool—and of course with a cool, Virginia Slims Menthol in hand. In this particular ad, the speaker scorns obsessiveness, not only over professional or interpersonal decision-making, but over food as well. Implicitly contrasting herself to those who worry and fret, she presents herself as utterly "easy" in her relationship with food. Unlike the FibreThin mother, she eats anytime she wants. But *like* the FibreThin mother (and this is the key similarity for my purposes), she has achieved a state beyond craving. Undominated by unsatisfied, internal need, she eats not only freely but without deep desire and without apparent consequence. It's "easy," she says. Presumably, without those forks in the road she might forget about food entirely.

The Virginia Slims woman is a fantasy figure, her cool attitude toward food as remote from the lives of most contemporary African American women as from any others. True, if we survey cultural attitudes toward women's appetites and body size, we find great variety—a variety shaped by ethnic, national, historical, class, and other factors. My eighty-year-old father, the child of immigrants, asks at the end of every meal if I "got enough to eat"; he considers me skinny unless I am plump by my own

Figure [1]

standards. His attitude reflects not only memories of economic struggle and a heritage of Jewish-Russian preference for zaftig women, but the lingering, well into this century, of a once more general Anglo-Saxon cultural appreciation for the buxom woman. In the mid-nineteenth century, hotels and bars were adorned with Bouguereau-inspired paintings of voluptuous female nudes; Lillian Russell, the most photographed woman in America in 1890, was known and admired for her hearty appetite, ample body (over two hundred pounds at the height of her popularity), and "challenging, fleshly arresting" beauty.[1] Even as such fleshly challenges became less widely appreciated in the twentieth century, men of Greek, Italian, Eastern European, and African descent, influenced by their own distinctive cultural heritages, were still likely to find female voluptuousness appealing. And even in the late 1960s and early 1970s, as Twiggy and Jean Shrimpton began to set a new norm for ultra-slenderness, lesbian cultures in the United States continued to be accepting—even celebrating—of fleshy, space-claiming female bodies.

Even more examples could be produced, of course, if we cast our glance more widely over the globe and back through history. Many cultures, clearly, have revered expansiveness in women's bodies and appetites. Some still do. But in the 1980s and 1990s an increasingly universal equation of slenderness with beauty and success has rendered the competing claims of cultural diversity ever feebler. Men who were teenagers from the mid-seventies on, whatever their ethnic roots or economic class, are likely to view long, slim legs, a flat stomach, and a firm rear end as essentials of female beauty. Unmuscled heft is no longer as acceptable as it once was in lesbian communities. Even Miss Soviet Union has become lean and tight, and the robust, earthy actresses who used to star in Russian films have been replaced by slender, Westernized types.

Arguably, a case could once be made for a contrast between (middle-class, heterosexual) white women's obsessive relations with food and a more accepting attitude toward women's appetites within African American communities. But in the nineties, features on diet, exercise, and body-image problems have grown increasingly prominent in magazines aimed at African American readers, reflecting the cultural reality that for most women today—whatever their racial or ethnic identity, and increasingly across class and sexual-orientation differences as well—free and easy relations with food are at best a relic of the past. (More frequently in *Essence* than in *Cosmo*, there may be a focus on health problems associated with overweight among African Americans, in addition to the glamorization of slenderness.) Almost all of us who can afford to be eating well are dieting—and hungry—almost all of the time.

It is thus Dexatrim, not Virginia Slims, that constructs the more realistic representation of women's subjective relations with food. In Dexatrim's commercial that shows a woman, her appetite-suppressant worn off, hurtling across the room, drawn like a living magnet to the breathing, menacing refrigerator, hunger is represented as an insistent, powerful force with a life of its own. This construction reflects the physiological reality of dieting, a state the body is unable to distinguish from starvation.[2] And it reflects its psychological reality as well; for dieters, who live in a state of constant denial, food is a perpetually beckoning presence, its power growing ever greater as the sanctions against gratification become more stringent. A slender body may be attainable through hard work, but a "cool" relation to food, the true "secret" of the beautiful "other" in the FibreThin commercial, is a tantalizing reminder of what lies beyond the reach of the inadequate and hungry self. (Of course, as the ads suggest, a psychocultural transformation remains possible, through FibreThin and Virginia Slims.)

Psyching out the Female Consumer

Sometimes, when I am analyzing and interpreting advertisements and commercials in class, students accuse me of a kind of paranoia about the significance of these representations as carriers and reproducers of culture. After all, they insist, these are just images, not "real life"; any fool knows that advertisers manipulate reality in the service of selling their products. I agree that on some level we "know" this. However, were it a meaningful or *usable* knowledge, it is unlikely that we would be witnessing the current spread of diet and exercise mania across racial and ethnic groups, or the explosion of technologies aimed at bodily "correction" and "enhancement."

Jean Baudrillard offers a more accurate description of our cultural estimation of the relation and relative importance of image and "reality." In *Simulations*, he recalls the Borges fable in which the cartographers of a mighty empire draw up a map so detailed that it ends up exactly covering the territory of the empire, a map which then frays and disintegrates as a symbol of the coming decline of the empire it perfectly represents. Today, Baudrillard suggests, the fable might be inverted: it is no longer the territory that provides the model for the map, but the map that defines the territory; and it is the *territory* "whose shreds are slowly rotting across the map." Thinking further, however, he declares even the inverted fable to be "useless." For what it still assumes is precisely that which is being lost today—namely, the distinction between the territory and its map, between reality and appearance. Today, all that we experience as meaningful are appearances.[3]

Thus, we all "know" that Cher and virtually every other female star over the age of twenty-five is the plastic product of numerous cosmetic surgeries on face and body. But, in the era of the "hyperreal" (as Baudrillard calls it), such "knowledge" is as faded and frayed as the old map in the Borges tale, unable to cast a shadow of doubt over the dazzling, compelling, authoritative images themselves. Like the knowledge of our own mortality when we are young and healthy, the knowledge that Cher's physical appearance is fabricated is an empty abstraction; it simply does not compute. It is the created image that has the hold on our most vibrant, immediate sense of what *is,* of what matters, of what we must pursue for ourselves.

In *constructing* the images, of course, continual use is made of knowledge (or at least what is imagined to be knowledge) of consumers' lives. Indeed, a careful reading of contemporary advertisements reveals continual and astute manipulation of problems that psychology and the popular media have targeted as characteristic dilemmas of the "contemporary woman," who is beset by conflicting role demands and pressures on her time. "Control"—a word that rarely used to appear in commercial contexts—has become a common trope in advertisements for products as disparate as mascara ("Perfect Pen Eyeliner. Puts *you* in control. And isn't that nice for a change?") and cat-box deodorant ("Control. I strive for it. My cat achieves it"). *"Soft felt tip gives you absolute control of your line"* [Fig. 2, p. 145]. It is virtually impossible to glance casually at this ad without reading "line" as "life"—which is, of course, the subliminal coding such ads intend. "Mastery" also frequently figures in ads for cosmetics and hair products: "Master your curls with new Adaptable Perm." The rhetoric of these ads is interestingly contrasted to the rhetoric of mastery and control directed at male consumers. Here, the message is almost always one of mastery and control over *others* rather than the self: "Now it's easier than ever to achieve a position of power in Manhattan" (an ad for a Manhattan health club), or "Don't just serve. Rule" (an ad for Speedo tennis shoes).

Advertisers are aware, too, of more specific *ways* in which women's lives are out of control, including our well-documented food disorders; they frequently incorporate the theme of food obsession into their pitch. The Sugar Free Jell-O Pudding campaign exemplifies a typical commercial strategy for exploiting women's eating problems while obscuring their dark realities. (The advertisers themselves would put this differently, of course.) In the "tip of my tongue" ad [Fig. 3, p. 146], the obsessive mental state of the compulsive eater is depicted fairly accurately, guaranteeing recognition from people with that problem: "If I'm not eating dessert, I'm talking about it. If I'm not talking about it, I'm eating it. And I'm always thinking about it . . . It's just always on my mind."

These thoughts, however, belong to a slender, confident, and—most important—decidedly not depressed individual, whose upbeat, open, and accepting attitude toward her constant hunger is far from that of most women who eat compulsively. "The inside of a binge," Geneen Roth writes, "is deep and dark. At the core . . . is deprivation, scarcity, a feeling that you can never get enough."[4] A student described her hunger as "a black hole that I had to fill up." In the Sugar Free Jell-O ad, by contrast, the mental state depicted is most like that of a growing teenage boy; to be continually hungry is represented as a normal, if somewhat humorous and occasionally annoying, state with no disastrous physical or emotional consequences.

The use of a male figure is one strategy, in contemporary ads, for representing compulsive eating as "natural" and even lovable. Men are *supposed* to have hearty, even voracious, appetites. It is a mark of the manly to eat spontaneously and expansively, and manliness is a frequent commercial code for amply portioned products: "Manwich," "Hungry Man Dinners," "Manhandlers." Even when men advertise diet products (as they more frequently do, now that physical perfection is increasingly being demanded of men as well as women), they brag about their appetites, as in the Tommy Lasorda commercials for Slim-Fast, which feature three burly football players (their masculinity beyond reproach) declaring that if Slim-Fast can satisfy *their* appetites, it can satisfy anyone's. The displacement of the female by a male figure (displacement when the targeted consumer is in fact a woman) thus dispels thoughts of addiction, danger, unhappiness,

Figure [2]

Figure [3]

and replaces them with a construction of compulsive eating (or thinking about food) as benign indulgence of a "natural" inclination. Consider the ad shown in Figure 4 [p. 147], depicting a male figure diving with abandon into the "tempered-to-full-flavor-consistency" joys of Häagen-Dazs deep chocolate.

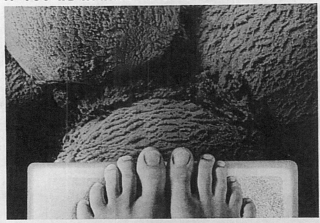

IF YOU'RE AFRAID OF EMOTIONAL HEIGHTS,

BEWARE OF HÄAGEN-DAZS®DEEP CHOCOLATE.

If intensity scares you, great pleasure upsets you or love makes you flee, please don't try our new Deep Chocolate Ice Creams. The shock of real Callebaut Belgian chocolate might be a tad overwhelming. And even if you can handle the thrill of Deep Chocolate alone, beware of Deep Chocolate Peanut Butter and Deep Chocolate Fudge. Or Belgian Chocolate Chocolate, found exclusively in our Shoppes. Häagen-Dazs Deep Chocolate. Surrender or stay away.

Available at participating Häagen-Dazs Ice Cream Shoppes and your favorite grocery.

© 1989 The Häagen-Dazs Company, Inc.

DEEP CHOCOLATE
THE FINEST ICE CREAM IN THE WORLD®

Figure [4]

Emotional heights, intensity, love, and thrills: it is women who habitually seek such experiences from food and who are most likely to be overwhelmed by their relationship to food, to find it dangerous and frightening (especially rich, fattening, soothing food like ice cream). The marketers
of Häagen-Dazs know this; they are aware of the well-publicized

prevalence of compulsive eating and binge behaviors among women. Indeed, this ad exploits, with artful precision, exactly the sorts of associations that are likely to resonate with a person for whom eating is invested with deep emotional meaning. Why, then, a male diver? In part, as I have been arguing, the displacement is necessary to insure that the grim actualities of women's eating problems remain obscured; the point, after all, is to sell ice cream, not to remind people of how dangerous food actually *is* for women. Too, the advertisers may reckon that women might enjoy seeing a man depicted in swooning surrender to ice cream, as a metaphor for the emotional surrender that so many women crave from their husbands and lovers.

Food, Sexuality, and Desire

I would argue, however, that more than a purely profit-maximizing, ideologically neutral, Madison Avenue mentality is at work in these ads. They must also be considered as gender ideology—that is, as specifically (consciously or unconsciously) servicing the cultural reproduction of gender difference and gender inequality, quite independent of (although at times coinciding with) marketing concerns. As gender ideology, the ads I have been discussing are not distinctively contemporary but continue a well-worn representational tradition, arguably inaugurated in the Victorian era, in which the depiction of women eating, particularly in sensuous surrender to rich, exciting food, is taboo.[5]

In exploring this dimension, we might begin by attempting to imagine an advertisement depicting a young, attractive woman indulging as freely, as salaciously as the man in the Post cereal ad shown in Figure 5 [p. 149]. Such an image would violate deeply sedimented expectations, would be experienced by many as disgusting and transgressive. When women are positively depicted as sensuously voracious about food (almost never in commercials, and only very rarely in movies and novels), their hunger for food is employed solely as a metaphor for their sexual appetite. In the eating scenes in *Tom Jones* and *Flashdance,* for example, the heroines' unrestrained delight in eating operates as sexual foreplay, a way of prefiguring the abandon that will shortly be expressed in bed. Women are permitted to lust for food itself only when they are pregnant or when it is clear they have been near starvation—as, for example, in *McCabe and Mrs. Miller,* in the scene in which Mrs. Miller, played by Julie Christie, wolfs down half a dozen eggs and a bowl of beef stew before the amazed eyes of McCabe. Significantly, the scene serves to establish Mrs. Miller's "manliness"; a woman who eats like this is to be taken seriously, is not to be trifled with, the movie suggests.

The metaphorical situation is virtually inverted in the representation of male eaters. Although voracious eating may occasionally code male sexual appetite (as in *Tom Jones*), we frequently also find *sexual* appetite operating as a metaphor for eating pleasure. In commercials that feature male eaters, the men are shown in a state of wild, sensual transport over

Figure [5]

heavily frosted, rich, gooey desserts. Their total lack of control is portrayed as appropriate, even adorable; the language of the background jingle is unashamedly aroused, sexual, and desiring.

> I'm thinking about you the whole day through [crooned to a Pillsbury cake]. I've got a passion for you.

> You're my one and only, my creamy deluxe [Betty Crocker frosting].

> You butter me up, I can't resist, you leave me breathless [Betty Crocker frosting].

> Your brownies give me fever. Your cake gives me chills [assorted Betty Crocker mixes].

> I'm a fool for your chocolate. I'm wild, crazy, out of control [assorted Betty Crocker mixes].

> I've got it bad, and I should know, 'cause I crave it from my head right down to my potato [for Pillsbury Potatoes Au Gratin].

> Can't help myself. It's Duncan Hines [assorted cake mixes] and nobody else.

In these commercials food is constructed as a sexual object of desire, and eating is legitimated as much more than a purely nutritive activity. Rather, food is *supposed* to supply sensual delight and succor—not as metaphorically standing for something else, but as an erotic experience in itself. Women are permitted such gratification from food only in measured doses. In another ad from the Diet Jell-O series, eating is metaphorically sexualized: "I'm a girl who just can't say no. I insist on dessert," admits the innocently dressed but flirtatiously posed model [Fig. 6, p. 151]. But at the same time that eating is mildly sexualized in this ad, it is also contained. She is permitted to "feel good about saying 'Yes'"—but ever so demurely, and to a harmless low-calorie product. Transgression beyond such limits is floridly sexualized, as an act of "cheating" [Fig. 7, p. 152]. Women may be encouraged (like the man on the Häagen-Dazs high board) to "dive in"—not, however, into a dangerous pool of Häagen-Dazs Deep Chocolate, but for a "refreshing dip" into Weight Watchers linguini [Fig. 8, p. 153]. Targeted at the working woman ("Just what you need to revive yourself from the workday routine"), this ad also exploits the aquatic metaphor to conjure up images of female independence and liberation ("Isn't it just like us to make waves?").

All of this may seem peculiarly contemporary, revolving as it does around the mass marketing of diet products. But in fact the same metaphorical universe, as well as the same practical prohibitions against female indulgence (for, of course, these ads are not only selling products but teaching appropriate behavior) were characteristic of Victorian gender ideology. Victorians did not have *Cosmo* and television, of course. But they did have conduct manuals, which warned elite women of the dangers of

Figure [6]

You'll think you're cheating

But you know you're not...
It's Wonder® Light bread.
Should you tell?
Should you tell your
friend that each full-size slice
of great tasting Wonder
Light is only 40 calories?
You can't just let her
suffer through carrot sticks
and rice cakes... Can you?

WONDER LIGHT   WONDER LIGHT

The lighter slice of America.

Figure [7]

indulgent and over-stimulating eating and advised how to consume in a feminine way (as little as possible and with the utmost precaution against unseemly show of desire). *Godey's Lady's Book* warned that it was vulgar for women to load their plates; young girls were admonished to "be frugal and plain in your tastes."[6] Detailed lexicons offered comparisons of the erotic and cooling effects of various foods, often with specific prescriptions for each sex.[7] Sexual metaphors permeate descriptions of potential transgression:

> Every luxurious table is a scene of temptation, which it requires fixed principles and an enlightened mind to withstand. . . . Nothing can be more seducing to the appetite than this arrangement of the viands which compose a feast; as the stomach is filled, and the natural desire for food subsides, the palate is tickled by more delicate and relishing dishes until it is betrayed into excess.[8]

Today, the same metaphors of temptation and fall appear frequently in advertisements for diet products [see Fig. 9, p. 154]. And in the Victorian era, as today, the forbiddenness of rich food often resulted in private binge behavior, described in *The Bazaar Book of Decorum* (1870) as the "secret luncheon," at which "many of the most abstemious at the open dinner are the most voracious . . . swallowing cream tarts by the dozen, and caramels and chocolate drops by the pound's weight."[9]

The emergence of such rigid and highly moralized restrictions on female appetite and eating are, arguably, part of what Bram Dijkstra has interpreted as a nineteenth-century "cultural ideological counter-offensive"

Figure [8]

Figure [9]

against the "new woman" and her challenge to prevailing gender arrangements and their constraints on women.[10] Mythological, artistic, polemical,
and scientific discourses from many cultures and eras certainly suggest
the symbolic potency of female hunger as a cultural metaphor for unleashed female power and desire, from the blood-craving Kali (who in one
representation is shown eating her own entrails) to the *Malleus Malificarum*
("For the sake of fulfilling the mouth of the womb, [witches] consort even
with the devil") to Hall and Oates's contemporary rock lyrics: "Oh, oh,
here she comes, watch out boys, she'll chew you up."[11]

   In *Tom Jones* and *Flashdance*, the trope of female hunger as female sexuality is embodied in attractive female characters; more frequently, however, female hunger as sexuality is represented by Western culture in
misogynist images permeated with terror and loathing rather than affec-

tion or admiration. In the figure of the man-eater the metaphor of the devouring woman reveals its deep psychological underpinnings. Eating is not really a metaphor for the sexual act; rather, the sexual act, when initiated and desired by a woman, is imagined as itself an act of eating, of incorporation and destruction of the object of desire. Thus, women's sexual appetites must be curtailed and controlled, because they threaten to deplete and consume the body and soul of the male. Such imagery, as Dijkstra has demonstrated, flourishes in the West in the art of the late nineteenth century. Arguably, the same cultural backlash (if not in the same form) operates today—for example, in the ascendancy of popular films that punish female sexuality and independence by rape and dismemberment (as in numerous slasher films), loss of family and children (*The Good Mother*), madness and death (*Fatal Attraction, Presumed Innocent*), and public humiliation and disgrace (*Dangerous Liaisons*).

Of course, Victorian prohibitions against women eating were not *only* about the ideology of gender. Or, perhaps better put, the ideology of gender contained other dimensions as well. The construction of "femininity" had not only a significant moral and sexual aspect (femininity as sexual passivity, timidity, purity, innocence) but a class dimension. In the reigning body symbolism of the day, a frail frame and lack of appetite signified not only spiritual transcendence of the desires of the flesh but *social* transcendence of the laboring, striving "economic" body. Then, as today, to be aristocratically cool and unconcerned with the mere facts of material survival was highly fashionable. The hungering bourgeois wished to appear, like the aristocrat, above the material desires that in fact ruled his life. The closest he could come was to possess a wife whose ethereal body became a sort of fashion statement of *his* aristocratic tastes. If he could not be or marry an aristocrat, he could have a wife who looked like one, a wife whose non-robust beauty and delicate appetite signified her lack of participation in the taxing "public sphere."[12]

Men Eat and Women Prepare

The metaphorical dualities at work here, whatever their class meanings, presuppose an idealized (and rarely actualized) gendered division of labor in which men strive, compete, and exert themselves in the public sphere while women are cocooned in the domestic arena (which is romanticized and mystified as a place of peace and leisure, and hence connotes transcendence of the laboring, bourgeois body). In the necessity to make such a division of labor appear natural we find another powerful ideological underpinning (perhaps the most important in the context of industrialized society) for the cultural containment of female appetite: the notion that women are most gratified by feeding and nourishing *others*, not themselves. As a literal activity, of course, women fed others long before the "home" came to be identified as women's special place; Caroline Bynum argues that there is reason to believe that food preparation was already a stereotypically female activity in the European Middle Ages.[13] But it was in the industrial era, with its idealization of the domestic arena as a place of nurture and comfort for men and children, that feeding others acquired the extended emotional meaning it has today.

In "An Ode to Mothers" columnist Bud Poloquin defines *Moms* as "those folks who, upon seeing there are only four pieces of pie for five people, promptly announce they never did care for the stuff."[14] Denial of self and the feeding of others are hopelessly enmeshed in this construction of the ideal mother, as they are in the nineteenth-century version of the ideal wife as "she who stands . . . famished before her husband, while he devours, stretched at ease, the produce of her exertions; waits his tardy permission without a word or a look of impatience, and feeds, with the humblest gratitude, and the shortest intermission of labor, on the scraps and offals which he disdains."[15] None of this self-sacrifice, however, is felt as such by the "paragon of womanhood" (as Charles Butler calls her), for it is here, in the care and feeding of others, that woman experiences the one form of desire that is appropriately hers: as Elias Canetti so succinctly puts it, "Her passion is to give food."[16]

Over a decade ago, John Berger trenchantly encapsulated the standard formula he saw as regulating the representation of gender difference, both throughout the history of art and in contemporary advertising: "Men act, and women appear."[17] Today, that opposition no longer seems to hold quite as rigidly as it once did (women are indeed objectified more than ever, but, in this image-dominated culture, men increasingly are too). But if this duality no longer strictly applies, the resilience of others is all the more instructive. Let me replace Berger's formulation with another, apparently more enduring one: "Men eat, and women prepare." At least in the sphere of popular representations, this division of labor is as prescriptive in 1991 as in 1891. Despite the increasing participation of women of all ages and classes in the "public" sphere, her "private" role of nurturer remains ideologically intact.

To be sure, we have inherited some of these representations from a former era—for example, the plump, generous Mammys and Grandmas who symbolically have prepared so many products: Aunt Jemima, Mrs. Smith, Mrs. Paul, Grandma Brown. But our cultural penchant for nostalgia does not get us off the hook here. At the start of the 1990s (and this seems to be even more striking now than five years ago), popular representations almost never depict a man *preparing* food as an everyday activity, routinely performed in the unpaid service of others. Occasionally, men *are* shown serving food—in the role of butler or waiter. They may be depicted roasting various items around a campfire, barbecuing meat, preparing a salad for a special company dinner, or making *instant* coffee (usually in a getaway cabin or vacation boat). But all of these are nonroutine, and their exceptional nature is frequently underscored in the ad. In one commercial, a man fixes instant coffee to serve to his wife in bed on her birthday. "How tough can it be?" he asks. "She makes breakfast every morning." In another ad, a man is shown preparing pancakes for his son's breakfast

Figure [10]

[Fig. 10, above]. "My pancakes deserve the rich maple flavor of Log Cabin Syrup," reads the bold type, suggesting ("my pancakes") male proprietorship and ease in the kitchen. The visual image of the father lovingly serving the son undoubtedly destabilizes cultural stereotypes (racial as well as gendered). But in the smaller print below the image we are told that this is a "special moment" with his son. Immediately the destabilizing image re-configures into a familiar one: like Dad's secret recipe for barbecue sauce, this father's pancakes make their appearance only on special occasions. Or perhaps it is the very fact that Dad is doing the cooking that *makes* this a significant, intimate occasion for sharing. (Imagine a woman instead of a man in the ad; would "special moment" not then seem odd?)

Continually, in representations that depict men preparing food, there will be a conspicuously absent wife or mother (for instance, in the hospital having a baby) who, it is implied, is *normally* responsible for the daily la-bor of food preparation and service. Even when men or boys are used to ad-vertise convenience foods, the product has usually been left for them with expert instructions added by Mom. In the Jell-O Heritage ad [Fig. 11, p. 159], this absent maternal figure (whether mother or grandmother is not clear) appears in the small insert to the upper right of the larger image, which depicts a young man away at college, well supplied with Jell-O pudding snacks. Significantly (although somewhat absurdly), she is asso-ciated with the provision of a "strong foundation" by virtue of the fact that *she* prepares instant pudding from a mix rather than merely opening up an already prepared pudding snack. Jell-O, of course, could not pre-sent nostalgic images of Grandma preparing *real* "scratch" pudding, since it does not want to evoke longing for a time when women did not depend on its products. But in terms of the oppositions exploited in this ad, instant pudding works just as well; compared to flipping the lid off a pudding snack, preparing instant pudding *is* a laborious task. It thus belongs to women's world. Men are almost *never* shown lavishing time on cooking. *Real* coffee is always prepared by women, as are all the cakes and casseroles that require more than a moment to put together. When men *are* shown cooking an elaborate meal, it is always *with* one or two other yup-pie men, converting the activity from an act of everyday service into a fes-tive, "Big Chill" occasion. But even these representations are rare. In all the many dinner parties that Hope and Michael hosted on "Thirtysome-thing," no man has ever appeared in the kitchen except to sneak a bit of the meal being prepared by Hope, Nancy, and Melissa.

Food and Love

At the beginning of the 1992 U.S. presidential campaign, Hillary Clin-ton, badgered by reporters' endless questions concerning her pursuit of a professional career, shot back defensively and sarcastically: "Well, I sup-pose I could have stayed home and baked cookies and had teas . . ." Media audiences never got to hear the end of her remark (or the question-ing that preceded it); the "cookies and teas" sound-bite became *the* gender-transgression of the campaign, replayed over and over, and presented by opponents as evidence of Hillary's rabid feminism and disdain for tradi-tional maternal values. Rightly protesting this interpretation, Hillary Clinton tried to prove her true womanhood by producing her favorite recipe for oatmeal chocolate chip cookies. Barbara Bush, apparently feel-

Figure [11]

ing that a gauntlet had been thrown down, responded in kind with a richer, less fibre-conscious recipe of her own. Newspapers across the country asked readers to prepare both and vote on which First Lady had the better cookie.

That the cookie itself should have become the symbol and center of the national debate about Hillary Clinton's adequacy as wife and mother is not surprising. Food is equated with maternal and wifely love throughout our culture. In nearly all commercials that feature men eating—such as the cake commercials whose sexualized rhetoric was quoted earlier—there is a woman in the background (either visible or implied) who has *prepared* the food. (The "Betty Crocker, You Sweet Talker" series has two women: the possessor of the clearly feminine hands offering the cakes, and Betty Crocker herself, to whom all the passionate croonings—"I'm a fool for your chocolate. I'm wild, crazy, out of control"—are addressed.) Most significantly, *always,* the woman in the background speaks the language of love and care through the offering of food: "Nothin' says lovin' like something from the oven"; "Give me that great taste of love"; "Nothing says 'Cookie, I love you' like Nestle's Toll House Cookies Do." In these commercials, male eating is inextricably tied to female offerings of love. This is not represented, however, as female self-abnegation. Rather, it is suggested that women receive *their* gratification through nourishing others, either in the old-fashioned way (taste and emotional pleasure) or in the health-conscious mode:

> *Her voice, heard off:* He's like a little boy—normally serious, *then* he eats English muffins with butter [shot of man's face trans-

ported with childlike delight] and *I* get to enjoy watching him.
A little butter brings a lot of joy.

> *He:* What are you doing?
> *She:* I'm listening to your heart.
> *He:* What does it say?
> *She:* It says that it's glad that you've started jogging, and
> that you're eating healthier. It's happy that I'm giving us new
> Promise margarine. Eating foods low in cholesterol is good for
> you and your heart.
> *He:* Know what else is good for me?
> *She:* What?
> *He:* You.
> *She beams, snuggling deeper into man's chest.*

My analysis, I want to emphasize, is not meant to disparage caring for
the physical and emotional well-being of others, "maternal" work that has
been scandalously socially undervalued even as it has been idealized and
sanctified. Nor am I counterposing to the argument of these ads the construction that women are simply oppressed by such roles. This would be
untrue to the personal experiences of many women, including myself. I remember the pride and pleasure that radiated from my mother, who was
anxious and unhappy in most other areas of her life, when her famous
stuffed cabbage was devoured enthusiastically and in voluminous quantities by my father, my sisters, and me. As a little girl, I loved watching her
roll each piece, enclosing just the right amount of filling, skillfully avoiding tearing the tender cabbage leaves as she folded them around the meat.
I never felt so safe and secure as at those moments. She was visibly
pleased when I asked her to teach me exactly how to make the dish and
thrilled when I even went so far as to write the quantities and instructions
down as she tried to formulate them into an official recipe (until then, it
had been passed through demonstration from mother to daughter, and
my mother considered that in writing it down I was conferring a higher
status on it). Those periods in my life when I have found myself too busy
writing, teaching, and traveling to find the time and energy to prepare
special meals for people that I love have been periods when a deep aspect
of my self has felt deprived, depressed.

Nor would I want my critique to be interpreted as effacing the collective,
historical experiences of those groups, forced into servitude for the families
of others, who have been systematically deprived of the freedom *to* care for
their own families. Bell hooks points out, for example, that black women's
creation of "home-place," of fragile and hard-won "spaces of care and nur-
turance" for the healing of deep wounds made by racism, sexism, and
poverty, was less a matter of obedience to a tyrannical gender-norm than
the construction of a "site of cultural resistance."[18] With this in mind, it is
clear that the Jell-O Heritage ad discussed earlier is more complex than my
interpretation has thus far allowed. Part of an extensive General Foods series aimed at the African American consumer and promoting America's

historically black colleges, the ad's association of the maternal figure with "strong foundations" runs far deeper than a nostalgic evocation of Mom's traditional cooking. In this ad, the maternal figure is linked with a black "heritage," with the preservation and communication of culture.

However, at the same time that hooks urges that contemporary black culture should honor the black woman's history of service to her family and her community, she also cautions against the ideological construction of such service as woman's natural role. (Despite the pleasure I take in cooking, in relationships where it has been expected of me I have resented it deeply.) It is this construction that is reinforced in the representations I have been examining, through their failure to depict males as "naturally" fulfilling that role, and—more perniciously—through their failure to depict females as appropriate *recipients* of such care. Only occasionally are little girls represented as being *fed;* more often, they (but never little boys) are shown learning how to feed others [Fig. 12, below]. In this way, caring

Figure [12]

is representationally "reproduced" as a quintessentially and exclusively female activity. It is significant and disquieting that the General Foods series does not include any ads that portray female students discovering their black heritage (or learning how to rely on convenience foods!) at college. It is possible that the ad series is very deliberate here, exploiting contemporary notions that the "crisis in black manhood" is the fault of black women and identifying its products with an imagined world in which opportunities for black men go hand in hand with "natural," prefeminist gender relations. Black men will find their way to college, it is suggested, so long as women remain in the background, encouraging and supporting rather than competing and undermining.

The ubiquitous configuration of woman-food-man, with food expressing the woman's love for the man and at the same time satisfying woman's desire to bestow love, establishes male hunger as thoroughly socially integrated into the network of heterosexual family and love relations. Men can eat *and* be loved; indeed, a central mode by which they receive love is through food from women. For women, by contrast (who are almost never shown being fed by others), eating—in the form of private, *self*-feeding—is represented as a *substitute* for human love. Weight Watchers transparently offers itself as such in its "Who says you can't live on love?" ad [Fig. 13, p. 163]. In other ads, it offers its low-cal spaghetti sauce as "A Friend." Diet Coke, emphasizing the sexual, insists that "sometimes the best relationships are purely fizzical." Miracle Whip Light offers itself as "a light that turns you on."

Notice that in these ads there is no partner, visible or implied, offering the food and thus operating as the true bestower of "love." In many ads— virtually a genre, in fact—the absence of the partner is explicitly thematized, a central aspect of the narrative of the ad. One commercial features a woman in bed, on the phone, refusing date after date in favor of an evening alone with her ice-cream bon bons: "Your Highness? Not tonight!" "The inauguration? Another year!" In another, a woman admits to spending a lot of time alone with her "latest obsession," a chocolate drink, because it gives her "the same feeling as being in love" and "satisfies her innermost cravings anytime [she] wants." She pleads with us, the viewers, not to tell Michael, her boyfriend.

These commercials hit a painful nerve for women. The bon bon commercial may seem merely silly, but the chocolate drink ad begins to evoke, darkly and disturbingly, the psychological and material realities of women's food problems. The talk of "obsession" and "innermost cravings," the furtiveness, the secrecy, the use of food to satisfy emotional needs, all suggest central elements of binge behavior. Frusen Glädjé supplies another piece and gives an important lie to the other, more upbeat commercials [Fig. 14, p. 164]: "He never called. So, Ben and I went out for a walk to pick up a pint of Frusen Glädjé. Ben's better looking anyway." Frusen Glädjé: "It feels so good." Here, as in the Häagen-Dazs ad discussed earlier, the sensuousness of the ice-cream experience is

Figure [13]

Figure [14]

emphasized; unlike the Häagen-Dazs ad, however, Frusen Glädjé offers solace from emotional depths rather than the thrill of emotional heights. This is, indeed, the prevailing gender reality. For women, the emotional comfort of self-feeding is rarely turned to in a state of pleasure and independence, but in despair, emptiness, loneliness, and desperation. Food is, as one woman put it, "the only thing that will take care of *me*."[19]

Food as Transgression

An extremely interesting fact about male bulimics: they rarely binge alone. They tend to binge at mealtime and in public places, whereas women almost always eat minimally at meals and gorge later, in private.[20] Even in our disorders (or perhaps especially in our disorders) we follow the gender rules. In the commercials I have been discussing, female eating is virtually always represented as private, secretive, illicit. The woman has stolen away from the world of husband, family, friends to a secret corner where she and the food can be alone. A "Do Not Disturb" sign hangs on the door to the room where the woman sits munching on her "purple passion," New York Deli Potato Chips. A husband returns home to discover that in his absence his wife, sitting on the floor, has eaten all the Frusen Glädjé; her voice is mildly defiant, although soft—"I ate all the Frusen Glädjé"—but her face is sheepish and her glance averted. Men sing openly of their wild cravings for Betty Crocker cakes; women's cravings are a dirty, shameful secret, to be indulged in only when no one is looking.

More often than not, however, women are not even permitted, even in private, indulgences so extravagant in scope as the full satisfaction of their hungers. Most commonly, women are used to advertise, *not* ice cream and potato chips (foods whose intake is very difficult to contain and control), but individually wrapped pieces of tiny, bite-size candies: Andes candies, Hershey's kisses, Mon Cheri bon bons. Instead of the mounds of cake and oozing frosting typical of commercials featuring male eaters, women are confined to a "tiny scoop" of flavor, a "tiny piece" of chocolate. As in the Weight Watchers linguini advertisement ("Dive in"), the rhetoric of indulgence is invoked, only to be contained by the product itself: "Indulge a little," urges Andes Candies. "Satisfy your urge to splurge in five delicious bite-size ways." The littleness of the candy and the amount of taste that is packed within its tiny boundaries are frequently emphasized: "Each bite-size piece packs a wallop of milk chocolate crunch." Instead of the emphasis on undifferentiated feelings of sensuous delight that we see in commercials showing men, the pitch aimed at women stresses the exquisite pleasure to be had from a sensually focused and limited experience. The message to women is explicit: "Indulge a *little*." (And only out of sight; even these minuscule bon bons are eaten privately, in isolation, behind closed doors.)

If one genre of commercials hints at the dark secrets of binge behavior—the refusal of female desire to remain circumscribed and repressed; the frustrations of "feeding" others and never being fed yourself—the "bite-size" candy genre represents female hunger as successfully contained within the bounds of appropriate feminine behavior. It is significant, surely, that in all these commercials the woman is found "indulging" only after a day spent serving others. In these commercials, it is permissible for women to feed the self (if such dainty nibbling merits this description) only after first feeding others:

For my angel, I sewed for days. Now I deserve a little praise.
I thank me very much with Andes Candies.

Chances are you spent the day doing things for others. Don't
you deserve something for yourself? Try a Mon Cheri. [The
woman is in the bathtub; in the background, dimly heard are
the voices of the day gone by: "Honey, did you pick up my dry
cleaning?" "Mrs. Jones, will you type this letter?" "Mommy,
we want to go to the park!" She sinks down into the tub, un-
wrapping the candy, in exquisite anticipation.]

These commercials, no less than the Victorian conduct manuals, offer a
virtual blueprint for disordered relations to food and hunger. The representation of unrestrained appetite as inappropriate for women, the depiction of female eating as a private, transgressive act, make restriction and
denial of hunger central features of the construction of femininity and set
up the compensatory binge as a virtual inevitability. Such restrictions on
appetite, moreover, are not merely about food intake. Rather, the social control of female hunger operates as a practical "discipline" (to use
Foucault's term) that trains female bodies in the knowledge of their limits
and possibilities. Denying oneself food becomes the central micro-practice
in the education of feminine self-restraint and containment of impulse.

Victorian women were told that it was vulgar to load their plates; in
1990, women students of mine complain of the tortures of the cafeteria—
the embarrassment of eating ice cream in front of the male students, the
pressure to take just a salad or, better yet, refuse food altogether. Later at
night, when they are alone, they confront the deprived and empty feeling
left in the wake of such a regimen. As in the commercials, the self-reward
and solace is food. The problem, however, after a day of restraint is the requirement for any further containment of the now ravenous self. Unlike
the women in the Andes candy commercials, few women who have spent
the day submerging their desires, either for the sake of their families or to
project the appropriately attractive lack of appetite to a cafeteria full of
adolescent boys, really feel rewarded by a bite-size piece of candy, no matter how much chocolate "wallop" it packs. In private, shamefully and
furtively, we binge.

Destabilizing Images?

When, in my classes, we discuss contemporary representations, I encourage my students to bring in examples that appear to violate traditional gender-dualities and the ideological messages contained in them.
Frequently, my students view our examination of these "subversive" representations as an investigation and determination of whether or not
"progress" has been made. My students want very much to believe that
progress is being made, and so do I. But "progress" is not an adequate description of the cultural status of the counter-examples they bring me.
Rather, they almost always display a complicated and bewitching tangle

of new possibilities and old patterns of representation. They reflect the instabilities that trouble the continued reproduction of the old dualities and ideologies, but they do not show clearly just where we are going.

A television commercial for Hormel microwaveable Kid's Kitchen Meals, for example, opens with two young girls trying to fix a bicycle. A little boy, watching them, offers to help, claiming that "I can fix anything. My dad lets me fix his car. My mom lets me fix dinner." When the girls are skeptical ("Yeah? Well, prove it!"), he fixes a Hormel's Kid's Kitchen Meal for them. Utterly impressed with his culinary skill and on the basis of this ready to trust his mechanical aptitude, they ask, "You know how to fix a bike?" "What? Yeah, I do!" he eagerly replies. Now, is this ad "progressive" or "regressive"? The little girls cannot fix their own bike, a highly traditional, "feminine" limitation. Yet they do not behave in helpless or coquettish ways in the commercial. Far from it. They speak in rough voices and challenging words to the boy, who is physically smaller (and, it appears, younger) than they; "Give me a break!" they mutter scornfully when he claims he can "fix anything." Despite their mechanical inability, they do not act deferential, and in a curious way this neutralizes the gendered meanings of the activities depicted. Not being able to fix a bike is something that could happen to anyone, they seem to believe. And so we may begin to see it this way too.

Then, too, there is the unusual representation of the male cooking for and serving the females. True, it only required a touch of the microwave panel. But this is, after all, only a little boy. One message this commercial may be delivering is that males can engage in traditionally "feminine" activities without threat to their manhood. Cooking for a woman does not mean that she won't respect you in the morning. She will still recognize your authority to fix her bike (indeed, she may become further convinced of it precisely by your mastery of "her" domain). The expansion of possibilities for boys thus extracts from girls the price of continued ineptitude in certain areas (or at least the show of it) and dependence on males. Yet, in an era in which most working women find themselves with two full-time jobs—their second shift beginning at five o'clock, when they return from work to meet their husband's expectations of dinner, a clean and comfortable home, a sympathetic ear—the message that cooking and serving others is not "sissy," though it may be problematic and nonprogressive in many ways, is perhaps the single most *practically* beneficial (to women) message we can convey to little boys.

In its provision of ambiguous and destabilizing imagery, the influx of women into the professional arena has had a significant effect on the representation of gender. Seeking to appeal to a population that wishes to be regarded (at least while on the job) as equal in power and ability to the men with whom they work, advertisers have tried to establish gender symmetry in those representations that depict or evoke the lives of professional couples. Minute Rice thus has two versions of its "I wonder what 'Minute' is cookin' up for dinner tonight?" commercial. In one, father and children come home from work and school to find mother "cookin' up" an

elaborate chicken stir-fry to serve over Minute Rice. In the other, a working woman returns to find her male partner "cookin' up" the dinner. The
configuration is indeed destabilizing, if only because it makes us aware of
how very rare it is to see. But, significantly, there are no children in this
commercial, as there are in the more traditional version; the absence of
children codes the fact that this is a yuppie couple, the group to which this
version is designed to appeal.

And now Häagen-Dazs, the original yuppie ice cream, has designed
an ad series for this market [Fig. 15, below, and Fig. 16, p. 169]. These ads

Figure [15]

Figure [16]

perfectly illustrate the unstable location of contemporary gender advertisements: they attempt to satisfy representational conventions that still
have a deep psychic grip on Western culture, while at the same time registering every new rhythm of the social heartbeat. "Enter the State of
Häagen-Dazs"—a clear invocation of the public world rather than the domestic domain. The man and woman are dressed virtually identically
(making small allowances for gender-tailoring) in equally no-nonsense,
dark business suits, styled for power. Their hair-styles are equivalent,
brushed back from the face, clipped short but not punky. They have similar expressions: slightly playful, caught in the act but certainly not feeling
guilty. They appear to be indulging in their ice-cream break in the middle
of a workday; this sets up both the fetching representational incongruity
of the ad and its realism. Ice cream has always been represented as relaxation food, to be *indulged* in; it belongs to a different universe than the
work ethic, performance principle, or spirit of competition. To eat it in a
business suit is like having "quickie" sex in the office, irregular and
naughty. Yet everyone knows that people *do* eat ice cream on their breaks
and during their lunch hours. The ad thus appears both realistic and *representationally* odd; we realize that we are seeing images we have not seen
before *except* in real life. And, of course, in real life, women *do* eat Häagen-
Dazs, as much as, if not more than, men.

And yet, intruding into this world of gender equality and eating realism that is designed to appeal to the sensibilities of "progressive" young
men and women is the inescapable disparity in how much and how the
man and woman are eating. He: an entire pint of vanilla fudge, with sufficient abandon to topple the carton, and greedy enough to suck the spoon.
She: a restrained Eve-bite (already taken; no licks or sucks in process
here), out of a single brittle bar (aestheticized as "artfully" nutty), in contrast to his bold, unaccessorized "Vanilla Fudge." Whether unconsciously
reproduced or deliberately crafted to appeal to the psychic contradictions
and ambivalence of its intended audience, the disparity comes from the
recesses of our most sedimented, unquestioned notions about gender.

NOTES

This essay grew out of a shorter piece, "How Television Teaches Women to Hate
Their Hungers," in *Mirror Images* (Newsletter of Anorexia Bulimia Support, Syracuse,
N.Y.) 4, no. 1 (1986): 8–9. An earlier version was delivered at the 1990 meetings of the
New York State Sociological Association, and some of the analysis has been presented in
various talks at Le Moyne and other colleges and community organizations. I owe
thanks to all my students who supplied examples.

[1] Journalist Beatrice Fairfax, quoted in Lois Banner, *American Beauty* (Chicago: University of Chicago Press, 1984), p. 136.

[2] "Starvation Stages in Weight-loss Patients Similar to Famine Victims," *International
Obesity Newsletter* 3 (April 1989).

[3] Jean Baudrillard, *Simulations* (New York: Semiotext(e), 1983), pp. 1–3; quotation is
on p. 2.

[4] Geneen Roth, *Feeding the Hungry Heart* (New York: New American Library, 1982),
p. 15.

[5]See Helena Mitchie, *The Flesh Made Word* (New York: Oxford University Press, 1987), for an extremely interesting discussion of this taboo in Victorian literature.

[6]Quoted from *Godey's* by Joan Jacobs Brumberg, *Fasting Girls* (Cambridge: Harvard University Press, 1988), p. 179.

[7]Mitchie, *The Flesh Made Word*, p. 15. Not surprisingly, red meat came under especial suspicion as a source of erotic inflammation. As was typical for the era, such anxieties were rigorously scientized: for example, in terms of the heat-producing capacities of red meat and its effects on the development of the sexual organs and menstrual flow. But, clearly, an irresistible associational overdetermination—meat as the beast, the raw, the primitive, the masculine—was the true inflammatory agent here. These associations survive today, put to commercial use by the American Beef Association, whose television ads feature James Garner and Cybil Shepard promoting "Beef: Real Food for Real People." Here the nineteenth-century link between meat aversion, delicacy, and refinement is exploited, this time in favor of the meat-eater, whose down-to-earth gutsiness is implicitly contrasted to the prissiness of the weak-blooded vegetarian.

[8]Mrs. H. O. Ward, *The Young Lady's Friend* (Philadelphia: Porter and Coates, 1880), p. 162, quoted in Mitchie, *The Flesh Made Word*, pp. 16–17.

[9]Quoted in Mitchie, *The Flesh Made Word*, p. 193.

[10]Bram Dijkstra, *Idols of Perversity* (New York: Oxford University Press, 1986), pp. 30–31.

[11]*Malleus Malificarum* quoted in Brian Easlea, *Witch-Hunting, Magic, and the New Philosophy* (Atlantic Highlands, N.J.: Humanities Press, 1980), p. 8; Hall and Oates, "Man-Eater."

[12]Women were thus warned that "gluttonous habits of life" would degrade their physical appearance and ruin their marriageability. "Gross eaters" could develop thick skin, broken blood vessels on the nose, cracked lips, and an unattractively "superanimal" facial expression (Brumberg, *Fasting Girls*, p. 179). Of course, the degree to which actual women were able to enact any part of these idealized and idolized constructions was highly variable (as it always is); but *all* women, of all classes and races, felt their effects as the normalizing measuring rods against which their own adequacy was judged (and, usually, found wanting).

[13]Caroline Walker Bynum, *Holy Feast and Holy Fast: The Religious Significance of Food to Medieval Women* (Berkeley: University of California Press, 1987), p. 191.

[14]*Syracuse Herald-American*, May 8, 1988, p. D1.

[15]Charles Butler, *The American Lady,* quoted in Dijkstra, *Idols of Perversity*, p. 18. Margery Spring Rice noted this same pattern of self-sacrifice among British working-class housewives in the 1930s. Faced with the task of feeding a family on an inadequate budget and cooking in cramped conditions, the housewife, according to Rice, often "takes one comparatively easy way out by eating much less than any other member of her family." She gives a multitude of examples from social workers' records, including "'Her food is quite insufficient owing to the claims of the family'"; "'She is . . . a good mother spending most of the housekeeping money on suitable food for the children and often goes without proper food for herself'"; "'Mrs. A . . . gives her family of eight children an excellent diet . . . but cannot eat herself as she is so exhausted by the time she has prepared the family meals'"; and, interestingly, "'the children look well fed and one cannot help believing that Mrs. F. is starving herself unnecessarily'" (*Working-Class Wives: Their Health and Conditions* [London: Virago, 1989; orig. pub. 1939], pp. 157, 160, 162, 167).

[16]Elias Canetti, *Crowds and Power* (New York: Viking, 1962), p. 221.

[17]John Berger, *Ways of Seeing* (London: Penguin, 1977).

[18]bell hooks, *Yearning* (Boston: South End Press, 1990), p. 42.

[19]Marcia Millman, *Such a Pretty Face: Being Fat in America* (New York: Norton, 1980), p. 106.

[20]John Schneider and W. Stewart Agras, "Bulimia in Males: A Matched Comparison with Females," *International Journal of Eating Disorders* 6, no. 2 (March 1987): 235–42.

· · · · · · · · · · · ·

QUESTIONS FOR A SECOND READING

1. Bordo's essay is designed to allow its readers to raise questions about food and advertising and the ways ads could be said to promote the "reproduction of gender difference and gender inequality." And yet, in the same breath, she says, "I would argue, however, that more than a purely profit-maximizing . . . Madison Avenue mentality is at work in these ads" (p. 148). If there is more at work here than a company's desire to make money, what is it? As Bordo invites you to think about this, whose interests are served in these ads? As you reread this selection, mark those moments in the text where you see Bordo identifying the cultural pressures that could be said to be at play in these advertisements. What are they? How might they be related? And who, or what, might they benefit?

2. Bordo brings a special training to the materials of popular culture. Among signs of this training in her prose are those terms and sources that are difficult or unfamiliar, particular to philosophy or to cultural studies. As you reread, underline or make a list of the key terms that seem to mark her expertise (to mark the difference between what she can say and what you can say). And mark those figures, like Berger or Baudrillard, who help her to say what she wants to say. Be prepared to identify those terms and references that mark the work of an expert. From their use and context in Bordo's essay, how might you explain or translate these passages for others? What could you add if you researched them in the library?

3. Bordo examines advertisements of different sorts—some sell food, for example, while others sell body images or psychological states—and she compares ads directed toward women with those designed for men. As you reread, make note of how she defines and establishes the differences in the ads designed for (or attractive to) men and those designed for (or attractive to) women. In what materials you have at hand (magazines, TV programs or ads, CD covers), find five or six images, images that *you* find powerful and attractive, images you can place alongside those provided by Bordo. How might they be "read" in her terms? Where and how might her terms be made to seem misguided, limited, or inadequate?

ASSIGNMENTS FOR WRITING

1. "Hunger as Ideology" begins with a section titled "The Woman Who Doesn't Eat Much" and ends with one titled "Destabilizing Images?" The opening section features several advertisements offering women "free and easy relations with food." The closing one features ads that Bordo suggests disrupt or destabilize the ideology or "commonsense" attitudes and values that we take for granted in our understanding of women, eating, and the body—that which "comes from the recesses of our most sedimented, unquestioned notions about gender." Between these two sec-

tions, she covers a range of subjects: "Food, Sexuality, and Desire," "Food and Love," "Food as Transgression."

For this assignment, write an essay in which you present and explain Bordo's argument. You should imagine that you are writing for someone who is interested in these issues but who has not read this particular essay. You will need, then, to be careful, fair, and detailed in your presentation. What are the significant examples for Bordo? How does she read them? And, finally, how does she pull these examples together? What does she conclude?

You should also, however, establish your perspective on the questions and materials at the center of "Hunger as Ideology." The purpose of the summary, in other words, is to establish a position you can attribute to "Bordo." You should do this strategically, in order that you can also establish a position in conversation with what she says. You can frame this other position or point of view in your name (as what, on reflection, *you* think) or in the name of a group you feel you can represent (people of your generation, your gender, your background, your set of commitments, identifications, and practice).

2. Bordo extends an invitation to her students "to bring in examples that appear to violate traditional gender-dualities and the ideological messages contained in them." These, she said, will "display a complicated and bewitching tangle of new possibilities and old patterns of representation" (pp. 166–67).

Write an essay in which you take up Bordo's invitation. On your own or with a group collect a set of advertisements (or images from other sources) that represent food and eating, women and men. Find examples and counterexamples to what she takes to be the traditional gender-dualities and the ideological messages contained in them. In order to present your project to others, write descriptions of the ads, as Bordo does, so that your readers will be able to "read" them (to see them and understand them) as you do. You'll need to place your examples in relation to Bordo's argument about the "old dualities and ideologies" and to what she says about images that "stabilize" and "destabilize." You will need, in other words, to put her terms to work on your examples. Make your goal not only to reproduce Bordo's project but to extend it, to refine it, to put it to the test.

3. Reread Bordo's essay and pay close attention to how she presents and reads her examples. What are the kinds of questions she routinely asks? And, as you look across her examples, think about the principles of selection and arrangement. What methods do you see in her work? What principles or assumptions? What defines her particular expertise?

You might also do this work as a work of criticism. You might think about what Bordo *doesn't* see in the ads she studies. What does she miss? and why? You might think about the questions she doesn't ask of the ads she studies. You might think about the ads she fails (or refuses) to include as part of her project. What is missing? What is unsaid or unnoticed?

Write an essay in which you choose two of Bordo's examples and use them to represent your study of her work. What does she do, as a writer and scholar, with her materials? What are her conclusions? What have you learned about her methods? How do you explain the kind of work represented by "Hunger as Ideology"? Assume that your audience is familiar with the essay but perhaps has not studied it as closely as you have and, as a consequence, could not understand it the way you do.

MAKING CONNECTIONS

1. In "Hunger as Ideology," Bordo refers to John Berger and his work in *Ways of Seeing*. Both Berger and Bordo are concerned with how we see and read images; both are concerned to correct the ways images are used and read; both trace the ways images serve the interests of money and power; both are writing to get the attention of the public and teach readers how and why they should pay a different kind of attention to the images around them.

   For this assignment, use Bordo's work in "Hunger as Ideology" to reconsider Berger's "Ways of Seeing" (p. 105). Write an essay in which you consider the two essays as examples of an ongoing project. Berger's essay precedes Bordo's by about a quarter of a century. If you look closely at one or two of their examples, and if you look at the larger concerns in their arguments, are they saying the same thing? doing the same work? If so, why? Why is such work still necessary? If not, how do their projects differ? And how might you account for those differences?

2. Robert Coles in "The Tradition: Fact and Fiction" (p. 176) is concerned with the representation of the female body—with what those images mean and what purposes they serve (or might serve). (See, in particular, his discussion of Dorothea Lange's photographs of the "migrant mother" [pp. 185–88] and his discussion of Walker Evans's photos of the tenant's daughter picking cotton [pp. 197–205].) Coles's descriptions are close and careful. They draw, however, on a very different vocabulary than those provided by Bordo.

   Write an essay in which you compare the methods and concerns of Bordo and Coles. You should think about how their projects differ; consider the ways they choose and present images, what they notice, and how they describe and analyze what they notice. Both are concerned with the social context of images. What does Coles offer in describing the larger forces at work in producing the meanings of images? What does he offer in place of Bordo's "ideology"?

ROBERT
COLES

*E*ARLY *IN HIS CAREER as a psychologist, Robert Coles spent seven years following migrant workers north from Florida to gather material for the second volume—*Migrants, Sharecroppers, Mountaineers—*of his remarkable, Pulitzer Prize–winning series of books,* Children of Crisis. *He learned about the workers' lives, he said, by visiting "certain homes week after week until it [had] come to pass that I [had] known certain families for many years." The sacrifice, patience, compassion, and discipline required for his massive documentary projects—the eight volumes of the* Children of Crisis *series and, later,* The Inner Lives of Children—*transform the usual business of research into something magnificent.*

Coles's project began when he was stationed at Keesler Air Force Base in Biloxi, Mississippi. He was, he says, a "rather smug and all too self-satisfied child psychiatrist, just out of medical training." He was in the South at the beginning of the civil rights movement, and the scenes he witnessed, the experience, for example, of black children taunted and threatened as they walked into newly desegregated schools, led him to abandon his plans to return to New England and to remain instead in the South to find out how children responded to crisis. He began with standard psychiatric questions, such as "How did these children respond to stress?" but soon realized, he said, "that I was meeting families whose assumptions, hopes, fears, and expectations were quite definitely strange to me. I realized, too, how arbitrarily I was fitting the lives of various individuals into my psychiatric categories—a useful practice under certain circumstances, but now, for me, a distinct hindrance. I was unwittingly setting severe, maybe crippling, limits on what I would allow myself to see, try to comprehend." He learned, through the children, to abandon his carefully rehearsed questions and to talk and listen. The stories he learned to tell are remarkable and moving and have an authority few writers achieve.

Born in 1929, Coles graduated from Harvard University in 1950, earned an M.D. degree from Columbia University in 1954, and began his career as a child psychiatrist. He is currently the James Agee Professor of Social Ethics at Harvard University and a founding member of the Center of Documentary Studies at Duke University. An essayist, poet, and scholar, Coles has published over fifty books, including Women of Crisis *(1978), coauthored with his wife, Jane Hallowell Coles,* The Call of Stories: Teaching and the Moral Imagination *(1989),* Harvard Diary *(1990),* The Call of Service: A Witness to Idealism *(1994),* School *(1998), and* The Children of Crisis Reader *(2001). Coles is also the editor of the documentary magazine* DoubleTake.

The essay that follows is a chapter from Coles's book Doing Documentary Work *(1997). Coles first presented it in 1996 in a series of lectures given at the New York Public Library. The chapter draws on the last twenty years of his teaching, including courses in the "literary-documentary tradition" at Harvard and at the Center for Documentary Studies at Duke. When Coles refers to "documentary work" he is referring to any attempt to engage, represent, and understand the lives of others. His reference, then, extends to journalists, poets, novelists, and filmmakers; to sociologists, anthropologists, and historians; to physicians, psychologists, and social workers; to anyone who is charged to know deeply and to speak and act for others. There is an urgency in Coles's work, a sense of mission and service, that is rare in academia and in contemporary intellectual life. You can feel this urgency in his conclusion to "The Tradition: Fact and Fiction":*

> *And so it goes, then—doing documentary work is a journey, and is a little more, too, a passage across boundaries (disciplines, occupational constraints, definitions, conventions all too influentially closed for traffic), a passage that can become a quest, even a pilgrimage, a movement toward the sacred truth enshrined not only on tablets of stone, but in the living hearts of those others whom we can hear, see, and get to understand. Thereby, we hope to be confirmed in our own humanity— the creature on this earth whose very nature it is to make just that kind of connection with others during the brief stay we are permitted here.*

The Tradition: Fact and Fiction

The heart of the matter for someone doing documentary work is the pursuit of what James Agee called "human actuality"—rendering and representing for others what has been witnessed, heard, overheard, or sensed. Fact is "the quality of being actual," hence Agee's concern with actuality.

All documentation, however, is put together by a particular mind whose capacities, interests, values, conjectures, suppositions and presuppositions, whose memories, and, not least, whose talents will come to bear directly or indirectly on what is, finally presented to the world in the form of words, pictures, or even music or artifacts of one kind or another. In shaping an article or a book, the writer can add factors and variables in two directions: social and cultural and historical on the one hand, individual or idiosyncratic on the other. As Agee reminds us in his long "country letter," his aria: "All that each person is, and experiences, and shall ever experience, in body and in mind, all these things are differing expressions of himself and of one root, and are identical: and not one of these things nor one of these persons is ever quite to be duplicated, nor replaced, nor has it ever quite had precedent: but each is a new and incommunicably tender life, wounded in every breath, and almost as hardly killed as easily wounded: sustaining, for a while, without defense, the enormous assaults of the universe."

Such an emphasis on human particularity would include the ups and downs of a life, even events (both internal and external) in that life that would seem to have nothing to do with the objectivity of, say, the world of central Alabama, but everything to do with the world of the writer or the photographer who will notice, ignore, take seriously, or find irrelevant Alabama's various moments, happenings, acts and deeds and comments, scenes. Events are filtered through a person's awareness, itself not uninfluenced by a history of private experience, by all sorts of aspirations, frustrations, and yearnings, by those elusive, significant "moods" as they can affect and even sway what we deem of interest or importance, not to mention how we assemble what we have learned into something to present to others—to editors, museum curators first of all, whose personal attitudes, not to mention the nature of their jobs or the values and desires of *their* bosses, all help shape their editorial or curatorial judgment. The web of one kind of human complexity (that of life in Hale County, Alabama) connects with, is influenced by, the web of another kind of human complexity (Agee and Evans and all that informs not only their lives but those of their magazine and book editors).

So often in our discussion of documentary work my students echo Agee, emphasize the "actuality" of the work—its responsibility to fact. They commonly pose for themselves the familiar alternative of fiction, as though we were dealing in clear-cut opposites: if not the true as against the false, at least the real as against the imaginary. But such opposites or alternatives don't quite do justice either conceptually or pragmatically to the aspect of "human actuality" that has to do with the vocational life of writers, photographers, folklorists, musicologists, and filmmakers, those who are trying to engage with people's words, their music, gestures, movements, and overall appearance and then let others know what they have learned. No one going anywhere, on a journalistic trip, on a documentary assignment, for social-science research, or to soak up the atmosphere of a place to aid in the writing of a story or a novel, will claim to be able to see and hear everything, or even claim to be able to notice all that truly matters. Who we are, to some variable extent, determines what we notice and, at another level of intellectual activity, what we regard as worthy of notice, what we find significant. Nor will technology help us all that decisively. I can arrive in America's Alabama or England's Yorkshire, I can find my way to a South Seas island or to central Africa, I can go visit a nearby suburban mall with the best tape recorder in the world, with cameras that take superb pictures, and even with a clear idea of what I am to do, and still I face the matter of looking *and* overlooking, paying instant heed *and* letting something slip by; and I face the matter of sorting out what I *have* noticed, of arranging it for emphasis—the matter, really, of *composition*, be it verbal or visual, the matter of re-presenting; and here that all-important word *narrative* enters. Stories heard or seen now have to turn into stories put together with some guiding intelligence and discrimination: I must select *what* ought to be present; decide on the *tone* of that presentation, its *atmosphere* or *mood*. These words can be as elusive as they are compelling to an essay, an exhibition of pictures, or a film.

Even if the strict limits of oral history are never suspended (*only* the taped interviews with informants are used in a given article or book, or any comments from the practitioner of oral history are confined to an introduction or to explanatory footnotes) there still remains that challenge of selection, with its implications for the narrative: which portions of which tapes are to be used, and with what assertive or clarifying or instructional agenda in mind (in the hope, for instance, of what popular or academic nod of comprehension or applause). How does one organize one's "material," with what topics in mind, what broader themes? How does one deal with the mix of factuality and emotionality that any taped interview presents, never mind a stock of them, and how does one arrange and unfold the events, the incidents: a story's pace, its plot, its coherence, its character development and portrayal, its suggestiveness, its degree of inwardness, its degree of connection to external action, and, all in all, its dramatic power, not to mention its moral authority?

The above words and phrases are summoned all the time by writers and teachers of fiction. Fictional devices, that is, inform the construction of nonfiction, and of course, fiction, conversely, draws upon the actual, the "real-life." A novelist uses his or her lived experience and the observations he or she has made and is making in the course of living a life as elements of a writing life. I remember William Carlos Williams pausing, after a home visit, to write down not only medical notes but a writer's notes: words heard; a revealing moment remembered; the appearance of a room on a particular day, or of a face brimming with surprise or happiness, a head lowered in dismay, a look of anticipation or alarm or dread, fear on a child's face, those details of life, of language, of appearance, of occurrence for which novelists are known, but which the rest of us also crave or require, as readers, of course, but also in our working lives: we all survive and prevail through a mastery of certain details, or fail by letting them slip through our fingers.

A novelist has to have those details at constant hand. He or she has had occasion in so-called real life to become aware of them but now has to fit this personal learning into a story, a narrative that requires both imagination and an idea of what will reach and touch readers persuasively. Nonfiction involves the same process, though we have to be careful of how we use words such as *experience, observation,* and, certainly, *imagination* when discussing nonfiction. A documentarian's report will be strengthened by what has been witnessed, but will be fueled, surely, by what those observations come to mean in his or her head: we absorb sights and sounds, and they become *our* experience, unique to us, in that we, their recipients, are unique. What we offer others in the way of our documentary reports, then, is *our* mix of what we have observed and experienced, as we have assembled it, that assembly having to do, again, with our imaginative capability, our gifts as writers, as editors, as storytellers, as artists. Oscar Lewis and Studs Terkel, working with taped interviews, pages and pages of transcripts, put all of that together in such a way that makes us readers marvel, not only at what we're told but at how it gets told—and, before that, at how it was elicited from the various individuals these two met and from anyone who worked with them (Lewis trained a team of colleagues to help him out). Others of us might have met the same people but obtained from them different stories, maybe fewer in number or less interesting, less revealing.

I remember well what one of my psychoanalytic supervisors, Elizabeth Zetzel, who was a rather solidly conventional physician with a mind George Eliot would have called "theoretic," told me as she contemplated my protocols (my daily notes of what I had heard from a particular patient). Psychoanalysis, she said, is not only the uncovering of psychological material; it is two people doing so. Therefore, anyone's analysis, undertaken with a particular analyst, is only one of a possible series of hypothetical analyses, depending on who *else* might be the analyst, and what might be looked at and concluded on the basis of that other person's presence as the analyst, rather than the one now being consulted. I had been zealously on the prowl for certain memories that would, frankly, confirm my clinical notion of what had happened earlier in a certain patient's life, and to what effect. Dr. Zetzel had realized (I would later realize) that this was not only *an* inquiry, or the "correct" inquiry, but *my* inquiry—that someone else might have had other clinical interests, other kinds of memories to pursue, other clinical destinations in mind and, very important, would no doubt have engaged with this patient in a different way. (Nietzsche's aphorism holds here: "It takes two to make a truth.")

Moreover, what I make of what I hear from any patient has to do with what I've learned, and with what I have brought from my life to what has been taught me. Psychoanalysis, then, is a person's continuing narrative, however "meandering" rather than formally structured, as it is prompted by and shaped by his or her life, of course, but also as it responds to a particular listener or observer who has his or her own narrative interests and capacities and intentions (his or her observations, experiences, and, as with artists, talent and imagination—ways of sensing and of phrasing what is sensed, skill at putting him- or herself in another's shoes). A profession also has its narrative as well as its intellectual and emotional demands, and it, too, affects a particular practitioner, here a psychoanalyst, in influential ways: an agreed-upon language; an agreed-upon story called a diagnosis or a clinical interpretation or summary, namely, how we (are trained to) tell ourselves what we're hearing before we get around to letting our patients know what we think. Put differently, we develop, as psychiatric or psychoanalytic listeners, a professional narrative, which is offered in response to the narratives we hear in that unusual room where matters of utter intimacy and privacy become a shared documentary experience limited to two people. Others may be brought into the "act," however, since patients talk to people they know, and so do we, in our professional lives (at meetings) and in our writing lives: we share case histories with our colleagues and stories with readers, and surely we tailor our stories to elicit readers' interest—a tradition that goes back to Freud's first books and accounts for those of the many who have followed throughout this profession's now hundred-year history.

All of the above is as intricate and knotty, but also as evident and ordinary, as what happens every day when any two people talk to each other. The words and the pictorial sense vary on both sides, depending upon who the people are; and if one or both of the two talks to a third or a fourth person, that "report" will also vary depending on the person then doing the listening. We have words for the gross distortions of this process: rumor, gossip. We are less likely to account for the almost infinite possible variations on an encounter that constitute a human exchange, or a human response to the nonhuman world of the landscape or the multihuman world of a social scene. Naturally, a novelist does go one significant step further—reserves the right to use his or her imagination more freely than a documentarian, and to call upon the imaginary as a matter of course: personal fantasies, made-up voices given to made-up characters with made-up names, and scenes described out of the mind's visual reveries, even as its verbal ones supply words. All of the above has to be done with judgment as well as provocative ingenuity and boldness. The imaginary life, like the real one, requires a teller's thoughtfulness, canniness, sensitivity, and talent for dealing with language, or with the visual. What emerges, if it is done successfully, is a kind of truth, sometimes (as in Tolstoy, George Eliot, Dickens; we each make our choices from among these storytellers) an enveloping and unforgettable wisdom that strikes the reader as realer than real, a truth that penetrates deep within one, that leaps beyond verisimilitude or incisive portrayal, appealing and recognizable characterization, and lands on a terrain where the cognitive, the emotional, the reflective, and the moral live side-by-side. "I make up stories all day," I hear a wonderfully able novelist say at a seminar on "documentary studies." "Some people would say I tell lies—my 'business' is to write them down and sell them, with the help of a publisher." We all demur, but he rejects what he hears as an evasive politeness on our part. "All right," he provokes us further, "I do a good job, so I get published, and you like what you read. But there are talented storytellers out there, let's call them that, who spend their lives telling stories, persuading people to get wrapped up in them, just like they talk of getting wrapped up in a good novel . . . and they are telling what you and I would call lies, a string of them, or falsehoods, or *un*truths. Some of them do enough of it that they become known chiefly, essentially, for what they tell *as*—they are 'con artists.' Am I a version of such a person, a successful, socially sanctioned, 'sublimated' version? Is that a useful way of thinking about stories and novels—cleverly or entertainingly put together lies?"

This writer, this novelist who was also a teacher and an effective conversationalist, was forcefully putting a big subject before us. He had, after a fashion, constructed a small story about the matter of storytelling in which he highlighted the matter of fiction as something made up—though often quite full of facts, observations, accurately recalled happenings, and also made up, potentially, of truth, even the highest kind of truth, as many of us would insist. Others in the seminar, of course, spoke of journalism and social science, their claims to another kind of truth, one that pertains to an observed world unconnected to an imagined one; though, again, the journalist's, the photographer's, the social scientist's imagination can all the time influence how a news story or a research project is done, what is obtained in the way of information, remarks, photographs, and how all of that is relayed to others.

I tried, in that seminar, to make sense of my own work, to figure out its nature, and so did we all: this was the purpose of the seminar. During the early 1960s, as I mentioned earlier, I was trying hard to learn how Southern schoolchildren, both black and white, were managing under the stresses of court-ordered desegregation in the South, and how civil rights activists were dealing with their special, often dangerous, even fatally dangerous lives of constant protest. I was doing psychiatric research and beginning to write up my findings for presentation to professional audiences and journals. By then, I'd also been interviewed by newspaper reporters, because I was immersed in a serious educational, social, and racial crisis. I was privileged (I only gradually realized) to be watching a moment of history. Soon I was not only taking what I heard from children, teachers, parents, and young activists and fitting it all into a language, a way of thinking, a theoretical or conceptual apparatus of sorts (lists of defense mechanisms, signs of various symptoms, evidence of successful adaptation); I was developing a general thesis on what makes for collapse in children under duress and what makes for "resiliency." I had developed a list of "variables," aspects of a life that tended to make a child worthy of being described as such by me: a resilient child. Eventually, with enough knowledge of enough children, I had in mind a broader claim, a more ambitious one, a statement on "*the* resilient child."

I was also seeing, in some newspapers, quotations correctly attributed to me that weren't always my words, and that seemed a bit foreign to me because they had been hurriedly scribbled as I talked. Even my exactly transcribed words, *taped* words, sometimes seemed strange to me, because they appeared out of context; they were deprived of the explanatory remarks, the narrative sequence, that had preceded and followed them. My wife would say, "You said *that?*" I would say yes, and then the refrain: "but the reporter used what I said for his purposes"—and I wasn't necessarily being critical. I had tried to explain something, had tried to speak with some qualifications or even with skepticism, second thoughts, or outright misgivings about my own thoughts, themselves being constantly modified by interviews, by conversations with colleagues, by *consideration* of this or that matter, the reflective aspect of what gets called experience.

The reporters, needless to say, had their own purposes to consider, their own experiences; they had gradually accumulated manners of hearing and remembering, of listening to tapes, based on notions of what they were meant to do professionally. I was meant to move from hearing children talk about what was on their minds to thinking about the *projections* these children summoned, the *denials* or *reaction-formations* to which they resorted; a journalist is used to hearing me, and soon enough, asking me pointed questions that aim for an opinion, an explanation, stated as plainly and unequivocally as possible. *Why* is this child doing so well, given the pressures she has to endure? Why is *that* child not doing so well? What is your explanation for the difference? If my explanation was too long-winded, evasive, abstract, or, finally, unconvincing, the reporter pressed, rephrased, got me to reconsider, to say things differently—until what I said helped him or her understand the subject at hand (and would presumably help his or her editor and readers, who inhabit his or her mind, understand). Sometimes I was not only surprised by the printed result, as my wife was, but grateful. Those reporters pushed me to think (and to put things) in ways not familiar to me, and when I remembered what I said, seeing it presented in the context of a story, a part of the reporter's own take on the subject, I found myself learning something, regarding matters with a different emphasis or point of view, responding, it can be said, to the "truth" of that particular interview. All interviews, one hopes, become jointly conducted!

The harder I struggled to make sense of my work, never mind make sense of what others might make of it, the more confused I became: what was I doing, what was I learning, what was I trying to say? I was a child psychiatrist and was learning to be a psychoanalyst, but I wasn't working with patients in an office or a clinic; I was visiting children and their parents in their homes, talking with teachers in schools, and, through SNCC [Student Nonviolent Coordinating Committee], doing things regarded by cities and states of the South as illegal, a challenge both to laws and to long-standing customs. On the one hand, I had to answer to a certain kind of psychiatric voice in me: why *are* you doing all this? On the other hand, I had to answer to the collective voices of civil rights workers: why are you concentrating your energies on *us*, when there's a "sick" society out there; for example, look at your own profession, the utterly segregated universities, medical schools, residency training programs, psychoanalytic institutes—why don't you study all that! Then, I had to contend with my great teacher Dr. W. C. Williams, to whom (1961, 1962) I'd sent some drafts of my psychiatric reports. "For God's sake," he told me once, "try to find a cure for that passive voice you use, for the third person, for all that technical language—it's a syndrome!" My apologies and chagrin and self-pity only elicited this: "Take your readers in hand, take them where you've been, tell them what you've seen, give them some stories you've heard. Most of all, write for *them,* the ordinary folks out there, not for yourself and your buddies in the profession of psychiatry." I can still recall my sense of futility and inadequacy as I thought about those admonishing remarks. I had always known that Dr. Williams could be irritable with people he knew and wanted to help (I'd seen him be so with patients), but now I felt critically judged, and unable to do anything in keeping with the advice given me—lest I lose my last link with my medical and psychiatric and psychoanalytic life: my capacity to write articles that would earn me (not to mention the work I was doing) a hearing, some acceptance.

What Dr. Williams urged, my wife, a high-school teacher of English and history, also urged. She began listening to the tapes we'd collected (she and I worked together, full-time, until our sons were born in 1964, 1966, and 1970). She marked up certain moments in the transcripts which she found interesting, pulled them together, and wrote from memory some descriptions of the scenes in which those comments were made: times, places, details such as the weather, the casual talk exchanged, the food so generously served us, the neighborhood excursions we took—to churches, to markets, a world explored with the help of embattled people who knew that if we were really to understand them, we had to go beyond those clinical questions that I wanted so much to ask them. In time Jane had assembled "moments," she called them, for me to read: a mix of descriptive writing and edited versions of interviews, with suggestions for what she called "personal reflection" on my part. "You'll have some old-fashioned essays," she wrote. "Nothing to be afraid of!"

Plenty to be afraid of, I thought. It took me a couple of years to overcome that apprehension and worry. I was taught and rallied and reassured by Jane, badgered by Dr. Williams, until he died (March 4, 1963), challenged by some of the friends I'd made in SNCC, who kept telling me I should "tell their stories," not try to "shrink" them, and encouraged by Margaret Long, a novelist who worked for the Southern Regional Council, an interracial group long devoted to standing up in many ways to segregation. In 1963 the Council published my first nonprofessional piece (as I thought of it back then) on the work I was doing: "Separate But Equal Lives." The very title signified a break for me, a departure from the heavy-weight jargon I'd learned to use as an expression of professional arrival. With this new kind of writing, I began to think differently about the very nature of the work I was doing. The point now was not only to analyze what children said, or the drawings they made, but to learn about their *lives*, in the hope of being able to describe them as knowingly and clearly as possible to anyone who cares to read of them rather than to my col-leagues in child psychiatry.

In 1970, well along in such writing, I heard this from one of my old su-pervisors at the Children's Hospital in Boston, George Gardner: "You're doing documentary work, documentary child psychiatry, I suppose you could call it." I was pleased, though also worried—haunted by the judg-mental self, its appearance often a measure of careerist anxiety. When I told my wife what Dr. Gardner had said, she laughed and said, "When Dr. Gardner settles for 'documentary work' alone, you'll be there!" But where is her "there"? We never discussed that question at the time. I was almost afraid to think about what she had in mind, even as I know in retrospect what she was suggesting—that I try to respond more broadly (less clini-cally) to these children, give them their due as individuals, as human be-ings, rather than patients. After all, they weren't "sick," or coming to me in a hospital or a clinical setting for "help"; they were "out there," living their lives, and I had come to them in an effort to learn how they "got along." Those two words increasingly became my methodological description of intent, my rationale of sorts: to try to ascertain as best I could the character of particular lives, the way they are lived, the assump-tions held, the hopes embraced, the fears and worries borne—in Flannery O'Connor's felicitous phrase, the particular "habit of being" that informs *this* person's existence, *that* one's. To render such lives requires that one take a stand with respect to them—that of the observer, first and foremost, so that they can be apprehended, but that of the *distanced* observer, the ed-itor, the critic (not of them, but of them as the subject of a story). What of their lives to offer others, and in what manner of delivery? As I asked that question I could hear one of Dr. Williams's refrains: "the language, the language!" Williams was forever trying to do justice both to what he heard from others, and to what he heard in his own head: the narrative side of documentary work, the exposition of a particular effort at exploration.

Documentary work, then, ultimately becomes, for most of us, docu-mentary writing, documentary photographs, a film, a taped series of folk songs, a collection of children's drawings and paintings: reports of what was encountered for the ears and eyes of others. Here we weed and choose from so very much accumulated. Here we connect ourselves criti-cally with those we have come to know—we arrange and direct their debut on the stage, and we encourage and discourage by selecting some segments and eliminating others. Moreover, to repeat, some of us add our own two cents (or more); we work what others have become to *us* into *our* narrative—the titles we give to photographs, the introductions we write for exhibitions, the statements we make with films. Even if our work is presented as only about *them*, we have been at work for weeks, for months, discarding and thereby concentrating what we retain: its significance mightily enhanced because so much else has been taken away.

It is not unfair, therefore, for an Oscar Lewis or a Studs Terkel or a Fred Wiseman to be known as the one who is "responsible" for what are supposedly documentary reports about all those others who were interviewed or filmed. Those others, in a certain way, have become "creations" of Lewis, Terkel, Wiseman—even if we have no explanatory comments from any of them about what they have done, and how, and with what purpose in mind. The stories such documentarians tell us are, in a way, the surviving remnants of so very much that has been left aside. We who cut, weave, edit, splice, crop, sequence, interpolate, interject, connect, pan, come up with our captions and comments, have our say (whenever and wherever and however) have thereby linked our lives to those we have attempted to document, creating a joint presentation for an audience that may or may not have been asked to consider all that has gone into what they are reading, hearing, or viewing.

I remember, a wonderfully enlightening afternoon spent with labor economist Paul Taylor in 1972, while I was working on a biographical study of Dorothea Lange. Jane and I sat in Taylor's spacious, comfortable Berkeley home, the one he and Dorothea Lange occupied together until her death of cancer in 1965. He took me, step by step, through their work together, the work that culminated in *American Exodus* (1939). We examined many of Lange's photographs, some of them prints that were never published or shown. We were looking at an artist's sensibility, as it informed the selections she had made—which picture really worked, really got across what the photographer intended for us to contemplate.

I studied her iconic "migrant mother," a picture known throughout the world, a visual rallying ground of sorts for those who want to be reminded and remind others of jeopardy's pensive life [Fig. 1, p. 186]. There she sits, her right hand touching her lower right cheek, the lady of Nipoma, caught gazing, in March of 1936, one of her children to her left, one to her right, head turned away from us, disinclined to look at the camera and, through it, the legions of viewers with whom it connects. The three figures seem so close, so "tight," it would be said in the South, yet each seems lost to the others: the children lost in the private world they secure by hiding their eyes, the mother lost in a look that is seemingly directed at no one and everyone, a look that is inward and yet that engages with us who look at her, and maybe with her, or through her, at the kind of life she has been living. But only minutes before Lange took that famous picture, she had taken others. At furthest remove [Fig. 2, p. 187] we are shown the same mother and her children in the makeshift tent that is their home; two others, a bit closer, show her with another child who has

Figure [1]

just been suckling at her breast and now has settled into a sleep. In one picture [Fig. 3, p. 188] the mother is alone with that child; in the next, [Fig. 4, p. 189] another of her children has come to her side, its face on her left shoulder. I return to the picture Lange has selected: now the older children are alongside their mother, but her appearance commands our attention—her hair lightly combed, her strong nose and broad forehead and

Figure [2]

wide mouth giving her face authority, her informally layered plainclothes, her worker's arms and fingers telling us that this is someone who every day has to take life on with no conviction of success around any corner.

Dorothea Lange has, in a sense, removed that woman from the very world she is meant, as a Farm Security Administration (FSA) photographer, to document. The tent is gone, and the land on which it is pitched, and the utensils. The children, in a way, are gone, their backs turned to us, their backs a sort of screen upon which we may project our sense of what is happening to them, what they feel. But one child's head is slightly lowered, and the other has covered her face with her right arm—and so a feeling of their sadness, become the viewer's sadness, has surely seized so many of us who have stared and stared at that woman, who is herself staring, and maybe, as in a Rodin sculpture, doing some serious thinking: struggling for a vision, dealing with an apprehension, experiencing a premonition or a nightmarish moment of foreboding. We are told by Lange that she is a "migrant mother," because otherwise she could be quite another kind of working (or nonworking) mother, yet she has been at least somewhat separated from sociological clues, and so she becomes psychologically more available to us, kin to us. A photographer has edited and cropped her work in order to make it more accessible to her anticipated

Figure [3]

viewers. As a documentarian, Lange snapped away with her camera, came back with a series of pictures that narrate a kind of white migrant life in the mid-1930s—and then, looking for one picture that would make the particular universal, that would bring us within a person's world rather than keep us out (as pitying onlookers), she decided upon a photograph that allows us to move from well-meant compassion to a sense of respect, even awe: we see a stoic dignity, a thoughtfulness whose compelling survival under such circumstances is itself something to ponder, something to find arresting, even miraculous.

Another well-known Lange picture that Paul Taylor and I studied was "Ditched, Stalled, and Stranded," taken in California's San Joaquin Valley in 1935. Taylor first showed me the uncropped version of that picture [Fig. 5, p. 190], with a man seated at the steering wheel of a car, his wife beside him. He has a wool cap on, of a kind today more commonly worn in Europe than here. He has a long face with a sturdy nose, and with wide eyes he stares past his wife (the right car door open) toward the viewer. The woman's right hand is in the pocket of her coat, which has a fur collar, and she is looking at an angle to the viewer. She has a round face, and seems to be of ample size. A bit of her dress and her right leg appear beyond the bottom limit of the coat. My dad, politically conservative, had

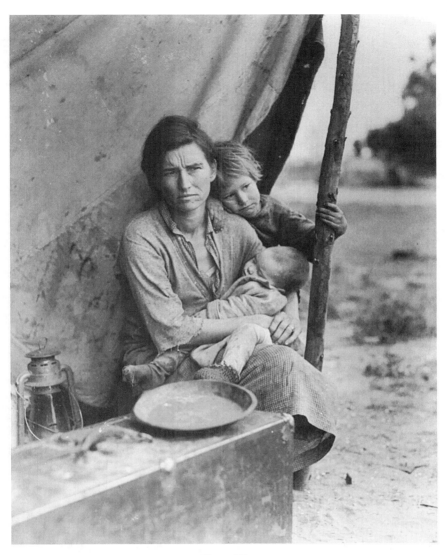

Figure [4]

seen that version of the picture years ago, and had pointed out to me that he was not impressed by Lange's title: here, after all, in the middle of the 1930s, at the height of the Great Depression, a worldwide phenomenon, were a couple who seemed well-clothed, well-fed—and who had a car. Did I realize, he wondered, how few people in the entire world, even in America, could be so described at that time? An automobile and a fur-collared coat to him meant something other than being "ditched, stalled, and stranded."

Figure [5]

Lange chose to crop that photograph for presentation in various exhibitions and books [Fig. 6, p. 191]. She removed the woman, save a touch of her coat (the cloth part), so the driver looks directly at us. Like the migrant mother, his gaze connects with our gaze, and we wonder who this man is, and where he wants to go, or is headed, and why he is described by the photographer as so thoroughly at an impasse. The photographer, in turn, tries to provide an answer. The man's left hand holds lightly onto the steering mechanism just below the wheel, and he seems almost an extension of that wheel, the two of them, along with the title given them, a metaphor for a troubled nation gone badly awry: whither his direction, and will he even be able to get going again, to arrive where he would like to be? Once more, Lange turns a photograph into a melancholy statement that embraces more than the population of a California agricultural re-

Figure [6]

gion. She does so by cropping (editing) her work, by denying us the possibility of a married couple in which one spouse seems reasonably contented, by reducing a scene to a driver who is readily seen as forlorn, and also as deeply introspective, eager for us, his fellow citizens, to return the intensity of his (moral) introspection.

I remember Paul Taylor gazing intently at the migrant mother and the man who was "ditched, stalled, and stranded"—a return on his part to a 1930s world, but also a moment's opportunity to reflect upon an entire documentary tradition, in which *American Exodus* figures importantly. No question, Paul and Jane reminded me, social observers and journalists have been journeying into poor neighborhoods, rural and urban, for generations, and in so doing have connected their written reports to a visual effort of one kind or another. Henry Mayhew's sensitively rendered *London Labour and the London Poor*, which describes nineteenth-century London, was accompanied by the drawings of Cruikshank, the well-known English illustrator—an inquiry that included a pictorial response. When George Orwell's *The Road to Wigan Pier* was first published in 1937, its text was supplemented by photographs, poorly reproduced, their maker unacknowledged—yet surely some who read Orwell's provocative and suggestive text were grateful for a glimpse of the world this great essayist had visited.

By the 1930s, under the auspices of the Farm Security Administration, and especially Roy Stryker, who had a keen sense of the relationship between politics and public awareness, a number of photographers were roaming the American land eager to catch sight of, and then, through their cameras, catch hold of a country struggling mightily with the consequences of the Great Depression—in the words of President Franklin Delano Roosevelt (1937) "one-third of a nation ill-housed, ill-clad, ill-nourished." So it is that Russell Lee and Ben Shahn and Arthur Rothstein and Walker Evans and Marion Post Wolcott, and, not least, Dorothea Lange became part of a significant photographic and cultural moment—the camera as an instrument of social awareness, of political ferment.

Though some photographers place great store by the titles they attach to their pictures, or write comments that help locate the viewer, help give him or her a sense of where the scene is or even provide a bit of context (how the person taking the picture happened to be at a particular place at a particular time), most photographers are content to let their work stand on its own, a silent confrontation of us all-too-wordy folk, for whom language (in the form of abstractions and recitations) can sometimes become an obstacle rather than a pathway to the lived truth of various lives. But Dorothea Lange's work in the 1930s, quite able, of course, to stand on its own, became part of something quite unique and important; and that connection (her photographs and the statements of some of the men and women whose pictures she took, joined to text written by Paul Taylor) would become a major achievement in the annals of fieldwork, of social-science research, of public information as rendered by a photographer and an academic (who in this case happened to be husband and wife).

It is possible to take much for granted as one goes through the pages of the 1939 edition of *American Exodus* (it was re-issued in 1969 with a foreword by Paul Taylor). The pictures are still powerful, even haunting, and some of them have become absorbed in an American iconography of sorts—the one titled "U.S. 54 in Southern New Mexico" [Fig. 7, p. 193], for instance, or the one taken in the Texas Panhandle in 1938 that shows a woman in profile, her right hand raised to her brow, her left to her neck: a portrait of perplexity, if not desperation [Fig. 8, p. 194]. That woman is

Figure [7]

quoted as saying "If you die, you're dead—that's all," and we, over half a century later, are apt to forget that in the 1930s there was no solid tradition of interviewing the subjects of a photographic study, linking what someone has to say to her or his evident circumstances as rendered by the camera. Again and again Dorothea Lange asked questions, wrote down what she heard (or overheard). Her sharp ears were a match for her shrewd and attentive eyes, and she knew to let both those aspects of her humanity connect with the people she had tried to understand.

Meanwhile, her husband was daring to do an original kind of explorative social science. As he accompanied her, he learned about the individuals, the locales she was photographing: how much workers got paid for picking crops, how much they paid for living in a migratory labor camp, and, more broadly, what had happened in the history of American agriculture from the earliest years of this century to the late 1930s. This was a study, after all, of a nation's fast-changing relationship to its land, of a major shift both in land usage and population: from the old South and the Plains states to California and Arizona, and from small farms or relatively genteel plantations to so-called factory-farms that now utterly dominate our grain and food (and animal) production. A combination of the economic collapse of the 1930s and the disastrous drought of that same time dislodged hundreds of thousands of Americans, some of whom sought jobs in cities, but many of whom embarked on the great trek westward, the last of the major migrations in that direction. For Paul Taylor, such an

Figure [8]

economic disaster was also a human one, and he knew how to do justice
to both aspects of what was truly a crisis for humble small-farm owners or
sharecroppers or tenant farmers or field hands. Taylor wanted to let his
fellow citizens know the broader social and economic and historical facts
and trends that had culminated in the 1930s "exodus"; Lange wanted us
to see both the world being left and the world being sought, and to attend
the words of the participants in a tragedy (for some) and an opportunity
(for others).

Although these two observers and researchers concentrated on the largely white families that departed the plains because a once enormously fertile expanse had become scorched earth, we are also asked to remember the Delta of the South, parts of Mississippi and Louisiana and Arkansas, and, by implication, the especially burdensome life of blacks, whose situation in the 1930s, even for progressives, was of far less concern than it would become a generation later, in the 1960s. The New Deal, it must be remembered, was very much sustained, politically, by the (white) powers-that-be of the South, and black folk, then, as now, on the very bottom of the ladder, were not even voters. Nevertheless, Lange and Taylor paid them heed, and did so prophetically—took us with them to the cities, to Memphis, to show us another exodus, that of millions of such people from the old rural South to its urban centers, or, more commonly, to those up North.

Also prophetically, these two original-minded social surveyors were at pains to attend what we today call the environment—what happens to the land, the water, that human beings can so cavalierly, so insistently take for granted. In picture after picture, we see not only human erosion—people becoming worn and vulnerable—but the erosion of the American land: farmland devastated by the bad luck of a serious drought, but also by years and years of use that become abuse. It was as if the prodigal land had been deemed beyond injury or misfortune. But suddenly the parched land said no to a people, to a nation, and suddenly the roads that covered that land bore an unprecedented kind of traffic: human travail on the move.

But Lange and Taylor go further, give us more to think about than the tragedy of the dust bowl become a major event in a nation already reeling from the collapse of its entire (manufacturing, banking) economy. Some of the pictures of California (the promised land!) tell us that new misfortunes, even catastrophes would soon enough follow what had taken place in Oklahoma and Texas and Kansas and Nebraska and the Dakotas. The lush Imperial Valley, where thousands came in hope of using their hands, their harvesting savvy, to pick crops and make a living, was already in the 1930s becoming a scene of litter, a place where the land had to bear a different kind of assault than that of a succession of plantings that aren't rotated, aren't planned in advance with consideration of what the earth needs as well as what it can enable. The debris, the junk that covers some of the California terrain was no doubt shown to us by Lange so that we could see how disorganized and bewildered and impoverished these would-be agricultural workers had become, see their down-and-out, even homeless lives: the bare earth all they had in the way of a place to settle, to be as families, at least for a while. Yet today we know how common such sights are across the nation—how those who live under far more comfortable, even affluent circumstances have their own ways of destroying one or another landscape, defacing fields, hills, and valleys that might otherwise be attractive to the eye, an aspect of nature untarnished.

These pictures remind us, yet again, that tragedies have a way of becoming contagious, that one of them can set in motion another, that the temptation to solve a problem quickly (let those people cross the country fast, and find much-needed work fast) can sometimes be costly indeed. There is something ever so desolate about the California of Lange's pictures—even though that state welcomed the people who flocked to it by providing jobs, and the hope that goes with work. Environmental problems to this day plague parts of the western states, problems that have to do with the way both land and water are used. Half a century ago, Lange and Taylor more than hinted at those problems, just as when they followed some of the South's black tenant farmers into the ghettos of a major city, Memphis, they gave us a peek at the urban crisis we would be having in a decade or two.

Also prophetic and important was the manner in which this project was done: informally, unpretentiously, inexpensively, with clear, lucid language and strong, direct, compelling photographs its instruments. For some of us, who still aim to learn from people out there in that so-called field, this particular piece of research stands out as a milestone: it offers us a guiding sense of what was (and presumably still is) possible—direct observation by people interested in learning firsthand from other people, without the mediation of statistics, theory, and endless elaborations of so-called methodology. Here were a man and a woman, a husband and a wife, who drove across our nation with paper, pen, and camera; who had no computers or questionnaires or "coding devices," no tape recorders, or movie cameras, no army of research assistants "trained" to obtain "data." Here were two individuals who would scorn that all-too-commonly upheld tenet of today's social-science research, the claim to be "value-free." They were, rather, a man and a woman of unashamed moral passion, of vigorous and proudly upheld subjectivity, anxious not to quantify or submit what they saw to conceptual assertion but to notice, to see and hear, and in so doing, to feel, then render so that others, too, would know in their hearts as well as their heads what it was that happened at a moment in American history, at a place on the American subcontinent. Here in Lange's photos, finally, the camera came into its own as a means of social and even economic and historical reflection. These pictures, in their powerfully unfolding drama, in their manner of arrangement and presentation and sequencing, in their narrative cogency and fluency, tell us so very much, offer us a gripping sense of where a social tragedy took place and how it shaped the lives of its victims. This is documentary study at its revelatory best—pictures and words joined together in a kind of nurturing interdependence that illustrates the old aphorism that the whole is greater than the sum of its parts.

American Exodus was not only a wonderfully sensitive, compellingly engaging documentary study; it challenged others to follow suit, to do their share in taking the measure, for good and bad, of our nation's twentieth-century fate. Dorothea Lange was an energetic ambitious photographer, but she also was a moral pilgrim of sorts, ever ready to give us a record of human experience that truly matters: our day-to-day struggles as members of a family, of a neighborhood, of a nation to make do, to take on life as best we can, no matter the obstacles we face. And so with Paul Taylor, a social scientist who dared pay a pastoral regard to his ordinary fellow citizens, even as he mobilized a broader kind of inquiry into the forces at work on them and on their nation. We can do no better these days than to look at their book, over half a century after it appeared, not only as an aspect of the past (a remarkable social record, an instance of careful collaborative inquiry), but as a summons to what might be done in the years ahead, what very much needs to be done: a humane and literate kind of social inquiry.

Speaking of such inquiry, Paul Taylor was quick to mention *Let Us Now Praise Famous Men* to Jane and me. He reminded us of Walker Evans's genius for careful, sometimes provocative cropping and editing of particular photographs—his ability to sequence his prints, look at their narrative momentum, and choose particular ones for presentation: the exactly memorable, summoning, kindling moments. Taylor made reference to Evans's photograph in *Let Us Now Praise Famous Men* that introduces one of the tenant farmers, a young man in overalls, his head slightly tilted to his right, his eyes (set in an unshaven face topped by curly hair) confronting the viewer head-on with an almost eerie combination of strength and pride on the one hand, and an unavoidable vulnerability on the other, as so many of us have felt [Fig. 9, p. 198]. That picture, now on the cover of the latest (1988) paperback edition of the book, signals to us the very point of the title, of the entire text as Agee conceived it: an ode to those hitherto unacknowledged, a salute to this man and others like him, this man whose fame has awaited a moral awakening of the kind this book hopes to inspire in us, just as the writer and photographer themselves were stirred from a certain slumber by all they witnessed during that Alabama time of theirs.

In the picture of this "famous man," as with certain of Lange's pictures, the viewer is given no room to wander, to be distracted. This is eye-to-eye engagement, a contrast to other possibilities available to Evans of the same man sitting at the same time in the same position. That farmer's daughter was actually sitting in a chair beside her father; one negative gives us a full-length portrait of him and her both, with the door and part of the side of their house and a portion of the porch also visible [Fig. 10, p. 199]. But Evans is struggling for an interiority, that of his subject and that of his subject's future viewer/visitor: let us not only praise this man, lift him to the ranks of the famous, but consider what might be going on within him, and let us, through the motions of our moral imagination, enter his life, try to understand it, and return with that understanding to our own, which is thereby altered. This is a tall order for a single picture, but then Evans and Agee were ambitious, as evidenced by their constant citation of the inadequacy of their project (vividly restless dreamers fearing the cold light of a morning).

Taylor also wanted us to look at a sequence of Evans's photographs of a tenant's daughter, bonneted, at work picking cotton. We who know the

Figure [9]

book remember her slouched, bent over the crops [Fig. 11, p. 200]. We don't see her face, don't really see any of *her*; she *is* her clothes, as if they were perched on an invisible person who is beyond our human approximations, who is of no apparent age or race. She is huddled over the fertile, flowering land to the point where she seems part of it, only barely above it, a lone assertion of our species and, too, a reminder of our incontestable dependence on the surrounding, the enveloping world of plants and

Figure [10]

shrubs. Yet, other negatives taken of that same scene at that same time reveal the girl standing upright [Fig. 12, p. 201], looking in profile at the surrounding terrain [Fig. 13, p. 202], or hunched over a part of it that hasn't the abundance of crops that we see in the picture Evans chose to show us [Fig. 14, p. 203]. There is one photograph, taken from above [Fig. 15, p. 204], that shows only the girl's straw hat, immersed in the foliage— an "arty" picture, an "interesting" one, a pretty image. With the circularity of straw (another crop!) imposed, so to speak, on the cotton field, the girl becomes a mere bearer of that hat (only a hump of her is evident).

Evans resists the aesthetic temptations of that last picture and of others in the series; he picks and chooses his way through a narrative sequence that might be titled in various ways: Alabama child labor; a young harvester; a girl at work picking cotton; or, drawing on Rupert Vance's wonderfully literate 1930s work at the University of North Carolina, an instance of a white child's connection to the "cotton culture." A photographer is carving out his own declaration based on his own survey research. He wants us, finally, to face facelessness, to see a child who isn't looking at us or at the nearby terrain (despite the fact that he had pictures of the girl doing both), but whose eyes were watching a row of plants, and whose body, whose very being, seems scarcely above them, tied to them, merging with them.

Figure [11]

Figure [12]

Figure [13]

Figure [14]

Figure [15]

There is, to be sure, an appealing beauty to the picture Evans selected from this sequence for the book: a graceful curve to the body, an elegance, a consequence of a learned, relaxed capability to pick and pick, as I saw in a migrant worker I once knew, who tried to teach me how to harvest celery. As I watched him look carefully, then make this cut, then the next one with his knife—swiftly, adroitly, with seeming ease and authority and exactitude—I caught myself thinking of his dignity, his full knowledge of a particular scene, while at the same time I worried that I was being a romantic: I was struggling with my own obvious lack of skill by ennobling his hard, tough, ill-paid labor (as, arguably, Orwell did when he went down into those mines in 1936). And so, perhaps, with this picture of Evans: we attempt to contemplate people's strenuous exertions even as we try to rescue them, at least partially, from those exertions. A miner can have his nobility, or be seen in a noble light by an observer, and that migrant can exact from his terribly burdened life moments of great, knowing competence, and this girl whom Evans noticed so painstakingly can also have her times of agility, balance, suppleness, the mystery of a lithe, enshrouded form as it "works on a row." Or are we to think of her only as an example of exploited child labor? When, that is, does our empathy and compassion ironically rob those whom we want so hard to understand of their loveliness, however tough the circumstances of their life? (I recognize the serious dangers, here, of an aesthetic that becomes a moral escape, a shameful avoidance of a grim actuality, a viewer's flight of willful blindness—hence, I think, Evans's refusal to let us dote on that hat, with its "interesting" setting.)

Walker Evans, in his own way, addressed the broader question of documentary expression in a lecture at Yale on March 11, 1964. He was sixty-one then; he had spent a lifetime traveling with his camera, planning and then executing various photographic expeditions. At Yale he said this: "My thought is that the term 'documentary' is inexact, vague, and even grammatically weak, as used to describe a style in photography which happens to be my style. Further, that what I believe is really good in the so-called documentary approach in photography is the addition of lyricism. Further, that the lyric is usually produced unconsciously and even unintentionally and accidentally by the cameraman—and with certain exceptions. Further, that when the photographer presses for the heightened documentary, he more often than not misses it. . . . The real thing that I'm talking about has purity and a certain severity, rigor, simplicity, directness, clarity, and it is without artistic pretension in a self-conscious sense of the word. That's the base of it."

So much there to applaud, especially the descriptive words "inexact" and "vague" and "grammatically weak": the difficulty we have in doing justice to the range and variation of writing and photography and film that a given tradition embraces. The word "documentary" is indeed difficult to pin down; is intended, really, as mentioned earlier, to fill a large space abutted on all sides by more precise and established and powerful

traditions: that of journalism or reportage, those of certain academic disciplines (sociology and anthropology in particular), and of late, a well-
organized, structured approach to folklore and filmmaking (as opposed to
an "unconscious" or "unintentional" or "accidental" approach)—university departments of "film studies" and "folklore studies." Evans's three
adjectives are themselves meant to be scattershot, if not "inexact" and
"vague"—a means of indicating a style, a manner of approach, or, in his
friend Agee's phrase, "a way of seeing," and also a way of doing: the one
who attempts documentary work as the willing, even eager beneficiary of
luck and chance, the contingent that in a second can open the doors of a
craftsman's imaginative life. Academics have their well-defined, carefully
established, and ever so highly sanctioned (and supported) routines,
procedures, requirements, "methodologies," their set language. Journalists are tied to the news closely or loosely. Nonfiction writing deals with
the consideration of ideas and concepts, with ruminations and reflections
of importance to a particular writer and his or her readers. Certain photographs follow suit, address *their* ideas and concepts: light, forms, the
spatial arrangements of objects—lines, say, rather than lives. In contrast,
even the word *documentarian* (never mind the nature of the work done)
may be imprecise, hard to pin down, at times misleading—in fact, no
"documents" need be gathered in the name of authenticity, in the name of
moving from a suspect (to some) "oral history" to a history of affidavits
and wills and letters, the older the better. But that is the way it goes—and
there are advantages: no deadline of tomorrow for the morning edition, or
three or four days for the Sunday one; no doctoral committee to drive one
crazy with nit-picking scrutiny of a language already sanitized and
watered-down and submitted to the test of departmental politics, a phenomenon that is surely a twentieth-century manifestation of original sin.

Instead, as Evans suggested, the doer of documentary work is out
there in this world of five billion people, free (at least by the nature of his
or her chosen manner of approach to people, places, events) to buckle
down, to try to find a congenial, even inspiring take on things. Evans cele-
brates a lyricism, and defines aspects of it nicely: a directness and a lack of
pretentiousness, a cleanness of presentation that he dares call severe and
pure. It is a lyricism, be it noted, that proved worthy (in its expression by
Evans) of companionship with Hart Crane's *The Bridge*, a lyricism that in
general bridges the observer, the observed, and the third party, as it were,
who is the second observer—a lyricism, Dr. Williams would insist, of
"things," a broad rubric for him that included human beings, and a rubric
meant to exclude only the rarefied, the insistently abstract. The document
in mind (mind you) can for a while be hungrily, ecstatically abstract—the
dreaming, the planning, the thinking out of a project—but down the line,
somehow, in some way, we have to get to "the thing itself."

Here is Evans being ambitiously abstract, as well as impressively in-
dustrious, aspiring, enterprising: "Projects: New York Society in the 1930s.
1. national groups 2. types of the time (b. and wh.) 3. children in streets

4. chalk drawings 5. air views of the city 6. subway 7. ship reporter (this project get police cards)." He continues, "the art audience at galleries, people at bars, set of movie ticket takers, set of newsstand dealers, set of shop windows, the props of upper class set, public schools faces and life." Those notes were, appropriately enough, scribbled on the reverse side of a Bank of Manhattan blank check in New York City during 1934–35. Another series of notes: "the trades, the backyards of N.Y., Harlem, bartenders, interiors of all sorts—to be filed and classified." A letter to Roy Stryker of the FSA in 1934: "Still photography, of general sociological nature." The point was to dream, to wander from topic to topic, and then, finally, to find the specific place and time, so that the eyes were free to follow the reasons of heart and mind both: a lyrical sociology; a journalism of the muse; a dramatic storytelling adventure that attends a scene in order to capture its evident life, probe its secrets, and turn it over as whole and complicated and concrete and elusive as it is has been found to those of us who care to be interested.

In a handsomely generous and affecting tribute to his colleague, his friend, his soulmate, James Agee, written in 1960 for a fresh edition of *Let Us Now Praise Famous Men*, Evans describes James Agee in 1936 as one who "worked in what looked like a rush and a rage." He also refers, in that vein, to Agee's "resolute, private rebellion." I do not think Evans himself was immune to this virus—an utter impatience with, even outrage at a sometimes stuffy and often callous world. As I read Evans or Agee I think of a motley assortment of others who fit in to this odd, cranky crowd—Studs Terkel and Oscar Lewis and George Orwell and Dorothea Lange and Paul Taylor, to name again some whom I've been calling in witness. Once, as I tried to get down to the specifics, a documentary mind preparing for a task, I remembered Evans's comments on what he hoped to do on, of all places, New York City's subways:

> The choice of the subway as locale for these pictures was arrived at not simply because of any particular atmosphere or background having to do with the subway in itself—but because that is where the people of the city range themselves at all hours under the most constant conditions for the work in mind. The work does not care to be "Life in the Subway" and obviously does not "cover" that subject.
>
> These people are everybody. These pictures have been selected and arranged, of course, but the total result of the lineup has claim to some kind of chance-average.
>
> The gallery page is a lottery, that is, the selection that falls there is determined by no *parti pris* such as, say, "I hate women," or "women are dressed foolishly," or "———." It *is* an arrangement, of course, as is the rest of the book, but the forces determining it have to do not only with such considerations as page composition, tone of picture, inferential interest of picture or face in itself.

> Speculations from such a page of sixteen women's faces and hats remains then an open matter, the loose privilege of the reader, and whoever chooses to decide from it that people are wonderful or that what America needs is a political revolution is at liberty to do so.

There he is, difficult and ungovernable for others, for his viewers and readers even, prepared to make substantial, maybe overwhelming demands on them. He'll have no truck with the most inviting and, alas, the most banal of titles for his work, even though one suspects that the abstraction "Life in the Subway" crossed his mind more than once as he thought about what he intended to do, its rationale, never mind its locale. He distances himself from all that is implied by the verb "cover," lest he be charged with the sin of inclusiveness, let alone that of a devouring topicality—as in a report or story that "covers" an issue by covering it with all sorts of facts, figures, opinions. Phrases like "chance-average" and "loose privilege" tell of the writer's venerable experience with both our language and this century's toll on our values. Who in the world today will settle for such informality, such a casual and relaxed attitude toward what is (or is not) an *average,* or a *privilege?* "Chance" and "loose" bespeak sipping whiskey in an armchair, with one of the big bands, Tommy Dorsey, maybe, playing "Whispering": a time before computer printouts arrived, or cocksure polls that have a plus or minus accuracy of—God knows what number. As for his concluding challenge (to himself, to all of us), it is one that laughs at ideology, that announces a sensibility contemptuous of singular interpretations, and that gives all of us splendid leeway to do as we damn please in what is volunteered unashamedly as an earnest, persistent, highly personal "visit" with some folks traveling underground.

There is evident discomfort in Evans's message, meant for himself above all; it never appeared in the foreword to the book showing his subway pictures. He wanted to define himself and his pictures so that they were not considered photojournalism, or part of yet another attempt to survey people or expose some (detrimental, damaging) aspect of their life. He was *there,* looking at men and women and children on their hurried way someplace. As the trains roared and sped, he presumably tried to catch hold of himself and others—literally as well as figuratively, a still moment in a quickly shifting scene of entrances and exits, a passing parade of technological and human activity. "I was pretty sure then, yes. I was sure that I was working in the documentary style. Yes, and I was doing social history, broadly speaking"—a cautious embrace at a point in a life's spectrum. But Evans would always qualify, circle around a purported professional location for himself, rather than hone in, dig in, *declare* without reservation. Here he is in a splendidly qualified and edifying further approach: "When you say 'documentary,' you have to have a sophisticated ear to receive that word. It should be documentary style, because documentary is police photography of a scene and a murder . . . that's a real document. You see, art is really useless, and a document has use. And therefore, art is never a document, but it can adopt that style. I do it. I'm called a documentary photographer. But that presupposes a quite subtle knowledge of this distinction."

A struggle there—to grasp, to adopt a style while reserving the artist's right of freedom to roam and select as he wishes. Others (in no way is this matter hierarchical) have their important and necessary obligations (the police photographer and, by extension, a host of people who work for or have joined a variety of institutions: newspapers, magazines, schools, universities). Evans's documentarian draws, in spirit, upon the earthy practicality of a police photographer, and also on the social and political indifference of an artist who, at a certain moment, has to be rid of all ideologies, even those he otherwise finds attractive, lest he become someone's parrot. The "style" he mentions here and elsewhere is nothing superficial; it refers to the connection an artist wants to have with, again, "human actuality," be it that of a police station, a subway, Alabama tenant farmers, Havana's 1930s street life—wherever it is that a Walker Evans imagines himself being, or ends up visiting. The rock-bottom issue is not only one's stated attitude toward "art" in general, but one's sense of oneself.

Once in a discussion at Dartmouth College in the 1970s, Evans took offense at questioners who wanted to know the mechanical details of his work, the kind of camera he used, and, beyond that, the way he developed and printed his photographs. He pointed out that what mattered to him was his intelligence, his taste, and his struggle for what such words imply and convey. Other photographers might have been eager to reply to such inquiries, men and women who are vitally interested in the technological possibilities of the machines they own and use, and who can get from them certain "effects": light or shadows amplified; appearances given new shape; the distortions, the "play" available to skilled men and women who, like Evans, are trying to be artists, photographic artists, but not artists and photographers in the "documentary style" or tradition, for which reality, however shaped and edited and narrated, has in some way to be an initial given. Hence the apprehension, the sorting of that reality in what Evans acknowledged to be a sociological manner, and hence his constantly moving presence in accordance with the demands of such a reality rather than those of a technological artistry, which certainly doesn't need central Alabama or the New York City subway for its expression, an artistry that can even confine itself to one room where the light arrives, moves about, and departs, all the while touching, in various ways, objects, human or inanimate.

William Carlos Williams was among Evans's admirers; he followed his work closely, wrote about it. He struggled, as Evans did, to be almost austere at times in his dispassionate insistence upon seeing many sides to whatever scene he was exploring—even as his big and generous heart could not help but press upon him as he sat at the typewriter, hence his gruff, tough moments followed by his fiery, exclamatory ones. In *Paterson* he struggled in that respect, struggled for a stance: the detached spectator, the informed but reserved onlooker as against the spy, the voyeur (and Evans, along with Agee, uses such imagery to indicate that side of himself: someone who has a lot at stake in what he's trying to do). Like Evans, Williams tried to come to grips with that word *documentary,* and made no bones about his belief that location and time mattered enormously: where one chose to stay and for how long, but also (he kept saying so in dozens of places and ways) the "language—and how it is used," by which he more broadly meant the relation of the watcher to the watched, of the one listening to those who fill his ears with words.

Williams was forever exploring in his mind the nature of a writer's, a photographer's, a filmmaker's dealings with those being called to what he once suggestively described as a "tentative alliance," one that might "fall apart at any minute." I asked for an explanation of that imagery (aware that in 1953, the Second World War and all the horror that preceded it, the pacts and agreements, the duplicities and betrayals, were still very much on his mind), and he was not loath to give it a try:

> When you're a doctor seeing a patient you're there by permission: the two of you have an agreement (or if it's a kid, the parents have signed you up, and the kid knows it). You can poke around; no other person in the world can poke around like that. You look and you listen and you poke some more, then you talk to yourself, you remember what you know and you compare notes with what you've seen in other patients (this silent talking, this recalling), and then you've made up your mind, so you start talking. Now, you're telling someone something, rather than asking; you're giving advice—orders, really. But the whole thing [the relationship] is based on that agreement: you can explore this body of mine, and you can ask me any damn thing you want, because that's who you are, a doctor, and that's who I am, a patient.
>
> Now, when I'm walking down the street there [in Paterson, where many of his patients lived] I'm trying to do another kind of "examination"—I'm still poking around, but I'm not doing it under the same terms. I'm hoping people will give me some access—talk with me and help me figure out what's going on around here [we were in Paterson]. I'm trying to look and listen, just as I do with the sick kids I see and their parents. I'm sizing up a place, a whole city, you could say: what is OK, what's working fine, and what's no good, and what "stinks out loud." A guy I know, I'll be standing there in the drugstore with him, and he's telling me "This positively stinks out loud," and I want to hear more. I'm excited, hearing him sound like he's Jeremiah's direct-line descendent. He can't do much more than sign his name. He has trouble reading the newspaper. He has to work to figure out those headlines. It's the radio that tells him everything. He hunkers down with it. He calls it his "friend" sometimes; [and] once I heard him call it his "source." Source of what, I wanted to know. "Everything," that's how

specific he could get! "What, for instance?" I asked, and he said, "The Guiding Light," and "Vic and Sade" [two soap operas], and then he said "the local news," he keeps up with it, and if he had another life, he'd like to be a "radio guy," he called it—he meant an announcer, the one who gives people the news. Then, he said: "Only I'd like to go see what's happening out there, and I'd know the people, I'd really know them, before I'd say anything about them. If you talk about people on radio, you should know them, otherwise it's not fair!"

I couldn't get him, what he said, out of my mind for a while. Days later, I'd think of him. It's not so easy to know people! I guess he'd find that out; he's ready to go try, in another life, if he could have it. But when I try to get him going more, about his own life, there's only so far he'll walk with me—and why should he? If you start thinking of yourself as a doctor examining a city, a diagnostician walking the streets, looking for people who can talk to you openly enough, so you can figure out what the illnesses are, the social illnesses, and what's "healthy" about it all—then you've got to *work* to get people to "sign up," to give you the trust you need for them to level with you, really level. Otherwise, you've got formality; you've got off-the-top-of-my-head stuff; you've got a quickie news story on that guy's radio, or the headline he struggles to make out. I feel like saying to him: save your energy, forget the damn headline and keep listening to that radio, if you can find something good on it, a big "if."

I've long felt that such "top-of-the head" ruminations, testy and splenetic, sometimes plaintive (if only it could be easier to learn what Williams so much wanted to learn about the "local pride" that was Paterson!) are themselves texts on documentary work for us to contemplate. Williams was anxious to connect his own thoughts to those of others, to let so-called ordinary people become his teachers, just as his patients all the time taught him. His profound distrust of all aestheticism ("The rest now run out after the rabbits") was prompted by his intuition that solipsistic art was not a suitable haven. He simply wasn't able to be indifferent to social reality in the ways that some of his poet friends found quite congenial. He knew the difficulties of apprehending that social reality, and, too, of finding the right words, the rhythms, the beat that would make his music somehow worthy of the music his ears picked up in Paterson: street music, tenement tunes, soul music and jazz and polkas and the tango and country music. He was always talking about the "American vein," which he tried to tap throughout his writing life—and to do so, he didn't only sit in his study and muse (though he wasn't at all averse to that kind of exploration). "Good luck to those who can keep their distance from the howl, the yell of things," he once said. Later, I'd wonder whether, by chewing out those writing colleagues every once in a while, he wasn't trying to exorcise his envy. But in the end he was who he was, and he more than settled for that existential fact. He built up, he wrote a *Paterson* that whispered and shouted, in good faith, stories of the chaste and bawdy Paterson, his witness to that city and its engagement with generations of needy seekers of all sorts: the words of honor spoken; the covenants abandoned; the people sold down the river; the victories won and lost; the folks who earned good dough, got a leg up; the folks who fell by the wayside. He gave us a chronicle, of course, but also a call to arms—and for him, the war was a struggle, against substantial odds, for a consciousness that isn't blunted and warped by the thousands of deceptions everywhere around. His version of Evans's "documentary style" was a vernacular not showily summoned out of a craving for distinction, but earned in the daily and various rounds of his several working lives (the doctor, the social observer, the historian and chronicler of the nearby, the poet and novelist and essayist, the painter even) whose simultaneity was a constant source of amazement to any of us lucky enough to catch sight of it all.

A precise definition is probably the last thing Walker Evans or William Carlos Williams would suggest for us today who want to consider, yet again, the nature of documentary work. Those two large spirits were unruly enough to scoff at the fantasy of control that informs a pretentiousness which won't allow for indefiniteness—that last word, for the documentarian, a necessity: the arm and leg room of exploration that has to take place, once one heeds the call, the refrain of "outside/outside myself/there is a world to explore," and the further instrumental refrain of "no ideas but in things." The one time I got Dr. Williams to consider the specific subject of "documentary research" or "documentary fieldwork," he laughed, and echoed Evans's wary refusal to get pinned down. He was more curt and gruff than, I suspect, Evans had ever desired to be, and so he dismissed the word documentary, in a way, by asking a rhetorical question, mimicking those who love to give themselves names, the more the better: "Would you want me to tell folks out there that I'm a documentary poet—and are you doing some documentary child psychiatry, now that you're visiting homes of people who haven't got the slightest interest in taking their kids to a clinic, and they don't need to?" He then laughed, to break the tension partially created by his remark, but also initiated by my floundering perplexity, and offered this, in a more gentle mode: "Lots of streets to walk, lots of ways to walk them"—a brief whistle, meant to signal the virtue of an elusive melody as about the best he could do.

To take Dr. Williams's hint, to remember the words of an Apocrypha rescued for our American century's time by James Agee and Walker Evans, let us praise the many "famous people" we can get to meet as we pursue a "documentary style," rather than keep trying to spell out authoritatively various essential characteristics; let the doing be a big part of the defining. Let us, that is, recount and depict, and thereby embody what we're aiming to do and, yes, to be. Let us think of those observers of their fellow human beings who have tried to hug hard what they also know can suddenly escape them, to their apprehending peril. Dr. Williams: "I'll be standing at the store counter talking to that loud-mouthed pest who is trying to con me into buying something stupid that I'll never need, and I should be enjoying the fun of hearing him out—what a *line!*—but instead I demolish him in my mind with *ideas,* ethnic and sociological and psychological, and pretty soon it's no fun for me, or for him either. I've forgotten him; he's disappeared under the withering fire of my clever thinking. I've left him for another ball game!"

To be less exhortative, more declarative, they are of many "sorts and conditions," documentarians (if that is what they want to be called—and we oughtn't be surprised if lots of people decline, say no to that word, maybe any word, any combination of words: "not the letter, but the spirit"). I think of writers or photographers or filmmakers, of musicologists who spend their time enraptured up Appalachian hollows or in Mississippi's Delta, of folklorists (Zora Neale Hurston was one) crazy for wonderfully wild stories told in odd and loony ways. I think of documentary work that is investigative or reportorial; that is muckraking; that is appreciative or fault-finding; that is pastoral or contemplative; that is prophetic or admonitory; that reaches for humor and irony, or is glad to be strictly deadpan and factually exuberant; that knows exactly where it is going and aims to take the rest of us along, or wants only to make an impression—with each of us defining its nature or intent. In a way, Orwell, in *Wigan Pier,* showed us the range of possibilities as he documented the life of the Brookers (and blasted them sky-high) and documented the life of certain miners (and put them on a tall pedestal), and, in between, wondered about the rest of us, himself and his buddies included: wondered about the way a study of others comes home to roost. In a way, as well, Williams was being more enlightening and helpful than a young listener of his comprehended when he jokingly referred to the documentary side of his prowling, roaming New Jersey patrol, and when he posed for me a consideration of how a clinician ought to think of the documentary work he is trying to do—home and school visits in which he talks with children who are of interest not because they have medical "problems," but because they are part of one or another larger (social or racial or national or economic) "problem." Journalists cover those children in their way; a documentarian will need to put in more time, and have a perspective at once broader and more detailed, one that is, maybe, a follow-up to the first, difficult, sometimes brave (and costly) forays of journalists.

How well, in that regard, I recall conversations with Ralph McGill of the Atlanta *Constitution* during the early years of the civil-rights struggle (1961–63). He had no small interest in the fate of the nine black students who initiated (high school) desegregation in Georgia's capital city during the autumn of 1961, even as my wife, Jane, and I were getting to know those black youths and their white classmates (Atlanta had managed to prevent the kind of riots that had plagued other Southern cities, such as Little Rock and New Orleans). The three of us would meet and talk, and from him, through his great storytelling generosity, Jane and I learned so very much. Often we discussed what Mr. McGill referred to as "the limits of journalism." He would remind us that "news" is the "commodity" his

reporters go everywhere to pursue, their words worked into the "product" that gets sold on the streets and delivered to stores and homes. But
those reporters (and photojournalists) are also great documentary teachers
and scholars: they know so very well how to go meet people, talk with
them, take pictures of them, right away take their measure, decide when
and how to go further, look for others to question. They know how to
make those utterly necessary first steps (find contacts, use them) that the
rest of us can be slow in realizing will make all the difference in whether a
particular project will unfold. They know, many of them, and they know
well, how to pose the toughest, most demanding and scrutinizing questions, at times utterly necessary questions, and ones that naïfs such as I
have certainly shirked entertaining, let alone asking. "How did you learn
to do your work?" students ask me all the time. I reply: from the great reporters I was lucky to meet and observe, from Pat Watters of the Atlanta
Journal, from Claude Sitton, the Southern corespondent of the *New York
Times,* from the ubiquitous and sometimes riotous Maggie Long, who
edited the *New South,* but called herself "an old newspaper hand," and
from Dorothy Day, who edited the *Catholic Worker* when I first met her,
but who had worked on journalistic assignments for newspapers for years
(in the 1920s) before she turned her life so radically around upon her conversion to Catholicism, and who, as she often reminded us, was the
daughter of a newspaperman and the sister of two of them.

Yet, as Mr. McGill sadly had to aver: "At a certain point we have to
stop"—meaning that a documentary inquiry ends, in favor of the requirements of another documentary initiative. It is then, he explained,
that "the magazine boys take over"—his way of referring to the greater
amount of space magazines allow, but also, of course, to the more
leisurely way of exercising Evans's "documentary style." We never got
into specifics, but because of his comparison, I began to think of the essays I read in various magazines (including those published by newspapers) in a different way: began to see the relative degree to which the author turns to people other than himself or herself as fellow bearers of a
story's burden, and the degree, as well, to which such people are allowed
(encouraged) to teach us by giving of themselves. Today, I think of Tru-
man Capote's *In Cold Blood,* of Ian Frazier's pieces, short and long, of
Alec Wilkinson's efforts with migrants in Florida, of his remarkable *A Violent Act;* and I remember *The New Yorker* of William Shawn as very
much, at times, given to a "documentary style." Among photographers
we can go back to Matthew Brady and the devastation of war that he
made a lasting part of our knowledge, if we care to remember; to Lewis
Hine and those children through whose condition he aroused our moral
sensibility (again, if we care to take notice); to, of course, the FSA men
and women; and today, Wendy Ewald, with her many brilliantly ingenious, spiritual explorations of childhood, aided by the children to whom
she gives cameras, and whose photographs and words she shares with
us. Photographers Alex Harris and Eugene Richards and Susan Meiselas
and Gilles Peress and Danny Lyon and Robert Frank and Thomas Roma

and Helen Levitt and Lee Friedlander; filmmakers Robert Flaherty and Pare Lorentz and Fred Wiseman and Robert Young and Michael Roemer and Ken Burns and Buddy Squires—all of these men and women are deservedly famous in the way Agee and Evans meant to signify for their Alabama teachers, known to the world as tenant farmers: humble by various criteria, but learned in ways any documentary tradition worth its name would aim to detail, to corroborate.

At a certain point in his research on Gandhi's life, Erik H. Erikson became dissatisfied. He had read many books and had spent a long time talking with a variety of scholars, historians, and political scientists, not to mention his psychoanalytic colleagues. He had obtained access to various library collections; he had attended a number of conferences; he had reviewed, courtesy of microfilm, journalistic accounts of Gandhi's various deeds and evaluations of the significance of his life. Nevertheless, this would-be biographer felt himself at an impasse. Why? I had no answer, despite the fact that I was teaching in his course then, helping him run a seminar, and trying to write about him, even as he was "struggling" with Gandhi (the phrase he often used)—almost as if the two were personally at odds, I sometimes thought.

We are sitting in Erikson's Widener study and I am interested, at the moment, in his work on Luther (my favorite of all his writings). He doesn't want to talk about that; he wants to talk about Gandhi's moral virtues, and, just as important, his flaws, if not vices: "I don't know whether I can proceed without in some way having it out with him [Gandhi]—how he fasted so honorably, risked his life for a just and merciful and fair political settlement, how he developed a decent and civilized manner of protest [nonviolence], and yet how he behaved as a husband and a father." Eventually, Erikson would write his well-known "letter," a breakthrough moment both in *Gandhi's Truth* and in psychoanalytic and historical thinking generally: a direct confrontation, a "having it out" with the spirit (the psychological "remains") of a figure who has left the living yet will endure through the ages. I listen, nod, try to steer us back to the fifteenth century, to *Luther*'s contradictions—it is, after all, *my* interview that are we are conducting! Few of my attempted subtleties miss my teacher's notice. Why am I now so interested in *Luther*? Well, Erik, why are *you* now so interested in Gandhi? That is the "line" of our reasoning together: mutual irritation expressed through a reductionist assault, by implication, on one another's motives, all under the dubious protection our shared profession provides. Finally, Erikson tells me, in annoyance at someone *else,* what he'd recently heard said by a distinguished cultural critic (and political philosopher)—that his *Young Man Luther* was a "marvelous novel"! I am taken aback; I keep silent; I worry about what my face wants to do, smile; I worry about what my voice wants to say (that such words are a high compliment), for I feel sure he wouldn't agree. He can sense, though, that I don't share his apparent chagrin. He puts this to me: "What do *you* think?" Lord, *that* question, the endlessly recurrent one of the late-twentieth-century, psychoanalyzed American *haute bourgeoisie!* I gulp. I feel my lips holding on tight to one another. I feel the inquiring openness of those wide blue eyes of this almost awesome figure. I find myself glancing at that shock of white hair flowing backward. I plunge: "Erik, it's a high compliment." I pause. I know I need to amplify, but I'm not prepared to, I'm afraid to. I settle for two more words, "the highest." He stares back at me. His face is immobile. I plead silently for the descent of compassionate understanding upon both of us. Continued silence; seconds become hours. I'm ready to speak, though I don't really know what I'll say—a dangerous situation, people like Erikson and me have long known: random conversational thoughts are a grist for an all-too-familiar (these days) mill, a gradual presentation by the unconscious of various unsettling thoughts.

But suddenly, amid a still persisting silence, the great one's face yields a broad smile. I immediately return it without having any prior thought that I should or would. He ribs me: "I know why you said that." I then pour out my explanation: that "novel" is not a pejorative word, certainly. I then make a statement about the revelatory nature of stories, not unlike the one I have tried to write here and elsewhere. I remind him that no one can know for *sure* what "young man Luther" thought and felt; that his story has to do with speculations, with informed guesses as well as facts, all told persuasively if not convincingly; that imagination is at work in such an effort; and that sometimes, in those "gray areas" or moments, the imagination appeals to or invokes the imaginary—a Luther who becomes more in a writer's mind than he can possibly be with respect to anyone's records, recollections, or reports. I tell him about a question I once heard William Shawn ask of an about-to-be *New Yorker* writer: how would you like us to present this piece? What did Shawn mean? As a factual piece, a profile, or a short story? But, the writer said, it's about someone who was real, who lived! Yes, it certainly is, the distinguished, knowing editor acknowledges, but he could imagine it being presented, with a few narrative changes, as a *story*, with that "someone" as a character in it. Erikson now goes beyond smiles; he laughs heartily and tells me that I seem to be "enjoying all this," and he goes further: "Now, you see why I want to go to India and interview those people who knew Gandhi and worked with him! You see why I want you to show me how you use your tape recorder!"

He stops; it is my turn to laugh. I tell him he'll become a "field worker." He gets irritated, and justifiably so; he reminds me of his expeditions to Indian reservations (the Sioux, the Yurok) in the 1930s and 1940s, trips I well know to have been brave and resourceful (and, yes, imaginative) actions, given the prevailing psychoanalytic orthodoxy then settling in on his generation in the United States. I apologize. He tells me he isn't asking that of me; he wants us, rather, to discuss the nature of those trips, of his forthcoming "visit" to the Indian subcontinent. I call them, cautiously (following his lead), "field trips." He wonders about the adjectival addition of "anthropological." I demur. I say that these days any conversation with a child or adult on one of our Indian reservations gets connected to the discipline of anthropology—an outcome that needs its own kind of historical inquiry, because conversations by Erikson or anyone else (who isn't an anthropologist) in this country ought not be so reflexively regarded. We sit quietly thinking—one of the joys, always, with him: a capacity, a willingness to put aside mere chatter, to endure those lulls which, after all, sometimes fall for a good reason. Finally, he smiles, asks me this: "What would your friend Agee call those 'trips'—or the one I'm going on?"

I have been teaching Agee in my weekly section of Erikson's course, and I have introduced the professor to some of the more compelling passages of *Let Us Now Praise Famous Men*. I smile; we banter. I observe that I don't know what Agee would say, because he's so hard to pin down on such matters, even in connection with his own Alabama trip, but Erikson asks me to surmise. I reply that whatever Agee would say, it would be long, constantly modified, and perhaps hard to fathom without a good deal of effort. Erikson laughs, and tells me that I need to learn to "speak on behalf of Agee," whom I admire and whose values and work and thoughts interest me. No way, I say.

Now I feel him headed toward his own research, toward our earlier discussion, and we get there with the help of his jesting self-criticism, meant also to put more bluntly on the record a perception of mine, maybe even a felt criticism of mine with respect to his work: "You don't seem to want to do with Agee what I may do with Gandhi, and did with Luther: try to figure out what was more or less likely to have happened in someone's life, and then say it—with the knowledge on your part, and [on that of] your readers, that we're not talking about letters or diaries or conversations recalled by someone, but that it's someone today doing the best he can with what *is* available." I think and think, let his words sink in. I take a stab: I say yes, maybe so. But then I try to embrace what I've hitherto kept at arm's length. I use the word *documentary*, and say that in the 1930s that word had a common usage among certain photographers and filmmakers, including Agee's friend Walker Evans. Perhaps, I suggest, Agee, were he to be "sent back" here by his Maker, might oblige us with that word— might allow Erikson's search for a firsthand *documentary* exposure to Indians here, and now Indians abroad, in the hope that what he saw and heard and then described would, in sum, be informative.

He likes the word *documentary*. I've seen him savor English words before, he who spoke German as his native language for over two decades, and who learned to speak such excellent English and write a beautifully flowing, even graceful and spirited English prose. He looks the word up in his much-used Oxford dictionary. I tell him that a dictionary "doesn't always help." Quickly he replies, "What does?" I'm slow in replying: "A word can gradually emerge in its meaning—can fill a gap." "What gap?" We're on to an extended discussion now, one that anticipates by a long three decades these lectures, this book. We speak, especially, about "seeing for oneself," as he keeps putting it—the importance of "making a record that you the writer can believe, before you ask someone else to believe it." I remember that way of saying it, will keep going back to those words, will regard them as helpful, as greatly "clarifying" (a word Erik loved to use): the documentary tradition as a continually developing "record" that is made in so many ways, with different voices and visions, intents and concerns, and with each contributor, finally, needing to meet a personal test, the hurdle of *you*, the would-be narrator, trying to ascertain what you truly believe *is*, though needing to do so with an awareness of the confines of your particular capability—that is, of your warts and wants, your various limits, and, too, the limits imposed upon you by the world around you, the time allotted you (and the historical time fate has given you) for your life to unfold.

When Erikson returned from that voyage to India, he was full of new energy, excited by what he'd been told, what he'd witnessed. He loved being back in his Widener study, but as often happens to us when we have gone on a long and important and memorable journey, he was finding it hard to "settle down." He was full of memories of what he'd experienced; he was trying to do justice to those memories; and he was recounting them, fitting them into a narrative, one the rest of us would soon read; he was speaking of his "colleagues," now not professors in a big-shot university, but rather hitherto (for him) nameless, faceless fellow human beings who would soon become (for us readers) developed characters with something to put on "record." He was, indeed, doing documentary work. And so it goes, then—doing documentary work is a journey, and is a little more, too, a passage across boundaries (disciplines, occupational constraints, definitions, conventions all too influentially closed for traffic), a passage that can become a quest, even a pilgrimage, a movement toward the sacred truth enshrined not only on tablets of stone, but in the living hearts of those others whom we can hear, see, and get to understand. Thereby, we hope to be confirmed in our own humanity—the creature on this earth whose very nature it is to make just that kind of connection with others during the brief stay we are permitted here.

• • • • • • • • • • • •

QUESTIONS FOR A SECOND READING

1. Early in his essay, Coles refers to his students' discussions of documentary work. His students, he says, "emphasize the 'actuality' of the work—its responsibility to fact." They think of documentaries as "the familiar alternative of fiction, as though we were dealing in clear-cut opposites: if not the true as against the false, at least the real as against the imaginary" (p. 177). Coles says that such opposites don't "do justice" to what writers, photographers, and other documentary artists do when they work with "people's words, their music, gestures, movements, and overall appearance" to represent to others what they have seen, heard, and learned.

So—what *is* the nature of documentary work? What *are* the issues, subtle rather than clear-cut, at the center of Coles's thinking? The essay could be said to be organized in five sections, each thinking through a different example: in the first, Coles talks about his own life and work, the second discusses the work of Dorothea Lange, the third the work of Walker Evans and James Agee, the fourth tells a story about the physician-poet William Carlos Williams, and the fifth a story about psychologist Erik Erikson. As you reread, stop at the end of each section to write notes on what you think it is "about." What is Coles saying about documentary work? What are the issues? When you get to the end, stop to write briefly on the progression of the essay. What is its train of thought? its beginning, middle, and end?

2. Coles offers three interesting examples of artists cropping or choosing photographic images of working class life (the couple in the car, the father and daughter on the porch, the girl picking cotton). Go back to those images and the discussions around them. Be sure that you can represent the argument Coles is making about Lange or Evans and the choices they made in producing or selecting a final image. Then take time to think about alternative arguments. (Coles provides one example in his father's response to "Ditched, Stalled, and Stranded.") How might you argue for one of the discarded images? or against the close-up view? You should think that the choices made by these artists are at least potentially controversial. What are the issues? What is at stake?

3. Coles says that "in shaping an article or a book, the writer can add factors and variables in two directions: social and cultural and historical on the one hand, individual or idiosyncratic on the other" (p. 177). As you reread, see where and how this distinction is stated or implied in Coles's discussions of the various artists or projects he treats in the essay. What examples does he provide of work that is social/cultural/historical and what examples does he provide of work that is individual/idiosyncratic? And where does Coles stand on these two directions? Which does he prefer or promote? And on what grounds?

4. Coles's essay assumes some knowledge of Dorothea Lange, Walker Evans, and James Agee. One way to work on the essay, then, would be to go to the library to get a copy of Lange's *American Exodus* or Agee's *Let Us Now Praise Famous Men*. You could also look for other works by or on these figures. One strategy for rereading would be to reread Coles once you have a better understanding of the materials he works with. This allows you a better sense of *his* agenda and point of view, the shaping force of his imagination.

ASSIGNMENTS FOR WRITING

1. One of the striking things about Coles's essay is the way it expands the range of what might be considered "documentary work." There is nothing unusual in thinking about Lange, Evans, and Agee; it is striking, however, to think about them in relation to Coles's work as a child psychiatrist and to

think then, about William Carlos Williams and Erik Erikson. This essay brings together a range of materials in order to think about a common issue. What is the issue? How does Coles think about it by using and arranging these materials? Where does he come out at the end?

Write an essay in which you represent this aspect of Coles's work as a writer in "The Tradition: Fact and Fiction." You will need to chart and summarize what he says. You will also need to think about how he does what he does. You could imagine that you are writing a review or writing a piece for a writing textbook or guidebook, one that wants to use Coles's essay as an example of how essays and essayists do their work.

2. It is possible to take Coles's essay as an invitation to do documentary work. The works he cites represent long-term projects and great commitments of time, energy, and spirit. One of the pleasures of being a student, however, is that you have the authority to try things out provisionally, tentatively, and on a smaller scale.

This assignment has two parts. For the first part, create a written documentary in which you represent some aspect of another person or, to use the language of the essay, in which you are in pursuit of a moment of "human actuality." The text you create can include photographs, interviews, observation—whatever is available. The point is for you to feel what it is like to be responsible, as a writer, for representing someone else, his or her thoughts, words, and actions. To those who do it for a living, this is a deep and deeply fraught responsibility.

Once you have completed your documentary (and perhaps once it has been read and evaluated by others), write a separate essay in which you use your work as a way of thinking back on and responding to Coles. Where and how, for example, did you serve as a "filter"? Where and how did you shape that material? What decisions did you have to make concerning foreground and background, the individual and idiosyncratic, or the social, cultural, and historical? What work would you need to do if you were to go back to this project and do an even better job with it? You could imagine this as a letter to Coles, a review of his book, or as a plan for future work of your own, perhaps the work of revising the documentary you have begun.

3. This assignment draws on the project outlined in the second of the "Questions for a Second Reading." Coles offers three examples of artists cropping or choosing photographic images of working class life (the couple in the car, the father and daughter on the porch, the girl picking cotton). These are relatively brief discussions, however, and these discussions do not engage with alternative points of view.

Write an essay in which you begin with Coles's account of the images, summarizing what he says for someone who has not read the essay or who read it a while ago and won't take time to pick it up again. You will need to represent the photographs, their history, and the points that Coles is making. Then, you will need to engage and extend the discussion. Coles, for example, seems to take for granted that the decisions the artists made were good decisions. Were they? What is at stake in choosing one photograph over another or in cropping the image to remove context and to focus in on the individual face? What was at stake for Coles?

And where and how might you enter this discussion? There should, in other words, be sections of your essay where you are speaking for Coles (and for Evans and Lange); there should also, however, be extended sections where you speak, thinking about the examples and engaging the issues raised by others.

4. "The Tradition: Fact and Fiction" is a chapter in Coles's book *Doing Documentary Work* (1997). The final chapter in the book presents materials from courses he and his colleagues have taught at Duke University's Center for Documentary Studies. Here is a brief selection of books and films used in their courses (his book has a full account):

> James Agee, *Let Us Now Praise Famous Men* (1941)
> Sherwood Anderson, *Home Town* (1940)
> John Berger, *A Seventh Man: Migrant Workers in Europe* (1975)
> Debbie Fleming Caffery, *Carry Me Home* (1990)
> Bruce Chatwin, *In Patagonia* (1977)
> Anton Chekhov, *The Island: A Journey to Sakhalin* (1895)
> W. E. B. Du Bois, *The Philadelphia Negro* (1899)
> George Eliot, *Scenes of Clerical Life* (1857)
> Martín Espada, *City of Coughing and Dead Radiators* (1993)
> Robert Flaherty, *Nanook of the North* (film) (1922)
> Lee Freidlander, *The Jazz People of New Orleans* (1992)
> Zora Neale Hurston, *Dust Tracks on a Road* (1942)
> Dorothea Lange, *American Exodus* (1941)
> Oscar Lewis, *The Children of Sanchez* (1961)
> Henry Mayhew, *London Labour and the London Poor* (1851)
> George Orwell, *The Road to Wigan Pier* (1958)
> Studs Terkel, *Working* (1975)
> William Carlos Williams, *Paterson* (1946)
> Frederick Wiseman, *Titicut Follies* (film) (1967); *High School*
> (film) (1968); *Blind* (film) (1986); *Deaf* (film) (1986)

Choose one of these to use as the basis for an essay in which you apply Coles's notion that any account of the "real," any documentary, is filtered through an individual's imagination and point of view, and his sense that documentaries either favor the long view (with emphasis on social, cultural, and historical contexts) or the short view (with emphasis on the individual or the idiosyncratic). What is the evidence of the filtering process in the work you have studied? What are the consequences? Where and how might you use the work you have done to add to or to speak back to what Coles has to say in "The Tradition: Fact and Fiction"?

MAKING CONNECTIONS

1. In "Hunger as Ideology" (p. 139), Susan Bordo examines representations of the female body in contemporary culture. In his discussion of Dorothea Lange's photographs of the migrant mother [pp. 185–88] and in his discussion of Walker Evans's photos of the tenant's daughter picking cotton [pp. 197–205], Coles is also concerned with the representation of the

female body—with what those images mean and the purposes they serve (or might serve). Coles's descriptions are close and careful. They draw, however, on a very different vocabulary than those provided by Bordo.

Write an essay in which you compare the methods and concerns of Bordo and Coles. You should think about how their projects differ; consider the ways they choose and present images, what they notice, and how they describe and analyze what they notice. Both are concerned with the social context of images. What does Coles offer in describing the larger forces at work in producing the meanings of images? What does he offer in place of Bordo's "ideology"?

2. In "Haunted America" (p. 471), Patricia Nelson Limerick writes about the "moral and spiritual muddles" of American history, referring to the complexity represented in any attempt to speak for and to understand the acts and motives of people distant from us in time and caught up in conflicts they themselves can neither fully control nor comprehend.

The historian does a form of documentary work that is often set alongside and offered as a supplement to the work of documentary photography, like that at the center of Coles's essay. ("Haunted America," in fact, was originally written to accompany a set of photographs collected in *Sweet Medicine: Sites of Indian Massacres, Battlefields, and Treaties*, Drex Brooks, 1995.)

Reread "Haunted America" and "The Tradition: Fact and Fiction" as a set, as part of a single project investigating the problems of representing the past. Write an essay in which you discuss the issues and problems at the center of each argument. While there are many similarities, focus primarily on the differences. Limerick and Coles have different training and occupy different places in the academy; they serve the culture differently as writers and scholars. How are those differences evident in these brief examples of their work?

power structure

efficiency
surveillance
- *prisoner feel like always being watched.*
- *watching someone is too much & too little.*
discipline — efficient.

- *society is a carceral continum, society based on structure*
  - *obvious / less obvious*

• *Discipline diff btw. ea. model.*

MICHEL
FOUCAULT

*M*ICHEL FOUCAULT (1926–1984) stands at the beginning of the twenty-first century as one of the world's leading intellectuals. He was trained as a philosopher, but much of his work, like that presented in Discipline and Punish: The Birth of the Prison (1975), traces the presence of certain ideas across European history. So he could also be thought of as a historian, but a historian whose goal is to revise the usual understanding of history—not as a progressive sequence but as a series of repetitions governed by powerful ideas, terms, and figures. Foucault was also a public intellectual, involved in such prominent issues as prison reform. He wrote frequently for French newspapers and reviews. His death from AIDS was front-page news in Le Monde, the French equivalent of the New York Times. He taught at several French universities and in 1970 was appointed to a professorship at the College de France, the highest position in the French system. He traveled widely, lecturing and visiting at universities throughout the world.*

Foucault's work is central to much current work in the humanities and the social sciences. In fact, it is hard to imagine any area of the academy that has not been influenced by his writing. There is a certain irony in all this, since Foucault argued persuasively that we need to give up thinking about knowledge as individually produced; we have to stop thinking the way we do about the "author" or the "genius," about individuality or creativity; we have to stop thinking as though there were truths that stand beyond the interests of a given moment. It is both dangerous and wrong, he argued, to assume that knowledge is disinterested. Edward Said had this to say of Foucault:

> His great critical contribution was to dissolve the anthropological models of identity and subjecthood underlying research in the humanistic and social sciences. Instead of seeing everything in culture and society as ultimately emanating from either a sort of unchanging Cartesian ego or a heroic solitary artist, Foucault proposed the much juster notion that all work, like social life itself, is collective. The principal task therefore is to circumvent or break down the ideological biases that prevent us from saying that what enables a doctor to practice medicine or a historian to write history is not mainly a set of individual gifts, but an ability to follow rules that are taken for granted as an unconscious a priori by all professionals. More than anyone before him, Foucault specified rules for those rules, and even more impressively, he showed how over long periods of time the rules became epistemological enforcers of what (as well as of how) people thought, lived, and spoke.

These rules, these unconscious enforcers, are visible in "discourse"—ways of thinking and speaking and acting that we take for granted as naturally or inevitably there but that are constructed over time and preserved by those who act without question, without stepping outside the discourse and thinking critically. But, says Foucault, there is no place "outside" the discourse, no free, clear space. There is always only another discursive position. A person in thinking, living, and speaking expresses not merely himself or herself but the thoughts and roles and phrases governed by the available ways of thinking and speaking. The key questions to ask, then, according to Foucault, are not Who said this? or Is it original? or Is it true? or Is it authentic? but Who talks this way? or What unspoken rules govern this way of speaking? or Where is this discourse used? Who gets to use it? when? and to what end?

The following selection is the third chapter of Discipline and Punish: The Birth of the Prison (translated from the French by Alan Sheridan). In this book, Foucault is concerned with the relationships between knowledge and power, arguing that knowledge is not pure and abstract but is implicated in networks of power relations. Or, as he puts it elsewhere, people govern themselves "through the production of truth." This includes the "truths" that determine how we imagine and manage the boundaries between the "normal" and the transgressive, the lawful and the delinquent. In a characteristic move, Foucault reverses our intuitive sense of how things are. He argues, for example, that it is not the case that prisons serve the courts and a system of justice but that the courts are the products, the servants of "the prison," the prison as an idea, as the central figure in a way of thinking about transgression, order, and the body, a way of thinking that is persistent and general, present, for example, through all efforts to produce the normal or "disciplined individual": "in the central position that [the prison] occupies, it is not alone, but linked to a whole series of 'carceral' mechanisms which seem distinct enough—since they are intended to alleviate pain, to cure, to

comfort—but which all tend, like the prison, to exercise a power of normaliza-
tion." Knowledge stands in an antagonistic role in Discipline and Punish; *it is*
part of a problem, not a route to a solution.

You will find "Panopticism" difficult reading. All readers find Foucault's
prose tough going. It helps to realize that it is necessarily difficult. Foucault,
remember, is trying to work outside of, or in spite of, the usual ways of thinking
and writing. He is trying not *to reproduce the standard discourse but to point to*
what it cannot or will not say. He is trying to make gestures beyond what is ordi-
narily, normally said. So his prose struggles with its own situation. Again, as
Edward Said says, "What [Foucault] was interested in . . . was 'the more' that
can be discovered lurking in signs and discourses but that is irreducible to lan-
guage and speech; 'it is this "more,"' he said, 'that we must reveal and describe.'
Such a concern appears to be both devious and obscure, yet it accounts for a lot
that is specially unsettling in Foucault's writing. There is no such thing as being
at home in his writing, neither for reader nor for writer." While readers find
Foucault difficult, he is widely read and widely cited. His books include The Birth
of the Clinic: An Archaeology of Medical Perception *(1963),* The Order of
Things: An Archaeology of the Human Sciences *(1966),* The Archaeology
of Knowledge *(1969),* Madness and Civilization *(1971), and the three-volume*
History of Sexuality *(1976, 1979, 1984).*

Panopticism

The following, according to an order published at the end of the seventeenth century, were the measures to be taken when the plague appeared
in a town.[1]

First, a strict spatial partitioning: the closing of the town and its outly-
ing districts, a prohibition to leave the town on pain of death, the killing of
all stray animals; the division of the town into distinct quarters, each governed by an intendant. Each street is placed under the authority of a syndic, who keeps it under surveillance; if he leaves the street, he will be condemned to death. On the appointed day, everyone is ordered to stay
indoors: it is forbidden to leave on pain of death. The syndic himself
comes to lock the door of each house from the outside; he takes the key
with him and hands it over to the intendant of the quarter; the intendant
keeps it until the end of the quarantine. Each family will have made its
own provisions; but, for bread and wine, small wooden canals are set up
between the street and the interior of the houses, thus allowing each person to receive his ration without communicating with the suppliers and
other residents; meat, fish, and herbs will be hoisted up into the houses
with pulleys and baskets. If it is absolutely necessary to leave the house, it
will be done in turn, avoiding any meeting. Only the intendants, syndics,

and guards will move about the streets and also, between the infected houses, from one corpse to another, the "crows," who can be left to die: these are "people of little substance who carry the sick, bury the dead, clean, and do many vile and abject offices." It is a segmented, immobile, frozen space. Each individual is fixed in his place. And, if he moves, he does so at the risk of his life, contagion, or punishment.

Inspection functions ceaselessly. The gaze is alert everywhere: "A considerable body of militia, commanded by good officers and men of substance," guards at the gates, at the town hall, and in every quarter to ensure the prompt obedience of the people and the most absolute authority of the magistrates, "as also to observe all disorder, theft and extortion." At each of the town gates there will be an observation post; at the end of each street sentinels. Every day, the intendant visits the quarter in his charge, inquires whether the syndics have carried out their tasks, whether the inhabitants have anything to complain of; they "observe their actions." Every day, too, the syndic goes into the street for which he is responsible; stops before each house: gets all the inhabitants to appear at the windows (those who live overlooking the courtyard will be allocated a window looking onto the street at which no one but they may show themselves); he calls each of them by name; informs himself as to the state of each and every one of them—"in which respect the inhabitants will be compelled to speak the truth under pain of death"; if someone does not appear at the window, the syndic must ask why: "In this way he will find out easily enough whether dead or sick are being concealed." Everyone locked up in his cage, everyone at his window, answering to his name and showing himself when asked—it is the great review of the living and the dead.

This surveillance is based on a system of permanent registration: reports from the syndics to the intendants, from the intendants to the magistrates or mayor. At the beginning of the "lock up," the role of each of the inhabitants present in the town is laid down, one by one; this document bears "the name, age, sex of everyone, notwithstanding his condition": a copy is sent to the intendant of the quarter, another to the office of the town hall, another to enable the syndic to make his daily roll call. Everything that may be observed during the course of the visits—deaths, illnesses, complaints, irregularities—is noted down and transmitted to the intendants and magistrates. The magistrates have complete control over medical treatment; they have appointed a physician in charge; no other practitioner may treat, no apothecary prepare medicine, no confessor visit a sick person without having received from him a written note "to prevent anyone from concealing and dealing with those sick of the contagion, unknown to the magistrates." The registration of the pathological must be constantly centralized. The relation of each individual to his disease and to his death passes through the representatives of power, the registration they make of it, the decisions they take on it.

Five or six days after the beginning of the quarantine, the process of purifying the houses one by one is begun. All the inhabitants are made to leave; in each room "the furniture and goods" are raised from the ground or suspended from the air; perfume is poured around the room; after carefully sealing the windows, doors, and even the keyholes with wax, the perfume is set alight. Finally, the entire house is closed while the perfume is consumed; those who have carried out the work are searched, as they were on entry, "in the presence of the residents of the house, to see that they did not have something on their persons as they left that they did not have on entering." Four hours later, the residents are allowed to reenter their homes.

This enclosed, segmented space, observed at every point, in which the individuals are inserted in a fixed place, in which the slightest movements are supervised, in which all events are recorded, in which an uninterrupted work of writing links the center and periphery, in which power is exercised without division, according to a continuous hierarchical figure, in which each individual is constantly located, examined, and distributed among the living beings, the sick, and the dead—all this constitutes a compact model of the disciplinary mechanism. The plague is met by order; its function is to sort out every possible confusion: that of the disease, which is transmitted when bodies are mixed together; that of the evil, which is increased when fear and death overcome prohibitions. It lays down for each individual his place, his body, his disease, and his death, his well-being, by means of an omnipresent and omniscient power that subdivides itself in a regular, uninterrupted way even to the ultimate determination of the individual, of what characterizes him, of what belongs to him, of what happens to him. Against the plague, which is a mixture, discipline brings into play its power, which is one of analysis. A whole literary fiction of the festival grew up around the plague: suspended laws, lifted prohibitions, the frenzy of passing time, bodies mingling together without respect, individuals unmasked, abandoning their statutory identity and the figure under which they had been recognized, allowing a quite different truth to appear. But there was also a political dream of the plague, which was exactly its reverse: not the collective festival, but strict divisions; not laws transgressed, but the penetration of regulation into even the smallest details of everyday life through the mediation of the complete hierarchy that assured the capillary functioning of power; not masks that were put on and taken off, but the assignment to each individual of his "true" name, his "true" place, his "true" body, his "true" disease. The plague as a form, at once real and imaginary, of disorder had as its medical and political correlative discipline. Behind the disciplinary mechanisms can be read the haunting memory of "contagions," of the plague, of rebellions, crimes, vagabondage, desertions, people who appear and disappear, live and die in disorder.

If it is true that the leper gave rise to rituals of exclusion, which to a certain extent provided the model for and general form of the great Confinement, then the plague gave rise to disciplinary projects. Rather than the massive, binary division between one set of people and another, it called for multiple separations, individualizing distributions, an organization in depth of surveillance and control, an intensification and a ramification of power. The leper was caught up in a practice of rejection, of exile-enclosure; he was left to his doom in a mass among which it was useless to differentiate; those sick of the plague were caught up in a meticulous tactical partitioning in which individual differentiations were the constricting effects of a power that multiplied, articulated, and subdivided itself; the great confinement on the one hand; the correct training on the other. The leper and his separation; the plague and its segmentations. The first is marked; the second analyzed and distributed. The exile of the leper and the arrest of the plague do not bring with them the same political dream. The first is that of a pure community, the second that of a disciplined society. Two ways of exercising power over men, of controlling their relations, of separating out their dangerous mixtures. The plague-stricken town, traversed throughout with hierarchy, surveillance, observation, writing; the town immobilized by the functioning of an extensive power that bears in a distinct way over all individual bodies—this is the utopia of the perfectly governed city. The plague (envisaged as a possibility at least) is the trial in the course of which one may define ideally the exercise of disciplinary power. In order to make rights and laws function according to pure theory, the jurists place themselves in imagination in the state of nature; in order to see perfect disciplines functioning, rulers dreamed of the state of plague. Underlying disciplinary projects the image of the plague stands for all forms of confusion and disorder; just as the image of the leper, cut off from all human contact, underlies projects of exclusion.

They are different projects, then, but not incompatible ones. We see them coming slowly together, and it is the peculiarity of the nineteenth century that it applied to the space of exclusion of which the leper was the symbolic inhabitant (beggars, vagabonds, madmen, and the disorderly formed the real population) the technique of power proper to disciplinary partitioning. Treat "lepers" as "plague victims," project the subtle segmentations of discipline onto the confused space of internment, combine it with the methods of analytical distribution proper to power, individualize the excluded, but use procedures of individualization to mark exclusion— this is what was operated regularly by disciplinary power from the beginning of the nineteenth century in the psychiatric asylum, the penitentiary, the reformatory, the approved school, and to some extent, the hospital. Generally speaking, all the authorities exercising individual control function according to a double mode; that of binary division and branding (mad/sane; dangerous/harmless; normal/abnormal); and that of coercive assignment, of differential distribution (who he is; where he must be; how he is to be characterized; how he is to be recognized; how a constant surveillance is to be exercised over him in an individual way, etc.). On the one hand, the lepers are treated as plague victims; the tactics of individualizing disciplines are imposed on the excluded; and, on the other hand, the universality of disciplinary controls makes it possible to brand the "leper" and to bring into play against him the dualistic mechanisms of exclusion. The constant division between the normal and the abnormal, to which every individual is subjected, brings us back to our own time, by applying the binary branding and exile of the leper to quite different objects; the existence of a whole set of techniques and institutions for measuring, supervising, and correcting the abnormal brings into play the disciplinary mechanisms to which the fear of the plague gave rise. All the mechanisms of power which, even today, are disposed around the abnormal individual, to brand him and to alter him, are composed of those two forms from which they distantly derive.

Bentham's *Panopticon* is the architectural figure of this composition. We know the principle on which it was based: at the periphery, an annular building; at the center, a tower; this tower is pierced with wide windows that open onto the inner side of the ring; the peripheric building is divided into cells, each of which extends the whole width of the building; they have two windows, one on the inside, corresponding to the windows of the tower; the other, on the outside, allows the light to cross the cell from one end to the other. All that is needed, then, is to place a supervisor

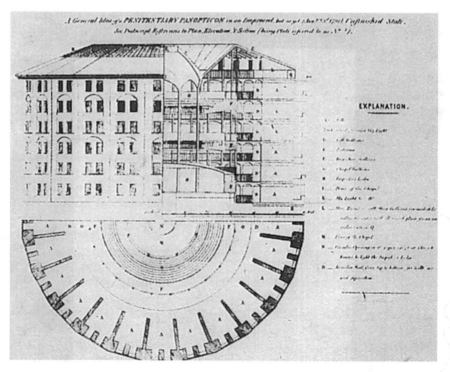

Plan of the Panopticon by J. Bentham (*The Works of Jeremy Bentham*, ed. Bowring, vol. IV, 1843, 172–73)

in a central tower and to shut up in each cell a madman, a patient, a condemned man, a worker, or a schoolboy. By the effect of backlighting, one can observe from the tower, standing out precisely against the light, the small captive shadows in the cells of the periphery. They are like so many cages, so many small theaters, in which each actor is alone, perfectly individualized and constantly visible. The panoptic mechanism arranges spatial unities that make it possible to see constantly and to recognize immediately. In short, it reverses the principle of the dungeon; or rather of its three functions—to enclose, to deprive of light, and to hide—it preserves only the first and eliminates the other two. Full lighting and the eye of a supervisor capture better than darkness, which is ultimately protected. Visibility is a trap.

To begin with, this made it possible—as a negative effect—to avoid those compact, swarming, howling masses that were to be found in places of confinement, those painted by Goya or described by Howard. Each individual, in his place, is securely confined to a cell from which he is seen from the front by the supervisor; but the side walls prevent him from coming into contact with his companions. He is seen, but he does not see; he is the object of information, never a subject in communication. The arrangement of his room, opposite the central tower, imposes on him an axial visibility; but the divisions of the ring, those separated cells, imply a lateral invisibility. And this invisibility is a guarantee of order. If the inmates are convicts, there is no danger of a plot, an attempt at collective escape, the planning of new crimes for the future, bad reciprocal influences; if they are patients, there is no danger of contagion; if they are madmen, there is no risk of their committing violence upon one another; if they are schoolchildren, there is no copying, no noise, no chatter, no waste of time; if they are workers, there are no disorders, no theft, no coalitions, none of those distractions that slow down the rate of work, make it less perfect, or cause accidents. The crowd, a compact mass, a locus of multiple exchanges, individualities merging together, a collective effect, is abolished and replaced by a collection of separated individualities. From the point of view of the guardian, it is replaced by a multiplicity that can be numbered and supervised; from the point of view of the inmates, by a sequestered and observed solitude (Bentham 60–64).

Hence the major effect of the Panopticon: to induce in the inmate a state of conscious and permanent visibility that assures the automatic functioning of power. So to arrange things that the surveillance is permanent in its effects even if it is discontinuous in its action; that the perfection of power should tend to render its actual exercise unnecessary; that this architectural apparatus should be a machine for creating and sustaining a power relation independent of the person who exercises it; in short, that the inmates should be caught up in a power situation of which they are themselves the bearers. To achieve this, it is at once too much and too little that the prisoner should be constantly observed by an inspector: too little, for what matters is that he knows himself to be observed; too much,

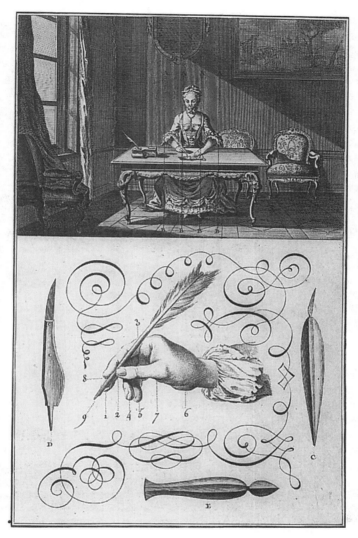

Handwriting model. *Collections historiques de l'I.N.R.D.P.*

because he has no need in fact of being so. In view of this, Bentham laid down the principle that power should be visible and unverifiable. Visible: the inmate will constantly have before his eyes the tall outline of the central tower from which he is spied upon. Unverifiable: the inmate must never know whether he is being looked at at any one moment; but he must be sure that he may always be so. In order to make the presence or absence of the inspector unverifiable, so that the prisoners, in their cells, cannot even see a shadow, Bentham envisaged not only venetian blinds

Interior of the penitentiary at Stateville, United States, twentieth century

on the windows of the central observation hall, but, on the inside, partitions that intersected the hall at right angles and, in order to pass from one
quarter to the other, not doors but zigzag openings; for the slightest noise,
a gleam of light, a brightness in a half-opened door would betray the presence of the guardian.[2] The Panopticon is a machine for dissociating the
see/being seen dyad: in the peripheric ring, one is totally seen, without
ever seeing; in the central tower, one sees everything without ever being
seen.[3]
     It is an important mechanism, for it automatizes and disindividualizes
power. Power has its principle not so much in a person as in a certain concerted distribution of bodies, surfaces, lights, gazes; in an arrangement
whose internal mechanisms produce the relation in which individuals are
caught up. The ceremonies, the rituals, the marks by which the sovereign's surplus power was manifested are useless. There is a machinery
that assures dissymmetry, disequilibrium, difference. Consequently, it
does not matter who exercises power. Any individual, taken almost at
random, can operate the machine: in the absence of the director, his family, his friends, his visitors, even his servants (Bentham 45). Similarly, it
does not matter what motive animates him: the curiosity of the indiscreet,
the malice of a child, the thirst for knowledge of a philosopher who
wishes to visit this museum of human nature, or the perversity of those

Lecture on the evils of alcoholism in the auditorium of Fresnes prison

who take pleasure in spying and punishing. The more numerous those anonymous and temporary observers are, the greater the risk for the inmate of being surprised and the greater his anxious awareness of being observed. The Panopticon is a marvelous machine which, whatever use one may wish to put it to, produces homogeneous effects of power.

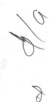

A real subjection is born mechanically from a fictitious relation. So it is not necessary to use force to constrain the convict to good behavior, the madman to calm, the worker to work, the schoolboy to application, the patient to the observation of the regulations. Bentham was surprised that panoptic institutions could be so light: there were no more bars, no more chains, no more heavy locks; all that was needed was that the separations should be clear and the openings well arranged. The heaviness of the old "houses of security," with their fortresslike architecture, could be replaced by the simple, economic geometry of a "house of certainty." The efficiency of power, its constraining force have, in a sense, passed over to the other side—to the side of its surface of application. He who is subjected to a field of visibility, and who knows it, assumes responsibility for the constraints of power; he makes them play spontaneously upon himself; he inscribes in himself the power relation in which he simultaneously plays both roles; he becomes the principle of his own subjection. By this very fact, the external power may throw off its physical weight; it tends to the noncorporal; and, the more it approaches this limit, the more constant, profound, and permanent are its effects: it is a perpetual victory that avoids any physical confrontation and which is always decided in advance.

Bentham does not say whether he was inspired, in his project, by Le Vaux's menagerie at Versailles: the first menagerie in which the different elements are not, as they traditionally were, distributed in a park (Loisel 104–7). At the center was an octagonal pavilion which, on the first floor, consisted of only a single room, the king's *salon*; on every side large windows looked out onto seven cages (the eighth side was reserved for the entrance), containing different species of animals. By Bentham's time, this menagerie had disappeared. But one finds in the program of the Panopticon a similar concern with individualizing observation, with characterization and classification, with the analytical arrangement of space. The Panopticon is a royal menagerie; the animal is replaced by man, individual distribution by specific grouping, and the king by the machinery of a furtive power. With this exception, the Panopticon also does the work of a naturalist. It makes it possible to draw up differences: among patients, to observe the symptoms of each individual, without the proximity of beds, the circulation of miasmas, the effects of contagion confusing the clinical tables; among schoolchildren, it makes it possible to observe performances (without there being any imitation or copying), to map aptitudes, to assess characters, to draw up rigorous classifications, and in relation to normal development, to distinguish "laziness and stubbornness" from "incurable imbecility"; among workers, it makes it possible to note the aptitudes of each worker, compare the time he takes to perform a task, and if they are paid by the day, to calculate their wages (Bentham 60–64).

So much for the question of observation. But the Panopticon was also a laboratory; it could be used as a machine to carry out experiments, to alter behavior, to train or correct individuals. To experiment with medicines and monitor their effects. To try out different punishments on prisoners, according to their crimes and character, and to seek the most effective ones. To teach different techniques simultaneously to the workers, to decide which is the best. To try out pedagogical experiments—and in particular to take up once again the well-debated problem of secluded education, by using orphans. One would see what would happen when, in their sixteenth or eighteenth year, they were presented with other boys or girls; one could verify whether, as Helvetius thought, anyone could learn anything; one would follow "the genealogy of every observable idea"; one could bring up different children according to different systems of thought, making certain children believe that two and two do not make four or that the moon is a cheese, then put them together when they are twenty or twenty-five years old; one would then have discussions that would be worth a great deal more than the sermons or lectures on which so much money is spent; one would have at least an opportunity of making discoveries in the domain of metaphysics. The Panopticon is a privileged place for experiments on men, and for analyzing with complete certainty the transformations that may be obtained from them. The Panopticon may even provide an apparatus for supervising its own mechanisms. In this central tower, the director may spy on all the employees that he has under his orders: nurses, doctors, foremen, teachers, warders; he will be able to judge them continuously, alter their behavior, impose upon them the methods he thinks best; and it will even be possible to observe the director himself. An inspector arriving unexpectedly at the center of the Panopticon will be able to judge at a glance, without anything being concealed from him, how the entire establishment is functioning. And, in any case, enclosed as he is in the middle of this architectural mechanism, is not the director's own fate entirely bound up with it? The incompetent physician who has allowed contagion to spread, the incompetent prison governor or workshop manager will be the first victims of an epidemic or a revolt. "'By every tie I could devise,' said the master of the Panopticon, 'my own fate had been bound up by me with theirs'" (Bentham 177). The Panopticon functions as a kind of laboratory of power. Thanks to its mechanisms of observation, it gains in efficiency and in the ability to penetrate into men's behavior; knowledge follows the advances of power, discovering new objects of knowledge over all the surfaces on which power is exercised.

The plague-stricken town, the panoptic establishment—the differences are important. They mark, at a distance of a century and a half, the transformations of the disciplinary program. In the first case, there is an exceptional situation: against an extraordinary evil, power is mobilized; it makes itself everywhere present and visible; it invents new mechanisms; it separates, it immobilizes, it partitions; it constructs for a time what is both a counter-city and the perfect society; it imposes an ideal functioning, but one that is reduced, in the final analysis, like the evil that it combats, to a simple dualism of life and death: that which moves brings death, and one kills that which moves. The Panopticon, on the other hand, must be understood as a generalizable model of functioning; a way of defining power relations in terms of the everyday life of men. No doubt Bentham presents it as a particular institution, closed in upon itself. Utopias, perfectly closed in upon themselves, are common enough. As opposed to the ruined prisons, littered with mechanisms of torture, to be seen in Piranese's engravings, the Panopticon presents a cruel, ingenious cage. The fact that it should have given rise, even in our own time, to so many variations, projected or realized, is evidence of the imaginary intensity that it has possessed for almost two hundred years. But the Panopticon must not be understood as a dream building: it is the diagram of a mechanism of power reduced to its ideal form; its functioning, abstracted from any obstacle, resistance, or friction, must be represented as a pure architectural and optical system: it is in fact a figure of political technology that may and must be detached from any specific use.

It is polyvalent in its applications; it serves to reform prisoners, but also to treat patients, to instruct schoolchildren, to confine the insane, to supervise workers, to put beggars and idlers to work. It is a type of location of bodies in space, of distribution of individuals in relation to one another, of hierarchical organization, of disposition of centers and channels of power, of definition of the instruments and modes of intervention of power, which can be implemented in hospitals, workshops, schools, prisons. Whenever one is dealing with a multiplicity of individuals on whom a task or a particular form of behavior must be imposed, the panoptic schema may be used. It is—necessary modifications apart—applicable "to all establishments whatsoever, in which, within a space not too large to be covered or commanded by buildings, a number of persons are meant to be kept under inspection" (Bentham 40; although Bentham takes the penitentiary house as his prime example, it is because it has many different functions to fulfill—safe custody, confinement, solitude, forced labor, and instruction).

In each of its applications, it makes it possible to perfect the exercise of power. It does this in several ways: because it can reduce the number of those who exercise it, while increasing the number of those on whom it is exercised. Because it is possible to intervene at any moment and because the constant pressure acts even before the offenses, mistakes, or crimes have been committed. Because, in these conditions, its strength is that it never intervenes, it is exercised spontaneously and without noise, it constitutes a mechanism whose effects follow from one another. Because, without any physical instrument other than architecture and geometry, it acts directly on individuals; it gives "power of mind over mind." The panoptic schema makes any apparatus of power more intense: it assures its economy (in material, in personnel, in time); it assures its efficacy by its preventative character, its continuous functioning and its automatic mechanisms. It is a way of obtaining from power "in hitherto unexampled quantity," "a great and new instrument of government . . . ; its great excellence consists in the great strength it is capable of giving to *any* institution it may be thought proper to apply it to" (Bentham 66).

It's a case of "it's easy once you've thought of it" in the political sphere. It can in fact be integrated into any function (education, medical treatment, production, punishment); it can increase the effect of this function, by being linked closely with it; it can constitute a mixed mechanism in which relations of power (and of knowledge) may be precisely adjusted, in the smallest detail, to the processes that are to be supervised; it can establish a direct proportion between "surplus power" and "surplus production." In short, it arranges things in such a way that the exercise of power is not added on from the outside, like a rigid, heavy constraint, to the functions it invests, but is so subtly present in them as to increase their efficiency by itself increasing its own points of contact. The panoptic mechanism is not simply a hinge, a point of exchange between a mechanism of power and a function; it is a way of making power relations function in a function, and of making a function function through these power relations. Bentham's preface to *Panopticon* opens with a list of the benefits to be obtained from his "inspection-house": "*Morals reformed—health preserved—industry invigorated—instruction diffused—public burthens lightened*—Economy seated, as it were, upon a rock—the gordian knot of the Poor-Laws not cut, but untied—all by a simple idea in architecture!" (Bentham 39).

Furthermore, the arrangement of this machine is such that its enclosed nature does not preclude a permanent presence from the outside: we have seen that anyone may come and exercise in the central tower the functions of surveillance, and that, this being the case, he can gain a clear idea of the way in which the surveillance is practiced. In fact, any panoptic institution, even if it is as rigorously closed as a penitentiary, may without difficulty be subjected to such irregular and constant inspections: and not only by the appointed inspectors, but also by the public; any member of society will have the right to come and see with his own eyes how the schools, hospitals, factories, prisons function. There is no risk, therefore, that the increase of power created by the panoptic machine may degenerate into tyranny; the disciplinary mechanism will be democratically controlled, since it will be constantly accessible "to the great tribunal committee of the world."[4] This Panopticon, subtly arranged so that an observer may observe, at a glance, so many different individuals, also enables everyone to come and observe any of the observers. The seeing machine was once a sort of dark room into which individuals spied; it has become a transparent building in which the exercise of power may be supervised by society as a whole.

The panoptic schema, without disappearing as such or losing any of its properties, was destined to spread throughout the social body; its vocation was to become a generalized function. The plague-stricken town provided an exceptional disciplinary model: perfect, but absolutely violent; to the disease that brought death, power opposed its perpetual threat of death; life inside it was reduced to its simplest expression; it was, against the power of death, the meticulous exercise of the right of the sword. The Panopticon, on the other hand, has a role of amplification; although it arranges power, although it is intended to make it more economic and more effective, it does so not for power itself, nor for the immediate salvation of a threatened society: its aim is to strengthen the social forces—to increase production, to develop the economy, spread education, raise the level of public morality; to increase and multiply.

How is power to be strengthened in such a way that, far from impeding progress, far from weighing upon it with its rules and regulations, it actually facilitates such progress? What intensificator of power will be able at the same time to be a multiplicator of production? How will power, by increasing its forces, be able to increase those of society instead of confiscating them or impeding them? The Panopticon's solution to this problem is that the productive increase of power can be assured only if, on the one hand, it can be exercised continuously in the very foundations of society, in the subtlest possible way, and if, on the other hand, it functions outside these sudden, violent, discontinuous forms that are bound up with the exercise of sovereignty. The body of the king, with its strange material and physical presence, with the force that he himself deploys or transmits to some few others, is at the opposite extreme of this new physics of power represented by panopticism; the domain of panopticism is, on the contrary, that whole lower region, that region of irregular bodies, with their details, their multiple movements, their heterogeneous forces, their spatial relations; what are required are mechanisms that analyze distributions, gaps, series, combinations, and which use instruments that render visible, record, differentiate, and compare: a physics of a relational and multiple power, which has its maximum intensity not in the person of the king, but in the bodies that can be individualized by these relations. At the theoretical level, Bentham defines another way of analyzing the social body and the power relations that traverse it; in terms of practice, he defines a procedure of subordination of bodies and forces that must increase the utility of power while practicing the economy of the prince. Panopticism is the general principle of a new "political anatomy" whose object and end are not the relations of sovereignty but the relations of discipline.

The celebrated, transparent, circular cage, with its high tower, powerful and knowing, may have been for Bentham a project of a perfect disciplinary institution; but he also set out to show how one may "unlock" the disciplines and get them to function in a diffused, multiple, polyvalent way throughout the whole social body. These disciplines, which the classical age had elaborated in specific, relatively enclosed places—barracks, schools, workshops—and whose total implementation had been imagined only at the limited and temporary scale of a plague-stricken town, Bentham dreamed of transforming into a network of mechanisms that would be everywhere and always alert, running through society without interruption in space or in time. The panoptic arrangement provides the formula for this generalization. It programs, at the level of an elementary

and easily transferable mechanism, the basic functioning of a society penetrated through and through with disciplinary mechanisms.

There are two images, then, of discipline. At one extreme, the disci-
pline-blockade, the enclosed institution, established on the edges of society, turned inwards towards negative functions: arresting evil, breaking
communications, suspending time. At the other extreme, with panopticism, is the discipline-mechanism: a functional mechanism that must improve the exercise of power by making it lighter, more rapid, more effective, a design of subtle coercion for a society to come. The movement from
one project to the other, from a schema of exceptional discipline to one of
a generalized surveillance, rests on a historical transformation: the gradual extension of the mechanisms of discipline throughout the seventeenth
and eighteenth centuries, their spread throughout the whole social body,
the formation of what might be called in general the disciplinary society.

A whole disciplinary generalization—the Benthamite physics of power
represents an acknowledgment of this—had operated throughout the classical age. The spread of disciplinary institutions, whose network was beginning to cover an ever larger surface and occupying above all a less and
less marginal position, testifies to this: what was an islet, a privileged
place, a circumstantial measure, or a singular model, became a general
formula; the regulations characteristic of the Protestant and pious armies
of William of Orange or of Gustavus Adolphus were transformed into regulations for all the armies of Europe; the model colleges of the Jesuits, or
the schools of Batencour or Demia, following the example set by Sturm,
provided the outlines for the general forms of educational discipline; the
ordering of the naval and military hospitals provided the model for the
entire reorganization of hospitals in the eighteenth century.

But this extension of the disciplinary institutions was no doubt only
the most visible aspect of various, more profound processes.

1. *The functional inversion of the disciplines.* At first, they were expected to
neutralize dangers, to fix useless or disturbed populations, to avoid the inconveniences of over-large assemblies; now they were being asked to play a
positive role, for they were becoming able to do so, to increase the possible
utility of individuals. Military discipline is no longer a mere means of preventing looting, desertion, or failure to obey orders among the troops; it has
become a basic technique to enable the army to exist, not as an assembled
crowd, but as a unity that derives from this very unity an increase in its
forces; discipline increases the skill of each individual, coordinates these
skills, accelerates movements, increases fire power, broadens the fronts of
attack without reducing their vigor, increases the capacity for resistance,
etc. The discipline of the workshop, while remaining a way of enforcing respect for the regulations and authorities, of preventing thefts or losses,
tends to increase aptitudes, speeds, output, and therefore profits; it still ex-
erts a moral influence over behavior, but more and more it treats actions in
terms of their results, introduces bodies into a machinery, forces into an

economy. When, in the seventeenth century, the provincial schools or the Christian elementary schools were founded, the justifications given for them were above all negative: those poor who were unable to bring up their children left them "in ignorance of their obligations: given the difficulties they have in earning a living, and themselves having been badly brought up, they are unable to communicate a sound upbringing that they themselves never had"; this involves three major inconveniences: ignorance of God, idleness (with its consequent drunkenness, impurity, larceny, brigandage), and the formation of those gangs of beggars, always ready to stir up public disorder and "virtually to exhaust the funds of the Hôtel-Dieu" (Demia 60–61). Now, at the beginning of the Revolution, the end laid down for primary education was to be, among other things, to "fortify," to "develop the body," to prepare the child "for a future in some mechanical work," to give him "an observant eye, a sure hand and prompt habits" (Talleyrand's Report to the Constituent Assembly, 10 September 1791, quoted by Léon 106). The disciplines function increasingly as techniques for making useful individuals. Hence their emergence from a marginal position on the confines of society, and detachment from the forms of exclusion or expiation, confinement, or retreat. Hence the slow loosening of their kinship with religious regularities and enclosures. Hence also their rooting in the most important, most central, and most productive sectors of society. They become attached to some of the great essential functions: factory production, the transmission of knowledge, the diffusion of aptitudes and skills, the war-machine. Hence, too, the double tendency one sees developing throughout the eighteenth century to increase the number of disciplinary institutions and to discipline the existing apparatuses.

2. *The swarming of disciplinary mechanisms.* While, on the one hand, the disciplinary establishments increase, their mechanisms have a certain tendency to become "deinstitutionalized," to emerge from the closed fortresses in which they once functioned and to circulate in a "free" state; the massive, compact disciplines are broken down into flexible methods of control, which may be transferred and adapted. Sometimes the closed apparatuses add to their internal and specific function a role of external surveillance, developing around themselves a whole margin of lateral controls. Thus the Christian School must not simply train docile children; it must also make it possible to supervise the parents, to gain information as to their way of life, their resources, their piety, their morals. The school tends to constitute minute social observatories that penetrate even to the adults and exercise regular supervision over them: the bad behavior of the child, or his absence, is a legitimate pretext, according to Demia, for one to go and question the neighbors, especially if there is any reason to believe that the family will not tell the truth; one can then go and question the parents themselves, to find out whether they know their catechism and the prayers, whether they are determined to root out the vices of their children, how many beds there are in the house and what the sleeping arrangements are; the visit may end with the giving of alms, the present of

a religious picture, or the provision of additional beds (Demia 39–40). Similarly, the hospital is increasingly conceived of as a base for the medical observation of the population outside; after the burning down of the Hôtel-Dieu in 1772, there were several demands that the large buildings, so heavy and so disordered, should be replaced by a series of smaller hospitals; their function would be to take in the sick of the quarter, but also to gather information, to be alert to any endemic or epidemic phenomena, to open dispensaries, to give advice to the inhabitants, and to keep the authorities informed of the sanitary state of the region.[5]

One also sees the spread of disciplinary procedures, not in the form of enclosed institutions, but as centers of observation disseminated throughout society. Religious groups and charity organizations had long played this role of "disciplining" the population. From the Counter-Reformation to the philanthropy of the July monarchy, initiatives of this type continued to increase; their aims were religious (conversion and moralization), economic (aid and encouragement to work), or political (the struggle against discontent or agitation). One has only to cite by way of example the regulations for the charity associations in the Paris parishes. The territory to be covered was divided into quarters and cantons and the members of the associations divided themselves up along the same lines. These members had to visit their respective areas regularly. "They will strive to eradicate places of ill-repute, tobacco shops, life-classes, gaming house, public scandals, blasphemy, impiety, and any other disorders that may come to their knowledge." They will also have to make individual visits to the poor; and the information to be obtained is laid down in regulations: the stability of the lodging, knowledge of prayers, attendance at the sacraments, knowledge of a trade, morality (and "whether they have not fallen into poverty through their own fault"); lastly, "one must learn by skillful questioning in what way they behave at home. Whether there is peace between them and their neighbors, whether they are careful to bring up their children in the fear of God . . . , whether they do not have their older children of different sexes sleeping together and with them, whether they do not allow licentiousness and cajolery in their families, especially in their older daughters. If one has any doubts as to whether they are married, one must ask to see their marriage certificate."[6]

3. *The state-control of the mechanisms of the discipline.* In England, it was private religious groups that carried out, for a long time, the functions of social discipline (cf. Radzinovitz 203–14); in France, although a part of this role remained in the hands of parish guilds or charity associations, another—and no doubt the most important part—was very soon taken over by the police apparatus.

The organization of a centralized police had long been regarded, even by contemporaries, as the most direct expression of royal absolutism; the sovereign had wished to have "his own magistrate to whom he might directly entrust his orders, his commissions, intentions, and who was entrusted with the execution of orders and orders under the King's private seal" (a note by Duval, first secretary at the police magistrature, quoted in Funck-Brentano I). In effect, in taking over a number of preexisting functions—the search for criminals, urban surveillance, economic and political supervision—the police magistratures and the magistrature-general that presided over them in Paris transposed them into a single, strict, administrative machine: "All the radiations of force and information that spread from the circumference culminate in the magistrate-general. . . . It is he who operates all the wheels that together produce order and harmony. The effects of his administration cannot be better compared than to the movement of the celestial bodies" (Des Essarts 344, 528).

But, although the police as an institution were certainly organized in the form of a state apparatus, and although this was certainly linked directly to the center of political sovereignty, the type of power that it exercises, the mechanisms it operates, and the elements to which it applies them are specific. It is an apparatus that must be coextensive with the entire social body and not only by the extreme limits that it embraces, but by the minuteness of the details it is concerned with. Police power must bear "over everything": it is not, however, the totality of the state nor of the kingdom as visible and invisible body of the monarch; it is the dust of events, actions, behavior, opinions—"everything that happens";[7] the police are concerned with "those things of every moment," those "unimportant things," of which Catherine II spoke in her Great Instruction (Supplement to the *Instruction for the Drawing Up of a New Code*, 1769, article 535). With the police, one is in the indefinite world of a supervision that seeks ideally to reach the most elementary particle, the most passing phenomenon of the social body: "The ministry of the magistrates and police officers is of the greatest importance; the objects that it embraces are in a sense definite, one may perceive them only by a sufficiently detailed examination" (Delamare, unnumbered preface): the infinitely small of political power.

And, in order to be exercised, this power had to be given the instrument of permanent, exhaustive, omnipresent surveillance, capable of making all visible, as long as it could itself remain invisible. It had to be like a faceless gaze that transformed the whole social body into a field of perception: thousands of eyes posted everywhere, mobile attentions ever on the alert, a long, hierarchized network which, according to Le Maire, comprised for Paris the forty-eight *commissaires*, the twenty *inspecteurs*, then the "observers," who were paid regularly, the *"basses mouches,"* or secret agents, who were paid by the day, then the informers, paid according to the job done, and finally the prostitutes. And this unceasing observation had to be accumulated in a series of reports and registers; throughout the eighteenth century, an immense police text increasingly covered society by means of a complex documentary organization (on the police registers in the eighteenth century, cf. Chassaigne). And, unlike the methods of judicial or administrative writing, what was registered in this way were forms of behavior, attitudes, possibilities, suspicions—a permanent account of individuals' behavior.

Now, it should be noted that, although this police supervision was entirely "in the hands of the king," it did not function in a single direction. It was in fact a double-entry system: it had to correspond, by manipulating the machinery of justice, to the immediate wishes of the king, but it was also capable of responding to solicitations from below; the celebrated *lettres de cachet*, or orders under the king's private seal, which were long the symbol of arbitrary royal rule and which brought detention into disrepute on political grounds, were in fact demanded by families, masters, local notables, neighbors, parish priests; and their function was to punish by confinement a whole infrapenality, that of disorder, agitation, disobedience, bad conduct; those things that Ledoux wanted to exclude from his architecturally perfect city and which he called "offenses of nonsurveillance." In short, the eighteenth-century police added a disciplinary function to its role as the auxiliary of justice in the pursuit of criminals and as an instrument for the political supervision of plots, opposition movements, or revolts. It was a complex function since it linked the absolute power of the monarch to the lowest levels of power disseminated in society; since, between these different, enclosed institutions of discipline (workshops, armies, schools), it extended an intermediary network, acting where they could not intervene, disciplining the nondisciplinary spaces; but it filled in the gaps, linked them together, guaranteed with its armed force an interstitial discipline and a metadiscipline. "By means of a wise police, the sovereign accustoms the people to order and obedience" (Vattel 162).

The organization of the police apparatus in the eighteenth century sanctioned a generalization of the disciplines that became coextensive with the state itself. Although it was linked in the most explicit way with everything in the royal power that exceeded the exercise of regular justice, it is understandable why the police offered such slight resistance to the rearrangement of the judicial power; and why it has not ceased to impose its prerogatives upon it, with ever-increasing weight, right up to the present day; this is no doubt because it is the secular arm of the judiciary; but it is also because, to a far greater degree than the judicial institution, it is identified, by reason of its extent and mechanisms, with a society of the disciplinary type. Yet it would be wrong to believe that the disciplinary functions were confiscated and absorbed once and for all by a state apparatus.

"Discipline" may be identified neither with an institution nor with an apparatus; it is a type of power, a modality for its exercise, comprising a whole set of instruments, techniques, procedures, levels of application, targets; it is a "physics" or an "anatomy" of power, a technology. And it may be taken over either by "specialized" institutions (the penitentiaries or "houses of correction" of the nineteenth century), or by institutions that use it as an essential instrument for a particular end (schools, hospitals), or by preexisting authorities that find in it a means of reinforcing or reorganizing their internal mechanisms of power (one day we should show how intrafamilial relations, essentially in the parents-children cell, have become "disciplined," absorbing since the classical age external schemata, first educational and military, then medical, psychiatric, psychological, which have made the family the privileged locus of emergence for the disciplinary question of the normal and the abnormal), or by apparatuses that have made discipline their principle of internal functioning (the disciplinarization of the administrative apparatus from the Napoleonic period), or finally by state apparatuses whose major, if not exclusive, function is to assure that discipline reigns over society as a whole (the police).

On the whole, therefore, one can speak of the formation of a disciplinary society in this movement that stretches from the enclosed disciplines, a sort of social "quarantine," to an indefinitely generalizable mechanism of "panopticism." Not because the disciplinary modality of power has replaced all the others; but because it has infiltrated the others, sometimes undermining them, but serving as an intermediary between them, linking them together, extending them, and above all making it possible to bring the effects of power to the most minute and distant elements. It assures an infinitesimal distribution of the power relations.

A few years after Bentham, Julius gave this society its birth certificate (Julius 384–86). Speaking of the panoptic principle, he said that there was much more there than architectural ingenuity: it was an event in the "history of the human mind." In appearance, it is merely the solution of a technical problem; but, through it, a whole type of society emerges. Antiquity had been a civilization of spectacle. "To render accessible to a multitude of men the inspection of a small number of objects": this was the problem to which the architecture of temples, theaters, and circuses responded. With spectacle, there was a predominance of public life, the intensity of festivals, sensual proximity. In these rituals in which blood flowed, society found new vigor and formed for a moment a single great body. The modern age poses the opposite problem: "To procure for a small number, or even for a single individual, the instantaneous view of a great multitude." In a society in which the principal elements are no longer the community and public life, but, on the one hand, private individuals and, on the other, the state, relations can be regulated only in a form that is the exact reverse of the spectacle: "It was to the modern age, to the ever-growing influence of the state, to its ever more profound intervention in all the details and all the relations of social life, that was reserved the task of increasing and perfecting its guarantees, by using and directing towards that great aim the building and distribution of buildings intended to observe a great multitude of men at the same time."

Julius saw as a fulfilled historical process that which Bentham had described as a technical program. Our society is one not of spectacle, but of surveillance; under the surface of images, one invests bodies in depth; behind the great abstraction of exchange, there continues the meticulous, concrete training of useful forces; the circuits of communication are the supports of an accumulation and a centralization of knowledge; the play of signs defines the anchorages of power; it is not that the beautiful totality of the individual is amputated, repressed, altered by our social order, it is rather that the individual is carefully fabricated in it, according to a whole technique of forces and bodies. We are much less Greeks than we believe. We are neither in the amphitheater, nor on the stage, but in the panoptic machine, invested by its effects of power, which we bring to ourselves since we are part of its mechanism. The importance, in historical mythology, of the Napoleonic character probably derives from the fact that it is at the point of junction of the monarchical, ritual exercise of sovereignty and the hierarchical, permanent exercise of indefinite discipline. He is the individual who looms over everything with a single gaze which no detail, however minute, can escape: "You may consider that no part of the Empire is without surveillance, no crime, no offense, no contravention that remains unpunished, and that the eye of the genius who can enlighten all embraces the whole of this vast machine, without, however, the slightest detail escaping his attention" (Treilhard 14). At the moment of its full blossoming, the disciplinary society still assumes with the Emperor the old aspect of the power of spectacle. As a monarch who is at one and the same time a usurper of the ancient throne and the organizer of the new state, he combined into a single symbolic, ultimate figure the whole of the long process by which the pomp of sovereignty, the necessarily spectacular manifestations of power, were extinguished one by one in the daily exercise of surveillance, in a panopticism in which the vigilance of intersecting gazes was soon to render useless both the eagle and the sun.

The formation of the disciplinary society is connected with a number of broad historical processes—economic, juridico-political, and lastly, scientific—of which it forms part.

1. Generally speaking, it might be said that the disciplines are techniques for assuring the ordering of human multiplicities. It is true that there is nothing exceptional or even characteristic in this: every system of power is presented with the same problem. But the peculiarity of the disciplines is that they try to define in relation to the multiplicities a tactics of power that fulfills three criteria: firstly, to obtain the exercise of power at the lowest possible cost (economically, by the low expenditure it involves; politically, by its discretion, its low exteriorization, its relative invisibility, the little resistance it arouses); secondly, to bring the effects of this social power to their maximum intensity and to extend them as far as possible, without either failure or interval; thirdly, to link this "economic" growth of power with the output of the apparatuses (educational, military, industrial, or medical) within which it is exercised; in short, to increase both the docility and the utility of all the elements of the system. This triple objective of the disciplines corresponds to a well-known historical conjuncture. One aspect of this conjuncture was the large demographic thrust of the eighteenth century; an increase in the floating population (one of the primary objects of discipline is to fix; it is an antinomadic technique); a change of quantitative scale in the groups to be supervised or manipulated (from the beginning of the seventeenth century to the eve of the French Revolution, the school population had been increasing rapidly, as

had no doubt the hospital population; by the end of the eighteenth century, the peacetime army exceeded 200,000 men). The other aspect of the conjuncture was the growth in the apparatus of production, which was becoming more and more extended and complex; it was also becoming more costly and its profitability had to be increased. The development of the disciplinary methods corresponded to these two processes, or rather, no doubt, to the new need to adjust their correlation. Neither the residual forms of feudal power nor the structures of the administrative monarchy, nor the local mechanisms of supervision, nor the unstable, tangled mass they all formed together could carry out this role: they were hindered from doing so by the irregular and inadequate extension of their network, by their often conflicting functioning, but above all by the "costly" nature of the power that was exercised in them. It was costly in several senses: because directly it cost a great deal to the Treasury; because the system of corrupt offices and farmed-out taxes weighed indirectly, but very heavily, on the population; because the resistance it encountered forced it into a cycle of perpetual reinforcement; because it proceeded essentially by levying (levying on money or products by royal, seigniorial, ecclesiastical taxation; levying on men or time by *corvées* of press-ganging, by locking up or banishing vagabonds). The development of the disciplines marks the appearance of elementary techniques belonging to a quite different economy: mechanisms of power which, instead of proceeding by deduction, are integrated into the productive efficiency of the apparatuses from within, into the growth of this efficiency and into the use of what it produces. For the old principle of "levying-violence," which governed the economy of power, the disciplines substitute the principle of "mildness-production-profit." These are the techniques that make it possible to adjust the multiplicity of men and the multiplication of the apparatuses of production (and this means not only "production" in the strict sense, but also the production of knowledge and skills in the school, the production of health in the hospitals, the production of destructive force in the army).

In this task of adjustment, discipline had to solve a number of problems for which the old economy of power was not sufficiently equipped. It could reduce the inefficiency of mass phenomena: reduce what, in a multiplicity, makes it much less manageable than a unity; reduce what is opposed to the use of each of its elements and of their sum; reduce everything that may counter the advantages of number. That is why discipline fixes; it arrests or regulates movements; it clears up confusion; it dissipates compact groupings of individuals wandering about the country in unpredictable ways; it establishes calculated distributions. It must also master all the forces that are formed from the very constitution of an organized multiplicity; it must neutralize the effects of counterpower that spring from them and which form a resistance to the power that wishes to dominate it: agitations, revolts, spontaneous organizations, coalitions—anything that may establish horizontal conjunctions. Hence the fact that the disciplines use procedures of partitioning and verticality, that they introduce, between the different elements at the same level, as solid separations as possible, that they define compact hierarchical networks, in short, that they oppose to the intrinsic, adverse force of multiplicity the technique of the continuous, individualizing pyramid. They must also increase the particular utility of each element of the multiplicity, but by means that are the most rapid and the least costly, that is to say, by using the multiplicity itself as an instrument of this growth. Hence, in order to extract from bodies the maximum time and force, the use of those overall methods known as timetables, collective training, exercises, total and detailed surveillance. Furthermore, the disciplines must increase the effect of utility proper to the multiplicities, so that each is made more useful than the simple sum of its elements: it is in order to increase the utilizable effects of the multiple that the disciplines define tactics of distribution, reciprocal adjustment of bodies, gestures, and rhythms, differentiation of capacities, reciprocal coordination in relation to apparatuses or tasks. Lastly, the disciplines have to bring into play the power relations, not above but inside the very texture of the multiplicity, as discreetly as possible, as well articulated on the other functions of these multiplicities and also in the least expensive way possible: to this correspond anonymous instruments of power, coextensive with the multiplicity that they regiment, such as hierarchical surveillance, continuous registration, perpetual assessment, and classification. In short, to substitute for a power that is manifested through the brilliance of those who exercise it, a power that insidiously objectifies those on whom it is applied; to form a body of knowledge about these individuals, rather than to deploy the ostentatious signs of sovereignty. In a word, the disciplines are the ensemble of minute technical inventions that made it possible to increase the useful size of multiplicities by decreasing the inconveniences of the power which, in order to make them useful, must control them. A multiplicity, whether in a workshop or a nation, an army or a school, reaches the threshold of a discipline when the relation of the one to the other becomes favorable.

If the economic take-off of the West began with the techniques that made possible the accumulation of capital, it might perhaps be said that the methods for administering the accumulation of men made possible a political take-off in relation to the traditional, ritual, costly, violent forms of power, which soon fell into disuse and were superseded by a subtle, calculated technology of subjection. In fact, the two processes—the accumulation of men and the accumulation of capital—cannot be separated; it would not have been possible to solve the problem of the accumulation of men without the growth of an apparatus of production capable of both sustaining them and using them; conversely, the techniques that made the cumulative multiplicity of men useful accelerated the accumulation of capital. At a less general level, the technological mutations of the apparatus of production, the division of labor and the elaboration of the disciplinary techniques sustained an ensemble of very close relations (cf. Marx, *Capital*, vol. I, chapter XIII and the very interesting analysis in Guerry and

Deleule). Each makes the other possible and necessary; each provides a model for the other. The disciplinary pyramid constituted the small cell of power within which the separation, coordination, and supervision of tasks was imposed and made efficient; and analytical partitioning of time, gestures, and bodily forces constituted an operational schema that could easily be transferred from the groups to be subjected to the mechanisms of production; the massive projection of military methods onto industrial organization was an example of this modeling of the division of labor following the model laid down by the schemata of power. But, on the other hand, the technical analysis of the process of production, its "mechanical" breaking-down, were projected onto the labor force whose task it was to implement it: the constitution of those disciplinary machines in which the individual forces that they bring together are composed into a whole and therefore increased is the effect of this projection. Let us say that discipline is the unitary technique by which the body is reduced as a "political" force at the least cost and maximized as a useful force. The growth of a capitalist economy gave rise to the specific modality of disciplinary power, whose general formulas, techniques of submitting forces and bodies, in short, "political anatomy," could be operated in the most diverse political regimes, apparatuses, or institutions.

2. The panoptic modality of power—at the elementary, technical, merely physical level at which it is situated—is not under the immediate dependence or a direct extension of the great juridico-political structures of a society; it is nonetheless not absolutely independent. Historically, the process by which the bourgeoisie became in the course of the eighteenth century the politically dominant class was masked by the establishment of an explicit, coded, and formally egalitarian juridical framework, made possible by the organization of a parliamentary, representative regime. But the development and generalization of disciplinary mechanisms constituted the other, dark side of these processes. The general juridical form that guaranteed a system of rights that were egalitarian in principle was supported by these tiny, everyday, physical mechanisms, by all those systems of micropower that are essentially nonegalitarian and asymmetrical that we call the disciplines. And although, in a formal way, the representative regime makes it possible, directly or indirectly, with or without relays, for the will of all to form the fundamental authority of sovereignty, the disciplines provide, at the base, a guarantee of the submission of forces and bodies. The real, corporal disciplines constituted the foundation of the formal, juridical liberties. The contract may have been regarded as the ideal foundation of law and political power; panopticism constituted the technique, universally widespread, of coercion. It continued to work in depth on the juridical structures of society, in order to make the effective mechanisms of power function in opposition to the formal framework that it had acquired. The "Enlightenment," which discovered the liberties, also invented the disciplines.

In appearance, the disciplines constitute nothing more than an infralaw. They seem to extend the general forms defined by law to the infinitesimal level of individual lives; or they appear as methods of training that enable individuals to become integrated into these general demands. They seem to constitute the same type of law on a different scale, thereby making it more meticulous and more indulgent. The disciplines should be regarded as a sort of counterlaw. They have the precise role of introducing insuperable asymmetries and excluding reciprocities. First, because discipline creates between individuals a "private" link, which is a relation of constraints entirely different from contractual obligation; the acceptance of a discipline may be underwritten by contract; the way in which it is imposed, the mechanisms it brings into play, the nonreversible subordination of one group of people by another, the "surplus" power that is always fixed on the same side, the inequality of position of the different "partners" in relation to the common regulation, all these distinguish the disciplinary link from the contractual link, and make it possible to distort the contractual link systematically from the moment it has as its content a mechanism of discipline. We know, for example, how many real procedures undermine the legal fiction of the work contract: workshop discipline is not the least important. Moreover, whereas the juridical systems define juridical subjects according to universal norms, the disciplines characterize, classify, specialize; they distribute along a scale, around a norm, hierarchize individuals in relation to one another and, if necessary, disqualify and invalidate. In any case, in the space and during the time in which they exercise their control and bring into play the asymmetries of their power, they effect a suspension of the law that is never total, but is never annulled either. Regular and institutional as it may be, the discipline, in its mechanism, is a "counterlaw." And, although the universal juridicism of modern society seems to fix limits on the exercise of power, its universally widespread panopticism enables it to operate, on the underside of the law, a machinery that is both immense and minute, which supports, reinforces, multiplies the asymmetry of power and undermines the limits that are traced around the law. The minute disciplines, the panopticisms of every day may well be below the level of emergence of the great apparatuses and the great political struggles. But, in the genealogy of modern society, they have been, with the class domination that traverses it, the political counterpart of the juridical norms according to which power was redistributed. Hence, no doubt, the importance that has been given for so long to the small techniques of discipline, to those apparently insignificant tricks that it has invented, and even to those "sciences" that give it a respectable face; hence the fear of abandoning them if one cannot find any substitute; hence the affirmation that they are at the very foundation of society, and an element in its equilibrium, whereas they are a series of mechanisms for unbalancing power relations definitively and everywhere; hence the persistence in regarding them as the humble, but concrete form of every morality, whereas they are a set of physico-political techniques.

To return to the problem of legal punishments, the prison with all the corrective technology at its disposal is to be resituated at the point where the codified power to punish turns into a disciplinary power to observe; at the point where the universal punishments of the law are applied selectively to certain individuals and always the same ones; at the point where the redefinition of the juridical subject by the penalty becomes a useful training of the criminal; at the point where the law is inverted and passes outside itself, and where the counterlaw becomes the effective and institutionalized content of the juridical forms. What generalizes the power to punish, then, is not the universal consciousness of the law in each juridical subject; it is the regular extension, the infinitely minute web of panoptic techniques.

3. Taken one by one, most of these techniques have a long history behind them. But what was new, in the eighteenth century, was that, by being combined and generalized, they attained a level at which the formation of knowledge and the increase of power regularly reinforce one another in a circular process. At this point, the disciplines crossed the "technological" threshold. First the hospital, then the school, then, later, the workshop were not simply "reordered" by the disciplines; they became, thanks to them, apparatuses such that any mechanism of objectification could be used in them as an instrument of subjection, and any growth of power could give rise in them to possible branches of knowledge; it was this link, proper to the technological systems, that made possible within the disciplinary element the formation of clinical medicine, psychiatry, child psychology, educational psychology, the rationalization of labor. It is a double process, then: an epistemological "thaw" through a refinement of power relations; a multiplication of the effects of power through the formation and accumulation of new forms of knowledge.

The extension of the disciplinary methods is inscribed in a broad historical process: the development at about the same time of many other technologies—agronomical, industrial, economic. But it must be recognized that, compared with the mining industries, the emerging chemical industries or methods of national accountancy, compared with the blast furnaces or the steam engine, panopticism has received little attention. It is regarded as not much more than a bizarre little utopia, a perverse dream—rather as though Bentham had been the Fourier of a police society, and the Phalanstery had taken on the form of the Panopticon. And yet this represented the abstract formula of a very real technology, that of individuals. There were many reasons why it received little praise; the most obvious is that the discourses to which it gave rise rarely acquired, except in the academic classifications, the status of sciences; but the real reason is no doubt that the power that it operates and which it augments is a direct, physical power that men exercise upon one another. An inglorious culmination had an origin that could be only grudgingly acknowledged. But it would be unjust to compare the disciplinary techniques with such inventions as the steam engine or Amici's microscope. They are much less; and yet, in a way, they are much more. If a historical equivalent or at least a point of comparison had to be found for them, it would be rather in the "inquisitorial" technique.

The eighteenth century invented the techniques of discipline and the examination, rather as the Middle Ages invented the judicial investigation. But it did so by quite different means. The investigation procedure, an old fiscal and administrative technique, had developed above all with the reorganization of the Church and the increase of the princely states in the twelfth and thirteenth centuries. At this time it permeated to a very large degree the jurisprudence first of the ecclesiastical courts, then of the lay courts. The investigation as an authoritarian search for a truth observed or attested was thus opposed to the old procedures of the oath, the ordeal, the judicial duel, the judgment of God, or even of the transaction between private individuals. The investigation was the sovereign power arrogating to itself the right to establish the truth by a number of regulated techniques. Now, although the investigation has since then been an integral part of Western justice (even up to our own day), one must not forget either its political origin, its link with the birth of the states and of monarchical sovereignty, or its later extension and its role in the formation of knowledge. In fact, the investigation has been the no doubt crude, but fundamental, element in the constitution of the empirical sciences; it has been the juridico-political matrix of this experimental knowledge, which, as we know, was very rapidly released at the end of the Middle Ages. It is perhaps true to say that, in Greece, mathematics were born from techniques of measurement; the sciences of nature, in any case, were born, to some extent, at the end of the Middle Ages, from the practices of investigation. The great empirical knowledge that covered the things of the world and transcribed them into the ordering of an indefinite discourse that observes, describes, and establishes the "facts" (at a time when the Western world was beginning the economic and political conquest of this same world) had its operating model no doubt in the Inquisition—that immense invention that our recent mildness has placed in the dark recesses of our memory. But what this politico-juridical, administrative, and criminal, religious and lay, investigation was to the sciences of nature, disciplinary analysis has been to the sciences of man. These sciences, which have so delighted our "humanity" for over a century, have their technical matrix in the petty, malicious minutiae of the disciplines and their investigations. These investigations are perhaps to psychology, psychiatry, pedagogy, criminology, and so many other strange sciences, what the terrible power of investigation was to the calm knowledge of the animals, the plants, or the earth. Another power, another knowledge. On the threshold of the classical age, Bacon, lawyer and statesman, tried to develop a methodology of investigation for the empirical sciences. What Great Observer will produce the methodology of examination for the human sciences? Unless, of course, such a thing is not possible. For, although it is true that, in becoming a technique for the empirical sciences, the investigation has detached itself from the inquisitorial procedure, in which it was historically rooted, the examination has remained extremely close to the disciplinary power that shaped it. It has always been and still is an intrinsic element of the disciplines. Of course it seems to have undergone a speculative purification by integrating itself with such sciences as psychology and psychiatry. And, in effect, its appearance in the form of tests, interviews, interrogations, and consultations is apparently in order to rectify the mechanisms of discipline: educational psychology is supposed to correct the rigors of the school, just as the medical or psychiatric interview is supposed to rectify the effects of the discipline of work. But we must not be misled; these techniques merely refer individuals from one disciplinary authority to another, and they reproduce, in a concentrated or formalized form, the schema of power-knowledge proper to each discipline (on this subject, cf. Tort). The great investigation that gave rise to the sciences of nature has become detached from its politico-juridical model; the examination, on the other hand, is still caught up in disciplinary technology.

In the Middle Ages, the procedure of investigation gradually superseded the old accusatory justice, by a process initiated from above; the disciplinary technique, on the other hand, insidiously and as if from below, has invaded a penal justice that is still, in principle, inquisitorial. All the great movements of extension that characterize modern penality—the problematization of the criminal behind his crime, the concern with a punishment that is a correction, a therapy, a normalization, the division of the act of judgment between various authorities that are supposed to measure, assess, diagnose, cure, transform individuals—all this betrays the penetration of the disciplinary examination into the judicial inquisition.

What is now imposed on penal justice as its point of application, its "useful" object, will no longer be the body of the guilty man set up against the body of the king; nor will it be the juridical subject of an ideal contract; it will be the disciplinary individual. The extreme point of penal justice under the Ancien Régime was the infinite segmentation of the body of the regicide: a manifestation of the strongest power over the body of the greatest criminal, whose total destruction made the crime explode into its truth. The ideal point of penality today would be an indefinite discipline: an interrogation without end, an investigation that would be extended without limit to a meticulous and ever more analytical observation, a judgment that would at the same time be the constitution of a file that was never closed, the calculated leniency of a penalty that would be interlaced with the ruthless curiosity of an examination, a procedure that would be at the same time the permanent measure of a gap in relation to an inaccessible norm and the asymptotic movement that strives to meet in infinity. The public execution was the logical culmination of a procedure governed by the Inquisition. The practice of placing individuals under "observation" is a natural extension of a justice imbued with disciplinary methods and examination procedures. Is it surprising that the cellular prison, with its regular chronologies, forced labor, its authorities of surveillance and registration, its experts in normality, who continue and multiply the functions of the judge, should have become the modern instrument of penalty? Is it surprising that prisons resemble factories, schools, barracks, hospitals, which all resemble prisons?

NOTES

[1] Archives militaires de Vincennes, A 1,516 91 sc. Pièce. This regulation is broadly similar to a whole series of others that date from the same period and earlier.

[2] In the *Postscript to the Panopticon,* 1791, Bentham adds dark inspection galleries painted in black around the inspector's lodge, each making it possible to observe two stories of cells.

[3] In his first version of the *Panopticon,* Bentham had also imagined an acoustic surveillance, operated by means of pipes leading from the cells to the central tower. In the *Postscript* he abandoned the idea, perhaps because he could not introduce into it the principle of dissymmetry and prevent the prisoners from hearing the inspector as well as the inspector hearing them. Julius tried to develop a system of dissymmetrical listening (Julius 18).

[4] Imagining this continuous flow of visitors entering the central tower by an underground passage and then observing the circular landscape of the Panopticon, was Bentham aware of the Panoramas that Barker was constructing at exactly the same period (the first seems to have dated from 1787) and in which the visitors, occupying the central place, saw unfolding around them a landscape, a city, or a battle. The visitors occupied exactly the place of the sovereign gaze.

[5] In the second half of the eighteenth century, it was often suggested that the army should be used for the surveillance and general partitioning of the population. The army, as yet to undergo discipline in the seventeenth century, was regarded as a force capable of instilling it. Cf., for example, Servan, *Le Soldat citoyen,* 1780.

[6] Arsenal, MS. 2565. Under this number, one also finds regulations for charity associations of the seventeenth and eighteenth centuries.

[7] Le Maire in a memorandum written at the request of Sartine, in answer to sixteen questions posed by Joseph II on the Parisian police. This memorandum was published by Gazier in 1879.

BIBLIOGRAPHY

Archives militaires de Vincennes, A 1,516 91 sc.
Bentham, J., *Works,* ed. Bowring, IV, 1843.
Chassaigne, M., *La Lieutenance générale de police,* 1906.
Delamare, N., *Traité de police,* 1705.
Demia, C., *Règlement pour les écoles de la ville de Lyon,* 1716.
Des Essarts, T. N., *Dictionnaire universel de police,* 1787.
Funck-Brentano, F., *Catalogue des manuscrits de la bibliothèque de l'Arsenal,* IX.
Guerry, F., and Deleule, D., *Le Corps productif,* 1973.
Julius, N. H., *Leçons sur les prisons,* I, 1831 (Fr. trans.).
Léon, A., *La Révolution française et l'éducation technique,* 1968.
Loisel, G., *Histoire des ménageries,* II, 1912.
Marx, Karl, *Capital,* vol. I, ed. 1970.
Radzinovitz, L., *The English Criminal Law,* II, 1956.
Servan, J., *Le Soldat citoyen,* 1780.
Tort, Michel, *Q.I.,* 1974.
Treilhard, J. B., *Motifs du code d'instruction criminelle,* 1808.
Vattel, E. de, *Le Droit des gens,* 1768.

•   •   •   •   •   •   •   •   •   •   •   •   •

QUESTIONS FOR A SECOND READING

1. Foucault's text begins with an account of a system enacted in the seventeenth century to control the spread of plague. After describing this system of surveillance, he compares it to the "rituals of exclusion" used to control lepers. He says, "The exile of the leper and the arrest of the plague do not bring with them the same political dream" (p. 228). At many points he sets up similar pairings, all in an attempt to understand the relations of power and knowledge in modern public life.

   As you reread, mark the various points at which Foucault works out the differences between a prior and the current "political dream" of order. What are the techniques or instruments that belong to each? What moments in history are defined by each? How and where are they visible in public life?

2. Toward the end of the chapter Foucault says, "The extension of the disciplinary methods is inscribed in a broad historical process." Foucault writes a difficult kind of history (at one point he calls it a genealogy), since it does not make use of the usual form of historical narrative—with characters, plots, scenes, and action. As you reread, take notes that will allow you to trace time, place, and sequence (and, if you can, agents and agency) in Foucault's account of the formation of the disciplinary society based on technologies of surveillance. Why do you think he avoids a narrative mode of presentation?

3. As you reread Foucault's text, bring forward the stages in his presentation (or the development of his argument). Mark those moments that you consider key or central to the working out of his argument concerning the panopticon. What sentences of his would you use to represent key moments in the text? The text at times turns to numbered sections. How, for example, do they function? Describe the beginning, middle, and end of the essay. Describe the skeleton or understructure of the chapter. What are its various stages or steps? How do they relate to each other?

ASSIGNMENTS FOR WRITING

1. About three-quarters of the way into this chapter, Foucault says,

   > Our society is one not of spectacle, but of surveillance; under the surface of images, one invests bodies in depth; behind the great abstraction of exchange, there continues the meticulous, concrete training of useful forces; the circuits of communication are the supports of an accumulation and a centralization of knowledge; the play of signs defines the anchorages of power; it is not that the beautiful totality of the individual is amputated, repressed, altered by our social order, it is rather that the individual is carefully fabricated in it, according to a whole technique of forces and bodies. (pp. 244–45)

This prose is eloquent and insists on its importance to our moment and our society; it is also very hard to read or to paraphrase. Who is doing what to whom? How do we think about the individual's being carefully fabricated in the social order?

Take this chapter as a problem to solve. What is it about? What are its key arguments? its examples and conclusions? Write an essay that summarizes "Panopticism." Imagine that you are writing for readers who have read the chapter (although they won't have the pages in front of them). You will need to take time to present and discuss examples from the text. Your job is to help your readers figure out what it says. You get the chance to take the lead and be the teacher. You should feel free to acknowledge that you don't understand certain sections even as you write about them.

So, how do you write about something you don't completely understand? Here's a suggestion. When you have completed your summary, read it over and treat it as a draft. Ask questions like these: What have I left out? What was I tempted to ignore or finesse? Go back to those sections of the chapter that you ignored and bring them into your essay. Revise by adding discussions of some of the very sections you don't understand. You can write about what you think Foucault *might* be saying—you can, that is, be cautious and tentative; you can admit that the text is what it is, hard to read. You don't have to master this text. You do, however, need to see what you can make of it.

2. About a third of the way through his text, Foucault asserts, "The Panopticon is a marvelous machine which, whatever use one may wish to put it to, produces homogeneous effects of power." Write an essay in which you explain the machinery of the panopticon as a mechanism of power. Paraphrase Foucault and, where it seems appropriate, use his words. Present Foucault's account as you understand it. As part of your essay, and in order to explain what he is getting at, turn to two examples—one of his, perhaps, and then one of your own.

3. Perhaps the most surprising thing about Foucault's argument in "Panopticism" is the way it equates prisons with schools, hospitals, and workplaces, sites we are accustomed to imagining as very different from a prison. Foucault argues against our commonly accepted understanding of such things.

At the end of the chapter Foucault asks two questions. These are rhetorical questions, strategically placed at the end. Presumably we are prepared to feel their force and to think of possible answers.

> Is it surprising that the cellular prison, with its regular chronologies, forced labor, its authorities of surveillance and registration, its experts in normality, who continue and multiply the functions of the judge, should have become the modern instrument of penality? Is it surprising that prisons resemble factories, schools, barracks, hospitals, which all resemble prisons? (pp. 252–53)

For this assignment, take the invitation of Foucault's conclusion. No, you want to respond, it is not surprising that "experts in normality, who continue and multiply the functions of the judge, should have become the modern instrument of penality." No, it is not surprising that "prisons

resemble factories, schools, barracks, hospitals, which all resemble prisons." Why isn't it surprising? Or, why isn't it surprising if you are thinking along with Foucault?

Write an essay in which you explore one of these possible resemblances. You may, if you choose, cite Foucault. You can certainly pick up
some of his key terms or examples and put them into play. You should
imagine, however, that it is your turn. With your work on Foucault behind you, you are writing to a general audience about "experts in normality" and the key sites of surveillance and control.

MAKING CONNECTIONS

1. Both John Berger in "Ways of Seeing" (p. 105) and Foucault in "Panopticism" discuss what Foucault calls "power relations." Berger claims that
   "the entire art of the past has now become a political issue," and he
   makes a case for the evolution of a "new language of images" which
   could "confer a new kind of power" if people were to understand history
   in art. Foucault argues that the Panopticon signals an "inspired" change
   in power relations. "It is," he says,

   > an important mechanism, for it automatizes and disindividualizes
   > power. Power has its principle not so much in a person as in a certain
   > concerted distribution of bodies, surfaces, lights, gazes; in an arrange-
   > ment whose internal mechanisms produce the relation in which indi-
   > viduals are caught up. (p. 232)

   Both Berger and Foucault create arguments about power, its methods
   and goals. As you read through their essays, mark passages you might
   use to explain how each author thinks about power—where it comes
   from, who has it, how it works, where you look for it, how you know
   when you see it, what it does, where it goes. You should reread the essays
   as a pair, as part of a single project in which you are looking to explain
   theories of power.

   Write an essay in which you present and explain "Ways of Seeing"
   and "Panopticism" as examples of Berger's and Foucault's theories of
   power. Both Berger and Foucault are arguing against usual understandings of power and knowledge and history. In this sense, their projects are
   similar. You should be sure, however, to look for differences as well as
   similarities.

2. Both "Projected Memory: Holocaust Photographs in Personal and Public
   Fantasy" (p. 400) by Marianne Hirsch and "Panopticism" by Foucault present difficulties to their readers. Let's assume that these essays are deliberately difficult, that they are difficult for all readers, not just for college
   students, and that the difficulty is necessary and strategic, not just an
   error in judgment or evidence of a writer's failure to be clear.

   Go to each selection and, as you review it, look for sections or examples you could use to define the peculiar difficulties each presents its
   readers—or to you as its reader. Think about the different demands the
   two essays make. And think about how you would explain the experience
   of reading these to someone getting ready to work on them for the first

time. What demands do they make of a reader? How do they ask to be read? Why would anyone want to read (or to write) this way? What have you learned about reading by having worked on these texts?

Write an essay in which you use these two selections as examples of the kinds of reading demanded at the university. What makes this material hard to read? How might one value (rather than regret) the work of reading as it is defined in these cases? What advice would you give to students who follow you, who might also be asked to read these selections?

3. In "Panopticism," Michel Foucault presents a disciplinary society based on technologies of surveillance. The image (and history) of the Panopticon stands at the center of Foucault's argument; it signals what he refers to as an "inspired" change in disciplinary practices since it "automizes and disindividualizes power." He says, "Power has its principle not so much in a person as in a certain concerned distribution of bodies, surfaces, lights, gazes; in an arrangement whose internal mechanisms produce the relation in which individuals are caught. . . . Consequently, it does not matter who exercises power" (p. 232).

Walter Benjamin (p. 75) is thinking about a different (a more recent) point in time and different technologies, but he is thinking about power and control and the shaping of minds and lives. At the center of his argument is film: "Thus, for contemporary man the representation of reality by the film is incomparably more significant than that of the painter, since it offers, precisely because of the thoroughgoing permeation of reality with mechanical equipment, an aspect of reality which is free of all equipment" (pp. 91–92). Benjamin is also interested in how power is exerted by art, by images, and by technologies of reproduction over the "masses."

Write an essay in which you consider the different representations of and attitudes toward power in Foucault's "Panopticism" and Benjamin's "The Work of Art in the Age of Mechanical Reproduction."

PAULO
FREIRE

*P*AULO FREIRE *(pronounce it "Fr-air-ah" unless you can make a Portuguese "r") was one of the most influential radical educators of our world. A native of Recife, Brazil, he spent most of his early career working in poverty-stricken areas of his homeland, developing methods for teaching illiterate adults to read and write and (as he would say) to think critically and, thereby, to take power over their own lives. Because he has created a classroom where teachers and students have equal power and equal dignity, his work has stood as a model for educators around the world. It led also to sixteen years of exile after the military coup in Brazil in 1964. During that time he taught in Europe and in the United States and worked for the Allende government in Chile, training the teachers whose job it would be to bring modern agricultural methods to the peasants.*

Freire (1921–1997) worked with the adult education programs of UNESCO, the Chilean Institute of Agrarian Reform, and the World Council of Churches. He was professor of educational philosophy at the Catholic University of São Paulo. He is the author of Education for Critical Consciousness, The Politics of Education, The Pedagogy of the Oppressed, Revised Edition *(from which the following essay is drawn), and* Learning to Question: A Pedagogy of Liberation *(with Antonio Faundez).*

For Freire, education is not an objective process, if by objective we mean "neutral" or "without bias or prejudice." Because teachers could be said to have something that their students lack, it is impossible to have a "neutral" classroom; and when teachers present a subject to their students they also present a point of view on that subject. The choice, according to Freire, is fairly simple: teachers either work "for the liberation of the people—their humanization—or for their domestication, their domination." The practice of teaching, however, is anything but simple. According to Freire, a teacher's most crucial skill is his or her ability to assist students' struggle to gain control over the conditions of their lives, and this means helping them not only to know but "to know that they know."

Freire edited, along with Henry A. Giroux of Miami University in Ohio, a series of books on education and teaching. In Literacy: Reading the Word and the World, a book for the series, Freire describes the interrelationship between reading the written word and understanding the world that surrounds us.

> My parents introduced me to reading the word at a certain moment in this rich experience of understanding my immediate world. Deciphering the word flowed naturally from reading my particular world; it was not something superimposed on it. I learned to read and write on the grounds of the backyard of my house, in the shade of the mango trees, with words from my world rather than from the wider world of my parents. The earth was my blackboard, the sticks my chalk.

For Freire, reading the written word involves understanding a text in its very particular social and historical context. Thus reading always involves "critical perception, interpretation, and rewriting of what is read."

The "Banking" Concept of Education

A careful analysis of the teacher-student relationship at any level, inside or outside the school, reveals its fundamentally *narrative* character. This relationship involves a narrating Subject (the teacher) and patient, listening objects (the students). The contents, whether values or empirical dimensions of reality, tend in the process of being narrated to become lifeless and petrified. Education is suffering from narration sickness.

The teacher talks about reality as if it were motionless, static, compartmentalized, and predictable. Or else he expounds on a topic completely alien to the existential experience of the students. His task is to "fill" the students with the contents of his narration—contents which are detached from reality, disconnected from the totality that engendered them and could give them significance. Words are emptied of their concreteness and become a hollow, alienated, and alienating verbosity.

The outstanding characteristic of this narrative education, then, is the sonority of words, not their transforming power. "Four times four is sixteen; the capital of Pará is Belém." The student records, memorizes, and repeats these phrases without perceiving what four times four really means, or realizing the true significance of "capital" in the affirmation "the capital of Pará is Belém," that is, what Belém means for Pará and what Pará means for Brazil.

Narration (with the teacher as narrator) leads the students to memorize mechanically the narrated content. Worse yet, it turns them into "containers," into "receptacles" to be "filled" by the teacher. The more completely she fills the receptacles, the better a teacher she is. The more meekly the receptacles permit themselves to be filled, the better students they are.

Education thus becomes an act of depositing, in which the students are the depositories and the teacher is the depositor. Instead of communicating, the teacher issues communiqués and makes deposits which the students patiently receive, memorize, and repeat. This is the "banking" concept of education, in which the scope of action allowed to the students extends only as far as receiving, filing, and storing the deposits. They do, it is true, have the opportunity to become collectors or cataloguers of the things they store. But in the last analysis, it is the people themselves who are filed away through the lack of creativity, transformation, and knowledge in this (at best) misguided system. For apart from inquiry, apart from the praxis, individuals cannot be truly human. Knowledge emerges only through invention and re-invention, through the restless, impatient, continuing, hopeful inquiry human beings pursue in the world, with the world, and with each other.

In the banking concept of education, knowledge is a gift bestowed by those who consider themselves knowledgeable upon those whom they consider to know nothing. Projecting an absolute ignorance onto others, a characteristic of the ideology of oppression, negates education and knowledge as processes of inquiry. The teacher presents himself to his students as their necessary opposite; by considering their ignorance absolute, he justifies his own existence. The students, alienated like the slave in the Hegelian dialectic, accept their ignorance as justifying the teacher's existence—but, unlike the slave, they never discover that they educate the teacher.

The *raison d'être* of libertarian education, on the other hand, lies in its drive towards reconciliation. Education must begin with the solution of the teacher-student contradiction, by reconciling the poles of the contradiction so that both are simultaneously teachers *and* students.

This solution is not (nor can it be) found in the banking concept. On the contrary, banking education maintains and even stimulates the contradiction through the following attitudes and practices, which mirror oppressive society as a whole:

a. the teacher teaches and the students are taught;
b. the teacher knows everything and the students know nothing;

c. the teacher thinks and the students are thought about;

d. the teacher talks and the students listen—meekly;

e. the teacher disciplines and the students are disciplined;

f. the teacher chooses and enforces his choice, and the students comply;

g. the teacher acts and the students have the illusion of acting through the action of the teacher;

h. the teacher chooses the program content, and the students (who were not consulted) adapt to it;

i. the teacher confuses the authority of knowledge with his or her own professional authority, which she and he sets in opposition to the freedom of the students;

j. the teacher is the Subject of the learning process, while the pupils are mere objects.

It is not surprising that the banking concept of education regards men as adaptable, manageable beings. The more students work at storing the deposits entrusted to them, the less they develop the critical consciousness which would result from their intervention in the world as transformers of that world. The more completely they accept the passive role imposed on them, the more they tend simply to adapt to the world as it is and to the fragmented view of reality deposited in them.

The capability of banking education to minimize or annul the students' creative power and to stimulate their credulity serves the interests of the oppressors, who care neither to have the world revealed nor to see it transformed. The oppressors use their "humanitarianism" to preserve a profitable situation. Thus they react almost instinctively against any experiment in education which stimulates the critical faculties and is not content with a partial view of reality but always seeks out the ties which link one point to another and one problem to another.

Indeed, the interests of the oppressors lie in "changing the consciousness of the oppressed, not the situation which oppresses them";[1] for the more the oppressed can be led to adapt to that situation, the more easily they can be dominated. To achieve this end, the oppressors use the banking concept of education in conjunction with a paternalistic social action apparatus, within which the oppressed receive the euphemistic title of "welfare recipients." They are treated as individual cases, as marginal persons who deviate from the general configuration of a "good, organized, and just" society. The oppressed are regarded as the pathology of the healthy society, which must therefore adjust these "incompetent and lazy" folk to its own patterns by changing their mentality. These marginals need to be "integrated," "incorporated" into the healthy society that they have "forsaken."

The truth is, however, that the oppressed are not "marginals," are not people living "outside" society. They have always been "inside"—inside the structure which made them "beings for others." The solution is not to "integrate" them into the structure of oppression, but to transform that structure so that they can become "beings for themselves." Such transformation, of course, would undermine the oppressors' purposes; hence their utilization of the banking concept of education to avoid the threat of student *conscientização*.°

The banking approach to adult education, for example, will never propose to students that they critically consider reality. It will deal instead with such vital questions as whether Roger gave green grass to the goat, and insist upon the importance of learning that, on the contrary, Roger gave green grass to the *rabbit*. The "humanism" of the banking approach masks the effort to turn women and men into automatons—the very negation of their ontological vocation to be more fully human.

Those who use the banking approach, knowingly or unknowingly (for there are innumerable well-intentioned bank-clerk teachers who do not realize that they are serving only to dehumanize), fail to perceive that the deposits themselves contain contradictions about reality. But, sooner or later, these contradictions may lead formerly passive students to turn against their domestication and the attempt to domesticate reality. They may discover through existential experience that their present way of life is irreconcilable with their vocation to become fully human. They may perceive through their relations with reality that reality is really a *process,* undergoing constant transformation. If men and women are searchers and their ontological vocation is humanization, sooner or later they may perceive the contradiction in which banking education seeks to maintain them, and then engage themselves in the struggle for their liberation.

But the humanist, revolutionary educator cannot wait for this possibility to materialize. From the outset, her efforts must coincide with those of the students to engage in critical thinking and the quest for mutual humanization. His efforts must be imbued with a profound trust in people and their creative power. To achieve this, they must be partners of the students in their relations with them.

The banking concept does not admit to such partnership—and necessarily so. To resolve the teacher-student contradiction, to exchange the role of depositor, prescriber, domesticator, for the role of student among students would be to undermine the power of oppression and serve the cause of liberation.

Implicit in the banking concept is the assumption of a dichotomy between human beings and the world: a person is merely *in* the world, not *with* the world or with others; the individual is spectator, not re-creator. In this view, the person is not a conscious being (*corpo consciente*); he or she is rather the possessor of *a* consciousness: an empty "mind" passively open to the reception of deposits of reality from the world outside. For example,

---

conscientização According to Freire's translator, "The term *conscientização* refers to learning to perceive social, political, and economic contradictions, and to take action against the oppressive elements of reality."

my desk, my books, my coffee cup, all the objects before me—as bits of the world which surrounds me—would be "inside" me, exactly as I am inside my study right now. This view makes no distinction between being accessible to consciousness and entering consciousness. The distinction, however, is essential: the objects which surround me are simply accessible to my consciousness, not located within it. I am aware of them, but they are not inside me.

It follows logically from the banking notion of consciousness that the educator's role is to regulate the way the world "enters into" the students. The teacher's task is to organize a process which already occurs spontaneously, to "fill" the students by making deposits of information which he or she considers to constitute true knowledge.[2] And since people "receive" the world as passive entities, education should make them more passive still, and adapt them to the world. The educated individual is the adapted person, because she or he is better "fit" for the world. Translated into practice, this concept is well suited to the purposes of the oppressors, whose tranquility rests on how well people fit the world the oppressors have created, and how little they question it.

The more completely the majority adapt to the purposes which the dominant minority prescribe for them (thereby depriving them of the right to their own purposes), the more easily the minority can continue to prescribe. The theory and practice of banking education serve this end quite efficiently. Verbalistic lessons, reading requirements,[3] the methods for evaluating "knowledge," the distance between the teacher and the taught, the criteria for promotion: everything in this ready-to-wear approach serves to obviate thinking.

The bank-clerk educator does not realize that there is no true security in his hypertrophied role, that one must seek to live *with* others in solidarity. One cannot impose oneself, nor even merely co-exist with one's students. Solidarity requires true communication, and the concept by which such an educator is guided fears and proscribes communication.

Yet only through communication can human life hold meaning. The teacher's thinking is authenticated only by the authenticity of the students' thinking. The teacher cannot think for her students, nor can she impose her thought on them. Authentic thinking, thinking that is concerned about *reality*, does not take place in ivory tower isolation, but only in communication. If it is true that thought has meaning only when generated by action upon the world, the subordination of students to teachers becomes impossible.

Because banking education begins with a false understanding of men and women as objects, it cannot promote the development of what Fromm calls "biophily," but instead produces its opposite: "necrophily."

> While life is characterized by growth in a structured, functional manner, the necrophilous person loves all that does not grow, all that is mechanical. The necrophilous person is driven by the desire to transform the organic into the inorganic, to approach

life mechanically, as if all living persons were things. . . . Memory, rather than experience; having, rather than being, is what counts. The necrophilous person can relate to an object—a flower or a person—only if he possesses it; hence a threat to his possession is a threat to himself; if he loses possession he loses contact with the world. . . . He loves control, and in the act of controlling he kills life.[4]

Oppression—overwhelming control—is necrophilic; it is nourished by love of death, not life. The banking concept of education, which serves the interests of oppression, is also necrophilic. Based on a mechanistic, static, naturalistic, spatialized view of consciousness, it transforms students into receiving objects. It attempts to control thinking and action, leads women and men to adjust to the world, and inhibits their creative power.

When their efforts to act responsibly are frustrated, when they find themselves unable to use their faculties, people suffer. "This suffering due to impotence is rooted in the very fact that the human equilibrium has been disturbed."[5] But the inability to act which causes people's anguish also causes them to reject their impotence, by attempting

> . . . to restore [their] capacity to act. But can [they], and how? One way is to submit to and identify with a person or group having power. By this symbolic participation in another person's life, [men have] the illusion of acting, when in reality [they] only submit to and become part of those who act.[6]

Populist manifestations perhaps best exemplify this type of behavior by the oppressed, who, by identifying with charismatic leaders, come to feel that they themselves are active and effective. The rebellion they express as they emerge in the historical process is motivated by that desire to act effectively. The dominant elites consider the remedy to be more domination and repression, carried out in the name of freedom, order, and social peace (that is, the peace of the elites). Thus they can condemn—logically, from their point of view—"the violence of a strike by workers and [can] call upon the state in the same breath to use violence in putting down the strike."[7]

Education as the exercise of domination stimulates the credulity of students, with the ideological intent (often not perceived by educators) of indoctrinating them to adapt to the world of oppression. This accusation is not made in the naïve hope that the dominant elites will thereby simply abandon the practice. Its objective is to call the attention of true humanists to the fact that they cannot use banking educational methods in the pursuit of liberation, for they would only negate that very pursuit. Nor may a revolutionary society inherit these methods from an oppressor society. The revolutionary society which practices banking education is either misguided or mistrusting of people. In either event, it is threatened by the specter of reaction.

Unfortunately, those who espouse the cause of liberation are themselves surrounded and influenced by the climate which generates the banking concept, and often do not perceive its true significance or its dehumanizing power. Paradoxically, then, they utilize this same instrument of alienation in what they consider an effort to liberate. Indeed, some "revolutionaries" brand as "innocents," "dreamers," or even "reactionaries" those who would challenge this educational practice. But one does not liberate people by alienating them. Authentic liberation—the process of humanization—is not another deposit to be made in men. Liberation is a praxis: the action and reflection of men and women upon their world in order to transform it. Those truly committed to the cause of liberation can accept neither the mechanistic concept of consciousness as an empty vessel to be filled, nor the use of banking methods of domination (propaganda, slogans—deposits) in the name of liberation.

Those truly committed to liberation must reject the banking concept in its entirety, adopting instead a concept of women and men as conscious beings, and consciousness as consciousness intent upon the world. They must abandon the educational goal of deposit-making and replace it with the posing of the problems of human beings in their relations with the world. "Problem-posing" education, responding to the essence of consciousness—*intentionality*—rejects communiqués and embodies communications. It epitomizes the special characteristic of consciousness: being *conscious of*, not only as intent on objects but as turned in upon itself in a Jasperian "split"—consciousness as consciousness *of* consciousness.

Liberating education consists in acts of cognition, not transferrals of information. It is a learning situation in which the cognizable object (far from being the end of the cognitive act) intermediates the cognitive actors—teacher on the one hand and students on the other. Accordingly, the practice of problem-posing education entails at the outset that the teacher-student contradiction be resolved. Dialogical relations—indispensable to the capacity of cognitive actors to cooperate in perceiving the same cognizable object—are otherwise impossible.

Indeed, problem-posing education, which breaks with the vertical patterns characteristic of banking education, can fulfill its function as the practice of freedom only if it can overcome the above contradiction. Through dialogue, the teacher-of-the-students and the students-of-the-teacher cease to exist and a new term emerges: teacher-student with students-teachers. The teacher is no longer merely the-one-who-teaches, but one who is himself taught in dialogue with the students, who in turn while being taught also teach. They become jointly responsible for a process in which all grow. In this process, arguments based on "authority" are no longer valid; in order to function, authority must be *on the side of* freedom, not *against* it. Here, no one teaches another, nor is anyone self-taught. People teach each other, mediated by the world, by the cognizable objects which in banking education are "owned" by the teacher.

The banking concept (with its tendency to dichotomize everything) distinguishes two stages in the action of the educator. During the first, he cognizes a cognizable object while he prepares his lessons in his study or his laboratory; during the second, he expounds to his students about that object. The students are not called upon to know, but to memorize the contents narrated by the teacher. Nor do the students practice any act of cognition, since the object towards which that act should be directed is the property of the teacher rather than a medium evoking the critical reflection of both teacher and students. Hence in the name of the "preservation of culture and knowledge" we have a system which achieves neither true knowledge nor true culture.

The problem-posing method does not dichotomize the activity of the teacher-student: she is not "cognitive" at one point and "narrative" at another. She is always "cognitive," whether preparing a project or engaging in dialogue with the students. He does not regard cognizable objects as his private property, but as the object of reflection by himself and the students. In this way, the problem-posing educator constantly re-forms his reflections in the reflection of the students. The students—no longer docile listeners—are now critical co-investigators in dialogue with the teacher. The teacher presents the material to the students for their consideration, and re-considers her earlier considerations as the students express their own. The role of the problem-posing educator is to create, together with the students, the conditions under which knowledge at the level of the *doxa* is superseded by true knowledge, at the level of the *logos*.

Whereas banking education anesthetizes and inhibits creative power, problem-posing education involves a constant unveiling of reality. The former attempts to maintain the *submersion* of consciousness; the latter strives for the *emergence* of consciousness and *critical intervention* in reality.

Students, as they are increasingly posed with problems relating to themselves in the world and with the world, will feel increasingly challenged and obliged to respond to that challenge. Because they apprehend the challenge as interrelated to other problems within a total context, not as a theoretical question, the resulting comprehension tends to be increasingly critical and thus constantly less alienated. Their response to the challenge evokes new challenges, followed by new understandings; and gradually the students come to regard themselves as committed.

Education as the practice of freedom—as opposed to education as the practice of domination—denies that man is abstract, isolated, independent, and unattached to the world; it also denies that the world exists as a reality apart from people. Authentic reflection considers neither abstract man nor the world without people, but people in their relations with the world. In these relations consciousness and world are simultaneous: consciousness neither precedes the world nor follows it.

> La conscience et le monde sont dormés d'un même coup: extérieur par essence à la conscience, le monde est, par essence relatif à elle.[8]

In one of our culture circles in Chile, the group was discussing (based on a codification) the anthropological concept of culture. In the midst of the discussion, a peasant who by banking standards was completely ignorant said: "Now I see that without man there is no world." When the educator responded: "Let's say, for the sake of argument, that all the men on earth were to die, but that the earth itself remained, together with trees, birds, animals, rivers, seas, the stars . . . wouldn't all this be a world?" "Oh no," the peasant replied emphatically. "There would be no one to say: 'This is a world.'"

The peasant wished to express the idea that there would be lacking the consciousness of the world which necessarily implies the world of consciousness. *I* cannot exist without a *non-I*. In turn, the *not-I* depends on that existence. The world which brings consciousness into existence becomes the world *of* that consciousness. Hence, the previously cited affirmation of Sartre: "*La conscience et le monde sont dormés d'un même coup.*"

As women and men, simultaneously reflecting on themselves and on the world, increase the scope of their perception, they begin to direct their observations towards previously inconspicuous phenomena:

> In perception properly so-called, as an explicit awareness [*Gewahren*], I am turned towards the object, to the paper, for instance. I apprehend it as being this here and now. The apprehension is a singling out, every object having a background in experience. Around and about the paper lie books, pencils, inkwell, and so forth, and these in a certain sense are also "perceived," perceptually there, in the "field of intuition"; but whilst I was turned towards the paper there was no turning in their direction, nor any apprehending of them, not even in a secondary sense. They appeared and yet were not singled out, were not posited on their own account. Every perception of a thing has such a zone of background intuitions or background awareness, if "intuiting" already includes the state of being turned towards, and this also is a "conscious experience," or more briefly a "consciousness of" all indeed that in point of fact lies in the co-perceived objective background.[9]

That which had existed objectively but had not been perceived in its deeper implications (if indeed it was perceived at all) begins to "stand out," assuming the character of a problem and therefore of challenge. Thus, men and women begin to single out elements from their "background awarenesses" and to reflect upon them. These elements are now objects of their consideration, and, as such, objects of their action and cognition.

In problem-posing education, people develop their power to perceive critically *the way they exist* in the world *with which* and *in which* they find themselves; they come to see the world not as a static reality, but as a reality in process, in transformation. Although the dialectical relations of women and men with the world exist independently of how these relations are perceived (or whether or not they are perceived at all), it is also true that the form of action they adopt is to a large extent a function of how they perceive themselves in the world. Hence, the teacher-student and the students-teachers reflect simultaneously on themselves and the world without dichotomizing this reflection from action, and thus establish an authentic form of thought and action.

Once again, the two educational concepts and practices under analysis come into conflict. Banking education (for obvious reasons) attempts, by mythicizing reality, to conceal certain facts which explain the way human beings exist in the world; problem-posing education sets itself the task of demythologizing. Banking education resists dialogue; problem-posing education regards dialogue as indispensable to the act of cognition which unveils reality. Banking education treats students as objects of assistance; problem-posing education makes them critical thinkers. Banking education inhibits creativity and domesticates (although it cannot completely destroy) the *intentionality* of consciousness by isolating consciousness from the world, thereby denying people their ontological and historical vocation of becoming more fully human. Problem-posing education bases itself on creativity and stimulates true reflection and action upon reality; thereby responding to the vocation of persons as beings who are authentic only when engaged in inquiry and creative transformation. In sum: banking theory and practice, as immobilizing and fixating forces, fail to acknowledge men and women as historical beings; problem-posing theory and practice take the people's historicity as their starting point.

Problem-posing education affirms men and women as beings in the process of *becoming*—as unfinished, uncompleted beings in and with a likewise unfinished reality. Indeed, in contrast to other animals who are unfinished, but not historical, people know themselves to be unfinished; they are aware of their incompletion. In this incompletion and this awareness lie the very roots of education as an exclusively human manifestation. The unfinished character of human beings and the transformational character of reality necessitate that education be an ongoing activity.

Education is thus constantly remade in the praxis. In order to *be*, it must *become*. Its "duration" (in the Bergsonian meaning of the word) is found in the interplay of the opposites *permanence* and *change*. The banking method emphasizes permanence and becomes reactionary; problem-posing education—which accepts neither a "well-behaved" present nor a predetermined future—roots itself in the dynamic present and becomes revolutionary.

Problem-posing education is revolutionary futurity. Hence, it is prophetic (and, as such, hopeful). Hence, it corresponds to the historical nature of humankind. Hence, it affirms women and men as beings who transcend themselves, who move forward and look ahead, for whom immobility represents a fatal threat, for whom looking at the past must only be a means of understanding more clearly what and who they are so that they can more wisely build the future. Hence, it identifies with the movement which engages people as beings aware of their incompletion—an historical movement which has its point of departure, its Subjects and its objective.

The point of departure of the movement lies in the people themselves. But since people do not exist apart from the world, apart from reality, the movement must begin with the human-world relationship. Accordingly, the point of departure must always be with men and women in the "here and now," which constitutes the situation within which they are submerged, from which they emerge, and in which they intervene. Only by starting from this situation—which determines their perception of it—can they begin to move. To do this authentically they must perceive their state not as fated and unalterable, but merely as limiting—and therefore challenging.

Whereas the banking method directly or indirectly reinforces men's fatalistic perception of their situation, the problem-posing method presents this very situation to them as a problem. As the situation becomes the object of their cognition, the naïve or magical perception which produced their fatalism gives way to perception which is able to perceive itself even as it perceives reality, and can thus be critically objective about that reality.

A deepened consciousness of their situation leads people to apprehend that situation as an historical reality susceptible of transformation. Resignation gives way to the drive for transformation and inquiry, over which men feel themselves to be in control. If people, as historical beings necessarily engaged with other people in a movement of inquiry, did not control that movement, it would be (and is) a violation of their humanity. Any situation in which some individuals prevent others from engaging in the process of inquiry is one of violence. The means used are not important; to alienate human beings from their own decision-making is to change them into objects.

This movement of inquiry must be directed towards humanization— the people's historical vocation. The pursuit of full humanity, however, cannot be carried out in isolation or individualism, but only in fellowship and solidarity; therefore it cannot unfold in the antagonistic relations between oppressors and oppressed. No one can be authentically human while he prevents others from being so. Attempting *to be more* human, individualistically, leads to *having more*, egotistically, a form of dehumanization. Not that it is not fundamental *to have* in order *to be* human. Precisely because it *is* necessary, some men's *having* must not be allowed to constitute an obstacle to others' *having*, must not consolidate the power of the former to crush the latter.

Problem-posing education, as a humanist and liberating praxis, posits as fundamental that the people subjected to domination must fight for their emancipation. To that end, it enables teachers and students to become Subjects of the educational process by overcoming authoritarianism and an alienating intellectualism; it also enables people to overcome their false perception of reality. The world—no longer something to be described with deceptive words—becomes the object of that transforming action by men and women which results in their humanization.

Problem-posing education does not and cannot serve the interests of the oppressor. No oppressive order could permit the oppressed to begin to question: Why? While only a revolutionary society can carry out this education in systematic terms, the revolutionary leaders need not take full power before they can employ the method. In the revolutionary process, the leaders cannot utilize the banking method as an interim measure, justi-fied on grounds of expediency, with the intention of *later* behaving in a genuinely revolutionary fashion. They must be revolutionary—that is to say, dialogical—from the outset.

NOTES

[1] Simone de Beauvoir, *La pensée de droite, aujourd'hui* (Paris); ST, *El pensamiento político de la derecha* (Buenos Aires, 1963), p. 34.

[2] This concept corresponds to what Sartre calls the "digestive" or "nutritive" con-cept of education, in which knowledge is "fed" by the teacher to the students to "fill them out." See Jean-Paul Sartre, "Une idée fundamentale de la phénomenologie de Husserl: L'intentionalité," *Situations* I (Paris, 1947).

[3] For example, some professors specify in their reading lists that a book should be read from pages 10 to 15—and do this to "help" their students!

[4] Eric Fromm, *The Heart of Man* (New York, 1966), p. 41.

[5] Ibid., p. 31.

[6] Ibid.

[7] Reinhold Niebuhr, *Moral Man and Immoral Society* (New York, 1960), p. 130.

[8] Sartre, op. cit., p. 32. [The passage is obscure but could be read as "Consciousness and the world are given at one and the same time: the exterior world as it enters con-sciousness is relative to our ways of seeing and understanding that world."—Editors' note]

[9] Edmund Husserl, *Ideas—General Introduction to Pure Phenomenology* (London, 1969), pp. 105–06.

• • • • • • • • • • • •

QUESTIONS FOR A SECOND READING

1. While Freire speaks powerfully about the politics of the classroom, he provides few examples of actual classroom situations. As you go back through the essay, try to ground (or to test) what he says with examples of your own. What would take place in a "problem-posing" class in English, history, psychology, or math? What is an "authentic form of thought and action"? How might you describe what Freire refers to as "reflection"? What, really, might teachers be expected to learn from their students? What example can you give of a time when you were "conscious of conscious-ness" and it made a difference to you with your schoolwork?

   You might also look for moments when Freire does provide examples of his own. On pages 262–63, for example, Freire makes the distinction between a student's role as a "spectator" and as "re-creator" by referring to his own relationship to the objects on his desk. How might you explain this distinction? Or, how might you use the example of his books and coffee cup to explain the distinction he makes between "being accessible to consciousness" and "entering consciousness"?

2. Freire uses two terms drawn from Marxist literature: *praxis* and *alienation*. From the way these words are used in the essay, how would you define them? And how might they be applied to the study of education?

3. A writer can be thought of as a teacher and a reader as a student. If you think of Freire as your teacher in this essay, does he enact his own principles? Does he speak to you as though he were making deposits in a bank? Or is there a way in which the essay allows for dialogue? Look for sections in the essay you could use to talk about the role Freire casts you in as a reader.

ASSIGNMENTS FOR WRITING

1. Surely all of us, anyone who has made it through twelve years of formal education, can think of a class, or an occasion outside of class, to serve as a quick example of what Freire calls the "banking" concept of education, where students were turned into "containers" to be "filled" by their teachers. If Freire is to be useful to you, however, he must do more than enable you to call up quick examples. He should allow you to say more than that a teacher once treated you like a container or that a teacher once gave you your freedom.

   Write an essay that focuses on a rich and illustrative incident from your own educational experience and read it (that is, interpret it) as Freire would. You will need to provide careful detail: things that were said and done, perhaps the exact wording of an assignment, a textbook, or a teacher's comments. And you will need to turn to the language of Freire's argument, to take key phrases and passages and see how they might be used to investigate your case.

   To do this you will need to read your account as not simply the story of you and your teacher, since Freire is not writing about individual personalities (an innocent student and a mean teacher, a rude teacher, or a thoughtless teacher) but about the roles we are cast in, whether we choose to be or not, by our culture and its institutions. The key question, then, is not who you were or who your teacher was but what roles you played and how those roles can lead you to better understand the larger narrative or drama of Education (an organized attempt to "regulate the way the world 'enters into' the students," p. 263).

   Freire would not want you to work passively or mechanically, however, as though you were following orders. He would want you to make your own mark on the work he has begun. Use your example, in other words, as a way of testing and examining what Freire says, *particularly those passages that you find difficult or obscure.*

2. Problem-posing education, according to Freire, "sets itself the task of demythologizing"; it "stimulates true reflection and action"; it allows students to be "engaged in inquiry and creative transformation." These are grand and powerful phrases, and it is interesting to consider what they might mean if applied to the work of a course in reading and writing.

If the object for study were Freire's essay, "The 'Banking' Concept of Education," what would Freire (or a teacher determined to adapt his practices) ask students to *do* with the essay? What writing assignment might he set for his students? Prepare that assignment, or a set of questions or guidelines or instructions (or whatever) that Freire might prepare for his class.

Once you've prepared the writing assignment, write the essay that you think would best fulfill it. And, once you've completed the essay, go on, finally, to write the teacher's comments on it—to write what you think Freire, or a teacher following his example, might write on a piece of student work.

MAKING CONNECTIONS

1. Freire says,

> Students, as they are increasingly posed with problems relating to themselves in the world and with the world, will feel increasingly challenged and obliged to respond to that challenge. Because they apprehend the challenge as interrelated to other problems within a total context, not as a theoretical question, the resulting comprehension tends to be increasingly critical and thus constantly less alienated. (p. 266)

Students learn to respond, Freire says, through dialogue with their teachers. Freire could be said to serve as your first teacher here. He has raised the issue for you and given you some language you can use to frame questions and to imagine the possibilities of response.

Using one of the essays in this book as a starting point, pose a problem that challenges you and makes you feel obliged to respond, a problem that, in Freire's terms, relates to you "in the world and with the world." This is a chance for you, in other words, to pose a Freirian question and then to write a Freirian essay, all as an exercise in the practice of freedom.

When you are done, you might reread what you have written to see how it resembles or differs from what you are used to writing. What are the indications that you are working with greater freedom? If you find evidence of alienation or "domination," to what would you attribute it and what, then, might you do to overcome it?

2. Freire writes about the distribution of power and authority in the classroom and argues that education too often alienates individuals from their own historical situation. Richard Rodriguez, in "The Achievement of Desire" (p. 652), writes about his education as a process of difficult but necessary alienation from his home, his childhood, and his family. And he

writes about power—about the power that he gained and lost as he became increasingly successful as a student.

But Freire and Rodriguez write about education as a central event in the shaping of an adult life. It is interesting to imagine what they might have to say to each other. Write a dialogue between the two in which they discuss what Rodriguez has written in "The Achievement of Desire." What would they say to each other? What questions would they ask? How would they respond to each other in the give-and-take of conversation?

Note: This should be a dialogue, not a debate. Your speakers are trying to learn something about each other and about education. They are not trying to win points or convince a jury.

SIMON
FRITH

*S*IMON FRITH *(b. 1946) is a professor of English at the University of Strath-clyde, Scotland. Frith was trained as a sociologist at Oxford and Berkeley. He has written a remarkable series of books on rock music and the study of contempo-rary popular culture:* Sociology of Rock *(1981),* Sound Effects *(1981),* Art into Pop *(with Howard Thorne, 1987),* Music for Pleasure *(1988),* Literary Studies as Cultural Studies: Whose Literature? Whose Culture? *(1991),* The Cambridge Companion to Pop and Rock *(edited with Will Straw and John Street, 2001), and* Performing Rites: On the Value of Popular Music *(1996), from which this selection is taken. He has written regular music reviews for the* Sunday Times of London *and* The Village Voice. *His has managed a se-rious career as a scholar without ever losing his passion as a fan, a collector, a pro-moter, and a consumer.*

*As the subtitle—*On the Value of Popular Music—*indicates, Frith's pri-mary concern is to make a case for the value of popular music. He knows, how-ever, that this requires more than just listing his favorite songs and singers; it re-quires him to bring popular music into the traditions of discussion about value and art. It is his goal to do this with a difference. It is already the case, he says, that discussions of popular culture can be found in the university and the univer-sity curriculum. English departments, among others, have been teaching film, television, advertising, and other forms of popular culture, including pop music,* *for decades. Frith argues that culture as an academic subject is different from "culture as a popular activity, a process, and the value terms which inform the latter are, it seems, irrelevant to the analysis of the former." He says,*

> *In universities . . . just as in high schools . . . there is still a split between . . . the discourse of the classroom (with its focus on a subject matter) and the discourse of the hallway (with its focus on oneself and one's opinions about a subject matter and one's opinions about other people's opinions about a subject matter and one's opinions about other people).*

The talk in the hallways is important; you can't study popular music without being engaged with its shifting energies and affiliations. Popular culture, Frith argues, is one of the ways we locate ourselves as part of the present and locate ourselves in relation to others. ("Who are you listening to? What do you like?") Think about how important it is for individuals or groups to identify with particular songs or artists; think of the role argument plays (arguments about teams, shows, or songs) in developing and knowing friends, in defining one's group, in remembering who we were last year and knowing where we are this year.

Performing Rites, *then, is an exercise in learning to talk about music in order to talk better, in a more informed way, about value, and to do so in order to think about music, about what makes it good and what it might be good for. Here, again, is Frith:*

> *To deny the significance of value judgments in popular culture (to ignore popular taste hierarchies) is . . . hypocritical. How often, I wonder, do popular cultural theorists celebrate popular cultural forms which they themselves soon find boring? How are their own feelings for the good and the bad coded into their own analyses? If, in my own cultural practice, I prefer Dickens to Barbara Cartland, Meat Loaf to U2, shouldn't I be prepared to argue the case for my values? Shouldn't I want other people to read Dickens rather than Cartland, to listen to Meat Loaf rather than U2? Shouldn't I be able to persuade them with classroom as well as hallway arguments? The problem is, precisely, how to do this. . . .*

And the book begins with two assumptions: "The first is that the essence of popular cultural practice is making judgments and assessing differences." The second is that "there is no reason to believe a priori that such judgments work differently in different cultural spheres. There are obvious differences between operas and soap operas, between classical and country music, but the fact that the objects of judgment are different doesn't mean that the processes of judgment are."

The second section of the book, from which "The Voice" is drawn, is about how a listener (an individual—the Audience) participates in the production of music. When we listen, he argues, we are not just listening to a performance; listening itself is a performance: "to understand how musical pleasure, meaning, and evaluation work, we have to understand how, as listeners, we perform the music for ourselves." Or, as he puts it elsewhere:

For sounds to be music we need to know how to hear them; we need "knowledge not just of musical forms but also of rules of behaviour in musical settings." The "meaning" of music describes, in short, not just an interpretive but a social process: musical meaning is not inherent . . . in the text.

"The Voice" articulates one area of the experience of listening, the experience of voice. It is remarkable for its range of reference (it seems as though Frith has listened to everything and remembered everything he's heard), and it is remarkable for its scholarship (he is engaged with the most serious and complicated issues in cultural studies); it is also a wonderful piece of writing—witty, smart, and surprising. Like all great works of criticism, it enacts as well as argues for its method.

The chapter preceding "The Voice" is titled "Songs as Texts." In that chapter, Frith presents his plan:

Most contemporary popular music takes the form of song (even acid house), and most people if asked what a song "means" refer to the words. In examining what the words do mean we can follow two obvious strategies, treating songs either as poems, literary objects which can be analyzed entirely separately from music, or as speech acts, words to be analyzed in performance. But in listening to the lyrics of pop songs we actually hear three things at once: words, which appear to give songs an independent source of semantic meaning; rhetoric, words being used in a special, musical way, a way which draws attention to features and problems of speech; and voices, words being spoken or sung in human tones which are themselves "meaningful," signs of persons and personality.

The following selection examines the ways we hear "voice." Because it is a chapter from a book, it moves toward a larger conclusion that will come later. We will provide a glimpse of that conclusion in the assignments that follow this selection. For now, you should read the chapter as self-contained, as an essay. It asks a fundamental question, "What is voice?" As you read the answer, you are invited into the practice of a remarkable listener.

The Voice

Let us imagine for this double function, localized in one and the same site, a single transgression, which would be generated by a simultaneous use of speech and kissing: *to kiss while embracing, to embrace while speaking*. It would appear that such a pleasure exists, since lovers incessantly "drink in speech upon the lips of the beloved," etc. What they delight in is, in the

erotic encounter, the play of meaning which opens and breaks off: the function *which is disturbed:* in a word: *the stammered body.*
— ROLAND BARTHES[1]

We came to listen to that voice of difference likely to bring us *what we can't have* and to divert us from the monotony of sameness.
— TRINH T. MINH-HA[2]

"Yeah," Scott said, "a singer like Ella says, 'My man's left me,' and you think the guy went down the street for a loaf of bread or something. But when Lady says, 'My man's gone' or 'My man's left me,' man, you can see the guy going down the street. His bags are packed, and he ain't never coming back. I mean like *never.*"
— TONY SCOTT on Billie Holiday[3]

Look at a song's lyrics on the page: whose "voice" is there? Who's talking? The answer seems to start with the pronouns, the "shifters," not just the "I," the apparent speaker, but the "you" and "we" and "she" which reveal various things about the speaker. Even without an explicit "I," that is, we have an implicit one, someone who's doing the addressing: "*you've* got a lot of nerve, to say that *you're* my friend." The "voice" in the printed lyrics is thus articulated by the text itself, by a process that is both self-expressive and self-revealing, both declared openly and implied by the narrative.[4]

But even from the reader's point of view there's more to the voice than this. The printed lyric is already a double act, both the communicative process it describes or enacts—the "I" of the lyric speaking to the "you" of the lyric—and the communicative process it entails, writing and reading. As readers do we necessarily become the "you" of the writer's "I"? Do we take onto ourselves her love or contempt? Do we have to take a place in her story? The answer is obviously no; or, at least, there are certainly other options. We can refuse to become involved at all, read the lyric as an overhead conversation between other people, take it to be reported speech, put quotation marks around it. Or we can read it as if speaking it, become the "I" ourselves. (I think it would be impossible to read Bob Dylan's "Positively 4th Street" as if we were the "you" at issue—and this is a song positively *obsessed* with the word. The pleasure of these lines is as a means of sounding our *own* feelings of contempt and hauteur.)

How we read lyrics is not a completely random or idiosyncratic choice. The lyricist sets up the situation—through her use of language, her construction of character—in a way that, in part, determines the response we make, the nature of our engagement. But once we say that, we admit that there's another "voice" here, the voice of the lyricist, the author, the person putting the words in the "I's" mouth, putting the protagonists into their lyrical situation. And the authorial voice can be more or less distinctive; we may recognize—respond to—that voice (Cole Porter, Elvis

Costello, Morrissey, P. J. Harvey) even when reading a lyric. "Voice" in this sense describes a sense of personality that doesn't involve shifters at all, but is familiar as the special way a person has with words: we immediately know who's speaking.

Now stop reading the lyrics, and listen to the song. Whose voice do we hear now? Again there's an obvious answer: the singer's, stupid! And what I argue in the rest of this chapter is that this is, in fact, the stupid answer. We hear the singer's voice, of course, but how that voice relates to the voices described above is the interesting question. To sing a lyric doesn't simplify the question of who is speaking to whom; it makes it more complicated.

In *The Composer's Voice*, Edward Cone asks whose voice we hear when we listen to a Schubert setting of a poem by Goethe. We hear a singer, Thomas Allen say, with a distinctive physical voice; we hear the protagonist of the song, the "I" of the narrative; we hear the poem's author, Goethe, in the distinctive organization of the words and their argument; and we hear Schubert, *in whose voice* the whole thing is composed.[5] And this last definition of voice, as the stylistic identity of the composer, is undoubtedly the dominant definition of "voice" in classical music criticism: a Schubert song is a Schubert song, regardless of whose words he has set to music and which singer is singing them. Schubert's "voice" thus refers to a personal quality—a quality of his personality—apparent in all his musical work.[6]

Even in this phrasing, though, a new question is raised. What is the relationship between Schubert's characteristics *as a composer* (his distinctive use of musical language which can be traced across different works, enabling us to speak of his musical "identity" and "development") and his characteristics *as a person?* This is, of course, to raise the long-debated question (long debated in literary criticism, at any rate) of the relationship between someone's life and their work. This issue tends to be put aside in music criticism because of the belief that music is a more directly emotional form of expression than literature, and is therefore more directly (or unconsciously) revealing of the composer's character. One of Anthony Storr's casual comments can thus be taken as typical: "The listener doesn't even have to be able to read music to recognize Haydn's robustness and humour, combined with his capacity for deep feeling."[7] Is music really so transparently expressive of personality? Is a voice?

The same questions can be addressed to popular music. What is the relationship between the "voice" we hear in a song and the author or composer of that song? Between the voice and the singer? This relationship has, of course, different complications in different genres, but two general issues arise immediately. First there is, as in classical music, the problem of biography: what is the relationship of life and art? On the whole, pop fans are less simple-minded than classical music critics about this. While one can certainly find Hollywood biopix of pop stars (Oliver Stone's *The Doors*, say) to match its biopix of classical composers—the life pouring out in the sounds—this tells us more about Hollywood (and the attempt to turn Jim Morrison into a Real Artist) than it does about pop music.

The up-front star system means that pop fans are well aware of the ways in which pop performers are inventions (and the pop biographer's task is usually therefore to expose the "real" Bob Dylan or Madonna who *isn't* in their music). And in pop, biography is used less to explain composition (the writing of the song) than expression (its performance): it is in real, material, singing voices that the "real" person is to be heard, not in scored stylistic or formulaic devices. The pop musician as interpreter (Billie Holiday, say) is therefore more likely to be understood in biographical terms than the pop musician as composer (Mark Knopfler, say), and when musicians are both, it is the performing rather than the composing voice that is taken to be the key to character. As Robert O'Meally asks about Billie Holiday, "She was the greatest jazz singer of all time. With Louis Armstrong, she invented modern jazz singing. Why do these accounts [all the books about her], which tell us so much about her drug problems, no-good men, and supposedly autobiographical sad songs, tell us so little about Billie Holiday, artist?"[8]

And the answer is because as listeners we assume that we can hear someone's life in their voice—a life that's there despite and not because of the singer's craft, a voice that says who they really are, an art that only exists because of what they've suffered. What makes Billie Holiday an artist from this perspective is that she was able to give *that which she couldn't help expressing* aesthetic shape and grace.[9] Compare Gregory Sandow on Frank Sinatra:

> Even before Kitty Kelley's unauthorized biography it was hardly a secret . . . that Sinatra hasn't always been the nicest of guys. So it's a commonplace of Sinatra criticism to separate Sinatra the artist from Sinatra the man. But I've always thought that his character slips through in his performance . . . And in fact it slips through precisely because of his art. Because he *is* an artist, he can't help telling a kind of truth; he can't help reaching towards the root of everything he's felt. He makes his living singing love songs; like any great popular singer, he can expand even a single sigh in those love songs into something vast. But he's also got his own story to tell, a story that goes far beyond what any love song could express: it's a story a little bit about triumph, partly about a lust for power, often about loss, and very much about humiliation and rage.[10]

The first general point to make about the pop voice, then, is that we hear singers as *personally* expressive (even, perhaps especially, when they are not singing "their own" songs) in a way that a classical singer, even a dramatic and "tragic" star like Maria Callas, is not. This is partly a matter of sound convention. As Libby Holman once put it, "My singing is like Flamenco. Sometimes, it's purposefully hideous. I try to convey anguish, anger, tragedy, passion. When you're expressing emotions like these, you cannot have a pure tone."[11]

In classical music, by contrast, the sound of the voice is determined by the score; the expression of anguish, anger, tragedy, and passion is a matter of musical organization. As Umberto Fiore writes, "In this context, the voice is in fact an instrument: bass, baritone, tenor, soprano and so forth. Individual styles can only *improve* these vocal masks, not really transgress them . . . the creation of a person, of a character, is substantially up to the music as such; if truth is there it is a *musical* truth."[12]

But if we hear the pop singer singing "her self," she is also singing a song, and so a second question arises: what is the relationship between the voice as a carrier of sounds, the singing voice, making "gestures," and the voice as a carrier of words, the speaking voice, making "utterances"? The issue is not meaning (words) versus absence of meaning (music), but the relationship between two different sorts of meaning-making, the tensions and conflicts between them. There's a question here of power: who is to be the master, words or music? And what makes the voice so interesting is that it makes meaning in these two ways simultaneously. We have, therefore, to approach the voice under four headings: as a *musical instrument*; as a *body*; as a *person*; and as a *character*.

I'll begin with the voice as a musical instrument. A voice obviously has a sound; it can be described in musical terms like any other instrument, as something with a certain pitch, a certain register, a certain timbral quality, and so forth. Voices can be used, like any other instrument, to make a noise of the right sort at the right time. Both these terms (right sort, right time) are apparent in the most instrumental use of the voice, as "backup." Here the singers' sound is more important than their words, which are either nonsensical or become so through repetition; and repetition is itself the key to how such voices work, as percussive instruments, marking out the regular time around which the lead singer can be quite irregular in matters of pitch and timing, quite inarticulate in terms of words or utterances.[13]

Even in this case, though, the voices can't be purely sound effects; at the very least they also indicate gender, and therefore gender relations (the aggressive-submissive attitude of the Raelettes to Ray Charles; the butch male choral support for Neil Tennant on the Pet Shop Boys' "Go West"), and it is notable that while rock conventionally uses other male voices, other members of the band, to sing close harmonies, backup singers are almost always female—and remarkably often black female at that.[14] This raises questions about the voice as body to which I'll return; but in talking about the voice as musical instrument I'm not just talking about sound, I'm also talking about skill and technique: neither backup nor lead singers simply stand on stage or in the studio and open their mouths. For the last sixty years or so, popular singers have had a musical instrument besides their voices: the electric microphone. The microphone made it possible for singers to make musical sounds—soft sounds, close sounds—that had not really been heard before in terms of public performance (just as the film closeup allowed one to see the bodies and faces of strangers in ways one would normally only see loved ones). The microphone allowed us to hear people in ways that normally implied intimacy—the whisper, the caress, the murmur. O'Meally notes the importance of the mike for the development of Billie Holiday's singing style, "as she moved from table to table in speakeasies . . . Whether in clubs or on recording dates, she continued to deliver her lyrics as if only for one or two listeners whom she addressed face to face."[15]

The appearance of the female torch singer and the male crooner had a number of consequences both for musical sexuality (crooners were initially heard as "effeminate" and unmanly, for example; the BBC even banned them for a time) and for what one might call musical seduction (radio advertisers took immediate note of "the performer's capacity to make each member of the audience perceive the song as an intimate, individual communication," and Rudy Vallee quickly became "one of the biggest radio and advertising successes").[16] As Bing Crosby, probably the greatest musical entrepreneur of the twentieth century (or at least the one with the best understanding of the implications of technology) realized, crooning made a singer the perfect salesman of his own song.[17]

This wasn't a matter of singers just going up to a microphone and opening their mouths, either. Mike technique had to be learned. Take the case of Frank Sinatra:

> As a young singer, he consciously perfected his handling of the microphone. "Many singers never learned to use one," he wrote later. "They never understood, and still don't, that a microphone is their instrument." A microphone must be deployed sparingly, he said, with the singer moving in and out of range of the mouth and suppressing excessive sibilants and noisy intakes of air. But Sinatra's understanding of the microphone went deeper than this merely mechanical level. He knew better than almost anyone else just what Henry Pleasants has maintained: that the microphone changes the very way that modern singers sing. It was his mastery of this instrument, the way he let its existence help shape his vocal production and singing style, that did much to make Sinatra the preeminent popular singer of our time.[18]

One effect of microphone use is to draw attention to the technique of singers *as singers* in ways that are not, I think, so obvious in classical music or opera, as they move with and around the instrument, as volume control takes on conversational nuances and vice versa.[19] Another is to draw attention to the *place* of the voice in music, to the arrangement of sounds behind and around it, as the microphone allows the voice to dominate other instruments whatever else is going on.[20] Consider these three descriptions of the popular musical voice.

Gregory Sandow on Alex Stordahl's arrangements for Frank Sinatra:

> I didn't know if I'd ever heard music at once so rapt and so shy.
> I searched for images. Could the arrangements be like waiters
> in a restaurant? They took on shape only when they emerged
> briefly into view to fill pauses in Sinatra's phrasing; they might
> have been clearing plates away, making room on the table for
> the next course to be served. Or better still, were they like a
> wife? That made sense. Stordahl's arrangements, I decided,
> were like an adoring wife who says nothing in public but
> works patiently at home, cooking, mending, tending a spotless
> refuge for her man . . . but it might be more accurate to say that
> they're like a perfect dance partner, or, better still, like a woman
> lost in a dream because she's dancing with a perfect man.
>   Violins introduce "Embraceable You," and I hear her open
> her arms to surrender. "Embrace me," he sings; she lets him
> guide her, and, after an all but imperceptible breath, nestles
> more closely in his embrace. Now he sings ". . . my sweet em-
> braceable you," and in response she whispers, almost to her-
> self, "Oh YES, Frank." "Embrace me," he goes on, and she an-
> ticipates his step, moving with him almost before he knows
> where he himself will go. Then she hears him pause for an in-
> stant as he sings "my silk . . . and laceable you"; she waits, sus-
> pended, secure that when he resumes he'll know exactly what
> to do. "I'm in love with you, I am," he croons, and when from
> far in the distance she hears him add "and verily so," she closes
> her eyes and dances almost in place, hardly moving in his
> arms.[21]

Aidan Day on Bob Dylan:

> Typically, the voice engages the line of the melody but its si-
> multaneous jarring, atonal separation from the music, together
> with the relentless subordination of musical elements to the ex-
> igencies of verbal order, opens a space which registers a dis-
> tance and unease involving both singer and listener. The
> singing voice at once solicits and rebuffs. The gratifications it
> offers are uncomfortable ones. It is a pattern of invitation and
> rejection in which the audience—alienated from easy absorp-
> tion into the music and denied relaxation—is required to attend
> closely to the transactions between voice and words. While the
> voice impinges distinctively on the listener, it simultaneously
> seeks to refuse an unthinking capitulation to itself and to the
> sense of what it is singing. It is a pattern which places special
> demands upon an audience, expecting it to participate ac-
> tively—and to risk itself—in the play of meaning.[22]

And Glenn Gould on Barbra Streisand:

> With Streisand . . . one becomes engaged by process, by a seem-
> ingly limitless array of available options . . . . Like [Elizabeth]
> Schwarzkopf, Streisand is one of the great italicizers; no phrase

is left solely to its own devices, and the range and diversity of her expressive gift is such that one is simply unable to chart an a priori stylistic course on her behalf. Much of the *Affekt* of intimacy—indeed, the sensation of eavesdropping on a private moment not yet wholly committed to its eventual public profile—is a direct result of our inability to anticipate her intentions.[23]

Although the voices described here are only ever heard, only exist, as musical instruments, as sounds in arrangements of sounds, each of these writers treats the voice as something which *has a relationship*—with an orchestra for Sinatra, with an audience for Dylan, with the music itself, the melody, for Streisand; the voice, that is to say, is described as if it existed—could be heard—apart from the sounds that it does make, apart from what we do hear. The implication is that all singers thus put "their own shape" on the music, and it is the meaning of "their own" that interests me.

What these critics hear, to put this more plainly, is a *willed sound,* a sound that is this way because it has been chosen so, could have been something else. As Edward Cone suggests, a voice can never really be heard as a wordless instrument; even when we listen to a singer in a language we do not understand, a singer making wordless sounds, scat singing, we still hear those sounds as words we do not understand, or as sounds made by someone who has *chosen* to be inarticulate.[24] "She accompanied herself on the piano," we observe; not "she accompanied herself on vocals." And the matching term, *unaccompanied,* which used to appear on popular concert bills, raises a broader question still: when singing, do you accompany the music, or does the music accompany you?

This helps explain, I think, the special status of the voice as a concept in both musical and literary analysis. On the one hand, a musician's "voice" need not be restricted to the voice in a physical sense: when jazz performers are said to "speak" with their instruments, it is this same quality of willed sound which is being described—which is why it is trickier to claim that classical musicians, constrained in some respects by the score, have individual "voices" (rather than styles): even Glenn Gould didn't really "speak" on his piano (even if he sang along with it). On the other hand, to hear or read a "voice" in a text is to assign *intention* to what we hear or read. "Authorless" texts are those—like newspaper headlines or advertising jingles—which however carefully crafted don't bear this imprint of individual articulation.

Even when treating the voice as an instrument, in short, we come up against the fact that it stands for the person more directly than any other musical device. Expression with the voice is taken to be more direct than expression on guitar or drum set, more revealing—which is why when drums and guitars are heard as directly expressive they are then heard as "voices." And this argument has legal sanction. Lawyers in cases of musical theft assume that a voice is a personal property, that it can be "stolen" in a way that other instrumental noises cannot (James Brown's vocal swoop is recognizably his immediately; a guitarist has to prove that a melodic riff, a composition rather than a sound, is unique). The most interesting legal rulings in this context concern soundalikes, cases in which the voices used ("Bette Midler," "Tom Waits") *weren't* actually theirs, and yet because they were recognizably "the same" could nevertheless be adjudged to invade the stars' "privacy," to steal their "personality." To recognize a voice, the courts ruled, is to recognize a person.[25]

Consider now the next element of this process, *the voice as body.* The starting point here is straightforward. The voice is a sound produced physically, by the movement of muscles and breath in the chest and throat and mouth; to listen to a voice is to listen to a physical event, to the sound of a body. This is, of course, true for the sound of other instruments too, but whereas what's involved there is the relationship between the body and something else—a string or reed or piano key or drum set—the voice draws our attention to something happening to the body itself; which is why we don't think of the microphone as a musical instrument: we don't expect voices to need anything outside the body in order to be heard. And this is clearly one reason why the voice seems particularly expressive of the body; it gives the listener access to it without mediation.

The effects of "the body in the singing voice" have been explored most famously by Roland Barthes, in his essay on the "grain" of the voice, where he argues that different timbral qualities have differential bodily implications. This point is usually taken up in rock criticism as a celebration of "the materiality of the body speaking its mother tongue," in terms of the "voluptuous pleasure of its signifier-sounds," but it is just as important to take note of the other side of Barthes's argument, his suggestion that there is such a thing as an "ungrained" voice, a voice that conceals its own means of physical production. This might, for example, be one way of describing those backup singers, further drawing attention to their peculiarity: here we have three smart, fleshly women, singing "grainlessly," while a physically awkward male star waxes *bodily.*[26]

In fact, though, there are further distinctions to be made here. We certainly do hear voices as physically produced: we assign them qualities of throatiness or nasality, and, more specifically, we listen by performing, by reproducing (even if only silently, tentatively) those muscular movements for ourselves, "sympathizing" with a singer by pushing the words up against the top of our mouths when she does. A "grained" voice might, then, simply describe a voice with which, for whatever reasons, we have physical sympathy: "I am sitting in the Met at Leontyne Price's recital in 1985 and Price's vibrations are *inside my body,* dressing it up with the accouterments of interiority."[27]

The voice as direct expression of the body, that is to say, is as important for the way we listen as for the way we interpret what we hear; we can sing along, reconstruct in fantasy our own sung versions of songs, in ways we can't even fantasize instrumental technique—however hard we may try with our air guitars—because with singing, *we feel we know what to do.*

We have bodies too, throats and stomachs and lungs. And even if we can't get the breathing right, the pitch, the note durations (which is why our performances only sound good to us), we still feel we understand what the singer is doing in physical principle (this is another reason why the voice seems so directly expressive an instrument: it doesn't take thought to know how that vocal noise was made).

This relates to a second point, that the voice *is* the sound of the body in a direct sense. Certain physical experiences, particularly extreme feelings, are given vocal sounds beyond our conscious control—the sounds of pain, lust, ecstasy, fear, what one might call inarticulate articulacy: the sounds, for example, of tears and laughter; the sounds made by soul singers around and between their notes, vocal noises that seem expressive of their deepest feelings because we hear them as if they've escaped from a body that the mind—language—can no longer control.[28]

Jonathan Swift put his own sardonic gloss on this three hundred years ago:

> Now the art of canting consists in skillfully adapting the voice to whatever words the spirit delivers, that each may strike the ears of the audience with its most significant cadence. The force or energy of this eloquence is not to be found, as among ancient orators, in the disposition of words to a sentence, or the turning of long periods; but, agreeably to the modern refinements in music, is taken up wholly in dwelling and dilating upon syllables and letters. Thus, it is frequent for a single vowel to draw sighs from a multitude, and for a whole assembly of saints to sob to the music of one solitary liquid. But these are trifles, when even sounds inarticulate are observed to produce as forcible effects. A master workman shall blow his nose so powerfully as to pierce the hearts of his people, who were disposed to receive the excrements of his brain with the same reverence as the issue of it. Hawking, spitting, and belching, the defects of other men's rhetoric, are the flowers, and figures, and ornaments of his. For the spirit being the same in all, it is of no import through what vehicle it is conveyed.[29]

One way in which we hear the body in the voice, to put this more positively, is in the sheer physical pleasure of singing itself, in the enjoyment a singer takes in particular movements of muscles, whether as a sense of oneness between mind and body, will and action (a singer may experience something of the joy of an athlete) or through the exploration of physical sensations and muscular powers one didn't know one had (and the listener, like the sports spectator, enjoys the experience partly by proxy, but also aesthetically, with awe at the sheer grace of, say, Aaron Neville not exactly singing "Tell It Like It Is," but *holding* its notes, turning them over for our admiration).[30]

One effect of such pleasure is that for many singers what they are singing, a word, is valued for its physical possibilities, what it allows the mouth or throat to do. The singer finds herself driven by the physical logic of the sound of the words rather than by the semantic meaning of the verse, and so creates a sense of spontaneity: the singing feels real rather than rehearsed; the singer is responding (like the listener) to the musical event of which they are part, being possessed by the music rather than possessing it. The most obvious device here (listen to Otis Redding live, for instance) is repetition, a syllable being savored, sung again, sung with different consonants, tossed up against different harmonies; but singers may slow things down as well—the young Elvis Presley, for example, seemed to bask (like one of Swift's cantors) in the sheer voluptuousness of his own vocal noise.[31]

Hovering around all of these approaches to the voice as body is the question (Bathes's question) of music and sexuality: what makes a voice *sexy?* What gives a voice its erotic charge? How does the attraction of a singing voice relate to sexual attraction? Gender is obviously one issue here. We've learned to hear voices as male and female (in terms of a biologically based but not determining low/high register, for example), and the singing voice carries these codings with it (which means that a performance artist like Laurie Anderson confuses the-body-in-the-voice no end by using a vocoder to give herself a "masculine" pitch, while Diamanda Galas threatens biological certainties with the sheer range of her vocals).[32]

What, then, is the significance of mainstream rock's generic preference for high-pitched male voices like Robert Plant's, for the articulation of a "hard" rock sound as a man straining to reach higher? In the spring of 1994 Canada's Crash Test Dummies had a worldwide hit with "Mmm Mmm Mmm Mmm," and no one doubted that a major reason for its success was the novelty of Brad Roberts's bass voice, his swollen vowels, the noise rumbling back down in his throat. This was manly singing, authoritative and a bit potbellied. And what made "Mmm Mmm Mmm Mmm" stand out was not that this sound is unusual as such (lots of men must sing in this deep-voiced way) but that it was unusual in today's radio soundscape. Roberts's voice is, by current pop standards, a freak.[33]

In other music contexts the high male voice has been regarded as freakish. Wayne Koestenbaum argues from his operatic perspective that the falsetto is "among the greatest of singing shames." "Long before anyone knew what a homosexual was," he writes, "entire cultures knew how to mock men who sang unconventionally high."[34] And Gary Giddins suggests that

> in American pop song and jazz, the baritone has ruled since the mid '20s, when Bing Crosby sang his first solos with Paul Whiteman and was celebrated for his virility and naturalness. The tenors he displaced were considered effete or affected—unnatural. The very few pop tenors who have appeared in recent decades were treated as novelties and worse: often they were adolescents (Wayne Newton, a castrato-manqué) or lunatic throwbacks (Tiny Tim and his ukulele).[35]

It's easy enough to spot the "unnatural" and "effeminate" rock use of the falsetto too: Frankie Valli's delirious high-pitched recollection of his father's advice in "Walk Like a Man"; Jimmy Somerville's appearance as a cherub in Sally Potter's *Orlando*. But the point is that such readings are matters of convention, not biology. A falsetto is, after all, a man's voice (there's no such thing as female falsetto); and the Crosby who, according to Giddins, "was celebrated for his virility and naturalness" was also the crooner the BBC sought to ban for "going against nature" and Cardinal O'Connell denounced for being "degenerate" and "effeminate."[36]

"Natural" voices, masculine and feminine, are defined culturally and must be understood structurally, as sounds heard against other sounds, and in rock history low, not high, voices have seemed structurally odder, a Captain Beefheart more idiosyncratic than a Jon Anderson. There are some obvious reasons for this. The high voice is heard as the young voice, and rock is a youth form—Frankie Lymon and Michael Jackson remain the teen male models. And one of the lasting effects of doo-wop was to break the male voice up into its component parts such that the combination of *all* its sounds, from low to high, defined masculinity. This remains the norm of male rock group singing, the boys in the band harmonizing above the lead, oohing and aahing just like a bunch of girls (but, of course, not heard like girls at all).

On the other hand, there have been few falsetto rappers so far, and if the youth and doo-wop roots of rock accustomed us to the sound of the high-pitched male voice, it was in a specific expressive context: as the sound of seduction, of intimacy, of the private man. For Britain's soul-inflected singers in particular (Mick Hucknell out of Jackie Wilson and Smokey Robinson) a high voice means not effeminacy (man as woman) but *a ladies' man*, and we now take it for granted that a male voice will move up a pitch to register more intense feeling, that the more strained the note, the more sincere the singer.

What seems odd about this is the relationship of body and voice and sex. It's as if in rock convention (*pace* Roland Barthes and the Barthians) the sexiest male voice is the least bodily—the heaving bosom of the Neapolitan baritone now seems "male" in a decidedly unsexy way (and Demis Roussos's high-pitched tremor thus comes across far more lasciviously than Pavarotti's big-chested tenor). But then Elvis Presley, probably as sexy a male pop singer as there has ever been, for a long time sought (via Dean Martin) to be an Italian balladeer; and what is apparent from his early records is that Presley was, in fact, his own doo-wop act, his bass no more unnatural than his falsetto. I'm perpetually seduced by his voice, and start to wonder: as a man-fan, what am I being seduced by? What am I being seduced for?

There's a simple point here: we hear voices as male or female and listen to what they say accordingly—according to our own sexual pleasures and preferences (which is why gay and lesbian singers can subvert pop standards by *not* changing the words: Ian Matthews bubbling that "I met him on a Monday and my heart stood still"; Mathilde Santing realizing that "I've grown accustomed to her face").[37] The possibilities for confusion here between "natural" and "conventional" voices of desire are well realized in X-Ray Spex's "Oh Bondage Up Yours!"[38] This is one of the most important tracks from the heyday of U.K. punk; its lyric refers both to the sexual bondage items worn by punks for shock value and to a generalized feminist anger. But the politics of the song lies in its voice—which is drawn to one's attention by the spoken intro: this is a "little girl" determined to be heard. And part of our "hearing" is negative, relates to what the voice is not. It is not "feminine"; it is not sweet or controlled or restrained. Such rawness also serves to register the track's punk authenticity—there is no need to assume that this sound reflects the limits of Poly Styrene's own voice; its "unmusicality" is crafted. It is necessary for the song's generic impact. There is, in short, a clear *collusion* here with the listener. The song addresses an "other"—"Up Yours!"—but on our behalf. We can only identify with the singer, with the voice, with the aggression. And if the politics here is a sexual politics, a gender politics, a politics of female identity and desire, then male listeners too are being offered the exhilaration of female de-bondage.

X-Ray Spex deliberately challenged the taken-for-granted reading of "male" and "female" voices both biologically—in terms of what girls do "naturally" sound like—and ideologically—in terms of what girls should naturally sound like. But there was a further question in their music too (or at least in their way of performing their music): does a voice have to be embodied? Must it be gendered? Can a singer *change sex?*

Sean Cubitt has made the point that the simultaneous emergence around the turn of the century of the telephone, the gramophone, and the radio meant that people became accustomed, for the first time ever, to hearing a voice without a body (previously such an experience would have meant the supernatural, the voice of God or the devil).[39]

But, of course, in practice we don't hear telephone or radio or recorded voices like this at all: we assign them bodies, we imagine their physical production. And this is not just a matter of sex and gender, but involves the other basic social attributes as well: age, race, ethnicity, class—everything that is necessary to put together a person to go with a voice. And the point to stress here is that when it comes to the singing voice *all* such readings have as much to do with conventional as "natural" expression, with the ways in which, in particular genres, singing voices are coded not just as female, but also as young, black, middle class, and so forth. In fact, the popular musician's hardest problem has been to develop conventional sounds for the *disembodied* voice—whether the ethereal voice (which is, nevertheless, female—the Cocteau Twins' Elizabeth Fraser) or the heavenly choir (ditto—Morricone's I Cantori Moderni d'Alessandroni); whether the computer voice (which is, nevertheless, male—Kraftwerk) or the collective voice of religious submission (ditto—the Stanley Brothers).[40]

This last strategy is the most interesting (and most successful) because it suggests that to disembody a voice is to rob it of individuality, and this leads directly to the question of vocal identity, to the *voice as a person*. How does a voice signify a person? What is the relationship of someone's vocal sound and their being? As I've already noted, the voice is usually taken to be the person (to imitate their voice is a way of becoming that person—hence the art of the impressionist), and the voice is certainly an important way in which we recognize people we already know (on the telephone, for example). But it is also a key factor in the way in which we assess and react to people we don't know, in the way we decide what sort of person they are, whether we like or dislike, trust or mistrust them. This is one reason why we often think we "know" a singer as part of what we mean by "liking" their voice (and why, similarly, we may feel we "know" the author of a book we like: we hear in it a particular sort of voice).

But having said this, I must add some qualifications. First, a voice is easy to change. As a matter of personal identity it is easier to change, indeed, than one's face (or one's body movements). And this is not just a matter of "acting" in the formal sense. People's voices change over time (as they adapt to the sounds of surrounding voices, to accents, and so forth; the shifting quality of people's voices in class terms, as they are upwardly or downwardly socially mobile, has often been noticed in Britain), and, more to the point, people's voices change according to circumstances—at home or in school, in the office or in bed, with friends or strangers (just listen to how people adapt their voice on the telephone, according to who is at the other end).

The voice, in short, may or may not be a key to someone's identity, but it is certainly a key to the ways in which we change identities, pretend to be something we're not, deceive people, lie. We use the voice, that is, not just to assess a person, but also, even more systematically, to asses that person's sincerity: the voice and how it is used (as well as words and how they are used) become a measure of someone's truthfulness.

In popular music, two points about this are striking. First, "truth" is a matter of sound conventions, which vary from genre to genre. What becomes clear in David Brackett's detailed comparison of Billie Holiday's and Bing Crosby's versions of "I'll Be Seeing You," for example, is that it is almost impossible to hear both of them as sincere: the assumptions that lie behind a reading of Holiday's voice as "witheringly" sad entail our hearing Crosby's voice as "shallow." If Holiday sings "for real," then Crosby, as Brackett puts it, gives "the impression of someone playing a role in a film"; while someone hearing Crosby as reassuringly direct and friendly could only hear Holiday as mannered. How we hear a musical voice, in other words, is tied into how we hear music.[41]

Second, one of pop's pleasures has always been singers taking on other people's voices, and I don't refer here simply to parody or pastiche but also to what Bernard Gendron describes as caricature, the taking on of another voice not as homage or mockery or pretense, but in order to draw attention to its specific characteristics (in the same way that a good comic impressionist doesn't just imitate someone's voice but uses its individual shape to reveal something about its owner). This is most obvious in the white use of black voices in rock and roll history, from Jerry Lee Lewis's "Whole Lotta Shakin' Goin' On," which, as Gendron says, "presents itself as white-boy-wildly-singing-and-playing-black," to Mick Jagger's "I'm a King Bee," which, we might say, presents itself as white-boy-lasciviously-slurring-and-playing-black-sex. No listener could have thought that either Lewis or Jagger was black; every listener realized that they wanted to be.[42]

Which leads me to my second general point about vocal deception: if a voice can be made to change to deceive other people, it can also be used to deceive ourselves. Our "internal" experience of the voice, that is to say, the way we hear ourselves, may not at all resemble how it sounds "externally," to other people (which is why most people are genuinely shocked—and appalled—when they first hear themselves on tape). "Putting on voices" is not something we only do as part of a specific public performance (in a *karaoke* bar, say), or in a specific act of deception; it is, rather, a normal part of our *imaginative* activity. And, as Jonathan Rée has suggested, it may in fact be difficult to know "one's own voice" amidst the babble of the different voices in which we talk to ourselves: "You glimpse the possibility that it is quite arbitrary to try to mark off certain of your vocal performances and nominate them as one voice, the voice that really belongs to you: do you really possess an ownmost, innermost voice which has the power to clamp quotation marks round the others and shrug them off as 'funny'?"[43]

This question seems pertinent too for our experience of hearing voices, of listening to song. The musical pleasure lies in the play we can make of both being addressed, responding to a voice as it speaks to us (caressingly, assertively, plaintively), and addressing, taking on the voice as our own, not just physically, as I've already discussed—singing along, moving our throat and chest muscles appropriately—but also emotionally and psychologically, taking on (in fantasy) *the vocal personality* too.

This is the context in which the voice as character becomes significant. In taking on a singer's vocal personality we are, in a sense, putting on a vocal costume, enacting the role that they are playing for ourselves. But a singer's act in this respect is complex. There is, first of all, the character presented as the protagonist of the song, its singer and narrator, the implied person controlling the plot, with an attitude and tone of voice; but there may also be a "quoted" character, the person whom the song is about (and singers, like lecturers, have their own mannered ways of indicating quote marks). On top of this there is the character of the singer as star, what we know about them, or are led to believe about them through their packaging and publicity, and then, further, an understanding of the singer as a person, what we like to imagine they are really like, what is revealed, *in the end*, by their voice.

Such a multiplicity of voices can be heard in *all* pop forms, whatever the generic differences in how they are registered—whether by Tom T. Hall or Johnny Rotten always "being themselves," by Dory Previn being "The Lady with the Braids" (complete with nervous laughter), or by Frank Sinatra being himself being a late-night melancholic in "One for My Baby"; whether, to be more dramatic, in Patti Smith's rock and roll chronicle, "Horses," in the Chi-Lites' strip cartoon, "Have You Seen Her," or in Meat Loaf's big brother act, "Objects in the Rear View Mirror May Appear Closer Than They Are."[44]

What we take for granted, listening to all these songs, is that they involve *layers* of interpretation, and that in pop it is therefore all but impossible to disentangle vocal realism, on the one hand, from vocal irony, on the other. How does one read, for example, Randy Newman's concert performance of "Lonely at the Top"? Here we have not just a cult singer/ songwriter pretending to be a superstar (listen to the audience laugh with him) but also a highly successful writer/composer pretending to be a failure (listen to him laugh at his audience). Or take Michelle Shocked's "Anchorage," the meaning of which, as Dai Griffiths argues, depends on "whether you hear in Anchorage, a place in Alaska, the natural voice of the letter writer, or in 'Anchorage,' a song by Michelle Shocked, the crafted voice of the songwriter." And the pleasure of this lies in the fact that we actually hear *both Anchorage and "Anchorage" at once*.[45]

This returns us to the point from which I started: all songs are narratives; genre conventions determine how such narratives work; words are used to define a voice and vice versa.[46] In one respect, then, a pop star is like a film star, taking on many parts but retaining an essential "personality" that is common to all of them and is the basis of their popular appeal. For the pop star the "real me" is a promise that lies in the way we hear the voice, just as for a film star the "real" person is to be found in the secret of their look. This naturally leads to the issue of performance, but first I want to address two final matters relating to the voice itself: the question of interpretation, and the use in pop music of voices speaking/singing to each other.

In his discussion of the classical song, Edward Cone, as we've seen, distinguishes a song's composer, performer, and protagonist. A number of analytic questions follow from this. For example, does a performer need to know what she's singing about? If she sings the notes correctly and expressively, according to classical convention, as instructed by the composer in the score, will this *in itself* have the character effect the composer intended?[47] Cone proposes an analytic distinction: a protagonist's character is determined by the composer (by the way the music is constructed) but interpreted by the performer, and the question becomes what the relationship is of these two processes: what does an interpreter *do*? Cone also suggests that in responding to this question for themselves, listeners effectively make a choice: either to focus on the music, the piece performed, the character as composed, or on the performance, the performer, the character as interpreted. And he implies that one of the key differences between the art and the pop aesthetic can be found here: the classical concert performance is designed to draw attention to the work; the pop performance is designed to draw attention to the performer.[48]

Does this distinction stand up to pop scrutiny? I would argue, rather, that the pop performer draws attention to performance itself, to the *relationship* between performer and work. Take the case of the torch song, the "elegy to unrequited love," which is, perhaps, the clearest example of the pop singer's interpretive art. John Moore has suggested that the torch singer is best heard as an emotional expert—not an expert on emotions as such (the assumption of the form was that such emotions were universal) but an expert on their expression. Although the torch singers presented particular feelings describing particular situations (romantic illusions and disillusion), our pleasure in the songs lies not in the drama of the event, but in the way the singers explore the nuances of the feeling; torch singing is for both singer and listener an essentially narcissistic art. Torch song lyrics were therefore just signs of the feelings that the singer was to explore through the way they were sung. The music set up a "sense of sadness," the words a "verbal space" within which a voice could tell a story; and the singer applied herself—her critical, musical faculties—to the pleasures and difficulties of interpreting feelings, atmosphere, verse.[49]

Torch singing, in short, was a highly disciplined skill; it was certainly not about "direct" emotional expression or self-abandon. It involved reflection on feeling, not the feelings themselves—Billie Holiday, writes Martin Williams, "had the ability of a great actress to keep a personal distance from both her material and her performance of it"—and part of the sexual charge of the torch song came from the fact that not only were these women singers, as the lyrical protagonists, almost always reflecting on the behavior of men, they were also, as interpreters, reflecting on the words of men. These songs, then (and perhaps this is Cone's point), clearly "belong" to their singers, not their writers. Interpretation in this context does not mean realizing what the composer (or, rather, his music) meant, but using the music to show what interpretation means. Billie Holiday's voice, writes Robert O'Meally, whatever the song she sang, "was always, *always* the heroine."[50]

"Is there actually such a thing as the love song," asks Edward Cone, "outside the conventions of the love song itself?" And the answer is no, with the proviso that conventions are only the beginning of musical expression, not its end, and thus different singers (Ruth Etting and Helen Morgan, Billie Holiday and Bryan Ferry) can take the same words, the same tune, the same situation ("Body and Soul," "These Foolish Things") and use them to provide quite different accounts of love itself, its permanence and transience, its sweetness and humiliation. Voices, not songs, hold the key to our pop pleasures; musicologists may analyze the art of the Gershwins or Cole Porter, but we hear Bryan Ferry or Peggy Lee.[51]

My final question concerns vocal difference: what is the relationship *between* voices in popular song? After all, since the mid-sixties the group (rather than the solo singer) has dominated Anglo-American popular music (at least in terms of male voices), and if such groups more often than not have a "lead" singer we rarely hear his voice completely unaccompanied. We are, that is, accustomed to the idea of a "group voice"— the appeal of both the Beatles and the Beach Boys rested on their (quite different) blend of male voices; while, to take a different genre example, the male vocal trio (on the model of the Impressions) was central to the development of reggae in the 1960s and 1970s.

Such use of voices (rather than voice) can be pushed in two directions. In male group tradition, whether traced from gospel, barbershop, doo-wop (or their intermingling), the emphasis has been, in Keir Keightley's words, on singing as "social co-operation, the submission of individuality to the service of a larger corporation structure," and the "rational" organization of male voices as *sounds*—Lennon and McCartney thus sang "as one" (and it was only later, when we and they wanted to take these songs seriously as art, not pop, that anyone could hear Beatles numbers as "a Lennon song," "a McCartney verse").[52]

In female group tradition, by contrast (and I am deliberately exaggerating this contrast here; in practice male and female groups are not so distinct), different voices are used differently, in a conversational way (which in another trajectory, out of insult ritual, also leads to rap). The voices on tracks like the Shangri-Las' "Leader of the Pack" or the Angels' "My Boyfriend's Back" function as each other's audience; the chorus, dramatically, comments on the story and the action, encouraging the lead singer, disbelieving her, egging her on. Here "corporate identity" is indicated less by harmony singing than by the sharing out of the lead voice itself, and there is a direct continuity between the Shirelles' 1958 "I Met Him on a Sunday" and Salt-n-Pepa's 1991 "Let's Talk About Sex."[53]

As a label, "girl groups" (which may include groups of boys) describes a form which is, by its nature, *dramatic:* girl group records feature—focus on—vocal rhetoric and its effects. And, though less obviously, so does the pop duet (a form which has been somewhat devalued by the current fashion of reviving old stars' careers by getting them to sing along with new stars to no dramatic effect at all). In country music, for example, the man/woman duet is usually conflictual; the male and female voices are registered separately, present their different points of view, with the chorus harmonies suggesting just a temporary truce (the classic pairing here was Conway Twitty and Loretta Lynn). In soul the duet was usually used as a way of intensifying feeling, as a means of seductive talk, male and female voices moving in and to musical and sexual union (listen, for example, to Marvin Gaye and Tammi Terrell).[54]

In rock the most effective duets work not so much with realist effects (a man and woman quarreling or making up) as with star quality and across genre lines. Sinead O'Connor, for example, has been used to brilliant effect as a voice *querying* what's being said by a rapper, on the one hand (in her song with M. C. Lyte, "I Want [Your Hands on Me]"), and by a country singer, on the other (on Willie Nelson's version of Peter Gabriel's "Don't Give Up")—and I defy anyone to listen to her first entry on the latter track without a shiver of recognition that *this* person (with all we know about her) should be telling Willie Nelson (with all we know about him), should be telling him, so surely, so sweetly, to survive.[55]

NOTES

[1]Roland Barthes, *Roland Barthes by Roland Barthes* [1975] (New York: Farrar, Straus and Giroux, 1977), p. 141. His emphases.

[2]Quoted in Ellie M. Hisama, "Postcolonialism on the Make: The Music of John Mellancamp, David Bowie and John Zorn," *Popular Music* 12(2) (1993): 99. Her emphasis.

[3]Quoted in Robert O'Meally, *Lady Day: The Many Faces of Billie Holiday* (New York: Arcade, 1991), p. 52.

[4]The song line is from Bob Dylan's "Positively 4th Street," 7" single, CBS, 1965. For the use of shifters see Alan Durant, *Conditions of Music* (London: Macmillan, 1984), pp. 201–206.

[5]I could add a further complication here: what is going on when a composer writes *in someone else's voice?* Elgar's *Enigma Variations,* for instance, originated in "a domestic evening" when the composer was messing around with a piece, "playing it in the different ways his friends might have done had they thought of it." As Elgar later explained: "I've written the variations each one to represent the mood of the 'party'—I've liked to imagine the 'party' writing the var[iation] him (or her) self and have written what I think they wd have written—if they were asses enough to compose—it's a quaint idea and the result is amusing to those behind the scene and won't affect the hearer who 'nose nuffin.'" Elgar was here using music not exactly to describe his friends but, in a sense, to be them—and this act of *impersonation* suggests that he, like Cone, did in the end think of music as being the composer's voice. See Francis Sparshott, "Portraits in Music—a Case Study: Elgar's 'Enigma' Variations," in Michael Krausz, *The Interpretation of Music* (Oxford: Clarendon Press, 1993), p. 234.

[6]Edward T. Cone, *The Composer's Voice* (Berkeley: University of California Press, 1972), chap. 1. But see also Carolyn Abbate, *Unsung Voices: Opera and Musical Narrative in the Nineteenth Century* (Princeton, N.J.: Princeton University Press, 1991): "To Cone's monologic and controlling 'composer's voice,' I prefer an aural vision of music animated by multiple, decentered voices localized in several invisible bodies" (p. 13). For Abbate, the "voices" in music "manifest themselves . . . as different *kinds* or modes of music that inhabit a single work. They are not uncovered by analyses that assume all music in a given work is stylistically or technically identical, originating from a single source in 'the Composer'" (p. 12; her emphasis). I return to this argument later in the chapter.

[7]Anthony Storr, *Music and the Mind* (London: HarperCollins, 1993), p. 117. Storr also tells us that "Wagner's personality was charismatic and so is his music" (p. 120).

[8]O'Meally, *Lady Day,* p. 97.

[9]As David Brackett notes, "It is difficult to determine whether our response [to her voice] is based on what we know about Holiday's life, or on a socially mediated construction of affect conveyed by certain musical gestures." Either way, to repeat O'Meally's point, few entries on her "in even the most scholarly jazz history books" fail to refer to "her struggles with drugs and personal relationships." See David Brackett, *Interpreting Popular Music* (Cambridge: Cambridge University Press, 1995), p. 62.

[10]Gregory Sandow, "Tough Love," *Village Voice,* January 13, 1987, p. 71.

[11]Quoted in John Moore, "'The Hieroglyphics of Love': The Torch Singers and Interpretation," *Popular Music* 8(1) (1989): 39.

[12]Umberto Fiore, "New Music, Popular Music, and Opera in Italy," unpublished paper, n.d., p. 4. His emphasis.

An opera buff like Wayne Koestenbaum might challenge this distinction. He has no doubts, for example, about Callas's individuality: "No note she sings remains the same; she changes voice *inside* the note, as if to say: 'Try to catch me, to name me, to confine me in your brutal classifications'" (his emphasis). But even for Koestenbaum the opera singer's "self" only emerges at moments of musical crisis: "at the moment of vulnerability and breakdown, the diva proves that the seamless singing has been masquerade, and now her cracked and decayed, raucous and undisguised self is coming out." Koestenbaum, *The Queen's Throat* (London: GMP, 1993), pp. 146, 127. In pop, "cracked and decayed" voices are always available.

It could also be argued that as Maria Callas became more obviously "personally expressive," so she became more of a pop than an opera singer (an effect of her marketing as a recording star). See Réal La Rochelle's illuminating *Callas: La Diva et le Vinyle* (Montréal: Les éditions Triptyque, 1987).

The problem of "how emotional expressivity is induced in song performance" when "the pitch parameter is restricted by the score" has interested psychologists too. How do we hear one performance as more "expressive" than another when the same notes have been sung? The point here seems to be that the singer's skill is "the ability to portray by acoustical means the particular emotional ambience embedded by the composer in the song," and not to bring their own, personal means of emotional expression to it (thus "dressing a song in an inappropriate ambience"). If classical singers do nevertheless use familiar rhetorical gestures ("expressive" singing is, in acoustic terms, more "agitated" than "unexpressive" singing), these are, in a sense, personally empty: the emotional meaning is in the music itself. We don't hear the singer as angry, anguished, and so forth, but the music. For an interesting discussion of these issues see Johan Sundberg, Jenny Iwarsson, and Håkon Hagegård, "A Singer's Expression of Emotions," paper presented to the Vocal Fold Physiology Conference, Korume, Japan, April 1994.

[13]I'm describing here the use of voices in rock's mainstream gospel-derived tradition. Ray Charles and the Raelettes were undoubtedly the key influence (listen, for example, to "I'm Moving On" on *The Genius Sings the Blues,* London-Atlantic, 1961); Van Morrison is probably the best rock exponent (live, at least), taking advantage of his consequent "freedom from utterance" to use his voice as if it were a saxophone.

[14]As was parodied by Lou Reed in "Walk on the Wild Side." There are male backup traditions too: not just the male voice choir used by the Pet Shop Boys, but also in black and white gospel—Elvis Presley used the Jordonnaires throughout his career, and even the vocally democratic doo-wop increasingly featured lead/backup male voices as it reached the pop charts (Dion and the Belmonts, for example; Frankie Lyman and the Teenagers). Gladys Knight's Pips, on the other hand, always came across as a simple gender role reversal. In country music the dominant gender convention is of the star male lead voice being tracked by an anonymous female backing voice, with the man all the way, but always just off center, a sweetener and a restraint—listen, for example, to how Emmylou Harris traces the desire behind Gram Parsons' voice on his "solo" LPs, *GP* (Reprise, 1973) and *Grievous Angel* (Reprise, 1974).

[15]O'Meally, *Lady Day,* pp. 31–32.

[16]For the BBC see my "Art *vs* Technology: The Strange Case of Popular Music," *Media Culture and Society* 8(3) (1986): 263. For advertising see Roland Marchand, *Advertising the American Dream: Making Way for Modernity, 1920–1940* (Berkeley: University of California Press, 1985), p. 109.

[17]"Significantly enough," as Bernard Gendron writes, "Crosby's singing style actually evoked the ire of spokespersons for moral purity, with Boston's Cardinal O'Connell referring to it as 'immoral and imbecile slush,' 'a degenerate low-down sort of interpretation of love,' and 'a sensuous effeminate luxurious sort of paganism.'" See Gendron's "Rock and Roll Mythology: Race and Sex in 'Whole Lotta Shakin' Going On,'" Working Paper 7 (Milwaukee: University of Wisconsin, Center for Twentieth Century Studies, 1985), p. 4.

[18]John Rockwell, *Sinatra* (New York: Random House, 1984), pp. 51–52.

[19]This generalization is perhaps too sweeping (Glenn Gould, for example, compares Barbra Streisand to Elizabeth Schwarzkopf in this respect), and there are clearly styles of classical singing—coloratura, for example—in which the performer draws attention to her vocal technique (and to not much else). But then that is probably the reason why Cecilia Bartoli is the only classical soprano I adore.

[20]One of the most obvious distinctions between pre- and post-microphone singing relates to this: in the original big bands the voice is featured as just a (minor) instrument, the words sung briefly, after one long instrumental workout and before another. By the end of the big band era, the instrumental break had become the punctuation, a fill between the second vocal chorus and the third vocal verse.

[21]Sandow, "Tough Love," pp. 71, 73.

[22]Aidan Day, *Jokerman* (Oxford: Blackwell, 1988), p. 2.

[23]Glenn Gould, "Streisand as Schwarzkopf," in *The Glenn Gould Reader*, pp. 309–310. Compare Gary Giddins on Ella Fitzgerald: "even when she recorded Tin Pan Alley muck, she could empower certain notes with a shivery reflex, *disassociating* the singer from the song yet giving the song a kick all the same." "Joy of Ella," *Village Voice*, April 27, 1993, p. 90. My emphasis.

[24]Cone, *The Composer's Voice*, p. 78.

[25]See Jane M. Gaines, "Bette Midler and the Piracy of Identity," in Simon Frith, ed., *Music and Copyright* (Edinburgh: Edinburgh University Press, 1993).

[26]Quotes from Barthes, "The Grain of the Voice," in *The Responsibility of Forms* (Berkeley: University of California Press, 1991), pp. 276, 270, 271.

[27]Koestenbaum, *The Queen's Throat*, p. 43. Barthes's essay does, in fact, read more like a heartfelt and elaborate defense of his taste (for Panzéra; against Fischer-Dieskau) than as a particularly convincing account of different vocal techniques as such.

[28]This relates, I suppose, to a Lacanian psychoanalytic view of musical pleasure, though I do not find Lacan's own words on music particularly illuminating. See, for example, his "De l'objet musical dans le champ de la psychoanalyse" [1974], *scilicet* 617 (1976). From the perspective of a kind of Lacanian socio-linguistics, Barbara Bradby and Brian Torode argue that: "the lyrics of the modern popular song permit a man to fantasise addressing a woman as love-object in terms of rocking a crying baby to hush it. This use of lullaby language exploits the words of the absent mother in order to silence the present lover." "Song-Work," paper presented at the British Sociological Association Conference, Manchester, 1982. And see their "Pity Peggy Sue," *Popular Music* 4 (1984), and, in the same issue, Sean Cubitt, "'Maybelline': Meaning and the Listening Subject"—"the real object of desire flees before us like Maybelline's Cadillac" (p. 222).

[29]Jonathan Swift, "A Discourse Concerning the Mechanical Operation of the Spirit" [1704], in *A Tale of the Tub and Other Satires* (London: J. M. Dent [Everyman], 1909), pp. 180–181.

[30]Aaron Neville's "Tell It Like It Is" was originally released as a single in 1966. A live version (recorded at Tipitina's, New Orleans, in 1982) is included on the Neville Brothers' *Neville-ization*, Black Top/Demon Records, 1984.

[31]For Otis Redding, listen to *Live in Europe*, Atlantic LP, 1972. Elvis Presley's pleasure in his own voice is best captured on *Elvis: The First Live Recordings* (RCA, 1984), live recordings from the Louisiana Hayride in 1955–56, and *Essential Elvis Presley*, vols. 1–3 (RCA, 1986, 1989, 1990), studio outtakes from his early RCA and Hollywood days. It is here (singers responding to themselves) rather than with backup singers (responding to a leader) that we get, paradoxically, the musical version of Erving Goffman's "response cries," the noises people make in conversation in response to someone else. Goffman suggests that such cries "do not mark a flooding of emotion outward, but a flooding of relevance in," but in musical terms the voice suggests both such movements simultaneously. See Erving Goffman, *Forms of Talk* (Oxford: Basil Blackwell, 1981), p. 121.

[32]We don't always get a singer's sex "right," though in my experience this is *not* usually an effect of pitch (the Laurie Anderson effect)—women's low voices and men's high voices are still heard as women's and men's voices; see the discussion of falsetto that fol-

lows in this chapter. The misjudgment seems, rather, to relate to genre expectation—the only singer I've known people systematically to misread is Jimmy Scott, and this seems to have more to do with his (torch singing) style than with his (not particularly high) pitch—listen, for example, to *Dream* (Sire, 1994).

[33]Crash Test Dummies, "Mmm Mmm Mmm Mmm" (RCA, 1993).

[34]Koestenbaum, *The Queen's Throat*, p. 165. He also suggests that "cultural folklore convinces us that we can tell someone is gay by voice alone" (p. 14).

[35]Giddins, "Joy of Ella," p. 90.

[36]Deborah Cameron has pointed out to me that there is actually a dispute among phoneticians concerning the "female falsetto"—how else would we describe what Minnie Riperton does with her voice on her 1974 Epic hit, "Lovin' You," for instance? And for a stimulating discussion of the special erotic appeal of the *low* female voice see Terry Castle, "In Praise of Brigitte Fassbaender (A Musical Emanation)" in her *The Apparitional Lesbian: Female Homosexuality and Modern Culture* (New York: Columbia University Press, 1993).

[37]Ian Matthews, "Da Doo Ron Ron," Philips 7" single, 1972; Mathilde Santing, "I've Grown Accustomed to Her Face," on *Mathilde Santing* 10" LP, Idiot, 1982.

[38]X-Ray Spex, "Oh Bondage Up Yours!" Virgin single, 1977.

[39]Sean Cubitt, "Note on the Popular Song," unpublished, 1983. Koestenbaum suggests that film musical ghosts (Marni Nixon singing for Audrey Hepburn in *My Fair Lady* and for Deborah Kerr in *The King and I*) are further examples of "singing without a body, singing from an erased place in the universe." *The Queen's Throat*, p. 11. And Wendy Wolf reminds me that part of the appeal of the pop video is that it re-embodies the pop voice.

[40]Record references: Cocteau Twins, "Aikea Guinea," 12" EP, 4AD 1985; Ennio Morricone, *Once Upon a Time in the West*, Soundtrack LP, RCA 1969; Kraftwerk, "The Robots," on *The Man Machine* LP, Capitol 1978; the Stanley Brothers and the Clinch Mountain Boys, *The Columbia Sessions, 1949–50*, Rounder LP, 1980.

[41]See Brackett, *Interpreting Popular Music*, chap. 2, for a detailed discussion of Crosby's and Holiday's contrasting "musical codes," and for critical responses to them. And compare Bernard Gendron's account of the white pop "dilution" of black rock 'n' roll songs in the 1950s: Gendron, "Rock and Roll Mythology," pp. 6–7.

I am reminded in this context of the wonderful moment when Martin Hatch, who had till then, as a good ethnomusicologist, sat equably through all the music I'd played during a course at Cornell on the "good and bad in popular culture," leapt out of his seat on hearing Bryan Ferry's version of "These Foolish Things" (one of my favorite ever tracks) and exclaimed: "*Now* I believe in bad music!"

[42]Gendron, "Rock and Roll Mythology," p. 7. Gendron suggests that we can also hear black performers like Chuck Berry, Little Richard, and Ray Charles caricaturing their own styles: "According to rock and roll mythology, they went from singing less black (like Nat King Cole or the Mills Brothers) to singing more black. In my judgement, it would be better to say that they adopted a more caricaturized version of singing black wildly, thus paving the way for soul music and the British invasion" (p. 10).

For a more general discussion of race and musical caricature, see Eric Lott, *Love and Theft: Blackface Minstrelsy and the American Working Class* (New York and Oxford: Oxford University Press, 1993). Record references here are Jerry Lee Lewis, "Whole Lotta Shakin' Goin' On" (Sun, 1957), and the Rolling Stones, "I'm a King Bee," on *The Rolling Stones* (Decca, 1964). There's no doubt too that white rock 'n' roll fans enjoyed the danger of sounding "black" in the safety of their own heads. The (much less obvious) phenomenon of black singers sounding "white" has hardly been studied.

[43]Jonathan Rée, "Funny Voices: Stories, Punctuation and Personal Identity," *New Literary History* 21 (1990): 1053.

[44]Record references are to Dory Previn, "Lady with the Braid," on *Mythical Kings and Iguanas* (UA, 1971); Frank Sinatra, "One for My Baby," on *Frank Sinatra Sings for Only the Lonely* (Capitol, 1958); Patti Smith, "Land," on *Horses* (Arista LP, 1975); the Chi-Lites, "Have You Seen Her" (Brunswick, 1971); Meat Loaf, "Objects in the Rear View Mirror May Appear Closer Than They Are," on *Bat out of Hell II* (Virgin, 1993).

[45]Dai Griffiths, "Talking About Popular Song: in Praise of 'Anchorage,'" in Rossana Dalmonte and Mario Baroni, eds., *Secondo Convegno Europeo di Analisi Musicale* (Trento: Universita degli Studi di Trento, 1992), p. 356. Record references: Randy Newman, "Lonely at the Top," on *Randy Newman/Live* (Reprise, 1971), and Michelle Shocked, "Anchorage," on *Short Sharp Shocked* (Cooking Vinyl, 1988).

[46]Carolyn Abbate suggests that in classical music "narrative" should be taken to describe a specific musical *act*, "a unique moment of performing narrative within a surrounding music" (*Unsung Voices*, p. 19). I've been suggesting here that in pop the voice always does this act, but that is not necessarily the case, and Abbate's argument could certainly be applied to pop's instrumental-narrative moments, whether they're performed by an improvising player like, say, Keith Richards, or by a calculating producer like, say, Phil Spector.

[47]Is it better, for example, for an opera to be sung in the language in which it was composed, which "sounds" right but may not be linguistically comprehensible to either singers or audience; or to translate the libretto into, say, English, which means that Anglophones now know what is being sung but the vocal *sounds* are no longer those in which the opera was originally composed? I would always opt for the first approach, but then words have always been the least of my musical pleasures.

[48]Cone, *The Composer's Voice*, pp. 119–121. For further consideration of this issue, with reference to instrumental interpretation, see Jerrold Levinson, "Performative *vs* Critical Interpretation in Music," in Krausz, *The Interpretation of Music.*

[49]See John Moore, "'The Hieroglyphics of Love.'" I take the concept of "verbal space" from Griffiths, "Talking About Popular Song," p. 353. For technical discussion of interpretive singing see Will Friedwald, *Jazz Singing: America's Great Voices from Bessie Smith to Bebop and Beyond* (New York: Scribners, 1990). For the torch singer's art listen to Chris Connor's "All About Ronnie" (1954), on *Out of This World* (Affinity, 1984), or Jerry Southern's "I Thought of You Last Night" (1952), on *When I Fall in Love* (MCA, 1984).

[50]O'Meally, *Lady Day*, p. 198. His emphasis. Martin Williams is quoted on p. 43.

[51]Cone, *The Composer's Voice*, p. 53. Record references: Billie Holiday, "These Foolish Things" (1936), on *The Billie Holiday Story Volume 1* (CBS, n.d.); Bryan Ferry, "These Foolish Things," on *These Foolish Things* (Island, 1973).

[52]Keightley's discussion concerns the Beach Boys—see "The History and Exegesis of Pop," p. 128.

[53]The Shangri-Las, "Leader of the Pack," Red Bird single, 1964; the Angels, "My Boyfriend's Back," smash single, 1963; the Shirelles, "I Met Him on a Sunday," Tiara/Decca single, 1958; Salt-n-Pepa, "Let's Talk About Sex," Next Plateau single, 1991.

[54]Record references: Loretta Lynn and Conway Twitty, *Lead Me On* (MCA, 1971); Marvin Gaye and Tammi Terrell, *Greatest Hits* (Motown, 1970).

[55]Records cited: Sinead O'Connor and M. C. Lyte, "I Want (Your Hands on Me)," Ensign 12" single, 1988; Willie Nelson, "Don't Give Up," on *Across the Borderline*, Columbia LP, 1993. For discussion of the former see Katrina Irving, "'I Want Your Hands On Me': Building Equivalences Through Rap Music," *Popular Music* 12(2) (1993): 117–120.

•   •   •   •   •   •   •   •   •   •   •   •

QUESTIONS FOR A SECOND READING

1. Four paragraphs into the essay Frith says,

   > Now stop reading the lyrics, and listen to the song. Whose voice do we hear now? Again there's an obvious answer: the singer's, stupid! And what I argue in the rest of this chapter is that this is, in fact, the stupid answer. (p. 278)

Well, it may be stupid, but it *is* the obvious answer (that is, the answer he suspects we would provide). As you reread the essay, what is the clever answer? And what do you need to know (or to know how to do) in order not to come up with a stupid response?

2. Toward the end of the essay, and speaking about Edward Cone and his account of the classical song, Frith says,

> Cone also suggests that in responding to this question for themselves [what does an interpreter *do*?], listeners effectively make a choice: either to focus on the music, the piece performed, the character as composed, or on the performance, the performer, the character as interpreted. And he implies that one of the key differences between the art and the pop aesthetic can be found here: the classical concert performance is designed to draw attention to the work; the pop performance is designed to draw attention to the performer. (p. 291–92)

And, Frith adds, "Does this distinction stand up to pop scrutiny? I would argue, rather, that the pop performer draws attention to performance itself, to the *relationship* between performer and work."

As you reread, highlight passages that you can use to explain the distinction Frith makes between the "performer" and "performance."

3. The essay is filled with references to performers in performance. The essay does not require (and Frith does not assume) that every reader is familiar with every reference to a singer or group, to a song or a performance. Still, there is interesting and useful work to do to fill in the details. Choose one of the key artists as a point of reference—Bing Crosby, Billie Holiday, Frank Sinatra, Bob Dylan, Meat Loaf, Patti Smith, Michelle Shocked, X-Ray Spex, Sinead O'Connor, or another—and find a recording of one of the songs he cites (the endnotes are quite precise on this). Prepare a presentation for class that includes both a recording and a discussion of "voice" in relation to the recording. Try to reproduce Frith's method for talking about and thinking about voice.

4. The final chapter of the book, "Toward a Popular Aesthetic," includes the following passage, a passage that seems like an appropriate conclusion to the argument you have read in "The Voice":

> It follows that an identity is always already an ideal, what we would like to be, not what we are. In taking pleasure from black or gay or female music I don't thus identify as black or gay or female (I don't actually experience these sounds as "black music" or "gay music" or "women's voices") but, rather, participate in imagined forms of democracy and desire, imagined forms of the social and the sexual. And what makes music special in this familiar cultural process is that musical identity is both fantastic—idealizing not just oneself but also the social world one inhabits—and real: it is enacted in activity. Music making and music listening, that is to say, are bodily matters; they involve what one might call *social movements*. In this respect, musical pleasure is not derived from fantasy—it is not mediated by daydreams—but is experienced directly: music gives us a real experience of what the ideal could be.

Reread with this conclusion in mind. Where and how might you see Frith preparing for a conclusion that is about identity, the ideal, democracy, and desire?

ASSIGNMENTS FOR WRITING

1. Frith provides three extended descriptions of musical voice: Gregory Sandow on Frank Sinatra (p. 282), Aidan Day on Bob Dylan (p. 282), and Glenn Gould on Barbra Streisand (pp. 282–83). Each of these voices, he says, "has a relationship" (with an orchestra, with an audience, with music itself); and each critic, he says, hears a "willed sound." He provides his own extended description of X-Ray Spex's "Oh Bondage Up Yours!" (p. 288). Choose a performer and a performance that matters to you, that you think is exemplary, and using these four passages as models, write descriptions of voice. (You should write more than one; if it works to follow the models closely, write four.)

   Once you have written these (perhaps as a first draft, a draft that can be read by others in your class), write an essay in which you use your examples in conversation with Frith and his arguments about voice.

2. Early in the essay, Frith says the following:

   > But if we hear the pop singer singing "her self," she is also singing a song, and so a second question arises: what is the relationship between the voice as a carrier of sounds, the singing voice, making "gestures," and the voice as a carrier of words, the speaking voice, making "utterances"? The issue is not meaning (words) versus an absence of meaning (music), but the relationship between two different sorts of meaning-making, the tensions and conflicts between them. There's a question here of power: who is to be the master, words or music? And what makes the voice so interesting is that it makes meaning in these two ways simultaneously. We have, therefore, to approach the voice under four headings: as *a musical instrument*; as *a body*; as *a person*; and as *a character*. (p. 280)

   "Gestures" and "utterances"; "instrument" and "body"; "person" and "character." There is an elaborate scheme here for description and analysis. Choose a performer and a performance that matters to you, that you think is exemplary, and using this scheme, write an account that puts into play the scheme and the terms used by Frith.

   Once you have written this (perhaps as a first draft, a draft that can be read by others in your class), write an essay in which you use your example to converse with Frith and his arguments about voice.

3. *Voice* is a word commonly used to describe style in writing. Writers are told that they need to find or, better yet, to develop their "own voice." Certain writers are said to have distinctive "voices" or to have the ability to play with or experiment with "voice." Frith says, "The voice, in short, may or may not be a key to someone's identity, but it is certainly a key to the ways in which we change identities, pretend to be something we're not, deceive people, lie" (p. 289). He offers these terms for the description of voice:

   > But if we hear the pop singer singing "her self," she is also singing a song, and so a second question arises: what is the relationship between the voice as a carrier of sounds, the singing voice, making "gestures," and the voice as a carrier of words, the speaking voice, making "utterances"? The issue is not meaning (words) versus an absence of mean-

ing (music), but the relationship between two different sorts of mean-ing-making, the tensions and conflicts between them. There's a question here of power: who is to be the master, words or music? And what makes the voice so interesting is that it makes meaning in these two ways simultaneously. We have, therefore, to approach the voice under four headings: as *a musical instrument*; as *a body*; as *a person*; and as *a character*. (p. 280)

"Gestures" and "utterances"; "instrument" and "body"; "person" and "character." There is an elaborate scheme here for description and analysis. It would need to be adapted, however, for a description of voice in prose performance. "Person" and "character" are recognizable. Something would need to be substituted for "instrument" (the word processor? the conventions of writing?) and/or "body" (language? syntax, sentences, paragraphs?).

Choose a distinctive example of prose style. You could use *Ways of Reading* for this; or you could look to pieces you have read and remembered, or to other anthologies. In an essay on "Voice," present this passage to your readers—that is, provide an introduction and include the passage as part of your essay. Then, use Frith's terms to talk about the presence, effect, and consequence of "voice."

4. Four paragraphs into the essay Frith says,

> Now stop reading the lyrics, and listen to the song. Whose voice do we hear now? Again there's an obvious answer: the singer's, stupid! And what I argue in the rest of this chapter is that this is, in fact, the stupid answer. (p. 278)

Well, it may be stupid, but it *is* the obvious answer (that is, the answer he suspects we would provide). Write an essay in which you present Frith's account of "voice" to someone not familiar with Frith's work or with this essay. You will need to provide summary and paraphrase, and you should provide some examples of extended quotation (so that your reader can get a sense of Frith's method and style). And, as you do this, find a place for examples and ideas of your own. These should be in response to Frith's—as extension, dialogue, qualification, homage, rebuttal.

5. Frith says that when we hear recorded voices (on telephone or radio), "we assign them bodies, we imagine their physical production. And this is not just a matter of sex and gender, but involves the other basic social attributes as well: age, race, ethnicity, class—everything that is necessary to put together a person to go with a voice" (p. 288). Everything necessary to put together a person—this sounds like science fiction. In Frith's analysis, however, the possibility of transformation is part of the promise and power of music and song; they enable the "negation of everyday life." The voice, he says, "may or may not be a key to someone's identity, but it is certainly a key to the ways in which we change identities . . ." (p. 289). We put together a person when we listen and we put together a person when we speak.

Write an essay in which you consider, first, how this makes sense from within the terms and arguments of Frith's essay and, second, how it does or does not make sense to you.

MAKING CONNECTIONS

1. Frith works from within the traditions of British cultural studies, which were formed in response to the Frankfurt school (the group that included Walter Benjamin). Benjamin (p. 73) writes primarily about film; Frith writes about music. Both are concerned with the ways popular culture shapes the lives (the thoughts, beliefs, and actions) of those who spend time with it; both are concerned with the ways popular culture does or does not enable people to resist, transform, or somehow improve the conditions of "everyday" life.

   Work first with "The Work of Art in the Age of Mechanical Reproduction" and then with "The Voice." Frith imagines that he is taking the argument one step further; that he is improving upon the conclusions of the Frankfurt school. With these two essays as your source, how would you describe the differences in their positions on the powers and effects of popular culture? If Frith speaks more clearly to our own age, how might this be so? And what do you think? Do you side with Frith?

   Question 4 in the "Questions for a Second Reading" might be useful to keep in mind as you think about Frith's position. It is also worth adding a passage from early in his book, at the end of the first chapter. He says,

   > I know this is where my own tastes will inform everything that follows, my own tastes, that is, for the *unpopular popular*, my own belief that the "difficult" appeals through traces it carries of another world in which it would be "easy." The utopian impulse, the *negation* of everyday life, the aesthetic impulse that Adorno recognized in high art, must be part of low art too.

2. *Voice* is a word commonly used to describe style in writing. Writers are told that they "need to find their own voice." Certain writers are said to have distinctive "voices" or to have the ability to play with or experiment with "voice." Frith says, "The voice, in short, may or may not be a key to someone's identity, but it is certainly a key to the ways in which we change identities, pretend to be something we're not, deceive people, lie" (p. 289). He offers these terms for the description of voice:

   > But if we hear the pop singer singing "her self," she is also singing a song, and so a second question arises: what is the relationship between the voice as a carrier of sounds, the singing voice, making "gestures," and the voice as a carrier of words, the speaking voice, making "utterances"? The issue is not meaning (words) versus an absence of meaning (music), but the relationship between two different sorts of meaning-making, the tensions and conflicts between them. There's a question here of power: who is to be the master, words or music? And what makes the voice so interesting is that it makes meaning in these two ways simultaneously. We have, therefore, to approach the voice under four headings: as *a musical instrument*; as *a body*; as *a person*; and as *a character*. (p. 280)

   Identity and change; "gestures" and "utterances"; "instrument" and "body"; "person" and "character." There is an elaborate scheme here for description and analysis. It would need to be adapted, however, for a description of voice in prose performance. "Person" and "character" are recognizable. Something would need to be substituted for "instrument" (the word processor? the conventions of writing?) and/or "body" (language? syntax, sentences, paragraphs?).

Gloria Anzaldúa, in "How to Tame a Wild Tongue" (p. 36), and John Edgar Wideman, in "Our Time" (p. 752), provide texts that foreground the importance and problem of voice and identity. Choose one of the two essays; read them with Frith's discussion in mind, and write an essay in which you talk about the presence, force, and consequence of voice in writing.

3. To introduce the four case studies in "The Photographic Essay" (p. 510), W. J. T. Mitchell says, "I want to examine four photo-essays that, in various ways, foreground the dialectic of exchange and resistance between photography and language." One of the case studies is the collaboration between Edward Said and Jean Mohr, *After the Last Sky: Palestinian Lives,* one chapter of which is represented in *Ways of Reading* ("States," p. 678). Frith is concerned with the dialectic of exchange and resistance between performance and descriptions (and evaluations) of performance.

Work closely with examples—Said writing about one of the photographs; Frith writing about a moment of performance—and write an essay that considers how each writer understands the problems of writing (writing about something that is not writing) and how each confronts the problems in practice.

CLIFFORD
GEERTZ

*C*LIFFORD GEERTZ *was born in San Francisco in 1926. After two years in the U.S. Navy Reserve, he earned a B.A. from Antioch College and a Ph.D. from Harvard. A Fellow of the National Academy of Science, the American Academy of Arts and Sciences, and the American Philosophical Society, Geertz has been a professor in the department of social science of the Institute for Advanced Study in Princeton, New Jersey, since 1970. He has written several books (mostly anthropological studies of Third World cultures) and published two collections of essays,* Interpretation of Cultures *(1977) and* Local Knowledge *(1985). Interpretation of Cultures, from which the following essay is drawn, became a classic and won for Geertz the rare distinction of being an academic whose scholarly work is eagerly read by people outside his academic discipline, even outside the academic community altogether. His book* Works and Lives: The Anthropologist as Author *(1989) won the National Book Critics Circle Award for Criticism. Geertz's most recent work is* Available Light: Anthropological Reflections on Philosophical Topics *(2000).*

"Deep Play" was first presented at a Paris conference organized by Geertz, the literary critic Paul de Man, and the American Academy of Arts and Sciences. The purpose of the conference was to bring together scholars from various academic departments (in the humanities, the social sciences, and the natural sciences) to see if they could find a way of talking to each other and, in doing so,

find a common ground to their work. The conference planners believed that there was a common ground, that all of these scholars were bound together by their participation in what they called "systematic study of meaningful forms." This is a grand phrase, but Geertz's essay clearly demonstrates what work of this sort requires of an anthropologist. The essay begins with a story, an anecdote, and the story Geertz tells is as open to your interpretation as it is to anyone else's. What follow, however, are Geertz's attempts to interpret the story he has told, first this way and then that. As you watch him work—finding patterns, making comparisons, drawing on the theories of experts, proposing theories of his own—you are offered a demonstration of how he finds meaningful forms and then sets out to study them systematically.

"Deep Play," in fact, was sent out as a model for all prospective conference participants, since it was a paper that showed not only what its author knew about his subject (cockfights in Bali) but what he knew about the methods and procedures that gave him access to his subject. It is a witty and sometimes dazzling essay with a wonderful story to tell—a story of both a Balinese cockfight and an anthropologist trying to write about and understand people whose culture seems, at first, so very different from his own.

Deep Play: Notes on the Balinese Cockfight

The Raid

Early in April of 1958, my wife and I arrived, malarial and diffident, in a Balinese village we intended, as anthropologists, to study. A small place, about five hundred people, and relatively remote, it was its own world. We were intruders, professional ones, and the villagers dealt with us as Balinese seem always to deal with people not part of their life who yet press themselves upon them: as though we were not there. For them, and to a degree for ourselves, we were nonpersons, specters, invisible men.

We moved into an extended family compound (that had been arranged before through the provincial government) belonging to one of the four major factions in village life. But except for our landlord and the village chief, whose cousin and brother-in-law he was, everyone ignored us in a way only a Balinese can do. As we wandered around, uncertain, wistful, eager to please, people seemed to look right through us with a gaze focused several yards behind us on some more actual stone or tree. Almost nobody greeted us; but nobody scowled or said anything unpleasant to us either, which would have been almost as satisfactory. If we ventured to approach someone (something one is powerfully inhibited from doing in such an atmosphere), he moved, negligently but definitively, away. If, seated or leaning against a wall, we had him trapped, he said nothing at all, or mumbled what for the Balinese is the ultimate non-word—"yes." The indifference, of course, was studied; the villagers were watching every move we made and they had an enormous amount of quite accurate information about who we were and what we were going to be doing. But they acted as if we simply did not exist, which, in fact, as this behavior was designed to inform us, we did not, or anyway not yet.

This is, as I say, general in Bali. Everywhere else I have been in Indonesia, and more latterly in Morocco, when I have gone into a new village people have poured out from all sides to take a very close look at me, and, often, an all-too-probing feel as well. In Balinese villages, at least those away from the tourist circuit, nothing happens at all. People go on pounding, chatting, making offerings, staring into space, carrying baskets about while one drifts around feeling vaguely disembodied. And the same thing is true on the individual level. When you first meet a Balinese, he seems virtually not to relate to you at all; he is, in the term Gregory Bateson and Margaret Mead made famous, "away."[1] Then—in a day, a week, a month (with some people the magic moment never comes)—he decides, for reasons I have never been quite able to fathom, that you *are* real, and then he becomes a warm, gay, sensitive, sympathetic, though, being Balinese, always precisely controlled person. You have crossed, somehow, some moral or metaphysical shadow line. Though you are not exactly taken as a Balinese (one has to be born to that), you are at least regarded as a human being rather than a cloud or a gust of wind. The whole complexion of your relationship dramatically changes to, in the majority of cases, a gentle, almost affectionate one—a low-keyed, rather playful, rather mannered, rather bemused geniality.

My wife and I were still very much in the gust of wind stage, a most frustrating, and even, as you soon begin to doubt whether you are really real after all, unnerving one, when, ten days or so after our arrival, a large cockfight was held in the public square to raise money for a new school.

Now, a few special occasions aside, cockfights are illegal in Bali under the Republic (as, for not altogether unrelated reasons, they were under the Dutch), largely as a result of the pretensions to puritanism radical nationalism tends to bring with it. The elite, which is not itself so very puritan, worries about the poor, ignorant peasant gambling all his money away, about what foreigners will think, about the waste of time better devoted to building up the country. It sees cockfighting as "primitive," "backward," "unprogressive," and generally unbecoming an ambitious nation. And, as with those other embarrassments—opium smoking, begging, or uncovered breasts—it seeks, rather unsystematically, to put a stop to it.

Of course, like drinking during prohibition or, today, smoking marihuana, cockfights, being a part of "The Balinese Way of Life," nonetheless go on happening, and with extraordinary frequency. And, like prohibition or marihuana, from time to time the police (who, in 1958 at least, were almost all not Balinese but Javanese) feel called upon to make a raid, confiscate the cocks and spurs, fine a few people, and even now and then expose some of them in the tropical sun for a day as object lessons which never, somehow, get learned, even though occasionally, quite occasionally, the object dies.

As a result, the fights are usually held in a secluded corner of a village in semisecrecy, a fact which tends to slow the action a little—not very much, but the Balinese do not care to have it slowed at all. In this case, however, perhaps because they were raising money for a school that the government was unable to give them, perhaps because raids had been few recently, perhaps, as I gathered from subsequent discussion, there was a notion that the necessary bribes had been paid, they thought they could take a chance on the central square and draw a larger and more enthusiastic crowd without attracting the attention of the law.

They were wrong. In the midst of the third match, with hundreds of people, including, still transparent, myself and my wife, fused into a single body around the ring, a superorganism in the literal sense, a truck full of policemen armed with machine guns roared up. Amid great screeching cries of "pulisi! pulisi!" from the crowd, the policemen jumped out, and, springing into the center of the ring, began to swing their guns around like gangsters in a motion picture, though not going so far as actually to fire them. The superorganism came instantly apart as its components scattered in all directions. People raced down the road, disappeared head first over walls, scrambled under platforms, folded themselves behind wicker screens, scuttled up coconut trees. Cocks armed with steel spurs sharp enough to cut off a finger or run a hole through a foot were running wildly around. Everything was dust and panic.

On the established anthropological principle, When in Rome, my wife and I decided, only slightly less instantaneously than everyone else, that the thing to do was run too. We ran down the main village street, northward, away from where we were living, for we were on that side of the ring. About halfway down another fugitive ducked suddenly into a compound—his own, it turned out—and we, seeing nothing ahead of us but rice fields, open country, and a very high volcano, followed him. As the three of us came tumbling into the courtyard, his wife, who had apparently been through this sort of thing before, whipped out a table, a tablecloth, three chairs, and three cups of tea, and we all, without any explicit communication whatsoever, sat down, commenced to sip tea, and sought to compose ourselves.

A few moments later, one of the policemen marched importantly into the yard, looking for the village chief. (The chief had not only been at the fight, he had arranged it. When the truck drove up he ran to the river, stripped off his sarong, and plunged in so he could say, when at length they found him sitting there pouring water over his head, that he had been away bathing when the whole affair had occurred and was ignorant of it. They did not believe him and fined him three hundred rupiah, which the village raised collectively.) Seeing my wife and I, "White Men," there in the yard, the policeman performed a classic double take. When he found his voice again he asked, approximately, what in the devil did we think we were doing there. Our host of five minutes leaped instantly to our defense, producing an impassioned description of who and what we were, so detailed and so accurate that it was my turn, having barely communicated with a living human being save my landlord and the village chief for more than a week, to be astonished. We had a perfect right to be there, he said, looking the Javanese upstart in the eye. We were American professors; the government had cleared us; we were there to study culture; we were going to write a book to tell Americans about Bali. And we had all been there drinking tea and talking about cultural matters all afternoon and did not know anything about any cockfight. Moreover, we had not seen the village chief all day, he must have gone to town. The policeman retreated in rather total disarray. And, after a decent interval, bewildered but relieved to have survived and stayed out of jail, so did we.

The next morning the village was a completely different world for us. Not only were we no longer invisible, we were suddenly the center of all attention, the object of a great outpouring of warmth, interest, and, most especially, amusement. Everyone in the village knew we had fled like everyone else. They asked us about it again and again (I must have told the story, small detail by small detail, fifty times by the end of the day), gently, affectionately, but quite insistently teasing us: "Why didn't you just stand there and tell the police who you were?" "Why didn't you just say you were only watching and not betting?" "Were you really afraid of those little guns?" As always, kinesthetically minded and, even when fleeing for their lives (or, as happened eight years later, surrendering them), the world's most poised people, they gleefully mimicked, also over and over again, our graceless style of running and what they claimed were our panic-stricken facial expressions. But above all, everyone was extremely pleased and even more surprised that we had not simply "pulled out our papers" (they knew about those too) and asserted our Distinguished Visitor status, but had instead demonstrated our solidarity with what were now our covillagers. (What we had actually demonstrated was our cowardice, but there is fellowship in that too.) Even the Brahmana priest, an old, grave, halfway-to-Heaven type who because of its associations with the underworld would never be involved, even distantly, in a cockfight, and was difficult to approach even to other Balinese, had us called into his courtyard to ask us about what had happened, chuckling happily at the sheer extraordinariness of it all.

In Bali, to be teased is to be accepted. It was the turning point so far as our relationship to the community was concerned, and we were quite literally "in." The whole village opened up to us, probably more than it ever would have otherwise (I might actually never have gotten to that priest, and our accidental host became one of my best informants), and certainly very much faster. Getting caught, or almost caught, in a vice raid is perhaps not a very generalizable recipe for achieving that mysterious necessity of anthropological field work, rapport, but for me it worked very well. It led to a sudden and unusually complete acceptance into a society extremely difficult for outsiders to penetrate. It gave me the kind of immediate, inside-view grasp of an aspect of "peasant mentality" that anthropologists not fortunate enough to flee headlong with their subjects from armed authorities normally do not get. And, perhaps most important of all, for the other things might have come in other ways, it put me very quickly on to a combination emotional explosion, status war, and philosophical drama of central significance to the society whose inner nature I desired to understand. By the time I left I had spent about as much time looking into cockfights as into witchcraft, irrigation, caste, or marriage.

Of Cocks and Men

Bali, mainly because it is Bali, is a well-studied place. Its mythology, art, ritual, social organization, patterns of child rearing, forms of law, even styles of trance, have all been microscopically examined for traces of that elusive substance Jane Belo called "The Balinese Temper."[2] But, aside from a few passing remarks, the cockfight has barely been noticed, although as a popular obsession of consuming power it is at least as important a revelation of what being a Balinese "is really like" as these more celebrated phenomena.[3] As much of America surfaces in a ball park, on a golf links, at a race track, or around a poker table, much of Bali surfaces in a cock ring. For it is only apparently cocks that are fighting there. Actually, it is men.

To anyone who has been in Bali any length of time, the deep psychological identification of Balinese men with their cocks is unmistakable. The double entendre here is deliberate. It works in exactly the same way in Balinese as it does in English, even to producing the same tired jokes, strained puns, and uninventive obscenities. Bateson and Mead have even suggested that, in line with the Balinese conception of the body as a set of separately animated parts, cocks are viewed as detachable, self-operating penises, ambulant genitals with a life of their own.[4] And while I do not have the kind of unconscious material either to confirm or disconfirm this intriguing notion, the fact that they are masculine symbols *par excellence* is about as indubitable, and to the Balinese about as evident, as the fact that water runs downhill.

The language of everyday moralism is shot through, on the male side of it, with roosterish imagery. *Sabung,* the word for cock (and one which appears in inscriptions as early as A.D. 922), is used metaphorically to mean "hero," "warrior," "champion," "man of parts," "political candidate," "bachelor," "dandy," "lady-killer," or "tough guy." A pompous man whose behavior presumes above his station is compared to a tailless cock who struts about as though he had a large, spectacular one. A desperate man who makes a last, irrational effort to extricate himself from an impossible situation is likened to a dying cock who makes one final lunge at his tormentor to drag him along to a common destruction. A stingy man, who promises much, gives little, and begrudges that is compared to a cock which, held by the tail, leaps at another without in fact engaging him. A marriageable young man still shy with the opposite sex or some-one in a new job anxious to make a good impression is called "a fighting cock caged for the first time."[5] Court trials, wars, political contests, inheritance disputes, and street arguments are all compared to cockfights.[6] Even the very island itself is perceived from its shape as a small, proud cock, poised, neck extended, back taut, tail raised, in eternal challenge to large, feckless, shapeless Java.[7]

But the intimacy of men with their cocks is more than metaphorical. Balinese men, or anyway a large majority of Balinese men, spend an enormous amount of time with their favorites, grooming them, feeding them, discussing them, trying them out against one another, or just gazing at them with a mixture of rapt admiration and dreamy self-absorption. Whenever you see a group of Balinese men squatting idly in the council shed or along the road in their hips down, shoulders forward, knees up fashion, half or more of them will have a rooster in his hands, holding it between his thighs, bouncing it gently up and down to strengthen its legs, ruffling its feathers with abstract sensuality, pushing it out against a neighbor's rooster to rouse its spirit, withdrawing it toward his loins to calm it again. Now and then, to get a feel for another bird, a man will fiddle this way with someone else's cock for a while, but usually by moving around to squat in place behind it, rather than just having it passed across to him as though it were merely an animal.

In the houseyard, the high-walled enclosures where the people live, fighting cocks are kept in wicker cages, moved frequently about so as to maintain the optimum balance of sun and shade. They are fed a special diet, which varies somewhat according to individual theories but which is mostly maize, sifted for impurities with far more care than it is when mere humans are going to eat it and offered to the animal kernel by kernel. Red pepper is stuffed down their beaks and up their anuses to give them spirit. They are bathed in the same ceremonial preparation of tepid water, medicinal herbs, flowers, and onions in which infants are bathed, and for a prize cock just about as often. Their combs are cropped, their plumage dressed, their spurs trimmed, their legs massaged, and they are inspected for flaws with the squinted concentration of a diamond merchant. A man who has a passion for cocks, an enthusiast in the literal sense of the term, can spend most of his life with them, and even those, the overwhelming majority, whose passion though intense has not entirely run away with them, can and do spend what seems not only to an outsider, but also to themselves, an inordinate amount of time with them. "I am cock crazy," my landlord, a quite ordinary *afficionado* by Balinese standards, used to moan as he went to move another cage, give another bath, or conduct another feeding. "We're all cock crazy."

The madness has some less visible dimensions, however, because although it is true that cocks are symbolic expressions or magnifications of their owner's self, the narcissistic male ego writ out in Aesopian terms, they are also expressions—and rather more immediate ones—of what the Balinese regard as the direct inversion, aesthetically, morally, and metaphysically, of human status: animality.

The Balinese revulsion against any behavior regarded as animal-like can hardly be overstressed. Babies are not allowed to crawl for that reason. Incest, though hardly approved, is a much less horrifying crime than bestiality. (The appropriate punishment for the second is death by drowning, for the first being forced to live like an animal.)[8] Most demons are represented—in sculpture, dance, ritual, myth—in some real or fantastic animal form. The main puberty rite consists in filing the child's teeth so they will not look like animal fangs. Not only defecation but eating is regarded as a disgusting, almost obscene activity, to be conducted hurriedly and privately, because of its association with animality. Even falling down or any form of clumsiness is considered to be bad for these reasons. Aside from cocks and a few domestic animals—oxen, ducks—of no emotional significance, the Balinese are aversive to animals, and treat their large number of dogs not merely callously but with a phobic cruelty. In identifying with his cock, the Balinese man is identifying not just with his ideal self, or even his penis, but also, and at the same time, with what he most fears, hates, and ambivalence being what it is, is fascinated by—The Powers of Darkness.

The connection of cocks and cockfighting with such Powers, with the animalistic demons that threaten constantly to invade the small, cleared off space in which the Balinese have so carefully built their lives and devour its inhabitants, is quite explicit. A cockfight, any cockfight, is in the first instance a blood sacrifice offered, with the appropriate chants and oblations, to the demons in order to pacify their ravenous, cannibal hunger. No temple festival should be conducted until one is made. (If it is omitted someone will inevitably fall into a trance and command with the voice of an angered spirit that the oversight be immediately corrected.) Collective responses to natural evils—illness, crop failure, volcanic eruptions—almost always involve them. And that famous holiday in Bali, The Day of Silence (*Njepi*), when everyone sits silent and immobile all day long in order to avoid contact with a sudden influx of demons chased momentarily out of hell, is preceded the previous day by large-scale cockfights (in this case legal) in almost every village on the island.

In the cockfight, man and beast, good and evil, ego and id, the creative power of aroused masculinity and the destructive power of loosened animality fuse in a bloody drama of hatred, cruelty, violence, and death. It is little wonder that when, as is the invariable rule, the owner of the winning cock takes the carcass of the loser—often torn limb from limb by its enraged owner—home to eat, he does so with a mixture of social embarrassment, moral satisfaction, aesthetic disgust, and cannibal joy. Or that a man who has lost an important fight is sometimes driven to wreck his family shrines and curse the gods, an act of metaphysical (and social) suicide. Or that in seeking earthly analogues for heaven and hell the Balinese compare the former to the mood of a man whose cock has just won, the latter to that of a man whose cock has just lost.

The Fight

Cockfights (*tetadjen; sabungan*) are held in a ring about fifty feet square. Usually they begin toward late afternoon and run three or four hours until sunset. About nine or ten separate matches (*sehet*) comprise a program. Each match is precisely like the others in general pattern: there is no main match, no connection between individual matches, no variation in their format, and each is arranged on a completely ad hoc basis. After a fight has ended and the emotional debris is cleaned away—the bets paid, the curses cursed, the carcasses possessed—seven, eight, perhaps even a dozen men slop negligently into the ring with a cock and seek to find there a logical opponent for it. This process, which rarely takes less than ten minutes and often a good deal longer, is conducted in a very subdued, oblique, even dissembling manner. Those not immediately involved give it at best but disguised, sidelong attention; those who, embarrassedly, are, attempt to pretend somehow that the whole thing is not really happening.

A match made, the other hopefuls retire with the same deliberate indifference, and the selected cocks have their spurs (*tadji*) affixed—razor-sharp, pointed steel swords, four or five inches long. This is a delicate job which only a small portion of men, a half-dozen or so in most villages, know how to do properly. The man who attaches the spurs also provides them, and if the rooster he assists wins its owner awards him the spur-leg of the victim. The spurs are affixed by winding a long length of string around the foot of the spur and the leg of the cock. For reasons I shall come to presently, it is done somewhat differently from case to case, and is an obsessively deliberate affair. The lore about spurs is extensive—they are sharpened only at eclipses and the dark of the moon, should be kept out of the sight of women, and so forth. And they are handled, both in use and out, with the same curious combination of fussiness and sensuality the Balinese direct toward ritual objects generally.

The spurs affixed, the two cocks are placed by their handlers (who may or may not be their owners) facing one another in the center of the ring.[9] A coconut pierced with a small hole is placed in a pail of water, in which it takes about twenty-one seconds to sink, a period known as a *tjeng* and marked at beginning and end by the beating of a slit gong. During these twenty-one seconds the handlers (*pengangkeb*) are not permitted to touch their roosters. If, as sometimes happens, the animals have not fought during this time, they are picked up, fluffed, pulled, prodded, and otherwise insulted, and put back in the center of the ring and the process begins again. Sometimes they refuse to fight at all, or one keeps running away, in which case they are imprisoned together under a wicker cage, which usually gets them engaged.

Most of the time, in any case, the cocks fly almost immediately at one another in a wing-beating, head-thrusting, leg-kicking explosion of animal fury so pure, so absolute, and in its own way so beautiful, as to be almost abstract, a Platonic concept of hate. Within moments one or the other drives home a solid blow with his spur. The handler whose cock has delivered the blow immediately picks it up so that it will not get a return blow, for if he does not the match is likely to end in a mutually mortal tie as the two birds wildly hack each other to pieces. This is particularly true if, as often happens, the spur sticks in its victim's body, for then the aggressor is at the mercy of his wounded foe.

With the birds again in the hands of their handlers, the coconut is now sunk three times after which the cock which has landed the blow must be set down to show that he is firm, a fact he demonstrates by wandering idly around the ring for a coconut sink. The coconut is then sunk twice more and the fight must recommence.

During this interval, slightly over two minutes, the handler of the wounded cock has been working frantically over it, like a trainer patching a mauled boxer between rounds, to get it in shape for a last, desperate try for victory. He blows in its mouth, putting the whole chicken head in his own mouth and sucking and blowing, fluffs it, stuffs its wounds with various sorts of medicines, and generally tries anything he can think of to arouse the last ounce of spirit which may be hidden somewhere within it. By the time he is forced to put it back down he is usually drenched in chicken blood, but, as in prize fighting, a good handler is worth his weight in gold. Some of them can virtually make the dead walk, at least long enough for the second and final round.

In the climactic battle (if there is one; sometimes the wounded cock simply expires in the handler's hands or immediately as it is placed down again), the cock who landed the first blow usually proceeds to finish off his weakened opponent. But this is far from an inevitable outcome, for if a cock can walk he can fight, and if he can fight, he can kill, and what counts is which cock expires first. If the wounded one can get a stab in and stagger on until the other drops, he is the official winner, even if he himself topples over an instant later.

Surrounding all this melodrama—which the crowd packed tight around the ring follows in near silence, moving their bodies in kinesthetic sympathy with the movement of the animals, cheering their champions on with wordless hand motions, shiftings of the shoulders, turnings of the head, falling back *en masse* as the cock with the murderous spurs careens toward one side of the ring (it is said that spectators sometimes lose eyes and fingers from being too attentive), surging forward again as they glance off toward another—is a vast body of extraordinarily elaborate and precisely detailed rules.

These rules, together with the developed lore of cocks and cockfighting which accompanies them, are written down in palm leaf manuscripts (*lontar; rontal*), passed on from generation to generation as part of the general legal and cultural tradition of the villages. At a fight, the umpire (*saja komong; djuru kembar*)—the man who manages the coconut—is in charge of their application and his authority is absolute. I have never seen an umpire's judgment questioned on any subject, even by the more despondent losers, nor have I ever heard, even in private, a charge of unfairness directed against one, or, for that matter, complaints about umpires in general. Only exceptionally well-trusted, solid, and, given the complexity of the code, knowledgeable citizens perform this job, and in fact men will bring their cocks only to fights presided over by such men. It is also the umpire to whom accusations of cheating, which, though rare in the extreme, occasionally arise, are referred; and it is he who in the not infrequent cases where the cocks expire virtually together decides which (if either, for, though the Balinese do not care for such an outcome, there can be ties) went first. Likened to a judge, a king, a priest, and a policeman, he is all of these, and under his assured direction the animal passion of the fight proceeds within the civic certainty of the law. In the dozens of cockfights I saw in Bali, I never once saw an altercation about rules. Indeed, I never saw an open altercation, other than those between cocks, at all.

This crosswise doubleness of an event which, taken as a fact of nature, is rage untrammeled and, taken as a fact of culture, is form perfected, defines the cockfight as a sociological entity. A cockfight is what, searching for a name for something not vertebrate enough to be called a group and not structureless enough to be called a crowd, Erving Goffman has called a "focused gathering"—a set of persons engrossed in a common flow of activity and relating to one another in terms of that flow.[10] Such gatherings meet and disperse; the participants in them fluctuate; the activity that focuses them is discreet—a particulate process that reoccurs rather than a continuous one that endures. They take their form from the situation that evokes them, the floor on which they are placed, as Goffman puts it; but it is a form, and an articulate one, nonetheless. For the situation, the floor is itself created, in jury deliberations, surgical operations, block meetings, sit-ins, cockfights, by the cultural preoccupations—here, as we shall see, the celebration of status rivalry—which not only specify the focus but, assembling actors and arranging scenery, bring it actually into being.

In classical times (that is to say, prior to the Dutch invasion of 1908), when there were no bureaucrats around to improve popular morality, the staging of a cockfight was an explicitly societal matter. Bringing a cock to an important fight was, for an adult male, a compulsory duty of citizenship; taxation of fights, which were usually held on market day, was a major source of public revenue; patronage of the art was a stated responsibility of princes; and the cock ring, or *wantilan*, stood in the center of the village near those other monuments of Balinese civility—the council house, the origin temple, the marketplace, the signal tower, and the banyan tree. Today, a few special occasions aside, the newer rectitude makes so open a statement of the connection between the excitements of collective life and those of blood sport impossible, but, less directly expressed, the connection itself remains intimate and intact. To expose it, however, it is necessary to turn to the aspect of cockfighting around which all the others pivot, and through which they exercise their force, an aspect I have thus far studiously ignored. I mean, of course, the gambling.

Odds and Even Money

The Balinese never do anything in a simple way that they can contrive to do in a complicated one, and to this generalization cockfight wagering is no exception.

In the first place, there are two sorts of bets, or *toh*.[11] There is the single axial bet on the center between the principals (*toh ketengah*), and there is the cloud of peripheral ones around the ring between members of the audience (*toh kesasi*). The first is typically large; the second typically small. The first is collective, involving coalitions of bettors clustering around the owner; the second is individual, man to man. The first is a matter of deliberate, very quiet, almost furtive arrangement by the coalition members and the umpire huddled like conspirators in the center of the ring; the second is a matter of impulsive shouting, public offers, and public acceptances by the excited throng around its edges. And most curiously, and as we shall see most revealingly, *where the first is always, without exception, even money, the second, equally without exception, is never such.* What is a fair coin in the center is a biased one on the side.

The center bet is the official one, hedged in again with a webwork of rules, and is made between the two cock owners, with the umpire as overseer and public witness.[12] This bet, which, as I say, is always relatively and sometimes very large, is never raised simply by the owner in whose name it is made, but by him together with four or five, sometimes seven or eight, allies—kin, village mates, neighbors, close friends. He may, if he is not especially well-to-do, not even be the major contributor, though, if only to show that he is not involved in any chicanery, he must be a significant one.

Of the fifty-seven matches for which I have exact and reliable data on the center bet, the range is from fifteen ringgits to five hundred, with a mean at eighty-five and with the distribution being rather noticeably trimodal: small fights (15 ringgits either side of 35) accounting for about 45 percent of the total number; medium ones (20 ringgits either side of 70) for about 25 percent; and large (75 ringgits either side of 175) for about 20 percent, with a few very small and very large ones out at the extremes. In a society where the normal daily wage of a manual laborer—a brickmaker, an ordinary farmworker, a market porter—was about three ringgits a day, and considering the fact that fights were held on the average about every two-and-a-half days in the immediate area I studied, this is clearly serious gambling, even if the bets are pooled rather than individual efforts.

The side bets are, however, something else altogether. Rather than the solemn, legalistic pactmaking of the center, wagering takes place rather in the fashion in which the stock exchange used to work when it was out on the curb. There is a fixed and known odds paradigm which runs in a continuous series from ten-to-nine at the short end to two-to-one at the long: 10-9, 9-8, 8-7, 7-6, 6-5, 5-4, 4-3, 3-2, 2-1. The man who wishes to back the *underdog cock* (leaving aside how favorites, *kebut,* and underdogs, *ngai,* are established for the moment) shouts the short-side number indicating the odds he wants *to be given.* That is, if he shouts *gasal,* "five," he wants the underdog at five-to-four (or, for him, four-to-five); if he shouts "four," he wants it at four-to-three (again, he putting up the "three"), if "nine," at nine-to-eight, and so on. A man backing the favorite, and thus considering giving odds if he can get them short enough, indicates the fact by crying out the color-type of that cock—"brown," "speckled," or whatever.[13]

As odds-takers (backers of the underdog) and odds-givers (backers of the favorite) sweep the crowd with their shouts, they begin to focus in on one another as potential betting pairs, often from far across the ring. The taker tries to shout the giver into longer odds, the giver to shout the taker into shorter ones.[14] The taker, who is the wooer in this situation, will signal how large a bet he wishes to make at the odds he is shouting by holding a number of fingers up in front of his face and vigorously waving them. If the giver, the wooed, replies in kind, the bet is made; if he does not, they unlock gazes and the search goes on.

The side betting, which takes place after the center bet has been made and its size announced, consists then in a rising crescendo of shouts as backers of the underdog offer their propositions to anyone who will accept them, while those who are backing the favorite but do not like the price being offered, shout equally frenetically the color of the cock to show they too are desperate to bet but want shorter odds.

Almost always odds-calling, which tends to be very consensual in that at any one time almost all callers are calling the same thing, starts off toward the long end of the range—five-to-four or four-to-three—and then moves, also consensually, toward the short end with greater or lesser speed and to a greater or lesser degree. Men crying "five" and finding themselves answered only with cries of "brown" start crying "six," either drawing the other callers fairly quickly with them or retiring from the scene as their too-generous offers are snapped up. If the change is made and partners are still scarce, the procedure is repeated in a move to "seven," and so on, only rarely, and in the very largest fights, reaching the ultimate "nine" or "ten" levels. Occasionally, if the cocks are clearly mismatched, there may be no upward movement at all, or even a movement down the scale to four-to-three, three-to-two, very, very rarely two-to-one, a shift which is accompanied by a declining number of bets as a shift upward is accompanied by an increasing number. But the general pattern is for the betting to move a shorter or longer distance up the scale toward the, for sidebets, nonexistent pole of even money, with the overwhelming majority of bets falling in the four-to-three to eight-to-seven range.[15]

As the moment for the release of the cocks by the handlers approaches, the screaming, at least in a match where the center bet is large, reaches almost frenzied proportions as the remaining unfulfilled bettors try desperately to find a last minute partner at a price they can live with. (Where the center bet is small, the opposite tends to occur: betting dies off, trailing into silence, as odds lengthen and people lose interest.) In a large-bet, well-made match—the kind of match the Balinese regard as "real cockfighting"—the mob scene quality, the sense that sheer chaos is about to break loose, with all those waving, shouting, pushing, clambering men is quite strong, an effect which is only heightened by the intense stillness that falls with instant suddenness, rather as if someone had turned off the current, when the slit gong sounds, the cocks are put down, and the battle begins.

When it ends, anywhere from fifteen seconds to five minutes later, *all bets are immediately paid.* There are absolutely no IOU's, at least to a betting opponent. One may, of course, borrow from a friend before offering or accepting a wager, but to offer or accept it you must have the money already in hand and, if you lose, you must pay it on the spot, before the next match begins. This is an iron rule, and as I have never heard of a disputed umpire's decision (though doubtless there must sometimes be some), I have also never heard of a welshed bet, perhaps because in a worked-up cockfight crowd the consequences might be, as they are reported to be sometimes for cheaters, drastic and immediate.

It is, in any case, this formal asymmetry between balanced center bets and unbalanced side ones that poses the critical analytical problem for a theory which sees cockfight wagering as the link connecting the fight to the wider world of Balinese culture. It also suggests the way to go about solving it and demonstrating the link.

The first point that needs to be made in this connection is that the higher the center bet, the more likely the match will in actual fact be an even one. Simple considerations of rationality suggest that. If you are betting fifteen ringgits on a cock, you might be willing to go along with even money even if you feel your animal somewhat the less promising. But if you are betting five hundred you are very, very likely to be loath to do so. Thus, in large-bet fights, which of course involve the better animals, tremendous care is taken to see that the cocks are about as evenly matched as to size, general condition, pugnacity, and so on as is humanly possible. The different ways of adjusting the spurs of the animals are often employed to secure this. If one cock seems stronger, an agreement will be made to position his spur at a slightly less advantageous angle—a kind of handicapping, at which spur affixers are, so it is said, extremely skilled. More care will be taken, too, to employ skillful handlers and to match them exactly as to abilities.

In short, in a large-bet fight the pressure to make the match a genuinely fifty-fifty proposition is enormous, and is consciously felt as such. For medium fights the pressure is somewhat less, and for small ones less yet, though there is always an effort to make things at least approximately equal, for even at fifteen ringgits (five days' work) no one wants to make an even money bet in a clearly unfavorable situation. And, again, what statistics I have tend to bear this out. In my fifty-seven matches, the favorite won thirty-three times overall, the underdog twenty-four, a 1.4 to 1 ratio. But if one splits the figures at sixty ringgits center bets, the ratios turn out to be 1.1 to 1 (twelve favorites, eleven underdogs) for those above this line, and 1.6 to 1 (twenty-one and thirteen) for those below it. Or, if you take the extremes, for very large fights, those with center bets over a hundred ringgits the ratio is 1 to 1 (seven and seven); for very small fights, those under forty ringgits, it is 1.9 to 1 (nineteen and ten).[16]

Now, from this proposition—that the higher the center bet the more exactly a fifty-fifty proposition the cockfight is—two things more or less immediately follow: (1) the higher the center bet, the greater is the pull on the side betting toward the short-odds end of the wagering spectrum and vice versa; (2) the higher the center bet, the greater the volume of side betting and vice versa.

The logic is similar in both cases. The closer the fight is in fact to even money, the less attractive the long end of the odds will appear and, therefore, the shorter it must be if there are to be takers. That this is the case is apparent from mere inspection, from the Balinese's own analysis of the matter, and from what more systematic observations I was able to collect. Given the difficulty of making precise and complete recordings of side betting, this argument is hard to cast in numerical form, but in all my cases the odds-giver, odds-taker consensual point, a quite pronounced minimax saddle where the bulk (at a guess, two-thirds to three-quarters in most cases) of the bets are actually made, was three or four points further along the scale toward the shorter end for the large-center-bet fights than for the small ones, with medium ones generally in between. In detail, the fit is not, of course, exact, but the general pattern is quite consistent: the power of the center bet to pull the side bets toward its own even-money pattern is directly proportional to its size, because its size is directly proportional to the degree to which the cocks are in fact evenly matched. As for the volume question, total wagering is greater in large-center-bet fights because such fights are considered more "interesting" not only in the sense that they are less predictable, but, more crucially, that more is at stake in them—in terms of money, in terms of the quality of the cocks, and consequently, as we shall see, in terms of social prestige.[17]

The paradox of fair coin in the middle, biased coin on the outside is thus a merely apparent one. The two betting systems, though formally incongruent, are not really contradictory to one another, but part of a single larger system in which the center bet is, so to speak, the "center of gravity," drawing, the larger it is the more so, the outside bets toward the short-odds end of the scale. The center bet thus "makes the game," or perhaps better, defines it, signals what, following a notion of Jeremy Bentham's, I am going to call its "depth."

The Balinese attempt to create an interesting, if you will, "deep," match by making the center bet as large as possible so that the cocks matched will be as equal and as fine as possible, and the outcome, thus, as unpredictable as possible. They do not always succeed. Nearly half the matches are relatively trivial, relatively uninteresting—in my borrowed terminology, "shallow"—affairs. But that fact no more argues against my interpretation than the fact that most painters, poets, and playwrights are mediocre argues against the view that artistic effort is directed toward profundity and, with a certain frequency, approximates it. The image of artistic technique is indeed exact: the center bet is a means, a device, for creating "interesting," "deep" matches, *not* the reason, at least not the main reason, *why* they are interesting, the source of their fascination, the substance of their depth. The question why such matches are interesting—indeed, for the Balinese, exquisitely absorbing—takes us out of the realm of formal concerns into more broadly sociological and social-psychological ones, and to a less purely economic idea of what "depth" in gaming amounts to.[18]

Playing with Fire

Bentham's concept of "deep play" is found in his *The Theory of Legislation*.[19] By it he means play in which the stakes are so high that it is, from his utilitarian standpoint, irrational for men to engage in it at all. If a man whose fortune is a thousand pounds (or ringgits) wages five hundred of it on an even bet, the marginal utility of the pound he stands to win is clearly less than the marginal disutility of the one he stands to lose. In genuine deep play, this is the case for both parties. They are both in over their heads. Having come together in search of pleasure they have entered into a relationship which will bring the participants, considered collectively, net pain rather than net pleasure. Bentham's conclusion was, therefore, that deep play was immoral from the first principles and, a typical step for him, should be prevented legally.

But more interesting than the ethical problem, at least for our concerns here, is that despite the logical force of Bentham's analysis men do engage in such play, both passionately and often, and even in the face of law's revenge. For Bentham and those who think as he does (nowadays mainly lawyers, economists, and a few psychiatrists), the explanation is, as I have said, that such men are irrational—addicts, fetishists, children, fools, savages, who need only to be protected against themselves. But for the Balinese, though naturally they do not formulate it in so many words, the explanation lies in the fact that in such play money is less a measure of utility, had or expected, than it is a symbol of moral import, perceived or imposed.

It is, in fact, in shallow games, ones in which smaller amounts of money are involved, that increments and decrements of cash are more nearly synonyms for utility and disutility, in the ordinary, unexpanded sense—for pleasure and pain, happiness and unhappiness. In deep ones, where the amounts of money are great, much more is at stake than material gain: namely esteem, honor, dignity, respect—in a word, though in Bali a profoundly freighted word, status.[20] It is at stake symbolically, for (a few cases of ruined addict gamblers aside) no one's status is actually altered by the outcome of a cockfight; it is only, and that momentarily, affirmed or insulted. But for the Balinese, for whom nothing is more pleasurable than an affront obliquely delivered or more painful than one obliquely received—particularly when mutual acquaintances, undeceived by surfaces, are watching—such appraisive drama is deep indeed.

This, I must stress immediately, is *not* to say that the money does not matter, or that the Balinese is no more concerned about losing five hundred ringgits than fifteen. Such a conclusion would be absurd. It is because money *does,* in this hardly unmaterialistic society, matter and matter very much that the more of it one risks the more of a lot of other things, such as one's pride, one's poise, one's dispassion, one's masculinity, one also risks, again only momentarily but again very publicly as well. In deep cockfights an owner and his collaborators, and, as we shall see, to a lesser but still quite real extent also their backers on the outside, put their money where their status is.

It is in large part *because* the marginal disutility of loss is so great at the higher levels of betting that to engage in such betting is to lay one's public self, allusively and metaphorically, through the medium of one's cock, on the line. And though to a Benthamite this might seem merely to increase the irrationality of the enterprise that much further, to the Balinese what it mainly increases is the meaningfulness of it all. And as (to follow Weber rather than Bentham) the imposition of meaning on life is the major end and primary condition of human existence, that access of significance more than compensates for the economic costs involved.[21] Actually, given the even-money quality of the larger matches, important changes in material fortune among those who regularly participate in them seem virtually nonexistent, because matters more or less even out over the long run. It is, actually, in the smaller, shallow fights, where one finds the handful of more pure, addict-type gamblers involved—those who *are* in it mainly for the money—that "real" changes in social position, largely downward, are affected. Men of this sort, plungers, are highly dispraised by "true cockfighters" as fools who do not understand what the sport is all about, vulgarians who simply miss the point of it all. They are, these addicts, regarded as fair game for the genuine enthusiasts, those who do understand, to take a little money away from, something that is easy enough to do by luring them, through the force of their greed, into irrational bets on mismatched cocks. Most of them do indeed manage to ruin themselves in a remarkably short time, but there always seem to be one or two of them around, pawning their land and selling their clothes in order to bet, at any particular time.[22]

This graduated correlation of "status gambling" with deeper fights and, inversely, "money gambling" with shallower ones is in fact quite general. Bettors themselves form a sociomoral hierarchy in these terms. As noted earlier, at most cockfights there are, around the very edges of the cockfight area, a large number of mindless, sheer-chance type gambling games (roulette, dice throw, coin-spin, pea-under-the-shell) operated by concessionaires. Only women, children, adolescents, and various other sorts of people who do not (or not yet) fight cocks—the extremely poor, the socially despised, the personally idiosyncratic—play at these games, at, of course, penny ante levels. Cockfighting men would be ashamed to go anywhere near them. Slightly above these people in standing are those who, though they do not themselves fight cocks, bet on the smaller matches around the edges. Next, there are those who fight cocks in small, or occasionally medium matches, but have not the status to join in the large ones, though they may bet from time to time on the side in those. And finally, there are those, the really substantial members of the community, the solid citizenry around whom local life revolves, who fight in the larger fights and bet on them around the side. The focusing element in these focused gatherings, these men generally dominate and define the sport as they dominate and define the society. When a Balinese male talks, in that almost venerative way, about "the true cockfighter," the *bebatoh* ("bettor") or *djuru kurung* ("cage keeper"), it is this sort of person, not those who bring the mentality of the pea-and-shell game into the quite different, inappropriate context of the cockfight, the driven gambler (*potét*, a word which has the secondary meaning of thief or reprobate), and the wistful hanger-on, that they mean. For such a man, what is really going on in a match is something rather close to an *affaire d'honneur* (though, with the Balinese talent for practical fantasy, the blood that is spilled is only figuratively human) than to the stupid, mechanical crank of a slot machine.

What makes Balinese cockfighting deep is thus not money in itself, but what, the more of it that is involved the more so, money causes to happen: the migration of the Balinese status hierarchy into the body of the cockfight. Psychologically an Aesopian representation of the ideal/demonic, rather narcissistic, male self, sociologically it is an equally Aesopian representation of the complex fields of tension set up by the controlled, muted, ceremonial, but for all that deeply felt, interaction of those selves in the context of everyday life. The cocks may be surrogates for their owners' personalities, animal mirrors of psychic form, but the cockfight is—or more exactly, deliberately is made to be—a simulation of the social matrix, the involved system of crosscutting, overlapping, highly corporate groups—villages, kingroups, irrigation societies, temple congregations, "castes"—in which its devotees live.[23] And as prestige, the necessity to affirm it, defend it, celebrate it, justify it, and just plain bask in it (but not, given the strongly ascriptive character of Balinese stratification, to seek it), is perhaps the central driving force in the society, so also—ambulant penises, blood sacrifices, and monetary exchanges aside—is it of the cockfight. This apparent amusement and seeming sport is, to take another phrase from Erving Goffman, "a status bloodbath."[24]

The easiest way to make this clear, and at least to some degree to demonstrate it, is to invoke the village whose cockfighting activities I observed the closest—the one in which the raid occurred and from which my statistical data are taken.

As all Balinese villages, this one—Tihingan, in the Klungkung region of southeast Bali—is intricately organized, a labyrinth of alliances and oppositions. But, unlike many, two sorts of corporate groups, which are also status groups, particularly stand out, and we may concentrate on them, in a part-for-whole way, without undue distortion.

First, the village is dominated by four large, patrilineal, partly endogamous descent groups which are constantly vying with one another and form the major factions in the village. Sometimes they group two and two, or rather the two larger ones versus the two smaller ones plus all the unaffiliated people; sometimes they operate independently. There are also subfactions within them, subfactions within the subfactions, and so on to rather fine levels of distinction. And second, there is the village itself, almost entirely endogamous, which is opposed to all the other villages round about in its cockfight circuit (which, as explained, is the market region), but which also forms alliances with certain of these neighbors against certain others in various supravillage political and social contexts. The exact situation is thus, as everywhere in Bali, quite distinctive; but the general pattern of a tiered hierarchy of status rivalries between highly corporate but various based groupings (and, thus, between the members of them) is entirely general.

Consider, then, as support of the general thesis that the cockfight, and especially the deep cockfight, is fundamentally a dramatization of status concerns, the following facts, which to avoid extended ethnographic description I will simply pronounce to be facts—though the concrete evidence—examples, statements, and numbers that could be brought to bear in support of them is both extensive and unmistakable:

1. A man virtually never bets against a cock owned by a member of his own kingroup. Usually he will feel obliged to bet for it, the more so the closer the kin tie and the deeper the fight. If he is certain in his mind that it will not win, he may just not bet at all, particularly if it is only a second cousin's bird or if the fight is a shallow one. But as a rule he will feel he must support it and, in deep games, nearly always does. Thus the great majority of the people calling "five" or "speckled" so demonstratively are expressing their allegiance to their kinsman, not their evaluation of his bird, their understanding of probability theory, or even their hopes of unearned income.

2. This principle is extended logically. If your kingroup is not involved you will support an allied kingroup against an unallied one in the same way, and so on through the very involved networks of alliances which, as I say, make up this, as any other, Balinese village.

3. So, too, for the village as a whole. If an outsider cock is fighting any cock from your village, you will tend to support the local one. If, what is a rare circumstance but occurs every now and then, a cock from outside your cockfight circuit is fighting one inside it you will also tend to support the "home bird."

4. Cocks which come from any distance are almost always favorites, for the theory is the man would not have dared to bring it if it was not a good cock, the more so the further he has come. His followers are, of course, obliged to support him, and when the more grand-scale legal cockfights are held (on holidays, and so on) the people of the village take what they regard to be the best cocks in the village, regardless of ownership, and go off to support them, although they will almost certainly have to give odds on them and to make large bets to show that they are not a cheapskate village. Actually, such "away games," though infrequent, tend to mend the ruptures between village members that the constantly occurring "home games," where village factions are opposed rather than united, exacerbate.

5. Almost all matches are sociologically relevant. You seldom get two outsider cocks fighting, or two cocks with no particular group backing, or with group backing which is mutually unrelated in any clear way. When you do get them, the game is very shallow, betting very slow, and the whole thing very dull, with no one save the immediate principals and an addict gambler or two at all interested.

6. By the same token, you rarely get two cocks from the same group, even more rarely from the same subfaction, and virtually never from the same sub-subfaction (which would be in most cases one extended family) fighting. Similarly, in outside village fights two members of the village will rarely fight against one another, even though, as bitter rivals, they would do so with enthusiasm on their home grounds.

7. On the individual level, people involved in an institutionalized hostility relationship, called *puik,* in which they do not speak or otherwise have anything to do with each other (the causes of this formal breaking of relations are many: wife-capture, inheritance arguments, political differences) will bet very heavily, sometimes almost maniacally, against one another in what is a frank and direct attack on the very masculinity, the ultimate ground of his status, of the opponent.

8. The center bet coalition is, in all but the shallowest games, *always* made up by structural allies—no "outside money" is involved. What is "outside" depends upon the context, of course, but given it, no outside money is mixed in with the main bet; if the principals cannot raise it, it is not made. The center bet, again especially in deeper games, is thus the most direct and open expression of social opposition, which is one

of the reasons why both it and match making are surrounded by such an air of unease, furtiveness, embarrassment, and so on.

9. The rule about borrowing money—that you may borrow *for* a bet but not *in* one—stems (and the Balinese are quite conscious of this) from similar considerations: you are never at the *economic* mercy of your enemy that way. Gambling debts, which can get quite large on a rather short-term basis, are always to friends, never to enemies, structurally speaking.

10. When two cocks are structurally irrelevant or neutral so far as *you* are concerned (though, as mentioned, they almost never are to each other) you do not even ask a relative or a friend whom he is betting on, because if you know how he is betting and he knows you know, and you go the other way, it will lead to strain. This rule is explicit and rigid; fairly elaborate, even rather artificial precautions are taken to avoid breaking it. At the very least you must pretend not to notice what he is doing, and he what you are doing.

11. There is a special word for betting against the grain, which is also the word for "pardon me" (*mpura*). It is considered a bad thing to do, though if the center bet is small it is sometimes all right as long as you do not do it too often. But the larger the bet and the more frequently you do it, the more the "pardon me" tack will lead to social disruption.

12. In fact, the institutionalized hostility relation, *puik*, is often formally initiated (though its causes always lie elsewhere) by such a "pardon me" bet in a deep fight, putting the symbolic fat in the fire. Similarly, the end of such a relationship and resumption of normal social intercourse is often signalized (but, again, not actually brought about) by one or the other of the enemies supporting the other's bird.

13. In sticky, cross-loyalty situations, of which in this extraordinarily complex social system there are of course many, where a man is caught between two more or less equally balanced loyalties, he tends to wander off for a cup of coffee or something to avoid having to bet, a form of behavior reminiscent of that of American voters in similar situations.[25]

14. The people involved in the center bet are, especially in deep fights, virtually always leading members of their group—kinship, village, or whatever. Further, those who bet on the side (including these people) are, as I have already remarked, the more established members of the village—the solid citizens. Cockfighting is for those who are involved in the everyday politics of prestige as well, not for youth, women, subordinates, and so forth.

15. So far as money is concerned, the explicitly expressed attitude toward it is that it is a secondary matter. It is not, as I have said, of no importance; Balinese are no happier to lose several weeks' income than anyone else. But they mainly look on the monetary aspects of the cockfight as self-balancing, a matter of just moving money around, circulating it among a fairly well-defined group of serious cockfighters. The really impor-

tant wins and losses are seen mostly in other terms, and the general attitude toward wagering is not any hope of cleaning up, of making a killing (addict gamblers again excepted), but that of the horseplayer's prayer: "O, God, please let me break even." In prestige terms, however, you do not want to break even, but, in a momentary, punctuate sort of way, win utterly. The talk (which goes on all the time) is about fights against such-and-such a cock of So-and-So which your cock demolished, not on how much you won, a fact people, even for large bets, rarely remember for any length of time, though they will remember the day they did in Pan Loh's finest cock for years.

16. You must bet on cocks of your own group aside from mere loyalty considerations, for if you do not people generally will say, "What! Is he too proud for the likes of us? Does he have to go to Java or Den Pasar [the capital town] to bet, he is such an important man?" Thus there is a general pressure to bet not only to show that you are important locally, but that you are not so important that you look down on everyone else as unfit even to be rivals. Similarly, home team people must bet against outside cocks or the outsiders will accuse it—a serious charge—of just collecting entry fees and not really being interested in cockfighting, as well as again being arrogant and insulting.

17. Finally, the Balinese peasants themselves are quite aware of all this and can and, at least to an ethnographer, do state most of it in approximately the same terms as I have. Fighting cocks, almost every Balinese I have ever discussed the subject with has said, is like playing with fire only not getting burned. You activate village and kingroup rivalries and hostilities, but in "play" form, coming dangerously and entrancingly close to the expression of open and direct interpersonal and intergroup aggression (something which, again, almost never happens in the normal course of ordinary life), but not quite, because, after all, it is "only a cockfight."

More observations of this sort could be advanced, but perhaps the general point is, if not made, at least well-delineated, and the whole argument thus far can be usefully summarized in a formal paradigm:

THE MORE A MATCH IS . . .

1. Between near status equals (and/or personal enemies)
2. Between high status individuals

THE DEEPER THE MATCH.

THE DEEPER THE MATCH . . .

1. The closer the identification of cock and man (or: more properly, the deeper the match the more the man will advance his best, most closely-identified-with cock).

2. The finer the cocks involved and the more exactly they will be matched.
3. The greater the emotion that will be involved and the more the general absorption in the match.
4. The higher the individual bets center and outside, the shorter the outside bet odds will tend to be, and the more betting there will be overall.
5. The less an "economic" and the more a "status" view of gaming will be involved, and the "solider" the citizens who will be gaming.[26]

Inverse arguments hold for the shallower the fight, culminating, in a reversed-signs sense, in the coin-spinning and dice-throwing amusements. For deep fights there are no absolute upper limits, though there are of course practical ones, and there are a great many legendlike tales of great Duel-in-the-Sun combats between lords and princes in classical times (for cockfighting has always been as much an elite concern as a popular one), far deeper than anything anyone, even aristocrats, could produce today anywhere in Bali.

Indeed, one of the great culture heroes of Bali is a prince, called after his passion for the sport, "The Cockfighter," who happened to be away at a very deep cockfight with a neighboring prince when the whole of his family—father, brothers, wives, sisters—were assassinated by commoner usurpers. Thus spared, he returned to dispatch the upstarts, regain the throne, reconstitute the Balinese high tradition, and build its most powerful, glorious, and prosperous state. Along with everything else that the Balinese see in fighting cocks—themselves, their social order, abstract hatred, masculinity, demonic power—they also see the archetype of status virtue, the arrogant, resolute, honor-mad player with real fire, the *ksatria* prince.[27]

Feathers, Blood, Crowds, and Money

"Poetry makes nothing happen," Auden says in his elegy of Yeats, "it survives in the valley of its saying . . . a way of happening, a mouth." The cockfight too, in this colloquial sense, makes nothing happen. Men go on allegorically humiliating one another and being allegorically humiliated by one another, day after day, glorying quietly in the experience if they have triumphed, crushed only slightly more openly by it if they have not. *But no one's status really changes.* You cannot ascend the status ladder by winning cockfights; you cannot, as an individual, really ascend it at all. Nor can you descend it that way.[28] All you can do is enjoy and savor, or suffer and withstand, the concocted sensation of drastic and momentary movement along an aesthetic semblance of that ladder, and kind of behind-the-mirror status jump which has the look of mobility without its actuality.

As any art form—for that, finally, is what we are dealing with—the cockfight renders ordinary, everyday experience comprehensible by presenting it in terms of acts and objects which have had their practical consequences removed and been reduced (or, if you prefer, raised) to the level of sheer appearances, where their meaning can be more powerfully articulated and more exactly perceived. The cockfight is "really real" only to the cocks—it does not kill anyone, castrate anyone, reduce anyone to animal status, alter the hierarchical relations among people, nor refashion the hierarchy; it does not even redistribute income in any significant way. What it does is what, for other peoples with other temperaments and other conventions, *Lear* and *Crime and Punishment* do; it catches up these themes—death, masculinity, rage, pride, loss, beneficence, chance—and, ordering them into an encompassing structure, presents them in such a way as to throw into relief a particular view of their essential nature. It puts a construction on them, makes them, to those historically positioned to appreciate the construction, meaningful—visible, tangible, graspable—"real," in an ideational sense. An image, fiction, a model, a metaphor, the cockfight is a means of expression; its function is neither to assuage social passions nor to heighten them (though, in its play-with-fire way, it does a bit of both), but, in a medium of feathers, blood, crowds, and money, to display them.

The question of how it is that we perceive qualities in things—paintings, books, melodies, plays—that we do not feel we can assert literally to be there has come, in recent years, into the very center of aesthetic theory.[29] Neither the sentiments of the artist, which remain his, nor those of the audience, which remain theirs, can account for the agitation of one painting or the serenity of another. We attribute grandeur, wit, despair, exuberance to strings of sounds; lightness, energy, violence, fluidity to blocks of stone. Novels are said to have strength, buildings eloquence, plays momentum, ballets repose. In this realm of eccentric predicates, to say that the cockfight, in its perfected cases at least, is "disquietful" does not seem at all unnatural, merely, as I have just denied it practical consequence, somewhat puzzling.

The disquietfulness arises, "somehow," out of a conjunction of three attributes of the fight: its immediate dramatic shape; its metaphoric content; and its social context. A cultural figure against a social ground, the fight is at once a convulsive surge of animal hatred, a mock war of symbolical selves, and a formal simulation of status tensions, and its aesthetic power derives from its capacity to force together these diverse realities. The reason it is disquietful is not that it has material effects (it has some, but they are minor); the reason that it is disquietful is that, joining pride to selfhood, selfhood to cocks, and cocks to destruction, it brings to imaginative realization a dimension of Balinese experience normally well-obscured from view. The transfer of a sense of gravity into what is in itself a rather blank and unvarious spectacle, a commotion of beating wings and throbbing legs, is effected by interpreting it as expressive of something unsettling in the way its authors and audience live, or, even more ominously, what they are.

As a dramatic shape, the fight displays a characteristic that does not seem so remarkable until one realizes that it does not have to be there: a radically atomistical structure.[30] Each match is a world unto itself, a particulate burst of form. There is the match making, there is the betting, there is the fight, there is the result—utter triumph and utter defeat—and there is the hurried, embarrassed passing of money. The loser is not consoled. People drift away from him, look through him, leave him to assimilate his momentary descent into nonbeing, reset his face, and return, scarless and intact, to the fray. Nor are winners congratulated, or events rehashed; once a match is ended the crowd's attention turns totally to the next, with no looking back. A shadow of the experience no doubt remains with the principals, perhaps even with some of the witnesses, of a deep fight, as it remains with us when we leave the theater after seeing a powerful play well-performed; but it quite soon fades to become at most a schematic memory—a diffuse glow or an abstract shudder—and usually not even that. Any expressive form lives only in its own present—the one it itself creates. But, here, that present is severed into a string of flashes, some more bright than others, but all of them disconnected, aesthetic quanta. Whatever the cockfight says, it says in spurts.

But, as I have argued lengthily elsewhere, the Balinese live in spurts.[31] Their life, as they arrange it and perceive it, is less a flow, a directional movement out of the past, through the present, toward the future than an on-off pulsation of meaning and vacuity, an arhythmic alternation of short periods when "something" (that is, something significant) is happening and equally short ones where "nothing" (that is, nothing much) is—between what they themselves call "full" and "empty" times, or, in another idiom, "junctures" and "holes." In focusing activity down to a burning-glass dot, the cockfight is merely being Balinese in the same way in which everything from the monadic encounters of everyday life, through the changing pointillism of *gamelan* music, to the visiting-day-of-the-gods temple celebrations are. It is not an imitation of the punctateness of Balinese social life, nor a depiction of it, nor even an expression of it; it is an example of it, carefully prepared.[32]

If one dimension of the cockfight's structure, its lack of temporal directionality, makes it seem a typical segment of the general social life, however, the other, its flat-out, head-to-head (or spur-to-spur) aggressiveness, makes it seem a contradiction, a reversal, even a subversion of it. In the normal course of things, the Balinese are shy to the point of obsessiveness of open conflict. Oblique, cautious, subdued, controlled, masters of indirection and dissimulation—what they call *alus*, "polished," "smooth"—they rarely face what they can turn away from, rarely resist what they can evade. But here they portray themselves as wild and murderous, manic explosions of instinctual cruelty. A powerful rendering of life as the Balinese most deeply do not want it (to adapt a phrase Frye has used of Gloucester's blinding) is set in the context of a sample of it as they do in fact have it.[33] And, because the context suggests that the rendering, if less than a straightforward description is nonetheless more than an idle fancy, it is here that the disquietfulness—the disquietfulness of the *fight,* not (or, anyway, not necessarily) its patrons, who seem in fact rather thoroughly to enjoy it—emerges. The slaughter in the cock ring is not a depiction of how things literally are among men, but, what is almost worse, of how, from a particular angle, they imaginatively are.[34]

The angle, of course, is stratificatory. What, as we have already seen, the cockfight talks most forcibly about is status relationships, and what it says about them is that they are matters of life and death. That prestige is a profoundly serious business is apparent everywhere one looks in Bali—in the village, the family, the economy, the state. A peculiar fusion of Polynesian title ranks and Hindu castes, the hierarchy of pride is the moral backbone of the society. But only in the cockfight are the sentiments upon which that hierarchy rests revealed in their natural colors. Enveloped elsewhere in a haze of etiquette, a thick cloud of euphemism and ceremony, gesture and allusion, they are here expressed in only the thinnest disguise of an animal mask, a mask which in fact demonstrates them far more effectively than it conceals them. Jealousy is as much a part of Bali as poise, envy as grace, brutality as charm; but without the cockfight the Balinese would have a much less certain understanding of them, which is, presumably, why they value it so highly.

Any expressive form works (when it works) by disarranging semantic contexts in such a way that properties conventionally ascribed to certain things are unconventionally ascribed to others, which are then seen actually to possess them. To call the wind a cripple, as Stevens does, to fix tone and manipulate timbre, as Schoenberg does, or, closer to our case, to picture an art critic as a dissolute bear, as Hogarth does, is to cross conceptual wires; the established conjunctions between objects and their qualities are altered and phenomena—fall weather, melodic shape, or cultural journalism—are clothed in signifiers which normally point to other referents.[35] Similarly, to connect—and connect, and connect—the collision of roosters with the divisiveness of status is to invite a transfer of perceptions from the former to the latter, a transfer which is at once a description and a judgment. (Logically, the transfer could, of course, as well go the other way; but, like most of the rest of us, the Balinese are a great deal more interested in understanding men than they are in understanding cocks.)

What sets the cockfight apart from the ordinary course of life, lifts it from the realm of everyday practical affairs, and surrounds it with an aura of enlarged importance is not, as functionalist sociology would have it, that it reinforces status discriminations (such reinforcement is hardly necessary in a society where every act proclaims them), but that it provides a metasocial commentary upon the whole matter of assorting human beings into fixed hierarchical ranks and then organizing the major part of collective existence around that assortment. Its function, if you want to call it that, is interpretive: it is a Balinese reading of Balinese experience; a story they tell themselves about themselves.

Saying Something of Something

To put the matter this way is to engage in a bit of metaphorical refocusing of one's own, for it shifts the analysis of cultural forms from an endeavor in general parallel to dissecting an organism, diagnosing a symptom, deciphering a code, or ordering a system—the dominant analogies in contemporary anthropology—to one in general parallel with penetrating a literary text. If one takes the cockfight, or any other collectively sustained symbolic structure, as a means of "saying something of something" (to invoke a famous Aristotelian tag), then one is faced with a problem not in social mechanics but social semantics.[36] For the anthropologist, whose concern is with formulating sociological principles, not with promoting or appreciating cockfights, the question is, what does one learn about such principles from examining culture as an assemblage of texts?

Such an extension of the notion of a text beyond written material, and even beyond verbal, is, though metaphorical, not, of course, all that novel. The *interpretatio naturae* tradition of the Middle Ages, which, culminating in Spinoza, attempted to read nature as Scripture, the Nietzschean effort to treat value systems as glosses on the will to power (or the Marxian one to treat them as glosses on property relations), and the Freudian replacement of the enigmatic text of the manifest dream with the plain one of the latent, all offer precedents, if not equally recommendable ones.[37] But the idea remains theoretically undeveloped; and the more profound corollary, so far as anthropology is concerned, that cultural forms can be treated as texts, as imaginative works built out of social materials, has yet to be systematically exploited.[38]

In the case at hand, to treat the cockfight as a text is to bring out a feature of it (in my opinion, the central feature of it) that treating it as a rite or a pastime, the two most obvious alternatives, would tend to obscure: its use of emotion for cognitive ends. What the cockfight says it says in a vocabulary of sentiment—the thrill of risk, the despair of loss, the pleasure of triumph. Yet what it says is not merely that risk is exciting, loss depressing, or triumph gratifying, banal tautologies of affect, but that it is of these emotions, thus exampled, that society is built and individuals put together. Attending cockfights and participating in them is, for the Balinese, a kind of sentimental education. What he learns there is what his culture's ethos and his private sensibility (or, anyway, certain aspects of them) look like when spelled out externally in a collective text; that the two are near enough alike to be articulated in the symbolics of a single such text; and— the disquieting part—that the text in which this revelation is accomplished consists of a chicken hacking another mindlessly to bits.

Every people, the proverb has it, loves its own form of violence. The cockfight is the Balinese reflection on theirs: on its look, its uses, its force, its fascination. Drawing on almost every level of Balinese experience, it brings together themes—animal savagery, male narcissism, opponent gambling, status rivalry, mass excitement, blood sacrifice—whose main connection is their involvement with rage and the fear of rage, and, binding them into a set of rules which at once contains them and allows them play, builds a symbolic structure in which, over and over again, the reality of their inner affiliation can be intelligibly felt. If, to quote Northrop Frye again, we go to see *Macbeth* to learn what a man feels like after he has gained a kingdom and lost his soul, Balinese go to cockfights to find out what a man, usually composed, aloof, almost obsessively self-absorbed, a kind of moral autocosm, feels like when, attacked, tormented, challenged, insulted, and driven in result to the extremes of fury, he has totally triumphed or been brought totally low. The whole passage, as it takes us back to Aristotle (though to the *Poetics* rather than the *Hermeneutics*), is worth quotation:

> But the poet [as opposed to the historian], Aristotle says, never makes any real statements at all, certainly no particular or specific ones. The poet's job is not to tell you what happened, but what happens: not what did take place, but the kind of thing that always does take place. He gives you the typical, recurring, or what Aristotle calls universal event. You wouldn't go to *Macbeth* to learn about the history of Scotland—you go to it to learn what man feels like after he's gained a kingdom and lost his soul. When you meet such a character as Micawber in Dickens, you don't feel that there must have been a man Dickens knew who was exactly like this: you feel that there's a bit of Micawber in almost everybody you know, including yourself. Our impressions of human life are picked up one by one, and remain for most of us loose and disorganized. But we constantly find things in literature that suddenly coordinate and bring into focus a great many such impressions, and this is part of what Aristotle means by the typical or universal human event.[39]

It is this kind of bringing of assorted experiences of everyday life to focus that the cockfight, set aside from that life as "only a game" and reconnected to it as "more than a game," accomplishes, and so creates what, better than typical or universal, could be called a paradigmatic human event—that is, one that tells us less what happens than the kind of thing that would happen if, as is not the case, life were art and could be as freely shaped by styles of feeling as *Macbeth* and *David Copperfield* are.

Enacted and reenacted, so far without end, the cockfight enables the Balinese, as, read and reread, *Macbeth* enables us, to see a dimension of his own subjectivity. As he watches fight after fight, with the active watching of an owner and a bettor (for cockfighting has no more interest as a pure spectator sport than croquet or dog racing do), he grows familiar with it and what it has to say to him, much as the attentive listener to string quartets or the absorbed viewer of still lifes grows slowly more familiar with them in a way which opens his subjectivity to himself.[40]

Yet, because—in another of those paradoxes, along with painted feel-ings and unconsequenced acts, which haunt aesthetics—that subjectivity does not properly exist until it is thus organized, art forms generate and regenerate the very subjectivity they pretend only to display. Quartets, still lifes, and cockfights are not merely reflections of a preexisting sensi-bility analogically represented; they are positive agents in the creation and maintenance of such a sensibility. If we see ourselves as a pack of Micaw-bers it is from reading too much Dickens (if we see ourselves as unillu-sioned realists, it is from reading too little); and similarly for Balinese, cocks, and cockfights. It is in such a way, coloring experience with the light they cast it in, rather than through whatever material effects they may have, that the arts play their role, as arts, in social life.[41]

In the cockfight, then, the Balinese forms and discovers his tempera-ment and his society's temper at the same time. Or, more exactly, he forms and discovers a particular face of them. Not only are there a great many other cultural texts providing commentaries on status hierarchy and self-regard in Bali, but there are a great many other critical sectors of Balinese life besides the stratificatory and the agonistic that receive such commen-tary. The ceremony consecrating a Brahmana priest, a matter of breath control, postural immobility, and vacant concentration upon the depths of being, displays a radically different, but to the Balinese equally real, prop-erty of social hierarchy—its reach toward the numinous transcendent. Set not in the matrix of the kinetic emotionality of animals, but in that of the static passionlessness of divine mentality, it expresses tranquillity not dis-quiet. The mass festivals at the village temples, which mobilize the whole local population in elaborate hostings of visiting gods—songs, dances, compliments, gifts—assert the spiritual unity of village mates against their status inequality and project a mood of amity and trust.[42] The cockfight is not the master key to Balinese life, any more than bullfighting is to Span-ish. What it says about that life is not unqualified nor even unchallenged by what other equally eloquent cultural statements say about it. But there is nothing more surprising in this than in the fact that Racine and Molière were contemporaries, or that the same people who arrange chrysanthe-mums cast swords.[43]

The culture of a people is an ensemble of texts, themselves ensembles, which the anthropologist strains to read over the shoulders of those to whom they properly belong. There are enormous difficulties in such an enterprise, methodological pitfalls to make a Freudian quake, and some moral perplexities as well. Nor is it the only way that symbolic forms can be sociologically handled. Functionalism lives, and so does psychologism. But to regard such forms as "saying something of something," and saying it to somebody, is at least to open up the possibility of an analysis which attends to their substance rather than to reductive formulas professing to account for them.

As in more familiar exercises in close reading, one can start anywhere in a culture's repertoire of forms and end up anywhere else. One can stay, as I have here, within a single, more or less bounded form and circle steadily within it. One can move between forms in search of broader unities or informing contrasts. One can even compare forms from different cultures to define their character in reciprocal relief. But whatever the level at which one operates, and however intricately, the guiding principle is the same: societies, like lives, contain their own interpretations. One has only to learn how to gain access to them.

REFERENCES

[1] Gregory Bateson and Margaret Mead, *Balinese Character: A Photographic Analysis* (New York: New York Academy of Sciences, 1942), p. 68.

[2] Jane Belo, "The Balinese Temper," in Jane Belo, ed., *Traditional Balinese Culture* (New York: Columbia University Press, 1970; originally published in 1935), pp. 85–110.

[3] The best discussion of cockfighting is again Bateson and Mead's (*Balinese Character*, pp. 24–25, 140), but it, too, is general and abbreviated.

[4] Ibid., pp. 25–26. The cockfight is unusual within Balinese culture in being a single-sex public activity from which the other sex is totally and expressly excluded. Sexual differentiation is culturally extremely played down in Bali and most activities, formal and informal, involve the participation of men and women on equal ground, commonly as linked couples. From religion, to politics, to economics, to kinship, to dress, Bali is a rather "uni-sex" society, a fact both its customs and its symbolism clearly express. Even in contexts where women do not in fact play much of a role—music, painting, certain agricultural activities—their absence, which is only relative in any case, is more a mere matter of fact than socially enforced. To this general pattern, the cockfight, entirely of, by, and for men (women—at least *Balinese* women—do not even watch), is the most striking exception.

[5] Christiaan Hooykaas, *The Lay of the Jaya Prana* (London, 1958), p. 39. The lay has a stanza (no. 17) with the reluctant bridegroom use. Jaya Prana, the subject of a Balinese Uriah myth, responds to the lord who has offered him the loveliest of six hundred servant girls: "Godly King, my Lord and Master/I beg you, give me leave to go/such things are not yet in my mind;/like a fighting cock encaged/indeed I am on my mettle/I am alone/as yet the flame has not been fanned."

[6] For these, see V. E. Korn, *Het Adatrecht van Bali,* 2d ed. ('S-Gravenhage: G. Naeff, 1932), index under *toh.*

[7] There is indeed a legend to the effect that the separation of Java and Bali is due to the action of a powerful Javanese religious figure who wished to protect himself against a Balinese culture hero (the ancestor of two Ksatria castes) who was a passionate cockfighting gambler. See Christiaan Hooykaas, *Agama Tirtha* (Amsterdam: Noord-Hollandsche, 1964), p. 184.

[8] An incestuous couple is forced to wear pig yokes over their necks and crawl to a pig trough and eat with their mouths there. On this, see Jane Belo, "Customs Pertaining to Twins in Bali," in Belo, ed., *Traditional Balinese Culture,* p. 49; on the abhorrence of animality generally, Bateson and Mead, *Balinese Character,* p. 22.

[9] Except for unimportant, small-bet fights (on the question of fight "importance," see below) spur affixing is usually done by someone other than the owner. Whether the owner handles his own cock or not more or less depends on how skilled he is at it, a consideration whose importance is again relative to the importance of the fight. When spur affixers and cock handlers are someone other than the owner, they are almost always a close relative—a brother or cousin—or a very intimate friend of his. They are thus almost extensions of his personality, as the fact that all three will refer to the cock as "mine," say "I" fought So-and-So, and so on, demonstrates. Also, owner-handler-affixer triads tend to be fairly fixed, though individuals may participate in several and often exchange roles within a given one.

[10] Erving Goffman, *Encounters: Two Studies in the Sociology of Interaction* (Indianapolis: Bobbs-Merrill, 1961), pp. 9–10.

[11] This word, which literally means an indelible stain or mark, as in a birthmark or a vein in a stone, is used as well for a deposit in a court case, for a pawn, for security offered in a loan, for a stand-in for someone else in a legal or ceremonial context, for an earnest advanced in a business deal, for a sign placed in a field to indicate its ownership is in dispute, and for the status of an unfaithful wife from whose lover her husband must gain satisfaction or surrender her to him. See Korn, *Het Adatrecht van Bali;* Theodoor Pigeaud, *Javaans-Nederlands Handwoordenbock* (Groningen: Wolters, 1938); H. H. Juynboll, *Oudjavaansche-Nederlandsche Woordenlijst* (Leiden: Brill, 1923).

[12] The center bet must be advanced in cash by both parties prior to the actual fight. The umpire holds the stakes until the decision is rendered and then awards them to the winner, avoiding, among other things, the intense embarrassment both winner and loser would feel if the latter had to pay off personally following his defeat. About 10 percent of the winner's receipts are subtracted for the umpire's share and that of the fight sponsors.

[13] Actually, the typing of cocks, which is extremely elaborate (I have collected more than twenty classes, certainly not a complete list), is not based on color alone, but on a series of independent, interacting, dimensions, which include, beside color, size, bone thickness, plumage, and temperament. (But *not* pedigree. The Balinese do not breed cocks to any significant extent, nor, so far as I have been able to discover, have they ever done so. The *asil,* or jungle cock, which is the basic fighting strain everywhere the sport is found, is native to southern Asia, and one can buy a good example in the chicken section of almost any Balinese market for anywhere from four or five ringgits up to fifty or more.) The color element is merely the one normally used as the type name, except when the two cocks of different types—as on principle they must be— have the same color, in which case a secondary indication from one of the other dimensions ("large speckled" v. "small speckled," etc.) is added. The types are coordinated with various cosmological ideas which help shape the making of matches, so that, for example, you fight a small, headstrong, speckled brown-on-white cock with flat-lying feathers and thin legs from the east side of the ring on a certain day of the complex Balinese calendar, and a large, cautious, all-black cock with tufted feathers and stubby legs from the north side on another day, and so on. All this is again recorded in palm-leaf manuscripts and endlessly discussed by the Balinese (who do not all have identical systems), and full-scale componential-cum-symbolic analysis of cock classifications would be extremely valuable both as an adjunct to the description of the cockfight and in itself. But my data on the subject, though extensive and varied, do not seem to be complete and systematic enough to attempt such an analysis here. For Balinese cosmological ideas more generally see Belo, ed., *Traditional Balinese Culture,* and J. L. Swellengrebel, ed., *Bali: Studies in Life, Thought, and Ritual* (The Hague: W. van Hoeve, 1960); for calendrical ones, Clifford Geertz, *Person, Time, and Conduct in Bali: An Essay in Cultural Analysis* (New Haven: Southeast Asia Studies, Yale University, 1966), pp. 45–53.

[14] For purposes of ethnographic completeness, it should be noted that it is possible for the man backing the favorite—the odds-giver—to make a bet in which he wins if his cock wins or there is a tie, a slight shortening of the odds (I do not have enough cases to be exact, but ties seem to occur about once every fifteen or twenty matches). He indicates his wish to do this by shouting *sapih* ("tie") rather than the cock-type, but such bets are in fact infrequent.

[15] The precise dynamics of the movement of the betting is one of the most intriguing, most complicated, and, given the heroic conditions under which it occurs, most difficult to study, aspects of the fight. Motion picture recording plus multiple observers would probably be necessary to deal with it effectively. Even impressionistically—the only approach open to a lone ethnographer caught in the middle of all this—it is clear that certain men lead both in determining the favorite (that is, making the opening cock-type calls which always initiate the process) and in directing the movement of the odds, these "opinion lead-

ers" being the more accomplished cockfighters-cum-solid-citizens to be discussed below. If these men begin to change their calls, others follow; if they begin to make bets, so do others and—though there is always a large number of frustrated bettors crying for shorter or longer odds to the end—the movement more or less ceases. But a detailed understanding of the whole process awaits what, alas, it is not very likely ever to get: a decision theorist armed with precise observations of individual behavior.

[16] Assuming only binominal variability, the departure from a fifty-fifty expectation in the sixty ringgits and below case is 1.38 standard deviations, or (in a one-direction test) an eight in one hundred possibility by chance alone; for the below forty ringgits case it is 1.65 standard deviations, or about five in one hundred. The fact that these departures though real are not extreme merely indicates, again, that even in the smaller fights the tendency to match cocks at least reasonably evenly persists. It is a matter of relative relaxation of the pressures toward equalization, not their elimination. The tendency for high-bet contests to be coin-flip propositions is, of course, even more striking, and suggests the Balinese know quite well what they are about.

[17] The reduction in wagering in smaller fights (which, of course, feeds on itself; one of the reasons people find small fights uninteresting is that there is less wagering in them, and contrariwise for large ones) takes place in three mutually reinforcing ways. First, there is a simple withdrawal of interest as people wander off to have a cup of coffee or chat with a friend. Second, the Balinese do not mathematically reduce odds, but bet directly in terms of stated odds as such. Thus, for a nine-to-eight bet, one man wagers nine ringgits, the other eight; for five-to-four, one wagers five, the other four. For any given currency unit, like the ringgit, therefore, 6.3 times as much money is involved in a ten-to-nine bet as in a two-to-one bet, for example, and, as noted, in small fights betting settles toward the longer end. Finally, the bets which are made tend to be one- rather than two-, three-, or in some of the very largest fights, four- or five-finger ones. (The fingers indicate the *multiples* of the stated bet odds at issue, not absolute figures. Two fingers in a six-to-five situation means a man wants to wager ten ringgits on the underdog against twelve, three in an eight-to-seven situation, twenty-one against twenty-four, and so on.)

[18] Besides wagering there are other economic aspects of the cockfight, especially its very close connection with the local market system which, though secondary both to its motivation and to its function, are not without importance. Cockfights are open events to which anyone who wishes may come, sometimes from quite distant areas, but well over 90 percent, probably over 95, are very local affairs, and the locality concerned is defined not by the village, nor even by the administrative district, but by the rural market system. Bali has a three-day market week with familiar "solar-system" type rotation. Though the markets themselves have never been very highly developed, small morning affairs in a village square, it is the microregion such rotation rather generally marks out—ten or twenty square miles, seven or eight neighboring villages (which in contemporary Bali is usually going to mean anywhere from five to ten to eleven thousand people) from which the core of any cockfight audience, indeed virtually all of it, will come. Most of the fights are in fact organized and sponsored by small combines of petty rural merchants under the general premise, very strongly held by them and indeed by all Balinese, that cockfights are good for trade because "they get money out of the house, they make it circulate." Stalls selling various sorts of things as well as assorted sheer-chance gambling games (see below) are set up around the edge of the area so that this even takes on the quality of a small fair. This connection of cockfighting with markets and market sellers is very old, as, among other things, their conjunction in inscriptions (Roelof Goris, *Prasasti Bali*, 2 vols. [Bandung: N. V. Masa Baru, 1954]) indicates. Trade has followed the cock for centuries in rural Bali and the sport has been one of the main agencies of the island's monetization.

[19] The phrase is found in the Hildreth translation, International Library of Psychology, 1931, note to p. 106; see L. L. Fuller, *The Morality of Law* (New Haven: Yale University Press, 1964), pp. 6ff.

[20] Of course, even in Bentham, utility is not normally confined as a concept to monetary losses and gains, and my argument here might be more carefully put in terms of a denial that for the Balinese, as for any people, utility (pleasure, happiness . . .) is merely identifiable with wealth. But such terminological problems are in any case secondary to the essential point: the cockfight is not roulette.

[21] Max Weber, *The Sociology of Religion* (Boston: Beacon Press, 1963). There is nothing specifically Balinese, of course, about deepening significance with money, as Whyte's description of corner boys in a working-class district of Boston demonstrates: "Gambling plays an important role in the lives of Cornerville people. Whatever game the corner boys play, they nearly always bet on the outcome. When there is nothing at stake, the game is not considered a real contest. This does not mean that the financial element is all-important. I have frequently heard men say that the honor of winning was much more important than the money at stake. The corner boys consider playing for money the real test of skill and, unless a man performs well when money is at stake, he is not considered a good competitor." W. F. Whyte, *Street Corner Society*, 2d ed. (Chicago: University of Chicago Press, 1955), p. 140.

[22] The extreme to which this madness is conceived on occasion to go—and the fact that it is considered madness—is demonstrated by the Balinese folktale *I Tuhung Kuning*. A gambler becomes so deranged by his passion that, leaving on a trip, he orders his pregnant wife to take care of the prospective newborn if it is a boy but to feed it as meat to his fighting cocks if it is a girl. The mother gives birth to a girl, but rather than giving the child to the cocks she gives them a large rat and conceals the girl with her own mother. When the husband returns the cocks, crowing a jingle, inform him of the deception and, furious, he sets out to kill the child. A goddess descends from heaven and takes the girl up to the skies with her. The cocks die from the food given them, the owner's sanity is restored, the goddess brings the girl back to the father and reunites him with his wife. The story is given as "Geel Komkommertje" in Jacoba Hooykaas-van Leeuwen Boomkamp, *Sprookjes en Verhalen van Bali* ('S-Gravenhage: Van Hoeve, 1956), pp. 19–25.

[23] For a fuller description of Balinese rural social structure, see Clifford Geertz, "Form and Variation in Balinese Village Structure," *American Anthropologist*, 61 (1959), 94–108; "Tihingan, A Balinese Village," in R. M. Koentjaraningrat, *Villages in Indonesia* (Ithaca: Cornell University Press, 1967), pp. 210–43; and, though it is a bit off the norm as Balinese villages go, V. E. Korn, *De Dorpsrepubliek tnganan Pagringsingan* (Santpoort [Netherlands]: C. A. Mees, 1933).

[24] Goffman, *Encounters*, p. 78.

[25] B. R. Berelson, P. F. Lazersfeld, and W. N. McPhee, *Voting: A Study of Opinion Formation in a Presidential Campaign* (Chicago: University of Chicago Press, 1954).

[26] As this is a formal paradigm, it is intended to display the logical, not the casual, structure of cockfighting. Just which of these considerations leads to which, in what order, and by what mechanisms, is another matter—one I have attempted to shed some light on in the general discussion.

[27] In another of Hooykaas-van Leeuwen Boomkamp's folk tales ("De Gast," *Sprookjes en Verhalen van Bali*, pp. 172–80), a low caste *Sudra*, a generous, pious, and carefree man who is also an accomplished cockfighter, loses, despite his accomplishment, fight after fight until he not only out of money but down to his last cock. He does not despair, however—"I bet," he says, "upon the Unseen World."

His wife, a good and hard-working woman, knowing how much he enjoys cockfighting, gives him her last "rainy day" money to go and bet. But, filled with misgivings due to his run of ill luck, he leaves his own cock at home and bets merely on the side. He soon loses all but a coin or two and repairs to a food stand for a snack, where he meets a decrepit, odorous, and generally unappetizing older beggar leaning on a staff. The old man asks for food, and the hero spends his last coins to buy him some. The old man then asks to pass the night with the hero, which the hero gladly invites him to do. As there is no food in the house, however, the hero tells his wife to kill the last cock for dinner. When the old man discovers this fact, he tells the hero he has three cocks in his own mountain hut and says the hero may have one of them for fighting. He also asks for the hero's son to accompany him as a servant, and, after the son agrees, this is done.

The old man turns out to be Siva and, thus, to live in a great palace in the sky, though the hero does not know this. In time, the hero decides to visit his son and collect the promised cock. Lifted up into Siva's presence, he is given the choice of three cocks. The first crows: "I have beaten fifteen opponents." The second crows, "I have beaten twenty-five opponents." The third crows, "I have beaten the King." "That one, the third, is my choice," says the hero, and returns with it to earth.

When he arrives at the cockfight, he is asked for an entry fee and replies, "I have no money; I will pay after my cock has won." As he is known never to win, he is let in because the king, who is there fighting, dislikes him and hopes to enslave him when he loses and cannot pay off. In order to insure that this happens, the king matches his finest cock against the hero's. When the cocks are placed down, the hero's flees, and the crowd, led by the arrogant king, hoots in laughter. The hero's cock then flies at the king himself, killing him with a spur stab in the throat. The hero flees. His house is encircled by the king's men. The cock changes into a Garuda, the great mythic bird of Indic legend, and carries the hero and his wife to safety in the heavens.

When the people see this, they make the hero king and his wife queen and they return as such to earth. Later his son, released by Siva, also returns and the hero-king announces his intention to enter a hermitage. ("I will fight no more cockfights. I have bet on the Unseen and won.") He enters the hermitage and his son becomes king.

[28] Addict gamblers are really less declassed (for their status is, as everyone else's, inherited) than merely impoverished and personally disgraced. The most prominent addict gambler in my cockfight circuit was actually a very high caste *satria* who sold off most of his considerable lands to support his habit. Though everyone privately regarded him as a fool and worse (some, more charitable, regarded him as sick), he was publicly treated with the elaborate deference and politeness due his rank. On the independence of personal reputation and public status in Bali, see Geertz, *Person, Time, and Conduct,* pp. 28–35.

[29] For four, somewhat variant treatments, see Susanne Langer, *Feeling and Form* (New York: Scribner's, 1953); Richard Wollheim, *Art and Its Objects* (New York: Harper and Row, 1968); Nelson Goodman, *Languages of Art* (Indianapolis: Bobbs-Merrill, 1968); Maurice Merleau-Ponty, "The Eye and the Mind," in his, *The Primacy of Perception* (Evanston: Northwestern University Press, 1964), pp. 159–90.

[30] British cockfights (the sport was banned there in 1840) indeed seem to have lacked it, and to have generated, therefore, a quite different family of shapes. Most British fights were "mains," in which a preagreed number of cocks were aligned into two teams and fought serially. Score was kept and wagering took place both on the individual matches and on the main as a whole. There were also "battle Royales," both in England and on the Continent, in which a large number of cocks were let loose at once with the one left standing at the end the victor. And in Wales, the so-called "Welsh main" followed an elimination pattern, along the lines of a present-day tennis tournament, winners proceeding to the next round. As a genre, the cockfight has perhaps less compositional flexibility than, say, Latin comedy, but it is not entirely without any. On cockfighting more generally, see Arch Ruport, *The Art of Cockfighting* (New York: Devin-Adair, 1949); G. R. Scott, *History of Cockfighting* (1957); and Lawrence Fitz-Barnard, *Fighting Sports* (London: Odhams Press, 1921).

[31] *Person, Time, and Conduct,* esp. pp. 42ff. I am, however, not the first person to have argued it: see G. Bateson, "Bali, the Value System of a Steady State," and "An Old Temple and a New Myth," in Belo, ed., *Traditional Balinese Culture,* pp. 384–402 and 111–36.

[32] For the necessity of distinguishing among "description," "representation," "exemplification," and "expression" (and the irrelevance of "imitation" to all of them), as modes of symbolic reference, see Goodman, *Languages of Art,* pp. 6–10, 45–91, 225–41.

[33] Northrop Frye, *The Educated Imagination* (Bloomington: University of Indiana Press, 1964), p. 99.

[34]There are two other Balinese values and disvalues which, connected with punctuate temporality on the one hand and unbridled aggressiveness on the other, reinforce
the sense that the cockfight is at once continuous with ordinary social life and a direct
negation of it: what the Balinese call *ramé*, and what they call *paling*. *Ramé* means
crowded, noisy, and active, and is a highly sought after social state: crowded markets,
mass festivals, busy streets are all *ramé*, as of course, is, in the extreme, a cockfight. *Ramé*
is what happens in the "full" times (its opposite, *sepi*, "quiet," is what happens in the
"empty" ones). *Paling* is social vertigo, the dizzy, disoriented, lost, turned around feeling one gets when one's place in the coordinates of social space is not clear, and it is a
tremendously disfavored, immensely anxiety-producing state. Balinese regard the exact
maintenance of spatial orientation ("not to know where north is" is to be crazy), balance,
decorum, status relationships, and so forth, as fundamental to ordered life (*krama*) and
paling, the sort of whirling confusion of position the scrambling cocks exemplify as its
profoundest enemy and contradiction. On *ramé*, see Bateson and Mead, *Balinese Character*, pp. 3, 64; on *paling*, ibid., p. 11, and Belo, ed., *Traditional Balinese Culture*, pp. 90ff.

[35]The Stevens reference is to his "The Motive for Metaphor" ("You like it under the
trees in autumn,/Because everything is half dead./The wind moves like a cripple
among the leaves/And repeats words without meaning"); the Schoenberg reference is
to the third of his *Five Orchestral Pieces* (Opus 16), and is borrowed from H. H. Drager,
"The Concept of 'Tonal Body,'" in Susanne Langer, ed., *Reflections of Art* (New York: Oxford University Press, 1961), p. 174. On Hogarth, and on this whole problem—there
called "multiple matrix matching"—see E. H. Gombrich, "The Use of Art for the Study
of Symbols," in James Hogg, ed., *Psychology and the Visual Arts* (Baltimore: Penguin
Books, 1969), pp. 149–70. The more usual term for this sort of semantic alchemy is
"metaphorical transfer," and good technical discussions of it can be found in M. Black,
Models and Metaphors (Ithaca: Cornell University Press, 1962), pp. 25ff; Goodman, *Languages of Art*, pp. 44ff; and W. Percy, "Metaphor as Mistake," *Sewanee Review*, 66 (1958),
78–99.

[36]The tag is from the second book of the *Organon, On Interpretation*. For a discussion
of it, and for the whole argument for freeing "the notion of text . . . from the notion of
scripture or writing," and constructing, thus, a general hermeneutics, see Paul Ricoeur,
Freud and Philosophy (New Haven: Yale University Press, 1970), pp. 20ff.

[37]Ibid.

[38]Lévi-Strauss's "structuralism" might seem an exception. But it is only an apparent
one, for, rather than taking myths, totem rites, marriage rules, or whatever as texts to interpret, Lévi-Strauss takes them as ciphers to solve, which is very much not the same
thing. He does not seek to understand symbolic forms in terms of how they function in
concrete situations to organize perceptions (meanings, emotions, concepts, attitudes); he
seeks to understand them entirely in terms of their internal structure, *indépendent de tout
sujet, de tout objet, et de toute contexte*. For my own view of this approach—that is suggestive and indefensible—see Clifford Geertz, "The Cerebral Savage: On the Work of Lévi-
Strauss," *Encounter*, 48 (1967), 25–32.

[39]Frye, *The Educated Imagination*, pp. 63–64.

[40]The use of the, to Europeans, "natural" visual idiom for perception—"see,"
"watches," and so forth—is more than usually misleading here, for the fact that, as mentioned earlier, Balinese follow the progress of the fight as much (perhaps, as fighting
cocks are actually rather hard to see except as blurs of motion, more) with their bodies
as with their eyes, moving their limbs, heads, and trunks in gestural mimicry of the
cocks' maneuvers, means that much of the individual's experience of the fight is kinesthetic rather than visual. If ever there was an example of Kenneth Burke's definition of a
symbolic act as "the dancing of an attitude" (*The Philosophy of Literary Form*, rev. ed.
[New York: Vintage Books, 1957], p. 9) the cockfight is it. On the enormous role of kinesthetic perception in Balinese life, [see] Bateson and Mead, *Balinese Character*, pp. 84–88;
on the active nature of aesthetic perception in general, [see] Goodman, *Languages of Art*,
pp. 241–44.

[41] All this coupling of the occidental great with the oriental lowly will doubtless disturb certain sorts of aestheticians as the earlier effort of anthropologists to speak of Christianity and totemism in the same breath disturbed certain sorts of theologians. But as ontological questions are (or should be) bracketed in the sociology of religion, judgmental ones are (or should be) bracketed in the sociology of art. In any case, the attempt to deprovincialize the concept of art is but part of the general anthropological conspiracy to deprovincialize all important social concepts—marriage, religion, law, rationality—and though this is a threat to aesthetic theories which regard certain works of art as beyond the reach of sociological analysis, it is no threat to the conviction, for which Robert Graves claims to have been reprimanded at his Cambridge tripos, that some poems are better than others.

[42] For the consecration ceremony, see V. E. Korn, "The Consecration of the Priest," in Swellengrebel, ed., *Bali*, pp. 131–54; for (somewhat exaggerated) village communion, Roelof Goris, "The Religious Character of the Balinese Village," ibid., pp. 79–100.

[43] That what the cockfight has to say about Bali is not altogether without perception and the disquiet it expresses about the general pattern of Balinese life is not wholly without reason is attested by the fact that in two weeks of December 1965, during the upheavals following the unsuccessful coup in Djakarta, between forty and eighty thousand Balinese (in a population of about two million) were killed, largely by one another—the worst outburst in the country. (John Hughes, *Indonesian Upheaval* [New York: McKay, 1967], pp. 173–83. Hughes's figures are, of course, rather casual estimates, but they are not the most extreme.) This is not to say, of course, that the killings were caused by the cockfight, could have been predicted on the basis of it, or were some sort of enlarged version of it with real people in the place of the cocks—all of which is nonsense. It is merely to say that if one looks at Bali not just through the medium of its dances, its shadowplays, its sculpture, and its girls, but—as the Balinese themselves do—also through the medium of its cockfight, the fact that the massacre occurred seems, if no less appealing, less like a contradiction to the laws of nature. As more than one real Gloucester has discovered, sometimes people actually get life precisely as they most deeply do not want it.

• • • • • • • • • • • •

QUESTIONS FOR A SECOND READING

1. Geertz says that the cockfight provides a "commentary upon the whole matter of sorting human beings into fixed hierarchical ranks and then organizing the major parts of collective existence around that assortment." The cockfights don't reinforce the patterns of Balinese life; they comment on them. Perhaps the first question to ask as you go back to the essay is "What is that commentary?" What do the cockfights say? And what don't they say?

2. "Deep Play: Notes on the Balinese Cockfight" is divided into seven sections. As you reread the essay, pay attention to the connections between these sections and the differences in the ways they are written. For each, think about what they propose to do (some, for example, tell stories, some use numbers, some have more footnotes than others).

What is the logic or system that makes one section follow another? Do you see the subtitles as seven headings on a topic outline?

If you look at the differences in the style or method of each section, what might they be said to represent? If each is evidence of something Geertz, as an anthropologist, knows how to do, what, in each case, is he doing? What is his expertise? And why, in each case, would it require this particular style of writing? The last two sections are perhaps the most difficult to read and understand. They also make repeated reference to literary texts. Why? What is Geertz doing here?

3. Throughout the essay Geertz is working very hard to *do* something with what he observed in Bali. (There are "enormous difficulties in such an enterprise," he says.) He is also, however, working hard *not* to do some things. (He doesn't want to be a "formalist," for example.) As you read the essay for the second time, look for passages that help you specifically define what it is Geertz wants to do and what it is he wants to be sure not to do.

4. It could be argued that "Deep Play" tells again the story of how white Western men have taken possession of the Third World, here with Geertz performing an act of intellectual colonization. In the opening section, for example, Geertz (as author) quickly turns both his wife and the Balinese people into stock characters, characters in a story designed to make him a hero. And, in the service of this story, he pushes aside the difficult political realities of Bali—the later killing of Balinese by the police is put in parentheses (so as not to disturb the flow of the happy story of how an anthropologist wins his way into the community). The remaining sections turn Balinese culture into numbers and theories, reducing the irreducible detail of people's lives into material for the production of goods (an essay furthering his career). And, one could argue, the piece ends by turning to Shakespeare and Dickens to "explain" the Balinese, completing the displacement of Balinese culture by Western culture.

This, anyway, is how such an argument might be constructed. As you reread the essay, mark passages you could use, as the author, to argue both for and against Geertz and his relationship to this story of colonization. To what extent can one say that Geertz is, finally, one more white man taking possession of the Third World? And to what extent can one argue that Geertz, as a writer, is struggling against this dominant, conventional narrative, working to revise it or to distance himself from it?

ASSIGNMENTS FOR WRITING

1. If this essay were your only evidence, how might you describe the work of an anthropologist? What do anthropologists do and how do they do it? Write an essay in which you look at "Deep Play" section by section, including the references, describing on the basis of each what it is that an anthropologist must be able to do. In each case, you have the chance to watch Geertz at work. (Your essay, then, might well have sections that correspond to Geertz's.) When you have worked through them all, write a

final section that discusses how these various skills or arts fit together to define the expertise of someone like Geertz.

2. Geertz says that "the culture of a people is an ensemble of texts, themselves ensembles, which the anthropologist strains to read over the shoulders of those to whom they properly belong." Anthropologists are expert at "reading" in this way. One of the interesting things about being a student is that you get to (or you have to) act like an expert, even though, properly speaking, you are not. Write an essay in which you prepare a Geertzian "reading" of some part of our culture you know well. Ideally, you should go out and observe the behavior you are studying, examining it and taking notes with your project in mind. You should imagine that you are working in Geertz's spirit, imitating his method and style and carrying out work that he has begun.

3. This is really a variation on the first assignment. This assignment, however, invites you to read against the grain of Geertz's essay. Imagine that someone has made the argument outlined briefly in the fourth "Question for a Second Reading"—that "Deep Play" is just one more version of a familiar story, a story of a white man taking possession of everything that is not already made in his own image. If you were going to respond to this argument—to extend it or to answer it—to what in the essay would you turn for evidence? And what might you say about what you find?

 Write an essay, then, in which you respond to the argument that says "Deep Play" is one more version of the familiar story of a white man taking possession of that which is not his.

MAKING CONNECTIONS

1. Susan Bordo in "Hunger as Ideology" (p. 139), Jane Tompkins in "Indians" (p. 718), and Susan Griffin in "Our Secret" (p. 345) could all be said to take an "anthropological" view of the people and practices they study. The worlds they describe are familiar (at least compared with Bali), and yet, as writers, they distance themselves from those worlds, make the familiar seem exotic, look at the people involved as "natives" whose behavior they choose to read as a strange and arbitrary text.

 Choose one of these selections—by Bordo, Tompkins, or Griffin—and read it along with Geertz's. Take the position that both authors read cultural patterns and cultural artifacts. Look at the characteristic examples of their ways of reading. What might you say about their methods? Do they look for the same things?

 Write an essay in which you explore and describe the different methods of the two writers. As researchers, what do they notice? What do they do with what they notice? Do they seek the same *kinds* of conclusions? How do they gather their materials, weight them, think them through? How, that is, do they do their work? And what might you conclude about the possibilities and limitations of each writer's project?

2. In "The Loss of the Creature" (p. 588), Walker Percy writes about tourists (actually several different kinds of tourists) and the difficulty they have

seeing what lies before them. Properly speaking, anthropologists are not tourists. There is a scholarly purpose to their travel, and presumably they have learned or developed the strategies necessary to get beyond the preformed "symbolic complexes" which would keep them from seeing the place or the people they have traveled to study. Geertz is an expert, in other words, not just any "layman seer of sights."

In his travels to Bali, Geertz seems to get just what he wants. He gets both the authentic experience and a complex understanding of that experience. If you read "Deep Play" from the perspective of Percy's essay, however, it is interesting to ask whether Percy would say that this was the case, and to ask how Percy would characterize the "strategies" that define Geertz's approach to his subject.

Write an essay in which you place Geertz in the context of Percy's tourists—not all of them, but the two or three whose stories seem most interesting when placed alongside Geertz's. The purpose of your essay should be to determine whether or not Geertz has solved the problem Percy defines for the tourist in "The Loss of the Creature."

Griffin

If Jew didn't exist then anti-sem couldn't have invented them.

∘ morbid projection → if you're afraid of something in yourself destroy in another what you fear in yourself.

Cell Nucleus ⟶ _Missile_ (violent, repressive)

• metaphor
∘ matrix
  – connectedness
  – narrative blend ideas ⟶

Himmler
missile lifted w/ force of a foreign memory
look at function but not ppl. around gun
→technical not social
historical

Matrix

she in some way like Him.
– history determining field
– multiple determination

Missile
technical not social
destructive
hate
himmler
grandfather.

SUSAN GRIFFIN

*S*USAN GRIFFIN *(b. 1943) is a well-known and respected feminist writer, poet, essayist, lecturer, teacher, playwright, and filmmaker. She has published more than twenty books, including an Emmy Award–winning play,* Voices, *with a preface by Adrienne Rich (1975); three books of poetry,* Like the Iris of an Eye *(1976),* Unremembered Country *(1987), and* Bending Home: Selected and New Poems *(1998), and four books of nonfiction that have become key feminist texts,* Women and Nature: The Roaring inside Her *(1978),* Rape: The Power of Consciousness *(1979),* Pornography and Silence: Culture's Revenge against Nature *(1981), and* A Chorus of Stones: The Private Life of War *(1992). Her most recent book is* What Her Body Thought: A Journey into the Shadows *(1999), on her battle with illness. The* Eros of Everyday Life *(1996) is a collection of essays on women in Western culture.*

"Our Secret" is a chapter from Susan Griffin's moving and powerful book A Chorus of Stones, *winner of the Bay Area Book Reviewers Association Award and a finalist for the Pulitzer Prize in nonfiction. The book explores the connections between present and past, public life and private life, an individual life and the lives of others. Griffin writes, for example, "I do not see my life as separate from history. In my mind my family secrets mingle with the secrets of statesmen and bombers." In one section of the book she writes of her mother's alcoholism and her father's response to it. In another she writes of her paternal grandmother, who*

was banished from the family for reasons never spoken. Next to these she thinks about Heinrich Himmler, head of the Nazi secret police, or Hugh Trenchard of the British Royal Air Force, who introduced the saturation bombing of cities and civilians to modern warfare, or Wernher von Braun and the development of rockets and rocketry. "As I held these [figures and scenes] in my mind," she writes, "a certain energy was generated between them. There were two subjects but one theme: denying and bearing witness."

A Chorus of Stones combines the skills of a careful researcher working with the documentary records of war, the imaginative powers of a novelist entering the lives and experiences of those long dead, and a poet's attention to language. It is a remarkable piece of writing, producing in its form and style the very experience of surprise and connectedness that Griffin presents as the product of her research. "It's not a historian's history," she once told an interviewer. "What's in it is true, but I think of it as a book that verges on myth and legend, because those are the ways we find the deepest meanings and significance of events."

Griffin's history is not a historian's history; her sociology is not a sociologist's; her psychology is not written in conventional forms or registers. She is actively engaged in the key research projects of our time, providing new knowledge and new ways of thinking and seeing, but she works outside the usual forms and boundaries of the academic disciplines. There are other ways of thinking about this, she seems to say. There are other ways to do this work. Her book on rape, for example, ends with a collage of women's voices, excerpts from public documents, and bits and pieces from the academy.

"Our Secret" has its own peculiar structure and features—the sections in italics, for example. As a piece of writing, it proceeds with a design that is not concerned to move quickly or efficiently from introduction to conclusion. It is, rather, a kind of collage or collection of stories, sketches, anecdotes, fragments. While the sections in the essay are presented as fragments, the essay is not, however, deeply confusing or disorienting. The pleasure of the text, in fact, is moving from here to there, feeling a thread of connection at one point, being surprised by a new direction at another. The writing is careful, thoughtful, controlled, even if this is not the kind of essay that announces its thesis and then collects examples for support. It takes a different attitude toward examples—and toward the kind of thinking one might bring to bear in gathering them and thinking them through. As Griffin says, "the telling and hearing of a story is not a simple act." It is not simple and, as her writing teaches us, it is not straightforward. As you read this essay, think of it as a lesson in reading, writing, and thinking. Think of it as a lesson in working differently. And you might ask why it is that this kind of writing is seldom taught in school.

Our Secret

The nucleus of the cell derives its name from the Latin nux, *meaning nut. Like the stone in a cherry, it is found in the center of the cell, and like this stone, keeps its precious kernel in a shell.*

She is across the room from me. I am in a chair facing her. We sit together in the late darkness of a summer night. As she speaks the space between us grows larger. She has entered her past. She is speaking of her childhood. Her father. The war. Did I know her father fought in the Battle of the Bulge? What was it for him, this great and terrible battle? She cannot say. He never spoke of it at home. They knew so little, her mother, her brothers, herself. Outside, the sea has disappeared. One finds the water now only by the city lights that cease to shine at its edges. California. She moved here with her family when her father became the commander of a military base. There were nuclear missiles standing just blocks from where she lived. But her father never spoke about them. Only after many years away from home did she learn what these weapons were.

The first guided missile is developed in Germany, during World War II. It is known as the Vergeltungswaffe, *or the Vengeance weapon. Later, it will be called the V-1 rocket.*

She is speaking of another life, another way of living. I give her the name Laura here. She speaks of the time after the war, when the cold war was just beginning. The way we are talking now, Laura tells me, was not possible in her family. I nod in recognition. Certain questions were never answered. She learned what not to ask. She begins to tell me a story. Once when she was six years old she went out with her father on a long trip. It was not even a year since the war ended. They were living in Germany.

They drove for miles and miles. Finally they turned into a small road at the edge of a village and drove through a wide gate in a high wall. The survivors were all gone. But there were other signs of this event beyond and yet still within her comprehension. Shoes in great piles. Bones. Women's hair, clothes, stains, a terrible odor. She began to cry a child's frightened tears and then to scream. She had no words for what she saw. Her father admonished her to be still. Only years later, and in a classroom, did she find out the name of this place and what had happened here.

The shell surrounding the nucleus is not hard and rigid; it is a porous membrane. These pores allow only some substances to pass through them, mediating the movement of materials in and out of the nucleus.

· · ·

Often I have looked back into my past with a new insight only to find that some old, hardly recollected feeling fits into a larger pattern of meaning. Time can be measured in many ways. We see time as moving forward and hope that by our efforts this motion is toward improvement. When the atomic bomb exploded, many who survived the blast say time stopped with the flash of light and was held suspended until the ash began to descend. Now, in my mind, I can feel myself moving backward in time. I am as if on a train. And the train pushes into history. This history seems to exist somewhere, waiting, a foreign country behind a border and, perhaps, also inside me. From the windows of my train, I can see what those outside do not see. They do not see each other, or the whole landscape through which the track is laid. This is a straight track, but still there are bends to fit the shape of the earth. There are even circles. And returns.

The missile is guided by a programmed mechanism. There is no electronic device that can be jammed. Once it is fired it cannot stop.

It is 1945 and a film is released in Germany. This film has been made for other nations to see. On the screen a train pulls into a station. The train is full of children. A man in a uniform greets the children warmly as they step off the train. Then the camera cuts to boys and girls who are swimming. The boys and girls race to see who can reach the other side of the pool first. Then a woman goes to a post office. A man goes to a bank. Men and women sit drinking coffee at a cafe. The film is called *The Führer Presents the Jews with a City.* It has been made at Terezin concentration camp.

Through the pores of the nuclear membrane a steady stream of ribonucleic acid, RNA, the basic material from which the cell is made, flows out.

It is wartime and a woman is writing a letter. *Everyone is on the brink of starvation,* she says. In the right-hand corner of the page she has written *Nordhausen, Germany 1944.* She is writing to Hans. *Do you remember,* she asks, the day this war was declared? The beauty of the place. The beauty of the sea. *And I bathed in it that day, for the last time.*

In the same year, someone else is also writing a letter. In the right-hand corner he has put his name followed by a title. *Heinrich Himmler. Reichsführer, SS. Make no mention of the special treatment of the Jews,* he says, use only the words Transportation of the Jews toward the Russian East.

A few months later this man will deliver a speech to a secret meeting of leaders in the district of Posen. *Now you know all about it, and you will keep quiet,* he will tell them. Now we share a secret and *we should take our secret to our graves.*

• • •

The missile flies from three to four thousand feet above the earth and this makes it difficult to attack from the ground.

The woman who writes of starvation is a painter in her seventy-seventh year. She has lost one grandchild to this war. And a son to the war before. Both boys were named Peter. Among the drawings she makes which have already become famous: a terrified mother grasps a child, *Death Seizes Children;* an old man curls over the bent body of an old woman, *Parents;* a thin face emerges white from charcoal, *Beggars.*

A small but critical part of the RNA flowing out of the pores holds most of the knowledge issued by the nucleus. These threads of RNA act as messengers.

Encountering such images, one is grateful to be spared. But is one ever really free of the fate of others? I was born in 1943, in the midst of this war. And I sense now that my life is still bound up with the lives of those who lived and died in this time. Even with Heinrich Himmler. All the details of his existence, his birth, childhood, adult years, death, still resonate here on earth.

The V-1 rocket is a winged plane powered by a duct motor with a pulsating flow of fuel.

It is April 1943, Heinrich Himmler, Reichsführer SS, has gained control of the production of rockets for the Third Reich. The SS Totenkampf stand guard with machine guns trained at the entrance to a long tunnel, two miles deep, fourteen yards wide and ten yards high, sequestered in the Harz Mountains near Nordhausen. Once an old mining shaft, this tunnel serves now as a secret factory for the manufacture of V-1 and V-2 missiles. The guards aim their machine guns at the factory workers who are inmates of concentration camp Dora.

Most of the RNA flowing out of the cell is destined for the construction of a substance needed to compensate for the continual wearing away of the cell.

It is 1925. Heinrich Himmler, who is now twenty-five years old, has been hired as a secretary by the chief of the Nazi Party in Landshut. He sits behind a small desk in a room overcrowded with party records, correspondence, and newspaper files. On the wall facing him he can see a portrait of Adolf Hitler. He hopes one day to meet the Führer. In anticipation of that day, while he believes no one watches, he practices speaking to this portrait.

It is 1922. Heinrich visits friends who have a three-year-old child. Before going to bed this child is allowed to run about naked. And this disturbs Heinrich. He writes in his diary, *One should teach a child a sense of shame.*

It is the summer of 1910. Heinrich begins his first diary. He is ten years old. He has just completed elementary school. His father tells him his childhood is over now. In the fall he will enter Wilhelms Gymnasium. There the grades he earns will determine his prospects for the future. From now on he must learn to take himself seriously.

Eight out of ten of the guided missiles will land within eight miles of their targets.

His father Gebhard is a schoolmaster. He knows the requirements. He provides the boy with pen and ink. Gebhard was once a tutor for Prince Heinrich of Wittelsbach. He has named his son Heinrich after this prince. He is grateful that the prince consented to be Heinrich's godparent. Heinrich is to write in his diary every day. Gebhard writes the first entry in his son's diary, to show the boy how it is to be done.

July 13 Departed at 11:50 and arrive safely on the bus in L. We have a very pretty house. In the afternoon we drink coffee at the coffee house.

I open the cover of the journal I began to keep just as I started my work on this book. I want to see what is on the first page. *It is here I begin a new life,* I wrote. Suffering many losses at once, I was alone and lonely. Yet suddenly I felt a new responsibility for myself. *The very act of keeping a journal,* I sensed, would help me into this life that would now be my own.

Inside the nucleus is the nucleolus where the synthesis of RNA takes place. Each nucleolus is filled with a small jungle of fern-like structures all of whose fronds and stalks move and rotate in perfect synchrony.

It is 1910. The twenty-second of July. Gebhard adds the words *first swim* to his son's brief entry, *thirteenth wedding anniversary of my dear parents.* 1911. Over several entries Heinrich lists each of thirty-seven times he takes a swim, in chronological order. *11:37 A.M. Departed for Lindau.* He does not write of his feelings. *August 8, Walk in the park.* Or dreams. *August 10, Bad weather.*

In the last few years I have been searching, though for what precisely I cannot say. Something still hidden which lies in the direction of Heinrich Himmler's life. I have been to Berlin and Munich on this search, and I have walked over the gravel at Dachau. Now as I sit here I read once again the fragments from Heinrich's boyhood diary that exist in English. I have begun to think of these words as ciphers. Repeat them to myself, hoping to find a door into the mind of this man, even as his character first forms so that I might learn how it is he becomes himself.

The task is not easy. The earliest entries in this diary betray so little. Like the words of a schoolboy commanded to write what the teacher requires of him, they are wooden and stiff. The stamp of his father's character is so heavy on this language that I catch not even a breath of a self here. It is easy to see how this would be true. One simply has to imagine Gebhard standing behind Heinrich and tapping his foot.

His father must have loomed large to him. Did Gebhard lay his hand on Heinrich's shoulder? The weight of that hand would not be comforting. It would be a warning. A reminder. Heinrich must straighten up now and be still. Yet perhaps he turns his head. Maybe there is a sound outside. A bird. Or his brother Gebhard's voice. But from the dark form behind him he hears a name pronounced. This is his name, *Heinrich.* The sound rolls sharply off his father's tongue. He turns his head back. He does not know what to write. He wants to turn to this form and beseech him, but this man who is his father is more silent than stone. And now when Heinrich can feel impatience all around him, he wants to ask, *What should I write?* The edge of his father's voice has gotten sharper. *Why can't you remember?* Just write what happened yesterday. And make sure you get the date right. *Don't you remember?* We took a walk in the park together and we ran into the duchess. Be certain you spell her name correctly. And look here, you must get the title right. That is extremely important. Cross it out. Do it again. *The title.*

The boy is relieved. His mind has not been working. His thoughts were like paralyzed limbs, immobile. Now he is in motion again. He writes the sentences as they are dictated to him. *The park.* He crosses out the name. He writes it again. Spelling it right. *The duchess.* And his father makes one more correction. The boy has not put down the correct time for their walk in the park.

And who is the man standing behind? In a photograph I have before me of the aging Professor and Frau Himmler, as they pose before a wall carefully composed with paintings and family portraits, Frau Himmler adorned with a demure lace collar, both she and the professor smiling kindly from behind steel-rimmed glasses, the professor somewhat rounded with age, in a dark three-piece suit and polka-dot tie, looks so ordinary.

The missile carries a warhead weighing 1,870 pounds. It has three different fuses to insure detonation.

Ordinary. What an astonishing array of images hide behind this word. The ordinary is of course never ordinary. I think of it now as a kind of mask, not an animated mask that expresses the essence of an inner truth, but a mask that falls like dead weight over the human face, making flesh a stationary object. One has difficulty penetrating the heavy mask that Gebhard and his family wore, difficulty piercing through to the creatures behind.

hi

It must not have been an easy task to create this mask. One detects the dimensions of the struggle in the advice of German child-rearing experts from this and the last century. *Crush the will,* they write. *Establish dominance. Permit no disobedience. Suppress everything in the child.*

I have seen illustrations from the books of one of these experts, perhaps the most famous of these pedagogues, Dr. Daniel Gottlieb Moritz Schreber. At first glance these pictures recall images of torture. But they are instead pictures of children whose posture or behavior is being corrected. A brace up the spine, a belt tied to a waist and the hair at the back of the neck so the child will be discouraged from slumping, a metal plate at the edge of a desk keeping the child from curling over her work, a child tied to a bed to prevent poor sleeping posture or masturbation. And there are other methods recommended in the text. An enema to be given before bedtime. The child immersed in ice-cold water up to the hips, before sleep.

The nightmare images of the German child-rearing practices that one discovers in this book call to mind the catastrophic events of recent German history. I first encountered this pedagogy in the writing of Alice Miller. At one time a psychoanalyst, she was haunted by the question, *What could make a person conceive the plan of gassing millions of human beings to death?* In her work, she traces the origins of this violence to childhood.

Of course there cannot be one answer to such a monumental riddle, nor does any event in history have a single cause. Rather a field exists, like a field of gravity that is created by the movements of many bodies. Each life is influenced and it in turn becomes an influence. Whatever is a cause is also an effect. Childhood experience is just one element in the determining field.

As a man who made history, Heinrich Himmler shaped many childhoods, including, in the most subtle of ways, my own. And an earlier history, a history of governments, of wars, of social customs, an idea of gender, the history of a religion leading to the idea of original sin, shaped Heinrich Himmler's childhood as certainly as any philosophy of child raising. One can take for instance any formative condition of his private life, the fact that he was a frail child, for example, favored by his mother, who could not meet masculine standards, and show that this circumstance derived its real meaning from a larger social system that gave inordinate significance to masculinity.

Yet to enter history through childhood experience shifts one's perspective not away from history but instead to an earlier time just before history has finally shaped us. Is there a child who existed before the conventional history that we tell of ourselves, one who, though invisible to us, still shapes events, even through this absence? How does our sense of history change when we consider childhood, and perhaps more important, why is it that until now we have chosen to ignore this point of origination, the birthplace and womb of ourselves, in our consideration of public events?

In the silence that reverberates around this question, an image is born in my mind. I can see a child's body, small, curled into itself, knees bent toward the chest, head bending softly into pillows and blankets, in a posture thought unhealthy by Dr. Schreber, hand raised to the face, delicate mouth making a circle around the thumb. There is comfort as well as sadness in this image. It is a kind of a self-portrait, drawn both from memory and from a feeling that is still inside me. As I dwell for a moment with this image I can imagine Heinrich in this posture, silent, curled, fetal, giving comfort to himself.

But now, alongside this earlier image, another is born. It is as if these two images were twins, always traveling in the world of thought together. One does not come to mind without the other. In this second portrait, which is also made of feeling and memory, a child's hands are tied into mittens. And by a string extending from one of the mittens, her hand is tied to the bars of her crib. She is not supposed to be putting her finger in her mouth. And she is crying out in rage while she yanks her hand violently trying to free herself of her bonds.

To most of existence there is an inner and an outer world. Skin, bark, surface of the ocean open to reveal other realities. What is inside shapes and sustains what appears. So it is too with human consciousness. And yet the mind rarely has a simple connection to the inner life. At a certain age we begin to define ourselves, to choose an image of who we are. I am this and not that, we say, attempting thus to erase whatever is within us that does not fit our idea of who we should be. In time we forget our earliest selves and replace that memory with the image we have constructed at the bidding of others.

One can see this process occur in the language of Heinrich's diaries. If in the earliest entries, except for the wooden style of a boy who obeys authority, Heinrich's character is hardly apparent, over time this stilted style becomes his own. As one reads on, one no longer thinks of a boy who is forced to the task, but of a prudish and rigid young man.

In Heinrich's boyhood diaries no one has been able to find any record of rage or of events that inspire such rage. Yet one cannot assume from this evidence that such did not exist. His father would have permitted neither anger nor even the memory of it to enter these pages. That there must be no visible trace of resentment toward the parent was the pedagogy of the age. Dr. Schreber believed that children should learn to be grateful. The pain and humiliation children endure are meant to benefit them. The parent is only trying to save the child's soul.

Now, for different reasons, I too find myself on the track of a child's soul. The dimensions of Heinrich Himmler's life have put me on this track. I am trying to grasp the inner state of his being. For a time the soul ceased to exist in the modern mind. One thought of a human being as a kind of machine, or as a cog in the greater mechanism of society, operating within another machine, the earth, which itself operates within the greater mechanical design of the universe.

When I was in Berlin, I spoke to a rabbi who had, it seemed to me, lost his faith. When I asked him if he still believed in God, he simply shook his head and widened his eyes as if to say, *How is this possible?* He had been telling me about his congregation: older people, many of Polish origin, survivors of the holocaust who were not able to leave Germany after the war because they were too ill to travel. He was poised in this painful place by choice. He had come to lead this congregation only temporarily but, once feeling the condition of his people, decided to stay. Still, despite his answer, and as much as the holocaust made a terrible argument for the death of the spirit, talking in that small study with this man, I could feel from him the light of something surviving.

The religious tradition that shaped Heinrich's childhood argues that the soul is not part of flesh but is instead a prisoner of the body. But suppose the soul is meant to live in and through the body and to know itself in the heart of earthly existence?

Then the soul is an integral part of the child's whole being, and its growth is thus part of the child's growth. It is, for example, like a seed planted underground in the soil, naturally moving toward the light. And it comes into its fullest manifestation thus only when seen, especially when self meeting self returns a gaze.

What then occurs if the soul in its small beginnings is forced to take on a secret life? A boy learns, for instance, to hide his thoughts from his father simply by failing to record them in his journals. He harbors his secrets in fear and guilt, confessing them to no one until in time the voice of his father chastising him becomes his own. A small war is waged in his mind. Daily implosions take place under his skin, by which in increments something in him seems to disappear. Gradually his father's voice subsumes the vitality of all his desires and even his rage, so that now what he wants most passionately is his own obedience, and his rage is aimed at his own failures. As over time his secrets fade from memory, he ceases to tell them, even to himself, so that finally a day arrives when he believes the image he has made of himself in his diaries is true.

The child, Dr. Schreber advised, *should be permeated by the impossibility of locking something in his heart.* The doctor who gave this advice had a son who was hospitalized for disabling schizophrenia. Another of his children committed suicide. But this was not taken as a warning against his approach. His methods of educating children were so much a part of the canon of everyday life in Germany that they were introduced into the state school system.

That this philosophy was taught in school gives me an interior view of the catastrophe to follow. It adds a certain dimension to my image of these events to know that a nation of citizens learned that no part of themselves could be safe from the scrutiny of authority, nothing locked in the heart, and at the same time to discover that the head of the secret police of this nation was the son of a schoolmaster. It was this man, after all, Heinrich Himmler, Reichsführer SS, who was later to say, speaking of the mass arrests of Jews, *Protective custody is an act of care.*

• • •

The polite manner of young Heinrich's diaries reminds me of life in my grandmother's home. Not the grandmother I lost and later found, but the one who, for many years, raised me. She was my mother's mother. The family would assemble in the living room together, sitting with a certain reserve, afraid to soil the surfaces. What was it that by accident might have been made visible?

All our family photographs were posed. We stood together in groups of three or four and squinted into the sun. My grandmother directed us to smile. I have carried one of these photographs with me for years without acknowledging to myself that in it my mother has the look she always had when she drank too much. In another photograph, taken near the time of my parents' divorce, I can see that my father is almost crying, though I could not see this earlier. I must have felt obliged to see only what my grandmother wanted us to see. Tranquil, domestic scenes.

In the matrix of the mitochondria all the processes of transformation join to-gether in a central vortex.

We were not comfortable with ourselves as a family. There was a great shared suffering and yet we never wept together, except for my mother, who would alternately weep and then rage when she was drunk. Together, under my grandmother's tutelage, we kept up appearances. Her effort was ceaseless.

When at the age of six I went to live with her, my grandmother worked to reshape me. I learned what she thought was correct grammar. The manners she had studied in books of etiquette were passed on to me, not by casual example but through anxious memorization and drill. Napkin to be lifted by the corner and swept onto the lap. Hand to be clasped firmly but not too firmly.

We were not to the manner born. On one side my great-grandfather was a farmer, and on the other a butcher newly emigrated from Ireland, who still spoke with a brogue. Both great-grandfathers drank too much, the one in public houses, the other more quietly at home. The great-grandfather who farmed was my grandmother's father. He was not wealthy but he aspired to gentility. My grandmother inherited both his aspiration and his failure.

We considered ourselves finer than the neighbors to our left with their chaotic household. But when certain visitors came, we were as if driven by an inward, secret panic that who we really were might be discovered. Inadvertently, by some careless gesture, we might reveal to these visitors who were our betters that we did not belong with them, that we were not real. Though of course we never spoke of this, to anyone, not even ourselves.

Gebhard Himmler's family was newly risen from poverty. Just as in my family, the Himmlers' gentility was a thinly laid surface, maintained no doubt only with great effort. Gebhard's father had come from a family of peasants and small artisans. Such a living etched from the soil, and by one's hands, is tenuous and hard. As is frequently the case with young men born to poverty, Johann became a soldier. And, like many young soldiers, he got himself into trouble more than once for brawling and general mischief. On one occasion he was reproved for what was called *immoral behavior with a low woman*. But nothing of this history survived in his son's version of him. By the time Gebhard was born, Johann was fifty-six years old and had reformed his ways. Having joined the royal police force of Bavaria, over the years he rose to the rank of sergeant. He was a respectable man, with a respectable position.

Perhaps Gebhard never learned of his father's less than respectable past. He was only three years old when Johann died. If he had the slightest notion, he did not breathe a word to his own children. Johann became the icon of the Himmler family, the heroic soldier who single-handedly brought his family from the obscurity of poverty into the warm light of the favored. Yet obscure histories have a way of casting a shadow over the present. Those who are born to propriety have a sense of entitlement, and this affords them some ease as they execute the correct mannerisms of their class. More recent members of the elect are less certain of themselves; around the edges of newly minted refinement one discerns a certain fearfulness, expressed perhaps as uncertainty, or as its opposite, rigidity.

One can sense that rigidity in Gebhard's face as a younger man. In a photograph of the Himmler family, Gebhard, who towers in the background, seems severe. He has the face of one who looks for mistakes. He is vigilant. Heinrich's mother looks very small next to him, almost as if she is cowering. She has that look I have seen many times on my father's face, which one can only describe as ameliorating. Heinrich is very small. He stands closest to the camera, shimmering in a white dress. His face is pretty, even delicate.

I am looking now at the etching called *Poverty*, made in 1897. Near the center, calling my attention, a woman holds her head in her hands. She stares through her hands into the face of a sleeping infant. Though the infant and the sheet and pillow around are filled with light, one recognizes that the child is dying. In a darker corner, two worried figures huddle, a father and another child. Room, mother, father, child exist in lines, a multitude of lines, and each line is filled with a rare intelligence.

Just as the physicist's scrutiny changes the object of perception, so does art transmute experience. One cannot look upon what Käthe Kollwitz has drawn without feeling. The lines around the child are bleak with unreason. Never have I seen so clearly that what we call poverty is simply a raw exposure to the terror and fragility of life. But there is more in this image. There is meaning in the frame. One can feel the artist's eyes. Her gaze is in one place soft, in another intense. Like the light around the infant, her attention interrupts the shadow that falls across the room.

The artist's choice of subject and the way she saw it were both radical departures, not only from certain acceptable assumptions in the world of art, but also from established social ideas because the poor were thought of as less than human. The death of a child to a poor parent was supposed to be a less painful event. In her depiction, the artist told a different story.

Heinrich is entering a new school now, and so his father makes a list of all his future classmates. Beside the name of each child he writes the child's father's name, what this father does for a living, and his social position. Heinrich must be careful, Gebhard tells him, to choose whom he befriends. In his diaries the boy seldom mentions his friends by name. Instead he writes that he played, for instance, with the landlord's child.

There is so much for Heinrich to learn. Gebhard must teach him the right way to bow. The proper forms of greeting. The history of his family; the history of his nation. Its heroes. His grandfather's illustrious military past. There is an order in the world and Heinrich has a place in this order which he must be trained to fill. His life is strictly scheduled. At this hour a walk in the woods so that he can appreciate nature. After that a game of chess to develop his mind. And after that piano, so that he will be cultured.

If a part of himself has vanished, that part of the self that feels and wants, and from which hence a coherent life might be shaped, Heinrich is not at sea yet. He has no time to drift or feel lost. Each moment has been spoken for, every move prescribed. He has only to carry out his father's plans for him.

But everything in his life is not as it should be. He is not popular among his classmates. Should it surprise us to learn that he has a penchant for listening to the secrets of his companions, and that afterward he repeats these secrets to his father, the schoolmaster? There is perhaps a secret he would like to learn and one he would like to tell, but this has long since been forgotten. Whatever he learns now he must tell his father. He must not keep anything from him. He must keep his father's good will at all costs. For, without his father, he does not exist.

And there is another reason Heinrich is not accepted by his classmates. He is frail. As an infant, stricken by influenza, he came close to perishing and his body still retains the mark of that illness. He is not strong. He is not good at the games the other boys play. At school he tries over and over to raise himself on the crossbars, unsuccessfully. He covets the popularity of his stronger, more masculine brother, Gebhard. But he cannot keep up with his brother. One day, when they go out for a simple bicycle ride together, Heinrich falls into the mud and returns with his clothes torn.

It is 1914. A war begins. There are parades. Young men marching in uniform. Tearful ceremonies at the railway station. Songs. Decorations. Heinrich is enthusiastic. The war has given him a sense of purpose in life. Like other boys, he plays at soldiering. He follows the war closely, writing in his diary of the progress of armies, *This time with 40 Army Corps and Russia and France against Germany.* The entries he makes do not seem so listless now; they have a new vigor. As the war continues, a new ambition gradually takes the shape of determination. Is this the way he will finally prove himself? Heinrich wants to be a soldier. And above all he wants a uniform.

It is 1915. In her journal Käthe Kollwitz records a disturbing sight. The night before at the opera she found herself sitting next to a young soldier. He was blinded. He sat *without stirring, his hands on his knees, his head erect.* She could not stop looking at him, and the memory of him, she writes now, *cuts her to the quick.*

It is 1916. As Heinrich comes of age he implores his father to help him find a regiment. He has many heated opinions about the war. But his thoughts are like the thoughts and feelings of many adolescents; what he expresses has no steady line of reason. His opinions are filled with contradictions, and he lacks that awareness of self which can turn ambivalence into an inner dialogue. Yet, beneath this amorphous bravado, there is a pattern. As if he were trying on different attitudes, Heinrich swings from harshness to compassion. In one place he writes, *The Russian prisoners multiply like vermin.* (Should I write here that this is a word he will one day use for Jews?) But later he is sympathetic to the same prisoners because they are so far away from home. Writing once of *the silly old women and petty bourgeois . . . who so dislike war,* in another entry, he remembers the young men he has seen depart on trains and he asks, *How many are alive today?*

Is the direction of any life inevitable? Or are there crossroads, points at which the direction might be changed? I am looking again at the Himmler family. Heinrich's infant face resembles the face of his mother. His face is soft. And his mother? In the photograph she is a fading presence. She occupied the same position as did most women in German families, secondary and obedient to the undisputed power of her husband. She has a slight smile which for some reason reminds me of the smile of a child I saw in a photograph from an album made by the SS. This child's image was captured as she stood on the platform at Auschwitz. In the photograph she emanates a certain frailty. Her smile is a very feminine smile. Asking, or perhaps pleading, *Don't hurt me.*

Is it possible that Heinrich, looking into that child's face, might have seen himself there? What is it in a life that makes one able to see oneself in others? Such affinities do not stop with obvious resemblance. There is a sense in which we all enter the lives of others.

It is 1917, and a boy who will be named Heinz is born to Catholic parents living in Vienna. Heinz's father bears a certain resemblance to Heinrich's father. He is a civil servant and, also like Gebhard, he is pedantic and correct in all he does. Heinrich will never meet this boy. And yet their paths will cross.

Early in the same year as Heinz's birth, Heinrich's father has finally succeeded in getting him into a regiment. As the war continues for one more year, Heinrich comes close to achieving his dream. He will be a soldier. He is sent to officer's training. Yet he is not entirely happy. *The food is bad,* he writes to his mother, *and there is not enough of it. It is cold. There are bedbugs. The room is barren.* Can she send him food? A blanket? Why doesn't she write him more often? Has she forgotten him? They are calling up troops. Suppose he should be called to the front and die?

But something turns in him. Does he sit on the edge of a neat, narrow military bunk bed as he writes in his diary that he does not want to be like a boy who whines to his mother? Now, he writes a different letter: *I am once more a soldier body and soul.* He loves his uniform; the oath he has learned to write; the first inspection he passes. He signs his letters now, *Miles Heinrich.* Soldier Heinrich.

I am looking at another photograph. It is of two boys. They are both in military uniform. Gebhard, Heinrich's older brother, is thicker and taller. Next to him Heinrich is still diminutive. But his face has become harder, and his smile, though faint like his mother's smile, has gained a new quality, harsh and stiff like the little collar he wears.

Most men can remember a time in their lives when they were not so different from girls, and they also remember when that time ended. In ancient Greece a young boy lived with his mother, practicing a feminine life in her household, until the day he was taken from her into the camp of men. From this day forward the life that had been soft and graceful became rigorous and hard, as the older boy was prepared for the life of a soldier.

My grandfather on my mother's side was a contemporary of Heinrich Himmler. He was the youngest boy in the family and an especially pretty child. Like Heinrich and all small boys in this period, he was dressed in a lace gown. His hair was long and curled about his face. Like Heinrich, he was his mother's favorite. She wanted to keep him in his finery. He was so beautiful in it, and he was her last child. My great-grandmother Sarah had a dreamy, artistic nature, and in his early years my grandfather took after her. But all of this made him seem girlish. And his father and older brothers teased him mercilessly. Life improved for him only when he graduated to long pants. With them he lost his dreamy nature too.

The soul is often imagined to be feminine. All those qualities thought of as soulful, a dreaminess or artistic sensibility, are supposed to come more naturally to women. Ephemeral, half seen, half present, nearly ghostly, with only the vaguest relation to the practical world of physical law, the soul appears to us as lost. The hero, with his more masculine virtues, must go in search of her. But there is another, older story of the soul. In this story she is firmly planted on the earth. She is incarnate and visible everywhere. Neither is she faint of heart, nor fading in her resolve. It is she, in fact, who goes bravely in search of desire.

1918. Suddenly the war is over. Germany has lost. Heinrich has failed to win his commission. He has not fought in a single battle. Prince Heinrich, his namesake, has died. The prince will be decorated for heroism, after his death. Heinrich returns home, not an officer or even a soldier any longer. He returns to school, completing his studies at the gymnasium and then the university. But he is adrift. Purposeless. And like the world he belongs to, dissatisfied. Neither man nor boy, he does not know what he wants.

Until now he could rely on a strict regimen provided by his father. Nothing was left uncertain or undefined for long in his father's house. The thoroughness of Gebhard's hold over his family comes alive for me through this procedure: every package, letter, or money order to pass through the door was by Gebhard's command to be duly recorded. And I begin to grasp a sense of Gebhard's priorities when I read that Heinrich, on one of his leaves home during the war, assisted his mother in this task. The shadow of his father's habits will stretch out over history. They will fall over an office in Berlin through which the SS, and the entire network of concentration camps, are administered. Every single piece of paper issued with regard to this office will pass over Heinrich's desk, and to each page he will add his own initials. Schedules for trains. Orders for building supplies. Adjustments in salaries. No detail will escape his surmise or fail to be recorded.

But at this moment in his life Heinrich is facing a void. I remember a similar void, when a long and intimate relationship ended. What I felt then was fear. And at times panic. In a journal I kept after this separation, I wrote, *Direct knowledge of the illusory nature of panic. The feeling that I had let everything go out of control.* I could turn in only one direction: inward. Each day I abated my fears for a time by observing myself. But what exists in that direction for Heinrich? He has not been allowed to inhabit that terrain. His inner life has been sealed off both from his father and himself.

I am not certain what I am working for, he writes, and then, not able to let this uncertainty remain, he adds, *I work because it is my duty.* He spends long hours in his room, seldom leaving the house at all. He is at sea. Still somewhat the adolescent, unformed, not knowing what face he should put on when going out into the world, in his journal he confesses that he still lacks that *naturally superior kind of manner that he would dearly like to possess.*

Is it any wonder then that he is so eager to rejoin the army? The army gave purpose and order to his life. He wants his uniform again. In his uniform he knows who he is. But his frailty haunts him. Over and over he shows up at recruiting stations throughout Bavaria only to be turned away each time, with the single word, *Untauglich.* Unfit. At night the echo of this word keeps him awake.

When he tries to recover his pride, he suffers another failure of a similar kind. A student of agriculture at the university, now he dreams of becoming a farmer. He believes he can take strength and vitality from the soil. After all his own applications are rejected, his father finds him a position in the countryside. He rides toward his new life on his motorcycle and is pelted by torrents of rain. Though he is cold and hungry, he is also exuberant. He has defeated his own weakness. But after only a few weeks his body fails him again. He returns home ill with typhus and must face the void once more.

What Germany needs now is a man of iron. How easy it is to hear the irony of these words Heinrich records in his journal. But at this moment in history, he is hearing another kind of echo. There are so many others who agree with him. The treaty of Versailles is taken as a humiliation. An unforgivable weakness, it is argued, has been allowed to invade the nation.

1920. 1922. 1923. Heinrich is twenty, twenty-two, twenty-three. He is growing up with the century. And he starts to adopt certain opinions popular at this time. As I imagine myself in his frame of mind, facing a void, cast into unknown waters, these opinions appear like rescue ships on the horizon, a promise of *terra firma*, the known.

It is for instance fashionable to argue that the emergence of female equality has drained the nation of its strength. At social gatherings Heinrich likes to discuss the differences between men and women. That twilight area between the certainties of gender, homosexuality, horrifies him. A man should be a man and a woman a woman. Sexually explicit illustrations in a book by Oscar Wilde horrify him. Uncomfortable with the opposite sex, so much so that one of his female friends believes he hates women, he has strong feelings about how men and women ought to relate. *A real man,* he sets down in his diary, *should love a woman as a child who must be admonished perhaps even punished, when she is foolish, though she must also be protected and looked after because she is so weak.*

As I try to enter Heinrich's experience, the feeling I sense behind these words is of immense comfort. I know who I am. My role in life, what I am to feel, what I am to be, has been made clear. I am a man. I am the strong protector. And what's more, I am needed. There is one who is weak. One who is weaker than I am. And I am the one who must protect her.

And yet behind the apparent calm of my present mood, there is an uneasiness. Who is this one that I protect? Does she tell me the truth about herself? I am beginning to suspect that she hides herself from me. There is something secretive in her nature. She is an unknown, even dangerous, territory.

The year is 1924. And Heinrich is still fascinated with secrets. He discovers that his brother's fiancée has committed one or maybe even two indiscretions. At his urging, Gebhard breaks off the engagement. But Heinrich is still not satisfied. He writes a friend who lives near his brother's former fiancée, *Do you know of any other shameful stories?* After this, he hires a private detective to look into her past.

Is it any coincidence that in the same year he writes in his diary that he has met a *great man, genuine and pure?* This man, he notes, may be the new leader Germany is seeking. He finds he shares a certain drift of thought with this man. He is discovering who he is now, partly by affinity and partly by negation. In his picture of himself, a profile begins to emerge cast in light and shadow. He knows now who he is and who he is not. He is not Jewish.

And increasingly he becomes obsessed with who he is not. In this pursuit, his curiosity is fed by best-selling books, posters, films, journals; he is part of a larger social movement, and this no doubt gives him comfort, and one cannot, in studying the landscape of his mind as set against the landscape of the social body, discover where he ends and the milieu of this time begins. He is perhaps like a particle in a wave, a wave which has only the most elusive relationship with the physical world, existing as an afterimage in the mind.

I can imagine him sitting at a small desk in his bedroom, still in his father's home. Is it the same desk where he was required to record some desultory sentences in his diary every day? He is bent over a book. It is evening. The light is on, shining on the pages of the book. Which book among the books he has listed in his journal does he read now? Is it *Das Liebnest* (*The Lovenest*), telling the story of a liaison between a Jewish man and a gentile woman? *Rasse?* Explaining the concept of racial superiority? Or is it *Judas Schuldsbach* (*The Book of Jewish Guilt*). Or *Die Sünde wider das Blut* (*The Sin Against the Blood*).

One can follow somewhat his train of thought here and there where he makes comments on what he reads in his journal. When he reads *Tscheka*, for instance, a history of the secret police in Russia, he says he is disappointed. *Everyone knows,* he writes, that the Jews control the secret police in Russia. But nowhere in the pages of this book does he find a mention of this "fact."

His mind has begun to take a definite shape, even a predictable pattern. Everywhere he casts his eyes he will discover a certain word. Wherever his thoughts wander he brings them back to this word. *Jew. Jude. Jew.* With this word he is on firm ground again. In the sound of the word, a box is closed, a box with all the necessary documents, with all the papers in order.

My grandfather was an anti-Semite. He had a long list of enemies that he liked to recite. Blacks were among them. And Catholics. And the English. He was Protestant and Irish. Because of his drinking he retired early (though we never discussed the cause). In my childhood I often found him sitting alone in the living room that was darkened by closed venetian blinds which kept all our colors from fading. Lonely myself, I would try to speak with him. His repertoire was small. When I was younger he would tell me stories of his childhood, and I loved those stories. He talked about the dog named Blackie that was his then. A ceramic statue of a small black dog resembling him stood near the fireplace. He loved this dog in a way that was almost painful to hear. But he could never enter that intricate world of expressed emotion in which the shadings of one's life as it is felt and experienced become articulated. This way of speaking was left to the women of our family. As I grew older and he could no longer tell me the story of his dog, he would talk to me about politics. It was then that, with a passion he revealed nowhere else, he would recite to me his long list filled with everyone he hated.

I did not like to listen to my grandfather speak this way. His face would get red, and his voice took on a grating tone that seemed to abrade not only the ears but some other slower, calmer velocity within the body of the room. His eyes, no longer looking at me, blazed with a kind of blindness. There was no reaching him at these moments. He was beyond any kind of touch or remembering. Even so, reciting the long list of those he hated, he came temporarily alive. Then, once out of this frame of mind, he lapsed into a kind of fog which we called, in the family, his retirement.

There was another part of my grandfather's mind that also disturbed me. But this passion was veiled. I stood at the borders of it occasionally catching glimpses. He had a stack of magazines by the chair he always occupied. They were devoted to the subject of crime, and the crimes were always grisly, involving photographs of women or girls uncovered in ditches, hacked to pieces or otherwise mutilated. I was never supposed to look in these magazines, but I did. What I saw there could not be reconciled with the other experience I had of my grandfather, fond of me, gentle, almost anachronistically protective.

Heinrich Himmler was also fascinated with crime. Along with books about Jews, he read avidly on the subjects of police work, espionage, torture. Despite his high ideals regarding chastity, he was drawn to torrid, even pornographic fiction, including *Ein Sadist im Priesterrock* (*A Sadist in Priestly Attire*) which he read quickly, noting in his journal that it was a book *about the corruption of women and girls . . . in Paris.*

Entering the odd and often inconsistent maze of his opinions, I feel a certain queasiness. I cannot find a balance point. I search in vain for some center, that place which is in us all, and is perhaps even beyond nationality, or even gender, the felt core of existence, which seems to be at the same time the most real. In Heinrich's morass of thought there are no connecting threads, no integrated whole. I find only the opinions themselves, standing in an odd relation to gravity, as if hastily formed, a rickety, perilous structure.

I am looking at a photograph. It was taken in 1925. Or perhaps 1926. A group of men pose before a doorway in Landshut. Over this doorway is a wreathed swastika. Nearly all the men are in uniform. Some wear shiny black boots. Heinrich is among them. He is the slightest, very thin. Heinrich Himmler. He is near the front. At the far left there is the blurred figure of a man who has been caught in motion as he rushes to join the other men. Of course I know his feeling. The desire to partake, and even to be part of memory.

Photographs are strange creations. They are depictions of a moment that is always passing; after the shutter closes, the subject moves out of the frame and begins to change outwardly or inwardly. One ages. One shifts to a different state of consciousness. Subtle changes can take place in an instant, perhaps one does not even feel them—but they are perceptible to the camera.

The idea we have of reality as a fixed quantity is an illusion. Everything moves. And the process of knowing oneself is in constant motion too, because the self is always changing. Nowhere is this so evident as in the process of art which takes one at once into the self and into *terra incognita*, the land of the unknown. *I am groping in the dark*, the artist Käthe Kollwitz writes in her journal. Here, I imagine she is not so much uttering a cry of despair as making a simple statement. A sense of emptiness always precedes creation.

Now, as I imagine Himmler, dressed in his neat uniform, seated behind his desk at party headquarters, I can feel the void he feared begin to recede. In every way his life has taken on definition. He has a purpose and a schedule. Even the place left by the cessation of his father's lessons has now been filled. He is surrounded by men whose ideas he begins to adopt. From Alfred Rosenberg he learns about the history of Aryan blood, a line Rosenberg traces back to thousands of years before Christ. From Walther Darré he learns that the countryside is a source of Nordic strength. (And that Jews gravitate toward cities.)

Yet I do not find the calmness of a man who has found himself in the descriptions I have encountered of Heinrich Himmler. Rather, he is filled with an anxious ambivalence. If there was once someone in him who felt strongly one way or the other, this one has long ago vanished. In a room filled with other leaders, he seems to fade into the woodwork, his manner obsequious, his effect inconsequential. He cannot make a decision alone. He is known to seek the advice of other men for even the smallest decisions. In the years to come it will be whispered that he is being led by his own assistant, Reinhard Heydrich. He has made only one decision on his own with a consistent resolve. Following Hitler with unwavering loyalty, he is known as *der treuer Heinrich*, true Heinrich. He describes himself as an instrument of the Führer's will.

But still he has something of his own. Something hidden. And this will make him powerful. He is a gatherer of secrets. As he supervises the sale of advertising space for the Nazi newspaper, *Der Völkischer Beobachter*, he instructs the members of his staff to gather information, not only on the party enemies, the socialists and the communists, but on Nazi Party members themselves. In his small office he sits surrounded by voluminous files that are filled with secrets. From this he will build his secret police. By 1925, with an order from Adolf Hitler, the Schutzstaffel, or SS, has become an official institution.

His life is moving now. Yet in this motion one has the feeling not of a flow, as in the flow of water in a cell, nor as the flow of rivers toward an ocean, but of an engine, a locomotive moving at high speed, or even a missile, traveling above the ground. History has an uncanny way of creating its own metaphors. In 1930, months after Himmler is elected to the Reichstag, Wernher von Braun begins his experiments with liquid fuel missiles that will one day soon lead to the development of the V-2 rocket.

The successful journey of a missile depends upon the study of ballistics. Gravitational fields vary at different heights. The relationship of a projectile to the earth's surface will determine its trajectory. The missile may give the illusion of liberation from the earth, or even abandon. Young men dreaming of space often invest the missile with these qualities. Yet, paradoxically, one is more free of the consideration of gravity while traveling the surface of the earth on foot. There is no necessity for mathematical calculation for each step, nor does one need to apply Newton's laws to take a walk. But the missile has in a sense been forced away from its own presence; the wisdom that is part of its own weight has been transgressed. It finds itself thus careening in a space devoid of memory, always on the verge of falling, but not falling and hence like one who is constantly afraid of illusion, gripped by an anxiety that cannot be resolved even by a fate that threatens catastrophe.

The catastrophes which came to pass after Heinrich Himmler's astonishing ascent to power did not occur in his own life, but came to rest in the lives of others, distant from him, and out of the context of his daily world. It is 1931. Heinz, the boy born in Vienna to Catholic parents, has just turned sixteen, and he is beginning to learn something about himself. All around him his school friends are falling in love with girls. But when he searches inside himself, he finds no such feelings. He is pulled in a different direction. He finds that he is still drawn to another boy. He does not yet know, or even guess, that these feelings will one day place him in the territory of a target.

It is 1933. Heinrich Himmler, Reichsführer SS, has become President of the Bavarian police. In this capacity he begins a campaign against *subversive elements.* Opposition journalists, Jewish business owners, Social Democrats, Communists—names culled from a list compiled on index cards by Himmler's deputy, Reinhard Heydrich—are rounded up and arrested. When the prisons become too crowded, Himmler builds temporary camps. Then, on March 22, the Reichsführer opens the first official and permanent concentration camp at Dachau.

It is 1934. Himmler's power and prestige in the Reich are growing. Yet someone stands in his way. Within the hierarchy of the state police forces, Ernst Röhm, Commandant of the SA, stands over him. But Himmler has made an alliance with Hermann Göring, who as President Minister of Prussia controls the Prussian police, known as the Gestapo. Through a telephone-tapping technique Göring has uncovered evidence of a seditious plot planned by Röhm against the Führer, and he brings this evidence to Himmler. The Führer, having his own reasons to proceed against Röhm, a notorious homosexual and a socialist, empowers the SS and the Gestapo to form an execution committee. This committee will assassinate Röhm, along with the other leaders of the SA. And in the same year, Göring transfers control of the Gestapo to the SS.

But something else less easy to conquer stands in the way of his dreams for himself. It is his own body. I can see him now as he struggles. He is on a playing field in Berlin. And he has broken out in a sweat. He has been trying once again to earn the Reich's sports badge, an honor whose requirements he himself established but cannot seem to fulfill. For three years he has exercised and practiced. On one day he will lift the required weights or run the required laps, but at every trial he fails to throw the discus far enough. His attempt is always a few centimeters short.

And once he is Reichsführer, he will set certain other standards for superiority that, no matter how heroic his efforts, he will never be able to meet. A sign of the *Übermensch*, he says, is blondness, but he himself is dark. He says he is careful to weed out any applicant for the SS who shows traces of a mongolian ancestry, but he himself has the narrow eyes he takes as a sign of such a descent. *I have refused to accept any man whose size was below six feet because I know only men of a certain size have the necessary quality of blood*, he declares, standing just five foot seven behind the podium.

It is the same year, and Heinz, who is certain now that he is a homosexual, has decided to end the silence which he feels to be a burden to him. From the earliest years of his childhood he has trusted his mother with all of his secrets. Now he will tell her another secret, the secret of whom he loves. *My dear child*, she tells him, *it is your life and you must live it*.

It is 1936. Though he does not know it, Himmler is moving into the sphere of Heinz's life now. He has organized a special section of the Gestapo to deal with homosexuality and abortion. On October 11, he declares in a public speech, *Germany's forebears knew what to do with homosexuals. They drowned them in bogs.* This was not punishment, he argues, but *the extermination of unnatural existence.*

As I read these words from Himmler's speech, they call to mind an image from a more recent past, an event I nearly witnessed. On my return from Berlin and after my search for my grandmother, I spent a few days in

Maine, close to the city of Bangor. This is a quiet town, not much used to violence. But just days before I arrived a young man had been murdered there. He was a homosexual. He wore an earring in one ear. While he walked home one evening with another man, three boys stopped him on the street. They threw him to the ground and began to kick him. He had trouble catching his breath. He was asthmatic. They picked him up and carried him to a railing of a nearby bridge. He told them he could not swim. Yet still, they threw him over the railing of the bridge into the stream, and he drowned. I saw a picture of him printed in the newspaper. That kind of beauty only very graceful children possess shined through his adult features. It was said that he had come to New England to live with his lover. But the love had failed, and before he died he was piecing his life back together.

When Himmler heard that one of his heroes, Frederick the Great, was a homosexual, he refused to believe his ears. I remember the year when my sister announced to my family that she was a lesbian. I can still recall the chill of fear that went up my spine at the sound of the word "queer." We came of age in the fifties; this was a decade of conformity, awash with mood both public and private, bearing on the life of the body and the body politic. Day after day my grandfather would sit in front of the television set watching as Joseph McCarthy interrogated witnesses about their loyalty to the flag. At the same time, a strict definition of what a woman or a man is had returned to capture the shared imagination. In school I was taught sewing and cooking, and I learned to carry my books in front of my chest to strengthen the muscles which held up my breasts.

I was not happy to hear that my sister was a homosexual. Moved from one member of my family to another, I did not feel secure in the love of others. As the child of divorce I was already different. *Where are your mother and father? Why don't you live with them?* I dreaded these questions. Now my sister, whom I adored and in many ways had patterned myself after, had become an outcast, moved even further out of the circle than I.

It is March 1938. Germany has invaded Austria. Himmler has put on a field-gray uniform for the occasion. Two hand grenades dangle from his Sam Browne belt. Accompanied by a special command unit of twenty-eight men armed with tommy guns and light machine guns, he proceeds to Vienna. Here he will set up Gestapo headquarters in the Hotel Metropole before he returns to Berlin.

It is a Friday, in March of 1939. Heinz, who is twenty-two years old now, and a university student, has received a summons. He is to appear for questioning at the Hotel Metropole. Telling his mother it can't be anything serious, he leaves. He enters a room and stands before a desk. The man behind the desk does not raise his head to nod. He continues to write. When he puts his pen down and looks up at the young man, he tells him,

concentration camps
missile a a metaphor for hate
opposing this is The nucleus

missile
vs.
nature

You are a queer, homosexual, admit it. Heinz tries to deny this. But the man behind the desk pulls out a photograph. He sees two faces here he knows. His own face and the face of his lover. He begins to weep.

I have come to believe that every life bears in some way on every other. The motion of cause and effect is like the motion of a wave in water, continuous, within and not without the matrix of being, so that all consequences, whether we know them or not, are intimately embedded in our experience. But the missile, as it hurls toward its target, has lost its context. It has been driven farther than the eye can see. How can one speak of direction any longer? Nothing in the space the missile passes through can seem familiar. In the process of flight, alienated by terror, this motion has become estranged from life, has fallen out of the natural rhythm of events.

I am imagining Himmler as he sits behind his desk in January of 1940. The procedures of introduction into the concentration camps have all been outlined or authorized by Himmler himself. He supervises every detail of these operations. Following his father's penchant for order, he makes many very explicit rules, and requires that reports be filed continually. Train schedules, orders for food supplies, descriptions of punishments all pass over his desk. He sits behind a massive door of carved wood, in his office, paneled in light, unvarnished oak, behind a desk that is normally empty, and clean, except for the bust of Hitler he displays at one end, and a little drummer boy at the other, between which he reads, considers and initials countless pieces of paper.

One should teach a child a sense of shame. These words of Himmler's journals come back to me as I imagine Heinz now standing naked in the snow. The weather is below zero. After a while he is taken to a cold shower, and then issued an ill-fitting uniform. Now he is ordered to stand with the other prisoners once more out in the cold while the commandant reads the rules. All the prisoners in these barracks are homosexuals. There are pink triangles sewn to their uniforms. They must sleep with the light on, they are told, and with their hands outside their blankets. This is a rule made especially for homosexual men. Any man caught with his hands under his blankets will be taken outside into the icy night where several bowls of water will be poured over him, and where he will he made to stand for an hour.

Except for the fact that this punishment usually led to death from cold and exposure, this practice reminds me of Dr. Schreber's procedure for curing children of masturbation. Just a few nights ago I woke up with this thought: *Was Dr. Schreber afraid of children?* Or the child he once was? Fear is often just beneath the tyrant's fury, a fear that must grow with the trajectory of his flight from himself. At Dachau I went inside a barrack. It was a standard design, similar in many camps. The plan of the camps too was standard, and resembled, so I was told by a German friend, the camp sites designed for the Hitler Youth. This seemed to me significant, not as a clue in an analysis, but more like a gesture that colors and changes a speaker's words.

It is the summer of 1940. After working for nearly a decade on liquid fuel rockets, Wernher von Braun begins to design a missile that can be used in the war. He is part of a team trying to meet certain military specifications. The missile must be carried through railway tunnels. It must cover a range of 275 kilometers and carry a warhead weighing one metric ton. The engineers have determined that the motor of this rocket, a prototype of the V-2, will need to be fueled by a pump, and now a pump has been made. Von Braun is free to turn his attention to the turbine drive.

When I think of this missile, or of men sleeping in a barrack, hands exposed, lying on top of worn blankets, an image of Himmler's hands comes to me. Those who remember him say that as he conducted a conversation, discussing a plan, for example, or giving a new order, his hands would lie on top of his desk, limp and inert. He did not like to witness the consequences of his commands. His plans were launched toward distant targets and blind to the consequences of flesh.

After a few months, in one of countless orders which mystify him, coming from a nameless source, and with no explanation, but which he must obey, Heinz is transferred from Sachsenhausen to Flossenbürg. The regime at this camp is the same, but here the commandant, unlike Himmler, does not choose to distance himself from the suffering of others. He is instead drawn to it. He will have a man flogged for the slightest infraction of the rules, and then stand to watch as this punishment is inflicted. The man who is flogged is made to call out the number of lashes as he is lashed, creating in him, no doubt, the feeling that he is causing his own pain. As the man's skin bursts open and he cries out in pain, the commandant's eyes grow excited. His face turns red. His hand slips into his trousers, and he begins to handle himself.

Was the commandant in this moment in any way an extension of the Reichsführer, living out a hidden aspect of this man, one who takes pleasure in the pain of others? This explanation must shed some light, except perhaps as it is intended through the category of an inexplicable perversity to put the crimes Himmler committed at a distance from any understanding of ourselves. The Reichsführer's sexuality is so commonplace. He was remarkable only for the extent of his prudery as a young man. Later, like so many men, he has a wife, who dominates him, and a mistress, younger, more docile, adoring, whom he in turn adores. It has been suggested that he takes pleasure in seeing the naked bodies of boys and young men. If he has a sexual fetish it is certainly this, the worship of physical perfection in the male body. And this worship has its sadistic aspects: his efforts to control reproduction, to force SS men to procreate with many women, the kidnapping from occupied countries of children deemed worthy. Under the veneer of his worship, an earlier rage must haunt him. The subject of cruel insults from other boys with hardier bodies, and the torturous methods his father used to raise him, does he not feel rage toward his persecutors, a rage that, in the course of time, enters history? Yet this is an essential part of the picture: he is dulled to rage. So many of his feelings are inaccessible to him. Like the concentration camps he commands, in many ways he remains absent to himself. And in this he is not so different from the civilization that produced him.

Writing this, I have tried to find my own rage. The memory is immediate. I am a child, almost nine years old. I sit on the cold pavement of a winter day in Los Angeles. My grandmother has angered me. There is a terrible injustice. A punishment that has enraged me. As I sit picking blades of grass and arranging them into piles, I am torturing her in my mind. I have tied her up and I am shouting at her. Threatening her. Striking her. I batter her, batter her as if with each blow, each landing of my hand against her flesh, I can force my way into her, I can be inside her, I can grab hold of someone inside her, someone who feels, who feels as I do, who feels the hurt I feel, the wound I feel, who feels pain as I feel pain. I am forcing her to feel what I feel. I am forcing her to know me. And as I strike her, blow after blow, a shudder of weeping is released in me, and I become utterly myself, the weeping in me becoming rage, the rage turning to tears, all the time my heart beating, all the time uttering a soundless, bitter, passionate cry, a cry of vengeance and of love.

Is this what is in the torturer's heart? With each blow of his whip does he want to make the tortured one feel as he himself has felt? The desire to know and be known is strong in all of us. Many years after the day I imagined myself as my grandmother's torturer I came to understand that, just as I had wanted my grandmother to feel what I had felt, she wanted me to feel as she had felt. Not what she felt as a woman, but what she had felt long ago as a child. Her childhood was lost to her, the feelings no longer remembered. One way or another, through punishment, severity, or even ridicule, she could goad me into fury and then tears. I expressed for her all she had held inside for so long.

One day, the commandant at Flossenbürg encounters a victim who will not cry and Heinz is a witness to this meeting. As usual this prisoner must count out the number of blows assigned to him. The beating commences. And the prisoner counts out the numbers. But otherwise he is silent. Except for the numbers, not a cry, not a sound, passes his lips. And this puts the commandant in a rage. He orders the guard to strike harder with the lash; he increases the number of lashes; he orders the prisoner to begin counting from zero again. Finally, the beating shall continue *until the swine starts screaming,* he shouts. And now, when the prisoner's blood is flowing to the ground, he starts to howl. And with this, the commandant's face grows red, and his hands slip into his trousers again.

A connection between violence and sexuality threads its way through many histories. As we sit in the living room together, looking out over the water, Laura's stories move in and out of the world of her family, and of our shared world, its habits, its wars. She is telling me another story about her father, the general. They were living on the missile base. She had been out late baby-sitting. When she returned home the house was dark. She had no key. It was raining hard. She rang. There was no answer. Then she began to pound on the door. Suddenly the door opened. The hallway was dark. She was yanked into this darkness by her father. He was standing naked. Without speaking to her he began to slap her hard across the face, again and again, and did not stop until her mother, appearing in the stairs in a bathrobe, stood between them. *I knew,* she told me, *they had been making love.*

What was the source of his rage? Did it come from childhood, or battle, or both, the battle awakening the panic of an earlier abuse? The training a soldier receives is to wreak his anger on others. Anyone near receives it. I have heard stories of a man waking at night screaming in terror, reaching for a gun hidden under the pillow, and pointing it or even firing at his own family. In a play about Heracles by Euripides, the great warrior, who has just returned from the underworld, thinking that he has vanquished death, is claimed by madness. He believes himself to be in the home of his enemy. But he is in his own home and, finding his own children, mistakes them for the children of his enemy, clubs one to death and then kills the other two with arrows.

But it is not only warriors who wreak vengeance on their own children. Suffering is passed on from parent to child unto many generations. Did I know as a child that my grandmother's unclaimed fury had made its way into my mother's psyche too? With all her will my mother tried not to repeat against her own children the crimes that had battered her. Where my grandmother was tyrannical, my mother was tolerant and gave free reign. Where my grandmother goaded with critical remarks, my mother was encouraging, and even elaborately praising. But, like my grandfather, my mother drank too much. It was a way of life for her. Sooner or later the long nights would come. Every time I returned home, either to live with her or to visit, I prayed she would not drink again, while I braced myself for what I knew to be inevitable. The evening would begin with a few beers at home, followed by an endless tour of several bars. Either I went along and waited in cars, or I waited at home. In the early morning she would return, her eyes wandering like moths in their sockets. We would sit in two chairs opposite each other, as if these were prearranged places, marked out for us on the stage by a powerful but invisible director. She would start by joking with me. She was marvelously witty when she was drunk. All her natural intelligence was released then and allowed to bloom. But this performance was brief. Her humor turned by dark degrees to meanness. What must have daily constricted her, a kind of sea monster, feeding beneath the waters of her consciousness, and strong, would rise up to stop her glee and mine. Then she would strike. If I was not in my chair to receive her words, she would come and get me. What she said was viperous to me, sank like venom into my veins, and burned a path inside me. Even today I can remember very few of the words she used. She said that my laugh was too loud, or ugly. That I was incapable of loving. I am thankful now that, because she was not in her right mind, I knew at least in a part of myself that these accusations were unfounded. Yet they produced a doubt in me, a lingering shadow, the sense that perhaps I deserved whatever suffering befell me, and that shadow lingers.

Even if a feeling has been made secret, even if it has vanished from memory, can it have disappeared altogether? A weapon is lifted with the force of a forgotten memory. The memory has no words, only the insistence of a pain that has turned into fury. A body, tender in its childhood or its nakedness, lies under this weapon. And this body takes up the rage, the pain, the disowned memory with each blow.

1893. *Self-portrait at Table.* An etching and aquatint, the first in a long series of self-portraits that span the artist's life. A single lamp illuminates her face, the upper part of the body and the table where she sits. Everything else is in darkness. At first glance one thinks of loneliness. But after a moment it is solitude one sees. And a single moment in that solitude, as if one note of music, resonant and deep, played uninterrupted, echoing from every surface, coming to full consciousness in this woman, who in this instant looks out to those who will return her gaze with a face that has taken in and is expressing the music in the air about her. Solemnly and with a quiet patience, her hands pause over the etching she makes, a form she is bringing into being, the one she recognizes as herself.

Who are we? The answer is not easy. There are so many strands to the story, and one must trace every strand. I begin to suspect each thread goes out infinitely and touches everything, everyone. I read these words from an ancient gnostic text, words that have been lost to us for a long time: *For I am the first and the last.* Though in another account we have heard the beginning of this speech spoken by Jesus, here these words come to us in the voice of the goddess. *I am the honored one and scorned one,* the older text goes on. *I am the whore and the holy one. I am the wife and the virgin. I am the barren one, and many are her sons.* These words take on a new meaning for me, as I remember them now. *I am the silence that is incomprehensible,* the text reads, and ends, *I am the utterance of my name.*

Were you to trace any life, and study even the minute consequences, the effect, for instance, of a three-minute walk over a patch of grass, of words said casually to a stranger who happens to sit nearby in a public place, the range of that life would extend way beyond the territory we imagine it to inhabit. This is of course less difficult to understand when imagining the boundaries of a life such as Heinrich Himmler had.

After my visit to Dachau, I went to Paris where, in the fourteenth arrondissement, in the Métro station, I met Hélène. She stopped to help me read my map. We found we were going in the same direction, and thus it was on our way there that we began to speak. Something told me she had survived a concentration camp. And she had. She too fell into the circle of Himmler's life and its consequences. Himmler never went to Paris. At the time of the first mass arrests there he was taking a group of high Nazi officials on a tour of Auschwitz. During the tour, by his orders, the prisoners were made to stand at attention for six hours under the hot sun, but that is another story. Under his command, the Gestapo in Paris began to prepare for the mass arrests of Jews.

Paris had fallen to the German armies in July 1940. By September of that year a notice went up in all the neighborhoods. *Avis aux Israélites*, it read. *Notice to Israelites. By the demand of the occupying authorities, Israelites must present themselves, by October 2, without delay, equipped with identification papers, to the office of the Censor, to complete an identity card.* The notice was signed by the mayor and threatened the most severe punishment for the failure to comply. Through this process vital information was recorded about each Jewish family. Names, ages, addresses, occupations, places of work. An index card was made up for each person. And each card was then duplicated and sent to the offices of the Gestapo on Avenue Foch. There, the cards were duplicated several more times so that the names could be filed by several categories, alphabetically by surname, by address, by arrondissement, occupation, and nationality. At this point in history, work that would be done by computer now was painstakingly completed by countless men and women. Their labor continued feverishly almost until the hour of the first mass arrests, the *rafles*, two years later.

One can trace every death to an order signed by Himmler, yet these arrests could never have taken place on such a massive scale without this vast system of information. What did they think, those who were enlisted for this work? They were civilians. French. There were of course Nazi collaborators, among them, those who shared the same philosophy, or who simply obeyed and profited from whoever might be in power. But among the men and women who did this work, my suspicion is, there were many who tried to keep from themselves the knowledge of what they did. Of course, the final purpose of their labors was never revealed to those who prepared the machinery of arrest. If a man allowed his imagination to stray in the direction of this purpose, he could no doubt comfort himself with the argument that he was only handling pieces of paper. He could tell himself that matters were simply being set in order. The men and women who manufacture the trigger mechanisms for nuclear bombs do not tell themselves they are making weapons. They say simply that they are metal forgers.

There are many ways we have of standing outside ourselves in ignorance. Those who have learned as children to become strangers to themselves do not find this a difficult task. Habit has made it natural not to feel. To ignore the consequences of what one does in the world becomes ordinary. And this tendency is encouraged by a social structure that makes fragments of real events. One is never allowed to see the effects of what one does. But this ignorance is not entirely passive. For some, blindness becomes a kind of refuge, a way of life that is chosen, even with stubborn volition, and does not yield easily even to visible evidence.

The arrests were accompanied by an elaborate procedure, needed on some level, no doubt, for practical reasons, but also serving another purpose. They garbed this violence in the cloak of legality. A mind separated from the depths of itself cannot easily tell right from wrong. To this mind, the outward signs of law and order signify righteousness. That Himmler had such a mind was not unique in his generation, nor, I suspect, in ours.

In a museum in Paris I found a mimeographed sheet giving instructions to the Parisian police on how to arrest Jews. They must always carry red pencils, the sheet admonished, because all records regarding the arrests of Jews must be written in red. And the instructions went on to specify that, regarding the arrests of Jews, all records must be made in triplicate. Finally, the sheet of instructions included a way to categorize those Jews arrested. I could not make any sense of the categories. I only knew them to be crucial. That they might determine life and death for a woman, or man, or child. And that in the mind that invented these categories they had to have had some hidden significance, standing, like the crudely shaped characters of a medieval play, for shades of feeling, hidden states of being, secret knowledge.

For the most part, the men who designed the first missiles were not interested in weapons so much as flight. In his account of the early work at Peenemünde laboratories, Wernher von Braun explains that the scientists there had discovered a way to fund their research by making rockets appeal to the military. Colonel Dornberger told the other scientists that they could not hope to continue if all they created were experimental rockets. All Wernher von Braun wanted was to design vehicles that would travel to the moon. In the early fifties, in a book he wrote with two other scientists, he speaks of the reasons for such a flight. Yes, he says, curiosity and adventure play a part. But the primary reason is *to increase man's knowledge of the universe.*

To tell a story, or to hear a story told, is not a simple transmission of information. Something else in the telling is given too, so that, once hearing, what one has heard becomes a part of oneself. Hélène and I went to the museum in Paris together. There, among photographs of the first mass arrests and the concentration camp at Drancy, she told me this story. Reading the notice signed by the mayor, she presented herself immediately at the office of the censor. She waited with others, patiently. But when her turn in line came, the censor looked at her carefully. She was blond and had blue eyes. *Are you really Jewish?* he asked her.

The question of who was and who was not Jewish was pivotal to the Nazi mind and much legal controversy hung in the balance of this debate. For a few years, anyone with three Jewish grandparents was considered Jewish. An ancestor who belonged to the faith, but was not of Jewish blood would be Jewish. One who did not belong to the faith, but was of Jewish blood, was also Jewish. At the heart of this controversy, I hear the whisper of ambivalence, and perhaps the smallest beginning of compassion. For, to this mind, the one who is not Jewish becomes recognizable as like oneself.

Yes, I am Jewish, she said. *But your mother,* he asked again. *Can you be certain? Yes,* she said. *Ask her, go home and ask her,* he said, putting his stamp away. *But my mother is dead,* she protested. Then, he said, keeping his stamp in the drawer, *Your father. Your father must not be Jewish. Go home and ask him. I know he is Jewish,* Hélène answered. *There is no doubt that he is Jewish. He has always been Jewish, and I am Jewish too.* Then the man was silent, he shook his head. And, looking past her, said, *Perhaps your father was not really your father. Have you thought of that? Perhaps he was not your father?* She was young. *Of course he's my father. How can you say that? Certainly he is my father,* she insisted. *He is Jewish and so am I.* And she demanded that her papers be stamped.

What was in this man's mind as he questioned her? Did he say to himself, Perhaps here is someone I can save? Did he have what Pierre Sauvage has called *a moment of goodness?* What we know as goodness is not a static quality but arrives through a series of choices, some imperceptible, which are continually presented to us.

It is 1941. And Heinrich Himmler pays a visit to the Russian front. He has been put in charge of organizing the *Einsatzgruppen,* moving groups of men who carry out the killing of civilians and partisans. He watches as a deep pit is dug by the captured men and women. Then, suddenly, a young man catches his eye. He is struck by some quality the man possesses. He takes a liking to him. He has the commandant of the *Einsatzgruppen* bring the young man to him. *Who was your father?* he asks. *Your mother? Your grandparents? Do you have at least one grandparent who was not Jewish?* He is trying to save the young man. But he answers no to all the questions. So Himmler, strictly following the letter of the law, watches as the young man is put to death.

The captured men, women, and children are ordered to remove their clothing then. Naked, they stand before the pit they have dug. Some scream. Some attempt escape. The young men in uniform place their rifles against their shoulders and fire into the naked bodies. They do not fall silently. There are cries. There are open wounds. There are faces blown apart. Stomachs opened up. The dying groan. Weep. Flutter. Open their mouths.

There is no photograph of the particular moment when Heinrich Himmler stares into the face of death. What does he look like? Is he pale? He is stricken, the accounts tell us, and more than he thought he would be. He has imagined something quieter, more efficient, like the even rows of numbers, the alphabetical lists of names he likes to put in his files. Something he might be able to understand and contain. But one cannot contain death so easily.

Death with Girl in Her Lap. One of many studies the artist did of death. A girl is drawn, her body dead or almost dead, in that suspended state where the breath is almost gone. There is no movement. No will. The lines the artist has drawn are simple. She has not rendered the natural form of head, arm, buttock, thigh exactly. But all these lines hold the feeling of a body in them. And as my eyes rest on this image, I can feel my own fear of death, and also, the largeness of grief, how grief will not let you remain insulated from your own feelings, or from life itself. It is as if I knew this girl. And death, too, appears to know her, cradling the fragile body with tenderness; she seems to understand the sorrow of dying. Perhaps this figure has taken into herself all the deaths she has witnessed. And in this way, she has become merciful.

Because Himmler finds it so difficult to witness these deaths, the commandant makes an appeal to him. If it is hard for you, he says, think what it must be for these young men who must carry out these executions, day after day. Shaken by what he has seen and heard, Himmler returns to Berlin resolved to ease the pain of these men. He will consult an engineer and set him to work immediately on new designs. Before the year has ended, he presents the *Einsatzgruppen* with a mobile killing truck. Now the young men will not have to witness death day after day. A hose from the exhaust pipe funnels fumes into a chamber built on the bed of a covered truck, which has a red cross painted on its side so its passengers will not be alarmed as they enter it.

To a certain kind of mind, what is hidden away ceases to exist.

Himmler does not like to watch the suffering of his prisoners. In this sense he does not witness the consequences of his own commands. But the mind is like a landscape in which nothing really ever disappears. What seems to have vanished has only transmuted to another form. Not wishing to witness what he has set in motion, still, in a silent part of himself, he must imagine what takes place. So, just as the child is made to live out the unclaimed imagination of the parent, others under Himmler's power were made to bear witness for him. Homosexuals were forced to witness and sometimes take part in the punishment of other homosexuals, Poles of other Poles, Jews of Jews. And as far as possible, the hands of the men of the SS were protected from the touch of death. Other prisoners were required to bury the bodies, or burn them in the ovens.

Hélène was turned in by a Jewish man who was trying, no doubt, to save his own life, and she was put under arrest by another Jewish man, an inmate of the same camp to which she was taken. She was grateful that she herself had not been forced to do harm. But something haunted her. A death that came to stand in place of her own death. As we walked through the streets of Paris she told me this story.

By the time of her arrest she was married and had a young son. Her husband was taken from their apartment during one of the mass arrests that began in July of 1942. Hélène was out at the time with her son. For some time she wandered the streets of Paris. She would sleep at night at the homes of various friends and acquaintances, leaving in the early morning so that she would not arouse suspicion among the neighbors. This was the hardest time, she told me, because there was so little food, even less than she was to have at Drancy. She had no ration card or any way of earning money. Her whole existence was illegal. She had to be as if invisible. She collected scraps from the street. It was on the street that she told me this story, as we walked from the fourth arrondissement to the fifth, crossing the bridge near Notre Dame, making our way toward the Boulevard St. Michel.

Her husband was a citizen of a neutral country and for this reason legally destined for another camp. From this camp he would not be deported. Instead he was taken to the French concentration camp at Drancy. After his arrest, hoping to help him, Hélène managed to take his papers to the Swiss Consulate. But the papers remained there. After her own arrest she was taken with her son to Drancy, where she was reunited with her husband. He told her that her efforts were useless. But still again and again she found ways to smuggle out letters to friends asking them to take her husband's papers from the Swiss Consulate to the camp at Drancy. One of these letters was to save their lives.

After a few months, preparations began to send Hélène and her family to Auschwitz. Along with many other women, she was taken to have her hair cut short, though those consigned to that task decided she should keep her long, blond hair. Still, she was herded along with the others to the train station and packed into the cars. Then, just two hours before the train was scheduled to leave, Hélène, her son, and her husband were pulled from the train. Her husband's papers had been brought by the Swiss consul to the camp. The Commandant, by assuming Hélène shared the same nationality with her husband, had made a fortuitous mistake.

But the train had to have a specific number of passengers before it could leave. In Hélène's place the guards brought a young man. She would never forget his face, she told me, or his name. Later she tried to find out whether he had lived or died but could learn nothing.

• • •

Himmler did not partake in the actual preparations for what he called "the final solution." Nor did he attend the Wannsee Conference where the decision to annihilate millions of human beings was made. He sent his assistant Heydrich. Yet Heydrich, who was there, did not count himself entirely present. He could say that each decision he made was at the bequest of Heinrich Himmler. In this way an odd system of insulation was created. These crimes, these murders of millions, were all carried out in absentia, as if by no one in particular.

This ghostlike quality, the strange absence of a knowing conscience, as if the living creature had abandoned the shell, was spread throughout the entire chain of command. So a French bureaucrat writing a letter in 1942 speaks in detail of the mass arrests that he himself supervised as if he had no other part in these murders except as a kind of spiritless cog in a vast machine whose force compelled him from without. *The German authorities have set aside especially for that purpose enough trains to transport 30,000 Jews,* he writes. *It is therefore necessary that the arrests made should correspond to the capacity of the trains.*

It is August 23, 1943. The first inmates of concentration camp Dora have arrived. Is there some reason why an unusually high percentage of prisoners ordered to work in this camp are homosexuals? They are set to work immediately, working with few tools, often with bare hands, to convert long tunnels carved into the Harz Mountains into a factory for the manufacture of missiles. They work for eighteen hours each day. Six of these hours are set aside for formal procedures, roll calls, official rituals of the camp. For six hours they must try to sleep in the tunnels, on the damp earth, in the same area where the machines, pickaxes, explosions, and drills are making a continually deafening noise, twenty-four hours of every day. They are fed very little. They see the daylight only once a week, at the Sunday roll call. The tunnels themselves are illuminated with faint light bulbs. The production of missiles has been moved here because the factories at Peenemünde were bombed. Because the secret work at Peenemünde had been revealed to the Allies by an informer, after the bombing the Reichsführer SS proposed that the factories should be installed in a concentration camp. Here, he argued, security could be more easily enforced; only the guards had any freedom, and they were subject to the harsh discipline of the SS. The labor itself could be hidden under the soil of the Harz Mountains.

Memory can be like a long, half-lit tunnel, a tunnel where one is likely to encounter phantoms of a self, long concealed, no longer nourished with the force of consciousness, existing in a tortured state between life and death. In his account of his years at Peenemünde, Wernher von Braun never mentions concentration camp Dora. Yet he was seen there more than once by inmates who remembered him. As the designing engineer, he had to supervise many details of production. Conditions at camp Dora

could not have escaped his attention. Dora did not have its own cremato-
rium. And so many men and women died in the course of a day that the
bodies waiting to be picked up by trucks and taken to the ovens of
Buchenwald were piled high next to the entrance to the tunnels.

Perhaps von Braun told himself that what went on in those tunnels
had nothing to do with him. He had not wished for these events, had not
wanted them. The orders came from someone who had power over him.
In the course of this writing I remembered a childhood incident that made
me disown myself in the same way. My best friend, who was my neighbor, had a mean streak and because of this had a kind of power over the
rest of us who played with her. For a year I left my grandmother's house
to live with my mother again. On my return I had been replaced by another little girl, and the two of them excluded me. But finally my chance
arrived. My friend had a quarrel with her new friend and enlisted me in
an act of revenge. Together we cornered her at the back of a yard, pushing
her into the garbage cans, yelling nasty words at her, throwing things at
her.

My friend led the attack, inventing the strategies and the words which
were hurled. With part of myself I knew what it was to be the object of this
kind of assault. But I also knew this was the way to regain my place with
my friend. Later I disowned my acts, as if I had not committed them. Because I was under the sway of my friend's power, I told myself that what I
did was really her doing. And in this way became unreal to myself. It was
as if my voice threatening her, my own anger, and my voice calling
names, had never existed.

I was told this story by a woman who survived the holocaust. The war
had not yet begun. Nor the exiles. Nor the mass arrests. But history was
on the point of these events, tipping over, ready to fall into the relentless
path of consequences. She was then just a child, playing games in the
street. And one day she found herself part of a circle of other children.
They had surrounded a little boy and were calling him names because he
was Jewish. He was her friend. But she thought if she left this circle, or
came to his defense, she herself would lose her standing among the others.
Then, suddenly, in an angry voice her mother called her in from the street.
As soon as the door shut behind her, her mother began to shout, words incomprehensible to her, and slapped her across the face. *Your father,* her
mother finally said, after crying, and in a quieter voice, *was Jewish.* Her father had been dead for three years. Soon after this day her mother too
would die. As the danger grew worse her gentile relatives would not harbor her any longer, and she joined the fate of those who tried to live in the
margins, as if invisible, as if mere shadows, terrified of a direct glance, of
recognition, existing at the unsteady boundary of consciousness.

In disowning the effects we have on others, we disown ourselves. My
father watched the suffering of my childhood and did nothing. He was

aware of my mother's alcoholism and the state of her mind when she drank. He knew my grandmother to be tyrannical. We could speak together of these things almost dispassionately, as if both of us were disinterested witnesses to a fascinating social drama. But after a day's visit with him, spent at the park, or riding horses, or at the movies, he would send me back into that world of suffering we had discussed so dispassionately.

His disinterest in my condition was not heartless. It reflected the distance he kept from his own experience. One could sense his suffering but he never expressed it directly. He was absent to a part of himself. He was closer to tears than many men, but he never shed those tears. If I cried he would fall into a frightened silence. And because of this, though I spent a great deal of time with him, he was always in a certain sense an absent father. Unknowingly I responded in kind, for years, feeling a vaguely defined anger that would neither let me love nor hate him.

My father learned his disinterest under the guise of masculinity. Boys don't cry. There are whole disciplines, institutions, rubrics in our culture which serve as categories of denial.

Science is such a category. The torture and death that Heinrich Himmler found disturbing to witness became acceptable to him when it fell under this rubric. He liked to watch the scientific experiments in the concentration camps. And then there is the rubric of military order. I am looking at a photograph. It was taken in 1941 in the Ukraine. The men of an *Einstazgruppen* are assembled in a group pose. In front of them their rifles rest in ceremonial order, composed into tripods. They stand straight and tall. They are clean-shaven and their uniforms are immaculate, in *apple-pie order*, as we would say in America.

It is not surprising that cleanliness in a profession that sheds blood would become a compulsion. Blood would evidence guilt and fear to a mind trying to escape the consequence of its decisions. It is late in the night when Laura tells me one more story. Her father is about to be sent to Europe, where he will fight in the Battle of the Bulge and become a general. For weeks her mother has prepared a party. The guests begin to arrive in formal dress and sparkling uniforms. The white-gloved junior officers stand to open the doors. Her mother, regal in satin and jewels, starts to descend the staircase. Laura sits on the top stair watching, dressed in her pajamas. Then suddenly a pool of blood appears at her mother's feet, her mother falls to the floor, and almost as quickly, without a word uttered, a junior officer sweeps up the stairs, removes her mother into a waiting car, while another one cleans up the blood. No one tells Laura that her mother has had a miscarriage, and the party continues as if no event had taken place, no small or large death, as if no death were about to take place, nor any blood be spilled.

But the nature of the material world frustrates our efforts to remain free of the suffering of others. The mobile killing van that Himmler summoned into being had some defects. Gas from the exhaust pipes leaked into the cabin where the drivers sat and made them ill. When they went to remove the bodies from the van they were covered with blood and excrement, and their faces bore expressions of anguish. Himmler's engineers fixed the leak, increased the flow of gas so the deaths would be quicker, and built in a drain to collect the bodily fluids that are part of death.

There are times when no engineers can contain death. Over this same landscape through which the mobile killing vans traveled, an invisible cloud would one day spread, and from it would descend a toxic substance that would work its way into the soil and the water, the plants and the bodies of animals, and into human cells, not only in this landscape of the Ukraine, but in the fjords of Norway, the fields of Italy and France, and even here, in the far reaches of California, bringing a death that recalled, more than forty years later, those earlier hidden deaths.

You can see pictures of them. Whole families, whole communities. The fabric on their backs almost worn through. Bodies as if ebbing away before your eyes. Poised on an edge. The cold visible around the thin joints of arms and knees. A bed made in a doorway. Moving then, over time, deeper and deeper into the shadows. Off the streets. Into back rooms, and then to the attics or the cellars. Windows blackened. Given less and less to eat. Moving into smaller and smaller spaces. Sequestered away like forbidden thoughts, or secrets.

Could he have seen in these images of those he had forced into hiding and suffering, into agony and death, an image of the outer reaches of his own consciousness? It is only now that I can begin to see he has become part of them. Those whose fate he sealed. Heinrich Himmler. A part of Jewish history. Remembered by those who fell into the net of his unclaimed life. Claimed as a facet of the wound, part of the tissue of the scar. A mark on the body of our minds, both those of us who know this history and those who do not.

For there is a sense in which we are all witnesses. Hunger, desperation, pain, loneliness, these are all visible in the streets about us. The way of life we live, a life we have never really chosen, forces us to walk past what we see. And out at the edge, beyond what we see or hear, we can feel a greater suffering, cries from a present or past starvation, a present or past torture, cries of those we have never met, coming to us in our dreams, and even if these cries do not survive in our waking knowledge, still, they live on in the part of ourselves we have ceased to know.

I think now of the missile again and how it came into being. Scientific inventions do not spring whole like Athena from the head of Zeus from the analytic implications of scientific discoveries. Technological advance takes shape slowly in the womb of society and is influenced and fed by our shared imagination. What we create thus mirrors the recesses of our own minds, and perhaps also hidden capacities. Television mimics the ability to see in the mind's eye. And the rocket? Perhaps the night flight of the soul, that ability celebrated in witches to send our thoughts as if through the air to those distant from us, to send images of ourselves, and even our secret feelings, out into an atmosphere beyond ourselves, to see worlds far flung from and strange to us becomes manifest in a sinister fashion in the missile.

Self-portrait in charcoal. Since the earliest rendering she made of her own image, much time has passed. The viewer here has moved closer. Now the artist's head fills the frame. She is much older in years and her features have taken on that androgyny which she thought necessary to the work of an artist. Her hair is white on the paper where the charcoal has not touched it. She is in profile and facing a definite direction. Her eyes look in that direction. But they do not focus on anyone or anything. The portrait is soft, the charcoal rubbed almost gently over the surface, here light, here dark. Her posture is one not so much of resolution as resignation. The portrait was drawn just after the First World War, the war in which her son Peter died. I have seen these eyes in the faces of those who grieve, eyes that are looking but not focused, seeing perhaps what is no longer visible.

After the war, German scientists who developed the V-1 and V-2 rocket immigrate to the United States where they continue to work on rocketry. Using the Vengeance weapon as a prototype, they develop the first ICBM missiles.

On the twenty-third of May 1945, as the war in Europe comes to an end, Heinrich Himmler is taken prisoner by the Allied command. He has removed the military insignia from his clothing, and he wears a patch over one eye. Disguised in this manner, and carrying the identity papers of a man he had condemned to death, he attempts to cross over the border at Bremervörde. No one at the checkpoint suspects him of being the Reichsführer SS. But once under the scrutiny of the guards, all his courage fails him. Like a trembling schoolboy, he blurts out the truth. Now he will be taken to a center for interrogation, stripped of his clothing and searched. He will refuse to wear the uniform of the enemy, so he will be given a blanket to wrap over his underclothing. Taken to a second center for interrogation, he will be forced to remove this blanket and his underclothes. The interrogators, wishing to make certain he has no poison hidden anywhere, no means by which to end his life and hence avoid giving testimony, will surround his naked body. They will ask him to open his mouth. But just as one of them sees a black capsule wedged between his teeth, he will jerk his head away and swallow. All attempts to save his life will fail. He will not survive to tell his own story. His secrets will die with him.

There were many who lived through those years who did not wish to speak of what they saw or did. None of the German rocket engineers bore witness to what they saw at concentration camp Dora. Common rank and file members of the Nazi Party, those without whose efforts or silent support the machinery could not have gone on, fell almost as a mass into silence. In Berlin and Munich I spoke to many men and women, in my generation or younger, who were the children of soldiers, or party members, or SS men, or generals, or simply believers. Their parents would not speak to them of what had happened. The atmosphere in both cities was as if a pall had been placed over memory. And thus the shared mind of this nation has no roots, no continuous link with what keeps life in a pattern of meaning.

Lately I have come to believe that an as yet undiscovered human need and even a property of matter is the desire for revelation. The truth within us has a way of coming out despite all conscious efforts to conceal it. I have heard stories from those in the generation after the war, all speaking of the same struggle to ferret truth from the silence of their parents so that they themselves could begin to live. One born the year the war ended was never told a word about concentration camps, at home or in school. She began to wake in the early morning hours with nightmares which mirrored down to fine and accurate detail the conditions of the camps. Another woman searching casually through some trunks in the attic of her home found a series of pamphlets, virulently and cruelly anti-Semitic, which had been written by her grandfather, a high Nazi official. Still another pieced together the truth of her father's life, a member of the Gestapo, a man she remembered as playful by contrast to her stern mother. He died in the war. Only over time could she put certain pieces together. How he had had a man working under him beaten. And then, how he had beaten her.

Many of those who survived the holocaust could not bear the memories of what happened to them and, trying to bury the past, they too fell into silence. Others continue to speak as they are able. The manner of speech varies. At an artist's retreat in the Santa Cruz Mountains I met a woman who survived Bergen Belsen and Auschwitz. She inscribes the number eight in many of her paintings. And the number two. This is the story she is telling with those numbers. It was raining the night she arrived with her mother, six brothers and sisters at Auschwitz. It fell very hard, she told me. We were walking in the early evening up a hill brown in the California fall. The path was strewn with yellow leaves illuminated by the sun in its descent. They had endured the long trip from Hungary to Poland, without food or water. They were very tired. Now the sky seemed very black but the platform, lit up with stadium lights, was blinding after the darkness of the train. She would never, she told me, forget the shouting. It is as if she still cannot get the sound out of her ears. The Gestapo gave one shrill order after another, in a language she did not yet understand. They were herded in confusion, blows coming down on them randomly from the guards, past a tall man in a cape. This was Dr. Mengele. He made a single gesture toward all her family and continued it toward her but in a different direction. For days, weeks, months after she had learned what their fate had been she kept walking in the direction of their parting and beyond toward the vanishing point of her vision of them.

There were seven from her family who died there that night. The eighth to die was her father. He was sent to a different camp and died on the day of liberation. Only two lived, she and one brother. The story of one life cannot be told separately from the story of other lives. Who are we? The question is not simple. What we call the self is part of a larger matrix of relationship and society. Had we been born to a different family, in a different time, to a different world, we would not be the same. All the lives that surround us are in us.

On the first day that I met Lenke she asked a question that stays with me still. Why do some inflict on others the suffering they have endured? What is it in a life that makes one choose to do this, or not? It is a question I cannot answer. Not even after several years pondering this question in the light of Heinrich Himmler's soul. Two years after my conversation with Lenke, as if there had been a very long pause in our dialogue, I was given a glimpse in the direction of an answer. Leo told me his story; it sounded back over time, offering not so much solution as response.

The nucleus of every cell in the human body contains the genetic plan for the whole organism.

We sat together in a large and noisy restaurant, light pouring through the windows, the present clamoring for our attention, even as we moved into the past. Leo was nine years old when the war entered his life. He remembers standing in a crowd, he told me, watching as a partisan was flogged and executed by the Germans. *What do you think I felt?* he asked me, the irony detectable in his voice. What he told me fell into his narration as part of a larger picture. The capture, the roughness, the laceration of flesh, the sight of death, all this excited him.

Violence was not new to him. Through bits and pieces surrounding the central line of his story I came to some idea of what his childhood must have been. His father was a cold man, given to rages over small errors. Leo was beaten often. Such attacks had already forced his older half brother out of the house. It was to this brother that Leo bonded and gave his love.

Leo remembered a party before the war. The room was lively with talk until his older brother arrived. Then a silence fell over everyone. The older men were afraid of this young man, even his father. And to Leo, his brother, with his air of power and command, was a hero. He could scarcely understand the roots of this power, moored in a political system of terror so effective, few even spoke of it. Leo's brother was a young member of Stalin's secret police. Cast into the streets while still a boy, he learned the arts of survival. Eventually he was arrested for assaulting and robbing a man. It was under this circumstance that he offered himself to the NKVD, the forerunner of the KGB, as an interrogator. He learned to torture men and women suspected of treason or of harboring secrets.

He wore high black leather boots and a black leather jacket, which impressed Leo. Leo followed him about, and they would take long walks together, his brother telling him the stories he could tell no one else. How he had tortured a woman. How he had made blood flow from the nipples of her breasts.

Everything he heard from his brother he took into himself. Such love as Leo had for his brother can be a forceful teacher. He did not see his brother often, nor was his intimacy with him great enough to create familiarity. What he had was a continual taste awakening hunger. Never did he know the daily presence of the beloved, or all his imperfections, the real person dwelling behind the mask of the ideal, the shiny and impervious leather. To fill the nearly perpetual absence of his brother he clung to this ideal. An appearance of strength. A certain arrogance in the face of violence, promising an even greater violence. Love always seeks a resting place.

I knew a similar attachment to my sister. Separated when I was six and she was thirteen, the experience of love I knew with her was longing, and over time this bonded me to longing itself. And to the books she brought me to read, the poems she read to me, worlds she pointed me toward.

And the German occupation of the Ukraine? The accident at Chernobyl had taken place just weeks before we met. But long before this event, the same land suffered other wounds. As the Soviet army retreated, they burned crops and killed livestock. Even before the German invasion, the land was charred and black for miles around. Then when the German army came, the executions began. And the deportations. Many were taken away to forced labor camps. Leo was among them.

His father was an agronomist with some knowledge of how to increase crop yields. The whole family was transported to Germany, but at the scientist's camp Leo was transported in another direction. His father watched him go, Leo told me, with no protest, not even the protestation of tears.

What was it like for him in the labor camp to which he was sent? His telling of the past existed in a framework of meaning he had built slowly over the years, and with great pain, forced to this understanding by events that he himself had brought into being, later in his life.

It is a question of passion, he told me. While he was in the camps, he began to worship the uniformed members of the SS and the SA, just as he had loved his brother. Their strength, their ideals, their willingness to do violence, to live for something beyond themselves, the black leather they wore, the way they were clean and polished and tall. He saw those who, like himself, were imprisoned as small and demeaned, caught in the ugliness of survival, lacking any heroism, cowardly, petty. Even now, as he looked back himself with another eye, his disdain for those who suffered persisted in a phantom form, in the timbre of his voice.

The punishment of the guards did not embitter him. In his mind he believed he himself was always justly punished. Once, against the rules, he stole food, honey, while he was working. He did not accept his own hunger as an argument for kindness. He admired the strength with which he was hit. Even the intimacy of the blows gave him a certain pride in himself. Loving the arms that hit him, he could think of this power as his own.

But there were two assaults which he could not forgive. They humiliated him. Now as I write I can see that to him his attackers must have been unworthy of his admiration. He was on a work detail in the neighboring village when a boy his own age slapped him. And later an old woman spat in his face.

This was all he told me of his time of imprisonment. After the liberation, he went into Germany to search for his family. Did he believe that perhaps, even now, something outside of the circle drawn by what he had suffered existed for him? Was there a seed of hope, a wish that made him, thin, weak, on shaking legs, travel the hundreds of miles, sleeping in trains and train stations, to search? He was exhausted, I can imagine, past that edge of weariness in which whatever is real ceases entirely to matter and existence itself is just a gesture, not aimed any longer at outcome, but just a simple expression of what remains and so can seem even brighter. He was making a kind of pilgrimage.

It is in this way, coldness beyond cold, frailty beyond endurance, that sorrow becomes a power. A light begins to shine past the fire of ovens, yet from them, as if stars, or turning leaves, falling and trapped in their fall, nevertheless kept their brilliance, and this brilliance a beacon, like a code, flashes out the precise language of human suffering. Then we know that what we suffer is not going to pass by without meaning.

Self-portrait, 1923. The artist's face is drawn of lines left white on the page which seem as if they were carved out of night. We are very close to her. It is only her face we see. Eye to eye, she looks directly at us. But her eyes are unfocused and weary with that kind of tiredness that has accumulated over so much time we think of it as aging. Her mouth, wide and frank, does not resist gravity any longer. This mouth smiles with an extraordinary subtlety. We can almost laugh with this mouth, drawn with lines which, like all the lines on the page, resemble scars, or tears in a fabric.

A story is told as much by silence as by speech. Like the white spaces in an etching, such silences render form. But unlike an etching in which the whole is grasped at once, the silence of a story must be understood over time. Leo described to me what his life was like after he found his parents, but he did not describe the moment, or even the day or week, when he found them. Only now as I write these words does the absence of joy in this reunion begin to speak to me. And in the space of this absence I can feel the kind of cold that can extinguish the most intense of fires.

Leo was soon streetwise. His family was near starvation. He worked the black market. Older men buying his goods would ask him for women, and he began to procure for them. He kept his family alive. His father, he told me, never acknowledged his effort. When they moved to America a few years later and Leo reminded him that his work had fed him, his father exclaimed, in a voice of shock and disparagement, *And what you did!*

In 1957, the Soviet Union develops the SS-6, a surface-to-surface missile. It is launched with thirty-two engines. Failing as a weapon, this device is used to launch the first satellite into space. In 1961, the Soviet Union develops the SS-7. These missiles carry nuclear warheads. They are launched from hardened silos to protect them from attack.

In America he was sent to high school. But he did not know how to be an ordinary boy among boys. He became a street fighter. Together with a group of boys among whom he was the toughest, he would look for something to happen. More than once they devised a trap for homosexual men. They would place the prettiest boy among them on a park bench and wait behind the trees and bushes. Usually a man would pull up in his car and go to sit on the bench next to the boy. When this man made any gesture of seduction, or suggested the boy leave with him, the boys would suddenly appear and, surrounding him, beat him and take his money.

I am thinking of these boys as one after another they forced the weight of their bodies into another man's body and tried to hurt him, to bloody him, to defeat him. I know it is possible to be a stranger to one's feelings. For the years after I was separated from my mother, I forgot that I missed her. My feeling was driven so deep, it was imperceptible, so much a part of me, I would not have called it grief. It is said that when boys or young men attack a man they find effeminate or believe to be homosexual they are trying to put at a distance all traces of homosexuality in themselves. But what does this mean? What is the central passion in this issue of manhood, proven or disproven? In my imagination I witness again the scene that Leo described to me. It is a passionate scene, edged by a love the boys feel for each other, and by something more, by a kind of grief, raging because it is buried so deep inside. Do they rage against this man's body because of what has been withheld from them, held back, like the food of intimacy, imprisoned and guarded in the bodies of older men, in the bodies of fathers? Is it this rage that fires the mettle of what we call manhood?

Yet, are we not all affected by this that is withheld in men? Are we not all forged in the same inferno? It was never said directly, but I know my great-grandfather beat my grandfather, and lectured him, drunkenly, humiliating and shaming him. I am told that as adults they quarreled violently over politics. No one in my family can remember the substance of the disagreement, only the red faces, the angry voices. Now, as I look back to imagine my grandfather passionately reciting the list of those he hated, our black neighbors, the Jews, the Communists, I follow the path of his staring eyes and begin to make out a figure. It is my great-grandfather Colvin, receiving even after his death too indifferently the ardent and raging pleas of his son. And hearing that voice again, I hear an echo from my grandfather's daughter, my mother, whose voice when she had been drinking too much had the same quality, as of the anguish of feeling held back for so long it has become monstrous, the furies inside her unleashed against me.

Leo's telling had a slightly bitter edge, a style which felt like the remnant of an older harshness. He kept looking at me as if to protect himself from any sign of shock in my face. Now he was not certain he would tell me the rest of his story. But he did.

Just after he graduated from high school, the Korean War began. He was drafted, and sent directly to Korea. Was he in combat? Leo shook his head. He was assigned to an intelligence unit. He spoke Russian. And he was directed to interrogate Russian prisoners who were captured behind enemy lines. He told me this story. He was given two men to question. With the first man he made every kind of threat. But he carried nothing out. The man was resolutely silent. And Leo learned nothing from him. He left the room with all his secrets. *You can never*, Leo told me later, *let any man get the better of you.* With the second man he was determined not to fail. He would get him to tell whatever he knew. He made the same threats again, and again met silence. Then, suddenly, using his thumb and finger, he put out the man's eye. And as the man was screaming and bleeding, he told him he would die one way or the other. He was going to be shot. But he had the choice now of seeing his executioners or not, of dying in agony or not. And then the man told him his secrets.

Self-portrait, 1927. She has drawn herself in charcoal again, and in profile. And she still looks out but now her eyes are focused. She is looking at something visible, distant, but perhaps coming slowly closer. Her mouth still turns down, and this must be a characteristic expression because her face is lined in that direction. The form of her face is drawn with soft strokes, blended into the page, as one life blends into another life, or a body into earth. There is something in the quality of her attention, fine lines sketched over her eyebrow. A deeper black circle under her eye. With a resolute, unhappy awareness, she recognizes what is before her.

The life plan of the body is encoded in the DNA molecule, a substance that has the ability to hold information and to replicate itself.

Self-portrait, 1934. As I look now I see in her face that whatever it was she saw before has now arrived. She looks directly at us again and we are even closer to her than before. One finger at the edge of the frame pulls against her eyebrow, against lines drawn there earlier, as if to relieve pain. All the lines lead downward, like rain. Her eyes are open but black, at once impenetrable and infinite. There is a weariness here again, the kind from which one never recovers. And grief? It is that grief I have spoken of earlier, no longer apart from the flesh and bone of her face.

After many years of silence, my mother and I were able to speak of what happened between us and in our family. It was healing for us, to hear and speak the truth, and made for a closeness we had not felt before. Both of us knew we were going to speak before we did.

Before a secret is told one can often feel the weight of it in the atmosphere. Leo gazed at me for a long moment. There was more he wanted to tell me and that I wanted to hear. The rest of his story was elsewhere, in the air, in our hands, the traffic on the street, felt. He shook his head again before he began. The war was over, but he had started in a certain direction and now he could not stop. He befriended a young man from the army. This man looked up to him the way he had to his brother. He wanted to teach the younger man what he knew. He had already committed several robberies, and he wanted an accomplice. They went out together, looking for an easy target for the young man to practice on. They found someone who was easy. He was old, and black. Leo showed his friend how to hold his gun, up close to the temple, pointing down. The boy did this. But the old man, terrified, simply ran. As Leo directed him, the younger man held the gun out in front of him to shoot and he pulled the trigger. But the cartridge of the bullet stuck in the chamber. So the man, still alive, kept running. Then, as Leo urged him on, his friend ran after the old man and, jumping on his back, began to hit him on the head with the butt of his pistol. The moment overtook him. Fear, and exhilaration at mastering fear, a deeper rage, all made a fuel for his fury. He hit and hit again and again. He drew blood. Then the man ceased to cry out, ceased to struggle. He lay still. And the younger man kept on hitting, so that the moment of the older man's death was lost in a frenzy of blows. Then finally there was silence. The young man, knowing he had caused a death, stood up shaking and walked away. He was stunned, as if he himself had been beaten. And Leo, who had been calling and shouting to encourage his friend, who had been laughing, he said, so hard he had to hold himself, was silent too. He went to stand by the body of the old man. Blood poured profusely from the wounds on his head. He stared into the face of this dead man. And now in his telling of the story he was crying. He paused. What was it there in that face for him, broken, afraid, shattered, flesh and bone past repair, past any effort, any strength? *I could see,* he told me, *that this man was just like me.*

In 1963 America develops a new missile, the Titan II. It has a larger range, a larger carrying capacity, a new guidance system, and an improved vehicle for re-entry. These missiles are still being deployed.

1938. *Self-portrait.* The artist is once again in profile. But now she faces another direction. The bones of her cheeks, mouth, nose, eyes are still all in shadow. Her eyebrows arch in tired anticipation. She has drawn herself with the simplest of strokes. Charcoal blending softly downward, all the strokes moving downward. This is old age. Not a single line drawn for vanity, or for the sake of pretense, protects us from her age. She is facing toward death.

We knew, both Leo and I, that now he was telling me what was most crucial to him. In the telling, some subtle change passed through him. Something unknown was taking shape here, both of us witnesses, both of us part of the event. This that he lived through was what I was seeking to understand. What he saw in the face of the dead man did not leave him. For a long time he was afraid of his own dreams. Every night, the same images returned to him, but images in motion, belonging to a longer narration. He dreamed that he entered a park and began to dig up a grave there. Each night he would plunge his hands in the earth and find the body buried there. But each night the body he found was more and more eroded. This erosion filled him with horror. He could not sleep alone. Every night he would find a different woman to sleep with him. Every night he would drink himself into insensibility. But the images of dreams began to come to him even in his waking hours. And so he began to drink ceaselessly. Finally he could not go on as before. Two months after the death he had witnessed he confessed his part in it.

For many reasons his sentence was light. Both he and his friend were young. They had been soldiers. He knew that, had the man he helped to kill not been black, his sentence would have been longer; or he may himself have been put to death. He said nothing of his years of imprisonment. Except that these years served to quiet the dreams that had haunted him. His wit, his air of toughness, all he had seen make him good at the work he does now with boys who have come into conflict with society, a work which must in some way be intended as restitution.

Yet, as he spoke, I began to see that he believed some part of his soul would never be retrieved. *There is a circle of humanity,* he told me, *and I can feel its warmth. But I am forever outside.*

I made no attempt to soften these words. What he said was true. A silence between us held what had been spoken. Then gradually we began to make small movements. Hands reaching for a key, a cigarette. By a quiet agreement, his story was over, and we were in the present again.

The telling and the hearing of a story is not a simple act. The one who tells must reach down into deeper layers of the self, reviving old feelings, reviewing the past. Whatever is retrieved is reworked into a new form, one that narrates events and gives the listener a path through these events that leads to some fragment of wisdom. The one who hears takes the story in, even to a place not visible or conscious to the mind, yet there. In this inner place a story from another life suffers a subtle change. As it enters the memory of the listener it is augmented by reflection, by other memories, and even the body hearing and responding in the moment of the telling. By such transmissions, consciousness is woven.

Over a year has passed now since I heard Leo's story. In my mind's eye, I see the events of his life as if they were carved out in woodblock prints, like the ones Käthe Kollwitz did. Of all her work, these most resemble Expressionist art. Was it intended that the form be so heavy, as if drawn centuries back into a mute untold history? Her work, and the work of the Expressionist movement, was called degenerate by the Nazis. These images, images of tumultuous inner feelings, or of suffering caused and hidden by social circumstance, were removed from the walls of museums and galleries.

When I was in Munich, a German friend told me that her generation has been deprived of German culture. What existed before the Third Reich was used in Nazi propaganda, and so has become as if dyed with the stain of that history. The artists and writers of the early twentieth century were silenced; they went into exile or perished. The link with the past was broken. Yet, even unremembered, the past never disappears. It exists still and continues under a mantle of silence, invisibly shaping lives.

The DNA molecule is made of long, fine, paired strands. These strands are helically coiled.

What is buried in the past of one generation falls to the next to claim. The children of Nazis and survivors alike have inherited a struggle between silence and speech.

The night I met Hélène at a Métro station in Paris I was returning from dinner with a friend. Ten years older than I, Jewish, French, in 1942, the year before my own birth, Natalie's life was put in danger. She was given false papers and shepherded with other children out of Paris through an underground movement. She lived out the duration of war in the countryside in the home of an ambassador who had diplomatic immunity. A woman who has remained one of her closest friends to this day was with her in this hiding place. The night we had dinner Natalie told me a story about her. This friend, she said, grew up determined to shed her past. She made Natalie promise never to reveal who she was or what had happened to her. She changed her name, denied that she was Jewish, and raised her children as gentiles. Then, opening her hands in a characteristic gesture, Natalie smiled at me. The story was to take a gently ironic turn. The past was to return. This summer, she told me, she had held one end of a bridal canopy, what in a Jewish wedding is called a chuppa, at the wedding of her friend's daughter. This girl was marrying the son of an Orthodox rabbi. And her son too, knowing nothing of his mother's past, had gravitated toward Judaism.

In 1975 the SS-19 missile is deployed in the Soviet Union. It carries several warheads, each with a different target. A computer within it controls and detects deviations from its programmed course.

One can find traces of every life in each life. There is a story from my own family history that urges its way onto the page here. Sometime in the eighteenth century three brothers migrated from Scotland to the United States. They came from Aberdeen and bore the name Marks, a name common in that city to Jewish families who had immigrated from Germany to escape the pogroms. Jacob Marks, who descended from these brothers, was my great-great-grandfather. The family story was that he was descended from Huguenots. In our family, only my sister and I speak of the possibility that he could have been Jewish. Jacob married Rosa and they gave birth to a daughter whom they named Sarah. She married Thomas Colvin, and their last son was Ernest Marks Colvin, my grandfather, the same grandfather who would recite to me his furious list of those he hated, including Jews.

Who would my grandfather, I wonder now, have been if he had known his own history. Could he then have seen the shape of his life as part of a larger configuration? Wasn't he without this knowledge like the missile, or the neutron torn away from gravity, the matrix that sustains and makes sense of experience?

In any given cell only a small fraction of the genes are active. Messages to awaken these genes are transmitted by the surrounding cytoplasm, messages from other cells, or from outside substances.

I cannot say for certain what our family history was. I know only that I did gravitate myself toward what seemed missing or lost in me. In my first years of high school I lived alone with my father. He was often gone, at work or staying with his girlfriend. I adopted the family of a school friend, spending hours with them, baby-sitting their younger children, helping with household tasks, sharing meals, spending an evening speaking of art or politics. Then one evening, as I returned home, I saw a strange man standing near my door. He had come to tell me my father was dead, struck by an automobile while he was crossing the street in the light of dusk. I turned for solace and finally shelter to my adopted family. In the short time we lived together, out of my love for them, I took on their gestures, the manner and rhythm of their thought, ways of cooking, cadences, a sprinkling of Yiddish vocabulary. I became in some ways Jewish.

In the late seventies the United States develops a circuitry for the Minuteman rocket which allows for a target to be changed in the midst of flight.

Is there any one of us who can count ourselves outside the circle circumscribed by our common past? Whether or not I was trying to reweave threads severed from my family history, a shared heritage of despair and hope, of destruction and sustenance, was within me. What I received from my adopted family helped me to continue my life. My suffering had been placed, even wordlessly, in a larger stream of suffering, and as if wrapped and held by a culture that had grown up to meet suffering, to retell the tales and place them in a larger context by which all life continues.

L'chayim. Life. Held to even at the worst times. The dream of a better world. The schoolbook, tattered, pages flying loose, gripped in the hands of a young student, his coat open at the shoulder and along the front where the fabric was worn. The ghetto of Slonim. 1938. The Passover cup, fashioned secretly by inmates at Terezin, the Passover plate, the menorah, made at the risk of death from purloined materials. Pictures drawn by those who were there. Despair, the attrition of pain, daily cold, hunger somehow entering the mark of pencil or brush. Butterflies painted by children who all later perished. Stitches made across Lenke's drawings, reminding us of the stitches she sustained in one operation after another, after her liberation, when she was stricken with tuberculosis of the spine. The prisoner forced to pick up discarded clothing of those sent to the gas chambers, who said that among this clothing, as he gathered it, he saw *Stars of David like a drift of yellow flowers.*

As the fertilized egg cell starts to divide, all the daughter cells have identical DNA, but the cells soon cease to look alike, and in a few weeks, a number of different kinds of cells can be recognized in the embryo.

I am thinking again of a child's body. Curled and small. Innocent. The skin soft like velvet to the touch. Eyes open and staring without reserve or calculation, quite simply, into the eyes of whoever appears in this field of vision. Without secrets. Arms open, ready to receive or give, just in the transpiration of flesh, sharing the sound of the heartbeat, the breath, the warmth of body on body.

In 1977 the Soviet Union puts the SS-NX-17 and SS N-18 into service. These are ballistic missiles to be launched from submarines. In 1978 the United States perfects the underwater launch system of the Tomahawk missile.

I could not, in the end, for some blessed reason, turn away from myself. Not at least in this place. The place of desire. I think now of the small lines etching themselves near the eyes of a woman's face I loved. And how, seeing these lines, I wanted to stroke her face. To lean myself, my body, my skin into her. A part of me unravels as I think of this, and I am taken toward longing, and beyond, into another region, past the walls of this house, or all I can see, stretching farther than the horizon where right now sea and sky blend. It is as if my cells are moving in a larger wave, a wave that takes in every history, every story.

At the end of nine months a multitude of different cells make up the newborn infant's body, including nerve cells, muscle cells, skin cells, retinal cells, liver cells, brain cells, cells of the heart that beats, cells of the mouth that opens, cells of the throat that cries . . .

When I think of that young man now, who died in the river near the island of my father's birth, died because he loved another man, I like to imagine his body bathed in the pleasure of that love. To believe that the hands that touched this young man's thighs, his buttocks, his penis, the mouth that felt its way over his body, the man who lay himself between his legs, or over, around his body did this lovingly, and that then the young man felt inside his flesh what radiated from his childlike beauty. Part angel. Bathed in a passionate sweetness. Tasting life at its youngest, most original center, the place of reason, where one is whole again as at birth.

In the last decade the Soviet Union improves its antiballistic missiles to make them maneuverable and capable of hovering in midair. The United States continues to develop and test the MX missile, with advanced inertial guidance, capable of delivering ten prearmed electronically guided warheads, each with maneuverability, possessing the power and accuracy to penetrate hardened silos. And the Soviet Union begins to design a series of smaller one-warhead mobile missiles, the SS-25, to be driven around by truck, and the SS-X-24, to be drawn on railroad tracks. And the United States develops a new warhead for the Trident missile carrying fourteen smaller warheads that can be released in a barrage along a track or a road.

A train is making its way through Germany. All along its route those who are in the cars can look out and see those who are outside the cars. And those who are outside can see those who are inside. Sometimes words are exchanged. Sometimes there is a plea for water. And sometimes, at the risk of life, water is given. Sometimes names are called out, or curses are spoken, under the breath. And sometimes there is only silence.

Who are those on the inside and where are they going? There are rumors. It is best not to ask. There are potatoes to buy with the last of the rations. There is a pot boiling on the stove. And, at any rate, the train has gone; the people have vanished. You did not know them. You will not see them again. Except perhaps in your dreams. But what do those images mean? Images of strangers. Agony that is not yours. A face that does not belong to you. And so in the daylight you try to erase what you have encountered and to forget those tracks that are laid even as if someplace in your body, even as part of yourself.

• • • • • • • • • • •

QUESTIONS FOR A SECOND READING

1. One of the challenges a reader faces with Griffin's text is knowing what to make of it. It's a long piece, but the reading is not difficult. The sections are short and straightforward. While the essay is made up of fragments, the arrangement is not deeply confusing or disorienting. Still, the piece has no single controlling idea; it does not move from thesis to conclusion.

One way of reading the essay is to see what one can make of it, what it might add up to. In this sense, the work of reading is to find an idea, passage, image, or metaphor—something in the text—and use this to organize the essay.

As you prepare to work back through the text, think about the point of reference you could use to organize your reading. Is the essay "about" Himmler? secrets? fascism? art? Germany? the United Sates? families and child-rearing? gay and lesbian sexuality? Can one of the brief sections be taken as a key to the text? What about the italicized sections—how are they to be used?

You should not assume that one of these is the right way to read. Assume, rather, that one way of working with the text is to organize it around a single point of reference, something you could say that Griffin "put there" for you to notice and to use.

Or you might want to do this in your name rather than Griffin's. That is, you might, as you reread, chart the connections *you* make, connections that you feel belong to you (to your past, your interests, your way of reading), and think about where and how you are drawn into the text (and with what you take to be Griffin's interests and desires). You might want to be prepared to talk about why you sum things up the way you do.

2. Although this is not the kind of prose you would expect to find in a textbook for a history course, and although the project is not what we usually think of as a "research" project, Griffin is a careful researcher. The project is serious and deliberate; it is "about" history, both family history and world history. Griffin knows what she is doing. So what *is* Griffin's project? As you reread, look to those sections where Griffin seems to be speaking to her readers about her work—about how she reads and how she writes, about how she gathers her materials and how she studies them. What is she doing? What is at stake in adopting such methods? How and why might you teach someone to do this work?

ASSIGNMENTS FOR WRITING

1. Griffin's text gathers together related fragments and works on them, but does so without yoking examples to a single, predetermined argument or thesis. In this sense, it is a kind of antiessay. One of the difficulties readers of this text face is in its retelling. If someone says to you, "Well, what was it about?" the answer is not easy or obvious. The text is so far-reaching, so carefully composed of interrelated stories and reflections, and so suggestive in its implications and in the connections it enables that it is difficult to summarize without violence, without seriously reducing the text.

But, imagine that somebody asks, "Well, what was it about?" Write an essay in which you present your reading of "Our Secret." You want to give your reader a sense of what the text is like (or what it is like to read the text), and you want to make clear that the account you are giving is your reading, your way of working it through. You might, in fact, want to suggest what you leave out or put to the side. (The first "Question for a Second Reading" might help you prepare for this.)

2. At several points in her essay, Griffin argues that we—all of us, especially all of us who read her essay—are part of a complex web of connections. At one point she says,

> Who are we? The question is not simple. What we call the self is part of a larger matrix of relationship and society. Had we been born to a different family, in a different time, to a different world, we would not be the same. All the lives that surround us are in us. (p. 382)

At another point she asks, "Is there any one of us who can count ourselves outside the circle circumscribed by our common past?" (p. 390). She speaks of a "field,"

> like a field of gravity that is created by the movements of many bodies. Each life is influenced and it in turn becomes an influence. Whatever is a cause is also an effect. Childhood experience is just one element in the determining field. (p. 350)

One way of thinking about this concept of the self (and of interrelatedness), at least under Griffin's guidance, is to work on the connections that she implies and asserts. As you reread the selection, look for powerful and surprising juxtapositions, fragments that stand together in interesting and suggestive ways. Think about the arguments represented by the blank space between those sections. (And look for Griffin's written statements about "relatedness.") Look for connections that seem important to the text (and to you) and representative of Griffin's thinking (and yours). Then, write an essay in which you use these examples to think through your understanding of Griffin's claims for this "larger matrix," the "determining field," or our "common past."

3. It is useful to think of Griffin's prose as experimental. She is trying to do something that she can't do in the "usual" essay form. She wants to make a different kind of argument or engage her reader in a different manner. And so she mixes personal and academic writing. She assembles fragments and puts seemingly unrelated material into surprising and suggestive relationships. She breaks the "plane" of the page with italicized intersections. She organizes her material, but not in the usual mode of thesis-example-conclusion. The arrangement is not nearly so linear. At one point, when she seems to be prepared to argue that German child-rearing practices produced the Holocaust, she quickly says:

> Of course there cannot be one answer to such a monumental riddle, nor does any event in history have a single cause. Rather a field exists, like a field of gravity that is created by the movements of many bodies. Each life is influenced and it in turn becomes an influence. Whatever is a cause is also an effect. Childhood experience is just one element in the determining field. (p. 350)

Her prose serves to create a "field," one where many bodies are set in relationship.

It is useful, then, to think about Griffin's prose as the enactment of a method, as a way of doing a certain kind of intellectual work. One way to study this, to feel its effects, is to imitate it, to take it as a model. For this assignment, write a Griffin-like essay, one similar in its methods of organization and argument. You will need to think about the stories you might tell, about the stories and texts you might gather (stories and texts not your own). As you write, you will want to think carefully about arrangement and about commentary (about where, that is, you will speak to your reader *as* the writer of the piece). You should not feel bound to Griffin's subject matter, but you should feel that you are working in her spirit.

MAKING CONNECTIONS

1. Is it surprising that prisons resemble factories, schools, barracks, hospitals, which all resemble prisons? (p. 253)

    —MICHEL FOUCAULT
    Panopticism

    The child, Dr. Schreber advised, *should be permeated by the impossibility of locking something in his heart.* . . . That this philosophy was taught in school gives me an interior view of the catastrophe to follow. It adds a certain dimension to my image of these events to know that a nation of citizens learned that no part of themselves could be safe from the scrutiny of authority, nothing locked in the heart, and at the same time to discover that the head of the secret police of this nation was the son of a schoolmaster. It was this man, after all, Heinrich Himmler, Reichsführer SS, who was later to say, speaking of the mass arrests of Jews, *Protective custody is an act of care.* (p. 352)

    —SUSAN GRIFFIN
    Our Secret

    Both Griffin and Foucault write about the "fabrication" of human life and desire within the operations of history and of specific social institutions—the family, the school, the military, the factory, the hospital. Both are concerned with the relationship between forces that are hidden, secret, and those that are obvious, exposed. Both write with an urgent concern for the history of the present, for the ways our current condition is tied to history, politics, and culture.

    And yet these are very different pieces to read. They are written differently—that is, they differently invite a reader's participation and understanding. They take different examples from history. They offer different accounts of the technologies of order and control. It can even be said that they do their work differently and that they work toward different ends.

    Write an essay in which you use one of the essays to explain and to investigate the other—where you use Griffin as a way of thinking about Foucault or Foucault as a way of thinking about Griffin. "To explain," "to investigate"—perhaps you would prefer to think of this encounter as a dialogue or a conversation, a way of bringing the two texts together. You should imagine that your readers are familiar with both texts, but have not yet thought of the two together. You should imagine that your readers do not have the texts in front of them, that you will need to do the work of presentation and summary.

2. Both Gloria Anzaldúa in the two chapters reprinted here from her book *Borderlands/La frontera* (p. 23) and Susan Griffin in "Our Secret" write mixed texts, or what might be called "montages." Neither of their pieces proceeds as simply a story or an essay, although both have elements of fiction and nonfiction in them (and, in Anzaldúa's case, poetry). They both can be said to be making arguments and to be telling stories. Anzaldúa, in her chapters, is directly concerned with matters of identity and the ways identity is represented through sexuality, religion, and culture. Griffin is concerned with the "self" as "part of a larger matrix of relationship and society."

   Write an essay in which you present and explain Anzaldúa's and Griffin's key arguments about the relation of identity, history, culture, and society. What terms and examples do they provide? What arguments or concerns? What different positions do they take? And what about their writing styles? How might their concerns be reflected in the ways they write?

3. Susan Griffin, in "Our Secret," is writing about the Holocaust and World War II. Early in her essay "Haunted America" (p. 471), Limerick says, "You can be the world's greatest enthusiast for narrative history, and you can still lose your nerve at the prospect of putting yourself and your readers at the mercy of one of these tales from hell." Griffin's is certainly a tale from hell. It may not be appropriate to say that she lost her nerve, but she is certainly unwilling to write the usual narrative history. Write an essay that reads Griffin's "Our Secret" through the lens of Limerick's "Haunted America." Is Griffin engaged in a Limerick-like project? or is she doing something different?

   You should assume that your audience is familiar with neither text. You will need to take care, in other words, to introduce, to summarize and paraphrase. You should provide enough material in quotation for a reader to get a sense of the formal experimentation in both essays.

4. Adrienne Rich, in "When We Dead Awaken: Writing as Re-Vision" (p. 627), and James Baldwin, in "Notes of a Native Son" (p. 52), use family history to think about and to represent forces beyond the family that shape human life and possibility—patriarchy and race. Susan Griffin is engaged in a similar project; she explains her motives this way, "One can find traces of every life in each life."

   Perhaps. It is a bold step to think that this is true and to believe that one can, or should, write the family into the national or international narrative. Write an essay in which you read "Our Secret" alongside one of these other two selections. Your goal is not only to discuss how these writers do what they do, and to what conclusions and to what ends, but also to discuss your sense of what is at stake in each project. How does a skilled writer handle such a project? What are the technical issues? What would lead a writer to write like this? Would you do the same? where and how? for whose benefit?

5. Early in her essay, "Projected Memory: Holocaust Photographs in Personal and Public Fantasy" (p. 400), Marianne Hirsch turns to a photograph by Lorie Novak, *Past Lives*. She says Lorie Novak "stages an uneasy confrontation of personal memory with public history." The phrase is an

apt one to use to describe the work of Susan Griffin in "Our Secret," a work about the Nazis, about the Holocaust, and about family history, all held together in a kind of collage-like or polyphonic prose. Griffin, too, could be said to stage an uneasy confrontation of personal memory with public history.

The project of postmemory, as defined by Hirsch, can be a writing project. In fact, to describe the individual's active engagement with the past that *is* postmemory, Hirsch uses metaphors of writing: "It is a question of adopting the traumatic experiences—and thus also the memories—of others as one's own, or, more precisely, as experiences one might oneself have had, and of inscribing them into one's own life story. It is a question of conceiving oneself as multiply interconnected with others of the same, of previous, and of subsequent generations, of the same and of other—proximate or distant—cultures and subcultures" (p. 407). We have the examples, early in the essay—Rymkiewicz and Agosín. Hirsch is also concerned about the problems that accompany such a task. It comes in the distinction she makes between "idiopathic" and "heteropathic" identification; her concern is cliché, sentimentality, a too-easy identification with that which is beyond you, even incomprehensible. She says,

> The challenge for the postmemorial artist is precisely to find the balance that allows the spectator [the reader] to enter the image, to imagine the disaster, but that disallows an overappropriate identification that makes the distances disappear, creating too available, too easy an access to this particular past.

Write an essay in which you consider Susan Griffin's "Our Secret" as the work of a postmemorial artist. How might Hirsch read, use, and value Griffin's writing? You will need to establish Hirsch's essay as an introduction and a point of reference. You will need to establish how she talks about writing and how she might talk about a project like Griffin's. And then you will need to turn with care to the text of "Our Secret."

[handwritten annotations:]

...pathy vs. identification

*...aren — easier to identify w, let go of baggage, evoke empathy
decrease distant btw. victim '*

identification:

acting out (melanch)
keep reaching trauma
- act out trauma
"return to repress"

Working Through
- being critical of past history.

Hybrid Now.

MARIANNE HIRSCH

continuity
memory

individ/grp collective
collective.

→ both have ethics.

displacement
exile
lack

M ARIANNE HIRSCH (b. 1949) is the Parents Distinguished Research Professor in the Humanities at Dartmouth College, where she teaches French and comparative literature. You can trace the development of her scholarly interests through the titles of her books: Beyond the Single Vision: Henry James, Michel Butler, Uwe Johnson (1981); The Voyage In: Fictions of Female Development (edited with Elizabeth Abel and Elizabeth Langland, 1983); The Mother/Daughter Plot: Narrative, Psychoanalysis, and Feminism (1989); Conflicts in Feminism (edited with Evelyn Fox Keller, 1990); Family Frames: Photography, Narrative, and Postmemory (1997); and The Familial Gaze (1999). Trained in literary theory and literary analysis, and with a particular interest in psychoanalysis and feminism, Hirsch turned her attention to the family and its representations. She was interested in the family as a concept, as a way of thinking and acting that arranges lives in the household and in society, and that has done so across time. Her work led her to everyday materials—to family records, letters, diaries, autobiographies, and photo albums. Like many trained in literary analysis, she has turned her methods and her attention to the materials of popular or everyday culture. The following essay, "Projected Memory: Holocaust Photographs in Personal and Public Fantasy," shows her interest in photography and memory—and in "postmemory," a term she coined to think about how memory is produced across generations.

The essay was originally included in a collection titled Acts of Memory: Cultural Recall in the Present *(edited by Mieke Bal, Jonathan Crewe, and Leo Spitzer, 1999). The argument of the book was that memory does not simply reside in individuals (stored in heads and hearts) or in institutional warehouses (libraries, museums, archives), but that memory is an active cultural project, one that represents our desire to link past and present. Or, as the editors note in the introduction, "This volume grew out of the authors' conviction that cultural recall is not merely something of which you happen to be a bearer but something that you actually* perform, *even if, in many instances, such acts are not consciously and willfully contrived."*

As you will see in the selection that follows, Marianne Hirsch is interested in "postmemory," memory that is not the product of direct or lived experience but that is produced by the stories and images that circulate from one generation to the next, evidenced in the ways children remember the memories of their parents. Her specific focus below is on how the children of Holocaust survivors remember the Holocaust; you could also think of the way today's generation of college freshmen "remember" the Vietnam War. This form of memory requires active participation—it must be an act of invention. Hirsch argues that it should also be a form of criticism (that is, a person needs to create the distance to know that what is remembered is invented). And, for its sources, it requires not only that which was heard at the dinner table but broader and more determined cultural productions—books, movies, magazines, television documentaries, and so on. Hirsch has written:

> *Postmemory is a powerful form of memory precisely because its connection to its object or source is mediated not through recollection but through an imaginative investment and creation. Postmemory characterizes the experience of those who grow up dominated by narratives that preceded their birth, whose own belated stories are evacuated by the stories of the previous generation, shaped by traumatic events that can be neither fully understood nor re-created. I have developed this notion in relation to children of Holocaust survivors, but I think it may usefully describe the second-generation memory of other cultural or collective traumatic events and experiences.*

And in a partially autobiographical essay, "Past Lives: Postmemories in Exile," Hirsch offers her own experience as a way of understanding this concept. Hirsch was born in Timisoara, Romania, in 1949, where her parents lived in exile from their native Czernowitz, once the capital of the Austrian Bukowina and annexed by the USSR in 1945. Czernowitz is a city she has never seen:

> *Still, the streets, buildings, and natural surroundings—the theater, restaurants, parks, rivers, and domestic settings of Czernowitz— none of which had I ever seen, heard, or smelled myself, occupy a monumental place in my childhood memories. All the while, as I was growing up hearing my parents' stories of life in Czernowitz before the war and the events during the wartime Russian and German occupations that culminated in their exile in 1945, I know that I would never see that place, and that my parents would never return there. I*

knew it not only because Czernowitz now belonged to the USSR and travel between there and Rumania was difficult; I knew it also from my parents' voice and demeanor, from the sense they projected that this world, their world, had been destroyed. . . . In our familial discourse, Czernowitz embodied the idea of home, of place, but to me it was, and would remain, out of reach.

And, she continues, "The Czernowitz of my postmemory is an imaginary city, but that makes it no less present, no less vivid, and perhaps because of the constructed and deeply invested nature of memory itself, no less accurate."

The essay that follows is a wonderful and evocative piece of writing. It invites you (it teaches you) to look at a series of photographs and through them to think about how we think about the past as memory (rather than as history), whether those memories are our own or not.

Projected Memory:
Holocaust Photographs
in Personal and Public Fantasy

I saw her wide-open eyes, and all of a sudden I knew: these eyes knew it all, they'd seen everything mine had, they knew infinitely more than anyone else in this country.

—BINJAMIN WILKOMIRSKI

Past Lives: Three Photographs

I. The photograph everyone knows: a boy in a peaked cap and knee-length socks, his hands raised. We do not know when it was taken. During the great extermination, in July or August 1942? Or during the Uprising in the ghetto in 1943? Or perhaps some other time. . . .

It is hard to say if the boy is standing in a courtyard or outside a house entrance in a street. . . . To the right stand four Germans. . . . Two of their faces, three even in good reproductions, are clearly visible. I have pored over that photo for so long and so often that if I were now after forty-five years to meet one of those Germans in the street I'd identify him instantly.

One of the Germans holds an automatic pistol under his arm, apparently aiming at the boy's back. . . . To the left there are several women, a few men, and about three children. All with their arms raised. . . . I have counted twenty-three people in this

Figure [1]   From the *Stroop Report* on the destruction of the Warsaw ghetto.

photo, though the figures on the left are so huddled together that I may have miscounted: nineteen Jews and four Germans. . . .

The boy in the center of the picture wears a short raincoat reaching just above his knees. His cap, tilted slightly askew, looks too big for him. Maybe it's his father's or his elder brother's? We have the boy's personal data: Artur Siematek, son of Leon and Sara née Dab, born in Lowicz. Artur is my contemporary: we were both born in 1935. We stand side by side, I in the photo taken on the high platform in Otwock. We may assume that both photographs were taken in the same month, mine a week or so earlier. We even seem to be wearing the same caps. Mine is of a lighter shade and also looks too big for my head. The boy is wearing knee-high socks, I am wearing white ankle socks. On the platform in Otwock I am smiling nicely. The boy's face—the photo was taken by an SS sergeant—betrays nothing.

"You're tired," I say to Artur. "It must be very uncomfortable standing like that with your arms in the air. I know what we'll do. I'll lift my arms up now, and you put yours down. They may not notice. But wait, I've got a better idea. We'll both stand with our arms up."

The above is a passage from Jarosław Rymkiewicz's novel, originally published in Poland in 1988, *The Final Station: Umschlagplatz*.[1] Earlier in the novel, the narrator is perusing his family photo album with his sister. "'Look,' he says to his sister, 'that is Swider, in the summer of 1942. That is you on the swing near the house. Here we are standing on the beach by the river. And here I am on the platform at Otwock. Cap and tie. The same white socks. But I can't for the life of me remember the house where we spent our holidays that year.'

"'Nor can I,' says my sister reading the inscription our mother has made on the page with the photo that was taken of me complete with tie, cap, and white socks on the high platform at Otwock. 'Church fair in Otwock, July 19, 1942.'

"'Did you know,' I say, 'that in the summer of 1942 there was still a ghetto in Otwock?'" (23–24).

> II. In my house in Santiago there were certain photographs that kept me good company, that watched over me like a constant presence. There were photographs of my great-grandfather Isidoro, whom we named the chocolate-covered soldier because he was so beautiful and exquisite; also there was a photograph of my aunt Emma who sang arias and spoke French; and there was a small photograph that my grandfather José had given me in the summer of 1970. . . .
>
> Anne Frank's presence in that little photograph was always at my side during my childhood nightmares. I knew that Anne had written a diary and that she had perished in the concentration camps only months before the arrival of the Allied Forces. There was something in her face, in her aspect, and in her age that reminded me of myself. I imagined her playing with my sisters and reading fragments of her diary to us. . . .
>
> I began my dialogue with Anne Frank from a simultaneous desire to remember and to forget. I wanted to know more about that curious girl's face that for so long had occupied a place on the wall of my room. . . . I wanted to speak with Anne Frank from an almost obsessive desire to revive her memory and make her return and enter our daily lives.

This is a passage from the introduction to a book of poems by Marjorie Agosín entitled *Dear Anne Frank* and published in a bilingual edition in 1994.[2] In the poems the poet addresses Anne Frank directly, thus hoping to "mak[e] her part of our daily lives." "Dear Anne," the first poem begins, invoking the Anne behind the photograph that "disperses your thirteen shrouded years, your thick bewitching eyebrows." "Is it you in that photo? Is it you in that diary . . . ?" Agosín asks; "you seem the mere shadow of a fantasy that names you" (15).

Both of these texts, a novel written by a Polish man (a non-Jew) and a volume of poems written by a Latin American Jewish woman, are inspired and motivated by encounters with images that have become generally familiar, perhaps even pervasive, in contemporary memory and discussion of the Holocaust. In both cases these are images of children. Indeed, if one had to name the visual images most frequently associated with the memory of the Holocaust, these two might well have been among them.

Figure [2]   *Past Lives*. Color photograph, 30 × 36″. © Lorie Novak, 1987.

III. Perhaps a third image—an image of a slightly different character—can illuminate the interactions that emerge in these two passages and help me to articulate the issues they raise. It will allow me to explore how camera images mediate the private and the public memory of the Holocaust, how they generate a memorial aesthetic for the second and even for subsequent generations, and what happens when they become overly familiar and iconic. Also what happens—as is frequently the case—if they are images of children.

Past Lives is the work of the Jewish-American artist Lorie Novak dated 1987. It is a photograph of a composite projection onto an interior wall: in the foreground is a picture of the children in Izieu—the Jewish children hidden in a French orphanage in Izieu who were eventually found and deported by Klaus Barbie. Nineteen eighty-seven was the year of the Barbie trial; this photograph appeared in a *New York Times Magazine* article on the Barbie affair. In the middle ground is a picture of Ethel Rosenberg's face. She, a mother of two young sons, was convicted of atomic espionage and executed by electrocution together with her husband Julius Rosenberg. In the background of Novak's composite image is a photograph of a smiling woman holding a little girl who clutches her mother's dress and seems about to burst into tears. This is the photographer Lorie Novak as a young child held by her mother. Novak was born in 1954 and thus this image dates from the mid-1950s.

By allowing her own childhood picture literally to be overshadowed by two public images, Novak stages an uneasy confrontation of personal memory with public history. Visually representing, in the 1980s, the memory of growing up in the United States in the 1950s, Novak includes not only family images but also those figures that might have populated her own or her mother's daydreams and nightmares: Ethel Rosenberg, the mother executed by the state, who, in Novak's terms, looks "hauntingly maternal"[3] but who is incapable of protecting her children or herself, and the children of Izieu, unprotected child victims of Nazi genocide. Unlike Rymkiewicz's narrator, Novak is not the contemporary of the children in the image: she is, like Agosín, a member of the second generation, connected to the child victims of the Holocaust through an intergenerational act of adoption and identification. Her mother, though younger, is indeed a contemporary of Ethel Rosenberg. Together they trace the trajectory of memory from the first to the second generation.

What drama is being enacted in Novak's *Past Lives?* If it is a drama of childhood fear and the inability to trust, about the desires and disappointments of mother-child relationships, then it is also, clearly, a drama about the power of public history to crowd out personal story, about the shock of the knowledge of *this* history: the Holocaust and the cold war, state power and individual powerlessness. Lorie, the little girl in the picture, is, after all, the only child who looks sad or unhappy: the other children are smiling, confidently looking toward a future they were never to have. The child who lives is crowded out by the children who were killed, the mother who lives, by the mother who was executed; their lives must take their shape in relation to the murderous breaks in these other, past, lives.

In *Past Lives,* space and time are conflated to reveal memory's material presence. As projected and superimposed camera images, the children of Izieu, Ethel Rosenberg, the young Lorie and her young mother are *all* ghostly revenants, indexical traces of a past projected into the present, seen in the present as overlays of memory. As her childhood image bleeds into the picture of the murdered children, as the picture of her mother merges with the image of the mother who was executed, Novak enacts a very particular kind of confrontation between the adult artist looking back to her childhood, the child she is in the image, and the victims projected onto them. This triangulation of looking, figured by the superimposition of images from disparate moments of personal and public history, is in itself an act of memory—not individual but cultural memory. It reveals memory to be an act in the *present* on the part of a subject who constitutes herself by means of a series of identifications across temporal, spatial, and cultural divides. It reveals memory to be *cultural,* fantasy to be *social and political,* in the sense that the representation of one girl's childhood includes, as a part of her own experience, the history into which she was born, the figures that inhabited her public life and perhaps also the life of her imagination. The present self, the artist who constructs the work, encounters in the image the past self and the other selves—the child and maternal victims, related to her through a cultural act of identification and affiliation—that define that past self, shaping her imagination and constituting her memories.[4]

These affiliations mark the subject of these memories as a member of her generation and a witness of her particular historical moment: born after World War II, as a Jew, she represents herself as branded by the harrowing memory of Nazi genocide, a memory that gets reinterpreted, repeatedly, throughout the subsequent half-century. Her text, shaped by identification with the victims, invites her viewers to participate with her in a cultural act of remembrance. Photographic projections make this marking literal and material as the image of Novak's body is inscribed with the story of those other children. Losing their physical boundaries, they merge with one another. The use of familiar public images, moreover—the children of Izieu, Anne Frank, the boy from Warsaw—facilitates this participation, in that viewers will *remember* seeing them before. When Agosín describes Anne Frank's photographic presence in her childhood, her readers will likely remember seeing the same image during theirs: their respective memories will trigger one another. As readers, we can thus enter the network of looks established in Agosín's poem: we imagine Marjorie looking at Anne's picture, which is looking back at her and at us; at the same time, we look at our own earlier selves looking at Anne's photograph, or thinking about her story. The memorial circle is enlarged, allowing for shared memories and shared fantasies. As we look at Novak's image, the image looks back at us, through multiple layers of eyes; by means of the mutual reflection and projection that characterizes the act of looking, we enter its space, the visual space of postmemory. Let me try to explain this term.

Postmemory and "Heteropathic Identification"

I have been haunted by *Past Lives* since I first saw it. When I look at it I see myself both in the sad little girl who is clutching her mother's dress and in the smiling girl who, at the very left of the picture, is half outside its frame, looking to a space beyond. I look at that bare corner wall and at the ghostly figures emerging from its depths and I am propelled back into my childhood daydreams. The dreams and fantasies of a child of survivors of Nazi persecution during World War II growing up in Eastern Europe in the 1950s were dominated by The War: Where would I have been, then? How would I have acted? The door bell rings in the middle of the night, the Gestapo is at the door, what do I do? The imbalance of Novak's image speaks to me most forcefully: in remembering my childhood, I too feel as though I were crouching in the corner of a bare room populated by larger-than-life ghosts: my parents' younger selves during the war, and those who were children like me and who had to face dangers I tried hard to experience in my imagination. *Past Lives* describes the very quality of my memories of my childhood, memories crowded out by the memories of others: stronger, more weighty memories, more vivid and more real than any scenes I can conjure up from my own childhood. Thinking about my childhood, I retrieve their memories more readily than my own; their memories *are* my memories. And yet, Novak's image also invites us to resist this equation.

In *Past Lives* Novak begins to articulate the aesthetic strategies of tragic identification, projection, and mourning that specifically characterize the second-generation memory of the Holocaust—what I have called *postmemory*.[5] She stages, retrospectively, a moment of knowledge for the Jewish child growing up in the 1950s whose needs, desires, and cares fade out in relation to the stories that surround her, the traumatic memories that preceded her birth but nevertheless define her own life's narrative. Like Agosín who spends her childhood in Chile conversing with Anne Frank's picture, Novak in *Past Lives* inscribes herself, through projection and identification, into the subject position of the child of survivors.

I use the term *postmemory* to describe the relationship of children of survivors of cultural or collective trauma to the experiences of their parents, experiences that they "remember" only as the stories and images with which they grew up, but that are so powerful, so monumental, as to constitute memories in their own right. The term is meant to convey its temporal and qualitative difference from survivor memory, its secondary or second-generation memory quality, its basis in displacement, its belatedness. Postmemory is a powerful form of memory precisely because its connection to its object or source is mediated not through recollection but through projection, investment, and creation. That is not to say that survivor memory itself is unmediated, but that it is more directly connected to the past. Postmemory characterizes the experience of those who grow up dominated by narratives that preceded their birth, whose own belated stories are displaced by the stories of the previous generation, shaped by traumatic events that they can neither understand nor re-create.

Not themselves children of Holocaust survivors, Novak and Agosín nevertheless speak from the position of postmemory. And although Rymkiewicz's protagonist is a contemporary of the boy from Warsaw, he is rewriting his own past in light of the knowledge that at the time he did not have; as he revises his childhood story he must take on the Jewish memories of his contemporaries as well as his own Polish ones. As I conceive of it, postmemory is not an identity position, but a space of remembrance, more broadly available through cultural and public, and not merely individual and personal, acts of remembrance, identification, and projection. It is a question of adopting the traumatic experiences—and thus also the memories—of others as one's own, or, more precisely, as experiences one might oneself have had, and of inscribing them into one's own life story. It is a question of conceiving oneself as multiply interconnected with others of the same, of previous, and of subsequent generations, of the same and of other—proximate or distant—cultures and subcultures. It is a question, more specifically, of an *ethical* relation to the oppressed or persecuted other for which postmemory can serve as a model: as I can "remember" my parents' memories, I can also "remember" the suffering of others, of the boy who lived in the same town in the ghetto while I was vacationing, of the children who were my age and who were deported. These lines of relation and identification need to be theorized more closely, however: how the familial and intergenerational identification with my parents can extend to the identification among children of different generations and circumstances and also perhaps to other, less proximate groups. And how, more important, identification can resist appropriation and incorporation, resist annihilating the distance between self and other, the otherness of the other.

In her recent *Threshold of the Visible World,* Kaja Silverman (borrowing the term from Max Scheler [*The Nature of Sympathy,* 1923]) has termed this process "heteropathic memory" and "identification"—a way of aligning the "not-me" with the "me" without interiorizing it, or, in her terms, "introduc[ing] the 'not-me' into my memory reserve."[6] Through "discursively 'implanted' memories" the subject can "participate in the desires, struggles, and sufferings of the other"—particularly, in Silverman's examples, the culturally devalued and persecuted other (185). Thus the subject can engage in what Silverman calls "identification-at-a-distance": identification that does not interiorize the other within the self but that goes out of one's self and out of one's own cultural norms in order to align oneself, through displacement, with another. Heteropathic memory (feeling and suffering with the other) means, as I understand it, the ability to say, "It could have been me; it was me, also," and, *at the same time,* "but it was not me." Postmemory in my terms is a form of heteropathic memory in which the self and the other are more closely connected through familial or group relation, for example, through what it means to be Jewish, or Polish. While postmemory implies a temporal distance between the self and the other—like Agosín and Anne Frank—Silverman's heteropathic recollection could depend solely on spatial or cultural distance, and temporal coincidence (as for the two Polish boys, for instance). In both cases, an enormous distance must be bridged and, in the specific case of

Holocaust memory, that distance *cannot* ultimately be bridged; the break between then and now, between the one who lived it and the one who did not, remains monumental and insurmountable, even as the heteropathic imagination struggles to overcome it.

Silverman's instrument of heteropathic recollection, like Lacan's vehicle of identification, is the look. Roland Barthes's distinction between *studium* and *punctum* dramatizes the relationship between these different forms of looking: while the *studium* inscribes the seen into the normative cultural script, the *punctum* finds in the image something so unfamiliar and unexpected that it acts like a "prick" or a "wound" interrupting any familiar relation to the visible world.[7] The productive look of heteropathic identification can see beyond "the given to be seen"; it can displace the incorporative, ingestive look of self-sameness and the familiar object it sees in favor of "an appetite for alterity" (181).

Camera images, particularly still photographs, are precisely the medium connecting first- and second-generation remembrance, memory and postmemory. Photographic images are stubborn survivors of death. We receive them, uncompromisingly, in the present tense. Inasmuch as they are instruments of memory, then, they expose its resolute but multilayered presentness. As objects of looking they lend themselves either to idiopathic *or* to heteropathic identification, to self-sameness *or* to displacement. Holocaust photographs, the leftovers and debris of a destroyed culture, made precious by the monumental losses they inscribe, certainly have the capacity to retain their radical otherness. The fragmentary sources and building blocks of the work of postmemory, they affirm the past's existence, its "having-been there," and, in their flat two-dimensionality, they also signal its insurmountable distance. In an image like *Past Lives,* however, so dependent on projection, these distances seem to disappear; within the image itself, past and present, self and other, appear to merge. In the form of projection, photographs can indeed lend themselves to the incorporative logic of narcissistic, idiopathic, looking. The challenge for the postmemorial artist is precisely to find the balance that allows the spectator to enter the image, to imagine the disaster, but that disallows an overappropriative identification that makes the distances disappear, creating too available, too easy an access to this particular past.

Images of Children

Why are such a large number of the archival images used in the texts documenting and memorializing the Holocaust images of children? The boy from Warsaw, for example, has appeared in numerous Holocaust films, novels, and poems; recently, he appears obsessively in advertising brochures for Holocaust histories, teaching aids, and books. The photograph is featured in both Alain Resnais's 1956 documentary *Night and Fog,* and Ingmar Bergman's 1966 film *Persona,* and, in 1990, it became the object of a documentary video (subtitled "a video about a photograph") entitled

Tsvi Nussbaum: A Boy from Warsaw.[8] Made for Finnish and French television, the video is devoted to examining the contention of Holocaust survivor Tsvi Nussbaum that he is the boy with his hands up and that the picture was not taken in the Warsaw ghetto at all but in the "Aryan" part of Warsaw where he was hiding. Although he doesn't remember the moment depicted very clearly, he brings photographs of himself as a boy as proof of his identity with the boy in the picture; thus his story draws on the emblematic role that the image has come to play. Rymkiewicz, in contrast, identified the boy as Artur Siematek, showing that the photograph's status as document is as questionable as its symbolic role can be determinative.[9]

Of this so frequently invoked image, Lucy Dawidowicz writes in her book *The War against the Jews:* "in the deluded German mind, every Jewish man, woman, and child became a panoplied warrior of a vast Satanic fighting machine. The most concrete illustration of this delusion is the now familiar photograph taken from the collection attached to Stroop's report of the Warsaw ghetto uprising. It shows uniformed German SS men holding guns to a group of women and children; in the foreground is a frightened boy of about six, his hands up. This was the face of the enemy."[10] Yala Korwin's poem "The Little Boy with His Hands Up" also voices the enormously influential role of this photograph to shape the visual memory and transmission of the Holocaust:

> Your image will remain with us,
> and grow and grow
> to immense proportions,
> to haunt the callous world,
> to accuse it, with ever stronger voice
> in the name of the million
> youngsters
> who lie, pitiful ragdolls,
> their eyes forever closed.[11]

The image has become the consummate space of projection: while Rymkiewicz's narrator contends that "the boy's face . . . betrays nothing," and Dawidowicz describes him as "frightened," Korwin writes:

> your face contorted with fear,
> grown old with knowledge beyond your years.
> . . . .
> All the torments of this harassed crowd
> are written on your face.

But the boy from Warsaw is only one of numerous children displayed in the photographic discourses of memory and postmemory. Anne Frank's image and her story are utterly pervasive—this to the great distress of commentators like Bruno Bettelheim who find it problematic that this young girl's strangely hopeful story should for a generation have constituted the only encounter with the knowledge of the Holocaust, an encounter engendering the type of adolescent identification we see in Marjorie Agosín's book of poems.[12] Anne Frank, Agosín insists, "had a name, had a face, . . . she was not just one more anonymous story among the countless stories of the Holocaust" (6–7). But many other children's faces dominate postmemorial texts to similar effect. The image of Richieu, Art Spiegelman's "ghost brother" to whom the second volume of *Maus* is dedicated, for example, elicits a very specific kind of investment by Spiegelman's readers. Richieu's face at the beginning of this book of schematic cartoon drawings of mice and cats jumps out of the covers to haunt us with its strange lifelike presence. When we open *Maus II* we already know that Richieu was killed and his photograph, one of three in the two volumes of *Maus,* acts like a ghostly apparition, materially recalling Richieu's absence. Like many other Holocaust photographs, this image stubbornly survived not only its young subject but the intended destruction of an entire culture down to its very objects and artifacts.

Other images of children are more anonymous but, like the children of Izieu in Novak's work, they invite a very specific kind of spectatorial look, a particular form of investment; thus they can help us to understand the particular kind of subject taking shape in the act of postmemory. In his memorial installations, the French artist Christian Boltanski invariably uses archival images of children, usually school pictures from Jewish schools in Vienna and Berlin in the 1930s.[13] Boltanski rephotographs and enlarges individual faces, installs them on top of tin biscuit boxes, mounts them on the wall or shrouds them with sheets, illuminating each with a black desk lamp that creates a large circle of light at the center of each picture. The faces are stripped of individuality. Even though their indexical, referential, function reemerges through the use of the class photos of a population the majority of which certainly ended up in Hitler's death camps, the images themselves, separate from the identifying label, blown up to enormous proportions and thus depersonalized, become icons of untimely death, icons of mourning. The power of the installations is ensured by the fact that these are images of children, looking forward to lives they were never to have.

Why children? Lucy Dawidowicz provides one answer: images of children bring home the utter senselessness of Holocaust destruction. Who could see the enemy in the face of a child? Children, moreover, were particularly vulnerable in Hitler's Europe: in the entire Nazi-occupied territory of Europe only 11 percent of Jewish children survived and thus the faces of children signal the unforgiving ferocity of the Nazi death machine.[14] It does not matter whether the boy from Warsaw survived or not for us to feel that vulnerability; with statistics of such enormity, every child whose image we see is, at least metaphorically, one who perished. Boltanski's technique of enlargement and "anonymization" provides another answer. "For me it's very important to start with a real image," he says. "Then I blow it up to make it universal."[15] But images of children readily lend themselves to such universalization anyway. Culturally, at the end of the twentieth century, the figure of the "child" is an adult construction, the site of adult fantasy, fear, and desire. As recent controversies suggest, our culture has a great deal invested in the children's innocence and vulnerability—and at the same time, in their eroticism and knowledge. Less individualized, less marked by the particularities of identity, moreover, children invite multiple projections and identifications. Their photographic images elicit an affiliative and identificatory as well as a protective spectatorial look marked by these investments. No wonder that the identity of the boy from Warsaw is contested.

To describe more specifically the visual encounter with the child victim, and to sort out the types of identification—idiopathic or heteropathic, based on appropriation or displacement—that shape it, requires an analysis of the *visual* work involved in these identifications. I approach this analysis by way of a very revealing scene from the recent film *Hatred* by Australian director Mitzi Goldman.[16] This film uses interviews, archival footage, and montage shot largely in New York's Harlem, in Germany, and in the Middle East, to explore hatred as an emotion. It contains a number of scenes in which Goldman returns with her father to Dessau, the German city from which he fled as a Jew in 1939. Her position as the child of this survivor shapes her inquiry into hatred in numerous ways, but this determining subject position is most clearly revealed in a scene in which the voice-over asks "What do I know about the Holocaust?" In this recurring scene a white child (at one time a boy, another time a girl) watches archival film footage of Nazi horror; in a similar scene an Asian boy watches television footage of the Vietnam war. The archival images projected are, again, overfamiliar images seen in many films or displays on the Holocaust and on Vietnam: the records of the Allied soldiers taken on the liberation of the camps, and the journalistic footage taken in Vietnam during the war. The voice-over continues: "The horror that was fed to us as children, I buried beneath a tough exterior. It was ancient history, not my life."

The three children in Goldman's film are secondary witnesses of horror; they are witnesses not to the event but to its visual documentary records. In Goldman's scene the child on the screen—the child we see—is not the victim but the witness, looking not at an individualized child victim but at the anonymous victims of the horrors of human brutality and hatred. Still, it seems to me that this representation of the child witness can tell us a great deal about the visual encounter with the child victim. As we see the children watching, it appears as if the images are projected right onto them. Strangely, the children are chewing as they watch. Mitzi Goldman has spoken of her strange memories of the Jewish school she attended, where, on rainy days when they could not go outside at lunchtime, the children were shown films about the Holocaust.[17] The children on the screen *feed* on images of horror, they have to ingest them with

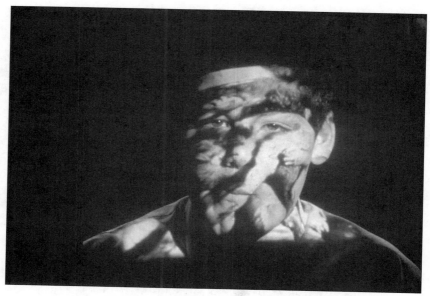

Figure [3]   Mitzi Goldman, *Hatred* (1996). Film still.

lunch; even more graphically, they are marked by them, bodily, as "Jewish" or as "Vietnamese." They watch and, like the film's narrator, they "feed on" images that do and do not impact on their present lives. Looking at the children watching we see them and the images they see on the same plane; thus the child witness is merged with the victims she or he sees. More than just specularity, looking produces the coalescence of spectator and spectacle; the object of the look is inscribed not only on the retina but on the entire body of the looking subject.

As we look at the face of the child victim—Anne Frank, or the little boy from Warsaw—do we not also see there what that child saw? By encountering the child victim, we also, by implication, encounter the atrocities he has seen. In her poem, Yala Korwin describes this confrontation:

> All the torments of this harassed
> crowd
> are written on your face.
> In your dark eyes—a vision of horror.
> You have seen death already
> on the ghetto streets, haven't you?
> (*To Tell the Story* 75)

As the child victim merges with the child witness, as we begin to recognize their identity, we ourselves, as spectators looking at the child victim, become witnesses, child witnesses, in our own right. Thus we see from both the adult, retrospective and more knowing, vantage point and from the vantage point of the uncomprehending child "grown old with knowledge beyond your years" (Korwin, *To Tell the Story* 75).

It is my argument that the visual encounter with the child victim is a triangular one, that identification occurs in a triangular field of looking. The adult viewer sees the child victim through the eyes of his or her own child self. The poet Marjorie Agosín looks at Anne Frank's photo through the adolescent in Chile who had fantasized about conversing with Anne and had asked her to join in her games. The adult narrator of Rymkiewicz's *The Final Station* confronts the picture of the boy from Warsaw with the Polish boy who wears white kneesocks and does not know what the Jewish boy knows. When the artist Lorie Novak finds the picture of the children of Izieu in the *New York Times* she superimposes it on a picture of herself as a child: it is only through that distant subject position that she can encounter these children. And the director Mitzi Goldman takes her father back to Dessau but she can only do so by way of her own childhood experience of feeding on images of hatred. The adult viewer who is also an artist shares the child viewing position with her own audience, which also enters the image in the position of child witness. The present tense of the photograph is a layered present on which several pasts are projected; at the same time, however, the present never recedes. The adult also encounters the child (the other child and his/her own child self) both as a child, through identification, and from the protective vantage point of the adult-looking subject. Identificatory looking and protective looking coexist in uneasy balance.

The split viewing subject that is evoked by the image of the child victim—both adult and child—is emblematic of the subject of memory and of fantasy. In the act of memory as well as the act of fantasy the subject is simultaneously actor and spectator, adult and child; we act and, concurrently, we observe ourselves acting.[18] It is a process of projection backward in time; in that sense, it is also a process of transformation from adult to child that produces an identification between two children.

But in the particular case of postmemory and "heteropathic recollection" where the subject is not split just between past and present, adult and child, but also between self and other, the layers of recollection and the subjective topography are even more complicated. The adult subject of postmemory encounters the image of the child victim *as* the child witness, and thus the split subjectivity characterizing the structure of memory is triangulated. And that triangulation identifies postmemory as necessarily cultural. Identification is group or generational identification. The two children whose mutual look defines the field of vision I am trying to map here are linked culturally and not necessarily personally: Marjorie and Anne as Jews, Jarosław and Artur as Poles. But that connection is facilitated, if not actually produced, by their mutual status as children and by the child's openness to identification. Through photographic projection, moreover, distances diminish even more, identities blur. When two children "look" at one another in the process of photographic witnessing, the otherness that separates them is diminished to the point where recollection could easily slide into the idiopathic away from the heteropathic—where displacement gives way to interiorization and appropriation. The image of the child, even the image of the child victim of incomprehensible horror, displaces "the appetite for alterity" with an urge toward identity. This could be the effect of the "it could have been me" created specifically by the image of the child. In the present political climate that constructs the child as an unexamined emblem of vulnerability and innocence, the image of the child lends itself too easily to trivialization and stereotype. It can only exacerbate the effect of oversaturation with visual images that, as Geoffrey Hartman, Julia Kristeva, and others charge, have made us immune to their effect.[19] Under what circumstances, then, can the image of the child victim preserve its alterity and thus also its power?

(Im)Possible Witnessing

In his recent work on Holocaust memory, Dominick LaCapra has enjoined us to recognize the transferential elements that interfere with efforts at working through this traumatic past. He has distinguished between two memorial positions: acting out (melancholia) and working through (mourning). Acting out is based on tragic identification and the constitution of one's self as a surrogate victim. It is based on overidentification and repetition. Keeping the wounds open, it results in retraumatization. Working through, on the other hand, involves self-reflexivity, a determination of responsibility, some amount of distance. A goal and not an end, it is a process of evolution that is never fully accomplished—and therefore never free of some element of acting out: "Acting out may well be necessary and unavoidable in the wake of extreme trauma, especially for victims," LaCapra says in *Representing the Holocaust*. But for "the interviewer and the analyst" (and, one might add, for the postmemorial generation), LaCapra urges that "one . . . attempt to put oneself in the other's position without taking the other's place." He further suggests, "one component of the process is the attempt to elaborate a hybridized narrative that does not avoid analysis, . . . it requires the effort to achieve a critical distance on experience."[20]

If the image of the child victim places the artist, the scholar, or the historian into the space of the child witness, then it would seem to impede working through unless distancing devices are introduced that would discourage an appropriative identification. What is disturbing, however, is precisely the obsessive repetition of these images of children—in itself, examples of acting out and the compulsion to repeat. The image of the child victim, moreover, facilitates an identification in which the viewer can too easily become a surrogate victim. Most important, the easy identification with children, their virtually universal availability for projection, risks the blurring of important areas of difference and alterity: context, specificity, responsibility, history. This is especially true of the images I have discussed in this paper, images of children who are not visibly wounded or in pain. In this light, one might contrast the boy from Warsaw with other images of emaciated, dirty, visibly suffering children taken in the Warsaw ghetto, images that have never achieved the same kind of visual prominence as the little boy with his hands up.

And yet, depending on the context into which they are inscribed and the narrative that they produce, these obsessively repeated pictures can be vehicles of a heteropathic memory; they can maintain their alterity and become part of a "hybridized narrative that does not avoid analysis." Clearly, the images' use and meaning vary significantly with the context in which they are inscribed and ultimately it is that context that must be closely examined.

Thus some of the works I have included rely on specific distancing devices that allow for the triangulated looking, for the displacement that qualifies identification. The fact, for example, that Rymkiewicz describes the photos but does not reproduce them, creates some significant distance. The inclusion of Rosenberg's face in *Past Lives* introduces a third term between the child victim and the child witness, and refocuses the attention onto the two adults in the text. Similarly, the introduction of the Asian child in the scene from *Hatred* creates a space of reflection, a form of displacement and thus a mediated identification not necessarily based on ethnic or national identity.

I shall distinguish these different forms of identification more closely by way of another image and the context in which it mysteriously appears not once but twice. This is the picture of Holocaust survivor Menachem S. [p. 416], whose testimony was taken at the Yale Fortunoff Video Archive for Holocaust testimonies by the psychoanalyst Dori Laub. In separate chapters of their coauthored book *Testimony*, Shoshana Felman and Dori Laub refer to Menachem's moving story to illustrate the very different points they each try to make in their essays: Felman to explore how her class received the testimonies they read and watched; Laub to comment on the role of the listener or witness to testimony.[21] Strangely, both reproduce this photograph in their chapters but neither of them makes even the most cursory reference to it. What is the work performed by this image of the victim child in the work of memory performed by *Testimony?*

At the age of five, Menachem was smuggled out of a detention camp by his parents so that he might survive. In Laub's account, "his mother wrapped him up in a shawl and gave him a passport photograph of herself as a student. She told him to turn to the picture whenever he felt he needed to do so. His parents both promised him that they would come and find him and bring him home after the war" (*Testimony* 86). The little boy was sent into the streets alone; he went first to a brothel where he found shelter and later to several Polish families who took him in and helped him to survive. After the war, however, his reunion with his parents destroyed his coping mechanisms. As Laub says, "His mother does not look like the person in the photograph. His parents have come back as death camp survivors, haggard

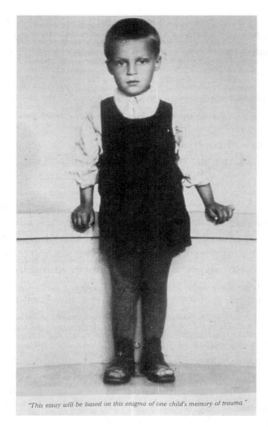

"This essay will be based on this enigma of one child's memory of trauma."

Figure [4]   Menachem S., age 4.

and emaciated, in striped uniforms, with teeth hanging loose in their gums" (88). The boy falls apart; he calls his parents Mr. and Mrs. and suffers from lifelong terrifying nightmares; only when he is able to tell his story in the testimonial context, after a thirty-five-year silence, does he gain some possibility of working through his traumatic past.

Felman cites several of Menachem's own reflections: "The thing that troubles me right now is the following: if we don't deal with our feelings, if we don't understand our experience, what are we doing to our children? . . . Are we transferring our anxieties, our fears, our problems, to the genera-tions to come? . . . We are talking here not only of *the lost generation* . . . this time we are dealing with *lost generations*" (46). For Felman's class "these reflections of the child survivor on the liberating, although frightening ef-fects of his own rebirth to speech in the testimonial process . . . were meant to conclude the course with the very eloquence of life, with a striking, vivid and extreme *real example* of the *liberating, vital function of the testimony*" (47). Note the repetition of terms like "speech," and "eloquence": it is precisely language and the ability to speak that get lost in the class after the students watch Menachem's videotaped account. To address the "crisis" that her class was going through as they watched the video testimonies, Felman decides that "what was called for was for me to reassume authority as the teacher of the class, and bring the students back into significance" (48). (Again, note this term and note the strictly differentiated adult/child roles that are assumed.) To "bring the students back into significance," Felman gives a half-hour lecture, an address to her class. "I first *reread* to them an excerpt from Celan's 'Bremen Speech' about what happened to the act of speaking, and to language, after the Holocaust." Felman stresses to her students their own "loss of language" in the face of what they were encountering, their feeling that "language was somehow incommensurate with it" (50). She concludes the course with an invitation for students to write their own testimony of the class itself. Citing some of their reflections, she concludes that "the crisis, in effect had been worked through and overcome. . . . The written work the class had finally submitted turned out to be an amazingly articulate, reflective, and profound statement of the trauma they had gone through and of the significance of their own position as a witness" (52). By implication, they have resumed their adult status, in language, in a language commensurate with their experiences. They have been able to work through the trauma, as adults.

Felman's strong insistence on language as *the* means of working through the crisis of witnessing returns me to her inclusion of the child's photograph and her own rather remarkable silence about it. Clearly, this included photo is not the picture that is at the crux of Menachem's story: the ID picture of his mother he carried with him throughout his years as a hidden child. Menachem went into hiding in 1942 at age four; the picture is labeled "the end of 1944 (age 5)." It was taken during the war when Menachem was in hiding, when, according to his own narrative, he spent every evening gazing at his mother's photo. In his eyes, in his serious face, we can imagine seeing the reflection of that other, shadow, photograph and the simultaneous loss and presence it signaled. And, we can also see, as in the eyes of all child victims, the atrocities the child has already witnessed at the age of five. Perhaps this image is performing the same work in Felman's account that the video testimonies did in her class. In the formulation of one student: "until now and throughout the texts we have been studying . . . we have been talking (to borrow Mallarmé's terms) about the *'testimony of an accident.'* We have been *talking* about the accident—and here all of a sudden *the accident happened* in the class, happened *to* the class. An accident *passed through* the class" (50). In the midst of Felman's own "amazingly articulate, reflective, and profound" analysis in her chapter, the little boy's picture, we might say, is that "accident" that passes through the book, allowing the crisis to be communicated, if in a different register. And, as Laub's own account demonstrates, the image projects the viewer, the subject of "heteropathic" memory, into the position of the child witness and thus into speechlessness.

Laub's own essay, as he explains, "proceeds from my autobiographical awareness as a child survivor" (75). He shares with other child survivors a very peculiar ability to remember: "The events are remembered and seem to have been experienced in a way that was far beyond the capacity of recall in a young child of my age. . . . These memories are like discrete islands of precocious thinking and feel almost like the remembrances of another child, removed yet connected to me in a complex way" (76). The essay indeed goes on to tell the story of another child—Menachem S.—and to discuss his silence, his struggle with witnessing, so as to illustrate a larger point about the impossibility of telling, about the Holocaust as "an event without a witness."

In Laub's essay this same photo is labeled differently: "This essay will be based on this enigma of one child's memory of trauma" (77). Had we not seen this picture earlier in the book, we would not know that this is not a childhood picture of Laub himself; it is placed in the midst of his own story and not Menachem's at all. In fact, every time I look at the picture and its generalized caption, I have to remind myself that this is not a picture of Dori Laub; it is as if the identities of the two subjects of Laub's essay, Menachem S. and Laub himself, were projected or superimposed onto one another. The essay includes three more photographs: *Menachem S. and his mother, Krakow, 1940*; *Menachem S., 1942*; and *Colonel Dr. Menachem S., 1988*. The fact that the first image carries no name reinforces this blurring of identities between Dori Laub and Menachem S.

Laub's essay rides on another picture, the ID picture of the mother, in Laub's reading the necessary witness, which allowed the five-year-old to survive by standing in as a listener to his story. In the essay itself, however, the 1944 picture of the child victim Menachem S. is playing that very same role: it is the silent witness that allows the analyst Dori Laub to perform his articulate analysis but that, with the child's serious and sad eyes, undercuts that wisdom—a reminder of incomprehensible horror, a space in which to experience uncomprehending speechlessness in the midst of articulate analysis. This photograph, we might argue, is the ground of indirect and paradoxical witnessing in this "event without a witness."

In the ways in which it is reproduced, repeated, and/or discussed in *Testimony,* this image of the boy Menachem S. maintains its alterity, an alterity from which both Felman and Laub quite resolutely try to distance themselves in the very space of their identification. In the particular context in which they place it, in the distancing discourse of scholarly discussion in which they embed it, the image of the child victim stands in for all that cannot be—and perhaps should not be—worked through. This image *is* the accident that happened in the midst of all the talking and writing that can only screen its effect. It is the *other child*, in his irreducible otherness, the one who has not yet, who might never be able to, translate memory into speech. A reminder of unspeakability, a vehicle of infantilization, it may well be the best medium of postmemory and heteropathic identification, of cultural memorialization of a past whose vivid pain is receding more and more into the distance. In his own analysis of working through,

Saul Friedlander explains why: "In fact, the numbing or distancing effect of intellectual work on the *Shoah* is unavoidable and necessary; the recurrence of strong emotional impact is also often unforeseeable and necessary. . . . But neither the protective numbing nor the disruptive emotion is entirely accessible to consciousness."[22] As my reading of Felman and Laub's texts suggests, in the right intertextual context, in the hybrid text, the image of the child victim can produce the disruptive emotion that prevents too easy a resolution of the work of mourning.

Two Endings

In a later scene from Mitzi Goldman's *Hatred,* an Israeli colonel—not Menachem S.—tells of a moment after his unit leveled a Palestinian household suspected of harboring terrorists. "Of course we had to destroy it," he says. When they are done, a little girl in a pink skirt walks out of the rubble, holding a doll. He describes her in such detail that we can visualize her face and dress and posture. "As a human being," the colonel concludes, "you see a small child and you think she can be your child. You cannot afford not to be a human being first." With his response—not identificatory, but protective—he elicits our sympathy, based on a shared humanity, on a universal identification with the image of the vulnerable child. Using the child as an alibi, the colonel erases his responsibility for the massacre that just occurred. He projects the image of the child between himself as agent and us as viewers, and it is the child who absorbs our attention. As a vehicle of an identificatory and protective look, the child screens out context, specificity, responsibility, agency. This scene contains all that is problematic about the pervasive use of the image of the child victim.

In her discussion of heteropathic memory, Kaja Silverman quotes a scene from Chris Marker's film *Sans Soleil:* "Who says that time heals all wounds? It would be better to say that time heals everything except wounds. With time the hurt of separation loses its real limits, with time the desired body will soon disappear, and if the desired body has already ceased to exist for the other then what remains is a wound, disembodied." Silverman adds: "If to remember is to provide the disembodied 'wound' with a psychic residence, then to remember other people's memories is to be wounded by their wounds" (*Threshold* 189). In the conclusion to his first essay in *Testimony,* Dori Laub speaks of the "hazards of listening" to the story of survivors, of becoming a secondary witness or the subject of heteropathic recollection. Those of us in the generation of postmemory watch survivors rebuild their lives; we watch them amass fortunes and erect castles. "Yet," says Laub, "in the center of this massive dedicated effort remains a danger, a nightmare, a fragility, a woundedness that defies all healing" (73). The image of the child witness, an image on which, figuratively at least, Laub projects his own childhood image, produces this woundedness in his writing and in our reading. It is a measure of the massive effort in which, as a culture, we have been engaged in the last half-century; to rebuild a world so massively destroyed without, however, denying the destruction or its wounds. The image of the child victim, which is also the image of the child witness, provides the disembodied wound of Holocaust destruction with a residence.[23]

NOTES

[1]Jarosław M. Rymkiewicz, *The Final Station: Umschlagplatz,* trans. Nina Taylor (New York: Farrar, Straus & Giroux, 1994), 324–26.

[2]Marjorie Agosín, *Dear Anne Frank,* trans. Richard Schaaf (Washington, D.C.: Azul Editions, 1994), 5–8. See also the new bilingual edition published by Brandeis University Press/University Press of New England (Hanover, N.H.: 1998).

[3]Artist talk, Hood Museum of Art, Dartmouth College, Hanover, New Hampshire, May 1996.

[4]For the definition of memory as an "act" see Pierre Janet, *Les Médications psychologiques* (1919–25; Paris: Société Pierre Janet, 1984, vol. 2), and the gloss on Janet's argument by Bessel A. van der Kolk and Otto van der Hart, "The Intrusive Past: The Flexibility of Memory and the Engraving of Trauma," in *Trauma: Explorations in Memory,* ed. Cathy Caruth (Baltimore: Johns Hopkins University Press, 1995).

[5]See Marianne Hirsch, *Family Frames: Photography, Narrative, and Postmemory* (Cambridge: Harvard University Press, 1997), esp. chaps. 1 and 6.

[6]Kaja Silverman, *The Threshold of the Visible World* (New York: Routledge, 1996), 185. Psychoanalytic theories of identification tend to stress its incorporative, appropriative logic based on idealization of the other. See in particular Diana Fuss's helpful discussion in *Identification Papers* (New York: Routledge, 1995). I appreciate Silverman's effort to theorize identification at a distance but what I find particularly helpful is her alignment, through the theorization of the look, of the structure of identification with the structure of memory, a process whereby we can "remember," through seeing, the memory of another.

[7]Roland Barthes, *Camera Lucida: Reflections on Photography,* trans. Richard Howard (New York: Hill and Wang, 1981). See Silverman's discussion of Barthes's terms, in *Threshold,* 181–85.

[8]Ilkaa Ahjopalo, dir., *Tsvi Nussbaum: A Boy from Warsaw* (1990), Ergo Media, Teaneck, N.J.

[9]The encounter between Rymkiewicz's narrator and Artur is in itself emblematic in Sidra DeKoven Ezrahi's "Representing Auschwitz," *History and Memory* 7, no. 2 (Fall–Winter 1996): 131.

[10]Lucy S. Dawidowicz, *The War Against the Jews: 1933–1945* (New York: Bantam, 1975), 166.

[11]Yala Korwin, *To Tell the Story: Poems of the Holocaust* (New York: Holocaust Library, 1987), 75. Other artists, writers, and critics have found this image equally inspiring. See especially the series of studies based on the photograph by painter Samuel Bak, which illustrates, yet again, the image's openness to identification. Samuel Bak, *Landscapes of Jewish Experience II* (Boston: Pucker Gallery, 1996). See also the long discussion of the image by Herman Rapaport in *Is There Truth in Art?* (Ithaca: Cornell University Press, 1997).

[12]Bruno Bettelheim, "The Ignored Lesson of Anne Frank," in *Surviving and Other Essays* (New York: Knopf, 1979).

[13]See Lynn Gumpert, *Christian Boltanski* (Paris: Flammarion, 1993). See also my own discussion of Boltanski's work in Hirsch, *Family Frames,* chap. 6.

[14]See Deboráh Dwork, *Children with a Star: Jewish Youth in Nazi Europe* (New Haven: Yale University Press, 1991), xxxiii. The most moving illustration of this is the monumental volume *French Children of the Holocaust: A Memorial,* ed. Susan Cohen, Howard Epstein, and Serge Klarsfeld, trans. Glorianne Depondt and Howard Epstein (New York: New York University Press, 1996), which lists the names of 11,400 deported French Jewish children and reproduces 2,500 of their photographs. The book, as the author writes in the introduction, is a "collective gravestone."

[15]Talk at the Institute for Contemporary Art, Boston, 25 January 1995.

[16]Mitzi Goldman, dir., *Hatred* (1996).

[17]Discussion following public showing of *Hatred* in Cape Town, South Africa, August 1996.

[18]On this split subject position, see Jean Laplanche and Jean-Bertrand Pontalis, "Fantasy and the Origins of Sexuality," in *Formation of Fantasy*, ed. Victor Burgin, James Donald, and Cora Kaplan (London: Routledge, 1989).

[19]See, among others, Julia Kristeva, "The Pain of Sorrow in the Modern World: The Works of Marguerite Duras," *PMLA* 102 (March 1987): 138–52, and Geoffrey Hartman, *The Longest Shadow: In the Aftermath of the Holocaust* (Bloomington: Indiana University Press, 1996), esp. "The Cinema Animal" and "Public Memory and Its Discontents."

[20]Dominick LaCapra, *Representing the Holocaust: History, Theory, Trauma* (Ithaca: Cornell University Press, 1994), 198–200. See Jacques Derrida's *Memoires, for Paul de Man*, trans. Cecile Lindsay, Jonathan Culler, Eduardo Cadava, and Peggy Kamuf (New York: Columbia University Press, 1988), for his reflections on the cannibalistic and appropriative modes of self/other relation that make mourning and identification after World War II impossible. See also Diana Fuss: "Trauma is another name for identification, the name we might give to the irrecoverable loss of a sense of human relatedness" (*Identification Papers*, 40).

[21]Shoshana Felman and Dori Laub, *Testimony: Crises of Witnessing in Literature, Psychoanalysis, and History* (New York: Routledge, 1992), chaps. 1 and 3.

[22]Saul Friedlander, "Trauma, Transference, and 'Working Through' in Writing the History of the *Shoah*," *History and Memory* 4 (1992): 51.

[23]I am grateful to the participants of the 1996 Dartmouth Humanities Institute on Cultural Memory and the Present for their ideas about cultural memory that have informed this argument and to audiences at the English Institute and the Comparative Literature Program at Dartmouth for their comments. Several colleagues have read earlier drafts of this paper and have made significant suggestions: Elizabeth Abel, Mieke Bal, Jonathan Crewe, Ivy Schweitzer, Leo Spitzer, Diana Taylor, Tom Trezise, Susanne Zantop. Mitzi Goldman and Lorie Novak have inspired this work with theirs; their encouragement is greatly appreciated.

●　●　●　●　●　●　●　●　●　●　●　●

QUESTIONS FOR A SECOND READING

1. At one point Hirsch refers to the work that is required to enter the "visual space" of postmemory. As you reread, pay close attention to how she defines this work and pay close attention to how this work is demonstrated in her use of (her "readings" of) the photographs she includes as part of her text. What terms does she use to define this work? What are its goals? What is at stake?

    And then you might ask: Does she demonstrate in her practice (in her use of the photos) the goals she defines in her argument? And, finally, what might this essay on looking at images have to do with writing—that is, how might you extrapolate a writing lesson?

2. About two-thirds of the way through, Hirsch says, "It is my argument that the visual encounter with the child victim is a triangular one, that identification occurs in a triangular field of looking" (p. 413). This sentence may come as a surprise (and perhaps is intended to), since the notion of a "triangular field" has not been front and center in the previous

discussions. Keep this sentence in mind as you reread. How are you prepared to think about a "triangular field of looking"? And, as you read on,
how are you being prepared for a "conclusion"?

3. The essay begins with three numbered sections (containing three images
   and two photographs). It concludes with two endings. The movement in
   the middle contains some surprising turns. The prose moves easily into first
   person. It relies heavily on images. This is not a conventional essay—introduction, body, conclusion. As you reread, pay close attention to the form of
   this essay—perhaps creating a chart or outline. Be prepared to use this to
   talk about the idea of the essay as it is represented in "Projected Memory."

4. The essay refers to a variety of sources: Rymkiewicz's novel, *The Final Station*; Marjorie Agosín's *Dear Anne Frank*; Art Spiegelman's *Maus* and
   Maus II; films by Resnais and Bergman (*Night and Fog* and *Persona*); a documentary, *Tsvi Nussbaum: A Boy from Warsaw*; a book of poetry by Yala
   Korwin; the *New York Times Magazine* article that included Lorie Novak's
   photograph *Past Lives*; a class taught by Shoshana Felman as reported in
   her book *Testimony*.

   There are others listed in the text and in the endnotes. Track one of
   these down and prepare a report for your class. What is it that would
   draw Hirsch to these examples (out of all the examples to represent the
   Holocaust)? Where and how is Hirsch's work suggested in them? How do
   you understand the work she did in bringing them into her essay?

ASSIGNMENTS FOR WRITING

1. The project of postmemory can be a writing project. In fact, to describe the
   individual's active engagement with the past that *is* postmemory, Hirsch
   uses metaphors of writing (or inscription): "It is a question of adopting
   the traumatic experiences—and thus also the memories—of others as
   one's own, or, more precisely, as experiences one might oneself have had,
   and of inscribing them into one's own life story. It is a question of conceiving oneself as multiply interconnected with others of the same, of previous, and of subsequent generations, of the same and of other—proximate
   or distant—cultures and subcultures" (p. 407).

   Use "Projected Memory" as an invitation to such a writing project,
   where you would write about a past that belongs to you but that is not
   yours. Hirsch is interested in stories of trauma and suffering. And there is,
   to be sure, much at stake (and much to be gained) by writing about the
   traumas that preoccupy us as a culture. You should not, however, feel that
   you must write about a traumatic past. You should write about what you
   have at hand—connections to the past through family, neighborhood, or
   (as Hirsch says) "group relation"—and as those memories can be
   prompted, assisted, and mediated by some documentary or photographic
   record (as in the case of the photos in "Projected Memory" and the story
   of Anne Frank for Rymkiewicz and Agosín). The past that you are tied to
   need not necessarily have national or international significance. The importance is that you can identify yourself with this past and with these
   memories (and that you can inscribe them into your own life story).

Since we are using Hirsch to invite you to write about the past, it is important to note where and how she identifies the problems that accompany such a task. It comes in the distinction she makes between "idiopathic" and "heteropathic" identification; her concern is cliché, sentimentality, a too-easy identification with that which is beyond you, even incomprehensible. She says,

> The challenge for the postmemorial artist is precisely to find the balance that allows the spectator [the reader] to enter the image, to imagine the disaster, but that disallows an overappropriate identification that makes the distances disappear, creating too available, too easy an access to this particular past. (p. 408)

2. In a sense, we have all been asked to remember the Holocaust. Its images, stories, reminders, words are regularly present in what we see, read, and hear. Our culture and European culture continue to rework and remember the attempt to exterminate the Jews in World War II. Choose an example that you remember or that you would like to know more about—a film or television show, an image, a work of art, a work of literature—and bring it under the sway of Hirsch's essay. You should assume that your readers are not familiar with Hirsch and her work and, even if they are familiar with your example, that they will need reminders.

   Once you establish Hirsch's work as your frame of reference, you will need to bring your example into the discussion. And your effort should be to do this in your voice and from your point of view. You want to show that you can use Hirsch's terms and bring her argument to bear; you also want to show that you have something to add to the discussion.

3. The essay begins with three numbered sections (containing three images and two photographs). It concludes with two endings. The movement in the middle contains some surprising turns. The prose moves easily into first person. It relies heavily on images. This is not a textbook essay.

   Reread the essay paying particular attention to its form and style, to what Hirsch is *doing* as well as what she is saying. While there is certainly an argument *in* Hirsch's essay, your concern should be with the argument represented *by* the essay, an argument about writing and scholarship and the relation of academic work to its potential audiences. Write an essay in which you discuss "Projected Memory" as a writing project. What might you learn from it as a writer? What might you learn from it about professors and about the academy? (You should assume that your readers have not read the essay; you can assume that they are students, like you, in a position to learn something about writing.)

4. As the title indicates, Hirsch's essay is about "projected memory" and it is about "Holocaust photographs in personal and public fantasy." It is not presented in the style of thesis, example, and conclusion. There is neither a conventional introduction nor a conventional summation. The arguments and demonstrations in between are rich, varied, and complicated.

   What, so far as you are concerned, is this essay about? And how does it speak to you—to your interests and concerns and projects and to your education? Write an essay, perhaps in the genre of a review, in which you present "Projected Memory: Holocaust Photographs in Personal and Public Fantasy" to those who have not yet read it. You will need to take care to give a thorough and accurate account of what Hirsch says and does.

You should also establish your position in relation to the essay, discussing where and how you found it useful or interesting.

MAKING CONNECTIONS

1. According to Hirsch, Lorie Novak *"stages an uneasy confrontation of personal memory with public history."* Hirsch studies, writes about (and stages) such confrontations herself. The phrase is an apt one to use to describe the work of Susan Griffin in "Our Secret" (p. 345), a work about the Nazis, about the Holocaust, and about family history, all held together in a kind of collage-like or polyphonic prose. Griffin, too, could be said to stage an uneasy confrontation of personal memory with public history.

   The project of postmemory, as defined by Hirsch, can be a writing project. In fact, to describe the individual's active engagement with the past that *is* postmemory, Hirsch uses metaphors of writing: "It is a question of adopting the traumatic experiences—and thus also the memories—of others as one's own, or, more precisely, as experiences one might oneself have had, and of inscribing them into one's own life story. It is a question of conceiving oneself as multiply interconnected with others of the same, of previous, and of subsequent generations; of the same and of other—proximate or distant—cultures and subcultures" (p. 407). We have the examples, early in the essay, of Rymkiewicz and Agosín. Hirsch is also concerned about the problems that accompany such a task. It comes in the distinction she makes between "idiopathic" and "heteropathic" identification; her concern is cliché, sentimentality, a too-easy identification with that which is beyond you, even incomprehensible. She says,

   > The challenge for the postmemorial artist is precisely to find the balance that allows the spectator [the reader] to enter the image, to imagine the disaster, but that disallows an overappropriate identification that makes the distances disappear, creating too available, too easy an access to this particular past. (p. 408)

   Write an essay in which you consider Susan Griffin's "Our Secret" as the work of a postmemorial artist. How might Hirsch read, use, and value Griffin's writing? You will need to establish Hirsch's essay as an introduction and a point of reference. You will need to establish how she talks about writing and how she might talk about a project like Griffin's. And then you will need to turn with care to the text of "Our Secret."

2. In his essay, "The Tradition: Fact and Fiction," Robert Coles (p. 176) comments on the documentary photography done by Dorothea Lange and Walker Evans during the Great Depression of the 1930s. Coles is interested in the ways photographs are both documentary records and works of art and so disrupt any clear distinction between fact and fiction. In his comments on one of Evans's photographs, he says,

   > But Evans is struggling for an interiority, that of his subject and that of his subject's future viewer/visitor: let us not only praise this man, lift him to the ranks of the famous, but consider what might be going on within him, and let us, through the motions of our moral imagination,

enter his life, try to understand it, and return with that understanding
to our own, which is thereby altered. (p. 197)

"This is a tall order for a single picture," he says, "but then Evans and
Agee were ambitious. . . ."

When he speaks of the viewer, the viewer Evans is assuming in his
photography, it is a viewer with a "moral imagination" who will do the
work to "enter [the subject's] life, try to understand it, and return with
that understanding" to his own life, a life which would, then, be altered.

Write an essay in which you read Coles's essay from the position of
Hirsch's argument. Both have the goal of teaching us how to use the photographic record. How are they different? Both speak with an urgency
about the necessity of paying attention to the records of the past and the
ethical issues involved. Again, how are they different? And, finally, if they
define two ways of approaching the photographic record, where do you
locate yourself within these issues?

You should imagine that you are writing for someone who can understand the issues but who is familiar with neither of these sources. You will
need to take care, in other words, to establish what the two authors say
and to give a sense of what it is like to read their prose.

3. Marianne Hirsch writes about memory; her training is in literature and
    literary theory. Patricia Nelson Limerick, in "Haunted America" (p. 471),
    writes about history; she is trained as a historian. Both, however, are con-
    cerned with the past, with how we preserve and understand the past,
    with the presence of the past, and with its bearing on our daily lives and
    affairs. Both write with a sense of urgency; both bring determined and
    passionate attention to their materials.

    Read the two essays together as a "set," as part of a single project in-
    vestigating the problems of confronting, using, and understanding the
    past. Write an essay in which you discuss the differences, focusing as
    closely as you can on specific examples from each essay. Examine the con-
    cerns or methods that belong to each but look, finally, to see the differ-
    ences. How would you account for those differences? What difference do
    they make to you as a reader, a writer, a person with an interest in under-
    standing the past?

HARRIET
JACOBS

*H*ARRIET JACOBS *was born in North Carolina in or around 1815. The selection that follows reproduces the opening chapters of her autobiography,*
Incidents in the Life of a Slave Girl, *and tells the story of her life from childhood to early adulthood, through the birth of her first child. In these chapters
Jacobs describes how she came to understand her identity as men's property—as a
slave and as a woman—as that identity was determined by her particular situation (her appearance, her education, the psychology of her owner, the values of her
family) and by the codes governing slavery in the South.*

*In the remaining chapters of her book, Jacobs tells of the birth of a second
child, of her escape from her owner, Dr. Flint, and of seven years spent hiding in a
crawl space under the roof of her grandmother's house. The father of her children,
Mr. Sands, did not, as she thought he might, purchase and free her, although he
eventually did purchase her children and allow them to live with her grandmother. He did not free the children, and they never bore his name.*

*Around 1842 Jacobs fled to New York, where she made contact with her chil-
dren and found work as a nursemaid in the family of Nathaniel P. Willis, a magazine editor who with his wife helped hide Jacobs from southern slaveholders and
eventually purchased Jacobs and her children and gave them their freedom.*

This is the end of Jacobs's story as it is reported in Incidents. *Recent research,
however, enables us to tell the story of the production of this autobiography, the*

text that represents its author's early life. Through her contact with the Willises, Jacobs met both black and white abolitionists and became active in the antislavery movement. She told her story to Amy Post, a feminist and abolitionist, and Post encouraged her to record it, which she did by writing in the evenings between 1853 and 1858. After unsuccessfully seeking publication in England, and with the help of the white abolitionist writer L. Maria Child, who read the manuscript and served as an editor (by rearranging sections and suggesting that certain incidents be expanded into chapters), Jacobs published Incidents in Boston in 1861 under the pseudonym "Linda Brent," along with Child's introduction, which is also reproduced here. During the Civil War, Jacobs left the Willises to be a nurse for black troops. She remained active, working with freed slaves for the next thirty years, and died in Washington, D.C., in 1897.

For years scholars questioned the authenticity of this autobiography, arguing that it seemed too skillful to have been written by a slave, and that more likely it had been written by white abolitionists as propaganda for their cause. The recent discovery, however, of a cache of letters and the research of Jean Fagan Yellin have established Jacobs's authorship and demonstrated that Child made only minor changes and assisted primarily by helping Jacobs find a publisher and an audience.

Still, the issue of authorship remains a complicated one, even if we can be confident that the writing belongs to Jacobs and records her struggles and achievements. The issue of authorship becomes complicated if we think of the dilemma facing Jacobs as a writer, telling a story that defied description to an audience who could never completely understand. There is, finally, a precarious relationship between the story of a slave's life, the story Jacobs had to tell, and the stories available to her and to her readers as models—stories of privileged, white, middle-class life: conventional narratives of family and childhood, love and marriage.

Houston Baker, one of our leading scholars of black culture, has described the situation of the slave narrator this way:

> But the slave narrator must also accomplish the almost unthinkable (since thought and language are inseparable) task of transmuting an authentic, unwritten self—a self that exists outside the conventional literary discourse structures of a white reading public—into a literary representation. . . . The voice of the unwritten self, once it is subjected to the linguistic codes, literary conventions, and audience expectations of a literate population, is perhaps never again the authentic voice of black American slavery. It is, rather, the voice of a self transformed by an autobiographical act into a sharer in the general public discourse about slavery.

The author of Incidents could be said to stand outside "the general public discourse," both because she was a slave and because she was a woman. The story she has to tell does not fit easily into the usual stories of courtship and marriage or the dominant attitudes toward sexuality and female "virtue." When you read Jacobs's concerns about her "competence," about her status as a woman or as a writer, concerns that seem strange in the face of this powerful text; when you hear her *addressing her readers, sometimes instructing them, sometimes apologizing, trying to bridge the gap between her experience and theirs, you should think not only of the trials she faced as a woman and a mother but also of her work as a writer. Here, too, she is struggling to take possession of her life.*

Incidents in the Life of a Slave Girl

Written by Herself

Northerners know nothing at all about Slavery. They think it is perpetual bondage only. They have no conception of the depth of *degradation* involved in that word, SLAVERY; if they had, they would never cease their efforts until so horrible a system was overthrown.

— A WOMAN OF NORTH CAROLINA

Rise up, ye women that are at ease! Hear my voice, ye careless daughters! Give ear unto my speech.

– Isaiah xxxii.9

Preface by the Author

Linda Brent

Reader, be assured this narrative is no fiction. I am aware that some of my adventures may seem incredible; but they are, nevertheless, strictly true. I have not exaggerated the wrongs inflicted by Slavery; on the contrary, my descriptions fall far short of the facts. I have concealed the names of places, and given persons fictitious names. I had no motive for secrecy on my own account, but I deemed it kind and considerate towards others to pursue this course.

I wish I were more competent to the task I have undertaken. But I trust my readers will excuse deficiencies in consideration of circumstances. I was born and reared in Slavery; and I remained in a Slave State twenty-seven years. Since I have been at the North, it has been necessary for me to work diligently for my own support, and the education of my children. This has not left me much leisure to make up for the loss of early opportunities to improve myself; and it has compelled me to write these pages at irregular intervals, whenever I could snatch an hour from household duties.

When I first arrived in Philadelphia, Bishop Paine advised me to publish a sketch of my life, but I told him I was altogether incompetent to such an undertaking. Though I have improved my mind somewhat since that time, I still remain of the same opinion; but I trust my motives will excuse what might otherwise seem presumptuous. I have not written my experiences in order to attract attention to myself; on the contrary, it would have been more pleasant to me to have been silent about my own history. Neither do I care to excite sympathy for my own sufferings. But I do earnestly desire to arouse the women of the North to a realizing sense of the condition of two millions of women at the South, still in bondage, suffering what I suffered, and most of them far worse. I want to add my testimony to that of abler pens to convince the people of the Free States what Slavery really is. Only by experience can any one realize how deep, and dark, and foul is that pit of abominations. May the blessing of God rest on this imperfect effort in behalf of my persecuted people!

Introduction by the Editor

L. Maria Child

The author of the following autobiography is personally known to me, and her conversation and manners inspire me with confidence. During the last seventeen years, she has lived the greater part of the time with a distinguished family in New York, and has so deported herself as to be highly esteemed by them. This fact is sufficient, without further credentials of her character. I believe those who know her will not be disposed to doubt her veracity, though some incidents in her story are more romantic than fiction.

At her request, I have revised her manuscript; but such changes as I have made have been mainly for purposes of condensation and orderly arrangement. I have not added any thing to the incidents, or changed the import of her very pertinent remarks. With trifling exceptions, both the ideas and the language are her own. I pruned excrescences a little, but otherwise I had no reason for changing her lively and dramatic way of telling her own story. The names of both persons and places are known to me; but for good reasons I suppress them.

It will naturally excite surprise that a woman reared in Slavery should be able to write so well. But circumstances will explain this. In the first place, nature endowed her with quick perceptions. Secondly, the mistress, with whom she lived till she was twelve years old, was a kind, considerate friend, who taught her to read and spell. Thirdly, she was placed in favorable circumstances after she came to the North; having frequent intercourse with intelligent persons, who felt a friendly interest in her welfare, and were disposed to give her opportunities for self-improvement.

I am well aware that many will accuse me of indecorum for presenting these pages to the public; for the experiences of this intelligent and much-injured woman belong to a class which some call delicate subjects, and others indelicate. This peculiar phase of Slavery has generally been kept veiled; but the public ought to be made acquainted with its monstrous features, and I willingly take the responsibility of presenting them with the veil withdrawn. I do this for the sake of my sisters in bondage, who are suffering wrongs so foul, that our ears are too delicate to listen to them. I do it with the hope of arousing conscientious and reflecting women at the North to a sense of their duty in the exertion of moral influence on the question of Slavery, on all possible occasions. I do it with the hope that every man who reads this narrative will swear solemnly before God that, so far as he has power to prevent it, no fugitive from Slavery shall ever be sent back to suffer in that loathsome den of corruption and cruelty.

Incidents in the Life of a Slave Girl, Seven Years Concealed

I
Childhood

I was born a slave; but I never knew it till six years of happy childhood had passed away. My father was a carpenter, and considered so intelligent and skilful in his trade, that, when buildings out of the common line were to be erected, he was sent for from long distances, to be head workman. On condition of paying his mistress two hundred dollars a year, and supporting himself, he was allowed to work at his trade, and manage his own affairs. His strongest wish was to purchase his children; but, though he several times offered his hard earnings for that purpose, he never succeeded. In complexion my parents were a light shade of brownish yellow, and were termed mulattoes. They lived together in a comfortable home; and, though we were all slaves, I was so fondly shielded that I never dreamed I was a piece of merchandise, trusted to them for safe keeping, and liable to be demanded of them at any moment. I had one brother, William, who was two years younger than myself—a bright, affectionate child. I had also a great treasure in my maternal grandmother, who was a remarkable woman in many respects. She was the daughter of a planter in South Carolina, who, at his death, left her mother and his three children free, with money to go to St. Augustine, where they had relatives. It was during the Revolutionary War; and they were captured on their passage, carried back, and sold to different purchasers. Such was the story my grandmother used to tell me; but I do not remember all the particulars. She was a little girl when she was captured and sold to the keeper of a large hotel. I have often heard her tell how hard she fared during childhood. But as she grew older she evinced so much intelligence, and was so faithful, that her master and mistress could not help seeing it was for their interest to take care of such a valuable piece of property. She became an indispensable personage in the household, officiating in all capacities, from cook and wet nurse to seamstress. She was much praised for her cooking; and her nice crackers became so famous in the neighborhood that many people were desirous of obtaining them. In consequence of numerous requests of this kind, she asked permission of her mistress to bake crackers at night, after all the household work was done; and she obtained leave to do it, provided she would clothe herself and her children from the profits. Upon these terms, after working hard all day for her mistress, she began her midnight bakings, assisted by her two oldest children. The business proved profitable; and each year she laid by a little, which was saved for a fund to purchase her children. Her master died, and the property was divided among his heirs. The widow had her dower in the hotel, which she continued to keep open. My grandmother remained in her service as a slave; but her children were divided among her master's children. As she had five, Benjamin, the youngest one, was sold, in order that each heir might have an equal portion of dollars and cents. There was so little difference in our ages that he seemed more like my brother than my uncle. He was a bright, handsome lad, nearly white; for he inherited the complexion my grandmother had derived from Anglo-Saxon ancestors. Though only ten years old, seven hundred and twenty dollars were paid for him. His sale was a terrible blow to my grandmother; but she was naturally hopeful, and she went to work with renewed energy, trusting in time to be able to purchase some of her children. She had laid up three hundred dollars, which her mistress one day begged as a loan, promising to pay her soon. The reader probably knows that no promise or writing given to a slave is legally binding; for, according to Southern laws, a slave, *being* property, can *hold* no property. When my grandmother lent her hard earnings to her mistress, she trusted solely to her honor. The honor of a slaveholder to a slave!

To this good grandmother I was indebted for many comforts. My brother Willie and I often received portions of the crackers, cakes, and preserves she made to sell; and after we ceased to be children we were indebted to her for many more important services.

Such were the unusually fortunate circumstances of my early childhood. When I was six years old, my mother died; and then, for the first time, I learned, by the talk around me, that I was a slave. My mother's mistress was the daughter of my grandmother's mistress. She was the foster sister of my mother; they were both nourished at my grandmother's breast. In fact, my mother had been weaned at three months old, that the babe of the mistress might obtain sufficient food. They played together as children; and, when they became women, my mother was a most faithful servant to her whiter foster sister. On her death-bed her mistress promised that her children should never suffer for any thing; and during her lifetime she kept her word. They all spoke kindly of my dead mother, who had been a slave merely in name, but in nature was noble and womanly. I grieved for her, and my young mind was troubled with the thought who would now take care of me and my little brother. I was told that my home was now to be with her mistress; and I found it a happy one. No toilsome or disagreeable duties were imposed upon me. My mistress was so kind to me that I was always glad to do her bidding, and proud to labor for her as much as my young years would permit. I would sit by her side for hours, sewing diligently, with a heart as free from care as that of any free-born white child. When she thought I was tired, she would send me out to run and jump; and away I bounded, to gather berries or flowers to decorate her room. Those were happy days—too happy to last. The slave child had no thought for the morrow; but there came that blight, which too surely waits on every human being born to be a chattel.

When I was nearly twelve years old, my kind mistress sickened and died. As I saw the cheek grow paler, and the eye more glassy, how earnestly I prayed in my heart that she might live! I loved her; for she had been almost like a mother to me. My prayers were not answered. She died, and they buried her in the little churchyard, where, day after day, my tears fell upon her grave.

I was sent to spend a week with my grandmother. I was now old enough to begin to think of the future; and again and again I asked myself what they would do with me. I felt sure I should never find another mistress so kind as the one who was gone. She had promised my dying mother that her children should never suffer for any thing; and when I remembered that, and recalled her many proofs of attachment to me, I could not help having some hopes that she had left me free. My friends were almost certain it would be so. They thought she would be sure to do it, on account of my mother's love and faithful service. But, alas! we all know that the memory of a faithful slave does not avail much to save her children from the auction block.

After a brief period of suspense, the will of my mistress was read, and we learned that she had bequeathed me to her sister's daughter, a child of five years old. So vanished our hopes. My mistress had taught me the precepts of God's Word: "Thou shalt love thy neighbor as thyself." "Whatsoever ye would that men should do unto you, do ye even so unto them." But I was her slave, and I suppose she did not recognize me as her neighbor. I would give much to blot out from my memory that one great wrong. As a child, I loved my mistress; and, looking back on the happy days I spent with her, I try to think with less bitterness of this act of injustice. While I was with her, she taught me to read and spell; and for this privilege, which so rarely falls to the lot of a slave, I bless her memory.

She possessed but few slaves; and at her death those were all distributed among her relatives. Five of them were my grandmother's children, and had shared the same milk that nourished her mother's children. Notwithstanding my grandmother's long and faithful service to her owners, not one of her children escaped the auction block. These God-breathing machines are no more, in the sight of their masters, than the cotton they plant, or the horses they tend.

II
The New Master and Mistress

Dr. Flint, a physician in the neighborhood, had married the sister of my mistress, and I was now the property of their little daughter. It was not without murmuring that I prepared for my new home; and what added to my unhappiness, was the fact that my brother William was purchased by the same family. My father, by his nature, as well as by the habit of transacting business as a skilful mechanic, had more of the feelings of a freeman than is common among slaves. My brother was a spirited boy; and being brought up under such influences, he early detested the name of master and mistress. One day, when his father and his mistress both happened to call him at the same time, he hesitated between the two; being perplexed to know which had the strongest claim upon his obedience. He finally concluded to go to his mistress. When my father reproved him for it, he said, "You both called me, and I didn't know which I ought to go to first."

"You are *my* child," replied our father, "and when I call you, you should come immediately, if you have to pass through fire and water."

Poor Willie! He was now to learn his first lesson of obedience to a master. Grandmother tried to cheer us with hopeful words, and they found an echo in the credulous hearts of youth.

When we entered our new home we encountered cold looks, cold words, and cold treatment. We were glad when the night came. On my narrow bed I moaned and wept, I felt so desolate and alone.

I had been there nearly a year, when a dear little friend of mine was buried. I heard her mother sob, as the clods fell on the coffin of her only child, and I turned away from the grave, feeling thankful that I still had something left to love. I met my grandmother, who said, "Come with me, Linda"; and from her tone I knew that something sad had happened. She led me apart from the people, and then said, "My child, your father is dead." Dead! How could I believe it? He had died so suddenly I had not even heard that he was sick. I went home with my grandmother. My heart rebelled against God, who had taken from me mother, father, mistress, and friend. The good grandmother tried to comfort me. "Who knows the ways of God?" said she. "Perhaps they have been kindly taken from the evil days to come." Years afterwards I often thought of this. She promised to be a mother to her grandchildren, so far as she might be permitted to do so; and strengthened by her love, I returned to my master's. I thought I should be allowed to go to my father's house the next morning; but I was ordered to go for flowers, that my mistress's house might be decorated for an evening party. I spent the day gathering flowers and weaving them into festoons, while the dead body of my father was lying within a mile of me. What cared my owners for that? he was merely a piece of property. Moreover, they thought he had spoiled his children, by teaching them to feel that they were human beings. This was blasphemous doctrine for a slave to teach; presumptuous in him, and dangerous to the masters.

The next day I followed his remains to a humble grave beside that of my dear mother. There were those who knew my father's worth, and respected his memory.

My home now seemed more dreary than ever. The laugh of the little slave-children sounded harsh and cruel. It was selfish to feel so about the joy of others. My brother moved about with a very grave face. I tried to comfort him, by saying, "Take courage, Willie; brighter days will come by and by."

"You don't know any thing about it, Linda," he replied. "We shall have to stay here all our days; we shall never be free."

I argued that we were growing older and stronger, and that perhaps we might, before long, be allowed to hire our own time, and then we could earn money to buy our freedom. William declared this was much easier to say than to do; moreover, he did not intend to *buy* his freedom. We held daily controversies upon this subject.

Little attention was paid to the slaves' meals in Dr. Flint's house. If they could catch a bit of food while it was going, well and good. I gave myself no trouble on that score, for on my various errands I passed my grandmother's house, where there was always something to spare for me. I was frequently threatened with punishment if I stopped there; and my grandmother, to avoid detaining me, often stood at the gate with something for my breakfast or dinner. I was indebted to *her* for all my comforts, spiritual or temporal. It was *her* labor that supplied my scanty wardrobe. I have a vivid recollection of the linsey-woolsey dress given me every winter by Mrs. Flint. How I hated it! It was one of the badges of slavery.

While my grandmother was thus helping to support me from her hard earnings, the three hundred dollars she had lent her mistress was never repaid. When her mistress died, her son-in-law, Dr. Flint, was appointed executor. When grandmother applied to him for payment, he said the estate was insolvent, and the law prohibited payment. It did not, however, prohibit him from retaining the silver candelabra, which had been purchased with that money. I presume they will be handed down in the family, from generation to generation.

My grandmother's mistress had always promised her that, at her death, she should be free; and it was said that in her will she made good the promise. But when the estate was settled, Dr. Flint told the faithful old servant that, under existing circumstances, it was necessary she should be sold.

On the appointed day, the customary advertisement was posted up, proclaiming that there would be a "public sale of negroes, horses, &c." Dr. Flint called to tell my grandmother that he was unwilling to wound her feelings by putting her up at auction, and that he would prefer to dispose of her at private sale. My grandmother saw through his hypocrisy; she understood very well that he was ashamed of the job. She was a very spirited woman, and if he was base enough to sell her, when her mistress intended she should be free, she was determined the public should know it. She had for a long time supplied many families with crackers and preserves; consequently, "Aunt Marthy," as she was called, was generally known, and every body who knew her respected her intelligence and good character. Her long and faithful service in the family was also well known, and the intention of her mistress to leave her free. When the day of sale came, she took her place among the chattels, and at the first call she sprang upon the auction-block. Many voices called out, "Shame! Shame! Who is going to sell *you*, Marthy? Don't stand there! That is no place for *you*." Without saying a word she quietly awaited her fate. No one bid for her. At last, a feeble voice, said, "Fifty dollars." It came from a maiden lady, seventy years old, the sister of my grandmother's deceased mistress. She had lived forty years under the same roof with my grandmother; she knew how faithfully she had served her owners, and how cruelly she had been defrauded of her rights; and she resolved to protect her. The auctioneer waited for a higher bid; but her wishes were respected; no one bid above her. She could neither read nor write; and when the bill of sale was made out, she signed it with a cross. But what consequence was that, when she had a big heart overflowing with human kindness? She gave the old servant her freedom.

At that time, my grandmother was just fifty years old. Laborious years had passed since then; and now my brother and I were slaves to the man who had defrauded her of her money, and tried to defraud her of her freedom. One of my mother's sisters, called Aunt Nancy, was also a slave in his family. She was a kind, good aunt to me; and supplied the place of both housekeeper and waiting maid to her mistress. She was, in fact, at the beginning and end of every thing.

Mrs. Flint, like many southern women, was totally deficient in energy. She had not strength to superintend her household affairs; but her nerves were so strong, that she could sit in her easy chair and see a woman whipped, till the blood trickled from every stroke of the lash. She was a member of the church; but partaking of the Lord's supper did not seem to put her in a Christian frame of mind. If dinner was not served at the exact time on that particular Sunday, she would station herself in the kitchen, and wait till it was dished, and then spit in all the kettles and pans that had been used for cooking. She did this to prevent the cook and her children from eking out their meagre fare with the remains of the gravy and other scrapings. The slaves could get nothing to eat except what she chose to give them. Provisions were weighed out by the pound and ounce, three times a day. I can assure you she gave them no chance to eat wheat bread from her flour barrel. She knew how many biscuits a quart of flour would make, and exactly what size they ought to be.

Dr. Flint was an epicure. The cook never sent a dinner to his table without fear and trembling; for if there happened to be a dish not to his liking, he would either order her to be whipped, or compel her to eat every mouthful of it in his presence. The poor, hungry creature might not have objected to eating it; but she did object to having her master cram it down her throat till she choked.

They had a pet dog, that was a nuisance in the house. The cook was ordered to make some Indian mush for him. He refused to eat, and when his head was held over it, the froth flowed from his mouth into the basin. He died a few minutes after. When Dr. Flint came in, he said the mush had not been well cooked, and that was the reason the animal would not eat it. He sent for the cook, and compelled her to eat it. He thought that the woman's stomach was stronger than the dog's; but her sufferings afterwards proved that he was mistaken. This poor woman endured many cruelties from her master and mistress; sometimes she was locked up, away from her nursing baby, for a whole day and night.

When I had been in the family a few weeks, one of the plantation slaves was brought to town, by order of his master. It was near night when he arrived, and Dr. Flint ordered him to be taken to the work house, and tied up to the joist, so that his feet would just escape the ground. In that situation he was to wait till the doctor had taken his tea. I shall never forget that night. Never before, in my life, had I heard hundreds of blows fall, in succession, on a human being. His piteous groans, and his "O, pray don't, massa," rang in my ear for months afterwards. There were many conjectures as to the cause of this terrible punishment. Some said master accused him of stealing corn; others said the slave had quarrelled with his wife, in presence of the overseer, and had accused his master of being the father of her child. They were both black, and the child was very fair.

I went into the work house next morning, and saw the cowhide still wet with blood, and the boards all covered with gore. The poor man lived, and continued to quarrel with his wife. A few months afterwards Dr. Flint handed them both over to a slave-trader. The guilty man put their value into his pocket, and had the satisfaction of knowing that they were out of sight and hearing. When the mother was delivered into the trader's hands, she said, "You *promised* to treat me well." To which he replied, "You have let your tongue run too far; damn you!" She had forgotten that it was a crime for a slave to tell who was the father of her child.

From others than the master persecution also comes in such cases. I once saw a young slave girl dying soon after the birth of a child nearly white. In her agony she cried out, "O Lord, come and take me!" Her mistress stood by, and mocked at her like an incarnate fiend. "You suffer, do you?" she exclaimed. "I am glad of it. You deserve it all, and more too."

The girl's mother said, "The baby is dead, thank God; and I hope my poor child will soon be in heaven, too."

"Heaven!" retorted the mistress. "There is no such place for the like of her and her bastard."

The poor mother turned away, sobbing. Her dying daughter called her, feebly, and as she bent over her, I heard her say, "Don't grieve so, mother; God knows all about it; and HE will have mercy upon me."

Her sufferings, afterwards, became so intense, that her mistress felt unable to stay; but when she left the room, the scornful smile was still on her lips. Seven children called her mother. The poor black woman had but the one child, whose eyes she saw closing in death, while she thanked God for taking her away from the greater bitterness of life.

III
The Slaves' New Year's Day

Dr. Flint owned a fine residence in town, several farms, and about fifty slaves, besides hiring a number by the year.

Hiring-day at the south takes place on the 1st of January. On the 2d, the slaves are expected to go to their new masters. On a farm, they work until the corn and cotton are laid. They then have two holidays. Some masters give them a good dinner under the trees. This over, they work until Christmas eve. If no heavy charges are meantime brought against them, they are given four or five holidays, whichever the master or overseer may think proper. Then comes New Year's eve; and they gather together their little alls, or more properly speaking, their little nothings, and wait anxiously for the dawning of day. At the appointed hour the grounds are thronged with men, women, and children, waiting, like criminals, to hear their doom pronounced. The slave is sure to know who is the most humane, or cruel master, within forty miles of him.

It is easy to find out, on that day, who clothes and feeds his slaves well; for he is surrounded by a crowd, begging, "Please, massa, hire me this year. I will work *very* hard, massa."

If a slave is unwilling to go with his new master, he is whipped, or locked up in jail, until he consents to go, and promises not to run away during the year. Should he chance to change his mind, thinking it justifiable to violate an extorted promise, woe unto him if he is caught! The whip is used till the blood flows at his feet; and his stiffened limbs are put in chains, to be dragged in the field for days and days!

If he lives until the next year, perhaps the same man will hire him again, without even giving him an opportunity of going to the hiring-ground. After those for hire are disposed of, those for sale are called up.

O, you happy free women, contrast *your* New Year's day with that of the poor bond-woman! With you it is a pleasant season, and the light of the day is blessed. Friendly wishes meet you every where, and gifts are showered upon you. Even hearts that have been estranged from you soften at this season, and lips that have been silent echo back, "I wish you a happy New Year." Children bring their little offerings, and raise their rosy lips for a caress. They are your own, and no hand but that of death can take them from you.

But to the slave mother New Year's day comes laden with peculiar sorrows. She sits on her cold cabin floor, watching the children who may all be torn from her the next morning; and often does she wish that she and they might die before the day dawns. She may be an ignorant creature, degraded by the system that has brutalized her from childhood; but she has a mother's instincts, and is capable of feeling a mother's agonies.

On one of these sale days, I saw a mother lead seven children to the auction-block. She knew that *some* of them would be taken from her; but they took *all*. The children were sold to a slave-trader, and their mother was bought by a man in her own town. Before night her children were all far away. She begged the trader to tell her where he intended to take them; this he refused to do. How *could* he, when he knew he would sell them, one by one, wherever he could command the highest price? I met that mother in the street, and her wild, haggard face lives to-day in my mind. She wrung her hands in anguish, and exclaimed, "Gone! All gone! Why *don't* God kill me?" I had no words wherewith to comfort her. Instances of this kind are of daily, yea, of hourly occurrence.

Slaveholders have a method, peculiar to their institution, of getting rid of *old* slaves, whose lives have been worn out in their service. I knew an old woman, who for seventy years faithfully served her master. She had become almost helpless, from hard labor and disease. Her owners moved to Alabama, and the old black woman was left to be sold to any body who would give twenty dollars for her.

IV
The Slave Who Dared to Feel Like a Man

Two years had passed since I entered Dr. Flint's family, and those years had brought much of the knowledge that comes from experience, though they had afforded little opportunity for any other kinds of knowledge.

My grandmother had, as much as possible, been a mother to her orphan grandchildren. By perseverance and unwearied industry, she was now mistress of a snug little home, surrounded with the necessaries of life. She would have been happy could her children have shared them with her. There remained but three children and two grandchildren, all slaves. Most earnestly did she strive to make us feel that it was the will of God: that He had seen fit to place us under such circumstances; and though it seemed hard, we ought to pray for contentment.

It was a beautiful faith, coming from a mother who could not call her children her own. But I, and Benjamin, her youngest boy, condemned it. We reasoned that it was much more the will of God that we should be situated as she was. We longed for a home like hers. There we always found sweet balsam for our troubles. She was so loving, so sympathizing! She always met us with a smile, and listened with patience to all our sorrows. She spoke so hopefully, that unconsciously the clouds gave place to sunshine. There was a grand big oven there, too, that baked bread and nice things for the town, and we knew there was always a choice bit in store for us.

But, alas! even the charms of the old oven failed to reconcile us to our hard lot. Benjamin was now a tall, handsome lad, strongly and gracefully made, and with a spirit too bold and daring for a slave. My brother William, now twelve years old, had the same aversion to the word master that he had when he was an urchin of seven years. I was his confidant. He came to me with all his troubles. I remember one instance in particular. It was on a lovely spring morning, and when I marked the sunlight dancing here and there, its beauty seemed to mock my sadness. For my master, whose restless, craving, vicious nature roved about day and night, seeking whom to devour, had just left me, with stinging, scorching words; words that scathed ear and brain like fire. O, how I despised him! I thought how glad I should be, if some day when he walked the earth, it would open and swallow him up, and disencumber the world of a plague.

When he told me that I was made for his use, made to obey his command in *every* thing; that I was nothing but a slave, whose will must and should surrender to his, never before had my puny arm felt half so strong.

So deeply was I absorbed in painful reflections afterwards, that I neither saw nor heard the entrance of any one, till the voice of William sounded close beside me. "Linda," said he, "what makes you look so sad? I love you. O, Linda, isn't this a bad world? Every body seems so cross and unhappy. I wish I had died when poor father did."

I told him that every body was *not* cross, or unhappy; that those who had pleasant homes, and kind friends, and who were not afraid to love them, were happy. But we, who were slave-children, without father or mother, could not expect to be happy. We must be good; perhaps that would bring us contentment.

"Yes," he said, "I try to be good; but what's the use? They are all the time troubling me." Then he proceeded to relate his afternoon's difficulty with young master Nicholas. It seemed that the brother of master Nicholas had pleased himself with making up stories about William. Master Nicholas said he should be flogged, and he would do it. Whereupon he went to work; but William fought bravely, and the young master, finding he was getting the better of him, undertook to tie his hands behind him. He failed in that likewise. By dint of kicking and fisting, William came out of the skirmish none the worse for a few scratches.

He continued to discourse on his young master's *meanness;* how he whipped the *little* boys, but was a perfect coward when a tussle ensued between him and white boys of his own size. On such occasions he always took to his legs. William had other charges to make against him. One was his rubbing up pennies with quicksilver, and passing them off for quarters of a dollar on an old man who kept a fruit stall. William was often sent to buy fruit, and he earnestly inquired of me what he ought to do under such circumstances. I told him it was certainly wrong to deceive the old man, and that it was his duty to tell him of the impositions practised by his young master. I assured him the old man would not be slow to comprehend the whole, and there the matter would end. William thought it might with the old man, but not with *him.* He said he did not mind the smart of the whip, but he did not like the *idea* of being whipped.

While I advised him to be good and forgiving I was not unconscious of the beam in my own eye. It was the very knowledge of my own shortcomings that urged me to retain, if possible, some sparks of my brother's God-given nature. I had not lived fourteen years in slavery for nothing. I had felt, seen, and heard enough, to read the characters, and question the motives, of those around me. The war of my life had begun; and though one of God's most powerless creatures, I resolved never to be conquered. Alas, for me!

If there was one pure, sunny spot for me, I believed it to be in Benjamin's heart, and in another's, whom I loved with all the ardor of a girl's first love. My owner knew of it, and sought in every way to render me miserable. He did not resort to corporal punishment, but to all the petty, tyrannical ways that human ingenuity could devise.

I remember the first time I was punished. It was in the month of February. My grandmother had taken my old shoes, and replaced them with a new pair. I needed them; for several inches of snow had fallen, and it still continued to fall. When I walked through Mrs. Flint's room, their creaking grated harshly on her refined nerves. She called me to her, and asked what I had about me that made such a horrid noise. I told her it was my new shoes. "Take them off," said she; "and if you put them on again, I'll throw them into the fire."

I took them off, and my stockings also. She then sent me a long distance, on an errand. As I went through the snow, my bare feet tingled. That night I was very hoarse; and I went to bed thinking the next day would find me sick, perhaps dead. What was my grief on waking to find myself quite well!

I had imagined if I died, or was laid up for some time, that my mistress would feel a twinge of remorse that she had so hated "the little imp," as she styled me. It was my ignorance of that mistress that gave rise to such extravagant imaginings.

Dr. Flint occasionally had high prices offered for me; but he always said, "She don't belong to me. She is my daughter's property, and I have no right to sell her." Good, honest man! My young mistress was still a child, and I could look for no protection from her. I loved her, and she returned my affection. I once heard her father allude to her attachment to me; and his wife promptly replied that it proceeded from fear. This put unpleasant doubts into my mind. Did the child feign what she did not feel? or was her mother jealous of the mite of love she bestowed on me? I concluded it must be the latter. I said to myself, "Surely, little children are true."

One afternoon I sat at my sewing, feeling unusual depression of spirits. My mistress had been accusing me of an offence, of which I assured her I was perfectly innocent; but I saw, by the contemptuous curl of her lip, that she believed I was telling a lie.

I wondered for what wise purpose God was leading me through such thorny paths, and whether still darker days were in store for me. As I sat musing thus, the door opened softly, and William came in. "Well, brother," said I, "what is the matter this time?"

"O Linda, Ben and his master have had a dreadful time!" said he.

My first thought was that Benjamin was killed. "Don't be frightened, Linda," said William; "I will tell you all about it."

It appeared that Benjamin's master had sent for him, and he did not immediately obey the summons. When he did, his master was angry, and began to whip him. He resisted. Master and slave fought, and finally the master was thrown. Benjamin had cause to tremble; for he had thrown to the ground his master—one of the richest men in town. I anxiously awaited the result.

That night I stole to my grandmother's house, and Benjamin also stole thither from his master's. My grandmother had gone to spend a day or two with an old friend living in the country.

"I have come," said Benjamin, "to tell you good by. I am going away."

I inquired where.

"To the north," he replied.

I looked at him to see whether he was in earnest. I saw it all in his firm, set mouth. I implored him not to go, but he paid no heed to my words. He said he was no longer a boy, and every day made his yoke more galling. He had raised his hand against his master, and was to be publicly whipped for the offence. I reminded him of the poverty and hardships he must encounter among strangers. I told him he might be caught and brought back; and that was terrible to think of.

He grew vexed, and asked if poverty and hardships with freedom, were not preferable to our treatment in slavery. "Linda," he continued, "we are dogs here; foot-balls, cattle, every thing that's mean. No, I will not stay. Let them bring me back. We don't die but once."

He was right; but it was hard to give him up. "Go," said I, "and break your mother's heart."

I repented of my words ere they were out.

"Linda," said he, speaking as I had not heard him speak that evening, "how *could* you say that? Poor mother! be kind to her, Linda; and you, too, cousin Fanny."

Cousin Fanny was a friend who had lived some years with us.

Farewells were exchanged, and the bright, kind boy, endeared to us by so many acts of love, vanished from our sight.

It is not necessary to state how he made his escape. Suffice it to say, he was on his way to New York when a violent storm overtook the vessel. The captain said he must put into the nearest port. This alarmed Benjamin, who was aware that he would be advertised in every port near his own town. His embarrassment was noticed by the captain. To port they went. There the advertisement met the captain's eye. Benjamin so exactly answered its description, that the captain laid hold on him, and bound him in chains. The storm passed, and they proceeded to New York. Before reaching that port Benjamin managed to get off his chains and throw them overboard. He escaped from the vessel, but was pursued, captured, and carried back to his master.

When my grandmother returned home and found her youngest child had fled, great was her sorrow; but, with characteristic piety, she said, "God's will be done." Each morning, she inquired if any news had been heard from her boy. Yes, news *was* heard. The master was rejoicing over a letter, announcing the capture of his human chattel.

That day seems but as yesterday, so well do I remember it. I saw him led through the streets in chains, to jail. His face was ghastly pale, yet full of determination. He had begged one of the sailors to go to his mother's house and ask her not to meet him. He said the sight of her distress would take from him all self-control. She yearned to see him, and she went; but she screened herself in the crowd, that it might be as her child had said.

We were not allowed to visit him; but we had known the jailer for years, and he was a kind-hearted man. At midnight he opened the jail door for my grandmother and myself to enter, in disguise. When we entered the cell not a sound broke the stillness. "Benjamin, Benjamin!" whispered my grandmother. No answer. "Benjamin!" she again faltered. There was a jingle of chains. The moon had just risen, and cast an uncertain light through the bars of the window. We knelt down and took Benjamin's cold hands in ours. We did not speak. Sobs were heard, and Benjamin's lips were unsealed; for his mother was weeping on his neck. How vividly does memory bring back that sad night! Mother and son talked together. He asked her pardon for the suffering he had caused her. She said she had nothing to forgive; she could not blame his desire for freedom. He told her that when he was captured, he broke away, and was about casting himself into the river, when thoughts of *her* came over him, and he desisted. She asked if he did not also think of God. I fancied I saw his face grow fierce in the moonlight. He answered, "No, I did not think of him. When a man is hunted like a wild beast he forgets there is a God, a heaven. He forgets every thing in his struggle to get beyond the reach of the bloodhounds."

"Don't talk so, Benjamin," said she. "Put your trust in God. Be humble, my child, and your master will forgive you."

"Forgive me for *what*, mother? For not letting him treat me like a dog? No! I will never humble myself to him. I have worked for him for nothing all my life, and I am repaid with stripes and imprisonment. Here I will stay till I die, or till he sells me."

The poor mother shuddered at his words. I think he felt it; for when he next spoke, his voice was calmer. "Don't fret about me, mother. I ain't worth it," said he. "I wish I had some of your goodness. You bear every thing patiently, just as though you thought it was all right. I wish I could."

She told him she had not always been so; once, she was like him; but when sore troubles came upon her, and she had no arm to lean upon, she learned to call on God, and he lightened her burdens. She besought him to do likewise.

We overstaid our time, and were obliged to hurry from the jail.

Benjamin had been imprisoned three weeks, when my grandmother went to intercede for him with his master. He was immovable. He said

Benjamin should serve as an example to the rest of his slaves; he should be kept in jail till he was subdued, or be sold if he got but one dollar for him. However, he afterwards relented in some degree. The chains were taken off, and we were allowed to visit him.

As his food was of the coarsest kind, we carried him as often as possible a warm supper, accompanied with some little luxury for the jailer.

Three months elapsed, and there was no prospect of release or of a purchaser. One day he was heard to sing and laugh. This piece of indecorum was told to his master, and the overseer was ordered to re-chain him. He was now confined in an apartment with other prisoners, who were covered with filthy rags. Benjamin was chained near them, and was soon covered with vermin. He worked at his chains till he succeeded in getting out of them. He passed them through the bars of the window, with a request that they should be taken to his master, and he should be informed that he was covered with vermin.

This audacity was punished with heavier chains, and prohibition of our visits.

My grandmother continued to send him fresh changes of clothes. The old ones were burned up. The last night we saw him in jail his mother still begged him to send for his master, and beg his pardon. Neither persuasion nor argument could turn him from his purpose. He calmly answered, "I am waiting his time."

Those chains were mournful to hear.

Another three months passed, and Benjamin left his prison walls. We that loved him waited to bid him a long and last farewell. A slave-trader had bought him. You remember, I told you what price he brought when ten years of age. Now he was more than twenty years old, and sold for three hundred dollars. The master had been blind to his own interest. Long confinement had made his face too pale, his form too thin; moreover, the trader had heard something of his character, and it did not strike him as suitable for a slave. He said he would give any price if the handsome lad was a girl. We thanked God that he was not.

Could you have seen that mother clinging to her child, when they fastened the irons upon his wrists; could you have heard her heart-rending groans, and seen her bloodshot eyes wander wildly from face to face, vainly pleading for mercy; could you have witnessed that scene as I saw it, you would exclaim, *Slavery is damnable!*

Benjamin, her youngest, her pet, was forever gone! She could not realize it. She had had an interview with the trader for the purpose of ascertaining if Benjamin could be purchased. She was told it was impossible, as he had given bonds not to sell him till he was out of the state. He promised that he would not sell him till he reached New Orleans.

With a strong arm and unvaried trust, my grandmother began her work of love. Benjamin must be free. If she succeeded, she knew they would still be separated; but the sacrifice was not too great. Day and night she labored. The trader's price would treble that he gave; but she was not discouraged.

She employed a lawyer to write to a gentleman, whom she knew, in New Orleans. She begged him to interest himself for Benjamin, and he willingly favored her request. When he saw Benjamin, and stated his business, he thanked him; but said he preferred to wait a while before making the trader an offer. He knew he had tried to obtain a high price for him, and had invariably failed. This encouraged him to make another effort for freedom. So one morning, long before day, Benjamin was missing. He was riding over the blue billows, bound for Baltimore.

For once his white face did him a kindly service. They had no suspicion that it belonged to a slave; otherwise, the law would have been followed out to the letter, and the *thing* rendered back to slavery. The brightest skies are often overshadowed by the darkest clouds. Benjamin was taken sick, and compelled to remain in Baltimore three weeks. His strength was slow in returning; and his desire to continue his journey seemed to retard his recovery. How could he get strength without air and exercise? He resolved to venture on a short walk. A by-street was selected, where he thought himself secure of not being met by any one that knew him; but a voice called out, "Halloo, Ben, my boy! what are you doing *here*?"

His first impulse was to run; but his legs trembled so that he could not stir. He turned to confront his antagonist, and behold, there stood his old master's next door neighbor! He thought it was all over with him now; but it proved otherwise. That man was a miracle. He possessed a goodly number of slaves, and yet was not quite deaf to that mystic clock, whose ticking is rarely heard in the slaveholder's breast.

"Ben, you are sick," said he. "Why, you look like a ghost. I guess I gave you something of a start. Never mind, Ben, I am not going to touch you. You had a pretty tough time of it, and you may go on your way rejoicing for all men. But I would advise you to get out of this place plaguy quick, for there are several gentlemen here from our town." He described the nearest and safest route to New York, and added, "I shall be glad to tell your mother I have seen you. Good by, Ben."

Benjamin turned away, filled with gratitude, and surprised that the town he hated contained such a gem—a gem worthy of a purer setting.

This gentleman was a Northerner by birth, and had married a southern lady. On his return, he told my grandmother that he had seen her son, and of the service he had rendered him.

Benjamin reached New York safely, and concluded to stop there until he had gained strength enough to proceed further. It happened that my grandmother's only remaining son had sailed for the same city on business for his mistress. Through God's providence, the brothers met. You may be sure it was a happy meeting. "O Phil," exclaimed Benjamin, "I am here at last." Then he told him how near he came to dying, almost in sight of free land, and how he prayed that he might live to get one breath of free air. He said life was worth something now, and it would be hard to die. In the old jail he had not valued it; once, he was tempted to destroy it; but something, he did not know what, had prevented him; perhaps it was fear. He had heard those who profess to be religious declare there was no heaven for self-murderers; and as his life had been pretty hot here, he did not desire a continuation of the same in another world. "If I die now," he exclaimed, "thank God, I shall die a freeman!"

He begged my uncle Phillip not to return south; but stay and work with him, till they earned enough to buy those at home. His brother told him it would kill their mother if he deserted her in her trouble. She had pledged her house, and with difficulty had raised money to buy him. Would he be bought?

"No, never!" he replied. "Do you suppose, Phil, when I have got so far out of their clutches, I will give them one red cent? No! And do you suppose I would turn mother out of her home in her old age? That I would let her pay all those hard-earned dollars for me, and never to see me? For you know she will stay south as long as her other children are slaves. What a good mother! Tell her to buy *you*, Phil. You have been a comfort to her, and I have been a trouble. And Linda, poor Linda; what'll become of her? Phil, you don't know what a life they lead her. She has told me something about it, and I wish old Flint was dead, or a better man. When I was in jail, he asked her if she didn't want *him* to ask my master to forgive me, and take me home again. She told him, No; that I didn't want to go back. He got mad, and said we were all alike. I never despised my own master half as much as I do that man. There is many a worse slaveholder than my master; but for all that I would not be his slave."

While Benjamin was sick, he had parted with nearly all his clothes to pay necessary expenses. But he did not part with a little pin I fastened in his bosom when we parted. It was the most valuable thing I owned, and I thought none more worthy to wear it. He had it still.

His brother furnished him with clothes, and gave him what money he had.

They parted with moistened eyes; and as Benjamin turned away, he said, "Phil, I part with all my kindred." And so it proved. We never heard from him again.

Uncle Phillip came home; and the first words he uttered when he entered the house were, "Mother, Ben is free! I have seen him in New York." She stood looking at him with a bewildered air. "Mother, don't you believe it?" he said, laying his hand softly upon her shoulder. She raised her hands, and exclaimed, "God be praised! Let us thank him." She dropped on her knees, and poured forth her heart in prayer. Then Phillip must sit down and repeat to her every word Benjamin had said. He told her all; only he forbore to mention how sick and pale her darling looked. Why should he distress her when she could do him no good?

The brave old woman still toiled on, hoping to rescue some of her other children. After a while she succeeded in buying Phillip. She paid eight hundred dollars, and came home with the precious document that secured his freedom. The happy mother and son sat together by the old hearthstone that night, telling how proud they were of each other, and how they would prove to the world that they could take care of themselves, as they had long taken care of others. We all concluded by saying, "He that is *willing* to be a slave, let him be a slave."

V
The Trials of Girlhood

During the first years of my service in Dr. Flint's family, I was accustomed to share some indulgences with the children of my mistress. Though this seemed to me no more than right, I was grateful for it, and tried to merit the kindness by the faithful discharge of my duties. But I now entered on my fifteenth year—a sad epoch in the life of a slave girl. My master began to whisper foul words in my ear. Young as I was, I could not remain ignorant of their import. I tried to treat them with indifference or contempt. The master's age, my extreme youth, and the fear that his conduct would be reported to my grandmother, made me bear this treatment for many months. He was a crafty man, and resorted to many means to accomplish his purposes. Sometimes he had stormy, terrific ways, that made his victims tremble; sometimes he assumed a gentleness that he thought must surely subdue. Of the two, I preferred his stormy moods, although they left me trembling. He tried his utmost to corrupt the pure principles my grandmother had instilled. He peopled my young mind with unclean images, such as only a vile monster could think of. I turned from him with disgust and hatred. But he was my master. I was compelled to live under the same roof with him—where I saw a man forty years my senior daily violating the most sacred commandments of nature. He told me I was his property; that I must be subject to his will in all things. My soul revolted against the mean tyranny. But where could I turn for protection? No matter whether the slave girl be as black as ebony or as fair as her mistress. In either case, there is no shadow of law to protect her from insult, from violence, or even from death; all these are inflicted by fiends who bear the shape of men. The mistress, who ought to protect the helpless victim, has no other feelings towards her but those of jealousy and rage. The degradation, the wrongs, the vices, that grow out of slavery, are more than I can describe. They are greater than you would willingly believe. Surely, if you credited one half the truths that are told you concerning the helpless millions suffering in this cruel bondage, you at the north would not help to tighten the yoke. You surely would refuse to do for the master, on your own soil, the mean and cruel work which trained bloodhounds and the lowest class of whites do for him at the south.

Every where the years bring to all enough of sin and sorrow; but in slavery the very dawn of life is darkened by these shadows. Even the little child, who is accustomed to wait on her mistress and her children, will learn, before she is twelve years old, why it is that her mistress hates such and such a one among the slaves. Perhaps the child's own mother is among those hated ones. She listens to violent outbreaks of jealous passion, and cannot help understanding what is the cause. She will become prematurely knowing in evil things. Soon she will learn to tremble when she hears her master's footfall. She will be compelled to realize that she is no longer a child. If God has bestowed beauty upon her, it will prove her greatest curse. That which commands admiration in the white woman only hastens the degradation of the female slave. I know that some are too much brutalized by slavery to feel the humiliation of their position; but many slaves feel it most acutely, and shrink from the memory of it. I cannot tell how much I suffered in the presence of these wrongs, nor how I am still pained by the retrospect. My master met me at every turn, reminding me that I belonged to him, and swearing by heaven and earth that he would compel me to submit to him. If I went out for a breath of fresh air, after a day of unwearied toil, his footsteps dogged me. If I knelt by my mother's grave, his dark shadow fell on me even there. The light heart which nature had given me became heavy with sad forebodings. The other slaves in my master's house noticed the change. Many of them pitied me; but none dared to ask the cause. They had no need to inquire. They knew too well the guilty practices under that roof; and they were aware that to speak of them was an offence that never went unpunished.

I longed for some one to confide in. I would have given the world to have laid my head on my grandmother's faithful bosom, and told her all my troubles. But Dr. Flint swore he would kill me, if I was not as silent as the grave. Then, although my grandmother was all in all to me, I feared her as well as loved her. I had been accustomed to look up to her with a respect bordering upon awe. I was very young, and felt shamefaced about telling her such impure things, especially as I knew her to be very strict on such subjects. Moreover, she was a woman of a high spirit. She was usually very quiet in her demeanor; but if her indignation was once roused, it was not very easily quelled. I had been told that she once chased a white gentleman with a loaded pistol, because he insulted one of her daughters. I dreaded the consequences of a violent outbreak; and both pride and fear kept me silent. But though I did not confide in my grandmother, and even evaded her vigilant watchfulness and inquiry, her presence in the neighborhood was some protection to me. Though she had been a slave, Dr. Flint was afraid of her. He dreaded her scorching rebukes. Moreover, she was known and patronized by many people; and he did not wish to have his villany made public. It was lucky for me that I did not live on a distant plantation, but in a town not so large that the inhabitants were ignorant of each other's affairs. Bad as are the laws and customs in a slaveholding community, the doctor, as a professional man, deemed it prudent to keep up some outward show of decency.

O, what days and nights of fear and sorrow that man caused me! Reader, it is not to awaken sympathy for myself that I am telling you truthfully what I suffered in slavery. I do it to kindle a flame of compassion in your hearts for my sisters who are still in bondage, suffering as I once suffered.

I once saw two beautiful children playing together. One was a fair white child; the other was her slave, and also her sister. When I saw them embracing each other, and heard their joyous laughter, I turned sadly away from the lovely sight. I foresaw the inevitable blight that would fall on the little slave's heart. I knew how soon her laughter would be changed to sighs. The fair child grew up to be a still fairer woman. From childhood to womanhood her pathway was blooming with flowers, and overarched by a sunny sky. Scarcely one day of her life had been clouded when the sun rose on her happy bridal morning.

How had those years dealt with her slave sister, the little playmate of her childhood? She, also, was very beautiful; but the flowers and sunshine of love were not for her. She drank the cup of sin, and shame, and misery, whereof her persecuted race are compelled to drink.

In view of these things, why are ye silent, ye free men and women of the north? Why do your tongues falter in maintenance of the right? Would that I had more ability! But my heart is so full, and my pen is so weak! There are noble men and women who plead for us, striving to help those who cannot help themselves. God bless them! God give them strength and courage to go on! God bless those, every where, who are laboring to advance the cause of humanity!

VI
The Jealous Mistress

I would ten thousand times rather that my children should be the half-starved paupers of Ireland than to be the most pampered among the slaves of America. I would rather drudge out my life on a cotton plantation, till the grave opened to give me rest, than to live with an unprincipled master and a jealous mistress. The felon's home in a penitentiary is preferable. He may repent, and turn from the error of his ways, and so find peace; but it is not so with a favorite slave. She is not allowed to have any pride of character. It is deemed a crime in her to wish to be virtuous.

Mrs. Flint possessed the key to her husband's character before I was born. She might have used this knowledge to counsel and to screen the young and the innocent among her slaves; but for them she had no sympathy. They were the objects of her constant suspicion and malevolence. She watched her husband with unceasing vigilance; but he was well practiced in means to evade it. What he could not find opportunity to say in words he manifested in signs. He invented more than were ever thought of in a deaf and dumb asylum. I let them pass, as if I did not understand what he meant; and many were the curses and threats bestowed on me for my stupidity. One day he caught me teaching myself to write. He frowned, as if he was not well pleased; but I suppose he came to the conclusion that such an accomplishment might help to advance his favorite

scheme. Before long, notes were often slipped into my hand. I would return them, saying, "I can't read them, sir." "Can't you?" he replied; "then I
must read them to you." He always finished the reading by asking, "Do
you understand?" Sometimes he would complain of the heat of the tea
room, and order his supper to be placed on a small table in the piazza. He
would seat himself there with a well-satisfied smile, and tell me to stand
by and brush away the flies. He would eat very slowly, pausing between
the mouthfuls. These intervals were employed in describing the happiness
I was so foolishly throwing away, and in threatening me with the penalty
that finally awaited my stubborn disobedience. He boasted much of the
forbearance he had exercised towards me, and reminded me that there
was a limit to his patience. When I succeeded in avoiding opportunities
for him to talk to me at home, I was ordered to come to his office, to do
some errand. When there, I was obliged to stand and listen to such language as he saw fit to address to me. Sometimes I so openly expressed my
contempt for him that he would become violently enraged, and I wondered why he did not strike me. Circumstanced as he was, he probably
thought it was better policy to be forbearing. But the state of things grew
worse and worse daily. In desperation I told him that I must and would
apply to my grandmother for protection. He threatened me with death,
and worse than death, if I made any complaint to her. Strange to say, I did
not despair. I was naturally of a buoyant disposition, and always I had a
hope of somehow getting out of his clutches. Like many a poor, simple
slave before me, I trusted that some threads of joy would yet be woven
into my dark destiny.

I had entered my sixteenth year, and every day it became more apparent that my presence was intolerable to Mrs. Flint. Angry words frequently passed between her and her husband. He had never punished me
himself, and he would not allow any body else to punish me. In that respect, she was never satisfied; but, in her angry moods, no terms were too
vile for her to bestow upon me. Yet I, whom she detested so bitterly, had
far more pity for her than he had, whose duty it was to make her life
happy. I never wronged her, or wished to wrong her; and one word of
kindness from her would have brought me to her feet.

After repeated quarrels between the doctor and his wife, he announced his intention to take his youngest daughter, then four years old,
to sleep in his apartment. It was necessary that a servant should sleep in
the same room, to be on hand if the child stirred. I was selected for that office, and informed for what purpose that arrangement had been made. By
managing to keep within sight of people, as much as possible, during the
day time, I had hitherto succeeded in eluding my master, though a [razor]
was often held to my throat to force me to change this line of policy. At
night I slept by the side of my great aunt, where I felt safe. He was too
prudent to come into her room. She was an old woman, and had been in
the family many years. Moreover, as a married man, and a professional
man, he deemed it necessary to save appearances in some degree. But he

resolved to remove the obstacle in the way of his scheme; and he thought he had planned it so that he should evade suspicion. He was well aware how much I prized my refuge by the side of my old aunt, and he determined to dispossess me of it. The first night the doctor had the little child in his room alone. The next morning, I was ordered to take my station as nurse the following night. A kind Providence interposed in my favor. During the day Mrs. Flint heard of this new arrangement, and a storm followed. I rejoiced to hear it rage.

After a while my mistress sent for me to come to her room. Her first question was, "Did you know you were to sleep in the doctor's room?"

"Yes, ma'am."

"Who told you?"

"My master."

"Will you answer truly all the questions I ask?"

"Yes, ma'am."

"Tell me, then, as you hope to be forgiven, are you innocent of what I have accused you?"

"I am."

She handed me a Bible, and said, "Lay your hand on your heart, kiss this holy book, and swear before God that you tell me the truth."

I took the oath she required, and I did it with a clear conscience.

"You have taken God's holy word to testify your innocence," said she. "If you have deceived me, beware! Now take this stool, sit down, look me directly in the face, and tell me all that has passed between your master and you."

I did as she ordered. As I went on with my account her color changed frequently, she wept, and sometimes groaned. She spoke in tones so sad, that I was touched by her grief. The tears came to my eyes; but I was soon convinced that her emotions arose from anger and wounded pride. She felt that her marriage vows were desecrated, her dignity insulted; but she had no compassion for the poor victim of her husband's perfidy. She pitied herself as a martyr; but she was incapable of feeling for the condition of shame and misery in which her unfortunate, helpless slave was placed.

Yet perhaps she had some touch of feeling for me; for when the conference was ended, she spoke kindly, and promised to protect me. I should have been much comforted by this assurance if I could have had confidence in it; but my experiences in slavery had filled me with distrust. She was not a very refined woman, and had not much control over her passions. I was an object of her jealousy, and, consequently, of her hatred; and I knew I could not expect kindness or confidence from her under the circumstances in which I was placed. I could not blame her. Slaveholders' wives feel as other women would under similar circumstances. The fire of her temper kindled from small sparks, and now the flame became so intense that the doctor was obliged to give up his intended arrangement.

I knew I had ignited the torch, and I expected to suffer for it afterwards; but I felt too thankful to my mistress for the timely aid she rendered me to care much about that. She now took me to sleep in a room adjoining her own. There I was an object of her especial care, though not of her especial comfort, for she spent many a sleepless night to watch over me. Sometimes I woke up, and found her bending over me. At other times she whispered in my ear, as though it was her husband who was speaking to me, and listened to hear what I would answer. If she startled me, on such occasions, she would glide stealthily away; and the next morning she would tell me I had been talking in my sleep, and ask who I was talking to. At last, I began to be fearful for my life. It had been often threatened; and you can imagine, better than I can describe, what an unpleasant sensation it must produce to wake up in the dead of night and find a jealous woman bending over you. Terrible as this experience was, I had fears that it would give place to one more terrible.

My mistress grew weary of her vigils; they did not prove satisfactory. She changed her tactics. She now tried the trick of accusing my master of crime, in my presence, and gave my name as the author of the accusation. To my utter astonishment, he replied, "I don't believe it; but if she did acknowledge it, you tortured her into exposing me." Tortured into exposing him! Truly, Satan had no difficulty in distinguishing the color of his soul! I understood his object in making this false representation. It was to show me that I gained nothing by seeking the protection of my mistress; that the power was still all in his own hands. I pitied Mrs. Flint. She was a second wife, many years the junior of her husband; and the hoary-headed miscreant was enough to try the patience of a wiser and better woman. She was completely foiled, and knew not how to proceed. She would gladly have had me flogged for my supposed false oath; but, as I have already stated, the doctor never allowed any one to whip me. The old sinner was politic. The application of the lash might have led to remarks that would have exposed him in the eyes of his children and grandchildren. How often did I rejoice that I lived in a town where all the inhabitants knew each other! If I had been on a remote plantation, or lost among the multitude of a crowded city, I should not be a living woman at this day.

The secrets of slavery are concealed like those of the Inquisition. My master was, to my knowledge, the father of eleven slaves. But did the mothers dare to tell who was the father of their children? Did the other slaves dare to allude to it, except in whispers among themselves? No, indeed! They knew too well the terrible consequences.

My grandmother could not avoid seeing things which excited her suspicions. She was uneasy about me, and tried various ways to buy me; but the never-changing answer was always repeated: "Linda does not belong to *me*. She is my daughter's property, and I have no legal right to sell her." The conscientious man! He was too scrupulous to *sell* me; but he had no scruples whatever about committing a much greater wrong against the helpless young girl placed under his guardianship, as his daughter's property. Sometimes my persecutor would ask me whether I would like to be sold. I told him I would rather be sold to any body than to lead such a life as I did. On such occasions he would assume the air of a very injured individual, and reproach me for my ingratitude. "Did I not take you into the house, and make you the companion of my own children?" he would say. "Have I ever treated you like a negro? I have never allowed you to be punished, not even to please your mistress. And this is the recompense I get, you ungrateful girl!" I answered that he had reasons of his own for screening me from punishment, and that the course he pursued made my mistress hate me and persecute me. If I wept, he would say, "Poor child! Don't cry! don't cry! I will make peace for you with your mistress. Only let me arrange matters in my own way. Poor, foolish girl! you don't know what is for your own good. I would cherish you. I would make a lady of you. Now go, and think of all I have promised you."

I did think of it.

Reader, I draw no imaginary pictures of southern homes. I am telling you the plain truth. Yet when victims make their escape from this wild beast of Slavery, northerners consent to act the part of bloodhounds, and hunt the poor fugitive back into his den, "full of dead men's bones, and all uncleanness." Nay, more, they are not only willing, but proud, to give their daughters in marriage to slaveholders. The poor girls have romantic notions of a sunny clime, and of the flowering vines that all the year round shade a happy home. To what disappointments are they destined! The young wife soon learns that the husband in whose hands she has placed her happiness pays no regard to his marriage vows. Children of every shade of complexion play with her own fair babies, and too well she knows that they are born unto him of his own household. Jealousy and hatred enter the flowery home, and it is ravaged of its loveliness.

Southern women often marry a man knowing that he is the father of many little slaves. They do not trouble themselves about it. They regard such children as property, as marketable as the pigs on the plantation; and it is seldom that they do not make them aware of this by passing them into the slave-trader's hands as soon as possible, and thus getting them out of their sight. I am glad to say there are some honorable exceptions.

I have myself known two southern wives who exhorted their husbands to free those slaves towards whom they stood in a "parental relation"; and their request was granted. These husbands blushed before the superior nobleness of their wives' natures. Though they had only counselled them to do that which it was their duty to do, it commanded their respect, and rendered their conduct more exemplary. Concealment was at an end, and confidence took the place of distrust.

Though this bad institution deadens the moral sense, even in white women, to a fearful extent, it is not altogether extinct. I have heard southern ladies say of Mr. Such a one, "He not only thinks it no disgrace to be the father of those little niggers, but he is not ashamed to call himself their master. I declare, such things ought not to be tolerated, in any decent society!"

VII
The Lover

Why does the slave ever love? Why allow the tendrils of the heart to twine around objects which may at any moment be wrenched away by the hand of violence? When separations come by the hand of death, the pious soul can bow in resignation, and say, "Not my will, but thine be done, O Lord!" But when the ruthless hand of man strikes the blow, regardless of the misery he causes, it is hard to be submissive. I did not reason thus when I was a young girl. Youth will be youth. I loved, and I indulged the hope that the dark clouds around me would turn out a bright lining. I forgot that in the land of my birth the shadows are too dense for light to penetrate. A land

> Where laughter is not mirth; nor thought the mind;
> Nor words a language; nor e'en men mankind.
> Where cries reply to curses, shrieks to blows,
> And each is tortured in his separate hell.

There was in the neighborhood a young colored carpenter; a free-born man. We had been well acquainted in childhood, and frequently met together afterwards. We became mutually attached, and he proposed to marry me. I loved him with all the ardor of a young girl's first love. But when I reflected that I was a slave, and that the laws gave no sanction to the marriage of such, my heart sank within me. My lover wanted to buy me; but I knew that Dr. Flint was too wilful and arbitrary a man to consent to that arrangement. From him, I was sure of experiencing all sorts of opposition, and I had nothing to hope from my mistress. She would have been delighted to have got rid of me, but not in that way. It would have relieved her mind of a burden if she could have seen me sold to some distant state, but if I was married near home I should be just as much in her husband's power as I had previously been,—for the husband of a slave has no power to protect her. Moreover, my mistress, like many others, seemed to think that slaves had no right to any family ties of their own; that they were created merely to wait upon the family of the mistress. I once heard her abuse a young slave girl, who told her that a colored man wanted to make her his wife. "I will have you peeled and pickled, my lady," said she, "if I ever hear you mention that subject again. Do you suppose that I will have you tending *my* children with the children of that nigger?" The girl to whom she said this had a mulatto child, of course not acknowledged by its father. The poor black man who loved her would have been proud to acknowledge his helpless offspring.

Many and anxious were the thoughts I revolved in my mind. I was at a loss what to do. Above all things, I was desirous to spare my lover the insults that had cut so deeply into my own soul. I talked with my grandmother about it, and partly told her my fears. I did not dare to tell her the worst. She had long suspected all was not right, and if I confirmed her suspicions I knew a storm would rise that would prove the overthrow of all my hopes.

This love-dream had been my support through many trials; and I could not bear to run the risk of having it suddenly dissipated. There was a lady in the neighborhood, a particular friend of Dr. Flint's, who often visited the house. I had a great respect for her, and she had always manifested a friendly interest in me. Grandmother thought she would have great influence with the doctor. I went to this lady, and told her my story. I told her I was aware that my lover's being a free-born man would prove a great objection; but he wanted to buy me; and if Dr. Flint would consent to that arrangement, I felt sure he would be willing to pay any reasonable price. She knew that Mrs. Flint disliked me; therefore, I ventured to suggest that perhaps my mistress would approve of my being sold, as that would rid her of me. The lady listened with kindly sympathy, and promised to do her utmost to promote my wishes. She had an interview with the doctor, and I believe she pleaded my cause earnestly; but it was all to no purpose.

How I dreaded my master now! Every minute I expected to be summoned to his presence; but the day passed, and I heard nothing from him. The next morning, a message was brought to me: "Master wants you in his study." I found the door ajar, and I stood a moment gazing at the hateful man who claimed a right to rule me, body and soul. I entered, and tried to appear calm. I did not want him to know how my heart was bleeding. He looked fixedly at me, with an expression which seemed to say, "I have half a mind to kill you on the spot." At last he broke the silence, and that was a relief to both of us.

"So you want to be married, do you?" said he, "and to a free nigger."

"Yes, sir."

"Well, I'll soon convince you whether I am your master, or the nigger fellow you honor so highly. If you *must* have a husband, you may take up with one of my slaves."

What a situation I should be in, as the wife of one of *his* slaves, even if my heart had been interested!

I replied, "Don't you suppose, sir, that a slave can have some preference about marrying? Do you suppose that all men are alike to her?"

"Do you love this nigger?" said he, abruptly.

"Yes, sir."

"How dare you tell me so!" he exclaimed, in great wrath. After a slight pause, he added, "I supposed you thought more of yourself; that you felt above the insults of such puppies."

I replied, "If he is a puppy I am a puppy, for we are both of the negro race. It is right and honorable for us to love each other. The man you call a puppy never insulted me, sir; and he would not love me if he did not believe me to be a virtuous woman."

He sprang upon me like a tiger, and gave me a stunning blow. It was the first time he had ever struck me; and fear did not enable me to control my anger. When I had recovered a little from the effects, I exclaimed, "You have struck me for answering you honestly. How I despise you!"

There was silence for some minutes. Perhaps he was deciding what should be my punishment; or, perhaps, he wanted to give me time to reflect on what I had said, and to whom I had said it. Finally, he asked, "Do you know what you have said?"

"Yes, sir; but your treatment drove me to it."

"Do you know that I have a right to do as I like with you,—that I can kill you, if I please?"

"You have tried to kill me, and I wish you had; but you have no right to do as you like with me."

"Silence!" he exclaimed, in a thundering voice. "By heavens, girl, you forget yourself too far! Are you mad? If you are, I will soon bring you to your senses. Do you think any other master would bear what I have borne from you this morning? Many masters would have killed you on the spot. How would you like to be sent to jail for your insolence?"

"I know I have been disrespectful, sir," I replied; "but you drove me to it; I couldn't help it. As for the jail, there would be more peace for me there than there is here."

"You deserve to go there," said he, "and to be under such treatment, that you would forget the meaning of the word *peace*. It would do you good. It would take some of your high notions out of you. But I am not ready to send you there yet, notwithstanding your ingratitude for all my kindness and forbearance. You have been the plague of my life. I have wanted to make you happy, and I have been repaid with the basest ingratitude; but though you have proved yourself incapable of appreciating my kindness, I will be lenient towards you, Linda. I will give you one more chance to redeem your character. If you behave yourself and do as I require, I will forgive you and treat you as I always have done; but if you disobey me, I will punish you as I would the meanest slave on my plantation. Never let me hear that fellow's name mentioned again. If I ever know of your speaking to him, I will cowhide you both; and if I catch him lurking about my premises, I will shoot him as soon as I would a dog. Do you hear what I say? I'll teach you a lesson about marriage and free niggers! Now go, and let this be the last time I have occasion to speak to you on this subject."

Reader, did you ever hate? I hope not. I never did but once; and I trust I never shall again. Somebody has called it "the atmosphere of hell"; and I believe it is so.

For a fortnight the doctor did not speak to me. He thought to mortify me; to make me feel that I had disgraced myself by receiving the honorable addresses of a respectable colored man, in preference to the base proposals of a white man. But though his lips disdained to address me, his eyes were very loquacious. No animal ever watched its prey more narrowly than he watched me. He knew that I could write, though he had failed to make me read his letters; and he was now troubled lest I should exchange letters with another man. After a while he became weary of silence; and I was sorry for it. One morning, as he passed through the hall, to leave the house, he contrived to thrust a note into my hand. I thought I had better read it, and spare myself the vexation of having him read it to me. It expressed regret for the blow he had given me, and reminded me that I myself was wholly to blame for it. He hoped I had become convinced of the injury I was doing myself by incurring his displeasure. He wrote that he had made up his mind to go to Louisiana; that he should take several slaves with him, and intended I should be one of the number. My mistress would remain where she was; therefore I should have nothing to fear from that quarter. If I merited kindness from him, he assured me that it would be lavishly bestowed. He begged me to think over the matter, and answer the following day.

The next morning I was called to carry a pair of scissors to his room. I laid them on the table, with the letter beside them. He thought it was my answer, and did not call me back. I went as usual to attend my young mistress to and from school. He met me in the street, and ordered me to stop at his office on my way back. When I entered, he showed me his letter, and asked me why I had not answered it. I replied, "I am your daughter's property, and it is in your power to send me, or take me, wherever you please." He said he was very glad to find me so willing to go, and that we should start early in the autumn. He had a large practice in the town, and I rather thought he had made up the story merely to frighten me. However that might be, I was determined that I would never go to Louisiana with him.

Summer passed away, and early in the autumn Dr. Flint's eldest son was sent to Louisiana to examine the country, with a view to emigrating. That news did not disturb me. I knew very well that I should not be sent with *him*. That I had not been taken to the plantation before this time, was owing to the fact that his son was there. He was jealous of his son; and jealousy of the overseer had kept him from punishing me by sending me into the fields to work. Is it strange that I was not proud of these protectors? As for the overseer, he was a man for whom I had less respect than I had for a bloodhound.

Young Mr. Flint did not bring back a favorable report of Louisiana, and I heard no more of that scheme. Soon after this, my lover met me at the corner of the street, and I stopped to speak to him. Looking up, I saw my master watching us from his window. I hurried home, trembling with fear. I was sent for, immediately, to go to his room. He met me with a blow. "When is mistress to be married?" said he, in a sneering tone. A shower of oaths and imprecations followed. How thankful I was that my lover was a free man! that my tyrant had no power to flog him for speaking to me in the street!

Again and again I revolved in my mind how all this would end. There was no hope that the doctor would consent to sell me on any terms. He had an iron will, and was determined to keep me, and to conquer me. My lover was an intelligent and religious man. Even if he could have obtained permission to marry me while I was a slave, the marriage would give him no power to protect me from my master. It would have made him miserable to witness the insults I should have been subjected to. And then, if we had children, I knew they must "follow the condition of the mother." What a terrible blight that would be on the heart of a free, intelligent father! For *his* sake, I felt that I ought not to link his fate with my own unhappy destiny. He was going to Savannah to see about a little property left him by an uncle; and hard as it was to bring my feelings to it, I earnestly entreated him not to come back. I advised him to go to the Free States, where his tongue would not be tied, and where his intelligence would be of more avail to him. He left me, still hoping the day would come when I could be bought. With me the lamp of hope had gone out. The dream of my girlhood was over. I felt lonely and desolate.

Still I was not stripped of all. I still had my good grandmother, and my affectionate brother. When he put his arms round my neck, and looked into my eyes, as if to read there the troubles I dared not tell, I felt that I still had something to love. But even that pleasant emotion was chilled by the reflection that he might be torn from me at any moment, by some sudden freak of my master. If he had known how we loved each other, I think he would have exulted in separating us. We often planned together how we could get to the north. But, as William remarked, such things are easier said than done. My movements were very closely watched, and we had no means of getting any money to defray our expenses. As for grandmother, she was strongly opposed to her children's undertaking any such project. She had not forgotten poor Benjamin's sufferings, and she was afraid that if another child tried to escape, he would have a similar or a worse fate. To me, nothing seemed more dreadful than my present life. I said to myself, "William *must* be free. He shall go to the north, and I will follow him." Many a slave sister has formed the same plans. . . .

X
A Perilous Passage in the Slave Girl's Life

After my lover went away, Dr. Flint contrived a new plan. He seemed to have an idea that my fear of my mistress was his greatest obstacle. In the blandest tones, he told me that he was going to build a small house for me, in a secluded place, four miles away from the town. I shuddered; but I was constrained to listen, while he talked of his intention to give me a home of my own, and to make a lady of me. Hitherto, I had escaped my dreaded fate, by being in the midst of people. My grandmother had already had high words with my master about me. She had told him pretty plainly what she thought of his character, and there was considerable gossip in the neighborhood about our affairs, to which the open-mouthed jealousy of Mrs. Flint contributed not a little. When my master said he was going to build a house for me, and that he could do it with little trouble and expense, I was in hopes something would happen to frustrate his scheme; but I soon heard that the house was actually begun. I vowed before my Maker that I would never enter it. I had rather toil on the plantation from dawn till dark; I had rather live and die in jail, than drag on, from day to day, through such a living death. I was determined that the master, whom I so hated and loathed, who had blighted the prospects of my youth, and made my life a desert, should not, after my long struggle with him, succeed at last in trampling his victim under his feet. I would do any thing, every thing, for the sake of defeating him. What *could* I do? I thought and thought, till I became desperate, and made a plunge into the abyss.

And now, reader, I come to a period in my unhappy life, which I would gladly forget if I could. The remembrance fills me with sorrow and shame. It pains me to tell you of it; but I have promised to tell you the truth, and I will do it honestly, let it cost me what it may. I will not try to screen myself behind the plea of compulsion from a master; for it was not so. Neither can I plead ignorance or thoughtlessness. For years, my master had done his utmost to pollute my mind with foul images, and to destroy the pure principles inculcated by my grandmother, and the good mistress of my childhood. The influences of slavery had had the same effect on me that they had on other young girls; they had made me prematurely knowing, concerning the evil ways of the world. I knew what I did, and I did it with deliberate calculation.

But, O, ye happy women, whose purity has been sheltered from childhood, who have been free to choose the objects of your affection, whose homes are protected by law, do not judge the poor desolate slave girl too severely! If slavery had been abolished, I, also, could have married the man of my choice; I could have had a home shielded by the laws; and I should have been spared the painful task of confessing what I am now about to relate; but all my prospects had been blighted by slavery. I wanted to keep myself pure; and, under the most adverse circumstances, I tried hard to preserve my self-respect; but I was struggling alone in the powerful grasp of the demon Slavery; and the monster proved too strong for me. I felt as if I was forsaken by God and man; as if all my efforts must be frustrated; and I became reckless in my despair.

I have told you that Dr. Flint's persecutions and his wife's jealousy had given rise to some gossip in the neighborhood. Among others, it chanced that a white unmarried gentleman had obtained some knowledge of the circumstances in which I was placed. He knew my grandmother, and often spoke to me in the street. He became interested for me, and asked questions about my master, which I answered in part. He expressed a great deal of sympathy, and a wish to aid me. He constantly sought opportunities to see me, and wrote to me frequently. I was a poor slave girl, only fifteen years old.

So much attention from a superior person was, of course, flattering; for human nature is the same in all. I also felt grateful for his sympathy, and encouraged by his kind words. It seemed to me a great thing to have such a friend. By degrees, a more tender feeling crept into my heart. He was an educated and eloquent gentleman; too eloquent, alas, for the poor slave girl who trusted in him. Of course I saw whither all this was tending. I knew the impassable gulf between us; but to be an object of interest to a man who is not married, and who is not her master, is agreeable to the pride and feelings of a slave, if her miserable situation has left her any pride or sentiment. It seems less degrading to give one's self, than to submit to compulsion. There is something akin to freedom in having a lover who has no control over you, except that which he gains by kindness and attachment. A master may treat you as rudely as he pleases, and you dare not speak; moreover, the wrong does not seem so great with an unmarried man, as with one who has a wife to be made unhappy. There may be sophistry in all this; but the condition of a slave confuses all principles of morality, and, in fact, renders the practice of them impossible.

When I found that my master had actually begun to build the lonely cottage, other feelings mixed with those I have described. Revenge, and calculations of interest, were added to flattered vanity and sincere gratitude for kindness. I knew nothing would enrage Dr. Flint so much as to know that I favored another; and it was something to triumph over my tyrant even in that small way. I thought he would revenge himself by selling me, and I was sure my friend, Mr. Sands, would buy me. He was a man of more generosity and feeling than my master, and I thought my freedom could be easily obtained from him. The crisis of my fate now came so near that I was desperate. I shuddered to think of being the mother of children that should be owned by my old tyrant. I knew that as soon as a new fancy took him, his victims were sold far off to get rid of them; especially if they had children. I had seen several women sold, with his babies at the breast. He never allowed his offspring by slaves to remain long in sight of himself and his wife. Of a man who was not my master I could ask to have my children well supported; and in this case, I felt confident I should obtain the boon. I also felt quite sure that they would be made free. With all these thoughts revolving in my mind, and seeing no other way of escaping the doom I so much dreaded, I made a headlong plunge. Pity me, and pardon me, O virtuous reader! You never knew what it is to be a slave; to be entirely unprotected by law or custom; to have the laws reduce you to the condition of a chattel, entirely subject to the will of another. You never exhausted your ingenuity in avoiding the snares, and eluding the power of a hated tyrant; you never shuddered at the sound of his footsteps, and trembled within hearing of his voice. I know I did wrong. No one can feel it more sensibly than I do. The painful and humiliating memory will haunt me to my dying day. Still, in looking back, calmly, on the events of my life, I feel that the slave woman ought not to be judged by the same standard as others.

The months passed on. I had many unhappy hours. I secretly mourned over the sorrow I was bringing on my grandmother, who had so tried to shield me from harm. I knew that I was the greatest comfort of her old age, and that it was a source of pride to her that I had not degraded myself, like most of the slaves. I wanted to confess to her that I was no longer worthy of her love; but I could not utter the dreaded words.

As for Dr. Flint, I had a feeling of satisfaction and triumph in the thought of telling *him.* From time to time he told me of his intended arrangements, and I was silent. At last, he came and told me the cottage was completed, and ordered me to go to it. I told him I would never enter it. He said, "I have heard enough of such talk as that. You shall go, if you are carried by force; and you shall remain there."

I replied, "I will never go there. In a few months I shall be a mother."

He stood and looked at me in dumb amazement, and left the house without a word. I thought I should be happy in my triumph over him. But now that the truth was out, and my relatives would hear of it, I felt wretched. Humble as were their circumstances, they had pride in my good character. Now, how could I look them in the face? My self-respect was gone! I had resolved that I would be virtuous, though I was a slave. I had said, "Let the storm beat! I will brave it till I die." And now, how humiliated I felt!

I went to my grandmother. My lips moved to make confession, but the words stuck in my throat. I sat down in the shade of a tree at her door and began to sew. I think she saw something unusual was the matter with me. The mother of slaves is very watchful. She knows there is no security for her children. After they have entered their teens she lives in daily expectation of trouble. This leads to many questions. If the girl is of a sensitive nature, timidity keeps her from answering truthfully, and this well-meant course has a tendency to drive her from maternal counsels. Presently, in came my mistress, like a mad woman, and accused me concerning her husband. My grandmother, whose suspicions had been previously awakened, believed what she said. She exclaimed, "O Linda! has it come to this? I had rather see you dead than to see you as you now are. You are a disgrace to your dead mother." She tore from my fingers my mother's wedding ring and her silver thimble. "Go away!" she exclaimed, "and never come to my house again." Her reproaches fell so hot and heavy, that they left me no chance to answer. Bitter tears, such as the eyes never shed but once, were my only answer. I rose from my seat, but fell back again, sobbing. She did not speak to me; but the tears were running down her furrowed cheeks, and they scorched me like fire. She had always been so kind to me! *So* kind! How I longed to throw myself at her feet, and tell her all the truth! But she had ordered me to go, and never to come there again. After a few minutes, I mustered strength, and started to obey her. With what feelings did I now close that little gate, which I used to open with such an eager hand in my childhood! It closed upon me with a sound I never heard before.

Where could I go? I was afraid to return to my master's. I walked on recklessly, not caring where I went, or what would become of me. When I had gone four or five miles, fatigue compelled me to stop. I sat down on the stump of an old tree. The stars were shining through the boughs above me. How they mocked me, with their bright, calm light! The hours passed by, and as I sat there alone a chilliness and deadly sickness came over me. I sank on the ground. My mind was full of horrid thoughts. I prayed to die; but the prayer was not answered. At last, with great effort I roused myself, and walked some distance further, to the house of a woman who had been a friend of my mother. When I told her why I was there, she spoke soothingly to me; but I could not be comforted. I thought I could bear my shame if I could only be reconciled to my grandmother. I longed to open my heart to her. I thought if she could know the real state of the case, and all I had been bearing for years, she would perhaps judge me less harshly. My friend advised me to send for her. I did so; but days of agonizing suspense passed before she came. Had she utterly forsaken me? No. She came at last. I knelt before her, and told her the things that had poisoned my life; how long I had been persecuted; that I saw no way of escape; and in an hour of extremity I had become desperate. She listened in silence. I told her I would bear any thing and do any thing, if in time I had hopes of obtaining her forgiveness. I begged of her to pity me, for my dead mother's sake. And she did pity me. She did not say, "I forgive you"; but she looked at me lovingly, with her eyes full of tears. She laid her old hand gently on my head, and murmured, "Poor child! Poor child!"

XI
The New Tie to Life

I returned to my good grandmother's house. She had an interview with Mr. Sands. When she asked him why he could not have left her one ewe lamb,—whether there were not plenty of slaves who did not care about character,—he made no answer; but he spoke kind and encouraging words. He promised to care for my child, and to buy me, be the conditions what they might.

I had not seen Dr. Flint for five days. I had never seen him since I made the avowal to him. He talked of the disgrace I had brought on myself; how I had sinned against my master, and mortified my old grandmother. He intimated that if I had accepted his proposals, he, as a physician, could have saved me from exposure. He even condescended to pity me. Could he have offered wormwood more bitter? He, whose persecutions had been the cause of my sin!

"Linda," said he, "though you have been criminal towards me, I feel for you, and I can pardon you if you obey my wishes. Tell me whether the fellow you wanted to marry is the father of your child. If you deceive me, you shall feel the fires of hell."

I did not feel as proud as I had done. My strongest weapon with him was gone. I was lowered in my own estimation, and had resolved to bear his abuse in silence. But when he spoke contemptuously of the lover who had always treated me honorably; when I remembered that but for *him* I might have been a virtuous, free, and happy wife, I lost my patience. "I have sinned against God and myself," I replied; "but not against you."

He clinched his teeth, and muttered, "Curse you!" He came towards me, with ill-suppressed rage, and exclaimed, "You obstinate girl! I could grind your bones to powder! You have thrown yourself away on some worthless rascal. You are weak-minded, and have been easily persuaded by those who don't care a straw for you. The future will settle accounts between us. You are blinded now; but hereafter you will be convinced that your master was your best friend. My lenity towards you is a proof of it. I might have punished you in many ways. I might have had you whipped till you fell dead under the lash. But I wanted you to live; I would have bettered your condition. Others cannot do it. You are my slave. Your mistress, disgusted by your conduct, forbids you to return to the house; therefore I leave you here for the present; but I shall see you often. I will call tomorrow."

He came with frowning brows, that showed a dissatisfied state of mind. After asking about my health, he inquired whether my board was paid, and who visited me. He then went on to say that he had neglected his duty; that as a physician there were certain things that he ought to have explained to me. Then followed talk such as would have made the most shameless blush. He ordered me to stand up before him. I obeyed. "I command you," said he, "to tell me whether the father of your child is white or black." I hesitated. "Answer me this instant!" he exclaimed. I did answer. He sprang upon me like a wolf, and grabbed my arm as if he would have broken it. "Do you love him?" said he, in a hissing tone.

"I am thankful that I do not despise him," I replied.

He raised his hand to strike me; but it fell again. I don't know what arrested the blow. He sat down, with lips tightly compressed. At last he spoke. "I came here," said he, "to make you a friendly proposition; but your ingratitude chafes me beyond endurance. You turn aside all my good intentions towards you. I don't know what it is that keeps me from killing you." Again he rose, as if he had a mind to strike me.

But he resumed. "On one condition I will forgive your insolence and crime. You must henceforth have no communication of any kind with the father of your child. You must not ask any thing from him, or receive any thing from him. I will take care of you and your child. You had better promise this at once, and not wait till you are deserted by him. This is the last act of mercy I shall show towards you."

I said something about being unwilling to have my child supported by a man who had cursed it and me also. He rejoined, that a woman who had sunk to my level had no right to expect any thing else. He asked, for the last time, would I accept his kindness? I answered that I would not.

"Very well," said he; "then take the consequences of your wayward course. Never look to me for help. You are my slave, and shall always be my slave. I will never sell you, that you may depend upon."

Hope died away in my heart as he closed the door after him. I had calculated that in his rage he would sell me to a slave-trader; and I knew the father of my child was on the watch to buy me.

About this time my uncle Phillip was expected to return from a voyage. The day before his departure I had officiated as bridesmaid to a young friend. My heart was then ill at ease, but my smiling countenance did not betray it. Only a year had passed; but what fearful changes it had wrought! My heart had grown gray in misery. Lives that flash in sunshine, and lives that are born in tears, receive their hue from circumstances. None of us know what a year may bring forth.

I felt no joy when they told me my uncle had come. He wanted to see me, though he knew what had happened. I shrank from him at first; but at last consented that he should come to my room. He received me as he always had done. O, how my heart smote me when I felt his tears on my burning cheeks! The words of my grandmother came to my mind,—"Perhaps your mother and father are taken from the evil days to come." My disappointed heart could now praise God that it was so. But why, thought I, did my relatives ever cherish hopes for me? What was there to save me from the usual fate of slave girls? Many more beautiful and more intelligent than I had experienced a similar fate, or a far worse one. How could they hope that I should escape?

My uncle's stay was short, and I was not sorry for it. I was too ill in mind and body to enjoy my friends as I had done. For some weeks I was unable to leave my bed. I could not have any doctor but my master, and I would not have him sent for. At last, alarmed by my increasing illness, they sent for him. I was very weak and nervous; and as soon as he entered the room, I began to scream. They told him my state was very critical. He had no wish to hasten me out of the world, and he withdrew.

When my babe was born, they said it was premature. It weighed only four pounds; but God let it live. I heard the doctor say I could not survive till morning. I had often prayed for death; but now I did not want to die, unless my child could die too. Many weeks passed before I was able to leave my bed. I was a mere wreck of my former self. For a year there was scarcely a day when I was free from chills and fever. My babe also was sickly. His little limbs were often racked with pain. Dr. Flint continued his visits, to look after my health; and he did not fail to remind me that my child was an addition to his stock of slaves.

I felt too feeble to dispute with him, and listened to his remarks in silence. His visits were less frequent; but his busy spirit could not remain quiet. He employed my brother in his office, and he was made the medium of frequent notes and messages to me. William was a bright lad, and of much use to the doctor. He had learned to put up medicines, to leech, cup, and bleed. He had taught himself to read and spell. I was proud of my brother; and the old doctor suspected as much. One day, when I had not seen him for several weeks, I heard his steps approaching the door. I dreaded the encounter, and hid myself. He inquired for me, of course; but I was nowhere to be found. He went to his office, and despatched William with a note. The color mounted to my brother's face when he gave it to me; and he said, "Don't you hate me, Linda, for bringing you these things?" I told him I could not blame him; he was a slave, and obliged to obey his master's will. The note ordered me to come to his office. I went. He demanded to know where I was when he called. I told him I was at home. He flew into a passion, and said he knew better. Then he launched out upon his usual themes,—my crimes against him, and my ingratitude for his forbearance. The laws were laid down to me anew, and I was dismissed. I felt humiliated that my brother should stand by, and listen to such language as would be addressed only to a slave. Poor boy! He was powerless to defend me; but I saw the tears, which he vainly strove to keep back. This manifestation of feeling irritated the doctor. William could do nothing to please him. One morning he did not arrive at the office so early as usual; and that circumstance afforded his master an opportunity to vent his spleen. He was put in jail. The next day my brother sent a trader to the doctor, with a request to be sold. His master was greatly incensed at what he called his insolence. He said he had put him there to reflect upon his bad conduct, and he certainly was not giving any evidence of repentance. For two days he harassed himself to find somebody to do his office work; but every thing went wrong without William. He was released, and ordered to take his old stand, with many threats, if he was not careful about his future behavior.

As the months passed on, my boy improved in health. When he was a year old, they called him beautiful. The little vine was taking deep root in my existence, though its clinging fondness excited a mixture of love and pain. When I was most sorely oppressed I found a solace in his smiles. I loved to watch his infant slumbers; but always there was a dark cloud over my enjoyment. I could never forget that he was a slave. Sometimes I wished that he might die in infancy. God tried me. My darling became very ill. The bright eyes grew dull, and the little feet and hands were so icy cold that I thought death had already touched them. I had prayed for his death, but never so earnestly as I now prayed for his life; and my prayer was heard. Alas, what mockery it is for a slave mother to try to pray back her dying child to life! Death is better than slavery. It was a sad thought that I had no name to give my child. His father caressed him and treated him kindly, whenever he had a chance to see him. He was not unwilling that he should bear his name; but he had no legal claim to it; and if I had bestowed it upon him, my master would have regarded it as a new crime, a new piece of insolence, and would, perhaps, revenge it on the boy. O, the serpent of Slavery has many and poisonous fangs!

• • • • • • • • • • • •

QUESTIONS FOR A SECOND READING

1. This text makes it difficult to say what we are prepared to say: that slaves were illiterate, uneducated, simple in their speech and thought. Jacobs's situation was not typical, to be sure, but she challenges the assumptions we bring to our imagination of this country's past and its people. This text has to be read carefully or it becomes familiar, a product of what we think we already know.

   As you reread, mark sentences or phrases or paragraphs you might use to illustrate Jacobs's characteristic style or skill as a writer. And mark those features of the text you might use to identify this text as the work of a woman held in slavery. Where and how is doing this difficult? surprising? a problem?

2. In her preface, Jacobs says that she doesn't care to excite sympathy for her suffering but to "arouse the women of the North to a realizing sense of the condition of two millions of women at the South." As you reread this selection, pay attention to the ways Jacobs addresses (and tries to influence) her readers. Why would she be suspicious of sympathy? What do you suppose she might have meant by "a realizing sense"? What kind of reader does she want? Why does she address women?

   Be sure to mark those sections that address the reader directly, and also those that seem to give evidence of Jacobs as a writer, working on the material, highlighting some incidents and passing over others (why do we get "incidents" and not the full story?), organizing our experience of the text, shaping scenes and sentences, organizing chapters. What is Jacobs doing in this text? What might her work as a writer have to do with her position (as a female slave) in relation to the world of her readers?

3. The emotional and family relations between people are difficult to chart in this selection, partly because they defy easy categorization. Can we, for example, assume that blacks and whites lived separately? that blacks were in bondage and whites were free? that family lines and color lines were distinct markers? that lovers were lovers and enemies were enemies? As you reread, pay close attention to the ways people are organized by family, love, community, and color. See what you can determine about the codes that govern relations in this representation of slave culture. And ask where and how Jacobs places herself in these various networks.

ASSIGNMENTS FOR WRITING

1. In the preface to her edition of *Incidents in the Life of a Slave Girl,* Jean Fagin Yellin says the following about Jacobs's narrative:

   > Contrasting literary styles express the contradictory thrusts of the story. Presenting herself as a heroic slave mother, Jacobs's narrator includes clear detail, uses straightforward language, and when

addressing the reader directly, utilizes standard abolitionist rhetoric to lament the inadequacy of her descriptions and to urge her audience to involve themselves in antislavery efforts. But she treats her sexual experiences obliquely, and when addressing the reader concerning her sexual behavior, pleads for forgiveness in the overwrought style of popular fiction. These melodramatic confessions are, however, subsumed within the text. What finally dominates is a new voice. It is the voice of a woman who, although she cannot discuss her sexual past without expressing deep conflict, nevertheless addresses this painful personal subject in order to politicize it, to insist that the forbidden topic of the sexual abuse of slave women be included in public discussions of the slavery question. By creating a narrator who presents her private sexual history as a subject of public political concern, Jacobs moves her book out of the world of conventional nineteenth-century polite discourse. In and through her creation of Linda Brent, who yokes her success story as a heroic slave mother to her confession as a woman who mourns that she is not a storybook heroine, Jacobs articulates her struggle to assert her womanhood and projects a new kind of female hero.

Yellin's account of the "voice" in Jacobs's text gives us a way to foreground the difference between life and narrative, a person (Harriet Jacobs) and a person rendered on the page ("Linda Brent," the "I" of the narrative), between the experience of slavery and the conventional ways of telling the story of slavery, between experience and the ways in which experience is shaped by a writer, readers, and a culture. It is interesting, in this sense, to read Yellin's account of *Incidents* along with Houston Baker's more general account of the "voice of the Southern slave" (quoted at length on p. 427). Baker, you may recall, said: "The voice of the unwritten self, once it is subjected to the linguistic codes, literary conventions, and audience expectations of a literate population, is perhaps never again the authentic voice of black American slavery. It is, rather, the voice of a self transformed by an autobiographical act into a sharer in the general public discourse about slavery."

Jacobs's situation as a writer could be said to reproduce her position as a slave, cast as a member of the community but not as a person. Write an essay in which you examine Jacobs's work as a writer. Consider the ways she works on her reader (a figure she both imagines and constructs) and also the ways she works on her material (a set of experiences, a language, and the conventional ways of telling the story of one's life). To do this, you will need to reread the text as something constructed (see the second "Question for a Second Reading").

2. We can take these opening chapters of *Incidents in the Life of a Slave Girl* as an account of a girl's coming of age, particularly in the sense that coming of age is a cultural (and not simply a biological) process. The chapters represent the ways in which Jacobs comes to be positioned as a woman in the community, and they represent her understanding of that process (and the necessary limits to her understanding, since no person can stand completely outside her culture and what it desires her to believe or to take as natural).

Read back through *Incidents*, paying particular attention to what Jacobs sees as the imposed structure of slave culture and what she takes as part of human nature. Remember that there are different ways of reading the codes that govern human relations. What Jacobs takes to be unnatural may well seem natural to Dr. Flint. Jacobs could be said to be reading "against" what Flint, or the Slave Owner as a generic type, would understand as naturally there.

Now read through again, this time reading against Jacobs, to see how her view of relationships could be said to be shaped also by a set of beliefs and interests. Look for a system governing Jacobs's understanding. You might ask, for instance, what system leads her to see Dr. Flint and Mr. Sands as different, since they could also be said to be similar—both slave owners, both after the same thing. How does Jacobs place herself in relation to other slaves? other blacks? Jacobs is light skinned. How does she fit into a system governed by color? Both Mrs. Flint and her grandmother react strongly to Jacobs. What system governs Jacobs's sense of the difference between these two women?

Write an essay in which you try to explain the codes that govern the relations between people in slave culture, at least as that culture is represented in "Incidents."

MAKING CONNECTIONS

1. Alice Walker's reading of the history of African American women in her essay, "In Search of Our Mothers' Gardens" (p. 739), pays particular attention to the "creative spirit" of these women in the face of oppressive working and living conditions. Of her mother, Walker writes:

   > Her face, as she prepares the Art that is her gift, is a legacy of respect she leaves to me, for all that illuminates and cherishes life. She has handed down respect for the possibilities—and the will to grasp them.
   > (p. 746)

   And to the poet Phillis Wheatley she writes: "It is not so much what you sang, as that you kept alive, in so many of our ancestors, *the notion of song*" (p. 743).

   Although Walker does not include Harriet Jacobs in her essay, one could imagine ways in which Jacobs's work as a writer is appropriate to Walker's discussion of African American women's creativity. As you reread Jacobs's selection, note the choices she makes as a writer: her language, her selection of incidents and details, her method of addressing an audience, the ways in which she negotiates a white literary tradition. Where, for instance, do you see her writing purposely negotiating a literary tradition that is not hers? Who does she imagine as her audience? How does she use language differently for different purposes? Why?

   How would you say that the writerly choices Jacobs makes and enacts allow her to express a creativity that otherwise would have been stifled? What type of legacy does she create in her narrative to pass on to her descendants? And, as Walker writes in honor of her mother and Wheatley, what might Walker or you write in honor of Jacobs?

   Write an essay in which you extend Walker's project by considering where and how Jacobs's work as a writer and artist would complement

Walker's argument for the "creative spirit" of African American women in the face of oppressive conditions.

2. In "When We Dead Awaken: Writing as Re-Vision" (p. 627), Adrienne Rich says, "Re-vision—the act of looking back, of seeing with fresh eyes, of entering an old text from a new critical direction—is for women more than a chapter in cultural history: it is an act of survival. Until we can understand the assumptions in which we are drenched we cannot know ourselves" (p. 629).

   Let's imagine that one of the difficulties we have in reading *Incidents* is that we approach it drenched in assumptions; we look with old eyes (or the wrong eyes). In honor of the challenge Rich sets for a reader—or, for that matter, in honor of Harriet Jacobs and the challenge she sets for a reader—write an essay in which you show what it would mean to revise your reading (or what you take to be most people's reading, the "common" reading) of *Incidents*. You will want to show both how the text would be read from this new critical direction and what effort (or method) would be involved in pushing against the old ways of reading.

3. Here, from "Arts of the Contact Zone" (p. 605), is Mary Louise Pratt on the "autoethnographic" text:

   > Guaman Poma's *New Chronicle* is an instance of what I have proposed to call an *autoethnographic* text, by which I mean a text in which people undertake to describe themselves in ways that engage with representations others have made of them. Thus if ethnographic texts are those in which European metropolitan subjects represent to themselves their others (usually their conquered others), autoethnographic texts are representations that the so-defined others construct *in response to* or in dialogue with those texts. . . . [T]hey involve a selective collaboration with and appropriation of idioms of the metropolis or the conqueror. These are merged or infiltrated to varying degrees with indigenous idioms to create self-representations intended to intervene in metropolitan modes of understanding. . . . Such texts often constitute a marginalized group's point of entry into the dominant circuits of print culture. It is interesting to think, for example, of American slave autobiography in its autoethnographic dimensions, which in some respects distinguish it from Euramerican autobiographical tradition. (pp. 608–09)

   Reread Jacobs's "Incidents in the Life of a Slave Girl" after reading Pratt's essay. Using the example of Pratt's work with the *New Chronicle*, write an essay in which you present a reading of Jacobs's text as an example of an autoethnographic and/or transcultural text. You should imagine that you are working to put Pratt's ideas to the test, but also to see what you can say on your own about *Incidents* as a text, as something written and read.

Memorial→ what we don't want to forget

Monument→ what we want to remember. *if* leader washing,

article

[Handwritten notes at top of page:]

- pop culture reduce complexity of ~~the~~ complx (victim/busnx) into momentary symbol
- history → narrative (beg, mid, end) temporal } both build consensus create consensus
- monument/mem. → static symbol

PATRICIA NELSON LIMERICK

[Handwritten notes:]

- multiple perspectives retelling history
- history is messy diff. narratives.

PATRICIA NELSON LIMERICK (b. 1951) is one of this country's most influential historians. She is certainly one of the most visible, with appearances on national radio and television and even a profile in People magazine. Limerick is a revisionist historian, revising the usual stories we tell of the American West (stories of open spaces, cowboys and Indians, the frontier, progress, our Manifest Destiny). These stories, she says, have a persistent power over the American imagination, affecting everything from movies and books to federal land management, the space program, and American foreign policy. Generations of Americans, she says, in a characteristically memorable formulation, grew up playing cowboys and Indians, while it was impossible to play masters and slaves. And the reason, she argues, is that southern historians did their job well and western historians did not. The West, as she defines it, was not an empty place but a meeting ground. The movement west was not a simple story of progress, of taming the frontier, but a complicated story of conquest and negotiation.

Limerick did her undergraduate work at the University of California at Santa Cruz and received her M.A. and Ph.D. from Yale University. She taught at Harvard University before moving to her current position as a professor of history and chair of the Center of the American West at the University of Colorado, Boulder. Her major work is her book The Legacy of Conquest: The Unbroken Past of the American West (1987). She is also the author of Desert Passages:

Encounters with the American Deserts *(1985)*, The Real West *(1996)*, and
Something in the Soil: Legacies and Reckonings in the New West *(2000)*.
She is coeditor of A Society to Match the Scenery *(1991)*, Trails: Toward a
New Western History *(1991)*, and One Foot on the Rockies: Women and
Creativity in the Modern American West *(with Joan M. Jensen, 1995)*, and
she wrote the text for Sweet Medicine: Sites of Indian Massacres, Battle-
fields, and Treaties *(photographs by Drex Brooks, 1995). In 1995, she was
named a fellow by the MacArthur Foundation.*

    *As a historian, Limerick is redirecting her profession's attention to the Ameri-
can West and changing the terms that govern the conception of its history. Her
ambitions, however, extend beyond the academy. Her work is "popular" in a way
that much of the work of academic historians is not. It has been her mission, in
fact, to speak to a broad constituency, not only meetings of historians, but the
Western Governors Association, the Western Association of Fish and Wildlife
Agencies, the Bureau of Land Management, the Society of American Foresters,
the International High-Level Radioactive Waste Management Conference, the
Colorado County Commissioners, and the National Conference of State Legisla-
tures. Her work is directed at changing the way Americans think—not only about
the past but about the present. And, unlike that of many contemporary intellectuals, Limerick's thinking is hopeful, utopian. This is the final paragraph of* The
Legacy of Conquest:

> *When Anglo-Americans look across the Mexican border or into an In-
> dian reservation, they are more likely to see stereotypes than recogniz-
> able individuals or particular groups; the same distortion of vision no
> doubt works the other way too. The unitary character known as "the
> white man" has never existed, nor has "the Indian." Yet the phrases
> receive constant use, as if they carried necessary meaning. Indians,
> Hispanics, Asians, Blacks, Anglos, businesspeople, workers, politi-
> cians, bureaucrats, natives, and newcomers, we share the same region
> and its history, but we wait to be introduced. The serious exploration
> of the historical process that made us neighbors provides that intro-
> duction.*

*The "serious exploration of the historical process" for Limerick, as you will see,
involves a serious attention to reading and writing. In this sense, her essay is particularly useful for an undergraduate writing course. We need to read carefully,
she argues, but also differently; we need, for example, to read not only Anglo-
American accounts of Native American history but also Native American accounts of that history, including their accounts of early contacts with European
settlers. And we need to write in ways that allow us to represent, rather than
erase, experiences and points of view that lie outside the standard narrative. As
Limerick says, "One skill essential to the writing of Western American history is
a capacity to deal with multiple points of view. It is as if one were a lawyer at a
trial designed on the principle of the Mad Hatter's tea party—as soon as one begins to understand and empathize with the plaintiff's case, it is time to move over
and empathize with the defendant." Yet it is even more complicated than this, for*

*"seldom are there only two parties or only two points of view." Part of the plea-
sure of reading Limerick's prose is the opportunity it provides to hear, in brief, a
variety of representative stories from the American West, stories told with style
and grace, and part of the pleasure is the opportunity it provides to witness her vision, spirit, and judgment.*

Haunted America

If there be one principle more deeply rooted than any other in
the mind of every American, it is that we should have nothing
to do with conquest.

> — THOMAS JEFFERSON,
> letter to William Short, 1791

... you will soon find it theologically and factually true that
man by nature is a damn mess.

> — NORMAN MACLEAN,
> *A River Runs Through It*

The Sharp Point of Conquest

If you place yourself at a distance, there is no clearer fact in American
history than the fact of conquest. In North America, just as much as in
South America, Africa, Asia, and Australia, Europeans invaded a land
fully occupied by natives. Sometimes by negotiations and sometimes by
warfare, the natives lost ground and the invaders gained it. From the
caves in the lava beds of Northern California, where the Modocs held off
the United States Army for months, to the site along the Mystic River in
Connecticut, where Puritans burned Pequots trapped in a stockade, the
landscape bears witness to the violent subordination of Indian people.
These haunted locations are not distant, exotic sites set apart from the turf
of our normal lives. Neither time nor space, it would seem, can insulate us
from these disturbing histories.

And yet distance makes these facts deceptively clear. Immerse yourself
in the story of the dispossession of any one group, and clarity dissolves.
There is nothing linear or direct in these stories. Only in rare circumstances were the affairs that we call "white-Indian wars" only matters of
whites against Indians. More often, Indians took part on both sides, tribe
against tribe or faction against faction, and whites sometimes played surprisingly peripheral roles in the working out of relationships between and
among Indian groups.

Moreover, if Indians were often divided against each other, the same
shortage of solidarity applied to the other side. In the tense and

unpredictable circumstances before, during, and after a war, whites often squabbled bitterly with each other, presenting something one would not begin to call a united front. In virtually every case, the story of how the war got started and how it proceeded is a long, detailed, and tangled business. These are narratives designed to break the self-esteem of storytellers. You can be the world's greatest enthusiast for narrative history, and you can still lose your nerve at the prospect of putting yourself and your readers at the mercy of one of these tales from hell.

They are tales from hell because they are stories so loaded with tiresome detail and pointless plot twists that narrative art bends and breaks under their weight. They are tales from hell, as well, because they are stories that drive their tellers and readers to a confrontation with the darkest and grimmest dimensions of human nature. Torture, maiming, rape, mutilation, murder—all of the worst injuries that human beings inflict on each other serve as the capstones to these stories. Whites did these things to Indians, and Indians did these things to whites. Invaded or invader, conquered or conqueror, nearly every group had occasion to use terror as a memorable method of communication.

The person who contemplates these tales ends up feeling a kind of nondiscriminatory moral shock, unnerved by nearly everybody's behavior. Of course, one can never lose sight of who started the whole business. Indians never invaded Europe; Indian tribes did not cross the Atlantic to seize the homes, fields, and sacred places of Europeans. It is perfectly clear who started this fight. And it is also perfectly clear who, when the dust had settled, had maneuvered whom into surrendering land, food, and the weapons of aggression and self-defense. But in between those two points of clarity lies a great stretch of historical turf in which people of all ethnicities and backgrounds embraced brutality and committed atrocities. In this disorienting turf, neither victims nor villains came with consistent labeling.

In the muddled events that lie between the beginning of invasion and the invaders' consolidated domination, historical lessons are hard to come by. Morals to the story that lift the spirit and inspire hope simply do not appear. On some occasions, historians are quick to make cheerful remarks about how the understanding of history will help us to understand ourselves and to cope with the dilemmas we have inherited from the past. It is hard to pipe up with one of those earnest declarations of faith in the value of historical knowledge when you are thinking of the water at the junction of the Mississippi River and the Bad Axe River. That water, on August 2, 1832, was reddened with the blood of the wounded Sauk and Fox people trying to escape the bullets of American troops. In Indian agent Joseph Street's description, "The Inds. were pushed literally into the Mississippi, the current of which was at one time perceptibly tinged with the blood of the Indians who were shot on its margin & in the stream. . . . It is impossible to say how many Inds. have been killed, as most of them were shot in the water or drowned in attempting to cross the Mississippi."[1] Those Indians who survived the crossing at Bad Axe did not leave brutality behind them when they escaped from the white soldiers. The survivors were attacked a few days later—by a party of Sioux.

What good can knowledge of this miserable story do? Is the principal lesson simply that the winning of Illinois was as tangled, brutal, and bloody a process as the winning of Massachusetts or the winning of Oregon? What exactly does knowledge of this event add to American self-understanding and well-being?

When I went to college, I had a fine professor in my freshman course in Western civilization. Jasper Rose was from England and given to the use of terms of address like "ducky." One day in class, we talked about the Calvinist belief in the evil that had lodged in the human soul after the fall of Adam. The way that Mr. Rose discussed the topic of human depravity puzzled me to my core.

"When you were talking about the way people used to believe in the evil in humans," I said to him after class, "you sounded as if *you* believed there is such a thing. But how could a modern person believe in human depravity?"

"Just wait, ducky," Mr. Rose sighed. "Just wait."

Jasper Rose was doing his best to get me braced for the Battle of Bad Axe. But there is no way to be truly braced for the dreadful reality of these events. The Mystic Fort Fire, the Ohio River Wars, Black Hawk's War, the Mountain Meadows Massacre, the Bear River Massacre, the Sand Creek Massacre, the Modoc War, and the Nez Perce War—all these events have me flummoxed. Yes, these stories are part of our national heritage; yes, they shaped us as a people; yes, we have to know our past to understand our present. But, by remembering these stories, what do we gain besides a revival and restoration of the misery?

A Twelve-Point Guide to War

In graduate school, we were trained to be finders of themes. Where others might see a bunch of unconnected facts, we were obligated to locate the underlying patterns. Like any exercise, this was hard at first but easier with practice. And, unlike many exercises, this one was addictive. In a world so overloaded with complexity and contradiction, the activity of getting a grip on themes and patterns is genuinely comforting and soothing. This ability of generalizations to bring calm is particularly appealing when one confronts ugly forms of human behavior. In that spirit, I now put forward twelve patterns of white-Indian wars. These are not universal laws; readers will, no doubt, think of many exceptions as they read. But the most that one can ask of one's historical patterns is that they are true more often than are not, and these easily meet that qualification.

To give these general patterns a clear tie to reality, I have prefaced each point with a story from the Modoc War of 1872–1873.[2] I have chosen this war because it clearly and directly embodies most of these patterns; because it makes a geographical break from the usual Great Plains–

centered tellings of the Indian wars, reminding us that these wars occurred all over the nation; and because it is a representatively agonizing war story.

Modoc Story, Part 1

The Modoc War began on November 29, 1872. Interaction between whites and Modocs began long before that. In the 1820s, traders from the Hudson's Bay Company came into Modoc territory, at the border of what are now the states of California and Oregon. Like many tribes, the Modocs enthusiastically adopted European-introduced horses. In the late 1840s, white settlers in Oregon laid out wagon roads through Modoc territory, providing both a route to and from California and a more southern line of access from the Oregon Trail. These roads provided opportunities for raiding and killing, as the Modocs and other Indians of the area responded to the presence of white travelers with livestock and well-packed wagons. Both civilian vigilante groups and federal troops reacted to these attacks, sometimes "punishing" Indians who had taken part in the raiding and sometimes simply attacking any Indians they could find. Gold discoveries brought miners into the area, and ranchers and farmers also settled in.

Newly founded towns were magnets for Indians as well as whites; Modocs were frequent visitors to the town of Yreka. Some Modoc women served as prostitutes, and both Modoc women and men proved susceptible to the appeal of alcohol. Modocs worked, as well, as cowboys on some of the local ranches. By the time of the war in 1872, the denim and calico clothes worn by many Modocs were only one of the marks of change in their habits. In battles during the war, the men shouted insults at white troops, expertly wielding their familiarity with the English language to rile up the enemy.

Pattern 1

Before a war happened, there was already a great deal of water under the bridge.

Before whites and Indians would feel inclined to fight each other in a sustained way, they had to get to know each other. Before prolonged violence came disease, exotic plants and animals, traders and trade dependence, intermarriage, missionaries, representatives of the federal government, and, often enough, white emigrants, farmers, miners, or ranchers. Before they took up arms against each other, Indians and whites had to go through a substantial "getting to know you" phase. But, unlike the pattern in the musical *The King and I*, "getting to know you" in these situations often meant "getting to dislike and distrust you," "getting to realize that, even though I thought I could use your presence for my benefit, it is not working out that way."

The "getting to know you" phase was often so long and consequential that the border between whites and Indians became blurred. Intermarriage was the most obvious example of this blurring. Where traders had been present for a while, children of mixed heritage became important figures in society, sometimes caught uncomfortably between groups, sometimes finding their status in between to be the source of considerable advantage. After a generation or two, the terms "Indian" and "white" had become more matters of political loyalty and cultural practice than lines of biological descent. Through intermarriage, natives and invaders had become, in the broadest sense, relatives; under those circumstances, Indian-white wars looked more like a quarrel between neighbors than a collision of strangers.

Interaction with whites, moreover, reshaped tribal economies and politics. Decades, sometimes centuries, of diplomacy, exchange, and negotiation preceded warfare, and Indian economies and forms of leadership showed the impact. Every time an Indian fired a gun in a battle, the use of a manufactured firearm offered another reminder of how intertwined the lives of the participants had already become.

Modoc Story, Part 2

In 1864, representatives of the federal government tried to negotiate an understanding with the Modocs and the other Indians of the area. But confusion was built into the process. In February of 1864, Elijah Steele, a judge and Indian agent for northern California, took part in discussions with the Modoc and two other tribes. By the terms of the Steele treaty, the Indians would cease to fight each other; they would not interfere with white settlers; and although they would retain the right to travel, they would agree to be regulated by the officers at Fort Klamath. The Steele treaty did not address the question of whether the Modocs would have a reservation near the Lost River, their home area; it did not, by the same token, suggest that this was impossible.

While the Steele treaty was at least moderately compatible with the Modocs' preference, it never received approval by the Indian Bureau or ratification by the United States Senate. Instead, in October of 1864, another negotiator—J. W. Pettit Huntington, superintendent of Indian affairs for Oregon—presided over a second set of discussions. The result was a second treaty, setting forth very different terms, terms much less acceptable to the Modocs, since this treaty would send them away from Lost River.

The second treaty created one reservation for both the Klamath and the Modocs. This land that made up the reservation was entirely Klamath land; the Modocs would have to leave their homes and move into the homeland of another, sometimes hostile tribe. The Modocs divided over this prospect: some of them followed the leader Old Schonchin to the reservation and agreed to live there, despite frequent friction with the

Klamath people. But another group left the reservation and returned to Lost River, repudiating the second treaty of 1864, while keeping their allegiance to the unratified Steele treaty. Kientpoos, or Captain Jack, emerged as the leader of this group.

White settlers in the Lost River country were not happy to see these original inhabitants return. Badgered by settlers' complaints of property damage and threats from the Modocs, federal officials succeeded in getting the Indians to return to the reservation—briefly. In the winter of 1869, A. B. Meacham, now the superintendent of Indian affairs for Oregon, persuaded Captain Jack and his fellows to go to the reservation. Then, in late April 1870, to the dismay of the settlers, Captain Jack's Modocs left the reservation and returned to Lost River. To Captain Jack and his party, the Steele treaty was the agreement with which they were still complying, and nothing in that treaty required them to live far from home in the company of the irritating Klamath. The treaty, the reservation, and all the various efforts to control the situation, launched by the officials of the United States Army and the Indian Bureau, had finally produced a perfect muddle.

Pattern 2

Before a war occurred, some men representing the federal government declared that they were going to settle everything and instead left everyone confused. That confusion was often the trigger for the war.

The Constitution declared the centrality of federal responsibility in Indian affairs, giving Congress the power "to regulate commerce with foreign nations, among the several states, and with the Indian tribes." Thus there was a constitutionally based reason for federal officials to swing into action in anticipation of conflict and to try to arrange a peace that would serve two not very compatible goals: the expansion of white commerce and settlement, and the protection and assimilation of the Indians.

And so a phalanx of territorial politicians, Indian agents, military officers, and humanitarians and reformers called for and attended hundreds of meetings with Indian people. At those meetings, the white officials declared their good intentions and their hopes for harmony between whites and Indians. While some of them were cheerful liars, veiling land grabs under the rhetoric of paternalistic helpfulness, many others believed the things they said.

Frequently the outcome of these councils and negotiations hinged on the honesty and efficiency of one person: the interpreter, who had to translate not only two very different languages but also two very different systems of property and law. Opportunities for confusion were unlimited. Merely identifying who, on either the tribal or federal side, had the authority to ratify and to enforce an agreement could be the most difficult part of these negotiations. White officials fell into the habit of selecting and identifying certain leaders as "chiefs," and then declaring that a whole tribe had agreed to cede territory and retreat to a reservation, when, in fact, only a few, not-always-respected individuals from the tribe had signed an agreement.

From these federal efforts to anticipate conflict and reach a resolution came agreements that carried very different meanings for different individuals and groups. With their multiple meanings, the agreements were very difficult to enforce. On the federal side, a breakdown of enforcement was built into a policy stretched to the point of snapping; an official goal of benevolence to Indians pulled in one direction, and an insistent white demand for lands and resources pulled in another.

Federal officials had visions of sharing the benefits of civilization and Christianity with grateful Indians; Indians had visions of maintaining their sovereignty and traditional economies; white settlers had visions of owning and using land without Indian interference. The federal negotiators and commissioners were placed exactly at the point where those visions clashed. It was not, therefore, unusual to find federal commissioners playing the part of the recipients of everyone's wrath, since both Indians and whites cast these negotiators as the bumblers whose negotiations had delivered everyone into confusion and conflict.

The effectiveness of federal intervention was undermined, as well, by the weakness of the government's power through the first century of the nation's existence. American citizens had a principled distrust of an established, well-funded army. Monarchies and tyrannies relied on standing armies. But democracies and republics called up citizen militias to deal with emergencies and then disbanded those militias when the emergencies were resolved. Here, then, was a curious reluctance to face up to the fact that the nation was engaged not in occasional military emergencies but in a prolonged and concerted war for the continent, a war that would not be won without a serious army, seriously funded. The ideology of expansion may have offered an image of inferior Indians who would simply melt away as white settlements expanded, but few tribes chose to melt and many chose to fight. The cost of war weighed on the federal treasury, principled opposition to a standing army or not. At the end of a war, the supporters of thrift would reappear, cutting back the army's funding and size and leaving the federal government in a chronic position of weakness when it came to enforcing its laws and standing by its promises.

Expenses aside, it was an awkward matter to use the United States Army against United States citizens. Even though the Army did sometimes try to remove white squatters and intruders from Indian territory, this was hardly the way to make the Army more popular. Unable to deliver on many of its promises and guarantees, the federal effort to get the jump on conflict and to negotiate peaceful agreements frequently added up to the achievement of giving all the partisans someone to blame when these agreements fell apart.

Modoc Story, Part 3

In November 1872, the pieces and parts of the federal government geared up for action. Replacing A. B. Meacham and too recently arrived in his job to know much about the Modocs, Thomas B. Odeneal, the new superintendent of Indian affairs for Oregon, asked Colonel John T. Green to send troops from Fort Klamath, to arrest Captain Jack and return him and his people to the Klamath Reservation. Selected by Green, Major James Jackson and thirty-eight soldiers took a long, miserable ride through rain and sleet. Several armed civilians joined in the enterprise.

Early on the morning of November 29, 1872, the Lost River Modocs were camped at two sites. The Army prepared to enter the larger of the two camps, the one with Captain Jack in it, while the civilians took on the smaller camp. Jackson and his men proposed to disarm the Modocs; the Modocs held on to their guns and rifles. In this tense situation, shooting suddenly started. Finding that they were in way over their heads, the civilians retreated—fast—from the smaller camp. The regular troops held on to the larger camp, but the Modocs fled and the troops did not pursue them. After burning the village, with Captain Jack now far beyond the reach of the Army, Major Jackson led a retreat of his own to a neighboring ranch.

While most of the Modocs headed off to take refuge in the nearby lava beds, a small group of men rode off to vent their anger on the nearby settlers. In his retreat, Major Jackson had not tried to warn settlers in the area, much less to offer them protection. A group including Hooker Jim, Boston Charley, Long Tim, and others—*but not Captain Jack*—stopped at several neighboring ranches, killing men and male children but sparing women. At their first stop, Hooker Jim and his allies killed a settler named William Boddy, along with Boddy's son-in-law, Nicholas Schira. Abruptly and terribly widowed, Mrs. Boddy and Mrs. Schira hid during the night and fled to refuge the next morning, while the Modoc party went on to attack other whites, killing fourteen altogether.

The bungled attempt to arrest Captain Jack triggered the war. The vengeance imposed by a few Modocs on the unwarned and unprepared white settlers made the momentum for war irreversible.

Pattern 3

The first acts of violence usually were more accidents of impulse and passion than the considered and chosen opening acts of an intended war.

At the end of a war, it was common for leaders—both white and Indian—to offer some version of this sentiment: "We did not want this war; it happened in spite of us." When they said this, they were not lying. On the contrary, they were recording the fact that at the start of the war, the preferences of the leaders did not carry nearly as much weight as the impatience and anger of a few individuals. On the Indian side, the first acts of violence were often committed by impulsive young men, driven by their ambition as warriors and defiant of the restraints imposed by their elders. Hunger was also a common provocation for violence. In the gritty details of daily life, invasion and conquest meant, at the bedrock, a loss of traditional sources for food for Indians, and there are few better triggers for desperate acts than the prospect of starvation. On the white side, the triggering acts of violence often came from a similar impatience in white settlers who felt that the United States Army was far too slow in coming to their aid and who therefore took it upon themselves to "punish" Indians for various "crimes," especially for theft. These acts of retaliation were often committed in defiance of white officials, who had a better grasp on the proposition that white American notions of "crime" and "punishment" made an uneven fit to the complex reality of incompatible groups with conflicting ambitions trying to live as neighbors.

Individualistic in their origins, these opening episodes of violence placed leaders in positions where their range of choice was much diminished. Repeatedly, the heated acts of a few individuals carried more weight than the restraint and caution that leaders had tried to maintain. Here came the turning point in the escalation of violence: white settlers and officials chose to take the acts of a few impatient Indian people to represent the will of the whole group. With that assumption embraced, everyone—women, children, and men who had not picked a fight—had to be punished for the actions of a few. Once that choice was made, the unrolling of the war might have seemed inevitable. But it is crucial to remember that there were *two* paths leading from this fork in the road, and neither was inevitable. Humans, in circumstances like these, have the capacity to distinguish individual actions from group actions and to calibrate their responses with that distinction in mind. Here is the clearest contribution of hindsight: if that capacity to make distinctions had been more often in play, the mortality and misery rate in these wars would have been much diminished.

Modoc Story, Part 4

When Hooker Jim's party, reacting to the soldiers' attack on their camp, killed some of their white neighbors, rumors spread in all directions. In towns and in ranch houses, settlers panicked, anticipating brutal surprises from all directions. From the security of hindsight, it is clear that whites who settled in Modoc territory had been taking a great risk, insisting on their right to live in contested terrain. But the killings committed by Hooker Jim's party cast the whites as undeserving victims, delivered by their innocence and trust to the knives and bullets of treacherous Indians. For most settlers in the area, the Lost River killings settled the question. *All* the nonreservation Modocs had to be punished, and what hindsight would call a war of conquest proved, at the time, to be a conflict in which the whites felt that *they* were the ones who had been mistreated and who were fully justified in defending themselves before the next outrage could occur.

Pattern 4

If Indians tried to terrorize settlers into leaving contested territory, whites instantly saw themselves as the innocent victims and Indians as the guilty aggressors, and thus the question of justification seemed settled.

Throughout history, humans have found various ways to communicate the message, "Get out; we don't want you here." Snubbing, shunning, segregation, economic boycotts, eviction notices, elimination of a food supply, threats, property destruction, torture, and murder—all of these gestures have been used to say to their recipients, "We'd just as soon you got out of here." When whites moved into territory that Indians claimed, and especially, when white settlement interfered with Indian food growing and food gathering, Indians turned to these various devices of communication to say, effectively and memorably, "Get out."

At various places and times, delivering this message to white intruders, Indian people used the full vocabulary of terror: fire, kidnapping, rape, murder, and mutilation. Because of the brutality practiced in these episodes, moral judgment of the Indian wars will never be pure or clear. Rather than trying to be saints of nonviolence and passive resistance, Indians could be cruel and arbitrary in their attacks on white families whose ambitions had led them to the wrong place at the wrong time.

Contemplating these attacks, historians become "equal opportunity cynics," seeing neither nobility nor brutality as the exclusive property of any group. While Indian attacks on white families have mixed and blurred the moral vision of historians, they sharpened and clarified the moral judgments of white settlers and officials. Once the Indians tried to terrorize settlers into leaving, in the minds of Anglo-Americans, the roles of aggressor and victim instantly reversed. Whites ceased to register as invaders and provokers of conflict and occupied, instead, the status of innocent victims. With this shift, the question of justification was settled: Indians had started the trouble and had asked for punishment, and whites could do whatever they had to do, in order to defend themselves.

Modoc Story, Part 5

After the violence at Lost River, the Modocs crossed Tule Lake and took refuge in an extraordinary place, the lava beds of northern California. When he heard the news of the bungled arrest and the flight of the Modocs, Colonel Frank Wheaton, Green's and Jackson's commanding officer, felt considerable confidence in his understanding of what to do next. He would assemble a force composed of units of both regulars and California and Oregon volunteers, and he would march into the lava beds toward the Modoc stronghold in the center, encircle the renegades, and defeat them. "I do not believe we need anticipate a continued resistance from this little band of Modocs," Wheaton told General E. R. S. Canby.[3] Canby, in turn, reported cheerfully: "I do not think the operations will be protracted."[4] In Washington, General William Tecumseh Sherman synthesized the various messages of confidence he had received from the West Coast and told the Secretary of War that Canby "is in actual command of all the troops and resources of the country and will doubtless bring this matter to a satisfactory end."[5]

In January 1873, Colonel Wheaton tried to put this confident plan into action. But a clumsy troop movement the night before had alerted the Modocs and sacrificed the advantage of surprise. On January 17, a dense fog covered the ground. The troops started forward and presented themselves as targets for Modoc bullets, often expertly delivered. The soldiers could see the injuries and deaths produced by these bullets, but with the thick fog and the rocky, ridge-broken landscape, they could seldom see the Indians who were firing on them. Demoralized, the troops ground to a halt; officers could not or would not follow the original plan to encircle the stronghold. By nightfall, the United States forces were in a disorderly retreat, leaving behind, for the Modocs' use, many of their firearms and much of their ammunition and abandoning many of the wounded. The January 17 attack proved to be a complete disaster for the whites, as the advantage shifted to the Modocs, who did not lose one warrior. Fewer than sixty Modoc men had defeated three hundred soldiers.

Pattern 5

The wars often began with an Indian victory, frequently because whites were overconfident and thought that fighting a primitive, unsophisticated enemy would be easy and quick.

By all the tenets of white American pride, it should have been easy to beat a set of disorderly, undisciplined primitives. That excess of confidence, however, often led to an initial defeat, as white troops plunged into battle confidently, certain that they had a clear advantage over a simple foe. A belief in one's own intrinsic superiority, these early battles demonstrated, could be a dangerous, even lethal delusion. The defeats put American forces through a rough period of reassessment, leading to the necessary recognition that Indian war was serious business, requiring substantial commitments of leadership, discipline, equipment, and, especially, funding. The defeats reinforced, moreover, the vision of the whites as the embattled, besieged victims, further obscuring the bedrock reality of white invasion, encroachment, and aggression. Perhaps most important, these losses made whites furious, determined on vengeance and unwilling to consider alternatives to the escalation of the war.

Modoc Story, Part 6

During the war, a significant number of Modocs stayed on the Klamath Reservation; some were sympathetic, some simply neutral, and some opposed to Captain Jack and his group. While the Army decided not to try to use Modocs against Modocs, some Klamath Indians took part in the January 17 attack on the lava beds. When the battle turned against the Army, officers placed some of the blame on the Klamaths for fighting half-heartedly. The Army then recruited a number of Indian auxiliaries from the Warm Springs Reservation. These Indians found cooperation with whites to be, on occasion, a life-threatening challenge. On one occasion, late in the war, the Warm Springs Indians tried to come to the aid of a group of soldiers who had been ambushed by Modocs. Panicked and unthinking, the soldiers fired on their rescuers. Despite every effort on the part of the Warm Springs Indians to identify themselves as friends, they could not get their allies to stop shooting at them.

By the end of the war, any notions of tribal solidarity had been shattered. Captain Jack had never been an enthusiastic advocate of war. The impulsive acts of Hooker Jim's party, in killing the Lost River settlers, had forced Captain Jack into a war he did not want. In the spring of 1873, as federal officials tried for a negotiated resolution to the war, the Modoc militants pressured Jack into taking part in a treacherous attack on the peace commissioners. On April 11, 1873, the Modocs killed Reverend Eleazar Thomas and General E. R. S. Canby (the only general killed in the Indian wars) and seriously wounded Albert Meacham. In May of 1873, Hooker Jim, Steamboat Frank, Shacknasty Jim, and Bogus Charley, members of the war party, left Captain Jack and surrendered to the Americans. Over the next weeks, the Modoc men who had pushed Captain Jack into war and assassination now served as his betrayers, helping the Army track him down for a final capture.

In July of 1873, Captain Jack and five others were tried and convicted for the murder of the commissioners. Hooker Jim and others of the original war advocates were not tried for either the murder of the Lost River settlers or the killings of the commissioners. On the contrary, the Army rewarded them for their betrayal of Captain Jack by exempting them from punishment, in order to set an example that would encourage other Indians to change sides. Captain Jack was obviously very much troubled by this chain of betrayal. "I didn't know anything of any settlers being killed until Hooker Jim came with his band and told me," he said at his trial. None of his own people "had killed any of the whites, and I had never told Hooker Jim and his party to murder any settlers; and I did not want them to stay with me." Hooker Jim was "the one that always wanted to fight, and commenced killing and murdering." But now, Captain Jack said, "I have to bear the blame for him and the rest of them."[6]

Pattern 6

The idea of an Indian war as a conflict of whites against Indians seldom had much to do with reality because Indians were usually on both sides of the conflict.

Intertribal conflict began long before the arrival of Europeans or Euro-Americans. In some areas, the introduction of horses and guns increased the stakes and intensity of intertribal raiding and war. All over North America, the expansion of white settlement escalated the conflict among tribes, as they struggled for control of a reduced supply of territory and re-sources. Under those circumstances, it made perfect sense for members of one tribe to see whites as helpful allies in campaigns against the common enemy of another tribe. It made sense, as well, to exercise a warrior's skills and take advantage of the opportunity presented by the Army's need for scouts and auxiliaries who knew the terrain and the ways of the enemy.

Divisions in war came, as well, from the presence of factions within tribes. The boundaries of identity and loyalty to a particular tribe were flexible; the band or the clan or the family was more likely to be the pri-mary unit of social cohesion. Conquest placed, moreover, a terrible strain on leadership. To some leaders, going along with whites and their treaties and reservations seemed like the wisest response to an unhappy situation; to leaders of a different persuasion, resistance—armed if necessary—seemed the best way to serve their people's interests. In some cases, mis-sionaries had split the tribe between those who had converted to Chris-tianity and those who held to the traditional beliefs and practices. And, true to human nature, conflicts of personality and of individual ambition played their role in dividing tribes.

Facing up to the divisions inside and among Indian groups requires one to pay attention to one's own unexamined sentimentality. Many late-twentieth-century Americans, of all ethnicities, remain susceptible to a ro-mantic wish that the victims of white American aggression had stood to-gether, measuring up to a standard for saintly, noble, heroic solidarity that any human population, living in perfectly happy and tranquil times, would have had a hard time meeting. Put humans under the terrible pres-sure of conquest, and the record discloses the great muddle that is human nature.

Modoc Story, Part 7

In the course of the Modoc War, the whites did not do much better than the Indians at maintaining solidarity. Blaming each other took nearly as much of their time and energy as did fighting Modocs. Before the war began, some federal officials put considerable effort into arguing that the whole situation had been produced by the actions of "bad" whites, who had given the Modocs bad advice and encouraged them in their resistance. When the plan to arrest Jack exploded into war, some whites blamed Superintendent Odeneal for acting in ill-considered haste (and for keeping himself at a safe distance from the scene of danger). Some blamed Major Jackson for letting the arrest action get out of control, for refusing to pursue the Modocs, and for failing to warn the neighboring settlers of their danger.

After the January 17 defeat of the Army, blamers and faultfinders launched into a second round of activity. After that debacle, Wheaton was replaced by Colonel Alvan C. Gillem. Not a particularly charismatic fellow, troubled by ill health, Gillem gained a reputation for reluctance to take on the Modocs and evoked considerable hostility from his officers. For the rest of the war, divisions ran in all directions: officers of the Army against representatives of the Indian Office; regulars against volunteers; the governor of Oregon against the appointed officials of the federal government; Oregonians against Californians (judged by the Oregonians to be too sympathetic to the Modocs); officers against local merchants and farmers who sold the Army provisions and supplies for a handsome profit; Eastern humanitarians standing up for the Modocs' rights against both the Army and the settlers.

The effort to form the Modoc Peace Commission was itself a fine demonstration of the disunity of whites. When A. B. Meacham was asked to serve with Thomas Odeneal, his successor as superintendent of Indian affairs in Oregon, Meacham, who felt Odeneal was responsible for the whole mess, held up the process until a commissioner more agreeable to Meacham could replace Odeneal. Long before they tried to negotiate with the Modocs, the peace commission had a hard enough time simply finding personnel who could peaceably talk with each other.

The Modoc War's most-distressing examples of the breakdown of white solidarity came in a few episodes in which uninjured soldiers refused to help the wounded during retreats. During the retreat from the January 17 defeat, the soldiers scrambled up a bluff to safety: "No one," Keith Murray notes, "helped anyone else, and the walking wounded were left to climb the hill as best they could." After another Army defeat, the soldiers lost their way in the night and those who could still walk "tried to avoid helping to carry the stretchers" of the wounded.[7] White Americans did not march in unity and harmony to the conquest of the continent. White Americans did not retreat in any better order.

Pattern 7

Whites were often quite disunited themselves, so disunited that white Americans sometimes looked as if they might kill each other before the Indians got a chance at them.

The impact of Indian war on white society resembled the impact of a rock on a window, a window that does not shatter entirely but still shows cracks that spread in all directions. The fractures ran right through the center of the federal government; the Office of Indian Affairs and the War Department were jealous of each other's turf and often opposed in their policies. The president often received conflicting advice from the various officials working in Indian affairs; these were not the circumstances to give rise to a coherent and consistent federal policy. In some cases, the lack of coordination and communication between Indian agents and Army officers was, directly and concretely, the cause of war.

The Army on its own was a fissured society. Personal rivalry and conflicting ambitions divided the officers. Personality conflicts were often heightened by the conditions of isolation and remoteness; it is not too much to say that some of these men truly hated each other. Young officers were often impatient with the restraints imposed by older officers; especially after the Civil War, as opportunities for promotion narrowed, a sense of frustrated ambition spread through the officer corps. Some of the most-heated conflicts centered on supplies, as officers out on the front lines struggled with inadequate food, firearms, clothing, and transportation. Enlisted men, in the meantime, felt varying degrees of enthusiasm and loyalty for their officers and for the whole cause and campaign in which they were employed. Sometimes the soldiers experienced true crises of confidence, convinced that they were trusting their lives to leaders without wisdom or sense. The most unmistakable expression of discontent and demoralization came in a high rate of desertion.

The greatest division in the fighting force was the gap between regulars and volunteers. Local citizens who joined militia units or who simply rode along as informal volunteers often saw the Army as plodding, cautious, and too easy on the Indians. Raids, retaliations, and acts of terror had built up strong currents of racial hostility; local volunteers often wanted to hit the Indians hard, fast, and indiscriminately. On the other hand, volunteers stood a good chance of being undrilled and undisciplined, susceptible to panic and flight at the most crucial moments. When volunteers complained about regulars, and regulars complained about volunteers in this tense and angry relationship between two elements of the white American population, there seemed to be little room left over for any attention to the Indian enemy.

Another important element of white disunity appeared in the dissenters, whites who for various reasons disapproved of the course of action taken by the Army. Sometimes these were settlers who had gotten to know Indians under tranquil and collaborative circumstances. Men and women like these sympathized with the misfortunes of their Indian neighbors, tried to help them secure permanent land claims, and complained of the Army's inflexibility and harshness. Another group of dissenters wore Army uniforms. It was not uncommon, after a massacre or vicious battle, to find a few soldiers or officers who were repelled by what they had seen or taken part in. In some cases, officers felt that their own honor had been violated; they had taken a group of Indians to be peaceful, had promised them safety, and then been unable to protect them from attack. These officers were surprisingly outspoken in expressing their dissent.

The loudest objections came from men and women far from the battlefield—humanitarians who registered their dismay and disapproval when they looked at the actions of the Army and hostile Western settlers. After the Civil War, these humanitarians coalesced as a significant lobby with real power. Army officers thus spent part of their time anticipating criticisms and denunciations from the humanitarians. These agents of Manifest Destiny could feel themselves to be besieged on all sides: constantly challenged and often outfoxed by the Indians, denounced by the Eastern humanitarians for their cruelty, and damned by Western settlers for their unwillingness to punish the Indians with proper harshness.

From time to time, the United States government has been denounced for its "genocidal" policies against Indians. But once you have examined the intensity and range of division within the white population, and even within the forces officially detailed to Indian affairs, then there is one clear defense against the accusations of genocide: even though some individuals did call for the extermination of the Indians, white Americans were simply too divided and disorganized to implement such a policy, even if a majority had supported it.

Modoc Story, Part 8

The Modoc people knew the landscape of the lava beds, and the whites did not. The lava beds provided the Indians with pockets of water and ice, with places to hide cattle, and with caves that could withstand bombardment. The landscape was shaped by parallel ridges of rocks which worked perfectly to the Modocs' advantage. The rock ridges were natural fortifications; the passages between the ridges served as corridors and pathways that permitted the Modocs to keep shifting their sparse number of warriors to new and unexpected locations. On January 17, 1873, as the regulars and the volunteers sat miserably in the mist and absorbed bullets that seemed to have been fired by the fog itself, the Indians' advantage in knowing the turf was the most compelling reality that the soldiers had to contemplate.

On April 26, 1873, a party of soldiers under Captain Evan Thomas went to the lava beds on a reconnaissance. In the early afternoon, the party sat down for an unguarded lunch. The Modoc ambush that came down upon them caught them completely by surprise. Many of the soldiers died on the spot; many more *would* have died if the Indians had not stopped the attack, when the Modoc leader Scarfaced Charley called out, "All you fellows that ain't dead had better go home. We don't want to kill you all in one day." Twenty-three of the Americans were killed, and nineteen wounded. Thomas's force, in historian Keith Murray's words, "had lost almost as many men in two hours as the entire army had lost thus far in the war." Just as they had during the January 17 battle, the Modocs "suffered no losses."[8]

The moment of the Modocs' cease-fire was by no means the end of the surviving soldiers' distress. Still to be reckoned with was the landscape. The relief party coming to their aid got lost. The doctor, traveling behind the relief party, also got lost. Walking the next night in a storm, carrying the wounded, the relief party tried to follow "guides" who "had no idea where they were going," putting the wounded through an awful, aimless ordeal of jostling and bumping against rocks. Knowing where you were, how to get out of there, and how to get to where you would rather be added up to a large element of success and survival in this campaign, and this was an element very much balanced toward the Modocs. "We seem," one of the Army's high-ranking officers telegraphed after the Thomas incident, "to be acting somewhat in the dark."[9]

Pattern 8

The fact that the Indians knew the landscape, terrain, food supply, and water sources put the whites at a considerable disadvantage.

A century after the Indian wars, "the lessons of Vietnam" became a commonly used phrase. The lessons of Vietnam hinged on the maddening realities of fighting a guerrilla war. The more confident Americans were of their technological superiority and greater wealth, the more vulnerable they were to an enemy who relied on other strengths entirely. In the jungles of Southeast Asia, Americans finally had to recognize the crippling disadvantages of being the intruders and strangers, trying to impose their will in a terrain the natives knew far better.

And yet it is no easy matter to distinguish the lessons of the Indian wars from the lessons of Vietnam. In the territory that would become the United States, the natives knew the terrain, the travel routes, the easily defensible locations, the climate, the location of water, and the sources of food. Their knowledge formed a great contrast with the ignorance, on all these topics, of most Army officers and soldiers. The Indian population could, moreover, shift back and forth between hostile and friendly, enemy and ally, in a way that left whites puzzled, jumpy, and frustrated. In the space of a few hours, a warrior raiding a settlement or fighting hard against the Army could become a family man, relaxed and at peace in his village.

Whatever whites may have thought about the superiority of their technology or their civilization, those assumptions of superiority did not do them much good on the battlefield. If anything, their excess of confidence played into the hands of the enemy. When full of confidence, whites were set up to fall for decoys and predisposed to cooperate with ambushes. Imagining the course of the war, far from the actual battlefield, officers could convince themselves of the effectiveness of their own grand plans and strategies, and then watch those visions dissolve under the pressure of difficult and disorienting terrain, impossible supply lines, and an enemy who simply knew more than they did about the place of contest.

The lessons of the Indian-white wars and the lessons of the Vietnam war were strikingly similar because they were both the lessons of guerrilla war, the kind of war in which the local, insider knowledge held by the natives gave them a great advantage. The invaders, by contrast, were decidedly out of their place. They had to work with the constant burden of overstretched and overstrained chains of communication and supply. At the most awkward moments, the invaders simply lost their bearings. Contemplating the Indian-white wars, one cannot avoid the conclusion that much of what we have taken to thinking of as the lessons of Vietnam was available for learning a century or more ago.

Modoc Story, Part 9

When the Modoc men fled Lost River for the lava beds, there was never a question of dividing families. Women and children went with the men; women and children occupied the stronghold along with the warriors; women and children, despite the close presence of soldiers, escaped from the stronghold with the warriors in April of 1873. There were no exemptions on the basis of gender or age from the migrations and hardships of this war.

For the first rounds of the war, the Army's inability to close with the Modocs limited any opportunity for injuring or killing noncombatants. On April 16, 1873, when the Modocs left the stronghold and the Army occupied it, hostility toward noncombatants boiled to the surface. Three old Modoc men were found alive in the stronghold, and one woman. Two of the men and the woman "were shot by soldiers," Modoc War historian Richard Dillon reports, "The third man was stoned to death by the Warm Springs" Indians. White soldiers "kicked the severed head of a Modoc like a soccer ball." Trooper Maurice Fitzgerald reported that he saw an aged "woman begging piteously for her life. 'Me no hurt no one, me no fight,' she whined." According to Fitzgerald's report, an officer then said, "'Is there anyone here who will put that old hag out of the way?' A Pennsylvania Dutchman stepped forward and said, 'I'll fix her, lieutenant.' He put the muzzle of his carbine to her head and blew it to pieces." Here, again, one has a hard time distinguishing the lessons of the Indian wars from the lessons of Vietnam.[10]

After Hooker Jim's party had killed the Lost River settlers at the start of the war, civilians in southern Oregon were wild for revenge. At the end of the war, one party of Modocs surrendered to a white man, John Fairchild, who had tried to be a peacemaker. John Fairchild's brother James started off with the captives in a wagon to take them to the Army. Two white men stopped the wagon, forced Fairchild away, and "fired into the wagon at almost point-blank range," killing four men and wounding one woman.[11] In circumstances like these, individual guilt or innocence could not be the determinant of one's fate; being Modoc and falling into the hands of vindictive whites were the two key components of a death sentence.

People writing with disapproval about violence toward noncombatants in wartime can, intentionally or not, come close to trivializing or dismissing the terrible effects of violence on actual combatants. It is, therefore, important to take a moment to remember what it might mean to be injured in legitimate, certified combat. This is a description of the ordeal of Jerry Crooks, a member of the California Volunteers, during the retreat from the January 17 defeat:

> He had taken a rifle ball in one leg, which broke the bone so badly he could not be carried in a blanket. So he rode a pony with his leg dangling loosely. When it struck boulders or even stubborn sagebrush, the pain was terrible. Finally, his comrades tied a rope around the leg so that it could be lifted when his mount came to an obstacle. Still, [a companion] wrote, "It was sickening to see the expression on his face, and the pain he must have endured was excruciating."[12]

Pattern 9

While some warriors and soldiers tried to keep a clear line between combatants and noncombatants, those efforts often broke down, in part because of confusion and in part because of pure hatred.

The conditions of guerrilla war carried their own grim logic. The invaders foundered in making distinctions—hostile from friendly, guilty from innocent, combatant from noncombatant. Demoralized and disoriented troops were men in the mood for scapegoating and not much interested in distinguishing between warriors and nonwarriors, men and women, adults and children. Moreover, Indian warriors were most often living in the midst of their families, because protecting the women and children was one of the principal obligations of the warriors and because the wars were taking place in their homelands, in the areas where these families lived. If the Army tried to make a surprise attack on the warriors, striking at dawn, women and children would be among the ones surprised. To the Army, fighting Indians who were often nomadic, the greatest challenge lay in locating them. Give them advance warning, try to separate the combatants from the noncombatants, and you could lose all the advantages of surprise; you could, for that matter, lose your entire opportunity to attack. Given the greater knowledge the natives had of the terrain, it might well be a long time before that opportunity arose again.

These reasons, in part, explain the violence inflicted on noncombatants. Beyond reason, however, lies passion—an intensity of hatred and an embrace of brutality that could make a man see a child or an infant as an appropriate target for murder. For many historians, writing of these wars, it has been tempting to avoid these troubling issues, by taking the position that we cannot permit ourselves any moral or emotional responses to these events, because we cannot judge the events of the past by the standards of today. According to this line of thought, the people who enthusiastically killed Indian women, children, and noncombatant men were simply men of their times, who operated under the standard attitudes and values of those times—attitudes and values that we, as creatures of another century, have no right to judge. But this argument is, finally, both inaccurate and dangerous.

It is inaccurate, because white American men of the nineteenth century had a wide range of attitudes and values, and we do them a considerable disservice when we write about them as if they had all submitted to the same, Manifest Destiny, attitudinal cookie cutter. Before adopting the "men of their times" model of moral homogeneity, one has an obligation to consider this haunting episode from the Bear River Massacre in 1863. Following the commands of his grandmother, the twelve-year-old Shoshone boy Yeager Timbimboo spent most of the day lying on the snow-covered ground, pretending to be dead. But at a crucial moment, he disobeyed his grandmother, and opened his eyes.

> A soldier came upon him and saw that he was alive and looking around. The military man stood over Yeager, his gun pointing at the young boy's head ready to fire. The soldier stared at the boy and the boy at the soldier. The second time the soldier raised his rifle the little boy knew his time to die was near. The soldier then lowered his gun and a moment later raised it again. For some reason he could not complete his task. He took his rifle down and walked away.[13]

"What went through this soldier's mind will never be known," said the Shoshone woman who told this story, but what went through this man's mind must be respected. It would be dangerous and chilling to say that we dare not use our own standards to respond to this man's moment of restraint and to find it heartening and impressive. If an ideal of historical detachment and objectivity requires us to hold to a scrupulous neutrality on the question of whether soldiers should shoot young children, then this is a professional ideal that corrodes the humanity of the historian.

The judgment of violence toward noncombatants is not, in any case, a matter of nineteenth-century standards in opposition to twentieth-century standards. It is just as much a matter of differences and conflicts among nineteenth-century white Americans themselves. In a number of the most violent episodes in this history, individual white officers and soldiers spoke out vigorously in opposition to what the majority had done. In Colorado in 1864, white officers opposed John Chivington's plan to attack at Sand Creek the day *before* the event; in the days and weeks after the massacre, some men in the Army and some civilians continued to speak out against Chivington and his supporters. In 1871, a Tucson citizen named William Oury led a massacre of Apache families at Camp Grant, Arizona. Royal Whitman, the officer at Camp Grant who had promised the families a sanctuary, instantly and persistently protested the attack. Twentieth-century Americans owe Royal Whitman the recognition that he was not a creation of twentieth-century moral hindsight. Royal Whitman, denouncer of the Camp Grant Massacre, was just as much a nineteenth-century man as William Oury, leader of the attack.

Modoc Story, Part 10

Captain Jack was a war leader who had not wanted war. He was, moreover, a leader with very limited power to impose his preferences on his people. On the contrary, he was often outmaneuvered by the war enthusiasts, pressured either to join them or admit to cowardice. Thus, even when the war had turned into a losing proposition, Captain Jack found it virtually impossible to persuade his people to reach a consensus for surrender. But Captain Jack confronted a relatively unusual situation in Indian war: a disposition, on the part of the federal government and its immediate representatives, to receive peace initiatives with some eagerness.

The result of these conditions was a pattern no doubt maddening to everyone involved: frequent indications, delivered through a variety of emissaries, that Captain Jack would like to surrender; optimism, on the part of some officials, that this might prove to be a route away from further carnage; and then a retreat on Jack's part, with the declaration that he could not surrender if it would mean that his people would have to leave Oregon or that some would be tried and executed for the killings of settlers or commissioners. Two propositions were clear and impossible to reconcile: Jack wanted out of the war, and yet he could find no way out.

Pattern 10

It was no easy matter to surrender; getting out of a war was a lot harder than getting one started.

When Indians decided they had had enough of a war, whites were often reluctant to receive that message. These are agonizing events to contemplate; in the Black Hawk War in 1832, the Sauk leader Black Hawk tried three times to tell the American troops that he wanted this struggle to end, and each time, he was rebuffed and his people were attacked again. Reaching the decision to surrender was by no means an easy one for an Indian leader, but getting the whites to agree to recognize that decision could often prove even tougher.

Why this reluctance to take white flags seriously? Differences of language and custom made it difficult to communicate clearly any message at all, whether of belligerence or of peace. Suspicions of treachery preoccupied both sides; a white flag could be, and sometimes was, a trick, a way of getting the opponent to drop his guard before a duplicitous attack. Perhaps more important, after investing many lives and much money in a war, whites wanted to get the most out of that investment. They wanted the enemy pushed to the margin, forced to make an unconditional surrender and to accept whatever terms the winners wished to impose. The clearest way to make certain that a group would never fight again was to reduce them, materially and psychologically, past the prospect of recovery. And, perhaps most important, a spirit of revenge and retaliation so powered white actions that the implied response to surrender was this: "You want to make peace *now*, but it is too late; you should have thought of this before you started fighting."

Modoc Story, Part 11

In July 1873, after some debates over the legality of a trial, a military hearing took place, with Captain Jack and five other Modoc men accused of murdering the peace commissioners in violation of a truce. The transcript of the hearing makes for painful reading. The presiding officer seemed willing to give the Modocs a chance to present their story, and an interpreter attended to translate for the accused. But the interpreter was also a witness for the prosecution, the Modocs had no attorney to represent them, and the whole procedure was clearly a foreign and discouraging process for them.

Early in the hearing, the transcript records this exchange: "The prisoners were then severally asked by the judge-advocate if they desired to introduce counsel; to which they severally replied in the negative; and that they had been unable to procure any." After each witness's testimony appears this notation: "The judge-advocate then asked the prisoners severally if they desired to cross-examine the witness, to which they replied in the negative." The feelings of men awaiting a life-or-death judgment from a process that was out of their control come through most strongly in Captain Jack's interruption in his address to the court. Speaking through an interpreter, Jack suddenly made this remark: "I hardly know how to talk here. I don't know how white people talk in such a place as this but I will do the best I can."[14]

Kept in a guardhouse at Fort Klamath after their conviction, Jack and his five comrades were taken out for hanging on October 3, 1873. When he was asked, the day before, if he had a last request, Captain Jack said, "I should like to live until I die a natural death."[15] Two of the younger Modocs had had their sentences commuted from death to life terms in Alcatraz, but the Army had adopted the curious custom of refusing to reveal this clemency until the moment scheduled for execution. All the Modocs were required to watch as Captain Jack, Boston Charley, Schonchin Jim, and Black Jim were hanged. That night, someone removed Captain Jack's body from its grave.

The rest of the nonreservation Modocs—thirty-nine men, fifty-four women, and sixty children—were put on a train, with their destination concealed from them. They were temporarily placed at Fort McPherson, Nebraska; then removed to Baxter Springs, Kansas; and then finally permitted to resettle in Seneca Springs, at the Quapaw Agency in Indian Territory (present-day Oklahoma). In 1909, thirty-six years after their defeat, the Modocs who so chose were permitted to return to the Klamath Reservation or, for those born in captivity, to go there for the first time.

If one goes by "the number of Indians involved," Keith Murray has observed, "this was the most expensive Indian war the United States ever fought."[16] In these matters, "expensive" carries a host of meanings.

Pattern 11

Exultation and a sense of achieved glory were hard emotions for the victors to feel at the end of a war; the Indians, at the time of the surrender, looked more like a pitiable and battered people than a fierce and terrifying enemy, valiantly defeated.

When the survivors of war decided to give up, they were likely to be hungry, tattered, demoralized, and, often enough, injured and wounded. Seeing them in this condition, some officials, officers, soldiers, and civilians responded to the end of the war with fits of regret and wishful hindsight, wondering, "Was all this really necessary?" The same outcome could have been reached, many participants would end up thinking, with much less in the way of expenses and suffering, using negotiations rather than bullets.

The moment of surrender creates an unsettling dilemma, as well, for historians. Brought together in Helen Hunt Jackson's *Century of Dishonor* (1881) and welded into place by Dee Brown's *Bury My Heart at Wounded Knee* (1971), the standard, sympathetic version of Indian-white history casts Indians as victims, passive people who stood frozen in place as a great wave of white expansion crashed down on them and left them broken and shattered. This story, of course, was of a piece with a broader approach to the history of people of color, an approach which accented the actions of whites toward the others, and virtually ignored anything that these others did for themselves and on their own terms.

In the last twenty years, the rejection of this model of passivity and victimization has become an article of faith among most American historians. Indians—and African Americans and Mexican Americans and Asian Americans—were not passive victims, we all recognize now; they were active participants in making and shaping their own history. We did Indian people a disservice when we adopted what one might call the "hanky at the eye" school of Indian history, thinking of Indians as melancholy victims, boohooing over the injuries of the past, lamenting the Indian plight, and seeing the whole story as very, very sad.

And yet, at the end of an Indian-white war, reduced by the hardships of life in chronic battle, sometimes betrayed by other Indians, often forcibly removed from the place they considered home, bullied into giving up ownership of that home, the Indians often *did* look like victims, and the whole story does indeed seem very, very sad. It would be silly to ride the pendulum swing back to the version of history in which the Indians were victims, and nothing but victims. As many of these twelve points of war suggest, these stories would not make an ounce of sense if one did not see Indians themselves as active forces in the shaping of history. But one ends up shaken in one's orthodoxy. Consider the condition of Indian people at the end of the wars, and the term "victim" keeps coming back to mind. Reciting a declaration of faith—"we just don't think of Indians as victims anymore"—will not drive the word out.

Modoc Story, Part 12

On November 29, 1872, Mrs. Boddy and Mrs. Schira were suddenly and bitterly widowed when Hooker Jim's group killed their husbands. In June 1873, while the Modocs were held as prisoners of war at Fort Klamath, Colonel Jefferson Davis, the commanding officer at the fort, responded to an alarm. Mrs. Boddy and Mrs. Schira had entered the prisoners' compound. "Mrs. Schira had a double-edged knife in her hand which she was trying to use on Hooker Jim. Mrs. Boddy had a gun which she did not know how to cock."[17] Colonel Davis restrained them and took away their weapons.

The depth of bitterness—Modoc to white and white to Modoc— seemed beyond any healing. And yet the American public's fascination with the West and with Indians offered an odd alternative to vengeance. Indians associated with wars of resistance were instant celebrities. Both the Nez Perce Chief Joseph and the Hunkpapa Sitting Bull had barely surrendered before they were being hosted and lionized, interviewed and celebrated, by white Americans. If Captain Jack had *not* taken part in the murder of commissioners during a truce, one suspects that instead of being hung in October 1873, he might well have been on a tour of the East Coast, watched by crowds in New York and hosted at a presidential reception in Washington, D.C.

Trying to capitalize on the commercial opportunity presented by the wars, the former superintendent of Indian affairs for Oregon and former peace commissioner Albert Meacham made the most of his injuries. When the Modocs killed Commissioner Eleazar Thomas and General E. R. S. Canby, Commissioner Meacham had been left for dead. Recovered from his many wounds, Meacham went on a prolonged lecture tour, displaying the wounds he had received from the Modocs and sometimes displaying the Modocs themselves. Shacknasty Jim, Steamboat Frank, and Scarfaced

Charley joined Meacham on his tours. The war turned colorful, quaint, and marketable in an amazingly short time.

Pattern 12

These Indian wars were often so bitter and so brutal that it is hard to imagine either how they ever turned romantic, picturesque, or fun in the works of American mythmakers or how the survivors and their descendants were ever able to live in peace with each other.

In the hands of novelists and filmmakers, the Indian-white wars became spectacles with great entertainment value. Here is one of the greatest mysteries of the commercial manipulation of the story of westward expansion: historical episodes in which human nature appeared at its worst provided novelists and moviemakers with the material for escapist fantasies. Escapist? In their true character, these stories raise profound questions about the reality of evil in human life, questions made even more compelling when they arise in a nation which has struggled to paint its history in shades of innocence. Rather than permitting the reader to escape the sorrows and troubles of the real world, these events force the reader's attention to the grimmest facts about American origins. They are moral and spiritual muddles, in which the lines between good guy and bad guy, victim and villain, twist and meander and intertwine. And yet by the powerful alchemy of selective storytelling, in American popular culture, narratives of great complexity became simple stories of adventure and heroism and triumph, with, perhaps, just a tinge of melancholy.

Just as mysterious is the process by which peace was restored and a kind of coexistence arranged. When you have been thinking about the injuries and outrages committed in the course of these wars, a century does not seem like enough time to restore the peace.

A story that Westerners tell to make fun of Easterners brings this issue to a focus. A car full of tourists from New Jersey pulls up at a gas station in a remote Western setting. "We notice there's an Indian reservation up ahead," the tourists say to the gas station attendant. "It's getting close to sunset; are we going to be safe if we try to cross the reservation after dark?"

"Well," says the gas station attendant, whose sister owns the motel next door, "I'd be very careful about that. But your timing is good; the weekly Army convoy leaves tomorrow at seven in the morning. If you wanted to get a room at the motel tonight, then you could be sure you'll be safe tomorrow."

This story usually presents a fine opportunity to laugh at the fools of the Eastern United States. But when you have been reading the stories of Indian-white warfare, considering the full measure of bitterness and brutality in those events and recognizing how short a period of time a century is, the notion of waiting for the 7 A.M. convoy does not seem like such a foolish idea.

And yet, at some point, the participants in these wars and their descendants broke the cycle of revenge and retaliation and ceased to think of each other's destruction as a desirable goal. In the United States of the late twentieth century, the descendants of the Modocs and the descendants of the white settlers of northern California and southern Oregon are not killing each other. We take that turn of events for granted, but for someone immersed in the history of the Indian-white wars, this outcome appears remarkable, surprising, and even illogical. Continued theft and manipulation of Indian resources, restrictions on Indian religious freedom, arbitrary and damaging federal intervention in reservation affairs, poverty, unemployment, alcoholism, discrimination, prejudice, and bitter memories—there is nothing cheering in those various manifestations of the legacy of conquest. But it is still a considerable relief when the flow of blood slows down, and the guns, by and large, fall silent.

After the Wars: The Character of American Sunlight

In America, the Indian is relegated to the obligatory first chapter—the "Once Great Nation" chapter—after which the Indian is cleared away as easily as brush, using a very sharp rhetorical tool called an "alas."

— RICHARD RODRIGUEZ,
Days of Obligation

Immerse yourself in the history of Indian-white wars, and you gain one advantage that others around you will not have. Along with your neighbors and associates, you may well be disheartened by the alarming violence of the late twentieth century—the urban gangs, the drug warfare, and the drive-by shootings that leave many feeling precarious and vulnerable. But while others imagine a happier age in the past, when times were less brutal and better values prevailed, the person who has been thinking about the Indian-white wars will waste no time in yearning for a prettier time in the past when humans treated each other better.

If you have been reading descriptions of the careful, detailed, exquisite, and very personal torture and mutilation that characterized Indian-white encounters on a number of occasions in the eighteenth and nineteenth centuries, then drive-by shootings acquire a different shading. They are terrible things, but they are not any more terrible than the killings of the Indian-white wars. By some measures, if you compare a nineteenth-century death by torture and mutilation to a twentieth-century death by a comparatively quick and impersonal shooting, the terribleness of violence may seem to be shrinking over time.

Readers may well find themselves rendered unhappy and unsettled by this line of reflection, and especially that curious word "measures." What, in heaven's name, are the proper measures for judging and comparing levels of horror and terror? Numbers are, for many people in the late twentieth century, the standard way of measuring everything: economic well-being, social values, educational achievement, the effectiveness of leaders, success or failure, progress or decline. But should number set the level of our response to brutality? Should there be some sort of direct correlation in which the numbers of dead and injured provide a precise setting for our horror and outrage?

Nearly everyone who writes about battles and massacres wrestles, at least briefly, with the problem of numbers. This episode of numerical reflection usually begins with the problem of disputed numbers: battles and massacres are occasions of passion, and passion works against precision in numerical records. Thus, calculating how many were killed, how many were injured, and how many in both of those categories were women and children is no easy matter.

There is a moment when this quantitative exercise strikes the more reflective writers as odd and troubling. Historian Juanita Brooks, writing about Utah's Mountain Meadows Massacre, offers what may well be the only clearheaded conclusion: "The total number [killed at Mountain Meadows] remains uncertain. We can be sure only that, however many there were, it was too many."[18]

While it certainly made a difference to the individuals involved, should it really make a difference to our judgment of an event if the total number of casualties at a given massacre added up to 214 or to 198? By the measure of numbers, the comparison between violence in the nineteenth century and violence in the twentieth century clearly works to the disadvantage of our times. In the wars of the twentieth century and the Holocaust in Nazi Germany, the numerical indices of brutality soared off the charts. If you went by the numbers, the violence of the Indian-white wars would hardly register when you put the totals of their casualties up against the millions in the twentieth century.

Whatever else we learn from numbers, we learn that twentieth-century human beings do not have much in the way of moral high ground. With its record of wars and holocausts and threatened atomic annihilation, the twentieth century provides no viewers' grandstand on which we can sit in self-righteous judgment of the cruelties of the nineteenth century. Thus, when the writers of a recent American history textbook tell us that "By twentieth-century standards, [Andrew] Jackson's Indian policy was both callous and brutal," one cannot help wondering, "And which twentieth-century standards are those?"[19]

There is, in any case, not much in the way of opportunity or originality left for late arrivals in the business of moral condemnation. By the 1970s, the federal government, the United States Army, the volunteer regiments, and the resource-grabbing settlers had taken just about every blow that printed words can inflict. The Modoc War, wrote historian Keith Murray in 1959, was "a perfect case study in American maladministration of its Indian affairs." This was "a government that did not know where it was going or what it was doing." The "most serious aspect" of the war, Murray concluded, was that "the federal government clearly learned nothing."[20] In a later history of the war, published in 1973, Richard Dillon was even more outspoken in his criticisms. The "land-lust of white settlers" gave the Modoc War its context, while the "immediate causes were the usual combination of civilian duplicity and pressure on government, a worthless treaty, Indian Bureau bungling (more stupidity than perfidy), and Army folly and overconfidence."[21]

Reading older, no-punches-pulled condemnations of the white-Indian wars, one feels a bit like the nineteenth-century prospectors who arrived late for a gold rush. Very much like a miner arriving at a placer site months after the first discoveries, one finds that earlier arrivals have already taken all the good lines. As much as the latter-day critic might like to land an original blow, the duplicitous federal government and the greedy white settlers have already been beaten around the post, and there is not much left for late arrivals to do, besides regret their timing.

The book reviews that responded to the publication of *Bury My Heart at Wounded Knee* in 1971 provide remarkable evidence of how completely condemnation of the wars had become a litany, a formula, a chant. The periodical *Book World* characterized *Bury My Heart* in these terms:

> Custer may have died for our sins, but Indians still have much to reproach the White Man for. A chronicle of lies, torture, and slaughter on the plains that exhausts anger, pity, and regret. Never again.[22]

Recommending Dee Brown's book as one of the "best books for young adults" for the year, the *Booklist* summed up its content:

> Battle by battle, massacre by massacre, broken treaty by broken treaty, this is a documented, gripping chronicle of the Indian struggle from 1860 to 1890 against the white man's systematic plunder.[23]

To a writer for *Newsweek*, the "appalling" story that Brown told, "with plenty of massacres and genocide overlooked by our traditional history texts," was "essential history for Americans, who must learn that this sort of thing was quite acceptable to the government in Washington."[24] Writing, as well, in *Newsweek*, Geoffrey Wolfe called *Bury My Heart at Wounded Knee* a "damning case against our national roots in greed, perfidy, ignorance, and malice."[25] For Peter Farb, in the *New York Review of Books*, Brown's "account of one horror after another endured by the reds at the hands of whites" showed the Indian wars "to be the dirty murders they were."[26] The book reads like "a crime file," *Life* magazine said, telling the story of the "thirty-year slaughter of Indians; the broken treaties that stole Indian hunting grounds; the inhumane treatment on reservations; . . . the systematic blood lettings, including the massacres of Sand Creek and Wounded Knee—Mylais of a century ago."[27]

These writers, it is clear, had Vietnam on their mind. But the United States got out of Vietnam and the recitation of wickedness hardly paused.

Even when you turn to the kind of historical writing in which blandness and inoffensiveness have been the most prized of virtues, the condemnation of white behavior in the Indian-white wars proves to be severe and unforgiving. Examine these quotations from recent college-level American history textbooks:

Grasping white men were guilty of many additional provocations. They flagrantly disregarded treaty promises, openly seized the land of the Indians, slaughtered their game, and occasionally debauched their women. . . . On several notorious occasions, innocent Indians were killed for outrages committed by their fellow tribesmen; sometimes they were shot just for "sport."[28]

The Western tribes were also victimized by the incompetence and duplicity of those white officials charged with protecting them. . . . The history of relations between the United States and the Native Americans was, therefore, one of nearly endless broken promises. . . . As usual, it was the whites who committed the most flagrant and vicious atrocities.[29]

The whites took away the tribes' sustenance, decimated their ranks, and shoved the remnants into remote and barren corners of their former domain. . . . No historical equation could have been more precise and implacable: The progress of the white settlers meant the death of the Indians. . . . The Indians had no chance against the overwhelming strength of the soldiers and the relentless white settlement of the land.[30]

The government showed little interest in honoring agreements with Indians. . . . [The attack at Sand Creek] was no worse than many incidents in earlier conflicts with Indians and not very different from what was later to occur in guerrilla wars involving American troops in the Philippines and more recently Vietnam.[31]

The whites cloaked their actions with high-sounding expressions like "civilization against savagery" and "Manifest Destiny." But the facts were simple: The whites came and took the Indians' land. . . . American policy towards the Indians was a calamity.[32]

Just a brief tour through these simple declarations from both book reviewers and textbook writers produces strange and unexpected results. "Now just a minute here," one surprises oneself by thinking. "Let's not get carried away; it's really quite a bit more complicated than that."

The biggest puzzle in these summations is, of course, their astonishing assumption of simplicity. The stories of the wars are narratives so tangled and dense that they defy clear telling. In these summations, every ounce of that complexity disappears. The diversity of white people and their responses to war are gone. Instead, a coherent, linear, and, most improbable of all, systematic process of eliminating Indians takes the place of the

actual jumble of motives and intentions, communications and miscommu-
nications, actions and reactions.

The most distressing element of these set pieces of condemnation is the
finality of their plots. Nearly every textbook crashes hard into the massacre at Wounded Knee in 1890; the bodies of the Lakota people left in the
snow stand for the end of the Indians as significant and distinctive figures
in American history. One textbook gives the section on the Indians in the
late nineteenth century the title "The End of Tribal Life." From this book,
students learn that, in the late nineteenth century, the Indians "lost their
special distinctiveness as a culture."[33] "In the end, blacks were oppressed,"
summarily declares one textbook published in 1989, while "Native Americans were exterminated."[34] In offering this picture of a strange and dreadful finality, the textbook writers no doubt think that they are showing
great sympathy for Indians. They are also, of course, killing them off with
a thoroughness that the United States Army did not, thank heavens,
match. This, surely, is what writer Richard Rodriguez had in mind when
he referred to the habit of getting rid of the Indians with "a very sharp
rhetorical tool called an 'alas.'"

Read some of these textbooks, and you want to shout, "Hold the
presses! These obituaries are premature!" But more surprising, even the
best-credentialed, sixties generation, consistent, white, liberal historian responds to the textbook litanies with an urge to defend the Army. Take this
summation from a Western American textbook published in 1984:

> The army was at the center of a vicious spiral of hatred, one
> level of fury escalating into a tier of bloodletting. The highest
> levels of command of the army should have been held account-
> able for not protecting Indians against white settlers. Though
> lesser officers and enlisted men often sympathized with the na-
> tive, there is not one significant example of the army protecting
> the Indian under the law.[35]

"Not one significant example"? It was a common pattern, after a war, for
white civilians to want to kill Indians who had surrendered and for the
Army to refuse to give them that opportunity. The characterization of the
wicked Army does not begin to acknowledge the many occasions on
which the soldiers ended up in the middle, trying to resist the settlers' demands for unrestrained violence while still trying to control the Indians.
The Army, of course, did terrible things, but the greater truth about the
Army was that it was inconsistent—equally inconsistent in both honor
and dishonor.

While the peaks of moral condemnation had already been climbed,
claimed, and occupied by the early 1970s, no one had made much of a
start on the project of fitting the wars into a broader understanding of
American history. On the contrary, some of the writers most committed to
lamentation over the injuries done to the Indians were also the most effective at declaring the topic closed and finished. With the massacre at

Wounded Knee, authors have drawn the curtain on the whole sad story of the conquest—drawn the curtain, driven the audience out of the theater, locked the doors, and put up a "CLOSED; WILL NOT REOPEN" sign. With the year 1890 standing not only for the end of the Indian wars but virtually for the end of the Indians, the whole subject is isolated, stripped of relevance, and denied any consequence for the present.

With Indian-white wars quarantined from significance, American history looks a great deal more appealing. Consider the portrait of westward expansion offered in 1993 by an American historian, called a "national treasure" by his interviewer. Here is Daniel Boorstin's declaration of faith in an inspiring and uplifting version of American history, resting on a cheerful rendering of westward expansion. In the midst of the divided and violent world of the 1990s, Boorstin said,

> community—an emphasis on what brings us together—is what I think is called for in our time. It's what built the American West: People coming by wagon trains, where they made their own systems of law and cooperated in going up and down the mountains and across the prairies to build new towns.[36]

To ask, "What's missing from this picture?" is to belabor the obvious. The tougher question by far is to ask how such a picture of history could carry any credibility at all. Knowledge of the brutality of the Indian wars has been widely distributed for centuries. And yet Daniel Boorstin carries considerable weight and influence when he places the opportunities and achievements of white people at the center of American history and pushes the conquest of Indians to the margins of the picture.

On behalf of those who join Boorstin in straining for a prettier picture of the nation's past, one has to say this: it is hard to find a way to tell the national story that does justice both to those who benefited from conquest and to those who literally lost ground. Consider what might seem to be the most remote subject from the history of the Indian-white wars: the history of white pioneer women. Men, conventional thinking goes, fight the wars; on this topic, of all topics, it ought to be permissible to concentrate on men's history to the exclusion of women. And vice versa: one ought to be able to write the history of white pioneer women with, at most, a few brief references to the unpleasantness of the Indian-white wars.

Indeed, separation and segregation have been the pattern in the writing of both the histories of Indian wars and of white pioneer women. Here, one can see the fragmentation of the history of the conquest of North America at its peak. That split appears most clearly and concretely in the writings of Dee Brown. Best known for *Bury My Heart at Wounded Knee*, Brown was also the author of another widely read book on the American West: *The Gentle Tamers: Women of the Old Wild West*, a set of portraits of pioneer women. Neither the word "Indian" nor the word "war" appears in the index of *Gentle Tamers*. In the chapter on "The Army Girls," the focus is on the hardships and travels of Army wives. There is no attention to the larger process of conquest which brought them those experiences, and no attention to the impact that the "Army Girls'" husbands had on Indian people.[37]

In Brown's strangely unconnected publications, we have the clearest and starkest example of a common pattern. The history of westward expansion has ended up divided into two, utterly separate stories: the sad and disheartening story of what whites did to the Indians, and the colorful and romantic story of what whites did for themselves. The very same writer can, on different occasions, write both of these stories, with no sense of self-contradiction or inconsistency.

These stories, however, move back together the moment one gives up the campaign to keep them apart. The history of pioneer women and the history of Indian war, to use the examples that seem the most separate, are very much intertwined. Women may have carried some technical status as noncombatants, but that status gave them no exemption from injury. Both white and Indian families were the targets of direct attack, and the deaths of soldiers and warriors in battle left widowed women on both sides facing very tough times. Women could, as well, be powerful forces in demanding revenge and retaliation. The seizure and rape of Indian women or the forced captivity of white women were often primary motivations for going to war. For Indian men, the mistreatment of Indian women could be the last straw in the insults of conquest; for white men, the idea of a white woman vulnerable to an Indian man's sexual desire could produce wild and irrational anger.

These connections between women and war are, however, the easy ideas to grasp. The tougher part is recognizing the connection between the wars and the white women settlers who were not direct participants in combat but who were nonetheless beneficiaries of the opportunities, resources, and lands opened up by the conquest and displacement of Indians. To call white pioneer women "beneficiaries of conquest" is by no means to say that their lives were easy or privileged; on the contrary, their hardships were often grueling. Moreover, many of the pioneer women, whose diaries and memoirs are now available to us, were likable women, women on whom the labels "cruel conqueror," "thoughtless invader," or "villainous displacer of native people" would sit awkwardly. They seem, truly, to have lived in a world apart from the world of massacre, mutilation, torture, and murder.

But did they?

"Although they do not ignore the reality of racist attitudes among white women," historian Antonia Castaneda has said of recent historians writing about white pioneer women, "their accounts are remarkably free of intercultural conflict in a land bloodied by three centuries of war and conquest." These writers ignore "the economic and other privileges that women of the conquering group derive from the oppression of women and men of the group being conquered." Conquest was not the exclusive enterprise of white men: "Within their gender spheres and based upon the power and privilege of their race and class," Castaneda writes, "Euro-American men and women expanded the geo-political–economic

area of the United States" and played their part in establishing the dominance of white Americans.[38]

Even if the vast majority of them never fired a gun on a battlefield,
much less took part in mutilation at a massacre, white pioneer women
were members of a civilian invading force and beneficiaries of the subordination of the natives. A recognition of the moral complexity of their position in history does these women no disservice; on the contrary, it gives a
much deeper meaning to their lives by restoring them to their full, tragic
context. Putting the history of white pioneer women back together with
the history of Indian war is in truth a matter of uniting American history,
not disuniting it.

Cease to quarantine the Indian-white wars, battles, and massacres, and
you take an essential step toward the uniting of American history.
Nineteenth-century white pioneer women and twentieth-century white career women, exploiters of natural resources and celebrators of natural
beauty, rural cowboys and urban businessmen, bluebloods of Boston whose
ancestors arrived in the 1620s and Mexican immigrants who arrived yesterday—a whole range of people who see each other as alien and who feel that
they have no common ground, benefit from the tragic events of conquest.
Conquest wove a web of consequences that does indeed unite the nation.
We live on haunted land, on land that is layers deep in human passion
and memory. There is, today, no longer any point in sorting out these passions and memories into starkly separate forms of ownership. Whether
the majority who died at any particular site were Indians or whites, these
places literally ground Americans of all backgrounds in their common history. In truth, the tragedies of the wars are our national joint property, and
how we handle that property is one test of our unity or disunity, maturity
or immaturity, as a people wearing the label "American."

For a century or two, white American intellectuals labored under the
notion that the United States was sadly disadvantaged when it came to the
joint property of history. The novelist Henry James gave this conviction of
American cultural inferiority its most memorable statement: "The past,
which died so young and had time to produce so little, attracts but scanty
attention." "The light of the sun seems fresh and innocent," James wrote,
"as if it knew as yet but few of the secrets of the world and none of the
weariness of shining."[39]

The sun that shines on North America has, it turns out, seen plenty. A
claim of innocence denies the meaning of the lives of those who died violently in the conquest of this continent, and that denial diminishes our souls.

NOTES

[1]Note 115 in *Black Hawk: An Autobiography,* ed. Donald Jackson (Urbana: University
of Illinois Press, 1964), 138–139.

[2]For this story, I am very much in debt to Keith A. Murray, *The Modocs and Their War*
(Norman: University of Oklahoma Press, 1959), Richard Dillon, *Burnt-Out Fires* (Engle-
wood Cliffs, N.J.: Prentice-Hall, 1973), and Francis S. Landrum, comp., *Guardhouse, Gallows, and Graves: The Trial and Execution of Indian Prisoners of the Modoc Indian War by the
U.S. Army* (Klamath Falls, Oreg.: Klamath County Museum, 1988).

[3]Dillon, *Burnt-Out Fires,* 157.

[4]Murray, *The Modocs and Their War,* 105.

[5]Dillon, *Burnt-Out Fires,* 158.

[6]"Proceedings of a Military Commission Convened at Fort Klamath, Oregon, for the Trial of Modoc Prisoners," Appendix B, in *Guardhouse, Gallows, and Graves,* Landrum, 126, 128.

[7]Murray, *The Modocs and Their War,* 125, 238.

[8]Ibid., 231, 236.

[9]Ibid., 237, 241.

[10]Dillon, *Burnt-Out Fires,* 260.

[11]Murray, *The Modocs and Their War,* 277.

[12]Dillon, *Burnt-Out Fires,* 178.

[13]Mae T. Parry, "Massacre at Boa Ogoi," Appendix B, in *The Shoshoni Frontier and the Bear River Massacre,* Brigham D. Madsen (Salt Like City: University of Utah Press, 1985), 235.

[14]"Proceedings," in *Guardhouse, Gallows, and Graves,* Landrum, 86, 95, 125.

[15]Murray, *The Modocs and Their War,* 301.

[16]Ibid., 309.

[17]Ibid., 274.

[18]Juanita Brooks, *The Mountain Meadows Massacre* (Norman: University of Oklahoma Press, 1964), xviii.

[19]James Kirby Martin, Randy Roberts, Steven Mintz, Linda O. McMurry, and James H. Jones, *America and Its People* (Glenview, Ill.: Scott, Foresman, 1989), 282.

[20]Murray, *The Modocs and Their War,* 313–316.

[21]Dillon, *Burnt-Out Fires,* vii.

[22]*Bookworld* 5 (December 5, 1971).

[23]*Booklist* 68 (April 1972): 663–664.

[24]*Newsweek* 78 (December 27, 1971): 57.

[25]*Newsweek* 77 (February 1, 1971): 69.

[26]Peter Farb, "Indian Corn," *New York Review of Books* 17 (December 16, 1971): 36–38.

[27]*Life* 70 (April 2, 1971): 9.

[28]Thomas A. Bailey and David M. Kennedy, *The American Pageant: A History of the Republic,* 9th ed. (Lexington, Mass.: Heath, 1991), 588.

[29]Alan Brinkley, Richard N. Current, Frank Freidel, and T. Harry Williams, *American History: A Survey,* 8th ed. (New York: McGraw-Hill, 1991), 501, 504.

[30]James A. Henretta, W. Elliott Brownlee, David Brody, and Susan Ware, *America's History* (Chicago: Dorsey, 1987), 597.

[31]John A. Garraty, *The American Nation: A History of the United States,* 7th ed. (New York: HarperCollins, 1991), 489.

[32]R. Jackson Wilson, James Gilbert, Stephen Nissenbaum, Karen Ordahl Kupperman, and Donald Scott, *The Pursuit of Liberty: A History of the American People,* 2d ed. (Belmont, Calif.: Wadsworth, 1990), 682, 688.

[33]Robert A. Divine, T. H. Bran, George M. Fredrickson, and R. Hal Williams, *America: Past and Present,* vol. 2, 3d ed. (New York: HarperCollins, 1991), 502–504.

[34]Martin et al., *America and Its People,* 503.

[35]Robert Hine, *The American West: An Interpretive History,* 2d ed. (Boston: Little, Brown, 1984), 212.

[36]Tad Szulc, "The Greatest Danger We Face," *Parade,* July 25, 1993, 4–7.

[37]Dee Brown, *Bury My Heart at Wounded Knee: An Indian History of the American West* (New York: Holt, Rinehart & Winston, 1971) and *The Gentle Tamers: Women of the Old Wild West* (1958; Lincoln: University of Nebraska Press, 1968).

[38]Antonia I. Castaneda, "Women of Color and the Rewriting of Western History: The Discourse, Politics, and Decolonization of History," *Pacific Historical Review* 61, no. 4 (November 1992): 520–521.

[39]Henry James, *Hawthorne* (1887; reprint, New York: AMS Press, 1968), 3, 12, 13.

. . . .

QUESTIONS FOR A SECOND READING

1. Early in the essay Limerick raises the question of the utility of historical research. "On some occasions," she says,

   > historians are quick to make cheerful remarks about how the understanding of history will help us to understand ourselves and to cope with the dilemmas we have inherited from the past. It is hard to pipe up with one of those earnest declarations of faith in the value of historical knowledge when you are thinking of the water at the junction of the Mississippi River and the Bad Axe River. (p. 472)

   What good is the knowledge of war, misery, greed, incompetence, and slaughter? Limerick later asks, "What do we gain besides a revival and restoration of the misery?" As you reread, note where and how Limerick provides a way of answering that question. In the example of her work, and in the ways she suggests its value and usefulness, how does she prepare a reader to answer it?

2. This selection offers a view of history as both an area of research and as something written, a writer's account of past events.

   > They are moral and spiritual muddles, in which the lines between good guy and bad guy, victim and villain, twist and meander and intertwine. And yet by the powerful alchemy of selective storytelling, in American popular culture, narratives of great complexity became simple stories of adventure and heroism and triumph, with, perhaps, just a tinge of melancholy. (p. 495)

   As you reread, look to see how she defines history as a writing problem. What are the problems? What examples does she offer? And how (through her example and in her analysis) does she suggest that these problems might be overcome?

3. Limerick says in her opening sentence, "If you place yourself at a distance, there is no clearer fact in American history than the fact of conquest." For students of your generation, for any reader at this point in time, the narrative of conquest, of white Europeans forcibly occupying native lands, is a familiar story. As you reread, note the surprises in the essay. Where does it provide surprising information or take a surprising turn? What do the surprises tell you about Limerick and her work?

ASSIGNMENTS FOR WRITING

1. One way to work on Limerick's essay is to take the challenge and write history—to write the kind of history, that is, that takes into account the problems she defines: the problems of myth, point of view, fixed ideas, simple narratives, selective storytelling, misery. You are not a professional historian, you are probably not using this book in a history course, and you don't have the time to produce a carefully researched history, one that

covers all the bases, but you can think of this as an exercise in history writing, a minihistory, a place to start. Here are two options:

a. Go to your college library or, perhaps, the local historical society, and find two or three first-person accounts of a single event, ideally accounts from different points of view. Or, if these are not available, look to the work of historians, but historians taking different positions on a single event. (This does not have to be a history of the American West.) Even if you work with published histories, try to include original documents and accounts in your essay. The more varied the accounts, the better. Then, working with these texts as your primary sources, write a history, one that you can offer as a response to "Haunted America."

b. While you can find materials in a library, you can also work with records that are closer to home. Imagine, for example, that you are going to write a family or neighborhood history. You have your own memories and experiences to work from, but for this to be a history (more than a "personal essay"), you will need to turn to other sources as well: interviews, old photos, newspaper clippings, letters, diaries,— whatever you can find. After gathering your materials, write a family or neighborhood history, one that you can offer as a response to "Haunted America."

If you have the time, you might stage the work out into several drafts, writing first from one position or point of view and then from another and then, perhaps, adding an overlay to indicate patterns you've detected (following Limerick's example).

2. Early in the essay Limerick raises the question of the utility of historical research. "On some occasions," she says,

> historians are quick to make cheerful remarks about how the understanding of history will help us to understand ourselves and to cope with the dilemmas we have inherited from the past. It is hard to pipe up with one of those earnest declarations of faith in the value of historical knowledge when you are thinking of the water at the junction of the Mississippi River and the Bad Axe River. (p. 472)

What good is the knowledge of war, misery, greed, incompetence, and slaughter? Limerick later asks, "What do we gain besides a revival and restoration of the misery?"

Write an essay in which you use "Haunted America" to answer that question. As you read the essay, what is Limerick's position on the usefulness of history, particularly for the general public? What might you argue on the basis of her example—that is, from this essay and your sense of its usefulness? You could imagine that you are writing an essay-review, something for a local magazine or newspaper.

3. After providing her "Twelve-Point Guide to War," Limerick turns to review some recent college-level American history textbooks. Turn to the books used on your campus (or that have been used on your campus over the last two decades). You could also turn to the textbook you used in high school, if it is available. Most college libraries shelve copies of the books used on campus, and the history department (or the bookstore) should be able to provide titles. Locate examples of accounts of contact and conflict: between whites and Indians, or whites and any of the other groups that have been

subject to "conquest"—African Americans, Asian Americans, Mexican Americans, and others. Choose only one group and only one period in history. In a project like this one, it is better to do close work with a limited sample.

Write an essay in which you test or extend Limerick's analysis by looking at additional textbooks. You should assume that you are writing for readers who have not read "Haunted America." You will, then, need to represent her argument and her examples. When you turn to your own, you should spend more time reading around in the textbook (including its introduction and preface) and talking about the examples you choose from the text. Limerick speaks as a professional historian; you should speak from the position of a textbook user, a student. What is at stake from your point of view?

MAKING CONNECTIONS

1. "Haunted America" was originally written as the text to accompany a book of photographs, photographs taken at the sites of major events in Indian-white relations (including battlefields): Drex Brooks, *Sweet Medicine: Sites of Indian Massacres, Battlefields, and Treaties* (Albuquerque: University of New Mexico Press, 1995). Find a copy and, using W. J. T. Mitchell's "The Photographic Essay: Four Case Studies" (p. 510) as introduction and point of reference, talk about the relationship between photographs and text.

2. Like Limerick, Jane Tompkins in "Indians" (p. 718) is writing about "textualism, morality, and the problem of history." And her focus is the historical representation of Indians. Tompkins, however, is not a historian, at least not in the strict, disciplinary sense of the word: she doesn't work in a history department. In this sense her commitments to and understanding of history is, perhaps, a bit different.

   Read the two essays together as a set, as part of a single project investigating the problems of writing history and understanding the past. Write an essay in which you discuss the differences, focusing as closely as you can on specific examples from each essay. Examine the concerns or methods that belong to both but look, finally, to see the differences. How would you account for those differences? What difference do they make to you as a reader, a writer, a person with an interest in understanding the past?

3. Susan Griffin, in "Our Secret" (p. 345), is writing about the Holocaust and World War II. Early in her essay, Limerick says, "You can be the world's greatest enthusiast for narrative history, and you can still lose your nerve at the prospect of putting yourself and your readers at the mercy of one of these tales from hell." Griffin's is certainly a tale from hell. It may not be appropriate to say that she lost her nerve, but she is certainly unwilling to write the usual narrative history. Write an essay that reads Griffin's "Our Secret" through the lens of Limerick's "Haunted America." Is Griffin engaged in a Limerick-like project? or is she doing something different?

   You should assume that your audience is familiar with neither text. You will need to take care, then, to introduce, to summarize and paraphrase. You should provide enough material in quotation for a reader to get a sense of the formal experimentation in both essays.

W. J. T.
MITCHELL

W. J. T. MITCHELL (b. 1941) is Gaylord Donnelley Distinguished Service Professor of English and Art History at the University of Chicago. His books include Iconology (1987), Blake's Composite Art (1978), The Language of Images (1980), Against Theory (1985), Art and the Public Sphere (1993), Landscape and Power (1994), and The Last Dinosaur Book: The Life and Times of a Cultural Icon (1998). He is the editor of one of the leading journals in the humanities, Critical Inquiry, and has received fellowships from the Guggenheim Foundation, the National Endowment for the Humanities, the Rockefeller Foundation, and the American Philosophical Society. Mitchell's career as a scholar and teacher is distinguished not only by its productivity and wide-reaching influence (his work, for example, is read beyond his discipline and outside the academy) but also for the ways it has brought together subjects usually treated as separate: literature and art, words and pictures, language and vision.

The following selection is taken from his 1994 prize-winning book, Picture Theory. Picture Theory is a massive, brilliant, and controversial book whose goal is to examine the interaction of words and images, verbal and visual representations, in a variety of media, including literature, painting, advertising, and film. It not only describes these interactions but traces their linkages to issues of knowledge, power, value, and human interest. (The following selection looks at the hybrid medium of the photographic essay.)

Picture Theory *brings together the materials and arguments of seminars Mitchell taught at the University of Chicago, seminars with titles like "Image and Text" and "Verbal and Visual Representation." His book is not, he says, so much a textbook as a "pedagogical primer or prompt-book for classroom experiments," experiments that would bring together the study of literature and the study of visual art under the general category of "representation." For Mitchell, this urgently needed form of study should be central to the undergraduate curriculum.*

Here is Mitchell in the introduction to Picture Theory:

> *W. E. B. Du Bois said "the problem of the Twentieth Century is the problem of the color-line." As we move into an era in which "color" and "line" (and the identities they designate) have become potently manipulable elements in pervasive technologies of simulation and mass mediation, we may find that the problem of the twenty-first century is the problem of the image. Certainly I would not be the first to suggest that we live in a culture dominated by pictures, visual simulations, stereotypes, illusions, copies, reproductions, imitations, and fantasies. Anxieties about the power of visual culture are not just the province of critical intellectuals. Everyone knows that television is bad for you and that its badness has something to do with the passivity and fixation of the spectator. But then people have always known, at least since Moses denounced the Golden Calf, that images were dangerous, that they can captivate the onlooker and steal the soul. . . . What we need is a critique of visual culture that is alert to the power of images for good and evil and that is capable of discriminating the variety and historical specificity of their uses.*

Mitchell's work is a contribution to that effort. A key word in Picture Theory, *one you will find in the chapter below, is "ekphrasis." Ekphrasis was originally used to name a minor literary genre, poems written about paintings; for Mitchell the term stands for the more general topic of "the verbal representation of visual representation" (words standing for images) and the human desire across time to believe that words can make us see or that they can give voice to (articulate, explain) something which is beyond or outside of language. In the chapter that follows, Mitchell looks at four "classic" texts of photojournalism to consider what is at stake in representing the world through picture and paragraph, and what is at stake in the arguments over which medium (photography or writing) can best make the claim to represent reality most truly, completely, or powerfully. Rather than choosing a side, Mitchell opens up the debate as a significant and useful contestation. His goal is to provide a practical example of how to think through particular texts, like a book of photojournalism, to larger questions of how we know what we know about the world, how we come to value what we value, and how power operates both through us and on us.*

The Photographic Essay:
Four Case Studies

Three questions:

1. *What is the relation of photography and language?*
2. *Why does it matter what this relation is?*
3. *How are these questions focused in the medium known as the "photographic essay"?*

Three answers:

1. *Photography is and is not a language; language also is and is not a "photography."*
2. *The relation of photography and language is a principal site of struggle for value and power in contemporary representations of reality; it is the place where images and words find and lose their conscience, their aesthetic and ethical identity.*
3. *The photographic essay is the dramatization of these questions in an emergent form of mixed, composite art.*

What follows is an attempt to connect these questions and answers.

Photography and Language

The totality of this relationship is perhaps best indicated by saying that appearances constitute a half-language.
— JOHN BERGER,
Another Way of Telling

The relationship of photography and language admits of two basic descriptions, fundamentally antithetical. The first stresses photography's difference from language, characterizing it as a "message without a code," a purely objective transcript of visual reality.[1] The second turns photography into a language, or stresses its absorption by language in actual usage. This latter view is currently in favor with sophisticated commentators on photography. It is getting increasingly hard to find anyone who will defend the view (variously labeled "positivist," "naturalistic," or "superstitious and naive") that photographs have a special causal and structural relationship with the reality that they represent. Perhaps this is due to the dominance of linguistic and semiotic models in the human sciences or to the skepticism, relativism, and conventionalism which dominates the world of advanced literary criticism. Whatever the reason, the dominant view of photography is now the kind articulated by Victor Burgin when he notes that "we rarely see a photograph *in use* which is not accompanied by language" and goes on to claim that the rare exceptions only confirm the domination of photography by language: "even the uncaptioned 'art' photograph," argues Burgin, "is invaded by language in the very moment it is looked at: in memory, in association, snatches of words and images continually intermingle and exchange one for the other."[2] Indeed, Burgin carries his argument well beyond looking at photography to "looking" as such, deriding the "naive idea of purely retinal vision," unaccompanied by language, a view which he associates with "an error of even greater consequence: that ubiquitous belief in 'the visual' as a realm of experience totally separated from, indeed antithetical to, 'the verbal' " (p. 53). Burgin traces "the idea that there are two quite distinct forms of communication, words and images" from the neoplatonic faith in a "divine language of things, richer than the language of words" to Ernst Gombrich's modern defense of the "natural" and "nonconventional" status of the photograph. "Today," concludes Burgin, "such relics are obstructing our view of photography" (p. 70).

What is it that troubles me about this conclusion? It isn't that I disagree with the claim that "language" (in some form) usually enters the experience of viewing photography or of viewing anything else. And it isn't the questioning of a reified distinction between words and images, verbal and visual representation; there seems no doubt that these different media interact with one another at numerous levels in cognition, consciousness, and communication. What troubles me, I suppose, is the confidence of tone, the assurance that we are able "today" to cast off certain "relics" that have mystified us for over two thousand years in favor of, presumably, a clear, unobstructed view of the matter. I'm especially struck by the figure of the "relic" as an obstructive image in contrast to the unobstructed view, since this is precisely the opposition which has (superstitiously) differentiated photography from more traditional forms of imagery and which formerly differentiated perspectival representation from "pre-scientific" modes of pictorial representation. Burgin's conclusions, in other words, are built upon a figurative opposition ("today/yesterday"; "clear view/obstructive relic") he has already dismissed as erroneous in its application to photography and vision. This return of an inconvenient figure suggests, at a minimum, that the relics are not quite so easily disposed of.

I'm also troubled by Burgin's confidence that "our view" can so easily be cleared up. Who is the "we" that has this "view"? It is implicitly divided between those who have overcome their superstitions about photography and those naifs who have not. "Our view" of photography is, in other words, far from homogeneous, but is the site of a struggle between the enlightened and the superstitious, moderns and ancients, perhaps even "moderns" and "postmoderns." Symptoms of this struggle emerge in Burgin's rhetoric when he speaks of the photograph as "invaded by language" (p. 51); what he seems not to consider is that this invasion might well provoke a resistance or that there might be some value at stake in such a resistance, some real motive for a defence of the non-linguistic character of the photograph. Burgin seems content to affirm the "fluidity" (p. 52) of the relation between photography and language and to treat photography as "a complex of exchanges between the verbal and the visual" (p. 58).

But why should we suppose this model of free and fluid "ex-changes" between photography and language to be true or desirable? How do we account for the stubbornness of the naive, superstitious view of photography? What could possibly motivate the persistence in erroneous beliefs about the radical difference between images and words and the special status of photography? Are these mistaken beliefs simply conceptual errors, like mistakes in arithmetic? Or are they more on the order of ideological beliefs, convictions that resist change by or-dinary means of persuasion and demonstration? What if it were the case that the "relics" which "obstruct" our view of photography also *consti-tute* that view? What if the only adequate formulation of the relation of photography and language was a paradox: photography both is and is not a language?

This, I take it, is what lies at the heart of what Roland Barthes calls "the photographic paradox," "the co-existence of two messages, the one with-out a code (the photographic analogue), the other with a code (the 'art,' or the treatment, or the 'writing,' or the rhetoric of the photograph)."[3] Barthes works through a number of strategies to clarify and rationalize this paradox. The most familiar is the division of the photographic "mes-sage" into "denotation" and "connotation," the former associated with the "mythical," nonverbal status of the photograph "in the perfection and plenitude of its analogy," the latter with the readability and textuality of the photograph. Barthes sometimes writes as if he believes that this divi-sion of the photographic message into "planes" or "levels" may solve the paradox:

> how, then, can the photograph be at once 'objective' and 'in-vested,' natural and cultural? It is through an understanding of the mode of imbrication of denoted and connoted messages that it may one day be possible to reply to that question. (p. 20)

But his more characteristic gesture is to reject easy answers predicted on a model of "free exchange" of verbal and visual messages, connoted or de-noted "levels": "structurally," he notes, "the paradox is clearly not the col-lusion of a denoted message and a connoted message . . . it is that the con-noted (or coded) message develops on the basis of a message *without a code*" (p. 19). To put the matter more fully: one connotation always present in the photograph is that it is a pure denotation; that is simply what it means to recognize it as a photograph rather than some other sort of image. Conversely, the denotation of a photograph, what we take it to rep-resent, is never free from what we take it to mean. The simplest snapshot of a bride and groom at a wedding is an inextricably woven network of denotation and connotation: we cannot divide it into "levels" which distinguish it as a "pure" reference to John and Mary, or a man and a woman, as opposed to its "connotations" of festivity. Connotation goes all the way down to roots of the photograph, to the motives for its production, to the selection of its subject matter, to the choice of angles and lighting. Similarly, "pure denotation" reaches all the way up to the most textually "readable" features of the photograph: the photograph is "read" *as if it were* the trace of an event, a "relic" of an occasion as laden with aura and mystery as the bride's garter or her fading bouquet. The distinction between connotation and denotation does not resolve the paradox of photography; it only allows us to restate it more fully.

Barthes emphasizes this point when he suggests that the "structural paradox" of photography "coincides with an ethical paradox: when one wants to be 'neutral,' 'objective,' one strives to copy reality meticulously, as though the analogical were a factor of resistance against the investment of values" (pp. 19–20). The "value" of photography resides precisely in its freedom from "values," just as, in cognitive terms, its principal connotation or "coded" implication is that it is pure denotation, without a code. The persistence of these paradoxes suggests that the "mode of imbrication" or overlapping between photography and language is best understood, not as a structural matter of "levels" or as a fluid exchange, but (to use Barthes's term) as a site of "resistance." This is not to suggest that resistance is always successful or that "collusion" and "exchange" between photography and language is impossible or automatically undesirable. It is to say that the exchanges which seem to make photography just another language, an adjunct or supplement to language, make no sense without an understanding of the resistance they overcome. What we need to explore now is the nature of this resistance and the values which have motivated it.

The Photographic Essay

The immediate instruments are two: the motionless camera and the printed word.

—JAMES AGEE,
Let Us Now Praise Famous Men[4]

The ideal place to study the interaction of photography and language is in that subgenre (or is it a medium within the medium?) of photography known as the "photographic essay." The classic examples of this form (Jacob Riis's *How the Other Half Lives,* Margaret Bourke-White and Erskine Caldwell's *You Have Seen Their Faces*) give us a literal conjunction of photographs and text—usually united by a documentary purpose, often political, journalistic, sometimes scientific (sociology). There is an argument by Eugene Smith that the photographic series or sequence, even without text,

can be regarded as a photo-essay,[5] and there are distinguished examples
of such works (Robert Frank's *The Americans*).[6] I want to concentrate, however, on the kinds of photographic essays which contain strong textual
elements, where the text is most definitely an "invasive" and even domi-
neering element. I also want to focus on the sort of photo-essay whose text
is concerned, not just with the subject matter in common between the two
media, but with the way in which the media address that subject matter.
Early in Jacob Riis's *How the Other Half Lives* he describes an incident in
which his flash powder almost set a tenement on fire. This event is not
represented in the photographs: what we see, instead, are scenes of tenement squalor in which dazed subjects (who have often been roused from
their sleep) are displayed in passive bedazzlement under the harsh illumi-
nation of Riis's flash powder [Figure 1]. Riis's textual anecdote reflects on
the scene of production of his images, characterizing and criticizing the
photographer's own competence, perhaps even his ethics. We might say
that Riis allows his text to subvert his images, call them into question. A
better argument would be that the text "enables" the images (and their
subjects) to take on a kind of independence and humanity that would be

[Figure 1]. Jacob Riis, *Lodgers in Bayard St. Tenement* . . . Page spread from *How the Other
Half Lives* (1890). Photo reproduced courtesy of the Museum of the City of New York.

unavailable under an economy of straightforward "exchange" between photographer and writer. The photographs may be "evidence" for propositions quite at odds with the official uses that Riis wants to put them. The beholder, in turn, is presented with an uncomfortable question: is the political, epistemological power of these images (their "shock" value) a justification for the violence that accompanies their production? (Riis worked as a journalist in close collaboration with the police; many of these photos were taken during nighttime raids; these are, in a real sense, surveillance photographs; they also had a profound effect on reform efforts in the New York slums.) Riis's joining of an inconvenient, disruptive text foregrounds this dilemma, draws us into it. A resistance arises in the text-photo relation; we move less easily, less quickly from reading to seeing. Admittedly, this resistance is exceptional in Riis, whose general practice is to assume a straightforward exchange of information between text and image. But its emergence even in this relatively homogeneous photo-essay alerts us to its possibility, its effect and motivations.

Another way to state this dilemma is as a tension between the claims of the ethical and the political, the aesthetic and the rhetorical. Photo-essays have been, by and large, the product of progressive, liberal consciences, associated with political reform and leftist causes. But the best of them, I want to suggest, do not treat photography or language simply as instruments in the service of a cause or an institution. Nor are they content to advertise the fine moral or artistic sensitivities of their producers. The problem is to mediate these disparate claims, to make the instrumentality of both writing and photography and their interactions serve the highest interests of "the cause" by subjecting it to criticism while advancing its banner. Agee distinguishes between the "immediate instruments" of the photo-essay, "the still camera and the printed word," and the "governing instrument—which is also one of the centers of the subject—[which] is individual, anti-authoritative human consciousness" (p. xiv). The production of the photo-essay, the actual labor that goes into it, should not be, in Agee's view, simply an instrumental application of media to politics, ideology, or any other subject matter. The "taking" of human subjects by a photographer (or a writer) is a concrete social encounter, often between a damaged, victimized, and powerless individual and a relatively privileged observer, often acting as the "eye of power," the agent of some social, political, or journalistic institution. The "use" of this person as instrumental subject matter in a code of photographic messages is exactly what links the political aim with the ethical, creating exchanges and resistances at the level of value that do not concern the photographer alone, but which reflect back on the writer's (relatively invisible) relation to the subject as well and on the exchanges between writer and photographer.[7]

One last question about the genre: why should it be called the "photographic *essay*"? Why not the photo novel or lyric or narrative or just the

"photo text"? There are, of course, examples of all these forms: Wright
Morris has used his photographs to illustrate his fiction; Paul Strand and
Nancy Newhall link photographs with lyric poems in *Time in New England*;
Jan Baetens has analyzed the emergent French genre of the "photographic
novel." What warrant is there for thinking of the "photo-essay"
as an especially privileged model for the conjunction of photography and
language? One reason is simply the dominance of the essay as the textual
form that conventionally accompanies photography in magazines and
newspapers. But there are, I think, some more fundamental reasons for a
decorum that seems to link the photograph with the essay in the way
that history painting was linked to the epic or landscape painting to the
lyric poem. The first is the presumption of a common referential reality:
not "realism" but "reality," nonfictionality, even "scientificity" are the
generic connotations that link the essay with the photograph.[8] The second
is the intimate fellowship between the informal or personal essay,
with its emphasis on a private "point of view," memory, and autobiography,
and photography's mythic status as a kind of materialized memory
trace imbedded in the context of personal associations and private
"perspectives." Third, there is the root sense of the essay as a partial, incomplete
"attempt," an effort to get as much of the truth about something
into its brief compass as the limits of space and writerly ingenuity
will allow. Photographs, similarly, seem necessarily incomplete in their
imposition of a frame that can never include everything that was there to
be, as we say, "taken." The generic incompleteness of the informal literary
essay becomes an especially crucial feature of the photographic
essay's relations of image and text. The text of the photo-essay typically
discloses a certain reserve or modesty in its claims to "speak for" or interpret
the images; like the photograph, it admits its inability to appropriate
everything that was there to be taken and tries to let the photographs
speak for themselves or "look back" at the viewer.

In the remainder of this essay I want to examine four photo-essays
that, in various ways, foreground the dialectic of exchange and resistance
between photography and language, the things that make it possible (and
sometimes impossible) to "read" the pictures, or to "see" the text illustrated
in them. I will limit myself to four main examples: the first, Agee
and Evans's *Let Us Now Praise Famous Men*, generally acknowledged as a
"classic" (and a modernist) prototype for the genre, will be used mainly
to lay out the principles of the form. The other three, exemplifying more
recent and perhaps "postmodern" strategies (Roland Barthes's *Camera
Lucida*, Malek Alloula's *The Colonial Harem*, and Edward Said and Jean
Mohr's *After the Last Sky*), will be analyzed in increasing detail to show
the encounter of principles with practice. The basic questions to be addressed
with each of these works are the same: what relationship between
photography and writing do they articulate? What tropes of differentiation
govern the division of labor between photographer and
writer, image and text, the viewer and the reader?

— boil down to saundbyk
— saundbyk is really
a thesis statement.

Spy and Counter-spy: Let Us Now Praise Famous Men

> Who are you who will read these words and study these pho-
> tographs, and through what cause, by what chance and for
> what purpose, and by what right do you qualify to, and what
> will you do about it.
>
> — JAMES AGEE

The central formal requirements of the photographic essay are memorably expressed in James Agee's introduction to *Let Us Now Praise Famous
Men:* "The photographs are not illustrative. They and the text are coequal,
mutually independent, and fully collaborative" (p. xv). These three requirements—equality, independence, and collaboration—are not simply
given by putting any text together with any set of photographs, and they
are not so easily reconcilable. Independence and collaboration, for instance, are values that may work at cross-purposes, and a "co-equality" of
photography and writing is easier to stipulate than it is to achieve or even
to imagine. Agee notes, for instance, that "the impotence of the reader's
eye" (p. xv) will probably lead to an underestimation of Evans's photographs; it is not hard to imagine a deafness or illiteracy underestimating
the text as well—a fate that actually befell *Let Us Now Praise Famous Men*
when it reached the editors of *Fortune* magazine, who had commissioned
it.[9] Agee's generic requirements are not only imperatives for the producers of an art form that seems highly problematic, they are also prescriptions for a highly alert reader/viewer that may not yet exist, that may in
fact have to be created.

It is easy enough to see how *Famous Men* satisfies the requirements of
independence and co-equality. The photographs are completely separate,
not only from Agee's text, but from any of the most minimal textual features that conventionally accompany a photo-essay: no captions, legends,
dates, names, locations, or even numbers are provided to assist a "reading" of the photographs. Even a relatively "pure" photographic essay like
Robert Frank's *The Americans* provides captions telling the subject and the
location. Frank's opening image, for instance, of shadowy figures at the
window of a flag-draped building [Figure 2, p. 518], is accompanied by
the caption "Parade—Hoboken, New Jersey" which immediately gives us
informational location not provided by the photograph and names a subject which it does not represent. Evans allows us no such clues or access
to his photographs. If we have studied Agee's text at some length, we
may surmise that the opening photograph is of Chester Bowles, and we
may think we can identify three different tenant families in Evans's pictures based on their descriptions in Agee's text, but all of these connections must be excavated; none of them are unequivocally given by any
"key" that links text to images. The location of Evans's photos at the front
of the volume is an even more aggressive declaration of photographic independence. In contrast to the standard practices of interweaving photos
with text or placing them in a middle or concluding section where they

Figure [2]. Robert Frank, *Parade—Hoboken, New Jersey* (1955–1956), from *The Americans* (1958). Copyright © Robert Frank. Courtesy, Pace/MacGill Gallery, New York.

can appear in the context provided by the text, Evans and Agee force us to confront the photographs without context, before we have had a chance to see a preface, table of contents, or even a title page. When we do finally reach the contents, we learn that we are already in "Book Two" and that the photographs are the "Book One," which we have already "read."

The "co-equality" of photos and text is, in one sense, a direct consequence of their independence, each medium being given a "book" of its own, each equally free of admixture with the other—Evans providing photos without text, Agee a text without photos. But equality is further suggested by the feeling that Evans's photos really do constitute, in W. Eugene Smith's phrase, an "essay" in their own right.[10] The sequence of Evans's photos does not tell a story but suggests rather a procession of general "topics" epitomized by specific figures—after the anomalous opening figure [Figure 3, p. 519] whose rumpled sport coat suggests a wealth and class somewhat above those of the tenant farmers, a survey of representative figures: Father [Figure 4, p. 520], Mother [Figure 5, p. 521], Bedroom [Figure 6, p. 522], House [Figure 7, p. 523], and Children (Girl-Boy-Girl) of descending ages [Figures 8, 9, 10, pp. 524–26].[11] It is possible to construct a master-narrative if we insist on one. Agee provides one some eighty pages later if we are alert to it: "a man and a woman are drawn together upon a bed and there is a child and there are children"

Figure [3]. Walker Evans, photograph from *Let Us Now Praise Famous Men* (1939) by James Agee and Walker Evans. Photograph courtesy of the Library of Congress.

(p. 55). We can even give these figures proper names: George and Annie Mae Gudger, their house, their children. But these text-image "exchanges" are not *given* to us by either the text or the images; if anything, the organization of the volume makes this difficult; it resists the straightforward collaboration of photo and text. And this resistance is not overcome by repeated readings and viewings, as if a secret code linking the photos to the

Figure [4]. Walker Evans, photograph from *Let Us Now Praise Famous Men* (1939) by
James Agee and Walker Evans. Photograph courtesy of the Library of Congress.

text were there to be deciphered. When all the "proper" names and places
are identified, we are reminded that these are fictional names: the
Gudgers, Rickettses, and Woodses do not exist by those names. We may
feel we "know" them through Evans's images, through Agee's intimate
meditations on their lives, but we never do, and we never will.

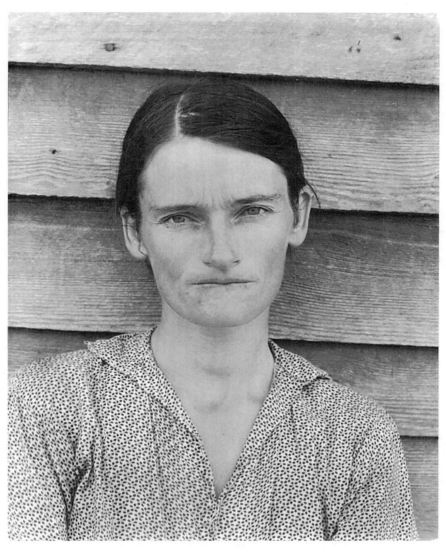

Figure [5]. Walker Evans, *Annie Mae Gudger,* photograph from *Let Us Now Praise Famous Men* (1939) by James Agee and Walker Evans. © Copyright, Estate of Walker Evans.

What is the meaning of this blockage between photo and text? One answer would be to link it with the aesthetics of a Greenbergian modernism, a search for the "purity" of each medium, uncontaminated by the mixing of pictorial and verbal codes. Evans's photos are like aggressively untitled abstract paintings, bereft of names, reference, and "literary" elements. They force us back onto the formal and material features of the images in

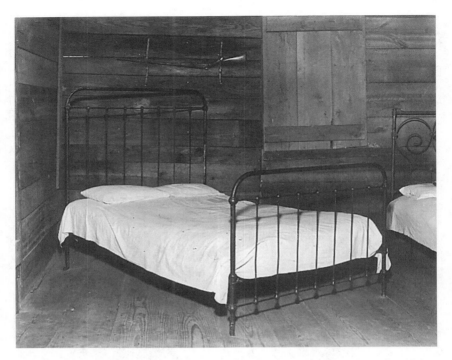

Figure [6]. Walker Evans, photograph from *Let Us Now Praise Famous Men* (1939) by James Agee and Walker Evans. Photograph courtesy of the Library of Congress.

themselves. The portrait of Annie Mae Gudger [see Figure 5, p. 521], for instance, becomes a purely formal study of flatness and worn, "graven" surfaces: the lines of her face, the weathered grain of the boards, the faded dress, the taut strands of her hair, the gravity of her expression all merge into a visual complex that is hauntingly beautiful and enigmatic. She becomes an "icon," arguably the most famous of all the anonymous men and women captured by Evans's camera, a pure aesthetic object, liberated from contingency and circumstance into a space of pure contemplation, the Mona Lisa of the Depression.

There is something deeply disturbing, even disagreeable, about this (unavoidable) aestheticizing response to what after all is a real person in desperately impoverished circumstances. Why should we have a right to look on this woman and find her fatigue, pain, and anxiety beautiful? What gives us the right to look upon her, as if we were God's spies? These questions are, of course, exactly the sorts of hectoring challenges Agee's text constantly confronts us with; they are also the questions that Evans's photos force on us when he shows us the tenant farmers as beautiful, formal studies filled with mystery, dignity, and presence. We can-

Figure [7]. Walker Evans, photograph from *Let Us Now Praise Famous Men* (1939) by James Agee and Walker Evans. Photograph courtesy of the Library of Congress.

not feel easy with our aesthetic appreciation of Annie Mae Gudger any more than we can pronounce her true name. Her beauty, like her identity, is held in reserve from us, at a distance: she looks back at us, withholding unreadable secrets. She asks as many questions of us as we of her: "who are you who will read these words and study these photographs?"

The aestheticizing separation of Evans's images from Agee's text is not, then, simply a formal characteristic but an ethical strategy, a way of preventing easy access to the world they represent. I call this an "ethical" strategy because it may well have been counterproductive for any political aims. The collaboration of Erskine Caldwell and Margaret Bourke-White in the representation of tenant farmers provides an instructive comparison. *You Have Seen Their Faces* offers unimpeded exchange between photos and text: Bourke-White's images interweave with Caldwell's essay; each photo is accompanied by a "legend" locating the shot and a "quotation" by the central figure. Consider *Hamilton, Alabama*/"We manage to get along" [Figure 11, p. 527].[12] The photograph restates the legend in its pictorial code, creating with its low-angle viewpoint and wide-angle lens an

Figure [8]. Walker Evans, photograph from *Let Us Now Praise Famous Men* (1939) by
James Agee and Walker Evans. Photograph courtesy of the Library of Congress.

impression of monumentality and strength (note especially how large the
figure's hands are made to seem). This sort of rhetorical reinforcement
and repetition is by far the more conventional arrangement of the photo-
essay, and it may explain the enormous popular success of *You Have Seen
Their Faces.*

It also illustrates vividly the kind of rhetorical relation of photo and
text that Evans and Agee were resisting. This is not to say that Evans and
Agee are "unrhetorical," but that their "collaboration" is governed by a
rhetoric of resistance rather than one of exchange and cooperation. Their
images and words are "fully collaborative" in the project of subverting
what they saw as a false and facile collaboration with governmental and
journalistic institutions (the Farm Security Administration, *Fortune* magazine).[13] The blockage between photo and text is, in effect, a sabotaging of
an effective surveillance and propaganda apparatus, one which creates
easily manipulable images and narratives to support political agendas.
Agee and Evans may well have agreed with many of the reformist political aims of Caldwell and Bourke-White and the institutions they represented: where they parted company is on what might be called the
"ethics of espionage." Agee repeatedly characterizes himself and Evans
as "spies": Agee is "a spy, traveling as a journalist"; Evans "a counter-

Figure [9]. Walker Evans, photograph from *Let Us Now Praise Famous Men* (1939) by James Agee and Walker Evans. Photograph courtesy of the Library of Congress.

spy, traveling as a photographer" (p. xxii). The "independence" of their collaboration is the strict condition for this spy/counter-spy relation; it is their way of keeping each other honest, playing the role of "conscience" to one another. Evans exemplifies for Agee the ruthless violence of their work and the possibility of doing it with some sort of honor. The visibility

[Figure 10]. Walker Evans, photograph from *Let Us Now Praise Famous Men* (1939) by James Agee and Walker Evans. Photograph courtesy of the Library of Congress.

of the photographic apparatus brings their espionage out into the open, and Agee admires the openness of Evans at work, his willingness to let his human subjects pose themselves, stage their own images in all their dignity and vulnerability, rather than treating them as material for pictorial self-expression. Agee, for his part, is all self-expression, as if the objectivity and restraint of Evans's work had to be countered by the fullest subjectivity and copiousness of confession. This division of labor

[Figure 11]. Margaret Bourke-White, *HAMILTON, ALABAMA. "We manage to get along."* From *You Have Seen Their Faces,* by Erskine Caldwell and Margaret Bourke-White. Courtesy of the Estate of Margaret Bourke-White.

is not just an ethics of production affecting the work of the writer and photographer;[14] it is, in a very real sense, an ethics of form imposed on the reader/viewer in the structural division of the photos and text. Our labor as beholders is as divided as that of Agee and Evans, and we find ourselves drawn, as they were, into a vortex of collaboration and resistance.[15]

Labyrinth and Thread: Camera Lucida

A labyrinthine man never seeks the truth, but only his Ariadne.
—NIETZSCHE
(quoted by Barthes)[16]

The strong, "agonistic" form of the photographic essay tends, as we have seen, to be as concerned with the nature of photography, writing, and the relation of the two, as with its represented subject matter (tenant farming, New York tenements, migrant workers, etc.). But most essays on photography (including this one) are not "photographic essays" in the sense I am giving the term here. Walter Benjamin's "A Short History of Photography" is not a photographic essay for the obvious reason that it is not illustrated. But even if it were, the photos would only be there to illustrate the text; they would not have the independence or co-equality that permits collaboration in a truly composite form.

One of the few "essays on photography" that approaches the status of a photographic essay is Barthes's *Camera Lucida*. The "independence" and "co-equality" of the photographs in Barthes's text is achieved, not by grouping them in a separate "book" where their own syntactical relations may emerge, but by a consistent subversion of the textual strategies that tend to incorporate photographs as "illustrative" or evidentiary examples. We open *Camera Lucida* to a frontispiece [Figure 12, p. 529], a color polaroid by Daniel Boudinet that never receives any commentary in the text. The only words of Barthes that might be applied to it are equivocal or negative ("Polaroid? Fun, but disappointing, except when a great photographer is involved" [p. 9]; "I am not very fond of Color . . . color is a coating applied *later on* to the original truth of the black-and-white photograph . . . an artifice, a cosmetic (like the kind used to paint corpses)" (p. 81). Are we to suppose, then, that Barthes simply "likes" this photograph and admires Boudinet's art? These criteria are continually subverted in Barthes's text by his seemingly capricious preferences, his refusal to assent to canonized masterpieces and masters: "there are moments when I detest Photographs: what have I to do with Atget's old tree trunks, with Pierre Boucher's nudes, with Germain Krull's double exposures (to cite only the old names)?" (p. 16). The Boudinet polaroid stands independent of Barthes's text: the best "reading" we can get it is perhaps simply as an emblem of the unreadability of photography, its occupation of a site forever prior to and outside Barthes's text. The photo presents an image of a veiled, intimate *boudoir,* simultaneously erotic and funereal, its tantalizingly partial revelation of light gleaming through the cleavage in the curtains like the secret at the center of a labyrinth. Barthes tells us that "it is a mistake to associate Photography . . . with the notion of a dark passage *(camera obscura).* It is *camera lucida* that we should say" (p. 106). But the darkened chamber of Barthes's frontispiece refuses to illustrate his text. If there is a *camera lucida* in this image it resides beyond the curtains of this scene, or perhaps in the luminous opening at its center, an evocation of the camera's aperture.[17]

[Figure 12]. Daniel Boudinet, *Polaroid, 1979,* in Roland Barthes, *Camera Lucida* (1981). © 1993 ARS, New York/SPADEM, Paris.

Most of the other photographs in Barthes's text seem, at first glance, purely illustrative, but a closer reading subverts this impression. Barthes's commentaries are doggedly resistant to the rhetoric of the *"studium,"* the "rational intermediary of an ethical or political culture" (p. 26) that allows photographs to be "read" or that would allow a scientific theory of the photograph to emerge. Instead, Barthes emphasizes what he calls the *"punctum,"* the stray, pointed detail that "pricks" or "wounds" him. These details (a necklace, bad teeth, folded arms, dirt streets) are accidental, uncoded, nameless features that open the photograph metonymically onto a contingent realm of memory and subjectivity: "it is what I add to the photograph and *what is nonetheless already there*" (p. 55), what is more often remembered about a photograph than what is seen in its actual presence.[18] The effect of this rhetoric is to render Barthes's text almost useless as a semiological theory of photography, while making it indispensable *to* such a theory. By insisting on his own personal experiences of photographs, by accepting the naive, primitive "astonishment," "magic," and "madness" of photography, Barthes makes his own experience the raw material of experimental data for a theory—a data, however, that is filled with consciousness of a skepticism about the theories that will be brought to it.[19]

The photograph that is of most importance to Barthes's text, a "private" picture of his mother taken in a glassed-in conservatory or "Winter Garden" when she was five years old, is not reproduced. "Something like the essence of the Photograph," says Barthes, "floated in this particular picture." If "all the world's photographs formed a Labyrinth, I knew at the center of this Labyrinth I should find nothing but this sole picture" (p. 73). But Barthes cannot take us into the center of the labyrinth except blindfolded, by ekphrasis, leading us with the thread of language. Barthes "cannot reproduce" the photograph of his mother because it "would be nothing but an indifferent picture" for anyone else. In its place he inserts a photograph by Nadar of *The Artist's Mother (or Wife)* [Figure 13, p. 531], which one "no one knows for certain" (p. 70).[20] This photograph receives only the most minimal, even banal commentary ("one of the loveliest photographs in the world" [p. 70]) and an equally banal caption which pretends to be quoted from the text, but (characteristically) is misquoted or constructed especially for this image: "'Who do you think is the world's greatest photographer?' 'Nadar'" (p. 68). Barthes's substitution of this maternal image for his own mother launches him into a series of increasingly general associative substitutions: this photograph becomes "*the* Photograph" becomes "*the* Image"; Barthes's mother becomes "The Artist's Mother" becomes "*the* Mother." The link between "Image" and "Mother" is then summarized as a universal cultural complex which has been reproduced in the particularity of Barthes's own experience of photography:

> Judaism rejected the image in order to protect itself from the risk of worshipping the Mother. . . . Although growing up in a religion-without-images where the Mother is not worshipped (Protestantism) but doubtless formed culturally by Catholic art, when I confronted the Winter Garden photograph I gave myself up to the Image, to the Image-Repertoire. (pp. 74–75)

Barthes is not a photographer; he made none of the photographs in his book, his only responsibility being to collect and arrange them within his text. He therefore has no collaborator in the usual sense. His collaborator is "Photography" itself, exemplified by an apparently miscellaneous collection of images, some private and personal, most the work of recognized

[Figure 13]. Nadar, *The Artist's Mother (or Wife)* (n.d.), in Roland Barthes, *Camera Lucida* (1981). © 1993 ARS, New York/SPADEM, Paris.

masters from Niepce to Stieglitz to Mapplethorpe and Avedon.[21] "All the world's photographs" are treated by Barthes as a labyrinth whose unrepresentable center conceals the Mother, *his* mother. A mother who, like the subjects of all photographs, "is dead and . . . is going to die" (p. 95) unites all the photographs in Barthes's text, endowing them with the independent unity that enables them to look back at us while withholding their secrets. The Nadar portrait, its maternal figure gazing abstractedly out of the photo, mouth discreetly covered by the rose she kisses, is the closest we come to an emblem of this self-possession and reserve.

The relation of the photographs to Barthes's text is, then, that of labyrinth and thread, the "maternal image-repertoire" and the umbilical cord of language. His role as a writer is not to master the photos, but to surrender himself as captivated observer, as naive subject of the idolatrous magic of images. The whole project is an attempt to suspend the appropriate "scientific" and "professional" discourse of photography in order to cultivate photography's resistance to language, allowing the photographs to "speak" their own language—not "its usual blah-blah: 'Technique,' 'Reality,' 'Reportage,' 'Art,' etc." but making "the image speak in silence" (p. 55). Barthes dismisses, therefore, much "sophisticated" commentary on photography, his own included:

> It is the fashion, nowadays, among Photography's commentators (sociologists and semiologists), to seize upon a semantic relativity: no "reality" (great scorn for the "realists" who do not see that the photograph is always coded) . . . the photograph, they say, is not an *analogon* of the world; what it represents is fabricated, because the photographic optic is subject to Albertian perspective (entirely historical) and because the inscription on the picture makes a three-dimensional object into a two-dimensional effigy. (p. 88)

Barthes declares this argument "futile," not just because photographs, like all images, are "analogical" in their coded structure, but because realism must be located in a different place: "the realists do not take the photograph for a 'copy' of reality, but for an emanation of *past reality: a magic,* not an art." This lost "magic" of photography, based in its naive realist stage (also its place in modernism), is what Barthes's text attempts to recover and why it must seem to efface itself, "give itself up to" its photographs, even as it weaves them into a labyrinth of theory and desire, science and autobiography.[22]

Voyeurism and Exorcism: The Colonial Harem

> It is as if the postcard photographer had been entrusted with a social mission: *put the collective phantasm into images.* He is the first to benefit from what he accomplishes through the delegation of power. The true voyeurism is that of the colonial society as a whole.
>
> —MALEK ALLOULA

The "magic" of photography can be the occasion of mystification as well as ecstasy, a point that is made by Malek Alloula's photographic essay on French colonial postcards of Algerian women.[23] Alloula dedicates his book to Barthes and adopts his basic vocabulary for the description of photographic magic, but he inverts Barthes's textual strategies in order to confront a body of images that exercised a detestable, pernicious magic over the representation of Algeria:

> What I read on these cards does not leave me indifferent. It demonstrates to me, were that still necessary, the desolate poverty of a gaze that I myself, as an Algerian, must have been the object of at some moment in my personal history. Among us, we believe in the nefarious effects of the evil eye (the evil gaze). We conjure them with our hand spread out like a fan. I close my hand back upon a pen to write *my* exorcism: *this text.* (p. 5)

There is no nostalgia here for a lost "primitive" or "realist" stage; there is no room for the *"punctum"* or ecstatic "wound" Barthes locates in the accidental detail. There is only the massive trauma of the "degrading fantasm" legitimating itself under the sign of photographic "reality." These photographs exclude all the "accidents" Barthes associates with the subversive "white magic" of the image. They stage for the voyeuristic French consumer the fantasy of "Oriental" luxury, lust, and indolence, as the unveiled "booty" before the colonial gaze. The critical text is counter-magic, a contrary incantation, repetitiously intoning its execrations on the filthy European pornographers with their ethnographic alibis.

Alloula's text fulfills the three conditions of the photographic essay in a quite unsuspected manner: his text is obviously independent of the images, that independence a direct result of Algeria's revolutionary independence of the French empire (Barbara Harlow's introduction places the book quite explicitly in the framework of Pontecorvo's film, *The Battle of Algiers*). There is "equality" of text and image in at least two senses. First, the text offers a point-by-point critical refutation of the implicit "argument" of the images. Second, it attempts to realize a contrary visual image or "staring back" into the face of the predatory colonial gaze. Alloula's text presents itself as a kind of substitute for a body of photographs that should have been taken, but never were:

> A reading of the sort that I propose to undertake would be entirely superfluous if there existed photographic traces of the gaze of the colonized upon the colonizer. In their absence, that is, in the absence of a confrontation of opposed gazes, I attempt here . . . to return this immense postcard to its sender. (p. 5)

Finally, there is "collaboration" in the sense that the postcards must be reproduced along with the text and thus forced to collaborate in their own deconstruction, their own "unveiling," much as the *algérienne* were forced to collaborate in the misrepresentation of Algerian women and their images forced to collaborate in a false textualizing—their insertion into a staged fantasy of exotic sexuality and unveiling, the colonial "chit-chat" (full of crude jokes) written on their backs, the colonial seal stamped across their faces, canceling the postage and their independent existence in one stroke.

Alloula's project is clearly beset on every side by contradictory impulses, the most evident being the necessity of reproducing the offending postcards in a book which may look to the casual observer like a coffee-table "collector's item" of exactly the sort he denounces. Occasional "classics" and "masterpieces" emerge, even in a pornographic genre:

> It is on "accomplishments" of this sort that a lucrative business of card collecting has been built and continues to thrive. It is also by means of this type of "accomplishment" that the occultation of meaning is effected, the meaning of the postcard that is of interest to us here. (p. 118)

"Aestheticization," far from being an antidote to the pornographic, is seen as an extension of it, a continuing cover-up of evil under the sign of beauty and rarity. This problem was also confronted by Agee, who dreaded the notion that his collaboration with Evans would be mystified by notions of special expertise or authority, chief among these the authority of the "artist": "the authors," he said, "are trying to deal with it not as journalists, sociologists, politicians, entertainers, humanitarians, priests, or artists, but seriously" (p. xv). "Seriousness" here means something quite antithetical to the notion of a canonical "classic" stamped with "aesthetic merit" and implies a sense of temporary, tactical intervention in an immediate human problem, not a claim on the indefinite future. That is why Agee wanted to print *Let Us Now Praise Famous Men* on newspaper stock. When told that "the pages would crumble to dust in a few years," he said, "that might not be a bad idea" (Stott, p. 264).

Let us add, then, to the generic criteria of the photographic essay a notion of seriousness which is frequently construed in anti-aesthetic terms, as a confrontation with the immediate, the local and limited, with the unbeautiful, the impoverished, the ephemeral, in a form that regards itself as simultaneously *indispensable* and *disposable.* The text of Alloula's *The Colonial Harem* sometimes reads as if it wanted to shred or incinerate the offending postcards it reproduces so well, to disfigure the pornographic beauty of the colonized women. But that would be, like most shreddings of historical documents, only a cover-up that would guarantee historical amnesia and a return of the repressed. Although Alloula can never quite say this, one feels that his essay is not simply a polemic against the French evil, but a tacit confession and purgation. Alloula reproduces the offending images, not just to aggressively "return an immense postcard to its sender," but to repossess and redeem those images, to "exorcise" an ideological spell that captivated mothers, wives, and sisters, as well as the "male society" that "no longer exists" (p. 122) in the colonial gaze. The rescue of women is an overcoming of impotence; the text asserts its manhood by freeing the images from the evil eye.

Barthes found the secret of photography in an image of his prepubescent mother at the center of a labyrinth. His text is the thread that takes us toward that center, a ritual surrender to the maternal image-repertoire. Alloula drives us out of the mystified labyrinth constructed by European representations of Arab women. He avenges the prostitution not only of the Mother, but of Photography itself, seeking to reverse the pornographic process.

What are we left with? Are the images redeemed, and if so, in what terms and for what sort of observer? How do we see, for instance, the final photograph of the book [Figure 14], which Alloula only mentions in passing, and whose symmetry approaches abstraction, reminiscent of an art nouveau fantasy? Can an American observer, in particular, see these

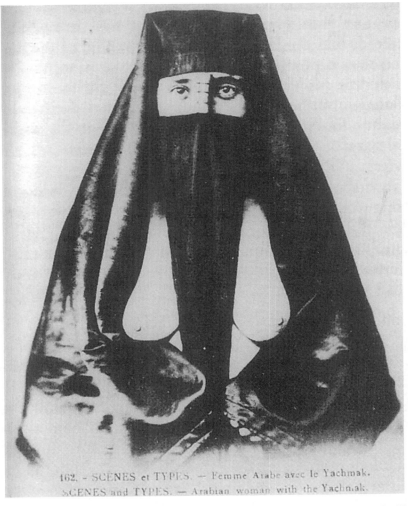

162. - SCENES et TYPES. — Femme Arabe avec le Yachmak.
SCENES and TYPES. — Arabian woman with the Yachmak.

[Figure 14]. *Scenes and Types: Arabian woman with the Yachmak* (n.d.), from *The Colonial Harem* (1986) by Malek Alloula, translated by Myrna and Wlad Godzich (French edition, 1981; English edition, Minneapolis: University of Minnesota Press, 1986).

photographs as anything more than quaint, archaic pornography, hauntingly beautiful relics of a lost colonial era, "collector's items" for a coffee-
table book? I don't have a simple answer to this question, but my first impulse is to register a feeling of *impotence* in the face of these women, whose
beauty is now mixed with danger, whose nakedness now becomes a veil
that has always excluded me from the labyrinth of their world.[24] I feel exiled from what I want to know, to understand, or (more precisely) what I
want to acknowledge and to be acknowledged by. In particular, Alloula's
text forces these acknowledgments from me: that I cannot read these photographs; that any narrative I might have brought to them is now shattered; that the labyrinth of photography, of the maternal image-repertoire,
defies penetration and colonization by any textual system, including
Malek Alloula's. The photographs, so long exchanged, circulated, inscribed, and traded, now assert their independence and equality, looking
at us as they collaborate in the undoing of the colonial gaze.

Exile and Return: After the Last Sky

> But I am the exile.
> Seal me with your eyes.
> —MAHMOUD DARWISH

Feelings of exile and impotence in the face of the imperial image are the
explicit subject of Edward Said and Jean Mohr's photographic essay on the
Palestinians. But instead of the aggressive "return of the repressed" in the
form of degraded, pornographic images, *After the Last Sky*[25] projects a new
set of images, self-representations of the colonized and dispossessed subjects, representations of their views of the colonizers: "our intention was to
show Palestinians through Palestinian eyes without minimizing the extent
to which even to themselves they feel different" (p. 6). The text is (as in *Camera Lucida*) a thread leading the writer and his readers back into the
labyrinth of otherness and the self-estrangement of exile. Its task is to see
that the "photographs are not" seen as "the exhibition of a foreign specimen" (p. 162), without, on the other hand, simply domesticating them.
Said's text is not, then, like Alloula's, a scourge to drive Western eyes out
the labyrinth. If Alloula treats the collaboration of text and image as a violent, coercive confrontation, Said and Mohr create a dialogical relation of
text and image that is collaborative in the classic (that is, modernist) sense
articulated by Agee and Evans, a cooperative endeavor by two like-minded
and highly talented professionals, writer and photographer.

The results of this "positive" collaboration are anything but straightforward. The independence of text and image is not asserted directly, as in
Agee and Evans, by a strict physical separation. Said and Mohr follow
something closer to the mode of *Camera Lucida*'s dialectical, intertwined relation of photos and essay, a complex of exchange and resistance.[26] Writer

and photographer both refuse the stereotyped division of labor that would produce a "text with illustrations" or an "album with captions." Said's text oscillates between supplementary relations to the images (commentary, meditations, reflections on photography) and "independent" material (the history of the Palestinians, autobiographical anecdotes, political criticism). Mohr's photographs oscillate between "illustrative" relations (pictures of boys lifting weights, for instance, document the "cult of physical strength" Said describes among Palestinian males) and "independent" statements that receive no direct commentary in the text, or play some kind of ironic counterpoint to it. An example: Said's discussion of his father's lifelong attempt to escape memories and material mementos of Jerusalem is juxtaposed (on the facing page) with an image that conveys just the opposite message and which receives no commentary, only a minimal caption: "the former mayor of Jerusalem and his wife, in exile in Jordan" [Figure 15, p. 538]. Behind them a photographic mural of the Mosque of Omar in Jerusalem occupies the entire wall of their living room. The collaboration of image and text here is not simply one of mutual support. It conveys the anxiety and ambivalence of the exile whose memories and mementos, the tokens of personal and national identity, may "seem . . . like encumbrances" (p. 14). The mural seems to tell us that the former mayor and his wife *cherish* these encumbrances, but their faces do not suggest that this in any way reduces their weight.

The relation of photographs and writing in *After the Last Sky* is consistently governed by the dialectic of *exile* and its overcoming, a double relation of estrangement and re-unification. If, as Said claims, "exile is a series of portraits without names, without context" (p. 12), return is figured in the attachment of names to photographs, contexts to images. But "return" is never quite so simple: sometimes the names are lost, unrecoverable; too often the attachment of text to an image can seem arbitrary, unsatisfactory. Neither pole in the dialectic of exile is univocally coded: estrangement is both imposed from without by historical circumstance and from within by the painfulness of memory, the will to forget and shed the "encumbrance" of Palestinian identity. "Re-unification," similarly, is the utopian object of desire and yet an object of potential aversion in its utopian impracticality. "Homecoming," says Said, "is out of the question. You learn to transform the mechanics of loss into a constantly postponed metaphysics of return" (p. 150). Where does the exile go "after the last sky" has clouded over, after Beirut, Cairo, Amman, the West Bank have failed to provide a home? What attitude do the physically exiled Palestinians take to the "exiles at home," the "present absentees" who live in "The Interior," inside Israel? The ambivalence expressed in these questions is also inscribed in the delicate, intricate, and precarious relations of text and image—the inside and outside, as it were, of this book.

The casual "Outsider," the beholder who takes this simply as an album of photographs, will have no difficulty grasping the major polemical point of the book, which is to counter the usual visual representation of

[Figure 15]. Jean Mohr, *Mayor of Jerusalem*, page spread from *After the Last Sky*, by
Edward W. Said. Copyright © 1986 by Edward W. Said. Reprinted by permission
of Pantheon Books, a division of Random House, Inc.

Palestinians as menacing figures with *kaffiyas* and ski-masks. Anonymous
"terrorists" are displaced by a set of visual facts that everyone knows in theory, but rarely acknowledges in practice—that Palestinians are also women,
children, businessmen, teachers, farmers, poets, shepherds, and auto mechanics. That the representation of Palestinians as ordinary human beings,
"capturable" by ordinary, domestic sorts of snapshots, should be in itself

remarkable is a measure of how extraordinarily limited the normal image of the Palestinian is. There is an acceptable "icon" of the Palestinian, as Said puts it, and the images in *After the Last Sky*—domestic, peaceful, ordinary— do not fit this decorum, as anyone will find who attempts to insert this book among the other photographic texts that adorn the typical coffee-table.

The history of this particular set of photographs suggests that this decorum is not simply natural or empirical but has to be reinforced by the most stringent prohibitions. Jean Mohr was commissioned to take the pictures for an exhibition at the International Conference on the Question of Palestine held by the United Nations in Geneva in 1983. "The official response," as Said notes

> was puzzling. . . . You can hang them up, we were told, but no writing can be displayed with them. No legends, no explanations. A compromise was finally negotiated whereby the name of the country or place (Jordan, Syria, West Bank, Gaza) could be affixed to the much-enlarged photographs, but not one word more. (p. 3)

The precise motives for this bureaucratic "prohibition on writing" never become clear. Said speculates that the various Arab states who participated in the conference (Israel and the United States did not) found the Palestinian cause "useful up to a point—for attacking Israel, for railing against Zionism, imperialism, and the United States," but the notion of considering the Palestinians *as a people* (that is, with a story, a text, an argument) was unacceptable. The prohibition on writing was perhaps a way of keeping these disturbing images from taking on an even more disturbing voice. Context, narrative, historical circumstances, identities, and places were repressed in favor of what might be seen as a parody of the abstract and "modernist" space of visual exhibition: minimal captions, no "legends," pure visual display without reference or representation. Exile is a series of photographs without texts.

After the Last Sky, then, is a violation of a double prohibition against a certain kind of image (nonbellicose, nonsublime) and against a writing joined to these images. This might seem an excessively formalistic point. But Said notes that "most literary critics . . . focus on what is said in Palestinian writing . . . [its] sociological and political meaning. But it is the *form* that should be looked at" (p. 38). This "form" is not something distinct from content; it *is* the content in its most material, particular sense, the specific places it carves out as the site of Palestinian existence. As such, it resists the reduction of the Palestinian question to a political issue, insisting on the ethical as well as aesthetic relation of text and image. The collaboration of photographer and writer in *After the Last Sky* cannot be seen, then, simply as corrective to the prohibition which segregates the Palestinian image from the Palestinian text. This collaboration is also embedded in a complex field of heterogeneities that can never quite be accommodated to traditional dialectical forms of aesthetic unity. We don't find a

Coleridgean "multeity in unity" in this book, but something more like a
multeity of glimpses of unity, seen as if through a pair of spectacles, one
lens of which is shattered. (This image, drawn from one of the most striking photographs in the book, is one I will return to later.)

The two lenses of this book are writing and photography, neither understood abstractly or generically but as constructions of specific histories,
places, and displacements. The photographer, a German born in Geneva,
naturalized as a Swiss citizen in 1939, has had concrete experience of intra-
European exile. The writer is a Palestinian Christian born in Jerusalem, exiled to Lebanon, Egypt, the United States. From one point of view the
writer is the insider, the clear, intact lens who can represent through his
own experience a focused image of "the Palestinian"; the photographer is
the alien, unable to speak the languages of Palestine or Israel, "seeing"
only the mute, inarticulate fragments of lives that the camera allows (thus,
many of the people in Mohr's photographs are anonymous, unidentified,
and photography re-doubles the exile of image from referent). From another point of view, the photographer is the clear, intact lens. His Swiss
neutrality allows him what was denied to the writer in the 1980s, the freedom to travel throughout Israel and the West Bank, to go "inside" Palestine and represent it with the transparent accuracy of photography. The
writer is the alien, the outsider, estranged from a land he dimly remembers as a child, a land in which he would have been, as an urbane, Christian intellectual, estranged from the rural, local culture of the Palestinian
masses. The writer acknowledges that he himself is the "cracked lens," unable to see, quite literally, the native country he longs for except in fragmentary glimpses provided by others.

The divisions of labor we have traced between writer and photographer—spy and counter-spy, thread and labyrinth, voyeur and exorcist—
are consistently undermined by the tightly woven collaboration of *After
the Last Sky*. But there is one vestige of traditional divisions of labor in the
way Said's meditations on gender difference suggest the collaboration of a
male text with a body of female images. Like Barthes, Said installs Woman
at the center of the photographic matrix. The section of the book called
"Interiors" (concerned with Palestinians who live inside Israel, with domestic spaces and the theme of privacy) is mainly devoted to images of
women. Said also follows Barthes in finding that the primal scene of the
photograph involves his mother. A British customs official rips up her
passport, destroying her legal identity and (presumably) her photographic
image in the same gesture. Like Alloula, Said is vindicating the disfigured
image of his mother; like Barthes, he is trying to re-assemble the fragments
of her identity. But he also portrays the women as the real preservers of
this identity, associated with "the land" and the idea of home, portrayed
as clinging irrationally, stubbornly, to "memories, title deeds, and legal
claims" (p. 81). The women are also the keepers of images in the Palestinian interior, the ones who hang up too many pictures too high on the
walls, who save the photograph albums and mementos that may encum-

ber the male Palestinian who wants to travel light. (Recall that Said's father "spent his life trying to escape these objects" [p. 14].) Yet Said acknowledges a "crucial absence of women" (p. 77) in the representation of Palestinians. The official icon is one of "automatic manhood," the macho terrorist who may feel himself both goaded and reproached by the "protracted discipline" (p. 79) of women's work.

Like Barthes, Said wants to preserve the feminine mystique of the image, its difference from the male writer's "articulate discourse" (p. 79). Thus, it sometimes seems as if he would prefer to leave the female images unidentified and therefore mysterious. Like Barthes, he does not reproduce an image of his mother, but substitutes an image of an elderly woman, generalized as an emblem—"a face, I thought when I first saw it, of our life at home" (p. 84). But six months later Said is reminded by his sister that this woman [Figure 16] is actually a distant relative whom he met in the forties and fifties, a reminder that produces mixed emotions:

> As soon as I recognized Mrs. Farraj, the suggested intimacy of the photograph's surface gave way to an explicitness with few secrets. She is a real person—Palestinian—with a real history at the interior of ours. But I do not know whether the photograph can, or does, say things as they really are. Something has been lost. But the representation is all we have. (p. 84)

[Figure 16]. Jean Mohr, *Amman, 1984. Mrs. Farraj.* In *After the Last Sky,* by Edward W. Said. Copyright © 1986 by Edward W. Said. Reprinted by permission of Pantheon Books, a division of Random House, Inc.

The uncharacteristic awkwardness of Said's writing here is, I think, a tacit acknowledgment of his ambivalence toward the associative complex, Woman/Image/Home, a confession of his complicity in the sentimental-izing of women and of the lost pastoral homeland that fixates the imagina-tion of the Palestinian male.[27] His candor about this ambivalence, his recognition that the photographic image has a life beyond the discursive, political uses he would make of it, allows the photograph to "look back" at him and us and assert the independence we associate with the strong form of the photo-essay. The poetic secrecy and intimacy he had hoped to find in this image is replaced by a prosaic familiarity and openness.

Jean Mohr provides Said with a striking emblem of his own ambiva-lence in a photograph which comes closer than any other in this book to supplying a portrait of the writer. Once again, the photo is an unidentified portrait, exiled from its referent, an image of an "elderly Palestinian vil-lager" with a broken lens in his glasses [Figure 17]. The photograph re-minds Said of Rafik Halabi, "a Palestinian-Druze-Israeli" whose book, *The West Bank Story*, is highly critical of Israeli occupation, but "who writes from the viewpoint of a loyal Israeli" who served in the army and "subscribes to Zionism." Said finds Halabi's position impossibly contradictory. Either he is "deluded" or "up to some elaborate rhetorical game" which Said does not understand. Either way, "the result is a book that runs on two completely different tracks" (p. 127). It occurs to Said, of course, that there is something

[Figure 17]. Jean Mohr, *Elderly Palestinian Villager. Ramallah, 1984.* In *After the Last Sky,* by Edward W. Said. Copyright © 1986 by Edward W. Said. Reprinted by permission of Pantheon Books, a division of Random House, Inc.

of himself, and perhaps of his own book, in this image: "Perhaps I am only describing *my* inability to order things coherently, sequentially, logically, and perhaps the difficulties of resolution I have discerned in Halabi's book and in the old man with broken glasses are mine, not theirs" (p. 130). First, the image is a double portrait of the Other as Insider, "a symbol, I said to myself, of some duality in our life that won't go away—refugees and terrorists, victims and victimizers, and so on" (p. 128). Not a bad reading, but Said is unhappy with it, as he is generally with emblematic readings that reduce the photograph to convenient verbal formulas. The man's face is "strong and gentle," the "blotch is on the lens, not in him" (p. 128). He has agreed to be photographed this way, so he can watch the camera and exert some control over his own image.

The resulting visual field (both for the wearer of the glasses and the beholder), Said notes, will always disclose a "small disturbance," a "curiously balanced imbalance" which is "very similar to the textual imbalance in Halabi's book" and, clearly, in Said and Mohr's. The Palestinians, a people without a geographic center and with only the most fragile cultural and historical identity have "no one central image," no "dominant theory," no "coherent discourse"; they are "without a center. Atonal" (p. 129). At moments like this, one glimpses Said's allegiance to the musical aesthetics of modernism, to that combination of pessimism and formalism we associate with Adorno. Said's composite, decentered, shifting, imbalanced collaboration with Mohr is nonetheless a shapely, congruent, and formal creation, a material embodiment of the reality he wants to represent, built out of a refusal to simplify, to sentimentalize or settle for polemic. Both writer and photographer could see themselves in this anonymous portrait, itself in exile from its subject: exile is indeed "a series of portraits without names, without contexts" (p. 12). But if photographs sundered from texts portray exile, photographs *with* text are images of return, sites of reconciliation, accommodation, acknowledgment. The delicate balancing act of a book "on two different tracks" may be a rhetorical game Said does not understand even as he is compelled to play it, but then he remarks that Palestinians sometimes "puzzle even ourselves" (p. 53).

The "central image" of the Palestinians is, for the moment, a double vision of just this sort—secular, rational, yet deeply involved in the emotions of victimage—figures in a rhetoric of paranoia which constructs them as the enemy of the victims of the Holocaust or as mere pawns in geopolitical schemes. Said and Mohr cannot be content, therefore, with a propaganda piece to "pretty up the image" of the Palestinians; they must work as well for an *internally directed* representation and critique, chiding not only the Arab and Israeli and Big Power interests, but the Palestinians themselves, Said included. The Palestinians' failings—their pursuit of inappropriate revolutionary models such as Cuba and Algeria, their impatient, macho romanticism, their failure to organize properly with the "protracted discipline" of women, their lack of a coherent history—are all part of the picture. The idea of the book, then, is ultimately to help bring the Palestinians into existence for themselves as much as for others; it is that most ambitious of books, a nation-making text.

Texts that make nations are, of course, what we call "classics," the worst fate (according to Agee) that can befall a book. It was a fate that befell *Let Us Now Praise Famous Men* after a period of neglect and misunderstanding. Our understanding of the thirties, particularly the Depression, is often seen as a product of Evans's and Agee's collaboration, and it helped to form an image of a nation in poverty, presented with dignity, sympathy, and truth. But Evans and Agee could never hope, as Said and Mohr do, to address the people they represent, to help bring them into being as a people. Whether this book fulfills such a hope is a question that will be settled beyond its pages: "there is no completely coherent discourse adequate to us, and I doubt whether at this point, if someone could fashion such a discourse, we could be adequate for it" (p. 129). It is at such moments of inadequacy, perhaps, that a mixed, hybrid discourse like that of the photographic essay emerges as a historical necessity.

Insofar as my own remarks here have been essays toward the definition of a genre or a medium, an attempt to articulate the formal principles of the photographic essay, they might be seen as a betrayal of the antiaesthetic, anticanonical experimentalism of this form. Why attempt to "classicize" by classifying and formalizing a medium that is so young and unpredictable? The photographic essay occupies a strange conceptual space in our understanding of representation, a place where "form" seems both indispensable and disposable. On the one hand, it seems to participate in what Stanley Cavell has described as the tendency of "modernist painting" to "break down the concept of genre altogether,"[28] as if the medium were not given naturally, but had to be re-invented, re-evaluated in each new instance; this is the tendency I've associated with the mutual "resistance" of photography and writing, the insistence on the distinctive character of each medium, the search for a "purity" of approach that is both aesthetic and ethical. On the other hand, the roots of the photo-essay in documentary journalism, newspapers, magazines, and the whole ensemble of visual-verbal interactions in mass media connect it to popular forms of communication that seem quite antithetical to modernism in their freedom of exchange between image and text and their material ephemerality. Perhaps this is just a way of placing the photographic essay at the crossroads between modernism and postmodernism, understanding it as a form in which the resistance to image-text exchange is (in contrast to painting) most crucial precisely because it has the most to overcome.[29] If this crossroads occupies a real place in our cultural history, it is one we cannot leave unmapped. To take literally the antiformalist rhetoric of the photographic essay would be to empty it of its specific, historical materiality as a representational practice and to neglect those labors of love in which we are enjoined to collaborate.

NOTES

[1] The phrase "message without a code" is from Roland Barthes's essay, "The Photographic Message," in *Image/Music/Text,* translated by Stephen Heath (New York: Hill and Wang, 1977), p. 19. I am grateful to David Antin and Alan Trachtenberg for their many intelligent suggestions and questions about an earlier version of this essay.

[2] Victor Burgin, "Seeing Sense," in *The End of Art Theory: Criticism and Post-Modernity* (Atlantic Highlands, NJ: Humanities Press, 1986), p. 51; further page references will be cited in the text.

[3] Roland Barthes, "The Photographic Message," in *Image/Music/Text,* p. 19; further page references will be cited in the text.

[4] James Agee and Walker Evans, *Let Us Now Praise Famous Men* (Originally published, 1939; New York: Houghton Mifflin, 1980), p. xiv; further page references will be cited in the text.

[5] See Tom Moran, *The Photo Essay: Paul Fusco and Will McBride,* in the Masters of Contemporary Photography series (Los Angeles, CA: Alskog, Inc., 1974). Eugene Smith's remarks on the genre of the photo-essay were made in conversation with the editors of this book and appear on pages 14–15.

[6] Robert Frank, *The Americans* (1st edition, 1959; rev. and enlarged ed., New York: Grossman Publishers, 1969). Frank's book is not entirely free of text, however. All the photographs are accompanied by brief captions, usually a designation of subject, time, or location, and there is an introduction by Jack Kerouac that emphasizes the implicit verbal coding of Frank's photographs: "What a poem this is, what poems can be written about this book of pictures some day by some young new writer . . ." (p. iii).

[7] For an excellent account of the way writers address the ethical issues of "approach to the subject" made visible by the photographic apparatus in action, see Carol Schloss, *In Visible Light: Photography and the American Writer: 1840–1940* (New York: Oxford University Press, 1987), p. 11.

[8] Recall the classic photo-essays based in scientific discourse such as geological surveys (Timothy O'Sullivan, for instance) and sociological studies (the work of Dorothea Lange and Paul Taylor). The modern discipline of art history is inconceivable without the illustrated slide lecture and the photographic reproduction of images. Any discourse that relies on the accurate mechanical reproduction of visual evidence engages with photography at some point.

[9] For a good account of the reception of Agee and Evans's work, see William Stott, *Documentary Expression and Thirties America* (New York: Oxford University Press, 1973), pp. 261–66.

[10] Eugene Smith argues that photojournalists tend to work within narrative conventions, producing "picture stories": "that's a form of its own, not an essay" (*The Photo Essay,* p. 15).

[11] This "topical" and nonnarrative format persists throughout the sequence of Evans's photos. The photos are divided into three sections, the first concentrating on the Gudgers and Woodses, the second on the Rickettses, and the third on the towns in their neighborhood.

[12] The reader who supposes that these quotations have some documentary authenticity, or even an expressive relation to the photographic subject, should heed Bourke-White's opening note: "the legends under the pictures are intended to express the authors' own conceptions of the sentiments of the individuals portrayed; they do not pretend to reproduce the actual sentiments of these persons." The candor of this admission is somewhat offset by the persistent fiction of the "quotation" throughout the text. This manipulation of verbal material is quite in keeping with Bourke-White's penchant for re-arranging the objects in the sharecroppers' households to conform with her own aesthetic tastes.

[13] Jefferson Hunter's book, *Image and Word: The Interaction of Twentieth Century Photographs and Texts* (Cambridge, MA: Harvard University Press, 1987) notes this

resistance but sees it merely as an "affront" to convention that made *Famous Men* "unsuccessful in 1941" and "uninfluential now" on the practice of photo-text collaboration. Hunter takes the "stylistic consistency" of Bourke-White and Caldwell as a model for the way "collaborative efforts succeed" (p. 79).

[14] For an excellent account of what I'm calling an "ethics of production," see Carol Schloss's chapter on Agee and Evans in her *In Visible Light.*

[15] I use the word "vortex" here to echo Agee's allusions to the Blakean vortex and to the presence of Blake as a presiding genius in *Famous Men.* I do not know how familiar Agee was with Blake's work as a composite artist, but if he knew the illuminated books, he must have been struck by the oft-remarked independence of Blake's engravings from his texts, an independence which is coupled, of course, with the most intimate collaboration. For more on Blakean text-image relations, see my *Blake's Composite Art* (Princeton, NJ: Princeton University Press, 1977), and chapter 4 above.

[16] Roland Barthes, *Camera Lucida* (French original, 1981; New York: Hill and Wang, 1981), p. 73; further page references will be cited in the text.

[17] The *camera lucida*, as Barthes knew, is not properly translated as a "light room" in opposition to a "dark room." It is "the name of that apparatus, anterior to Photography, which permitted drawing an object through a prism, one eye on the model, the other on the paper" (p. 106). The opening in the curtains, as optical aperture, plays precisely this role.

[18] "I may know better a photograph I remember than a photograph I am looking at, as if direct vision oriented its language wrongly, engaging it in an effort of description which will always miss its point of effect, the *punctum*" (p. 53). The opposition between *studium* and *punctum* is coordinated, in Barthes's discussion, with related distinctions between the public and the private, the professional and the amateur. The captions further reinforce what Barthes calls "the two ways of the Photograph," dividing themselves into a scholarly, bibliographic identification of photographer, subject, date, etc. and an italicized quotation registering Barthes's personal response, the *punctum*. This practice of double captioning is, I think, a pervasive convention in photographic essays, often signaled by hyphenation (as in Robert Frank's *The Americans*), or contrasting type-styles (as in *You Have Seen Their Faces*): Hamilton, Alabama/ "We manage to get along."

[19] Victor Burgin regards the antiscientific rhetoric of *Camera Lucida* with dismay: "The passage in *Camera Lucida* where Barthes lambasts the scientist of the sign (his own other self) has become widely quoted amongst precisely the sorts of critics Barthes opposed" ("Re-reading *Camera Lucida*," in *The End of Art Theory*, p. 91). Burgin's reduction of this to a straightforward political clash ignores the fact that the "sorts of critics" Barthes "opposed" included *himself,* and this opposition is precisely what gives his criticism ethical and political force.

[20] Joel Snyder informs me that these identifications are confused. The photograph was taken by Paul Nadar, the artist's son, and is of his mother, Nadar's wife. Given the use Barthes makes of the photograph, the confusion of father and son, wife and mother, is hardly surprising. The manifest uncertainty of the caption and its misquotation of Barthes's own text suggest that Barthes was deliberately attaching a confused "legend" to this photo.

[21] The twenty-five European and American photos in *Camera Lucida* range from journalism to art photos to personal family photographs and include examples of "old masters" (the "first photograph"—by Niepce; Charles Clifford, "The Alhambra"; G. W. Wilson, "Queen Victoria") from the nineteenth century as well as twentieth-century works. The effort is clearly to suggest "Photography" in its full range without making any effort to be comprehensive or systematic.

[22] This respect for the "naive realism" of photography is also a crucial feature of Agee's text. Agee notes "how much slower white people are to catch on than negroes, who understand the meaning of a camera, a weapon, a stealer of images and souls, a gun, an evil eye" (p. 362).

[23] Malek Alloula, *The Colonial Harem,* translated by Myrna and Wlad Godzich (French edition, 1981; English edition, Minneapolis: University of Minnesota Press, 1986); further page references will be cited in the text.

[24] This impotence is perhaps nothing more than the familiar liberal guilt of the white male American becoming conscious of complicity in the ethos of imperialism. But it is also a more personal reaction which stems from a not altogether pleasant failure to react "properly" to the pornographic image, a failure which I can't take credit for as a matter of moral uprightness (morality, I suspect, only enters in when the proper reaction is there to be resisted). I had registered this feeling at the first perusal of the photographs in *The Colonial Harem.* Needless to say, a sensation of the uncanny attended my reading of the final paragraph of Alloula's text: "Voyeurism turns into an obsessive neurosis. The great erotic dream, ebbing from the sad faces of the wage earners in the poses, lets appear, in the flotsam perpetuated by the postcard, another figure: that of *impotence*" (p. 122).

[25] Edward Said and Jean Mohr, *After the Last Sky* (London: Pantheon, 1986); further page references will be cited in the text.

[26] Mohr's earlier collaborations with John Berger are clearly an important precedent also. See especially *The Seventh Man* (Originally published, Penguin, 1975; London: Writers and Readers, 1982), a photographic essay on migrant workers in Europe.

[27] "I can see the women everywhere in Palestinian life, and I see how they exist between the syrupy sentimentalism of roles we ascribe to them (mothers, virgins, martyrs) and the annoyance, even dislike that their unassimilated strength provokes in our warily politicized, automatic manhood" (p. 77).

[28] Stanley Cavell, *The World Viewed: Reflections on the Ontology of Film,* enlarged edition (Cambridge, MA: Harvard University Press, 1979), p. 106.

[29] I say "in contrast to painting" because the emancipation of painting from language, or at least the rhetoric of emancipation, has dominated the sophisticated understanding of painting for most of this century. For a fuller version of this argument, see chapter 7. . . .

• • • • • • • • • • • •

QUESTIONS FOR A SECOND READING

1. Mitchell's essay is very straightforward and helpful in its structure. It opens with three questions and three answers. These are followed by six sections. The first two raise issues and questions related to photography and language and to the medium of the "photographic essay"; the last four present the case studies, the readings of particular texts from the point of view of the issues and questions raised at the opening. With all of this assistance, "The Photographic Essay" is still not easy to read. The arguments are subtle (and in some cases counterintuitive), and they refer constantly to other books and ideas, to a conversation among scholars and artists with a long history and, at times, a specialized vocabulary.

   As you reread, let the structure of the essay organize your work. When you finish the first two sections, stop to summarize and restate the argument. Underline or write down the key terms and questions. Mitchell, for example, alludes to naive and sophisticated responses to photos. What are they? What is Mitchell's position?

The "case studies" work with books that you may not have seen or read and may not have at hand. And yet they require you to know something about them. Mitchell, in other words, must provide summary, example, and illustration as part of his discussion. After each of the case studies, stop, go back, and be ready to provide an account of the book at the center of each case study. Who wrote it? What is its project? And then be ready to provide an account of Mitchell's discussion. What use is Mitchell making of this book? What point? How does it serve his project?

2. This is an essay written by a scholar, a specialist in literature, art history, critical theory, and cultural studies. The specialized terms he uses are drawn from these fields of study. Sometimes he uses them as though they were familiar; in other cases he locates them in relation to a particular text and author. As you reread, underline or create a list of those terms that seem significant and particular to Mitchell's project, terms like "code," "trope," "dialectical," "figurative," "non-linguistic," "modernism," and "post-modernism." As an exercise, create a glossary of terms for use by other readers of this text. From their use and context, or (as a last resort) from other sources you can find, prepare definitions of these terms. Or, better yet, write summary sentences about "The Photographic Essay" that put these terms to work.

3. At the end of the second section, Mitchell says, "In the remainder of this essay I want to examine four photo-essays that, in various ways, fore-ground the dialectic of exchange and resistance between photography and language, the things that make it possible (and sometimes impos-sible) to 'read' the pictures, or to 'see' the text illustrated in them." As you reread, locate and mark those moments in the four case studies where Mitchell foregrounds "the dialectic of exchange and resistance between photography and language." What are the examples? How do the texts differ? Why, for Mitchell, is this interesting or important?

4. There are four books that serve as central examples to Mitchell's study: *Let Us Now Praise Famous Men,* James Agee and Walker Evans; *Camera Lucida,* Roland Barthes; *The Colonial Harem,* Malek Alloula; and *After the Last Sky,* Edward Said and Jean Mohr. Jacob Riis's *How the Other Half Lives* also provides an important illustration in the second section of the essay. Go to the library to study one of these texts. Find one or two examples you can copy and bring to class to extend or challenge Mitchell's discussion of that text. Be sure to bring words as well as images.

ASSIGNMENTS FOR WRITING

1. To introduce the four case studies in "The Photographic Essay," Mitchell says, "I want to examine four photo-essays that, in various ways, fore-ground the dialectic of exchange and resistance between photography and language." For this assignment, work closely with the four case stud-ies to bring forward what remains implied in Mitchell's text, the *differences* in the four cases. What *are* the "various ways" they foreground the dialec-tic of exchange and resistance between photography and language? What position does Mitchell seem to take on the value or achievement of each of

the four books? What seems to you to be the significant or interesting differences? Mitchell's essay is designed to prepare you to be a reader of the photographic essay. From the examples Mitchell gives, what sorts of books would you be hoping to find?

You should imagine that you are writing for someone who has not read "The Photographic Essay." You will need, then, to be sure to represent and summarize the text. (See the first "Question for a Second Reading.") The point of the summary, however, is to define a position from which you can begin to do your work. And, to repeat what was said above, your work is to bring forward what Mitchell does not foreground—his sense of the differences between the four cases and the implication or value of those differences. And, in relation to what you see in Mitchell, your job is to articulate your own position on the range, importance, and possibility of the genre of the photo-essay.

2. These four books provide the central examples for Mitchell's study: *Let Us Now Praise Famous Men,* James Agee and Walker Evans; *Camera Lucida,* Roland Barthes; *The Colonial Harem,* Malek Alloula; and *After the Last Sky,* Edward Said and Jean Mohr. Jacob Riis's *How the Other Half Lives* also provides an important illustration in the second section of the essay. Go to the library to study one of these texts. Or, find an example of a "photographic essay" that you could put alongside Mitchell's examples.

For this assignment, take up Mitchell's project by extending his work in "The Photographic Essay" and considering new or additional examples. You should assume that you are writing for a reader who is familiar with Mitchell's essay (but who does not have the book open on his or her desk). Your work is to put Mitchell to the test—to extend, test, and perhaps challenge or qualify his account of the genre. As with his project, the basic questions are these: What relationship between photography and writing do these examples articulate? What tropes of differentiation govern the division of labor between photographer and writer, image and text, the viewer and the reader?

3. In the introduction to *Picture Theory,* Mitchell says,

> What we need is a critique of visual culture that is alert to the power of images for good and evil and that is capable of discriminating the variety and historical specificity of their uses.

One way to think about the "variety and historical specificity" of the use of images is to look at the examples Mitchell provides in this chapter, examples of writers using images as the subjects of their writing, but also the example of his own use and "reading" of those images.

At times, Mitchell is quick to include us in his ways of reading. In response to the Walker Evans photograph of Annie Mae Gudger, he says:

> There is something deeply disturbing, even disagreeable, about this (unavoidable) aestheticizing response to what after all is a real person in desperately impoverished circumstances. Why should we have a right to look on this woman and find her fatigue, pain, and anxiety beautiful? (p. 522)

His readers are written into the "we" of such sentences. At times he highlights the "reading" represented by the writer of the photo-essay, as he does, for example, in his account of Roland Barthes's use of Nadar's *The Artist's Mother (or Wife)*. And at times he singles himself out as an individual case, as, for example, when he says of the postcard image of the "Arabian Woman with the Yachmak":

> Can an American observer, in particular, see these photographs as anything more than quaint, archaic pornography, hauntingly beautiful relics of a lost colonial era, "collector's items" for a coffee-table book? I don't have a simple answer to this question, but my first impulse is to register a feeling of *impotence* in the face of these women, whose beauty is now mixed with danger, whose nakedness now becomes a veil that has always excluded me from the labyrinth of their world. (pp. 535–36)

Write an essay in which you present a close reading of Mitchell's text, looking specifically at the ways it figures (or represents) readers reading. What variety of readings does he chart? Where and how are they historically specific? What lessons are there to be learned from these examples? What does Mitchell seem to be saying about appropriate ways of reading? What about you—what's your position?

MAKING CONNECTIONS

1. In "Ways of Seeing" (p. 105), John Berger says, "Original paintings are silent and still in a sense that information never is." Both Berger and Mitchell are interested in the use of images, what happens to them when they are packaged, deployed, reproduced, turned into text. For both, the use of images is a sign of the health of the individual and the health of the culture.

   Write an essay in which you use Berger's essay to weigh, evaluate, and understand Mitchell's. You will need, of course, to take time to summarize what Berger says and to establish his position. Once you have established his point of view, turn to Mitchell, particularly the example he provides of someone trying to understand what is at stake when we speak for images. Would Berger see Mitchell, for example, as someone who justifies and practices "mystification"?

   Or, write an essay in which you use Mitchell's essay to weigh, evaluate, and understand Berger, both the Berger of "Ways of Seeing" and the Berger who speaks for Rembrandt's *Woman in Bed* (p. 129) and on Caravaggio's *The Calling of St. Matthew* (p. 131). You will need, of course, to take time to summarize what Mitchell says and to establish his position on the relationship of words and images. And you will need to think (as Mitchell might think) about the difference between photographs and paintings and what is at stake in providing a written account of a painted image. Once you have established his point of view, turn to Berger, particularly the example he provides of someone who places words next to images. Perhaps the questions to ask would be these: What relationship between painting and writing do these examples articulate? What tropes of differentiation govern the division of labor between painter and writer, image and text, the viewer and the reader?

2. Both Robert Coles, in "The Tradition: Fact and Fiction" (p. 176), and Mitchell, in "The Photographic Essay," write about the genre of the photo-essay and, in particular, about *Let Us Now Praise Famous Men,* the "classic" text by James Agee and Walker Evans. Write an essay in which you elaborate the differences in their approaches to and accounts of this text. You can imagine that you are writing for a reader who has read none of the texts at hand, so you will need to be careful in summary (perhaps reproducing some of the illustrations). What does each notice or choose to notice in the text? How are these decisions related to the larger projects of the two authors? to their underlying commitments and concerns? And, finally, where are you on the differences between the two? Would you align yourself with one or the other writer? From their example, is there a position you would define as your own or as an alternative?

   Note: Your work with this project would be greatly enhanced by your reviewing, as well, the full text of *Let Us Now Praise Famous Men.* With the text, you can establish a more complete sense of context, including what both writers miss or leave out. You can think about the agenda or desires that led to their selection of exemplary material.

3. Mitchell is concerned with the ways both words and images take possession of their subjects. And, in his account, there is a political dimension to this. It is a matter of the rich looking at and describing the poor in *Let Us Now Praise Famous Men,* of colonial power and the colonized in *The Colonial Harem* and *After the Last Sky.* (It is harder to name the victims and agents of appropriation in *Camera Lucida.* It would be worth your time to read that section carefully to see what terms Barthes offers.) In Mary Louise Pratt's terms in "Arts of the Contact Zone" (p. 605), both the photos and the texts represent moments of contact between persons of different cultures and unequal status.

   Write an essay in which you consider two of the "cases" in "The Photographic Essay" in terms of Pratt's discussion of the contact zone. How would she understand the status and meaning of the words and images used to represent the "other"? How is her understanding different from Mitchell's? Both could be said to be interested in the role of power, the political, and history in the use and formation of texts. Which account seems most useful to you? most useful for what?

- Defn. genre of photo essay "series of picts linked together by a series of wds."
- relati of text & image - one can't fully convey, photo have hidden text
- Photography & essay writing emerge at the same time.
- Referentiality → essay refer to something in reality.
- P.O.V photographer have a POV.
- Perspective is everything

  Conotation   Denot.
  implied mean.   defn. mean.

- Connotation of a photograph is pure denotation "in success my think it we tend to look at a photo in a certain way" tend to see facts. is reality. "a piece of reality "tend to see facts. conotation is pure referentiality, always true & fact.

ALICE
MUNRO

A LICE MUNRO (b. 1931) is one of the most prolific, most admired, and most widely read writers of short fiction at work today. Since the 1970s her stories have appeared regularly in The New Yorker. *She has published nine collections of short stories:* Dance of the Happy Shades *(1968);* Lives of Girls and Women *(1971);* Something I've Been Meaning to Tell You *(1974);* Who Do You Think You Are? *(1978);* The Moons of Jupiter *(1982);* The Progress of Love *(1986);* Friend of My Youth *(1990);* Open Secrets *(1994), the collection that includes "The Albanian Virgin"; and* Hateship, Friendship, Courtship, Loveship, Marriage *(2001).*

Munro, a Canadian, lives in rural Canada, the setting for most of her fiction. Ted Solotaroff, in a review of Open Secrets *for* The Nation *magazine, said, "Her purview is the private history of women's life in the small towns of the Ottawa Valley, where she has lived most of hers, with occasional sweeps to Toronto and Vancouver. Her provincial steadiness and clarity are set against an urbane sophistication, like that of the great stylist of 1920s realism, Katherine Anne Porter, brought up to date." Munro has said that her models were writers of the American South—Flannery O'Connor, Eudora Welty, Carson McCullers—all writers who have created southern, small-town settings, characters, and idioms. The central characters in Munro's stories are almost always women, often betrayed and cut loose (or cutting loose) from husbands or lovers, often on the move and* settling into a rural or provincial setting, usually trying to make some sense out of the past, struggling to account for the present, and generally learning that they can do OK, make a life, and make some sense out of it on their own. We like the characters because they seem real. Munro will set stories in the past, with careful attention to history and detail, and we are tempted to read those, too, as though they were history rather than fiction.

"The Albanian Virgin" is one of two truly great stories in Open Secrets (the other, "Carried Away," takes place during World War I and consists partly of letters). "The Albanian Virgin" is among her best work and deserves to be in any anthology of twentieth-century fiction. At once jarring, dazzling, and difficult, it runs two narratives side by side. One is the story of the narrator, Claire, whose circumstances are familiar in Munro's fiction. The second is the story of the Albanian Virgin, a story that sometimes seems made up (that is, made up by the character) and sometimes seems real. One of the tasks set for the reader is to follow these two parallel stories, at least until the end. (In the interview cited below, Munro said that "the two stories combined there are a romantic fairy tale and a sort of romance worked out in real life.")

In a 1994 interview (published in the New York Times Book Review), Munro spoke at length about "The Albanian Virgin." The story moves far away from her usual settings. "I got interested in Albania," she said, "because I heard a story, which I've never been able to verify, that a librarian in Clinton [Clinton, Ontario, Munro's home], traveling in Europe in the 1920s, was captured by bandits in Albania." The interviewer further explains:

> Ms. Munro's research led her to a book called High Albania, in which she came upon a chapter called "The Albanian Virgin" that set forth the restrictions imposed on women in some of the remote villages of that time. It also described an escape route: by forswearing sex and marriage, a woman could become a kind of honorary man, living as she pleased. "She could smoke and booze and spend her life polishing her weapons," Ms. Munro remarked with a laugh.

As you read the story you will need to be patient. It is presented in pieces, or fragments; it is confusing at first, as you are forced to try to figure out who is speaking and what is going on. There are surprises along the way. These difficulties are part of the story's design and central to the way it chooses to engage or define its reader.

The Albanian Virgin

In the mountains, in Maltsia e madhe, she must have tried to tell them her name, and "Lottar" was what they made of it. She had a wound in her leg, from a fall on sharp rocks when her guide was shot. She had a fever. How long it took them to carry her through the mountains, bound up in a rug and strapped to a horse's back, she had no idea. They gave her water to drink now and then, and sometimes *raki*, which was a kind of brandy, very strong. She could smell pines. At one time they were on a boat and she woke up and saw the stars, brightening and fading and changing places—unstable clusters that made her sick. Later she understood that they must have been on the lake. Lake Scutari, or Sckhoder, or Skodra. They pulled up among the reeds. The rug was full of vermin, which got under the rag tied around her leg.

At the end of her journey, though she did not know it was the end, she was lying in a small stone hut that was an out-building of the big house, called the *kula*. It was the hut of the sick and dying. Not of giving birth, which these women did in the cornfields, or beside the path when they were carrying a load to market.

She was lying, perhaps for weeks, on a heaped-up bed of ferns. It was comfortable, and had the advantage of being easily changed when fouled and bloodied. The old woman named Tima looked after her. She plugged up the wound with a paste made of beeswax and olive oil and pine resin. Several times a day the dressing was removed, the wound washed out with *raki*. Lottar could see black lace curtains hanging from the rafters, and she thought she was in her room at home, with her mother (who was dead) looking after her. "Why have you hung up those curtains?" she said. "They look horrible."

She was really seeing cobwebs, all thick and furry with smoke—ancient cobwebs, never disturbed from year to year.

Also, in her delirium, she had the sensation of some wide board being pushed against her face—something like a coffin plank. But when she came to her senses she learned that it was nothing but a crucifix, a wooden crucifix that a man was trying to get her to kiss. The man was a priest, a Franciscan. He was a tall, fierce-looking man with black eyebrows and mustache and a rank smell, and he carried, besides the crucifix, a gun that she learned later was a Browning revolver. He knew by the look of her that she was a giaour—not a Muslim—but he did not understand that she might be a heretic. He knew a little English but pronounced it in a way that she could not make out. And she did not then know any of the language of the Ghegs. But after her fever subsided, when he tried a few words of Italian on her, they were able to talk, because she had learned Italian at school and had been travelling for six months in Italy. He understood so much more than anyone else around her that she expected him, at first, to understand everything. What is the nearest city? she asked him, and he said, Skodra. So go there, please, she said—go and find the British Consulate, if there is one. I belong to the British Empire. Tell them I am here. Or if there is no British Consul, go to the police.

She did not understand that under no circumstances would anybody go to the police. She didn't know that she belonged now to this tribe, this *kula*, even though taking her prisoner had not been their intention and was an embarrassing mistake.

It is shameful beyond belief to attack a woman. When they had shot and killed her guide, they had thought that she would turn her horse around and fly back down the mountain road, back to Bar. But her horse took fright at the shot and stumbled among the boulders and she fell, and her leg was injured. Then they had no choice but to carry her with them, back across the border between the Crna Gora (which means Black Rock, or Montenegro) and Maltsia e madhe.

"But why rob the guide and not me?" she said, naturally thinking robbery to be the motive. She thought of how starved they looked, the man and his horse, and of the fluttering white rags of his headdress.

"Oh, they are not robbers!" said the Franciscan, shocked. "They are honest men. They shot him because they were in blood with him. With his house. It is their law."

He told her that the man who had been shot, her guide, had killed a man of this *kula*. He had done that because the man he had killed had killed a man of his *kula*. This would go on, it had been going on for a long time now, there were always more sons being born. They think they have more sons than other people in the world, and it is to serve this necessity.

"Well, it is terrible," the Franciscan concluded. "But it is for their honor, the honor of their family. They are always ready to die for their honor."

She said that her guide did not seem to be so ready, if he had fled to Crna Gora.

"But it did not make any difference, did it?" said the Franciscan. "Even if he had gone to America, it would not have made any difference."

At Trieste she had boarded a steamer, to travel down the Dalmatian Coast. She was with her friends Mr. and Mrs. Cozzens, whom she had met in Italy, and their friend Dr. Lamb, who had joined them from England. They put in at the little port of Bar, which the Italians call Antivari, and stayed the night at the European Hotel. After dinner they walked on the terrace, but Mrs. Cozzens was afraid of a chill, so they went indoors and played cards. There was rain in the night. She woke up and listened to the rain and was full of disappointment, which gave rise to a loathing for these middle-aged people, particularly for Dr. Lamb, whom she believed the Cozzenses had summoned from England to meet her. They probably thought she was rich. A transatlantic heiress whose accent they could almost forgive. These people ate too much and then they had to take pills. And they worried about being in strange places—what had they come for? In the morning she would have to get back on the boat with them or they would make a fuss. She would never take the road over the mountains to Cetinge, Montenegro's capital city—they had been told that it was not wise. She would never see the bell tower where the heads of Turks used to hang, or the plane tree under which the Poet-Prince held audience with the people. She could not get back to sleep, so she decided to go downstairs with the first light, and, even if it was still raining, to go a little way up the road behind the town, just to see the ruins that she knew were there, among the olive trees, and the Austrian fortress on its rock and the dark face of Mount Lovchen.

The weather obliged her, and so did the man at the hotel desk, producing almost at once a tattered but cheerful guide and his underfed horse. They set out—she on the horse, the man walking ahead. The road was steep and twisting and full of boulders, the sun increasingly hot and the intervening shade cold and black. She became hungry and thought she must turn back soon. She would have breakfast with her companions, who got up late.

No doubt there was some sort of search for her, after the guide's body was found. The authorities must have been notified—whoever the authorities were. The boat must have sailed on time, her friends must have gone with it. The hotel had not taken their passports. Nobody back in Canada would think of investigating. She was not writing regularly to anyone, she had had a falling-out with her brother, her parents were dead. You won't come home till all your inheritance is spent, her brother had said, and then who will look after you?

When she was being carried through the pine forest, she awoke and found herself suspended, lulled—in spite of the pain and perhaps because of the *raki*—into a disbelieving surrender. She fastened her eyes on the bundle that was hanging from the saddle of the man ahead of her and knocking against the horse's back. It was something about the size of a cabbage, wrapped in a stiff and rusty-looking cloth.

I heard this story in the old St. Joseph's Hospital in Victoria from Charlotte, who was the sort of friend I had in my early days there. My friendships then seemed both intimate and uncertain. I never knew why people told me things, or what they meant me to believe.

I had come to the hospital with flowers and chocolates. Charlotte lifted her head, with its clipped and feathery white hair, toward the roses. "Bah!" she said. "They have no smell! Not to me, anyway. They are beautiful, of course.

"You must eat the chocolates yourself," she said. "Everything tastes like tar to me. I don't know how I know what tar tastes like, but this is what I think."

She was feverish. Her hand, when I held it, felt hot and puffy. Her hair had all been cut off, and this made her look as if she had actually lost flesh around her face and neck. The part of her under the hospital covers seemed as extensive and lumpy as ever.

"But you must not think I am ungrateful," she said. "Sit down. Bring that chair from over there—she doesn't need it."

There were two other women in the room. One was just a thatch of yellow-gray hair on the pillow, and the other was tied into a chair, wriggling and grunting.

"This is a terrible place," said Charlotte. "But we must just try our best to put up with it. I am so glad to see you. That one over there yells all night long," she said, nodding toward the window bed. "We must thank Christ she's asleep now. I don't get a wink of sleep, but I have been putting the time to very good use. What do you think I've been doing? I've been making up a story, for a movie! I have it all in my head and I want you to hear it. You will be able to judge if it will make a good movie. I think it will. I would like Jennifer Jones to act in it. I don't know, though. She does not seem to have the same spirit anymore. She married that mogul.

"Listen," she said. "(Oh, could you haul that pillow up more, behind my head?) It takes place in Albania, in northern Albania, which is called Maltsia e madhe, in the nineteen-twenties, when things were very primitive. It is about a young woman travelling alone. Lottar is her name in the story."

I sat and listened. Charlotte would lean forward, even rock a little on her hard bed, stressing some point for me. Her puffy hands flew up and down, her blue eyes widened commandingly, and then from time to time she sank back onto the pillows, and she shut her eyes to get the story in focus again. Ah, yes, she said. Yes, yes. And she continued.

"Yes, yes," she said at last. "I know how it goes on, but that is enough for now. You will have to come back. Tomorrow. Will you come back?"

I said, yes, tomorrow, and she appeared to have fallen asleep without hearing me.

The *kula* was a great, rough stone house with a stable below and the living quarters above. A veranda ran all the way around, and there would always be an old woman sitting there, with a bobbin contraption that flew like a bird from one hand to the other and left a trail of shiny black braid, mile after mile of black braid, which was the adornment of all the men's trousers. Other women worked at the looms or sewed together the leather sandals. Nobody sat there knitting, because nobody would think to sit down to knit. Knitting was what they did while they trotted back and forth to the spring with their water barrels strapped to their backs, or took the path to the fields or to the beech wood, where they collected the fallen branches. They knitted stockings—black and white, red and white, with zigzag patterns like lightning strokes. Women's hands must never be idle. Before dawn they pounded the bread dough in its blackened wooden trough, shaped it into loaves on the backs of shovels, and baked it on the hearth. (It was corn bread, unleavened and eaten hot, which would swell up like a puffball in your stomach.) Then they had to sweep out the *kula* and dump the dirty ferns and pile up armloads of fresh ferns for the next night's sleep. This was often one of Lottar's jobs, since she was so unskilled at everything else. Little girls stirred the yogurt so that lumps would not form as it soured. Older girls might butcher a kid and sew up its stomach, which they had stuffed with wild garlic and sage and apples. Or they would go together, girls and women, all ages, to wash the men's white head scarves in the cold little river nearby, whose waters were clear as glass. They tended the tobacco crop and hung the ripe leaves to dry in the darkened shed. They hoed the corn and cucumbers, milked the ewes.

The women looked stern but they were not so, really. They were only preoccupied, and proud of themselves, and eager for competition. Who could carry the heaviest load of wood, knit the fastest, hoe the most rows of cornstalks? Tima, who had looked after Lottar when she was sick, was the most spectacular worker of all. She would run up the slope to the *kula* with a load of wood bound to her back that looked ten times as big as herself. She would leap from rock to rock in the river and pound the scarves as if they were the bodies of enemies. "Oh, Tima, Tima!" the other women cried out in ironic admiration, and "Oh, Lottar, Lottar!" in nearly the same tones, when Lottar, at the other end of a scale of usefulness, let the clothes drift away downstream. Sometimes they whacked Lottar with a stick, as they would a donkey, but this had more exasperation in it than cruelty. Sometimes the young ones would say, "Talk your talk!" and for their entertainment she would speak English. They wrinkled up their faces and spat, at such peculiar sounds. She tried to teach them words—"hand," "nose," and so on. But these seemed to them jokes, and they would repeat them to each other and fall about laughing.

Women were with women and men were with men, except at times in the night (women teased about such times were full of shame and denial, and sometimes there would be a slapping) and at meals, when the women served the men their food. What the men did all day was none of women's business. Men made their ammunition, and gave a lot of care to their guns, which were in some cases very beautiful, decorated with engraved silver. They also dynamited rocks to clear the road, and were responsible for the horses. Wherever they were, there was a lot of laughing, and sometimes singing and firing off of blanks. While they were at home they seemed to be on holiday, and then some of them would have to ride off on an expedition of punishment, or to attend a council called to put an end to some particular bout of killing. None of the women believed it would work—they laughed and said that it would only mean twenty more shot. When a young man was going off on his first killing, the women made a great fuss over his clothes and his haircut, to encourage him. If he didn't succeed, no woman would marry him—a woman of any worth would be ashamed to marry a man who had not killed—and everyone was anxious to have new brides in the house, to help with the work.

One night, when Lottar served one man his food—a guest; there were always guests invited for meals around the low table, the *sofra*—she noticed what small hands he had, and hairless wrists. Yet he was not young, he was not a boy. A wrinkled, leathery face, without a mustache. She listened for his voice in the talk, and it seemed to her hoarse but womanish. But he smoked, he ate with the men, he carried a gun.

"Is that a man?" Lottar said to the woman serving with her. The woman shook her head, not willing to speak where the men might hear them. But the young girls who overheard the question were not so careful. "Is that a man? Is that a man?" they mimicked Lottar. "Oh, Lottar, you are so stupid! Don't you know when you see a Virgin?"

So she did not ask them anything else. But the next time she saw the Franciscan, she ran after him to ask him her question. What is a Virgin? She had to run after him, because he did not stop and talk to her now as he had when she was sick in the little hut. She was always working when he came to the *kula,* and he could not spend much time with the women anyway—he sat with the men. She ran after him when she saw him leaving, striding down the path among the sumac trees, heading for the bare wooden church and the lean-to church house, where he lived.

He said it was a woman, but a woman who had become like a man. She did not want to marry, and she took an oath in front of witnesses that she never would, and then she put on men's clothes and had her own gun, and her horse if she could afford one, and she lived as she liked. Usually she was poor, she had no woman to work for her. But nobody troubled her, and she could eat at the *sofra* with the men.

Lottar no longer spoke to the priest about going to Skodra. She understood now that it must be a long way away. Sometimes she asked if he had heard anything, if anybody was looking for her, and he would say, sternly, no one. When she thought of how she had been during those first weeks—giving orders, speaking English without embarrassment, sure that her special case merited attention—she was ashamed at how little she had understood. And the longer she stayed at the *kula,* the better she spoke the language and became accustomed to the work, the stranger was the thought of leaving. Someday she must go, but how could it be now? How could she leave in the middle of the tobacco-picking or the sumac harvest, or during the preparations for the feast of the Translation of St. Nicholas?

In the tobacco fields they took off their jerkins and blouses and worked half naked in the sun, hidden between the rows of tall plants. The tobacco juice was black and sticky, like molasses, and it ran down their arms and was smeared over their breasts. At dusk they went down to the river and scrubbed themselves clean. They splashed in the cold water, girls and big, broad women together. They tried to push each other off balance, and Lottar heard her name cried then, in warning and triumph, without contempt, like any other name: "Lottar, watch out! Lottar!"

They told her things. They told her that children died here because of the *Striga.* Even grown-up people shrivel and die sometimes, when the *Striga* has put her spell on them. The *Striga* looks like a normal woman, so you do not know who she is. She sucks blood. To catch her, you must lay a cross on the threshold of the church on Easter Sunday when everybody is inside. Then the woman who is the *Striga* cannot come out. Or you can follow the woman you suspect, and you may see her vomit up the blood. If you can manage to scrape up some of this blood on a silver coin, and carry that coin with you, no *Striga* can touch you, ever.

Hair cut at the time of the full moon will turn white.

If you have pains in your limbs, cut some hair from your head and your armpits and burn it—then the pains will go away.

The *oras* are the devils that come out at night and flash false lights to bewilder travellers. You must crouch down and cover your head, else they will lead you over a cliff. Also they will catch the horses and ride them to death.

The tobacco had been harvested, the sheep brought down from the slopes, animals and humans shut up in the *kula* through the weeks of snow and cold rain, and one day, in the early warmth of the spring sun, the women brought Lottar to a chair on the veranda. There, with great ceremony and delight, they shaved off the hair above her forehead. Then they combed some black, bubbling dye through the hair that remained. The dye was greasy—the hair became so stiff that they could shape it into wings and buns as firm as blood puddings. Everybody thronged about, criticizing and admiring. They put flour on her face and dressed her up in clothes they had pulled out of one of the great carved chests. What for, she asked, as she found herself disappearing into a white blouse with gold embroidery, a red bodice with fringed epaulets, a sash of striped silk a yard wide and a dozen yards long, a black-and-red wool skirt, with chain after chain of false gold being thrown over her hair and around her neck. For beauty, they said. And they said when they had finished, "See! She is beautiful!" Those who said it seemed triumphant, challenging others who must have doubted that the transformation could be made. They squeezed the muscles in her arms, which she had got from hoeing and wood-carrying, and patted her broad, floured forehead. Then they shrieked, because they had forgotten a very important thing—the black paint that joins the eyebrows in a single line over the nose.

"The priest is coming!" shouted one of the girls, who must have been placed as a lookout, and the woman who was painting the black line said, "Ha, he will not stop it!" But the others drew aside.

The Franciscan shot off a couple of blanks, as he always did to announce his arrival, and the men of the house fired off blanks also, to welcome him. But he did not stay with the men this time. He climbed at once to the veranda, calling, "Shame! Shame! Shame on you all! Shame!

"I know what you have dyed her hair for," he said to the women. "I know why you have put bride's clothes on her. All for a pig of a Muslim!

"You! You sitting there in your paint," he said to Lottar. "Don't you know what it is for? Don't you know they have sold you to a Muslim? He is coming from Vuthaj. He will be here by dark!"

"So what of it?" said one of the women boldly. "All they could get for her was three napoleons. She has to marry somebody."

The Franciscan told her to hold her tongue. "Is this what you want?" he said to Lottar. "To marry an infidel and go to live with him in Vuthaj?"

Lottar said no. She felt as if she could hardly move or open her mouth, under the weight of her greased hair and her finery. Under this weight she struggled as you do to rouse yourself to a danger, out of sleep. The idea of marrying the Muslim was still too distant to be the danger—what she understood was that she would be separated from the priest, and would never be able to claim an explanation from him again.

"Did you know you were being married?" he asked her. "Is it something you want, to be married?"

No, she said. No. And the Franciscan clapped his hands. "Take off that gold trash!" he said. "Take those clothes off her! I am going to make her a Virgin!

"If you become a Virgin, it will be all right," he said to her. "The Muslim will not have to shoot anybody. But you must swear you will never go with a man. You must swear in front of witnesses. *Per quri e per kruch.* By the stone and by the Cross. Do you understand that? I am not going to let them marry you to a Muslim, but I do not want more shooting to start on this land."

It was one of the things the Franciscan tried so hard to prevent—the selling of women to Muslim men. It put him into a frenzy, that their religion could be so easily set aside. They sold girls like Lottar, who would bring no price anywhere else, and widows who had borne only girls.

Slowly and sulkily the women removed all the rich clothes. They brought out men's trousers, worn and with no braid, and a shirt and head scarf. Lottar put them on. One woman with an ugly pair of shears chopped off most of what remained of Lottar's hair, which was difficult to cut because of the dressing.

"Tomorrow you would have been a bride," they said to her. Some of them seemed mournful, some contemptuous. "Now you will never have a son."

The little girls snatched up the hair that had been cut off and stuck it on their heads, arranging various knots and fringes.

Lottar swore her oath in front of twelve witnesses. They were, of course, all men, and looked as sullen as the women about the turn things had taken. She never saw the Muslim. The Franciscan berated the men and said that if this sort of thing did not stop he would close up the churchyard and make them bury their dead in unholy ground. Lottar sat at a distance from them all, in her unaccustomed clothes. It was strange and unpleasant to be idle. When the Franciscan had finished his harangue, he came over and stood looking down at her. He was breathing hard because of his rage, or the exertions of the lecture.

"Well, then," he said. "Well." He reached into some inner fold of his clothing and brought out a cigarette and gave it to her. It smelled of his skin.

. . .

A nurse brought in Charlotte's supper, a light meal of soup and canned peaches. Charlotte took the cover off the soup, smelled it, and turned her head away. "Go away, don't look at this slop," she said. "Come back tomorrow—you know it's not finished yet."

The nurse walked with me to the door, and once we were in the corridor she said, "It's always the ones with the least at home who turn the most critical. She's not the easiest in the world, but you can't help kind of admiring her. You're not related, are you?"

Oh, no, I said. No.

"When she came in it was amazing. We were taking her things off and somebody said, oh, what lovely bracelets, and right away she wanted to sell them! Her *husband* is something else. Do you know him? They are really quite the characters."

Charlotte's husband, Gjurdhi, had come to my bookstore by himself one cold morning less than a week earlier. He was pulling a wagon full of books, which he had wrapped up in a blanket. He had tried to sell me some books once before, in their apartment, and I thought perhaps these were the same ones. I had been confused then, but now that I was on my own ground I was able to be more forceful. I said no, I did not handle secondhand books, I was not interested. Gjurdhi nodded brusquely, as if I had not needed to tell him this and it was of no importance to our conversation. He continued to pick up the books one by one, urging me to run my hands over the bindings, insisting that I note the beauty of the illustrations and be impressed by the dates of publication. I had to repeat my refusal over and over again, and I heard myself begin to attach some apologies to it, quite against my own will. He chose to understand each rejection as applying to an individual book and would simply fetch out another, saying vehemently, "This, too! This is very beautiful. You will notice. And it is very old. Look what a beautiful old book!"

They were travel books, some of them, from the turn of the century. Not so very old, and not so beautiful, either, with their dim, grainy photographs. *A Trek Through the Black Peaks. High Albania. Secret Lands of Southern Europe.*

"You will have to go to the Antiquarian Bookstore," I said. "The one on Fort Street. It isn't far to take them."

He made a sound of disgust, maybe indicating that he knew well enough where it was, or that he had already made an unsuccessful trip there, or that most of these books had come from there, one way or another, in the first place.

"How is Charlotte?" I said warmly. I had not seen her for a while, although she used to visit the store quite often. She would bring me little presents—coffee beans coated with chocolate to give me energy; a bar of pure glycerine soap to counteract the drying effects, on the skin, of having to handle so much paper. A paperweight embedded with samples of rocks found in British Columbia, a pencil that lit up in the dark (so that I could see to write up bills if the lights should go out). She drank coffee with me, talked, and strolled about the store, discreetly occupied, when I was busy. Through the dark, blustery days of fall she wore the velvet cloak that I had first seen her in, and kept the rain off with an oversized, ancient black umbrella. She called it her tent. If she saw that I had become too involved with a customer, she would tap me on the shoulder and say, "I'll just silently steal away with my tent now. We'll talk another day."

Once, a customer said to me bluntly, "Who is that woman? I've seen her around town with her husband. I guess he's her husband. I thought they were peddlers."

Could Charlotte have heard that, I wondered. Could she have detected a coolness in the attitude of my new clerk? (Charlotte was certainly cool to her.) There might have been just too many times when I was busy. I did not actually think that the visits had stopped. I preferred to think that an interval had grown longer, for a reason that might have nothing to do with me. I was busy and tired, anyway, as Christmas loomed. The number of books I was selling was a pleasant surprise.

"I don't want to be any kind of character assassin," the clerk had said to me. "But I think you should know that that woman and her husband have been banned from a lot of stores in town. They're suspected of lifting things. I don't know. He wears that rubber coat with the big sleeves and she's got her cloak. I do know for sure that they used to go around at Christmastime and snip off holly that was growing in people's gardens. Then they took it round and tried to sell it in apartment buildings."

On that cold morning, after I had refused all the books in his wagon, I asked Gjurdhi again how Charlotte was. He said that she was sick. He spoke sullenly, as if it were none of my business.

"Take her a book," I said. I picked out a Penguin light verse. "Take her this—tell her I hope she enjoys it. Tell her I hope she'll be better very soon. Perhaps I can get around to see her."

He put the book into his bundle in the wagon. I thought that he would probably try to sell it immediately.

"Not at home," he said. "In the hospital."

I had noticed, each time he bent over the wagon, a large, wooden crucifix that swung down outside his coat and had to be tucked back inside. Now this happened again, and I said, thoughtlessly, in my confusion and contrition, "Isn't that beautiful! What beautiful dark wood! It looks medieval."

He pulled it over his head, saying, "Very old. Very beautiful. Oak wood. Yes."

He pushed it into my hand, and as soon as I realized what was happening I pushed it back.

"*Wonderful* wood," I said. As he put it away I felt rescued, though full of irritable remorse.

"Oh, I hope Charlotte is not very sick!" I said.

He smiled disdainfully, tapping himself on the chest—perhaps to show me the source of Charlotte's trouble, perhaps only to feel for himself the skin that was newly bared there.

Then he took himself, the crucifix, the books, and the wagon out of my store. I felt that insults had been offered, humiliations suffered, on both sides.

Up past the tobacco field was a beech wood, where Lottar had often gone to get sticks for the fire. Beyond that was a grassy slope—a high meadow—and at the top of the meadow, about half an hour's climb from the *kula*, was a small stone shelter, a primitive place with no window, a low doorway and no door, a corner hearth without a chimney. Sheep took cover there; the floor was littered with their droppings.

That was where she went to live after she became a Virgin. The incident of the Muslim bridegroom had taken place in the spring, just about a year after she first came to Maltsia e madhe, and it was time for the sheep to be driven to their higher pastures. Lottar was to keep count of the flock and see that they did not fall into ravines or wander too far away. And she was to milk the ewes every evening. She was expected to shoot wolves, if any came near. But none did, no one alive now at the *kula* had ever seen a wolf. The only wild animals Lottar saw were a red fox, once, by the stream, and the rabbits, which were plentiful and unwary. She learned to shoot and skin and cook them, cleaning them out as she had seen the butcher girls do at the *kula* and stewing the meatier parts in her pot over the fire, with some bulbs of wild garlic.

She did not want to sleep inside the shelter, so she fixed up a roof of branches outside, against the wall, this roof an extension of the roof of the building. She had her heap of ferns underneath, and a felt rug she had been given, to spread on the ferns when she slept. She no longer took any notice of the bugs. There were some spikes pushed into the wall between the dry stones. She did not know why they were there, but they served her well for hanging up the milk pails and the few pots she had been provided with. She brought her water from the stream, in which she washed her own head scarf, and herself sometimes, more for relief from the heat than out of concern about her dirtiness.

Everything was changed. She no longer saw the women. She lost her habits of constant work. The little girls came up in the evenings to get the milk. This far away from the *kula* and their mothers, they became quite wild. They climbed up on the roof, often smashing through the arrangement of branches which Lottar had contrived. They jumped into the ferns and sometimes snatched an armful of them to bind into a crude ball, which they threw at one another until it fell apart. They enjoyed themselves so much that Lottar had to chase them away at dusk, reminding them of how frightened they got in the beech wood after dark. She believed that they ran all the way through it and spilled half the milk on their way.

Now and then they brought her corn flour, which she mixed with water and baked on her shovel by the fire. Once they had a treat, a sheep's head—she wondered if they had stolen it—for her to boil in her pot. She was allowed to keep some of the milk, and instead of drinking it fresh she usually let it go sour, and stirred it to make yogurt to dip her bread in. That was how she preferred it now.

The men often came up through the wood shortly after the little girls had run through it on their way down. It seemed that this was a custom of theirs, in the summer. They liked to sit on the banks of the stream and fire off blanks and drink *raki* and sing, or sometimes just smoke and talk. They were not making this expedition to see how she was getting on. But since they were coming anyway, they brought her presents of coffee and tobacco and were full of competing advice on how to fix up the roof of her shelter so it wouldn't fall down, how to keep her fire going all night, how to use her gun.

Her gun was an old Italian Martini, which had been given to her when she left the *kula*. Some of the men said that gun was unlucky, since it had belonged to a boy who had been killed before he himself had even shot anybody. Others said that Martinis in general were unlucky, hardly any use at all.

Mausers were what you needed, for accuracy and repeating power.

But Mauser bullets were too small to do enough damage. There were men walking around full of Mauser holes—you could hear them whistle as they passed by.

Nothing can really compare with a heavy flintlock that has a good packing of powder, a bullet, and nails.

When they weren't talking about guns, the men spoke of recent killings, and told jokes. One of them told a joke about a wizard. There was a wizard held in prison by a Pasha. The Pasha brought him out to do tricks in front of guests. Bring a bowl of water, said the wizard. Now, this water is the sea. And what port shall I show you on the sea? Show a port on the island of Malta, they said. And there it was. Houses and churches and a steamer ready to sail. Now would you like to see me step on board that steamer? And the Pasha laughed. Go ahead! So the wizard put his foot in the bowl of water and stepped on board the steamer and went to America! What do you think of that!

"There are no wizards, anyway," said the Franciscan, who had climbed up with the men on this evening, as he often did. "If you had said a saint, you might have made some sense." He spoke severely, but Lottar thought he was happy, as they all were, as she, too, was permitted to be, in their presence and in his, though he paid no attention to her. The strong tobacco that they gave her to smoke made her dizzy and she had to lie down on the grass.

The time came when Lottar had to think about moving inside her house. The mornings were cold, the ferns were soaked with dew, and the grape leaves were turning yellow. She took the shovel and cleaned the sheep droppings off the floor, in preparation for making up her bed inside. She began to stuff grass and leaves and mud into the chinks between the stones.

When the men came they asked her what she was doing that for. For the winter, she said, and they laughed.

"Nobody can stay here in the winter," they said. They showed her how deep the snow was, putting hands against their breastbones. Besides, all the sheep would have been taken down.

"There will be no work for you—and what will you eat?" they said. "Do you think the women will let you have bread and yogurt for nothing?"

"How can I go back to the *kula?*" Lottar said. "I am a Virgin, where would I sleep? What kind of work would I do?"

"That is right," they said kindly, speaking to her and then to each other. "When a Virgin belongs to the *kula* she gets a bit of land, usually, where she can live on her own. But this one doesn't really belong to the *kula,* she has no father to give her anything. What will she do?"

Shortly after this—and in the middle of the day, when visitors never came—the Franciscan climbed the meadow, all alone.

"I don't trust them," he said. "I think they will try again to sell you to a Muslim. Even though you have been sworn. They will try to make some money out of you. If they could find you a Christian, it might not be so bad, but I am sure it will be an infidel."

They sat on the grass and drank coffee. The Franciscan said, "Do you have any belongings to take with you? No. Soon we will start."

"Who will milk the ewes?" said Lottar. Some of the ewes were already working their way down the slope; they would stand and wait for her.

"Leave them," said the Franciscan.

In this way she left not only the sheep but her shelter, the meadow, the wild grape and the sumac and mountain ash and juniper bushes and scrub oak she had looked at all summer, the rabbit pelt she had used as a pillow and the pan she had boiled her coffee in, the heap of wood she had gathered only that morning, the stones around her fire—each one of them known to her by its particular shape and color. She understood that she was leaving, because the Franciscan was so stern, but she did not understand it in a way that would make her look around, to see everything for the last time. That was not necessary, anyway. She would never forget any of it.

As they entered the beech wood the Franciscan said, "Now we must be very quiet. I am going to take another path, which does not go so near the *kula.* If we hear anybody on the path, we will hide."

Hours, then, of silent walking, between the beech trees with their smooth elephant bark, and the black-limbed oaks and the dry pines. Up and down, crossing the ridges, choosing paths that Lottar had not known existed. The Franciscan never hesitated and never spoke of a rest. When they came out of the trees at last, Lottar was very surprised to see that there was still so much light in the sky.

The Franciscan pulled a loaf of bread and a knife from some pocket in his garment, and they ate as they walked.

They came to a dry riverbed, paved with stones that were not flat and easily walkable but a torrent, a still torrent of stones between fields of corn and tobacco. They could hear dogs barking, and sometimes people's voices. The corn and tobacco plants, still unharvested, were higher than their heads, and they walked along the dry river in this shelter, while the daylight entirely faded. When they could not walk anymore and the darkness would conceal them, they sat down on the white stones of the riverbed.

"Where are you taking me?" Lottar finally asked. At the start she had thought they must be going in the direction of the church and the priest's house, but now she saw that this could not be so. They had come much too far.

"I am taking you to the Bishop's house," said the Franciscan. "He will know what to do with you."

"Why not to your house?" said Lottar. "I could be a servant in your house."

"It isn't allowed—to have a woman servant in my house. Or in any priest's house. This Bishop now will not allow even an old woman. And he is right, trouble comes from having a woman in the house."

After the moon rose they went on. They walked and rested, walked and rested, but never fell asleep, or even looked for a comfortable place to lie down. Their feet were tough and their sandals well worn, and they did not get blisters. Both of them were used to walking long distances—the Franciscan in his far-flung parish and Lottar when she was following the sheep.

The Franciscan became less stern—perhaps less worried—after a while and talked to her almost as he had done in the first days of their acquaintance. He spoke Italian, though she was now fairly proficient in the language of the Ghegs.

"I was born in Italy," he said. "My parents were Ghegs, but I lived in Italy when I was young, and that was where I became a priest. Once I went back for a visit, years ago, and I shaved off my mustache, I do not know why. Oh, yes, I do know—it was because they laughed at me in the village. Then when I got back I did not dare show my face in the *madhe.* A hairless man there is a disgrace. I sat in a room in Skodra until it grew again."

"It is Skodra we are going to?" said Lottar.

"Yes, that is where the Bishop is. He will send a message that it was right to take you away, even if it is an act of stealing. They are barbarians, in the *madhe.* They will come up and pull on your sleeve in the middle of Mass and ask you to write a letter for them. Have you seen what they put up on the graves? The crosses? They make the cross into a very thin man with a rifle across his arms. Haven't you seen that?" He laughed and shook his head and said, "I don't know what to do with them. But they are good people all the same—they will never betray you."

"But you thought they might sell me in spite of my oath."

"Oh, yes. But to sell a woman is a way to get some money. And they are so poor."

Lottar now realized that in Skodra she would be in an unfamiliar position—she would not be powerless. When they got there, she could run away from him. She could find someone who spoke English, she could find the British Consulate. Or, if not that, the French.

The grass was soaking wet before dawn and the night got very cold. But when the sun came up Lottar stopped shivering and within an hour she was hot. They walked on all day. They ate the rest of the bread and drank from any stream they found that had water in it. They had left the dry river and the mountains far behind. Lottar looked back and saw a wall of jagged rocks with a little green clinging around their bases. That green was the woods and meadows which she had thought so high. They followed paths through the hot fields and were never out of the sound of barking dogs. They met people on the paths.

At first the Franciscan said, "Do not speak to anybody—they will wonder who you are." But he had to answer when greetings were spoken.

"Is this the way to Skodra? We are going to Skodra to the Bishop's house. This is my servant with me, who has come from the mountains.

"It is all right, you look like a servant in these clothes," he said to Lottar. "But do not speak—they will wonder, if you speak."

I had painted the walls of my bookstore a clear, light yellow. Yellow stands for intellectual curiosity. Somebody must have told me that. I opened the store in March of 1964. This was in Victoria, in British Columbia.

I sat there at the desk, with my offerings spread out behind me. The publishers' representatives had advised me to stock books about dogs and horses, sailing and gardening, bird books and flower books—they said that was all anybody in Victoria would buy. I flew against their advice and brought in novels and poetry and books that explained about Sufism and relativity and Linear B. And I had set out these books, when they came, so that Political Science could shade into Philosophy and Philosophy into Religion without a harsh break, so that compatible poets could nestle together, the arrangement of the shelves of books—I believed—reflecting a more or less natural ambling of the mind, in which treasures new and forgotten might be continually surfacing. I had taken all this care, and now what? Now I waited, and I felt like somebody who had got dramatically dressed up for a party, maybe even fetching jewels from the pawnshop or the family vault, only to discover that it was just a few neighbors playing cards. It was just meat loaf and mashed potatoes in the kitchen, and a glass of fizzy pink wine.

The store was often empty for a couple of hours at a time, and then when somebody did come in, it would be to ask about a book remembered from the Sunday-school library or a grandmother's bookcase or left behind twenty years ago in a foreign hotel. The title was usually forgotten, but the person would tell me the story. It is about this little girl who goes out to Australia with her father to mine the gold claims they have inherited. It is about the woman who had a baby all alone in Alaska. It is about a race between one of the old clipper ships and the first steamer, way back in the 1840s.

Oh, well. I just thought I'd ask.

They would leave without a glance at the riches around them.

A few people did exclaim in gratitude, said what a glorious addition to the town. They would browse for half an hour, an hour, before spending seventy-five cents.

It takes time.

I had found a one-room apartment with a kitchenette in an old building at a corner called the Dardanelles. The bed folded up into the wall. But I did not usually bother to fold it up, because I never had any company. And the hook seemed unsafe to me. I was afraid that the bed might leap out of the wall sometime when I was eating my tinned soup or baked-potato supper. It might kill me. Also, I kept the window open all the time, because I believed I could smell a whiff of escaping gas, even when the two burners and the oven were shut off. With the window open at home and the door open at the store, to entice the customers, it was necessary for me to be always bundled up in my black woolly sweater or my red corduroy dressing gown (a garment that had once left its pink tinge on all my forsaken husband's handkerchiefs and underwear). I had difficulty separating myself from these comforting articles of clothing so that they might be washed. I was sleepy much of the time, underfed and shivering.

But I was not despondent. I had made a desperate change in my life, and in spite of the regrets I suffered every day, I was proud of that. I felt as if I had finally come out into the world in a new, true skin. Sitting at the desk, I made a cup of coffee or of thin red soup last an hour, clasping my hands around the cup while there was still any warmth to be got from it. I read, but without purpose or involvement. I read stray sentences from the books that I had always meant to read. Often these sentences seemed so satisfying to me, or so elusive and lovely, that I could not help abandoning all the surrounding words and giving myself up to a peculiar state. I was alert and dreamy, closed off from all particular people but conscious all the time of the city itself—which seemed a strange place.

A small city, here at the western edge of the country. Pockets of fakery for tourists. The Tudor shop fronts and double-decker buses and flowerpots and horse-drawn rides: almost insulting. But the sea light in the street, the spare and healthy old people leaning into the wind as they took their daily walks along the broom-topped cliffs, the shabby, slightly bizarre bungalows with their monkey-puzzle trees and ornate shrubs in the gardens. Chestnut trees blossom as spring comes on, hawthorn trees along the streets bear red-and-white flowers, oily-leaved bushes put out lush pink and rose-red blooms such as you would never see in the hinterlands. Like a town in a story, I thought—like the transplanted seaside town of the story set in New Zealand, in Tasmania. But something North

American persists. So many people, after all, have come here from Winnipeg or Saskatchewan. At noon a smell of dinners cooking drifts out of poor, plain apartment buildings. Frying meat, boiling vegetables—farm dinners being cooked, in the middle of the day, in cramped kitchenettes.

How could I tell what I liked so much? Certainly it was not what a new merchant might be looking for—bustle and energy to raise the hope of commercial success. *Not much doing* was the message the town got across to me. And when a person who is opening a store doesn't mind hearing the message *Not much doing*, you could ask, What's going on? People open shops in order to sell things, they hope to become busy so that they will have to enlarge the shop, then to sell more things, and grow rich, and eventually not have to come into the shop at all. Isn't that true? But are there other people who open a shop with the hope of being sheltered there, among such things as they most value—the yarn or the teacups or the books—and with the idea only of making a comfortable assertion? They will become a part of the block, a part of the street, part of everybody's map of the town, and eventually of everybody's memories. They will sit and drink coffee in the middle of the morning, they will get out the familiar bits of tinsel at Christmas, they will wash the windows in spring before spreading out the new stock. Shops, to these people, are what a cabin in the woods might be to somebody else— a refuge and a justification.

Some customers are necessary, of course. The rent comes due and the stock will not pay for itself. I had inherited a little money—that was what had made it possible for me to come out here and get the shop going—but unless business picked up to some extent I could not last beyond the summer. I understood that. I was glad that more people started coming in as the weather warmed up. More books were sold, survival began to seem possible. Book prizes were due to be awarded in the schools at the end of term, and that brought the schoolteachers with their lists and their praise and their unfortunate expectation of discounts. The people who came to browse were buying regularly, and some of them began to turn into friends—or the sort of friends I had here, where it seemed I would be happy to talk to people day after day and never learn their names.

When Lottar and the priest first saw the town of Skodra, it seemed to float above the mud flats, its domes and steeples shining as if they were made of mist. But when they entered it in the early evening all this tranquility vanished. The streets were paved with big, rough stones and were full of people and donkey carts, roving dogs, pigs being driven somewhere, and smells of fires and cooking and dung and something terrible— like rotten hides. A man came along with a parrot on his shoulder. The bird seemed to be shrieking curses in an unknown language. Several times the Franciscan stopped people and asked the way to the Bishop's house, but they pushed by him without answering or laughed at him or said some words he didn't understand. A boy said that he would show the way, for money.

"We have no money," the Franciscan said. He pulled Lottar into a doorway and there they sat down to rest. "In Maltsia e madhe," he said, "many of these who think so well of themselves would soon sing a different tune."

Lottar's notion of running away and leaving him had vanished. For one thing, she could not manage to ask directions any better than he could. For another, she felt that they were allies who could not survive in this place out of sight of each other. She had not understood how much she depended on the smell of his skin, the aggrieved determination of his long strides, the flourish of his black mustache.

The Franciscan jumped up and said he had remembered—he had remembered now the way to the Bishop's house. He hurried ahead of her through narrow, high-walled back streets where nothing of houses or courtyards could be seen—just walls and gates. The paving stones were thrust up so that walking here was as difficult as in the dry riverbed. But he was right, he gave a shout of triumph, they had come to the gate of the Bishop's house.

A servant opened the gate and let them in, but only after some high-pitched argument. Lottar was told to sit on the ground just inside the gate, and the Franciscan was led into the house to see the Bishop. Soon someone was sent through the streets to the British Consulate (Lottar was not told this), and he came back with the Consul's manservant. It was dark by then, and the Consul's servant carried a lantern. And Lottar was led away again. She followed the servant and his lantern to the consulate.

A tub of hot water for her to bathe in, in the courtyard. Her clothes taken away. Probably burned. Her greasy black, vermin-infested hair cut off. Kerosene poured on her scalp. She had to tell her story—the story of how she came to Maltsia e madhe—and this was difficult, because she was not used to speaking English, also because that time seemed so far away and unimportant. She had to learn to sleep on a mattress, to sit on a chair, to eat with a knife and fork.

As soon as possible they put her on a boat.

Charlotte stopped. She said, "That part is not of interest."

I had come to Victoria because it was the farthest place I could get to from London, Ontario, without going out of the country. In London, my husband, Donald, and I had rented a basement apartment in our house to a couple named Nelson and Sylvia. Nelson was an English major at the university and Sylvia was a nurse. Donald was a dermatologist, and I was doing a thesis on Mary Shelley—not very quickly. I had met Donald when I went to see him about a rash on my neck. He was eight years older than I was—a tall, freckled, blushing man, cleverer than he looked. A dermatologist sees grief and despair, though the problems that bring people to him may not be in the same class as tumors and blocked arteries. He sees sabotage from within, and truly unlucky fate. He sees how matters like love and happiness can be governed by a patch of riled-up cells. Experience of this sort had made Donald kind, in a cautious, impersonal way.

He said that my rash was probably due to stress, and that he could see that I was going to be a wonderful woman, once I got a few problems under control.

We invited Sylvia and Nelson upstairs for dinner, and Sylvia told us about the tiny town they both came from, in Northern Ontario. She said that Nelson had always been the smartest person in their class and in their school and possibly in the whole town. When she said this, Nelson looked at her with a perfectly flat and devastating expression, an expression that seemed to be waiting with infinite patience and the mildest curiosity for some explanation, and Slyvia laughed and said, "Just kidding, of course."

When Sylvia was working late shifts at the hospital, I sometimes asked Nelson to share a meal with us in a more informal way. We got used to his silences and his indifferent table manners and to the fact that he did not eat rice or noodles, eggplant, olives, shrimp, peppers, or avocados, and no doubt a lot of other things, because those had not been familiar foods in the town in Northern Ontario.

Nelson looked older than he was. He was short and sturdily built, sallow-skinned, unsmiling, with a suggestion of mature scorn and handy pugnaciousness laid over his features, so that it seemed he might be a hockey coach, or an intelligent, uneducated, fair-minded, and foul-mouthed foreman of a construction gang, rather than a shy, twenty-two-year-old student.

He was not shy in love. I found him resourceful and determined. The seduction was mutual, and it was a first affair for both of us. I had once heard somebody say, at a party, that one of the nice things about marriage was that you could have real affairs—an affair before marriage could always turn out to be nothing but courtship. I was disgusted by this speech, and frightened to think that life could be so bleak and trivial. But once my own affair with Nelson started, I was amazed all the time. There was no bleakness or triviality about it, only ruthlessness and clarity of desire, and sparkling deception.

Nelson was the one who first faced up to things. One afternoon he turned on his back and said hoarsely and defiantly, "We are going to have to leave."

I thought he meant that he and Sylvia would have to leave, they could not go on living in this house. But he meant himself and me. "We" meant himself and me. Of course he and I had said "we" of our arrangements, of our transgression. Now he had made it the "we" of our decision—perhaps of a life together.

My thesis was supposed to be on Mary Shelley's later novels, the ones nobody knows about. *Lodore, Perkin Warbeck, The Last Man*. But I was really more interested in Mary's life before she learned her sad lessons and buckled down to raising her son to be a baronet. I loved to read about the other women who had hated or envied or traipsed along: Harriet, Shelley's first wife, and Fanny Imlay, who was Mary's half-sister and may have been in love with Shelley herself, and Mary's stepsister, Mary Jane

Clairmont, who took my own name—Claire—and joined Mary and Shelley on their unwed honeymoon so that she could keep on chasing Byron. I had often talked to Donald about impetuous Mary and married Shelley and their meetings at Mary's mother's grave, about the suicides of Harriet and Fanny and the persistence of Claire, who had a baby by Byron. But I never mentioned any of this to Nelson, partly because we had little time for talk and partly because I did not want him to think that I drew some sort of comfort or inspiration from this mishmash of love and despair and treachery and self-dramatizing. I did not want to think so myself. And Nelson was not a fan of the nineteenth century or the Romantics. He said so. He said that he wanted to do something on the Muckrakers. Perhaps he meant that as a joke.

Sylvia did not behave like Harriet. Her mind was not influenced or impeded by literature, and when she found out what had been going on, she went into a wholesome rage.

"You blithering idiot," she said to Nelson.

"You two-faced twit," she said to me.

The four of us were in our living room. Donald went on cleaning and filling his pipe, tapped it and lit it, nursed and inspected it, drew on it, lit it again—all so much the way someone would do in a movie that I was embarrassed for him. Then he put some books and the latest copy of *Macleans* into his briefcase, went to the bathroom to get his razor and to the bedroom to get his pajamas, and walked out.

He went straight to the apartment of a young widow who worked as a secretary at his clinic. In a letter he wrote to me later, he said that he had never thought of this woman except as a friend until that night, when it suddenly dawned on him what a pleasure it would be to love a kind and sensible, *unwracked-up* sort of person.

Sylvia had to be at work at eleven o'clock. Nelson usually walked her over to the hospital—they did not have a car. On this night she told him that she would rather be escorted by a skunk.

That left Nelson and me alone together. The scene had lasted a much shorter time than I had expected. Nelson seemed gloomy but relieved, and if I felt that short shrift had been given to the notion of love as a capturing tide, a glorious and harrowing event, I knew better than to show it.

We lay down on the bed to talk about our plans and ended up making love, because that was what we were used to doing. Sometime during the night Nelson woke up and thought it best to go downstairs to his own bed.

I got up in the dark, dressed, packed a suitcase, wrote a note, and walked to the phone at the corner, where I called a taxi. I took the six-o'clock train to Toronto, connecting with the train to Vancouver. It was cheaper to take the train, if you were willing to sit up for three nights, which I was.

So there I sat, in the sad, shambling morning in the day coach, coming down the steep-walled Fraser Canyon into the sodden Fraser Valley, where smoke hung over the small, dripping houses, the brown vines, the thorny bushes and huddled sheep. It was in December that this earthquake in my life had arrived. Christmas was cancelled for me. Winter with its snowdrifts and icicles and invigorating blizzards was cancelled by this blurred season of muck and rain. I was constipated, I knew that I had bad breath, my limbs were cramped, and my spirits utterly bleak. And did I not think then, What nonsense it is to suppose one man so different from another when all that life really boils down to is getting a decent cup of coffee and room to stretch out in? Did I not think that even if Nelson were sitting here beside me, he would have turned into a gray-faced stranger whose desolation and unease merely extended my own?

No. No. Nelson would still be Nelson to me. I had not changed, with regard to his skin and his smell and his forbidding eyes. It seemed to be the outside of Nelson which came most readily to my mind, and in the case of Donald it was his inner quakes and sympathies, the labored-at kindness and those private misgivings that I had got knowledge of by wheedling and conniving. If I could have my love of these two men together, and settle it on one man, I would be a happy woman. If I could care for everybody in the world as minutely as I did for Nelson, and as calmly, as uncarnally as I now did for Donald, I would be a saint. Instead, I had dealt a twofold, a wanton-seeming, blow.

The regular customers who had changed into something like friends were: a middle-aged woman who was a chartered accountant but preferred such reading as *Six Existentialist Thinkers,* and *The Meaning of Meaning;* a provincial civil servant who ordered splendid, expensive works of pornography such as I had not known existed (their elaborate Oriental, Etruscan connections seemed to me grotesque and uninteresting, compared to the simple, effective, longed-for rituals of myself and Nelson); a Notary Public who lived behind his office at the foot of Johnson Street ("I live in the slums," he told me. "Some night I expect a big bruiser of a fellow to lurch around the corner hollering '*Ste-el-la.*'"); and the woman I knew later as Charlotte—the Notary Public called her the Duchess. None of these people cared much for one another, and an early attempt that I made to bring the accountant and the Notary Public into conversation was a fizzle.

"Spare me the females with the withered, painted faces," the Notary Public said, the next time he came in. "I hope you haven't got her lurking around anywhere tonight."

It was true that the accountant painted her thin, intelligent, fifty-year-old face with a heavy hand, and drew on eyebrows that were like two strokes of India ink. But who was the Notary Public to talk, with his stumpy, nicotined teeth and pocked cheeks?

"I got the impression of a rather superficial fellow," the accountant said, as if she had guessed and bravely discounted the remarks made about herself.

So much for trying to corral people into couples, I wrote to Donald. *And who am I to try?* I wrote to Donald regularly, describing the store, and the city, and even, as well as I could, my own unaccountable feelings. He was living with Helen, the secretary. I wrote also to Nelson, who might or might not be living alone, might or might not be reunited with Sylvia. I didn't think he was. I thought she would believe in inexcusable behavior and definite endings. He had a new address. I had looked it up in the London phone book at the public library. Donald, after a grudging start, was writing back. He wrote impersonal, mildly interesting letters about people we both knew, events at the clinic. Nelson did not write at all. I started sending registered letters. Now I knew at least that he picked them up.

Charlotte and Gjurdhi must have come into the store together, but I did not understand that they were a couple until it was time for them to leave. Charlotte was a heavy, shapeless, but quick-moving woman, with a pink face, bright blue eyes, and a lot of glistening white hair, worn like a girl's, waving down over her shoulders. Though the weather was fairly warm, she was wearing a cape of dark-gray velvet with a scanty gray fur trim—a garment that looked as if it belonged, or had once belonged, on the stage. A loose shirt and a pair of plaid wool slacks showed underneath, and there were open sandals on her broad, bare, dusty feet. She clanked as if she wore hidden armor. An arm reaching up to get a book showed what caused the clanking. Bracelets—any number of them, heavy or slender, tarnished or bright. Some were set with large, square stones, the color of toffee or blood.

"Imagine this old fraud being still on the go," she said to me, as if continuing some desultory and enjoyable conversation.

She had picked up a book by Anaïs Nin.

"Don't pay any attention," she said. "I say terrible things. I'm quite fond of the woman, really. It's him I can't stand."

"Henry Miller?" I said, beginning to follow this.

"That's right." She went on talking about Henry Miller, Paris, California, in a scoffing, energetic, half-affectionate way. She seemed to have been neighbors, at least, with the people she was talking about. Finally, naïvely, I asked her if this was the case.

"No, no. I just feel I know them all. Not personally. Well—personally. Yes, personally. What other way is there to know them? I mean, I haven't met them, face-to-face. But in their books? Surely that's what they intend? I know them. I know them to the point where they bore me. Just like anybody you know. Don't you find that?"

She drifted over to the table where I had laid out the New Directions paperbacks.

"Here's the new bunch, then," she said. "Oh, my," she said, widening her eyes at the photographs of Ginsberg and Corso and Ferlinghetti. She began reading, so attentively that I thought the next thing she said must be part of some poem.

"I've gone by and I've seen you here," she said. She put the book down and I realized she meant me. "I've seen you sitting in here, and I've thought a young woman would probably like to be outside some of the time. In the sun. I don't suppose you'd consider hiring me to sit there, so you could get out?"

"Well, I would like to—" I said.

"I'm not so dumb. I'm fairly knowledgeable, really. Ask me who wrote Ovid's *Metamorphoses*. It's all right, you don't have to laugh."

"I would like to, but I really can't afford to."

"Oh, well. You're probably right. I'm not very chic. And I would probably foul things up. I would argue with people if they were buying books I thought were dreadful." She did not seem disappointed. She picked up a copy of *The Dud Avocado* and said, "There! I have to buy this, for the title."

She gave a little whistle, and the man it seemed to be meant for looked up from the table of books he had been staring at, near the back of the store. I had known he was there but had not connected him with her. I thought he was just one of those men who wander in off the street, alone, and stand looking about, as if trying to figure out what sort of place this is or what the books are for. Not a drunk or a panhandler, and certainly not anybody to be worried about—just one of a number of shabby, utterly un-communicative old men who belong to the city somewhat as the pigeons do, moving restlessly all day within a limited area, never looking at people's faces. He was wearing a coat that came down to his ankles, made of some shiny, rubberized, liver-colored material, and a brown velvet cap with a tassle. The sort of cap a doddery old scholar or a clergyman might wear in an English movie. There was, then, a similarity between them—they were both wearing things that might have been discards from a cos-tume box. But close up he looked years older than she. A long, yellowish face, drooping tobacco-brown eyes, an unsavory, straggling mustache. Some faint remains of handsomeness, or potency. A quenched ferocity. He came at her whistle—which seemed half serious, half a joke—and stood by, mute and self-respecting as a dog or a donkey, while the woman pre-pared to pay.

At that time, the government of British Columbia applied a sales tax to books. In this case it was four cents.

"I can't pay that," she said. "A tax on books. I think it is immoral. I would rather go to jail. Don't you agree?"

I agreed. I did not point out—as I would have done with anybody else—that the store would not be let off the hook on that account.

"Don't I sound appalling?" she said. "See what this government can do to people? It makes them into *orators*."

She put the book in her bag without paying the four cents, and never paid the tax on any future occasion.

I described the two of them to the Notary Public. He knew at once who I meant.

"I call them the Duchess and the Algerian," he said. "I don't know what the background is. I think maybe he's a retired terrorist. They go around the town with a wagon, like scavengers."

I got a note asking me to supper on a Sunday evening. It was signed *Charlotte,* without a surname, but the wording and handwriting were quite formal.

My husband Gjurdhi and I would be delighted—

Up until then I had not wished for any invitations of this sort and would have been embarrassed and disturbed to get one. So the pleasure I felt surprised me. Charlotte held out a decided promise; she was unlike the others whom I wanted to see only in the store.

The building where they lived was on Pandora Street. It was covered with mustard stucco and had a tiny, tiled vestibule that reminded me of a public toilet. It did not smell, though, and the apartment was not really dirty, just horrendously untidy. Books were stacked against the walls, and pieces of patterned cloth were hung up droopily to hide the wallpaper. There were bamboo blinds on the window, sheets of colored paper—surely flammable—pinned over the light bulbs.

"What a darling you are to come," cried Charlotte. "We were afraid you would have tons more interesting things to do than visiting ancient old us. Where can you sit down? What about here?" She took a pile of magazines off a wicker chair. "Is that comfortable? It makes such interesting noises, wicker. Sometimes I'll be sitting here alone and that chair will start creaking and cracking exactly as if someone were shifting around in it. I could say it was a presence, but I'm no good at believing in that rubbish. I've tried."

Gjurdhi poured out a sweet yellow wine. For me a long-stemmed glass that had not been dusted, for Charlotte a glass tumbler, for himself a plastic cup. It seemed impossible that any dinner could come out of the little kitchen alcove, where foodstuffs and pots and dishes were piled helter-skelter, but there was a good smell of roasting chicken, and in a little while Gjurdhi brought out the first course—platters of sliced cucumber, dishes of yogurt. I sat in the wicker chair and Charlotte in the single armchair. Gjurdhi sat on the floor. Charlotte was wearing her slacks, and a rose-colored T-shirt which clung to her unsupported breast. She had painted her toenails to match the T-shirt. Her bracelets clanked against the plate as she picked up the slices of cucumber. (We were eating with our fingers.) Gjurdhi wore his cap and a dark-red silky dressing gown over his trousers. Stains had mingled with its pattern.

After the cucumber, we ate chicken cooked with raisins in golden spices, and sour bread, and rice. Charlotte and I were provided with forks, but Gjurdhi scooped the rice up with the bread. I would often think of this meal in the years that followed, when this kind of food, this informal way of sitting and eating, and even some version of the style and the untidiness of the room, would become familiar and fashionable. The people I knew, and I myself, would give up—for a while—on dining-room tables, matching wineglasses, to some extent on cutlery or chairs. When I was being entertained, or making a stab at entertaining people, in this way, I would think of Charlotte and Gjurdhi and the edge of true privation, the risky authenticity that marked them off from all these later imitations. At the time, it was all new to me, and I was both uneasy and delighted. I hoped to be worthy of such exoticism but not to be tried too far.

Mary Shelley came to light shortly. I recited the titles of the later novels, and Charlotte said dreamily, "Per-kin War-beck. Wasn't he the one—wasn't he the one who pretended to be a little Prince who was murdered in the Tower?"

She was the only person I had ever met—not a historian, not a *Tudor* historian—who had known this.

"That would make a movie," she said. "Don't you think? The question I always think about Pretenders like that is who do *they* think they are? Do they believe it's true, or what? But Mary Shelley's own life is the movie, isn't it? I wonder there hasn't been one made. Who would play Mary, do you think? No. No, first of all, start with Harriet. Who would play Harriet?

"Someone who would look well drowned," she said, ripping off a golden chunk of chicken. "Elizabeth Taylor? Not a big enough part. Susannah York?

"Who was the father?" she wondered, referring to Harriet's unborn baby. "I don't think it was Shelley. I've never thought so. Do you?"

This was all very well, very enjoyable, but I had hoped we would get to explanations—personal revelations, if not exactly confidences. You did expect some of that, on occasions like this. Hadn't Sylvia, at my own table, told about the town in Northern Ontario and about Nelson's being the smartest person in the school? I was surprised at how eager I found myself, at last, to tell my story. Donald and Nelson—I was looking forward to telling the truth, or some of it, in all its wounding complexity, to a person who would not be surprised or outraged by it. I would have liked to puzzle over my behavior, in good company. Had I taken on Donald as a father figure—or as a parent figure, since both my parents were dead? Had I deserted him because I was angry at *them* for deserting *me*? What did Nelson's silence mean, and was it now permanent? (But I did not think, after all, that I would tell anybody about the letter that had been returned to me last week, marked "Not Known at This Address.")

This was not what Charlotte had in mind. There was no opportunity, no exchange. After the chicken, the wineglass and the tumbler and cup were taken away and filled with an extremely sweet pink sherbet that was easier to drink than to eat with a spoon. Then came small cups of desperately strong coffee. Gjurdhi lit two candles as the room grew darker, and I was given one of these to carry to the bathroom, which turned out to be a toilet with a shower. Charlotte said the lights were not working.

"Some repairs going on," she said. "Or else they have taken a whim. I really think they take whims. But fortunately we have our gas stove. As long as we have a gas stove we can laugh at their whims. My only regret is that we cannot play any music. I was going to play some old political songs—'I dreamed I saw Joe Hill last night,'" she sang in a mocking baritone. "Do you know that one?"

I did know it. Donald used to sing it when he was a little drunk. Usually the people who sang "Joe Hill" had certain vague but discernible political sympathies, but with Charlotte I did not think this would be so. She would not operate from sympathies, from principles. She would be playful about what other people took seriously. I was not certain what I felt about her. It was not simple liking or respect. It was more like a wish to move in her element, unsurprised. To be buoyant, self-mocking, gently malicious, unquenchable.

Gjurdhi, meanwhile, was showing me some of the books. How had this started? Probably from a comment I made—how many of them there were, something of that sort—when I stumbled over some on my way back from the toilet. He was bringing forward books with bindings of leather or imitation leather—how could I know the difference?—with marbled endpapers, watercolor frontispieces, steel engravings. At first, I believed admiration might be all that was required, and I admired everything. But close to my ear I heard the mention of money—was that the first distinct thing I had ever heard Gjurdhi say?

"I only handle new books," I said. "These are marvellous, but I don't really know anything about them. It's a completely different business, books like these."

Gjurdhi shook his head as if I had not understood and he would now try, firmly, to explain again. He repeated the price in a more insistent voice. Did he think I was trying to haggle with him? Or perhaps he was telling me what he had paid for the book? We might be having a speculative conversation about the price it might be sold for—not about whether I should buy it.

I kept saying no, and yes, trying to juggle these responses appropriately. *No*, I cannot take them for my store. *Yes*, they are very fine. *No*, truly, I'm sorry, I am not the one to judge.

"If we had been living in another country, Gjurdhi and I might have done something," Charlotte was saying. "Or even if the movies in this country had ever got off the ground. That's what I would love to have done. Got work in the movies. As extras. Or maybe we are not bland enough types to be extras, maybe they would have found bit parts for us. I believe extras have to be the sort that don't stand out in a crowd, so you can use them over and over again. Gjurdhi and I are more memorable than that. Gjurdhi in particular—you could *use* that face."

She paid no attention to the second conversation that had developed, but continued talking to me, shaking her head indulgently at Gjurdhi now and then, to suggest that he was behaving in a way she found engaging, though perhaps importunate. I had to talk to him softly, sideways, nodding all the while in response to her.

"Really you should take them to the Antiquarian Bookstore," I said. "Yes, they are quite beautiful. Books like these are out of my range."

Gjurdhi did not whine, his manner was not ingratiating. Peremptory, rather. It seemed as if he would give me orders, and would be most disgusted if I did not capitulate. In my confusion I helped myself to more of the yellow wine, pouring it into my unwashed sherbet glass. This was probably a dire offense. Gjurdhi looked horridly displeased.

"Can you imagine illustrations in modern novels?" said Charlotte, finally consenting to tie the two conversations together. "For instance, in Norman Mailer? They would have to be abstracts. Don't you think? Sort of barbed wire and blotches?"

I went home with a headache and a feeling of jangled inadequacy. I was a prude, that was all, when it came to mixing up buying and selling with hospitality. I had perhaps behaved clumsily, I had disappointed them. And they had disappointed me. Making me wonder why I had been asked.

I was homesick for Donald, because of "Joe Hill."

I also had a longing for Nelson, because of an expression on Charlotte's face as I was leaving. A savoring and contended look that I knew had to do with Gjurdhi, though I hardly wanted to believe that. It made me think that after I walked downstairs and left the building and went into the street, some hot and skinny, slithery, yellowish, indecent old beast, some mangy but urgent old tiger, was going to pounce among the books and the dirty dishes and conduct a familiar rampage.

A day or so later I got a letter from Donald. He wanted a divorce, so that he could marry Helen.

I hired a clerk, a college girl, to come in for a couple of hours in the afternoon, so I could get to the bank, and do some office work. The first time Charlotte saw her she went up to the desk and patted a stack of books sitting there, ready for quick sale.

"Is this what the office managers are telling their minions to buy?" she said. The girl smiled cautiously and didn't answer.

Charlotte was right. It was a book called *Psycho-Cybernetics,* about having a positive self-image.

"You were smart to hire her instead of me," Charlotte said. "She is much niftier-looking, and she won't shoot her mouth off and scare the customers away. She won't have *opinions.*"

"There's something I ought to tell you about that woman," the clerk said, after Charlotte left.

That part is not of interest.

"What do you mean?" I said. But my mind had been wandering, that third afternoon in the hospital. Just at the last part of Charlotte's story I had thought of a special-order book that hadn't come in, on Mediterranean cruises. Also I had been thinking about the Notary Public, who had been beaten about the head the night before, in his office on Johnson Street. He was not dead but he might be blinded. Robbery? Or an act of revenge, outrage, connected with a layer of his life that I hadn't guessed at?

Melodrama and confusion made this place seem more ordinary to me, but less within my grasp.

"Of course it is of interest," I said. "All of it. It's a fascinating story."

"Fascinating," repeated Charlotte in a mincing way. She made a face, so she looked like a baby vomiting out a spoonful of pap. Her eyes, still fixed on me, seemed to be losing color, losing their childish, bright, and self-important blue. Fretfulness was changing into disgust. An expression of vicious disgust, she showed, of unspeakable weariness—such as people might show to the mirror but hardly ever to one another. Perhaps because of the thoughts that were already in my head, it occurred to me that Charlotte might die. She might die at any moment. At this moment. Now.

She motioned at the water glass, with its crooked plastic straw. I held the glass so that she could drink, and supported her head. I could feel the heat of her scalp, a throbbing at the base of her skull. She drank thirstily, and the terrible look left her face.

She said, "Stale."

"I think it would make an excellent movie," I said, easing her back onto the pillows. She grabbed my wrist, then let it go.

"Where did you get the idea?" I said.

"From life," said Charlotte indistinctly. "Wait a moment." She turned her head away, on the pillow, as if she had to arrange something in private. Then she recovered, and she told a little more.

Charlotte did not die. At least she did not die in the hospital. When I came in rather late, the next afternoon, her bed was empty and freshly made up. The nurse who had talked to me before was trying to take the temperature of the woman tied in the chair. She laughed at the look on my face.

"Oh, no!" she said. "Not that. She checked out of here this morning. Her husband came and got her. We were transferring her to a long-term place out in Saanich, and he was supposed to be taking her there. He said he had the taxi outside. Then we get this phone call that they never showed up! They were in great spirits when they left. He brought her a pile of money, and she was throwing it up in the air. I don't know—maybe it was only dollar bills. But we haven't a clue where they've got to."

I walked around to the apartment building on Pandora Street. I thought they might simply have gone home. They might have lost the instructions about how to get to the nursing home and not wanted to ask. They might have decided to stay together in their apartment no matter what. They might have turned on the gas.

At first I could not find the building and thought that I must be in the wrong block. But I remembered the corner store and some of the houses.

The building had been changed—that was what had happened. The stucco had been painted pink; large, new windows and French doors had been put in; little balconies with wrought-iron railings had been attached. The fancy balconies had been painted white, the whole place had the air of an ice-cream parlor. No doubt it had been renovated inside as well, and the rents increased, so that people like Charlotte and Gjurdhi could have no hope of living there. I checked the names by the door, and of course theirs were gone. They must have moved out some time ago.

The change in the apartment building seemed to have some message for me. It was about vanishing. I knew that Charlotte and Gjurdhi had not actually vanished—they were somewhere, living or dead. But for me they had vanished. And because of this fact—not really because of any loss of them— I was tipped into dismay more menacing than any of the little eddies of regret that had caught me in the past year. I had lost my bearings. I had to get back to the store so my clerk could go home, but I felt as if I could as easily walk another way, just any way at all. My connection was in danger—that was all. Sometimes our connection is frayed, it is in danger, it seems almost lost. Views and streets deny knowledge of us, the air grows thin. Wouldn't we rather have a destiny to submit to, then, something that claims us, anything instead of such flimsy choices, arbitrary days?

I let myself slip, then, into imagining a life with Nelson. If I had done so accurately, this is how it would have gone.

He comes to Victoria. But he does not like the idea of working in the store, serving the public. He gets a job teaching at a boys' school, a posh place where his look of lower-class toughness, his bruising manners, soon make him a favorite.

We move from the apartment at the Dardanelles to a roomy bungalow a few blocks from the sea. We marry.

But this is the beginning of a period of estrangement. I become pregnant. Nelson falls in love with the mother of a student. I fall in love with an intern I meet in the hospital during labor.

We get over all this—Nelson and I do. We have another child. We acquire friends, furniture, rituals. We go to too many parties at certain seasons of the year, and talk regularly about starting a new life, somewhere far away, where we don't know anybody.

We become distant, close—distant, close—over and over again.

As I entered the store, I was aware of a man standing near the door, half looking in the window, half looking up the street, then looking at me. He was a short man dressed in a trenchcoat and a fedora. I had the impression of someone disguised. Jokingly disguised. He moved toward me and bumped my shoulder, and I cried out as if I had received the shock of my life, and indeed it was true that I had. For this really was Nelson, come to claim me. Or at least to accost me, and see what would happen.

We have been very happy.

I have often felt completely alone.

There is always in this life something to discover.

The days and the years have gone by in some sort of blur.
On the whole, I am satisfied.

When Lottar was leaving the Bishop's courtyard, she was wrapped in
a long cloak they had given her, perhaps to conceal her ragged clothing, or
to contain her smell. The Consul's servant spoke to her in English, telling
her where they were going. She could understand him but could not reply.
It was not quite dark. She could still see the pale shapes of roses and oranges in the Bishop's garden.

The Bishop's man was holding the gate open.

She had never seen the Bishop at all. And she had not seen the Franciscan since he had followed the Bishop's man into the house. She called out
for him now, as she was leaving. She had no name to call, so she called,
"Xoti! Xoti! Xoti," which means "leader" or "master" in the language of
the Ghegs. But no answer came, and the Consul's servant swung his
lantern impatiently, showing her the way to go. Its light fell by accident on
the Franciscan standing half concealed by a tree. It was a little orange tree
he stood behind. His face, pale as the oranges were in that light, looked
out of the branches, all its swarthiness drained away. It was a wan face
hanging in the tree, its melancholy expression quite impersonal and unde-
manding, like the expression you might see on the face of a devout but
proud apostle in a church window. Then it was gone, taking the breath out
of her body, as she knew too late.

She called him and called him, and when the boat came into the harbor
at Trieste he was waiting on the dock.

• • • • • • • • • • • •

QUESTIONS FOR A SECOND READING

1. The story is arranged in pieces, or fragments. As a reader works through
   them, they become two story lines: one set in the 1920s in Albania, on the
   Dalmatian coast; the other is set in the 1960s in Canada, on the Pacific
   coast. The first story, about a woman called Lottar, is told by Charlotte to
   Claire; the second is told by Claire to us (and, we learn, includes all these
   stories). But it takes some time for the pattern to establish itself and we
   might be lost at first, or confused.

   As you reread, pay attention to how Munro handles—orchestrates—
   the unfolding. How does she position the reader? How does she organize
   our attention and allow us access to the two story lines? What are the effects? How would you explain or define her strategy?

2. This is a different question from the first, but it begins the same way. The
   story is arranged in pieces, or fragments. As a reader works through

them, they become two story lines: one set in the 1920s in Albania, on the Dalmatian coast; the other is set in the 1960s in Canada, on the Pacific coast. The first story, about a woman called Lottar, is told by Charlotte to Claire; the second is told by Claire to us (and, we learn, includes all these stories). But it takes some time for the pattern to establish itself and we might be lost at first, or confused.

As you reread, pay attention to the connections between the parallel stories—similarities and differences. It is safe to assume that in asking us to think of them together, the story asks us to use them in tandem, one commenting on or highlighting or providing a counterpoint to the other. What are the connections? If you think through them, where are you led or what kinds of conclusions are you invited to draw?

3. The story positions us to ask this question: Is Charlotte telling the story of her own life? Is she Lottar? Or is the story an invention, something made up? And if it is an invention, to what end? Early on Charlotte says that she is making up a story for a movie, but this does not seem convincing or adequate.

   As you reread, look to see how the story, "The Albanian Virgin," positions you in relation to Charlotte and her story. How does the story want us to think this question through?

4. Mary Shelley, Harriet Shelley, Fanny Imlay, Mary Jane Clairmont, Shelley, and Bryon: these are the authors and figures that have captured Claire's imagination. They are offered to us as a sign of her intellectual and literary character. Mary Wollstonecraft Shelley, Percy Bysshe Shelley, Lord Byron (George Gordon)—these figures can be found in any British literature anthology. The others can be tracked down with a little more legwork in the library (and perhaps on the Internet). Choose one and prepare a report for your class. Then, as you reread, think about the information Munro is providing at this point in the narrative.

ASSIGNMENTS FOR WRITING

1. At one point in the story Claire, commenting on her attempt to bring together two of her customers in the bookstore, writes in a letter to Donald, *"So much for trying to corral people into couples . . . And who am I to try?"* Coupling is clearly a concern of this story, a story that is filled with couples and with storytellers who are trying to bring them together. There are the two storytellers *in* the story, Charlotte and Claire. Munro, the storyteller, stands behind it all, not identifying herself with any of the characters or as a presence in the narrative, although she too is busy corralling people into couples.

   Write an essay on "The Albanian Virgin" as a story about storytelling, as the occasion for an established writer to think about stories—where they come from, what they do, and what they are good for. As a reader, you should find space in your essay to speak on your own behalf, or on behalf of your generation, readers of your age, positioned as you are. Speak about your sense of *this* story, where it comes from, what it does and what it is good for, and about stories more generally.

2. "The Albanian Virgin" is arranged in pieces, or fragments. As a reader works through them, they become two story lines: one set in the 1920s in Albania, on the Dalmatian coast; the other is set in the 1960s in Canada, on the Pacific coast. The first story, about a woman called Lottar, is told by Charlotte to Claire; the second is told by Claire to us (and, we learn, includes all these stories). But it takes some time for the pattern to establish itself and we might be lost at first, or confused.

Try your hand at writing a story like this one. You can imagine that you are writing fiction, or you can imagine that you are writing a memoir, or any story drawn from life that has (or could have) two story lines. You should begin by rereading "The Albanian Virgin" and thinking about how Munro does what she does. (The first two "Questions for a Second Reading" provide a way of rereading with this thought in mind.) You should try to catch the rhythm and swing of the arrangement in her story, to control your readers' attention in a similar way and to put the two story lines to work in a similar fashion.

3. The central characters in this story are women: Claire, Charlotte, and, in Charlotte's story, Lottar. In the story of Lottar, the men are represented schematically—they drink, they shoot their guns, they kill each other, they don't work very hard. Lottar is concerned with escape, freedom. There is an invitation to read the story through its representation of women and men and you are asked to think through the point of view of women.

Write an essay on "The Albanian Virgin" as a story about women. If there is an argument here, what is it? And where is it? How is it arranged through the various characters and story lines? And if there is an argument, how does the story (or its author, Alice Munro) position you as a reader in relation to that argument? How are we to read it? What are we supposed to do with it?

MAKING CONNECTIONS

1. "The Albanian Virgin" is arranged in pieces, or fragments. As a reader works through them, they become two story lines: one set in the 1920s in Albania, on the Dalmatian coast; the other is set in the 1960s in Canada, on the Pacific coast. The first story, about a woman called Lottar, is told by Charlotte to Claire; the second is told by Claire to us (and, we learn, includes all these stories). But it takes some time for the pattern to establish itself and we might be lost at first, or confused. (The first two "Questions for a Second Reading" provide a way of rereading with this thought in mind.)

The formal experimentation here is part of the story's work or project. Other selections in *Ways of Reading* experiment with form: Susan Griffin's "Our Secret" (p. 345), John Edgar Wideman's "Our Time" (p. 752), Gloria Anzaldúa's "Entering into the Serpent" (p. 23) and "How to Tame a Wild Tongue" (p. 36). If we put aside the distinctions made between fiction and nonfiction, it is interesting to think about these as similar projects, similarly motivated.

Choose one of the other selections and read it next to "The Albanian Virgin." Write an essay in which you think about writing in relation to formal conventions and formal expectations. What are the "standard" forms against which these two texts can be read? What do they do that the standard forms can't do? How do you understand the work of these writers? What lessons in their work might there be for you as a writer?

2. The central characters in this story are women: Claire, Charlotte, and, in Charlotte's story, Lottar. In the story of Lottar, the men are represented schematically—they drink, they shoot their guns, they kill each other, they don't work very hard. Lottar is concerned with escape, freedom. There is an invitation to read the story through its representation of women and men and to think from the point of view of the women. (If there is an argument here, what is it? And where is it? How is it arranged through the various characters and story lines? And if there is an argument, how does the story—or its author, Alice Munro—position you as a reader in relation to that argument?)

Susan Bordo, in "Hunger as Ideology" (p. 139), writes about women and the representation of women in advertising. This, too, considers the ways in which women are positioned inside a patriarchal culture. The argument here is up front; it is foregrounded in the text. (You might, however, use the "Questions for a Second Reading" to help focus your attention on this.)

Write an essay in which you consider these two texts and these two arguments. You should assume that your readers are not familiar with either the story or the essay. You will, then, need to take care to introduce them, to summarize and paraphrase the arguments, to provide a sense of what it is like to read these texts, to think about how a reader is positioned. As you work this out, use the occasion to think about the difference between story and essay. (It is really not enough, perhaps not even accurate, to say that one is true and the other is an invention.) Think about the different ways they address their audiences, the different ways they work on subject and form and argument, the different commitments they have to persuasion.

WALKER
PERCY

W *ALKER PERCY, in his midforties, after a life of relative obscurity and after a career as, he said, a "failed physician," wrote his first novel,* The Movie-goer. *It won the National Book Award for fiction in 1962, and Percy emerged as one of this country's leading novelists. Little in his background would have predicted such a career*

After graduating from Columbia University's medical school in 1941, Percy (b. 1916) went to work at Bellevue Hospital in New York City. He soon contracted tuberculosis from performing autopsies on derelicts and was sent to a sanitorium to recover, where, as he said, "I was in bed so much, alone so much, that I had nothing to do but read and think. I began to question everything I had once believed." He returned to medicine briefly but suffered a relapse and during his long recovery began "to make reading a full-time occupation." He left medicine, but not until 1954, almost a decade later, did he publish his first essay, "Symbol as Need."

The essays that followed, including "The Loss of the Creature," all dealt with the relationships between language and understanding or belief, and they were all published in obscure academic journals. In the later essays, Percy seemed to turn away from academic forms of argument and to depend more and more on stories or anecdotes from daily life—to write, in fact, as a storyteller and to be wary of abstraction or explanation. Robert Coles has said that it was Percy's failure to find a form that would reach a larger audience that led him to try his hand at a novel. You will notice in the essay that follows that Percy delights in piling example upon example; he never seems to settle down to a topic sentence, or any sentence for that matter that sums everything up and makes the examples superfluous.

In addition to The Moviegoer, *Percy has written five other novels, including* Lancelot *(1977),* Love in the Ruins *(1971), and* The Thanatos Syndrome *(1987). He has published two books of essays,* The Message in the Bottle: How Queer Man Is, How Queer Language Is, and What One Has to Do with the Other *(1975, from which "The Loss of the Creature" is taken), and* Lost in the Cosmos: The Last Self-help Book *(1983). Walker Percy died at his home in Covington, Louisiana, on May 10, 1990, leaving a considerable amount of unpublished work, some of which has been gathered into a posthumous collection,* Signposts in a Strange Land *(1991). The* Correspondence of Shelby Foote and Walker Percy *was published in 1996.*

The Loss of the Creature

I

Every explorer names his island Formosa, beautiful. To him it is beautiful because, being first, he has access to it and can see it for what it is. But to no one else is it ever as beautiful—except the rare man who manages to recover it, who knows that it has to be recovered.

Garcia López de Cárdenas discovered the Grand Canyon and was amazed at the sight. It can be imagined: One crosses miles of desert, breaks through the mesquite, and there it is at one's feet. Later the government set the place aside as a national park, hoping to pass along to millions the experience of Cárdenas. Does not one see the same sight from the Bright Angel Lodge that Cárdenas saw?

The assumption is that the Grand Canyon is a remarkably interesting and beautiful place and that if it had a certain value P for Cárdenas, the same value P may be transmitted to any number of sightseers—just as Banting's discovery of insulin can be transmitted to any number of diabetics. A counterinfluence is at work, however, and it would be nearer the truth to say that if the place is seen by a million sightseers, a single sightseer does not receive value P but a millionth part of value P.

It is assumed that since the Grand Canyon has the fixed interest value P, tours can be organized for any number of people. A man in Boston decides to spend his vacation at the Grand Canyon. He visits his travel bureau, looks at the folder, signs up for a two-week tour. He and his family take the tour, see the Grand Canyon, and return to Boston. May we say that this man has seen the Grand Canyon? Possibly he has. But it is more likely that what he has done is the one sure way not to see the canyon.

Why is it almost impossible to gaze directly at the Grand Canyon under these circumstances and see it for what it is—as one picks up a strange object from one's back yard and gazes directly at it? It is almost impossible because the Grand Canyon, the thing as it is, has been appropriated by the symbolic complex which has already been formed in the sightseer's mind. Seeing the canyon under approved circumstances is seeing the symbolic complex head on. The thing is no longer the thing as it confronted the Spaniard; it is rather that which has already been formulated—by picture postcard, geography book, tourist folders, and the words *Grand Canyon*. As a result of this preformulation, the source of the sightseer's pleasure undergoes a shift. Where the wonder and delight of the Spaniard arose from his penetration of the thing itself, from a progressive discovery of depths, patterns, colors, shadows, etc., now the sightseer measures his satisfaction *by the degree to which the canyon conforms to the preformed complex.* If it does so, if it looks just like the postcard, he is pleased; he might even say, "Why it is every bit as beautiful as a picture postcard!" He feels he has not been cheated. But if it does not conform, if the colors are somber, he will not be able to see it directly; he will only be conscious of the disparity between what it is and what it is supposed to be. He will say later that he was unlucky in not being there at the right time. The highest point, the term of the sightseer's satisfaction, is not the sovereign discovery of the thing before him; it is rather the measuring up of the thing to the criterion of the preformed symbolic complex.

Seeing the canyon is made even more difficult by what the sightseer does when the moment arrives, when sovereign knower confronts the thing to be known. Instead of looking at it, he photographs it. There is no confrontation at all. At the end of forty years of preformulation and with the Grand Canyon yawning at his feet, what does he do? He waives his right of seeing and knowing and records symbols for the next forty years. For him there is no present; there is only the past of what has been formulated and seen and the future of what has been formulated and not seen. The present is surrendered to the past and the future.

The sightseer may be aware that something is wrong. He may simply be bored; or he may be conscious of the difficulty: that the great thing yawning at his feet somehow eludes him. The harder he looks at it, the less he can see. It eludes everybody. The tourist cannot see it; the bellboy at the Bright Angel Lodge cannot see it: for him it is only one side of the space he lives in, like one wall of a room; to the ranger it is a tissue of everyday signs relevant to his own prospects—the blue haze down there means that he will probably get rained on during the donkey ride.

How can the sightseer recover the Grand Canyon? He can recover it in any number of ways, all sharing in common the stratagem of avoiding the approved confrontation of the tour and the Park Service.

It may be recovered by leaving the beaten track. The tourist leaves the tour, camps in the back country. He arises before dawn and approaches the South Rim through a wild terrain where there are no trails and no railed-in lookout points. In other words, he sees the canyon by avoiding all the facilities for seeing the canyon. If the benevolent Park Service hears about this fellow and thinks he has a good idea and places the following notice in the Bright Angel Lodge: *Consult ranger for information on getting off the beaten track*—the end result will only be the closing of another access to the canyon.

It may be recovered by a dialectical movement which brings one back to the beaten track but at a level above it. For example, after a lifetime of avoiding the beaten track and guided tours, a man may deliberately seek out the most beaten track of all, the most commonplace tour imaginable: he may visit the canyon by a Greyhound tour in the company of a party from Terre Haute—just as a man who has lived in New York all his life may visit the Statue of Liberty. (Such dialectical savorings of the familiar as the familiar are, of course, a favorite stratagem of *The New Yorker* magazine.) The thing is recovered from familiarity by means of an exercise in familiarity. Our complex friend stands behind his fellow tourists at the Bright Angel Lodge and sees the canyon through them and their predicament, their picture taking and busy disregard. In a sense, he exploits his fellow tourists; he stands on their shoulders to see the canyon.

Such a man is far more advanced in the dialectic than the sightseer who is trying to get off the beaten track—getting up at dawn and approaching the canyon through the mesquite. This stratagem is, in fact, for our complex man the weariest, most beaten track of all.

It may be recovered as a consequence of a breakdown of the symbolic machinery by which the experts present the experience to the consumer. A family visits the canyon in the usual way. But shortly after their arrival, the park is closed by an outbreak of typhus in the south. They have the canyon to themselves. What do they mean when they tell the home folks of their good luck: "We had the whole place to ourselves"? How does one see the thing better when the others are absent? Is looking like sucking: the more lookers, the less there is to see? They could hardly answer, but by saying this they testify to a state of affairs which is considerably more complex than the simple statement of the schoolbook about the Spaniard and the millions who followed him. It is a state in which there is a complex distribution of sovereignty, of zoning.

It may be recovered in a time of national disaster. The Bright Angel Lodge is converted into a rest home, a function that has nothing to do with the canyon a few yards away. A wounded man is brought in. He regains consciousness; there outside his window is the canyon.

The most extreme case of access by privilege conferred by disaster is the Huxleyan novel of the adventures of the surviving remnant after the great wars of the twentieth century. An expedition from Australia lands in Southern California and heads east. They stumble across the Bright Angel Lodge, now fallen into ruins. The trails are grown over, the guard rails fallen away, the dime telescope at Battleship Point rusted. But there is the canyon, exposed at last. Exposed by what? By the decay of those facilities which were designed to help the sightseer.

This dialectic of sightseeing cannot be taken into account by planners, for the object of the dialectic is nothing other than the subversion of the efforts of the planners.

The dialectic is not known to objective theorists, psychologists, and the like. Yet it is quite well known in the fantasy-consciousness of the popular arts. The devices by which the museum exhibit, the Grand Canyon, the ordinary thing, is recovered have long since been stumbled upon. A movie shows a man visiting the Grand Canyon. But the movie maker knows something the planner does not know. He knows that one cannot take the sight frontally. The canyon must be approached by the stratagems we have mentioned: the Inside Track, the Familiar Revisited, the Accidental Encounter. Who is the stranger at the Bright Angel Lodge? Is he the ordinary tourist from Terre Haute that he makes himself out to be? He is not. He has another objective in mind, to revenge his wronged brother, counterespionage, etc. By virtue of the fact that he has other fish to fry, he may take a stroll along the rim after supper and then we can see the canyon through him. The movie accomplishes its purpose by concealing it. Overtly the characters (the American family marooned by typhus) and we the onlookers experience pity for the sufferers, and the family experience anxiety for themselves; covertly and in truth they are the happiest of people and we are happy through them, for we have the canyon to ourselves. The movie cashes in on the recovery of sovereignty through disaster. Not only is the canyon now accessible to the remnant: the members of the remnant are now accessible to each other, a whole new ensemble of relations becomes possible—friendship, love, hatred, clandestine sexual adventures. In a movie when a man sits next to a woman on a bus, it is necessary either that the bus break down or that the woman lose her memory. (The question occurs to one: Do you imagine there are sightseers who see sights just as they are supposed to? a family who live in Terre Haute, who decide to take the canyon tour, who go there, see it, enjoy it immensely, and go home content? a family who are entirely innocent of all the barriers, zones, losses of sovereignty I have been talking about? Wouldn't most people be sorry if Battleship Point fell into the canyon, carrying all one's fellow passengers to their death, leaving one alone on the South Rim? I cannot answer this. Perhaps there are such people. Certainly a great many American families would swear they had no such problems, that they came, saw, and went away happy. Yet it is just these families who would be happiest if they had gotten the Inside Track and been among the surviving remnant.)

It is now apparent that as between the many measures which may be taken to overcome the opacity, the boredom, of the direct confrontation of the thing or creature in its citadel of symbolic investiture, some are less authentic than others. That is to say, some stratagems obviously serve other purposes than that of providing access to being—for example, various unconscious motivations which it is not necessary to go into here.

Let us take an example in which the recovery of being is ambiguous, where it may under the same circumstances contain both authentic and unauthentic components. An American couple, we will say, drives down into Mexico. They see the usual sights and have a fair time of it. Yet they are never without the sense of missing something. Although Taxco and Cuernavaca are interesting and picturesque as advertised, they fall short of "it." What do the couple have in mind by "it"? What do they really hope for? What sort of experience could they have in Mexico so that upon their return, they would feel that "it" had happened? We have a clue: Their hope has something to do with their own role as tourists in a foreign country and the way in which they conceive this role. It has something to do with other American tourists. Certainly they feel that they are very far from "it" when, after traveling five thousand miles, they arrive at the plaza in Guanajuato only to find themselves surrounded by a dozen other couples from the Midwest.

Already we may distinguish authentic and unauthentic elements. First, we see the problem the couple faces and we understand their efforts to surmount it. The problem is to find an "unspoiled" place. "Unspoiled" does not mean only that a place is left physically intact; it means also that it is not encrusted by renown and by the familiar (as in Taxco), that it has not been discovered by others. We understand that the couple really want to get at the place and enjoy it. Yet at the same time we wonder if there is not something wrong in their dislike of their compatriots. Does access to the place require the exclusion of others?

Let us see what happens.

The couple decide to drive from Guanajuato to Mexico City. On the way they get lost. After hours on a rocky mountain road, they find themselves in a tiny valley not even marked on the map. There they discover an Indian village. Some sort of religious festival is going on. It is apparently a corn dance in supplication of the rain god.

The couple know at once that this is "it." They are entranced. They spend several days in the village, observing the Indians and being themselves observed with friendly curiosity.

Now may we not say that the sightseers have at last come face to face with an authentic sight, a sight which is charming, quaint, picturesque, unspoiled, and that they see the sight and come away rewarded? Possibly this may occur. Yet it is more likely that what happens is a far cry indeed from an immediate encounter with being, that the experience, while masquerading as such, is in truth a rather desperate impersonation. I use the word *desperate* advisedly to signify an actual loss of hope.

The clue to the spuriousness of their enjoyment of the village and the festival is a certain restiveness in the sightseers themselves. It is given expression by their repeated exclamations that "this is too good to be true," and by their anxiety that it may not prove to be so perfect, and finally by their downright relief at leaving the valley and having the experience in the bag, so to speak—that is, safely embalmed in memory and movie film.

What is the source of their anxiety during the visit? Does it not mean that the couple are looking at the place with a certain standard of performance in mind? Are they like Fabre, who gazed at the world about him with wonder, letting it be what it is; or are they not like the overanxious mother who sees her child as one performing, now doing badly, now doing well? The village is their child and their love for it is an anxious love because they are afraid that at any moment it might fail them.

We have another clue in their subsequent remark to an ethnologist friend. "How we wished you had been there with us! What a perfect goldmine of folkways! Every minute we would say to each other, if only you were here! You must return with us." This surely testifies to a generosity of spirit, a willingness to share their experience with others, not at all like their feelings toward their fellow Iowans on the plaza at Guanajuato!

I am afraid this is not the case at all. It is true that they longed for their ethnologist friend, but it was for an entirely different reason. They wanted him, not to share their experience, but to certify their experience as genuine.

"This is it" and "Now we are really living" do not necessarily refer to the sovereign encounter of the person with the sight that enlivens the mind and gladdens the heart. It means that now at last we are having the acceptable experience. The present experience is always measured by a prototype, the "it" of their dreams. "Now I am really living" means that now I am filling the role of sightseer and the sight is living up to the prototype of sights. This quaint and picturesque village is measured by a Platonic ideal of the Quaint and the Picturesque.

Hence their anxiety during the encounter. For at any minute something could go wrong. A fellow Iowan might emerge from a 'dobe hut; the chief might show them his Sears catalog. (If the failures are "wrong" enough, as these are, they might still be turned to account as rueful conversation pieces. "There we were expecting the chief to bring us a churinga and he shows up with a Sears catalog!") They have snatched victory from disaster, but their experience always runs the danger of failure.

They need the ethnologist to certify their experience as genuine. This is borne out by their behavior when the three of them return for the next corn dance. During the dance, the couple do not watch the goings-on; instead they watch the ethnologist! Their highest hope is that their friend should find the dance interesting. And if he should show signs of true absorption, an interest in the goings-on so powerful that he becomes oblivious of his friends—then their cup is full. "Didn't we tell you?" they say at last. What they want from him is not ethnological explanations; all they want is his approval.

What has taken place is a radical loss of sovereignty over that which is as much theirs as it is the ethnologist's. The fault does not lie with the ethnologist. He has no wish to stake a claim to the village; in fact, he desires the opposite: he will bore his friends to death by telling them about the village and the meaning of the folkways. A degree of sovereignty has been surrendered by the couple. It is the nature of the loss, moreover, that they are not aware of the loss, beyond a certain uneasiness. (Even if they read this and admitted it, it would be very difficult for them to bridge the gap in their confrontation of the world. Their consciousness of the corn dance cannot escape their consciousness of their consciousness, so that with the onset of the first direct enjoyment, their higher consciousness pounces and certifies: "Now you are doing it! Now you are really living!" and, in certifying the experience, sets it at nought.)

Their basic placement in the world is such that they recognize a priority of title of the expert over his particular department of being. The whole horizon of being is staked out by "them," the experts. The highest satisfaction of the sightseer (not merely the tourist but any layman seer of sights) is that his sight should be certified as genuine. The worst of this impoverishment is that there is no sense of impoverishment. The surrender of title is so complete that it never even occurs to one to reassert title. A poor man may envy the rich man, but the sightseer does not envy the expert. When a caste system becomes absolute, envy disappears. Yet the caste of layman-expert is not the fault of the expert. It is due altogether to the eager surrender of sovereignty by the layman so that he may take up the role not of the person but of the consumer.

I do not refer only to the special relation of layman to theorist. I refer to the general situation in which sovereignty is surrendered to a class of privileged knowers, whether these be theorists or artists. A reader may surrender sovereignty over that which has been written about, just as a consumer may surrender sovereignty over a thing which has been theorized about. The consumer is content to receive an experience just as it has been presented to him by theorists and planners. The reader may also be content to judge life by whether it has or has not been formulated by those who know and write about life. A young man goes to France. He too has a fair time of it, sees the sights, enjoys the food. On his last day, in fact as he sits in a restaurant in Le Havre waiting for his boat, something happens. A group of French students in the restaurant get into an impassioned argument over a recent play. A riot takes place. Madame la concierge joins in, swinging her mop at the rioters. Our young American is transported. This is "it." And he had almost left France without seeing "it"!

But the young man's delight is ambiguous. On the one hand, it is a pleasure for him to encounter the same Gallic temperament he had heard about from Puccini and Rolland. But on the other hand, the source of his pleasure testifies to a certain alienation. For the young man is actually barred from a direct encounter with anything French excepting only that which has been set forth, authenticated by Puccini and Rolland—those who know. If he had encountered the restaurant scene without reading Hemingway, without knowing that the performance was so typically, charmingly French, he would not have been delighted. He would only have been anxious at seeing things get so out of hand. The source of his delight is the sanction of those who know.

This loss of sovereignty is not a marginal process, as might appear from my example of estranged sightseers. It is a generalized surrender of the horizon to those experts within whose competence a particular segment of the horizon is thought to lie. Kwakiutls are surrendered to Franz Boas; decaying Southern mansions are surrendered to Faulkner and Tennessee Williams. So that, although it is by no means the intention of the expert to expropriate sovereignty—in fact he would not even know what sovereignty meant in this context—the danger of theory and consumption is a seduction and deprivation of the consumer.

In the New Mexico desert, natives occasionally come across strange-looking artifacts which have fallen from the skies and which are stenciled: *Return to U.S. Experimental Project, Alamogordo. Reward.* The finder returns the object and is rewarded. He knows nothing of the nature of the object he has found and does not care to know. The sole role of the native, the highest role he can play, is that of finder and returner of the mysterious equipment.

The same is true of the laymen's relation to *natural* objects in a modern technical society. No matter what the object or event is, whether it is a star, a swallow, a Kwakiutl, a "psychological phenomenon," the layman who confronts it does not confront it as a sovereign person, as Crusoe confronts a seashell he finds on the beach. The highest role he can conceive himself as playing is to be able to recognize the title of the object, to return it to the appropriate expert and have it certified as a genuine find. He does not even permit himself to see the thing—as Gerard Hopkins could see a rock or a cloud or a field. If anyone asks him why he doesn't look, he may reply that he didn't take that subject in college (or he hasn't read Faulkner).

This loss of sovereignty extends even to oneself. There is the neurotic who asks nothing more of his doctor than that his symptoms should prove interesting. When all else fails, the poor fellow has nothing to offer but his own neurosis. But even this is sufficient if only the doctor will show interest when he says, "Last night I had a curious sort of dream; perhaps it will be significant to one who knows about such things. It seems I was standing in a sort of alley—" (I have nothing else to offer you but my own unhappiness. Please say that it, at least, measures up, that it is a *proper* sort of unhappiness.)

II

A young Falkland Islander walking along a beach and spying a dead dogfish and going to work on it with his jackknife has, in a fashion wholly unprovided in modern educational theory, a great advantage over the Scarsdale high-school pupil who finds the dogfish on his laboratory desk. Similarly the citizen of Huxley's *Brave New World* who stumbles across a volume of Shakespeare in some vine-grown ruins and squats on a potsherd to read it is in a fairer way of getting at a sonnet than the Harvard sophomore taking English Poetry II.

The educator whose business it is to teach students biology or poetry is unaware of a whole ensemble of relations which exist between the student and the dogfish and between the student and the Shakespeare sonnet. To put it bluntly: A student who has the desire to get at a dogfish or a Shakespeare sonnet may have the greatest difficulty in salvaging the creature itself from the educational package in which it is presented. The great difficulty is that he is not aware that there is a difficulty; surely, he thinks, in such a fine classroom, with such a fine textbook, the sonnet must come across! What's wrong with me?

The sonnet and the dogfish are obscured by two different processes. The sonnet is obscured by the symbolic package which is formulated not by the sonnet itself but by the *media* through which the sonnet is transmitted, the media which the educators believe for some reason to be transparent. The new textbook, the type, the smell of the page, the classroom, the aluminum windows and the winter sky, the personality of Miss Hawkins—these media which are supposed to transmit the sonnet may only succeed in transmitting themselves. It is only the hardiest and cleverest of students who can salvage the sonnet from this many-tissued package. It is only the rarest student who knows that the sonnet must be salvaged from the package. (The educator is well aware that something is wrong, that there is a fatal gap between the student's learning and the student's life: the student reads the poem, appears to understand it, and gives all the answers. But what does he recall if he should happen to read a Shakespeare sonnet twenty years later? Does he recall the poem or does he recall the smell of the page and the smell of Miss Hawkins?)

One might object, pointing out that Huxley's citizen reading his sonnet in the ruins and the Falkland Islander looking at his dogfish on the beach also receive them in a certain package. Yes, but the difference lies in the fundamental placement of the student in the world, a placement which makes it possible to extract the thing from the package. The pupil at Scarsdale High sees himself placed as a consumer receiving an experience-package; but the Falkland Islander exploring his dogfish is a person exercising the sovereign right of a person in his lordship and mastery of creation. He too could use an instructor and a book and a technique, but he would use them as his subordinates, just as he uses his jackknife. The biology student does not use his scalpel as an instrument, he uses it as a magic wand! Since it is a "scientific instrument," it should do "scientific things."

The dogfish is concealed in the same symbolic package as the sonnet. But the dogfish suffers an additional loss. As a consequence of this double deprivation, the Sarah Lawrence student who scores A in zoology is apt to know very little about a dogfish. She is twice removed from the dogfish, once by the symbolic complex by which the dogfish is concealed, once again by the spoliation of the dogfish by theory which renders it invisible. Through no fault of zoology instructors, it is nevertheless a fact that the zoology laboratory at Sarah Lawrence College is one of the few places in the world where it is all but impossible to see a dogfish.

The dogfish, the tree, the seashell, the American Negro, the dream, are rendered invisible by a shift of reality from concrete thing to theory which Whitehead has called the fallacy of misplaced concreteness. It is the mistaking of an idea, a principle, an abstraction, for the real. As a consequence of the shift, the "specimen" is seen as less real than the theory of the specimen. As Kierkegaard said, once a person is seen as a specimen of a race or a species, at that very moment he ceases to be an individual. Then there are no more individuals but only specimens.

To illustrate: A student enters a laboratory which, in the pragmatic view, offers the student the optimum conditions under which an educational experience may be had. In the existential view, however—that view of the student in which he is regarded not as a receptacle of experience but as a knowing being whose peculiar property it is to see himself as being in a certain situation—the modern laboratory could not have been more effectively designed to conceal the dogfish forever.

The student comes to his desk. On it, neatly arranged by his instructor, he finds his laboratory manual, a dissecting board, instruments, and a mimeographed list:

> *Exercise 22: Materials*
> 1 dissecting board
> 1 scalpel
> 1 forceps
> 1 probe
> 1 bottle india ink and syringe
> 1 specimen of *Squalus acanthias*

The clue of the situation in which the student finds himself is to be found in the last item: 1 specimen of *Squalus acanthias.*

The phrase *specimen of* expresses in the most succinct way imaginable the radical character of the loss of being which has occurred under his very nose. To refer to the dogfish, the unique concrete existent before him, as a "specimen of *Squalus acanthias*" reveals by its grammar the spoliation of the dogfish by the theoretical method. This phrase, *specimen of,* example of, instance of, indicates the ontological status of the individual creature in the eyes of the theorist. The dogfish itself is seen as a rather shabby expression of an ideal reality, the species *Squalus acanthias.* The result is the radical devaluation of the individual dogfish. (The *reductio ad absurdum* of Whitehead's shift is Toynbee's employment of it in his historical method. If a gram of NaCl is referred to by the chemist as a "sample of" NaCl, one may think of it as such and not much is missed by the oversight of the act of being of this particular pinch of salt, but when the Jews and the Jewish religion are understood as—in Toynbee's favorite phrase—a "classical example of" such and such a kind of *Voelkerwanderung,* we begin to suspect that something is being left out.)

If we look into the ways in which the student can recover the dogfish (or the sonnet), we will see that they have in common the stratagem of avoiding the educator's direct presentation of the object as a lesson to be learned and restoring access to sonnet and dogfish as beings to be known, reasserting the sovereignty of knower over known.

In truth, the biography of scientists and poets is usually the story of the discovery of the indirect approach, the circumvention of the educator's presentation—the young man who was sent to the *Technikum* and on his way fell into the habit of loitering in book stores and reading poetry; or the young man dutifully attending law school who on the way became curious about the comings and goings of ants. One remembers the scene in *The Heart Is a Lonely Hunter* where the girl hides in the bushes to hear the Capehart in the big house play Beethoven. Perhaps she was the lucky one after all. Think of the unhappy souls inside, who see the record, worry about scratches, and most of all worry about whether they are *getting it*, whether they are bona fide music lovers. What is the best way to hear Beethoven: sitting in a proper silence around the Capehart or eavesdropping from an azalea bush?

However it may come about, we notice two traits of the second situation: (1) an openness of the thing before one—instead of being an exercise to be learned according to an approved mode, it is a garden of delights which beckons to one; (2) a sovereignty of the knower—instead of being a consumer of a prepared experience, I am a sovereign wayfarer, a wanderer in the neighborhood of being who stumbles into the garden.

One can think of two sorts of circumstances through which the thing may be restored to the person. (There is always, of course, the direct recovery: A student may simply be strong enough, brave enough, clever enough to take the dogfish and the sonnet by storm, to wrest control of it from the educators and the educational package.) First by ordeal: The Bomb falls; when the young man recovers consciousness in the shambles of the biology laboratory, there not ten inches from his nose lies the dogfish. Now all at once he can see it directly and without let, just as the exile or the prisoner or the sick man sees the sparrow at his window in all its inexhaustibility; just as the commuter who has had a heart attack sees his own hand for the first time. In these cases, the simulacrum of everydayness and of consumption has been destroyed by disaster; in the case of the bomb, literally destroyed. Secondly, by apprenticeship to a great man: one day a great biologist walks into the laboratory; he stops in front of our student's desk; he leans over, picks up the dogfish, and, ignoring instruments and procedure, probes with a broken fingernail into the little carcass. "Now here is a curious business," he says, ignoring also the proper jargon of the speciality. "Look here how this little duct reverses its direction and drops into the pelvis. Now if you would look into a coelacanth, you would see that it—" And all at once the student can see. The technician and the sophomore who loves his textbooks are always offended by the genuine research man because the latter is usually a little vague and always humble before the thing; he doesn't have much use for the equipment or the jargon. Whereas the technician is never vague and never humble before the thing; he holds the thing disposed of by the principle, the formula, the textbook outline; and he thinks a great deal of equipment and jargon.

But since neither of these methods of recovering the dogfish is pedagogically feasible—perhaps the great man even less so than the Bomb—I wish to propose the following educational technique which should prove equally effective for Harvard and Shreveport High School. I propose that English poetry and biology should be taught as usual, but that at irregular intervals, poetry students should find dogfishes on their desks and biology students should find Shakespeare sonnets on their dissection boards. I am serious in declaring that a Sarah Lawrence English major who began poking about in a dogfish with a bobby pin would learn more in thirty minutes than a biology major in a whole semester; and that the latter upon reading on her dissecting board

> That time of year Thou may'st in me behold
> When yellow leaves, or none, or few, do hang
> Upon those boughs which shake against the cold—
> Bare ruin'd choirs where late the sweet birds sang

might catch fire at the beauty of it.

The situation of the tourist at the Grand Canyon and the biology student are special cases of a predicament in which everyone finds himself in a modern technical society—a society, that is, in which there is a division between expert and layman, planner and consumer, in which experts and planners take special measures to teach and edify the consumer. The measures taken are measures appropriate to the consumer: the expert and the planner *know* and *plan*, but the consumer *needs* and *experiences*.

There is a double deprivation. First, the thing is lost through its packaging. The very means by which the thing is presented for consumption, the very techniques by which the thing is made available as an item of need-satisfaction, these very means operate to remove the thing from the sovereignty of the knower. A loss of title occurs. The measures which the museum curator takes to present the thing to the public are self-liquidating. The upshot of the curator's efforts are not that everyone can see the exhibit but that no one can see it. The curator protests: Why are they so indifferent? Why do they even deface the exhibit? Don't they know it is theirs? But it is not theirs. It is his, the curator's. By the most exclusive sort of zoning, the museum exhibit, the park oak tree, is part of an ensemble, a package, which is almost impenetrable to them. The archaeologist who puts his find in a museum so that everyone can see it accomplishes the reverse of his expectations. The result of his action is that no one can see it now but the archaeologist. He would have done better to keep it in his pocket and show it now and then to strangers.

The tourist who carves his initials in a public place, which is theoretically "his" in the first place, has good reasons for doing so, reasons which the exhibitor and planner know nothing about. He does so because in his role of consumer of an experience (a "recreational experience" to satisfy a "recreational need") he knows that he is disinherited. He is deprived of his title over being. He knows very well that he is in a very special sort of zone in which his only rights are the rights of a consumer. He moves like a ghost through schoolroom, city streets, trains, parks, movies. He carves his initials as a last desperate measure to escape his ghostly role of consumer. He is saying in effect: I am not a ghost after all; I am a sovereign person. And he establishes title the only way remaining to him, by staking his claim over one square inch of wood or stone.

Does this mean that we should get rid of museums? No, but it means that the sightseer should be prepared to enter into a struggle to recover a sight from a museum.

The second loss is the spoliation of the thing, the tree, the rock, the swallow, by the layman's misunderstanding of scientific theory. He believes that the thing is *disposed of* by theory, that it stands in the Platonic relation of being a *specimen* of such and such an underlying principle. In the transmission of scientific theory from theorist to layman, the expectation of the theorist is reversed. Instead of the marvels of the universe being made available to the public, the universe is disposed of by theory. The loss of sovereignty takes this form: as a result of the science of botany, trees are not made available to every man. On the contrary. The tree loses its proper density and mystery as a concrete existent and, as merely another *specimen* of a species, becomes itself nugatory.

Does this mean that there is no use taking biology at Harvard and Shreveport High? No, but it means that the student should know what a fight he has on his hands to rescue the specimen from the educational package. The educator is only partly to blame. For there is nothing the educator can do to provide for this need of the student. Everything the educator does only succeeds in becoming, for the student, part of the educational package. The highest role of the educator is the maieutic role of Socrates: to help the student come to himself not as a consumer of experience but as a sovereign individual.

The thing is twice lost to the consumer. First, sovereignty is lost: it is theirs, not his. Second, it is radically devalued by theory. This is a loss which has been brought about by science but through no fault of the scientist and through no fault of scientific theory. The loss has come about as a consequence of the seduction of the layman by science. The layman will be seduced as long as he regards beings as consumer items to be experienced rather than prizes to be won, and as long as he waives his sovereign rights as a person and accepts his role of consumer as the highest estate to which the layman can aspire.

As Mounier said, the person is not something one can study and provide for; he is something one struggles for. But unless he also struggles for himself, unless he knows that there is a struggle, he is going to be just what the planners think he is.

. . . .

QUESTIONS FOR A SECOND READING

1. Percy's essay proceeds by adding example to example, one after another. If all the examples were meant to illustrate the same thing, the same general point or idea, then one would most likely have been enough. The rest would have been redundant. It makes sense, then, to assume that each example gives a different view of what Percy is saying, that each modifies the others, or qualifies them, or adds a piece that was otherwise lacking. It's as though Percy needed one more to get it right or to figure out what was missing along the way. As you read back through the essay, pay particular attention to the *differences* between the examples (between the various tourists going to the Grand Canyon, or between the tourists at the Grand Canyon and the tourists in Mexico). Also note the logic or system that leads from one to the next. What progress of thought is represented by the movement from one example to another, or from tourists to students?

2. The essay is filled with talk about "loss"—the loss of sovereignty, the loss of the creature—but it is resolutely ambiguous about what it is that we have lost. As you work your way back through, note the passages that describe what we are missing and why we should care. Are we to believe, for example, that Cárdenas actually had it (whatever "it" is)—that he had no preconceived notions when he saw the Grand Canyon? Mightn't he have said, "I claim this for my queen" or "There I see the glory of God" or "This wilderness is not fit for man"? To whom, or in the name of what, is this loss that Percy chronicles such a matter of concern? If this is not just Percy's peculiar prejudice, if we are asked to share his concerns, whose interests or what interests are represented here?

3. The essay is made up of stories or anecdotes, all of them fanciful. Percy did not, in other words, turn to first-person accounts of visitors to the Grand Canyon or to statements by actual students or teachers. Why not, do you suppose? What does this choice say about his "method"—about what it can and can't do? As you reread the essay, look for sections you could use to talk about the power and limits of Percy's method.

ASSIGNMENTS FOR WRITING

1. Percy tells several stories—some of them quite good stories—but it is often hard to know just what he is getting at, just what point it is he is trying to make. If he's making an argument, it's not the sort of argument that is easy to summarize. And if the stories (or anecdotes) are meant to serve

as examples, they are not the sort of examples that lead directly to a single, general conclusion or that serve to clarify a point or support an obvious thesis. In fact, at the very moment when you expect Percy to come forward and pull things together, he offers yet another story, as though another example, rather than any general statement, would get you closer to what he is saying.

There are, at the same time, terms and phrases to suggest that this is an essay with a point to make. Percy talks, for example, about "the loss of sovereignty," "symbolic packages," "consumers of experience," and "dialectic," and it seems that these terms and phrases are meant to name or comment on key scenes, situations, or characters in the examples.

For this assignment, tell a story of your own, one that is suggested by the stories Percy tells—perhaps a story about a time you went looking for something or at something, or about a time when you did or did not find a dogfish in your Shakespeare class. You should imagine that you are carrying out a project that Walker Percy has begun, a project that has you looking back at your own experience through the lens of "The Loss of the Creature," noticing what Percy would notice and following the paths that he would find interesting. Try to bring the terms that Percy uses—like "sovereign," "consumer," "expert," and "dialectic"—to bear on the story you have to tell. Feel free to imitate Percy's style and method in your essay.

2. Percy charts several routes to the Grand Canyon: you can take the packaged tour, you can get off the beaten track, you can wait for a disaster, you can follow the "dialectical movement which brings one back to the beaten track but at a level above it." This last path (or stratagem), he says, is for the complex traveler.

> Our complex friend stands behind his fellow tourists at the Bright Angel Lodge and sees the canyon through them and their predicament, their picture taking and busy disregard. In a sense, he exploits his fellow tourists; he stands on their shoulders to see the canyon. (p. 590)

The complex traveler sees the Grand Canyon through the example of the common tourists with "their predicament, their picture taking and busy disregard." He "stands on their shoulders" to see the canyon. This distinction between complex and common approaches is an important one in the essay. It is interesting to imagine how the distinction could be put to work to define ways of reading.

Suppose that you read "The Loss of the Creature" as a common reader. What would you see? What would you identify as key sections of the text? What would you miss? What would you say about what you see?

If you think of yourself, now, as a complex reader, modeled after any of Percy's more complex tourists or students, what would you see? What would you identify as key sections of the text? What would you miss? What would you say about what you see?

For this assignment, write an essay with three sections. You may number them, if you choose. The first section should represent the work of a common reader with "The Loss of the Creature," and the second should represent the work of a complex reader. The third section should look back and comment on the previous two. In particular, you might address these questions: Why might a person prefer one reading over the other? What is to be gained or lost with both?

MAKING CONNECTIONS

1. In "The Loss of the Creature," Percy writes about tourists and the difficulty they have seeing that which lies before them. In "Deep Play: Notes on the Balinese Cockfight" (p. 305), Clifford Geertz tells the story of his travels in Bali. Anthropologists, properly speaking, are not tourists. There is a scholarly purpose to their travel and, presumably, they have learned or developed the strategies necessary to get beyond the preformed "symbolic complex" that would keep them from seeing the place or the people they have traveled to study. They are experts, in other words, not common sightseers.

   In his travels to Bali, Geertz seems to get just what he wants. He gets both the authentic experience and a complex understanding of that experience. If you read "Deep Play" from the perspective of Percy's essay, however, it is interesting to ask whether Percy would say that this was the case (whether Percy might say that Geertz has gone as far as one can go after Cárdenas), and it is interesting to ask how Percy would characterize the "strategies" that define Geertz's approach to his subject.

   Write an essay in which you place Geertz in the context of Percy's tourists (not all of them, but two or three whose stories seem most interesting when placed alongside Geertz's). The purpose of your essay is to offer a Percian reading of Geertz's essay—to study his text, that is, in light of the terms and methods Percy has established in "The Loss of the Creature."

2. But the difference lies in the fundamental placement of the student in the world. . . . (Walker Percy, p. 596)

   What I am about to say to you has taken me more than twenty years to admit: *A primary reason for my success in the classroom was that I couldn't forget that schooling was changing me and separating me from the life I enjoyed before becoming a student.* (Richard Rodriguez, p. 654)

   Both Percy and Richard Rodriguez, in "The Achievement of Desire" (p. 652), write about students and how they are "placed" in the world by teachers and by the way schools characteristically represent knowledge, the novice, and the expert. And both tell stories to make their points, stories of characteristic students in characteristic situations. Write an essay in which you tell a story of your own, one meant to serve as a corrective or a supplement to the stories Percy and Rodriguez tell. You will want both to tell your story and to use it as a way of returning to and commenting on Percy and Rodriguez and the arguments they make. Your authority can rest on the fact that you are a student and as a consequence have ways of understanding that position that they do not.

anthropological defn. of culture → set of trait/belief/rituals
that define a grp of ppl.

- high culture → beck, find in museum
- mass culture → culture that massed produced ex] holly wd movie
- pop culture → rebellion against industry norms/stds.
    ~~rebellion ag~~. parody - high/mass culture.
        make fun of others art to make
        coherence btw. high + mass culture.

MARY LOUISE
PRATT

- contact zone → 2/more cultures come together in
    assymtememic relationship of power

- community → community never given always _imagined_
        community imagines, ~~and~~ reinforced by law (first
            - frat will defend ea. other   sover_
            - limited — got boundaries
- autoethnography → describing   something new about self in
        a dominant   lang. talk about self using
        dominant lang.

M ARY LOUISE PRATT (b. 1948) grew up in Listowel, Ontario, a small
Canadian farm town. She got her B.A. at the University of Toronto and
her Ph.D. from Stanford University, where she is now a professor in the departments of comparative literature and Spanish and Portuguese. At Stanford, she
was one of the cofounders of the new freshman culture program, a controversial
series of required courses that replaced the old Western civilization core courses.
The course she is particularly associated with is called "Europe and the Americas"; it brings together European representations of the Americas with indigenous American texts. As you might guess from the essay that follows, the new
program at Stanford expands the range of countries, languages, cultures, and
texts that are seen as a necessary introduction to the world; it also, however, revises the very idea of culture that many of us take for granted—particularly the
idea that culture, at its best, expresses common values in a common language.

Pratt is the author of Toward a Speech Act Theory of Literary Discourse
(1977) and coauthor of Women, Culture, and Politics in Latin America
(1990), the textbook Linguistics for Students of Literature (1980), Amor
Brujo: The Images and Culture of Love in the Andes (1990), and Imperial
Eyes: Studies in Travel Writing and Transculturation (1992). The essay that
follows was revised to serve as the introduction to Imperial Eyes, which is particularly about European travel writing in the eighteenth and nineteenth

- carries risk b/c it may not be interpretable
by others.
- antique of way we usually write

centuries, when Europe was "discovering" Africa and the Americas. It argues that travel writing produced "the rest of the world" for European readers. It didn't "report" on Africa or South America; it produced an "Africa" or an "America" for European consumption. Travel writing produced places that could be thought of as barren, empty, undeveloped, inconceivable, needful of European influence and control, ready to serve European industrial, intellectual, and commercial interests. The reports of travelers or, later, scientists and anthropologists are part of a more general process by which the emerging industrial nations took possession of new territory.

The European understanding of Peru, for example, came through European accounts, not from attempts to understand or elicit responses from Andeans, Peruvian natives. When such a response was delivered, when an Andean, Guaman Poma, wrote to King Philip III of Spain, his letter was unreadable. Pratt is interested in just those moments of contact between peoples and cultures. She is interested in how King Philip read (or failed to read) a letter from Peru, but also in how someone like Guaman Poma prepared himself to write to the king of Spain. To fix these moments, she makes use of a phrase she coined, the "contact zone," which, she says,

> I use to refer to the space of colonial encounters, the space in which peoples geographically and historically separated come into contact with each other and establish ongoing relations, usually involving conditions of coercion, radical inequality, and intractable conflict. . . . By using the term "contact," I aim to foreground the interactive, improvisational dimensions of colonial encounters so easily ignored or suppressed by diffusionist accounts of conquest and domination. A "contact" perspective emphasizes how subjects are constituted in and by their relations to each other. It treats the relations among colonizers and colonized, or travelers and "travelees," not in terms of separateness or apartheid, but in terms of copresence, interaction, interlocking understandings and practices.

Like Adrienne Rich's "When We Dead Awaken: Writing as Re-Vision" (and, for that matter, Clifford Geertz's "Deep Play"), "Arts of the Contact Zone" was first written as a lecture. It was delivered as a keynote address at the second Modern Language Association Literacy Conference, held in Pittsburgh, Pennsylvania, in 1990.

Arts of the Contact Zone

Whenever the subject of literacy comes up, what often pops first into my mind is a conversation I overheard eight years ago between my son Sam and his best friend, Willie, aged six and seven, respectively: "Why don't you trade me Many Trails for Carl Yats . . . Yesits . . . Ya-strum-scrum." "That's not how you say it, dummy, it's Carl Yes . . . Yes . . . oh, I don't know." Sam and Willie had just discovered baseball cards. Many Trails was their decoding, with the help of first-grade English phonics, of the name Manny Trillo. The name they were quite rightly stumped on was Carl Yastremski. That was the first time I remembered seeing them put their incipient literacy to their own use, and I was of course thrilled.

Sam and Willie learned a lot about phonics that year by trying to decipher surnames on baseball cards, and a lot about cities, states, heights, weights, places of birth, stages of life. In the years that followed, I watched Sam apply his arithmetic skills to working out batting averages and subtracting retirement years from rookie years; I watched him develop senses of patterning and order by arranging and rearranging his cards for hours on end, and aesthetic judgment by comparing different photos, different series, layouts, and color schemes. American geography and history took shape in his mind through baseball cards. Much of his social life revolved around trading them, and he learned about exchange, fairness, trust, the importance of processes as opposed to results, what it means to get cheated, taken advantage of, even robbed. Baseball cards were the medium of his economic life too. Nowhere better to learn the power and arbitrariness of money, the absolute divorce between use value and exchange value, notions of long- and short-term investment, the possibility of personal values that are independent of market values.

Baseball cards meant baseball card shows, where there was much to be learned about adult worlds as well. And baseball cards opened the door to baseball books, shelves and shelves of encyclopedias, magazines, histories, biographies, novels, books of jokes, anecdotes, cartoons, even poems. Sam learned the history of American racism and the struggle against it through baseball; he saw the Depression and two world wars from behind home plate. He learned the meaning of commodified labor, what it means for one's body and talents to be owned and dispensed by another. He knows something about Japan, Taiwan, Cuba, and Central America and how men and boys do things there. Through the history and experience of baseball stadiums he thought about architecture, light, wind, topography, meteorology, the dynamics of public space. He learned the meaning of expertise, of knowing about something well enough that you can start a conversation with a stranger and feel sure of holding your own. Even with an adult—especially with an adult. Throughout his preadolescent years, baseball history was Sam's luminous point of contact with grown-ups, his lifeline to caring. And, of course, all this time he was also playing baseball, struggling his way through the stages of the local Little League system, lucky enough to be a pretty good player, loving the game and coming to know deeply his strengths and weaknesses.

Literacy began for Sam with the newly pronounceable names on the picture cards and brought him what has been easily the broadest, most varied, most enduring, and most integrated experience of his thirteen-year life. Like many parents, I was delighted to see schooling give Sam the tools with which to find and open all these doors. At the same time I found it unforgivable that schooling itself gave him nothing remotely as meaningful to do, let alone anything that would actually take him beyond the referential, masculinist ethos of baseball and its lore.

However, I was not invited here to speak as a parent, nor as an expert on literacy. I was asked to speak as an MLA [Modern Language Association] member working in the elite academy. In that capacity my contribution is undoubtedly supposed to be abstract, irrelevant, and anchored outside the real world. I wouldn't dream of disappointing anyone. I propose immediately to head back several centuries to a text that has a few points in common with baseball cards and raises thoughts about what Tony Sarmiento, in his comments to the conference, called new visions of literacy. In 1908 a Peruvianist named Richard Pietschmann was exploring in the Danish Royal Archive in Copenhagen and came across a manuscript. It was dated in the city of Cuzco in Peru, in the year 1613, some forty years after the final fall of the Inca empire to the Spanish and signed with an unmistakably Andean indigenous name: Felipe Guaman Poma de Ayala. Written in a mixture of Quechua and ungrammatical, expressive Spanish, the manuscript was a letter addressed by an unknown but apparently literate Andean to King Philip III of Spain. What stunned Pietschmann was that the letter was twelve hundred pages long. There were almost eight hundred pages of written text and four hundred of captioned line drawings. It was titled *The First New Chronicle and Good Government.* No one knew (or knows) how the manuscript got to the library in Copenhagen or how long it had been there. No one, it appeared, had ever bothered to read it or figured out how. Quechua was not thought of as a written language in 1908, nor Andean culture as a literate culture.

Pietschmann prepared a paper on his find, which he presented in London in 1912, a year after the rediscovery of Machu Picchu by Hiram Bingham. Reception, by an international congress of Americanists, was apparently confused. It took twenty-five years for a facsimile edition of the work to appear in Paris. It was not till the late 1970s, as positivist reading habits gave way to interpretive studies and colonial elitisms to postcolonial pluralisms, that Western scholars found ways of reading Guaman Poma's *New Chronicle and Good Government* as the extraordinary intercultural tour de force that it was. The letter got there, only 350 years too late, a miracle and a terrible tragedy.

I propose to say a few more words about this erstwhile unreadable text, in order to lay out some thoughts about writing and literacy in what I like to call the *contact zones.* I use this term to refer to social spaces where cultures meet, clash, and grapple with each other, often in contexts of highly asymmetrical relations of power, such as colonialism, slavery, or their aftermaths as they are lived out in many parts of the world today. Eventually I will use the term to reconsider the models of community that many of us rely on in teaching and theorizing and that are under challenge today. But first a little more about Guaman Poma's giant letter to Philip III.

Insofar as anything is known about him at all, Guaman Poma exemplified the sociocultural complexities produced by conquest and empire. He was an indigenous Andean who claimed noble Inca descent and who had adopted (at least in some sense) Christianity. He may have worked in the Spanish colonial administration as an interpreter, scribe, or assistant to a Spanish tax collector—as a mediator, in short. He says he learned to write from his half brother, a mestizo whose Spanish father had given him access to religious education.

Guaman Poma's letter to the king is written in two languages (Spanish and Quechua) and two parts. The first is called the *Nueva corónica,* "New Chronicle." The title is important. The chronicle of course was the main writing apparatus through which the Spanish presented their American conquests to themselves. It constituted one of the main official discourses. In writing a "new chronicle," Guaman Poma took over the official Spanish genre for his own ends. Those ends were, roughly, to construct a new picture of the world, a picture of a Christian world with Andean rather than European peoples at the center of it—Cuzco, not Jerusalem. In the *New Chronicle* Guaman Poma begins by rewriting the Christian history of the world from Adam and Eve (Fig. 1 [p. 609]), incorporating the Amerindians into it as offspring of one of the sons of Noah. He identifies five ages of Christian history that he links in parallel with the five ages of canonical Andean history—separate but equal trajectories that diverge with Noah and reintersect not with Columbus but with Saint Bartholomew, claimed to have preceded Columbus in the Americas. In a couple of hundred pages, Guaman Poma constructs a veritable encyclopedia of Inca and pre-Inca history, customs, laws, social forms, public offices, and dynastic leaders. The depictions resemble European manners and customs description, but also reproduce the meticulous detail with which knowledge in Inca society was stored on *quipus* and in the oral memories of elders.

Guaman Poma's *New Chronicle* is an instance of what I have proposed to call an *autoethnographic* text, by which I mean a text in which people undertake to describe themselves in ways that engage with representations others have made of them. Thus if ethnographic texts are those in which European metropolitan subjects represent to themselves their others (usually their conquered others), autoethnographic texts are representations that the so-defined others construct *in response to* or in dialogue with those texts. Autoethnographic texts are not, then, what are usually thought of as autochthonous forms of expression or self-representation (as the Andean *quipus* were). Rather they involve a selective collaboration with and appropriation of idioms of the metropolis or the conqueror. These are merged or infiltrated to varying degrees with indigenous idioms to create self-representations intended to intervene in metropolitan modes of understanding. Autoethnographic works are often addressed to both metropolitan audiences and the speaker's own community. Their reception is thus highly indeterminate. Such texts often constitute a marginalized group's point of entry into the dominant circuits of print culture. It is interesting to think, for example, of American slave autobiography in its autoethnographic dimensions, which in some respects distinguish it from Euramerican autobiographical tradition. The concept might help explain why some of the earliest published writing by Chicanas took the form of folkloric manners and customs sketches written in English and published in English-language newspapers or folklore magazines (see Treviño). Autoethnographic representation often involves concrete collaborations between people, as between literate ex-slaves and abolitionist intellectuals, or between Guaman Poma and the Inca elders who were his informants. Often, as in Guaman Poma, it involves more than one language. In recent decades autoethnography, critique, and resistance have reconnected with writing in a contemporary creation of the contact zone, the *testimonio*.

Guaman Poma's *New Chronicle* ends with a revisionist account of the Spanish conquest, which, he argues, should have been a peaceful

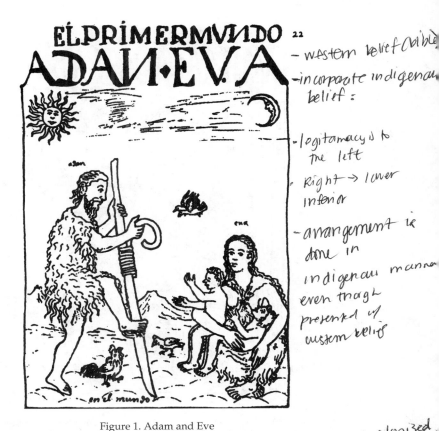

Figure 1. Adam and Eve

encounter of equals with the potential for benefiting both, but for the mindless greed of the Spanish. He parodies Spanish history. Following contact with the Incas, he writes, "In all Castille, there was a great commotion. All day and at night in their dreams the Spaniards were saying, 'Yndias, yndias, oro, plata, oro, plata del Piru'" ("Indies, Indies, gold, silver, gold, silver from Peru") (Fig. 2). The Spanish, he writes, brought nothing of value to share with the Andeans, nothing "but armor and guns con la codicia de oro, plata oro y plata, yndias, a las Yndias, Piru" ("with the lust for gold, silver, gold and silver, Indies, the Indies, Peru") (372). I quote these words as an example of a conquered subject using the conqueror's language to construct a parodic, oppositional representation of the conqueror's own speech. Guaman Poma mirrors back to the Spanish (in their language, which is alien to him) an image of themselves that they often suppress and will therefore surely recognize. Such are the dynamics of language, writing, and representation in contact zones.

The second half of the epistle continues the critique. It is titled *Buen gobierno y justicia*, "Good Government and Justice," and combines a descrip-

Figure 2. Conquista. Meeting of Spaniard and Inca. The Inca says in Quechua, "You eat this gold?" Spaniard replies in Spanish, "We eat this gold."

tion of colonial society in the Andean region with a passionate denunciation of Spanish exploitation and abuse. (These, at the time he was writing, were decimating the population of the Andes at a genocidal rate. In fact, the potential loss of the labor force became a main cause for reform of the system.) Guaman Poma's most implacable hostility is invoked by the clergy, followed by the dreaded *corregidores,* or colonial overseers (Fig. 3). He also praises good works, Christian habits, and just men where he finds them, and offers at length his views as to what constitutes "good government and justice." The Indies, he argues, should be administered through a collaboration of Inca and Spanish elites. The epistle ends with an imaginary question-and-answer session in which, in a reversal of hierarchy, the king is depicted asking Guaman Poma questions about how to reform the empire—a dialogue imagined across the many lines that divide the Andean scribe from the imperial monarch, and in which the subordinated subject single-handedly gives himself authority in the colonizer's language and verbal repertoire. In a way, it worked—this extraordinary text did get written—but in a way it did not, for the letter never reached its addressee.

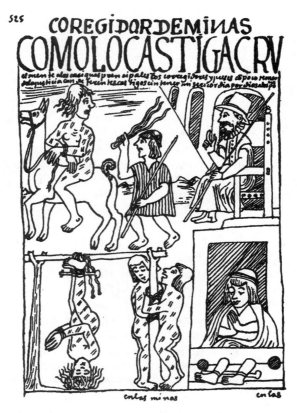

Figure 3. Corregidor de minas. Catalog of Spanish abuses
of indigenous labor force.

To grasp the import of Guaman Poma's project, one needs to keep in mind that the Incas had no system of writing. Their huge empire is said to be the only known instance of a full-blown bureaucratic state society built and administered without writing. Guaman Poma constructs his text by appropriating and adapting pieces of the representational repertoire of the invaders. He does not simply imitate or reproduce it; he selects and adapts it along Andean lines to express (bilingually, mind you) Andean interests and aspirations. Ethnographers have used the term *transculturation* to describe processes whereby members of subordinated or marginal groups select and invent from materials transmitted by a dominant or metropolitan culture. The term, originally coined by Cuban sociologist Fernando Ortiz in the 1940s, aimed to replace overly reductive concepts of acculturation and assimilation used to characterize culture under conquest. While subordinate peoples do not usually control what emanates from the dominant culture, they do determine to varying extents what gets absorbed into their own and what it gets used for. Transculturation, like autoethnography, is a phenomenon of the contact zone.

As scholars have realized only relatively recently, the transcultural character of Guaman Poma's text is intricately apparent in its visual as well as its written component. The genre of the four hundred line drawings is European—there seems to have been no tradition of representational drawing among the Incas—but in their execution they deploy specifically Andean systems of spatial symbolism that express Andean values and aspirations.[1]

In figure 1, for instance, Adam is depicted on the left-hand side below the sun, while Eve is on the right-hand side below the moon, and slightly lower than Adam. The two are divided by the diagonal of Adam's digging stick. In Andean spatial symbolism, the diagonal descending from the sun marks the basic line of power and authority dividing upper from lower, male from female, dominant from subordinate. In figure 2, the Inca appears in the same position as Adam, with the Spaniard opposite, and the two at the same height. In figure 3, depicting Spanish abuses of power, the symbolic pattern is reversed. The Spaniard is in a high position indicating dominance, but on the "wrong" (right-hand) side. The diagonals of his lance and that of the servant doing the flogging mark out a line of illegitimate, though real, power. The Andean figures continue to occupy the left-hand side of the picture, but clearly as victims. Guaman Poma wrote that the Spanish conquest had produced *"un mundo al reves,"* "a world in reverse."

In sum, Guaman Poma's text is truly a product of the contact zone. If one thinks of cultures, or literatures, as discrete, coherently structured, monolingual edifices, Guaman Poma's text, and indeed any autoethnographic work, appears anomalous or chaotic—as it apparently did to the European scholars Pietschmann spoke to in 1912. If one does not think of cultures this way, then Guaman Poma's text is simply heterogeneous, as the Andean region was itself and remains today. Such a text is heterogeneous on the reception end as well as the production end: it will read very differently to people in different positions in the contact zone. Because it deploys

European and Andean systems of meaning making, the letter necessarily means differently to bilingual Spanish-Quechua speakers and to monolingual speakers in either language; the drawings mean differently to monocultural readers, Spanish or Andean, and to bicultural readers responding to the Andean symbolic structures embodied in European genres.

In the Andes in the early 1600s there existed a literate public with considerable intercultural competence and degrees of bilingualism. Unfortunately, such a community did not exist in the Spanish court with which Guaman Poma was trying to make contact. It is interesting to note that in the same year Guaman Poma sent off his letter, a text by another Peruvian was adopted in official circles in Spain as the canonical Christian mediation between the Spanish conquest and Inca history. It was another huge encyclopedic work, titled the *Royal Commentaries of the Incas*, written, tellingly, by a mestizo, Inca Garcilaso de la Vega. Like the mestizo half brother who taught Guaman Poma to read and write, Inca Garcilaso was the son of an Inca princess and a Spanish official, and had lived in Spain since he was seventeen. Though he too spoke Quechua, his book is written in eloquent, standard Spanish, without illustrations. While Guaman Poma's life's work sat somewhere unread, the *Royal Commentaries* was edited and reedited in Spain and the New World, a mediation that coded the Andean past and present in ways thought unthreatening to colonial hierarchy.[2] The textual hierarchy persists; the *Royal Commentaries* today remains a staple item on Ph.D. reading lists in Spanish, while the *New Chronicle and Good Government*, despite the ready availability of several fine editions, is not. However, though Guaman Poma's text did not reach its destination, the transcultural currents of expression it exemplifies continued to evolve in the Andes, as they still do, less in writing than in storytelling, ritual, song, dance-drama, painting and sculpture, dress, textile art, forms of governance, religious belief, and many other vernacular art forms. All express the effects of long-term contact and intractable, unequal conflict.

Autoethnography, transculturation, critique, collaboration, bilingualism, mediation, parody, denunciation, imaginary dialogue, vernacular expression—these are some of the literate arts of the contact zone. Miscomprehension, incomprehension, dead letters, unread masterpieces, absolute heterogeneity of meaning—these are some of the perils of writing in the contact zone. They all live among us today in the transnationalized metropolis of the United States and are becoming more widely visible, more pressing, and, like Guaman Poma's text, more decipherable to those who once would have ignored them in defense of a stable, centered sense of knowledge and reality.

Contact and Community

The idea of the contact zone is intended in part to contrast with ideas of community that underlie much of the thinking about language, communication, and culture that gets done in the academy. A couple of years ago, thinking about the linguistic theories I knew, I tried to make sense of a utopian quality that often seemed to characterize social analyses of language by the academy. Languages were seen as living in "speech communities," and these tended to be theorized as discrete, self-defined, coherent entities, held together by a homogeneous competence or grammar shared identically and equally among all the members. This abstract idea of the speech community seemed to reflect, among other things, the utopian way modern nations conceive of themselves as what Benedict Anderson calls "imagined communities."[3] In a book of that title, Anderson observes that with the possible exception of what he calls "primordial villages," human communities exist as *imagined* entities in which people "will never know most of their fellow-members, meet them or even hear of them, yet in the mind of each lives the image of their communion." "Communities are distinguished," he goes on to say, "not by their falsity/genuineness, but by *the style in which they are imagined*" (15; emphasis mine). Anderson proposes three features that characterize the style in which the modern nation is imagined. First, it is imagined as *limited*, by "finite, if elastic, boundaries"; second, it is imagined as *sovereign;* and, third, it is imagined as *fraternal*, "a deep, horizontal comradeship" for which millions of people are prepared "not so much to kill as willingly to die" (15). As the image suggests, the nation-community is embodied metonymically in the finite, sovereign, fraternal figure of the citizen-soldier.

Anderson argues that European bourgeoisies were distinguished by their ability to "achieve solidarity on an essentially imagined basis" (74) on a scale far greater than that of elites of other times and places. Writing and literacy play a central role in this argument. Anderson maintains, as have others, that the main instrument that made bourgeois nation-building projects possible was print capitalism. The commercial circulation of books in the various European vernaculars, he argues, was what first created the invisible networks that would eventually constitute the literate elites and those they ruled as nations. (Estimates are that 180 million books were put into circulation in Europe between the years 1500 and 1600 alone.)

Now obviously this style of imagining of modern nations, as Anderson describes it, is strongly utopian, embodying values like equality, fraternity, liberty, which the societies often profess but systematically fail to realize. The prototype of the modern nation as imagined community was, it seemed to me, mirrored in ways people thought about language and the speech community. Many commentators have pointed out how modern views of language as code and competence assume a unified and homogeneous social world in which language exists as a shared patrimony—as a device, precisely, for imagining community. An image of a universally shared literacy is also part of the picture. The prototypical manifestation of language is generally taken to be the speech of individual adult native speakers face-to-face (as in Saussure's famous diagram) in monolingual, even monodialectal situations—in short, the most homogeneous case linguistically and socially. The same goes for written communication. Now one could certainly imagine a theory that assumed different things— that argued, for instance, that the most revealing speech situation for understanding language was one involving a gathering of people each of whom spoke two languages and understood a third and held only one language in common with any of the others. It depends on what workings of language you want to see or want to see first, on what you choose to define as normative.

In keeping with autonomous, fraternal models of community, analyses of language use commonly assume that principles of cooperation and shared understanding are normally in effect. Descriptions of interactions between people in conversation, classrooms, medical and bureaucratic settings, readily take it for granted that the situation is governed by a single set of rules or norms shared by all participants. The analysis focuses then on how those rules produce or fail to produce an orderly, coherent exchange. Models involving games and moves are often used to describe interactions. Despite whatever conflicts or systematic social differences might be in play, it is assumed that all participants are engaged in the same game and that the game is the same for all players. Often it is. But of course it often is not, as, for example, when speakers are from different classes or cultures, or one party is exercising authority and another is submitting to it or questioning it. Last year one of my children moved to a new elementary school that had more open classrooms and more flexible curricula than the conventional school he started out in. A few days into the term, we asked him what it was like at the new school. "Well," he said, "they're a lot nicer, and they have a lot less rules. But know *why* they're nicer?" "Why?" I asked. "So you'll obey all the rules they don't have," he replied. This is a very coherent analysis with considerable elegance and explanatory power, but probably not the one his teacher would have given.

When linguistic (or literate) interaction is described in terms of orderliness, games, moves, or scripts, usually only legitimate moves are actually named as part of the system, where legitimacy is defined from the point of view of the party in authority—regardless of what other parties might see themselves as doing. Teacher-pupil language, for example, tends to be described almost entirely from the point of view of the teacher and teaching, not from the point of view of pupils and pupiling (the word doesn't even exist, though the thing certainly does). If a classroom is analyzed as a social world unified and homogenized with respect to the teacher, whatever students do other than what the teacher specifies is invisible or anomalous to the analysis. This can be true in practice as well. On several occasions my fourth grader, the one busy obeying all the rules they didn't have, was given writing assignments that took the form of answering a series of questions to build up a paragraph. These questions often asked him to identify with the interests of those in power over him—parents, teachers, doctors, public authorities. He invariably sought ways to resist or subvert these assignments. One assignment, for instance, called for imagining "a helpful invention." The students were asked to write single-sentence responses to the following questions:

> What kind of invention would help you?
> How would it help you?
> Why would you need it?
> What would it look like?
> Would other people be able to use it also?
> What would be an invention to help your teacher?
> What would be an invention to help your parents?

Manuel's reply read as follows:

> A grate adventchin
>
> Some inventchins are GRATE!!!!!!!!!!! My inventchin would be a shot that would put every thing you learn at school in your brain. It would help me by letting me graduate right now!! I would need it because it would let me play with my friends, go on vacachin and, do fun a lot more. It would look like a regular shot. Ather peaple would use to. This inventchin would help my teacher parents get away from a lot of work. I think a shot like this would be GRATE!

Despite the spelling, the assignment received the usual star to indicate the task had been fulfilled in an acceptable way. No recognition was available, however, of the humor, the attempt to be critical or contestatory, to parody the structures of authority. On that score, Manuel's luck was only slightly better than Guaman Poma's. What is the place of unsolicited oppositional discourse, parody, resistance, critique in the imagined classroom community? Are teachers supposed to feel that their teaching has been most successful when they have eliminated such things and unified the social world, probably in their own image? Who wins when we do that? Who loses?

Such questions may be hypothetical, because in the United States in the 1990s, many teachers find themselves less and less able to do that even if they want to. The composition of the national collectivity is changing and so are the styles, as Anderson put it, in which it is being imagined. In the 1980s in many nation-states, imagined national syntheses that had retained hegemonic force began to dissolve. Internal social groups with histories and lifeways different from the official ones began insisting on those histories and lifeways *as part of their citizenship,* as the very mode of their membership in the national collectivity. In their dialogues with dominant institutions, many groups began asserting a rhetoric of belonging that made demands beyond those of representation and basic rights granted from above. In universities we started to hear, "I don't just want you to let me be here, I want to belong here; this institution should belong to me as much as it does to anyone else." Institutions have responded with, among other things, rhetorics of diversity and multiculturalism whose import at this moment is up for grabs across the ideological spectrum.

These shifts are being lived out by everyone working in education today, and everyone is challenged by them in one way or another. Those of us committed to educational democracy are particularly challenged as that notion finds itself besieged on the public agenda. Many of those who govern us display, openly, their interest in a quiescent, ignorant, manipulable electorate. Even as an ideal, the concept of an enlightened citizenry seems to have disappeared from the national imagination. A couple of years ago the university where I work went through an intense and wrenching debate over a narrowly defined Western-culture requirement that had been instituted there in 1980. It kept boiling down to a debate over the ideas of national patrimony, cultural citizenship, and imagined community. In the end, the requirement was transformed into a much more broadly defined course called Cultures, Ideas, Values.[4] In the context of the change, a new course was designed that centered on the Americas and the multiple cultural histories (including European ones) that have intersected here. As you can imagine, the course attracted a very diverse student body. The classroom functioned not like a homogeneous community or a horizontal alliance but like a contact zone. Every single text we read stood in specific historical relationships to the students in the class, but the range and variety of historical relationships in play were enormous. Everybody had a stake in nearly everything we read, but the range and kind of stakes varied widely.

It was the most exciting teaching we had ever done, and also the hardest. We were struck, for example, at how anomalous the formal lecture became in a contact zone (who can forget Atahuallpa throwing down the Bible because it would not speak to him?). The lecturer's traditional (imagined) task—unifying the world in the class's eyes by means of a monologue that rings equally coherent, revealing, and true for all, forging an ad hoc community, homogeneous with respect to one's own words—this task became not only impossible but anomalous and unimaginable. Instead, one had to work in the knowledge that whatever one said was going to be systematically received in radically heterogeneous ways that we were neither able nor entitled to prescribe.

The very nature of the course put ideas and identities on the line. All the students in the class had the experience, for example, of hearing their culture discussed and objectified in ways that horrified them; all the students saw their roots traced back to legacies of both glory and shame; all the students experienced face-to-face the ignorance and incomprehension, and occasionally the hostility, of others. In the absence of community values and the hope of synthesis, it was easy to forget the positives; the fact, for instance, that kinds of marginalization once taken for granted were gone. Virtually every student was having the experience of seeing the world described with him or her in it. Along with rage, incomprehension, and pain, there were exhilarating moments of wonder and revelation, mutual understanding, and new wisdom—the joys of the contact zone. The sufferings and revelations were, at different moments to be sure, experienced by every student. No one was excluded, and no one was safe.

The fact that no one was safe made all of us involved in the course appreciate the importance of what we came to call "safe houses." We used the term to refer to social and intellectual spaces where groups can constitute themselves as horizontal, homogeneous, sovereign communities with high degrees of trust, shared understandings, temporary protection from legacies of oppression. This is why, as we realized, multicultural curricula should not seek to replace ethnic or women's studies, for example. Where there are legacies of subordination, groups need places for healing and mutual recognition, safe houses in which to construct shared understandings, knowledges, claims on the world that they can then bring into the contact zone.

Meanwhile, our job in the Americas course remains to figure out how to make that crossroads the best site for learning that it can be. We are looking for the pedagogical arts of the contact zone. These will include, we are sure, exercises in storytelling and in identifying with the ideas, interests, histories, and attitudes of others; experiments in transculturation and collaborative work and in the arts of critique, parody, and comparison (including unseemly comparisons between elite and vernacular cultural forms); the redemption of the oral; ways for people to engage with suppressed aspects of history (including their own histories), ways to move *into and out of* rhetorics of authenticity; ground rules for communication across lines of difference and hierarchy that go beyond politeness but maintain mutual respect; a systematic approach to the all-important concept of *cultural mediation*. These arts were in play in every room at the extraordinary Pittsburgh conference on literacy. I learned a lot about them there, and I am thankful.

WORKS CITED

Adorno, Rolena. *Guaman Poma de Ayala: Writing and Resistance in Colonial Peru.* Austin: U of Texas P, 1986.

Anderson, Benedict. *Imagined Communities: Reflections on the Origins and Spread of Nationalism.* London: Verso, 1984.

Garcilaso de la Vega, El Inca. *Royal Commentaries of the Incas.* 1613. Austin: U of Texas P, 1966.

Guaman Poma de Ayala, Felipe. *El primer nueva corónica y buen gobierno.* Manuscript. Ed. John Murra and Rolena Adorno. Mexico: Siglo XXI, 1980.

Pratt, Mary Louise. "Linguistic Utopias." *The Linguistics of Writing.* Ed. Nigel Fabb et al. Manchester: Manchester UP, 1987. 48–66.

Treviño, Gloria. "Cultural Ambivalence in Early Chicano Prose Fiction." Diss. Stanford U, 1985.

NOTES

[1]For an introduction in English to these and other aspects of Guaman Poma's work, see Rolena Adorno. Adorno and Mercedes Lopez-Baralt pioneered the study of Andean symbolic systems in Guaman Poma.

[2] It is far from clear that the *Royal Commentaries* was as benign as the Spanish seemed to assume. The book certainly played a role in maintaining the identity and aspirations of indigenous elites in the Andes. In the mid–eighteenth century, a new edition of the *Royal Commentaries* was suppressed by Spanish authorities because its preface included a prophecy by Sir Walter Raleigh that the English would invade Peru and restore the Inca monarchy.

[3] The discussion of community here is summarized from my essay "Linguistic Utopias."

[4] For information about this program and the contents of courses taught in it, write Program in Cultures, Ideas, Values (CIV), Stanford Univ., Stanford, CA 94305.

●　●　●　●　●　●　●　●　●　●　●　●　●

QUESTIONS FOR A SECOND READING

1. Perhaps the most interesting question "Arts of the Contact Zone" raises for its readers is how to put together the pieces: the examples from Pratt's children, the discussion of Guaman Poma and the *New Chronicle and Good Government,* the brief history of European literacy, and the discussion of curriculum reform at Stanford. The terms that run through the sections are, among others, these: "contact," "community," "autoethnography," "transculturation." As you reread, mark those passages you might use to trace the general argument that cuts across these examples.

2. This essay was originally delivered as a lecture. Before you read her essay again, create a set of notes on what you remember as important, relevant, or worthwhile. Imagine yourself as part of her audience. Then reread the essay. Where would you want to interrupt her? What questions could you ask her that might make "Arts of the Contact Zone" more accessible to you?

3. This is an essay about reading and writing and teaching and learning, about the "literate arts" and the "pedagogical arts" of the contact zone. Surely the composition class, the first-year college English class, can be imagined as a contact zone. And it seems in the spirit of Pratt's essay to identify (as a student) with Guaman Poma. As you reread, think about how and where this essay might be said to speak directly to you about your education as a reader and writer in a contact zone.

4. There are some difficult terms in this essay: "autochthonous," "autoethnography," "transculturation." The last two are defined in the text; the first you will have to look up. (We did.) In some ways, the slipperiest of the key words in the essay is "culture." At one point Pratt says,

    > If one thinks of cultures, or literatures, as discrete, coherently structured, monolingual edifices, Guaman Poma's text, and indeed any autoethnographic work, appears anomalous or chaotic—as it apparently did to the European scholars Pietschmann spoke to in 1912. If one does not think of cultures this way, then Guaman Poma's text is simply heterogeneous, as the Andean region was itself and remains today. Such a text is heterogeneous on the reception end as well as the production

end: it will read very differently to people in different positions in the
contact zone. (p. 612)

If one thinks of cultures as "coherently structured, monolingual edifices,"
the text appears one way; if one thinks otherwise the text is "simply heterogeneous." What might it mean to make this shift in the way one thinks
of culture? Can you do it—that is, can you read the *New Chronicle* from
both points of view, make the two points of view work in your own imagining? Can you, for example, think of a group that you participate in as a
"community"? Then can you think of it as a "contact zone"? Which one
seems "natural" to you? What does Pratt assume to be the dominant point
of view now, for *her* readers?

As you reread, not only do you want to get a sense of how to explain
these two attitudes toward culture, but you need to practice shifting your
point of view from one to the other. Think, from inside the position of
each, of the things you would be expected to say about Poma's text,
Manuel's invention, and your classroom.

ASSIGNMENTS FOR WRITING

Here, briefly, are two descriptions of the writing one might find or expect in the "contact zone." They serve as an introduction to the three writing assignments.

> Autoethnography, transculturation, critique, collaboration, bilingual-
> ism, mediation, parody, denunciation, imaginary dialogue, vernacular
> expression—these are some of the literate arts of the contact zone. Mis-
> comprehension, incomprehension, dead letters, unread masterpieces,
> absolute heterogeneity of meaning—these are some of the perils of
> writing in the contact zone. They all live among us today in the
> transnationalized metropolis of the United States and are becoming
> more widely visible, more pressing, and, like Guaman Poma's text,
> more decipherable to those who once would have ignored them in de-
> fense of a stable, centered sense of knowledge and reality. (p. 613)

> We are looking for the pedagogical arts of the contact zone. These will
> include, we are sure, exercises in storytelling and in identifying with
> the ideas, interests, histories, and attitudes of others; experiments in
> transculturation and collaborative work and in the arts of critique, par-
> ody, and comparison (including unseemly comparisons between elite
> and vernacular cultural forms); the redemption of the oral; ways for
> people to engage with suppressed aspects of history (including their
> own histories), ways to move *into and out of* rhetorics of authenticity;
> ground rules for communication across lines of difference and hierar-
> chy that go beyond politeness but maintain mutual respect; a system-
> atic approach to the all-important concept of *cultural mediation.* (p. 618)

1. One way of working with Pratt's essay, of extending its project, would
   be to conduct your own local inventory of writing from the contact zone.
   You might do this on your own or in teams with others from your class.
   You will want to gather several similar documents, your "archive," before you make your final selection. Think about how to make that choice.

What makes one document stand out as representative? Here are two ways you might organize your search:

a. You could look for historical documents. A local historical society might have documents written by Native Americans ("Indians") to the white settlers. There may be documents written by slaves to masters or to northern whites explaining their experience with slavery. There may be documents by women (like suffragettes) trying to negotiate for public positions and rights. There may be documents from any of a number of racial or ethnic groups—Hispanic, Jewish, Irish, Italian, Polish, Swedish—trying to explain their positions to the mainstream culture. There may, perhaps at union halls, be documents written by workers to owners. Your own sense of the heritage of your area should direct your search.

b. Or you could look for contemporary documents in the print that is around you, things that you might otherwise overlook. Pratt refers to one of the characteristic genres of the Hispanic community, the *"testimonio."* You could look at the writing of any marginalized group, particularly writing intended, at least in part, to represent the experience of outsiders to the dominant culture (or to be in dialogue with that culture or to respond to that culture). These documents, if we follow Pratt's example, would encompass the work of young children or students, including college students.

Once you have completed your inventory, choose a document you would like to work with and present it carefully and in detail (perhaps in even greater detail than Pratt's presentation of the *New Chronicle*). You might imagine that you are presenting this to someone who would not have seen it and would not know how to read it, at least not as an example of the literate arts of the contact zone.

2. Another way of extending the project of Pratt's essay would be to write your own autoethnography. It should not be too hard to locate a setting or context in which you are the "other"—the one who speaks from outside rather than inside the dominant discourse. Pratt says that the position of the outsider is marked not only by differences of language and ways of thinking and speaking but also by differences in power, authority, status. In a sense, she argues, the only way those in power can understand you is in *their* terms. These are terms you will need to use to tell your story, but your goal is to describe your position in ways that "engage with representations others have made of [you]" without giving in or giving up or disappearing in their already formed sense of who you are.

This is an interesting challenge. One of the things that will make the writing difficult is that the autoethnographic or transcultural text calls upon skills not usually valued in American classrooms: bilingualism, parody, denunciation, imaginary dialogue, vernacular expression, storytelling, unseemly comparisons of high and low cultural forms—these are some of the terms Pratt offers. These do not fit easily with the traditional genres of the writing class (essay, term paper, summary, report) or its traditional values (unity, consistency, sincerity, clarity, correctness, decorum).

You will probably need to take this essay (or whatever it should be called) through several drafts. It might be best to begin as Pratt's student, using her description as a preliminary guide. Once you get a sense of your own project, you may find that you have terms or examples to add to her list of the literate arts of the contact zone.

3. Citing Benedict Anderson and what he calls "imagined communities," Pratt argues that our idea of community is "strongly utopian, embodying values like equality, fraternity, liberty, which the societies often profess but systematically fail to realize." Against this utopian vision of community, Pratt argues that we need to develop ways of understanding (even noticing) social and intellectual spaces that are not homogeneous, unified; we need to develop ways of understanding and valuing difference.

Think of a community of which you are a member, a community that is important to you. And think about the utopian terms you are given to name and describe this community. Think, then, about this group in Pratt's terms—as a "contact zone." How would you name and describe this social space? Write an essay in which you present these alternate points of view on a single social group. You will need to present this discussion fully, so that someone who is not part of your group can follow what you say, and you should take time to think about the consequences (for you, for your group) of this shift in point of view, in terms.

MAKING CONNECTIONS

1. In "The Photographic Essay: Four Case Studies" (p. 510), W. J. T. Mitchell is concerned with the ways both words and images take possession of their subjects. And, in his account, there is a political dimension to this. It is a matter of the rich looking at and describing the poor in *Let Us Now Praise Famous Men*, of colonial power and the colonized in *The Colonial Harem* and *After the Last Sky*. (It is harder to name the victims and agents of appropriation in *Camera Lucida*. It would be worth your time to read that section carefully to see what terms Barthes offers.) In Pratt's terms in "Arts of the Contact Zone," both the photos and the texts represent moments of contact between persons of different cultures and unequal status.

Write an essay in which you consider two of the cases in "The Photographic Essay" in terms of Pratt's discussion of the contact zone. How would she understand the status and meaning of the words and images used to represent the "other"? How is her understanding different from Mitchell's? Both could be said to be interested in the role of power, the political, and history in the use and formation of texts. Which account seems most useful to you? Useful for what?

2. Here, from "Arts of the Contact Zone" (p. 605), is Mary Louise Pratt on the "autoethnographic" text:

> Guaman Poma's *New Chronicle* is an instance of what I have proposed to call an *autoethnographic* text, by which I mean a text in which people undertake to describe themselves in ways that engage with representations others have made of them. Thus if ethnographic texts are those in

which European metropolitan subjects represent to themselves their others (usually their conquered others), autoethnographic texts are representations that the so-defined others construct *in response to* or in dialogue with those texts. . . . [T]hey involve a selective collaboration with and appropriation of idioms of the metropolis or the conqueror. These are merged or infiltrated to varying degrees with indigenous idioms to create self-representations intended to intervene in metropolitan modes of understanding. . . . Such texts often constitute a marginalized group's point of entry into the dominant circuits of print culture. It is interesting to think, for example, of American slave autobiography in its autoethnographic dimensions, which in some respects distinguish it from Euramerican autobiographical tradition. (pp. 608-09)

Harriet Jacobs's "Incidents in the Life of a Slave Girl" (p. 428) is an example of an American slave autobiography. James Baldwin's "Notes of a Native Son" (p. 52) could serve as its twentieth-century counterpart. Read both and, working closely with the terms of Pratt's analysis in "Arts of the Contact Zone," discuss them as examples of autoethnographic and/or transcultural texts. You should imagine that you are working to put Pratt's ideas to the test (*do* they do what she says such texts must do?), but also add what you have to say on these two examples of African American autobiography.

ADRIENNE
RICH

conclusion

*A*DRIENNE RICH *(b. 1929) once said that whatever she knows, she wants to "know it in [her] own nerves." As a writer, Rich found it necessary to acknowledge her anger at both the oppression of women and her immediate experience of that oppression. She needed to find the "anger that is creative." "Until I could tap into the very rich ocean," she said, "I think that my work was constrained in certain ways. There's this fear of anger in women, which is partly because we've been told it was always destructive, it was always unseemly, and unwomanly, and monstrous."*

Rich's poetry combines passion and anger with a "yen for order." She wrote her first book of poems, A Change of World, *while an undergraduate at Radcliffe College. The book won the 1951 Yale Younger Poets Award and a generous introduction from W. H. Auden, who was one of the judges. In 1991 she won the Commonwealth Award in Literature and in 1992 the Robert Frost Medal from the Poetry Society of America for a lifetime of achievement in literature. Her other works, which include* The Diamond Cutters *(1955),* Snapshots of a Daughter-in-Law *(1963, 1967),* Necessities of Life *(1966),* Leaflets *(1969),* The Will to Change *(1970), and* Diving into the Wreck *(1973), show an increasing concern for the political and psychological consequences of life in patriarchal society. When offered the National Book Award for* Diving into the Wreck, *Rich refused it as an individual but accepted it, in a statement written with two other nominees—Audre Lorde and Alice Walker (whose essay "In Search of Our Mothers' Gardens" appears on p. 739)—in the name of all women:*

> We . . . together accept this award in the name of all the women whose voices have gone and still go unheard in a patriarchal world, and in the name of those who, like us, have been tolerated as token women in this culture, often at great cost and in great pain. . . . We dedicate this occasion to the struggle for self-determination of all women, of every color, identification, or derived class, . . . the women who will understand what we are doing here and those who will not understand yet; the silent women whose voices have been denied us, the articulate women who have given us the strength to do our work.

After graduating from Radcliffe in 1951, Rich married and raised three sons. One of her prose collections, Of Woman Born: Motherhood as Experience and Institution *(1976), treats her experience as both mother and daughter with eloquence, even as it calls for the destruction of motherhood as an institution. In 1970 Rich left her marriage, and six years later she published a book of poems that explore a lesbian relationship. But the term "lesbian" for Rich referred to "nothing so simple and dismissible as the fact that two women might go to bed together." As she says in "It Is the Lesbian in Us," a speech reprinted in* On Lies, Secrets, and Silence: Selected Prose *(1979), it refers also to "a sense of desiring oneself; above all, of choosing oneself; it was also a primary intensity; between women, an intensity which in the world at large was trivialized, caricatured, or invested with evil. . . . It is the lesbian in us who drives us to feel imaginatively, render in language, grasp, the full connection between woman and woman."*

The essay "When We Dead Awaken: Writing as Re-Vision" was written in 1971. In an introduction to a recent collection of her essays, Arts of the Possible, *Rich says,*

> In selecting a few essays from my earlier work . . . , I sometimes had a rueful sense of how one period's necessary strategies can mutate into the monsters of a later time. The accurate feminist perceptions that women's lives, historically and individually, were mostly unrecorded and that the personal is political are cases in point. Feminism has depended heavily on the concrete testimony of individual women, a testimony that was meant to accumulate toward collective understanding and practice. . . . In "When We Dead Awaken," I borrowed a title from Ibsen's last play, written in 1900. Certainly the issues Ibsen had dramatized were very much alive. I "used myself" to illustrate a woman writer's journey, rather tentatively. In 1971, this still seemed a questionable, even illegitimate, approach, especially in a paper to be given at an academic convention. . . .
>
> By the late 1900s, in mainstream American public discourse, personal anecdote was replacing critical argument, true confessions were foregrounding the discussion of ideas. A feminism that sought to engage race and colonialism, the global monoculture of United States corporate and military interests, the specific locations and agencies of women within all this was being countered by the marketing of a

United States model of female—or feminine—self-involvement and
self-improvement, devoid of political context or content.

One way of working on her essay is to move from it to the later work, using
"When We Dead Awaken" as a framework for further reading. We have provided
a selection of poems that can serve as preparation for such a project. These poems
are selected from Rich's 1986 book, Your Native Land, Your Life, a book that
addresses questions of legacy, heritage, and inheritance. The poems are drawn
from the opening section, which is titled "Sources." One of the poems contains the
phrase "split at the root." This is a phrase Rich has used before to refer to her
own formation as the daughter of a Jewish man and a Gentile woman. It appears
for the fist time in a long poem, "Readings of History," included in Snapshots of
a Daughter-in-Law, where she describes herself as "Split at the root, neither
Gentile nor Jew, Yankee nor Rebel."

And, in a 1982 essay, "Split at the Root: An Essay on Jewish Identity," she
says of that poem: "I was still trying to have it both ways: to be neither/nor, trying to live (with my Jewish husband and three children more Jewish in ancestry
than I) in the predominantly gentile, Yankee academic world of Cambridge, Massachusetts." The essay, "Split at the Root," concludes with these paragraphs:

> Sometimes I feel I have seen too long from too many disconnected
> angles: white, Jewish, anti-Semite, racist, anti-racist, once-married,
> lesbian, middle-class, feminist, exmatriate Southerner, split at the
> root: *that I will never bring them whole. I would have liked, in this*
> *essay, to bring together the meanings of anti-Semitism and racism as*
> *I have experienced them and as I believe they intersect in the world*
> *beyond my life. But I am not able to do this yet.*

And:

> This essay, then, has no conclusions: it is another beginning, for me.
> Not just a way of saying, in 1982 Right-wing America, I too will
> wear the yellow star. *It's a moving into accountability, enlarging*
> *the range of accountability. I know that in the rest of my life, the next*
> *half-century or so, every aspect of my identity will have to be en-*
> *gaged. The middle-class white girl taught to trade obedience for privi-*
> *lege. The Jewish lesbian raised to be a heterosexual Gentile. The*
> *woman who first heard oppression named and analyzed in the Black*
> *civil rights struggle. The woman with three sons, the feminist who*
> *hates male violence. The woman limping with a cane, the woman who*
> *has stopped bleeding, are also accountable. The poet who knows that*
> *beautiful language can lie, that the oppressor's language sometimes*
> *sounds beautiful. The woman trying, as part of her resistance, to*
> *clean up her act.*

Adrienne Rich has published fifteen books of poetry and four collections of
prose. They include Blood, Bread, and Poetry: Selected Prose *(1986);* An
Atlas of the Difficult World: Poems, 1988–91 *(1991), which was awarded the*
1992 Los Angeles Times Book Prize for poetry and was a finalist for both the Na-
tional Book Award and the National Book Critics Circle Award; Collected Early

Poems: 1950–1970 *(1993);* Dark Fields of the Republic: Poems 1991–1995 *(1995);* Midnight Salvage: Poems 1995–1998 *(1999); and* Arts of the Possible: Essays and Conversations *(2001). Rich has taught at Columbia, Brandeis, Cornell, Rutgers, and Stanford universities, Swarthmore College, and the City College of New York. Among her many awards and honors she has held two Guggenheim Fellowships and an Amy Lowell Traveling Fellowship. She has been a member of the department of literature of the American Academy and Institute of Arts and Letters since 1990. In 1997 Rich was awarded the Academy's Wallace Stevens Award for outstanding and proven mastery in the art of poetry, and in 1999 she was elected a Chancellor of the Academy. In 1999 she received the Lifetime Achievement Award from the Lannan Foundation. She lives in northern California.*

After the essay "When We Dead Awaken," we have included a selection of poems from Rich's 1986 book, Your Native Land, Your Life, *a book that addresses questions of legacy, heritage, and inheritance.*

When We Dead Awaken: Writing as Re-Vision°

The Modern Language Association is both marketplace and funeral parlor for the professional study of Western literature in North America. Like all gatherings of the professions, it has been and remains a "procession of the sons of educated men" (Virginia Woolf): a congeries of old-boys' networks, academicians rehearsing their numb canons in sessions dedicated to the literature of white males, junior scholars under the lash of "publish or perish" delivering papers in the bizarrely lit drawing-rooms of immense hotels: a ritual competition veering between cynicism and desperation.

However, in the interstices of these gentlemanly rites (or, in Mary Daly's words, on the boundaries of this patriarchal space),[1] some feminist scholars, teachers, and graduate students, joined by feminist writers, editors, and publishers, have for a decade been creating more subversive occasions, challenging the sacredness of the gentlemanly canon, sharing the rediscovery of buried works by women, asking women's questions, bringing literary history and criticism back to life in both senses. The Commission of the Status of Women in the Profession was formed in 1969, and held its first public event in 1970. In 1971 the Commission

---

As Rich explains, this essay—written in 1971—was first published in 1972 and then included in her volume *On Lies, Secrets, and Silence* (1979). At that time she added the introductory note reprinted here, as well as some notes, identified as *"A.R., 1978."* [Editor's note in the Norton edition.]

asked Ellen Peck Killoh, Tillie Olsen, Elaine Reuben, and myself, with Elaine Hedges as moderator, to talk on "The Woman Writer in the Twentieth Century." The essay that follows was written for that forum, and later published, along with the other papers from the forum and workshops, in an issue of College English *edited by Elaine Hedges ("Women Writing and Teaching," vol. 34, no. 1, October 1972). With a few revisions, mainly updating, it was reprinted in* American Poets *in 1976, edited by William Heyen (New York: Bobbs-Merrill, 1976). That later text is the one published here.*

The challenge flung by feminists at the accepted literary canon, at the methods of teaching it, and at the biased and astigmatic view of male "literary scholarship," has not diminished in the decade since the first Women's Forum; it has become broadened and intensified more recently by the challenges of black and lesbian feminists pointing out that feminist literary criticism itself has overlooked or held back from examining the work of black women and lesbians. The dynamic between a political vision and the demand for a fresh vision of literature is clear: without a growing feminist movement, the first inroads of feminist scholarship could not have been made; without the sharpening of a black feminist consciousness, black women's writing would have been left in limbo between misogynist black male critics and white feminists still struggling to unearth a white women's tradition; without an articulate lesbian/feminist movement, lesbian writing would still be lying in that closet where many of us used to sit reading forbidden books "in a bad light."

Much, much more is yet to be done; and university curricula have of course changed very little as a result of all this. What *is* changing is the availability of knowledge, of vital texts, the visible effects on women's lives of seeing, hearing our wordless or negated experience affirmed and pursued further in language.

Ibsen's *When We Dead Awaken* is a play about the use that the male artist and thinker—in the process of creating culture as we know it—has made of women, in his life and in his work; and about a woman's slow struggling awakening to the use to which her life has been put. Bernard Shaw wrote in 1900 of this play:

> [Ibsen] shows us that no degradation ever devised or permitted is as disastrous as this degradation; that through it women can die into luxuries for men and yet can kill them; that men and women are becoming conscious of this; and that what remains to be seen as perhaps the most interesting of all imminent social developments is what will happen "when we dead awaken."[2]

It's exhilarating to be alive in a time of awakening consciousness; it can also be confusing, disorienting, and painful. The awakening of dead or sleeping consciousness has already affected the lives of millions of women, even those who don't know it yet. It is also affecting the lives of men, even those who deny its claims upon them. The argument will go on whether an oppressive economic class system is responsible for the oppressive nature of male/female relations, or whether, in fact, patriarchy— the domination of males—is the original model of oppression on which all others are based. But in the last few years the women's movement has drawn inescapable and illuminating connections between our sexual lives and our political institutions. The sleepwalkers are coming awake, and for the first time this awakening has a collective reality; it is no longer such a lonely thing to open one's eyes.

Re-vision—the act of looking back, of seeing with fresh eyes, of entering an old text from a new critical direction—is for women more than a chapter in cultural history: it is an act of survival. Until we can understand the assumptions in which we are drenched we cannot know ourselves. And this drive to self-knowledge, for women, is more than a search for identity: it is part of our refusal of the self-destructiveness of male-dominated society. A radical critique of literature, feminist in its impulse, would take the work first of all as a clue to how we live, how we have been living, how we have been led to imagine ourselves, how our language has trapped as well as liberated us, how the very act of naming has been till now a male prerogative, and how we can begin to see and name—and therefore live—afresh. A change in the concept of sexual identity is essential if we are not going to see the old political order reassert itself in every new revolution. We need to know the writing of the past, and know it differently than we have ever known it; not to pass on a tradition but to break its hold over us.

For writers, and at this moment for women writers in particular, there is the challenge and promise of a whole new psychic geography to be explored. But there is also a difficult and dangerous walking on the ice, as we try to find language and images for the consciousness we are just coming into, and with little in the past to support us. I want to talk about some aspect of this difficulty and this danger.

Jane Harrison, the great classical anthropologist, wrote in 1914 in a letter to her friend Gilbert Murray:

> By and by, about "Women," it has bothered me often—why do women never want to write poetry about Man as a sex—why is Woman a dream and a terror to man and not the other way around? . . . Is it mere convention and propriety, or something deeper?[3]

I think Jane Harrison's question cuts deep into the myth-making tradition, the romantic tradition; deep into what women and men have been to each other; and deep into the psyche of the woman writer. Thinking about that question, I began thinking of the work of two twentieth-century women poets, Sylvia Plath and Diane Wakoski. It strikes me that in the work of both Man appears as, if not a dream, a fascination and a terror; and that the source of the fascination and the terror is, simply, Man's power—to dominate, tyrannize, choose, or reject the woman. The charisma of Man seems to come purely from his power over her and his control of the world by force, not from anything fertile or life-giving in him. And, in the work of both these poets, it is finally the woman's sense of *herself*—embattled, possessed—that gives the poetry its dynamic charge, its rhythms of struggle, need, will, and female energy. Until recently this female anger and this furious awareness of the Man's power over her were not available materials to the female poet, who tended to write of Love as the source of her suffering, and to view that victimization by Love as an almost inevitable fate. Or, like Marianne Moore and Elizabeth Bishop, she kept sexuality at a measured and chiseled distance in her poems.

One answer to Jane Harrison's question has to be that historically men and women have played very different parts in each others' lives. Where woman has been a luxury for man, and has served as the painter's model and the poet's muse, but also as comforter, nurse, cook, bearer of his seed, secretarial assistant, and copyist of manuscripts, man has played a quite different role for the female artist. Henry James repeats an incident which the writer Prosper Mérimée described, of how, while he was living with George Sand,

> he once opened his eyes, in the raw winter dawn, to see his companion, in a dressing-gown, on her knees before the domestic hearth, a candle-stick beside her and a red *madras* round her head, making bravely, with her own hands the fire that was to enable her to sit down betimes to urgent pen and paper. The story represents him as having felt that the spectacle chilled his ardor and tried his taste; her appearance was unfortunate, her occupation an inconsequence, and her industry a reproof—the result of all which was a lively irritation and an early rupture.[4]

The specter of this kind of male judgment, along with the misnaming and thwarting of her needs by a culture controlled by males, has created problems for the woman writer: problems of contact with herself, problems of language and style, problems of energy and survival.

In rereading Virginia Woolf's *A Room of One's Own* (1929) for the first time in some years, I was astonished at the sense of effort, of pains taken, of dogged tentativeness, in the tone of that essay. And I recognized that tone. I had heard it often enough, in myself and in other women. It is the tone of a woman almost in touch with her anger, who is determined not to appear angry, who is *willing* herself to be calm, detached, and even charming in a roomful of men where things have been said which are attacks on her very integrity. Virginia Woolf is addressing an audience of women, but she is acutely conscious—as she always was—of being overheard by men: by Morgan and Lytton and Maynard Keynes and for that matter by her father, Leslie Stephen.[5] She drew the language out into an exacerbated thread in her determination to have her own sensibility yet protect it from those masculine presences. Only at rare moments in that essay do you hear the passion in her voice; she was trying to sound as cool as Jane Austen, as Olympian as Shakespeare, because that is the way the men of the culture thought a writer should sound.

No male writer has written primarily or even largely for women, or with the sense of women's criticism as a consideration when he chooses his materials, his theme, his language. But to a lesser or greater extent, every woman writer has written for men even when, like Virginia Woolf, she was supposed to be addressing women. If we have come to the point when this balance might begin to change, when women can stop being haunted, not only by "convention and propriety" but by internalized fears of being and saying themselves, then it is an extraordinary moment for the woman writer—and reader.

I have hesitated to do what I am going to do now, which is to use myself as an illustration. For one thing, it's a lot easier and less dangerous to talk about other women writers. But there is something else. Like Virginia Woolf, I am aware of the women who are not with us here because they are washing the dishes and looking after the children. Nearly fifty years after she spoke, that fact remains largely unchanged. And I am thinking also of women whom she left out of the picture altogether—women who are washing other people's dishes and caring for other people's children, not to mention women who went on the streets last night in order to feed their children. We seem to be special women here, we have liked to think of ourselves as special, and we have known that men would tolerate, even romanticize us as special, as long as our words and actions didn't threaten their privilege of tolerating or rejecting us and our work according to *their* ideas of what a special woman ought to be. An important insight of the radical women's movement has been how divisive and how ultimately destructive is this myth of the special woman, who is also the token woman. Every one of us here in this room has had great luck—we are teachers, writers, academicians; our own gifts could not have been enough, for we all know women whose gifts are buried or aborted. Our struggles can have meaning and our privileges—however precarious under patriarchy—can be justified only if they can help to change the lives of women whose gifts—and whose very being—continue to be thwarted and silenced.

My own luck was being born white and middle-class into a house full of books, with a father who encouraged me to read and write. So for about twenty years I wrote for a particular man, who criticized and praised me and made me feel I was indeed "special." The obverse side of this, of course, was that I tried for a long time to please him, or rather, not to displease him. And then of course there were other men—writers, teachers—the Man, who was not a terror or a dream but a literary master and a master in other ways less easy to acknowledge. And there were all those poems about women, written by men: it seemed to be a given that men wrote poems and women frequently inhabited them. These women were almost always beautiful, but threatened with the loss of beauty, the loss of youth—the fate worse than death. Or, they were beautiful and died young, like Lucy and Lenore. Or, the woman was like Maud Gonne, cruel and disastrously mistaken, and the poem reproached her because she had refused to become a luxury for the poet.

A lot is being said today about the influence that the myths and images of women have on all of us who are products of culture. I think it has been a peculiar confusion to the girl or woman who tries to write because she is peculiarly susceptible to language. She goes to poetry or fiction looking for *her* way of being in the world, since she too has been putting words and images together; she is looking eagerly for guides, maps, possibilities; and over and over in the "words' masculine persuasive force" of literature she comes up against something that negates everything she is about: she meets the image of Woman in books written by men. She finds a terror and a dream, she finds a beautiful pale face, she finds La Belle Dame Sans Merci, she finds Juliet or Tess or Salomé, but precisely what she does not find is that absorbed, drudging, puzzled, sometimes inspired creature, herself, who sits at a desk trying to put words together.

So what does she do? What did I do? I read the older women poets with their peculiar keenness and ambivalence: Sappho, Christina Rossetti, Emily Dickinson, Elinor Wylie, Edna Millay, H. D. I discovered that the woman poet most admired at the time (by men) was Marianne Moore, who was maidenly, elegant, intellectual, discreet. But even in reading these women I was looking in them for the same things I had found in the poetry of men, because I wanted women poets to be the equals of men, and to be equal was still confused with sounding the same.

I know that my style was formed first by male poets: by the men I was reading as an undergraduate—Frost, Dylan Thomas, Donne, Auden, MacNeice, Stevens, Yeats. What I chiefly learned from them was craft.[6] But poems are like dreams: in them you put what you don't know you know. Looking back at poems I wrote before I was twenty-one, I'm startled because beneath the conscious craft are glimpses of the split I even then experienced between the girl who wrote poems, who defined herself in writing poems, and the girl who was to define herself by her relationships with men. "Aunt Jennifer's Tigers" (1951), written while I was a student, looks with deliberate detachment at this split.

> Aunt Jennifer's tigers stride across a screen,
> Bright topaz denizens of a world of green.

They do not fear the men beneath the tree;
They pace in sleek chivalric certainty.

Aunt Jennifer's fingers fluttering through her wool
Find even the ivory needle hard to pull.
The massive weight of Uncle's wedding band
Sits heavily upon Aunt Jennifer's hand.

When Aunt is dead, her terrified hands will lie
Still ringed with ordeals she was mastered by.
The tigers in the panel that she made
Will go on striding, proud and unafraid.

In writing this poem, composed and apparently cool as it is, I thought I
was creating a portrait of an imaginary woman. But this woman suffers
from the opposition of her imagination, worked out in tapestry, and her
lifestyle, "ringed with ordeals she was mastered by." It was important to
me that Aunt Jennifer was a person as distinct from myself as possible—
distanced by the formalism of the poem, by its objective, observant tone—
even by putting the woman in a different generation.

In those years formalism was part of the strategy—like asbestos
gloves, it allowed me to handle materials I couldn't pick up barehanded.
A later strategy was to use the persona of a man, as I did in "The Loser"
(1958):

> *A man thinks of the woman he once loved:*
> *first, after her wedding, and then nearly a*
> *decade later.*

> I
> I kissed you, bride and lost, and went
> home from that bourgeois sacrament,
> your cheek still tasting cold upon
> my lips that gave you benison
> with all the swagger that they knew—
> as losers somehow learn to do.

> Your wedding made my eyes ache; soon
> the world would be worse off for one
> more golden apple dropped to ground
> without the least protesting sound,
> and you would windfall lie, and we
> forget your shimmer on the tree.

> Beauty is always wasted: if
> not Mignon's song sung to the deaf,
> at all events to the unmoved.
> A face like yours cannot be loved
> long or seriously enough.
> Almost, we seem to hold it off.

II
Well, you are tougher than I thought.
Now when the wash with ice hangs taut
this morning of St. Valentine,
I see you strip the squeaking line,
your body weighed against the load,
and all my groans can do no good.

Because you still are beautiful,
though squared and stiffened by the pull
of what nine windy years have done.
You have three daughters, lost a son.
I see all your intelligence
flung into that unwearied stance.

My envy is of no avail.
I turn my head and wish him well
who chafed your beauty into use
and lives forever in a house
lit by the friction of your mind.
You stagger in against the wind.

   I finished college, published my first book by a fluke, as it seemed to
me, and broke off a love affair. I took a job, lived alone, went on writing,
fell in love. I was young, full of energy, and the book seemed to mean
that others agreed I was a poet. Because I was also determined to prove
that as a woman poet I could also have what was then defined as a "full"
woman's life, I plunged in my early twenties into marriage and had three
children before I was thirty. There was nothing overt in the environment
to warn me: these were the fifties, and in reaction to the earlier wave of
feminism, middle-class women were making careers of domestic perfection, working to send their husbands through professional schools, then
retiring to raise large families. People were moving out to the suburbs,
technology was going to be the answer to everything, even sex; the family was in its glory. Life was extremely private; women were isolated
from each other by the loyalties of marriage. I have a sense that women
didn't talk to each other much in the fifties—not about their secret empti-
nesses, their frustrations. I went on trying to write; my second book and
first child appeared in the same month. But by the time that book came
out I was already dissatisfied with those poems, which seemed to me
mere exercises for poems I hadn't written. The book was praised, however, for its "gracefulness"; I had a marriage and a child. If there were
doubts, if there were periods of null depression or active despairing,
these could only mean that I was ungrateful, insatiable, perhaps a monster.
   About the time my third child was born, I felt that I had either to consider myself a failed woman and a failed poet, or to try to find some synthesis by which to understand what was happening to me. What frightened me most was the sense of drift, of being pulled along a current which

called itself my destiny, but in which I seemed to be losing touch with whoever I had been, with the girl who had experienced her own will and energy almost ecstatically at times, walking around a city or riding a train at night or typing in a student room. In a poem about my grandmother I wrote (of myself): "A young girl, thought sleeping, is certified dead" ("Halfway"). I was writing very little, partly from fatigue, that female fatigue of suppressed anger and loss of contact with my own being; partly from the discontinuity of female life with its attention to small chores, errands, work that others constantly undo, small children's constant needs. What I did write was unconvincing to me; my anger and frustration were hard to acknowledge in or out of poems because in fact I cared a great deal about my husband and my children. Trying to look back and understand that time I have tried to analyze the real nature of the conflict. Most, if not all, human lives are full of fantasy—passive day-dreaming which need not be acted on. But to write poetry or fiction, or even to think well, is not to fantasize, or to put fantasies on paper. For a poem to coalesce, for a character or an action to take shape, there has to be an imaginative transformation of reality which is in no way passive. And a certain freedom of the mind is needed—freedom to press on, to enter the currents of your thought like a glider pilot, knowing that your motion can be sustained, that the buoyancy of your attention will not be suddenly snatched away. Moreover, if the imagination is to transcend and transform experience it has to question, to challenge, to conceive of alternatives, perhaps to the very life you are living at that moment. You have to be free to play around with the notion that day might be night, love might be hate; nothing can be too sacred for the imagination to turn into its opposite or to call experimentally by another name. For writing is renaming. Now, to be maternally with small children all day in the old way, to be with a man in the old way of marriage, requires a holding-back, a putting-aside of that imaginative activity, and demands instead a kind of conservatism. I want to make it clear that I am *not* saying that in order to write well, or think well, it is necessary to become unavailable to others, or to become a devouring ego. This has been the myth of the masculine artist and thinker; and I do not accept it. But to be a female human being trying to fulfill traditional female functions in a traditional way *is* in direct conflict with the subversive function of the imagination. The word traditional is important here. There must be ways, and we will be finding out more and more about them, in which the energy of creation and the energy of relation can be united. But in those years I always felt the conflict as a failure of love in myself. I had thought I was choosing a full life; the life available to most men, in which sexuality, work, and parenthood could coexist. But I felt, at twenty-nine, guilt toward the people closest to me, and guilty toward my own being.

I wanted, then, more than anything, the one thing of which there was never enough: time to think, time to write. The fifties and early sixties were years of rapid revelations: the sit-ins and marches in the South, the Bay of

Pigs, the early antiwar movement, raised large questions—questions for which the masculine world of the academy around me seemed to have expert and fluent answers. But I needed to think for myself—about pacifism and dissent and violence, about poetry and society, and about my own relationship to all these things. For about ten years I was reading in fierce snatches, scribbling in notebooks, writing poetry in fragments; I was looking desperately for clues, because if there were no clues then I thought I might be insane. I wrote in a notebook about this time:

> Paralyzed by the sense that there exists a mesh of relationships—e.g., between my anger at the children, my sensual life, pacifism, sex (I mean sex in its broadest significance, not merely sexual desire)—an interconnectedness which, if I could see it, make it valid, would give me back myself, make it possible to function lucidly and passionately. Yet I grope in and out among these dark webs.

I think I began at this point to feel that politics was not something "out there" but something "in here" and of the essence of my condition.

In the late fifties I was able to write, for the first time, directly about experiencing myself as a woman. The poem was jotted in fragments during children's naps, brief hours in a library, or at 3:00 A.M. after rising with a wakeful child. I despaired of doing any continuous work at this time. Yet I began to feel that my fragments and scraps had a common consciousness and a common theme, one which I would have been very unwilling to put on paper at an earlier time because I had been taught that poetry should be "universal," which meant, of course, nonfemale. Until then I had tried very much *not* to identify myself as a female poet. Over two years I wrote a ten-part poem called "Snapshots of a Daughter-in-Law" (1958–1960), in a longer looser mode than I'd ever trusted myself with before. It was an extraordinary relief to write that poem. It strikes me now as too literary, too dependent on allusion; I hadn't found the courage yet to do without authorities, or even to use the pronoun "I"—the woman in the poem is always "she." One section of it, No. 2, concerns a woman who thinks she is going mad; she is haunted by voices telling her to resist and rebel, voices which she can hear but not obey.

2.
Banging the coffee-pot into the sink
she hears the angels chiding, and looks out
past the raked gardens to the sloppy sky.
Only a week since They said: *Have no patience.*

The next time it was: *Be insatiable.*
Then: *Save yourself; others you cannot save.*
Sometimes she's let the tapstream scald her arm,
a match burn to her thumbnail,

or held her hand above the kettle's snout
right in the woolly steam. They are probably angels,
since nothing hurts her anymore, except
each morning's grit blowing into her eyes.

The poem "Orion," written five years later, is a poem of reconnection
with a part of myself I had felt I was losing—the active principle, the energetic imagination, the "half-brother" whom I projected, as I had for many
years, into the constellation Orion. It's no accident that the words "cold
and egotistical" appear in this poem, and are applied to myself.

Far back when I went zig-zagging
through tamarack pastures
you were my genius, you
my cast-iron Viking, my helmed
lion-heart king in prison.
Years later now you're young

my fierce half-brother, staring
down from that simplified west
your breast open, your belt dragged down
by an oldfashioned thing, a sword
the last bravado you won't give over
though it weighs you down as you stride

and the stars in it are dim
and maybe have stopped burning.
But you burn, and I know it;
as I throw back my head to take you in
an old transfusion happens again:
divine astronomy is nothing to it.

Indoors I bruise and blunder,
break faith, leave ill enough
alone, a dead child born in the dark.
Night cracks up over the chimney,
pieces of time, frozen geodes
come showering down in the grate.

A man reaches behind my eyes
and finds them empty
a woman's head turns away
from my head in the mirror
children are dying my death
and eating crumbs of my life.

Pity is not your forte.
Calmly you ache up there
pinned aloft in your crow's nest,
my speechless pirate!
You take it all for granted
and when I look you back

it's with a starlike eye
shooting its cold and egotistical spear
where it can do least damage.
Breathe deep! No hurt, no pardon
out here in the cold with you
you with your back to the wall.

The choice still seemed to be between "love"—womanly, maternal love, altruistic love—a love defined and ruled by the weight of an entire culture; and egotism—a force directed by men into creation, achievement, ambition, often at the expense of others, but justifiably so. For weren't they men, and wasn't that their destiny as womanly, selfless love was ours? We know now that the alternatives are false ones—that the word "love" is itself in need of re-vision.

There is a companion poem to "Orion," written three years later, in which at last the woman in the poem and the woman writing the poem become the same person. It is called "Planetarium," and it was written after a visit to a real planetarium, where I read an account of the work of Caroline Herschel, the astronomer, who worked with her brother William, but whose name remained obscure, as his did not.

Thinking of Caroline Herschel, 1750–1848,
astronomer, sister of William; and others

A woman in the shape of a monster
a monster in the shape of a woman
the skies are full of them

a woman   'in the snow
among the Clocks and instruments
or measuring the ground with poles'

in her 98 years to discover
8 comets

she whom the moon ruled
like us
levitating into the night sky
riding the polished lenses

Galaxies of women, there
doing penance for impetuousness
ribs chilled
in those spaces   of the mind

An eye,

  'virile, precise and absolutely certain'
from the mad webs of Uranusborg

                 encountering the NOVA

every impulse of light exploding
from the core

as life flies out of us

    Tycho whispering at last
    'Let me not seem to have lived in vain'

What we see, we see
and seeing is changing

the light that shrivels a mountain
and leaves a man alive

Heartbeat of the pulsar
heart sweating through my body

The radio impulse
pouring in from Taurus

    I am bombarded yet   I stand

I have been standing all my life in the
direct path of a battery of signals
the most accurately transmitted most
untranslateable language in the universe
I am a galactic cloud so deep   so invo-
luted that a light wave could take 15
years to travel through me   And has
taken   I am an instrument in the shape
of a woman trying to translate pulsations
into images   for the relief of the body
and the reconstruction of the mind.

In closing I want to tell you about a dream I had last summer. I dreamed I was asked to read my poetry at a mass women's meeting, but when I began to read, what came out were the lyrics of a blues song. I share this dream with you because it seemed to me to say something about the problems and the future of the woman writer, and probably of women in general. The awakening of consciousness is not like the crossing of a frontier—one step and you are in another country. Much of woman's poetry has been of the nature of the blues song: a cry of pain, of victimization, or a lyric of seduction.[7] And today, much poetry by women—and prose for that matter—is charged with anger. I think we need to go through that anger, and we will betray our own reality if we try, as Virginia Woolf was trying, for an objectivity, a detachment, that would make us sound more like Jane Austen or Shakespeare. We know more than Jane Austen or Shakespeare knew: more than Jane Austen because our lives are more complex, more than Shakespeare because we know more about the lives of women—Jane Austen and Virginia Woolf included.

Both the victimization and the anger experienced by women are real, and have real sources, everywhere in the environment, built into society, language, the structures of thought. They will go on being trapped and explored by poets, among others. We can neither deny them, nor will we rest there. A new generation of women poets is already working out of the psychic energy released when women begin to move out towards what the feminist philosopher Mary Daly has described as the "new space" on the boundaries of patriarchy.[8] Women are speaking to and of women in these poems, out of a newly released courage to name, to love each other, to share risk and grief and celebration.

To the eye of a feminist, the work of Western male poets now writing reveals a deep, fatalistic pessimism as to the possibilities of change, whether societal or personal, along with a familiar and threadbare use of women (and nature) as redemptive on the one hand, threatening on the other; and a new tide of phallocentric sadism and overt woman-hating which matches the sexual brutality of recent films. "Political" poetry by men remains stranded amid the struggles for power among male groups; in condemning U.S. imperialism or the Chilean junta the poet can claim to speak for the oppressed while remaining, as male, part of a system of sexual oppression. The enemy is always outside the self, the struggle somewhere else. The mood of isolation, self-pity, and self-imitation that pervades "nonpolitical" poetry suggests that a profound change in masculine consciousness will have to precede any new male poetic—or other—inspiration. The creative energy of patriarchy is fast running out; what remains is its self-generating energy for destruction. As women, we have our work cut out for us.

NOTES

[1] Mary Daly, *Beyond God the Father* (Boston: Beacon, 1973), pp. 40–41.

[2] G. B. Shaw, *The Quintessence of Ibsenism* (New York: Hill & Wang, 1922), p. 139.

[3] J. G. Stewart, *Jane Ellen Harrison: A Portrait from Letters* (London: Merlin, 1959), p. 140.

[4] Henry James, "Notes on Novelists," in *Selected Literary Criticism of Henry James,* Morris Shapira, ed. (London: Heinemann, 1963), pp. 157–58.

[5] *A. R., 1978:* This intuition of mine was corroborated when, early in 1978, I read the correspondence between Woolf and Dame Ethel Smyth (Henry W. and Albert A. Berg Collection, The New York Public Library, Astor, Lenox and Tilden Foundations); in a letter dated June 8, 1933, Woolf speaks of having kept her own personality out of *A Room of One's Own* lest she not be taken seriously: "... how personal, so will they say, rubbing their hands with glee, women always are; *I even hear them as I write.*" (Italics mine.)

[6] *A. R., 1978:* Yet I spent months, at sixteen, memorizing and writing imitations of Millay's sonnets; and in notebooks of that period I find what are obviously attempts to imitate Dickinson's metrics and verbal compression. I knew H. D. only through anthologized lyrics; her epic poetry was not then available to me.

[7] *A. R., 1978:* When I dreamed that dream, was I wholly ignorant of the tradition of Bessie Smith and other women's blues lyrics which transcended victimization to sing of resistance and independence?

[8] Mary Daly, *Beyond God the Father: Towards a Philosophy of Women's Liberation* (Boston: Beacon, 1973).

Sources

I

Sixteen years.   The narrow, rough-gullied backroads
almost the same.   The farms: almost the same,
a new barn here, a new roof there, a rusting car,
collapsed sugar-house, trailer, new young wife
trying to make a lawn instead of a dooryard,
new names, old kinds of names: Rocquette, Desmarais,
Clark, Pierce, Stone.   Gossier.   No names of mine.

The vixen I met at twilight on Route 5
south of Willoughby: long dead.   She was an omen
to me, surviving, herding her cubs
in the silvery bend of the road
in nineteen sixty-five.

Shapes of things: so much the same
they feel like eternal forms: the house and barn
on the rise above May Pond; the bow of Pisgah;
the face of milkweed blooming,
brookwater pleating over slanted granite,
boletus under pine, the half-composted needles
it broke through patterned on its skin.
Shape of queen anne's lace, with the drop of blood.
Bladder-campion veined with purple.
Multifoliate heal-all.

II

I refuse to become a seeker for cures.
Everything that has ever
helped me has come through what already
lay stored in me.   Old things, diffuse, unnamed, lie strong
across my heart.
                 This is from where
my strength comes, even when I miss my strength
even when it turns on me
like a violent master.

III

From where?   the voice asks coldly.

This is the voice in cold morning air
that pierces dreams.   *From where does your strength come?*

Old things . . .

From where does your strength come, you Southern Jew?
split at the root, raised in a castle of air?

Yes.   I expected this.   I have known for years
the question was coming.   *From where*

(not from these, surely,
Protestant separatists, Jew-baiters, nightriders

who fired in Irasburg in nineteen-sixty-eight
on a black family newly settled in these hills)

From where

the dew grows thick late August on the fierce green grass
and on the wooden sill and on the stone

the mountains stand in an extraordinary
point of no return   though still are green

collapsed shed-boards gleam like pewter in the dew
the realms of touch-me-not   fiery with tiny tongues

cover the wild ground of the woods

IV

With whom do you believe your lot is cast?
From where does your strength come?

I think somehow, somewhere
every poem of mine must repeat those questions

which are not the same.   There is a *whom*, a *where*
that is not chosen   that is given   and sometimes falsely given

in the beginning we grasp whatever we can
to survive

V

All during World War II
I told myself I had some special destiny:
there had to be a reason
I was not living in a bombed-out house
or cellar   hiding out with rats

there had to be a reason
I was growing up safe, American
with sugar rationed in a Mason jar

split at the root   white-skinned social christian
neither gentile nor Jew

through the immense silence
of the Holocaust

I had no idea of what I had been spared

still less of the women and men   my kin
the Jews of Vicksburg or Birmingham
whose lives must have been strategies no less
than the vixen's on Route 5

VI

If they had played the flute, or chess
I was told   I was not told what they told
their children when the Klan rode
how they might have seen themselves

a chosen people

of shopkeepers
clinging by strategy to a way of life
that had its own uses for them

proud of their length of sojourn in America
deploring the late-comers   the peasants from Russia

I saw my father building
his rootless ideology

his private castle in air

in that most dangerous place, the family home
we were the chosen people

In the beginning we grasp whatever we can

VII

For years I struggled with you: your categories, your theories,
your will, the cruelty which came inextricable from your love.   For
years all arguments I carried on in my head were with you.   I saw
myself, the eldest daughter raised as a son, taught to study but not
to pray, taught to hold reading and writing sacred: the eldest daughter
in a house with no son, she who must overthrow the father, take
what he taught her and use it against him.   All this in a castle of
air, the floating world of the assimilated who know and deny they
will always be aliens.
    After your death I met you again as the face of patriarchy, could
name at last precisely the principle you embodied, there was an
ideology at last which let me dispose of you, identify the suffering
you caused, hate you righteously as part of a system, the kingdom
of the fathers.   I saw the power and arrogance of the male as your
true watermark; I did not see beneath it the suffering of the Jew,

the alien stamp you bore, because you had deliberately arranged that it should be invisible to me. It is only now, under a powerful, womanly lens, that I can decipher your suffering and deny no part of my own.

XVIII

There is something more than self-hatred. That still outlives
these photos of the old Ashkenazi life:
we are gifted children at camp in the country
or orphaned children in kindergarten
we are hurrying along the rare book dealers' street
with the sunlight striking one side
we are walking the wards of the Jewish hospital
along diagonal squares   young serious nurses
we are part of a family group
formally taken in 1936
with tables, armchairs, ferns
(behind us, in our lives, the muddy street
and the ragged shames
the street-musician, the weavers lined for strike)
we are part of a family wearing white head-bandages
we were beaten in a pogrom

The place where all tracks end
is the place where history was meant to stop
but does not stop   where thinking
was meant to stop but does not stop
where the pattern was meant to give way at last
                                                    but only

becomes a different pattern
                                terrible, threadbare
strained   familiar   on-going

XX

The faithful drudging child
the child at the oak desk whose penmanship,
hard work, style will win her prizes
becomes the woman with a mission, not to win prizes
but to change the laws of history.
How she gets this mission
is not clear, how the boundaries of perfection
explode, leaving her cheekbone grey with smoke
a piece of her hair singed off, her shirt
spattered with earth . . . Say that she grew up in a house
with talk of books, ideal societies—

she is gripped by a blue, a foreign air,
a desert absolute: dragged by the roots of her own will
into another scene of choices.

XXII

I have resisted this for years, writing to you as if you could hear me. It's been different with my father: he and I always had a kind of rhetoric going with each other, a battle between us, it didn't matter if one of us was alive or dead.   But, you, I've had a sense of protecting your existence, not using it merely as a theme for poetry or tragic musings; letting you dwell in the minds of those who have reason to miss you, in your way, or their way, not mine. The living, writers especially, are terrible projectionists. I hate the way they use the dead.

Yet I can't finish this without speaking to you, not simply of you. You knew there was more left than food and humor. Even as you said that in 1953 I knew it was a formula you had found, to stand between you and pain. The deep crevices of black pumpernickel under the knife, the sweet butter and red onions we ate on those slices; the lox and cream cheese on fresh onion rolls; bowls of sour cream mixed with cut radishes, cucumber, scallions; green tomatoes and kosher dill pickles in half-translucent paper; these, you said, were the remnants of the culture, along with the fresh *challah* which turned stale so fast but looked so beautiful.

That's way I want to speak to you now. To say: no person, trying to take responsibility for her or his identity, should have to be so alone. There must be those among whom we can sit down and weep, and still be counted as warriors. (I make up this strange, angry packet for you, threaded with love.) I think you thought there was no such place for you, and perhaps there was none then, and perhaps there is none now; but we will have to make it, we who want an end to suffering, who want to change the laws of history, if we are not to *give ourselves away.*

•   •   •

I have wished I could rest among the beautiful and common weeds I can name, both here and in other tracts of the globe. But there is no finite knowing, no such rest. Innocent birds, deserts, morning-glories, point to choices, leading away from the familiar. When I speak of an end to suffering I don't mean anesthesia. I mean knowing the world, and my place in it, not in order to stare with bitterness or detachment, but as a powerful and womanly series of choices: and   here   I   write   the   words,   in   their   fullness: powerful;   womanly.

August 1981–
August 1982

•   •   •   •   •   •   •   •   •   •   •   •   •

QUESTIONS FOR A SECOND READING

1. Rich says, "We need to know the writing of the past, and know it differently than we have ever known it; not to pass on a tradition but to break its hold over us." In what ways does this essay, as an example of a woman writing, both reproduce and revise the genre? As she is writing here, what does Rich *do* with the writing of the past—with the conventions of the essay or the public lecture? As you reread the essay, mark sections that illustrate the ways Rich is either reproducing or revising the conventions of the essay or the public lecture. Where and how does she revise the genre? Where and how does she not? Where does Rich resist tradition? Where does she conform? How might you account for the differences?

2. It is a rare pleasure to hear a poet talk in detail about her work. As you read back through the essay, pay particular attention to what Rich notices in her poems. What *does* she notice? What does she say about what she notices? What does this allow you to say about poems or the making of poems? What does it allow you to say about the responsibilities of a reader?

3. As Rich writes her essay, she refers to a number of literary figures like Morgan, Lytton, and Maynard Keynes, Lucy and Lenore and Maude Gonne, and Plath, Bishop, and Wakoski. Reading through her essay again, make a complete list of the names Rich draws into her discussion. Who are these people? To answer this question you will need to do some library investigation checking such sources as a biographical index, *Who's Who*, and literary texts, or consulting with a reference librarian on how to find such information.

    Once you've identified the names on your list, the next question to consider is how this knowledge influences your reading of Rich. What does each individual represent that merits her or his inclusion? To answer this question you will need to have located and read through at least one text by the individuals—one "primary source," that is—or one text about the individuals—a "secondary source"—you are researching. Why might Rich have chosen to include particular references at particular moments? What differences do they make in her arguments? in your reading of her arguments?

4. "When We Dead Awaken: Writing as Re-Vision" was written in 1971. The poem "Planetarium," the last of those she uses as an example (p. 638), was written in (or around) 1968. The work does not end there, however. Rich has had, and she continues to have, a productive career as a writer. An interesting project would be to find and read a book of poems chosen from a later point in her career. To begin, reread the essay, with particular attention to the trajectory indicated by her treatment of the three poems she offers as examples of "re-vision": the excerpt from

"Snapshots of a Daughter-in-Law" (p. 636), "Orion" (p. 637), and "Planetarium" (p. 638). Think about the direction that is implied, the questions that are raised, and how those questions relate not only to subject matter but to point of view, form, and style. Prepare a discussion for class on how the later book you chose can be seen as a continuation of the process of "re-vision." Be sure to bring copies of one or two new poems to class.

ASSIGNMENTS FOR WRITING

1. Rich says,

   > For a poem to coalesce, for a character or an action to take shape, there has to be an imaginative transformation of reality which is in no way passive. . . . Moreover, if the imagination is to transcend and transform experience it has to question, to challenge, to conceive of alternatives, perhaps to the very life you are living at that moment. You have to be free to play around with the notion that day might be night, love might be hate; nothing can be too sacred for the imagination to turn into its opposite or to call experimentally by another name. For writing is re-naming. (p. 635)

   This is powerful language, and it is interesting to imagine how it might work for a person trying to read and understand one of Rich's poems. For this assignment, begin with a close reading of the quotation from Rich: What is your understanding of her term "imaginative transformation"? What does it allow a writer to do? And why might that be important? Then, as a way of testing Rich's term and your reading of it, choose one of the poems Rich includes in the essay and write an essay of your own that considers the poem as an act of "imaginative transformation." What is transformed into what? and to what end? or to what consequence? What can you say about the poem as an act of "renaming"? as a form of political action?

2. In "When We Dead Awaken: Writing as Re-Vision," Rich chooses five of her poems to represent stages in her history as a poet; however, it is a history not charted entirely (or mostly) by conscious decisions on her part as she tells us when she writes: "poems are like dreams: in them you put what you don't know you know." It is through the act of "re-vision"—of entering the old text of her poems from a new critical direction—that patterns in her work as a writer begin to emerge.

   Write an essay in which you explore Rich's term—"re-vision"—by describing what you consider to be a significant pattern of change in Rich's poems. As you do this work, you will want to attend closely to and quote from the language of her poems and what she has to say about them. You might want to consider such questions as: How does her explanation of herself as a poet inform your reading of her poems? What did she put into her poems that she didn't yet know on a conscious level? What does her poetry reveal about the evolution of Rich as a poet? as a woman?

3.   I have hesitated to do what I am going to do now, which is to use my-
      self as an illustration. For one thing, it's a lot easier and less dangerous
      to talk about other[s]. (p. 631)

      Until we can understand the assumptions in which we are drenched
      we cannot know ourselves. (p.629)

Although Rich tells a story of her own, she does so to provide an illustration of an even larger story—one about what it means to be a woman and
a writer. Tell a story of your own about the ways you might be said to
have been named or shaped or positioned by an established and powerful
culture. Like Rich does (and perhaps with similar hesitation), use your
own experience as an illustration, as a way of investigating both your
own situation and the situation of people like you. You should imagine
that this assignment is a way for you to use (and put to the test) some of
Rich's terms, words like "re-vision," "renaming," and "structure." You
might also want to consider defining key terms specific to your story (for
Rich, for example, a defining term is "patriarchy").

4.   Rich says, "We need to know the writing of the past, and know it differ-
      ently than we have ever known it; not to pass on a tradition but to break
      its hold over us." That "us" includes you too. Look back over your own
      writing (perhaps the drafts and revisions you have written for this
      course), and think back over comments teachers have made, textbooks
      you've seen; think about what student writers do and what they are told
      to do, about the secrets students keep and the secrets teachers keep. You
      can assume, as Rich does, that there are ways of speaking about writing
      that are part of the culture of schooling and that they are designed to pre-
      serve certain ways of writing and thinking and to discourage others.

          One might argue, in other words, that there are traditions here. As
      you look at the evidence of the "past" in your own work, what are its sig-
      nificant features? What might you name this tradition (or these tradi-
      tions)? How would you illustrate its hold on your work or the work of
      students generally? What might you have to do to begin to "know it dif-
      ferently," "to break its hold," or to revise? And, finally, why would some-
      one want (or not want) to break its hold?

5.   Reread the essay "When We Dead Awaken" so that it can provide a
      framework as you read the poems from *Your Native Land, Your Life*
      (p. 641). As you reread, pay particular attention to the trajectory indicated
      by her treatment of the three poems she offers as examples of "re-vision":
      the excerpt from "Snapshots of a Daughter-in-Law" (p. 636), "Orion"
      (p. 637), and "Planetarium" (p. 638). And remember the dates: "When We
      Dead Awaken" was written in 1971; "Split at the Root" was written in
      1982; the poems from *Your Native Land, Your Life* date from around 1986.
      You should be sure to attend to changes in form, style, and presentation
      as well as to variations in subject matter and point of view.

          Write an essay in which you think *from* "When We Dead Awaken" *to*
      these later poems. You could imagine that you are extending the original
      essay, adding paragraphs to the end of the discussion of the poems. That
      discussion is followed by the essay's conclusion: "In closing, I want to tell
      you about a dream I had last summer." You might also consider how Rich

might have revised the conclusion. Or you could use these poems to be in conversation with the Rich of "When We Dead Awaken," in dialogue with her and with her argument, thinking about what she is not yet ready or willing or able to say, to think, or to do.

MAKING CONNECTIONS

1. Adrienne Rich in "When We Dead Awaken: Writing as Re-Vision," Susan Griffin in "Our Secret" (p. 345), and James Baldwin in "Notes of a Native Son" (p. 52) uses each family history to think about and to represent forces beyond the family that shape human life and possibility—patriarchy, war, and race. Susan Griffin explains her motives this way, "One can find traces of every life in each life."

   Perhaps. It is a bold step to think that this is true and to believe that one can, or should, write the family into the national or international narrative. Write an essay in which you read "When We Dead Awaken" alongside one of the other two essays. Your goal is not only to discuss how these writers do what they do, and to what conclusions and to what ends, but also to discuss your sense of what is at stake in such a project. What are the technical issues? How does a skilled writer handle this project? What would lead a writer to write something like this? Would you do it? where and how? for whose benefit?

2. Susan Bordo (p. 139) and Gloria Anzaldúa (p. 23, 36) make strong statements about the situation of women—in relation to the past, to language, politics, and culture. Their essays have certain similarities, but it is also interesting to consider the differences and what these differences might be said to represent. Choose one selection to compare with "When We Dead Awaken," read the two together, marking passages you might use in a discussion, and write an essay in which you examine the interesting differences between these essays. Consider the essays as different forms or schools of feminist thought, different ways of thinking critically about the situations of women. Assume that there is more to say than "different people have different opinions," or "different people write about different subjects." How else might you account for these differences? their significance?

3. In "The Albanian Virgin" (p. 554), Alice Munro plots a story of women in patriarchal culture. Reread this story as an argument, as an example of how fiction and fiction writers do work that could be said to be similar to the work of an essay, like "When We Dead Awaken."

   The central characters in "The Albanian Virgin" are women: Claire, Charlotte, and, in Charlotte's story, Lottar. In the story of Lottar, the men are represented schematically—they drink, they shoot their guns, they kill each other, they don't work very hard. Lottar is concerned with escape, freedom. There is an invitation to read the story through its representation of women and men and to think from the point of view of the women. If there is an argument here, what is it? And where is it? How is it arranged through the various characters and story lines? And if there is an argument, how does the story—or its author, Alice Munro—position you as a reader in relation to that argument?

In "When We Dead Awaken," Adrienne Rich considers the ways in which women are positioned inside a patriarchal culture. The argument here is up front; it is foregrounded in the text.

Write an essay in which you consider these two texts and these two arguments. You should assume that your readers are not familiar with either the story or the essay. You will, then, need to take care to introduce them, to summarize and paraphrase the arguments, to provide a sense of what it is like to read these texts, to think about how a reader is positioned. As you work this out, use the occasion to think about the difference between story and essay. (It is really not enough, perhaps not even accurate, to say that one is true and the other is an invention.) Think about the different ways they address their audiences, the different ways they work on subject and form and argument, and the different commitments they have to persuasion.

RICHARD
RODRIGUEZ

*R*ICHARD RODRIGUEZ, *the son of Mexican immigrants, was born in San Francisco in 1944. He grew up in Sacramento, where he attended Catholic schools before going on to Stanford University, Columbia University, the War-burg Institute in London, and the University of California at Berkeley, eventually completing a Ph.D. in English Renaissance literature. His essays have been pub-lished in* Saturday Review, The American Scholar, Change, *and elsewhere. He now lives in San Francisco and works as a lecturer, educational consultant, and freelance writer. He has published several books:* Days of Obligation: An Argument with My Mexican Father *(1992),* The Ethics of Change *(1992), and* Hunger of Memory *(1981).*

In Hunger of Memory, *a book of autobiographical essays that the* Chris-tian Science Monitor *called "beautifully written, wrung from a sore heart," Rodriguez tells the story of his education, paying particular attention to both the meaning of his success as a student and, as he says, "its consequent price—the loss." Rodriguez's loss is represented most powerfully by his increased alienation from his parents and the decrease of intimate exchanges in family life. His par-ents' primary language was Spanish; his, once he became eager for success in school, was English. But the barrier was not only a language barrier. Rodriguez discovered that the interests he developed at school and through his reading were interests he did not share with those at home—in fact, his desire to speak of them tended to threaten and humiliate his mother and father.*

This separation, Rodriguez argues, is a necessary part of every person's development, even though not everyone experiences it so dramatically. We must leave home and familiar ways of speaking and understanding in order to participate in public life. On these grounds, Rodriguez has been a strong voice against bilingual education, arguing that classes conducted in Spanish will only reinforce Spanish-speaking students' separateness from mainstream American life. Rodriguez's book caused a great deal of controversy upon publication, particularly in the Hispanic community. As one critic argued, "It is indeed painful that Mr. Rodriguez has come to identify himself so completely with the majority culture that he must propagandize for a system of education which can only produce other deprived and impoverished souls like himself."

The selection that follows, Chapter 2 of Hunger of Memory, *deals with Rodriguez's experiences in school. "If," he says, "because of my schooling I had grown culturally separated from my parents, my education finally had given me ways of speaking and caring about that fact." This essay is a record of how he came to understand the changes in his life. A reviewer writing in the* Atlantic Monthly *concluded that* Hunger of Memory *will survive in our literature "not because of some forgotten public issues that once bisected Richard Rodriguez's life, but because his history of that life has something to say about what it means to be American . . . and what it means to be human."*

The Achievement of Desire

I stand in the ghetto classroom—"the guest speaker"—attempting to lecture on the mystery of the sounds of our words to rows of diffident students. "Don't you hear it? Listen! The music of our words. '*Sumer is icumen in. . . .*' And songs on the car radio. We need Aretha Franklin's voice to fill plain words with music—her life." In the face of their empty stares, I try to create an enthusiasm. But the girls in the back row turn to watch some boy passing outside. There are flutters of smiles, waves. And someone's mouth elongates heavy, silent words through the barrier of glass. Silent words—the lips straining to shape each voiceless syllable: "*Meet meee late errr.*" By the door, the instructor smiles at me, apparently hoping that I will be able to spark some enthusiasm in the class. But only one student seems to be listening. A girl, maybe fourteen. In this gray room her eyes shine with ambition. She keeps nodding and nodding at all that I say; she even takes notes. And each time I ask a question, she jerks up and down in her desk like a marionette, while her hand waves over the bowed heads of her classmates. It is myself (as a boy) I see as she faces me now (a man in my thirties).

The boy who first entered a classroom barely able to speak English, twenty years later concluded his studies in the stately quiet of the reading room in the British Museum. Thus with one sentence I can summarize my academic career. It will be harder to summarize what sort of life connects the boy to the man.

With every award, each graduation from one level of education to the next, people I'd meet would congratulate me. Their refrain [was] always the same: "Your parents must be very proud." Sometimes then they'd ask me how I managed it—my "success." (How?) After a while, I had several quick answers to give in reply. I'd admit, for one thing, that I went to an excellent grammar school. (My earliest teachers, the nuns, made my success their ambition.) And my brother and both my sisters were very good students. (They often brought home the shiny school trophies I came to want.) And my mother and father always encouraged me. (At every graduation they were behind the stunning flash of the camera when I turned to look at the crowd.)

As important as these factors were, however, they account inadequately for my academic advance. Nor do they suggest what an odd success I managed. For although I was a very good student, I was also a very bad student. I was a "scholarship boy," a certain kind of scholarship boy. Always successful, I was always unconfident. Exhilarated by my progress. Sad. I became the prized student—anxious and eager to learn. Too eager, too anxious—an imitative and unoriginal pupil. My brother and two sisters enjoyed the advantages I did, and they grew to be as successful as I, but none of them ever seemed so anxious about their schooling. A second-grade student, I was the one who came home and corrected the "simple" grammatical mistakes of our parents. ("Two negatives make a positive.") Proudly I announced—to my family's startled silence—that a teacher had said I was losing all trace of a Spanish accent. I was oddly annoyed when I was unable to get parental help with a homework assignment. The night my father tried to help me with an arithmetic exercise, he kept reading the instructions, each time more deliberately, until I pried the textbook out of his hands, saying, "I'll try to figure it out some more by myself."

When I reached the third grade, I outgrew such behavior. I became more tactful, careful to keep separate the two very different worlds of my day. But then, with ever-increasing intensity, I devoted myself to my studies. I became bookish, puzzling to all my family. Ambition set me apart. When my brother saw me struggling home with stacks of library books, he would laugh, shouting: "Hey, Four Eyes!" My father opened a closet one day and was startled to find me inside, reading a novel. My mother would find me reading when I was supposed to be asleep or helping around the house or playing outside. In a voice angry or worried or just curious, she'd ask: "What do you see in your books?" It became the family's joke. When I was called and wouldn't reply, someone would say I must be hiding under my bed with a book.

(How did I manage my success?)

What I am about to say to you has taken me more than twenty years to admit: *A primary reason for my success in the classroom was that I couldn't forget that schooling was changing me and separating me from the life I enjoyed before becoming a student.* That simple realization! For years I never spoke to anyone about it. Never mentioned a thing to my family or my teachers or classmates. From a very early age, I understood enough, just enough about my classroom experiences to keep what I knew repressed, hidden beneath layers of embarrassment. Not until my last months as a graduate student, nearly thirty years old, was it possible for me to think much about the reasons for my academic success. Only then. At the end of my schooling, I needed to determine how far I had moved from my past. The adult finally confronted, and now must publicly say, what the child shuddered from knowing and could never admit to himself or to those many faces that smiled at his every success. ("Your parents must be very proud. . . .")

I

At the end, in the British Museum (too distracted to finish my dissertation) for weeks I read, speed-read, books by modern educational theorists, only to find infrequent and slight mention of students like me. (Much more is written about the more typical case, the lower-class student who barely is helped by his schooling.) Then one day, leafing through Richard Hoggart's *The Uses of Literacy*, I found, in his description of the scholarship boy, myself. For the first time I realized that there were other students like me, and so I was able to frame the meaning of my academic success, its consequent price—the loss.

Hoggart's description is distinguished, at least initially, by deep understanding. What he grasps very well is that the scholarship boy must move between environments, his home and the classroom, which are at cultural extremes, opposed. With his family, the boy has the intense pleasure of intimacy, the family's consolation in feeling public alienation. Lavish emotions texture home life. *Then,* at school, the instruction bids him to trust lonely reason primarily. Immediate needs set the pace of his parents' lives. From his mother and father the boy learns to trust spontaneity and nonrational ways of knowing. *Then,* at school, there is mental calm. Teachers emphasize the value of a reflectiveness that opens a space between thinking and immediate action.

Years of schooling must pass before the boy will be able to sketch the cultural differences in his day as abstractly as this. But he senses those differences early. Perhaps as early as the night he brings home an assignment from school and finds the house too noisy for study.

> He has to be more and more alone, if he is going to "get on."
> He will have, probably unconsciously, to oppose the ethos of

the hearth, the intense gregariousness of the working-class family group. Since everything centres upon the living-room, there is unlikely to be a room of his own; the bedrooms are cold and inhospitable, and to warm them or the front room, if there is one, would not only be expensive, but would require an imaginative leap—out of the tradition—which most families are not capable of making. There is a corner of the living-room table. On the other side Mother is ironing, the wireless is on, someone is singing a snatch of song or Father says intermittently whatever comes into his head. The boy has to cut himself off mentally, so as to do his homework, as well as he can.[1]

The next day, the lesson is as apparent at school. There are even rows of desks. Discussion is ordered. The boy must rehearse his thoughts and raise his hand before speaking out in a loud voice to an audience of classmates. And there is time enough, and silence, to think about ideas (big ideas) never considered at home by his parents.

Not for the working-class child alone is adjustment to the classroom difficult. Good schooling requires that any student alter early childhood habits. But the working-class child is usually least prepared for the change. And, unlike many middle-class children, he goes home and sees in his parents a way of life not only different but starkly opposed to that of the classroom. (He enters the house and hears his parents talking in ways his teachers discourage.)

Without extraordinary determination and the great assistance of others—at home and at school—there is little chance for success. Typically most working-class children are barely changed by the classroom. The exception succeeds. The relative few become scholarship students. Of these, Richard Hoggart estimates, most manage a fairly graceful transition. Somehow they learn to live in the two very different worlds of their day. There are some others, however, those Hoggart pejoratively terms "scholarship boys," for whom success comes with special anxiety. Scholarship boy: good student, troubled son. The child is "moderately endowed," intellectually mediocre, Hoggart supposes—though it may be more pertinent to note the special qualities of temperament in the child. High-strung child. Brooding. Sensitive. Haunted by the knowledge that one *chooses* to become a student. (Education is not an inevitable or natural step in growing up.) Here is a child who cannot forget that his academic success distances him from a life he loved, even from his own memory of himself.

Initially, he wavers, balances allegiance. ("The boy is himself [until he reaches, say, the upper forms] very much of *both* the worlds of home and school. He is enormously obedient to the dictates of the world of school, but emotionally still strongly wants to continue as part of the family circle.") Gradually, necessarily, the balance is lost. The boy needs to spend more and more time studying, each night enclosing himself in the silence permitted and required by intense concentration. He takes his first step toward academic success, away from his family.

From the very first days, through the years following, it will be with his parents—the figures of lost authority, the persons toward whom he feels deepest love—that the change will be most powerfully measured. A separation will unravel between them. Advancing in his studies, the boy notices that his mother and father have not changed as much as he. Rather, when he sees them, they often remind him of the person he once was and the life he earlier shared with them. He realizes what some Romantics also know when they praise the working class for the capacity for human closeness, qualities of passion and spontaneity, that the rest of us experience in like measure only in the earliest part of our youth. For the Romantic, this doesn't make working-class life childish. Working-class life challenges precisely because it is an *adult* way of life.

The scholarship boy reaches a different conclusion. He cannot afford to admire his parents. (How could he and still pursue such a contrary life?) He permits himself embarrassment at their lack of education. And to evade nostalgia for the life he has lost, he concentrates on the benefits education will bestow upon him. He becomes especially ambitious. Without the support of old certainties and consolations, almost mechanically, he assumes the procedures and doctrines of the classroom. The kind of allegiance the young student might have given his mother and father only days earlier, he transfers to the teacher, the new figure of authority. "[The scholarship boy] tends to make a father-figure of his form-master," Hoggart observes.

But Hoggart's calm prose only makes me recall the urgency with which I came to idolize my grammar school teachers. I began by imitating their accents, using their diction, trusting their every direction. The very first facts they dispensed, I grasped with awe. Any book they told me to read, I read—then waited for them to tell me which books I enjoyed. Their every casual opinion I came to adopt and to trumpet when I returned home. I stayed after school "to help"—to get my teacher's undivided attention. It was the nun's encouragement that mattered most to me. (She understood exactly what—my parents never seemed to appraise so well—all my achievements entailed.) Memory gently caressed each word of praise bestowed in the classroom so that compliments teachers paid me years ago come quickly to mind even today.

The enthusiasm I felt in second-grade classes I flaunted before both my parents. The docile, obedient student came home a shrill and precocious son who insisted on correcting and teaching his parents with the remark: "My teacher told us. . . ."

I intended to hurt my mother and father. I was still angry at them for having encouraged me toward classroom English. But gradually this anger was exhausted, replaced by guilt as school grew more and more attractive to me. I grew increasingly successful, a talkative student. My hand was raised in the classroom; I yearned to answer any question. At home, life was less noisy than it had been. (I spoke to classmates and teachers more often each day than to family members.) Quiet at home, I sat with my papers for hours each night. I never forgot that schooling had irretrievably changed my family's life. That knowledge, however, did not weaken ambition. Instead, it strengthened resolve. Those times I remembered the loss of my past with regret, I quickly reminded myself of all the things my teachers could give me. (They could make me an educated man.) I tightened my grip on pencil and books. I evaded nostalgia. Tried hard to forget. But one does not forget by trying to forget. One only remembers. I remembered too well that education had changed my family's life. I would not have become a scholarship boy had I not so often remembered.

Once she was sure that her children knew English, my mother would tell us, "You should keep up your Spanish." Voices playfully groaned in response. "¡*Pochos!*" my mother would tease. I listened silently.

After a while, I grew more calm at home. I developed tact. A fourth-grade student, I was no longer the show-off in front of my parents. I became a conventionally dutiful son, politely affectionate, cheerful enough, even—for reasons beyond choosing—my father's favorite. And much about my family life was easy then, comfortable, happy in the rhythm of our living together: hearing my father getting ready for work; eating the breakfast my mother had made me; looking up from a novel to hear my brother or one of my sisters playing with friends in the backyard; in winter, coming upon the house all lighted up after dark.

But withheld from my mother and father was any mention of what most mattered to me: the extraordinary experience of first-learning. Late afternoon: in the midst of preparing dinner, my mother would come up behind me while I was trying to read. Her head just over mine, her breath warmly scented with food. "What are you reading?" Or, "Tell me all about your new courses." I would barely respond, "Just the usual things, nothing special." (A half smile, then silence. Her head moving back in the silence. Silence! Instead of the flood of intimate sounds that had once flowed smoothly between us, there was this silence.) After dinner, I would rush to a bedroom with papers and books. As often as possible, I resisted parental pleas to "save lights" by coming to the kitchen to work. I kept so much, so often, to myself. Sad. Enthusiastic. Troubled by the excitement of coming upon new ideas. Eager. Fascinated by the promising texture of a brand-new book. I hoarded the pleasures of learning. Alone for hours. Enthralled. Nervous. I rarely looked away from my books—or back on my memories. Nights when relatives visited and the front rooms were warmed by Spanish sounds, I slipped quietly out of the house.

It mattered that education was changing me. It never ceased to matter. My brother and sisters would giggle at our mother's mispronounced words. They'd correct her gently. My mother laughed girlishly one night, trying not to pronounce *sheep* as *ship*. From a distance I listened sullenly. From that distance, pretending not to notice on another occasion, I saw my father looking at the title pages of my library books. That was the scene on my mind when I walked home with a fourth-grade companion and heard him say that his parents read to him every night. (A strange-sounding book—*Winnie the Pooh*.) Immediately, I wanted to know, "What is it like?" My companion, however, thought I wanted to know about the plot of the book. Another day, my mother surprised me by asking for a "nice" book to read. "Something not too hard you think I might like." Carefully I chose one, Willa Cather's *My Ántonia*. But when, several weeks later, I happened to see it next to her bed unread except for the first few pages, I was furious and suddenly wanted to cry. I grabbed up the book and took it back to my room and placed it in its place, alphabetically on my shelf.

"Your parents must be very proud of you." People began to say that to me about the time I was in sixth grade. To answer affirmatively, I'd smile. Shyly I'd smile, never betraying my sense of the irony: I was not proud of my mother and father. I was embarrassed by their lack of education. It was not that I ever thought they were stupid, though stupidly I took for granted their enormous native intelligence. Simply, what mattered to me was that they were not like my teachers.

But, "Why didn't you tell us about the award?" my mother demanded, her frown weakened by pride. At the grammar school ceremony several weeks after, her eyes were brighter than the trophy I'd won. Pushing back the hair from my forehead, she whispered that I had "shown" the *gringos*. A few minutes later, I heard my father speak to my teacher and felt ashamed of his labored, accented words. Then guilty for the shame. I felt such contrary feelings. (There is no simple road-map through the heart of the scholarship boy.) My teacher was so soft-spoken and her words were edged sharp and clean. I admired her until it seemed to me that she spoke too carefully. Sensing that she was condescending to them, I became nervous. Resentful. Protective. I tried to move my parents away. "You both must be very proud of Richard," the nun said. They responded quickly. (They were proud.) "We are proud of all our children." Then this after-thought: "They sure didn't get their brains from us." They all laughed. I smiled.

Tightening the irony into a knot was the knowledge that my parents were always behind me. They made success possible. They evened the path. They sent their children to parochial schools because the nuns "teach better." They paid a tuition they couldn't afford. They spoke English to us.

For their children my parents wanted chances they never had—an easier way. It saddened my mother to learn that some relatives forced their children to start working right after high school. To *her* children she would say, "Get all the education you can." In schooling she recognized the key to job advancement. And with the remark she remembered her past.

As a girl new to America my mother had been awarded a high school diploma by teachers too careless or busy to notice that she hardly spoke English. On her own, she determined to learn how to type. That skill got her jobs typing envelopes in letter shops, and it encouraged in her an optimism about the possibility of advancement. (Each morning when her sisters put on uniforms, she chose a bright-colored dress.) The years of young womanhood passed, and her typing speed increased. She also became an excellent speller of words she mispronounced. "And I've never been to college," she'd say, smiling, when her children asked her to spell words they were too lazy to look up in a dictionary.

Typing, however, was dead-end work. Finally frustrating. When her youngest child started high school, my mother got a full-time office job once again. (Her paycheck combined with my father's to make us—in fact—what we had already become in our imagination of ourselves—middle class.) She worked then for the (California) state government in numbered civil service positions secured by examinations. The old ambition of her youth was rekindled. During the lunch hour, she consulted bulletin boards for announcements of openings. One day she saw mention of something called an "anti-poverty agency." A typing job. A glamorous job, part of the governor's staff. "A knowledge of Spanish required." Without hesitation she applied and became nervous only when the job was suddenly hers.

"Everyone comes to work all dressed up," she reported at night. And didn't need to say more than that her co-workers wouldn't let her answer the phones. She was only a typist, after all, albeit a very fast typist. And an excellent speller. One morning there was a letter to be sent to a Washington cabinet officer. On the dictating tape, a voice referred to urban guerrillas. My mother typed (the wrong word, correctly): "gorillas." The mistake horrified the anti-poverty bureaucrats who shortly after arranged to have her returned to her previous position. She would go no further. So she willed her ambition to their children. "Get all the education you can; with an education you can do anything." (With a good education *she* could have done anything.)

When I was in high school, I admitted to my mother that I planned to become a teacher someday. That seemed to please her. But I never tried to explain that it was not the occupation of teaching I yearned for as much as it was something more elusive: I wanted to *be* like my teachers, to possess their knowledge, to assume their authority, their confidence, even to assume a teacher's persona.

In contrast to my mother, my father never verbally encouraged his children's academic success. Nor did he often praise us. My mother had to remind him to "say something" to one of his children who scored some academic success. But whereas my mother saw in education the opportunity for job advancement, my father recognized that education provided an even more startling possibility: it could enable a person to escape from a life of mere labor.

In Mexico, orphaned when he was eight, my father left school to work as an "apprentice" for an uncle. Twelve years later, he left Mexico in frustration and arrived in America. He had great expectations then of

becoming an engineer. ("Work for my hands and my head.") He knew a
Catholic priest who promised to get him money enough to study full time
for a high school diploma. But the promises came to nothing. Instead there
was a dark succession of warehouse, cannery, and factory jobs. After work
he went to night school along with my mother. A year, two passed. Nothing much changed, except that fatigue worked its way into the bone; then
everything changed. He didn't talk anymore of becoming an engineer. He
stayed outside on the steps of the school while my mother went inside to
learn typing and shorthand.

By the time I was born, my father worked at "clean" jobs. For a time he
was a janitor at a fancy department store. ("Easy work; the machines do it
all.") Later he became a dental technician. ("Simple.") But by then he was
pessimistic about the ultimate meaning of work and the possibility of ever
escaping its claims. In some of my earliest memories of him, my father already seems aged by fatigue. (He has never really grown old like my
mother.) From boyhood to manhood, I have remembered him in a single
image: seated, asleep on the sofa, his head thrown back in a hideous
corpselike grin, the evening newspaper spread out before him. "But look
at all you've accomplished," his best friend said to him once. My father
said nothing. Only smiled.

It was my father who laughed when I claimed to be tired by reading
and writing. It was he who teased me for having soft hands. (He seemed
to sense that some great achievement of leisure was implied by my papers
and books.) It was my father who became angry while watching on television some woman at the Miss America contest tell the announcer that she
was going to college. ("Majoring in fine arts.") "College!" he snarled. He
despised the trivialization of higher education, the inflated grades and
cheapened diplomas, the half education that so often passed as mass education in my generation.

It was my father again who wondered why I didn't display my awards
on the wall of my bedroom. He said he liked to go to doctors' offices and
see their certificates and degrees on the wall. ("Nice.") My citations from
school got left in closets at home. The gleaming figure astride one of my
trophies was broken, wingless, after hitting the ground. My medals were
placed in a jar of loose change. And when I lost my high school diploma,
my father found it as it was about to be thrown out with the trash. Without telling me, he put it away with his own things for safekeeping.

These memories slammed together at the instant of hearing that refrain familiar to all scholarship students: "Your parents must be
proud. . . ." Yes, my parents were proud. I knew it. But my parents regarded my progress with more than mere pride. They endured my early
precocious behavior—but with what private anger and humiliation? As
their children got older and would come home to challenge ideas both of
them held, they argued before submitting to the force of logic or superior
factual evidence with the disclaimer, "It's what we were taught in our
time to believe." These discussions ended abruptly, though my mother re-

membered them on other occasions when she complained that our "big ideas" were going to our heads. More acute was her complaint that the family wasn't close anymore, like some others she knew. Why weren't we close, "more in the Mexican style"? Everyone is so private, she added. And she mimicked the yes and no answers she got in reply to her questions. Why didn't we talk more? (My father never asked.) I never said.

I was the first in my family who asked to leave home when it came time to go to college. I had been admitted to Stanford, one hundred miles away. My departure would only make physically apparent the separation that had occurred long before. But it was going too far. In the months preceding my leaving, I heard the question my mother never asked except indirectly. In the hot kitchen, tired at the end of her workday, she demanded to know, "Why aren't the colleges here in Sacramento good enough for you? They are for your brother and sister." In the middle of a car ride, not turning to face me, she wondered, "Why do you need to go so far away?" Late at night, ironing, she said with disgust, "Why do you have to put us through this big expense? You know your scholarship will never cover it all." But when September came there was a rush to get everything ready. In a bedroom that last night I packed the big brown valise, and my mother sat nearby sewing initials onto the clothes I would take. And she said no more about my leaving.

Months later, two weeks of Christmas vacation: the first hours home were the hardest. ("What's new?") My parents and I sat in the kitchen for a conversation. (But, lacking the same words to develop our sentences and to shape our interests, what was there to say? What could I tell them of the term paper I had just finished on the "universality of Shakespeare's appeal"?) I mentioned only small, obvious things: my dormitory life; weekend trips I had taken; random events. They responded with news of their own. (One was almost grateful for a family crisis about which there was much to discuss.) We tried to make our conversation seem like more than an interview.

II

From an early age I knew that my mother and father could read and write both Spanish and English. I had observed my father making his way through what, I now suppose, must have been income tax forms. On other occasions I waited apprehensively while my mother read onion-paper letters airmailed from Mexico with news of a relative's illness or death. For both my parents, however, reading was something done out of necessity and as quickly as possible. Never did I see either of them read an entire book. Nor did I see them read for pleasure. Their reading consisted of work manuals, prayer books, newspaper, recipes.

Richard Hoggart imagines how, at home,

> [the scholarship boy] sees strewn around, and reads regularly himself, magazines which are never mentioned at school,

which seem not to belong to the world to which the school introduces him; at school he hears about and reads books never mentioned at home. When he brings those books into the house they do not take their place with other books which the family are reading, for often there are none or almost none; his books look, rather, like strange tools.

In our house each school year would begin with my mother's careful instruction: "Don't write in your books so we can sell them at the end of the year." The remark was echoed in public by my teachers, but only in part: "Boys and girls, don't write in your books. You must learn to treat them with great care and respect."

OPEN THE DOORS OF YOUR MIND WITH BOOKS, read the red and white poster over the nun's desk in early September. It soon was apparent to me that reading was the classroom's central activity. Each course had its own book. And the information gathered from a book was unquestioned. READ TO LEARN, the sign on the wall advised in December. I privately wondered: What was the connection between reading and learning? Did one learn something only by reading it? Was an idea only an idea if it could be written down? In June, CONSIDER BOOKS YOUR BEST FRIENDS. Friends? Reading was, at best, only a chore. I needed to look up whole paragraphs of words in a dictionary. Lines of type were dizzying, the eye having to move slowly across the page, then down, and across. . . . The sentences of the first books I read were coolly impersonal. Toned hard. What most bothered me, however, was the isolation reading required. To console myself for the loneliness I'd feel when I read, I tried reading in a very soft voice. Until: "Who is doing all that talking to his neighbor?" Shortly after, remedial reading classes were arranged for me with a very old nun.

At the end of each school day, for nearly six months, I would meet with her in the tiny room that served as the school's library but was actually only a storeroom for used textbooks and a vast collection of *National Geographics*. Everything about our sessions pleased me: the smallness of the room; the noise of the janitor's broom hitting the edge of the long hallway outside the door; the green of the sun, lighting the wall; and the old woman's face blurred white with a beard. Most of the time we took turns. I began with my elementary text. Sentences of astonishing simplicity seemed to me lifeless and drab: "The boys ran from the rain. . . . She wanted to sing. . . . The kite rose in the blue." Then the old nun would read from her favorite books, usually biographies of early American presidents. Playfully she ran through complex sentences, calling the words alive with her voice, making it seem that the author somehow was speaking directly to me. I smiled just to listen to her. I sat there and sensed for the very first time some possibility of fellowship between a reader and a writer, a communication, never *intimate* like that I heard spoken words at home convey, but one nonetheless *personal*.

One day the nun concluded a session by asking me why I was so reluctant to read by myself. I tried to explain; said something about the way written words made me feel all alone—almost, I wanted to add but didn't, as when I spoke to myself in a room just emptied of furniture. She studied my face as I spoke; she seemed to be watching more than listening. In an uneventful voice she replied that I had nothing to fear. Didn't I realize that reading would open up whole new worlds? A book could open doors for me. It could introduce me to people and show me places I never imagined existed. She gestured toward the bookshelves. (Bare-breasted African women danced, and the shiny hubcaps of automobiles on the back covers of the *Geographic* gleamed in my mind.) I listened with respect. But her words were not very influential. I was thinking then of another consequence of literacy, one I was too shy to admit but nonetheless trusted. Books were going to make me "educated." *That* confidence enabled me, several months later, to overcome my fear of the silence.

In fourth grade I embarked upon a grandiose reading program. "Give me the names of important books," I would say to startled teachers. They soon found out that I had in mind "adult books." I ignored their suggestion of anything I suspected was written for children. (Not until I was in college, as a result, did I read *Huckleberry Finn* or *Alice's Adventures in Wonderland.*) Instead, I read *The Scarlet Letter* and Franklin's *Autobiography.* And whatever I read I read for extra credit. Each time I finished a book, I reported the achievement to a teacher and basked in the praise my effort earned. Despite my best efforts, however, there seemed to be more and more books I needed to read. At the library I would literally tremble as I came upon whole shelves of books I hadn't read. So I read and I read and I read: *Great Expectations;* all the short stories of Kipling; *The Babe Ruth Story;* the entire first volume of the *Encyclopedia Britannica* (A–ANSTEY); the *Iliad; Moby Dick; Gone with the Wind; The Good Earth; Ramona; Forever Amber; The Lives of the Saints; Crime and Punishment; The Pearl. . . .* Librarians who initially frowned when I checked out the maximum ten books at a time started saving books they thought I might like. Teachers would say to the rest of the class, "I only wish the rest of you took reading as seriously as Richard obviously does."

But at home I would hear my mother wondering, "What do you see in your books?" (Was reading a hobby like her knitting? Was so much reading even healthy for a boy? Was it the sign of "brains"? Or was it just a convenient excuse for not helping about the house on Saturday mornings?) Always, "What do you see . . . ?"

What *did* I see in my books? I had the idea that they were crucial for my academic success, though I couldn't have said exactly how or why. In the sixth grade I simply concluded that what gave a book its value was some major idea or theme it contained. If that core essence could be mined and memorized, I would become learned like my teachers. I decided to record in a notebook the themes of the books that I read. After reading *Robinson Crusoe,* I wrote that its theme was "the value of learning to live by oneself." When I completed *Wuthering Heights,* I noted the danger of "letting emotions get out of control." Rereading these brief moralistic appraisals usually left me disheartened. I couldn't believe that they were really the source of reading's value. But for many more years, they constituted the only means I had of describing to myself the educational value of books.

In spite of my earnestness, I found reading a pleasurable activity. I came to enjoy the lonely good company of books. Early on weekday mornings, I'd read in my bed. I'd feel a mysterious comfort then, reading in the dawn quiet—the blue-gray silence interrupted by the occasional churning of the refrigerator motor a few rooms away or the more distant sounds of a city bus beginning its run. On weekends I'd go to the public library to read, surrounded by old men and women. Or, if the weather was fine, I would take my books to the park and read in the shade of a tree. A warm summer evening was my favorite reading time. Neighbors would leave for vacation and I would water their lawns. I would sit through the twilight on the front porches or in backyards, reading to the cool, whirling sounds of the sprinklers.

I also had favorite writers. But often those writers I enjoyed most I was least able to value. When I read William Saroyan's *The Human Comedy*, I was immediately pleased by the narrator's warmth and the charm of his story. But as quickly I became suspicious. A book so enjoyable to read couldn't be very "important." Another summer I determined to read all the novels of Dickens. Reading his fat novels, I loved the feeling I got—after the first hundred pages—of being at home in a fictional world where I knew the names of the characters and cared about what was going to happen to them. And it bothered me that I was forced away at the conclusion, when the fiction closed tight, like a fortune-teller's fist—the futures of all the major characters neatly resolved. I never knew how to take such feelings seriously, however. Nor did I suspect that these experiences could be part of a novel's meaning. Still, there were pleasures to sustain me after I'd finish my books. Carrying a volume back to the library, I would be pleased by its weight. I'd run my fingers along the edge of the pages and marvel at the breadth of my achievement. Around my room, growing stacks of paperback books reenforced my assurance.

I entered high school having read hundreds of books. My habit of reading made me a confident speaker and writer of English. Reading also enabled me to sense something of the shape, the major concerns, of Western thought. (I was able to say something about Dante and Descartes and Engels and James Baldwin in my high school term papers.) In these various ways, books brought me academic success as I hoped that they would. But I was not a good reader. Merely bookish, I lacked a point of view when I read. Rather, I read in order to acquire a point of view. I vacuumed books for epigrams, scraps of information, ideas, themes—anything to fill the hollow within me and make me feel educated. When one of my teachers suggested to his drowsy tenth-grade English class that a person could not have a "complicated idea" until he had read at least two thousand books, I heard the remark without detecting either its irony or its very complicated truth. I merely determined to compile a list of all the books I had ever read. Harsh with myself, I included only once a title I might have read several times. (How, after all, could one read a book more than once?) And I included only those books over a hundred pages in length. (Could anything shorter be a book?)

There was yet another high school list I compiled. One day I came across a newspaper article about the retirement of an English professor at a nearby state college. The article was accompanied by a list of the "hundred most important books of Western Civilization." "More than anything else in my life," the professor told the reporter with finality, "these books have made me all that I am." That was the kind of remark I couldn't ignore. I clipped out the list and kept it for the several months it took me to read all of the titles. Most books, of course, I barely understood. While reading Plato's *Republic,* for instance, I needed to keep looking at the book jacket comments to remind myself what the text was about. Nevertheless, with the special patience and superstition of a scholarship boy, I looked at every word of the text. And by the time I reached the last word, relieved, I convinced myself that I had read *The Republic.* In a ceremony of great pride, I solemnly crossed Plato off my list.

III

The scholarship boy pleases most when he is young—the working-class child struggling for academic success. To his teachers, he offers great satisfaction; his success is their proudest achievement. Many other persons offer to help him. A businessman learns the boy's story and promises to underwrite part of the cost of his college education. A woman leaves him her entire library of several hundred books when she moves. His progress is featured in a newspaper article. Many people seem happy for him. They marvel. "How did you manage so fast?" From all sides, there is lavish praise and encouragement.

In his grammar school classroom, however, the boy already makes students around him uneasy. They scorn his desire to succeed. They scorn him for constantly wanting the teacher's attention and praise. "Kiss Ass," they call him when his hand swings up in response to every question he hears. Later, when he makes it to college, no one will mock him aloud. But he detects annoyance on the faces of some students and even some teachers who watch him. It puzzles him often. In college, then in graduate school, he behaves much as he always has. If anything is different about him it is that he dares to anticipate the successful conclusion of his studies. At last he feels that he belongs in the classroom, and this is exactly the source of the dissatisfaction he causes. To many persons around him, he appears too much the academic. There may be some things about him that recall his beginnings—his shabby clothes; his persistent poverty; or his dark skin (in those cases when it symbolizes his parents' disadvantaged condition)—but they only make clear how far he has moved from his past. He has used education to remake himself.

It bothers his fellow academics to face this. They will not say why exactly. (They sneer.) But their expectations become obvious when they are disappointed. They expect—they want—a student less changed by his schooling. If the scholarship boy, from a past so distant from the classroom, could remain in some basic way unchanged, he would be able to prove that it is possible for anyone to become educated without basically changing from the person one was.

Here is no fabulous hero, no idealized scholar-worker. The scholarship boy does not straddle, cannot reconcile, the two great opposing cultures of his life. His success is unromantic and plain. He sits in the classroom and offers those sitting beside him no calming reassurance about their own lives. He sits in the seminar room—a man with brown skin, the son of working-class Mexican immigrant parents. (Addressing the professor at the head of the table, his voice catches with nervousness.) There is no trace of his parents' in his speech. Instead he approximates the accents of teachers and classmates. Coming from *him* those sounds seem suddenly odd. Odd too is the effect produced when *he* uses academic jargon—bubbles at the tip of his tongue: "*Topos* . . . negative capability . . . vegetation imagery in Shakespearean comedy." He lifts an opinion from Coleridge, takes something else from Frye or Empson or Leavis. He even repeats exactly his professor's earlier comment. All his ideas are clearly borrowed. He seems to have no thought of his own. He chatters while his listeners smile—their look one of disdain.

When he is older and thus when so little of the person he was survives, the scholarship boy makes only too apparent his profound lack of *self*-confidence. This is the conventional assessment that even Richard Hoggart repeats:

> [The scholarship boy] tends to over-stress the importance of examinations, of the piling-up of knowledge and of received opinions. He discovers a technique of apparent learning, of the acquiring of facts rather than of the handling and use of facts. He learns how to receive a purely literate education, one using only a small part of the personality and challenging only a limited area of his being. He begins to see life as a ladder, as permanent examination with some praise and some further exhortation at each stage. He becomes an expert imbiber and doler-out; his competence will vary, but will rarely be accompanied by genuine enthusiasms. He rarely feels the reality of knowledge, of other men's thoughts and imaginings, on his own pulses. . . . He has something of the blinkered pony about him. . . .

But this is criticism more accurate than fair. The scholarship boy is a very bad student. He is the great mimic; a collector of thoughts, not a thinker; the very last person in class who ever feels obliged to have an opinion of his own. In large part, however, the reason he is such a bad student is because he realizes more often and more acutely than most other students—than Hoggart himself—that education requires radical self-reformation. As a very young boy, regarding his parents, as he struggles with an early homework assignment, he knows this too well. That is why he lacks self-assurance. He does not forget that the classroom is responsible for remaking him. He relies on his teacher, depends on all that he hears in the classroom and reads in his books. He becomes in every obvious way the worst student, a dummy mouthing the opinions of others. But he would not be so bad—nor would he become so successful, a *scholarship* boy—if he did not accurately perceive that the best synonym for primary "education" is "imitation."

Those who would take seriously the boy's success—and his failure—would be forced to realize how great is the change any academic undergoes, how far one must move from one's past. It is easiest to ignore such considerations. So little is said about the scholarship boy in pages and pages of educational literature. Nothing is said of the silence that comes to separate the boy from his parents. Instead, one hears proposals for increasing the self-esteem of students and encouraging early intellectual independence. Paragraphs glitter with a constellation of terms like *creativity* and *originality*. (Ignored altogether is the function of imitation in a student's life.) Radical educationalists meanwhile complain that ghetto schools "oppress" students by trying to mold them, stifling native characteristics. The truer critique would be just the reverse: not that schools change ghetto students too much, but that while they might promote the occasional scholarship student, they change most students barely at all.

From the story of the scholarship boy there is no specific pedagogy to glean. There is, however, a much larger lesson. His story makes clear that education is a long, unglamorous, even demeaning process—*a nurturing never natural to the person one was before one entered a classroom*. At once different from most other students, the scholarship boy is also the archetypal "good student." He exaggerates the difficulty of being a student, but his exaggeration reveals a general predicament. Others are changed by their schooling as much as he. They too must re-form themselves. They must develop the skill of memory long before they become truly critical thinkers. And when they read Plato for the first several times, it will be with awe more than deep comprehension.

The impact of schooling on the scholarship boy is only more apparent to the boy himself and to others. Finally, although he may be laughable—a blinkered pony—the boy will not let his critics forget their own change. He ends up too much like them. When he speaks, they hear themselves echoed. In his pedantry, they trace their own. His ambitions are theirs. If his failure were singular, they might readily pity him. But he is more troubling than that. They would not scorn him if this were not so.

IV

Like me, Hoggart's imagined scholarship boy spends most of his years in the classroom afraid to long for his past. Only at the very end of his schooling does the boy-man become nostalgic. In this sudden change of heart, Richard Hoggart notes:

> He longs for the membership he lost, "he pines for some Nameless Eden where he never was." The nostalgia is the stronger and the more ambiguous because he is really "in quest of his own absconded self yet scared to find it." He both wants to go back and yet thinks he has gone beyond his class, feels himself weighted with knowledge of his own and their situation, which hereafter forbids him the simpler pleasures of his father and mother. . . .

According to Hoggart, the scholarship boy grows nostalgic because he remains the uncertain scholar, bright enough to have moved from his past, yet unable to feel easy, a part of a community of academics.

This analysis, however, only partially suggests what happened to me in my last year as a graduate student. When I traveled to London to write a dissertation on English Renaissance literature, I was finally confident of membership in a "community of scholars." But the pleasure that confidence gave me faded rapidly. After only two or three months in the reading room of the British Museum, it became clear that I had joined a lonely community. Around me each day were dour faces eclipsed by large piles of books. There were the regulars, like the old couple who arrived every morning, each holding a loop of the shopping bag which contained all their notes. And there was the historian who chattered madly to herself. ("Oh dear! Oh! Now, what's this? What? Oh, my!") There were also the faces of young men and women worn by long study. And everywhere eyes turned away the moment our glance accidentally met. Some persons I sat beside day after day, yet we passed silently at the end of the day, strangers. Still, we were united by a common respect for the written word and for scholarship. We did form a union, though one in which we remained distant from one another.

More profound and unsettling was the bond I recognized with those writers whose books I consulted. Whenever I opened a text that hadn't been used for years, I realized that my special interests and skills united me to a mere handful of academics. We formed an exclusive—eccentric!—society, separated from others who would never care or be able to share our concerns. (The pages I turned were stiff like layers of dead skin.) I began to wonder: Who, beside my dissertation director and a few faculty members, would ever read what I wrote? And: Was my dissertation much more than an act of social withdrawal? These questions went unanswered in the silence of the Museum reading room. They remained to trouble me after I'd leave the library each afternoon and feel myself shy—unsteady, speaking simple sentences at the grocer's or the butcher's on my way back to my bed-sitter.

Meanwhile my file cards accumulated. A professional, I knew exactly how to search a book for pertinent information. I could quickly assess and summarize the usability of the many books I consulted. But whenever I started to write, I knew too much (and not enough) to be able to write anything but sentences that were overly cautious, timid, strained brittle under the heavy weight of footnotes and qualifications. I seemed unable to dare a passionate statement. I felt drawn by professionalism to the edge of sterility, capable of no more than pedantic, lifeless, unassailable prose.

Then nostalgia began.

After years spent unwilling to admit its attractions, I gestured nostalgically toward the past. I yearned for that time when I had not been so alone. I became impatient with books. I wanted experience more immediate. I feared the library's silence. I silently scorned the gray, timid faces around me. I grew to hate the growing pages of my dissertation on genre and Renaissance literature. (In my mind I heard relatives laughing as they tried to make sense of its title.) I wanted something—I couldn't say exactly what. I told myself that I wanted a more passionate life. And a life less thoughtful. And above all, I wanted to be less alone. One day I heard some Spanish academics whispering back and forth to each other, and their sounds seemed ghostly voices recalling my life. Yearning became preoccupation then. Boyhood memories beckoned, flooded my mind. (Laughing intimate voices. Bounding up the front steps of the porch. A sudden embrace inside the door.)

For weeks after, I turned to books by educational experts. I needed to learn how far I had moved from my past—to determine how fast I would be able to recover something of it once again. But I found little. Only a chapter in a book by Richard Hoggart. . . . I left the reading room and the circle of faces.

I came home. After the year in England, I spent three summer months living with my mother and father, relieved by how easy it was to be home. It no longer seemed very important to me that we had little to say. I felt easy sitting and eating and walking with them. I watched them, nevertheless, looking for evidence of those elastic, sturdy strands that bind generations in a web of inheritance. I thought as I watched my mother one night: of course a friend had been right when she told me that I gestured and laughed just like my mother. Another time I saw for myself: my father's eyes were much like my own, constantly watchful.

But after the early relief, this return, came suspicion, nagging until I realized that I had not neatly sidestepped the impact of schooling. My desire to do so was precisely the measure of how much I remained an academic. *Negatively* (for that is how this idea first occurred to me): my need to think so much and so abstractly about my parents and our relationship was in itself an indication of my long education. My father and mother did not pass their time thinking about the cultural meanings of their experience. It was I who described their daily lives with airy ideas. And yet, *positively:* the ability to consider experience so abstractly allowed me to shape into desire what would otherwise have remained indefinite, meaningless longing in the British Museum. If, because of my schooling, I had grown culturally separated from my parents, my education finally had given me ways of speaking and caring about that fact.

My best teachers in college and graduate school, years before, had tried to prepare me for this conclusion, I think, when they discussed texts of aristocratic pastoral literature. Faithfully, I wrote down all that they said. I memorized it: "The praise of the unlettered by the highly educated is one of the primary themes of 'elitist' literature." But, "the importance of the praise given the unsolitary, richly passionate and spontaneous life is that it simultaneously reflects the value of a reflective life." I heard it all. But there was no way for any of it to mean very much to me. I was a scholarship boy at the time, busily laddering my way up the rungs of education. To pass an examination, I copied down exactly what my teachers told me. It would require many more years of schooling (an inevitable miseducation) in which I came to trust the silence of reading and the habit of abstracting from immediate experience—moving away from a life of closeness and immediacy I remembered with my parents, growing older—before I turned unafraid to desire the past, and thereby achieved what had eluded me for so long—the end of education.

NOTE

[1] All quotations in this essay are from Richard Hoggart, *The Uses of Literacy* (London: Chatto and Windus, 1957), chapter 10. [Author's note]

•   •   •   •   •   •   •   •   •   •   •

QUESTIONS FOR A SECOND READING

1. In *Hunger of Memory,* the book from which "The Achievement of Desire" is drawn, Rodriguez says several times that the story he tells, although it is very much his story, is also a story of our common experience—growing up, leaving home, becoming educated, entering the world. When you reread this essay, look particularly for sections or passages you might bring forward as evidence that this is, in fact, an essay which can give you a way of looking at your own life, and not just his. And look for sections that defy universal application. To what degree *is* his story the story of our common experience? Why might he (or his readers) want to insist that his story is everyone's story?

2. At the end of the essay, Rodriguez says:

> It would require many more years of schooling (an inevitable miseducation) in which I came to trust the silence of reading and the habit of abstracting from immediate experience—moving away from a life of closeness and immediacy I remembered with my parents, growing older—before I turned unafraid to desire the past, and thereby achieved what had eluded me for so long—the end of education.

What do you think, as you reread this essay, is the "end of education"? And what does that end (that goal? stopping point?) have to do with "miseducation," "the silence of reading," "the habit of abstracting from immediate experience," and "desiring the past"?

ASSIGNMENTS FOR WRITING

1. You could look at the relationship between Richard Rodriguez and Richard Hoggart as a case study of the relation of a reader to a writer or a student to a teacher. Look closely at Rodriguez's references to Hoggart's book, *The Uses of Literacy,* and at the way Rodriguez made use of that book to name and describe his own experience as a student. (An extended selection of *The Uses of Literacy* can be found on pages 891–99. What did he find in the book? How did he use it? How does he use it in his own writing?

   Write an essay in which you discuss Rodriguez's use of Hoggart's *The Uses of Literacy.* How, for example, would you compare Rodriguez's version of the "scholarship boy" with Hoggart's? (At one point, Rodriguez says that Hoggart's account is "more accurate than fair." What might he have meant by that?) And what kind of reader is the Rodriguez who is writing "The Achievement of Desire"—is he still a "scholarship boy," or is that description no longer appropriate?

   Note: You might begin your research with what may seem to be a purely technical matter, examining how Rodriguez handles quotations and works Hoggart's words into paragraphs of his own. On the basis of Rodriguez's use of quoted passages, how would you describe the relationship between Hoggart's words and Rodriguez's? Who has the greater authority? Who is the expert, and under what conditions? What "rules" might Rodriguez be said to follow or to break? Do you see any change in the course of the essay in how Rodriguez uses block quotations? in how he comments on them?

2. Rodriguez insists that his story is also everyone's story. Take an episode from your life, one that seems in some way similar to one of the episodes in "The Achievement of Desire," and cast it into a shorter version of Rodriguez's essay. Your job here is to look at your experience in Rodriguez's terms, which means thinking the way he does, noticing what he would notice, interpreting details in a similar fashion, using his key terms, seeing through his point of view; it could also mean imitating his style of writing, doing whatever it is you see him doing characteristically while he writes. Imitation, Rodriguez argues, is not necessarily a bad thing; it can, in fact, be one of the powerful ways in which a person learns.

Note: This assignment can also be used to read against "The Achievement of Desire." Rodriguez insists on the universality of his experience leaving home and community and joining the larger public life. You could highlight the differences between your experience and his. You should begin by imitating Rodriguez's method; you do not have to arrive at his conclusions, however.

3.   What I am about to say to you has taken me more than twenty years to admit: *A primary reason for my success in the classroom was that I couldn't forget that schooling was changing me and separating me from the life I enjoyed before becoming a student.* (p. 654)

    If, because of my schooling, I had grown culturally separated from my parents, my education finally had given me ways of speaking and caring about that fact. (p. 670)

As you reread Rodriguez's essay, what would you say are his "ways of speaking and caring"? One way to think about this question is to trace how the lessons he learned about reading, education, language, family, culture, and class shifted as he moved from elementary school through college and graduate school to his career as a teacher and a writer. What scholarly abilities did he learn that provided him with "ways of speaking and caring" valued in the academic community? Where and how do you see him using them in his essay?

Write an essay in which you discuss how Rodriguez reads (reviews, summarizes, interprets) his family, his teachers, his schooling, himself, and his books. What differences can you say such reading makes to those ways of speaking and caring that you locate in the text?

MAKING CONNECTIONS

1. Paulo Freire, in "The 'Banking' Concept of Education" (p. 259), discusses the political implications of the relations between teachers and students. Some forms of schooling, he says, can give students control over their lives, but most schooling teaches students only to submit to domination by others. If you look closely at the history of Rodriguez's schooling from the perspective of Freire's essay, what do you see? Write an essay describing how Freire might analyze Rodriguez's education. How would he see the process as it unfolds throughout Rodriguez's experience, as a student, from his early schooling (including the study he did on his own at home), through his college and graduate studies, to the position he takes, finally, as the writer of "The Achievement of Desire"?

2. Here, from "Arts of the Contact Zone" (p. 605), is Mary Louise Pratt on the "autoethnographic" text:

    Guaman Poma's *New Chronicle* is an instance of what I have proposed to call an *autoethnographic* text, by which I mean a text in which people undertake to describe themselves in ways that engage with representations others have made of them. Thus if ethnographic texts are those in which European metropolitan subjects represent to themselves their others (usually their conquered others), autoethnographic texts are representations that the so-defined others construct *in response to* or in dialogue with those texts. . . . [T]hey involve a selective collaboration with and appropriation of idioms of the metropolis or the conqueror. These are merged or infiltrated to varying degrees with indigenous idioms to create self-representations intended to intervene in metropolitan modes of understanding. . . . Such texts often constitute a marginalized group's point of entry into the dominant circuits of print culture. (pp. 608-09)

Richard Rodriguez's "The Achievement of Desire" could be considered "autoethnography." He is clearly working to explain himself, to account for who he is and who he has become. But to whom? Who is identified as his audience? Can you talk here about "indigenous idioms" or the "idioms of the metropolis"?

Reread "The Achievement of Desire" with Pratt's essay in mind. And write an essay in which you discuss "The Achievement of Desire" as an example of an autoethnographic and/or a transcultural text. You should imagine that you are working to put Pratt's ideas to the test (does it present itself as a convenient example?), but also add what you have to say about the ways this autobiography defines its audience, speaker, and purpose.

3. Richard Rodriguez in "The Achievement of Desire," Adrienne Rich in "When We Dead Awaken: Writing as Re-Vision" (p. 627), Susan Griffin in "Our Secret" (p. 345), and James Baldwin in "Notes of a Native Son" (p. 52) each use family history to think about and to represent forces beyond the family that shape human life and possibility—class, patriarchy, war, and race. Susan Griffin explains her motives this way, "One can find traces of every life in each life."

Perhaps. It is a bold step to think that this is true and to believe that one can, or should, write the family into the national or international narrative. Write an essay in which you read "The Achievement of Desire" alongside one of the other three essays. Your goal is not only to discuss how these writers do what they do, and to what conclusions and to what ends, but also to discuss your sense of what is at stake in such a project. How are their accounts of family different? How do they connect the structure of the family to larger structural concerns? What are the key differences, and how might you explain them?

Good photoessay makes you look at issues of power, placement
pic tell about exile
exile → not having a history, ghostliness / series of portraits w/o context

- place, history = identity
- recreating space of memory through photos — lack of land
- no cultural identification, bc everything at one only
   commonality (exile).

EDWARD
SAID

- displacement :
   - personal reading
   - experience discontinuity
   - locus of identity & memory vls. not having it.

   - memory
   - identification
   - oppression
   - children

E DWARD SAID (b. 1935) is one of the world's most distinguished literary
critics and scholars, distinguished (among other things) for his insistence on
the connectedness of art and politics, literature and history. As he argues in his
influential essay "The World, the Text, the Critic,"

> Texts have ways of existing, both theoretical and practical, that even
> in their most rarefied form are always enmeshed in circumstance,
> time, place, and society—in short, they are in the world, and hence
> worldly. The same is doubtless true of the critic, as reader and as
> writer.

Said (pronounced "sigh-eed") has been a "worldly" reader and writer and the selection that follows is a case in point. It is part of his long-term engagement with
the history and politics of the Middle East, particularly of the people we refer to as
Palestinians. His critical efforts, perhaps best represented by his most influential
book, Orientalism (1978), examine the ways the West has represented and understood the East ("They cannot represent themselves; they must be represented"),
demonstrating how Western journalists, writers, artists, and scholars have created and preserved a view of Eastern cultures as mysterious, dangerous, unchanging, and inferior.

674

Said was born in Jerusalem, in what was at that time Palestine, to parents who were members of the Christian Palestinian community. In 1947, as the United Nations was establishing Israel as a Jewish state, his family fled to Cairo. In the introduction to After the Last Sky: Palestinian Lives *(1986), the book from which the following selection was taken, he says,*

> *I was twelve, with the limited awareness and memory of a relatively sheltered boy. By the mid-spring of 1948 my extended family in its entirety had departed, evicted from Palestine along with almost a million other Palestinians. This was the* nakba, *or catastrophe, which heralded the destruction of our society and our dispossession as a people.*

Said was educated in English-speaking schools in Cairo and Massachusetts; he completed his undergraduate training at Princeton and received his Ph.D. from Harvard in 1964. Since 1963 he has been a member of the English department at Columbia University in New York. In the 1970s, he began writing to a broad public on the situation of the Palestinians; from 1977 to 1991 he served on the Palestinian National Council, an exile government. In 1991 he split from the Palestinian Liberation Organization (PLO) over its Gulf War policy (Yasir Arafat's support of Saddam Hussein) and, as he says, for "what I considered to be its new defeatism."

The peculiar and distinctive project represented by After the Last Sky *began in the 1980s, in the midst of this political engagement. "In 1983," Said writes in the introduction,*

> *while I was serving as a consultant to the United Nations for its International Conference on the Question of Palestine (ICQP), I suggested that photographs of Palestinians be hung in the entrance hall to the main conference site in Geneva. I had of course known and admired Mohr's work with John Berger, and I recommended that he be commissioned to photograph some of the principal locales of Palestinian life. Given the initial enthusiasm for the idea, Mohr left on a special UN-sponsored trip to the Near East. The photographs he brought back were indeed wonderful; the official response, however, was puzzling and, to someone with a taste for irony, exquisite. You can hang them up, we were told, but no writing can be displayed with them.*

In response to a UN mandate, Said had also commissioned twenty studies for the participants at the conference. Of the twenty, only three were accepted as "official documents." The others were rejected "because one after another Arab state objected to this or that principle, this or that insinuation, this or that putative injury to its sovereignty." And yet, Said argues, the complex experience, history, and identity of the people known as Palestinians remained virtually unknown, particularly in the West (and in the United States). To most, Said says, "Palestinians are visible principally as fighters, terrorists, and lawless pariahs." When Jean Mohr, the photographer, told a friend that he was preparing an exhibition on the Palestinians, the friend responded, "Don't you think the subject's a bit dated? Look, I've taken photographs of Palestinians too, especially in the refugee camps . . . it's really sad! But these days, who's interested in people who eat off the ground with their hands? And then there's all that terrorism . . . I'd have thought you'd be better off using your energy and capabilities on something more worthwhile."

For both Said and Mohr, these rejections provided the motive for After the Last Sky. Said's account, from the book's introduction, is worth quoting at length for how well it represents the problems of writing:

> Let us use photographs and a text, we said to each other, to say something that hasn't been said about Palestinians. Yet the problem of writing about and representing—in all senses of the word—Palestinians in some fresh way is part of a much larger problem. For it is not as if no one speaks about or portrays the Palestinians. The difficulty is that everyone, including the Palestinians themselves, speaks a very great deal. A huge body of literature has grown up, most of it polemical, accusatory, denunciatory. At this point, no one writing about Palestine—and indeed, no one going to Palestine—starts from scratch: We have all been there before, whether by reading about it, experiencing its millennial presence and power, or actually living there for periods of time. It is a terribly crowded place, almost too crowded for what it is asked to be by way of history or interpretation of history.

The resulting book is quite a remarkable document. The photos are not the photos of a glossy coffee-table book and yet they are compelling and memorable. The prose at times leads to the photos; at times it follows as meditation or explanation, an effort to get things right—"things like exile, dispossession, habits of expression, internal and external landscapes, stubbornness, poignancy, and heroism." It is a writing with pictures, not a writing to which photos were later added. Said had, in fact, been unable to return to Israel/Palestine for several years. As part of this project, he had hoped to be able to take a trip to the West Bank and Gaza in order to see beyond Mohr's photographs, but such a trip proved to be unsafe and impossible—both Arab and Israeli officials had reason to treat him with suspicion. The book was written in exile; the photos, memories, books, and newspapers, these were the only vehicles of return.

After the Last Sky is, Said wrote in 1999, "an unreconciled book, in which the contradictions and antinomies of our lives and experiences remain as they are, assembled neither (I hope) into neat wholes nor into sentimental ruminations about the past. Fragments, memories, disjointed scenes, intimate particulars." The Palestinians, Said wrote in the introduction, fall between classifications. "We are at once too recently formed and too variously experienced to be a population of articulate exiles with a completely systematic vision and too voluble and trouble making to be simply a pathetic mass of refugees." And he adds, "The whole point of this book is to engage this difficulty, to deny the habitually simple, even harmful representations of Palestinians, and to replace them with something more capable of capturing the complex reality of their experience."

Furthermore, he says, "just as Jean Mohr and I, a Swiss and a Palestinian, collaborated in the process, we would like you—Palestinians, Europeans, Americans,

Africans, Latin Americans, Asians—to do so also." This is both an invitation and a challenge. While there is much to learn about the Palestinians, the people and their history, the opening moment in the collaborative project is to learn to look and to read in the service of a complex and nuanced act of understanding.

Said is the author of many books and collections, including Joseph Conrad and the Fiction of Autobiography *(1966),* Beginnings: Intention and Method *(1975),* Orientalism *(1978),* The Question of Palestine *(1979),* Covering Islam: How the Media and the Experts Determine How We See the Rest of the World *(1981),* Blaming the Victims *(1988),* Musical Elaborations *(1991),* Culture and Imperialism *(1993),* The Politics of Dispossession: The Struggle for Palestinian Self-Determination, 1989–1994 *(1994),* Representations of the Intellectual *(1994),* Peace and Its Discontents: Essays on Palestine in the Middle East Peace Process *(1995),* Out of Place: A Memoir *(2000),* The End of the Peace Process: Oslo and After *(2001), and* Mona Hatoum: The Entire World as a Foreign Land *(2001).*

Jean Mohr has worked as a photographer for UNESCO, the World Health Organization, and the International Red Cross. He has collaborated on four books with John Berger, Ways of Seeing *(1972; see excerpt on p. 105),* A Seventh Man *(1975),* Another Way of Telling *(1982), and* A Fortunate Man *(1967).*

States

Caught in a meager, anonymous space outside a drab Arab city, outside a refugee camp, outside the crushing time of one disaster after another, a wedding party stands, surprised, sad, slightly uncomfortable [p. 678]. Palestinians—the telltale mixture of styles and attitudes is so evidently theirs—near Tripoli in northern Lebanon. A few months after this picture was taken their camp was ravaged by intra-Palestinian fighting. Cutting across the wedding party's path here is the ever-present Mercedes, emblazoned with its extra mark of authenticity, the proud *D* for *Deutschland*. A rare luxury in the West, the Mercedes—usually secondhand and smuggled in—is the commonest of cars in the Levant. It has become what horse, mule, and camel were, and then much more. Universal taxi, it is a symbol of modern technology domesticated, of the intrusion of the West into traditional life, of illicit trade. More important, the Mercedes is the all-purpose conveyance, something one uses for everything—funerals, weddings, births, proud display, leaving home, coming home, fixing, stealing, reselling, running away in, hiding in. But because Palestinians have no state of their own to shield them, the Mercedes, its provenance and destination obscure, seems like an intruder, a delegate of the forces that both dislocate and hem them in. "The earth is closing on us, pushing us through the last passage," writes the poet Mahmoud Darwish.

Tripoli, Badawi camp, May 1983.

The paradox of mobility and insecurity. Wherever we Palestinians are, we are not in our Palestine, which no longer exists. You travel, from one end of the Arab world to the other, in Europe, Africa, the Americas, Australia, and there you find Palestinians like yourself who, like yourself, are subject to special laws, a special status, the markings of a force and violence not yours. Exiles at home as well as abroad, Palestinians also still inhabit the territory of former Palestine (Israel, the West Bank, Gaza), in sadly reduced circumstances. They are either "the Arabs of Judea and Samaria," or, in Israel, "non-Jews." Some are referred to as "present absentees." In Arab countries, except for Jordan, they are given special cards identifying them as "Palestinian refugees," and even where they are respectable engineers, teachers, business people, or technicians, they know that in the eyes of their host country they will always be aliens. Inevitably, photographs of Palestinians today include this fact and make it visible.

Memory adds to the unrelieved intensity of Palestinian exile. Palestine is central to the cultures of Islam, Christianity, and Judaism; Orient and Occident have turned it into a legend. There is no forgetting it, no way of overlooking it. The world news is often full of what has happened in Palestine-Israel, the latest Middle East crisis, the most recent Palestinian exploits. The sights, wares, and monuments of Palestine are the objects of commerce, war, pilgrimage, cults, the subjects of literature, art, song, fan-

Tel Sheva, 1979. A village of settled nomads near Bersheeba. Some years ago, these
people still lived in a tent, under the desert sky. The carpet on the ground
is the only reminder of that earlier period.

tasy. East and West, their high and their commercial cultures, have descended on Palestine. Bride and groom wear the ill-fitting nuptial cos-
tumes of Europe, yet behind and around them are the clothes and objects
of their native land, natural to their friends and attendants. The happiness
of the occasion is at odds with their lot as refugees with nowhere to go.
The children playing nearby contrast starkly with the unappealing sur-
roundings; the new husband's large workman's hands clash with his
wife's delicate, obscuring white. When we cross from Palestine into other
territories, even if we find ourselves decently in new places, the old ones
loom behind us as tangible and unreal as reproduced memory or absent
causes for our present state.

Sometimes the poignancy of resettlement stands out like bold script
imposed on faint pencil traces. The fit between body and new setting is
not good. The angles are wrong. Lines supposed to decorate a wall instead
form an imperfectly assembled box in which we have been put. We perch
on chairs uncertain whether to address or evade our interlocutor. This
child is held out, and yet also held in. Men and women re-express the un-
attractiveness around them: The angle made across her face by the
woman's robe duplicates the ghastly wall pattern, the man's crossed feet
repeat and contradict the outward thrust of the chair leg. He seems unsettled, poised for departure. Now what? Now where? All at once it is our
transience and impermanence that our visibility expresses, for we can be

[handwritten: Identity difficult to maintain but Palestinians have to show iden. for roots]

seen as figures forced to push on to another house, village, or region. Just as we once were taken from one "habitat" to a new one, we can be moved again.

Exile is a series of portraits without names, without contexts. Images that are largely unexplained, nameless, mute. I look at them without precise anecdotal knowledge, but their realistic exactness nevertheless makes a deeper impression than mere information. I cannot reach the actual people who were photographed, except through a European photographer who saw them for me. And I imagine that he, in turn, spoke to them through an interpreter. The one thing I know for sure, however, is that they treated him politely but as someone who came from, or perhaps acted at the direction of, those who put them where they so miserably are. There was the embarrassment of people uncertain why they were being looked at and recorded. Powerless to stop it.

When A. Z.'s father was dying, he called his children, one of whom is married to my sister, into his room for a last family gathering. A frail, very old man from Haifa, he had spent his last thirty-four years in Beirut in a state of agitated disbelief at the loss of his house and property. Now he murmured to his children the final faltering words of a penniless, helpless patriarch. "Hold on to the keys and the deed," he told them, pointing to a battered suitcase near his bed, a repository of the family estate salvaged from Palestine when Haifa's Arabs were expelled. These intimate mementos of a past irrevocably lost circulate among us, like the genealogies and fables of a wandering singer of tales. Photographs, dresses, objects severed from their original locale, the rituals of speech and custom: Much reproduced, enlarged, thematized, embroidered, and passed around, they are strands in the web of affiliations we Palestinians use to tie ourselves to our identity and to each other.

Sometimes these objects, heavy with memory—albums, rosary beads, shawls, little boxes—seem to me like encumbrances. We carry them about, hang them up on every new set of walls we shelter in, reflect lovingly on them. Then we do not notice the bitterness, but it continues and grows nonetheless. Nor do we acknowledge the frozen immobility of our attitudes. In the end the past owns us. My father spent his life trying to escape these objects, "Jerusalem" chief among them—the actual place as much as its reproduced and manufactured self. Born in Jerusalem, as were his parents, grandparents, and all his family back in time to a distant vanishing point, he was a child of the Old City who traded with tourists in bits of the true cross and crowns of thorn. Yet he hated the place; for him, he often said, it meant death. Little of it remained with him except a fragmentary story or two, an odd coin or medal, one photograph of his father on horseback, and two small rugs. I never even saw a picture of my grandmother's face. But as he grew older, he reverted to old Jerusalemite expressions that I did not understand, never having heard them during the years of my youth.

Amman, 1984. A visit to the former mayor of Jerusalem and his wife, in exile in Jordan.

• • •

Identity—who we are, where we come from, what we are—is difficult to maintain in exile. Most other people take their identity for granted. Not the Palestinian, who is required to show proofs of identity more or less constantly. It is not only that we are regarded as terrorists, but that our existence as native Arab inhabitants of Palestine, with primordial rights there (and not elsewhere), is either denied or challenged. And there is

Ramallah, 1979. An everyday street scene, banal and reassuring. And yet, the
tension is constant. A passing military jeep, a flying stone—the incident,
the drama, can occur at any moment.

more. Such as it is, our existence is linked negatively to encomiums about
Israel's democracy, achievements, excitement; in much Western rhetoric
we have slipped into the place occupied by Nazis and anti-Semites; collectively, we can aspire to little except political anonymity and resettlement;
we are known for no actual achievement, no characteristic worthy of es-

teem, except the effrontery of disrupting Middle East peace. Some Israeli settlers on the West Bank say: "The Palestinians can stay here, with no rights, as resident aliens." Other Israelis are less kind. We have no known Einsteins, no Chagall, no Freud or Rubinstein to protect us with a legacy of glorious achievements. We have had no Holocaust to protect us with the world's compassion. We are "other," and opposite, a flaw in the geometry of resettlement and exodus. Silence and discretion veil the hurt, slow the body searches, soothe the sting of loss.

A zone of recollected pleasure surrounds the few unchanged spots of Palestinian life in Palestine. The foodsellers and peddlers—itinerant vendors of cakes or corn—are still there for the casual eye to see, and they still provoke the appetite. They seem to travel not only from place to place, but from an earlier time to the present, carrying with them the same clientele—the young girls and boys, the homeward-bound cyclist, the loitering student or clerk—now as then. We buy their wares with the same surreptitiously found change (who can remember the unit? was it a piaster? fils? shilling?) spent on the same meager object, neither especially good nor especially well prepared. The luxurious pleasure of tasting the vendor's *simsim,* the round sesame cakes dipped in that tangy mixture of thyme and sumac, or his *durra,* boiled corn sprayed with salt, surpasses the mere act of eating and opens before us the altogether agreeable taste of food not connected with meals, with nourishment, with routine. But what a

distance now actually separates me from the concreteness of that life. How easily traveled the photographs make it seem, and how possible to suspend the barriers keeping me from the scenes they portray.

For the land is further away than it has ever been. Born in Jerusalem in late 1935, I left mandatory Palestine permanently at the end of 1947. In the spring of 1948, my last cousin evacuated our family's house in West Jerusalem; Martin Buber subsequently lived there till his death, I have been told. I grew up in Egypt, then came to the United States as a student. In 1966 I visited Ramallah, part of the Jordanian West Bank, for a family wedding. My father, who was to die five years later, accompanied my sister and me. Since our visit, all the members of my family have resettled— in Jordan, in Lebanon, in the United States, and in Europe. As far as I know, I have no relatives who still live in what was once Palestine. Wars, revolutions, civil struggles have changed the countries I have lived in— Lebanon, Jordan, Egypt—beyond recognition. Until thirty-five years ago I could travel from Cairo to Beirut overland, through territories held or in other ways controlled by rival colonial powers. Now, although my mother lives in Beirut, I have not visited her since the Israeli invasion of 1982: Palestinians are no longer welcome there. The fact is that today I can neither return to the places of my youth, nor voyage freely in the countries and places that mean the most to me, nor feel safe from arrest or violence even in the countries I used to frequent but whose governments and policies have changed radically in recent times. There is little that is more unpleasant for me these days than the customs and police check upon entering an Arab country.

Consider the tremendous upheavals since 1948 each of which effectively destroyed the ecology of our previous existence. When I was born, we in Palestine felt ourselves to be part of a small community, presided over by the majority community and one or another of the outside powers holding sway over the territory. My family and I, for example, were members of a tiny Protestant group within a much larger Greek Orthodox Christian minority, within the larger Sunni Islam majority; the important outside power was Britain, with its great rival France a close second. But then after World War II Britain and France lost their hold, and for the first time we directly confronted the colonial legacy—inept rulers, divided populations, conflicting promises made to resident Arabs and mostly European Jews with incompatible claims. In 1948 Israel was established; Palestine was destroyed, and the great Palestinian dispossession began. In 1956 Egypt was invaded by Britain, France, and Israel, causing what was left of the large Levantine communities there (Italian, Greek, Jewish, Armenian, Syrian) to leave. The rise of Abdel Nasser fired all Arabs—especially Palestinians—with the hope of a revived Arab nationalism, but after the union of Syria with Egypt failed in 1961, the Arab cold war, as it has been called, began in earnest; Saudi Arabia versus Egypt, Jordan versus Syria, Syria versus Iraq. . . . A new population of refugees, migrant workers, and traveling political parties crisscrossed the Arab world. We Pal-

[handwritten at top: literally geography / exile in them of stability / continuity of land has disappeared.]

estinians immersed ourselves in the politics of Baathism in Syria and Iraq, of Nasserism in Egypt, of the Arab Nationalist Movement in Lebanon.

The 1967 war was followed shortly after by the Arab oil boom. For the first time, Palestinian nationalism arose as an independent force in the Middle East. Never did our future seem more hopeful. In time, however, our appearance on the political scene stimulated, if it did not actually cause, a great many less healthy phenomena: fundamentalist Islam, Maronite nationalism, Jewish zealotry. The new consumer culture, the computerized economy, further exacerbated the startling disparities in the Arab world between rich and poor, old and new, privileged and disinherited. Then, starting in 1975, the Lebanese civil war pitted the various Lebanese sects, the Palestinians, and a number of Arab and foreign powers against each other. Beirut was destroyed as the intellectual and political nerve center of Arab life; for us, it was the end of our only important, relatively independent center of Palestinian nationalism, with the Palestinian Liberation Organization at its heart. Anwar Sadat recognized Israel, and Camp David further dismantled the region's alliances and disrupted its balance. After the Iranian revolution in 1979 came the Iran-Iraq war. Israel's 1982 invasion of Lebanon put more Palestinians on the move, as the massacres in the Palestinian refugee camps of Sabra and Shatila reduced the community still further. By the end of 1983, Palestinians were fighting each other, and Syria and Libya were directly involved, supporting Palestinian dissidents against PLO loyalists. With the irony typical of our political fate, however, in mid-1985 we were united together in Sabra and Shatila to fight off a hostile Shi'ite militia patronized by Syria.

The stability of geography and the continuity of land—these have completely disappeared from my life and the life of all Palestinians. If we are not stopped at borders, or herded into new camps, or denied reentry and residence, or barred from travel from one place to another, more of our land is taken, our lives are interfered with arbitrarily, our voices are prevented from reaching each other, our identity is confined to frightened little islands in an inhospitable environment of superior military force sanitized by the clinical jargon of pure administration. On the West Bank and in Gaza we confront several Zionist "master plans"—which, according to Meron Benvenisti, ex-deputy mayor of Jerusalem, are "explicitly sectarian." He continues:

[handwritten: too much distance]

> The criteria established to determine priorities of settlement regions are "*interconnection* [*havirah*] between existing Jewish areas for the creation of [Jewish] settlement continuity" and "*separation* [*hayitz*] to restrict uncontrolled Arab settlement and the prevention of Arab settlement blocs"; "*scarcity* [*hesech*] refers to areas devoid of Jewish settlement." In these criteria "pure planning and political planning elements are included."
>
>   *(The West Bank Data Project:*
>   *A Survey of Israeli Policies)*

Continuity for *them*, the dominant population; discontinuity for *us*, the dispossessed and dispersed.

The circle is completed, though, when we Palestinians acknowledge that much the same thesis is adhered to by Arab and other states where sizable Palestinian communities exist. There too we are in dispersed camps, regions, quarters, zones; but unlike their Israeli counterparts, these places are not the scientific product of "pure planning" or "political planning." The Baqa'a camp in Amman, the Palestinian quarter of Hawaly in Kuwait, are simply there.

All forms of Palestinian activity, all attempts at unity, are suspect. On the West Bank and Gaza, "development" (the systematic strengthening of Palestinian economic and social life) is forbidden, whereas "improvement" is tolerated so long as there isn't too much of it; so long as it doesn't become development. The colors of the Palestinian flag are outlawed by Israeli military law; Fathi Gabin of Gaza, an artist, was given a six-month prison sentence for using black, green, red, and white in one of his works. An exhibit of Palestinian culture at al-Najah University in Nablus earned the school a four-month closing. Since our history is forbidden, narratives are rare; the story of origins, of home, of nation is underground. When it appears it is broken, often wayward and meandering in the extreme, always coded, usually in outrageous forms—mock-epics, satires, sardonic parables, absurd rituals—that make little sense to an outsider. Thus Palestinian life is scattered, discontinuous, marked by the artificial and im-

Tyre, South Lebanon, 1983. Bourj el-Shemali camp. The car bears witness to a drama, circumstances unknown. The flowers: the month of May, it is spring. The children: wearing smart clothes, almost certainly donated by a charity. They are refugees—the children of refugees.

Bedouin encampment near Bersheeba, 1979.

posed arrangements of interrupted or confined space, by the dislocations and unsynchronized rhythms of disturbed time. Across our children's lives, in the open fields in which they play, lie the ruins of war, of a borrowed or imported industrial technology, of cast-off or abandoned forms. How odd the conjuncture, and yet for Palestinians, how fitting. For where no straight line leads from home to birthplace to school to maturity, all events are accidents, all progress is a digression, all residence is exile. We linger in nondescript places, neither here nor there; we peer through windows without glass, ride conveyances without movement or power. Resourcefulness and receptivity are the attitudes that serve best.

The difference between the new generation of Palestinians and that of 1948 is striking. Our parents bore on their faces the marks of disaster uncomprehended. Suddenly their past had been interrupted, their society obliterated, their existence radically impoverished. Refugees, all of them. Our children know no such past. Cars are equally for riding or, ruined, for playing in. Everything around them seems expendable, impermanent, unstable, especially where—as in Lebanon—Palestinian communities have been disastrously depleted or destroyed, where much of their life is undocumented, where they themselves are uncounted.

No Palestinian census exists. There is no line that can be drawn from one Palestinian to another that does not seem to interfere with the political designs of one or another state. While all of us live among "normal" people, people with complete lives, they seem to us hopelessly out of reach, with their countries, their familial continuity, their societies intact. How does a Palestinian father tell his son and daughter that Lebanon (Egypt, Syria, Jordan, New York) is where we are, but not where we are *from*? How does a mother confirm her intimate recollections of childhood in Palestine to her children, now that the facts, the places, even the names, are no longer allowed to exist?

So we borrow and we patch things together. Palestinians retain the inflections of Jaffa, of Hebron, of Jerusalem and other cities left behind, even as their dialect becomes that of Beirut, Detroit, or Paris. I have found out much more about Palestine and met many more Palestinians than I ever did, or perhaps could have, in pre-1948 Palestine. For a long time I thought that this was so because I was a child then, somewhat sheltered, a member of a minority. But my experience is confirmed by my oldest and closest Palestinian friend, Ibrahim Abu-Lughod. Although he was more in and of pre-1948 Palestine—because older, more conscious and active—than I ever was, he too says that he is much more in contact with Palestinians today than when he was in Palestine. He writes, "Thanks to modern technological progress, Palestinian families, and Palestinian society as a whole, have been able to forge very numerous human, social, and political links. By getting on a plane I can see the majority of my friends. It's because of this that our family has remained unified. I see all the members of my family at least once or twice a year. Being in Jaffa, I could never have seen relatives who lived in Gaza, for example." But Ibrahim does not celebrate this sociability: "I constantly experience the sense that something is missing for me. To compensate for this lack, I multiply and intensify human contacts."

Over the missing "something" are superimposed new realities. Plane travel and phone conversations nourish and connect the fortunate; the symbols of a universal pop culture enshroud the vulnerable.

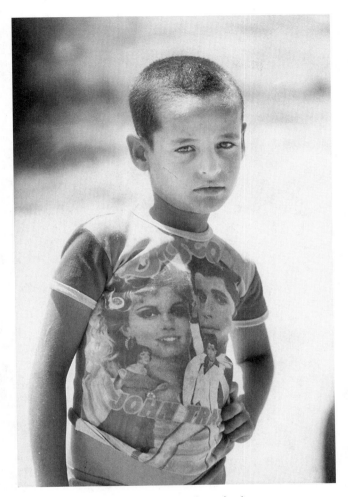

Gaza, 1979. Refugee camp. A boy of unknown age.

There can be no orderly sequence of time. You see it in our children who seem to have skipped a phase of growth or, more alarming, achieved an out-of-season maturity in one part of their body or mind while the rest remains childlike. None of us can forget the whispers and occasional proclamations that our children are "the population factor"—to be feared, and hence to be deported—or constitute special targets for death. I heard it said in Lebanon that Palestinian children in particular should be killed because each of them is a potential terrorist. Kill them before they kill you.

How rich our mutability, how easily we change (and are changed) from one thing to another, how unstable our place—and all because of the missing foundation of our existence, the lost ground of our origin, the broken link with our land and our past. There are no Palestinians. Who are

Tel Sheva, 1979. A group portrait, taken at the request of the children.

the Palestinians? "The inhabitants of Judea and Samaria." Non-Jews. Terrorists. Troublemakers. DPs.° Refugees. Names on a card. Numbers on a list. Praised in speeches—*el pueblo palestino, il popolo palestino, le peuple palestinien*—but treated as interruptions, intermittent presences. Gone from Jordan in 1970, now from Lebanon.

   None of these departures and arrivals is clean, definitive. Some of us leave, others stay behind. Remnants, new arrivals, old residents. Two great images encapsulate our unresolved existence. One is the identity card (passport, travel document, laissez-passer), which is never Palestin-

---

DPs   Displaced persons or displaced people. [Editors' note]

ian but always something else; it is the subject of our national poem, Mahmoud Darwish's "Bitaqit Hawia": "Record! I am an Arab / Without a name—without title / patient in a country / with people enraged." And the second is Emil Habiby's invention the Pessoptimist (*al-mutasha 'il*), the protagonist of a disorderly and ingenious work of Kafkaesque fiction, which has become a kind of national epic. The Pessoptimist is being half here, half not here, part historical creature, part mythological invention, hopeful and hopeless, everyone's favorite obsession and scapegoat. Is Habiby's character fiction, or does his extravagant fantasy only begin to approximate the real? Is he a made-up figure or the true essence of our existence? Is Habiby's jamming-together of words—*mutafa'il* and *mutasha'im* into *mutasha'il*, which repeats the Palestinian habit of combining opposites like *la* ("no") and *na'am* ("yes") into *la'am*—a way of obliterating distinctions that do not apply to us, yet must be integrated into our lives?

Emil Habiby is a craggy, uncompromisingly complex, and fearsomely ironic man from Haifa, son of a Christian family, Communist party stalwart, longtime Knesset member, journalist, editor. His novel about the Pessoptimist (whose first name, incidentally, is Said) is chaotic because it mixes time, characters, and places; fiction, allegory, history, and flat statement, without any thread to guide the reader through its complexities. It is the best work of Palestinian writing yet produced, precisely because the

Bersheeba, 1979. Near a Bedouin encampment, a little kitchen garden—and its scarecrow of bits and pieces.

most seemingly disorganized and ironic. In it we encounter characters whose names are of particular significance to Palestinians: The name of Yuaad, the work's female lead, means "it shall be repeated," a reference to the string of defeats that mark our history, and the fatalistic formulae that color our discourse. One of the other characters is Isam al-Bathanjani—Isam the Eggplant, a lawyer who is not very helpful to Said but who keeps turning up just the same. So it is with eggplants in Palestine. My family—my father in particular—has always been attached to eggplants from Battir, and during the many years since any of us had Battiri eggplants the seal of approval on good eggplants was that "they're almost as good as the Battiris."

Today when I recall the tiresome paeans to Battiris, or when in London and Paris I see the same Jaffa oranges or Gaza vegetables grown in the *bayarat* ("orchards") and fields of my youth, but now marketed by Israeli export companies, the contrast between the inarticulate rich *thereness* of what we once knew and the systematic export of the produce into the hungry mouths of Europe strikes me with its unkind political message. The land and the peasants are bound together through work whose products seem always to have meant something to other people, to have been destined for consumption elsewhere. This observation holds force not just because the Carmel boxes and the carefully wrapped eggplants are emblems of the power that rules the sprawling fertility and enduring human labor of Palestine, but also because the discontinuity between me, out here, and the actuality there is so much more compelling now than my receding memories and experiences of Palestine.

Another, far more unusual, item concerning this vegetable appears in an article by Avigdor Feldman, "The New Order of the Military Government: State of Israel Against the Eggplant," which appeared in the journal *Koteret Rashit*, August 24, 1983. Laws 1015 and 1039, Feldman reports, stipulate that any Arab on the West Bank and Gaza who owns land must get written permission from the military governor before planting either a new vegetable—for example, an eggplant—or fruit tree. Failure to get permission risks one the destruction of the tree or vegetable plus one year's imprisonment.

Exile again. The facts of my birth are so distant and strange as to be about someone I've heard of rather than someone I know. Nazareth—my mother's town. Jerusalem—my father's. The pictures I see display the same produce, presented in the same carelessly plentiful way, in the same rough wooden cases. The same people walk by, looking at the same posters and trinkets, concealing the same secrets, searching for the same profits, pleasures, and goals. The same as what? There is little that I can truly remember about Jerusalem and Nazareth, little that is specific, little that has the irreducible durability of tactile, visual, or auditory memories that concede nothing to time, little—and this is the "same" I referred to—

Gaza, 1979. Farm using refugee labor.

that is not confused with pictures I have seen or scenes I have glimpsed elsewhere in the Arab world.

Palestine is exile, dispossession, the inaccurate memories of one place slipping into vague memories of another, a confused recovery of general wares, passive presences scattered around in the Arab environment. The story of Palestine cannot be told smoothly. Instead, the past, like the present, offers only occurrences and coincidences. Random. The man enters a quiet alley where he will pass cucumbers on his right, tomatoes on his left; a priest walks down the stairs, the boy dashes off, satchel under arm, other boys loiter, shopkeepers look out for business; carrying an airline bag, a man advances past a display of trinkets, a young man disappears around the corner, two boys idle aimlessly. Tomatoes, watermelons, arcades, cucumbers, posters, people, eggplants—not simply there, but represented by photographs as being there—saturated with meaning and memory, and still very far away. Look more closely and think through these possibilities: The poster is about Egypt. The trinkets are made in Korea or Hong Kong. The scenes are surveyed, enclosed, and surrounded by Israelis. European and Japanese tourists have more access to Jerusalem and Nazareth than I do. Slowly, our lives—like Palestine itself—dissolve into something else. We can't hold to the center for long.

Exile. At a recent conference in America featuring a "dialogue" between Israeli and Palestinian intellectuals with reconciliation high on the agenda, a man rises from the audience to pose a question. "I am a Palestinian, a peas-

Nazareth, 1979. Portrait of Om Kalsoum.

Jerusalem, 1979. A snapshot.

Jerusalem, 1979. A snapshot.

ant. Look at my hands. I was kicked out in 1948 and went to Lebanon. Then I was driven out, and went to Africa. Then to Europe. Then to here. Today [he pulls out an envelope] I received a paper telling me to leave this country. Would one of you scholars tell me please: Where am I supposed to go now?" No one had anything to tell him. He was an embarrassment, and I have no idea what in fact he did, what became of him. My shame.

Old City of Jerusalem, 1984. A tourist shop. Customers are rare. Will they be American, Swiss, or Israeli?

Jerusalem, 1979.

The Palestinian's claims on Israel are generally unacknowledged, much less seen as directly connected to the founding of the state. On the Arabs there is an ambivalent Palestinian claim, recognized in Arab countries by countless words, gestures, threats, and promises. Palestine, after all, is the centerpiece of Arab nationalism. No Arab leader since World War II has failed to make Palestine a symbol of his country's nationalist foreign policy. Yet, despite the avowals, we have no way of knowing really how they—all the "theys"—feel about us. Our history has cost every one of our friends a great deal. It has gone on too long.

Let Ghassan Kanafani's novella *Men in the Sun* stand for the fear we have that unless we press "them" they will allow us to disappear, and the equal worry that if we press them they will either decry our hectoring presence, and quash it in their states, or turn us into easy symbols of their nationalism. Three refugees concealed in the belly of a tanker truck are being transported illegally across the border into Kuwait. As the driver converses with the guards, the men (Palestinians) die of suffocation—in the sun, forgotten. It is not the driver's forgetfulness that nags at him. It is their silence. "Why didn't you knock on the sides of the tank? Why didn't you bang the sides of the tank? Why? Why? Why?" Our fear to press.

The Palestinians as commodity. Producing ourselves much as the *masabih,* lamps, tapestries, baskets, embroideries, mother-of-pearl trinkets are produced. We turn ourselves into objects not for sale, but for scrutiny. People ask us, as if looking into an exhibit case, "What is it you Palestinians want?"—as if we can put our demands into a single neat phrase. All

of us speak of *awdah*, "return," but do we mean that literally, or do we mean "we must restore ourselves to ourselves"? The latter is the real point, I think, although I know many Palestinians who want their houses and their way of life back, exactly. But is there any place that fits us, together with our accumulated memories and experiences?

Do we exist? What proof do we have?

The further we get from the Palestine of our past, the more precarious our status, the more disrupted our being, the more intermittent our presence. When did we become "a people"? When did we stop being one? Or are we in the process of becoming one? What do those big questions have to do with our intimate relationships with each other and with others? We frequently end our letters with the mottoes "Palestinian love" or "Palestinian kisses." Are there really such things as Palestinian intimacy and embraces, or are they simply intimacy and embraces, experiences common to everyone, neither politically significant nor particular to a nation or a people?

The politics of such a question gets very close to our central dilemma: We all know that we are Arabs, and yet the concept, not to say the lived actuality, of Arabism—once the creed and the discourse of a proud Arab nation, free of imperialism, united, respected, powerful—is fast disappearing, cut up into the cautious defensiveness of relatively provincial Arab states, each with its own traditions—partly invented, partly real—each with its own nationality and restricted identity. In addition, Palestine has been replaced by an Israel whose aggressive sense of itself as the state of the Jewish people fuels the exclusivity of a national identity won and maintained to a great extent at our expense. We are not Jews, we have no place there except as resident aliens, we are outsiders. In the Arab states we are in a different position. There we are Arabs, but it is the process of nationalization that excludes us: Egypt is for and by Egyptians, Iraq is for and by Iraqis, in ways that cannot include Palestinians whose intense national revival is a separate phenomenon. Thus we are the same as other Arabs, and yet different. We cannot exist except as Arabs, even though "the Arabs" exist otherwise as Lebanese, Jordanians, Moroccans, Kuwaitis, and so forth.

Add to this the problems we have of sustaining ourselves as a collective unit and you then get a sense of how *abstract,* how very solitary and unique, we tend to feel.

Strip off the occasional assertiveness and stridency of the Palestinian stance and you may catch sight of a much more fugitive, but ultimately quite beautifully representative and subtle, sense of identity. It speaks in languages not yet fully formed, in settings not completely constituted, like the shy glance of a child holding her father's knee while she curiously and tentatively examines the stranger who photographs her. Her look conjures up the unappreciated fact of birth, that sudden, unprepared-for depositing of a small bundle of self on the fields of the Levant after which comes the

Village of Ramah, Galilee, 1979. A secular high school with students from thirty-six
neighboring villages.

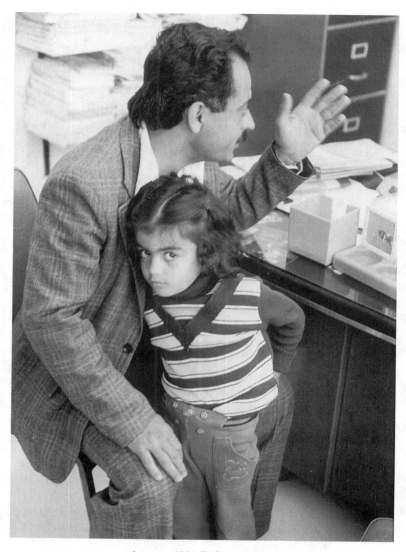

Amman, 1984. Pediatric clinic.

trajectory of dispossession, military and political violence, and that constant, mysterious entanglement with monotheistic religion at its most profound—the Christian Incarnation and Resurrection, the Ascension to heaven of the Prophet Mohammed, the Covenant of Yahweh with his people—that is knotted definitively in Jerusalem, center of the world, *locus classicus* of Palestine, Israel, and Paradise.

A secular world of fatigue and miraculously renewed energies, the world of American cigarettes and an unending stream of small papers

Sidon, South Lebanon, 1983. A refugee writes out a message destined for her husband, a prisoner in the camp at Ansar.

pulled out of miscellaneous notebooks or "blocnotes," written on with disposable pens, messages of things wanted, of people missing, of requests to the bureaucracy. The Palestinian predicament: finding an "official" place for yourself in a system that makes no allowances for you, which means endlessly improvising solutions for the problem of finding a missing loved one, of planning a trip, of entering a school, on whatever bit of paper is at hand. Constructed and deconstructed, ephemera are what we negotiate with, since we authorize no part of the world and only influence increasingly small bits of it. In any case, we keep going.

The striking thing about Palestinian prose and prose fiction is its formal instability: Our literature in a certain very narrow sense *is* the elusive, resistant reality it tries so often to represent. Most literary critics in Israel and the West focus on what is said in Palestinian writing, who is described, what the plot and contents deliver, their sociological and political meaning. But it is *form* that should be looked at. Particularly in fiction, the struggle to achieve form expresses the writer's efforts to construct a coherent scene, a narrative that might overcome the almost metaphysical impossibility of representing the present. A typical Palestinian work will always be concerned with this peculiar problem, which is at once a problem of plot and an enactment of the writer's enterprise. In Kanafani's *Men in the Sun* much of the action takes place on the dusty streets of an Iraqi town where three Palestinian men must petition, plead, and bargain with "specialists" to smuggle them across the border into Kuwait. Impelled by exile and dislocation, the Palestinians need to carve a path for themselves in existence, which for them is by no means a given or stable reality. Like the history of the lands they left, their lives seem interrupted just before they could come to maturity and satisfaction; thus each man leaves behind family and responsibilities, to whose exigencies he must answer—unsuccessfully—here in the present. Kanafani's very sentences express instability and fluctuation—the present tense is subject to echoes from the past, verbs of sight give way to verbs of sound or smell, and one sense interweaves with another—in an effort to defend against the harsh present and to protect some particularly cherished fragment of the past. Thus, the precarious actuality of these men in the sun reproduces the precarious status of the writer, each echoing the other.

Our characteristic mode, then, is not a narrative, in which scenes take place *seriatim*, but rather broken narratives, fragmentary compositions, and self-consciously staged testimonials, in which the narrative voice keeps stumbling over itself, its obligations, and its limitations.

Each Palestinian structure presents itself as a potential ruin. The theme of the formerly proud family house (village, city, camp) now wrecked, left behind, or owned by someone else, turns up everywhere in our literature and cultural heritage. Each new house is a substitute, supplanted in turn by yet another substitute. The names of these places extend all the way from the private (my friend Mohammed Tarbush expatiates nobly on the beauties of Beit Natif, a village near Bethlehem that was wiped out of existence by Israeli bulldozers in 1948; his widowed mother now lives in Jarash, Jordan, he in Paris) to the official, or institutionalized, sites of ruin—Deir Yassin, Tell el-Zaatar, Birim and Ikrit, Ein el-Hilwé, Sabra, Shatila, and more. Even "Palestine" itself is such a place and, curiously, al-

Sidon, South Lebanon, 1983. Camp at Ein el-Hilwé. Time passes: destruction, reconstruction, redestruction.

ready appears as a subject of elegy in journalism, essays, and literature of the early twentieth century. In the works of Halim Nassar, Ezzat Darwaza, Khallil Beidas, and Aref el-Aref, Palestine's destruction is predicted.

All cultures spin out a dialectic of self and other, the subject "I" who is native, authentic, at home, and the object "it" or "you," who is foreign, perhaps threatening, different, out there. From this dialectic comes the series of heroes and monsters, founding fathers and barbarians, prized masterpieces and despised opponents that express a culture from its deepest sense of national self-identity to its refined patriotism, and finally to its coarse jingoism, xenophobia, and exclusivist bias. For Palestinian culture, the odd thing is that its own identity is more frequently than not perceived as "other." "Palestine" is so charged with significance for others that Palestinians cannot perceive it as intimately theirs without a simultaneous sense of its urgent importance for others as well. "Ours" but not yet fully "ours." Before 1948, Palestine had a central agonistic meaning both for Arab nationalism and for the Zionist movement. After 1948, the parts of Palestine still inhabited by Arabs took on the additional label of the "non-Jewish" part of the Jewish state. Even a picture of an Arab town—like Nazareth where my mother was born and grew up—may express this alienating perspective. Because it is taken from outside Nazareth (in fact, from Upper Nazareth, a totally Jewish addition to the town, built on the surrounding hills), the photograph renders Palestine as "other." I never knew Nazareth, so this is my only image of it, an image of the "other," from the "outside," Upper Nazareth.

Thus the insider becomes the outsider. Not only have the interpositions between us and Palestine grown more formidable over time, but, to make matters worse, most of us pass our lives separated from each other. Yet we live in comradely communication despite the barriers. Today the Palestinian genius expresses itself in crossings-over, in clearing hurdles, activities that do not lessen the alienation, discontinuity, and dispossession, but that dramatize and clarify them instead. We have remained; in the words of Tawfik Zayyad's famous poem, "The Twenty Impossibles," it would be easier "to catch fried fish in the Milky Way,/to plow the sea,/to teach the alligator speech" than to make us leave. To the Israelis, whose incomparable military and political power dominates us, we are at the periphery, the image that will not go away. Every assertion of our nonexistence, every attempt to spirit us away, every new effort to prove that we were never really there, simply raises the question of why so much denial of, and such energy expended on, what was not there? Could it be that even as alien outsiders we dog their military might with our obdurate moral claim, our insistence (like that of Bartleby the Scrivener) that "we would prefer not to," not to leave, not to abandon Palestine forever?

The proof of whatever small success we have had is not that we have regained a homeland, or acquired a new one; rather, it is that some Israelis

Arab Nazareth, 1979. Viewed from Upper Nazareth.

Tyre, South Lebanon, 1983. Rashidyé camp: A local official
collects messages from the relations of refugees for the
International Red Cross.

have admitted the possibility of sharing a common space with us, in Palestine. The proposed modes of such a sharing are adventurous and utopian in the present context of hostility between Arabs and Jews, but on an intellectual level they are actual, and to some of us—on both sides—they make sense. Most Palestinians have their own special instance of the Israeli who reached out across the barricade most humanly. For some it is the intrepid Israeli lawyer defending Palestinian political prisoners, or trying to prevent land expropriations and collective punishment; for others it is—the testimony of Salah Ta'amari, leader of the Palestinian prisoners rounded up during the Israeli invasion and put in the Ansar prison camp, comes to

Kalandia (near Ramallah), 1967. A few days after the end of the June
War: in the foreground, an Israeli officer, lost in thought. Behind the
window, a young villager.

mind—an Israeli in a position of authority (prison guard or army officer)
who prevented some atrocity or showed some clear sign of humanity and
fellow feeling. For my part, removed from the terrible pressures of the
scene, I think of all the Israeli (or non-Israeli) Jews whose articulate witness to the injustice of their people against mine has marked out a communal territory. The result has usually been a friendship whose depth is
directly proportional to the admiration I feel for their tenacity of conscience and belief in the face of the most slanderous attacks. Surely few
have equaled the courage and principle of Israel Shahak, of Leah Tsemal
and Felicia Langer, of Noam Chomsky, of Izzy Stone, of Elmer Berger, of

Jerusalem, 1979. A dialogue between left-wing Israeli and Arab intellectuals.

Matti Peled, of so many others who stood up bravely during the events in Lebanon.

There are few opportunities for us Palestinians, or us Palestinians *and* Israelis, to learn anything about the world we live in that is *not* touched by, indeed soaked in, the hostilities of our struggle. And if it isn't the Palestinian-Zionist struggle, there are the pressures of religion, of every conceivable ideology, of family, peers, and compatriots, each of them bearing down upon us, pushing, kneading, prodding every one of us from childhood to maturity.

In such an environment, learning itself is a chancy, hybrid activity, laced with the unresolvable antitheses of our age. The child is full of the curious hope and undirected energy that attract the curatorial powers of both church and state. Fortunately, here the spirit of the creative urge in all human activity asserts itself—neither church nor state can ultimately exhaust, or control, the possibilities latent in the classroom, playground, or family. An orderly row of chairs and tables, a disciplined recitation circle in a Catholic school with a nun in charge, are also places for the absorption of more knowledge and experience than authorities impart—places where the child explores here and there, his/her mind and body wandering in space and time despite the constraints in each. In a school where the teacher is a devout Muslim, the child's propensity for disturbing or opposing the schemes of knowledge and discipline causes him/her to leave the table, disrupt the pattern, seek unthought-of possibilities. The tension between teachers and students remains, but better the tension than the peace of passivity, or the unresisting assent to authority.

Nazareth, 1979. A municipal kindergarten, looked after by nuns.

The pressures of the here and now require an answer to the Palestinian crisis here and now. Whereas our interlocutors, our "others"—the Arab states, the United States, the USSR, Israel, our friends and enemies—have the luxury of a state in which institutions do their work undisturbed by the question of existence-or-not, we lead our lives under a sword of Damocles, whose dry rhetorical form is the query "When are you Palestinians going to accept a solution?"—the implication being that if we don't, we'll disappear. This, then, is our midnight hour.

It is difficult to know how much the often stated, tediously reiterated worries about us, which include endless lectures on the need for a clear

Amman, 1984. Camp at Baqa'a, one of the oldest in Jordan. The YWCA looks after some of the kindergartens.

Palestinian statement of the desire for peace (as if we controlled the decisive factors!), are malicious provocation and how much genuine, if sympathetic, ignorance. I don't think any of us reacts as impatiently to such
things as we did, say, five years ago. True, our collective situation is more
precarious now than it was, but I detect a general turning inward among
Palestinians, as if many of us feel the need to consolidate and collect the
shards of Palestinian life still present and available to us. This is not qui-
etism at all, nor is it resignation. Rather, it springs from the natural impulse to stand back when the headlong rush of events gets to be too much,
perhaps, for us to savor life as life, to reflect at some distance from politics
on where we came from and where we are, to regrasp, revise, recompre-
hend the tumultuous experiences at whose center, quite without our consent, we have been made to stand.

Jean Mohr's photograph of a small but clearly formed human group
surrounded by a dense and layered reality expresses very well what we
experience during that detachment from an ideologically saturated world.
This image of four people seen at a distance near Ramallah, in the middle
of and yet separated from thick foliage, stairs, several tiers of terraces and
houses, a lone electricity pole off to the right, is for me a private, crystal-
lized, almost Proustian evocation of Palestine. Memory: During the summer of 1942—I was six—we rented a house in Ramallah. My father, I recall, was ill with high blood pressure and recovering from a nervous
breakdown. I remember him as withdrawn and constantly smoking. My
mother took me to a variety show at the local Friends school. During the
second half I left the hall to go to the toilet, but for reasons I could not (and

Jerusalem, 1984.

Near Senjel, a village between Ramallah and Nablus, 1979.

still do not) grasp, the boy-scout usher would not let me back in. I recall with ever-renewed poignancy the sudden sense of distance I experienced from what was familiar and pleasant—my mother, friends, the show; all at once the rift introduced into the cozy life I led taught me the meaning of separation, of solitude, and of anguished boredom. There was nothing to do but wait, although my mother did appear a little later to find out what had happened to me. We left immediately, but not before I furtively took a quick look back through the door window at the lighted stage. The telescoped vision of small figures assembled in a detached space has remained with me for over forty years, and it reappears in the adjusted and transformed center of Jean's 1983 picture. I never ventured anywhere near that part of Ramallah again. I would no more know it than I would the precise place of this photo; and yet I am sure it would be familiar, the way this one immediately seemed.

My private past is inscribed on the surface of this peaceful but somehow brooding pastoral scene in the contemporary West Bank. I am not the only one surveying the scene. There is the child on the left who looks on. There are also the Swiss photographer, compassionate, curious, silent, and of course the ever-present Israeli security services, who hold the West

Bank and its population in the vise of occupation. As for those terraces and multiple levels: Do they serve the activities of daily life or are they the haunted stairs of a prison which, like Piranesi's, lead nowhere, confining their human captives? The dense mass of leaves, right and left, lend their bulk to the frame, but they too impinge on the slender life they surround, like memory or a history too complex to be sorted out, bigger than its subject, richer than any consciousness one might have of it.

The power grid recalls the Mercedes in Tripoli. Unassimilated, its modernity and power have been felt with considerable strength in our lives here and there throughout the Third World. Another childhood memory: Driving through the Sinai from Egypt into Palestine, we would see the row of telephone and electricity pylons partnering the empty macadamized road that cut through an even emptier desert. Who are they, I would ask myself. What do they think when we are not here? When we stopped to stretch our legs, I would go up to a pole and look at its dull brown surface for some sign of life, identity, or awareness. Once I marked one with my initials EWS, hoping to find it again on the trip back. All of them looked exactly the same as we hurtled by. We never stopped. I never drove there again, nor can I now. Futile efforts to register my presence on the scene.

Intimate memory and contemporary social reality seem connected by the little passage between the child, absorbed in his private, silent sphere, and the three older people, who are the public world of adults, work, and community. It is a vacant, somewhat tenuously maintained space, however; sandy, pebbly, and weedy. All the force in the photograph moves dramatically from trees left to trees right, from the visible enclave of domesticity (stairs, houses, terrace) to the unseen larger world of power and authority beyond. I wonder whether the four people are in fact connected, or whether as a group they simply happen to be in the way of unseen forces totally indifferent to the dwelling and living space these people inhabit. This is also, then, a photograph of latent, of impending desolation, and once again I am depressed by the transience of Palestinian life, its vulnerability and all too easy dislocation. But another movement, another feeling, asserts itself in response, set in motion by the two strikingly marked openings in the buildings, openings that suggest rich, cool interiors which outsiders cannot penetrate. Let us enter.

•   •   •   •   •   •   •   •   •   •   •   •

QUESTIONS FOR A SECOND READING

1. The first three paragraphs provide a "reading" of the opening photograph, "Tripoli, Badawi camp, May 1983." Or, to put it another way, the writing evolves from and is in response to that photograph. As you reread these paragraphs, pay close attention to what Said is doing, to what he

notices, to what prompts or requires commentary. How would you describe and explain the writing that follows? What is he doing with the photo? What is he doing as a writer? What is he doing for a reader? (How does he position a reader?)

It might be useful to begin by thinking about what he is *not* doing. It is not, for example, the presentation one might expect in a slide show on travel in Lebanon. Nor is it the kind of presentation one might expect while seeing the slides of family or friends, or slides in an art history or art appreciation class.

Once you have worked through the opening three paragraphs, reread the essay paying attention to Said's work with all the photographs. Is there a pattern? Do any of the commentaries stand out for their force, variety, innovation?

2. Here is another passage from the introduction to *After the Last Sky:*

> Its style and method—the interplay of text and photos, the mixture of genres, modes, styles—do not tell a consecutive story, nor do they constitute a political essay. Since the main features of our present existence are dispossession, dispersion, and yet also a kind of power incommensurate with our stateless exile, I believe that essentially unconventional, hybrid, and fragmentary forms of expression should be used to represent us. What I have quite consciously designed, then, is an alternative mode of expression to the one usually encountered in the media, in works of social science, in popular fiction.

And later:

> The multifaceted vision is essential to any representation of us. Stateless, dispossessed, de-centered, we are frequently unable either to speak the "truth" of our experience or to make it heard. We do not usually control the images that represent us; we have been confined to spaces designed to reduce or stunt us; and we have often been distorted by pressures and powers that have been too much for us. An additional problem is that our language, Arabic, is unfamiliar in the West and belongs to a tradition and civilization usually both misunderstood and maligned. Everything we write about ourselves, therefore, is an interpretive translation—of our language, our experience, our senses of self and others.

And from "States":

> The striking thing about Palestinian prose and prose fiction is its formal instability: Our literature in a certain very narrow sense *is* the elusive, resistant reality it tries so often to represent. Most literary critics in Israel and the West focus on what is said in Palestinian writing, who is described, what the plot and contents deliver, their sociological and political meaning. But it is *form* that should be looked at. Particularly in fiction, the struggle to achieve form expresses the writer's efforts to construct a coherent scene, a narrative that might overcome the almost metaphysical impossibility of representing the present. (p. 702)

As you reread, think about form—organization, arrangement, and genre. What *is* the order of the writing in this essay? (We will call it an "essay" for lack of a better term.) How might you diagram or explain its organization? By what principle(s) is it ordered and arranged? The essay shifts genres—memoir, history, argument. It is, as Said says, "hybrid." What surprises are there? or disappointments? How might you describe the writer's strategy as he works on his audience, on readers? And, finally, do you find Said's explanation sufficient or useful—does the experience of exile produce its own inevitable style of report and representation?

3. The essay is filled with references to people (including writers), places, and events that are, most likely, foreign to you. Choose one that seems interesting or important, worth devoting time to research. Of course the Internet will be a resource, but you should also use the library, if only to become aware of the different opportunities and materials it provides. Compile a report of the additional information; be prepared to discuss how the research has served or changed your position as a reader of "States."

4. The final chapter of *After the Last Sky* ends with this:

> I would like to think, though, that such a book not only tells the reader about us, but in some way also reads the reader. I would like to think that we are not just the people seen or looked at in these photographs: We are also looking at our observers.

Read back through Said's essay by looking at the photos with this reversal in mind—looking in order to see yourself as the one who is being looked at, as the one observed. How are you positioned by the photographer, Jean Mohr? How are you positioned by the person in the scene, always acknowledging your presence? What are you being told?

Once you have read through the photographs, reread the essay itself, with a similar question in mind. This time, however, look for evidence of how Said positions you, defines you, invents you as a presence in the scene.

ASSIGNMENTS FOR WRITING

1. Compose a similar project, a Said-like reading of a set of photos. These can be photos prepared for the occasion (by you or a colleague); they could also be photos already available. Whatever their source, they should represent people and places, a history and/or geography that you know well, that you know to be complex and contradictory, and that you know will not be easily or readily understood by others, both the group for whom you will be writing (most usefully the members of your class) and readers more generally. You must begin with a sense that the photos cannot speak for themselves; you must speak for them.

   In preparation, you should reread closely to come to a careful understanding of Said's project. (The first and second "Questions for a Second Reading," should be useful for this.) To prepare a document that is Said-like (one that shows your understanding of what Said is doing), you will need to have an expert's sense of how to write from and to photographs, and you will need to consider questions of form—of order, arrangement, and genre.

2. While "States" does not present itself as polemical writing—an argument in defense of Palestinian rights, an argument designed to locate blame or propose national or international policy—it is, still, writing with a pur-

pose. It has an argument, it has a particular project in mind, and it wants something to happen.

Write an essay that represents the argument or the project of "States" for someone who has not read it. You will need, in other words, to establish a context and to summarize. You should also work from passages (and images)—that is, you will want to give your reader a sense of the text, its key terms and language. And write about "States" as though it has something to do with you.

Your essay is not just summary, in other words, but summary in service of statement, response, or extension. As you are invited to think about the Palestinians, or about exile more generally, or about the texts and images that are commonly available, what do you think? What do you have to add?

3. The final chapter of *After the Last Sky* ends with this:

> I would like to think, though, that such a book not only tells the reader about us, but in some way also reads the reader. I would like to think that we are not just the people seen or looked at in these photographs: We are also looking at our observers.

The fourth question in "Questions for a Second Reading" sets a strategy for rereading with this passage in mind—looking in order to see yourself as the one who is being looked at, as the one observed. Write an essay in which you think this through by referring specifically to images and to text. How are you positioned? By whom and to what end?

MAKING CONNECTIONS

1. Edward Said talks about the formal problems in the writing of "States" (and for more on this, see the second of the "Questions for a Second Reading"):

> The striking thing about Palestinian prose and prose fiction is its formal instability: Our literature in a certain very narrow sense *is* the elusive, resistant reality it tries so often to represent. Most literary critics in Israel and the West focus on what is said in Palestinian writing, who is described, what the plot and contents deliver, their sociological and political meaning. But it is *form* that should be looked at. Particularly in fiction, the struggle to achieve form expresses the writer's efforts to construct a coherent scene, a narrative that might overcome the almost metaphysical impossibility of representing the present. (p. 702)

And here is a similar discussion from the introduction to *After the Last Sky:*

> The multifaceted vision is essential to any representation of us. Stateless, dispossessed, de-centered, we are frequently unable either to speak the "truth" of our experience or to make it heard. We do not usually control the images that represent us; we have been confined to spaces designed to reduce or stunt us; and we have often been distorted by pressures and powers that have been too much for us. An additional problem is that our language, Arabic, is unfamiliar in the West and belongs to a tradition and civilization usually both misunderstood and maligned. Everything we write about ourselves, therefore, is an

interpretive translation—of our language, our experience, our senses of self and others.

Edward Said's sense of his project as a writing project, a writing project requiring formal experimentation, is similar to Gloria Anzaldúa's in *Borderlands/La frontera*. In the two chapters represented in *Ways of Reading,* "Entering into the Serpent" (p. 23) and "How to Tame a Wild Tongue" (p. 36), Anzaldúa is also writing (and resisting) "interpretive translation." In place of the photographs in "States," she offers poems, stories and myths, passages in Spanish.

Write an essay in which you consider these selections as writing projects. The formal experimentation in each are said by the writers to be fundamental, necessary, a product of the distance between a particular world of experience and the available modes of representation. In what ways are the essays similar? In what ways are they different? Where and how is a reader (where and how are you) positioned in each? What is the experience of reading them? What does one need to learn to be their ideal reader?

2. *After the Last Sky: Palestinian Lives* is one of the central "cases" in W. J. T. Mitchell's "The Photographic Essay: Four Case Studies"(p. 510). Mitchell's essay examines the "dialectic of exchange and resistance that make it possible (and sometimes impossible) to 'read' the pictures, or to 'see' the text illustrated in them."

    Before reading Mitchell, take time to work on "States" and to write a draft addressing the relationship of image to text. (The first of the "Questions for a Second Reading" provides a way of preparing for this.)

    Once you have worked through the opening three paragraphs, reread the essay with an eye to the accumulating relationships between image and text. Is there a pattern? Do any stand out for their force, variety, innovation?

    Once you've written that draft, read Mitchell and bring his analysis into the conversation. You will want to refer to the general frame and the terms of his argument and to the specific discussion of images in *After the Last Sky*. What does Mitchell bring to the essay? How would you define his expertise? What do you see that he doesn't? How might you define your position or point of view in relation to his?

3. Jean Mohr's collaboration with John Berger (see p. 105) was important to Said, particularly in the 1975 book *A Seventh Man,* a photographic essay on migrant workers in Europe. You'll need to use the library or the bookstore for this assignment. Find a copy of *A Seventh Man* and write an essay on what you think it was in Mohr's work, and in his collaboration with Berger, that was most compelling to Said.

historical relativism→ history is a matter of
style as much as events
—what we see is determind
by what we think we know.

· absence primitivism → civil right (identity) → pro activ his.
trajectory changing notions of what really happens.

JANE
TOMPKINS

· epistemology → study of nature of knowledge

*J*ANE TOMPKINS (b. 1940) received her B.A. from Bryn Mawr and completed both an M.A. and a Ph.D. at Yale. She has taught at Temple University, Connecticut College, Duke University, and the University of Illinois at Chicago. Among her publications are Sensational Designs: The Cultural Work of American Fiction, 1790–1860 (1985) and West of Everything: The Inner Life of Westerns (1992). She is also editor of Reader-Response Criticism: From Formalism to Post-Structuralism (1980). Her most recent book, A Life in School: What the Teacher Learned (1997) is a first-person critical account of American higher education.

In Sensational Designs Tompkins suggests that novels and short stories ought to be studied "not because they manage to escape the limitations of their particular time and place, but because they offer powerful examples of the way a culture thinks about itself, articulating and proposing solutions for the problems that shape a particular historical moment." This perspective leads Tompkins to conclude that the study of literature ought to focus not merely on those texts we call masterpieces but also on the texts of popular or best-selling authors. By studying these popular texts, Tompkins believes we can learn more of the "work" of novels and short stories, the influence they exert over the society in which they have been produced.

"Indians" was first published in 1986 in the influential journal of literary criticism Critical Inquiry. It is an unusual essay in many ways, not the least of *which is how it turns, as Tompkins's work often does, to anecdote and personal example. This is a surprising essay, perhaps even more surprising to faculty than to undergraduates. It is as though Tompkins was not willing to hide the "limitation of [her] particular time and place," limitations most scholars are more than happy to hide. In fact, Tompkins's selection could be said to take the reader behind the scenes of the respectable drama of academic research, offering a powerful example of how contemporary academic culture thinks about itself, articulating and proposing solutions for the problems that shape its particular historical moment. If individual interpretations are made and not found—if, for that matter, the "truths" of history or the background to American literature are made and not found—then there is every reason to acknowledge the circumstances of their making. And this is what Tompkins does. "Indians" is both a report on Tompkins's research and a reflection on the ways knowledge is produced, defended, and revised in academic life.*

"Indians": Textualism, Morality, and the Problem of History

When I was growing up in New York City, my parents used to take me to an event in Inwood Park at which Indians—real American Indians dressed in feathers and blankets—could be seen and touched by children like me. This event was always a disappointment. It was more fun to imagine that you *were* an Indian in one of the caves in Inwood Park than to shake the hand of an old man in a headdress who was not overwhelmed at the opportunity of meeting you. After staring at the Indians for a while, we would take a walk in the woods where the caves were, and once I asked my mother if the remains of a fire I had seen in one of them might have been left by the original inhabitants. After that, wandering up some stone steps cut into the side of the hill, I imagined I was a princess in a rude castle. My Indians, like my princesses, were creatures totally of the imagination, and I did not care to have any real exemplars interfering with what I already knew.

I already knew about Indians from having read about them in school. Over and over we were told the story of how Peter Minuit had bought Manhattan Island from the Indians for twenty-four dollars' worth of glass beads. And it was a story we didn't mind hearing because it gave us the rare pleasure of having someone to feel superior to, since the poor Indians had not known (as we eight-year-olds did) how valuable a piece of property Manhattan Island would become. Generally, much was made of the Indian presence in Manhattan; a poem in one of our readers began: "Where we walk to school today/Indian children used to play," and we were encouraged to write poetry on this topic ourselves. So I had a fairly rich relationship with Indians before I ever met the unprepossessing people in Inwood Park. I felt that I had a lot in common with them. They, too, liked animals (they were often named after animals); they, too, made mistakes—they liked the brightly colored trinkets of little value that the white men were always offering them; they were handsome, warlike, and brave and had led an exciting, romantic life in the forest long ago, a life such as I dreamed of leading myself. I felt lucky to be living in one of the places where they had definitely been. Never mind where they were or what they were doing now.

My story stands for the relationship most non-Indians have to the people who first populated this continent, a relationship characterized by narcissistic fantasies of freedom and adventure, of a life lived closer to nature and to spirit than the life we lead now. As Vine Deloria, Jr., has pointed out, the American Indian Movement in the early seventies couldn't get people to pay attention to what was happening to Indians who were alive in the present, so powerful was this country's infatuation with people who wore loincloths, lived in tepees, and roamed the plains and forest long ago.[1] The present essay, like these fantasies, doesn't have much to do with actual Indians, though its subject matter is the histories of European-Indian relations in seventeenth-century New England. In a sense, my encounter with Indians as an adult doing "research" replicates the childhood one, for while I started out to learn more about Indians, I ended up preoccupied with a problem of my own.

This essay enacts a particular instance of the challenge poststructuralism poses to the study of history. In simpler language, it concerns the difference that point of view makes when people are giving accounts of events, whether at first or second hand. The problem is that if all accounts of events are determined through and through by the observer's frame of reference, then one will never know, in any given case, what really happened.

I encountered this problem in concrete terms while preparing to teach a course in colonial American literature. I'd set out to learn what I could about the Puritans' relations with American Indians. All I wanted was a general idea of what happened between the English settlers and the natives in seventeenth-century New England; poststructuralism and its dilemmas were the furthest thing from my mind. I began, more or less automatically, with Perry Miller, who hardly mentions the Indians at all, then proceeded to the work of historians who had dealt exclusively with the European-Indian encounter. At first, it was a question of deciding which of these authors to believe, for it quickly became apparent that there was no unanimity on the subject. As I read on, however, I discovered that the problem was more complicated than deciding whose version of events was correct. Some of the conflicting accounts were not simply contradictory, they were completely incommensurable, in that their assumptions about what counted as a valid approach to the subject, and what the subject itself was, diverged in fundamental ways. Faced with an array of mutually irreconcilable points of view, points of view which determined what was being discussed as well as the terms of the discussion, I decided to turn to primary sources for clarification, only to discover that the primary sources reproduced the problem all over again. I found myself, in other words, in an epistemological quandary, not only unable to decide among conflicting versions of events but also unable to believe that any such decision could, in principle, be made. It was a moral quandary as well. Knowledge of what really happened when the Europeans and the Indians first met seemed particularly important, since the result of that encounter was virtual genocide. This was the kind of past "mistake" which, presumably, we studied history in order to avoid repeating. If studying history couldn't put us in touch with actual events and their causes, then what was to prevent such atrocities from happening again?

For a while, I remained at this impasse. But through analyzing the process by which I had reached it, I eventually arrived at an understanding which seemed to offer a way out. This essay records the concrete experience of meeting and solving the difficulty I have just described (as an abstract problem, I thought I had solved it long ago). My purpose is not to throw new light on antifoundationalist epistemology—the solution I reached is not a new one—but to dramatize and expose the troubles antifoundationalism gets you into when you meet it, so to speak, in the road.

My research began with Perry Miller. Early in the preface to *Errand into the Wilderness*, while explaining how he came to write his history of the New England mind, Miller writes a sentence that stopped me dead. He says that what fascinated him as a young man about his country's history was "the massive narrative of the movement of European culture into the vacant wilderness of America."[2] "Vacant"? Miller, writing in 1956, doesn't pause over the word "vacant," but to people who read his preface thirty years later, the word is shocking. In what circumstances could someone proposing to write a history of colonial New England *not* take account of the Indian presence there?

The rest of Miller's preface supplies an answer to this question, if one takes the trouble to piece together its details. Miller explains that as a young man, jealous of older compatriots who had had the luck to fight in World War I, he had gone to Africa in search of adventure. "The adventures that Africa afforded," he writes, "were tawdry enough, but it became the setting for a sudden epiphany" (p. vii). "It was given to me," he writes, "disconsolate on the edge of a jungle of central Africa, to have thrust upon me the mission of expounding what I took to be the innermost propulsion of the United States, while supervising, in that barbaric tropic, the unloading of drums of case oil flowing out of the inexhaustible wilderness of America" (p. viii). Miller's picture of himself on the banks of the Congo furnishes a key to the kind of history he will write and to his mental image of a vacant wilderness; it explains why it was just there, under precisely these conditions, that he should have had his epiphany.

The fuel drums stand, in Miller's mind, for the popular misconception of what this country is about. They are "tangible symbols of [America's] appalling power," a power that everyone but Miller takes for the ultimate reality (p. ix). To Miller, "the mind of man is the basic factor in human history," and he will plead, all unaccommodated as he is among the fuel drums, for the intellect—the intellect for which his fellow historians, with their chapters on "stoves or bathtubs, or tax laws," "the Wilmot Proviso" and "the chain store," "have so little respect" (p. viii, ix). His preface seethes with a hatred of the merely physical and mechanical, and this hatred, which is really a form of moral outrage, explains not only the contempt with which he mentions the stoves and bathtubs but also the nature of his experience in Africa and its relationship to the "massive narrative" he will write.

Miller's experiences in Africa are "tawdry," his tropic is barbaric because the jungle he stands on the edge of means nothing to him, no more, indeed something less, than the case oil. It is the nothingness of Africa that precipitates his vision. It is the barbarity of the "dark continent," the obvious (but superficial) parallelism between the jungle at Matadi and America's "vacant wilderness" that releases in Miller the desire to define and vindicate his country's cultural identity. To the young Miller, colonial Africa and colonial America are—but for the history he will bring to light—mirror images of one another. And what he fails to see in the one landscape is the same thing he overlooks in the other: the human beings who people it. As Miller stood with his back to the jungle, thinking about the role of mind in human history, his failure to see that the land into which European culture had moved was not vacant but already occupied by a varied and numerous population, is of a piece with his failure, in his portrait of himself at Matadi, to notice *who* was carrying the fuel drums he was supervising the unloading of.

The point is crucial because it suggests that what is invisible to the historian in his own historical moment remains invisible when he turns his gaze to the past. It isn't that Miller didn't "see" the black men, in a literal sense, any more than it's the case that when he looked back he didn't "see" the Indians, in the sense of not realizing they were there. Rather, it's that neither the Indians nor the blacks *counted* for him, in a fundamental way. The way in which Indians can be seen but not counted is illustrated by an entry in Governor John Winthrop's journal, three hundred years before, when he recorded that there had been a great storm with high winds "yet through God's great mercy it did no hurt, but only killed one Indian with the fall of a tree."[3] The juxtaposition suggests that Miller shared with Winthrop a certain colonial point of view, a point of view from which Indians, though present, do not finally matter.

• • •

A book entitled *New England Frontier: Puritans and Indians, 1620–1675,* written by Alden Vaughan and published in 1965, promised to rectify Miller's omission. In the outpouring of work on the European-Indian encounter that began in the early sixties, this book is the first major landmark, and to a neophyte it seems definitive. Vaughan acknowledges the absence of Indian sources and emphasizes his use of materials which catch the Puritans "off guard."[4] His announced conclusion that "the New England Puritans followed a remarkably humane, considerate, and just policy in their dealings with the Indians" seems supported by the scope, documentation, and methodicalness of his project (*NEF,* p. vii). The author's fair-mindedness and equanimity seem everywhere apparent, so that when he asserts "the history of interracial relations from the arrival of the Pilgrims to the outbreak of King Philip's War is a credit to the integrity of both peoples," one is positively reassured (*NEF,* p. viii).

But these impressions do not survive an admission that comes late in the book, when, in the course of explaining why works like Helen Hunt Jackson's *Century of Dishonor* had spread misconceptions about Puritan treatment of the Indians, Vaughan finally lays his own cards on the table.

> The root of the misunderstanding [about Puritans and Indians] . . . lies[s] in a failure to recognize the nature of the two societies that met in seventeenth-century New England. One was unified, visionary, disciplined, and dynamic. The other was divided, self-satisfied, undisciplined, and static. It would be unreasonable to expect that such societies could live side by side indefinitely with no penetration of the more fragmented and passive by the more consolidated and active. What resulted, then, was not—as many have held—a clash of dissimilar ways of life, but rather the expansion of one into the areas in which the other was lacking. [*NEF,* p. 323]

From our present vantage point, these remarks seem culturally biased to an incredible degree, not to mention inaccurate: Was Puritan society unified? If so, how does one account for its internal dissensions and obsessive need to cast out deviants? Is "unity" necessarily a positive culture trait? From what standpoint can one say that American Indians were neither disciplined nor visionary, when both these characteristics loom so large in the ethnographies? Is it an accident that ways of describing cultural strength and weakness coincide with gender stereotypes— active/passive, and so on? Why is one culture said to "penetrate" the other? Why is the "other" described in terms of "lack"?

Vaughan's fundamental categories of apprehension and judgment will not withstand even the most cursory inspection. For what looked like evenhandedness when he was writing *New England Frontier* does not look that way anymore. In his introduction to *New Directions in American Intellectual History,* John Higham writes that by the end of the sixties the entire conceptual foundation on which [this sort of work] rested [had] crumbled away. . . . Simultaneously, in sociology, anthropology, and history, two working assumptions . . . came under withering attack: first, the assumption that societies tend to be integrated, and second, that a shared culture maintains that integration. . . . By the late 1960s all claims issued in the name of an "American mind" . . . were subject to drastic skepticism.[5]

"Clearly," Higham continues, "the sociocultural upheaval of the sixties created the occasion" for this reaction.[6] Vaughan's book, it seemed, could only have been written before the events of the sixties had sensitized scholars to questions of race and ethnicity. It came as no surprise, therefore, that ten years later there appeared a study of European-Indian relations which reflected the new awareness of social issues the sixties had engendered. And it offered an entirely different picture of the European-Indian encounter.

Francis Jennings's *The Invasion of America* (1975) rips wide open the idea that the Puritans were humane and considerate in their dealings with the Indians. In Jennings's account, even more massively documented than Vaughan's, the early settlers lied to the Indians, stole from them, murdered them, scalped them, captured them, tortured them, raped them, sold them into slavery, confiscated their land, destroyed their crops, burned their homes, scattered their possessions, gave them alcohol, undermined their systems of belief, and infected them with diseases that wiped out 90 percent of their numbers within the first hundred years after contact.[7]

Jennings mounts an all-out attack on the essential decency of the Puritan leadership and their apologists in the twentieth century. The Pequot War, which previous historians had described as an attempt on the part of Massachusetts Bay to protect itself from the fiercest of the New England tribes, becomes, in Jennings's painstakingly researched account, a deliberate war of extermination, waged by whites against Indians. It starts with trumped-up charges, is carried on through a series of increasingly bloody reprisals, and ends in the massacre of scores of Indian men, women, and children, all so that Massachusetts Bay could gain political and economic control of the southern Connecticut Valley. When one reads this and then turns over the page and sees a reproduction of the Bay Colony seal, which depicts an Indian from whose mouth issue the words "Come over and help us," the effect is shattering.[8]

But even so powerful an argument as Jennings's did not remain unshaken by subsequent work. Reading on, I discovered that if the events of the sixties had revolutionized the study of European-Indian relations, the events of the seventies produced yet another transformation. The American Indian Movement, and in particular the founding of the Native American Rights Fund in 1971 to finance Indian litigation, and a court decision in 1975 which gave the tribes the right to seek redress for past injustices in federal court, created a climate within which historians began to focus on the Indians themselves. "Almost simultaneously," writes James Axtell, "frontier and colonial historians began to discover the necessity of considering the American natives as real determinants of history and the utility of ethnohistory as a way of ensuring parity of focus and impartiality of judgment."[9] In Miller, Indians had been simply beneath notice; in Vaughan, they belonged to an inferior culture; and in Jennings, they were the more or less innocent prey of power-hungry whites. But in the most original and provocative of the ethnohistories, Calvin Martin's *Keepers of the Game,* Indians became complicated, purposeful human beings, whose lives were spiritually motivated to a high degree.[10] Their relationship to the animals they hunted, to the natural environment, and to the whites with whom they traded became intelligible within a system of beliefs that formed the basis for an entirely new perspective on the European-Indian encounter.

Within the broader question of why European contact had such a devastating effect on the Indians, Martin's specific aim is to determine why Indians participated in the fur trade which ultimately led them to the brink of annihilation. The standard answer to this question had always been that once the Indian was introduced to European guns, copper kettles, woolen blankets, and the like, he literally couldn't keep his hands off them. In order to acquire these coveted items, he decimated the animal populations on which his survival depended. In short, the Indian's motivation in participating in the fur trade was assumed to be the same as the white European's—a desire to accumulate material goods. In direct opposition to this thesis, Martin argues that the reason why Indians ruthlessly exploited their own resources had nothing to do with supply and demand, but stemmed rather from a breakdown of the cosmic worldview that tied them to the game they killed in a spiritual relationship of parity and mutual obligation.

The hunt, according to Martin, was conceived not primarily as a physical activity but as a spiritual quest, in which the spirit of the hunter must overmaster the spirit of the game animal before the kill can take place. The animal, in effect, *allows* itself to be found and killed, once the hunter has mastered its spirit. The hunter prepared himself through rituals of fasting, sweating, or dreaming which revealed the identity of his prey and where he can find it. The physical act of killing is the least important element in the process. Once the animal is killed, eaten, and its parts used for clothing or implements, its remains must be disposed of in ritually prescribed fashion, or the game boss, the "keeper" of that species, will not permit more animals to be killed. The relationship between Indians and animals, then, is contractual; each side must hold up its end of the bargain, or no further transactions can occur.

What happened, according to Martin, was that as a result of diseases introduced into the animal population by Europeans, the game suddenly disappeared, began to act in inexplicable ways, or sickened and died in plain view, and communicated their diseases to the Indians. The Indians, consequently, believed that their compact with the animals had been broken and that the keepers of the game, the tutelary spirits of each animal species whom they had been so careful to propitiate, had betrayed them. And when missionization, wars with the Europeans, and displacement from their tribal lands had further weakened Indian society and its belief structure, the Indians, no longer restrained by religious sanctions, in effect, turned on the animals in a holy war of revenge.

Whether or not Martin's specific claim about the "holy war" was correct, his analysis made it clear to me that, given the Indians' understanding of economic, religious, and physical processes, an Indian account of what transpired when the European settlers arrived here would look nothing like our own. Their (potential, unwritten) history of the conflict could bear only a marginal resemblance to Eurocentric views. I began to think that the key to understanding European-Indian relations was to see them as an encounter between wholly disparate cultures, and that therefore either defending or attacking the colonists was beside the point since, given the cultural disparity between the two groups, conflict was inevitable and in large part a product of mutual misunderstanding.

But three years after Martin's book appeared, Shepard Krech III edited a collection of seven essays called *Indians, Animals, and the Fur Trade*, attacking Martin's entire project. Here the authors argued that we don't need an ideological or religious explanation for the fur trade. As Charles Hudson writes,

> The Southeastern Indians slaughtered deer (and were prompted to enslave and kill each other) because of their position on the outer fringes of an expanding modern world-system. . . . In the modern world-system there is a core region which establishes *economic* relations with its colonial periphery. . . . If the Indians could not produce commodities, they were on the road to cultural extinction. . . . To maximize his chances for survival, an eighteenth-century Southeastern Indian had to . . . live in the interior, out of range of European cattle, forestry, and agriculture. . . . He had to produce a commodity which was valuable enough to earn him some protection from English slavers.[11]

Though we are talking here about Southeastern Indians, rather than the subarctic and Northeastern tribes Martin studied, what really accounts for these divergent explanations of why Indians slaughtered the game are the assumptions that underlie them. Martin believes that the Indians acted on the basis of perceptions made available to them by their own cosmology; that is, he explains their behavior as the Indians themselves would have explained it (insofar as he can), using a logic and a set of values that are not Eurocentric but derived from within Amerindian culture. Hudson, on the other hand, insists that the Indians' own beliefs are irrelevant to an explanation of how they acted, which can only be understood, as far as he is concerned, in the terms of a Western materialist economic and political analysis. Martin and Hudson, in short, don't agree on what counts as an explanation, and this disagreement sheds light on the preceding accounts as well. From this standpoint, we can see that Vaughan, who thought that the Puritans were superior to the Indians, and Jennings, who thought the reverse, are both, like Hudson, using Eurocentric criteria of description and evaluation. While all three critics (Vaughan, Jennings and Hudson) acknowledge that Indians and Europeans behave differently from one another, the behavior differs, as it were, within the order of the same: all three assume, though only Hudson makes the assumption explicit, that an understanding of relations between the Europeans and the Indians must be elaborated in European terms. In Martin's analysis, however, what we have are not only two different sets of behavior but two incommensurable ways of describing and assigning meaning to events. This difference at the level of explanation calls into question the possibility of obtaining any theory-independent account of interaction between Indians and Europeans.

At this point, dismayed and confused by the wildly divergent views of colonial history the twentieth-century historians had provided, I decided to look at some primary materials. I thought, perhaps, if I looked at some firsthand accounts and at some scholars looking at those accounts, it would be possible to decide which experts were right and which were wrong by comparing their views with the evidence. Captivity narratives seemed a good place to begin, since it was logical to suppose that the records left by whites who had been captured by Indians would furnish the sort of firsthand information I wanted.

I began with two fascinating essays based on these materials written by the ethnohistorian James Axtell, "The White Indians of Colonial America" and "The Scholastic Philosophy of the Wilderness."[12] These essays suggest that it would have been a privilege to be captured by North American Indians and taken off to Canada to dwell in a wigwam for the rest of one's life. Axtell's reconstruction of the process by which Indians taught European captives to feel comfortable in the wilderness, first taking their shoes away and giving them moccasins, carrying the children on their backs, sharing the scanty food supply equally, ceremonially cleansing them of their old identities, giving them Indian clothes and jewelry, assiduously teaching them the Indian language, finally adopting them into their families, and even visiting them after many years if, as sometimes happened, they were restored to white society—all of this creates a compelling portrait of Indian culture and helps to explain the extraordinary attraction that Indian culture apparently exercised over Europeans.

But, as I had by now come to expect, this beguiling portrait of the Indians' superior humanity is called into question by other writings on Indian captivity—for example, Norman Heard's *White into Red*, whose summation of the comparative treatment of captive children east and west of the Mississippi seems to contradict some of Axtell's conclusions:

> The treatment of captive children seems to have been similar in initial stages.... Most children were treated brutally at the time of capture. Babies and toddlers usually were killed immediately and other small children would be dispatched during the rapid retreat to the Indian villages if they cried, failed to keep the pace, or otherwise indicated a lack of fortitude needed to become a worthy member of the tribe. Upon reaching the village, the child might face such ordeals as running the gauntlet or dancing in the center of a throng of threatening Indians. The prisoner might be so seriously injured at this time that he would no longer be acceptable for adoption.[13]

One account which Heard reprints is particularly arresting. A young girl captured by the Comanches who had not been adopted into the family but used as a slave had been peculiarly mistreated. When they wanted to wake her up the family she belonged to would take a burning brand from the fire and touch it to her nose. When she was returned to her parents, the flesh of her nose was completely burned away, exposing the bone.[14]

Since the pictures drawn by Heard and Axtell were in certain respects irreconcilable, it made sense to turn to a firsthand account to see how the Indians treated their captives in a particular instance. Mary Rowlandson's "The Soveraignty and Goodness of God," published in Boston around 1680, suggested itself because it was so widely read and had set the pattern for later narratives. Rowlandson interprets her captivity as God's punishment on her for failing to keep the Sabbath properly on several occasions. She sees everything that happens to her as a sign from God. When the Indians are kind to her, she attributes her good fortune to Divine Providence; when they are cruel, she blames her captors. But beyond the question of how Rowlandson interprets events is the question of what she saw in the first place and what she considered worth reporting. The following passage, with its abrupt shifts of focus and peculiar emphases, makes it hard to see her testimony as evidence of anything other than the Puritan point of view:

> Then my heart began to fail: and I fell weeping, which was the first time to my remembrance, that I wept before them. Although I had met with so much Affliction, and my heart was many times ready to break, yet could I not shed one tear in their sight: but rather had been all this while in a maze, and like one astonished: but now I may say as, Psal. 137.1. *By the Rivers of Babylon, there we sate down; yea, we wept when we remembered Zion.* There one of them asked me, why I wept, I could hardly tell what to say: yet I answered, they would kill me: No, said he, none will hurt you. Then came one of them and gave me two spoon-fulls of Meal to comfort me, and another gave

me half a pint of Pease; which was more worth than many
Bushels at another time. Then I went to see King Philip, he
bade me come in and sit down, and asked me whether I woold
smoke it (a usual Complement nowadayes among Saints and
Sinners) but this no way suited me. For though I had formerly
used Tobacco, yet I had left it ever since I was first taken. It
seems to be a Bait, the Devil layes to make men loose their
precious time: I remember with shame, how formerly, when I
had taken two or three pipes, I was presently ready for another,
such a bewitching thing it is: But I thank God, he has now
given me power over it; surely there are many who may be better imployed than to ly sucking a stinking Tobacco-pipe.[15]

Anyone who has ever tried to give up smoking has to sympathize with
Rowlandson, but it is nonetheless remarkable, first, that a passage which
begins with her weeping openly in front of her captors, and comparing
herself to Israel in Babylon, should end with her railing against the vice of
tobacco; and, second, that it has not a word to say about King Philip, the
leader of the Indians who captured her and mastermind of the campaign
that devastated the white population of the English colonies. The fact that
Rowlandson has just been introduced to the chief of chiefs makes hardly
any impression on her at all. What excites her is a moral issue which was
being hotly debated in the seventeenth century: to smoke or not to smoke
(Puritans frowned on it, apparently, because it wasted time and presented
a fire hazard). What seem to us the peculiar emphases in Rowlandson's relation are not the result of her having *screened out* evidence she couldn't
handle, but of her way of constructing the world. She saw what her
seventeenth-century English Separatist background made visible. It is
when one realizes that the biases of twentieth-century historians like
Vaughan or Axtell cannot be corrected for simply by consulting the primary materials, since the primary materials are constructed according to
their authors' biases, that one begins to envy Miller his vision at Matadi.
Not for what he didn't see—the Indian and the black—but for his epistemological confidence.

Since captivity narratives made a poor source of evidence for the nature of European-Indian relations in early New England because they
were so relentlessly pietistic, my hope was that a better source of evidence
might be writings designed simply to tell Englishmen what the American
natives were like. These authors could be presumed to be less severely biased, since they hadn't seen their loved ones killed by Indians or been
made to endure the hardships of captivity, and because they weren't writing propaganda calculated to prove that God had delivered his chosen
people from the hands of Satan's emissaries.

The problem was that these texts were written with aims no less specific than those of the captivity narrative, though the aims were of a
different sort. Here is a passage from William Wood's *New England's
Prospect,* published in London in 1634.

To enter into a serious discourse concerning the natural conditions of these Indians might procure admiration from the people of any civilized nations, in regard of their civility and good natures. . . . These Indians are of affable, courteous and well disposed natures, ready to communicate the best of their wealth to the mutual good of one another; . . . so . . . perspicuous is their love . . . that they are as willing to part with a mite in poverty as treasure in plenty. . . . If it were possible to recount the courtesies they have showed the English, since their first arrival in those parts, it would not only steady belief, that they are a loving people, but also win the love of those that never saw them, and wipe off that needless fear that is too deeply rooted in the conceits of many who think them envious and of such rancorous and inhumane dispositions, that they will one day make an end of their English inmates.[16]

However, in a pamphlet published twenty-one years earlier, Alexander Whitaker of Virginia has this to say of the natives:

These naked slaves . . . serve the divell for feare, after a most base manner, sacrificing sometimes (as I have heere heard) their own Children to him. . . . They live naked in bodie, as if their shame of their sinne deserved no covering: Their names are as naked as their bodie: They esteem it a virtue to lie, deceive and steale as their master the divell teacheth to them.[17]

According to Robert Berkhofer in *The White Man's Indian*, these divergent reports can be explained by looking at the authors' motives. A favorable report like Wood's, intended to encourage new emigrants to America, naturally represented Indians as loving and courteous, civilized and generous, in order to allay the fears of prospective colonists. Whitaker, on the other hand, a minister who wishes to convince his readers that the Indians are in need of conversion, paints them as benighted agents of the devil. Berkhofer's commentary constantly implies that white men were to blame for having represented the Indians in the image of their own desires and needs.[18] But the evidence supplied by Rowlandson's narrative, and by the accounts left by early reporters such as Wood and Whitaker, suggests something rather different. Though it is probably true that in certain cases Europeans did consciously tamper with the evidence, in most cases there is no reason to suppose that they did not record faithfully what they saw. And what they saw was not an illusion, was not determined by selfish motives in any narrow sense, but was there by virtue of a *way* of seeing which they could no more consciously manipulate than they could choose not to have been born. At this point, it seemed to me, the ethnocentric bias of the firsthand observers invited an investigation of the cultural situation they spoke from. Karen Kupperman's *Settling with the Indians* (1980) supplied just such an analysis.

Kupperman argues that Englishmen inevitably looked at Indians in exactly the same way that they looked at other Englishmen. For instance, if they looked down on Indians and saw them as people to be exploited, it was not because of racial prejudice or antique notions about savagery, it was because they looked down on ordinary English men and women and saw them as subjects for exploitation as well.[19] According to Kupperman, what concerned these writers most when they described the Indians were the insignia of social class, of rank, and of prestige. Indian faces are virtually never described in the earliest accounts, but clothes and hairstyles, tattoos and jewelry, posture and skin color are. "Early modern Englishmen believed that people can create their own identity, and that therefore one communicates to the world through signals such as dress and other forms of decoration who one is, what group or category one belongs to."[20]

Kupperman's book marks a watershed in writings on European-Indian relations, for it reverses the strategy employed by Martin two years before. Whereas Martin had performed an ethnographic analysis of Indian cosmology in order to explain, from within, the Indians' motives for engaging in the fur trade, Kupperman performs an ethnographic study of seventeenth-century England in order to explain, from within, what motivated Englishmen's behavior. The sympathy and understanding that Martin, Axtell, and others extend to the Indians are extended in Kupperman's work to the English themselves. Rather than giving an account of "what happened" between Indians and Europeans, like Martin, she reconstructs the worldview that gave the experience of one group its context. With her study, scholarship on European-Indian relations comes full circle.

It may well seem to you at this point that, given the tremendous variation among the historical accounts, I had no choice but to end in relativism. If the experience of encountering conflicting versions of the "same" events suggests anything certain it is that the attitude a historian takes up in relation to a given event, the way in which he or she judges and even describes "it"—and the "it" has to go in quotation marks because, depending on the perspective, that event either did or did not occur—this stance, these judgments and descriptions are a function of the historian's position in relation to the subject. Miller, standing on the banks of the Congo, couldn't see the black men he was supervising because of his background, his assumptions, values, experiences, goals. Jennings, intent on exposing the distortions introduced into the historical record by Vaughan and his predecessors stretching all the way back to Winthrop, couldn't see that Winthrop and his peers were not racists but only Englishmen who looked at other cultures in the way their own culture had taught them to see one another. The historian can never escape the limitations of his or her own position in history and so inevitably gives an account that is an extension of the circumstances from which it springs. But it seems to me that when one is confronted with this particular succession of stories, cultural and historical relativism is not a position that one can comfortably assume. The phenomena to which these histories testify—conquest, massacre, and genocide, on the one hand; torture, slavery, and murder on the other—cry out for judgment. When faced with claims and counterclaims of this magnitude one feels obligated to reach an understanding of what actually did occur. The dilemma posed by the study of European-Indian relations in early America is that the highly charged nature of the materials demands a moral decisiveness which the succession of conflicting accounts effectively precludes. That is the dilemma I found myself in at the end of this course of reading, and which I eventually came to resolve as follows.

After a while it began to seem to me that there was something wrong with the way I formulated the problem. The statement that the materials on European-Indian relations were so highly charged that they demanded moral judgment, but that the judgment couldn't be made because all possible descriptions of what happened were biased, seemed to contain an internal contradiction. The statement implied that in order to make a moral judgment about something, you have to know something else first—namely, the facts of the case you're being called upon to judge. My complaint was that their perspectival nature would disqualify any facts I might encounter and that therefore I couldn't judge. But to say as I did that the materials I had read were "highly charged" and therefore demanded judgment suggests both that I was reacting to something real—to some facts—*and* that I judged them. Perhaps I wasn't so much in the lurch morally or epistemologically as I had thought. If you—or I—react with horror to the story of the girl captured and enslaved by Comanches who touched a firebrand to her nose every time they wanted to wake her up, it's because we read this as a story about cruelty and suffering, and not as a story about the conventions of prisoner exchange or the economics of Comanche life. The *seeing* of the story as a cause for alarm rather than a droll anecdote or a piece of curious information is evidence of values we already hold, of judgments already made, of facts already perceived as facts.

My problem presupposed that I couldn't judge because I didn't know what the facts were. All I had, or could have, was a series of different perspectives, and so nothing that would count as an authoritative source on which moral judgments could be based. But, as I have just shown, I did judge, and that is because, as I now think, I did have some facts. I seemed to accept as facts that ninety percent of the native American population of New England died after the first hundred years of contact, that tribes in eastern Canada and the northeastern United States had a compact with the game they killed, that Comanches had subjected a captive girl to casual cruelty, that King Philip smoked a pipe, and so on. It was only where different versions of the same event came into conflict that I doubted the text was a record of something real. And even then, there was no question about certain major catastrophes. I believed that four hundred Pequots were killed near Saybrook, that Winthrop was the Governor of the Massachusetts Bay Colony when it happened, and so on. My sense that certain events, such as the Pequot War, did occur in no way reflected the indecisiveness that overtook me when I tried to choose among the various historical versions. In fact, the need I felt to make up my mind was impelled by the conviction that certain things *had* happened that shouldn't have happened. Hence it was never the case that "what happened" was completely unknowable or un-available. It's rather that in the process of reading so many different approaches to the same phenomenon I became aware of the difference in the attitudes that informed these approaches. The awareness of the interests motivating each version cast suspicion over everything, in retrospect, and I ended by claiming that there was nothing I could know. This, I now see, was never really the case. But how did it happen?

Someone else, confronted with the same materials, could have decided that one of these historical accounts was correct. Still another person might have decided that more evidence was needed in order to decide among them. Why did I conclude that none of the accounts was accurate because they were all produced from some particular angle of vision? Presumably there was something in my background that enabled me to see the problem in this way. That something, very likely, was poststructuralist theory. I let my discovery that Vaughan was a product of the fifties, Jennings of the sixties, Rowlandson of a Puritan worldview, and so on lead me to the conclusion that all facts are theory dependent because that conclusion was already a thinkable one for me. My inability to come up with a true account was not the product of being situated nowhere; it was the product of certitude that existed *somewhere else*, namely, in contemporary literary theory. Hence, the level at which my indecision came into play was a function of particular beliefs I held. I was never in a position of epistemological indeterminacy, I was never *en abyme*. The idea that all accounts are perspectival seemed to me a superior standpoint from which to view all the versions of "what happened," and to regard with sympathetic condescension any person so old-fashioned and benighted as to believe that there really was some way of arriving at the truth. But this skeptical standpoint was just as firm as any other. The fact that it was also seriously disabling—it prevented me from coming to any conclusion about what I had read—did not render it any less definite.

At this point something is beginning to show itself that has up to now been hidden. The notion that all facts are only facts within a perspective has the effect of emptying statements of their content. Once I had Miller and Vaughan and Jennings, Martin and Hudson, Axtell and Heard, Rowlandson and Wood and Whitaker, and Kupperman; I had Europeans and Indians, ships and canoes, wigwams and log cabins, bows and arrows and muskets, wigs and tattoos, whiskey and corn, rivers and forts, treaties and battles, fire and blood—and then suddenly all I had was a metastatement about perspectives. The effect of bringing perspectivism to bear on history was to wipe out completely the subject matter of history. And it follows that bringing perspectivism to bear in this way on any subject matter would have a similar effect; everything is wiped out and you are left with nothing but a single idea—perspectivism itself.

But—and it is a crucial but—all this is true only if you believe that there is an alternative. As long as you think that there are or should be facts that exist outside of any perspective, then the notion that facts are perspectival will have this disappearing effect on whatever it touches. But if you are convinced that the alternative does not exist, that there really are no facts except as they are embedded in some particular way of seeing the world, then the argument that a set of facts derives from some particular worldview is no longer an argument against that set of facts. If all facts share this characteristic, to say that any one fact is perspectival doesn't change its factual nature in the slightest. It merely reiterates it.

This doesn't mean that you have to accept just anybody's facts. You can show that what someone else asserts to be a fact is false. But it does mean that you can't argue that someone else's facts are not facts *because they are only the product of a perspective*, since this will be true of the facts that you perceive as well. What this means then is that arguments about "what happened" have to proceed much as they did before poststructuralism broke in with all its talk about language-based reality and culturally produced knowledge. Reasons must be given, evidence adduced, authorities cited, analogies drawn. Being aware that all facts are motivated, believing that people are always operating inside some particular interpretive framework or other is a pertinent argument when what is under discussion is the way beliefs are grounded. But it doesn't give one any leverage on the facts of a particular case.[21]

What this means for the problem I've been addressing is that I must piece together the story of European-Indian relations as best I can, believing this version up to a point, that version not at all, another almost entirely, according to what seems reasonable and plausible, given everything else that I know. And this, as I've shown, is what I was already doing in the back of my mind without realizing it, because there was nothing else I *could* do. If the accounts don't fit together neatly, that is not a reason for rejecting them all in favor of a metadiscourse about epistemology; on the contrary, one encounters contradictory facts and divergent points of view in practically every phase of life, from deciding whom to marry to choosing the right brand of cat food, and one decides as best one can given the evidence available. It is only the nature of the academic situation which makes it appear that one can linger on the threshold of decision in the name of an epistemological principle. What has really happened in such a case is that the subject of debate has changed from the question of what happened in a particular instance to the question of how knowledge is arrived at. The absence of pressure to decide what happened creates the possibility for this change of venue.

The change of venue, however, is itself an action taken. In diverting attention from the original problem and placing it where Miller did, on "the mind of man," it once again ignores what happened and still is happening to American Indians. The moral problem that confronts me now is not that

I can never have any facts to go on, but that the work I do is not directed toward solving the kinds of problems that studying the history of European-Indian relations has awakened me to.

NOTES

[1] See Vine Deloria, Jr., *God Is Red* (New York, 1973), pp. 39–56.

[2] Perry Miller, *Errand into the Wilderness* (Cambridge, Mass., 1964), p. vii; all further references will be included in the text.

[3] This passage from John Winthrop's *Journal* is excerpted by Perry Miller in his anthology *The American Puritans: Their Prose and Poetry* (Garden City, N.Y., 1956), p. 43. In his headnote to the selections from the *Journal*, Miller speaks of Winthrop's "characteristic objectivity" (p. 37).

[4] Alden T. Vaughan, *New England Frontier: Puritans and Indians, 1620–1675* (Boston, 1965), pp. vi–vii; all further references to this work, abbreviated *NEF*, will be included in the text.

[5] John Higham, intro. to *New Directions in American Intellectual History*, ed. Higham and Paul K. Conkin (Baltimore, 1979), p. xii.

[6] Ibid.

[7] See Francis Jennings, *The Invasion of America: Indians, Colonialism, and the Cant of Conquest* (New York, 1975), pp. 3–31. Jennings writes: "The so-called settlement of America was a *re*settlement, reoccupation of a land made waste by the diseases and demoralization introduced by the newcomers. Although the source data pertaining to populations have never been compiled, one careful scholar, Henry D. Dobyns, has provided a relatively conservative and meticulously reasoned estimate conforming to the known effects of conquest catastrophe. Dobyns has calculated a total aboriginal population for the western hemisphere within the range of 90 to 112 million, of which 10 to 12 million lived north of the Rio Grande" (p. 30).

[8] Jennings, fig. 7, p. 229; and see pp. 186–229.

[9] James Axtell, *The European and the Indian: Essays in the Ethnohistory of Colonial North America* (Oxford, 1981), p. viii.

[10] See Calvin Martin, *Keepers of the Game: Indian-Animal Relationships and the Fur Trade* (Berkeley and Los Angeles, 1978).

[11] See the essay by Charles Hudson in *Indians, Animals, and the Fur Trade: A Critique of "Keepers of the Game,"* ed. Shepard Krech III (Athens, Ga., 1981), pp. 167–69.

[12] See Axtell, "The White Indians of Colonial America" and "The Scholastic Philosophy of the Wilderness," *The European and the Indian*, pp. 168–206 and 131–67.

[13] J. Norman Heard, *White into Red: A Study of the Assimilation of White Persons Captured by Indians* (Metuchen, N.J., 1973), p. 97.

[14] See ibid., p. 98.

[15] Mary Rowlandson, "The Sovereignty and Goodness of God, Together with the Faithfulness of His Promises Displayed; Being a Narrative of the Captivity and Restauration of Mrs. Mary Rowlandson (1676)," in *Held Captive by Indians: Selected Narratives, 1642–1836*, ed. Richard VanDerBeets (Knoxville, Tenn., 1973), pp. 57–58.

[16] William Wood, *New England's Prospect*, ed. Vaughan (Amherst, Mass., 1977), pp. 88–89.

[17] Alexander Whitaker, *Goode Newes from Virginia* (1613), quoted in Robert F. Berkhofer, Jr., *The White Man's Indian: Images of the American Indian from Columbus to the Present* (New York, 1978), p. 19.

[18] See, for example, Berkhofer's discussion of the passages he quotes from Whitaker (*The White Man's Indian*, pp. 19, 20).

[19] See Karen Ordahl Kupperman, *Settling with the Indians: The Meeting of English and Indian Cultures in America, 1580–1640* (Totowa, N.J., 1980), pp. 3, 4.

[20] Ibid., p. 35.

[21] The position I've been outlining is a version of neopragmatism. For an exposition, see *Against Theory: Literary Studies and the New Pragmatism*, ed. W. J. T. Mitchell (Chicago, 1985).

. . . .

QUESTIONS FOR A SECOND READING

1. Tompkins's essay can be divided into three parts: the account of her childhood understanding of Indians; the account of her research into scholarly and first-person accounts of the relations between the Indians and the settlers in New England; and a final conclusion (beginning on p. 731). The conclusion, in many ways, is the hardest part of the essay to understand. Like the conclusion to Clifford Geertz's "Deep Play: Notes on the Balinese Cockfight" (p. 305), it assumes not only that you have followed a chain of reasoning but that you have access to the larger philosophical questions that have preoccupied the academic community. In this sense the conclusion presents special problems for a student reader. Why might one be dissatisfied with "metadiscourse"? What kind of work is Tompkins talking about, for example, when she says, "The moral problem that confronts me now is . . . that the work I do is not directed toward solving the kinds of problems that studying the history of European-Indian relations has awakened me to"?

   As you reread the essay, look to see how the first two sections might be seen as a preparation for the conclusion. And as you reread the concluding section (which you may have to do several times), try to imagine the larger, unspoken issues it poses for those who teach American literature or who are professionally involved in reading and researching the past.

2. One of the things to notice about Tompkins's essay is how neatly all the pieces fit together in her narrative. If you wanted to read against this essay, you might say that they fit together *too* neatly. The seemingly "natural" progression from book to book or step to step in this account of her research and her thinking could be said to reveal the degree to which the story was shaped or made, constructed for the occasion. Real experience is never quite so tidy.

   As you reread the essay, be aware of the narrative as something made and ask yourself, How does she do that? What is she leaving out? Where is she working hard to get her material to fit? This is partly a matter of watching how Tompkins does her work—looking at paragraphs, for instance, and seeing how they represent her material and her reading of that material. It is also a matter of looking for what is not there, for seams that indicate necessary or unconscious omissions (as though while writing this essay, too, she "did not care to have any real exemplars interfering with what I already knew").

ASSIGNMENTS FOR WRITING

1. Tompkins's essay tells the story of a research project. It also, however, "reads" that narrative—that is, not only does Tompkins describe what she did, or what other people said, but she reflects on what her actions or the work of others might be said to represent. She writes about "point of view" or "frame of reference" and the ways they might be said to determine how people act, what they write, and what they know.

   Write an essay that tells a similar story, one of your own, using Tompkins's essay as a model. There are two ways you might do this:

   a. You could tell the story of a research project, a paper (most likely a term paper) you prepared for school. This does not have to be a pious or dutiful account. Tompkins, after all, is writing against what she takes to be the predictable or expected account of research as the disinterested pursuit of truth—in which a student would go to the library to "find" the truth about the Indians and the settlers. And she writes in a style that is not solemnly academic. Like Tompkins, you can tell what you take to be the untold story of term-paper research, you can reflect on the "problem" of such research by turning to your own account.

      Your account should begin well before your work in the library—that is, you too will want to show the "prehistory" of your project, the possible connections between school work and your life outside school. It should also tell the story of your work with other people's writing. The purpose of all this is to reflect on how knowledge is constructed and how you, as a student, have been expected to participate (and how you have, in fact, participated) in that process.

   b. You could tell the story of a discovery that did not involve reading or library research; in fact, you could tell the story of a discovery that did not involve school at all. In this sense you would be working in response to the first section of Tompkins's essay, in which what she knows about Indians is constructed from a combination of cultural models and personal desire.

2. In her essay Tompkins offers her experience as a representative case. Her story is meant to highlight a problem central to teaching, learning, and research—central, that is, to academic life. As a student, you can read this essay as a way of looking in on the work and concerns of your faculty (a group represented not only by Tompkins but by those against whom she is arguing). Write an essay directed to someone who has not read "Indians," someone who will be entering your school as a first-year student next semester. Your job is to introduce an incoming freshman to the academy, using Tompkins as your guide. You will need to present her argument and her conclusion in such a way as to make clear the consequences of what she says for someone about to begin an undergraduate education. Remember, you are writing to an incoming student; you will want to capture that audience's attention.

MAKING CONNECTIONS

1. Like Jane Tompkins in "Indians," Patricia Limerick in "Haunted Amer-
    ica" (p. 471) is writing about "textualism, morality, and the problem of
    history." She is a professional historian and her specialty is the American
    West. Tompkins, however, is not a historian, at least not in the strict, dis-
    ciplinary sense of the word. She doesn't work in a history department; in
    this sense her commitments to and understanding of history are, perhaps,
    a bit different from Limerick's.

    Read the two essays together, as a set, as part of a single project inves-
    tigating the problems writing history and understanding the past. Write
    an essay in which you discuss the differences, focusing as closely as you
    can on specific examples from each essay. Examine the concerns or meth-
    ods that belong to each but look, finally, to see the differences. How
    would you account for those differences? What difference do they make
    to you as a reader, a writer, a person with an interest in understanding the
    past?

2. In "Our Time" (p. 752), John Edgar Wideman writes about the problems
    he has "knowing" and writing about his brother Robby. In this sense,
    both "Our Time" and "Indians" are about the problems of understanding,
    about the different relationship between "real exemplars" and what we
    know. Write an essay in which you compare these two selections, looking
    in particular at the differences in the ways each author represents this
    problem and its possible solutions. Although you are working from only
    two sources, you could imagine that your essay is a way of investigat-
    ing the differences between the work of a "creative" writer and that of
    a scholar.

3. Jane Tompkins in "Indians" offers her experience as a representative case.
    "This essay enacts a particular instance of the challenge poststructuralism
    poses to the study of history. In simpler language, it concerns the differ-
    ence that point of view makes when people are giving accounts of events,
    whether at first or second hand." Marianne Hirsch, in "Projected Mem-
    ory: Holocaust Photographs in Personal and Public Fantasy"(p. 400), is
    also concerned with point of view, with how we can most appropriately
    read and use the records of the past.

    Read "Indians" and "Projected Memory" as part of a single project.
    (They are, in fact, both responses to the challenge poststructuralism poses
    to the study of history.) How does each represent the problems of getting
    access to, then reading and understanding the records of the past? What is
    at stake for each writer—what makes the project such an urgent one
    (more than "merely" academic)? How does memory function for each?
    What are the crucial documentary records? What are the critical or
    methodological skills required for the task? And, as you imagine your
    own commitments to the past (as a student, as a citizen), where do you
    position yourself in relation to the issues these essays represent and to the
    projects they suggest?

ALICE
WALKER

A LICE WALKER, *the youngest of eight children in a sharecropping family, was born in 1944 in Eatonton, Georgia. She is now one of the most widely read contemporary American novelists. In her work, she frequently returns to scenes of family life—some violent, some peaceful. "I was curious to know," she writes, "why people of families (specifically black families) are often cruel to each other and how much of this cruelty is caused by outside forces. . . . Family relationships are sacred. No amount of outside pressure and injustice should make us lose sight of that fact." In her nonfiction, Walker has helped to define a historical context for the contemporary black artist, a legacy that has had to be recovered from libraries and archives. The essay that follows, "In Search of Our Mothers' Gardens," defines black history as a family matter. It begins by charting the violence done to women who "died with their real gifts stifled within them" and concludes with Walker's recollection of her own mother, a recollection that enables her to imagine generations of black women handing on a "creative spark" to those who follow.*

In addition to In Search of Our Mothers' Gardens *(1983), Walker has written novels, including* The Third Life of Grange Copeland *(1970) and* The Color Purple *(1982), which won the Pulitzer Prize; collections of poems, including* Revolutionary Petunias *(1973) and* Good Night, Willie Lee, I'll See You in the Morning *(1979); two collections of short stories,* In Love and Trouble

(1973) and You Can't Keep a Good Woman Down *(1981), and a biography of* Langston Hughes. *She has also served as an editor at* Ms. *magazine. After graduating from Sarah Lawrence College in 1965, she taught at a number of colleges and universities, including Wellesley College and Yale University. She has held a Guggenheim Fellowship and a National Endowment for the Arts fellowship. She lives in San Francisco and teaches at the University of California at Berkeley.*

While pursuing her own career as a writer, Walker has fought to win recognition for the work of Zora Neale Hurston, a black woman author and anthropologist whose best-known work is the novel Their Eyes Were Watching God *(1937). Hurston died penniless in a Florida welfare home. Walker's recent work includes* Living by the Word *(1988), a collection of essays, letters, journal entries, lectures, and poems on the themes of race, gender, sexuality, and political freedom;* To Hell with Dying *(1988), a children's picture book;* The Temple of My Familiar *(1989), and* Possessing the Secret of Joy *(1992), both novels; and* Her Blue Body Everything We Know: Earthling Poems, 1965–1990 *(1991), a collection of poems. Walker has also co-written, with Michael Meade, the introduction to a sound recording by Sobonfu Some titled* We Have No Word for Sex *(1994), an African oral tale. Her latest books are* Anything We Love Can Be Saved: A Writer's Activism *(1997), a collection of essays;* By the Light of My Father's Smile *(1998), a novel; and* The Way Forward Is with a Broken Heart *(2000), a collection of stories based in part on Walker's failed early marriage.*

In Search of
Our Mothers' Gardens

> I described her own nature and temperament. Told how they
> needed a larger life for their expression. . . . I pointed out that
> in lieu of proper channels, her emotions had overflowed into
> paths that dissipated them. I talked, beautifully I thought,
> about an art that would be born, an art that would open the
> way for women the likes of her. I asked her to hope, and build
> up an inner life against the coming of that day. . . . I sang, with
> a strange quiver in my voice, a promise song.
>
> —"AVEY," JEAN TOOMER, *Cane*
> *The poet speaking to a prostitute who falls
> asleep while he's talking*

When the poet Jean Toomer walked through the South in the early twenties, he discovered a curious thing: black women whose spirituality was so intense, so deep, so *unconscious*, they were themselves unaware of the richness they held. They stumbled blindly through their lives:

creatures so abused and mutilated in body, so dimmed and confused by pain, that they considered themselves unworthy even of hope. In the self-less abstractions their bodies became to the men who used them, they became more than "sexual objects," more even than mere women: they became "Saints." Instead of being perceived as whole persons, their bodies became shrines: what was thought to be their minds became temples suitable for worship. These crazy Saints stared out at the world, wildly, like lunatics—or quietly, like suicides; and the "God" that was in their gaze was as mute as a great stone.

Who were these Saints? These crazy, loony, pitiful women?

Some of them, without a doubt, were our mothers and grandmothers.

In the still heat of the post-Reconstruction South, this is how they seemed to Jean Toomer: exquisite butterflies trapped in an evil honey, toiling away their lives in an era, a century, that did not acknowledge them, except as "the *mule* of the world." They dreamed dreams that no one knew—not even themselves, in any coherent fashion—and saw visions no one could understand. They wandered or sat about the countryside crooning lullabies to ghosts, and drawing the mother of Christ in charcoal on courthouse walls.

They forced their minds to desert their bodies and their striving spirits sought to rise, like frail whirlwinds from the hard red clay. And when those frail whirlwinds fell, in scattered particles, upon the ground, no one mourned. Instead, men lit candles to celebrate the emptiness that remained, as people do who enter a beautiful but vacant space to resurrect a God.

Our mothers and grandmothers, some of them: moving to music not yet written. And they waited.

They waited for a day when the unknown thing that was in them would be made known; but guessed, somehow in their darkness, that on the day of their revelation, they would be long dead. Therefore to Toomer they walked, and even ran, in slow motion. For they were going nowhere immediate, and the future was not yet within their grasp. And men took our mothers and grandmothers, "but got no pleasure from it." So complex was their passion and their calm.

To Toomer, they lay vacant and fallow as autumn fields, with harvest time never in sight; and he saw them enter loveless marriages, without joy; and become prostitutes, without resistance; and become mothers of children, without fulfillment.

For these grandmothers and mothers of ours were not Saints, but Artists; driven to a numb and bleeding madness by the springs of creativity in them for which there was no release. They were Creators, who lived lives of spiritual waste, because they were so rich in spirituality—which is the basis of Art—that the strain of enduring their unused and unwanted talent drove them insane. Throwing away this spirituality was their pathetic attempt to lighten the soul to a weight their work-worn, sexually abused bodies could bear.

What did it mean for a black woman to be an artist in our grandmothers' time? In our great-grandmothers' day? It is a question with an answer cruel enough to stop the blood.

Did you have a genius of a great-great-grandmother who died under some ignorant and depraved white overseer's lash? Or was she required to bake biscuits for a lazy backwater tramp, when she cried out in her soul to paint watercolors of sunsets, or the rain falling on the green and peaceful pasturelands? Or was her body broken and forced to bear children (who were more often than not sold away from her)—eight, ten, fifteen, twenty children—when her one joy was the thought of modeling heroic figures of rebellion, in stone or clay?

How was the creativity of the black woman kept alive, year after year and century after century, when for most of the years black people have been in America, it was a punishable crime for a black person to read or write? And the freedom to paint, to sculpt, to expand the mind with action did not exist. Consider, if you can bear to imagine it, which might have been the result if singing, too, had been forbidden by law. Listen to the voices of Bessie Smith, Billie Holiday, Nina Simone, Roberta Flack, and Aretha Franklin, among others, and imagine those voices muzzled for life. Then you may begin to comprehend the lives of our "crazy," "Sainted" mothers and grandmothers. The agony of the lives of women who might have been Poets, Novelists, Essayists, and Short-Story Writers (over a period of centuries), who died with their real gifts stifled within them.

And, if this were the end of the story, we would have cause to cry out in my paraphrase of Okot p'Bitek's great poem:

> O, my clanswomen
> Let us all cry together!
> Come,
> Let us mourn the death of our mother,
> The death of a Queen
> The ash that was produced
> By a great fire!
> O, this homestead is utterly dead
> Close the gates
> With *lacari* thorns,
> For our mother
> The creator of the Stool is lost!
> And all the young women
> Have perished in the wilderness!

But this is not the end of the story, for all the young women—our mothers and grandmothers, *ourselves*—have not perished in the wilderness. And if we ask ourselves why, and search for and find the answer, we will know beyond all efforts to erase it from our minds, just exactly who, and of what, we black American women are.

One example, perhaps the most pathetic, most misunderstood one, can provide a backdrop for our mothers' work: Phillis Wheatley, a slave in the 1700s.

Virginia Woolf, in her book *A Room of One's Own,* wrote that in order for a woman to write fiction she must have two things, certainly: a room of her own (with key and lock) and enough money to support herself.

What then are we to make of Phillis Wheatley, a slave, who owned not even herself? This sickly, frail black girl who required a servant of her own at times—her health was so precarious—and who, had she been white, would have been easily considered the intellectual superior of all the women and most of the men in the society of her day.

Virginia Woolf wrote further, speaking of course not of our Phillis, that "any woman born with a great gift in the sixteenth century [insert "eighteenth century," insert "black woman," insert "born or made a slave"] would certainly have gone crazed, shot herself, or ended her days in some lonely cottage outside the village, half witch, half wizard [insert "Saint"], feared and mocked at. For it needs little skill and psychology to be sure that a highly gifted girl who had tried to use her gift of poetry would have been so thwarted and hindered by contrary instincts [add "chains, guns, the lash, the ownership of one's body by someone else, submission to an alien religion"], that she must have lost her health and sanity to a certainty."

The key words, as they relate to Phillis, are "contrary instincts." For when we read the poetry of Phillis Wheatley—as when we read the novels of Nella Larsen or the oddly false-sounding autobiography of that freest of all black women writers, Zora Hurston—evidence of "contrary instincts" is everywhere. Her loyalties were completely divided, as was, without question, her mind.

But how could this be otherwise? Captured at seven, a slave of wealthy, doting whites who instilled in her the "savagery" of the Africa they "rescued" her from . . . one wonders if she was even able to remember her homeland as she had known it, or as it really was.

Yet, because she did try to use her gift for poetry in a world that made her a slave, she was "so thwarted and hindered by . . . contrary instincts, that she . . . lost her health. . . ." In the last years of her brief life, burdened not only with the need to express her gift but also with a penniless, friendless "freedom" and several small children for whom she was forced to do strenuous work to feed, she lost her health, certainly. Suffering from malnutrition and neglect and who knows what mental agonies, Phillis Wheatley died.

So torn by "contrary instincts" was black, kidnapped, enslaved Phillis that her description of "the Goddess"—as she poetically called the Liberty she did not have—is ironically, cruelly humorous. And, in fact, has held Phillis up to ridicule for more than a century. It is usually read prior to hanging Phillis's memory as that of a fool. She wrote:

> The Goddess comes, she moves divinely fair,
> Olive and laurel binds her *golden* hair.
> Wherever shines this native of the skies,
> Unnumber'd charms and recent graces rise. [My italics]

It is obvious that Phillis, the slave, combed the "Goddess's" hair every morning, prior, perhaps, to bringing in the milk, or fixing her mistress's lunch. She took her imagery from the one thing she saw elevated above all others.

With the benefit of hindsight we ask, "How could she?"

But at last, Phillis, we understand. No more snickering when your stiff, struggling, ambivalent lines are forced on us. We know now that you were not an idiot or a traitor; only a sickly little black girl, snatched from your home and country and made a slave; a woman who still struggled to sing the song that was your gift, although in a land of barbarians who praised you for your bewildered tongue. It is not so much what you sang, as that you kept alive, in so many of our ancestors, *the notion of song.*

Black women are called, in the folklore that so aptly identified one's status in society, "the *mule* of the world," because we have been handed the burdens that everyone else—*everyone* else—refused to carry. We have also been called "Matriarchs," "Superwomen," and "Mean and Evil Bitches." Not to mention "Castraters" and "Sapphire's Mama." When we have pleaded for understanding, our character has been distorted, when we have asked for simple caring, we have been handed empty inspirational appellations, then stuck in the farthest corner. When we have asked for love, we have been given children. In short, even our plainer gifts, our labors of fidelity and love, have been knocked down our throats. To be an artist and a black woman, even today, lowers our status in many respects, rather than raises it: and yet, artists we will be.

Therefore we must fearlessly pull out of ourselves and look at and identify with our lives the living creativity some of our great-grandmothers were not allowed to know. I stress *some* of them because it is well known that the majority of our great-grandmothers knew, even without "knowing" it, the reality of their spirituality, even if they didn't recognize it beyond what happened in the singing at church—and they never had any intention of giving it up.

How they did it—those millions of black women who were not Phillis Wheatley, or Lucy Terry or Frances Harper or Zora Hurston or Nella Larsen or Bessie Smith; or Elizabeth Catlett, or Katherine Dunham, either—brings me to the title of this essay, "In Search of Our Mothers' Gardens," which is a personal account that is yet shared, in its theme and its meaning, by all of us. I found, while thinking about the far-reaching world of the creative black woman, that often the truest answer to a question that really matters can be found very close.

• • •

In the late 1920s my mother ran away from home to marry my father. Marriage, if not running away, was expected of seventeen-year-old girls. By the time she was twenty, she had two children and was pregnant with a third. Five children later, I was born. And this is how I came to know my mother: she seemed a large, soft, loving-eyed woman who was rarely impatient in our home. Her quick, violent temper was on view only a few times a year, when she battled with the white landlord who had the misfortune to suggest to her that her children did not need to go to school.

She made all the clothes we wore, even my brothers' overalls. She made all the towels and sheets we used. She spent the summers canning vegetables and fruits. She spent the winter evenings making quilts enough to cover all our beds.

During the "working" day, she labored beside—not behind—my father in the fields. Her day began before sunup, and did not end until late at night. There was never a moment for her to sit down, undisturbed, to unravel her own private thoughts; never a time free from interruption—by work or the noisy inquiries of her many children. And yet, it is to my mother—and all our mothers who were not famous—that I went in search of the secret of what has fed that muzzled and often mutilated, but vibrant, creative spirit that the black woman has inherited, and that pops out in wild and unlikely places to this day.

But when, you will ask, did my overworked mother have time to know or care about feeding the creative spirit?

The answer is so simple that many of us have spent years discovering it. We have constantly looked high, when we should have looked high—and low.

For example: in the Smithsonian Institution in Washington, D.C., there hangs a quilt unlike any other in the world. In fanciful, inspired, and yet simple and identifiable figures, it portrays the story of the Crucifixion. It is considered rare, beyond price. Though it follows no known pattern of quilt-making, and though it is made of bits and pieces of worthless rags, it is obviously the work of a person of powerful imagination and deep spiritual feeling. Below this quilt I saw a note that says it was made by "an anonymous black woman in Alabama, a hundred years ago."

If we could locate this "anonymous" black woman from Alabama, she would turn out to be one of our grandmothers—an artist who left her mark in the only materials she could afford, and in the only medium her position in society allowed her to use.

As Virginia Woolf wrote further, in *A Room of One's Own*:

> Yet genius of a sort must have existed among women as it must have existed among the working class. [Change this to "slaves" and the "wives and daughters of sharecroppers."] Now and again an Emily Brontë or a Robert Burns [change this to "a Zora Hurston or a Richard Wright"] blazes out and proves its presence. But certainly it never got itself on to paper. When, however, one reads of a witch being ducked, of a woman pos-

sessed by devils [or "Sainthood"], of a wise woman selling herbs [our root workers], or even a very remarkable man who had a mother, then I think we are on the track of a lost novelist, a suppressed poet, or some mute and inglorious Jane Austen. . . . Indeed, I would venture to guess that Anon, who wrote so many poems without singing them, was often a woman. . . .

And so our mothers and grandmothers have, more often than not anonymously, handed on the creative spark, the seed of the flower they themselves never hoped to see: or like a sealed letter they could not plainly read.

And so it is, certainly, with my own mother. Unlike "Ma" Rainey's songs, which retained their creator's name even while blasting forth from Bessie Smith's mouth, no song or poem will bear my mother's name. Yet so many of the stories that I write, that we all write, are my mother's stories. Only recently did I fully realize this: that through years of listening to my mother's stories of her life, I have absorbed not only the stories themselves, but something of the manner in which she spoke, something of the urgency that involves the knowledge that her stories—like her life—must be recorded. It is probably for this reason that so much of what I have written is about characters whose counterparts in real life are so much older than I am.

But the telling of these stories, which came from my mother's lips as naturally as breathing, was not the only way my mother showed herself as an artist. For stories, too, were subject to being distracted, to dying without conclusion. Dinners must be started, and cotton must be gathered before the big rains. The artist that was and is my mother showed itself to me only after many years. This is what I finally noticed.

Like Mem, a character in *The Third Life of Grange Copeland,* my mother adorned with flowers whatever shabby house we were forced to live in. And not just your typical straggly country stand of zinnias, either. She planted ambitious gardens—and still does—with over fifty different varieties of plants that bloom profusely from early March until late November. Before she left home for the fields, she watered her flowers, chopped up the grass, and laid out new beds. When she returned from the fields she might divide clumps of bulbs, dig a cold pit, uproot and replant roses, or prune branches from her taller bushes or trees—until night came and it was too dark to see.

Whatever she planted grew as if by magic, and her fame as a grower of flowers spread over three counties. Because of her creativity with her flowers, even my memories of poverty are seen through a screen of blooms—sunflowers, petunias, roses, dahlias, forsythia, spirea, delphiniums, verbena . . . and on and on.

And I remember people coming to my mother's yard to be given cuttings from her flowers; I hear again the praise showered on her because whatever rocky soil she landed on, she turned into a garden. A garden so brilliant with colors, so original in its design, so magnificent with life and creativity, that to this day people drive by our house in Georgia—perfect strangers and imperfect strangers—and ask to stand or walk among my mother's art.

I notice that it is only when my mother is working in her flowers that she is radiant, almost to the point of being invisible—except as Creator: hand and eye. She is involved in work her soul must have. Ordering the universe in the image of her personal conception of Beauty.

Her face, as she prepares the Art that is her gift, is a legacy of respect she leaves to me, for all that illuminates and cherishes life. She has handed down respect for the possibilities—and the will to grasp them.

For her, so hindered and intruded upon in so many ways, being an artist has still been a daily part of her life. This ability to hold on, even in very simple ways, is work black women have done for a very long time.

This poem is not enough, but it is something, for the woman who literally covered the holes in our walls with sunflowers.

> They were women then
> My mama's generation
> Husky of voice—Stout of
> Step
> With fists as well as
> Hands
> How they battered down
> Doors
> And ironed
> Starched white
> Shirts
> How they led
> Armies
> Headragged Generals
> Across mined
> Fields
> Booby-trapped
> Kitchens
> To discover books
> Desks
> A place for us
> How they knew what we
> *Must* know
> Without knowing a page
> Of it
> Themselves

Guided by my heritage of a love of beauty and a respect for strength— in search of my mother's garden, I found my own.

And perhaps in Africa over two hundred years ago, there was just such a mother; perhaps she painted vivid and daring decorations in oranges and yellows and greens on the walls of her hut; perhaps she sang— in a voice like Roberta Flack's—*sweetly* over the compounds of her village;

perhaps she wove the most stunning mats or told the most ingenious stories of all the village storytellers. Perhaps she was herself a poet— although only her daughter's name is signed to the poems that we know.

Perhaps Phillis Wheatley's mother was also an artist.

Perhaps in more than Phillis Wheatley's biological life is her mother's signature made clear.

. . . .

QUESTIONS FOR A SECOND READING

1. In the essay, Walker develops the interesting notion of "contrary in-stincts," particularly when she discusses Phillis Wheatley. The problem for Walker (and others) is that Wheatley would idolize a fair-haired white woman as a goddess of liberty rather than turn to herself as a model, or to the black women who struggled mightily for their identities and liberty. Walker asks, "How could she?" As you reread the essay, pay attention to the sections in which Walker discusses "contrary instincts." How would you define this term? What kind of answers does this essay make possible to the question "How could she?"

2. Bessie Smith, Roberta Flack, Phillis Wheatley, Zora Neale Hurston— Walker's essay is filled with allusions to black women artists; in fact, the essay serves as a kind of book list or reader's guide; it suggests a program of reading. Jean Toomer, however, is a man, and Virginia Woolf, a white woman; the references aren't strictly to black women. As you reread this essay, pay attention to the names (go to the library and track down some you don't know; you can use the bibliographical index in a good dictio-nary or ask a reference librarian to help you look up the information). What can you make of the collection of writers, poets, singers, and artists Walker sets down as a heritage? What use does she make of them?

3. As you reread the essay, note the sections in which Walker talks about herself. How does she feel about her mother, the history of black women in America, and "contrary instincts"? How would you describe Walker's feelings and attitudes toward herself, the past, and the pressures of living in a predominantly white culture? In considering these questions, don't settle for big words like "honest," "sensitive," or "compassionate." They are accurate, to be sure, but they are imprecise and don't do justice to Walker's seriousness and individuality.

ASSIGNMENTS FOR WRITING

1. Virginia Woolf, a white British writer from the early twentieth century, plays a key role in Walker's essay. Not only does Walker cite Woolf's work, but she revises a long passage to bring it to bear on her experience

or to make it serve her argument. This is a bold move on her part. How do you understand it? How do you understand it as a way of indicating her relationship to this writer and the intellectual heritage she represents? Why bring Virginia Woolf into this essay at all?

(You might, as an exercise, perform similar revisions of passages from "In Search of Our Mothers' Gardens," or of other selections in *Ways of Reading*, of other texts in courses you are taking this term, or from books that you've kept with you over the years. You might think about other, similar acts of revision familiar to you from current literary or popular culture—music, film, TV, art, and advertising. How and why are these artists making use of the past?)

Write an essay in which you focus attention on Walker's revision of Woolf. Use it as a way of thinking about the essay, both what it says and what it does. Use it as a way of thinking out from the essay to the situation of African American writers. And use it as a way of thinking about the relationship of those in the present, including yourself, to the work of the past.

2. Walker's essay poses a number of questions about the history of African American women in America, including how their "creative spirit" survived in the face of oppressive working and living conditions. At one point, Walker describes her mother's life in the late 1920s, after she ran away from home to marry Walker's father. Her mother's difficult life was filled with unrelenting work, yet she managed to keep a "vibrant, creative spirit" alive. At another point, Walker writes, "Our mothers and grandmothers, some of them: moving to music not yet written. And they waited . . . for a day when the unknown thing that was in them would be made known; but guessed, somehow in their darkness, that on the day of their revelation, they would be long dead" (p. 740).

Write an essay in which you discuss Walker's project as a creative endeavor, one in which she reconceives, or rewrites, texts from the past. What would you say, in other words, that Walker creates as she writes her essay?

3. In her essay Walker raises the question of what it meant (and what it still means) to be a black woman and an artist, and her response proceeds from examples that take her mother and herself, among others, into account. As you read her essay, observe Walker's methods of working. How does she build her arguments? Where does her evidence come from? her authority? To whom is she appealing? What do her methods allow her to see (and say) and not to see? And, finally, how might her conclusions be related to her methods?

Write a paper in which you examine Walker's essay in terms of the methods by which it proceeds. Consider the connections among her arguments, evidence, supposed audience, and conclusions, and feel free to invent names and descriptions for what you would call her characteristic ways of working. Remember that your job is to invent a way of describing how Walker works and how her methods—her ways of gathering materials, of thinking them through, of presenting herself and her thoughts, of imagining a world of speakers and listeners—might be related to the issues she raises and the conclusions she draws.

MAKING CONNECTIONS

1. Throughout "Our Time" (p. 752) by John Edgar Wideman, Robby talks about his contrary instincts, his ambivalent feelings toward making it in the "square" world. How can you consider Robby in light of Walker's observations about contrary instincts and the way black women lived in the past? Write an essay in which you explore how Wideman's understanding of his brother Robby's contrary instincts is different from Walker's understanding of her mother's contrary instincts.

2. Like Alice Walker, Marianne Hirsch is concerned with understanding, promoting, and preserving her relationship to the past, a past that is both her family's past and part of twentieth-century history. Write an essay in which you present both projects: Walker's in "In Search of Our Mothers' Gardens" and Marianne Hirsch's in "Projected Memory: Holocaust Photographs in Personal and Public Fantasy" (p. 400).0 You should assume that your readers are familiar with neither. You will need, then, to carefully present the arguments of the essays but also a sense of how they are written, of how they do their work. How do they justify a looking backward? What is the most productive relationship of present to past? What examples can you bring to the discussion—that is, as you look to the culture of your own moment (to movies and television, music, art, advertising, literature), what are the interesting or significant examples of the use of the past? How might you bring them into a discussion of Walker and Hirsch? How might you speak for your generation and its use of the past?

JOHN EDGAR
WIDEMAN

*J*OHN EDGAR WIDEMAN *was born in 1941 in Washington, D.C., but spent most of his youth in Homewood, a neighborhood in Pittsburgh. He earned a B.A. from the University of Pennsylvania, taught at the University of Wyoming, and is currently a professor of English at the University of Massachusetts at Amherst. In addition to the nonfiction work* Brothers and Keepers *(1984), from which this selection is drawn, Wideman has published a number of critically acclaimed works of fiction, including* The Lynchers; Reuben; Philadelphia Fire: A Novel; Fever: Twelve Stories; *and a series of novels set in Homewood:* Damballah; Hiding Place; *and* Sent for You Yesterday *(which won the 1984 PEN/Faulkner Award). The latter novels have been reissued as a set, titled* The Homewood Trilogy. *His most recent books include* Fever *(1996),* The Cattle Killing *(1996),* Hiding Place *(1998), and* Two Cities *(1998). In 1994, Wideman published another work of nonfiction,* Fatheralong: A Meditation on Fathers and Sons, Race and Society.

In the preface to this collection, Wideman writes,

> *The value of black life in America is judged, as life generally in this country is judged, by external, material signs of success. Urban ghettoes are dangerous, broken-down, economically marginal pockets of real estate infected with drugs, poverty, violence, crime, and since*

black life is seen as rooted in the ghetto, black people are identified with the ugliness, danger, and deterioration surrounding them. This logic is simpleminded and devastating, its hold on the American imagination as old as slavery; in fact, it recycles the classic justification for slavery, blaming the cause and consequences of oppression on the oppressed. Instead of launching a preemptive strike at the flawed assumptions that perpetuate racist thinking, blacks and whites are doomed to battle endlessly with the symptoms of racism.

In these three books again bound as one I have set myself to the task of making concrete those invisible planes of existence that bear witness to the fact that black life, for all its material impoverishment, continues to thrive, to generate alternative styles, redemptive strategies, people who hope and cope. But more than attempting to prove a "humanity," which should be self-evident anyway to those not blinded by racism, my goal is to celebrate and affirm. Where did I come from? Who am I? Where am I going?

Brothers and Keepers *is a family story; it is about Wideman and his brother Robby. John went to Oxford as a Rhodes scholar, and Robby went to prison for his role in a robbery and a murder. In the section that follows, "Our Time," Wideman tries to understand his brother, their relationship, where they came from, where they are going. In this account, you will hear the voices of Robby, John, and people from the neighborhood, but also the voice of the writer, speaking about the difficulty of writing and the dangers of explaining away Robby's life.*

Brothers and Keepers *is not the first time Wideman has written to or about his brother. The first of the Homewood series,* Damballah *(1981), is dedicated to Robby. The dedication reads:*

Stories are letters. Letters sent to anybody or everybody. But the best kind are meant to be read by a specific somebody. When you read that kind you know you are eavesdropping. You know a real person somewhere will read the same words you are reading and the story is that person's business and you are a ghost listening in.

Remember. I think it was Geral I first heard call a watermelon a letter from home. After all these years I understand a little better what she meant. She was saying the melon is a letter addressed to us. A story for us from down home. Down Home being everywhere we've never been, the rural South, the old days, slavery, Africa. That juicy, striped message with red meat and seeds, which always looked like roaches to me, was blackness as cross and celebration, a history we could taste and chew. And it was meant for us. Addressed to us. We were meant to slit it open and take care of business.

Consider all these stories as letters from home. I never liked watermelon as a kid. I think I remember you did. You weren't afraid of becoming instant nigger, of sitting barefoot and goggle-eyed and Day-Glo black and drippy-lipped on massa's fence if you took one bite of the forbidden fruit. I was too scared to enjoy watermelon. Too self-conscious. I let people rob me of a simple pleasure. Watermelon's still tainted for me. But I know better now. I can play with the idea even if I can't get down and have a natural ball eating a real one.

Anyway . . . these stories are letters. Long overdue letters from
me to you. I wish they could tear down the walls. I wish they could
snatch you away from where you are.

Our Time

You remember what we were saying about young black men in the street-
world life. And trying to understand why the "square world" becomes completely
unattractive to them. It has to do with the fact that their world is the GHETTO
and in that world all the glamour, all the praise and attention is given to the slick
guy, the gangster especially, the ones that get over in the "life." And it's because
we can't help but feel some satisfaction seeing a brother, a black man, get over on
these people, on their system without playing by their rules. No matter how much
we have incorporated these rules as our own, we know that they were forced on us
by people who did not have our best interests at heart. So this hip guy, this gangster or player or whatever label you give these brothers that we like to shun because of the poison that they spread, we, black people, still look at them with some
sense of pride and admiration, our children openly, us adults somewhere deep inside. We know they represent rebellion—what little is left in us. Well, having
lived in the "life," it becomes very hard—almost impossible—to find any contentment in joining the status quo. Too hard to go back to being nobody in a world
that hates you. Even if I had struck it rich in the life, I would have managed to
throw it down the fast lane. Or have lost it on a revolutionary whim. Hopefully
the latter.

I have always burned up in my fervent passions of desire and want. My
senses at times tingle and itch with my romantic, idealistic outlook on life, which
has always made me keep my distance from reality, reality that was a constant insult to my world, to my dream of happiness and peace, to my people-for-people
kind of world, my easy-cars-for-a-nickel-or-a-dime sorta world. And these driving
passions, this sensitivity to the love and good in people, also turned on me because
I used it to play on people and their feelings. These aspirations of love and desire
turned on me when I wasn't able to live up to this sweet-self morality, so I began
to self-destruct, burning up in my sensitivity, losing direction, because nowhere
could I find this world of truth and love and harmony.

In the real world, the world left for me, it was unacceptable to be "good," it
was square to be smart in school, it was jive to show respect to people outside the
street world, it was cool to be cold to your woman and the people that loved you.
The things we liked we called "bad." "Man, that was a bad girl." The world of the
angry black kid growing up in the sixties was a world in which to be in was to be
out—out of touch with the square world and all of its rules on what's right and

wrong. The thing was to make your own rules, do your own thing, but make sure it's contrary to what society says or is.

I SHALL ALWAYS PRAY

I

Garth looked bad. Real bad. Ichabod Crane anyway, but now he was a skeleton. Lying there in the bed with his bones poking through his skin, it made you want to cry. Garth's barely able to talk, his smooth, medium-brown skin yellow as pee. Ichabod legs and long hands and long feet, Garth could make you laugh just walking down the street. On the set you'd see him coming a far way off. Three-quarters leg so you knew it had to be Garth the way he was split up higher in the crotch than anybody else. Wilt the Stilt with a lean bird body perched on top his high waist. Size-fifteen shoes. Hands could palm a basketball easy as holding a pool cue. Fingers long enough to wrap round a basketball, but Garth couldn't play a lick. Never could get all that lankiness together on the court. You'd look at him sometimes as he was trucking down Homewood Avenue and think that nigger ain't walking, he's trying to remember how to walk. Awkward as a pigeon on roller skates. Knobby joints out of whack, arms and legs flailing, going their separate ways, his body jerking to keep them from going too far. Moving down the street like that wouldn't work, didn't make sense if you stood back and watched, if you pretended you hadn't seen Garth get where he was going a million times before. Nothing funny now, though. White hospital sheets pulled to his chest. Garth's head always looked small as a tennis ball way up there on his shoulders. Now it's a yellow, shrunken skull.

Ever since Robby had entered the ward, he'd wanted to reach over and hide his friend's arm under the covers. For two weeks Gar had been wasting away in the bed. Bad enough knowing Gar was dying. Didn't need that pitiful stick arm reminding him how close to nothing his main man had fallen. So fast. It could happen so fast. If Robby tried to raise that arm it would come off in his hand. As gentle as he could would not be gentle enough. The arm would disintegrate, like a long ash off the end of a cigarette.

Time to leave. No sense in sitting any longer. Garth not talking, no way of telling whether he was listening either. And Robby has nothing more to say. Choked up the way he gets inside hospitals. Hospital smell and quiet, the bare halls and bare floors, the echoes, something about all that he can't name, wouldn't try to name, rises in him and chills him. Like his teeth are chattering the whole time he's inside a hospital. Like his entire body is trembling uncontrollably, only nobody can see it or hear it but him. Shaking because he can't breathe the stuffy air. Hot and cold at the same time. He's been aching to leave since he entered the ward. Aching to get up and bust through the big glass front doors. Aching to pounce on that spidery arm flung back behind Gar's head. The arm too wasted to belong to his friend. He wants to grab it and hurl it away.

Robby pulls on tight white gloves the undertaker had dealt out to him and the rest of the pallbearers. His brown skin shows through the thin material, turns the white dingy. He's remembering that last time in Garth's ward. The hospital stink. Hot, chilly air. A bare arm protruding from the sleeve of the hospital gown, more dried-up toothpick than arm, a withered twig, with Garth's fingers like a bunch of skinny brown bananas drooping from the knobby tip.

Robby had studied the metal guts of the hospital bed, the black scuff marks swirling around the chair's legs. When he'd finally risen to go, his chair scraping against the vinyl floor broke a long silence. The noise must have roused Garth's attention. He'd spoken again.

You're good, man. Don't ever forget, Rob. You're the best.

Garth's first words since the little banter back and forth when Robby had entered the ward and dragged a chair to the side of Gar's bed. A whisper scarcely audible now that Robby was standing. Garth had tried to grin. The best he could manage was a pained adjustment of the bones of his face, no more than a shadow scudding across the yellow skull, but Robby had seen the famous smile. He hesitated, stopped rushing toward the door long enough to smile back. Because that was Gar. That was the way Gar was. He always had a smile and a good word for his cut buddies. Garth's grin was money in the bank. You could count on it like you could count on a good word from him. Something in his face would tell you you were alright, better than alright, that he believed in you, that you were, as he'd just whispered, "the best." You could depend on Garth to say something to make you feel good, even though you knew he was lying. With that grin greasing the lie you had to believe it, even though you knew better. Garth was the gang's dreamer. When he talked, you could see his dreams. That's why Robby had believed it, seen the grin, the bright shadow lighting Garth's face an instant. Out of nothing, out of pain, fear, the certainty of death gripping them both, Garth's voice had manufactured the grin.

Now they had to bury Garth. A few days after the visit to the hospital the phone rang and it was Garth's mother with the news of her son's death. Not really news. Robby had known it was just a matter of time. Of waiting for the moment when somebody else's voice would pronounce the words he'd said to himself a hundred times. *He's gone. Gar's dead.* Long gone before the telephone rang. Gar was gone when they stuck him up in the hospital bed. By the time they'd figured out what ailed him and admitted him to the hospital, it was too late. The disease had turned him to a skeleton. Nothing left of Garth to treat. They hid his messy death under white sheets, perfumed it with disinfectant, pumped him full of drugs so he wouldn't disturb his neighbors.

The others had squeezed into their pallbearers' gloves. Cheap white cotton gloves so you could use them once and throw them away like the rubber ones doctors wear when they stick their fingers up your ass. Michael, Cecil, and Sowell were pallbearers, too. With Robby and two men from Garth's family they would carry the coffin from Gaines Funeral Parlor to the hearse. Garth had been the dreamer for the gang. Robby counted four black fingers in the white glove. Garth was the thumb. The hand would be clumsy, wouldn't work right without him. Garth was different. But everybody else was different, too. Mike, the ice man, supercool. Cecil indifferent, ready to do most anything or nothing and couldn't care less which it was. Sowell wasn't really part of the gang; he didn't hang with them, didn't like to take the risks that were part of the "life." Sowell kept a good job. The "life" for him was just a way to make quick money. He didn't shoot up; he thought of himself as a businessman, an investor not a partner in their schemes. They knew Sowell mostly through Garth. Perhaps things would change now. The four survivors closer after they shared the burden of Gar's coffin, after they hoisted it and slid it on steel rollers into the back of Gaines's Cadillac hearse.

Robby was grateful for the gloves. He'd never been able to touch anything dead. He'd taken a beating once from his father rather than touch the bloody mousetrap his mother had nudged to the back door with her toe and ordered him to empty. The brass handle of the coffin felt damp through the glove. He gripped tighter to stop the flow of blood or sweat, whatever it was leaking from him or seeping from the metal. Garth had melted down to nothing by the end so it couldn't be him nearly yanking off Robby's shoulder when the box shifted and its weight shot forward. Felt like a coffin full of bricks. Robby stared across at Mike but Mike was a soldier, eyes front, riveted to the yawning rear door of the hearse. Mike's eyes wouldn't admit it, but they'd almost lost the coffin. They were rookie pallbearers and maneuvering down the carpeted front steps of Gaines Funeral Parlor they'd almost let Garth fly out their hands. They needed somebody who knew what he was doing. An old, steady head to show them the way. They needed Garth. But Garth was long gone. Ashes inside the steel box.

They began drinking later that afternoon in Garth's people's house. Women and food in one room, men hitting the whiskey hard in another. It was a typical project apartment. The kind everybody had stayed in or visited one time or another. Small, shabby, featureless. Not a place to live. No matter what you did to it, how clean you kept it or what kind of furniture you loaded it with, the walls and ceilings were not meant to be home for anybody. A place you passed through. Not yours, because the people who'd been there before you left their indelible marks everywhere and you couldn't help adding your bruises and knots for the next tenants. You could rent a kitchen and bedroom and a bathroom and a living room, the project flats were laid out so you had a room for each of the things people did in houses. Problem was, every corner was cut. Living cramped is one thing and people can get cozy in the closest quarters. It's another thing to live in a place designed to be just a little less than adequate. No slack, no space to personalize, to stamp the flat with what's peculiar to your style. Like a man sitting on a toilet seat that's too small and the toilet too close to the bathtub so his knees shove against the enamel edge. He can move his bowels that way and plenty of people in the world have a lot less but he'll never enjoy sitting there, never feel the deep down comfort of belonging where he must squat.

Anyway, the whiskey started flowing in that little project apartment. Robby listened, for Garth's sake, as long as he could to old people reminiscing about funerals they'd attended, about all the friends and relatives they'd escorted to the edge of Jordan, old folks sipping good whiskey and moaning and groaning till it seemed a sin to be left behind on this side of the river after so many saints had crossed over. He listened to people express their grief, tell sad, familiar stories. As he got high he listened less closely to the words. Faces and gestures revealed more than enough. When he split with Mike and Cecil and their ladies, Sowell tagged along. By then the tacky, low-ceilinged rooms of the flat were packed. Loud talk, laughter, storytellers competing for audiences. Robby half expected the door he pushed shut behind himself to pop open again, waited for bottled-up noise to explode into the funky hallway.

Nobody thinking about cemeteries now. Nobody else needs to be buried today, so it was time to get it on. Some people had been getting close to rowdy. Some people had been getting mad. Mad at one of the guests in the apartment, mad at doctors and hospitals and whites in general who had the whole world in their hands but didn't have the slightest idea what to do with it. A short, dark man, bubble-eyed, immaculately dressed in a three-piece, wool, herringbone suit, had railed about the callousness, the ignorance of white witch doctors who, by misdiagnosing Garth's illness, had sealed his doom. His harangue had drawn a crowd. He wasn't just talking, he was testifying, and a hush had fallen over half the room as he dissected the dirty tricks of white folks. If somebody ran to the hospital and snatched a white-coated doctor and threw him into the circle surrounding the little fish-eyed man, the mourners would tear the pale-faced devil apart. Robby wished he could feed them one. Remembered Garth weak and helpless in the bed and the doctors and nurses flitting around in the halls, jiving the other patients, ignoring Gar like he wasn't there. Garth was dead because he had believed them. Dead because he had nowhere else to turn when the pain in his gut and the headaches grew worse and worse. Not that he trusted the doctors or believed they gave a flying fuck about him. He'd just run out of choices and had to put himself in their hands. They told him jaundice was his problem, and while his liver rotted away and pain cooked him dizzy Garth assured anyone who asked that it was just a matter of giving the medicine time to work. To kill the pain he blew weed as long as he had strength to hold a joint between his lips. Take a whole bunch of smoke to cool me out these days. Puffing like a chimney till he lost it and fell back and Robby scrambling to grab the joint before Garth torched hisself.

When you thought about it, Garth's dying made no sense. And the more you thought the more you dug that nothing else did neither. The world's a stone bitch. Nothing true if that's not true. The man had you coming and going. He owned everything worth owning and all you'd ever get was what he didn't want anymore, what he'd chewed and spit out and left in the gutter for niggers to fight over. Garth had pointed to the street and said, If we ever make it, it got to come from there, from the curb. We got to melt that rock till we get us some money. He grinned then, Ain't no big thing. We'll make it, brother man. We got what it takes. It's our time.

Something had crawled in Garth's belly. The man said it wasn't nothing. Sold him some aspirins and said he'd be alright in no time. The man killed Garth. Couldn't kill him no deader with a .357 magnum slug, but ain't no crime been committed. Just one those things. You know, everybody makes mistakes. And a dead nigger ain't really such a big mistake when you think about it. Matter of fact you mize well forget the whole thing. Nigger wasn't going nowhere, nohow. I mean he wasn't no brain surgeon or astronaut, no movie star or big-time athlete. Probably a dope fiend or gangster. Wind up killing some innocent person or wasting another nigger. Shucks. That doctor ought to get a medal.

Hey, man. Robby caught Mike's eye. Then Cecil and Sowell turned to him. They knew he was speaking to everybody. Late now. Ten, eleven, because it had been dark outside for hours. Quiet now. Too quiet in his pad. And too much smoke and drink since the funeral. From a bare bulb in the kitchen ceiling light seeped down the hallway and hovered dimly in the doorway of the room where they sat. Robby wondered if the others felt as bad as he did. If the cemetery clothes itched their skin. If they could smell grave dust on their shoes. He hoped they'd finish this last jug of wine and let the day be over. He needed sleep, downtime to get the terrible weight of Garth's death off his mind. He'd been grateful for the darkness. For the company of his cut buddies after the funeral. For the Sun Ra tape until it ended and plunged them into a deeper silence than any he'd ever known. Garth was gone. In a few days people would stop talking about him. He was in the ground. Stone-cold dead. Robby had held a chunk of crumbly ground in his white-gloved fingers and mashed it and dropped the dust into the hole. Now the ground had closed over Garth and what did it mean? Here one day and gone the next and that was that. They'd bury somebody else out of Gaines tomorrow. People would dress up and cry and get drunk and tell lies and next day it'd be somebody else's turn to die. Which one of the shadows in this black room would go first? What did it matter? Who cared? Who would remember their names; they were ghosts already. Dead as Garth already. Only difference was, Garth didn't have it to worry about no more. Garth didn't have to pretend he was going anywhere cause he was there. He'd made it to the place they all were headed fast as their legs could carry them. Every step was a step closer to the stone-cold ground, the pitch-black hole where they'd dropped Garth's body.

Hey, youall. We got to drink to Garth one last time.

They clinked glasses in the darkness. Robby searched for something to say. The right words wouldn't come. He knew there was something proper and precise that needed to be said. Because the exact words eluded him, because only the right words would do, he swallowed his gulp of heavy, sweet wine in silence.

He knew he'd let Garth down. If it had been one of the others dead, Michael or Cecil or Sowell or him, Garth wouldn't let it slide by like this, wouldn't let it end like so many other nights had ended, the fellows nodding off one by one, stupefied by smoke and drink, each one beginning to shop around in his mind, trying to figure whether or not he should turn in or if there was a lady somewhere who'd welcome him in her bed. No. Garth would have figured a way to make it special. They wouldn't be hiding in the bushes. They'd be knights in shining armor around a big table. They'd raise their giant, silver cups to honor the fallen comrade. Like in the olden days. Clean, brave dudes with gold rings and gold chains. They'd draw their blades. Razor-edged swords that gleam in the light with jewels sparkling in the handles. They'd make a roof over the table when they stood and raised their swords and the points touched in the sky. A silver dagger on a satin pillow in the middle of the table. Everybody roll up their sleeves and prick a vein and go round, each one touching everybody else so the blood runs together and we're brothers forever, brothers as long as blood flows in anybody's arm. We'd ride off and do unbelievable shit. The dead one always with us cause we'd do it all for him. Swear we'd never let him down.

It's our time now. We can't let Garth down. Let's drink this last one for him and promise him we'll do what he said we could. We'll be the best. We'll make it to the top for him. We'll do it for Garth.

Glasses rattled together again. Robby empties his and thinks about smashing it against a wall. He'd seen it done that way in movies but it was late at night and these crazy niggers might not know when to stop throwing things. A battlefield of broken glass for him to creep through when he gets out of bed in the morning. He doesn't toss the empty glass. Can't see a solid place anyway where it would strike clean and shatter to a million points of light.

My brother had said something about a guy named Garth during one of my visits to the prison. Just a name mentioned in passing. *Garth* or *Gar*. I'd asked Robby to spell it for me. Garth had been a friend of Robby's, about Robby's age, who died one summer of a mysterious disease. Later when Robby chose to begin the story of the robbery and killing by saying, "It all started with Gar dying," I remembered that first casual mention and remembered a conversation with my mother. My mom and I were in the kitchen of the house on Tokay Street. My recollection of details was vague at first but something about the conversation had made a lasting impression because, six years later, hearing Robby say the name *Garth* brought back my mother's words.

My mother worried about Robby all the time. Whenever I visited home, sooner or later I'd find myself alone with Mom and she'd pour out her fears about Robby's *wildness*, the deep trouble he was bound for, the web of entanglements and intrigues and bad company he was weaving around himself with a maddening disregard for the inevitable consequences.

I don't know. I just don't know how to reach him. He won't listen. He's doing wrong and he knows it but nothing I say makes any difference. He's not like the rest of youall. You'd misbehave but I could talk to you or smack you if I had to and you'd straighten up. With Robby it's like talking to a wall.

I'd listen and get angry at my brother because I registered not so much the danger he was bringing on himself, but the effect of his escapades on the woman who'd brought us both into the world. After all, Robby was no baby. If he wanted to mess up, nobody could stop him. Also Robby was my brother, meaning that his wildness was just a stage, a chaotic phase of his life that would only last till he got his head together and decided to start doing right. Doing as the rest of us did. He was my brother. He couldn't fall too far. His brushes with the law (I'd had some, too), the time he'd spent in jail, were serious but temporary setbacks. I viewed his troubles, when I thought about them at all, as a form of protracted juvenile delinquency, and fully expected Robby would learn his lesson sooner or later and return to the fold, the prodigal son, chastened, perhaps a better person for the experience. In the meantime the most serious consequence of his wildness was Mom's devastating unhappiness. She couldn't sustain the detachment, the laissez-faire optimism I had talked myself into. Because I was two thousand miles away, in Wyoming, I didn't have to deal with the day-to-day evidence of Robby's trouble. The syringe Mom found under his bed. The twenty-dollar bill missing from her purse. The times he'd cruise in higher than a kite, his pupils reduced to pinpricks, with his crew and they'd raid the refrigerator and make a loud, sloppy feast, all of them feeling so good they couldn't imagine anybody not up there on cloud nine with them enjoying the time of their lives. Cruising in, then disappearing just as abruptly, leaving their dishes and pans and mess behind. Robby covering Mom with kisses and smiles and drowning her in babytalk hootchey-coo as he staggers through the front door. Her alone in the ravaged, silent kitchen, listening as doors slam and a car squeals off on the cobblestones of Tokay, wondering where they're headed next, wishing, praying Robby will return and eat and eat and eat till he falls asleep at the table so she can carry him upstairs and tuck him in and kiss his forehead and shut the door gently on his sleep.

I wasn't around for all that. Didn't want to know how bad things were for him. Worrying about my mother was tough enough. I could identify with her grief, I could blame my brother. An awful situation, but simple too. My role, my responsibilities and loyalties were clear. The *wildness* was to blame, and it was a passing thing, so I just had to help my mother survive the worst of it, then everything would be alright. I'd steel myself for the moments alone with her when she'd tell me the worst. In the kitchen, usually, over a cup of coffee with the radio playing. When my mother was alone in the house on Tokay, either the TV or a radio or both were always on. Atop the kitchen table a small clock radio turned to WAMO, one of Pittsburgh's soul stations, would background with scratchy gospel music whatever we said in the morning in the kitchen. On a morning like that in 1975, while I drank a cup of coffee and part of me, still half-asleep, hidden, swayed to the soft beat of gospel, my mother had explained how upset Robby was over the death of his friend, Garth.

It was a terrible thing. I've known Garth's mother for years. He was a good boy. No saint for sure, but deep down a good boy. Like your brother. Not a mean bone in his body. Out there in the street doing wrong, but that's where most of them are. What else can they do, John? Sometimes I can't blame them. No jobs, no money in their pockets. How they supposed to feel like men? Garth did better than most. Whatever else he was into, he kept that little job over at Westinghouse and helped out his mother. A big, playful kid. Always smiling. I think that's why him and Robby were so tight. Neither one had good sense. Giggled and acted like fools. Garth no wider than my finger. Straight up and down. A stringbean if I ever saw one. When Robby lived here in the house with me, Garth was always around. I know how bad Robby feels. He hasn't said a word but I know. When Robby's quiet, you know something's wrong. Soon as his eyes pop open in the morning he's looking for the party. First thing in the morning he's chipper and chattering. Looking for the party. That's your brother. He had a match in Garth.

Shame the way they did that boy. He'd been down to the clinic two or three times but they sent him home. Said he had an infection and it would take care of itself. Something like that anyway. You know how they are down there. Have to be spitting blood to get attention. Then all they give you is a Band-Aid. He went back two times, but they kept telling him the same dumb thing. Anybody who knew Garth could see something awful was wrong. Circles under his eyes. Sallow look to his skin. Losing weight. And the poor thing didn't have any weight to lose. Last time I saw him I was shocked. Just about shocked out my shoes. Wasn't Garth standing in front of me. Not the boy I knew.

Well, to make a long story short, they finally took him in the hospital but it was too late. They let him walk the streets till he was dead. It was wrong. Worse than wrong how they did him, but that's how those dogs do us every day God sends here. Garth's gone, so nothing nobody can say will do any good. I feel so sorry for his mother. She lived for that boy. I called her and tried to talk but what can you say? I prayed for her and prayed for Garth and prayed for Robby. A thing like that tears people up.

It's worse if you keep it inside. And that's your brother's way. He'll let it eat him up and then go out and do something crazy.

Until she told me Garth's story I guess I hadn't realized how much my mother had begun to change. She had always seemed to me to exemplify the tolerance, the patience, the long view epitomized in her father. John French's favorite saying was, Give 'em the benefit of the doubt. She could get as ruffled, as evil as the rest of us, cry and scream or tear around the house fit to be tied. She had her grudges and quarrels. Mom could let it all hang out, yet most of the time she radiated a deep calm. She reacted strongly to things but at the same time held judgment in abeyance. Events, personalities always deserved a second, slower appraisal, an evaluation outside the sphere of everyday hassles and vexations. You gave people the benefit of the doubt. You attempted to remove your ego, acknowledge the limitations of your individual view of things. You consulted as far as you were equipped by temperament and intelligence a broader, more abiding set of relationships and connections.

You tried on the other person's point of view. You sought the other, better person in yourself who might talk you into relinquishing for a moment your selfish interest in whatever was at issue. You stopped and considered the long view, possibilities other than the one that momentarily was leading you by the nose. You gave yourself and other people the benefit of the doubt.

My mother had that capacity. I'd admired, envied, and benefited infinitely from its presence. As she related the story of Garth's death and my brother's anger and remorse, her tone was uncompromisingly bitter. No slack, no margin of doubt was being granted to the forces that destroyed Garth and still pursued her son. She had exhausted her reserves of understanding and compassion. The long view supplied the same ugly picture as the short. She had an enemy now. It was that revealed truth that had given the conversation its edge, its impact. *They* had killed Garth, and his dying had killed part of her son; so the battle lines were drawn. Irreconcilably. Absolutely. The backside of John French's motto had come into play. Giving someone the benefit of the doubt was also giving him enough rope to hang himself. If a person takes advantage of the benefit of the doubt and keeps on taking and taking, one day the rope plays out. The piper must be paid. If you've been the one giving, it becomes incumbent on you to grip your end tight and take away. You turn the other cheek, but slowly, cautiously, and keep your fist balled up at your side. If your antagonist decides to smack rather than kiss you or leave you alone, you make sure you get in the first blow. And make sure it's hard enough to knock him down.

Before she told Garth's story, my mother had already changed, but it took years for me to realize how profoundly she hated what had been done to Garth and then Robby. The gentleness of my grandfather, like his fair skin and good French hair, had been passed down to my mother. Gentleness styled the way she thought, spoke, and moved in the world.

Her easy disposition and sociability masked the intensity of her feelings. Her attitude to authority of any kind, doctors, clerks, police, bill collectors, newscasters, whites in general partook of her constitutional gentleness. She wasn't docile or cowed. The power other people possessed or believed they possessed didn't frighten her; she accommodated herself, offered something they could accept as deference but that was in fact the same resigned, alert attention she paid to roaches or weather or poverty, any of the givens outside herself that she couldn't do much about. She never engaged in public tests of will, never pushed herself or her point of view on people she didn't know. Social awkwardness embarrassed her. Like most Americans she didn't like paying taxes, was suspicious of politicians, resented the disparity between big and little people in our society and the double standard that allowed big shots to get away with murder. She paid particular attention to news stories that reinforced her basic political assumption that power corrupts. On the other hand she knew the world was a vale of tears and one's strength, granted by God to deal with life's inevitable calamities, should not be squandered on small stuff.

In spite of all her temperamental and philosophic resistance to extremes, my mother would be radicalized. What the demonstrations, protest marches, and slogans of the sixties had not effected would be accomplished by Garth's death and my brother's troubles. She would become an aggressive, acid critic of the status quo in all its forms: from the President ("If it wasn't for that rat I'd have a storm door to go with the storm windows but he cut the program") on down to bank tellers ("I go there every Friday and I'm one of the few black faces she sees all day and she knows me as well as she knows that wart on her cheek but she'll still make me show my license before she'll cash my check"). A son she loved would be pursued, captured, tried, and imprisoned by the forces of law and order. Throughout the ordeal her love for him wouldn't change, couldn't change. His crime tested her love and also tested the nature, the intent of the forces arrayed against her son. She had to make a choice. On one side were the stark facts of his crime: robbery, murder, flight; her son an outlaw, a fugitive; then a prisoner. On the other side the guardians of society, the laws, courts, police, judges, and keepers who were responsible for punishing her son's transgression.

She didn't invent the two sides and initially didn't believe there couldn't be a middle ground. She extended the benefit of the doubt. Tried to situate herself somewhere in between, acknowledging the evil of her son's crime while simultaneously holding on to the fact that he existed as a human being before, after, and during the crime he'd committed. He'd done wrong but he was still Robby and she'd always be his mother. Strangely, on the dark side, the side of the crime and its terrible consequences, she would find room to exercise her love. As negative as the elements were, a life taken, the grief of the survivors, suffering, waste, guilt, remorse, the scale was human; she could apply her sense of right and wrong. Her life to that point had equipped her with values, with tools for sorting out and coping with disaster. So she would choose to make her fight there, on treacherous yet familiar ground—familiar since her son was there—and she could place herself, a woman, a mother, a grieving, bereaved human being, there beside him.

Nothing like that was possible on the other side. The legitimacy of the other side was grounded not in her experience of life, but in a set of rules seemingly framed to sidestep, ignore, or replace her sense of reality. Accepting the version of reality encoded in *their* rules would be like stepping into a cage and locking herself in. Definitions of her son, herself, of need and frailty and mercy, of blackness and redemption and justice had all been neatly formulated. No need here for her questions, her uncertainty, her fear, her love. Everything was clean and clear. No room for her sense that things like good and evil, right and wrong bleed into each other and create a dreadful margin of ambiguity no one could name but could only enter, enter at the risk of everything because everything is at stake and no one on earth knows what it means to enter or what will happen if and when the testing of the margin is over.

She could love her son, accept his guilt, accept the necessity of punishment, suffer with him, grow with him past the stage of blaming everyone but himself for his troubles, grieve with him when true penitence began to exact its toll. Though she might wish penance and absolution could be achieved in private, without the intervention of a prison sentence, she understood dues must be paid. He was her son but he was also a man who had committed a robbery in the course of which another woman's son had been killed. What would appall her and what finally turned her against the forces of law and order was the incapacity of the legal system to grant her son's humanity. "Fair" was the word she used—a John French word. She expected them to treat Robby fair. Fairness was what made her willing to give him up to punishment even though her love screamed no and her hands clung to his shoulders. Fairness was what she expected from the other side in their dealings with her and her son.

She could see their side, but they steadfastly refused to see hers. And when she realized fairness was not forthcoming, she began to hate. In the lack of reciprocity, in the failure to grant that Robby was first a man, then a man who had done wrong, the institutions and individuals who took over control of his life denied not only his humanity but the very existence of the world that had nurtured him and nurtured her—the world of touching, laughing, suffering black people that established Robby's claim to something more than a number.

Mom expects the worst now. She's peeped their hole card. She understands they have a master plan that leaves little to accident, that most of the ugliest things happening to black people are not accidental but the predictable results of the working of the plan. What she learned about authority, about law and order didn't make sense at first. It went against her instincts, what she wanted to believe, against the generosity she'd observed in her father's interactions with other Homewood people. He was fair. He'd pick up the egg rolls he loved from the back kitchen door of Mr. Wong's restaurant and not blame Wong, his old talking buddy and card-playing crony, for not serving black people in his restaurant. Wong had a family and depended on white folks to feed them, so Wong didn't have any choice and neither did John French if he wanted those incredible egg rolls. He treated everyone, high and low, the same. He said what he meant and meant what he said. John French expected no more from other people than he expected from himself. And he'd been known to mess up many a time, but that was him, that was John French, no better, no worse than any man who pulls on his britches one leg at a time. He needed a little slack, needed the benefit of that blind eye people who love, or people who want to get along with other people, must learn to cast. John French was grateful for the slack, so was quick to extend it to others. Till they crossed him.

My mother had been raised in Homewood. The old Homewood. Her relations with people in that close-knit, homogeneous community were based on trust, mutual respect, common spiritual and material concerns. Face-to-face contact, shared language and values, a large fund of communal experience rendered individual lives extremely visible in Homewood. Both a person's self-identity ("You know who you are") and accountability ("Other people know who you are") were firmly established.

If one of the Homewood people said, "That's the French girl" or, "There goes John French's daughter," a portrait with subtle shading and complex resonance was painted by the words. If the listener addressed was also a Homewood resident, the speaker's voice located the young woman passing innocently down Tioga Street in a world invisible to outsiders. A French girl was somebody who lived in Cassina Way, somebody you didn't fool with or talk nasty to. Didn't speak to at all except in certain places or on certain occasions. French girls were church girls, Homewood African Methodist Episcopal Zion Sunday-school-picnic and social-event young ladies. You wouldn't find them hanging around anywhere without escorts or chaperones. French girls had that fair, light, bright, almost white redbone complexion and fine blown hair and nice big legs but all that was to be appreciated from a distance because they were nice girls and because they had this crazy daddy who wore a big brown country hat and gambled and drank wine and once ran a man out of town, ran him away without ever laying a hand on him or making a bad-mouthed threat, just cut his eyes a certain way when he said the man's name and the word went out and the man who had cheated a drunk John French with loaded dice was gone. Just like that. And there was the time Elias Brown was cleaning his shotgun in his backyard. Brown had his double-barreled shotgun across his knees and a jug of Dago Red on the ground beside him and it was a Saturday and hot and Brown was sweating through his BVD undershirt and paying more attention to the wine than he was to the gun. Next thing you know, *Boom!* Off it goes and buckshot sprayed down Cassina Way, and it's Saturday and summer like I said, so chillens playing everywhere but God watches over fools and babies so nobody hit bad. Nobody hit at all except the little French girl, Geraldine, playing out there in the alley and she got nicked in her knee. Barely drew blood. A sliver of that buckshot musta ricocheted off the cobblestones and cut her knee. Thank Jesus she the only one hit and she ain't hit bad. Poor Elias Brown don't quite know what done happened till some the mens run over in his yard and snatch the gun and shake the wine out his head. What you doing, fool? Don't you know no better all those children running round here? Coulda killed one these babies. Elias stone drunk and don't hear nothing, see nothing till one the men say French girl. Nicked the little French girl, Geraldine. Then Elias woke up real quick. His knees, his dusty butt, everything he got starts to trembling and his eyes get big as dinner plates. Then he's gone like a turkey through the corn. Nobody seen Elias for a week. He's in Ohio at his sister's next time anybody hear anything about Elias. He's cross there in Ohio and still shaking till he git word John French ain't after him. It took three men gon over there telling the same story to get Elias back to Homewood. John French ain't mad. He *was* mad but he ain't mad now. Little girl just nicked is all and French ain't study-ing you, Brown.

You heard things like that in Homewood names. Rules of etiquette, thumbnail character sketches, a history of the community. A dire warning to get back could be coded into the saying of a person's name, and a fur-ther inflection of the speaker's voice could tell you to ignore the facts, for-get what he's just reminded you to remember and go on. Try your luck.

Because Homewood was self-contained and possessed such a strong personality, because its people depended less on outsiders than they did on each other for so many of their most basic satisfactions, they didn't no-tice the net settling over their community until it was already firmly in place. Even though the strands of the net—racial discrimination, economic exploitation, white hate and fear—had existed time out of mind, what people didn't notice or chose not to notice was that the net was being drawn tighter, that ruthless people outside the community had the power to choke the life out of Homewood, and as soon as it served their interests would do just that. During the final stages, as the net closed like a fist around Homewood, my mother couldn't pretend it wasn't there. But in-stead of setting her free, the truth trapped her in a cage as tangible as the iron bars of Robby's cell.

Some signs were subtle, gradual. The A & P started to die. Nobody mopped filth from the floors. Nobody bothered to restock empty shelves. Fewer and fewer white faces among the shoppers. A plate-glass display window gets broken and stays broken. When they finally close the store, they paste the going-out-of-business notice over the jagged, taped crack. Other signs as blatant, as sudden as fire engines and patrol cars breaking your sleep, screaming through the dark Homewood streets. First Garth's death, then Robby's troubles brought it all home. My mother realized her personal unhappiness and grief were inseparable from what was happening *out there*. Out there had never been further away than the thousand insults and humiliations she had disciplined herself to ignore. What she had deemed petty, not worth bothering about, were strings of the net just as necessary, as effective as the most dramatic intrusions into her life. She decided to stop letting things go by. No more benefit of the doubt. Doubt had been cruelly excised. She decided to train herself to be as wary, as unforgiving as she'd once been ready to live and let live. My mother wouldn't become paranoid, not even overtly prickly or bristling. That would have been too contrary to her style, to what her blood and upbringing had instilled. The change was inside. What she thought of people. How she judged situations. Things she'd say or do startled me, set me back on my heels because I didn't recognize my mother in them. I couldn't account for the stare of pure unadulterated hatred she directed at the prison guard when he turned away from her to answer the phone before handing her the rest-room key she'd requested, the vehemence with which she had cussed Richard Nixon for paying no taxes when she, scraping by on an income of less than four thousand dollars a year, owed the IRS three hundred dollars.

Garth's death and Robby's troubles were at the center of her new vision. Like a prism, they caught the light, transformed it so she could trace the seemingly random inconveniences and impositions coloring her life to their source in a master plan.

I first heard Garth's story in the summer of 1975, the summer my wife carried our daughter Jamila in her belly, the summer before the robbery and killing. The story contained all the clues I'm trying to decipher now. Sitting in the kitchen vaguely distracted by gospel music from the little clock radio atop the table, listening as my mother expressed her sorrow, her indignation at the way Garth was treated, her fears for my brother, I was hearing a new voice. Something about the voice struck me then, but I missed what was novel and crucial. I'd lost my Homewood ear. Missed all the things unsaid that invested her words with special urgency. People in Homewood often ask: You said that to say what? The impacted quality of an utterance either buries a point too obscurely or insists on a point so strongly that the listener wants the meat of the message repeated, wants it restated clearly so it stands alone on its own two feet. If I'd been alert enough to ask that question, to dig down to the root and core of Garth's story after my mother told it, I might have understood sooner how desperate and dangerous Homewood had become. Six years later my brother was in prison, and when he began the story of his troubles with Garth's death, a circle completed itself; Robby was talking to me, but I was still on the outside, looking in.

That day six years later, I talked with Robby three hours, the maximum allotted for weekday visits with a prisoner. It was the first time in life we'd ever talked that long. Probably two and a half hours longer than the longest, unbroken, private conversation we'd ever had. And it had taken guards, locks, and bars to bring us together. The ironies of the situation, the irony of that fact, escaped neither of us.

I listened mostly, interrupting my brother's story a few times to clarify dates or names. Much of what he related was familiar. The people, the places. Even the voice, the words he chose were mine in a way. We're so alike, I kept thinking, anticipating what he would say next, how he would say it, filling in naturally, easily with my words what he left unsaid. Trouble was our minds weren't interchangeable. No more than our bodies. The guards wouldn't have allowed me to stay in my brother's place. He was the criminal. I was the visitor from outside. Different as night and day. As Robby talked I let myself forget that difference. Paid too much attention to myself listening and lost some of what he was saying. What I missed would have helped define the difference. But I missed it. It was easy to half listen. For both of us to pretend to be closer than we were. We needed the closeness. We were brothers. In the prison visiting lounge I acted toward my brother the way I'd been acting toward him all my life, heard what I wanted to hear, rejected the rest.

When Robby talked, the similarity of his Homewood and mine was a trap. I could believe I knew exactly what he was describing. I could relax into his story, walk down Dunfermline or Tioga, see my crippled grandmother sitting on the porch of the house on Finance, all the color her pale face had lost blooming in the rosebush beneath her in the yard, see Robby in the downstairs hall of the house on Marchand, rapping with his girl on the phone, which sat on a three-legged stand just inside the front door. I'd slip unaware out of his story into one of my own. I'd be following him, an obedient shadow, then a cloud would blot the sun and I'd be gone, unchained, a dark form still skulking behind him but no longer in tow.

The hardest habit to break, since it was the habit of a lifetime, would be listening to myself listen to him. That habit would destroy any chance of seeing my brother on his terms; and seeing him in his terms, learning his terms, seemed the whole point of learning his story. However numerous and comforting the similarities, we were different. The world had seized on the difference, allowed me room to thrive, while he'd been forced into a cage. Why did it work out that way? What was the nature of the difference? Why did it haunt me? Temporarily at least, to answer these questions, I had to root my fiction-writing self out of our exchanges. I had to teach myself to listen. Start fresh, clear the pipes, resist too facile an identification, tame the urge to take off with Robby's story and make it my own.

I understood all that, but could I break the habit? And even if I did learn to listen, wouldn't there be a point at which I'd have to take over the telling? Wasn't there something fundamental in my writing, in my capacity to function, that depended on flight, on escape? Wasn't another person's skin a hiding place, a place to work out anxiety, to face threats too intimidating to handle in any other fashion? Wasn't writing about people a way of exploiting them?

A stranger's gait, or eyes, or a piece of clothing can rivet my attention. Then it's like falling down to the center of the earth. Not exactly fear or panic but an uneasy, uncontrollable momentum, a sense of being swallowed, engulfed in blackness that has no dimensions, no fixed points. That boundless, incarcerating black hole is another person. The detail grabbing me functions as a door and it swings open and I'm drawn, sucked, pulled in head over heels till suddenly I'm righted again, on track again and the peculiarity, the ordinariness of the detail that usurped my attention becomes a window, a way of seeing out of another person's eyes, just as for a second it had been my way in. I'm scooting along on short, stubby legs and the legs are not anybody else's and certainly not mine, but I feel for a second what it's like to motor through the world atop these peculiar duck thighs and foreshortened calves and I know how wobbly the earth feels under those run-over-at-the-heel, split-seamed penny loafers. Then just as suddenly I'm back. I'm me again, slightly embarrassed, guilty because I've been trespassing and don't know how long I've been gone or if anybody noticed me violating somebody else's turf.

Do I write to escape, to make a fiction of my life? If I can't be trusted with the story of my own life, how could I ask my brother to trust me with his?

The business of making a book together was new for both of us. Difficult. Awkward. Another book could be constructed about a writer who goes to a prison to interview his brother but comes away with his own story. The conversations with his brother would provide a stage for dramatizing the writer's tortured relationship to other people, himself, his craft. The writer's motives, the issue of exploitation, the inevitable conflict between his role as detached observer and his responsibility as a brother would be at the center of such a book. When I stopped hearing Robby and listened to myself listening, that kind of book shouldered its way into my consciousness. I didn't like the feeling. That book compromised the intimacy I wanted to achieve with my brother. It was as obtrusive as the Wearever pen in my hand, the little yellow sheets of Yard Count paper begged from the pad of the guard in charge of overseeing the visiting lounge. The borrowed pen and paper (I was not permitted into the lounge with my own) were necessary props. I couldn't rely on memory to get my brother's story down and the keepers had refused my request to use a tape recorder, so there I was. Jimmy Olson, cub reporter, poised on the edge of my seat, pen and paper at ready, asking to be treated as a brother.

We were both rookies. Neither of us had learned very much about sharing our feelings with other family members. At home it had been assumed that each family member possessed deep, powerful feelings and that very little or nothing at all needed to be said about these feelings because we all were stuck with them and talk wouldn't change them. Your particular feelings were a private matter and family was a protective fence around everybody's privacy. Inside the perimeter of the fence each family member resided in his or her own quarters. What transpired in each dwelling was mainly the business of its inhabitant as long as nothing generated within an individual unit threatened the peace or safety of the whole. None of us knew how traditional West African families were organized or what values the circular shape of their villages embodied, but the living arrangements we had worked out among ourselves resembled the ancient African patterns. You were granted emotional privacy, independence, and space to commune with your feelings. You were encouraged to deal with as much as you could on your own, yet you never felt alone. The high wall of the family, the collective, communal reality of other souls, other huts like yours eliminated some of the dread, the isolation experienced when you turned inside and tried to make sense out of the chaos of your individual feelings. No matter how grown you thought you were or how far you believed you'd strayed, you knew you could cry *Mama* in the depths of the night and somebody would tend to you. Arms would wrap round you, a soft soothing voice lend its support. If not a flesh-and-blood mother then a mother in the form of song or story or a surrogate, Aunt Geral, Aunt Martha, drawn from the network of family numbers.

Privacy was a bridge between you and the rest of the family. But you had to learn to control the traffic. You had to keep it uncluttered, resist the temptation to cry wolf. Privacy in our family was a birthright, a union card granted with family membership. The card said you're one of us but also certified your separateness, your obligation to keep much of what defined your separateness to yourself.

An almost aesthetic consideration's involved. Okay, let's live together. Let's each build a hut and for security we'll arrange the individual dwellings in a circle and then build an outer ring to enclose the whole village. Now your hut is your own business, but let's in general agree on certain outward forms. Since we all benefit from the larger pattern, let's compromise, conform to some degree on the materials, the shape of each unit. Because symmetry and harmony please the eye. Let's adopt a style, one that won't crimp anybody's individuality, one that will buttress and enhance each member's image of what a living place should be.

So Robby and I faced each other in the prison visiting lounge as familiar strangers, linked by blood and time. But how do you begin talking about blood, about time? He's been inside his privacy and I've been inside mine, and neither of us in thirty-odd years had felt the need to exchange more than social calls. We shared the common history, values, and style developed within the tall stockade of family, and that was enough to make us care about each other, enough to insure a profound depth of mutual regard, but the feelings were undifferentiated. They'd seldom been tested specifically, concretely. His privacy and mine had been exclusive, sanctioned by family traditions. Don't get too close. Don't ask too many questions or give too many answers. Don't pry. Don't let what's inside slop out on the people around you.

The stories I'd sent to Robby were an attempt to reveal what I thought about certain matters crucial to us both. Our shared roots and destinies. I wanted him to know what I'd been thinking and how that thinking was drawing me closer to him. I was banging on the door of his privacy. I believed I'd shed some of my own.

We were ready to talk. It was easy to begin. Impossible. We were neophytes, rookies. I was a double rookie. A beginner at this kind of intimacy, a beginner at trying to record it. My double awkwardness kept getting in the way. I'd hidden the borrowed pen by dropping my hand below the level of the table where we sat. Now when in hell would be the right moment to raise it? To use it? I had to depend on my brother's instincts, his generosity. I had to listen, listen.

Luckily there was catching up to do. He asked me about my kids, about his son, Omar, about the new nieces and nephews he'd never seen. That helped. Reminded us we were brothers. We got on with it. Conditions in the prisons. Robby's state of mind. The atmosphere behind the prison walls had been particularly tense for over a year. A group of new, younger guards had instituted a get-tough policy. More strip searches, cell shakedowns, strict enforcement of penny-ante rules and regulations. Grown men treated like children by other grown men. Inmates yanked out of line and punished because a button is undone or hair uncombed. What politicians demanded in the free world was being acted out inside the prison. A crusade, a war on crime waged by a gang of gung-ho guards against men who were already certified casualties, prisoners of war. The walking wounded being beaten and shot up again because they're easy targets. Robby's closest friends, including Cecil and Mike, are in the hole. Others who were considered potential troublemakers had been transferred to harsher prisons. Robby was warned by a guard. We ain't caught you in the shit yet, but we will. We know what you're thinking and we'll catch you in it. Or put you in it. Got your buddies and we'll get you.

The previous summer, 1980, a prisoner, Leon Patterson, had been asphyxiated in his cell. He was an asthma sufferer, a convicted murderer who depended on medication to survive the most severe attacks of his illness. On a hot August afternoon when the pollution index had reached its highest count of the summer, Patterson was locked in his cell in a cell block without windows and little air. At four o'clock, two hours after he'd been confined to the range, he began to call for help. Other prisoners raised the traditional distress signal, rattling tin cups against the bars of their cells. Patterson's cries for help became screams, and his fellow inmates beat on the bars and shouted with him. Over an hour passed before any guards arrived. They carted away Patterson's limp body. He never revived and was pronounced dead at 10:45 that evening. His death epitomized the polarization in the prison. Patterson was seen as one more victim of the guards' inhumanity. A series of incidents followed in the ensuing year, hunger strikes, melees between guards and prisoners, culminating in a near massacre when the dog days of August hung once more over the prison.

One of the favorite tactics of the militant guards was grabbing a man from the line as the prisoners moved single-file through an archway dividing the recreation yard from the main cell blocks. No reason was given or needed. It was a simple show of force, a reminder of the guards' absolute power, their right to treat the inmates any way they chose, and do it with impunity. A sit-down strike in the prison auditorium followed one of the more violent attacks on an inmate. The prisoner who had resisted an arbitrary seizure and strip search was smacked in the face. He punched back and the guards jumped him, knocked him to the ground with their fists and sticks. The incident took place in plain view of over a hundred prisoners and it was the last straw. The victim had been provoked, assaulted, and surely would be punished for attempting to protect himself, for doing what any man would and should do in similar circumstances. The prisoner would suffer again. In addition to the physical beating they'd administered, the guards would attack the man's record. He'd be written up. A kangaroo court would take away his *good time*, thereby lengthening the period he'd have to wait before becoming eligible for probation or parole. Finally, on the basis of the guards' testimony he'd probably get a sixty-day sojourn in the hole. The prisoners realized it was time to take a stand. What had happened to one could happen to any of them. They rushed into the auditorium and locked themselves in. The prisoners held out till armed state troopers and prison guards in riot gear surrounded the building. Given the mood of that past year and the unmistakable threat in the new warden's voice as he repeated through a loudspeaker his refusal to meet with the prisoners and discuss their grievances, everybody inside the building knew that the authorities meant business, that the forces of law and order would love nothing better than an excuse to turn the auditorium into a shooting gallery. The strike was broken. The men filed out. A point was driven home again. Prisoners have no rights the keepers are bound to respect.

That was how the summer had gone. Summer was bad enough in the penitentiary in the best of times. Warm weather stirred the prisoners' blood. The siren call of the streets intensified. Circus time. The street blooming again after the long, cold winter. People outdoors. On their stoops. On the corners. In bright summer clothes or hardly any clothes at all. The free-world sounds and sights more real as the weather heats up. Confinement a torture. Each cell a hotbox. The keepers take advantage of every excuse to keep you out of the yard, to deprive you of the simple pleasure of a breeze, the blue sky. Why? So that the pleasant weather can be used as a tool, a boon to be withheld. So punishment has a sharper edge. By a perverse turn of the screw something good becomes something bad. Summer a bitch at best, but this past summer as the young turks among the guards ran roughshod over the prisoners, the prison had come close to blowing, to exploding like a piece of rotten fruit in the sun. And if the lid blew, my brother knew he'd be one of the first to die. During any large-scale uprising, in the first violent, chaotic seconds no board of inquiry would ever be able to reconstruct, scores would be settled. A bullet in the back of the brain would get rid of troublemakers, remove potential leaders, uncontrollable prisoners the guards hated and feared. You were supremely eligible for a bullet if the guards couldn't press your button. If they hadn't learned how to manipulate you, if you couldn't be bought or sold, if you weren't into drug and sex games, if you weren't cowed or depraved, then you were a threat.

Robby understood that he was sentenced to die. That all sentences were death sentences. If he didn't buckle under, the guards would do everything in their power to kill him. If he succumbed to the pressure to surrender dignity, self-respect, control over his own mind and body, then he'd become a beast, and what was good in him would die. The death sentence was unambiguous. The question for him became: How long could he survive in spite of the death sentence? Nothing he did would guarantee his safety. A disturbance in a cell block halfway across the prison could provide an excuse for shooting him and dumping him with the other victims. Anytime he was ordered to go with guards out of sight of other prisoners, his escorts could claim he attacked them, or attempted to escape. Since the flimsiest pretext would make murdering him acceptable, he had no means of protecting himself. Yet to maintain sanity, to minimize their opportunities to destroy him, he had to be constantly vigilant. He had to discipline himself to avoid confrontations, he had to weigh in terms of life and death every decision he made; he had to listen and obey his keepers' orders, but he also had to determine in certain threatening situations whether it was better to say no and keep himself out of a trap or take his chances that this particular summons was not the one inviting him to his doom. Of course to say no perpetuated his reputation as one who couldn't be controlled, a bad guy, a guy you never turn your back on, one of the prisoners out to get the guards. That rap made you more dangerous in the keepers' eyes and therefore increased the likelihood they'd be frightened into striking first. Saying no put you in no less jeopardy than going along with the program. Because the program was contrived to kill you. Directly or indirectly, you knew where you were headed. What you didn't know was the schedule. Tomorrow. Next week. A month. A minute. When would one of them get itchy, get beyond waiting a second longer? Would there be a plan, a contrived incident, a conspiracy they'd talk about and set up as they drank coffee in the guards' room or would it be the hair-trigger impulse of one of them who held a grudge, harbored an antipathy so elemental, so irrational that it could express itself only in a burst of pure, unrestrained violence?

If you're Robby and have the will to survive, these are the possibilities you must constantly entertain. Vigilance is the price of survival. Beneath the vigilance, however, is a gnawing awareness boiling in the pit of your stomach. You can be as vigilant as you're able, you can keep fighting the good fight to survive, and still your fate is out of your hands. If they decide to come for you in the morning, that's it. Your ass is grass and those minutes, and hours, days and years you painfully stitched together to put off the final reckoning won't matter at all. So the choice, difficult beyond words, to say yes or say no is made in light of the knowledge that in the end neither your yes nor your no matters. Your life is not in your hands.

The events, the atmosphere of the summer had brought home to Robby the futility of resistance. Power was absurdly apportioned all on one side. To pretend you could control your own destiny was a joke. You learned to laugh at your puniness, as you laughed at the stink of your farts lighting up your cell. Like you laughed at the seriousness of the masturbation ritual that romanticized, cloaked in darkness and secrecy, the simple, hungry shaking of your penis in your fist. You had no choice, but you always had to decide to go on or stop. It had been a stuttering, stop, start, maybe, fuck it, bitch of a summer, and now, for better or worse, we were starting up something else. Robby backtracks his story from Garth to another beginning, the house on Copeland Street in Shadyside where we lived when he was born.

I know that had something to do with it. Living in Shadyside with only white people around. You remember how it was. Except for us and them couple other families it was a all-white neighborhood. I got a thing about black. See, black was like the forbidden fruit. Even when we went to Freed's in Homewood, Geraldine and them never let me go no farther than the end of the block. All them times I stayed over there I didn't go past Mr. Conrad's house by the vacant lot or the other corner where Billy Shields and them stayed. Started to wondering what was so different about a black neighborhood. I was just a little kid and I was curious. I really wanted to know why they didn't want me finding out what was over there. Be playing with the kids next door to Freed, you know, Sonny and Gumpy and them, but all the time I'm wondering what's round the corner, what's up the street. Didn't care if it was *bad* or good or dangerous or what, I had to find out. If it's something bad I figured they would have told me, tried to scare me off. But nobody said nothing except, No. Don't you go no farther than the corner. Then back home in Shadyside nothing but white people so I couldn't ask nobody what was special about black. Black was a mystery and in my mind I decided I'd find out what it was all about. Didn't care if it killed me, I was going to find out.

One time, it was later, I was close to starting high school, I overheard Mommy and Geraldine and Sissy talking in Freed's kitchen. They was talking about us moving from Shadyside back to Homewood. The biggest thing they was worried about was me. How would it be for me being in Homewood and going to Westinghouse? I could tell they was scared. Specially Mom. You know how she is. She didn't want to move. Homewood scared her. Not so much the place but how I'd act if I got out there in the middle of it. She already knew I was wild, hard to handle. There'd be too much mess for me to get into in Homewood. She could see trouble coming.

And she was right. Me and trouble hooked up. See, it was a question of being somebody. Being my own person. Like youns had sports and good grades sewed up. Wasn't nothing I could do in school or sports that youns hadn't done already. People said, Here comes another Wideman. He's gon be a good student like his brothers and sister. That's the way it was spozed to be. I was another Wideman, the last one, the baby, and everybody knew how I was spozed to act. But something inside me said no. Didn't want to be like the rest of youns. Me, I had to be a rebel. Had to get out from under youns' good grades and do. Way back then I decided I wanted to be a star. I wanted to make it big. My way. I wanted the glamour. I wanted to sit high up.

Figured out school and sports wasn't the way. I got to thinking my brothers and sister was squares. Loved youall but wasn't no room left for me. Had to figure out a new territory. I had to be a rebel.

Along about junior high I discovered Garfield. I started hanging out up on Garfield Hill. You know, partying and stuff in Garfield cause that's where the niggers was. Garfield was black, and I finally found what I'd been looking for. That place they was trying to hide from me. It was heaven. You know. Hanging out with the fellows. Drinking wine and trying anything else we could get our hands on. And the ladies. Always a party on the weekends. Had me plenty sweet little soft-leg Garfield ladies. Niggers run my butt off that hill more than a couple times behind messing with somebody's piece but I'd be back next weekend. Cause I'd found heaven. Looking back now, wasn't much to Garfield. Just a rinky-dink ghetto up on a hill, but it was the street. I'd found my place.

Having a little bit of a taste behind me I couldn't wait to get to Homewood. In a way I got mad with Mommy and the rest of them. Seemed to me like they was trying to hold me back from a good time. Seemed like they just didn't want me to have no fun. That's when I decided I'd go on about my own business. Do it my way. Cause I wasn't getting no slack at home. They still expected me to be like my sister and brothers. They didn't know I thought youns was squares. Yeah. I knew I was hipper and groovier than youns ever thought of being. Streetwise, into something. Had my own territory and I was bad. I was a rebel. Wasn't following in nobody's footsteps but my own. And I was a hip cookie, you better believe it. Wasn't a hipper thing out there than your brother, Rob. I couldn't wait for them to turn me loose in Homewood.

Me being the youngest and all, the baby in the family, people always said, ain't he cute. That Robby gon be a ladykiller. Been hearing that mess since day one so ain't no surprise I started to believing it. Youns had me pegged as a lady's man so that's what I was. The girls be talking the same trash everybody else did. Ain't he cute. Be petting me and spoiling me like I'm still the baby of the family and I sure ain't gon tell them stop. Thought I was cute as the girls be telling me. Thought sure enough, I'm gon be a star. I loved to get up and show my behind. Must have been good at it too cause the teacher used to call me up in front of the class to perform. The kids'd get real quiet. That's probably why the teacher got me up. Keep the class quiet while she nods off. Cause they'd listen to me. Sure nuff pay attention.

Performing always come natural to me. Wasn't nervous or nothing. Just get up and do my thing. They liked for me to do impressions. I could mimic anybody. You remember how I'd do that silly stuff around the house. Anybody I'd see on TV or hear on a record I could mimic to a T. Bob Hope, Nixon, Smokey Robinson, Ed Sullivan. White or black. I could talk just like them or sing a song just like they did. The class yell out a famous name and I'd do the one they wanted to hear. If things had gone another way I've always believed I could have made it big in show business. If you could keep them little frisky kids in Liberty School quiet you could handle any audience. Always could sing and do impressions. You remember Mom asking me to do them for you when you came home from college.

I still be performing. Read poetry in the hole. The other fellows get real quiet and listen. Sing down in there too. Nothing else to do, so we entertain each other. They always asking me to sing or read. "Hey, Wideman. C'mon man and do something." Then it gets quiet while they waiting for me to start. Quiet and it's already dark. You in your own cell and can't see nobody else. Barely enough light to read by. The other fellows can hear you but it's just you and them walls so it feels like being alone much as it feels like you're singing or reading to somebody else.

Yeah. I read my own poems sometimes. Other times I just start in on whatever book I happen to be reading. One the books you sent me, maybe. Fellows like my poems. They say I write about the things they be thinking. Say it's like listening to their own self thinking. That's cause we all down there together. What else you gonna do but think of the people on the outside. Your woman. Your kids or folks, if you got any. Just the same old sad shit we all be thinking all the time. That's what I write and the fellows like to hear it.

Funny how things go around like that. Go round and round and keep coming back to the same place. Teacher used to get me up to pacify the class and I'm doing the same thing in prison. You said your teachers called on you to tell stories, didn't they? Yeah. It's funny how much we're alike. In spite of everything I always believed that. Inside. The feeling side. I always believed we was the most alike out of all the kids. I see stuff in your books. The kinds of things I be thinking or feeling.

Your teachers got you up, too. To tell stories. That's funny, ain't it.

I listen to my brother Robby. He unravels my voice. I sit with him in the darkness of the Behavioral Adjustment Unit. My imagination creates something like a giant seashell, enfolding, enclosing us. Its inner surface is velvet-soft and black. A curving mirror doubling the darkness. Poems are Jean Toomer's petals of dusk, petals of dawn. I want to stop. Savor the sweet, solitary pleasure, the time stolen from time in the hole. But the image I'm creating is a trick of the glass. The mirror that would swallow Robby and then chime to me: You're the fairest of them all. The voice I hear issues from a crack in the glass. I'm two or three steps ahead of my brother, making fiction out of his words. Somebody needs to snatch me by the neck and say, Stop. Stop and listen, listen to him.

The Behavioral Adjustment Unit is, as one guard put it, "a maximum-security prison within a maximum-security prison." The "Restricted Housing Unit" or "hole" or "Home Block" is a squat, two-story cement building containing thirty-five six-by-eight-foot cells. The governor of Pennsylvania closed the area in 1972 because of "inhumane conditions," but within a year the hole was reopened. For at least twenty-three hours a day the prisoners are confined to their cells. An hour of outdoor exercise is permitted only on days the guards choose to supervise it. Two meals are served three hours apart, then nothing except coffee and bread for the next twenty-one. The regulation that limits the time an inmate can serve in the BAU for a single offense is routinely sidestepped by the keepers. "Administrative custody" is a provision allowing officials to cage men in the BAU indefinitely. Hunger strikes are one means the prisoners have employed to protest the harsh conditions of the penal unit. Hearings prompted by the strikes have produced no major changes in the way the hole operates. Law, due process, the rights of the prisoners are irrelevant to the functioning of this prison within a prison. Robby was sentenced to six months in the BAU because a guard suspected he was involved in an attempted escape. The fact that a hearing, held six months later, established Robby's innocence, was small consolation since he'd already served his time in the hole.

Robby tells me about the other side of being the youngest: Okay, you're everybody's pet and that's boss, but on the other hand you sometimes feel you're the least important. Always last. Always bringing up the rear. You learn to do stuff on your own because the older kids are always busy, off doing their things, and you're too young, left behind because you don't fit, or just because they forget you're back here, at the end, bringing up the rear. But when orders are given out, you sure get your share. "John's coming home this weekend. Clean up your room." Robby remembers being forced to get a haircut on the occasion of one of my visits. Honor thy brother. Get your hair cut, your room rid up, and put on clean clothes. He'll be here with his family and I don't want the house looking like a pigpen.

I have to laugh at the image of myself as somebody to get a haircut for. Robby must have been fit to be tied.

Yeah, I was hot. I mean, you was doing well and all that, but shit, you were my brother. And it was my head. What's my head got to do with you? But you know how Mommy is. Ain't no talking to her when her mind gets set. Anything I tried to say was "talking *back*," so I just went ahead to the man and got my ears lowered.

I was trying to be a rebel but back then the most important thing still was what the grown-ups thought about me. How they felt meant everything.

Everything. Me and Tish and Dave were the ones at home then. You was gone and Gene was gone so it was the three of us fighting for attention. And we fought. Every crumb, everytime something got cut up or parceled out or it was Christmas or Easter, we so busy checking out what the other one got wasn't hardly no time to enjoy our own. Like a dogfight or cat fight all the time. And being the youngest I'm steady losing ground most the time. Seemed like to me, Tish and Dave the ones everybody talked about. Seemed like my time would never come. That ain't the way it really was, I know. I had my share cause I was the baby and ain't he cute and lots of times I know I got away with outrageous stuff or got my way cause I could play that baby mess to the hilt. Still it seemed like Dave and Tish was the ones really mattered. Mommy and Daddy and Sis and Geral and Big Otie and Ernie always slipping some change in their pockets or taking them to the store or letting them stay over all night in Homewood. I was a jealous little rascal. Sometimes I thought everybody thought I was just a spoiled brat. I'd say damn all youall. I'd think, Go on and love those square turkeys, but one day I'll be the one coming back with a suitcase full of money and a Cadillac. Go on and love them good grades. Robby gon do it his own way.

See, in my mind I was Superfly. I'd drive up slow to the curb. My hog be half a block long and these fine foxes in the back. Everybody looking when I ease out the door clean and mean. Got a check in my pocket to give to Mom. Buy her a new house with everything in it new. Pay her back for the hard times. I could see that happening as real as I can see your face right now. Wasn't no way it wasn't gon happen. Rob was gon make it big. I'd be at the door, smiling with the check in my hand and Mommy'd be so happy she'd be crying.

Well, it's a different story ain't it. Turned out different from how I used to think it would. The worst thing I did, the thing I feel most guilty behind is stealing Mom's life. It's like I stole her youth. Can't nothing change that. I can't give back what's gone. Robbing white people didn't cause me to lose no sleep back then. Couldn't feel but so bad about that. How you gon feel sorry when society's so corrupt, when everybody got their hand out or got their hand in somebody else's pocket and ain't no rules nobody listens to if they can get away with breaking them? How you gon apply the rules? It was dog eat dog out there, so how was I spozed to feel sorry if I was doing what everybody else doing. I just got caught is all. I'm sorry about that, and damned sorry that guy Stavros got killed, but as far as what I did, as far as robbing white people, ain't no way I was gon torture myself over that one.

I tried to write Mom a letter. Not too long ago. Should say I did write the letter and put it in a envelope and sent it cause that's what I did, but I be crying so much trying to write it I don't know what wound up in that letter. I wanted Mom to know I knew what I'd done. In a way I wanted to say I was sorry for spoiling her life. After all she did for me I turned around and made her life miserable. That's the wrongest thing I've done and I wanted to say I was sorry but I kept seeing her face while I was

writing the letter. I'd see her face and it would get older while I was looking. She'd get this old woman's face all lined and wrinkled and tired
about the eyes. Wasn't nothing I could do but watch. Cause I'd done it
and knew I done it and all the letters in the world ain't gon change her
face. I sit and think about stuff like that all the time. It's better now. I think
about other things too. You know like trying to figure what's really right
and wrong, but there be days the guilt don't never go away.

I'm the one made her tired, John. And that's my greatest sorrow. All
the love that's in me she created. Then I went and let her down.

When you in prison you got plenty of time to think, that's for damned
sure. Too much time. I've gone over and over my life. Every moment.
Every little thing again and again. I lay down on my bed and watch it happening over and over. Like a movie. I get it all broke down in pieces then I
break up the pieces then I take the pieces of the pieces and run them
through my hands so I remember every word a person said to me or what
I said to them and weigh the words till I think I know what each and
every one meant. Then I try to put it back together. Try to understand
where I been. Why I did what I did. You got time for that in here. Time's
all you got in here.

Going over and over things sometimes you can make sense. You
know. Like the chinky-chinky Chinaman sittin' on the fence. You put it together and you think, yes. That's why I did thus and so. Yeah. That's why
I lost that job or lost that woman or broke that one's heart. You stop thinking in terms of something being good or being evil, you just try to say this
happened because that happened because something else came first. You
can spend days trying to figure out just one little thing you did. People out
there in the world walk around in a daze cause they ain't got time to
think. When I was out there, I wasn't no different. Had this Superfly thing
and that was the whole bit. Nobody could tell me nothing.

Seems like I should start the story back in Shadyside. In the house on
Copeland Street. Nothing but white kids around. Them little white kids
had everything, too. That's what I thought, anyway. Nice houses, nice
clothes. They could buy pop and comic books and candy when they
wanted to. We wasn't that bad off, but compared to what them little white
kids had I always felt like I didn't have nothing. It made me kinda quiet
and shy around them. Me knowing all the time I wanted what they had.
Wanted it bad. There was them white kids with everything and there was
the black world Mommy and them was holding back from me. No place
to turn, in a way. I guess you could say I was stuck in the middle.
Couldn't have what the white kids in Shadyside had, and I wasn't allowed to look around the corner for something else. So I'd start the story
with Shadyside, the house on Copeland.

Another place to start could be December 29, 1950—the date of
Robby's birth. For some reason—maybe my mother and father were feud-
ing, maybe we just happened to be visiting my grandmother's house
when my mother's time came—the trip to the hospital to have Robby

began from Finance Street, from the house beside the railroad tracks in Homewood. What I remember is the bustle, people rushing around, yelling up and down the stairwell, doors slammed, drawers being opened and shut. A cold winter day so lots of coats and scarves and galoshes. My mother's face was very pale above the dark cloth coat that made her look even bigger than she was, carrying Robby the ninth month. On the way out the front door she stopped and stared back over her shoulder like she'd forgotten something. People just about shoving her out the house. Lots of bustle and noise getting her through the crowded hallway into the vestibule. Somebody opened the front door and December rattled the glass panes. Wind gusting and whistling, everybody calling out last-minute instructions, arrangements, goodbyes, blessings, prayers. My mother's white face calm, hovering a moment above it all as she turned back toward the hall, the stairs where I was planted, halfway to the top. She didn't find me, wasn't looking for me. A thought had crossed her mind and carried her far away. She didn't know why so many hands were rushing her out the door. She didn't hear the swirl of words, the icy blast of wind. Wrapped in a navy-blue coat, either Aunt Aida's or an old one of my grandmother's, which didn't have all its black buttons but stretched double over her big belly, my mother was wondering whether or not she'd turned off the water in the bathroom sink and deciding whether or not she should return up the stairs to check. Something like that crossing her mind, freeing her an instant before she got down to the business of pushing my brother into the world.

Both my grandfathers died on December 28. My grandmother died just after dawn on December 29. My sister lost a baby early in January. The end of the year has become associated with mournings, funerals; New Year's Day arrives burdened by a sense of loss, bereavement. Robby's birthday became tainted. To be born close to Christmas is bad enough in and of itself. Your birthday celebration gets upstaged by the orgy of gift giving on Christmas Day. No matter how many presents you receive on December 29, they seem a trickle after the Christmas flood. Plus there's too much excitement in too brief a period. Parents and relatives are exhausted, broke, still hung over from the Christmas rush, so there just isn't very much left to work with if your birthday comes four short days after Jesus'. Almost like not having a birthday. Or even worse, like sharing it with your brothers and sister instead of having the private oasis of your very own special day. So Robby cried a lot on his birthdays. And it certainly wasn't a happy time for my mother. Her father, John French, died the year after Robby was born, one day before Robby's birthday. Fifteen years and a day later Mom would lose her mother. The death of the baby my sister was carrying was a final, cruel blow, scaring my mother, jinxing the end of the year eternally. She dreaded the holiday season, expected it to bring dire tidings. She had attempted at one point to consecrate the sad days, employ them as a period of reflection, quietly, privately memorialize the passing of the two people who'd loved her most in the world. But the death of my father's father, then the miscarriage within this jinxed span of days burst the fragile truce my mother had effected with the year's end. She withdraws into herself, anticipates the worse as soon as Christmas decorations begin appearing. In 1975, the year of the robbery and murder, Robby was on the run when his birthday fell. My mother was sure he wouldn't survive the deadly close of the year.

Robby's birthday is smack dab in the middle of the hard time. Planted like a flag to let you know the bad time's arrived. His adult life, the manhood of my mother's last child, begins as she is orphaned, as she starts to become nobody's child.

I named Robby. Before the women hustled my mother out the door into a taxi, I jumped down the stairs, tugged on her coattail, and reminded her she'd promised it'd be Robby. No doubt in my mind she'd bring me home a baby brother. Don't ask me why I was certain. I just was. I hadn't even considered names for a girl. Robby it would be. Robert Douglas. Where the Douglas came from is another story, but the Robert came from me because I liked the sound. Robert was formal, dignified, important. Robert. And that was nearly as nice as the chance I'd have to call my little brother Rob and Robby.

He weighed seven pounds, fourteen ounces. He was born in Allegheny Hospital at 6:30 in the evening, December 29, 1950. His fingers and toes were intact and quite long. He was a plump baby. My grandfather, high on Dago Red, tramped into the maternity ward just minutes after Robby was delivered. John French was delighted with the new baby. Called him Red. A big fat little red nigger.

December always been a bad month for me. One the worst days of my life was in December. It's still one the worst days in my life even after all this other mess. Jail. Running. The whole bit. Been waiting to tell you this a long time. Ain't no reason to hold it back no longer. We into this telling-the-truth thing so mize well tell it all. I'm still shamed, but there it is. You know that TV of youall's got stolen from Mommy's. Well, I did it. Was me and Henry took youall's TV that time and set the house up to look like a robbery. We did it. Took my own brother's TV. Couldn't hardly look you in the face for a long time after we done it. Was pretty sure youall never knowed it was me, but I felt real bad round youns anyway. No way I was gon confess though. Too shamed. A junkie stealing from his own family. See. Used to bullshit myself. Say I ain't like them other guys. They stone junkies, they hooked. Do anything for a hit. But me, I'm Robby. I'm cool. I be believing that shit, too. Fooling myself. You got to bullshit yourself when you falling. Got to do it to live wit yourself. See but where it's at is you be doing any goddam thing for dope. You hooked and that's all's to it. You a stone junkie just like the rest.

Always wondered if you knew I took it.

Mom was suspicious. She knew more than we did then. About the dope. The seriousness of it. Money disappearing from her purse when nobody in the house but the two of you. Finding a syringe on the third floor. Stuff like that she hadn't talked about to us yet. So your stealing the TV was a possibility that came up. But to me it was just one of many. One of the things that could have happened along with a whole lot of other possibilities we sat around talking about. An unlikely possibility as far as I was concerned. Nobody wanted to believe it was you. Mom tried to tell us how it *could* be but in my mind you weren't the one. Haven't thought about it much since then. Except as one of those things that make me worry about Mom living in the house alone. One of those things making Homewood dangerous, tearing it down.

I'm glad I'm finally getting to tell you. I never could get it out. Didn't want you to think I'd steal from my own brother. Specially since all youall done to help me out. You and Judy and the kids. Stealing youall's TV. Don't make no sense, does it? But if we gon get the story down mize well get it all down.

It was a while ago. Do you remember the year?

Nineteen seventy-one was Greens. When we robbed Greens and got in big trouble so it had to be the year before that, 1970. That's when it had to be. Youns was home for Christmas. Mommy and them was having a big party. A reunion kinda cause all the family was together. Everybody home for the first time in a long time. Tish in from Detroit. David back from Philly. Youns in town. My birthday, too. Party spozed to celebrate my birthday too, since it came right along in there after Christmas. Maybe that's why I was feeling so bad. Knowing I had a birthday coming and knowing at the same time how fucked up I was.

Sat in a chair all day. I was hooked for the first time. Good and hooked. Didn't know how low you could feel till that day. Cold and snowing outside. And I got the stone miseries inside. Couldn't move. Weak and sick. Henry too. He was wit me in the house feeling bad as I was. We was two desperate dudes. Didn't have no money and that Jones down on us.

Mommy kept asking, What's wrong with you two? She was on my case all day. What ails you, Robby? Got to be about three o'clock. She come in the room again: You better get up and get some decent clothes on. We're leaving for Geral's soon. See cause it was the day of the big Christmas party. Geral had baked a cake for me. Everybody was together and they'd be singing Happy Birthday Robby and do. The whole bit an I'm spozed to be guest of honor and can't even move out the chair. Here I go again disappointing everybody. Everybody be at Geral's looking for me and Geral had a cake and everything. Where's Robby? He's home dying cause he can't get no dope.

Feeling real sorry for myself but I'm hating me too. Wrapped up in a blanket like some damned Indin. Shivering and wondering how the hell Ima go out in this cold and hustle up some money. Wind be howling. Snow pitching a bitch. There we is. Stuck in the house. Two pitiful junkies.

Scheming how we gon get over. Some sorry-assed dudes. But it's comical
in a way too, when you look back. To get well we need to get money. And
no way we gon get money less we go outside and get sicker than we already is. Mom peeking in the room, getting on my case. Get up out that
chair, boy. What are you waiting for? We're leaving in two minutes.

So I says, Go on. I ain't ready. Youns go on. I'll catch up with youns at
Geral's.

Mommy standing in the doorway. She can't say too much, cause
youns is home and you ain't hip to what's happening. C'mon now. We
can't wait any longer for you. Please get up. Geral baked a cake for you.
Everybody's looking forward to seeing you.

Seem like she stands there a hour begging me to come. She ain't mad
no more. She's begging. Just about ready to cry. Youall in the other room.
You can hear what she's saying but you can't see her eyes and they tearing
me up. Her eyes begging me to get out the chair and it's tearing me up to
see her hurting so bad, but ain't nothing I can do. Jones sitting on my chest
and ain't no getup in me.

Youns go head, Mommy. I'll be over in a little while. Be there to blow
them candles out and cut the cake.

She knew better. Knew if I didn't come right then, chances was I
wasn't coming at all. She knew but wasn't nothing she could do. Guess I
knew I was lying too. Nothing in my mind cept copping that dope. Yeah,
Mom. Be there to light them candles. I'm grinning but she ain't smiling
back. She knows I'm in trouble, deep trouble. I can see her today standing
in the doorway begging me to come with youns.

But it ain't meant to be. Me and Henry thought we come up with a
idea. Henry's old man had some pistols. We was gon steal em and hock
em. Take the money and score. Then we be better. Wouldn't be no big
thing to hustle some money, get the guns outa hock. Sneak the pistols
back in Henry's house, everything be alright. Wouldn't even exactly be
stealing from his old man. Like we just borrowing the pistols till we score
and take care business. Henry's old man wouldn't even know his pistols
missing. Slick. Sick as we was, thinking we slick.

A hundred times. Mom musta poked her head in the room a hundred
times.

What's wrong with you?

Like a drum beating in my head. What's wrong with you? But the
other thing is stronger. The dope talking to me louder. It says get you
some. It says you ain't never gon get better less you cop.

We waited long as we could but it didn't turn no better outside. Still
snowing. Wind shaking the whole house. How we gon walk to Henry's
and steal them pistols? Henry live way up on the hill. And the way up
Tokay then you still got a long way to go over into the projects. Can't
make it. No way we gon climb Tokay. So then what? Everybody's left for
Geral's. Then I remembers the TV youns brought. A little portable Sony
black-and-white, right? You and Judy sleeping in Mom's room and she

has her TV already in there, so the Sony ain't unpacked. Saw it sitting with youall's suitcases over by the dresser. On top the dresser in a box. Remembered it and soon's I did I knew we had to have it. Sick as I was that TV had to go. Wouldn't really be stealing. Borrow it instead of borrowing the pistols. Pawn it. Get straight. Steal some money and buy it back. Just borrowing youall's TV.

Won't take me and Henry no time to rob something and buy back the TV. We stone thieves. Just had to get well first so we could operate. So we took youns TV and set the house up to look like a robbery.

I'm remembering the day. Wondering why it had slipped completely from my mind. I feel like a stranger. Yet as Robby talks, my memory confirms details of his recollection. I admit, yes. I was there. That's the way it was. But *where* was I? Who was I? How did I miss so much?

His confessions make me uncomfortable. Instead of concentrating on what he's revealing, I'm pushed into considering all the things I could be confessing, should be confessing but haven't and probably won't ever. I feel hypocritical. Why should I allow my brother to repose a confidence in me when it's beyond my power to reciprocate? Shouldn't I confess that first? My embarrassment, my uneasiness, the clinical, analytic coldness settling over me when I catch on to what's about to happen.

I have a lot to hide. Places inside myself where truth hurts, where incriminating secrets are hidden, places I avoid, or deny most of the time. Pulling one piece of that debris to the surface, airing it in the light of day doesn't accomplish much, doesn't clarify the rest of what's buried down there. What I feel when I delve deeply into myself is chaos. Chaos and contradiction. So how up front can I get? I'm moved by Robby's secrets. The heart I have is breaking. But what that heart is and where it is I can't say. I can't depend on it, so he shouldn't. Part of me goes out to him. Heartbreak is the sound of ice cracking. Deep. Layers and layers muffling the sound.

I listen but I can't trust myself. I have no desire to tell everything about myself so I resist his attempt to be up front with me. The chaos at my core must be in his. His confession pushes me to think of all the stuff I should lay on him. And that scares the shit out of me. I don't like to feel dirty, but that's how I feel when people try to come clean with me.

Very complicated and very simple too. The fact is I don't believe in clean. What I know best is myself and, knowing what I know about myself, clean seems impossible. A dream. One of those better selves occasionally in the driver's seat but nothing more. Nothing to be depended upon. A self no more or less in control than the countless other selves who each, for a time, seem to be running things.

Chaos is what he's addressing. What his candor, his frankness, his confession echo against. Chaos and time and circumstances and the old news, the bad news that we still walk in circles, each of us trapped in his own little world. Behind bars. Locked in our cells.

But my heart can break, does break listening to my brother's pain. I just remember differently. Different parts of the incident he's describing come back. Strange thing is my recollections return through the door he opened. My memories needed his. Maybe the fact that we recall different things is crucial. Maybe they are foreground and background, propping each other up. He holds on to this or that scrap of the past and I listen to what he's saved and it's not mine, not what I saw or heard or felt. The pressure's on me then. If his version of the past is real, then what's mine? Where does it fit? As he stitches his memories together they bridge a vast emptiness. The time lost enveloping us all. Everything. And hearing him talk, listening to him try to make something of the nothing, challenges me. My sense of the emptiness playing around his words, any words, is intensified. Words are nothing and everything. If I don't speak I have no past. Except the nothing, the emptiness. My brother's memories are not mine, so I have to break into the silence with my own version of the past. My words. My whistling in the dark. His story freeing me, because it forces me to tell my own.

I'm sorry you took so long to forgive yourself. I forgave you a long time ago, in advance for a sin I didn't even know you'd committed. You lied to me. You stole from me. I'm in prison now listening because we committed those sins against each other countless times. I want your forgiveness. Talking about debts you owe me makes me awkward, uneasy. We remember different things. They set us apart. They bring us together searching for what is lost, for the meaning of difference, of distance.

For instance, the Sony TV. It was a present from Mort, Judy's dad. When we told him about the break-in and robbery at Mom's house, he bought us another Sony. Later we discovered the stolen TV was covered by our homeowner's policy even though we'd lost it in Pittsburgh. A claim was filed and eventually we collected around a hundred bucks. Not enough to buy a new Sony but a good portion of the purchase price. Seemed a lark when the check arrived. Pennies from heaven. One hundred dollars free and clear since we already had the new TV Mort had surprised us with. About a year later one of us, Judy or I, was telling the story of the robbery and how well we came out of it. Not until that very moment when I caught a glimpse of Mort's face out of the corner of my eye did I realize what we'd done. Judy remembers urging me to send Mort that insurance check and she probably did, but I have no recollection of an argument. In my mind there had never been an issue. Why shouldn't we keep the money? But when I saw the look of surprise and hurt flash across Mort's face, I knew the insurance check should have gone directly to him. He's a generous man and probably would have refused to accept it, but we'd taken advantage of his generosity by not offering the check as soon as we received it. Clearly the money belonged to him. Unasked, he'd replaced the lost TV. I had treated him like an institution, one of those faceless corporate entities like the gas company or IRS. By then, by the time I saw the surprise in Mort's face and understood how selfishly, thoughtlessly, even corruptly I'd behaved, it was too late. Offering Mort a hundred dollars at that point would have been insulting. Anything I could think of saying sounded hopelessly lame, inept. I'd fucked up. I'd injured someone who'd been nothing but kind and generous to me. Not intentionally, consciously, but that only made the whole business worse in a way because I'd failed him instinctively. The failure was a measure of who I was. What I'd unthinkingly done revealed something about my relationship to Mort I'm sure he'd rather not have discovered. No way I could take my action back, make it up. It reflected a truth about who I was.

That memory pops right up. Compromising, ugly. Ironically, it's also about stealing from a relative. Not to buy dope, but to feed a habit just as self-destructive. The habit of taking good fortune for granted, the habit of blind self-absorption that allows us to believe the world owes us everything and we are not responsible for giving anything in return. Spoiled children. The good coming our way taken as our due. No strings attached.

Lots of other recollections were triggered as Robby spoke of that winter and the lost TV. The shock of walking into a burgled house. How it makes you feel unclean. How quickly you lose the sense of privacy and security a house, any place you call home, is supposed to provide. It's a form of rape. Forced entry, violation, brutal hands defiling what's personal, and precious. The aftershock of seeing your possessions strewn about, broken. Fear gnawing at you because what you thought was safe isn't safe at all. The worst has happened and can happen again. Your sanctuary has been destroyed. Any time you walk in your door you may be greeted by the same scene. Or worse. You may stumble upon the thieves themselves. The symbolic rape of your dwelling place enacted on your actual body. Real screams. Real blood. A knife at your throat. A stranger's weight bearing down.

Mom put it in different words but she was as shaken as I was when we walked into her house after Geral's party. Given what I know now, she must have been even more profoundly disturbed than I imagined. A double bind. Bad enough to be ripped off by anonymous thieves. How much worse if the thief is your son? For Mom the robbery was proof Robby was gone. Somebody else walking round in his skin. Mom was wounded in ways I hadn't begun to guess at. At the root of her pain were your troubles, the troubles stealing you away from her, from all of us. The troubles thick in the air as that snow you are remembering, the troubles falling on your head and mine, troubles I refused to see. . . .

Snowing and the hawk kicking my ass but I got to have it. TV's in a box under my arm and me and Henry walking down Bennett to Homewood Avenue. Need thirty dollars. Thirty dollars buy us two spoons. Looking for One-Arm Ralph, the fence. Looking for him or that big white Cadillac he drives.

Wind blowing snow all up in my face. Thought I's bout to die out there. Nobody on the avenue. Even the junkies and dealers inside today.

Wouldn't put no dog out in weather like that. So cold my teeth is chattering, talking to me. No feeling in my hands but I got to hold on to that TV. Henry took it for a little while so's I could put both my hands in my pockets. Henry lookin bad as I'm feeling. Thought I was gon puke. But it's too goddamn cold to puke.

Nobody in sight. Shit and double shit's what I'm thinking. They got to be somewhere. Twenty-four hours a day, seven days a week somebody doing business. Finally we seen One-Arm Ralph come out the Hi Hat.

This TV, man, Lemme hold thirty dollars on it.

Ralph ain't goin for it. Twenty-five the best he say he can do. Twenty-five don't do us no good. It's fifteen each for a spoon. One spoon ain't enough. We begging the dude now. We got to have it, man. Got to get well. We good for the money. Need thirty dollars for two hits. You get your money back.

Too cold to be standing around arguing. The dude go in his pocket and give us the thirty. He been knowing us. He know we good for it. I'm telling him don't sell the TV right away. Hold it till tomorrow we have his money. He say, You don't come back tonight you blow it. Ralph a hard motherfucker and don't want him changing his mind again about the thirty so I say, We'll have the money tonight. Hold the TV till tonight, you get your money.

Now all we got to do is find Goose. Goose always be hanging on the set. Ain't nobody else dealing, Goose be out there for his people. Goose an alright dude, but even Goose ain't out in the street on no day like this. I know the cat stays over the barbershop on Homewood Avenue. Across from Murphy's five-and-ten. I goes round to the side entrance, the alleyway tween Homewood and Kelly. That's how you get to his place. Goose lets me in and I cop. For some reason I turn up the alley and go toward Kelly instead of back to Homewood the way I came in. Don't know why I did it. Being slick. Being scared. Henry's waiting on the avenue for me so I go round the long way just in case somebody pinned him. I can check out the scene before I come back up the avenue. That's probably what I'm thinking. But soon's I turn the corner of Kelly, Bam. Up pops the devil.

Up against the wall, Squirrel.

It's Simon and Garfunkel, two jive undercover cops. We call them that, you dig. Lemme tell you what kind of undercover cops these niggers was. Both of em wearing Big Apple hats and jackets like people be wearing then but they both got on police shoes. Police brogans you could spot a mile away. But they think they slick. They disguised, see. Apple hats and hippy-dip jackets. Everybody knew them chumps was cops. Ride around in a big Continental. Going for bad. Everybody hated them cause everybody knew they in the dope business. They bust a junkie, take his shit and sell it. One them had a cousin. Biggest dealer on the Hill. You know where he getting half his dope. Be selling again what Simon and Garfunkel stole from junkies. Some rotten dudes. Liked to beat on people too. Wasn't bad enough they robbing people. They whipped heads too.

Soon's I turn the corner they got me. Bams me up against the wall. They so lame they think they got Squirrel. Think I'm Squirrel and they gon make a big bust. We got you, Squirrel. They happy, see, cause Squirrel dealing heavy then. Thought they caught them a whole shopping bag of dope.

Wearing my double-breasted pea coat. Used to be sharp but it's raggedy now. Ain't worth shit in cold weather like that. Pockets got holes and the dope dropped down in the lining so they don't find nothing the first time they search me. Can tell they mad. Thought they into something big and don't find shit. Looking at each other like, What the fuck's going on here? We big-time undercover supercops. This ain't spozed to be happening to us. They roughing me up too. Pulling my clothes off and shit. Hands all down in my pockets again. It's freezing and I'm shivering but these fools don't give a fuck. Rip my goddamn pea coat off me. Shaking it. Tearing it up. Find the two packs of dope inside the lining this time. Ain't what they wanted but they pissed off now. Take what they can get now.

What's this, Squirrel? Got your ass now.

Slinging me down the alley. I'm stone sick now. Begging these cats for mercy. Youall got me. You got your bust. Lemme snort some the dope, man. Little bit out each bag. You still got your bust. I'm dying. Little taste fore you lock me up.

Rotten motherfuckers ain't going for it. They see I'm sick as a dog. They know what's happening. Cold as it is, the sweat pouring out me. It's sweat but it's like ice. Like knives cutting me. They ain't give back my coat. Snowing on me and I'm shaking and sweating and sick. They can see all this. They know what's happening but ain't no mercy in these dudes. Henry's cross the street watching them bust me. Tears in his eyes. Ain't nothing he can do. The street's empty. Henry's bout froze too. Watching them sling my ass in their Continental. Never forget how Henry looked that day. All alone on the avenue. Tears froze in his eyes. Seeing him like that was a sad thing. Last thing I saw was him standing there across Homewood Avenue before they slammed me up in the car. Like I was in two places. That's me standing there in the snow. That's me so sick and cold I'm crying in the empty street and ain't a damn thing I can do about it.

By the time they get me down to the Police Station, down to No. 5 in East Liberty, I ain't no more good, sure nuff. Puking. Begging them punks not to bust me. Just bout out my mind. Must have been a pitiful sight. Then's when Henry went to Geral's house and scratched on the window and called David out on the porch. That's when youall found out I was in trouble and had to come down and get me. Right in the middle of the party and everything. Henry's sick too and he been walking round Homewood in the cold didn't know what to do. But he's my man. He got to Geral's so youall could come down and help me. Shamed to go in so he scratched on the window to get Dave on the porch.

Party's over and youns go to Mommy's and on top everything else find the house broke in and the TV gone. All the stuff's going through my mind. I'm on the bottom now. Low as you can go. Had me in a cell and I was lying cross the cot staring at the ceiling. Bars all round. Up cross the ceiling too. Like in a cage in the zoo. Miserable as I could be. All the shit staring me in the face. You're a dope fiend. You stole your brother's TV. You're hurting Mommy again. Hurting everybody. You're sick. You're nothing. Looking up at the bars on the ceiling and wondering if I could tie my belt there. Stick my neck in it. I wanted to be dead.

Tied my belt to the ceiling. Then this guard checking on me he starts to hollering.

What you doing? Hey, Joe. This guy's trying to commit suicide.

They take my clothes. Leave me nothing but my shorts. I'm lying there shivering in my underwear and that's the end. In a cage naked like some goddamn animal. Shaking like a leaf. Thinking maybe I can beat my head against the bars or maybe jump down off the bed head first on the concrete and bust my brains open. Dead already. Nothing already. Low as I can go.

Must have passed out or gone to sleep or something, cause it gets blurry round in here. Don't remember much but they gave back my clothes and took me Downtown and there was a arraignment next morning.

Mommy told me later, one the cops advised her not to pay my bond. Said the best thing for him be to stay in jail awhile. Let him see how it is inside. Scare im. But I be steady beggin. Please, please get me out here. Youns got soft-hearted. Got the money together and paid the bond.

What would have happened if you left me to rot in there till my hearing? Damned if I know. I probably woulda went crazy, for one thing. I do know that. Know I was sick and scared and cried like a baby for Mommy and them to get me out. Don't think it really do no good letting them keep me in there. I mean the jail's a terrible place. You can get everything in jail you get in the street. No different. Cept in jail it's more dangerous cause you got a whole bunch of crazies locked up in one little space. Worse than the street. Less you got buddies in there they tear you up. Got to learn to survive quick. Cause jail be the stone jungle. Call prison the House of Knowledge cause you learns how to be a sure nuff criminal. Come in lame you leave knowing all kinds of evil shit. You learn quick or they eats you up. That's where it's at. So you leave a person in there, chances are they gets worse. Or gets wasted.

But Mom has that soft heart anyway and she ain't leaving her baby boy in no miserable jail. Right or wrong, she ain't leaving me in no place like that. Daddy been talking to Simon and Garfunkel. Daddy's hip, see. He been out there in the street all his life and he knows what's to it. Knows those guys and knows how rotten they is. Ain't no big thing they catch one pitiful little junkie holding two spoons. They wants dealers. They wants to look good Downtown. They wants to bust dealers and cop beaucoup dope so's they can steal it and get rich. Daddy makes a deal with them rats. Says if they drop the charges he'll make me set up Goose. Finger Goose and then stay off Homewood Avenue. Daddy says I'll do that so they let me go.

No way Ima squeal on Goose but I said okay, it's a deal. Soon's I was loose I warned Goose. Pretend like I'm trying to set him up so the cops get off my ass but Goose see me coming know the cops is watching. Helped him, really. Like a lookout. Them dumb motherfuckers got tired playing me. Simon got greedy. Somebody set him up. He got busted for drugs. Still see Garfunkel riding round in his Continental but they took him off the avenue. Too dangerous. Everybody hated them guys.

My lowest day. Didn't know till then I was strung out. That's the first time I was hooked. Started shooting up with Squirrel and Bugs Johnson when Squirrel be coming over to Mom's sometimes. Get up in the morning, go up to the third floor, and shoot up. They was like my teachers. Bugs goes way back. He started with Uncle Carl. Been shooting ever since. Dude's old now. Call him King of the Junkies, he been round so long. Bugs seen it all. You know junkies don't hardly be getting old. Have their day then they gone. Don't see em no more. They in jail or dead. Junkie just don't have no long life. Fast life but your average dopehead ain't round long. Bugs different. He was a pal of Uncle Carl's back in the fifties. Shot up together way back then. Now here he is wit Squirrel and me, still doing this thing. Everybody knows Bugs. He the King.

Let me shoot up wit em but they wouldn't let me go out in the street and hustle wit em. Said I was too young. Too green.

Learning from the King, see. That's how I started the heavy stuff. Me and Squirrel and Bugs first thing in the morning when I got out of bed. Mom was gone to work. They getting themselves ready to hit the street. Make that money. Just like a job. Wasn't no time before I was out there, too. On my own learning to get money for dope. Me and my little mob. We was ready. Didn't take us no time fore we was gangsters. Gon be the next Bugs Johnson. Gon make it to the top.

Don't take long. One day you the King. Next day dope got you and it's the King. You ain't nothing. You lying there naked bout to die and it don't take but a minute. You fall and you gone in a minute. That's the life. That's how it is. And I was out there. I know. Now they got me jammed up in the slammer. That's the way it is. But nobody could tell me nothing then. Hard head. You know. Got to find out for myself. Nobody could tell me nothing. Just out of high school and my life's over and I didn't even know it. Too dumb. Too hardheaded. I was gon do it my way. Youns was square. Youns didn't know nothing. Me, I was gon make mine from the curb. Hammer that rock till I was a supergangster. Be the one dealing the shit. Be the one running the junkies. That's all I knew. Street smarts. Stop being a chump. Forget that nickel-dime hoodlum bag. Be a star. Rise to the top.

You know where that got me. You heard that story. Here I sit today behind that story. Nobody to blame but my ownself. I know that now. But things was fucked up in the streets. You could fall in them streets, Brother. Low. Them streets could snatch you bald-headed and turn you around and wring you inside out. Streets was a bitch. Wake up some mornings and you think you in hell. Think you died and went straight to hell. I know cause I been there. Be days I wished I was dead. Be days worser than that.

•   •   •   •   •   •   •   •   •   •   •   •

QUESTIONS FOR A SECOND READING

1. Wideman frequently interrupts this narrative to talk about the problems he is having as a writer. He says, for example, "The hardest habit to break, since it was the habit of a lifetime, would be listening to myself listen to him. That habit would destroy any chance of seeing my brother on his terms; and seeing him in his terms, learning his terms, seemed the whole point of learning his story" (p. 767). What might Wideman mean by this—listening to himself listen? As you reread "Our Time," note the sections in which Wideman speaks to you directly as a writer. What is he saying? Where and how are you surprised by what he says?

   Wideman calls attention to the problems he faces. How does he try to solve them? Are you sympathetic? Do the solutions work, so far as you are concerned?

2. Wideman says that his mother had a remarkable capacity for "[trying] on the other person's point of view." Wideman tries on another point of view himself, speaking to us in the voice of his brother Robby. As you reread this selection, note the passages spoken in Robby's voice and try to infer Robby's point of view from them. If you look at the differences between John and Robby as evidenced by the ways they use language to understand and represent the world, what do you notice?

3. Wideman talks about three ways he could start Robby's story: with Garth's death, with the house in Shadyside, and with the day of Robby's birth. What difference would it make in each case if he chose one and not the others? What's the point of presenting all three?

ASSIGNMENTS FOR WRITING

1. At several points in the essay, Wideman discusses his position as a writer, telling Robby's story, and he describes the problems he faces in writing this piece (or in "reading" the text of his brother's life). You could read this selection, in other words, as an essay about reading and writing.

   Why do you think Wideman talks about these problems here? Why not keep quiet and hope that no one notices? Choose three or four passages in which Wideman refers directly or indirectly to his work as a writer, and write an essay defining the problems Wideman faces and explaining why you think he raises them as he does. Finally, what might this have to do with your work as a writer—or as a student in this writing class?

2. Wideman tells Robby's story in this excerpt, but he also tells the story of his neighborhood, Homewood; of his mother; and of his grandfather John

French. Write an essay retelling one of these stories and explaining what it might have to do with Robby and John's.

3. "Our Time" is a family history, but it is also a meditation on the problems of writing family histories—or, more generally, the problems of writing about the "real" world. There are sections in "Our Time" where Wideman speaks directly about the problems he faces as a writer. And the unusual features in the prose stand as examples of how he tried to solve these problems—at certain points Wideman writes as an essayist, at others like a storyteller; at certain points he switches voices and/or typeface; the piece breaks up into sections, it doesn't move from introduction to conclusion. Think of these as part of Wideman's method, as his way of working on the problems of writing as practical problems, where he is trying to figure out how to do justice to his brother and his story.

As you prepare to write this assignment, read back through the selection to think about it as a way of doing one's work, as a project, as a way of writing. What are the selection's key features? What is its shape or design? How does Wideman, the writer, do what he does? And you might ask: What would it take to learn to write like this? How is this writing related to the writing taught in school? Where and how might it serve you as a student?

Once you have developed a sense of Wideman's method, write a Wideman-like piece of your own, one that has the rhythm and the moves, the shape and the design of "Our Time." As far as subject matter is concerned, let Wideman's text stand as an invitation (inviting you to write about family and neighborhood) but don't feel compelled to follow his lead. You can write about anything you want. The key is to follow the essay as an example of a *way* of writing—moving slowly, turning this way and that, combining stories and reflection, working outside of a rigid structure of thesis and proof.

MAKING CONNECTIONS

1. Various selections in this book can be said to be "experimental" in their use of nonfiction prose. These are essays that don't do what essays are supposed to do. They break the rules. They surprise. The writers work differently than most writers. They imagine a different project (or they imagine their project differently).

Although any number of the selections in *Ways of Reading* might be read alongside "Our Time," here are some that have seemed interesting to our students: Gloria Anzaldúa, the essays from *Borderlands/La frontera* (pp. 23, 36); Susan Griffin, "Our Secret" (p. 345); Alice Munro, "The Albanian Virgin" (p. 554); and Marianne Hirsch, "Projected Memory: Holocaust Photographs in Personal and Public Fantasy" (p. 400).

Choose one selection to compare with Wideman's and write an essay in which you both explain and explore the projects represented by the two pieces of writing. How do they address a reader's expectations? How do they manipulate the genre? How do they reimagine the features we take for granted in the genre of the essay—sentences and paragraphs; introductions and conclusions; argument, narrative, and exposition? And what is to be gained (or what is at stake) in writing this way? (Would you, for example, argue that these forms of writing should be taught in college?) You should assume that you are writing for someone who is a sophisticated reader but who is not familiar with these particular essays. You will need, that is, to be careful in choosing and presenting examples.

2. Both Harriet Jacobs, in "Incidents in the Life of a Slave Girl" (p. 428), and Wideman speak directly to the reader. They seem to feel that there are problems of understanding in the stories they have to tell and in their relations to their subjects and audiences. Look back over both stories and mark the passages in which the authors address you as a reader. Ask yourself why the authors might do this. What do they reveal about their work as writers at such moments? How would you describe the relationship each writer has with her or his subject matter? As a reader of each of these stories, how would you describe the relationship between the authors and yourself as the "audience"?

   After you have completed this preliminary research, write an essay in which you discuss these two acts of writing *as* acts of writing—that is, as stories in which the writers are self-conscious about their work as writers and make their audience aware of their self-consciousness. What differences or connections exist between you, the authors, and their subject matter? How do these differences or connections influence you as a reader?

3. Toward the end of his essay "Notes of a Native Son" (p. 52), after talking about the riot in Harlem in 1943, James Baldwin says,

   > If ever, indeed, the violence which fills Harlem's churches, pool halls, and bars erupts outward in a more direct fashion, Harlem and its citizens are likely to vanish in an apocalyptic flood. That this is not likely to happen is due to a great many reasons, most hidden and powerful among them the Negro's real relation to the white American. This relation prohibits, simply, anything as uncomplicated and satisfactory as pure hatred. (p. 66)

   We are still, as a country and as a culture, trying to explain to ourselves the real relationship between white Americans and what we now refer to as "African Americans." "Our Time" is written in the tradition of "Notes of a Native Son." You should imagine, that is, that John Edgar Wideman cannot *not* have Baldwin in mind when he writes (just as Baldwin could not *not* have had Richard Wright in mind); you should also imagine that Wideman sees himself representing the next generation, that he has worked hard to develop his own style, projects, and point of view.

   Read "Notes of a Native Son" and then reread "Our Time," thinking about tradition, looking for differences and similarities, listening for echoes, imaging that one author is making silent reference to the other. And write an essay about the two as they stand in relation to each other. Assume that your reader is familiar with neither of your selections. You will need to introduce and present both documents (present through summary, paraphrase, and quotation). The purpose of the comparison should be to think about the history and the problems of representing what Baldwin refers to as "the Negro's real relation to the white American."

Assignment
Sequences

WORKING WITH
ASSIGNMENT
SEQUENCES

*T*HE *ASSIGNMENT SEQUENCES* that follow are different from the single writing assignments at the end of each essay. The single writing assignments are designed to give you a way back into the works you have read. They define the way you, the reader, can work on an essay by writing about it—testing its assumptions, probing its examples, applying its way of thinking to a new setting or to new material. A single assignment might ask you to read what Paulo Freire has to say about education and then, as a writer, to use Freire's terms and methods to analyze a moment from your own schooling. The single assignments are designed to demonstrate how a student might work on an essay, particularly an essay that is long or complex, and they are designed to show how pieces that might seem daunting are open, manageable, and managed best by writing.

The assignment sequences have a similar function, but with one important difference. Instead of writing one paper, or working on one or two selections from the book, you will be writing several essays and reading several selections. Your work will be sequential as well as cumulative. The work you do on Freire, for example, will give you a way of beginning with Mary Louise Pratt, or Adrienne Rich. It will give you an angle of vision. You won't be a newcomer to such discussions. Your previous reading will make the new essay rich with association. Passages or examples will jump out, as if magnetized, and demand your attention. And by reading these essays in context, you will see each writer as a single voice in a larger discussion. Neither Freire, nor Pratt, nor Rich, after all, has had the last word on the subject of education. It is not as though, by working on one of the essays, you have wrapped the subject up, ready to be put on the shelf.

The sequences are designed, then, so that you will be working not only on essays but on a subject, like education (or history, or culture, or the autobiography), a subject that can be examined, probed, and understood through the various frames provided by your reading. Each essay becomes a way of seeing a problem or a subject; it becomes a tool for thinking, an example of how a mind might work, a way of using language to make a subject rich and alive. In the assignment sequences, your reading is not random. Each sequence provides a set of readings that can be pulled together into a single project.

The sequences allow you to participate in an extended academic project, one with several texts and several weeks' worth of writing. You are not just adding one essay to another (Freire + Pratt = ?) but trying out an approach to a subject by revising it, looking at new examples, hearing what someone else has to say, and beginning again to take a position of your own. Projects like these take time. It is not at all uncommon for professional writers to devote weeks or even months to a single essay, and the essay they write marks not the end of their thinking on the subject, but only one stage. Similarly, when readers are working on a project, the pieces they read accumulate on their desks and in their minds and become part of an extended conversation with several speakers, each voice offering a point of view on a subject, a new set of examples, or a new way of talking that resonates with echoes from earlier reading.

A student may read many books, take several courses, write many papers; ideally each experience becomes part of something larger, an education. The work of understanding, in other words, requires time and repeated effort. The power that comes from understanding cannot be acquired quickly—by reading one essay or working for a few hours. A student, finally, is a person who choreographs such experiences, not someone who passes one test only to move on to another. And the assignment sequences are designed to reproduce, although in a condensed period of time, the rhythm and texture of academic life. They invite you to try on its characteristic ways of seeing, thinking, and writing. The work you do in one week will not be lost when it has bearing on the work you do in the next. If an essay by Patricia Nelson Limerick has value for you, it is not because you proved to a teacher that you read it, but because you have put it to work and made it a part of your vocabulary as a student.

Working with a Sequence

Here is what you can expect as you work with a sequence. You begin by working with a single story or essay. You will need to read each piece twice, the second time with the "Questions for a Second Reading" and the assignment sequence in mind. Before rereading the selection, in other words, you should read through the assignments to get a sense of where you will be headed. And you should read the questions at the end of each selection. (You can use those questions to help frame questions of your own.) The purpose of all these questions, in a sense, is to prepare the text to speak—to bring it to life and insist that it respond to your attention, answer your questions. If you think of the authors as people you can talk to, if you think of their pages as occasions for dialogue (as places where you get to ask questions and insist on responses)—if you prepare your return to those pages in these ways, you are opening up the essays or stories (not closing them down or finishing them off) and creating a scene where you get to step forward as a performer.

While each sequence moves from selection to selection in *Ways of Reading,* the most significant movement in the sequence is defined by the essays you write. Your essays provide the other major text for the course. In fact, when we teach these sequences, we seldom have any discussion of the assigned readings before our students have had a chance to write. When we talk as a group about Rich's "When We Dead Awaken: Writing as Re-Vision," for example, we begin by reproducing one or two student essays, handing them out to the class, and using them as the basis for discussion. We want to start, in other words, by looking at ways of reading Rich's essay—not at her essay alone.

The essays you write for each assignment in a sequence might be thought of as work-in-progress. Your instructor will tell you the degree to which each essay should be finished—that is, the degree to which it should be revised and copyedited and worked into a finished performance. In our classes, most writing assignments go through at least one revision. After we have had a chance to see a draft (or after a draft has been seen by others in the class), and after we have had some discussion of sample student essays we ask students to read the assigned essay or story one more time and to rework their essays to bring their work one step further—not necessarily to finish the essays (as though there would be nothing else to say) but to finish up this stage in their work and to feel their achievement in a way a writer simply cannot the first time through. Each assignment, then, really functions as two assignments in the schedule for the course. As a consequence, we don't "cover" as many essays in a semester as students might in another class. But coverage is not our goal. In a sense, we are teaching our students how to read slowly and closely, to return to a text rather than set it aside, to take the time to reread and rewrite and to reflect on what these activities entail. Some of these sequences, then, contain more readings or more writing assignments than you can address in a quarter or semester. Different courses work at different paces. It is important, however, to preserve time for rereading and rewriting. The sequences were written with the assumption that they would be revised to meet the needs of teachers, students, and programs. As you look at your syllabus, you may find, then, that reading or writing assignments have been changed, added, or dropped.

You will be writing papers that can be thought of as single essays. But you will also be working on a project, something bigger than its individual parts. From the perspective of the project, each piece you write is part of a larger body of work that evolves over the term. You might think of each sequence as a revision exercise, where the revision looks forward to what comes next as well as backward to what you have done. This form of revision asks you to do more than complete a single paper; it invites you to resee a subject or reimagine what you might say about it from a new point of view. You should feel free, then, to draw on your earlier essays when you work on one of the later assignments. There is every reason for you to reuse ideas, phrases, sentences, even paragraphs as your work builds from one week to the next. The advantage of work-in-progress is that you are not starting over completely every time you sit down to write. You've been over this territory before. You've developed some expertise in your subject. There is a body of work behind you.

Most of the sequences bring together several essays from the text and ask you to imagine them as an extended conversation, one with several speakers. The assignments are designed to give you a voice in the conversation as well, to allow you to speak in turn and to take your place in the company of other writers. This is the final purpose of the assignment sequence: after several weeks' work on the essays and on the subject that draws them together, you will begin to establish your own point of view. You will develop a position from which you can speak with authority, drawing strength from the work you have done as well as from your familiarity with the people who surround you.

This book brings together some of the most powerful voices of our culture. They speak in a manner that asks for response. The assignments at the end of each selection and, with a wider range of reference, the assignment sequences here at the end of the book demonstrate that there is no reason for a student, in such company, to remain silent.

SEQUENCE ONE

The Aims of Education

Paulo Freire

Adrienne Rich

Mary Louise Pratt

Susan Griffin

YOU HAVE BEEN in school for several years, long enough for your experiences in the classroom to seem natural, inevitable. The purpose of this sequence is to invite you to step outside a world you may have begun to take for granted, to look at the ways you have been taught and at the unspoken assumptions behind your education. The eight assignments that follow bring together four essays that discuss how people (and particularly students) become trapped inside habits of thought. These habits of thought (they are sometimes referred to as "structures" of thought; Adrienne Rich calls them the "assumptions in which we are drenched") become invisible (or seem natural) because of the ways our schools work or because of the ways we have traditionally learned to use language when we speak, read, or write.

The essays brought together in this sequence provide powerful critiques of the usual accounts of education. The first two (by Paulo Freire and Adrienne Rich) argue that there are, or should be, ways of using language that can enable a person to break free from limited or limiting ways of thinking. The next, by Mary Louise Pratt, examines the classroom as an imagined community and discusses the nature of a student's participation in that community. The last reading in this sequence, the selection from Susan Griffin's *A Chorus of Stones*, is presented as an example of an alternative intellectual or academic project, one driven by a desire to know and understand the past but written outside the usual conventions of history or the social sciences. The writing assignments that accompany the readings provide an opportunity for you to test the arguments in the individual essays by weighing them against scenes and episodes from your own schooling. Some ask you to work within a specific argument (Rich's account of patriarchy, for example), and some ask you to experiment with the conventions of academic prose. (In some classes, students may be asked to work with a selection of these assignments.) The final assignment provides an occasion for you to draw material from all the essays you have written for this sequence into a final and more comprehensive statement on schools and schooling.

•   •   •   •   •   •   •   •   •   •   •   •

A S S I G N M E N T   1

Applying Freire to Your Own Experience as a Student [Freire]

> The teacher talks about reality as if it were motionless, static, compartmentalized, and predictable. Or else he expounds on a topic completely alien to the existential experience of the students. His task is to "fill" the students with the contents of his narration—contents which are detached from reality, disconnected from the totality that engendered them and could give them significance. Words are emptied of their concreteness and become a hollow, alienated, and alienating verbosity. (p. 259)
>
> — PAULO FREIRE
> *The "Banking" Concept of Education*

Surely, anyone who has made it through twelve years of formal education can think of a class, or an occasion outside of class, to serve as a quick example of what Freire calls the "banking" concept of education, where students are turned into "containers" to be "filled" by their teachers. If Freire is to be useful to you, however, he must do more than call up quick examples. He should allow you to say more than that a teacher once treated you like a container (or that a teacher once gave you your freedom).

Write an essay that focuses on a rich and illustrative incident from your own educational experience and read it (that is, interpret it) as Freire would. You will need to provide careful detail: things that were said and done, perhaps the exact wording of an assignment, a textbook, or a teacher's comments. And you will need to turn to the language of Freire's argument, to take key phrases and passages from his argument and see how they might be used to investigate your case.

To do this you will need to read your account as not simply the story of you and your teacher, since Freire is not writing about individual personalities (an innocent student and a mean teacher, a rude teacher, or a thoughtless teacher) but about the roles we are cast in, whether we choose to be or not, by our culture and its institutions. The key question, then, is not who you were or who your teacher was but what roles you played and how those roles can lead you to better understand the larger narrative or drama of Education (an organized attempt to "regulate the way the world 'enters into' the students").

Note: Freire would not want you to work passively or mechanically, as though you were merely following orders. He would want you to make your own mark on the work he has begun. Use your example, in other words, as a way of testing and examining what Freire says, particularly those passages that you find difficult or obscure.

* * * * * * * * * * *

ASSIGNMENT **2**

Studying Rich as a Case in Point [Freire, Rich]

The truth is, however, that the oppressed are not "marginals," are not men living "outside" society. They have always been "inside"—inside the structure which made them "beings for others." The solution is not to "integrate" them into the structure of oppression, but to transform that structure so that they can become "beings for themselves." Such transformation, of course, would undermine the oppressors' purposes. . . . (pp. 261–62)

— PAULO FREIRE
The "Banking" Concept of Education

For a poem to coalesce, for a character or an action to take shape, there has to be an imaginative transformation of reality which is in no way passive. . . . Moreover, if the imagination is to transcend and transform experience it has to question, to challenge, to conceive of alternatives, perhaps to the very life you are living at that moment. You have to be free to play

around with the notion that day might be night, love might be
hate; nothing can be too sacred for the imagination to turn into
its opposite or to call experimentally by another name. For
writing is renaming. (p. 635)

—ADRIENNE RICH
When We Dead Awaken: Writing as Re-Vision

Both Freire and Rich talk repeatedly about transformations—about
transforming structures, transforming the world, transforming the way
language is used, transforming the relations between people. In fact, the
changes in Rich's poetry might be seen as evidence of her transforming
the structures from within which she worked. And, when Freire takes a
situation we think of as "natural" (teachers talking and students sitting
silent) and names it "banking education," he makes it possible for students and their teachers to question, challenge, conceive of alternatives,
and transform experience. Each, in other words, can be framed as an example in the language of the other—Freire in Rich's terms, Rich in Freire's.
For both, this act of transformation is something that takes place within
and through the use of language.

Rich's essay could be read as a statement about the aims of education,
particularly if the changes in her work are taken as evidence of something
the poet learned to do. Rich talks about teachers, about people who helped
her to reimagine her situation as a woman and a poet, and about the work
she had to do on her own.

For this assignment, take three of the poems Rich offers as examples of
change in her writing—"Aunt Jennifer's Tigers," the section from "Snapshots of a Daughter-in-Law," and "Planetarium,"as well as the additional
poems reprinted in "Sources"—and use them as a way of talking about re-
vision. What, to your mind, are the key differences between these poems?
What might the movement they mark be said to represent? And what do
these poems, as examples, have to do with the argument about writing,
culture, and gender in the rest of the essay?

As you prepare to write, you might also ask some questions in Freire's
name. For example: What problems did Rich pose for herself? How might
this be taken as an example of a problem-posing education? In what ways
might Rich be said to have been having a "dialogue" with her own work?
Who was the teacher (or the teachers) here and what did the poet learn
to do?

You are not alone as you read these poems, in other words. In fact,
Rich provides her own commentary on the three poems, noting what for
her are key changes and what they represent. You will want to acknowledge what Rich has to say, to be sure, but you should not be bound by it.
You, too, are a person with a point of view on this issue. Rich (with Freire)
provides a powerful language for talking about change, but you want to
be sure to carve out space where you have the opportunity to speak
as well.

• • • • • • • • • • • •

A S S I G N M E N T **3**

Tradition and the Writing
of the Past [Rich]

> We need to know the writing of the past, and know it differ-
> ently than we have ever known it; not to pass on a tradition but
> to break its hold over us. (p. 629)
> — ADRIENNE RICH
> *When We Dead Awaken: Writing as Re-Vision*

"We need to know the writing of the past," Rich says. The "we" of that
sentence can be read as an invitation to you. Look back over your own
writing (perhaps the drafts and revisions you have written for this
course), and think back over comments teachers have made, textbooks
you have seen; think about what student writers do and what they are
told to do, about the secrets students keep and the secrets teachers keep.
You can assume, as Rich does, that there are ways of speaking about writing that are part of the culture of schooling and that they are designed to
preserve certain ways of writing and thinking and to discourage others.
Write an essay in which you reflect on the writing of the past and its presence in your own work as a writer.

One might argue, in other words, that there are ways of writing that
are part of schooling. There are traditions here, too. As you look at the evidence of the "past" in your own work, what are its significant features:
What might you name this tradition (or these traditions)? What are the
"official" names? What do these names tell us? What do they hide? What
difference might it make to name tradition in terms of gender and call it
"patriarchal"?

How would you illustrate the hold this tradition has on your work or
the work of students generally? What might you have to do to begin to
"know it differently," "to break its hold," or to revise? And, finally, why
would someone want (or not want) to make such a break?

. . . .

A S S I G N M E N T **4**

The Contact Zone [Pratt]

The idea of the contact zone is intended in part to contrast with ideas of community that underlie much of the thinking about language, communication, and culture that gets done in the academy. (p. 613)

— MARY LOUISE PRATT
Arts of the Contact Zone

Citing Benedict Anderson and what he calls "imagined communities," Pratt argues that our idea of community is "strongly utopian, embodying values like equality, fraternity, liberty, which the societies often profess but systematically fail to realize." Against this utopian vision of community, Pratt argues that we need to develop ways of understanding (even noticing) social and intellectual spaces that are not homogeneous, unified; we need to develop ways of understanding and valuing difference. And, for Pratt, the argument extends to schooling. "What is the place," she asks,

> of unsolicited oppositional discourse, parody, resistance, critique in the imagined classroom community? Are teachers supposed to feel that their teaching has been most successful when they have eliminated such things and unified the social world, probably in their own image? Who wins when we do that? Who loses? (p. 616)

Such questions, she says, "may be hypothetical, because in the United States in the 1990s, many teachers find themselves less and less able to do that even if they want to."

"In the United States in the 1990s." "The imagined classroom." From your experience, what scenes might be used to represent schooling in the 1990s and beyond? How are they usually imagined (idealized, represented, interpreted, valued)? What are the implications of Pratt's argument?

Write an essay in which you use Pratt's terms to examine a representative scene from your own experience with schools and schooling. What examples, stories, or images best represent your experience? How might they be interpreted as examples of community? as examples of "contact zones"? As you prepare your essay, you will want to set the scene as carefully as you can, so that someone who was not there can see it fully. Think about how someone who has not read Pratt might interpret the scene. And think through the various ways *you* might interpret your example. And you should also think about your position in an argument about school as a "contact zone." What do you (or people like you) stand to gain or lose when you adopt Pratt's point of view?

. . . .

ASSIGNMENT **5**

The Pedagogical Arts
of the Contact Zone [Pratt]

> Meanwhile, our job in the Americas course remains to figure out how to make that crossroads the best site for learning that it can be. We are looking for the pedagogical arts of the contact zone. These will include, we are sure, exercises in storytelling and in identifying with the ideas, interests, histories, and atti-tudes of others; experiments in transculturation and collabora-tive work and in the arts of critique, parody, and comparison (including unseemly comparisons between elite and vernacular cultural forms); the redemption of the oral; ways for people to engage with suppressed aspects of history (including their own histories), ways to move *into and out of* rhetorics of authenticity; ground rules for communication across lines of difference and hierarchy that go beyond politeness but maintain mutual re-spect; a systematic approach to the all-important concept of *cul-tural mediation.* (p. 618)
>
> — MARY LOUISE PRATT
> *Arts of the Contact Zone*

Pratt writes generally about culture and history, but also about read-ing and writing and teaching and learning, about the "literate" and "peda-gogical" arts of this place she calls the "contact zone." Think about the class you are in—its position in the curriculum, in the institution. Think about its official goals (and its unofficial goals). Think about the positions represented by the students, the teacher. Think about how to think about the class, in Pratt's terms, as a "contact zone."

And think about the unusual exercises represented by her list: "story-telling," "experiments in transculturation," "critique," "parody," "un-seemly comparisons," moving into and out of "rhetorics of authentic-ity"—these are some of them. Take one of these suggested exercises, explain what you take it to mean, and then go on to discuss how it might be put into practice in a writing class. What would students do? to what end? How would their work be evaluated? What place would the exercise have in the larger sequence of assignments over the term, quarter, or semester? In your terms, and from your point of view, what might you learn from such an exercise?

Or you could think of the question this way: What comments would a teacher make on one of the papers you have written so far in order that its revision might stand as one of these exercises? How would the revision be different from what you are used to doing?

Write an essay in which you present and discuss an exercise designed to serve the writing class as a "contact zone."

•   •   •   •   •   •   •   •   •   •   •   •

ASSIGNMENT 6

Writing against the Grain [Griffin]

As you reread "Our Secret," think of Griffin's prose as experimental, as deliberate and crafted. She is trying to do something that she can't do in the "usual" essay form. She wants to make a different kind of argument and engage her reader in a different manner. And so she mixes personal and academic writing. She assembles fragments and juxtaposes seemingly unrelated material in surprising and suggestive relationships. She breaks the "plane" of the page with italicized inter-sections. She organizes her material, that is, but not in the usual mode of thesis-example-conclusion. The arrangement is not nearly so linear. At one point, when she seems to be prepared to argue that German child-rearing practices produced the Holocaust, she quickly says:

> Of course there cannot be one answer to such a monumental riddle, nor does any event in history have a single cause. Rather a field exists, like a field of gravity that is created by the movements of many bodies. Each life is influenced and it in turn becomes an influence. Whatever is a cause is also an effect. Childhood experience is just one element in the determining field. (p. 350)

Her prose serves to create a "field," one where many bodies are set in relationship.

It is useful, then, to think about Griffin's prose as the enactment of a method, as a way of doing a certain kind of intellectual work. One way to study this, to feel its effects, is to imitate it, to take it as a model. For this assignment, write a Griffin-like essay, one similar in its methods or organization and argument. You will need to think about the stories you might tell, about the stories and texts you might gather (stories and texts not your own). As you write, you will want to think carefully about arrangement and about commentary (about where, that is, you will speak to your reader *as* the writer of the piece). You should not feel bound to Griffin's subject matter, but you should feel that you are working in her spirit.

• • • • • • • • • • •

A S S I G N M E N T **7**

The Task of Attention [Griffin]

I am looking now at the etching called *Poverty*, made in 1897. Near the center, calling my attention, a woman holds her head in her hands. (p. 354)

> —SUSAN GRIFFIN
> *Our Secret*

This is one of the many moments where Griffin speaks to us as though in the midst of her work. The point of this assignment is to think about that work—what it is, how she does it, and what it might have to do with schools and schooling. She is, after all, doing much of the traditional work of scholars—going to the archive, studying old materials, traveling and interviewing subjects, learning and writing history.

And yet this is not the kind of prose you would expect to find in a textbook for a history course. Even if the project is not what we usually think of as a "research" project, Griffin is a careful researcher. Griffin knows what she is doing. Having experimented with a Griffin-like essay, go back now to look again (this time with a writer's eye) at both the features of Griffin's prose and the way she characterizes her work as a scholar, gathering and studying her materials.

Write an essay in which you present an account of *how* Griffin does her work. You should use her words and examples from the text, but you should also feel that it is your job to explain what you present and to comment on it from the point of view of a student. As you reread, look to those sections where Griffin seems to be speaking to her readers about her work—about how she reads and how she writes, about how she gathers her materials and how she studies them. What is she doing? What is at stake in adopting such methods? How might they be taught? Where in the curriculum might (should?) such lessons be featured?

· · · · · · · · · · · · ·

A S S I G N M E N T **8**

Putting Things Together
[Freire, Rich, Pratt, Griffin]

This is the final assignment of this sequence, and it is the occasion for you to step back and take stock of all that you have done. Perhaps the best way for you to do this is by making a statement of your own about the role of reading and writing in an undergraduate education. You might, for example, write a document for students who will be entering your school for the first time, telling them what they should expect or what they should know about reading and writing if they want to make the most of their education. Or this might be an essay written for an alumni magazine or a paper for a faculty committee charged with reviewing undergraduate education. Or you might want to think of this essay as primarily autobiographical, as that chapter of your autobiography where you think through your experiences with schooling.

You should feel free to draw as much as you can from the papers you have already written, making your points through examples you have already examined, perhaps using your own work with these assignments as an example of what students might be expected to do.

The Arts of the Contact Zone

Mary Louise Pratt

Gloria Anzaldúa

Harriet Jacobs

James Baldwin

*T*HIS SEQUENCE allows you to work closely with the argument of Mary Louise Pratt's "Arts of the Contact Zone," not so much through summary (repeating the argument) as through extension (working under its influence, applying its terms and protocols). In particular, you are asked to try your hand at those ways of reading and writing Pratt defines as part of the "literate arts of the contact zone," ways of reading and writing that have not historically been taught or valued in American schools.

Pratt is one of the country's most influential cultural critics. In "Arts of the Contact Zone," she makes the argument that our usual ways of reading and writing assume identification—that is, we learn to read and write the texts that express our own position and point of view. As a result, texts that reproduce different ways of thinking, texts that allude to different cultural systems, seem flawed, wrong, or inscrutable. As a counterposition, Pratt asks us to imagine scenes of reading, writing, teaching, and learning as "contact zones," places of contact between people who can't or don't or won't necessarily identify with one another.

In the first assignment, you are asked to search for or produce a document to exemplify the arts of the contact zone, working in library archives, searching the streets, surfing the Internet, or writing an "autoethnography." This is a big job, and probably new to most students; it is a project you will want to come back to and revise. The next assignments ask you to look at three selections in *Ways of Reading* that exemplify or present movements of cultural contact: Gloria Anzaldúa's *Borderlands/La frontera*, a text that announces itself as the product of a mixed, *mestiza* cultural position; Harriet Jacobs's "Incidents in the Life of a Slave Girl," a slave narrative (or "autoethnography"); and James Baldwin's account of a "native son." The final assignment asks you to think back over both Pratt's argument and your work to make a more general statement about the arts of the contact zone.

• • • • • • • • • • •

ASSIGNMENT 1

The Literate Arts of the Contact Zone [Pratt]

Here, briefly, are two descriptions of the writing one might find or expect in the "contact zone":

> Autoethnography, transculturation, critique, collaboration, bilingualism, mediation, parody, denunciation, imaginary dialogue, vernacular expression—these are some of the literate arts of the contact zone. Miscomprehension, incomprehension, dead letters, unread masterpieces, absolute heterogeneity of meaning—these are some of the perils of writing in the contact zone. They all live among us today in the transnationalized metropolis of the United States and are becoming more widely visible, more pressing, and, like Guaman Poma's text, more decipherable to those who once would have ignored them in defense of a stable, centered sense of knowledge and reality. (p. 613)

> We are looking for the pedagogical arts of the contact zone. These will include, we are sure, exercises in storytelling and in identifying with the ideas, interests, histories, and attitudes of others; experiments in transculturation and collaborative work and in the arts of critique, parody, and comparison (including unseemly comparisons between elite and vernacular cultural forms); the redemption of the oral; ways for people to engage with suppressed aspects of history (including their own histories), ways to move *into and out of* rhetorics of authenticity; ground rules for communication across lines of difference and hierarchy that go beyond politeness but maintain mutual respect; a systematic approach to the all-important concept of *cultural mediation*. (p. 618)

Here are two ways of working on Pratt's idea of the "contact zone." Choose one.

1. One way of working with Pratt's essay, of extending its project, would be to conduct your own local inventory of writing from the contact zone. You might do this on your own or in teams, with others from your class. You will want to gather several similar documents, your "archive," before you make a final selection. Think about how to make that choice. What makes one document stand out as representative? Here are two ways you might organize your search:

   a. You could look for historical documents. A local historical society might have documents written by Native Americans ("Indians") to the white settlers. There may be documents written by slaves to masters or to northern whites explaining their experience. There may be documents written by women (suffragettes, for example) trying to negotiate for public positions or rights. There may be documents from any of a number of racial or ethnic groups—Hispanic, Jewish, Irish, Italian, Polish, Swedish—trying to explain their positions to the mainstream culture. There may, perhaps at union halls, be documents written by workers to owners. Your own sense of the heritage of your area should direct your search.

   b. Or you could look at contemporary documents in the print that is around you, texts that you might otherwise overlook. Pratt refers to one of the characteristic genres of the Hispanic community, the *"testimonio."* You could look for songs, testimonies, manifestos, statements by groups on campus, stories, autobiographies, interviews, letters to the editor, Web pages. You could look at the writing of any marginalized group, particularly writing intended, at least in part, to represent the experience of outsiders to the dominant culture (or to be in dialogue with that culture or to respond to that culture). These documents, if we follow Pratt's example, would encompass the work of young children or students, including college students.

   Once you have completed your inventory, choose a document you would like to work with and write an essay that presents it carefully and in detail (perhaps in even greater detail than Pratt's presentation of the *New Chronicle*). You will, in other words, need to set the scene, summarize, explain, and work block quotations into your essay. You might imagine that you are presenting this to someone who would not have seen it and would not know how to read it, at least not as an example of the literate arts of the contact zone.

2. Another way of extending the project of Pratt's essay would be to write your own autoethnography. It should not be too hard to locate a setting or context in which you are the "other"—the one who speaks from outside rather than inside the dominant discourse. Pratt says that the

position of the outsider is marked not only by differences of language and ways of thinking and speaking but also by differences in power, authority, status. In a sense, she argues, the only way those in power can understand you is in *their* terms. These are terms you will need to use to tell your story, but your goal is to describe your position in ways that "engage with representations others have made of [you]" without giving in or giving up or disappearing in their already formed sense of who you are.

This is an interesting challenge. One of the things that will make the writing difficult is that the autoethnographic or transcultural text calls upon skills not usually valued in American classrooms: bilingualism, parody, denunciation, imaginary dialogue, vernacular expression, storytelling, unseemly comparisons of high and low cultural forms—these are some of the terms Pratt offers. These do not fit easily with the traditional genres of the writing class (essay, term paper, summary, report) or its traditional values (unity, consistency, sincerity, clarity, correctness, decorum).

You will probably need to take this essay (or whatever it should be called) through several drafts. (In fact, you might revise this essay after you have completed assignments 2 and 3.) It might be best to begin as Pratt's student, using her description as a preliminary guide. Once you get a sense of your own project, you may find that you have terms or examples to add to her list of the literate arts of the contact zone.

•   •   •   •   •   •   •   •   •   •   •   •

ASSIGNMENT 2

Borderlands [Pratt, Anzaldúa]

In "Arts of the Contact Zone," Pratt talks about the "autoethnographic" text, "a text in which people undertake to describe themselves in ways that engage with representations others have made of them," and about "transculturation," the "processes whereby members of subordinated or marginal groups select and invent from the materials transmitted by a dominant or metropolitan culture."

Write an essay in which you present a reading of *Borderlands/La frontera* as an example of an autoethnographic and/or transcultural text. You should imagine that you are writing to someone who is not familiar with either Pratt's argument or Anzaldúa's thinking. Part of your work, then, is to present Anzaldúa's text to readers who don't have it in front of them. You have the example of Pratt's reading of Guaman Poma's *New Chronicle and Good Government.* And you have her discussion of the "literate arts of the contact zone." Think about how Anzaldúa's text might be similarly read, and about how her text does and doesn't fit Pratt's description. Your goal should be to add an example to Pratt's discussion and to qualify it, to alter or reframe what she has said now that you have had a chance to look at an additional example.

• • • • • • • • • • •

ASSIGNMENT 3

Autoethnography [Pratt, Jacobs]

Here is Mary Louise Pratt on the "autoethnographic" text:

> Guaman Poma's *New Chronicle* is an instance of what I have proposed to call an *autoethnographic* text, by which I mean a text in which people undertake to describe themselves in ways that engage with representations others have made of them. Thus if ethnographic texts are those in which European metropolitan subjects represent to themselves their others (usually their conquered others), autoethnographic texts are representations that the so-defined others construct *in response to* or in dialogue with those texts. . . . [T]hey involve a selective collaboration with and appropriation of idioms of the metropolis or the conqueror. These are merged or infiltrated to varying degrees with indigenous idioms to create self-representations intended to intervene in metropolitan modes of understanding. Autoethnographic works are often addressed to both metropolitan audiences and the speaker's own community. Their reception is thus highly indeterminate. Such texts often constitute a marginalized group's point of entry into the dominant circuits of print culture. It is interesting to think, for example, of American slave autobiography in its autoethnographic dimensions, which in some respects distinguish it from Euramerican autobiographical tradition. (pp. 608–09)

Reread Harriet Jacobs's "Incidents in the Life of a Slave Girl" after reading Pratt's essay. Using the example of Pratt's work with the *New Chronicle,* write an essay presenting a reading of Jacobs's text as an autoethnographic and/or transcultural text. You should think about not only how it might be read from this point of view but also how, without this perspective, it might (in Pratt's terms) be misread or unread. Imagine that you are working to put Pratt's ideas to the test but also to see what you can say on your own about "Incidents" as a text, as something written and read.

• • • • • • • • • • • •

ASSIGNMENT 4

Writing from Within [Pratt, Baldwin]

Here, from "Arts of the Contact Zone," is Mary Louise Pratt on the "autoethnographic" text:

> Guaman Poma's *New Chronicle* is an instance of what I have proposed to call an *autoethnographic* text, by which I mean a text in which people undertake to describe themselves in ways that engage with representations others have made of them. Thus if ethnographic texts are those in which European metropolitan subjects represent to themselves their others (usually their con-quered others), autoethnographic texts are representations that the so-defined others construct *in response to* or in dialogue with those texts. . . . [T]hey involve a selective collaboration with and appropriation of idioms of the metropolis or the con-queror. These are merged or infiltrated to varying degrees with indigenous idioms to create self-representations intended to in-tervene in metropolitan modes of understanding. . . . Such texts often constitute a marginalized group's point of entry into the dominant circuits of print culture. (pp. 608–09)

James Baldwin's essay, "Notes of a Native Son," presents an interest-ing opportunity to think about Pratt's concept of the "autoethnographic text." The essay was written in 1955 and published in *Harper's Magazine.* By this point in his career Baldwin was emerging as a distinctive presence in American letters; one role he played (and it was partly a role he defined for himself) was as a person who could speak from experience about "the Negro's real relation to the white American." Baldwin's relation to his subject is not a simple one, and one way to examine this is to think about the position of the speaker in "Notes of a Native Son." As Baldwin defines (in his writing) a place from which he can speak (about his family and to his readers), what is that place? Where is it in relation to the city? Where is it in relation to his family? Where is it in relation to white America?

Using the example of Pratt's work with the *New Chronicle*, write an essay in which you present a reading of "Notes of a Native Son." In what ways is it useful to think of "collaboration" and "appropriation" in de-scribing Baldwin's achievements as a writer, a thinker, and a narrator? In what ways is it not?

And what does this example allow you to add to Pratt's discussion of the autoethnographic and/or transcultural text? How does Baldwin define a position from which he can speak to (and be read by) white America?

black America? Where do you see him working to establish his integrity and the integrity of his subjects—where, that is, do you see him establishing his authority? Where and how does he anticipate misreadings?

. . . .

A S S I G N M E N T 5

On Culture
[Pratt, Anzaldúa, Jacobs, Baldwin]

In some ways, the slipperiest of the key words in Pratt's essay "Arts of the Contact Zone" is "culture." At one point Pratt says,

> If one thinks of cultures, or literatures, as discrete, coherently structured, monolingual edifices, Guaman Poma's text, and indeed any autoethnographic work, appears anomalous or chaotic—as it apparently did to the European scholars Pietschmann spoke to in 1912. If one does not think of cultures this way, then Guaman Poma's text is simply heterogeneous, as the Andean region was itself and remains today. Such a text is heterogeneous on the reception end as well as the production end: it will read very differently to people in different positions in the contact zone. (p. 612)

If one thinks of cultures as "coherently structured, monolingual edifices," the text appears one way; if one thinks otherwise, the text is "simply heterogeneous." What might it mean to make this shift in the way one thinks of culture? Can you do it—that is, can you read the *New Chronicle* (or its excerpts) from both points of view? Better yet—what about your own culture and its key texts? Can you, for example, think of a group that you participate in as a "community"? Where and how does it represent itself to others? Where and how does it do this in writing? What are its "literate arts"?

The assignments in this sequence are an exercise in reading texts as heterogeneous, as contact zones. As a way of reflecting back over your work in this sequence, write an essay in which you explain the work you have been doing to someone not in the course, someone who is interested in reading, writing, and learning, but who has not read Pratt, Anzaldúa, Jacobs, or Baldwin.

○—○—○—○—○—○—○—○—○—○—○—○—○—○—○—○

SEQUENCE THREE

Autobiographical Explorations

James Baldwin

Richard Rodriguez

Edward Said

Jane Tompkins

*A*UTOBIOGRAPHICAL WRITING has been a regular feature of writing courses since the nineteenth century. There are a variety of reasons for the prevalence of autobiography, not the least of which is the pleasure students take in thinking about and writing about their lives and their world. There is also a long tradition of published autobiographical writing, particularly in the United States. The title of this sequence puts a particular spin on that tradition, since it points to a more specialized use of autobiography, phrased here as "exploration." What is suggested by the title is a use of writing (and the example of one's experience, including intellectual experience) to investigate, question, explore, inquire. Often the genre is not used for these purposes at all. Autobiographical writing is often used for purposes of display or self-promotion, or to further (rather than question) an argument (about success, about how to live a good or proper or fulfilling life).

There are two threads to this sequence. The first is to invite you to experiment with the genre of "autobiographical exploration." The second is to foreground the relationship between your work and the work of others, to think about how and why and where you are prepared to write autobiographically (prepared not only by the lessons you've learned in school but by the culture and the way it invites you to tell—and live—the story of your life). And, if you are working inside a conventional field, a predictable way of writing, the sequence asks where and how you might make your mark or assert your position—your identity as a person (a character in a life story) and as a writer (someone working with the conventions of life-writing).

The first five assignments ask you to write from within the example of other writers, writers engaged in "revisionary" projects: James Baldwin, Richard Rodriguez, Edward Said, and Jane Tompkins. One of the difficulties, for a student, of an extended project like this is finding a way of writing differently. An autobiographical project *without* the readings (where, in a sense, you were writing on your own) might well produce each week only more of the same, the same story written in the same style. Our goal is to make you aware of the options available to you as a writer as you think about, write, and represent your life. You should think of these assignments as asking not for mere or mechanical imitation, but as invitations to think about areas of your life as these authors have and to imagine the problems and potential of life-writing through the example of their prose, its style and methods.

The last assignment in the sequence is a retrospective assignment. Here you are asked to think back over what you have done and to write a "Preface" to your work, a short essay to prepare other readers to understand what you have been working on and best appreciate the problems and achievements of your work. We will be asking you to think of yourself as an author, to read what you have written and to write about your texts, as, perhaps, you have sometimes been asked to write *about* the works of other authors.

This sequence is followed by a minisequence, "Autobiographical Explorations (II)," on page 823. This alternative sequence provides similar assignments but with different readings. They can be substituted for assignments in the first "Autobiographical Explorations" sequence or added to those assignments.

. . . .

ASSIGNMENT **1**

Exploring Character [Baldwin]

The title of the essay "Notes of a Native Son," alludes to *Native Son*, the 1940 novel by Richard Wright. The central character of *Native Son* is Bigger Thomas, an angry young black man who kills two women, one white and one black; his actions ignite a race riot in Chicago. Bigger Thomas is characterized by his inarticulateness, his inability to speak from or about his situation and his anger. Here is a brief passage from *Native Son*. Bigger Thomas, imprisoned and sentenced to death, is in conversation with his lawyer, Max:

> Max opened his mouth to say something and Bigger drowned out his voice. "I ain't trying to forgive nobody and I ain't asking for nobody to forgive me. I ain't going to cry. They wouldn't let me live and I killed. Maybe it ain't fair to kill, and I reckon I really didn't want to kill. But when I think of why all the killing was, I begin to feel what I wanted, what I am. . . .
>
> Bigger saw Max back away from him with compressed lips. But he felt he had to make Max understand how he saw things now.
>
> "I didn't want to kill!" Bigger shouted. "But what I killed for, I *am*! It must've been pretty deep in me to make me kill! I must have felt it awful hard to murder."

One way of reading "Notes of a Native Son" is as a revision of Wright's novel, an attempt to create a counterpoint to Bigger Thomas. Bigger struggles to speak. The narrator in "Notes of a Native Son" speaks at great length and with apparent ease. "Notes" could be said to represent a narrative where Baldwin, a writer of the next generation, provides a voice for Bigger, for his anger and rage, a voice Max could listen to and understand. It tells the story of a native son, born to poverty and discrimination, that does not end in murder and imprisonment.

The speaker in "Notes of a Native Son," like the "Thoreau" in *Walden*, is one of the exemplary characters of American letters. Write an essay on the character of the speaker, or narrator, in "Notes of a Native Son." What is his story? How does he think and speak? How does he make his way in the world? What promise might he offer to a culture still struggling to understand the position of the black man? Can you think of a comparable twenty-first-century voice?

•   •   •   •   •   •   •   •   •   •   •

A S S I G N M E N T   2

Autobiographical Exploration [Baldwin]

Irving Howe, a distinguished writer and critic, said that Baldwin brought a "new luster" to the essay as an art form, "a form with possibilities for discursive reflection and concrete drama." And, he said, "The style of these essays is a remarkable instance of the way in which a grave and sustained eloquence . . . can be employed in an age deeply suspicious of rhetorical prowess."

"Discursive reflection and concrete drama." "Notes of a Native Son" is a mix of narrative (or story) and argument (or commentary). This is not the kind of argument that works from thesis statement through example to conclusion. It works slowly, indirectly, by accretion and apposition, and with a careful, determined attention to detail. As a way of rereading Baldwin's essay, write a Baldwin-like essay of your own.

This is an invitation to carry out a similar project, one that reproduces his method and style, extends his example to a new set of materials. You can choose any subject (or person, or occurrence) as your narrative center; your goal should be to connect the local with the national, to connect personal history with larger issues or concerns, and to use concrete drama as the occasion for discursive reflection. It is also an invitation to formal experimentation, to try out Baldwin-like sentences, paragraphs, and chapters (or subsections).

. . . .

A S S I G N M E N T   3

Desire, Reading, and the Past [Rodriguez]

In "The Achievement of Desire," Richard Rodriguez tells stories of home but also stories of reading, of moments when things he read allowed him a way of reconsidering or revising ("framing," he calls it) the stories he would tell himself about himself. It is a very particular account of neighborhood, family, ethnicity, and schooling.

At the same time, Rodriguez insists that his story is also everyone's story—that his experience is universal. Take an episode from your life, one that seems in some ways similar to one of the episodes in "The Achievement of Desire," and cast it into a shorter version of Rodriguez's essay. Try to make use of your reading in ways similar to his. Think about what you have read lately in school, perhaps in this anthology.

In general, however, your job in this assignment is to look at your experience in Rodriguez's terms, which means thinking the way he does, noticing what he would notice, interpreting details in a similar fashion, using his key terms, seeing through his point of view; it could mean imitating his style of writing, doing whatever it is you see him doing characteristically when he writes. Imitation, Rodriguez argues, is not necessarily a bad thing; it can, he argues, be one of the powerful ways a person learns. Let this assignment serve as an exercise.

• • • • • • • • • • • •

ASSIGNMENT 4

A Photographic Essay [Said]

Edward Said, in the introduction to *After the Last Sky*, says of his method in "States":

> Its style and method—the interplay of text and photos, the mixture of genres, modes, styles—do not tell a consecutive story, nor do they constitute a political essay. Since the main features of our present existence are dispossession, dispersion, and yet also a kind of power incommensurate with our stateless exile, I believe that essentially unconventional, hybrid, and fragmentary forms of expression should be used to represent us. What I have quite consciously designed, then, is an alternative mode of expression to the one usually encountered in the media, in works of social science, in popular fiction.

And later:

> The multifaceted vision is essential to any representation of us. Stateless, dispossessed, de-centered, we are frequently unable either to speak the "truth" of our experience or to make it heard. We do not usually control the images that represent us; we have been confined to spaces designed to reduce or stunt us; and we have often been distorted by pressures and powers that have been too much for us. An additional problem is that our language, Arabic, is unfamiliar in the West and belongs to a tradition and civilization usually both misunderstood and maligned. Everything we write about ourselves, therefore, is an interpretive translation—of our language, our experience, our senses of self and others.

Reread "States," paying particular attention to the relationship of text and photograph, and paying attention to form. What *is* the order of the writing in this essay? (We will call it an "essay" for lack of a better term.) How might you diagram or explain its organization? By what principle(s) is it ordered and arranged? The essay shifts genres—memoir, history, argument. It is, as Said comments, "hybrid." What surprises are there? or disappointments? How might you describe the writer's strategy as he works on his audience, on readers? And, finally, do you find Said's explanation sufficient or useful—does the experience of exile produce its own inevitable style of report and representation?

For this assignment, compose a similar project, a Said-like reading of a set of photos. These can be photos prepared for the occasion (by you or a colleague); they could also be photos already available. Whatever their source, they should represent people and places, a history and/or geography that you know well, that you know to be complex and contradictory, and that you know will not be easily or readily understood by others, both the group for whom you will be writing (most usefully the members of your class) and readers more generally. You must begin with a sense that the photos cannot speak for themselves; you must speak for them.

In preparation, you should reread closely to come to a careful understanding of Said's project. (The first and second "Questions for a Second Reading" should be useful for this.)

. . . .

ASSIGNMENT **5**

Personal Experience as Intellectual Experience [Tompkins]

Jane Tompkins's essay "Indians" tells the story of a research project, one undertaken as a professor prepares to teach a course, but with reference to its own prehistory, way back to the author's childhood in New York City. Tompkins provides an example of how personal experience is not simply action in the world but also (and often) intellectual experience, a narrative defined by books read, courses taken, changes of mind, new understandings.

Using Tompkins's essay as a model, write a personal essay that tells a similar story, one drawing on your own experiences. You could tell the story of a research project, a paper (most likely a term paper) you prepared for school. This does not have to be a pious or dutiful account. Tompkins, after all, is writing *against* what she takes to be the predictable or expected account of research as the disinterested pursuit of truth—in which a student would go to the library to "find" the truth about the Indians and the settlers. And she writes in a style that is not solemnly academic. Like Tompkins, you can tell what you take to be the untold story of term-paper research, you can reflect on the problem of such research as a story of learning. Or you could tell the story of any important experience you have had as a student or, out of school, as a person who observes, reads, and thinks. Your goal should be to think of your story *as* a story, with characters and scenes (and, perhaps, dialogue), with action, suspense, and surprises.

•   •   •   •   •   •   •   •   •   •   •   •   •

ASSIGNMENT **6**

The "I" of the Personal Essay
[Baldwin, Rodriguez, Said, Tompkins]

The assignments in this sequence have been designed to prompt autobiographical writing. They have been invitations for you to tell your story
and to think about the ways stories represent a person and a life. They
have also, of course, been exercises in imitation, in writing "like" Baldwin,
Rodriguez, Said, and Tompkins, in casting your story in their terms. These
exercises highlight the ways in which your story is never just your own
but also written through our culture's sense of what it means to be a person, to live, grow, change, learn, experience. No writer simply gets to invent childhood. Childhood, like adulthood, is a category already determined by hundreds of thousands of representations of life—in books, in
songs, on TV, in paintings, in the stories we tell ourselves about ourselves.
As you have written these four personal narratives, you have, of course,
been "telling the truth," just as you have also, of course, been creating a
character, setting scenes, providing certain representations that provide a
version of (but that don't begin to sum up) your life.

Read back over the four essays you have written (and perhaps revised). As you read, look for examples of where you feel you were doing
your best work, where you are proud of the writing and interested in
what it allows you to see or to think (where the "investigations" seem
most worthwhile).

And think about what is *not* contained in these essays. What experiences are missing? What point of view? What ways of speaking or thinking or writing? If you were to go back to assemble these pieces into a
longer essay, what would you keep and what would you add or change?
What are the problems facing a writer, like you, trying to write a life, to
take experience and represent it in sentences?

With these questions in mind, reread the four essays you have written
and write a "Preface," a short piece introducing a reader to what you have
written (to your work—and perhaps work you may do on these essays in
the future).

o—o—o—o—o—o—o—o—o—o—o—o—o—o

SEQUENCE FOUR

Autobiographical Explorations (II)

Adrienne Rich
Alice Munro
John Edgar Wideman
Simon Frith

*T*HIS SEQUENCE provides an alternative set of readings for sequence three (p. 816). Assignments can be mixed, added, or substituted. All of these can be used to represent personal narrative as a writing problem, as something risky, even dangerous, as something to work on and to work on carefully, not as something simple or easy or to be taken for granted.

. . . .

ASSIGNMENT 1

A Moment of Hesitation [Rich]

I have hesitated to do what I am going to do now, which is to use myself as an illustration. For one thing, it's a lot easier and less dangerous to talk about other[s]. (p. 631)

Until we can understand the assumptions in which we are
drenched we cannot know ourselves. (p. 629)
        — ADRIENNE RICH
        When We Dead Awaken: Writing as Re-Vision

Write an essay in which you, like Rich (and perhaps with similar hesitation), use your experience as an illustration, as a way of investigating
not just your situation but the situations of people like you. Tell a story
from your recent past and use it to talk about the ways you might be said
to have been shaped or named or positioned by an established and powerful culture. You could imagine that this assignment is a way for you to use
(and put to the test) some of Rich's key terms, words like "re-vision," "renaming," "structure," and "patriarchy."

•   •   •   •   •   •   •   •   •   •   •

A S S I G N M E N T   2

Adjacency [Munro]

"The Albanian Virgin" is arranged in pieces, or fragments. As a reader
works through them, they become two story lines: one set in the 1920s in
Albania, on the Dalmatian coast; the other is set in the 1960s in Canada, on
the Pacific coast. The first story, about a woman called Lottar, is told by
Charlotte to Claire; the second is told by Claire to us (and, we learn, includes all these stories). But it takes some time for the pattern to establish
itself and we might be lost at first, or confused.

Try your hand at writing a story like this one. You can imagine that
you are writing fiction, or you can imagine that you are writing a memoir,
or any story drawn from life that has (or could have) two story lines. You
should begin by rereading "The Albanian Virgin" and thinking about how
Munro accomplishes what she does. (The first two "Questions for a Second Reading" provide a way of rereading with this thought in mind.) You
should try to catch the rhythm and swing of the arrangement in her story,
to control your readers' attention in a similar way, and to put the two
story lines to work in a similar fashion.

. . . .

ASSIGNMENT 3

Old Habits [Wideman]

Wideman frequently interrupts the narrative in "Our Time" to talk about the problems he is having as a writer. He says, for example, "The hardest habit to break, since it was the habit of a lifetime, would be listening to myself listen to him. That habit would destroy any chance of seeing my brother on his terms; and seeing him in his terms, learning his terms, seemed the whole point of learning his story" (p. 767).

Wideman gives you the sense of a writer who is aware from the inside, while writing, of the problems inherent in the personal narrative. This genre always shades and deflects; it is always partial and biased; in its very attempts to be complete, to understand totally, it reduces its subject in ways that are unacceptable. And so you can see Wideman's efforts to overcome these problems—he writes in Robby's voice; he starts his story three different times, first with Garth, later with the neighborhood, hoping that a variety of perspectives will overcome the limits inherent in each; he stops and speaks to us not as the storyteller but as the writer, thinking about what he is doing and not doing.

Let Wideman's essay provide a kind of writing lesson. It highlights problems; it suggests alternatives. Using Wideman, then, as your writing teacher, write a family history of your own. Yours will most likely be shorter than Wideman's, but let its writing be the occasion for you also to work on a personal narrative as a writing problem, an interesting problem that forces a writer to think about the limits of representation and point of view (about who gets to speak and in whose terms, about who sums things up and what is left out in this accounting).

. . . .

ASSIGNMENT 4

Voice [Frith]

"Voice" is a word commonly used to describe style in writing. Writers are told that they need to find or, better yet, to develop their "own voice." Certain writers are said to have distinctive voices or to have the ability to play with or experiment with voice. In his essay on popular music, Simon

Frith says, "The voice, in short, may or may not be a key to someone's identity, but it is certainly a key to the ways in which we change identities, pretend to be something we're not, deceive people, lie."

Frith offers these terms for the description of voice:

> But if we hear the pop singer singing "her self," she is also singing a song, and so a second question arises: what is the relationship between the voice as a carrier of sounds, the singing voice, making "gestures," and the voice as a carrier of words, the speaking voice, making "utterances"? The issue is not meaning (words) versus absence of meaning (music), but the relationship between two different sorts of meaning-making, the tensions and conflicts between them. There's a question here of power: who is to be the master, words or music? And what makes the voice so interesting is that it makes meaning in these two ways simultaneously. We have, therefore, to approach the voice under four headings: as *a musical instrument*; as *a body*; as *a person*; and as *a character*. (p. 280)

"Gestures" and "utterances"; "instrument" and "body"; "person" and "character." There is an elaborate scheme here for description and analysis. It would need to be adapted, however, for a description of voice in prose performance. "Person" and "character" are recognizable. Something would need to be substituted for "instrument" (the word processor? the conventions of writing?) and/or "body" (language? syntax, sentences, paragraphs?).

Look to the presence of voice in the selections you have read in this assignment sequence. Choose some interesting and representative passages, perhaps putting one or two writers in comparison with another. And write an essay on voice, presenting these passages to your readers—that is, provide an introduction and include the passage as part of your essay. Then, use Frith's terms to talk about the presence, effects, and consequence of voice.

· · · · · · · · · · ·

ASSIGNMENT 5

The "I" of the Personal Essay
[Rich, Munro, Wideman]

The assignments in this sequence have been designed to prompt autobiographical writing and your thinking about it. They have been invitations for you to tell your story and to think about the ways stories represent a person and life. They have also, of course, been exercises in imitation, in writing "like" Rich, Munro, and Wideman, in casting your story in their terms. These exercises highlight the ways in which your story is never just your own but also written through our culture's sense of what it means to be a person, to live, grow, change, learn, experience. No writer simply gets to invent childhood. Childhood, like adulthood, is a category already determined by hundreds of thousands of representations of life— in books, in songs, on TV, in paintings, in the stories we tell ourselves about ourselves. As you have written these personal narratives, you have, of course, been "telling the truth," just as you have also, of course, been creating a character, setting scenes, providing certain representations that provide a version of (but that don't begin to sum up) your life.

Read back over the essays you have written (and perhaps revised). As you read, look for examples of where you feel you were doing your best work, where you are proud of the writing and interested in what it allows you to see or to think (where the "investigations" seem most worthwhile).

And think about what is not contained in these essays. What experiences are missing? What point of view? What ways of speaking or thinking or writing? If you were to go back to assemble these pieces into a longer essay, what would you keep and what would you add or change? What are the problems facing a writer like you, trying to write a life, to take experience and represent it in sentences?

With these questions in mind, reread the essays you have written for this sequence and write a preface, a short piece introducing a reader to what you have written (or perhaps to related work you might do in the future).

○—○—○—○—○—○—○—○—○—○—○—○—○—○—○

Close Reading/Close Writing

John Edgar Wideman
James Baldwin
John Berger
Susan Griffin

*T*HIS SEQUENCE is a set of exercises designed to encourage close attention to detail. Skilled readers need to know how to read closely for
meaning and effect—to see detail and not just the gist of the text, or the
"big picture." (The exercises will help you to be a better reader of
Wideman, Baldwin, Berger, and Griffin.) Skilled writers need to know
how to attend to subtleties in phrasing and punctuation that assist in the
organization of complex, multivocal sentences.

Each exercise provides (or asks you to select) a sample sentence or
paragraph from the text, one that is characteristic or exemplary of the author's style. It asks you to imitate that sentence or paragraph (that is, to
write in parallel). And it asks you to describe sentences, not through textbook terms (subject, predicate, direct object), but in terms of what the sentence *does*. The prose statement calls attention to writing as *action*, as a way
of doing something with words.

The examples below can be extended to any of the selections in *Ways of
Reading*. They serve both to prepare readers to read closely and as writing
exercises.

. . . .

ASSIGNMENT 1

Language, Rhythm, Tone [Wideman]

To read Wideman's prose, a reader needs to learn to pay close attention to his "rules of etiquette," his "thumbnail character sketches," his "history of the community"—that is, Homewood. At several points in "Our Time," Wideman comments on the importance of language to life in Homewood ("a further inflection of the speaker's voice could tell you to ignore the facts, forget what he's just reminded you to remember").

Below are two passages from "Our Time." Listen for tone and inflection; pay attention to the rhythm and shape of the sentences.

> Garth looked bad. Real bad. Ichabod Crane anyway, but now he was a skeleton. Lying there in the bed with his bones poking through his skin, it made you want to cry. Garth's barely able to talk, his smooth, medium-brown skin yellow as pee. Ichabod legs and long hands and long feet, Garth could make you laugh just walking down the street. On the set you'd see him coming a far way off. Three-quarters leg so you knew it had to be Garth the way he was split up higher in the crotch than anybody else. Wilt the Stilt with a lean bird body perched on top his high waist. Size-fifteen shoes. Hands could palm a basketball easy as holding a pool cue. Fingers long enough to wrap round a basketball, but Garth couldn't play a lick. Never could get all that lankiness together on the court. You'd look at him sometimes as he was trucking down Homewood Avenue and think that nigger ain't walking, he's trying to remember how to walk.
> (p. 753)

Wideman writes carefully here, paying attention to rhythm and idiom, and placing his speaker carefully in relation to Garth and to his community. The language moves from writing to speech and back again. How would you place the language—is this Black English? Homewood English? Wideman's English? And the fragments (the incomplete sentences), why are they there? What is Wideman doing?

Here is a second example. In this one Wideman presents the French girls. If the previous passage was built from fragments, in this one a sentence seems to run past its boundaries. And again, the language moves from writing to speech and back again.

> A French girl was somebody who lived in Cassina Way, somebody you didn't fool with or talk nasty to. Didn't speak to at all except in certain places or on certain occasions. French girls were church girls, Homewood African Methodist Episcopal

Zion Sunday-school-picnic and social-event young ladies. You wouldn't find them hanging around anywhere without escorts or chaperones. French girls had that fair, light, bright, almost white redbone complexion and fine blown hair and nice big legs but all that was to be appreciated from a distance because they were nice girls and because they had this crazy daddy who wore a big brown country hat and gambled and drank wine and once ran a man out of town, ran him away without ever laying a hand on him or making a bad-mouthed threat, just cut his eyes a certain way when he said the man's name and the word went out and the man who had cheated a drunk John French with loaded dice was gone. Just like that. (p. 764)

Write two passages with exactly the same number of words, the same phrasing, and the same punctuation as these two. (We'll call them parallel passages and sentences.) You provide the subject matter. The words, of course, should be different. When you are done, write a one-sentence description of what you are *doing* in those passages.

Finally, go back to "Our Time"; choose two or three additional examples that seem characteristic of Wideman's prose, examples you find interesting and worth discussion. Be prepared to say something about why you think Wideman's project would require (or produce) such writing.

. . . .

A S S I G N M E N T **2**

Punctuation [Baldwin]

Here is a characteristic passage from the first section of "Notes of a Native Son." As you reread it, think of the punctuation as part of an expressive project, part of an attempt to order and arrange and control what must be said but cannot be said easily:

He was not a young man when we were growing up and he had already suffered many kinds of ruin; in his outrageously demanding and protective way he loved his children, who were black like him and menaced, like him; and all these things sometimes showed in his face when he tried, never to my knowledge with any success, to establish contact with any of us. When he took one of his children on his knee to play, the child always became fretful and began to cry; when he tried to help one of us with our homework the absolutely unabating tension which emanated from him caused our minds and our tongues to become paralyzed, so that he, scarcely knowing

why, flew into a rage and the child, not knowing why, was
punished. (p. 53)

If this is done for effect, what *is* the effect?

One way to work on this question is to write parallel sentences, each
with the exact number of words in the same order and with the same
punctuation. You can fill in any content you want. Once you get inside the
sentences, see where they will lead you (or where you must go).

Another way is to find other passages in Baldwin's essay (perhaps
pairs of sentences) that you can set beside the passage above. Be prepared
in class to lead a discussion of not only what the words say but also what
the arrangement says (or seems to say).

• • • • • • • • • • • •

ASSIGNMENT **3**

Character, Point of View [Berger]

In *Ways of Seeing*, John Berger argues that in order to understand art
from the past, we should situate ourselves in it. He demonstrates what he
means by that in his essay with his reading of the Frans Hals paintings. He
also demonstrates what it means in the two additional selections, "On
Rembrandt's *Woman in Bed*" and "On Caravaggio's *The Calling of St.
Matthew*." Here's a lengthy passage from the latter:

> *The Calling of St. Matthew* depicts five men sitting round their
> usual table, telling stories, gossiping, boasting of what one day
> they will do, counting money. The room is dimly lit. Suddenly
> the door is flung open. The two figures who enter are still part
> of the violent noise and light of the invasion. (Berenson wrote
> that Christ, who is one of the figures, comes in like a police in-
> spector to make an arrest.)
>
> Two of Matthew's colleagues refuse to look up, the other
> two younger ones stare at the strangers with a mixture of cu-
> riosity and condescension. Why is he proposing something so
> mad? Who's protecting him, the thin one who does all the talk-
> ing? And Matthew, the tax-collector with a shifty conscience
> which has made him more unreasonable than most of his col-
> leagues, points at himself and asks: Is it really I who must go?
> Is it really I who must follow you?
>
> How many thousands of decisions to leave have resembled
> Christ's hand here! The hand is held out towards the one who
> has to decide, yet it is ungraspable because so fluid. It orders
> the way, yet offers no direct support. Matthew will get up and
> follow the thin stranger from the room, down the narrow

streets, out of the district. He will write his gospel, he will travel to Ethiopia and the South Caspian and Persia. Probably he will be murdered.

And behind the drama of this moment of decision in the room at the top of the stairs, there is a window, giving onto the outside world. Traditionally in painting, windows were treated either as sources of light or as frames framing nature or framing an exemplary event outside. Not so this window. No light enters by it. The window is opaque. We see nothing. Mercifully we see nothing because what is outside is bound to be threatening. It is a window through which only the worst news can come. (p. 132)

Berger is trying to do what he claims a viewer of art should do. The act, as represented here, is an act of writing. Berger stages a dialogue between a viewer and a painting, and he does this to provide a lesson in seeing. It is also, of course, a writing lesson.

Write a brief essay of your own in imitation of (or as a critical revision of) Berger's brief essays on *Woman in Bed* and *The Calling of St. Matthew*. You'll need to find a painting as your subject, and you'll need to make that painting available in some way as part of your essay. (You could include a photo or a postcard or a reproduction.)

After you have written your passage, briefly discuss its writing. What were you expected to do? What, for example, were its pleasures and possibilities, the risks or liabilities of writing this way?

•   •   •   •   •   •   •   •   •   •   •

ASSIGNMENT 4

The Paragraph, the Essay [Griffin]

It is useful to think of Griffin's prose as experimental. She is trying to do something that she can't do in the "usual" essay form. She wants to make a different kind of argument or engage her reader in a different manner. And so she mixes personal and academic writing. She assembles fragments and puts seemingly unrelated material into surprising and suggestive relationships. She breaks the "plane" of the page with italicized intersections. She organizes her material, but not in the usual mode of thesis-example-conclusion. The arrangement is not nearly so linear. At one point, when she seems to be prepared to argue that German child-rearing practices produced the Holocaust, she quickly says:

Of course there cannot be one answer to such a monumental riddle, nor does any event in history have a single cause.

> Rather a field exists, like a field of gravity that is created by the movements of many bodies. Each life is influenced and it in turn becomes an influence. Whatever is a cause is also an effect. Childhood experience is just one element in the determining field. (p. 350)

Her prose serves to create a "field," one where many bodies are set in relationship.

It is useful, then, to think about Griffin's prose as the enactment of a method, as a way of doing a certain kind of intellectual work. One way to study this, to feel its effects, is to imitate it, to take it as a model. For this assignment, write a Griffin-like essay, one similar in its methods of organization and argument. You will need to think about the stories you might tell, about the stories and texts you might gather (stories and texts not your own). As you write, you will want to think carefully about arrangement and about commentary (about where, that is, you will speak to your reader *as* the writer of the piece). You should not feel bound to Griffin's subject matter, but you should feel that you are working in her spirit.

• • • • • • • • • • • •

A S S I G N M E N T 5

The Paragraph, the Essay [Baldwin]

Irving Howe, a distinguished writer and critic, said that Baldwin brought a "new luster" to the essay as an art form, "a form with possibilities for discursive reflection and concrete drama." And, he said, "The style of these essays is a remarkable instance of the way in which a grave and sustained eloquence . . . can be employed in an age deeply suspicious of rhetorical prowess."

"Discursive reflection and concrete drama." "Notes of a Native Son" is a mix of narrative (or story) and argument (or commentary). This is not the kind of argument that works from thesis statement through example to conclusion. It works slowly, indirectly, by accretion and apposition, and with a careful, determined attention to detail. As a way of rereading Baldwin's essay, write a Baldwin-like essay of your own.

This is an invitation to carry out a similar project, one that reproduces his method and style, extends his example to a new set of materials. You can choose any subject (or person, or occurrence) as your narrative center; your goal should be to connect the local with the national, to connect personal history with larger issues or concerns, and to use concrete drama as the occasion for discursive reflection. It is also an invitation to formal experimentation, to try out Baldwin-like sentences, paragraphs, and chapters (or subsections).

•   •   •   •   •   •   •   •   •   •   •   •

A S S I G N M E N T **6**

A Classroom Lesson

Most composition courses require a handbook of rules and models for writers. And most writers keep a handbook as a ready desk reference. Here is a sample from *A Writer's Reference,* Fourth Edition (1999), by Diana Hacker.

E1

Parallelism

If two or more ideas are parallel, they are easier to grasp when expressed in parallel grammatical form. Single words should be balanced with single words, phrases with phrases, clauses with clauses.

A kiss can be a comma, a question mark, or an exclamation point.
—Mistinguett

This novel is not to be tossed lightly aside, but to be hurled with great force.   —Dorothy Parker

In matters of principle, stand like a rock; in matters of taste, swim with the current.   —Thomas Jefferson

E3-b Place phrases and clauses so that readers can see at a glance what they modify.

Although phrases and clauses can appear at some distance from the words they modify, make sure that your meaning is clear. When phrases or clauses are oddly placed, absurd misreadings can result.

MISPLACED   The king returned to the clinic where he underwent heart surgery in 1992 in a limousine sent by the White House.

REVISED   Traveling in a limousine sent by the White House, the king returned to the clinic where he underwent heart surgery in 1992.

The king did not undergo heart surgery in a limousine. The revision corrects this false impression.

Given the work you have done with these exercises, prepare a response to the handbook as a writer's guide. You could write a brief review, perhaps directed at college students who will be using a handbook; you could write your own alternative or parodic handbook entries. Your goal is to bring together what you have done in the form of advice for writers that can stand next to the advice provided by the handbook.

SEQUENCE SIX

The Documentary Tradition

Robert Coles
W. J. T. Mitchell
Edward Said
Marianne Hirsch

*D*OCUMENTARY WORK has traditionally combined words and images in an attempt to capture and bring forward areas of the world or areas of human experience that would otherwise remain hidden from view. The impulse is thought to be generous and politically progressive— that is, those doing documentary work have assumed that by providing accounts of, for example, the conditions of poverty, this knowledge would lead those with money and power to act to ameliorate those conditions. This sequence is designed to both introduce you to a key text in the history of documentary work, James Agee and Walker Evans's *Let Us Now Praise Famous Men* (as it is featured in two recent books, Robert Coles's *Doing Documentary Work* and W. J. T. Mitchell's *Picture Theory*), and to raise questions about the past and present of the documentary tradition. Coles and Mitchell situate Agee and Evans's project in the history of documentary and the theoretical issues surrounding current debates about the use of words and images to represent the "real" world. The first three assignments ask you to work with their arguments. The fourth turns to the work of Edward Said and Jean Mohr, subjects in W. J. T. Mitchell's *Picture Theory*. The fifth considers Marianne Hirsch's work on memory, and the final assignment returns you to Coles and Mitchell and their theories of representation.

. . . .

A S S I G N M E N T **1**

Images [Coles]

In "The Tradition: Fact and Fiction," Robert Coles offers three interesting examples of artists cropping or framing photographic images of working class life (the couple in the car, the father and daughter on the porch, the girl picking cotton). Go back to those images and the discussions around them. Be sure that you can represent the argument Coles is making about Lange or Evans and the choices they made in producing or selecting a final image. Then, take time to think about alternative arguments. (Coles provides one example in his father's response to "Ditched, Stalled, and Stranded.") How might you argue for one of the discarded images? Against the close-up view?

Write an essay in which you begin with Coles's account of the images, summarizing what he says for someone who has not read the essay (or who read it a while ago and won't take time to pick it up again). You will need to represent the photographs, their history, and the points that Coles is making. Then, you will need to engage and extend the discussion. Coles, for example, seems to take for granted that the decisions the artists made were good decisions. Were they? What is at stake in choosing one photograph over another or in cropping the image to remove context and to focus in on the individual face? What was at stake for Coles?

And where and how might you enter this discussion? There should, in other words, be sections of your essay where you are speaking for Coles (and for Evans and Lange); there should also, however, be extended sections where you speak for yourself, thinking about the examples and engaging the issues raised by others.

. . . .

A S S I G N M E N T **2**

Image and Text [Mitchell]

To introduce the four case studies in "The Photographic Essay: Four Case Studies," Mitchell says, "I want to examine four photo-essays that, in various ways, foreground the dialectic of exchange and resistance between photography and language." For this assignment, work closely with the four case studies to bring forward what remains implied in Mitchell's text, the *differences* in the four cases. What *are* the "various ways" they foreground the dialectic of exchange and resistance between photography and language? What position does Mitchell seem to take on the value or achievement of each of the four books? What seems to you to be the important or significant or interesting differences? Mitchell's essay is designed to prepare you to be a reader of the photographic essay. From the examples Mitchell gives, what sorts of books would you be hoping to find?

You should imagine that you are writing for someone who has not read "The Photographic Essay." You will need, then, to be sure to represent and summarize the text. The point of the summary, however, is to define a position from which you can begin to do your work. And, to repeat what was said above, your work is to bring forward what Mitchell does not foreground—his sense of the differences between the four cases and the implication or value of those differences. And, in relation to what you see in Mitchell, your job is to articulate your own position on the range, importance, and possibility of the genre of the photo-essay.

．　．　．　．　．　．　．　．　．　．　．

A S S I G N M E N T   **3**

Let Us Now Praise Famous Men
[Coles, Mitchell]

Both Coles and Mitchell write about the genre of the photo-essay and, in particular, about *Let Us Now Praise Famous Men*, the "classic" text by James Agee and Walker Evans. Write an essay in which you elaborate the differences in their approaches to and accounts of this text. You can imagine that you are writing for a reader who has read none of the texts at hand, so you will need to be careful in summary (perhaps reproducing some of the illustrations). What does each notice or choose to notice in the text? How are these decisions related to the larger projects of the two authors? to their underlying commitments and concerns? And, finally, where are you on the differences between the two? Would you align yourself with one or the other writer? From their example, is there a position you would define as your own or as an alternative?

Note: Your work with this project would be greatly enhanced by your reviewing the full text of *Let Us Now Praise Famous Men*. With the text, you can establish a more complete sense of context, including what both writers miss or leave out. You can think about the agenda or desires that led to their selection of exemplary material.

. . . .

A S S I G N M E N T **4**

States
[Said, Mitchell]

After the Last Sky: Palestinian Lives is one of the central "cases" in W. J. T. Mitchell's "The Photographic Essay: Four Case Studies." Mitchell's essay examines the "dialectic of exchange and resistance that make it possible (and sometimes impossible) to 'read' the pictures, or to 'see' the text illustrated in them."

Before rereading Mitchell, take time to work on "States" and to write a draft addressing the relationship of image to text. (The first of the "Questions for a Second Reading" [see pp. 712–13] provides a way of preparing for this.)

Once you have worked through the opening three paragraphs, reread the essay with an eye to the accumulating relationships between image and text. Is there a pattern? Do any stand out for their force, variety, innovation?

Once you've written that draft, read Mitchell and bring his analysis into the conversation. You will want to refer to the general frame and the terms of his argument and to the specific discussion of images in *After the Last Sky*. What does Mitchell bring to the essay? How does he understand the differences between Said/Mohr and Agee/Evans? How would you define Mitchell's expertise? What can he allow you to say or do? And, in return, what do you see that he doesn't? How might you define your position or point of view in relation to his?

. . . .

A S S I G N M E N T **5**

Projected Memory
[Hirsch, Coles]

In his essay "The Tradition: Fact and Fiction," Robert Coles comments on the documentary photography done by Dorothea Lange and Walker Evans during the Great Depression of the 1930s. Coles is interested in the ways photographs are both documentary records and works of art and thus disrupt any clear distinction between fact and fiction. In his comments on one of Evans's photographs, he says,

> But Evans is struggling for an interiority, that of his subject and that of his subject's future viewer/visitor: let us not only praise this man, lift him to the ranks of the famous, but consider what might be going on within him, and let us, through the motions of our moral imagination, enter his life, try to understand it, and return with that understanding to our own, which is thereby altered. (p. 197)

This is a tall order for a single picture, he continues, "but then Evans and Agee were ambitious."

When he speaks of the viewer, the viewer Evans is assuming in his photography, it is a viewer with a "moral imagination" who will do the work to "enter [the subject's] life, try to understand it, and return with that understanding" to his own life, a life which would, then, be altered.

Write an essay in which you read Coles's essay from the position of Hirsch's argument. Both have the goal of teaching us how to use the photographic record. How are they different? Both speak with an urgency about the necessity of paying attention to the records of the past and the ethical issues involved. Again, how are they different? And, finally, if they define two ways of approaching the photographic record, where do you locate yourself with these issues?

•   •   •   •   •   •   •   •   •   •   •   •

ASSIGNMENT 6

A Final View
[Coles, Mitchell]

Compose a photo-essay of your own. The photographs can be prepared for the occasion (by you or a colleague); they could also be photos already available. Whatever their source, they should represent people and places, a history and/or geography that you know well, that you know to be complex and contradictory, and that you know will not be easily or readily understood by others, both the group for whom you will be writing (most usefully the members of your class) and readers more generally. You must begin with a sense that the photos cannot speak for themselves; you must speak for them.

In preparation, you should think about the examples you've studied: Evans and Agee, Said and Mohr, Hirsch. Something in their work can help you at this point to choose and arrange the images, to think about the relation of words to photographs, to think about the purpose and direction of your writing.

When you are done, write a brief preface in which you situate your project in relation to the reading you have done in this sequence, particularly in relation to the issues defined by Coles and Mitchell.

Experimental Readings and Writings

Susan Griffin

Marianne Hirsch

John Edgar Wideman

Gloria Anzaldúa

*T*HIS SEQUENCE offers you opportunities to work with selections that are striking both for what they have to say and for the ways they use writing. In each case the writer is experimenting, pushing against or stepping outside of conventional ways of writing and thinking. The sequence is an opportunity to learn about these experimental ways of writing from the inside, as a practitioner, as someone who learns from doing the very thing that he or she is studying. You will be asked to try out the kinds of writing you've read in the course. For example, the first assignment asks you to step into Susan Griffin's shoes, to mix personal and academic writing, and in doing so, you are challenged to do a kind of intellectual work on subject matter to which you feel strong (though maybe contrary and paradoxical) ties.

The second assignment invites you to work on a set of photographs in a manner similar to Marianne Hirsch in her essay, "Projected Memory: Holocaust Photographs in Personal and Public Fantasy." The third assignment asks you to study Griffin's and Hirsch's essays as examples of methods, as ways of doing intellectual work.

In assignment 4, you're asked to write a memoir, or family or neighborhood history, as a way of thinking about writers' methods through John Edgar Wideman's essay "Our Time." Assignment 5 then moves you to the most unconventional text in the series, chapters from Gloria

Anzaldúa's mixed-language book, *Borderlands/La frontera*. She describes her writing as "a crazy dance," "an assemblage, a montage, a beaded work." Here again you are asked to work from inside this unconventional project. The sixth and final assignment asks you to step back and study the experimental work you have completed.

* * * * * * * * * * * *

ASSIGNMENT 1

A Mix of Personal and Academic Writing [Griffin]

> To tell a story, or to hear a story told, is not a simple transmission of information. Something else in the telling is given too, so that, once hearing, what one has heard becomes a part of oneself. (p. 372)
>
> I have come to believe that every life bears in some way on every other. The motion of cause and effect is like the motion of a wave in water, continuous, within and not without the matrix of being, so that all consequences, whether we know them or not, are intimately embedded in our experience. (p. 366)
>
> — SUSAN GRIFFIN
> *Our Secret*

It is useful to think of Griffin's prose as experimental. She is trying to do something that she can't do in the "usual" essay form. She wants to make a different kind of argument or engage her reader in a different manner. And so she mixes personal and academic writing. She assembles fragments and puts seemingly unrelated material into surprising and suggestive relationships. She breaks the "plane" of the page with italicized inter-sections. She organizes her material, that is, but not in the usual mode of thesis-example-conclusion. Nor does she only represent people's stories, including her own. The arrangement is not nearly so linear. At one point, when she seems to be prepared to argue that German child-rearing practices produced the Holocaust, she quickly says:

> Of course there cannot be one answer to such a monumental riddle, nor does any event in history have a single cause. Rather a field exists, like a field of gravity that is created by the movements of many bodies. Each life is influenced and it in turn becomes an influence. Whatever is a cause is also an effect.

Childhood experience is just one element in the determining field. (p. 350)

Her prose serves to create a "field," one where many bodies are set in relationship.

It is useful, then, to think about Griffin's prose as the enactment of a method, as a way of doing a certain kind of intellectual work, a work to which she has strong personal and emotional ties. One way to study this, to feel its effects, is to imitate it, to take it as a model. For this assignment, write a Griffin-like essay, one similar to "Our Secret" in its methods of organization and argument. You will need to think about the stories you might tell, about the stories and texts you might gather (stories and texts not your own), stories to which you are drawn by an emotional and intellectual curiosity. As you write, you will want to think carefully about arrangement and about commentary (about where, that is, you will speak to your reader *as* the writer of the piece). You should not feel bound to Griffin's subject matter, but you should feel that you are working in her spirit with subjects that matter to you.

· · · · · · · · · · · ·

ASSIGNMENT 2

Postmemory [Hirsch]

The project of postmemory can be a writing project. In fact, to describe the individual's active engagement with the past that *is* postmemory, Hirsch uses metaphors of writing (or inscription): "It is a question of adopting the traumatic experiences—and thus also the memories—of others as one's own, or, more precisely, as experiences one might oneself have had, and of inscribing them into one's own life story. It is a question of conceiving oneself as multiply interconnected with others of the same, of previous, and of subsequent generations, of the same and of other—proximate or distant—cultures and subcultures" (p. 407).

Use "Projected Memory" as invitation to such a writing project, where you would write about a past that belongs to you but that is not yours. Hirsch is interested in stories of trauma and suffering. And there is, to be sure, much at stake (and much to be gained) by writing about the traumas that preoccupy us as a culture. You should not, however, feel that you must write about a traumatic past. You should write about what you have at hand—connections to the past through family, neighborhood, or (as Hirsch says) "group relation"—and as those memories can be prompted, assisted, and mediated by some documentary or photographic record (as in the case of the photos in "Projected Memory" and the story of Anne

Frank for Rymkiewicz and Agosín). The past that you are tied to need not necessarily have national or international significance. The importance is that you can identify yourself with this past and with these memories (and that you can inscribe them into your own life story).

Since we are using Hirsch to invite you to write about the past, it is important to note where and how she identifies the problems that accompany such a task. It comes in the distinction she makes between "idiopathic" and "heteropathic" identification; her concern is cliché, sentimental, a too-easy identification with that which is beyond you, even incomprehensible. She says,

> The challenge for the postmemorial artist is precisely to find the balance that allows the spectator [the reader] to enter the image, to imagine the disaster, but that disallows an overappropriate identification that makes the distances disappear, creating too available, too easy an access to this particular past. (p. 408)

. . . .

ASSIGNMENT **3**

Writing the Past
[Griffin, Hirsch]

Susan Griffin is trained as a historian, and Marianne Hirsch is a research professor in the humanities. Both write as historians. Both are committed to studying and understanding the past. The prose of "Projected Memory: Holocaust Photographs in Personal and Public Fantasy" and "Our Secret," however, demonstrate that for both writers, the writing of history is a difficult rather than a straightforward task. The difficulty is not simply a matter of having accurate records or significant recall; the difficulty is present in (a part of) writing and the relationship of the writer to language and, through language, to the past; the problems are formal problems: where to begin, how to end, how to put stories together in a way that is meaningful, that they might add up to something.

Write an essay in which you use one of these selections to investigate another—where, perhaps, you use Griffin to think about Hirsch or Hirsch to think about Griffin. Given what one author is doing, how do you see the work of the other? How are these projects in dialogue or conversation? Where and how do they go in completely different directions? What, as examples, do they have to say to a student of writing about the "rules" most often taken for granted in writing class—rules governing sentences and paragraphs; introductions, bodies, and conclusions; narrative, argument, and exposition?

You should imagine that your readers are familiar with both texts but have not thought of bringing them together and do not have the texts handy. You will, then, need to do the work of presentation and summary as you establish the points of comparison.

· · · · · · · · · · · · ·

A S S I G N M E N T   4

Turning This Way and That [Wideman]

"Our Time" is a family history, but it is also a meditation on the problems of writing family histories—or, more generally, the problems of writing about the "real" world. There are sections in "Our Time" where Wideman speaks directly about the problems he faces as a writer. And the unusual features in the prose stand as examples of how he tried to solve these problems—at certain points Wideman writes as an essayist, at others like a storyteller; at certain points he switches voices and/or typeface; the piece breaks up into sections, it doesn't move from introduction to conclusion. Think of these as part of Wideman's method, as his way of working on the problems of writing as practical problems, where he is trying to figure out how to do justice to his brother and his story.

As you prepare to write this assignment, read back through the selection to think about it as a way of doing one's work, as a project, as a way of writing. What are the selection's key features? What is its shape or design? How does Wideman, the writer, do what he does? And you might ask: What would it take to learn to write like this? How is this writing related to the writing taught in school? Where and how might it serve you as a student?

Once you have developed a sense of Wideman's method, write a Wideman-like piece of your own, one that has the rhythm and the moves, the shape and the design of "Our Time." As far as subject matter is concerned, let Wideman's text stand as an invitation (inviting you to write about family and neighborhood) but don't feel compelled to follow his lead. You can write about anything you want. The key is to follow the essay as an example of a *way* of writing—moving slowly, turning this way and that, combining stories and reflection, working outside of a rigid structure of thesis and proof.

. . . .

ASSIGNMENT 5

A Crazy Dance [Anzaldúa]

> In looking at this book that I'm almost finished writing, I see a
> mosaic pattern (Aztec-like) emerging, a weaving pattern, thin
> here, thick there. . . . This almost finished product seems an as-
> semblage, a montage, a beaded work with several leitmotifs
> and with a central core, now appearing, now disappearing in a
> crazy dance. The whole thing has had a mind of its own, escap-
> ing me and insisting on putting together the pieces of its own
> puzzle with minimal direction from my will. It is a rebellious,
> willful entity, a precocious girl-child forced to grow up too
> quickly, rough, unyielding, with pieces of feather sticking out
> here and there, fur, twigs, clay. My child, but not for much
> longer. This female being is angry, sad, joyful, is Coatlicue,
> dove, horse, serpent, cactus. Though it is a flawed thing—
> clumsy, complex, groping blind thing, for me it is alive, infused
> with spirit. I talk to it; it talks to me.
>
> — GLORIA ANZALDÚA
> *Borderlands/La frontera*

Gloria Anzaldúa has described her text in *Borderlands/La frontera* as a
kind of crazy dance; it is, she says, a text with a mind of its own, "putting
together the pieces of its own puzzle with minimal direction from my
will." Hers is a prose full of variety and seeming contradictions; it is a
writing that could be said to represent the cultural "crossroads" which is
her experience/sensibility.

As an experiment whose goal is the development of an alternate (in
Anzaldúa's terms, a mixed or *mestiza*) understanding, write an autobiographical text whose shape and motives could be described in her terms: a
mosaic, woven, with numerous overlays; a montage, a beaded work, a
crazy dance, drawing upon the various ways of thinking, speaking, understanding that might be said to be part of your own mixed cultural position, your mixed sensibility.

To prepare for this essay, think about the different positions you could
be said to occupy, the different voices that are part of your background or
present, the competing ways of thinking that make up your points of view.
Imagine that your goal is to present your world and your experience to
those who are not necessarily prepared to be sympathetic or to understand.
And, following Anzaldúa, you should work to construct a mixed text, not a
single unified one. This will be hard, since you will be writing what might
be called a "forbidden" text, one you have not been prepared to write.

. . . .

A S S I G N M E N T   6

Writing and Schooling
[Griffin, Hirsch, Wideman, Anzaldúa]

You have written five assignments so far, and all of them, with perhaps the exception of the third—the one in which you were asked to write about Griffin's and Hirsch's methods—could be described as experimental. (It might be worth asking: Did you write a conventional essay for the third? Did you have a choice?)

The selections you took as models, writing by Griffin, Hirsch, Wideman, and Anzaldúa, certainly did not follow the usual guidelines for school writing. They broke some rules. They pushed the limits. They didn't do what essays are supposed to do, at least by certain standards. They were frustrated by limits of the usual ways of doing things with words. In a sense, they saw "good" writing as a problem, a problem they could work on as writers. Most likely, the same things could be said about your writing in this sequence. You did things that stood outside of (or that stood against) the forms of writing most often taught in school.

Read over your work. What were you able to do that you wouldn't, or couldn't, have done if you had written in a more conventional style? Be as precise as you can. How and where does this writing differ from the writing you have been taught in school? Again, be as precise as you can—go to old papers, textbooks, or syllabi to look for examples of "good writing" and the standard advice to young writers. Given what you have seen, where and how might more experimental writing be used in the schools (or in schooling)? What role might it play in courses that are not writing courses? What role might it play in a young writer's education?

Write an essay in which you use the example of your work in this sequence to think about writing and the teaching of writing in our schools.

o—o—o—o—o—o—o—o—o—o—o—o—o

SEQUENCE EIGHT

Experts and Expertise

W. J. T. Mitchell

Adrienne Rich

Clifford Geertz

John Edgar Wideman

Walker Percy

*T*HE *FIRST FOUR ASSIGNMENTS* in this sequence give you the chance to think about familiar settings or experiences through the work of writers who have had a significant effect on contemporary culture: W. J. T. Mitchell, Adrienne Rich, Clifford Geertz, and John Edgar Wideman.

In "The Photographic Essay: Four Case Studies," W. J. T. Mitchell asks his readers to think about the power of words and images through the example of the photographic essay as they can be seen to represent a "dialectic of exchange and resistance between photography and language." In "When We Dead Awaken: Writing as Re-Vision," Adrienne Rich examines the history and possibility of women's writing. Clifford Geertz, in "Deep Play: Notes on the Balinese Cockfight," provides an extended account and interpretation of the cockfight as a feature of Balinese culture. And John Edgar Wideman, in "Our Time," uses a family story to investigate the conditions of life in a black, urban neighborhood.

In each case, you will be given the opportunity to work alongside these thinkers as an apprentice, carrying out work they have begun. The final assignment in the sequence will ask you to look back on what you have done, to take stock, and with Walker Percy's account of the oppressive nature of expertise in mind, to draw some conclusions about the potential and consequences of this kind of intellectual apprenticeship.

• • • • • • • • • • •

ASSIGNMENT 1

Words and Images [Mitchell]

These four books provide the central examples for Mitchell's study: *Let Us Now Praise Famous Men,* James Agee and Walker Evans; *Camera Lucida,* Roland Barthes; *The Colonial Harem,* Malek Alloula; and *After the Last Sky,* Edward Said and Jean Mohr. Jacob Riis's *How the Other Half Lives* also provides an important illustration in the second section of the essay. Go to the library to study one of these texts. Or, find an example of a "photographic essay" that you could put alongside Mitchell's examples. (A chapter from *After the Last Sky* appears on pp. 677–712.)

For this assignment, take up Mitchell's project by extending his work in "The Photographic Essay" and considering new or additional examples. You should assume that you are writing for a reader who is familiar with Mitchell's essay. (This reader, however, will not have the book open on his or her desk.) Your work is to put Mitchell to the test—to extend, test, and perhaps challenge or qualify his account of the genre. As with his project, the basic questions are these: What relationship between photography and writing do [these examples] articulate? What tropes of differentiation govern the division of labor between photographer and writer, image and text, the viewer and the reader?

• • • • • • • • • • •

ASSIGNMENT 2

Looking Back [Rich]

Re-vision—the act of looking back, of seeing with fresh eyes, of entering an old text from a new critical direction—is for women more than a chapter in cultural history: it is an act of survival. Until we can understand the assumptions in which we are drenched we cannot know ourselves. (p. 629)

I have hesitated to do what I am going to do now, which is to use myself as an illustration. For one thing, it's a lot easier and less dangerous to talk about other[s]. (p. 631)

— ADRIENNE RICH
When We Dead Awaken: Writing as Re-Vision

In "When We Dead Awaken," Rich is writing not to tell her story but to tell a collective story, the story of women or women writers, a story in which she figures only as a representative example. In fact, the focus on individual experience might be said to run against the argument she has to make about the shaping forces of culture and history, in whose context knowing oneself means knowing the assumptions in which one is "drenched."

Yet Rich tells her story—offering poems, anecdotes, details from her life. Write an essay in which you too (and perhaps with similar hesitation) use your own experience as an illustration, as a way of investigating not just your situation but the situation of people like you. (Think about what materials you might have to offer in place of her poems.) Tell a story of your own and use it to talk about the ways you might be said to have been shaped or named or positioned by an established and powerful culture. You should imagine that this assignment is a way for you to use (and put to the test) some of Rich's key terms, words like "re-vision," "renaming," "structure," and "patriarchy."

● ● ● ● ● ● ● ● ● ● ●

ASSIGNMENT **3**

Seeing Your World through
Geertz's Eyes [Geertz]

The culture of a people is an ensemble of texts, themselves ensembles, which the anthropologist strains to read over the
shoulders of those to whom they properly belong. (p. 332)
— CLIFFORD GEERTZ
Deep Play: Notes on the Balinese Cockfight

Geertz talks about "reading" a culture while peering over the shoulders of those to whom it properly belongs. In "Deep Play," he "reads" the
cockfight over the shoulders of the Balinese. But the cockfight is not a
single event to be described in isolation. It is itself a "text," one that must
be understood in context. Or, as Geertz says, the cockfight is a "Balinese
reading of Balinese experience; a story they tell themselves about
themselves."

The job of the anthropologist, Geertz says, is "formulating sociological
principles, not . . . promoting or appreciating cockfights." And the question for the anthropologist is this: "What does one learn about such principles from examining culture as an assemblage of texts?" Societies, he

says, "like lives, contain their own interpretations. One has only to learn how to gain access to them."

Anthropologists are experts at gaining access to cultures and at performing this kind of complex reading. One of the interesting things about being a student is that you get to (or you have to) act like an expert even though, properly speaking, you are not. Write an essay in which you prepare a Geertzian "reading" of some part of our culture you know well (sorority rush, window shopping in a shopping mall, slam dancing, studying in the library, decorating a dorm room, tailgate parties at the football game, whatever). Ideally, you should go out and observe the behavior you are studying, looking at the players and taking notes with your project in mind. You should imagine that you are working in Geertz's spirit, imitating his method and style and carrying out work that he has begun.

• • • • • • • • • • • •

ASSIGNMENT 4

Wideman as a Case in Point
[Wideman]

The hardest habit to break, since it was the habit of a lifetime, would be listening to myself listen to him. That habit would destroy any chance of seeing my brother on his terms; and seeing him in his terms, learning his terms, seemed the whole point of learning his story. However numerous and comforting the similarities, we were different. The world had seized on the difference, allowed me room to thrive, while he'd been forced into a cage. (p. 767)

— JOHN EDGAR WIDEMAN
Our Time

At several points in this selection, Wideman discusses his position as a writer, researching and telling Robby's story, and he describes the problems he faces in writing this piece (and in "reading" the text of his brother's life). You could read this excerpt, in other words, as an essay on reading and writing.

Why do you think Wideman brings himself and these problems into the text? Why not keep quiet and hope no one notices? Choose three or four passages where Wideman refers directly or indirectly to the work he is doing as he writes this piece, and write an essay describing this work and why you think Wideman refers to it as he does. If he confronts problems, what are they and how does he go about solving them? If Wideman is an expert, how might you describe his expertise? And what might his example say to you as you think about your work as a student? as a writer?

• • • • • • • • • • •

ASSIGNMENT **5**

On Experts and Expertise
[Mitchell, Rich, Geertz, Wideman, Percy]

The whole horizon of being is staked out by "them," the experts. The highest satisfaction of the sightseer (not merely the tourist but any layman seer of sights) is that his sight should be certified as genuine. The worst of this impoverishment is that there is no sense of impoverishment. (p. 594)

I refer to the general situation in which sovereignty is surrendered to a class of privileged knowers, whether these be theorists or artists. A reader may surrender sovereignty over that which has been written about, just as a consumer may surrender sovereignty over a thing which has been theorized about. The consumer is content to receive an experience just as it has been presented to him by theorists and planners. The reader may also be content to judge life by whether it has or has not been formulated by those who know and write about life. (p. 594)

— WALKER PERCY
The Loss of the Creature

In the last four assignments you were asked to try on other writers' ways of seeing the world. You looked at what you had read or done, and at scenes from your own life, casting your experience in the terms of others.

Percy, in "The Loss of the Creature," offers what might be taken as a critique of such activity. "A reader," he says, "may surrender sovereignty over that which has been written about, just as a consumer may surrender sovereignty over a thing which has been theorized about." Mitchell, Rich, Geertz, and Wideman have all been presented to you as, in a sense, "privileged knowers." You have been asked to model your own work on their examples.

It seems safe to say that, at least so far as Percy is concerned, surrendering sovereignty is not a good thing to do. If Percy were to read over your work in these assignments, how do you think he would describe what you have done? If he were to take your work as an example in his essay, where might he place it? And how would his reading of your work fit with your sense of what you have done? Would Percy's assessment be accurate, or is there something he would be missing, something he would fail to see?

Write an essay in which you describe and comment on your work in this sequence, looking at it both from Percy's point of view and from your own, but viewing that work as an example of an educational practice, a way of reading (and writing) that may or may not have benefits for the reader.

Note: You will need to review carefully those earlier papers and mark sections that you feel might serve as interesting examples in your discussion. You want to base your conclusions on the best evidence you can. When you begin writing, it might be useful to refer to the writer of those earlier papers as a "he" or a "she" who played certain roles and performed his or her work in certain characteristic ways. You can save the first person, the "I," for the person who is writing this assignment and looking back on those texts.

History and Ethnography:
Reading the Lives
of Others

Clifford Geertz

Patricia Nelson Limerick

John Edgar Wideman

Mary Louise Pratt

W*RITING REMAINS* one of the most powerful tools we have for preserving and understanding the past and the present. This is simple to say. What good writing is, and what writing is good for—these questions are constantly debated by writers and academics. There are big philosophical questions here (what is the borderline between the truth and fiction, between what is there and what is a product of imagination or point of view?). There are practical questions (how do you learn to write history or ethnography? how do you revise it to make it better?). And both the philosophical questions and the practical questions have bearing on the work a student performs in the undergraduate curriculum, where students are constantly called upon to read and write textual accounts of human experience. This sequence is designed to give you a chance to do the work firsthand, to write a history or ethnography, and to think about and revise that work through the work of critics and theorists.

The first two assignments ask you to prepare first drafts of an ethnography and a history, written in response to the examples of Clifford Geertz (an anthropologist) and Patricia Nelson Limerick (a historian). The third assignment asks you to read "Our Time," by John Edgar Wideman. Wideman, in professional terms, is neither an anthropologist nor a historian. He is, rather, a fiction writer who has turned his hand to nonfiction, to write about African American culture and his family. With Wideman as a lever for thinking about issues of representation, you are asked to turn to all three essays to prepare a guide for writers, and, in the fourth assignment, you are asked to revise one of your earlier essays. The next assignment takes an additional theoretical step, looking (through Mary Louise Pratt's essay "Arts of the Contact Zone") at problems of representation as they are rooted more generally in culture, history, and ideology (and not just in the work of an individual writer and his or her text). The last assignment is an opportunity for a further revision, one that includes a section of reflection on the work you have done.

•   •   •   •   •   •   •   •   •   •   •   •   •

ASSIGNMENT 1

Ethnography [Geertz]

As in more familiar exercises in close reading, one can start anywhere in a culture's repertoire of forms and end up anywhere else. One can stay, as I have here, within a single, more or less bounded form and circle steadily within it. One can move between forms in search of broader unities or informing contrasts. One can even compare forms from different cultures to define their character in reciprocal relief. But whatever the level at which one operates, and however intricately, the guiding principle is the same: societies, like lives, contain their own interpretations. One has only to learn how to gain access to them. (pp. 332–33)

— CLIFFORD GEERTZ
Deep Play: Notes on the Balinese Cockfight

Geertz says that "the culture of a people is an ensemble of texts, themselves ensembles, which the anthropologist strains to read over the shoulders of those to whom they properly belong." Anthropologists are expert at "reading" in this way; they are trained to do it.

One of the interesting things about being a student is that you get to (or you have to) act like an expert even though you are not "officially" credentialed. Write an essay in which you prepare a Geertzian "reading" of the activities of some subgroup or some part of our culture you know well. Ideally, you should go out and observe the behavior you are studying ("straining to read over the shoulders" of those to whom this "text" properly belongs), examining it and taking notes with your project in mind. You should imagine that you are working in Geertz's spirit, imitating his method and style and carrying out work that he has begun. (It might be wise, however, to focus more locally than he does. He writes about a national culture—the Balinese cockfight as a key to Bali. You should probably not set out to write about "America" but about something more local. And you should write about some group of which you are not already a part, a group which you can imagine as "foreign," different, other.)

• • • • • • • • • • •

A S S I G N M E N T **2**

History [Limerick]

One skill essential to the writing of Western American history is a capacity to deal with multiple points of view. It is as if one were a lawyer at a trial designed on the principle of the Mad Hatter's tea party—as soon as one begins to understand and empathize with the plaintiff's case, it is time to move over and empathize with the defendant. Seldom are there only two parties or only two points of view.

—PATRICIA NELSON LIMERICK
Empire of Innocence

One way to work on Limerick's essay "Haunted America" is to take the challenge and write history—to write the kind of history, that is, that takes into account the problems she defines: the problems of myth, point of view, fixed ideas, simple narratives, selective storytelling, misery. You are not a professional historian, you are probably not using this book in a history course, and you don't have the time to produce a carefully researched history, one that covers all the bases, but you can think of this as an exercise in history writing, a minihistory, a place to start. Here are two options:

1. Go to your college library or, perhaps, the local historical society, and find two or three first-person accounts of a single event, ideally accounts from different points of view. Or, if these are not available, look to the work of historians, but historians taking different positions on a single event. (This does not have to be a history of the American West.) Even if you work with published histories, try to include original documents and accounts in your essay. The more varied the accounts, the better. Then, working with these texts as your primary

sources, write a history, one that you can offer as a response to
"Haunted America."

2. While you can find materials in a library, you can also work with
records that are closer to home. Imagine, for example, that you are
going to write a family or neighborhood history. You have your own
memories and experiences to work from, but for this to be a history
(more than a "personal essay"), you will need to turn to other sources
as well: interviews, old photos, newspaper clippings, letters, diaries,
interviews—whatever you can find. After gathering your materials,
write a family or neighborhood history, one that you can offer as a response to "Haunted America."

If you have the time, you might stage the work out into drafts, writing
first from one position or point of view and then from another and then,
perhaps, adding an overlay to indicate patterns you've detected (following Limerick's example).

•   •   •   •   •   •   •   •   •   •   •

ASSIGNMENT 3

A Writer's Guide
[Wideman, Geertz, Limerick]

While John Edgar Wideman is not writing history or ethnography in
"Our Time," at least not in the strict sense of the terms, he is writing about
others and about the past—he is trying to recover, represent, and understand the story of his brother Robby, his family, and their neighborhood.
He is trying to recover all those factors that might be said to have led to or
produced his brother's present situation.

It is interesting to read "Our Time," Geertz's "Deep Play," and
Limerick's "Haunted America" as alternate ways of thinking about the
problems of history and ethnography. As you reread these selections,
mark passages you might use to illustrate the styles, methods, and/or
concerns of each writer. You should reread the essays as a group, as part
of a single project investigating the problems of writing about other
people and about the past. Each essay could be read as both a reflection on
writing and a practical guide for those who follow. What do they say
about method? What tips do they offer, directly or through their examples? What cautions?

Write an essay in which you present, as though for a textbook or manual, a "Practical Guide for the Writer of History and Ethnography," drawn
from the work of Wideman, Geertz, and Limerick.

• • • • • • • • • • • •

ASSIGNMENT 4

Revision
[Geertz, Limerick, Wideman]

Go back to the first two essays you wrote for this sequence, the ethnography and the history, and choose one to revise. As always with revision, you should select the best essay, the one you care about the most. Your goal in revising this paper should be to take it on to its next step, not necessarily to fix it or clean it up or finish it, but to see how you can open up and add to what you have begun. As you prepare, you should consider the guidelines you wrote in assignment 3.

• • • • • • • • • • • •

ASSIGNMENT 5

Reading Others [Pratt]

Pratt, in "Arts of the Contact Zone," makes the case for the difficulties of reading, as well as writing, the "other":

> Autoethnography, transculturation, critique, collaboration, bilingualism, mediation, parody, denunciation, imaginary dialogue, vernacular expression—these are some of the literate arts of the contact zone. Miscomprehension, incomprehension, dead letters, unread masterpieces, absolute heterogeneity of meaning—these are some of the perils of writing in the contact zone. They all live among us today in the transnationalized metropolis of the United States and are becoming more widely visible, more pressing, and, like Guaman Poma's text, more decipherable to those who once would have ignored them in defense of a stable, centered sense of knowledge and reality. (p. 613)

> We are looking for the pedagogical arts of the contact zone. These will include, we are sure, exercises in storytelling and in identifying with the ideas, interests, histories, and attitudes of others; experiments in transculturation, and collaborative work

and in the arts of critique, parody, and comparison (including unseemly comparisons between elite and vernacular cultural forms); the redemption of the oral; ways for people to engage with suppressed aspects of history (including their own histories), ways to move *into and out of* rhetorics of authenticity; ground rules for communication across lines of difference and hierarchy that go beyond politeness but maintain mutual respect; a systematic approach to the all-important concept of *cultural mediation.* (p. 618)

One way of working with Pratt's essay, of extending its project, would be to conduct your own local inventory of writing from the contact zone. You might do this on your own or in teams, with others from your class. Here are two ways you might organize your search:

1. You could look for historical documents. A local historical society might have documents written by Native Americans ("Indians") to the white settlers. There may be documents written by slaves to masters or to northern whites. There may be documents written by women to men (written by the suffragettes, for example) negotiating public positions or rights. There may be documents from any of a number of racial or ethnic groups—Hispanic, Jewish, Irish, Italian, Polish, Swedish—trying to explain their positions to the mainstream culture. There may, perhaps at union halls, be documents written by workers to owners. Your own sense of the heritage of your area should direct your search.

2. Or you could look at contemporary documents in the print that is around you, texts that you might otherwise overlook. Pratt refers to one of the characteristic genres of the Hispanic community, the *"testimonio."* You could look for songs, testimonies, manifestos, statements by groups on campus, stories, autobiographies, interviews, letters to the editor, Web pages. You could look at the writing of any marginalized group, particularly writing intended, at least in part, to represent the experience of outsiders to the dominant culture (or to be in dialogue with that culture or to respond to that culture). These documents, if we follow Pratt's example, would include the work of young children or students, including college students.

Once you have completed your inventory, choose a document you would like to work with and present it carefully and in detail (perhaps in even greater detail than Pratt's presentation of the *New Chronicle*). You might imagine that you are presenting this to someone who would not have seen it and would not know how to read it, at least not as an example of the literate arts of the contact zone.

• • • • • • • • • • • •

ASSIGNMENT **6**

Revision (Again)
[Geertz, Limerick, Wideman, Pratt]

Pratt has provided a way to think about the problems of writing about the past or present as they are rooted in culture, history, and ideology (and not simply in the work of an individual writer on his or her text). You can't escape your position in the scene of contact, she argues—there is, in other words, no place outside of history or culture that is pure or free, offering a clear view of the past or others. This does not mean, however, that there is nothing to do. Behind Pratt's essay is a clear concern for improving the "literate arts" of the contact zone, for improving reading or writing.

Go back to the revision you prepared in assignment 4 and take it through one more revision. For the purposes of this sequence, it is a final draft, although few writers ever assume that their work is "finished." For this draft, your goal should be to bring your work to some provisional close. You want to make it as elegant and eloquent (and nicely produced) as you can. You also want to make it as thoughtful and responsible as it can be—that is, you want to show, in your practice, that you are conscious of the problems inherent in writing ethnography or history.

For this draft, whether you are writing an ethnography or a history, you should also add a short final reflective section (like Geertz's "Saying Something of Something"), in which you think about your work in the essay, reflecting not so much on what you have learned as on what you have done. This is a space where you can step out of your role as historian or ethnographer to think about the writing and your work as a writer.

SEQUENCE TEN

On Difficulty

Marianne Hirsch
Michel Foucault
John Edgar Wideman
Alice Munro
Walter Benjamin

*T*HE SIX ASSIGNMENTS in this sequence invite you to consider the nature of difficult texts and how the problems they pose might be said to belong simultaneously to language, to readers, and to writers. The sequence presents five difficult essays. The assumption the sequence makes is that they are difficult for all readers, not just students, and that the difficulty is necessary, strategic, not a mistake or evidence of a writer's failure.

The first assignment asks you to look closely at Marianne Hirsch's "Projected Memory: Holocaust Photographs in Personal and Public Fantasy" in order to discuss the ways in which she works with her sources. The second asks you to look at Michel Foucault's "Panopticism," particularly as it could be said to present an argument that is at once eloquent yet hard to understand. The third, fourth, and fifth assignments ask you to look at texts with unusual modes of development (John Edgar Wideman's "Our Time," Alice Munro's "The Albanian Virgin," and Walter Benjamin's "The Work of Art in the Age of Mechanical Reproduction"). All of these texts argue for different ways of reading and writing, work that stands outside the usual ways of doing things with words. The last assignment is a retrospective. It asks you to read back over your work and pull together what you've learned into a "theory of difficulty."

• • • • • • • • • • • •

ASSIGNMENT **1**

Uneasy Confrontations [Hirsch]

According to Marianne Hirsch, Lorie Novak "stages an uneasy confrontation of personal memory with public history." Hirsch studies, writes about (and stages) such confrontations herself. She begins her essay with a photograph, "From the *Stroop Report* on the destruction of the Warsaw ghetto," then an epigraph from Binjamin Wilkomirski followed by a long quotation from Jarosław Rymkiewicz's novel, *The Final Station: Umschlagplatz,* which is followed by a passage from the introduction to a book of poems by Marjorie Agosín titled *Dear Anne Frank.* All of this occurs in the first two pages.

As the title indicates, Hirsch's essay is about "projected memory" and it is about "holocaust photographs in personal and public fantasy." Like her beginning, her essay turns frequently to materials she has gathered. They could be thought of as part of her argument about the relationship of personal and public images of Holocaust victims in what she terms *postmemory.* From the very beginning, her essay stands contrary to conventional expectations—perhaps especially to conventional school expectations—about style, development, and presentation.

What, so far as you are concerned, is this essay about? And why is it constructed as it is? While there is certainly an argument *in* Hirsch's essay, there is also an argument represented *by* the essay, an argument enacted in a way of writing. How might this way of writing be necessary, necessary to Hirsch and her project?

Write an essay, perhaps in the genre of a review, in which you present "Projected Memory" to those who have not yet read it. You will need to take care to give a thorough and accurate account of what Hirsch says and does. You should also establish your position in relation to the essay, discussing where and how you found it useful or interesting.

•   •   •   •   •   •   •   •   •   •   •   •   •

ASSIGNMENT 2

Foucault's Fabrication [Foucault]

About three-quarters of the way into "Panopticism," Foucault says,

> Our society is one not of spectacle, but of surveillance; under
> the surface of images, one invests bodies in depth; behind the
> great abstraction of exchange, there continues the meticulous,
> concrete training of useful forces; the circuits of communication
> are the supports of an accumulation and a centralization of
> knowledge; the play of signs defines the anchorages of power;
> it is not that the beautiful totality of the individual is ampu-
> tated, repressed, altered by our social order, it is rather that the
> individual is carefully fabricated in it, according to a whole
> technique of forces and bodies. (pp. 244–45)

This prose is eloquent and insists on its importance to our moment and
our society; it is also very hard to read or to paraphrase. Who is doing
what to whom? How do we think about the individual being carefully
fabricated in the social order?

Take this selection as a problem to solve. What is it about? What are its
key arguments, its examples and conclusions? Write an essay that summarizes "Panopticism." Imagine that you are writing for readers who have
read the chapter (although they won't have the pages in front of them)
and who are at sea as to its argument. You will need to take time to present and discuss examples from the text. Your job is to help your readers
figure out what it says. You get the chance to take the lead and be the
teacher. In addition, you should feel free to acknowledge that you don't
understand certain sections even as you write about them.

So how do you write about something you don't completely understand? Here's a suggestion. When you have completed your summary,
read it over and treat it as a draft. Ask questions like these: What have I left
out? What was I tempted to ignore or finesse? Go back to those sections of
the chapter that you ignored and bring them into your essay. Revise by
adding discussions of some of the very sections you don't understand. You
can write about what you think Foucault might be saying—you can, that
is, be cautious and tentative; you can admit that the text is what it is, hard
to read. You don't have to master this text. You do, however, need to see
what you can make of it.

. . . .

A S S I G N M E N T **3**

A Story of Reading [Wideman]

At several points in "Our Time," Wideman interrupts the narrative to discuss his position as a writer telling Robby's story. He describes the problems he faces in writing this piece (or in "reading" the text of his brother's life). You could read this selection, in other words, as an essay about reading and writing. It is Wideman's account of his work.

And, as a narrative, "Our Time" is made up of sections, fragments, different voices. It is left to the reader, in a sense, to put the pieces together and complete the story. There is work for a reader to do, in other words, and one way to account for that work is to call it "practice" or "training." Wideman wants to force a reader's attention by offering a text that makes unusual demands, a text that teaches a reader to read differently. If you think of your experience with the text, of how you negotiated its terrain, what is the story of reading you might tell? In what way do your difficulties parallel Wideman's—at least those he tells us about when he stops to talk about the problems he faces as a writer?

Write an essay in which you tell the story of what it was like to read "Our Time" and compare your experience working with this text with Wideman's account of his own.

A story of reading—this is not a usual school exercise. Usually you are asked what texts mean, not what it was like to read them. As you prepare for this assignment, think back as closely as you can to your experience the first time through. And you will want to reread, looking for how and where Wideman seems to be deliberately working on his reader, defying expectation and directing response. You want to tell a story that is rich in detail, precise in accounting for moments in the text. You want to bring forward the features that can make your story a good story to read—suspense, action, context, drama. Since this is your story, you are one of the characters. You will want to refer to yourself as you were at the moment of reading while also reserving a space for you to speak from your present position, as a person thinking about what it was like to read the text, and as a person thinking about Wideman and about reading. You are telling a story, but you will need to break the narrative (as Wideman breaks his) to account in more general terms for the demands Wideman makes on readers. What habits does he assume a reader will bring to this text? How and why does he want to break them?

. . . .

ASSIGNMENT 4

Story Lines [Munro]

The story "The Albanian Virgin" is arranged in pieces, or fragments. As a reader works through them, they become two story lines: one set in the 1920s in Albania, on the Dalmatian coast; the other is set in the 1960s in Canada, on the Pacific coast. The first story, about a woman called Lottar, is told by Charlotte to Claire; the second is told by Claire to us (and, we learn, includes all these stories). But it takes some time for the pattern to establish itself and we might be lost at first, or confused.

As you reread, pay attention to how Munro handles, or orchestrates, the unfolding. How does she position the reader? How does she organize our attention and allow us access to the two story lines? What are the effects? How would you explain or define her strategy? Why does she make it so hard?

Write an essay on "The Albanian Virgin" as an argument about stories (and storytelling) and readers (and reading). As a reader, you should find space in your essay to speak on your own behalf, or on behalf of your generation, readers of your age, positioned as you are. Speak about your sense of *this* story, where it comes from, what it does, and what it might be good for.

. . . .

ASSIGNMENT 5

A Sense of an Ending [Benjamin]

In the epilogue, Walter Benjamin offers two accounts of war. Write an essay in which you explain the epilogue as a conclusion. Where and how does the essay prepare a reader for this conclusion? It will be important to work with the complete essay and not to take as final (or without further context) things said in earlier pages.

How would you paraphrase the two positions Benjamin presents? And where do you locate Benjamin in the epilogue—what is *he* saying? For this essay, you can imagine a reader who has read "The Work of Art in the Age of Mechanical Reproduction." Your reader will not, however, have the book in hand.

. . . .

ASSIGNMENT **6**

A Theory of Difficulty
[Hirsch, Foucault, Wideman, Munro, Benjamin]

Now that you have worked with these five texts, you are in a good position to review what you have written about each of them in order to say something more general about difficulty—difficulty in writing, difficulty in reading.

Write an essay in which you present a theory of difficulty, a kind of guide, something that might be useful to students who are regularly asked to confront difficult assignments. You will want to work from your previous essays—pulling out sections, revising, reworking examples for this new essay. Don't let your earlier work go unacknowledged. But, at the same time, feel free to move out from these readings to other materials, examples, or situations.

S E Q U E N C E   E L E V E N

Reading Culture

John Berger

Susan Bordo

Michel Foucault

W. J. T. Mitchell

*I*N *THIS SEQUENCE,* you will be reading and writing about culture. Not Culture, something you get if you go to the museum or a concert on Sunday, but culture—the images, words, and sounds that pervade our lives and organize and represent our common experience. This sequence invites your reflection on the ways culture "works" in and through the lives of individual consumers.

The difficulty of this sequence lies in the way it asks you to imagine that you are not a sovereign individual, making your own choices and charting the course of your life. This is conceptually difficult, but it can also be distasteful, since we learn at an early age to put great stock in imagining our own freedom. Most of the readings that follow ask you to imagine that you are the product of your culture; that your ideas, feelings, and actions, your ways of thinking and being, are constructed for you by a large, organized, pervasive force (sometimes called history, sometimes called culture, sometimes called ideology). You don't feel this to be the case, but that is part of the power of culture, or so the argument goes. These forces hide themselves. They lead you to believe that their constructions are naturally, inevitably there, that things are the way they are because that is just "the way things are." The assignments in this sequence ask you to read against your common sense. You will be expected to try on the role of the critic—to see how and where it might be useful to recognize complex motives in ordinary expressions.

The authors in this sequence all write as though, through great effort, they could step outside culture to see and criticize its workings. The assignments in this sequence will ask you both to reflect on this type of criticism and to participate in it. The first assignment is an exercise in the kind of historical reading represented by the work of John Berger, a reading designed to take a painting from the context of The Museum or High Culture and to put it back (Berger would say) into the context of history and of the images that dominate daily life. The second and third assignments draw on Susan Bordo's essay, "Hunger as Ideology." Like Berger, Bordo investigates the relationship of images to our sense of the past and our understanding of the present. The fourth assignment turns to Foucault to bring the terms and examples of *Discipline and Punish* into the discussion of ideology, power, and contemporary culture. The fifth turns to W. J. T. Mitchell's study of the photographic essay, a study that allows him a different angle from which to consider the power of words and images. The final assignment is a retrospective and asks you to revise and reconsider the work you have done in this sequence.

This sequence is followed by a minisequence, "Reading Culture (II)," on page 875. This alternative sequence provides readings and assignments that follow a parallel line of thought and allow for similar projects. They can be substituted for assignments in the first "Reading Culture" sequence or added to them.

. . . .

A S S I G N M E N T **1**

Looking at Pictures [Berger]

Original paintings are silent and still in a sense that information never is. Even a reproduction hung on the wall is not comparable in this respect for in the original the silence and stillness permeate the actual material, the paint, in which one follows the traces of the painter's immediate gestures. This has the effect of closing the distance in time between the painting of the picture and one's own act of looking at it. . . . What we make of that painted moment when it is before our eyes depends upon what we expect of art, and that in turn depends today upon how we have already experienced the meaning of paintings through reproductions. (p. 125)

— JOHN BERGER
Ways of Seeing

While Berger describes original paintings as silent in this passage, it is clear that these paintings begin to speak if one approaches them properly, if one learns to ask "the right questions of the past." Berger demonstrates one route of approach, for example, in his reading of the Hals paintings, where he asks questions about the people and objects and their relationship to the painter and the viewer. What the paintings might be made to say, however, depends upon the viewer's expectations, his or her sense of the questions that seem appropriate or possible. Berger argues that, because of the way art is currently displayed, discussed, and reproduced, the viewer expects only to be mystified.

For this assignment, imagine that you are working against the silence and mystification Berger describes. Go to a museum—or, if that is not possible, to a large-format book of reproductions in the library (or, if that is not possible, to the reproductions in "Ways of Seeing")—and select a painting that seems silent and still, yet invites conversation. Your job is to figure out what sorts of questions to ask, to interrogate the painting, to get it to speak, to engage with the past in some form of dialogue. Write an essay in which you record this process and what you have learned from it. Somewhere in your essay, perhaps at the end, turn back to Berger's chapter to talk about how this process has or hasn't confirmed what you take to be Berger's expectations.

Note: If possible, include with your essay a reproduction of the painting you select. (Check the postcards at the museum gift shop.) In any event, you want to make sure that you describe the painting in sufficient detail for your readers to follow what you say.

· · · · · · · · · · · ·

A S S I G N M E N T 2

The Ideology of Hunger [Bordo]

Bordo extends an invitation to her students to "bring in examples that appear to violate traditional gender-dualities and the ideological messages contained in them." These, she said, will "display a complicated and bewitching tangle of new possibilities and old patterns of representation."

Write an essay in which you take up Bordo's invitation. On your own, or with a group, collect a set of advertisements (or images from other sources) that represent food and eating, women and men. Find examples and counterexamples to what she takes to be the traditional gender-dualities and the ideological messages contained in them. To present your project to others, you'll need to write descriptions of the ads, as Bordo does, so that your readers will be able to read them (to see them and understand them) as you do. You'll need to place your examples in relation to Bordo's argument about the "old dualities and ideologies" and to what she says about images that "stabilize" and "destabilize." You will need, in other words, to put her terms to work on your examples. Your goal should be to not only reproduce Bordo's project but to extend it, to refine it, to put it to the test. You should find yourself moving toward a statement of your own about the ideology of hunger in present-day America. And you should imagine that you are writing for a reader unfamiliar with Bordo's essay and its key terms.

• • • • • • • • • • •

ASSIGNMENT 3

Ideology and Agency [Bordo, Berger]

In "Hunger as Ideology," Bordo refers to John Berger and his work in *Ways of Seeing*. Both Berger and Bordo are concerned with how we see and read images; both are concerned to correct the ways images are used and read; both trace the ways images serve the interests of money and power; both are writing to get the attention of the public and teach readers how and why they should pay a different kind of attention to the images around them.

For this assignment, use Bordo's work in "Hunger as Ideology" to reconsider Berger's "Ways of Seeing." Write an essay in which you consider the two essays as examples of an ongoing project. As each considers the uses of images, who is doing what to whom? to what end? by what means?

Berger's essay precedes Bordo's by about a quarter of a century. If you look closely at one or two of their examples, and if you look at the larger concerns in their arguments, are they saying the same thing? doing the same work? If so, why? Why is such work still necessary? If not, how do their projects differ? And how might you account for those differences?

• • • • • • • • • • •

ASSIGNMENT 4

On Agency [Foucault]

[The Panopticon] is an important mechanism, for it automatizes and disindividualizes power. Power has its principle not so much in a person as in a certain concerted distribution of bodies, surfaces, lights, gazes; in an arrangement whose internal mechanisms produce the relation in which individuals are caught up. The ceremonies, the rituals, the marks by which the sovereign's surplus power was manifested are useless. There is a machinery that assures dissymmetry, disequilibrium, difference. Consequently, it does not matter who exercises power. Any individual, taken almost at random, can operate the machine: in the absence of the director, his family, his friends, his visitors, even his servants. Similarly, it does not matter what motive animates him: the curiosity of the indiscreet, the malice of a child, the thirst for knowledge of a philosopher who wishes to visit this museum of human nature, or the perversity of those who take pleasure in spying and punishing. The more numerous those anonymous and temporary observers are, the greater the risk for the inmate of being surprised and the greater his anxious awareness of being observed. The Panopticon is a marvelous machine which, whatever use one may wish to put it to, produces homogeneous effects of power. (pp. 232–33)

— MICHEL FOUCAULT
Panopticism

Foucault's work has changed our ways of thinking about "who is doing what to whom." Write an essay in which you explain Foucault's understanding of the Panopticon as a mechanism of power. You will need to paraphrase Foucault's argument, translate his terms, and, where appropriate, cite and deploy his terms. Present Foucault's account as you understand it, and be willing to talk about what you don't understand—or don't quite understand.

As part of your essay, and in order to examine his argument and his terms, use Foucault as a way of thinking about Bordo and Berger. How might Foucault treat the material they select for their examples? (As you write, it would be strategically useful to limit yourself to one example from each.) How does each of the three writers account for *agency* in their descriptions of the workings of power? What do you make of the differences in their accounts of power and knowledge? What do they imply about how one might live in or understand the world? What might they have to do with the ways you, or people like you, live in and understand the world?

. . . .

A S S I G N M E N T   **5**

Reading Images [Mitchell]

In the introduction to *Picture Theory,* W. J. T. Mitchell says,

> What we need is a critique of visual culture that is alert to the
> power of images for good and evil and that is capable of dis-
> criminating the variety and historical specificity of their uses.

One way to think about the "variety and historical specificity" of the use
of images is to look at the examples Mitchell provides in this chapter, examples of writers using images as the subjects of their writing, but also the
example of his own use and "reading" of those images.

At times, Mitchell is quick to include us in his ways of reading. In response to the Walker Evans photograph of Annie Mae Gudger, he says:

> There is something deeply disturbing, even disagreeable, about
> this (unavoidable) aestheticizing response to what after all is a
> real person in desperately impoverished circumstances. Why
> should we have a right to look on this woman and find her fa-
> tigue, pain, and anxiety beautiful? (p. 522)

His readers are written into the "we" of such sentences. At times he highlights the "reading" represented by the writer of the photo-essay, as he
does, for example, in his account of Roland Barthes use of Nadar's *The
Artist's Mother (or Wife).* And at times he singles himself out as an individual case, as, for example, when he says of the postcard image of the *Arabian Woman with the Yachmak:*

> Can an American observer, in particular, see these pho-
> tographs as anything more than quaint, archaic pornography,
> hauntingly beautiful relics of a lost colonial era, "collector's
> items" for a coffee-table book? I don't have a simple answer to
> this question, but my first impulse is to register a feeling of
> *impotence* in the face of these women, whose beauty is now
> mixed with danger, whose nakedness now becomes a veil that
> has always excluded me from the labyrinth of their world.
> (pp. 535–36)

Write an essay in which you present a close reading of Mitchell's text,
looking specifically at the ways it figures (or represents) readers reading.
What variety of readings does he chart? Where and how are they histori-
cally specific? What lessons are there to be learned from these examples?
What does Mitchell seem to be saying about appropriate ways of reading?
Where would you position him in relation to Berger and Bordo?

•   •   •   •   •   •   •   •   •   •   •   •   •

ASSIGNMENT   6

Visual Culture
[Berger, Bordo, Foucault, Mitchell]

Three of the writers you have been reading—Berger, Bordo, and Mitchell—are concerned about the use and status of images, concerned with what happens to them (and to us) when they are packaged, deployed, reproduced, turned into text. For all of these writers, the use of images is a sign of the health of the individual and the health of the culture.

Write an essay in which you revise and bring together the essays you have written for this sequence. You can treat them as individual statements, revising each, ordering them, writing an introduction, conclusion, and necessary transitions. Or you can revise more radically and combine what you have into some other form.

Your goal should be to bring the writers into conversation with each other, to use one selection to weigh, evaluate, and understand another. And your goal should be to find a way, yourself, to enter the conversation—to find a space, a voice, a set of examples and concerns. Where and how do these issues touch you and people like you (some group for whom you feel authorized to speak)? Where do you feel a similar urgency? Where and how would you qualify or challenge the position of these other writers? Where and how would you join them?

SEQUENCE TWELVE

Reading Culture (II)

Walter Benjamin
John Berger
Simon Frith

*T*HIS SEQUENCE provides an alternative set of readings for sequence eleven (p. 868). It begins with the work of Walter Benjamin, a key source for John Berger and, though not cited directly in *Performing Rites*, an important figure for British cultural studies and, by extension, for Simon Frith.

.   .   .   .

ASSIGNMENT 1

The Work of Art in the Age of Mechanical Reproduction [Benjamin]

Walter Benjamin's argument depends upon the concepts of "authenticity" and "aura." He says,

> [T]hat which withers in the age of mechanical reproduction is the aura of the work of art. This is a symptomatic process whose significance points beyond the realm of art. One might

generalize by saying: the technique of reproduction detaches the reproduced object from the domain of tradition. By making many reproductions it substitutes a plurality of copies for a unique existence. And in permitting the reproduction to meet the beholder or listener in his own particular situation, it reactivates the object reproduced. These two processes lead to a tremendous shattering of tradition which is the obverse of the contemporary crisis and renewal of mankind. Both processes are intimately connected with the contemporary mass movements. Their most powerful agent is the film. Its social significance, particularly in its most positive form, is inconceivable without its destructive, cathartic aspect, that is, the liquidation of the traditional value of the cultural heritage. (p. 79)

For this assignment, imagine that you are writing for someone who has not read Benjamin's essay. What is he saying here? What does this have to do with the essay as a whole? What examples can you bring to bear from the text? It will be important to work with the complete essay and not to take as final (or without further context) things said in earlier pages.

•   •   •   •   •   •   •   •   •   •   •   •   •

A S S I G N M E N T   2

Thinking about Cases [Benjamin]

Benjamin writes in 1936. He is not a visionary and he is not writing science fiction and so he does not imagine all the developments in technical reproduction (and the developmental tendencies of art) that are present in our own historical moment. Write an essay in which you extend "The Work of Art in the Age of Mechanical Reproduction" into the twenty-first century. You should focus your work in a single area: film and video, painting, architecture, music, or literature and writing. You will need to provide a careful account of Benjamin's argument, focusing close attention on a particular discussion of your genre.

Once you have provided the Benjaminian background, you can see what happens as you work forward to the present time. You can imagine that you are extending Benjamin's work, that you are in conversation with it, or that you are putting him to the test. You can, if it makes sense to you, continue in his style—writing short sections, numbered in sequence, with similar internal design.

• • • • • • • • • • • •

ASSIGNMENT 3

Ways of Seeing [Berger, Benjamin]

John Berger offers his essay, "Ways of Seeing," as a reading of "The Work of Art in the Age of Mechanical Reproduction." Rather than a footnote or a series of footnotes or passages in quotation, he acknowledges Benjamin's precedence and influence by including his picture and a brief reference at the end of his text. It is a lovely gesture.

After reading "The Work of Art," read "Ways of Seeing" with an eye (or ear) to where and how it draws upon or speaks back to Benjamin's work. Think not only about the large sweep of the argument, but about particular ideas, terms, or phrases that adhere from or echo or allude to the prior text.

With this preparation, write an essay in which you present and discuss Berger's use of Benjamin. Where and how does he draw from him? Where and how does he extend, refute, or exceed him? And, from this example, what conclusions can you draw about the work of scholarship and the relations between scholars?

• • • • • • • • • • • •

ASSIGNMENT 4

Ways of Listening [Frith]

Three paragraphs into his chapter titled, "The Voice," Simon Frith says,

> Now stop reading the lyrics, and listen to the song. Whose voice do we hear now? Again there's an obvious answer: the singer's, stupid! And what I argue in the rest of this chapter is that this is, in fact, the stupid answer. (p. 278)

Well, it may be stupid, but it *is* the obvious answer (that is, the answer he suspects we would provide).

Frith provides three extended descriptions of musical voice: Gregory Sandow on Frank Sinatra (p. 279), Aidan Day on Bob Dylan (p. 282), and Glenn Gould on Barbra Streisand (pp. 282–83). Each of these voices, he says, "has a relationship" (with an orchestra, with an audience, with music itself); and each critic, he says, hears a "willed sound." He provides his own extended description of X-Ray Spex's "Oh Bondage Up Yours!" (p. 288). Choose a performer and a performance that matters to you, that you think is exemplary, and using these four passages as models, write descriptions of voice. (You should write more than one; if it works to follow the models closely, write four.)

Once you have written these (perhaps as a first draft, a draft that can be read by others in your class), write an essay in which you use your examples in conversation with Frith and his arguments about voice.

* * * * * * * * * * * *

A S S I G N M E N T   **5**

Back to Benjamin [Frith, Benjamin]

Frith works from within the traditions of British cultural studies, which were formed in response to the Frankfurt school (the group that included Walter Benjamin). Benjamin writes primarily about film; Frith writes about music. Both are concerned with the ways popular culture shapes the lives (the thoughts, beliefs, and actions) of those who spend time with it; both are concerned with the ways popular culture does or does not enable people to resist, transform, or somehow improve the conditions of "everyday" life.

Work first with "The Work of Art in the Age of Mechanical Reproduction" and then with "The Voice." Frith imagines that he is taking the argument one step further, that he is improving on the conclusions of the Frankfurt school. With these two essays as your source, how would you describe the differences in their two positions on the powers and effects of popular culture? If Frith speaks more clearly to our own age, how might this be so? And what do you think? Do you side with Frith?

Question 4 in the "Questions for a Second Reading" (p. 299) might be useful as you think about Frith's position. It is also worth adding a passage from early in his book, at the end of the first chapter, where he says,

> I know this is where my own tastes will inform everything that follows, my own tastes, that is, for the *unpopular popular*, my own belief that the "difficult" appeals through traces it carries of another world in which it would be "easy." The utopian impulse, the *negation* of everyday life, the aesthetic impulse that Adorno recognized in high art, must be part of low art too. (*Performing Rites* 20)

. . . .

ASSIGNMENT **6**

Conclusions [Benjamin, Berger, Frith]

The final chapter of Frith's book (*Performing Rites: On the Value of Popular Music*), titled "Toward a Popular Aesthetic," includes the following passage, a passage that seems like an appropriate conclusion to the argument you have read in "The Voice":

> It follows that an identity is always already an ideal, what we would like to be, not what we are. In taking pleasure from black or gay or female music I don't thus identify as black or gay or female (I don't actually experience these sounds as "black music" or "gay music" or "women's voices") but, rather, participate in imagined forms of democracy and desire, imagined forms of the social and the sexual. And what makes music special in this familiar cultural process is that musical identity is both fantastic—idealizing not just oneself but also the social world one inhabits—and real: it is enacted in activity. Music making and music listening, that is to say, are bodily matters; they involve what one might call *social movements*. In this respect, musical pleasure is not derived from fantasy—it is not mediated by daydreams—but is experienced directly: music gives us a real experience of what the ideal could be.

Go to the final two paragraphs of John Berger's "Ways of Seeing" and to the epilogue of "The Work of Art in the Age of Mechanical Reproduction." You are working from limited sources, a small piece of the work of each of these scholars and critics. Still, from these conclusions, what can you say about the goals and desires of the critical work they represent?

Write an essay in which you discuss these conclusions both together and in relation to the arguments that precede them. How are they similar? How are they different? How do they imagine the relationship of art, criticism, culture, and history? And where do you locate yourself, and your generation (or the people for whom you feel authorized to speak), in relation to these accounts of history and culture?

SEQUENCE THIRTEEN

The Uses of Reading

Richard Rodriguez and Richard Hoggart
Walter Benjamin
Alice Walker
David Bartholomae and Anthony Petrosky

THIS SEQUENCE focuses attention on authors as readers, on the use of sources, and on the art of reading as a writer. It combines technical lessons with lessons on the practice and rhetoric of citation. The first assignment, for example, calls attention to the block quotations in Richard Rodriguez's essay, "The Achievement of Desire." These allow him to work the words of another writer, Richard Hoggart, into his text; they also demonstrate the ways he (Rodriguez) locates himself, his ideas, and his experience in relation to a figure who provides a powerful prior example. At some points he takes Hoggart's words as his own; at others he works to define his position against or beyond what Hoggart has to say. The next two assignments look at two writers from significantly different moments in history—Walter Benjamin and Alice Walker. Both are writers in difficult relation to their sources and to the culture represented by those sources. The assignments ask you to think again about how writers use the writing that precedes them in order to move forward, to get work done, to define a position for writing and thinking. The final assignment returns attention to attitudes toward reading and writing in contemporary American education, with *Ways of Reading* offered as an example.

• • • • • • • • • • • • •

A S S I G N M E N T **1**

The Scholarship Boy [Rodriguez, Hoggart]

You could look at the relationship between Richard Rodriguez and Richard Hoggart as a case study of the relation of a reader to a writer or a student to a teacher. Look closely at Rodriguez's references to Hoggart's book, *The Uses of Literacy,* and at the way Rodriguez made use of that book to name and describe his own experience as a student. (An extended selection of *The Uses of Literacy* can be found on pp. 891–99.) What did he find in the book? How did he use it? How does he use it in his own writing?

Write an essay in which you discuss Rodriguez's use of Hoggart's *The Uses of Literacy.* How, for example, would you compare Rodriguez's version of the "scholarship boy" with Hoggart's? (At one point, Rodriguez says that Hoggart's account is "more accurate than fair." What might he have meant by that?) And what kind of reader is the Rodriguez who is writing "The Achievement of Desire"—is he still a "scholarship boy," or is that description no longer appropriate?

Note: You might begin your research with what may seeem to be a purely technical matter, examining how Rodriguez handles quotations and works Hoggart's words into paragraphs of his own. On the basis of Rodriguez's use of quoted passages, how would you describe the relationship between Hoggart's words and Rodriguez's? Who has the greater authority? Who is the expert, and under what conditions? What "rules" might Rodriguez be said to follow or to break? Do you see any change in the course of the essay in how Rodriguez uses block quotations? in how he comments on them?

• • • • • • • • • • • •

A S S I G N M E N T **2**

Sources [Benjamin]

One of the interesting features of Walter Benjamin's essay, "The Work of Art in the Age of Mechanical Reproduction," is the use of footnotes. As you reread, pay particular attention to the way each note functions—functions for you as a reader, functions (or might have functioned) for

Benjamin as a writer. Choose one or two that seem to you to be particularly interesting or illustrative. Write an essay in which you provide a reader unfamiliar with "The Work of Art in the Age of Mechanical Reproduction" with a way of seeing and understanding Benjamin's use of the footnote. And offer this not only as an interesting spectacle but as evidence of a style of writing or a theory of writing, one that might have potential uses for you and your colleagues.

According to political theorist Hannah Arendt, editor of his *Illuminations* (1968, Schocken Books), Benjamin's ideal was a work that would consist entirely of quotations, prepared so masterfully that "it could dispense with any accompanying text." She says,

> To the extent that an accompanying text by the author proved unavoidable, it was a matter of fashioning it in such a way as to preserve "the intention of such investigations," namely, "to plumb the depths of language and thought . . . by drilling rather than excavating," so as not to ruin everything with explanations that seek to provide a causal or systematic connection. . . . What mattered to him above all was to avoid anything that might be reminiscent of empathy, as though a given subject of investigation had a message in readiness which easily communicated itself, or could be communicated, to the reader or spectator. (*Illuminations* 47–48)

• • • • • • • • • • • •

A S S I G N M E N T   **3**

Contrary Instincts [Walker]

In "In Search of Our Mothers' Gardens," Alice Walker uses the term "contrary instincts" when she discusses Phillis Wheatley. The problem for Walker (and others) is that Wheatley would idolize a fair-haired white woman as a goddess of liberty rather than turn to herself as a model or to the black women who struggled mightily for their identities and their liberty.

Walker's essay is filled with allusions to black women artists: Bessie Smith, Roberta Flack, Phillis Wheatley, Zora Neale Hurston; in fact, the essay serves as a kind of book list or reader's guide; it suggests a program of reading. (The references aren't strictly to black women. Jean Toomer was a man and Virginia Woolf was white.)

As you reread this essay, pay attention to the names. (Go to the library and track down some you don't know and take a look at some of their work; skimming is fine.) Write an essay in which you reflect on the use

Walker makes of writers and their writing. You might ask yourself how and where her use of the past is similar to or different from what you saw in Rodriguez or Benjamin. Can they provide useful points of reference as you think about (and write about) Alice Walker?

* * * * * * * * * * * *

Ways of Reading
[Bartholomae and Petrosky]

Reread the introduction to *Ways of Reading*. Given the work that you have done in this sequence, you are prepared to read it not as a simple statement of "how things are" but as a position taken in a tradition of concern over the role of reading in the preparation of Americans. Write an essay in which you consider the introduction in relation to Rodriguez, Hoggart, Benjamin, and the ways they articulate the proper uses of reading.

And what about you—do you see your own interests and concerns, the values you hold (or those held by people you admire), the abilities you might need or hope to gain—do you see these represented in what you have read?

SEQUENCE FOURTEEN

Ways of Seeing

John Berger
W. J. T. Mitchell

*T*HIS SEQUENCE works closely with John Berger's "Ways of Seeing" and his argument about the relationship between a spectator (one who sees and "reads" a painting) and knowledge, in his case a knowledge of history. The opening assignment asks for a summary account of Berger's argument. Assignment 2 then asks you to put Berger to the test by extending his project and producing a "reading" of a painting of your own choice. The third assignment turns again to Berger, this time to his use of paintings by Rembrandt and Caravaggio. You are asked in assignment 4 to turn to W. J. T. Mitchell's argument about words and images as a way of providing context to Berger (and an additional set of terms and concerns). The final assignment is a revision of your reading of a painting, this time with additional commentary to theorize and contextualize the work that you have done.

•   •   •   •   •   •   •   •   •   •   •

ASSIGNMENT 1

Ways of Seeing [Berger]

We are not saying that there is nothing left to experience before original works of art except a sense of awe because they have survived. The way original works of art are usually approached—through museum catalogues, guides, hired cassettes, etc.—is not the only way they might be approached. When the art of the past ceases to be viewed nostalgically, the works will cease to be holy relics—although they will never re-become what they were before the age of reproduction. We are not saying original works of art are now useless. (pp. 124–25)

— JOHN BERGER
Ways of Seeing

Berger argues that there are barriers to vision, problems in the ways we see or don't see original works of art, problems that can be located in and overcome by strategies of approach. For Berger, what we lose if we fail to see properly is history: "If we 'saw' the art of the past, we would situate ourselves in history. When we are prevented from seeing it, we are being deprived of the history which belongs to us" (p. 108). It is not hard to figure out who, according to Berger, prevents us from seeing the art of the past. He says it is the ruling class. It *is* difficult, however, to figure out what he believes gets in the way and what all this has to do with history.

For this assignment, write an essay explaining what, as you read Berger, gets in the way when we look at paintings, and what it is that we might do to overcome the barriers to vision (and to history). Imagine that you are writing for someone interested in art, perhaps preparing to go to a museum, but someone who has not read Berger's essay. You will, that is, need to be careful in summary and paraphrase.

· · · · · · · · · · ·

ASSIGNMENT 2

A Painting in Writing [Berger]

Original paintings are silent and still in a sense that information never is. Even a reproduction hung on a wall is not comparable in this respect for in the original the silence and stillness permeate the actual material, the paint, in which one follows the traces of the painter's immediate gestures. This has the effect of closing the distance in the time between the painting of the picture and one's own act of looking at it.... What we make of that painted moment when it is before our eyes depends upon what we expect of art, and that in turn depends today upon how we have already experienced the meaning of paintings through reproductions. (p. 125)

— JOHN BERGER
Ways of Seeing

While Berger describes original paintings as silent in this passage, it is clear that these paintings begin to speak if one approaches them properly, if one learns to ask "the right questions of the past." Berger demonstrates one route of approach, for example, in his reading of the Hals paintings, where he asks questions about the people and objects and their relationships to the painter and the viewer. What the paintings might be made to say, however, depends upon the viewer's expectations, his or her sense of the questions that seem appropriate or possible. Berger argues that, because of the way art is currently displayed, discussed, and reproduced, the viewer expects only to be mystified.

For this paper, imagine that you are working against the silence and mystification Berger describes. Go to a museum—or, if that is not possible, to a large-format book of reproductions in the library (or, if that is not possible, to the reproductions in this essay)—and select a painting that seems silent and still, yet invites conversation. Your job is to figure out what sorts of questions to ask, to interrogate the painting, to get it to speak, to engage with the past in some form of dialogue. Write an essay in which you record this process and what you have learned from it. Somewhere in your paper, perhaps at the end, turn back to Berger's essay and speak to it about how this process has or hasn't confirmed what you take to be Berger's expectations.

Note: If possible, include with your essay a reproduction of the painting you select. (Check the postcards at the museum gift shop.) In any event, you want to make sure that you describe the painting in sufficient detail for your readers to follow what you say.

● ● ● ● ● ● ● ● ● ● ●

ASSIGNMENT 3

Berger Writing [Berger]

If the new language of images were used differently, it would, through its use, confer a new kind of power. Within it we could begin to define our experiences more precisely in areas where words are inadequate. . . . Not only personal experience, but also the essential historical experience of our relation to the past: that is to say the experience of seeking to give meaning to our lives, of trying to understand the history of which we can become the active agents. (p. 127)

—JOHN BERGER
Ways of Seeing

As a writer, Berger is someone who uses images (including some of the great paintings of the Western tradition) "to define . . . experience more precisely in areas where words are inadequate."

In a wonderful book, *And Our Faces, My Heart, Brief as Photos,* a book that is both a meditation on time and space and a long love letter (if you can imagine such a combination), Berger writes about paintings to say what he wants to say to his lover. We have included two examples, descriptions of Rembrandt's *Woman in Bed* and Caravaggio's *The Calling of St. Matthew.*

Read these as examples, as lessons in how and why to look at, to value, to think with, to write about paintings. Then use these (or one of them) as a way of thinking about the concluding section of "Ways of Seeing" (pp. 125–27). You can assume that your readers have read Berger's essay but have difficulty grasping what he is saying in that final section, particularly since it is a section that seems to call for action, asking the reader to do something. Of what use might Berger's example be in trying to understand what we might do with and because of paintings? How is his writing different from yours? Would you attribute these differences to training and education? What else?

. . . .

ASSIGNMENT **4**

Picture Theory [Berger, Mitchell]

In "Ways of Seeing," John Berger says "original paintings are silent and still in a sense that information never is." Both Berger and W. J. T. Mitchell, in "The Photographic Essay: Four Case Studies," are interested in the use of images, what happens to them when they are packaged, deployed, reproduced, turned into text. For both, the use of images is a sign of the health of the individual and the health of the culture.

Write an essay in which you use Mitchell's essay to weigh, evaluate, and understand Berger, both the Berger of "Ways of Seeing" and the Berger who speaks for Rembrandt's *Woman in Bed* and Caravaggio's *The Calling of St. Matthew.* You will need, of course, to take time to summarize what Mitchell says and to establish his position on the relationship of words and images. And you will need to think (as Mitchell might think) about the difference between photographs and paintings and what is at stake in providing a written account of a painted image.

Once you have established his point of view, turn to Berger, particularly the example he provides of someone who places words next to images. Perhaps the questions to ask would be these: What relationship between painting and writing do [these examples] articulate? What tropes of differentiation govern the division of labor between photographer [or painter] and writer, image and text, the viewer and the reader?

• • • • • • • • • • • •

A S S I G N M E N T **5**

Revision [Mitchell, Berger]

For this assignment, go back to the essay you wrote for assignment 2, your representation of a painting, and revise it. You should imagine that your work is both the work of reconsideration (rethinking, looking again, changing what you have written) and addition (filling in the gaps, considering other positions and points of view, moving in new directions, completing what you have begun). As you do this work, you can draw on the comments you have received from your instructor and (perhaps) from other students in your class.

As you work on addition, please also add a section of commentary in which you bring Mitchell and Berger, their terms and arguments, to bear on what you have written. You can imagine that as part of your essay; or you can imagine it as a separate piece, as an introduction, afterword, or coda.

SEQUENCE FIFTEEN

Working with the Past

Richard Rodriguez and Richard Hoggart

Marianne Hirsch

Harriet Jacobs

Alice Walker

*T*HIS SEQUENCE takes a close and extended look at the relations between a writer and the past, including that part of the past which is represented by other books and by tradition and convention. The point of the sequence is to examine instances where authors directly or indirectly work under the influence of others. Much of the usual talk about "creativity" and "originality" hides the ways in which all texts allude to others, the ways all draw upon (and sometimes, revise) the work of the past. By erasing the past, readers give undue attention to an author's "genius" or independence, losing sight of the larger cultural and historical field within which (and sometimes against which) a writer works. (And, while this connection is not highlighted in the sequence, it is possible for you to see your own work with *Ways of Reading* mirrored in the work of these other writers. As you write in response to their work, they write in response to others'.)

The first assignment gives precise, material definition to the past, representing it in an extended passage from Richard Hoggart's *The Uses of Literacy*. Hoggart is a British cultural critic, the son of working class parents, who writes in the section included here about "the scholarship boy"—that is, the working class boy in a more elite educational environment. Richard Rodriguez, in "The Achievement of Desire," alludes to and quotes from this section of Hoggart's book. The assignment asks you to look at the larger text from which Rodriguez drew to ask questions about what he missed, what he left out, and how he read.

The next two assignments consider the "prior text" as something written more deeply, broadly, and generally into the culture and its memory. Marianne Hirsch writes, for example, about how memory is reproduced across generations. She argues that memory does not simply reside in individuals (stored in heads and hearts) or in institutional warehouses (libraries, museums, archives), but that memory is an active cultural project, one that represents our desire to link past and present.

The final three assignments work with Harriet Jacobs's autobiographical narrative, "Incidents in the Life of a Slave Girl," and Alice Walker's "In Search of Our Mothers' Gardens." Readers are often tempted to read the Jacobs narrative as, in a sense, coming from nowhere, since the stereotypical figure of the slave is of someone who cannot read and write. It is hard for readers to place Jacobs in relation to either slave culture or the culture of American literacy. These assignments ask you to imagine both Jacobs's representation of her own past through the collection of "incidents" that make up her narrative and her relationship to other texts, represented by the assumptions she makes about her readers and the way they will read. With Walker, we return to a more direct discussion of tradition and legacy, this time with particular reference to the legacy of African American women's writing.

This sequence is followed by a minisequence, "Working with the Past (II)," on page 904. This alternative sequence provides similar assignments but with different readings. They can be substituted for assignments in the first "Working with the Past" sequence.

• • • • • • • • • • • •

A S S I G N M E N T 1

The Scholarship Boy [Rodriguez, Hoggart]

At the end of this assignment, you will find an extended section from Richard Hoggart's *The Uses of Literacy*. This is the book Rodriguez found in the British Museum, the book he used, he says, to "frame the meaning of my academic success." The section here is the one that surrounds the passages Rodriguez cites in "The Achievement of Desire." Read the Hoggart excerpt and think about these questions: How might you compare Rodriguez's version of the "scholarship boy" with Hoggart's? How might you explain the importance of Hoggart's book to Rodriguez? What kind of reader is the Rodriguez who is writing "The Achievement of Desire"—is he still a "scholarship boy" or is that description no longer appropriate?

You could look at the relationship between Rodriguez and Hoggart as a case study in the possible relations between a writer and a prior text or between a student and a teacher. Read the two together, taking notes to assist such a comparative reading. As you read Rodriguez's discussion of Hoggart's book, pay attention to both the terms and passages Rodriguez selects and those he ignores, and pay attention to what Rodriguez *does* with what he selects. Look closely at how Rodriguez reads and presents Hoggart's text.

As you read Hoggart's account of the scholarship boy, try to read from outside Rodriguez's point of view. How else might these passages be read? In what ways might Hoggart be said to be saying what Rodriguez says he is saying? In what ways might he be said to be saying something else, something Rodriguez misses or ignores? In what ways might Hoggart be said to be making a different argument, telling a different story? What position or point of view or set of beliefs would authorize this other reading, the reading from outside Rodriguez's point of view? And, if you can establish this "alternative" reading, what does that tell you about the position or point of view or set of beliefs that authorize Rodriguez's use of the text?

As you prepare to write about Rodriguez's use of Hoggart, think about how you will describe his performance. What, for example, might you attribute to strategy, to Rodriguez's intent? What might you attribute to blindness (a failure to see or notice something in the text)? What might you attribute to the unconscious (a fear of the text, a form of repression, a desire to transform the text into something else)? These are conventional ways of telling the story of reading. What use are they to your project? Can you imagine others?

Write an essay in which you discuss Rodriguez as an example of a reader and writer working with a prior text. Your goal should be to understand Rodriguez and "The Achievement of Desire" better but also to think about the implications of his "case" for readers and writers in the undergraduate curriculum.

. . .

A Scholarship Boy

For my part I am very sorry for him. It is an uneasy lot at best, to be what we call highly taught and yet not to enjoy: to be present at this great spectacle of life and never to be liberated from a small hungry shivering self.

— GEORGE ELIOT

This is a difficult chapter to write, though one that should be written. As in other chapters, I shall be isolating a group of related trends: but the consequent dangers of over-emphasis are here especially acute. The three immediately preceding chapters have discussed attitudes which could from one point of view appear to represent a kind of poise. But the people most affected by the attitudes now to be examined—the "anxious and the uprooted"—are to be recognised primarily by their lack of poise, by their uncertainty. About the self-indulgences which seem to satisfy many in their class they tend to be unhappily superior: they are much affected by the cynicism which affects almost everyone, but this is likely to increase their lack of purpose rather than tempt them to "cash in" or to react into further indulgence.

In part they have a sense of loss which affects some in all groups. With them the sense of loss is increased precisely because they are emotionally uprooted from their class, often under the stimulus of a stronger critical intelligence or imagination, qualities which can lead them into an unusual self-consciousness before their own situation (and make it easy for a sympathiser to dramatise their *"Angst"*). Involved with this may be a physical uprooting from their class through the medium of the scholarship system. A great many seem to me to be affected in this way, though only a very small proportion badly; at one boundary the group includes psychotics; at the other, people leading apparently normal lives but never without an underlying sense of some unease.

It will be convenient to speak first of the nature of the uprooting which some scholarship boys experience. I have in mind those who, for a number of years, perhaps for a very long time, have a sense of no longer really belonging to any group. We all know that many do find a poise in their new situations. There are "declassed" experts and specialists who go into their own spheres after the long scholarship climb has led them to a Ph.D. There are brilliant individuals who become fine administrators and officials, and find themselves thoroughly at home. There are some, not necessarily so gifted, who reach a kind of poise which is yet not a passivity nor even a failure in awareness, who are at ease in their new group without any ostentatious adoption of the protective colouring of that group, and who have an easy relationship with their working-class relatives, based not on a form of patronage but on a just respect. Almost every working-class boy who goes through the process of further education by scholarships finds himself chafing against his environment during adolescence. He is at the friction-point of two cultures; the test of his real education lies in his ability, by about the age of twenty-five, to smile at his father with his whole face and to respect his flighty young sister and his slower brother. I shall be concerned with those for whom the uprooting is particularly troublesome, not because I underestimate the gains which this kind of selection gives, nor because I wish to stress the more depressing features in contemporary life, but because the difficulties of some people illuminate much in the wider discussion of cultural change. Like transplanted stock, they react to a widespread drought earlier than those who have been left in their original soil.

I am sometimes inclined to think that the problem of self-adjustment is, in general, especially difficult for those working-class boys who are only moderately endowed, who have talent sufficient to separate them from the majority of their working-class contemporaries, but not to go much farther. I am not implying a correlation between intelligence and lack of unease; intellectual people have their own troubles: but this kind of anxiety often seems most to afflict those in the working-classes who have been pulled one stage away from their original culture and yet have not the intellectual equipment which would then cause them to move on to join the "declassed" professionals and experts. In one sense, it is true, no one is ever "declassed"; and it is interesting to see how this occasionally obtrudes (particularly today, when ex-working-class boys move in all the managing areas of society)—in the touch of insecurity, which often appears as an undue concern to establish "presence" in an otherwise quite professional professor, in the intermittent rough homeliness of an important executive and committee-man, in the tendency to vertigo which betrays a lurking sense of uncertainty in a successful journalist.

But I am chiefly concerned with those who are self-conscious and yet not self-aware in any full sense, who are as a result uncertain, dissatisfied, and gnawed by self-doubt. Sometimes they lack will, though they have intelligence, and "it takes will to cross this waste." More often perhaps, though they have as much will as the majority, they have not sufficient to resolve the complex tensions which their uprooting, the peculiar problems of their particular domestic settings, and the uncertainties common to the time create.

As childhood gives way to adolescence and that to manhood, this kind of boy tends to be progressively cut off from the ordinary life of his group. He is marked out early: and here I am thinking not so much of his teachers in the "elementary" school as of fellow-members of his family. " 'E's got brains," or " 'E's bright," he hears constantly; and in part the tone is one of pride and admiration. He is in a way cut off by his parents as much as by his talent which urges him to break away from his group. Yet on their side this is not altogether from admiration: " 'E's got brains," yes, and he is expected to follow the trail that opens. But there can also be a limiting quality in the tone with which the phrase is used; character counts more. Still, he has brains—a mark of pride and almost a brand; he is heading for a different world, a different sort of job.

He has to be more and more alone, if he is going to "get on." He will have, probably unconsciously, to oppose the ethos of the hearth, the intense gregariousness of the working-class family group. Since everything centres upon the living-room, there is unlikely to be a room of his own; the bedrooms are cold and inhospitable, and to warm them or the front room, if there is one, would not only be expensive, but would require an imaginative leap—out of the tradition—which most families are not

capable of making. There is a corner of the living-room table. On the other
side Mother is ironing, the wireless is on, someone is singing a snatch of
song, or Father says intermittently whatever comes into his head. The boy
has to cut himself off mentally, so as to do his homework, as well as he
can. In summer, matters can be easier; bedrooms are warm enough to
work in: but only a few boys, in my experience, take advantage of this. For
the boy is himself (until he reaches, say, the upper forms) very much of
both the worlds of home and school. He is enormously obedient to the dictates of the world of school, but emotionally still strongly wants to continue as part of the family circle.

So the first big step is taken in the progress towards membership of a
different sort of group or to isolation, when such a boy has to resist the
central domestic quality of working-class life. This is true, perhaps particularly true, if he belongs to a happy home, because the happy homes are
often the more gregarious. Quite early the stress on solitariness, the encouragement towards strong self-concern, is felt; and this can make it
more difficult for him to belong to another group later.

At his "elementary" school, from as early as the age of eight, he is
likely to be in some degree set apart, though this may not happen if his
school is in an area which each year provides a couple of dozen boys from
"the scholarship form" for the grammar-schools. But probably he is in an
area predominantly working-class and his school takes up only a few
scholarships a year. The situation is altering as the number of scholarships
increases, but in any case human adjustments do not come as abruptly as
administrative changes.

He is similarly likely to be separated from the boys' groups outside the
home, is no longer a full member of the gang which clusters round the
lamp-posts in the evenings; there is homework to be done. But these are
the male groups among which others in his generation grew up, and his
detachment from them is emotionally linked with one more aspect of his
home situation—that he now tends to be closer to the women of the house
than to the men. This is true, even if his father is not the kind who dismisses books and reading as "a woman's game." The boy spends a large
part of his time at the physical centre of the home, where the woman's
spirit rules, quietly getting on with his work whilst his mother gets on
with her jobs—the father not yet back from work or out for a drink with
his mates. The man and the boy's brothers are outside, in the world of
men; the boy sits in the women's world. Perhaps this partly explains why
many authors from the working-classes, when they write about their
childhood, give the women in it so tender and central a place. There is
bound to be occasional friction, of course—when they wonder whether
the boy is "getting above himself," or when he feels a strong reluctance to
break off and do one of the odd jobs a boy is expected to do. But predominantly the atmosphere is likely to be intimate, gentle, and attractive. With
one ear he hears the women discussing their worries and ailments and
hopes, and he tells them at intervals about his school and the work and

what the master said. He usually receives boundless uncomprehending sympathy: he knows they do not understand, but still he tells them; he would like to link the two environments.

This description simplifies and overstresses the break; in each individual case there will be many qualifications. But in presenting the isolation in its most emphatic form the description epitomises what is very frequently found. For such a boy is between two worlds, the worlds of school and home; and they meet at few points. Once at the grammar-school, he quickly learns to make use of a pair of different accents, perhaps even two different apparent characters and differing standards of value. Think of his reading-material, for example: at home he sees strewn around and reads regularly himself, magazines which are never mentioned at school, which seem not to belong to the world to which the school introduces him; at school he hears about and reads books never mentioned at home. When he brings those books into the house they do not take their place with other books which the family are reading, for often there are none or almost none; his books look, rather, like strange tools.

He will perhaps, especially today, escape the worst immediate difficulties of his new environment, the stigma of cheaper clothes, of not being able to afford to go on school-holiday trips, of parents who turn up for the grammar-school play looking shamefully working-class. But as a grammar-school boy, he is likely to be anxious to do well, to be accepted or even to catch the eye as he caught the eye, because of his brains, at the "elementary" school. For brains are the currency by which he has bought his way, and increasingly brains seem to be the currency that tells. He tends to make his schoolmasters over-important, since they are the cashiers in the new world of brain-currency. In his home-world his father is still his father; in the other world of school his father can have little place: he tends to make a father-figure of his form-master.

Consequently, even though his family may push him very little, he will probably push himself harder than he should. He begins to see life, for as far as he can envisage it, as a series of hurdle-jumps, the hurdles of scholarships which are won by learning how to amass and manipulate the new currency. He tends to over-stress the importance of examinations, of the piling-up of knowledge and of received opinions. He discovers a technique of apparent learning, of acquiring of facts rather than of the handling and use of facts. He learns how to receive a purely literate education, one using only a small part of the personality and challenging only a limited area of his being. He begins to see life as a ladder, as a permanent examination with some praise and some further exhortation at each stage. He becomes an expert imbiber and doler-out; his competence will vary, but will rarely be accompanied by genuine enthusiasms. He rarely feels the reality of knowledge, of other men's thoughts and imaginings, on his own pulses; he rarely discovers an author for himself and on his own. In this half of his life he can respond only if there is a direct connection with the system of training. He has something of the blinkered pony about him;

sometimes he is trained by those who have been through the same regimen, who are hardly unblinkered themselves, and who praise him in the degree to which he takes comfortably to their blinkers. Though there is a powerful, unidealistic, unwarmed realism about his attitude at bottom, that is his chief form of initiative; of other forms—the freely-ranging mind, the bold flying of mental kites, the courage to reject some "lines" even though they are officially as important as all the rest—of these he probably has little, and his training does not often encourage them. This is not a new problem; Herbert Spencer spoke of it fifty years ago: but it still exists: "The established systems of education, whatever their matter may be, are fundamentally vicious in their manner. They encourage *submissive receptivity* instead of *independent activity*."

There is too little stress on action, on personal will and decision; too much goes on in the head, with the rather-better-than-normal intellectual machine which has brought him to his grammar-school. And because so often the "good" boy, the boy who does well, is the one who with his conscientious passivity meets the main demand of his new environment, he gradually loses spontaneity so as to acquire examination-passing reliability. He can snap his fingers at no one and nothing; he seems set to make an adequate, reliable, and unjoyous kind of clerk. He has been too long "afraid of all that has to be obeyed." Hazlitt, writing at the beginning of the nineteenth century, made a wider and more impassioned judgment on trends in his society; but it has some relevance here and now:

> Men do not become what by nature they are meant to be, but what society makes them. The generous feelings, and high propensities of the soul are, as it were, shrunk up, seared, violently wrenched, and amputated, to fit us for our intercourse with the world, something in the manner that beggars maim and mutilate their children, to make them fit for their future situation in life.

Such a scholarship boy has lost some of the resilience and some of the vitality of his cousins who are still knocking about the streets. In an earlier generation, as one of the quicker-witted persons born into the working-classes, he would in all probability have had those wits developed in the jungle of the slums, where wit had to ally itself to energy and initiative. He plays little on the streets; he does not run round delivering newspapers: his sexual growth is perhaps delayed. He loses something of the gamin's resilience and carelessness, of his readiness to take a chance, of his perkiness and boldness, and he does not acquire the unconscious confidence of many a public-school-trained child of the middle-classes. He has been trained like a circus-horse, for scholarship winning.

As a result, when he comes to the end of the series of set-pieces, when he is at last put out to raise his eyes to a world of tangible and unaccommodating things, of elusive and disconcerting human beings, he finds himself with little inner momentum. The driving-belt hangs loosely, disconnected from the only machine it has so far served, the examination-passing machine. He finds difficulty in choosing a direction in the world where there is no longer a master to please, a toffee-apple at the end of each stage, a certificate, a place in the upper half of the assessable world. He is unhappy in a society which presents largely a picture of disorder, which is huge and sprawling, not limited, ordered, and centrally-heated; in which the toffee-apples are not accurately given to those who work hardest nor even to the most intelligent: but in which disturbing imponderables like "character," "pure luck," "ability to mix," and "boldness" have a way of tipping the scales.

His condition is made worse because the whole trend of his previous training has made him care too much for marked and ticketed success. This world, too, cares much for recognisable success, but does not distribute it along the lines on which he has been trained to win it. He would be happier if he cared less, if he could blow the gaff for himself on the world's success values. But they too closely resemble the values of school; to reject them he would have first to escape the inner prison in which the school's tabulated rules for success have immured him.

He does not wish to accept the world's criterion—get on at any price (though he has an acute sense of the importance of money). But he has been equipped for hurdle-jumping; so he merely dreams of getting-on, but somehow not in the world's way. He has neither the comforts of simply accepting the big world's values, nor the recompense of feeling firmly critical towards them.

He has moved away from his "lower" origins, and may move farther. If so, he is likely to be nagged underneath by a sense of how far he has come, by the fear and shame of a possible falling-back. And this increases his inability to leave himself alone. Sometimes the kind of job he gets only increases this slightly dizzy sense of still being on the ladder; unhappy on it, but also proud and, in the nature of his condition, usually incapable of jumping-off, of pulling-out of that particular race:

> Pale, shabby, tightly strung, he had advanced from post to post in his insurance office with the bearing of a man about to be discharged. . . . Brains had only meant that he must work harder in the elementary school than those born free of them. At night he could still hear the malicious chorus telling him that he was a favourite of the master. . . . Brains, like a fierce heat, had turned the world to a desert round him, and across the sands in the occasional mirage he saw the stupid crowds, playing, laughing, and without thought enjoying the tenderness, the compassion, the companionship of love.

That is over-dramatised, not applicable to all or even to most—but in some way affecting many. It affects also that larger group, to which I now turn, of those who in some ways ask questions of themselves about their society, who are because of this, even though they may never have been to grammar-schools, "between two worlds, one dead, the other powerless to be born." They are the "private faces in public places" among the working-classes; they are Koestler's "thoughtful corporals"; they are among those, though not the whole of those, who take up many kinds of self-improvement. They may be performing any kind of work, from manual labour to teaching; but my own experience suggests that they are to be found frequently among minor clerks and similarly black-coated workers, and among elementary school-teachers, especially in the big cities. Often their earnestness for improvement shows itself as an urge to act like some people in the middle-classes; but this is not a political betrayal: it is much nearer to a mistaken idealism.

This kind of person, and we have seen that this is his first great loss, belongs now to no class, usually not even to what is called, loosely enough, the "classless intelligentsia." He cannot face squarely his own working-class, for that, since the intuitive links have gone, would require a greater command in facing himself than he is capable of. Sometimes he is ashamed of his origins; he has learned to "turn up his nose," to be a bit superior about much in working-class manners. He is often not at ease about his own physical appearance which speaks too clearly of his birth; he feels uncertain or angry inside when he realises that that, and a hundred habits of speech and manners, can "give him away" daily. He tends to visit his own sense of inadequacy upon the group which fathered him; and he provides himself with a mantle of defensive attitudes. Thus he may exhibit an unconvincing pride in his own gaucheness at practical things—"brain-workers" are never "good with their hands." Underneath he knows that his compensatory claim to possess finer weapons, to be able to handle "book-knowledge," is insecurely based. He tries to read all the good books, but they do not give him that power of speech and command over experience which he seeks. He is as gauche there as with the craftsman's tools.

He cannot go back; with one part of himself he does not want to go back to a homeliness which was often narrow: with another part he longs for the membership he has lost, "he pines for some Nameless Eden where he never was." The nostalgia is the stronger and the more ambiguous because he is really "in quest of his own absconded self yet scared to find it." He both wants to go back and yet thinks he has gone beyond his class, feels himself weighted with knowledge of his own and their situation, which hereafter forbids him the simpler pleasures of his father and mother. And this is only one of his temptations to self-dramatisation.

If he tries to be "pally" with working-class people, to show that he is one of them, they "smell it a mile off." They are less at ease with him than with some in other classes. With them they can establish and are prepared to honour, seriously or as a kind of rather ironical game, a formal relationship; they "know where they are with them." But they can immediately detect the uncertainty in his attitudes, that he belongs neither to them nor to one of the groups with which they are used to performing a hierarchical play of relations; the odd man out is still the odd man out.

He has left his class, at least in spirit, by being in certain ways unusual; and he is still unusual in another class, too tense and overwound. Sometimes the working-classes and the middle-classes can laugh together. He rarely laughs; he smiles constrainedly with the corner of his mouth. He is usually ill at ease with the middle-classes because with one side of himself he does not want them to accept him; he mistrusts or even a little despises them. He is divided here as in so many other ways. With one part of himself he admires much he finds in them: a play of intelligence, a breadth of outlook, a kind of style. He would like to be a citizen of that well-polished, prosperous, cool, book-lined, and magazine-discussing world of the successful intelligent middle-class which he glimpses through doorways or feels awkward among on short visits, aware of his grubby finger-nails. With another part of himself he develops an asperity towards that world: he turns up his nose at its self-satisfactions, its earnest social concern, its intelligent coffee-parties, its suave sons at Oxford, and its Mrs. Miniverish or Mrs. Ramseyish cultural pretensions. He is rather over-ready to notice anything which can be regarded as pretentious or fanciful, anything which allows him to say that these people do not know what life is really like. He wavers between scorn and longing.

— RICHARD HOGGART
The Uses of Literacy (1957)

.   .   .   .

A S S I G N M E N T   2

Projected Memory [Hirsch]

As its title indicates, Hirsch's essay is about "projected memory" and it is about "holocaust photographs in personal and public fantasy." It is not presented in the style of thesis, example, and conclusion. There is neither a conventional introduction nor a conventional summing up. The arguments and demonstrations in between are rich, varied, and complex.

What, so far as you are concerned, is this essay about? And how does it speak to you—to your interests, concerns, projects, and to your education? Write an essay, perhaps in the genre of a review, in which you present "Projected Memory: Holocaust Photographs in Personal and Public Fantasy" to those who have not yet read it. You will need to take care to give a thorough and accurate account of what Hirsch says and does. You should also establish your position in relation to the essay, discussing where and how you found it useful or interesting.

• • • • • • • • • • • •

A S S I G N M E N T **3**

The Project of Postmemory [Hirsch]

The project of postmemory can be a writing project. In fact, to describe the individual's active engagement with the past that *is* postmemory, Hirsch uses metaphors of writing (or inscription):

> It is a question of adopting the traumatic experiences—and thus also the memories—of others as one's own, or, more precisely, as experiences one might oneself have had, and of inscribing them into one's own life story. It is a question of conceiving oneself as multiply interconnected with others of the same, of previous, and of subsequent generations, of the same and of other—proximate or distant—cultures and subcultures. (p. 407)

Use "Projected Memory" as invitation to such a writing project, where you would write about a past that belongs to you but that is not yours. Hirsch is interested in stories of trauma and suffering. And there is, to be sure, much at stake (and much to be gained) by writing about the traumas that preoccupy us as a culture. You should not, however, feel that you must write about a traumatic past. You should write about what you have at hand—connections to the past through family, neighborhood, or (as Hirsch says) "group relation"—and as those memories can be prompted, assisted, and mediated by some documentary or photographic record (as in the case of the photos in "Projected Memory" and the story of Anne Frank for Rymkiewicz and Agosín). The past that you are tied to need not necessarily have national or international significance. The importance is that you can identify yourself with this past and with these memories (and that you can inscribe them into your own life story).

Since we are using Hirsch to invite you to write about the past, it is important to note where and how she identifies the problems that accompany such a task. It comes in the distinction she makes between "idiopathic" and "heteropathic" identification; her concern is cliché, sentimental, a too-easy identification with that which is beyond you, even incomprehensible. She says,

> The challenge for the postmemorial artist is precisely to find the balance that allows the spectator [the reader] to enter the

image, to imagine the disaster, but that disallows an overappropriate identification that makes the distances disappear, creating too available, too easy an access to this particular past. (p. 408)

• • • • • • • • • • •

ASSIGNMENT 4

A Life Story [Jacobs]

By creating a narrator who presents her private sexual history as a subject of public political concern, Jacobs moves her book out of the world of conventional nineteenth-century polite discourse. In and through her creation of Linda Brent, who yokes her success story as a heroic slave mother to her confession as a woman who mourns that she is not a storybook heroine, Jacobs articulates her struggle to assert her womanhood and projects a new kind of female hero.

—JEAN FAGIN YELLIN
"Introduction," *Incidents in the Life of a Slave Girl*

In an essay titled "The Voice of the Southern Slave," literary critic Houston Baker says,

The voice of the unwritten self, once it is subjected to the linguistic codes, literary conventions, and audience expectations of a literate population, is perhaps never again the authentic voice of black American slavery. It is, rather, the voice of a self transformed by an autobiographical act into a sharer in the general public discourse about slavery.

This voice shares not only in the general public discourse about slavery but also in the general public discourse representing family, growing up, love, marriage, virtue, childbirth. It shares in the discourse of "normal" life—that is, life outside of slavery. For a slave, the self and its relations to others had a different public construction. A slave was property. A mother didn't have the right to her children, a woman to her body. While some may say that this was true generally of women in the nineteenth century (and the twentieth), slavery enacted and enforced the most extreme social reservations about a woman's rights and selfhood.

The passage from Baker's essay allows us to highlight the gap between a life and a narrative, between a person (Harriet Jacobs) and a person rendered on the page (Linda Brent), between the experience of slavery and the conventional ways of telling the story of life, between experience and the ways experience is shaped by a writer, readers, and a culture.

Write an essay in which you examine Jacobs's work as a writer. Consider the ways she works on her reader (a figure she both imagines and constructs) and also the ways she works on her material (a set of experiences but also a language and the story and conventional ways of representing a young woman's life). Where *is* Jacobs in this text? What is her work? What can you say about the sources of her work, the models or conventions it draws upon, deploys, or transforms? The narrative was written in retrospect when Jacobs was older and free, as a series of incidents. You can read the text as a writer's reconstruction of the past. What can you say about the ways Jacobs, as a writer, works with the past?

•   •   •   •   •   •   •   •   •   •   •   •

A S S I G N M E N T   **5**

Working with the Past [Walker]

In her essay "In Search of Our Mothers' Gardens," Walker views the "creative spirit" of African American women as a legacy passed down from generation to generation, in spite of societal barriers:

> Our mothers and grandmothers, some of them: moving to music not yet written. And they waited . . . for a day when the unknown thing that was in them would be made known; but guessed, somehow in their darkness, that on the day of their revelation they would be long dead. (p. 740)

Walker (much like Rodriguez, who "borrows" from Hoggart) uses Virginia Woolf's term "contrary instincts" to explain this legacy. And her essay is filled with passages from other texts. How does she use these? Why? What is the relationship of the "creative spirit" to the work of the past, at least as that relationship is both argued and represented in Walker's prose?

Write an essay in which you discuss Walker's project as a "creative" endeavor. What work does she do when she borrows the term "contrary instincts" from Woolf? What about the other allusions to the past, to texts written and unwritten? How might you characterize this work? Taking Walker's position as an African American artist of today into consideration, how might this essay be read as part of the tradition of creativity she charts? How might it be read as part of a tradition? How might it be read as an example of "creativity"? Or, to pose the question in different terms, what might you say Walker "creates" as she writes this essay?

. . . .

A S S I G N M E N T **6**

Legacies [Walker, Jacobs]

Walker's reading of the history of African American women focuses on the "creative spirit" of these women in the face of oppression. Of her mother, Walker writes:

> Her face, as she prepares the Art that is her gift, is a legacy of respect she leaves to me, for all that illuminates and cherishes life. She has handed down respect for the possibilities—and the will to grasp them. (p. 746)

And to the poet Phillis Wheatley, she writes,

> But at last, Phillis, we understand. No more snickering when your stiff, struggling, ambivalent lines are forced on us. We know now that you were not an idiot or a traitor; only a sickly little black girl, snatched from your home and country and made a slave; a woman who still struggled to sing the song that was your gift, although in a land of barbarians who praised you for your bewildered tongue. It is not so much what you sang, as that you kept alive, in so many of our ancestors, *the notion of song.* (p. 743)

Although Walker chooses to focus on artists other than Harriet Jacobs in her essay, one could imagine ways in which Jacobs's example is appropriate to Walker's discussion of African American women's creativity.

Write an essay in which you extend Walker's project by considering how and where Jacobs's work as a writer would or would not serve Walker's argument. You can draw on the essays you wrote for assignments 4 and 5 for this essay, but you should treat them as material for a revision. You should reread Jacobs, and you should reread your essay with a mind to sections that you can rework. What legacy might Jacobs be said to create? What kind of example might she provide? How would it serve or alter Walker's argument? Why might Jacobs be overlooked?

SEQUENCE SIXTEEN

Working with the Past (II)

Alice Munro

James Baldwin

Edward Said

Walter Benjamin

*T*HIS SEQUENCE provides a variation on sequence fifteen. For a full description of the rationale behind the sequence, see the introduction to sequence fifteen (p. 889).

• • • • • • • • • • •

ASSIGNMENT 1

The Albanian Virgin [Munro]

The story "The Albanian Virgin" is arranged in pieces, or fragments. As a reader works through them, they become two story lines: one set in the 1920s in Albania, on the Dalmatian coast; the other is set in the 1960s in Canada, on the Pacific coast. The first story, about a woman called Lottar, is told by Charlotte to Claire; the second is told by Claire to us (and, we learn, includes all these stories). But it takes some time for the pattern to establish itself and we might be lost or confused. As you reread, pay attention to how Munro handles, or orchestrates, the unfolding. How does she position the reader? How does she organize our attention and allow us access to the two story lines? How would you explain or define her strategy?

One effect of the two story lines is to place past against present,

Charlotte's story (Lottar's story) next to Claire's. To what effect? To what ends? Write an essay in which you discuss the presence of the past in "The Albanian Virgin." How does the story position you in relation to Charlotte and Claire, past and present? How does the story want us to think about the two?

• • • • • • • • • • •

ASSIGNMENT **2**

Notes of a Native Son [Baldwin]

In "Notes of a Native Son," Baldwin says this about the eulogy at his father's funeral:

> Every man in the chapel hoped that when his hour came he, too, would be eulogized, which is to say forgiven, and that all of his lapses, greeds, errors, and strayings from the truth would be invested with coherence and looked upon with charity. This was perhaps the last thing human beings could give each other and it was what they demanded, after all, of the Lord. (p. 63)

At this moment in the essay a reader is invited to think about "Notes of a Native Son." It is not a eulogy, at least not technically, since it was written long after the funeral and not read at the ceremony. The essay is, among other things, a son's public account of his father.

Write an essay in which you contextualize, examine, and explain Baldwin's representation of his father in "Notes of a Native Son." What does Baldwin say, in the end, about his father? How are we asked to understand this man in relation to his family? to history? What use is Baldwin making of his father and his story? How does this serve his attempt to understand past and present?

• • • • • • • • • • •

ASSIGNMENT **3**

States [Said]

The first three paragraphs in this essay provide a "reading" of the opening photograph, "Tripoli, Badawi camp, May 1983." Or, to put it another way, the writing evolves from and is in response to that photograph.

As you reread these paragraphs, pay close attention to what Said is doing, to what he notices, to what prompts or requires commentary. How would you describe and explain the writing that follows? What is he doing with the photo? What is he doing as a writer? What is he doing for a reader? (How does he position a reader?)

It might be useful to begin by thinking about what he is *not* doing. It is not, for example, the presentation one might expect in a slide show on travel in Lebanon. Nor is it the kind of presentation one might expect while seeing the slides of family or friends, or slides in an art history or art appreciation class.

Once you have worked through the opening three paragraphs, reread the essay paying attention to Said's work with all the photographs. Is there a pattern? Do any of the commentaries stand out for their force, variety, innovation?

Write an essay in which you discuss Said's use of the photographs. How does he define a relationship to the Palestinians and their history? How is it defined for him? How is it defined for us?

• • • • • • • • • • •

ASSIGNMENT 4

The Work of Art in the Age of Mechanical Reproduction [Benjamin]

Benjamin writes in 1936. He is not a visionary and he is not writing science fiction and so he does not imagine all the developments in technical reproduction (and the developmental tendencies of art) that are present in our own historical moment. He is, however, trying to imagine the age in which we continue to live, the age of mechanical reproduction.

Write an essay in which you extend "The Work of Art in the Age of Mechanical Reproduction" into the twenty-first century. You should focus your work in a single area: film and video, painting, architecture, music, or literature and writing. You will need to provide a careful account of Benjamin's argument, focusing close attention on a particular discussion of your genre.

Once you have provided the Benjaminian background, you can see what happens as you work forward to the present time. You can imagine that you are extending Benjamin's work, that you are in conversation with it, or that you are putting him to the test. How does he imagine (and invite you to imagine) the continuity between his time and ours?

Writing History

Patricia Nelson Limerick
Jane Tompkins

*T*HIS SHORT SEQUENCE has two goals: to present two views of the "problem of history" (the problem of representing and understanding the past) and to use these accounts as an introduction to academic life (or to the forms of theorizing particular to that branch of the academy preoccupied by the problems of understanding the past). The first two assignments ask you to translate articles by Patricia Nelson Limerick and Jane Tompkins for an audience of beginning undergraduates. Your goal is to teach your audience something about the essays but also to use the essays as an introduction to the ways academics think and work. The final assignment asks you to write a short history (a local, family, or neighborhood history) and to think about your work in the context of problems of method presented by Limerick and Tompkins. You are working as a novice; they are working as professionals. The questions the sequence ends with are these: What would Limerick and Tompkins have to say to you about your work? What do you have to say to them about theirs?

· · · · · · · · · · · ·

ASSIGNMENT 1

Haunted America [Limerick]

In her essay "Haunted America," Patricia Nelson Limerick presents episodes from the history of the American West, and she thinks out loud about history as something written (about the problems of history as reading and writing problems). In it, Limerick offers criticism and advice, an account of the problems of western history and how they might be addressed (problems of narrative, detail, and point of view, for example). As you reread, look for passages that define both the problems and the possible solutions for those who read and write about the past.

Write an essay in which you present Limerick's account of the problems of history to a novice, someone new to Limerick and new to the academy. You should assume that your reader has not read the selection in this textbook—you will, that is, need to set the scene, to summarize, paraphrase, quote, and explain. Your goal is to give your reader not only a sense of what Limerick says but also an idea of why it might be important to a student in the early stages of a college or university career.

· · · · · · · · · · · ·

A S S I G N M E N T **2**

"Indians" [Tompkins]

In "Indians," Tompkins offers her experience researching and writing about Native Americans in colonial America as a representative case. Her story is meant to highlight a problem central to teaching, learning, and research—central, that is, to academic life. As a student, you can read this essay as a way of looking in on the work and concerns of your faculty (a group represented not only by Tompkins but by those against whom she is arguing). Write an essay directed to someone who has not read "Indians," someone who will be entering your school as a first-year student next semester. Your job is to introduce an incoming freshman to the academy, using Tompkins as your guide. (Since you've already written about Limerick, and since you can assume that the same readers will read both essays, you can bring Limerick in as a point of reference or comparison.) You will need to present Tompkins's argument and her conclusion in such a way as to make clear the consequences of what she says for someone about to begin an undergraduate education.

. . . .

ASSIGNMENT **3**

Writing History [Limerick, Tompkins]

One way to work on these selections is to take the challenge and write history—to write the kind of history, that is, that takes into account the problems defined by Limerick and Tompkins: the problems of myth, point of view, fixed ideas, facts and perspective, morality. You are not a professional historian, you are probably not using this book in a history course, and you probably don't have the time to produce a carefully researched history, one that covers all the bases, but you can think of this as an exercise in history writing, a minihistory, a place to start. Here are two options:

1. Go to your college library or, perhaps, the local historical society and find two or three first-person accounts of a single place, person, or event in your community. Try to work with original documents. The more varied the accounts, the better. Then, working with these texts as your primary sources, write a history, one that you can offer as a response to Limerick and Tompkins.
2. While you can find materials in a library, you can also work with records that are closer to home. Imagine, for example, that you are going to write a family or a neighborhood history. You have your own memories and experiences to work from, but for this to be a history (and not a "personal essay"), you will need to turn to other sources as well: interviews, old photos, newspaper clippings, letters, diaries—whatever you can find. After gathering your materials, write a family or neighborhood history, one that you can offer as a response to Limerick and Tompkins.

Choose one of the two projects. When you are done, write a quick one-page memo to the experts, Limerick and Tompkins. What can you tell them about the experience of a novice historian that they might find useful or interesting?

Writing Projects

Edward Said

Alice Munro

James Baldwin

Adrienne Rich

*T*HE PURPOSE of this sequence is to invite you to work closely with pieces of writing that call attention to themselves as writing, that make visible writing as a problem, a fundamental problem of representation and understanding. The five assignments that follow bring together works of nonfiction that question their ability to represent the "real." The opening assignments direct your work with those readings. While you will be writing separate essays, you can choose to work on related subject matter. (The projects can become pieces of something larger, in other words.) Connecting the essays is not necessary, however. (Some students, in fact, have found this to be a burden.) The final assignment asks you to revise and to reflect on the work you have done.

· · · · · · · · · ·

ASSIGNMENT 1

Words and Images [Said]

The first three paragraphs of Edward Said's essay "States" provide a "reading" of the opening photograph, "Tripoli, Badawi camp, May 1983." Or, to put it another way, the writing evolves from and is in response to that photograph. As a way of preparing for this assignment, reread these paragraphs and pay close attention to what Said is doing, to what he notices, to what prompts or requires commentary. How would you describe and explain the writing that follows? What is he doing with the photo? What is he doing as a writer? What is he doing for a reader? (How does he position a reader?)

It might be useful to begin by thinking about what he is *not* doing. It is not, for example, the presentation one might expect in a slide show on travel in Lebanon. Nor is it the kind of presentation one might expect while seeing the slides of family or friends, or slides in an art history or art appreciation class.

Once you have worked through the opening three paragraphs, reread the essay paying attention to Said's work with all the photographs. Is there a pattern? Do any of the commentaries stand out for their force, variety, innovation?

For this assignment, compose a similar project, a Said-like reading of a set of photos. These can be photos prepared for the occasion (by you or a colleague); they could also be photos already available. Whatever their source, they should represent people and places, a history and/or geography that you know well, that you know to be complex and contradictory, and that you know will not be easily or readily understood by others, both the group for whom you will be writing (most usefully the members of your class) and readers more generally.

You must begin with a sense that the photos cannot speak for themselves—you must speak for them.

• • • • • • • • • • •

ASSIGNMENT 2

Story Lines [Munro]

"The Albanian Virgin" is arranged in pieces, or fragments. As a reader works through them, they become two story lines: one set in the 1920s in Albania, on the Dalmatian coast; the other is set in the 1960s in Canada, on the Pacific coast. The first story, about a woman called Lottar, is told by Charlotte to Claire; the second is told by Claire to us (and, we learn, includes all these stories). But it takes some time for the pattern to establish itself and we might be lost at first, or confused.

Try your hand at writing a story like this one. You can imagine that you are writing fiction, or you can imagine that you are writing a memoir, or any story drawn from life that has (or could have) two story lines. You should begin by rereading "The Albanian Virgin" and thinking about how

Munro accomplishes what she does. (The first two "Questions for a Second Reading" [pp. 583–84] provide a way of rereading with this thought in mind.) You should try to catch the rhythm and swing of the arrangement in her story, to control your reader's attention in a similar way, and to put the two story lines to work in a similar fashion.

•   •   •   •   •   •   •   •   •   •   •   •   •

A S S I G N M E N T   3

Writing the Present [Baldwin]

Irving Howe, a distinguished writer and critic, said that Baldwin brought a "new luster" to the essay as an art form, "a form with possibilities for discursive reflection and concrete drama." And, he said, "The style of these essays is a remarkable instance of the way in which a grave and sustained eloquence . . . can be employed in an age deeply suspicious of rhetorical prowess."

"Discursive reflection and concrete drama." "Notes of a Native Son" is a mix of narrative (or story) and argument (or commentary). This is not the kind of argument that works from thesis statement through example to conclusion. It works slowly, indirectly, by accretion and apposition, and with a careful, determined attention to detail. As a way of rereading Baldwin's essay, write a Baldwin-like essay of your own.

This is an invitation to carry out a similar project, one that reproduces his method and style, extends his example to a new set of materials. You can choose any subject (or person, or occurrence) as your narrative center; your goal should be to connect the local with the national, to correct personal history with larger issues or concerns, and to use concrete drama as the occasion for discursive reflection. It is also an invitation to formal experimentation, to try out Baldwin-like sentences, paragraphs, and chapters (or subsections).

•   •   •   •   •   •   •   •   •   •   •   •   •

A S S I G N M E N T   4

A Project [Rich]

I have hesitated to do what I am going to do now, which is to use myself as an illustration. For one thing, it's a lot easier and less dangerous to talk about other[s]. (p. 631)

> Until we can understand the assumptions in which we are
> drenched we cannot know ourselves. (p. 629)

Although Rich tells a story of her own, she does so to provide an illustration of an even larger story—one about what it means to be a woman and a writer. Tell a story of your own about the ways you might be said to have been named or shaped or positioned by an established and powerful culture. Like Rich does (and perhaps with similar hesitation), use your own experience as an illustration, as a way of investigating both your own situation and the situation of people like you. You should imagine that this assignment is a way for you to use (and put to the test) some of Rich's terms, words like "re-vision," "renaming," and "structure." You might also want to consider defining key terms specific to your story (for Rich, for example, a defining term is "patriarchy").

• • • • • • • • • • • •

ASSIGNMENT 5

Commentary [Said, Munro, Baldwin, Rich]

This is the final assignment in the sequence. It is the occasion for you to revise and reflect on the assignments on which you have worked. Gather the writing you have prepared into a folder. These may be chapters in a linked piece; they may be separate pieces collected as part of a more general project on writing and representation.

Write a brief essay in which you comment on the work you have done, perhaps on its reception by others in your class, and through it to your work as a writer in relation to the work of Said, Munro, Baldwin, and Rich.

You could think of this essay as a kind of introduction or afterword to the work in your folder. Or you could think of it as a plan for revision. You could also think of it as the occasion to write about the relationship of this kind of writing to the world you imagine outside this classroom—the world of work, the rest of the curriculum, the community, the circle of family, lovers, and friends

(continued from p. iv)

John Berger, "Ways of Seeing." From *Ways of Seeing* by John Berger. Copyright © 1972 by Penguin Books Ltd. Used by permission of Viking Penguin, a division of Penguin Putnam, Inc. "On Rembrandt's 'Woman in Bed'" and "On Caravaggio's 'The Calling of St. Matthew.'" From *And Our Faces, My Heart, Brief as Photos* by John Berger. Copyright © 1984 by John Berger. Reprinted by permission of Pantheon Books, a division of Random House, Inc. Botticelli, "Venus and Mars"; Leonardo da Vinci, "Virgin of the Rocks" and "The Virgin and Child with St. Anne and St. John the Baptist. Alinari/Art Resource, New York. Reproduced by courtesy of the Trustees, The National Gallery, London. Leonardo da Vinci, "Virgin of the Rocks." Scala/Art Resource, NY. Pierre Bourdieu and Alain Darbel, from *L'Amour de l'Art*. Reprinted by permission of Éditions de Minuit. Peter Breughel the Elder, "The Procession to Calvary." Erich Lessing/Art Resource, NY. Details of Peter Breughel the Elder, "The Procession to Calvary." Erich Lessing/Art Resource, NY. Frans Hals, "Regents of the Old Men's Alms House" and "Regentesses of the Old Men's Alms House." Reprinted by permission of Frans Halsmuseum. Vincent Van Gogh, "Wheatfield with Crows." Amsterdam, Van Gogh Museum (Vincent Van Gogh Foundation). Jan Vermeer, "The Kitchenmaid." Rijksmuseum, Amsterdam. Rembrandt, "Woman in Bed." Reprinted with permission of the National Galleries of Scotland. Caravaggio, "The Calling of St. Matthew." Scala/Art Resource, NY.

Susan Bordo, "Hunger as Ideology." From *Unbearable Weight: Feminism, Western Culture, and the Body* by Susan Bordo. Copyright © 1993 The Regents of the University of California Press. Used by permission.

Robert Coles, "The Tradition: Fact and Fiction." From *Doing Documentary Work* by Robert Coles. Copyright © 1997 by Robert Coles. Used by permission of Oxford University Press, Inc. Lange and Evans photographs courtesy of the Library of Congress.

Michel Foucault, "Panopticism." From *Discipline and Punish* (New York: Pantheon Books, 1977). Originally published in French as *Surveiler et Punir* by Alan Sheridan. Reprinted by permission of Georges Borchardt, Inc. *L'art d'écrire* engraved by Prévost, from *L'Encyclopédie*, 1763. Musée National de l'Education—I.N.R.P.-Rouen.

Paulo Freire, "The 'Banking' Concept of Education." From *Pedagogy of the Oppressed* by Paulo Freire. Copyright © 1970, 1993 by Paulo Freire. Reprinted by permission of The Continuum Publishing Company.

Simon Frith, "The Voice." Reprinted by permission of the publisher from *Performing Rites: On The Value of Popular Music* by Simon Frith (Cambridge, Mass: Harvard University Press). Copyright © 1996 by Simon Frith.

Clifford Geertz, "Deep Play: Notes on the Balinese Cockfight." Reprinted by permission of *Daedalus*, Journal of the American Academy of Arts and Sciences, from the issue titled "Myth, Symbol, and Culture," Winter 1972, vol. 101, no. 1.

Susan Griffin, "Our Secret." From *A Chorus of Stones* by Susan Griffin. Copyright © 1992 by Susan Griffin. Used by permission of Doubleday, a division of Bantam Doubleday Dell Publishing Group, Inc.

Marianne Hirsch, excerpt from "Projected Memory: Holocaust Photographs in Personal and Public Fantasy." From *Acts of Memory*, edited by Mieke Bal, Jonathan Crewe, and Leo Spitzer. Copyright © 1998 by the Trustees of Dartmouth College, reprinted by permission of University Press of New England. "From the *Stroop Report* on the Destruction of the Warsaw ghetto." Liaison Agency/Getty Images. "Past Lives (for the Children of Izieu)," © Lorie Novak, 1987, color photograph.

Richard Hoggart, "A Scholarship Boy." Excerpt from *The Uses of Literacy* by Richard Hoggart, published by Chatto & Windus. Used by permission of The Random House Group Limited.

Patricia Nelson Limerick, "Haunted America." From *Sweet Medicine: Sites of Indian Massacres, Battlefields, and Treaties* (Albuquerque: University of New Mexico Press, 1995) by Drex Brooks. Reprinted by permission of University of New Mexico Press.

W. J. T. Mitchell, "The Photographic Essay: Four Case Studies." From *Picture Theory* by W. J. T. Mitchell. Reprinted by permission of The University of Chicago Press. Jacob Riis, "Lodgers in Bayard St. Tenement," from *How the Other Half Lives* (1890). Photo reproduced courtesy of the Museum of the City of New York. "Parade—Hoboken, New Jersey," copyright *The Americans*, Robert Frank, courtesy PaceWildensteinMacGill Gallery, New York. Walker Evans, photographs from *Let Us Now Praise Famous Men* (1939) by James Agee and Walker Evans. Photographs courtesy of the Library of Congress. Walker Evans, "Annie Mae Gudger." Copyright © Walker Evans Archive, The Metropolitan Museum of Art. Margaret Bourke-White, "HAMILTON, ALABAMA." Courtesy of Jonathan Toby White, PLC. Daniel Boudinet, "Polaroid, 1979," from Roland Barthes, *Camera Lucida* (1981). Patrimoine Photographique, Paris. Nadar, "The Artist's Mother (Or Wife)," in Roland Barthes, *Camera Lucida* (1981). Cliché Paul Nadar/Arch.Phot. © Centre des monuments nationaux, Paris. Courtesy of the University of Minnesota Press. "Scenes and Types: Arabian Woman with the Yachmak" from *The Colonial Harem* by Malek Alloula. Jean Mohr, "Mayor of Jerusalem," "Amman, 1984. Mrs. Farraj," and "Elderly Palestinian Villager, Ramallah, 1984," from *After the Last Sky* by Edward Said. Photographs by Jean Mohr, Geneva.

Alice Munro, "The Albanian Virgin." From *Open Secrets* by Alice Munro. Copyright © 1994 by Alice Munro. Used by permission of Alfred A. Knopf, a division of Random House, Inc.

Walker Percy, "The Loss of the Creature." From *The Message in the Bottle* by Walker Percy. Copyright © 1975 by Walker Percy. Reprinted by permission of Farrar, Straus & Giroux, Inc.

Mary Louise Pratt, "Arts of the Contact Zone." From *Profession 91*. Copyright © 1991. Reprinted by permission of the Modern Language Association of America.

Adrienne Rich, "When We Dead Awaken: Writing as Re-Vision." From *On Lies, Secrets, and Silence: Selected Prose 1966–1978* by Adrienne Rich. Copyright © 1979 by W. W. Norton & Company, Inc. Used by permission of the author and W. W. Norton & Company, Inc. "Aunt Jennifer's Tigers." Copyright © 1993, 1951 by Adrienne Rich, "The Loser." Copyright © 1993, 1967, 1963 by Adrienne Rich, the lines from "Snapshots of a Daughter-in-Law." Copyright © 1993, 1967, 1963 by Adrienne Rich, "Orion." Copyright © 1993 by Adrienne Rich. Copyright © 1969 by W. W. Norton & Company, Inc. "Planetarium." Copyright © 1993 by Adrienne Rich. Copyright © 1971 by W.W. Norton & Company, Inc. From *Collected Early Poems: 1950–1970* by Adrienne Rich. Used by permission of the author and W. W. Norton & Company, Inc. Parts I, II, III, IV, V, VI, VII, XVIII, XX, XXII, and an excerpt from Part XXIII of "Sources," from *Your Native Land, Your Life: Poems by Adrienne Rich*. Copyright © 1986 by Adrienne Rich. Used by permission of the author and W. W. Norton & Company, Inc.

Richard Rodriguez, "The Achievement of Desire." From *Hunger of Memory* by Richard Rodriguez. Copyright © 1982 by Richard Rodriguez. Reprinted by permission of David R. Godine, Publisher, Inc.

Edward Said, "States." From *After the Last Sky* by Edward Said. Copyright © 1986 by Edward Said. Reprinted with permission from the Wylie Agency. Photographs by Jean Mohr, Geneva.

Jane Tompkins, "'Indians': Textualism, Morality, and the Problem of History." From *Critical Inquiry*, vol. 13, no. 1 (Autumn 1986). Reprinted in Henry Louis Gates, ed., *Race, Writing, and Difference* (1986), pp. 101–19. Copyright © The University of Chicago. All rights reserved. Reprinted by permission of the publisher.

Alice Walker, "In Search of Our Mothers' Gardens." From *In Search of Our Mothers' Gardens: Womanist Prose*, copyright © 1974 by Alice Walker. Reprinted by permission of Harcourt Brace & Company. "Women" (internal poem) from *Revolutionary Petunias and Other Poems*, copyright © 1970 by Alice Walker. Reprinted by permission of Harcourt Brace & Company.

John Edgar Wideman, "Our Time." From *Brothers and Keepers* by John Edgar Wideman. Copyright © 1984 by John Edgar Wideman. Reprinted by permission of Henry Holt and Co., Inc.

RESEARCH AND WRITING ONLINE

Whether you want to investigate ideas behind a thought-provoking essay or conduct in-depth research for a paper, the Web resources for *Ways of Reading* can help you find what you need on the Web—and then use it once you find it.

The English Research Room for Navigating the Web

www.bedfordstmartins.com/english_research

The Web brings a flood of information to your screen, but it still takes skill to track down the best sources. Not only does *The English Research Room* point you to some reliable starting places for Web investigations, it also lets you tune up your skills with interactive tutorials.

- Want to improve your skill at searching electronic databases, online catalogs, and the Web? Try the *Interactive Tutorials* for some hands-on practice.

- Need quick access to online search engines, reference sources, and research sites? Explore *Research Links* for some good starting places.

- Have questions on evaluating the sources you find, navigating the Web, or conducting research in general? Consult our *Reference Units* for authoritative advice.

Research and Documentation Online for Including Sources in Your Writing

www.bedfordstmartins.com/resdoc

Including sources correctly in a paper is often a challenge, and the Web has made it even more complex. This online version of the popular booklet *Research and Documentation in the Electronic Age*, by Diana Hacker, provides clear advice for the humanities, social sciences, history, and the sciences on

- which Web and library sources are relevant to your topic (with links to Web sources)

- how to integrate outside material into your paper

- how to cite sources correctly, using the appropriate documentation style

- what the format for the final paper should be